Occupational Outlook Handbook

Occupational Outlook Handbook

2000–01 Edition

Compiled by

The United States Department of Labor

VGM Career Books
NTC/Contemporary Publishing Group

Publisher's Preface

NTC/Contemporary Publishing Group is proud to bring you this special version of the *Occupational Outlook Handbook*. This important government publication, like the *Dictionary of Occupational Titles*, is an essential tool for all jobseekers.

First-time jobseekers can use *Occupational Outlook Handbook* to find out more about nearly 250 different types of careers. Vital information is given for each career field, including nature of the work, working conditions, employment, training, advancement opportunities, job outlook, earnings, and sources of additional information.

Experienced jobseekers should use this book to find the latest employment statistics for their career fields and the projected employment opportunities over the next several years. Those wishing to change careers will find helpful information on occupations related to their current experience; this information may indicate which new career areas to pursue.

Everyone can benefit from using the *Occupational Outlook Handbook*. Before making important career decisions, be sure to consult this publication for concise, comprehensive coverage of the employment picture in America today.

The Editors
VGM CAREER BOOKS

This VGM edition is an unabridged publication of Bulletin 2500, the *Occupational Outlook Handbook*, compiled by the United Sates Department of Labor, Bureau of Labor Statistics.

Published by VGM Career Books
A division of NTC/Contemporary Publishing Group, Inc.
4255 West Touhy Avenue, Lincolnwood (Chicago), Illinois 60712-1975 U.S.A.

Printed in the United States of America
International Standard Book Number: 0-658-00226-0 (cloth)
0-658-00227-9 (paper)
International Standard Serial Number: 0082-9072
2 3 4 5 6 7 8 9 0 VLP VLP 0 5 4 3 2 1

Acknowledgments

The Bureau of Labor Statistics produced the *Handbook* under the general guidance and direction of Neal H. Rosenthal, Associate Commissioner for Employment Projections, and Mike Pilot, Chief, Division of Occupational Outlook. Chester C. Levine and Jon Q. Sargent, Managers of Occupational Outlook Studies, provided planning and day-to-day direction.

Supervisors overseeing the research and preparation of material were Theresa Cosca, Mark Mittelhauser, Kristina Shelley, and Carolyn Veneri. Occupational analysts who contributed material were Hall Dillon, Arlene Dohm, Eric B. Figueroa, Chad M. Fleetwood, Jeffrey C. Gruenert, Jonathan Kelinson, R. Sean Kirby, T. Alan Lacey, Kevin M. McCarron, Andrew J. Nelson, Erik A. Savisaar, Terry Schau, Jill Silver, Gary Steinberg, Tiffany T. Stringer, and Patricia A. Tate.

Word processing support was provided by Beverly A. Williams. Cover and other art work were designed by Keith Tapscott.

Note

Many trade associations, professional societies, unions, industrial organizations, and government agencies provide career information that is valuable to counselors and jobseekers. For the convenience of *Handbook* users, some of these organizations and, in some cases, their Internet addresses are listed at the end of each occupational statement. Although these references were carefully compiled, the Bureau of Labor Statistics has neither authority nor facilities for investigating the organizations or the information or publications that may be sent in response to a request and cannot guarantee the accuracy of such information. The listing of an organization, therefore, does not constitute in any way an endorsement or recommendation by the Bureau either of the organization and its activities or of the information it may supply. Each organization has sole responsibility for whatever information it may issue.

The *Handbook* describes the job outlook over a projected 10-year period for occupations across the Nation; consequently, short-term labor market fluctuations and regional differences in job outlook generally are not discussed. Similarly, the *Handbook* provides a general, composite description of jobs and cannot be expected to reflect work situations in specific establishments or localities. The *Handbook*, therefore, is not intended and should not be used as a guide for determining wages, hours, the right of a particular union to represent workers, appropriate bargaining units, or formal job evaluation systems. Nor should earnings data in the *Handbook* be used to compute future loss of earnings in adjudication proceedings involving work injuries or accidental deaths.

 Comments about the contents of this publication and suggestions for improving it are welcome. Please address them to Chief, Division of Occupational Outlook, Bureau of Labor Statistics, U.S. Department of Labor, Washington, DC 20212. Phone: **(202) 691-5700.** Fax: **(202) 691-5745.** E-mail: **oohinfo@bls.gov.** Additional information is available on the Internet: **http://stats.bls.gov/ocohome.htm.**

Photograph Credits

The Bureau of Labor Statistics wishes to express its appreciation for the cooperation and assistance of the many government and private sources—listed below—that either contributed photographs or made their facilities available to photographers working under contract to the U.S. Department of Labor. Photographs may not be free of every possible safety or health hazard. Depiction of company or trade name in no way constitutes endorsement by the Department of Labor.

Adas Israel Congregation, Washington, DC; Air Traffic Controllers, Dulles International Airport; Allen-Mitchell & Company Machine Shop, Washington, DC; Amaco Refinery, Yorktown, VA; American Association of Retired Persons, Legal Counsel for the Elderly, Washington, DC; American University, including Washington College of Law, Washington, DC; Amtrak, Washington, DC; Animal Disease Center of the State of Illinois, Galesburg, IL; Appalachian Spring; Association of Flight Attendants; Audiophone, Washington, DC; Backyard Boat, Alexandria, VA; Baltimore Specialty Steels, Baltimore, MD; Baltimore Homesteading Program; Behnke Nurseries, Inc., Beltsville, MD; Black Magic Film Company; Brown Honda; Carlotta Joyner and Staff, U.S. General Accounting Office; Children's Hospital, Washington, DC; City Paper, Washington, DC; Columbia Gardens Memorials, Arlington, VA; Craddock-Terry, Farmville, Virginia Plant; Cultural Affairs Program, Arlington, VA; Cumberland Memorial Hospital, Cumberland, MD; Dance Place, Washington, DC; D.C. Vending Company, Washington, DC; Detective Agency, Washington, DC; District Cable of Washington, DC; Dixon's Pest Control Service; D.L. Boyd, Hyattsville, MD; Dr. Bruce L. Lazerow, Sears Optical, White Oak, MD; Dr. David Walls-Kaufman, Capitol Hill Chiropractic, Washington, DC; Dr. Gerald Lipps, D.D.S., Rockville, MD; Fannie Mae; Fire Department of District of Columbia; George Meany Labor Studies Center and Archives, Silver Spring, MD; George Washington University Hospital, Washington, DC; Giant Food Stores, Silver Spring, MD; H. & H. Bindery, Hyattsville, MD; Hospice of Washington, DC; Hurly Company; Industrial Photo, Silver Spring, MD; Iona House for Senior Citizens, Washington, DC; Johns Hopkins Hospital, Baltimore, MD; Jolles Brothers, Inc., Beltsville, MD; Joseph Passonneau, F.A.I.A., A.S.C.E.; Kath Keler; Kevin Hassett, State Farm Insurance, Washington, DC; Knox Veterinary Clinic, Galesburg, IL; Kop-Flex, Inc., Baltimore, MD; La Pierre and Company Design Studio, Alexandria, VA; Legg, Mason, Walker, Wood, Inc.; Litton Systems, Inc., Amecom Division, College Park, MD; Mar, Inc., Naval Engineering Group, Rockville, MD; Marc Rubenstein, Advanced Tool and Machine Service, Washington, DC; Martek Biosciences Corporation, Inc., Columbia, MD; Marriott Corporation; Martha Tabor, Working Images Photographs; Maryann Honakar, D.D.S.; Maryland Semiconductor, Inc., Clarksburg, MD; Maryland State Department of Forestry; Medical Records Corporation, Vienna, VA; Mt. Ranier Police Department, Mt. Ranier, MD; National Weather Service Forecast Office, Washington, DC; National Zoological Park, Washington, DC; Norfolk Naval Base, Norfolk, VA; Northwestern Illinois Research and Demonstration Center, University of Illinois at Champaign-Urbana; Pastor Laureen E. Smith, Western Presbyterian Church, Washington, DC; Population Reference Bureau, Inc., Washington, DC; President's Committee on Employment of People With Disabilities; Providence Opticians, Washington, DC; Rapp Funeral Home, Silver Spring, MD; Red Cross Blood Bank, Baltimore, MD; Riggs National Bank, Dupont Circle Branch, Washington, DC; Robert Schwartz Associates, Architects; Rock Terrace High School, Montgomery County, MD; Sandy Springs Friends School, Sandy Springs, MD; Seely Pine Furniture, Berkeley Springs, WV; Sheraton Washington Hotel, Washington, DC; Southern States Cooperative, Lothian, MD; State Farm Insurance Company, Frederick, MD; St. Martin's Catholic Church, Washington, DC; Suburban Dental Laboratories, Rockville, MD; Theodolphus Brooks Upholstery, Washington, DC; Thrifty Rental Cars; TJ's Auto Body Repair Shop, Washington, DC; Travel Bound, Fairfax, VA; United Airlines, Dulles International Airport Terminal; University of Delaware, Lewes, DE; University of Maryland, Chemical Engineering, Electrical Engineering, Materials Engineering, Mathematics, and Nuclear Engineering Departments; U.S. Air Force, Andrews Air Force Base, MD; U.S. Army Corps of Engineers, Fort Belvoir, VA; U.S. Census Bureau, Suitland, MD; U.S. Coast Guard, Annapolis, MD; U.S. Customs Officers, Dulles International Airport; US Elevator; U.S. Office of Personnel Management; U.S. Post Office, Galesburg, IL; Vandy L. Jamison, Jr., Attorney; Violin House of Weaver, Bethesda, MD; Walter Reed Army Hospital, Washington, DC; Washington Area Metropolitan Transit Authority; Washington Gas Company, Washington, DC; Washington Home, Washington, DC; Washington Times; Wendy Bayard, M.S.W., National Rehabilitation Hospital, Washington, DC; WETA, Alexandria, VA; William Maquire, USDA Agricultural Research Station, Beltsville, MD; WMATA, Washington, DC; Woodley House, Washington, DC; Wyatt Company, Washington, DC; Zsuzsi Wolf Jewelry, Alexandria, VA.

Contents

Special Features

Occupational Coverage

Executive, Administrative, and Managerial

Professional and Technical

Marketing and Sales

Administrative Support, Including Clerical

Service

Occupational Outlook Handbook

Tomorrow's Jobs

Making informed career decisions requires reliable information about opportunities in the future. Opportunities result from the relationships between the population, labor force, and the demand for goods and services.

Population ultimately limits the size of the labor force—individuals working or looking for work—which constrains how much can be produced. Demand for various goods and services determines employment in the industries providing them. Occupational employment opportunities, in turn, result from skills needed within specific industries. Opportunities for computer engineers and other computer-related occupations, for example, have surged in response to rapid growth in demand for computer services.

Examining the past and projecting changes in these relationships are the foundation of the Occupational Outlook Program. This chapter presents highlights of Bureau of Labor Statistics projections of the labor force and occupational and industry employment that can help guide your career plans. Sources of detailed information about the projections appear on the preceding page.

Population

Population trends affect employment opportunities in a number of ways. Changes in population influence the demand for goods and services. For example, a growing and aging population has increased the demand for health services. Equally important, population changes produce corresponding changes in the size and demographic composition of the labor force.

The U.S. population is expected to increase 23 million over the 1998-2008 period, at roughly the same rate of growth as during the 1988-98 period but much slower than over the 1978-88 period (chart 1). Continued growth will mean more consumers of goods and services, spurring demand for workers in a wide range of occupations and industries. The effects of population growth in various occupations will differ. The differences are partially accounted for by the age distribution of the future population.

The youth population, ages 16 to 24, is expected to increase as a share of the population for the first time since the 1970s. Overall, the 25 to 54 age group is expected to decrease as a share of the population. Within this group, however, the 45 and over age group will grow as a percent of the population. The 55 and over age group will grow the fastest, increasing from 26.6 to 30 percent over the 1998-2008 period.

Minorities and immigrants will constitute a larger share of the U.S. population in 2008 than they do today. Substantial increases in the Hispanic, black, and Asian populations are forecasted, reflecting high birth rates as well as a continued flow of immigrants.

Labor Force

Population is the single most important factor in determining the size and composition of the labor force—comprised of people who are either working or looking for work. The civilian labor force is expected to increase by 17 million, or 12 percent, to 154.6 million over the 1998-2008 period. This increase is almost the same as the 13 percent increase during the 1988-98 period but much less than the 19 percent increase during the 1978-88 period.

The U.S. workforce will become more diverse by 2008. White, non-Hispanic persons will make up a decreasing share of the labor force, from 73.9 to 70.7 percent. Hispanics, non-Hispanic blacks, and Asians and other racial groups are projected to comprise an increasing share of the labor force

Chart 1. **Population and labor force growth – 1978-88, 1988-98, and projected 1998-2008**

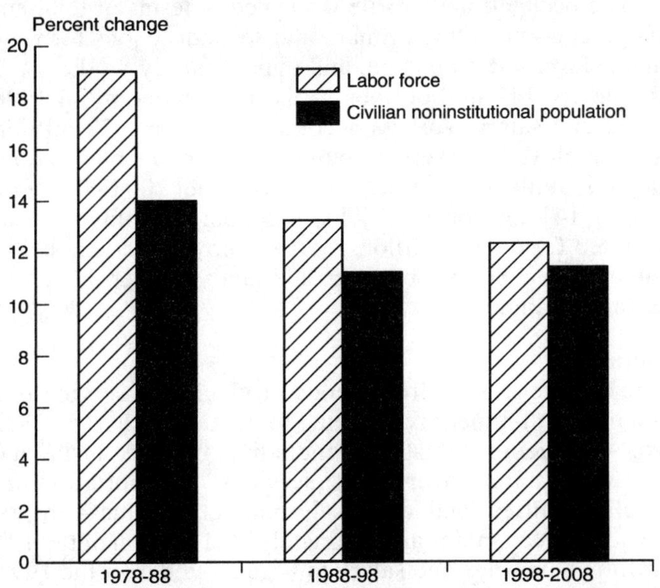

Chart 2. **Percent of labor force by race and ethnic origin, 1998 and projected 2008**

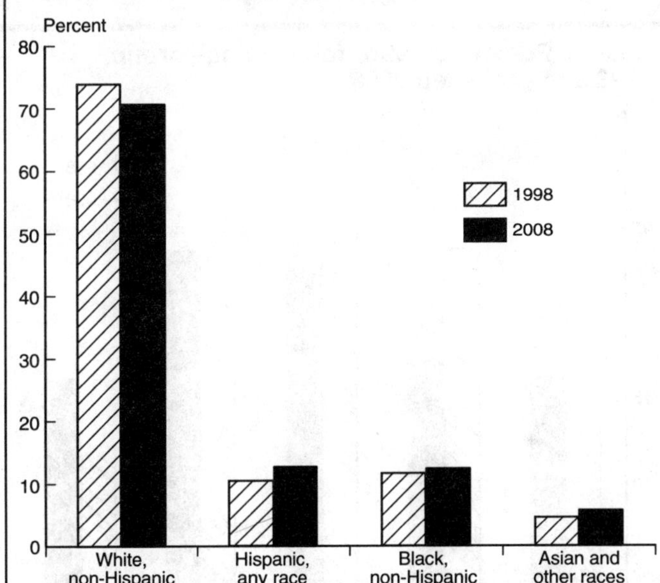

by 2008—10.4 to 12.7 percent, 11.6 to 12.4 percent, and 4.6 to 5.7 percent, respectively (chart 2). However, despite relatively slow growth, white non-Hispanics will have the largest numerical growth in the labor force between 1998 and 2008, reflecting the large size of this group.

The number of men and women in the labor force will grow, but the number of men will grow at a slower rate than in the past. Between 1998 and 2008, men's share of the labor force is expected to decrease from 53.7 to 52.5 percent while women's share is expected to increase from 46.3 to 47.5 percent.

The youth labor force, ages 16 to 24, is expected to slightly increase its share of the labor force to 16 percent in 2008, growing more rapidly than the overall labor force for the first time in 25 years. The large group of workers 25 to 44 years old, who comprised 51 percent of the labor force in 1998, is projected to decline to 44 percent of the labor force by 2008. Workers 45 and older, on the other hand, are projected to increase from 33 to 40 percent of the labor force between 1998 and 2008, due to the aging baby-boom generation (chart 3).

Education and Training

Projected job growth varies widely by education and training requirements. Five out of the six education and training categories projected to have the highest percent change require at least a bachelor's degree (chart 4). These five categories will account for one-third of all employment growth over the 1998-2008 period. Employment in occupations that do not require postsecondary education are projected to grow by about 12 percent while occupations that require at least a bachelor's degree are projected to grow by almost 22 percent, compared to 14 percent for all occupations combined.

Education is essential in getting a high paying job. In fact, all but a few of the 50 highest paying occupations require a college degree. However, a number of occupations—for example, blue-collar worker supervisors, electricians, and police patrol officers—do not require a college degree, yet offer higher than average earnings.

Chart 3. **Percent of labor force by age group, 1998 and projected 2008**

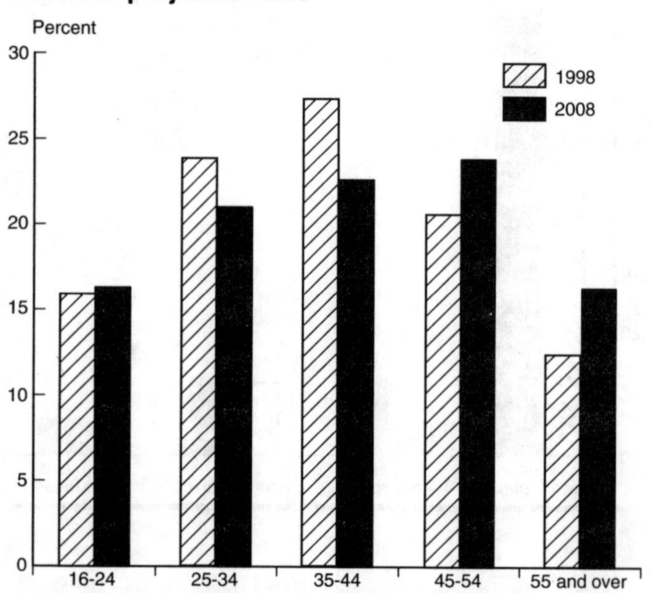

Chart 4. **Growth rates by most significant source of education and training, projected 1998-2008**

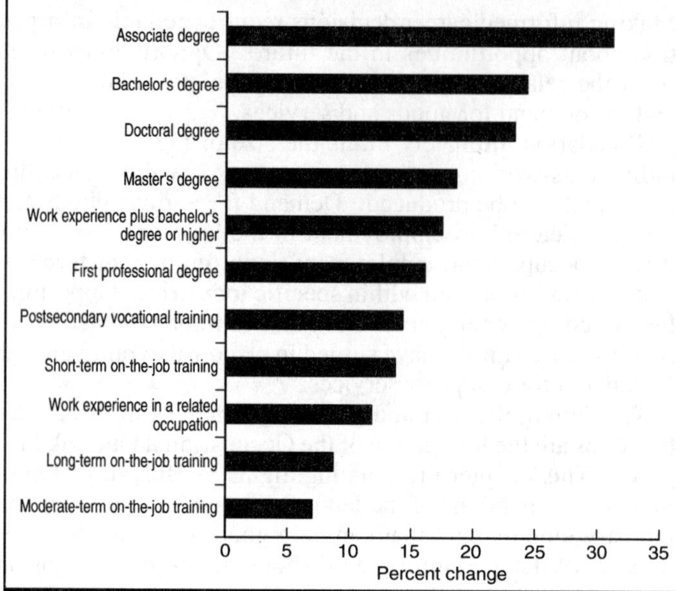

Employment

Total employment is expected to increase from 141 million in 1998 to 161 million in 2008, or by 14 percent. The 20 million jobs that will be added by 2008 will not be evenly distributed across major industrial and occupational groups. Changes in consumer demands, technology, and many other factors will contribute to the continually changing employment structure in the U.S. economy.

The following two sections examine projected employment change from both industrial and occupational perspectives. The industrial profile is discussed in terms of primary wage and salary employment; primary employment excludes secondary jobs for those who hold multiple jobs. The exception is agriculture, which includes self-employed and unpaid family workers in addition to salaried workers.

The occupational profile is viewed in terms of total employment—including primary and secondary jobs for wage and salary, self-employed, and unpaid family workers. Of the nearly 141 million jobs in the U.S. economy in 1998, wage and salary workers accounted for over 128 million; self-employed workers accounted for over 12 million; and unpaid family workers accounted for about 200,000. Of the nearly 141 million total jobs, secondary employment accounted for over 2 million. Self-employed workers held 9 out of 10 secondary jobs; wage and salary workers held most of the remainder.

Industry

The long-term shift from goods-producing to service-producing employment is expected to continue (chart 5). Service-producing industries—including finance, insurance, and real estate; government; services; transportation and public utilities; and wholesale and retail trade—are expected to account for approximately 19.1 million of the 19.5 million new wage and salary jobs generated over the 1998-2008 period. The services and retail trade industry sectors will account for nearly three-fourths of total wage and salary job growth, a continuation of the employment growth pattern of the 1988-98 period.

Chart 5. **Percent change in wage and salary employment, service-producing industries, 1988-98 and projected 1998-2008**

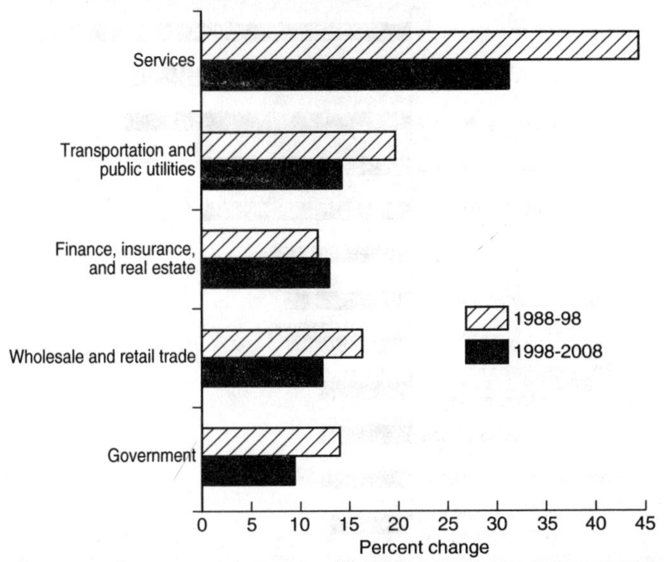

Services. The largest and fastest growing major industry group—services—is expected to add 11.8 million new jobs by 2008. Nearly three-fourths of this projected job growth is concentrated in three sectors of services—business, health, and professional and miscellaneous services. Business services—including personnel supply and computer and data processing services, among other detailed industries—will add 4.6 million jobs. Health services—including home health care services and nursing and personal care facilities, among other detailed industries—will add 2.8 million jobs. Professional and miscellaneous services—including management and public relations and research and testing services, among other detailed industries—will add 1.1 million jobs. Employment in computer and data processing services is projected to grow 117 percent between 1998 and 2008, ranking as the fastest growing industry.

Transportation and public utilities. Overall employment is expected to increase by 674,000 jobs, or 14 percent. Employment in the transportation sector is expected to increase by 16 percent, from 4.3 to 5 million jobs. Air, truck, and local and interurban passenger transportation will account for 32, 30, and 23 percent, respectively, of the job growth in this industry. Employment in communications is expected to grow about as fast as average through 2008, adding about 300,000 new jobs. Employment in utilities is expected to decline by about 4 percent. However, faster than average growth is expected in water supply and sanitary services with the creation of about 67,000 jobs.

Finance, insurance, and real estate. Employment is expected to increase by 13 percent—adding 960,000 jobs to the 1998 level of 7.4 million. Demand for financial services is expected to continue. The security and commodity brokers segment of the industry is expected to grow by 40 percent, creating about 255,000 jobs. Nondepository institutions will add 193,000 jobs and have a growth rate of 29 percent, fueled by increased demand for nonbank corporations that offer bank-like services. Continued demand for real estate will create 179,000 new jobs, at a growth rate of about 12 percent. The insurance carriers segment is expected to grow by nearly 10 percent—adding 154,000 jobs.

Wholesale and retail trade. Employment is expected to increase by 7 and 14 percent, respectively, growing from 6.8 to 7.3 million in wholesale trade and from 22.3 to 25.4 million in retail trade. With the addition of 1.3 million jobs, the eating and drinking places segment of the retail industry is projected to have the largest numerical increase in employment.

Government. Between 1998 and 2008, government employment, including public education and public hospitals, is expected to increase by over 9 percent, from 19.8 to 21.7 million jobs. State and local government, particularly education, will drive employment growth. Federal Government employment is expected to decline by 165,000 jobs.

Employment in the goods-producing industries has been relatively stagnant since the early 1980s. Overall, this sector is expected to grow by 1.6 percent over the 1998-2008 period. Although employment growth is expected to show little change, projected growth within the sector varies considerably (chart 6).

Construction. Construction is expected to increase by 9 percent from 5.9 to 6.5 million. Demand for new housing and an increase in road, bridge, and tunnel construction will account for the bulk of employment growth in this industry.

Agriculture, forestry, and fishing. Overall employment in agriculture, forestry, and fishing is expected to increase by nearly 5 percent from 2.2 to 2.3 million. Strong growth in agricultural services will more than offset an expected continued decline in crops and livestock and livestock products.

Manufacturing. Manufacturing employment is expected to decline by less than 1 percent from the 1998 level of 18.8 million. The projected loss of jobs reflects improved production methods, advances in technology, and increased trade.

Mining. Mining employment is expected to decrease by 19 percent from 590,000 to 475,000. The continued decline is partly due to laborsaving machinery and increased imports.

Chart 6. **Percent change in wage and salary employment, goods-producing industries, 1988-98 and projected 1998-2008**

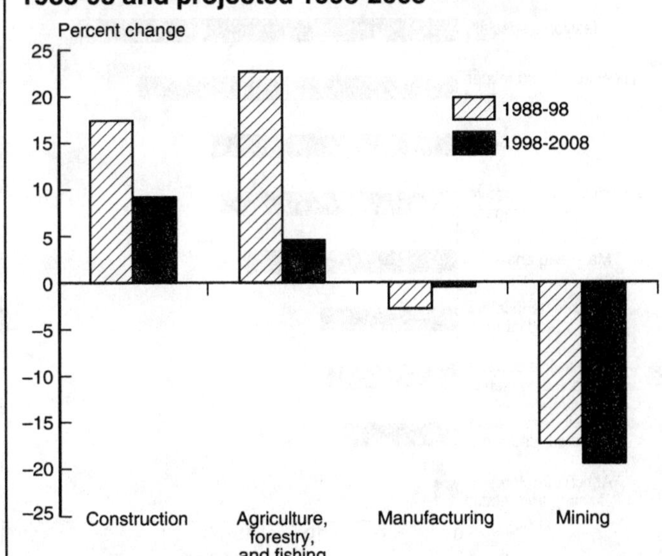

Occupation

Expansion of the service-producing sector is expected to continue, creating demand for many occupations. However, projected job growth varies among major occupational groups (chart 7).

Professional specialty. Professional specialty occupations comprise the fastest growing group. Over the 1998-2008 period, a 27-percent increase in the number of new professional specialty jobs is projected, an increase of 5.3 million. Professional specialty workers perform a wide variety of duties, and are employed throughout private industry and government. Computer systems analysts, computer engineers and scientists, special education teachers, and social and recreation workers are among the fastest growing occupations in this group.

Technicians and related support. Employment of technicians and related support occupations is projected to grow by 22 percent, adding 1.1 million jobs by 2008. Workers in this group provide technical assistance to engineers, scientists, physicians, and other professional specialty workers, and operate and program technical equipment. Over half of the projected employment growth among technicians—about 616,000 jobs—is among health technicians and technologists. Considerable growth is also expected among computer programmers and paralegals and legal assistants.

Service. Employment in service occupations is projected to increase by 3.9 million, or 17 percent, by 2008, the second largest numerical gain among the major occupational groups. Over half of the new jobs are in the rapidly growing services industry division, led by business services, health services, and social services.

Executive, administrative, and managerial. Executive, administrative, and managerial occupations are projected to increase by 16 percent, or 2.4 million, over the 1998-2008 period. Workers in this group establish policies, make plans, determine staffing requirements, and direct the activities of businesses, government agencies, and other organizations. The services industry division is expected to account for half of the job growth, adding 1.2 million jobs. The number of self-employed executive, administrative, and managerial workers is expected to increase by 361,000—

Chart 7. **Percent change in total employment by major occupational group, projected 1998-2008**

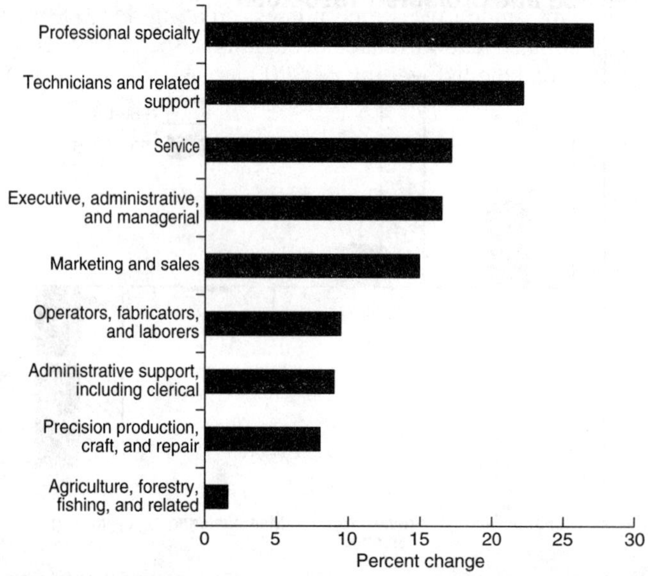

Chart 8. **Occupations with fast growth and high pay that have the largest numerical growth, projected 1998-2008**

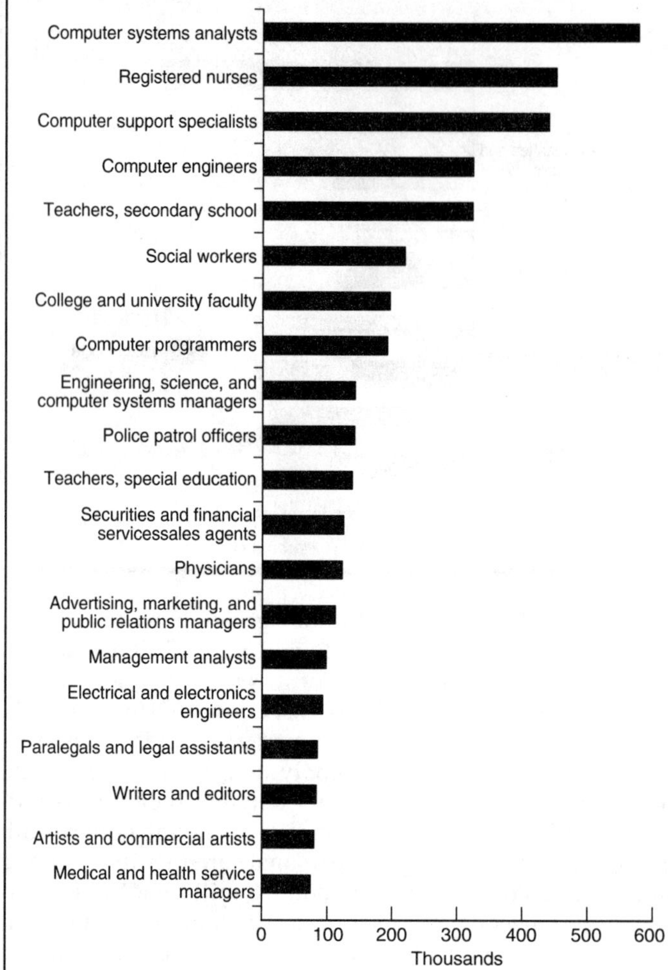

more than any other major occupational group—to almost 2.5 million by 2008.

Marketing and sales. Workers in marketing and sales occupations sell goods and services, purchase commodities and property for resale, and stimulate consumer interest. Employment in this group is projected to increase by 15 percent, or 2.3 million, from 1998 to 2008. The services industry division is expected to add the most marketing and sales jobs—719,000—by 2008, followed by an additional 92,000 jobs in the transportation and public utilities industry division.

Operators, fabricators, and laborers. Employment of operators, fabricators, and laborers is expected to increase by 1.8 million workers, or 9.4 percent, from 1998 to 2008. Most new jobs in this group are expected among transportation and material moving machine and vehicle operators; helpers, laborers, and material movers, hand; and hand workers, including assemblers and fabricators, adding 745,000, 626,000, and 290,000 jobs, respectively.

Administrative support, including clerical. The number of workers in administrative support occupations, including clerical is projected to increase by 9 percent from 1998 to 2008, adding 2.2 million new jobs. With 24.5 million workers, this is the largest major occupational group. Workers perform a wide variety of administrative tasks necessary to keep organizations functioning efficiently. Due mostly to technological change, several large occupations within this group—for example,

Chart 9. **Occupations projected to grow fastest, 1998-2008**

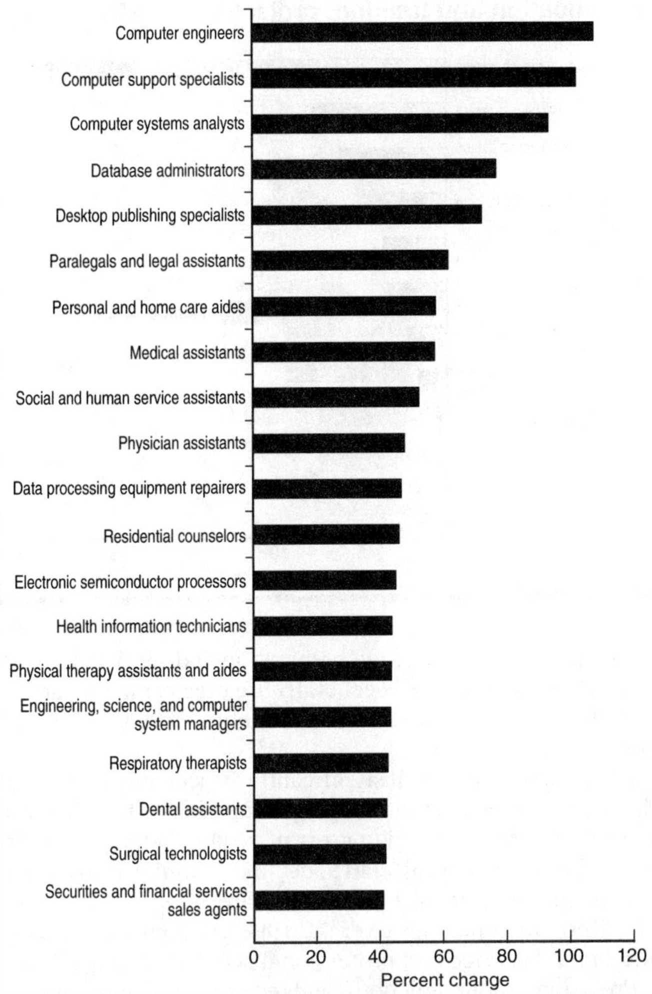

Chart 10. **Occupations with the largest numercial decrease in employment, projected 1998-2008**

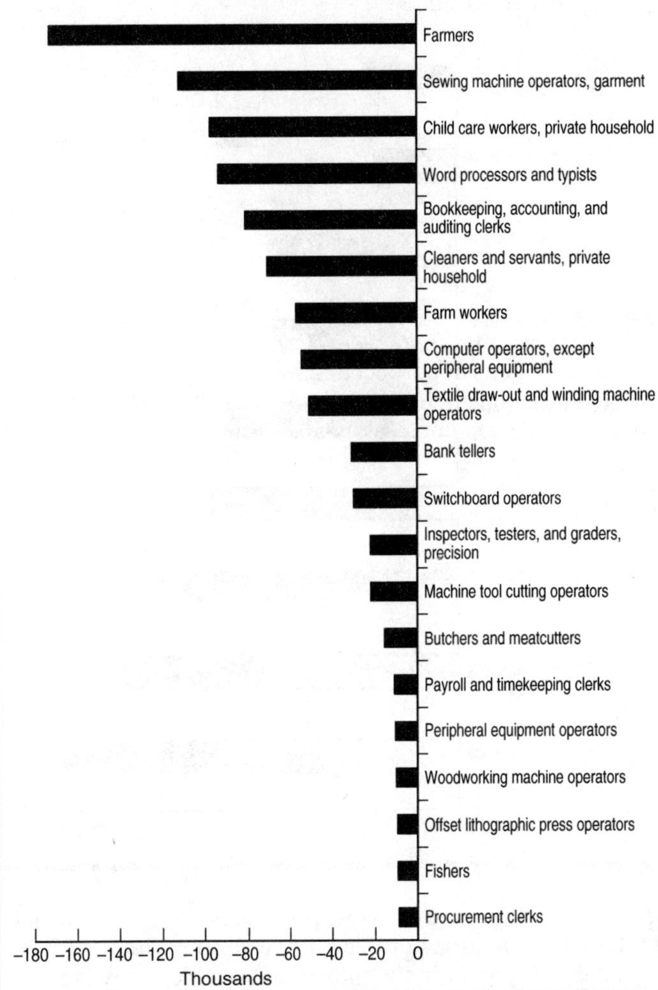

bookkeeping, accounting, and auditing clerks—are expected to decline. However, other occupations less affected by technological change are expected to increase. These occupations include teacher assistants, adding 375,000 jobs; office and administrative support supervisors and managers, adding 313,000 jobs; receptionists and information clerks, adding 305,000 jobs; and adjusters, investigators, and collectors, adding 302,000 jobs.

Precision production, craft, and repair. Employment in precision production, craft, and repair occupations is projected to grow 8 percent, creating almost 1.3 million new jobs, over the 1998-2008 period. Mechanics, installers, and repairers are expected to add 588,000 new jobs by 2008; construction trades workers are expected to add 390,000 new jobs; and blue-collar worker supervisors are expected to add 196,000 new jobs.

Agriculture, forestry, fishing, and related. Agriculture, forestry, fishing, and related occupations are projected to grow only by only 2 percent, adding 71,000 new jobs. Workers in these occupations cultivate plants, breed and raise livestock, and catch animals. Within this major group, job losses are expected for farmers and farm workers. In contrast, landscaping, groundskeeping, nursery, greenhouse, and lawn service occupations are expected to add 262,000 new jobs by 2008.

The 20 occupations listed in chart 8 are among those projected to grow fast and produce large numbers of new jobs, in addition to having higher than average earnings. Half of these occupations are involved with computer technology, health care, and education. Systems analysts top this list, adding over 577,000 jobs between 1998 and 2008, reflecting high demand for computer services. Among other computer-related occupations, computer support specialists and computer engineers are expected to add 439,000 and 323,000 new jobs, respectively. Similarly, strong demand for health care services will fuel growth among registered nurses, creating 451,000 new jobs. Among education-related occupations, secondary school teachers head the list, adding 322,000 jobs.

Computer-related jobs are expected to grow the fastest over the projection period (chart 9). In fact, these jobs make up the four fastest growing occupations in the economy. Computer engineers, computer support specialists, computer systems analysts, and database administrators are expected to increase by 108, 102, 94, and 77 percent, respectively. Many other occupations projected to grow the fastest are in health care.

Table 1 lists occupations projected to grow the fastest and to generate the largest number of new jobs over the 1998-2008 period, by level of education and training.

Declining occupational employment stems from declining industry employment, technological advances, organizational changes, and other factors. For example, increased productivity and farm consolidations are expected to result in a decline of 173,000 farmers over the 1998-2008 period (chart 10). Office automation and the increased use of word processing equipment by professionals and managerial employees will

Chart 11. **Job openings due to growth and replacement needs by major occupational group, projected 1998-2008**

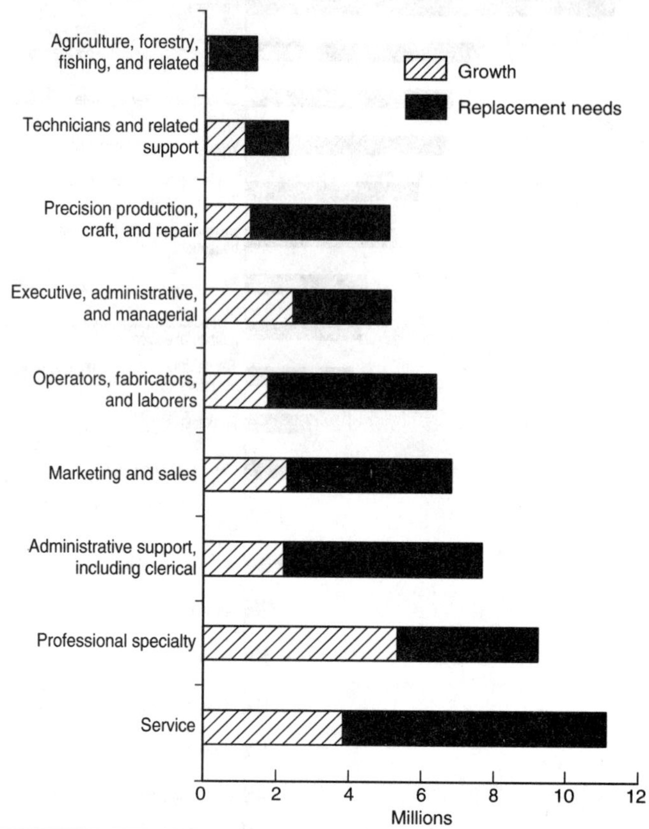

Chart 12. **Job openings due to growth and replacement needs by most significant source of education and training, projected 1998-2008**

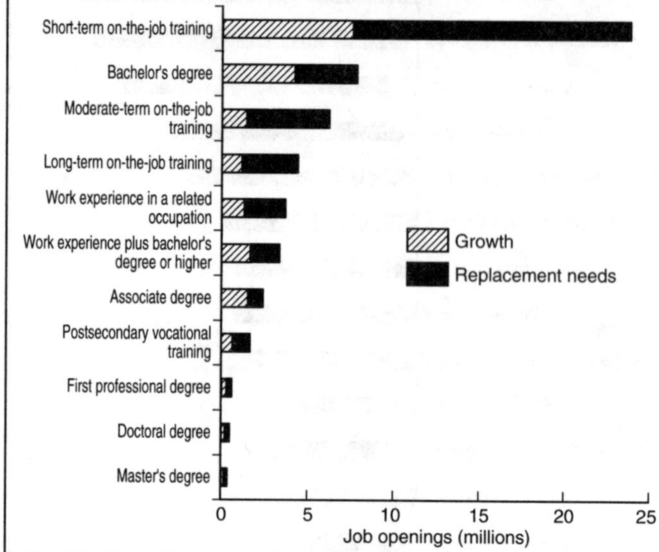

lead to a decline among word processors and typists. Examples of occupations projected to lose jobs along with declining employment in the industries in which they are concentrated include farm workers; sewing machine operators, garment; and child-care workers, private household.

Total Job Openings

Job openings stem from both employment growth and replacement needs (chart 11). Replacement needs arise as workers leave occupations. Some transfer to other occupations while others retire, return to school, or quit to assume household responsibilities. Replacement needs are projected to account for 63 percent of the approximately 55 million job openings between 1998 and 2008. Thus, even occupations with slower than average growth or little or no change in employment may still offer many job openings.

Professional specialty occupations are projected to grow faster and add more jobs than any major occupational group, with 5.3 million new jobs by 2008. Two-thirds of this job growth is expected among teachers, librarians, and counselors; computer, mathematical, and operations research occupations; and health assessment and treating occupations. With 3.9 million job openings due to replacement needs, professional specialty occupations comprise the only major group projected to generate more openings from job growth than from replacement needs.

Due to high replacement needs, service occupations are projected to have the largest number of total job openings, 11.1 million. A large number of replacements are expected to arise as young workers leave food preparation and service occupations. Replacement needs generally are greatest in the largest occupations and in those with relatively low pay or limited training requirements.

Office automation will significantly affect many individual administrative and clerical support occupations. Overall, these occupations are projected to grow more slowly than the average, while some are projected to decline. Administrative support, including clerical occupations, are projected to create 7.7 million job openings over the 1998-2008 period, ranking third behind service and professional specialty occupations.

Precision production, craft, and repair occupations and operators, fabricators, and laborers are projected to grow more slowly than the average for all occupations through 2008, due mostly to advances in technology and changes in production methods. Replacement needs are projected to account for almost three-fourths of all the job openings in these groups.

Employment in occupations requiring an associate degree is projected to increase 31 percent, faster than any other occupational group categorized by education and training. However, this category only ranks seventh among the 11 education and training categories in terms of total job openings. The largest number of job openings will be among occupations requiring short-term on-the-job training, a bachelor's degree, and moderate-term on-the-job training (chart 12).

Almost two-thirds of the projected job openings over the 1998-2008 period will be in occupations that require on-the-job training, due mostly to replacement needs. These jobs will account for 34.5 million of the projected 55 million total job openings through 2008. However, many of these jobs typically offer low pay and benefits; this is particularly true of jobs requiring only short-term on-the-job training, which account for 24 million job openings, far more than any other occupational group.

Jobs requiring at least a bachelor's degree will account for about 12.7 million job openings through 2008. Most of these openings will result from job growth and usually offer higher pay and benefits.

Table 1. Fastest growing occupations projected to have the largest numerical increase in employment between 1998 and 2008 by level of education and training

Fastest growing occupations	Education/training category	Occupations having the largest numerical increase in employment
	First-professional degree	
Veterinarians		Physicians
Chiropractors		Lawyers
Physicians		Clergy
Lawyers		Veterinarians
Clergy		Pharmacists
	Doctoral degree	
Biological scientists		College and university faculty
Medical scientists		Biological scientists
College and university faculty		Medical scientists
Physicists and astronomers		Physicists and astronomers
	Master's degree	
Speech-language pathologists and audiologists		Counselors
Physical therapists		Physical therapists
Counselors		Speech-language pathologists and audiologists
Urban and regional planners		Psychologists
Archivists, curators, and conservators		Librarians
	Work experience plus bachelor's or higher degree	
Engineering, science, and computer systems managers		General managers and top executives
Medical and health services managers		Engineering, science, and computer systems managers
Management analysts		Advertising, marketing, and public relations managers
Artists and commercial artists		Management analysts
Advertising, marketing, and public relations managers		Financial managers
	Bachelor's degree	
Computer engineers		Computer systems analysts
Computer systems analysts		Computer engineers
Database administrators		Teachers, secondary school
Physicians assistants		Social workers
Residential counselors		Teachers, elementary school
	Associate degree	
Computer support specialists		Registered nurses
Paralegals and legal assistants		Computer support specialists
Health information technicians		Paralegals and legal assistants
Physical therapy assistants and aides		Dental hygienists
Respiratory therapists		Electrical and electronic technicians and technologists
	Postsecondary vocational training	
Data processing equipment repairers		Licensed practical nurses
Surgical technologists		Automotive mechanics
Central office and PBX installers and repairers		Hairstylists and cosmetologists
Emergency medical technicians		Emergency medical technicians
Manicurists		Data processing equipment repairers
	Work experience in a related occupation	
Private detectives and investigators		Office and administrative support supervisors
Detectives and criminal investigators		Marketing and sales worker supervisors
Instructors, adult (nonvocational) education		Blue-collar worker supervisors
Lawn service managers		Food service and lodging managers
Office and administrative support supervisors		Teachers and instructors, vocational education and training
	Long-term on-the-job training (more than 12 months)	
Desktop publishing specialists		Correction officers
Correctional officers		Cooks, restaurant
Sheriffs and deputy sheriffs		Police patrol officers
Police patrol officers		Maintenance repairers, general utility
Telephone and cable TV line installers		Carpenters
	Moderate-term on-the-job training (1 to 12 months)	
Medical assistants		Medical assistants
Social and human services assistants		Social and human services assistants
Electronic semiconductor processors		Instructors and coaches, sports and physical training
Dental assistants		Dental assistants
Models, demonstrators, and product promoters		Packaging and filling machine operators
	Short-term on-the-job training (up to 1 month)	
Personal care and home health aides		Retail salespersons
Bill and account collectors		Cashiers
Ambulance drivers and attendants, except emergency medical technicians		Truck drivers, except driver/sales workers
Adjustment clerks		Office clerks, general
Teacher assistants		Personal care and home health aides

Sources of Career Information

This section identifies sources of information about career planning, counseling, training, education, and financial aid. *Handbook* statements also include a section on sources of additional information, which lists organizations that can be contacted for more information about particular occupations as well as the required training and education.

Career information

Listed below are several places to begin collecting information on careers and job opportunities.

Personal contacts. The people close to you—your family and friends—can be extremely helpful in providing career information. They may be able to answer your questions directly or put you in touch with someone else who can. Networking can lead to meeting someone who can answer your questions about a specific career or company, and who can provide inside information and other helpful hints. It is an effective way to learn the type of training necessary for a certain position, how someone in that position entered the field, the prospects for advancement, and what they like and dislike about the work.

Public libraries, career centers, and guidance offices. These institutions maintain a great deal of up-to-date material. To begin your library search, look at the computer listings under "vocations" or "careers" and then under specific fields. Check the periodicals section, where trade and professional magazines and journals about specific occupations and industries are located. Become familiar with the concerns and activities of potential employers by skimming their annual reports and other public documents. Occupational information on video cassettes and through computerized information systems or the Internet can be valuable. Don't forget the librarians; they can be a great source and can save you valuable time by directing you to relevant information.

Check your school's career centers for resources such as individual counseling and testing, guest speakers, field trips, books, career magazines, and career days.

Always assess career guidance materials carefully. The information should be current and objective. Beware of materials that seem to glamourize the occupation, overstate the earnings, or exaggerate the demand for workers.

Counselors. These professionals are trained to help you discover your strengths and weaknesses, evaluate your goals and values, and help you determine what you would like in a career. Counselors will not tell you what to do. However, they may administer interest inventories and aptitude tests, interpret the results, and help you explore various options. Counselors also may discuss local job markets and the entry requirements and costs of schools, colleges, or training programs. Counselors are found in:

- High school guidance offices
- College career planning and placement offices
- Placement offices in private vocational or technical schools and institutions
- Vocational rehabilitation agencies
- Counseling services offered by community organizations
- Private counseling agencies and private practices
- State employment service offices

Before employing the services of a private counselor or agency, you may want to seek recommendations and check their credentials. The International Association of Counseling Services (IACS) accredits counseling services throughout the country. To receive a listing of accredited services for your region, send a self-addressed, stamped, business-size envelope to:

☛ IACS, 101 South Whiting St., Suite 211, Alexandria, VA 22304. Internet: **http://mason.gmu.edu/~iacs**

The *Directory of Counseling Services*, an IACS publication providing employment counseling and other assistance, may be available in your library or school career counseling center. A list of certified career counselors by city or State is available from:

☛ The National Board of Certified Counselors, 3 Terrace Way, Suite D, Greensboro, NC 27403-3660. Phone: (334) 547-0607. Internet: **http://www.nbcc.org**

Internet networks and resources. The growth of on-line listings has made countless resources instantly available at any time. Most companies, professional societies, academic institutions, and government agencies maintain Internet sites that highlight the organization's latest information and activities.

Listings may include information such as government documents, schedules of events, and job openings. Listings for academic institutions often provide links to career counseling and placement services through career resource centers, as well as information on financing your education. Colleges and universities also offer on-line guides to campus facilities and admission requirements and procedures.

The variety of career information available through the internet provide much of the same information available through libraries, career centers, and guidance offices. However, no single network or resource will contain all desired information, so be prepared to search a variety of places. As in a library search, look through various lists by field or discipline, or by using keywords.

Career sites can be an excellent place to obtain information about job opportunities. They provide a forum for employers to list job openings and for individuals to post their resumés. Some Internet sites may also provide an opportunity to research a particular industry or company.

America's Job Bank (AJB), administered by the U.S. Department of Labor, lists as many as 1 million job openings on any given day. These job openings are compiled by State employment service offices throughout the Nation. AJB is accessible at: **http://www.ajb.dni.us**

Professional societies, trade associations, labor unions, business firms, and educational institutions. These organizations provide a variety of free or inexpensive career material. Many of these are in an additional information section of the *Handbook.* For information on occupations not covered in the *Handbook*, consult directories in your library's reference section for the names of potential sources. You may start with *The Guide to American Directories* or *The Directory of Directories*. Another useful resource is *The Encyclopedia of Associations*, an annual publication listing trade associations, professional societies, labor unions, and fraternal and patriotic organizations.

The National Technical Information Service Audiovisual Center, a central source for audiovisual material produced by the U.S. Government, sells material on jobs and careers. For a catalog, contact:

☛ NTIS Audiovisual Center, Springfield, VA 22161. Phone: (800) 553-6847. Internet: **http://www.ntis.gov/nac**

Federal Government. Information on employment with the Federal Government is available from the Office of Personnel Management. Consult your telephone directory under U.S. Government for a local number or call (912) 757-3100; TDD (912) 744-2299.

☛ Internet: **http://www.usajobs.opm.gov**

Organizations for specific groups. The organizations listed below provide information on career planning, training, or job opportunities prepared for specific groups. Consult directories in your library's reference center or a career guidance office for information on additional organizations associated with specific groups.

Disabled workers:
Counseling, training, and placement services for those with disabilities is available from:

☛ The National Business and Disability Council, 201 I.U. Willets Rd., Albertson, NY 11507. Phone: (516) 465-1515.
Internet: **http://www.business-disability.com**

Blind workers:
Information on the free national reference and referral service for the blind can be obtained by contacting:

☛ National Federation of the Blind, Job Opportunities for the Blind (JOB), 1800 Johnson St., Baltimore, MD 21230. Phone: (410) 659-9314. Internet: **http://www.nfb.org**

Older workers:

☛ National Association of Older Workers Employment Services, c/o National Council on the Aging, 409 3rd St. SW., Suite 200, Washington, DC 20024. Phone: (202) 479-1200.

☛ National Caucus and Center on Black Aged, Inc., 1424 K St. NW., Suite 500, Washington, DC 20005. Phone: (202) 637-8400. Internet: **http://www.ncba-blackaged.org**

☛ Asociación Nacional pro Personas Mayores (National Association for Hispanic Elderly), 234 East Colorado Blvd., Pasadena, CA 91101. Phone: (626) 564-1988.

Veterans:
Contact the nearest regional office of the U.S. Department of Labor Veterans' Employment and Training Service or:

☛ Veterans' Employment and Training Service (VETS), 200 Constitution Ave. NW., Room S-1315, Washington, DC 20210. Phone: (202) 219-9116. Internet: **http://www.dol.gov/dol/vets**

Women:

☛ Department of Labor, Women's Bureau Clearinghouse, 200 Constitution Ave. NW., Washington, DC 20210. Phone: (800) 827-5335. Internet: **http://www.dol.gov/dol/wb**

☛ Wider Opportunities for Women, 815 15th St. NW., Suite 916, Washington, DC 20005. Phone: (202) 638-3143.
Internet: **http://www.wowonline.org**

Federal laws, executive orders, and selected Federal grant programs bar discrimination in employment based on race, color, religion, sex, national origin, age, and handicap. Information on how to file a charge of discrimination is available from U.S. Equal Employment Opportunity Commission offices around the country. Their addresses and telephone numbers are listed in telephone directories under U.S. Government, EEOC.

☛ Internet: **http://www.eeoc.gov**

Education and training information

Colleges, schools, and training institutes readily reply to requests for information about their programs. When contacting these institutions, you may want to keep in mind the following items:

- Admission requirements
- Courses offered
- Certificates or degrees awarded
- Cost
- Available financial aid
- Location and size of school
- Placement rate of graduates

Check with professional and trade associations for lists of schools that offer career preparation in a field in which you are interested. High school guidance offices and libraries usually have copies of the directories listed below, as well as college catalogs that can provide more information on specific institutions. Helpful resources include the *Directory of Private Career Schools and Colleges of Technology*, put out by the Accrediting Commission of Career Schools and Colleges of Technology. Be sure to use the latest edition because these directories and catalogs are revised periodically.

Information about home or correspondence study programs appears in the *Directory of Accredited Institutions*. Send requests for the *Directory* and a list of other publications to:

☛ Distance Education and Training Council, 1601 18th St. NW., Washington, DC 20009. Phone: (202) 234-5100. Internet: **http://www.detc.org**

Information about apprenticeships is available from local labor unions, school guidance counselors, and State employment offices or from:

☛ Bureau of Apprenticeship and Training, U.S. Department of Labor, 200 Constitution Ave. NW., Room N-4649, Washington, DC 20210. Phone: (202) 219-5921. Internet: **http://www.doleta.gov/individ/apprent.htm**

Completing an internship is an excellent way for students and others to learn about an occupation and to make valuable contacts. Many employers offer internships that provide short-term or part-time job experience that can lead to a permanent position. Contact your school's career guidance center or employers directly regarding internship opportunities.

Financial aid information

Information about financial aid is available from a variety of sources. Contact your high school guidance counselor and college financial aid officer for information concerning qualifications and applications for scholarships, fellowships, grants, loans, and work-study programs. Every State administers financial aid programs; contact State Departments of Education for information. Banks and credit unions will provide information about student loans. You also may want to consult the directories and guides available in guidance offices and public libraries for sources of student financial aid.

The Federal Government provides grants, loans, work-study programs, and other benefits to students. Information about programs administered by the U.S. Department of Education is presented in *The Student Guide to Federal Financial Aid Programs*, updated annually. To receive a copy, write to:

☛ Federal Student Aid Information Center, c/o Federal Student Aid Programs, P.O. Box 84, Washington, DC 20044-0084. Phone: (800) 433-3243. Internet: **http://www.ed.gov/offices/OSFAP/Students**

The U.S. Department of Health and Human Services offers loan, scholarship, and faculty loan repayment programs.

☛ Phone: (301) 443-4776.
Internet: **http://www.hrsa.dhhs.gov/bhpr/dsa/dsa.htm**

Copies of *The Student Guide*, a guide to financial aid, are available from the U.S. Department of Education, Federal Student Aid Information Center.

☛ Phone: (800) 433-3243.
Internet: **http://www.ed.gov/prog_info/sfa/studentguide**

College is Possible—a resource guide prepared by the Coalition of America's Colleges and Universities and the U.S. Department of Education—lists books, pamphlets, and Internet sites to help students prepare for, choose, and pay for college. It includes information on scholarships and is available in English and Spanish.

☛ Phone: (800) 433-3243. Internet: **http://www.collegeispossible.org**

The Armed Forces have several educational assistance programs. These include the Reserve Officers' Training Corps (ROTC), the new G.I. bill, and tuition assistance. Information can be obtained from military recruiting centers, located in most cities.

☛ Internet: **http://www.defenselink.mil/other_info/careers.html**

State and local information

The *Handbook* provides information for the Nation as a whole. State or local area information is available from:

State employment security agencies. These agencies develop detailed information about local labor markets, such as current and projected employment by occupation and industry, characteristics of the work force, and changes in State and local area economic activity. Listed below are addresses and telephone numbers of the directors of research and analysis in these agencies and, in most cases, Internet addresses of these agencies.

Most States have career information delivery systems (CIDS). Look for these systems in secondary schools, postsecondary institutions, libraries, job training sites, vocational rehabilitation centers, and employment service offices. The public can use the systems' computers, printed material, microfiche, and toll-free hotlines to obtain information on occupations, educational opportunities, student financial aid, apprenticeships, and military careers. Ask counselors for specific locations.

State occupational projections are also available on the Internet: **http://www.dws.state.ut.us/bls**

Alabama
Chief, Labor Market Information, Alabama Department of Industrial Relations, 649 Monroe St., Room 422, Montgomery, AL 36130. Phone: (334) 242-8800. Internet: **http://www.dir.state.al.us/lmi**

Alaska
Chief, Research and Analysis, Alaska Department of Labor, P.O. Box 25501, Juneau, AK 99802-5501. Phone: (907) 465-4500.
Internet: **http://www.labor.state.ak.us**

Arizona
Research Administrator, Arizona Department of Economic Security, P.O. Box 6123, Site Code 733A, Phoenix, AZ 85005. Phone: (602) 542-3871.
Internet: **http://www.de.state.az.us/links/economic/webpage/page6.html**

Arkansas
Labor Market Information Director, Arkansas Employment Security Department, P.O. Box 2981, Little Rock, AR 72203-2981. Phone: (501)682-3159. Internet: **http://www.state.ar.us/esd**

California
Chief, Labor Market Information Division, California Employment Development Department, P.O. Box 826880, MIC 57, Sacramento, CA 94280-0001. Phone: (916) 262-2160. Internet: **http://www.calmis.cahwnet.gov**

Colorado
Director, Labor Market Information, Colorado Department of Labor and Employment, 1515 Arapahoe St., Tower 2, Suite 400, Denver, CO 80202-2117. Phone: (303) 620-4977. Internet: **http://lmi.cdle.state.co.us**

Connecticut
Director, Office of Research and Information, Connecticut Labor Department, 200 Folly Brook Blvd., Wethersfield, CT 06109-1114. Phone: (860) 263-6255. Internet: **http://www.ctdol.state.ct.us/lmi/index.htm**

Delaware
Labor Market Information Director, Delaware Department of Labor, 4425 N. Market St., Wilmington, DE 19802. Phone: (302) 761-8060.
Internet: **http://www.oolmi.net**

District of Columbia
Chief of Labor Market Information, District of Columbia Department of Employment Services, 500 C St. NW., Room 201, Washington, DC 20001. Phone: (202) 724-7214.

Florida
Chief, Bureau of Labor Market and Performance Information, Florida Department of Labor and Employment Security, 2012 Capitol Circle SE., Hartman Bldg., Suite 200, Tallahassee, FL 32399-2151. Phone: (850) 488-1048. Internet: **http://lmi.floridajobs.org**

Georgia
Director, Labor Market Information, Georgia Department of Labor, 148 International Boulevard NE., Atlanta, GA 30303-1751. Phone: (404) 656-3177. Internet: **http://www.dol.state.ga.us/lmi**

Guam
Administrator, Department of Labor, Guam Employment Services, P.O. Box 9970, Tamuning, Guam 96931. Phone: (671) 475-0111. Internet: **http://gu.jobsearch.org**

Hawaii
Chief, Research and Statistics Office, Hawaii Department of Labor and Industrial Relations, 830 Punchbowl St., Room 304, Honolulu, HI 96813. Phone: (808) 586-8999. Internet: **http://dlir.state.hi.us**

Idaho
Bureau Chief, Research and Analysis, Idaho Department of Labor, 317 Main St., Boise, ID 83735-0001. Phone: (208) 334-6170. Internet: **http://www.sde.state.id.us/cis**

Illinois
Economic Information and Analysis Manager, Illinois Department of Employment Security, 401 South State St., Suite 743, Chicago, IL 60605. Phone: (312) 793-2316. Internet: **http://www.ioicc.state.il.us/LMI/default.htm**

Indiana
Director, Labor Market Information, Indiana Department of Workforce Development, Indiana Government Center, South , E211, 10 North Senate Ave., Indianapolis, IN 46204-2277. Phone: (317) 232-7460. Internet: **http://www.dwd.state.in.us**

Iowa
Division Administrator, Research and Information Services, Iowa Workforce Development, 1000 East Grand Ave., Des Moines, IA 50319-0209. Phone: (515) 281-6647. Internet: **http://www.state.ia.us/iwd**

Kansas
Chief, Kansas Department of Human Resources, 401 SW Topeka Blvd., Topeka, KS 66603-3182. Phone: (785) 296-5058. Internet: **http://entkdhr.ink.org/cgi-dir/newjob.cgi**

Kentucky
Manager, LMI Branch, Division of Administration/Financial Mngt, Kentucky Department of Employment Services, 275 East Main St., Suite 2-C, Frankfort, KY 40621. Phone: (502) 564-7976. Internet: **http://www.des.state.ky.us/agencies/wforce/des/lmi/lmi.htm**

Louisiana
Director, Research and Statistics Division, Louisiana Department of Labor, P.O. Box 94094, Baton Rouge, LA 70804-9094. Phone: (225) 342-3140. Internet: **http://www.ldol.state.la.us/lmipage.htm**

Maine
Director, Labor Market Information Services, Maine Department of Labor, 20 Union St., Augusta, ME 04330. Phone: (207) 287-2271. Internet: **http://www.state.me.us/labor/lmis/frdef.htm**

Maryland
Director, Office of Labor Market Analysis and Information, Maryland Department of Labor, Licensing and Regulations, 1100 North Eutaw St., Room 601, Baltimore, MD 21201. Phone: (410) 767-2250. Internet: **http://www.dllr.state.md.us/lmi/index.htm**

Massachusetts
Labor Market Information and Research Director, Massachusetts Division of Employment and Training, 19 Staniford St., 5th Floor, Boston, MA 02114. Phone: (617) 626-6560. Internet: **http://www.detma.org/lmiinfo.htmb**

Michigan
Director, Office of Labor Market Information, Michigan Jobs Commission, Employment Service Agency, 7310 Woodward Ave., Room 520, Detroit, MI 48202. Phone: (313) 872-5904. Internet: **http://www.michlmi.org**

Minnesota
Director, BLS Programs, Research and Statistical Office, Minnesota Department of Economic Security, 390 North Robert St., St. Paul, MN 55104. Phone: (612) 296-4087. Internet: **http://www.des.state.mn.us/lmi/careers**

Mississippi
Labor Market Information Director, Mississippi Employment Security Commission, P.O. Box 1699, Jackson, MS 39215-1699. Phone: (601) 961-7424. Internet: **http://208.137.131.31/lmi/index.html**

Missouri
Chief Administrator, Research and Analysis, Missouri Department of Labor and Industrial Relations, 421 East Dunkin St., P.O. Box 59, Jefferson City, MO 65104-0059. Phone: (573) 751-3637. Internet: **http://www.works.state.mo.us/lmi**

Montana
Director, Office of Research and Analysis, Montana Department of Labor and Industry, P.O. Box 1728, Helena, MT 59624-1728. Phone: (406) 444-2430; within Montana at (800) 633-0229; outside Montana at (800) 541-3904. Internet: **http://rad.dli.state.mt.us**

Nebraska
Labor Market Information Administrator, Nebraska Department of Labor, 550 South 16th St., Lincoln, NE 68509-4600. Phone: (402) 471-9964. Internet: **http://www.dol.state.ne.us/nelmi.htm**

Nevada
Chief, DETR, Bureau of Research and Analysis, Information Development and Processing Division, 500 East Third St., Carson City, NV 89713-0001. Phone: (775) 687-4550, ext. 228. Internet: **http://www.state.nv.us/detr/lmi/index.htm**

New Hampshire
Director, Economic and Labor Market Information Bureau, New Hampshire Department of Employment Security, 32 South Main St., Concord, NH 03301. Phone: (603) 228-4123. Internet: **http://www.nhworks.state.nh.us/LMIpage.htm**

New Jersey
Assistant Commissioner, Labor Planning and Analysis, New Jersey Department of Labor, P.O. Box 56, 5th Floor, Trenton, NJ 08625-0056. Phone: (609) 292-2643. Internet: **http://www.state.nj.us/labor/lra/**

New Mexico
Chief, Economic Research and Analysis Bureau, New Mexico Department of Labor, 401 Broadway Blvd. NE, P.O. Box 1928, Albuquerque, NM 87103. Phone: (505) 841-8645. Internet: **http://www3.state.nm.us/dol/dol_lmif.html**

New York
Director, Division of Research and Statistics, New York Department of Labor, State Office Building Campus, Room 400, Albany, NY 12240. Phone: (518) 457-6369. Internet: **http://www.labor.state.ny.us/html/atool/lmiatool.htm**

North Carolina
Director, Labor Market Information, North Carolina Employment Security Commission, P.O. Box 25903, Raleigh, NC 27611. Phone: (919) 733-2936. Internet: **http://www.esc.state.nc.us**

North Dakota
Program Support Area Manager, North Dakota Job Service, 1000 East Divide Ave., P.O. Box 5507, Bismarck, ND 58506-5507. Phone: (701) 328-2868. Internet: **http://www.state.nd.us/jsnd/lmi.htm**

Ohio
Director, Ohio Bureau of Employment Services, Labor Market Information Division, 145 South Front St., P.O. Box 1618, Columbus, OH 43216-1618. Phone: (614) 752-9494. Internet: **http://lmi.state.oh.us**

Oklahoma
Director, Labor Market Information, Oklahoma Employment Security Commission, 2401 North Lincoln, Will Rogers Memorial Office Bldg., Oklahoma City, OK 73105. Phone: (405) 525-7265.
Internet: **http://www.oesc.state.ok.us/lmi/default.htm**

Oregon
Labor Market Information Director, Oregon Employment Department, 875 Union St. NE., Salem, OR 97311. Phone: (503) 947-1212.
Internet: **http://olmis.emp.state.or.us**

Pennsylvania
Director, Bureau of Research and Statistics, Pennsylvania Department of Labor and Industry, 7th and Forester Streets, Room 101, Harrisburg, PA 17120-0001. Phone: (717) 787-3266. Internet: **http://www.lmi.state.pa.us**

Puerto Rico
Director, Research and Statistics Division, Puerto Rico Bureau of Employment Security, 505 Munoz Rivera Ave., 20th Floor, Hato Rey, PR 00918. Phone: (787) 754-5385.

Rhode Island
Director, Labor Market Information, Rhode Island Department of Employment and Training, 101 Friendship St., Providence, RI 02903-3740. Phone: (401) 222-3730.
Internet: **http://www.det.state.ri.us/webdev/lmi/rioicchm.html**

South Carolina
Director, Labor Market Information, South Carolina Employment Security Commission, 610 Hampton St., P.O. Box 995, Columbia, SC 29202. Phone: (803) 737-2660. Internet: **http://www.sces.org/lmi/index.htm**

South Dakota
Director, Labor Market Center, South Dakota Department of Labor, P.O. Box 4730, Aberdeen, SD 57402-4730. Phone: (605) 626-2314.
Internet: **http://www.state.sd.us/dol/lmic/index.htm**

Tennessee
Director, Research and Statistics Division, Tennessee Department of Employment Security, 500 James Robertson Pkwy., Davy Crockett Tower, 11th Floor, Nashville, TN 37245-1000. Phone: (615) 741-2284.
Internet: **http://www.state.tn.us/empsec/lmi.htm**

Texas
Director of Labor Market Information, Texas Workforce Commission, 9001 North IH-35, Suite 103A, Austin, TX 78778. Phone: (512) 491-4802. Internet: **http://www.twc.state.tx.us/lmi/lmi.html**

Utah
Director, Labor Market Information, Utah Department of Workforce Services, 140 East 300 South, P.O. Box 45249, Salt Lake City, UT 84145-0249. Phone: (801) 526-9401. Internet: **http://www.dws.state.ut.us**

Vermont
Chief, Research and Analysis, Vermont Department of Employment and Training, 5 Green Mountain Dr., P.O. Box 488, Montpelier, VT 05601-0488. Phone: (802) 828-4153. Internet: **http://www.det.state.vt.us**

Virgin Islands
Chief, Bureau of Labor Statistics, Virgin Islands Department of Labor, 53A and 54B Kronprindsens Gade, Charlotte Amalie, St. Thomas, VI 00820. Phone: (340) 776-3700.

Virginia
Director, Economic Information and Services Division, Virginia Employment Commission, 703 East Main St., P.O. Box 1358, Richmond, VA 23218-1358. Phone: (804) 786-7496.
Internet: **http://www.vec.state.va.us/lbrmkt/lmi.htm**

Washington
Director, Labor Market and Economic Analysis, Employment Security Division, Mail Stop 6000—P.O. Box 9046, Olympia, WA 98507-9046. Phone: (360) 438-4804. Internet: **http://www.wa.gov/esd/lmea**

West Virginia
Director, Research, Information and Analysis, West Virginia Bureau of Employment Programs, 112 California Ave., Charleston, WV 25305-0112. Phone: (304) 558-2660.
Internet: **http://www.state.wv.us/bep/lmi/default.htm**

Wisconsin
Chief, LMI Data Development, Wisconsin Department of Workforce Development, 201 East Washington Ave., Room 2214, Madison, WI 53702. Phone: (608) 266-2930. Internet: **http://www.dwd.state.si.us/dwelmi**

Wyoming
Manager, Research and Planning, Division of Administration, Wyoming Department of Employment, P.O. Box 2760, Casper, WY 82602-2760. Phone: (307) 473-3801. Internet: **http://wydoe.state.wy.us**

Finding a Job and Evaluating a Job Offer

Finding Information on Job Availability

It takes some people a great deal of time and effort to find a job they enjoy. Others may walk right into an ideal employment situation. Do not be discouraged if you have to pursue many leads. Friends, neighbors, teachers, and counselors may know of available jobs in your field of interest. Read the classified ads. Consult State employment service offices and consider private employment agencies. You may also contact employers directly.

Where To Learn About Job Openings

Personal contacts
College career planning and placement offices
Classified ads
—National and local newspapers
—Professional journals
—Trade magazines
Internet networks and resources
State employment service offices
Federal Government
Professional associations
Labor unions
Employers
Employment agencies and career consultants
Community agencies

Job Search Methods

Personal contacts. Your family, friends, and acquaintances may offer one of the most effective ways to find a job. They may help you directly or put you in touch with someone else who can. Such networking can lead to information about specific job openings.

College career planning and placement offices. College placement offices help their students and alumni find jobs. They set up appointments and allow recruiters to use their facilities for interviews. Placement offices usually have a list of part-time, temporary, and summer jobs offered on campus. They may also have lists of jobs for regional, nonprofit, and government organizations. Students can receive career counseling and testing and job search advice. At career resource libraries they may attend workshops on such topics as job search strategy, resume writing, letter writing, and effective interviewing; critique drafts of resumes and watch videotapes of mock interviews; explore files of resumes and references; and attend job fairs conducted by the placement office.

Classified ads. The "Help Wanted" ads in newspapers list numerous jobs. You should realize, however, that many other job openings are not listed, and that the classified ads sometimes do not give all of the important information. They may offer little or no description of the job, working conditions, or pay. Some ads do not identify the employer. They may simply give a post office box to mail your resume to, making follow-up inquiries very difficult. Some ads offer out-of-town jobs; others advertise employment agencies rather than actual employment opportunities.

When using classified ads, keep the following in mind:

- Do not rely solely on the classifieds to find a job; follow other leads as well.
- Answer ads promptly, because openings may be filled quickly, even before the ad stops appearing in the paper.
- Read the ads every day, particularly the Sunday edition, which usually includes the most listings.
- Beware of "no experience necessary" ads. These ads often signal low wages, poor working conditions, or commission work.
- Keep a record of all ads to which you have responded, including the specific skills, educational background, and personal qualifications required for the position.

Internet networks and resources. The Internet, which is available 7 days a week, 24 hours a day, provides a variety of information, including job listings and job search resources and techniques. However, no single network or resource will contain all of the information available on employment or career opportunities, so be prepared to search for what you need. Remember that job listings may be posted by field or discipline, so begin your search using keywords.

When searching employment databases on the Internet, it is sometimes possible to send your resume to an employer by e-mail or to post it on-line. Some sources allow you to send e-mail free of charge, but be careful that you are not going to incur any additional charges for postings or updates.

State employment service offices. The State employment service, sometimes called Job Service, operates in coordination with the U.S. Department of Labor's Employment Service. Local offices, found nationwide, help jobseekers find jobs and help employers find qualified workers at no cost to either. To find the office nearest you, look in the State government telephone listings under "Job Service" or "Employment."

Job matching and referral. At the State employment service office, an interviewer will determine if you are "job ready" or if you need help from counseling and testing services to assess your occupational aptitudes and interests and to help you choose and prepare for a career. After you are "job ready," you may examine available job listings and select openings that interest you. A staff member can then describe the job openings in detail and arrange for interviews with prospective employers.

America's Job Bank, run by the U.S. Department of Labor's Employment and Training Administration, provides: Information on preparing your resume and using the Internet for your job search; trends in the U.S. job market; State occupational projections; and a list of approximately 1 million job openings. The list contains a wide range of mostly full-time private sector jobs that are available all over the country. Jobseekers can access this list on the Internet at: **http://www.ajb.dni.us**. Computers with access to the Internet are available to the public in any local public employment service office, as well as in schools, libraries, and military installations.

Tips for Finding the Right Job, a U.S. Department of Labor pamphlet, offers advice on determining your job skills, organizing your job search, writing a resume, and making the most of an interview. *Job Search Guide: Strategies For Professionals*, another U.S. Department of Labor publication, discusses specific steps that jobseekers can follow to identify employment opportunities. This publication includes sections on handling job loss, managing personal resources, assessing personal skills and interests, researching the job market, conducting the job search, and networking. Check with your State employment service office, or order a copy of these and other publications from the U.S. Government Printing Office's Superintendent of Documents by telephone: (202) 512-1800 or via the Internet at: **http://www.gpo.gov** or at: **http://www.dol.gov**

Services for special groups. By law, veterans are entitled to priority for job placement at State employment service centers. If you are a veteran, a veterans' employment representative can inform you of available assistance and help you deal with problems.

State service centers refer youths between 16 and 21 and economically disadvantaged applicants to opportunities available under the Job Training Partnership Act (JTPA) of 1982. They also help prepare individuals facing employment barriers for jobs.

Federal Government. Information on Federal Government jobs is available from the Office of Personnel Management through a telephone-based system. Consult your telephone directory under U.S. Government for a local number or call (912) 757-3100; TDD (912) 744-2299. Information also is available on the Internet at: **http://www.usajobs.opm.gov**

Professional associations. Many professions have associations that offer employment information, including career planning, educational programs, job listings, and job placement. To use these services, associations usually require that you be a member of their association; information can be obtained directly from an association through the Internet, by telephone, or by mail.

Labor unions. Labor unions provide various employment services to members, including apprenticeship programs that teach a specific trade or skill. Contact the appropriate labor union or State apprenticeship council for more information.

Employers. It is possible to apply directly to employers without a referral. You may locate a potential employer in the *Yellow Pages*, in local chambers of commerce directories, and in other directories that provide information about employers. When you find an employer that interests you, send a cover letter and resume even if you are not certain that an opening exists.

Private employment agencies and career consultants. These agencies can be helpful, but they are in business to make money. Most operate on a commission basis, with the fee dependent upon a percentage of the salary paid to a successful applicant. You or the hiring company will pay a fee. Find out the exact cost and who is responsible for paying associated fees before using the service.

Although employment agencies can help you save time and contact employers who otherwise might be difficult to locate, the costs may outweigh the benefits if you are responsible for the fee. Consider any guarantees the agency offers when determining if the service is worth the cost.

Community agencies. Many nonprofit organizations, including religious institutions and vocational rehabilitation agencies, offer counseling, career development, and job placement services, generally targeted to a particular group, such as women, youth, minorities, ex-offenders, or older workers.

Applying for a Job

Resumes and application forms. Resumes and application forms are two ways to provide employers with written evidence of your qualifications and skills. Generally, the same information appears on both the resume and the application form, but the way it is presented differs. Some employers prefer a resume and others require an application form. The accompanying box presents the basic information you should include in your resume.

There are many ways of organizing a resume. Depending on the job, you should choose the format that best highlights your skills, training, and experience. It may be helpful to look in a variety of books and publications at your local library or bookstore for different examples.

What Usually Goes Into a Resume

- Name, address, and telephone number.
- Employment objective. State the type of work or specific job you are seeking.
- Education, including school name and address, dates of attendance, curriculum, and highest grade completed or degree awarded.
- Experience, paid and volunteer. Include the following for each job: Job title, name and location of employer, and dates of employment. Briefly describe your job duties.
- Special skills, proficiency in foreign languages, achievements, and membership in organizations.
- References, when requested.

When you fill out an application form, make sure you fill it out completely and follow all instructions. Do not omit any requested information and make sure that the information you provide is correct.

Cover letters. A cover letter is sent with a resume or application form, as a way of introducing yourself to perspective employers. It should capture the employer's attention, follow a business letter format, and should usually include the following information:

- The name and address of the specific person to whom the letter is addressed.
- The reason for your interest in the company or position.
- Your main qualifications for the position (in brief).
- A request for an interview.
- Your home and work phone numbers.

Interviewing. An interview gives you the opportunity to showcase your qualifications to an employer, so it pays to be well prepared. The information in the accompanying box provides some helpful hints.

Job Interview Tips

Preparation:
Learn about the organization.
Have a specific job or jobs in mind.
Review your qualifications for the job.
Prepare answers to broad questions about yourself.
Review your resume.
Practice an interview with a friend or relative.
Arrive before the scheduled time of your interview.

Personal Appearance:
Be well groomed.
Dress appropriately.
Do not chew gum or smoke.

The Interview:
Relax and answer each question concisely.
Respond promptly.
Use good manners. Learn the name of your interviewer and shake hands as you meet.
Use proper English—avoid slang.
Be cooperative and enthusiastic.
Ask questions about the position and the organization.
Thank the interviewer when you leave and, as a follow up, in writing.

Test (if employer gives one):
Listen closely to instructions.
Read each question carefully.
Write legibly and clearly.
Budget your time wisely and don't dwell on one question

Information to Bring to an Interview:
Social Security number.
Driver's license number.
Resume. Although not all employers require applicants to bring a resume, you should be able to furnish the interviewer information about your education, training, and previous employment.
References. An employer usually requires three references. Get permission before using anyone as a reference. Make sure they will give you a good reference. Try to avoid using relatives.

Evaluating a Job Offer

Once you receive a job offer, you are faced with a difficult decision and must evaluate the offer carefully. Fortunately, most organizations will not expect you to accept or reject an offer immediately.

There are many issues to consider when assessing a job offer. Will the organization be a good place to work? Will the job be interesting? Are there opportunities for advancement? Is the salary fair? Does the employer offer good benefits? If you have not already figured out exactly what you want, the following discussion may help you develop a set of criteria for judging job offers, whether you are starting a career, reentering the labor force after a long absence, or planning a career change.

The organization. Background information on an organization can help you decide whether it is a good place for you to work. Factors to consider include the organization's business or activity, financial condition, age, size, and location.

You can generally get background information on an organization, particularly a large organization, by telephoning its public relations office. A public company's annual report to the stockholders tells about its corporate philosophy, history, products or services, goals, and financial status. Most government agencies can furnish reports that describe their programs and missions. Press releases, company newsletters or magazines, and recruitment brochures also can be useful. Ask the organization for any other items that might interest a prospective employee.

If possible, speak to current or former employees of the organization. Background information on the organization may be available on the Internet or at your public or school library. If you cannot get an annual report, check the library for reference directories that may provide basic facts about the company, such as earnings, products and services, and number of employees. Some directories widely available in libraries include:

- *Dun & Bradstreet's Million Dollar Directory*
- *Standard and Poor's Register of Corporations*
- *Moody's Industrial Manual*
- *Thomas' Register of American Manufacturers*
- *Ward's Business Directory*

Stories about an organization in magazines and newspapers can tell a great deal about its successes, failures, and plans for the future. You can identify articles on a company by looking under its name in periodical or computerized indexes in libraries. However, it probably will not be useful to look back more than 2 or 3 years.

The library also may have government publications that present projections of growth for the industry in which the organization is classified. Long-term projections of employment and output for more than 200 industries, covering the entire economy, are developed by the Bureau of Labor Statistics and revised every two years—see the November 1999 *Monthly Labor Review* for the most recent projections. The *U.S. Industry and Trade Outlook*, published annually by the U.S. Department of Commerce, presents detailed analyses of the globalization of U.S. industry and growth prospects for some industrial sectors. Trade magazines also have periodic articles on the trends for specific industries.

Career centers at colleges and universities often have information on employers that is not available in libraries. Ask a career center representative how to find out about a particular organization.

Does the organization's business or activity match your own interests and beliefs?
It is easier to apply yourself to the work if you are enthusiastic about what the organization does.

How will the size of the organization affect you?
Large firms generally offer a greater variety of training programs and career paths, more managerial levels for advancement, and better employee benefits than small firms. Large employers may also have more advanced technologies. However, jobs in large firms may tend to be highly specialized.

Jobs in small firms may offer broader authority and responsibility, a closer working relationship with top management, and a chance to clearly see your contribution to the success of the organization.

Should you work for a relatively new organization or one that is well established?
New businesses have a high failure rate, but for many people, the excitement of helping create a company and the potential for sharing in its success more than offset the risk of job loss. However, it may be just as exciting and rewarding to work for a young firm that already has a foothold on success.

Does it make a difference if the company is private or public?
An individual or a family may control a privately owned company and key jobs may be reserved for relatives and friends. A board of directors responsible to the stockholders controls a publicly owned company and key jobs are usually open to anyone.

Is the organization in an industry with favorable long-term prospects?
The most successful firms tend to be in industries that are growing rapidly.

Nature of the job. Even if everything else about the job is attractive, you will be unhappy if you dislike the day-to-day work. Determining in advance whether you will like the work may be difficult. However, the more you find out about the job before accepting or rejecting the offer, the more likely you are to make the right choice. Actually working in the industry and, if possible, for the company would provide considerable insight. You can gain work experience through part-time, temporary, or summer jobs, or through internship or work-study programs while in school, all of which can lead to permanent job offers.

Where is the job located?
If the job is in another section of the country, you need to consider the cost of living, the availability of housing and transportation, and the quality of educational and recreational facilities in that section of the country. Even if the job location is in your area, you should consider the time and expense of commuting.

Does the work match your interests and make good use of your skills?
The duties and responsibilities of the job should be explained in enough detail to answer this question.

How important is the job in this company?
An explanation of where you fit in the organization and how you are supposed to contribute to its overall objectives should give you an idea of the job's importance.

Are you comfortable with the hours?
Most jobs involve regular hours—for example, 40 hours a week, during the day, Monday through Friday. Other jobs require night, weekend, or holiday work. In addition, some jobs routinely require overtime to meet deadlines or sales or production goals, or to better serve customers. Consider the effect the work hours will have on your personal life.

How long do most people who enter this job stay with the company?
High turnover can mean dissatisfaction with the nature of the work or something else about the job.

Opportunities offered by employers. A good job offers you opportunities to learn new skills, increase your earnings, and rise to positions of greater authority, responsibility, and prestige. A lack of opportunities can dampen interest in the work and result in frustration and boredom.

The company should have a training plan for you. What valuable new skills does the company plan to teach you?

The employer should give you some idea of promotion possibilities within the organization. What is the next step on the career ladder? If you have to wait for a job to become vacant before you can be promoted, how long does this usually take? When opportunities for advancement do arise, will you compete with applicants from outside the company? Can you apply for jobs for which you qualify elsewhere within the organization, or is mobility within the firm limited?

Salaries and benefits. Wait for the employer to introduce these subjects. Some companies will not talk about pay until they have decided to hire you. In order to know if their offer is reasonable, you need a rough estimate of what the job should pay. You may have to go to several sources for this information. Try to find family, friends, or acquaintances who recently were hired in similar jobs. Ask your teachers and the staff in placement offices about starting pay for graduates with your qualifications. Help-wanted ads in newspapers sometimes give salary ranges for similar positions. Check the library or your school's career center for salary surveys such as those conducted by the National Association of Colleges and Employers or various professional associations.

If you are considering the salary and benefits for a job in another geographic area, make allowances for differences in the cost of living, which may be significantly higher in a large metropolitan area than in a smaller city, town, or rural area.

You also should learn the organization's policy regarding overtime. Depending on the job, you may or may not be exempt from laws requiring the employer to compensate you for overtime. Find out how many hours you will be expected to work each week and whether you receive overtime pay or compensatory time off for working more than the specified number of hours in a week.

Also take into account that the starting salary is just that—the start. Your salary should be reviewed on a regular basis; many organizations do it every year. How much can you expect to earn after 1, 2, or 3 or more years? An employer cannot be specific about the amount of pay if it includes commissions and bonuses.

Benefits can also add a lot to your base pay, but they vary widely. Find out exactly what the benefit package includes and how much of the costs you must bear.

National, State, and metropolitan area data from the National Compensation Survey, which integrates data from three existing Bureau of Labor Statistics programs—the Employment Cost Index, the Occupational Compensation Survey, and the Employee Benefits Survey—are available from:

☛ Bureau of Labor Statistics, Office of Compensation and Working Conditions, 2 Massachusetts Ave. NE., Room 4130, Washington, DC 20212-0001. Telephone: (202) 691-6199.
Internet: **http://stats.bls.gov/comhome.htm**

Data on earnings by detailed occupation from the Occupational Employment Statistics (OES) Survey are available from:

☛ Bureau of Labor Statistics, Office of Employment and Unemployment Statistics, Occupational Employment Statistics, 2 Massachusetts Ave. NE., Room 4840, Washington, DC 20212-0001. Telephone: (202) 691-6569.
Internet: **http://stats.bls.gov/oeshome.htm**

Occupational Information Included in the *Handbook*

The *Occupational Outlook Handbook* is best used as a reference; it is not meant to be read from cover to cover. Instead, start by looking at the table of contents, where related occupations are grouped in clusters, or look in the alphabetical index in the back of the *Handbook* for specific occupations that interest you. For any occupation that sounds interesting, use the *Handbook* to learn about the type of work; education and training requirements and advancement possibilities; earnings; job outlook; and related occupations. Each occupational statement, or description, in the *Handbook* follows a standard format, making it easier for you to compare occupations.

Two previous sections—Tomorrow's Jobs and Sources of Career Information—highlight the forces that are likely to determine employment opportunities in industries and occupations through the year 2008, and indicate where to obtain additional information. This section is an overview of how the occupational statements are organized. It highlights information presented in each section of a *Handbook* statement, gives examples of specific occupations in some cases, and offers some hints on how to interpret the information provided.

Unless otherwise noted, the source of employment and earnings data presented in the *Handbook* is the Bureau of Labor Statistics. Many *Handbook* statements cite earnings data from the Occupational Employment Statistics (OES) survey, while other statements include earnings data from outside sources. OES data may be used to compare earnings among occupations; however, outside data may not be used in this manner because characteristics of these data vary widely.

About those numbers at the beginning of each statement

The numbers in parentheses that appear just below the title of most occupational statements are from the Occupational Information Network (O*NET), which has replaced the Dictionary of Occupational Titles (D.O.T.). Like the D.O.T. in the past, the O*NET is used by State employment service offices to classify applicants and job openings, and by some career information centers and libraries to file occupational information.

An index beginning on page 530 cross-references O*NET codes to occupations covered in the *Handbook*. The O*NET is also cross-referenced to the revised 1998 Standard Occupational Classification (SOC). All Federal Government agencies that collect occupational data are expected to adopt the new SOC over the next few years.

Significant Points

This section highlights key occupational characteristics.

Nature of the Work

This section discusses what workers do. Individual job duties may vary by industry or employer. For instance, workers in larger firms tend to be more specialized whereas those in smaller firms often have a wider variety of duties. Most occupations have several levels of skills and responsibilities through which workers may progress. Beginners may start as trainees performing routine tasks under close supervision. Experienced workers usually undertake more difficult tasks and are expected to perform with less supervision.

The influence of technological advancements on the way work is done is mentioned. For example, the Internet allows purchasers to acquire supplies with a click of the mouse, saving time and money. This section of *Handbook* statements also discusses emerging specialties. For instance, sales engineers—who combine the education of an engineer with the challenge of sales—comprise a specialty within manufacturers' and wholesale sales representatives.

Working Conditions

This section identifies the typical hours worked, the workplace environment, susceptibility to injury, special equipment, and physical activities and the extent of travel required. In many occupations people work regular business hours—40 hours a week, Monday through Friday—but many do not. For example, waiters and waitresses often work evenings and weekends.

The work setting can range from a hospital, to a mall, to an off-shore oil rig. Truckdrivers might be susceptible to injury, while paramedics have high job-related stress. Electronic semiconductor processors may wear protective clothing or equipment, some construction craft laborers do physically demanding work, and top executives may travel frequently.

Employment

This section reports the number of jobs the occupation provided in 1998 and the key industries where these jobs are found. When significant, the geographic distribution of jobs and the proportion of part-time (less than 35 hours a week) and self-employed workers in the occupation are mentioned. Self-employed workers accounted for nearly 9 percent of the workforce in 1998; however, they were concentrated in a small number of occupations, such as lawyers, health practitioners, and construction craft workers.

Training, Other Qualifications, and Advancement

After knowing what a job is all about, it is important to understand how to train for it. This section describes the most significant sources of training, including the training preferred by employers, the typical length of training, and advancement possibilities. Job skills are sometimes acquired through high school, informal on-the-job training, formal training (including apprenticeships), the Armed Forces, home study, hobbies, or previous work experience. For example, sales experience is particularly important for many sales jobs. Many professional and technical jobs, on the other hand, require formal postsecondary education—

Key phrases in the *Handbook*

This box explains how to interpret the key phrases used to describe projected changes in employment. It also explains the terms used to describe the relationship between the number of job openings and the number of jobseekers. The descriptions of this relationship in a particular occupation reflects the knowledge and judgment of economists in the Bureau's Office of Employment Projections.

Changing employment between 1998 and 2008

If the statement reads:	Employment is projected to:
Grow much faster than average	increase 36 percent or more
Grow faster than average	increase 21 to 35 percent
Grow about as fast as average	increase 10 to 20 percent
Grow more slowly than average, or little or no change	increase 0 to 9 percent
Decline	decrease 1 percent or more

Opportunities and competition for jobs

If the statement reads:	Job openings compared to jobseekers may be:
Very good to excellent opportunities	More numerous
Good or favorable opportunities	In rough balance
May face keen competition or can expect keen competition	Fewer

postsecondary vocational or technical training, or college, postgraduate, or professional education.

In addition to training requirements, the *Handbook* also mentions desirable skills, aptitudes, and personal characteristics. For some entry-level jobs, personal characteristics are more important than formal training. Employers generally seek people who read, write, and speak well; compute accurately; think logically; learn quickly; get along with others; and demonstrate dependability.

Some occupations require certification or licensing to enter the field, to advance, or to practice independently. Certification or licensing generally involves completing courses and passing examinations. Many occupations increasingly have continuing education or skill improvement requirements to keep up with the changing economy or to improve advancement opportunities.

Job Outlook

In planning for the future, it is important to consider potential job opportunities. This section describes the factors that will result in growth or decline in the number of jobs. In some cases, the *Handbook* mentions the relative number of job openings an occupation is likely to provide. Occupations which are large and have high turnover rates, such as food and beverage service occupations, generally provide the most job openings—reflecting the need to replace workers who transfer to other occupations or stop working.

Some *Handbook* statements discuss the relationship between the number of jobseekers and job openings. In some occupations, there is a rough balance between jobseekers and openings, whereas other occupations are characterized by shortages or surpluses. Limited training facilities, salary regulations, or undesirable aspects of the work—as in the case of private household workers—can cause shortages of entrants. On the other hand, glamorous or potentially high paying occupations, such as actors or musicians, generally have surpluses of jobseekers. Variation in job opportunities by industry, size of firm, or geographic location also may be discussed. Even in crowded fields, job openings do exist. Good students or well-qualified individuals should not be deterred from undertaking training or seeking entry.

Susceptibility to layoffs due to imports, slowdowns in economic activity, technological advancements, or budget cuts are also addressed in this section. For example, employment of construction craft workers is sensitive to slowdowns in construction activity, while employment of government workers is sensitive to budget cuts.

Earnings

This section discusses typical earnings and how workers are compensated—annual salaries, hourly wages, commissions, piece rates, tips, or bonuses. Within every occupation, earnings vary by experience, responsibility, performance, tenure, and geographic area. Earnings data from the Bureau of Labor Statistics and, in some cases, from outside sources are included. Data may cover the entire occupation or a specific group within the occupation.

Benefits account for more than a quarter of total compensation costs to employers. Benefits such as paid vacation, health insurance, and sick leave generally are not mentioned because thay are so widespread. Less common benefits include child care, tuition for dependents, housing assistance, summers off, and free or discounted merchandise or services. Though not as common as traditional benefits such as paid vacation, employers increasingly offer flexible hours and profit sharing plans to attract and retain highly qualified workers.

Related Occupations

Occupations involving similar aptitudes, interests, education, and training are listed.

Sources of Additional Information

No single publication can completely describe all aspects of an occupation. Thus, the *Handbook* lists mailing addresses for associations, government agencies, unions, and other organizations that can provide occupational information. In some cases, tollfree phone numbers and Internet addresses also are listed. Free or relatively inexpensive publications offering more information may be mentioned; some of these may also be available in libraries, school career centers, guidance offices, or on the Internet.

For additional sources of information, read the earlier chapter, Sources of Career Information.

Executive, Administrative, and Managerial Occupations

Accountants and Auditors

(O*NET 21114A and 21114B)

Significant Points

- Most jobs require at least a bachelor's degree in accounting or a related field.
- Jobseekers who obtain professional recognition through certification or licensure, a master's degree, proficiency in accounting and auditing computer software, or specialized expertise will have an advantage in the job market.
- Competition will remain keen for the most prestigious jobs in major accounting and business firms.

Nature of the Work

Accountants and auditors help to ensure that the Nation's firms are run more efficiently, its public records kept more accurately, and its taxes paid properly and on time. They perform these vital functions by offering an increasingly wide array of business and accounting services to their clients. Broadly, these services include public, management, and government accounting, as well as internal auditing. In each of these major fields, however, accountants and auditors continue to carry out the fundamental tasks of the occupation—prepare, analyze, and verify financial documents in order to provide information to clients.

Specific job duties vary widely in the four major fields of accounting. Public accountants perform a broad range of accounting, auditing, tax, and consulting activities for their clients, who may be corporations, governments, nonprofit organizations, or individuals. For example, some public accountants concentrate on tax matters, such as advising companies of the tax advantages and disadvantages of certain business decisions and preparing individual income tax returns. Others are consultants who offer advice in areas such as compensation or employee health care benefits; the design of accounting and data processing systems; and the selection of controls to safeguard assets. Some specialize in forensic accounting—investigating and interpreting bankruptcies and other complex financial transactions. Still others audit a client's financial statements and report to investors and authorities that they have been prepared and reported correctly. Public accountants, many of whom are Certified Public Accountants (CPAs), generally have their own businesses or work for public accounting firms.

Management accountants—also called industrial, corporate, or private accountants—record and analyze the financial information of the companies for which they work. Other responsibilities include budgeting, performance evaluation, cost management, and asset management. They are usually part of executive teams involved in strategic planning or new product development. Management accountants analyze and interpret the financial information corporate executives need to make sound business decisions. They also prepare financial reports for non-management groups, including stockholders, creditors, regulatory agencies, and tax authorities. Within accounting departments, they may work in areas including financial analysis, planning and budgeting, and cost accounting.

Many persons with an accounting background work in the public sector. Government accountants and auditors maintain and examine the records of government agencies and audit private businesses and individuals whose activities are subject to government regulations or taxation. Accountants employed by Federal, State, and local governments guarantee that revenues are received and expenditures are made in accordance with laws and regulations. Those who are employed by the Federal Government may work as Internal Revenue Service agents or in financial management, financial institution examination, or budget analysis and administration.

An increasingly important area of accounting and auditing is internal auditing. Internal auditors verify the accuracy of their organization's records and check for mismanagement, waste, or fraud. Specifically, they examine and evaluate their firms' financial and information systems, management procedures, and internal controls to ensure that records are accurate and controls are adequate to protect against fraud and waste. They also review company operations—evaluating their efficiency, effectiveness, and compliance with corporate policies and procedures, laws, and government regulations. There are many types of highly specialized auditors, such as electronic data processing, environmental, engineering, legal, insurance premium, bank, and health care auditors. As computer systems make information more timely, internal auditors help managers to base their decisions on actual data, rather than personal observation. Internal auditors may also recommend controls for their organization's computer system to ensure the reliability of the system and the integrity of the data.

Computers are rapidly changing the nature of the work for most accountants and auditors. With the aid of special software packages, accountants summarize transactions in standard formats for financial records and organize data in special formats for financial analysis. These accounting packages greatly reduce the amount of tedious manual work associated with data and recordkeeping. Personal and laptop computers enable accountants and auditors to be more mobile and to use their clients' computer systems to extract information from large mainframe computers. As a result of these trends, a growing number of accountants and auditors have extensive computer skills and specialize in correcting problems with software or developing software to meet unique data needs.

Working Conditions

Most accountants and auditors work in a typical office setting. Self-employed accountants may be able to do part of their work at home. Accountants and auditors employed by public accounting firms and

Accountants and auditors prepare, analyze, and verify financial information.

government agencies may travel frequently to perform audits at clients' places of business, branches of their firm, or government facilities.

Most accountants and auditors generally work a standard 40-hour week, but many work longer hours, particularly if they are self-employed and have numerous clients. Tax specialists often work long hours during the tax season.

Employment

Accountants and auditors held over 1,080,000 jobs in 1998. They worked throughout private industry and government, but about 1 out of 4 worked for accounting, auditing, and bookkeeping firms. Approximately 1 out of 10 accountants or auditors were self-employed.

Many accountants and auditors are unlicensed management accountants, internal auditors, or government accountants and auditors. However, a large number are licensed Certified Public Accountants, Public Accountants (PAs), Registered Public Accountants (RPAs), and Accounting Practitioners (APs). Most accountants and auditors work in urban areas, where public accounting firms and central or regional offices of businesses are concentrated.

Some individuals with backgrounds in accounting and auditing are full-time college and university faculty; others teach part time while working as self-employed accountants, or as salaried accountants for private industry or government. (See the *Handbook* statement on college and university faculty.)

Training, Other Qualifications, and Advancement

Most accountant and internal auditor positions require at least a bachelor's degree in accounting or a related field. Beginning accounting and auditing positions in the Federal Government, for example, usually require 4 years of college (including 24 semester hours in accounting or auditing) or an equivalent combination of education and experience. Some employers prefer applicants with a master's degree in accounting or a master's degree in business administration with a concentration in accounting.

Previous experience in accounting or auditing can help an applicant get a job. Many colleges offer students an opportunity to gain experience through summer or part-time internship programs conducted by public accounting or business firms. In addition, practical knowledge of computers and their applications in accounting and internal auditing is a great asset for jobseekers in the accounting field.

Professional recognition through certification or licensure provides a distinct advantage in the job market. All CPAs must have a certificate and the partners in their firm must have licenses issued by a State Board of Accountancy. The vast majority of States require CPA candidates to be college graduates, but a few States substitute a number of years of public accounting experience for the college degree. Based on recommendations made by the American Institute of Certified Public Accountants, 17 States currently require CPA candidates to complete 150 semester hours of college coursework—an additional 30 hours beyond the usual 4-year bachelor's degree. Most States have adopted similar legislation that will become effective in the future. Many schools have altered their curricula accordingly, and prospective accounting majors should carefully research accounting curricula and the requirements for any States in which they hope to become licensed.

All States use the four-part Uniform CPA Examination prepared by the American Institute of Certified Public Accountants. The 2-day CPA examination is rigorous, and only about one-quarter of those who take it each year pass every part they attempt. Candidates are not required to pass all four parts at once, but most States require candidates to pass at least two parts for partial credit and all four sections within a certain period of time. Most States also require applicants for a CPA certificate to have some accounting experience.

The designations PA or RPA are also recognized by most States, and several States continue to issue these licenses. With the growth in the number of CPA's, however, the majority of States are phasing out non-CPA designations—PA, RPA, and AP—by not issuing new licenses. Accountants who hold PA or RPA designations have legal rights, duties, and obligations similar to those of CPAs, but their qualifications for licensure are less stringent. AP designation requires less formal training and covers a more limited scope of practice than the CPA.

Nearly all States require CPAs and other public accountants to complete a certain number of hours of continuing professional education before their licenses can be renewed. The professional associations representing accountants sponsor numerous courses, seminars, group study programs, and other forms of continuing education.

Professional societies bestow other forms of credentials on a voluntary basis. Voluntary certification can attest to professional competence in a specialized field of accounting and auditing. It can also certify that a recognized level of professional competence has been achieved by accountants and auditors who acquired some skills on the job, without the formal education or public accounting work experience needed to meet the rigorous standards required to take the CPA examination.

The Institute of Management Accountants (IMA) confers the Certified Management Accountant (CMA) designation upon applicants who complete a bachelor's degree or attain a minimum score on specified graduate school entrance exams. Applicants must also pass a four-part examination, agree to meet continuing education requirements, comply with standards of professional conduct, and have worked at least 2 years in management accounting. The CMA program is administered through the Institute of Certified Management Accountants, an affiliate of the IMA.

Graduates from accredited colleges and universities who have worked for 2 years as internal auditors and have passed a four-part examination may earn the designation Certified Internal Auditor (CIA) from the Institute of Internal Auditors. Similarly, the Information Systems Audit and Control Association confers the designation Certified Information Systems Auditor (CISA) upon candidates who pass an examination and have 5 years of experience in auditing electronic data processing systems. Auditing or data processing experience and college education may be substituted for up to 3 years of work experience in this program. The Accreditation Council for Accountancy and Taxation, a satellite organization of the National Society of Public Accountants, confers three designations—Accredited in Accountancy (AA), Accredited Tax Advisor (ATA), and Accredited Tax Preparer (ATP). Candidates for the AA must pass an exam, while candidates for the ATA and ATP must complete the required coursework and pass an exam. Other organizations, such as the National Association of Certified Fraud Examiners and the Bank Administration Institute, confer specialized auditing designations. Often a practitioner will hold multiple licenses and designations. For instance, an internal auditor might be a CPA, CIA, and CISA.

Persons planning a career in accounting should have an aptitude for mathematics and be able to analyze, compare, and interpret facts and figures quickly. They must be able to clearly communicate the results of their work to clients and managers. Accountants and auditors must be good at working with people as well as with business systems and computers. Because millions of financial statement users rely on their services, accountants and auditors should have high standards of integrity.

Capable accountants and auditors may advance rapidly; those having inadequate academic preparation may be assigned routine jobs and find promotion difficult. Many graduates of junior colleges and business and correspondence schools, as well as bookkeepers and accounting clerks who meet the education and experience requirements set by their employers, can obtain junior accounting positions and advance to positions with more responsibilities by demonstrating their accounting skills on the job.

Beginning public accountants usually start by assisting with work for several clients. They may advance to positions with more responsibility in 1 or 2 years, and to senior positions within another few years. Those who excel may become supervisors, managers, partners, open their own public accounting firms, or transfer to executive positions in management accounting or internal auditing in private firms.

Management accountants often start as cost accountants, junior internal auditors, or as trainees for other accounting positions. As they rise through the organization, they may advance to accounting manager, chief cost accountant, budget director, or manager of internal auditing. Some become controllers, treasurers, financial vice presidents, chief financial officers, or corporation presidents. Many senior corporation executives have a background in accounting, internal auditing, or finance.

In general, there is a large degree of mobility among public accountants, management accountants, and internal auditors. Practitioners often shift into management accounting or internal auditing from public accounting, or between internal auditing and management accounting. However, it is less common for accountants and auditors to move from either management accounting or internal auditing into public accounting.

Job Outlook

Employment of accountants and auditors is expected to grow about as fast as the average for all occupations through the year 2008. In addition to openings resulting from growth, the need to replace accountants and auditors who retire or transfer to other occupations will produce thousands of job openings annually in this large occupation.

As the economy grows, the number of business establishments will increase, requiring more accountants and auditors to set up books, prepare taxes, and provide management advice. As these businesses grow, the volume and complexity of information developed by accountants and auditors regarding costs, expenditures, and taxes will increase as well. More complex requirements for accountants and auditors also arise from changes in legislation related to taxes, financial reporting standards, business investments, mergers, and other financial matters. In addition, businesses will increasingly need quick, accurate, and individually tailored financial information due to the demands of growing international competition. These trends will positively affect the employment of accountants and auditors.

The changing role of accountants and auditors also will spur job growth. In response to market demand, these professionals will offer more management and consulting services as they take on a greater advisory role and develop more sophisticated and flexible accounting systems. By focusing more on analyzing operations rather than just providing financial data, accountants will help to increase the demand for their services. Also, internal auditors will increasingly be needed to discover and eliminate waste and fraud.

However, this trend will be counteracted somewhat by a decrease in the demand for traditional services and growing use of accounting software. Accountants will spend less time performing audits due to potential liability and relatively low profits, and will shift away from tax preparation due to the increasing popularity of tax preparation firms. As computer programs continue simplifying some accounting-related tasks, clerical staff will increasingly handle many routine calculations.

Accountants and auditors who have earned professional recognition through certification or licensure should have the best job prospects. For example, CPAs should continue to enjoy a wide range of job opportunities, especially as more States enact the 150-hour requirement, making it more difficult to obtain this certification. Similarly, CMAs should be in demand as their management advice is increasingly sought. Applicants with a master's degree in accounting, or a master's degree in business administration with a concentration in accounting, will also have an advantage in the job market.

Proficiency in accounting and auditing computer software, or expertise in specialized areas such as international business, specific industries, or current legislation, may also be helpful in landing certain accounting and auditing jobs. In addition, employers increasingly seek applicants with strong interpersonal and communication skills. Regardless of one's qualifications, however, competition will remain keen for the most prestigious jobs in major accounting and business firms.

Earnings

In 1998, the median annual earnings of accountants and auditors were $37,860. The middle half of the occupation earned between $29,840 and $49,460. The top 10 percent of accountants and auditors earned more than $76,160, and the bottom decile earned less than $23,800. Accountants and auditors earn slightly more in urban areas. In 1997, median annual earnings in the industries employing the largest numbers of accountants and auditors were:

Industry	Earnings
Accounting, auditing, and bookkeeping	$38,100
State government, except education and hospitals	35,900
Federal government	43,100
Local government, except education and hospitals	36,400
Commercial banks	35,700

According to a salary survey conducted by the National Association of Colleges and Employers, bachelor's degree candidates in accounting received starting offers averaging $34,500 a year in 1999; master's degree candidates in accounting, $36,800.

According to a salary survey conducted by Robert Half International, a staffing services firm specializing in accounting and finance, accountants and auditors with up to 1 year of experience earned between $26,000-$36,250 in 1999. Those with 1 to 3 years of experience earned between $29,250-$41,250. Senior accountants and auditors earned between $34,750-$51,000; managers earned between $41,750-$68,500; and directors of accounting and auditing earned between $56,250-$91,000 a year. The variation in salaries reflects differences in size of firm, location, level of education, and professional credentials.

In the Federal Government, the starting annual salary for junior accountants and auditors was about $20,600 in 1999. Candidates who had a superior academic record might start at $25,500, while applicants with a master's degree or 2 years of professional experience usually began at $31,200. Beginning salaries were slightly higher in selected areas where the prevailing local pay level was higher. Accountants employed by the Federal Government in nonsupervisory, supervisory, and managerial positions averaged about $58,200 a year in 1999; auditors averaged $62,500.

Related Occupations

Accountants and auditors design internal control systems and analyze financial data. Others for whom training in accounting is invaluable include appraisers, budget officers, loan officers, financial analysts and managers, bank officers, actuaries, underwriters, tax collectors and revenue agents, FBI special agents, securities sales representatives, and purchasing agents.

Sources of Additional Information

Information about careers in certified public accounting and about CPA standards and examinations may be obtained from:

☛ American Institute of Certified Public Accountants, Harborside Financial Center, 201 Plaza III, Jersey City, NJ 07311-3881.
Internet: **http://www.aicpa.org**

Information on careers in management accounting and the CMA designation may be obtained from:

☛ Institute of Management Accountants, 10 Paragon Dr., Montvale, NJ 07645-1760. Internet: **http://www.imanet.org**

Information on the Accredited in Accountancy/Accredited Business Accountant, Accredited Tax Advisor, or Accredited Tax Preparer designations may be obtained from:

☛ National Society of Accountants and the Accreditation Council for Accountancy and Taxation, 1010 North Fairfax St., Alexandria, VA 22314.
Internet: **http://www.acatcredentials.org**

Information on careers in internal auditing and the CIA designation may be obtained from:

☛ The Institute of Internal Auditors, 249 Maitland Ave., Altamonte Springs, FL 32701-4201. Internet: **http://www.theiia.org**

Information on careers in information systems auditing and the CISA designation may be obtained from:

☛ The Information Systems Audit and Control Association, 3701 Algonquin Rd., Suite 1010, Rolling Meadows, IL 60008.
Internet: **http://www.isaca.org**

For information on accredited programs in accounting and business, contact:

☛ American Assembly of Collegiate Schools of Business—The International Association for Management Education, 605 Old Ballas Rd., Suite 220, St. Louis, MO 63141. Internet: **http://www.aacsb.edu**

Administrative Services and Facility Managers

(O*NET 13014B)

Significant Points

- Administrative services and facility managers work in private industry and government and have varied responsibilities, experience, earnings, and education.
- Despite projected employment growth, especially among facility managers, competition should remain keen due to the substantial supply of competent, experienced workers seeking managerial jobs.

Nature of the Work

Administrative services and facility managers perform a broad range of duties in virtually every sector of the economy. *Administrative services managers,* for example, coordinate and direct support services to organizations as diverse as insurance companies, computer manufacturers, and government offices. These workers manage the many services that allow organizations to operate efficiently, such as secretarial and reception; administration; payroll; conference planning and travel; information and data processing; mail; materials scheduling and distribution; printing and reproduction; records management; telecommunications management; personal property procurement, supply, and disposal; security; and parking.

Specific duties for these managers vary by degree of responsibility and authority. First-line administrative services managers directly supervise a staff that performs various support services. Mid-level managers, on the other hand, develop departmental plans, set goals and deadlines, implement procedures to improve productivity and customer service, and define the responsibilities of supervisory-level managers. Some mid-level administrative services managers oversee first-line supervisors from various departments, including the clerical staff. Mid-level managers also may be involved in the hiring and dismissal of employees, but they generally have no role in the formulation of personnel policy. Some of these managers advance to upper-level positions such as vice president of administrative services, which are discussed in the *Handbook* statement on general managers and top executives.

In small organizations, a single administrative services manager may oversee all support services. In larger ones, however, first-line administrative services managers often report to mid-level managers who, in turn, report to owners or top-level managers. As the size of the firm increases, administrative services managers are more likely to specialize in specific support activities. For example, some administrative services managers work primarily as office managers, contract administrators, or unclaimed property officers. In many cases, the duties of these administrative services managers are similar to those of other managers and supervisors, some of whom are discussed in other *Handbook* statements.

Because of the range of administrative services required by organizations, the nature of many of these managers' jobs also varies significantly. Administrative services managers who work as contract administrators, for instance, oversee the preparation, analysis, negotiation, and review of contracts related to the purchase or sale of equipment, materials, supplies, products, or services. In addition, some

Administrative services and facility managers must be able to coordinate several activities at once.

administrative services managers acquire, distribute, and store supplies; while others dispose of surplus property or oversee the disposal of unclaimed property.

Facility managers are assigned a wide range of tasks in planning, designing, and managing facilities. They are responsible for coordinating the physical workplace with the people and work of an organization. This task requires integrating the principles of business administration, architecture, as well as the behavioral and engineering sciences. Although the specific tasks assigned to facility managers vary substantially depending on the organization, the duties fall into several categories. They include operations and maintenance, real estate, project planning and management, communication, finance, quality assessment, facility function, and human and environmental factors. Tasks within these broad categories may include space and workplace planning, budgeting, the purchase and sale of real estate, lease management, renovations, or architectural planning and design. Facility managers may suggest and oversee renovation projects for a variety of reasons, ranging from improving efficiency to ensuring that facilities meet government regulations and environmental, health, and security standards. Additionally, facility managers continually monitor the facility to ensure that it remains safe, secure, and well-maintained. Often, the facility manager is responsible for directing staff including maintenance, grounds, and custodial workers.

Working Conditions

Administrative services and facility managers generally work in comfortable offices. However, managers involved in contract administration and personal property procurement, use, and disposal may travel extensively between their home office, branch offices, vendors' offices, and property sales sites. Also, facility managers who are responsible for the design of workspaces may spend time at construction sites and may travel between different facilities while monitoring the work of maintenance, grounds, and custodial staffs.

Most administrative services and facility managers work a standard 40-hour week. However, uncompensated overtime is often required to resolve problems and meet deadlines. Facility managers are often on call to address a variety of problems that can arise in a facility during non-work hours. Because of frequent deadlines and the challenges of managing staff and resources, the work of administrative services and facility managers can be stressful.

Employment

Administrative services and facility managers held about 364,000 jobs in 1998. Over half worked in service industries, including management, business, social, and health services. The remaining workers were widely dispersed throughout the economy.

Training, Other Qualifications, and Advancement

Educational requirements for these managers vary widely, depending on the size and complexity of the organization. In small organizations, experience may be the only requirement needed to enter a position as office manager. When an opening in administrative services management occurs, the office manager may be promoted to the position based on past performance. In large organizations, however, administrative services managers are normally hired from outside and each position has formal education and experience requirements. Some administrative services managers have advanced degrees.

Specific requirements vary by job responsibility. For first-line administrative services managers of secretarial, mailroom, and related support activities, many employers prefer an associate degree in business or management, although a high school diploma may suffice when combined with appropriate experience. For managers of audiovisual, graphics, and other technical activities, postsecondary technical school training is preferred. Managers of highly complex services such as contract administration generally need a bachelor's degree in business, human resources, or finance. Regardless of major, the curriculum should include courses in office technology, accounting, business mathematics, computer applications, human resources, and business law. Most facility managers have an undergraduate or graduate degree in engineering, architecture, business administration, or facility management. Many have a background in real estate, construction or interior design, in addition to managerial experience. Whatever the manager's educational background, it must be accompanied by related work experience reflecting demonstrated ability. For this reason, many administrative services managers have advanced through the ranks of their organization, acquiring work experience in various administrative positions before assuming first-line supervisory duties. All managers who oversee departmental supervisors should be familiar with office procedures and equipment. Managers of personal property acquisition and disposal need experience in purchasing and sales, and knowledge of a variety of supplies, machinery, and equipment. Managers concerned with supply, inventory, and distribution should be experienced in receiving, warehousing, packaging, shipping, transportation, and related operations. Contract administrators may have worked as contract specialists, cost analysts, or procurement specialists. Managers of unclaimed property often have experience in insurance claims analysis and records management.

Persons interested in becoming administrative services or facility managers should have good communication skills and be able to establish effective working relationships with many different people, ranging from managers, supervisors, and professionals, to clerks and blue-collar workers. They should be analytical, detail oriented, flexible, and decisive. The ability to coordinate several activities at once, quickly analyze and resolve specific problems, and cope with deadlines is also important.

Most administrative services managers in small organizations advance by moving to other management positions or to a larger organization. Advancement is easier in large firms that employ several levels of administrative services managers. Attainment of the Certified Administrative Manager (CAM) designation offered by the Institute of Certified Professional Managers through work experience and successful completion of examinations can increase a manager's advancement potential. In addition, a bachelor's degree enhances a first-level manager's opportunities to advance to a mid-level management position, such as director of administrative services, and eventually to a top-level management position, such as executive vice president for administrative services. Those with the required capital and experience can establish their own management consulting firm.

Advancement of facility managers is based on the practices and size of individual companies. Some facility managers transfer from other departments within the organization or work their way up from technical positions. Others advance through a progression of facility management positions that offer additional responsibilities. Completion of the competency-based professional certification program offered by the International Facility Management Association can give prospective candidates an advantage. In order to qualify for this Certified Facility Manager (CFM) designation, applicants must meet certain educational and experience requirements.

Job Outlook

Employment of administrative services and facility managers is expected to grow about as fast as the average for all occupations through 2008. Demand should be especially strong for facility managers, and for administrative services managers in management services and management consulting as public and private organizations continue to contract out and streamline administrative services in an effort to cut costs. Many additional job openings will stem from the need to replace workers who transfer to other jobs, retire, or stop working for other reasons. Nevertheless, competition should remain keen due to the large number of competent, experienced workers seeking managerial jobs.

Continuing corporate restructuring and increasing utilization of office technology should result in a flatter organizational structure with fewer levels of the management, reducing the need for some middle management positions. This should adversely affect administrative services managers who oversee first-line mangers. Because many administrative managers have a variety of functions, however, the effects of these changes on employment should be less severe than for other middle managers who specialize in certain functions.

Earnings

Earnings of administrative services and facility managers vary greatly depending on their employer, specialty, and geographic area in which they work. In general, however, median annual earnings of administrative services and facility managers in 1998 were $44,370. The middle 50 percent earned between $31,980 and $68,840. The lowest 10 percent earned less than $24,100, and the highest 10 percent earned more than $89,850. Median annual earnings in the industries employing the largest numbers of these workers in 1997 are shown below:

Hospitals	$49,000
Commercial banks	47,500
Colleges and universities	44,500
Local government, except education and hospitals	40,900
Management and public relations	36,900

In the Federal Government, contract specialists in nonsupervisory, supervisory, and managerial positions averaged $55,300 a year in early 1999; facilities managers, $53,100; industrial property managers, $52,100; property disposal specialists, $48,000; administrative officers, $53,100, and support services administrators, $43,900.

According to the International Facility Management Association, facility managers had annual earnings of approximately $66,000 in 1998. Entry level positions in facility management offered salaries ranging from $27,000 to $42,000 a year. However, facility directors can earn more than $80,000 per year, and top facility executives can earn in excess of $160,000. These salaries vary depending on level of education, exact position, company size, and geographic location.

Related Occupations

Administrative services and facility managers direct and coordinate support services and oversee the purchase, use, and disposal of personal property. Occupations with similar functions include appraisers, buyers, office and administrative support supervisors, contract specialists, cost estimators, procurement services managers, property and real estate managers, purchasing managers, and personnel managers.

Sources of Additional Information

For information about careers in facility management, facility management education and degree programs, as well as the Certified Facility Manager (CFM) designation, contact:

☛ International Facility Management Association, 1 East Greenway Plaza, Suite 1100, Houston, TX 77046-0194. Internet: **http://www.ifma.org**

General information regarding facility management and a list of facility management educational and degree programs may be obtained from:

☛ The Association of Higher Education Facilities Officers, 1643 Prince St., Alexandria, VA 22314-2818. Internet: **http://www.appa.org**

For information about the Certified Administrative Manager designation, contact:

☛ Institute of Certified Professional Managers, James Madison University, College of Business, Harrisonburg, VA 22807. Internet: **http://www.cob.jmu.edu/icpm**

Advertising, Marketing, and Public Relations Managers

(O*NET 13011A, 13011B, 13011C, 13011D)

Significant Points

- Employment is projected to increase rapidly, but competition for jobs is expected to be intense.
- Advertising, marketing, and public relations managers have high earnings, but substantial travel and long hours, including evenings and weekends, are common.
- A college degree with almost any major is suitable for entering this occupation, but most people enter these jobs after acquiring experience in related positions.

Nature of the Work

The objective of any firm is to market its products or services profitably. In small firms, the owner or chief executive officer might assume all advertising, promotions, marketing, sales, and public relations responsibilities. In large firms, which may offer numerous products and services nationally or even worldwide, an executive vice president directs overall advertising, promotions, marketing, sales, and public relations policies. (Executive vice presidents are included in the *Handbook* statement on general managers and top executives.) Advertising, marketing, and public relations managers coordinate the market research, marketing strategy, sales, advertising, promotion, pricing, product development, and public relations activities. Middle and supervisory managers oversee and supervise staffs of professionals and technicians.

Advertising and promotion staffs usually are small except in the largest firms. In a small firm, they may serve as a liaison between the firm and the advertising or promotion agency to which many advertising or promotional functions are contracted out. In larger firms, advertising managers oversee in-house account services, creative services, and media services departments. The *account executive* manages the account services department, assesses the need for advertising and, in advertising agencies, maintains the accounts of clients. The creative services department develops the subject matter and presentation of advertising. The *creative director* oversees the copy chief, art director, and their respective staffs. The *media director* oversees planning groups that select the communication media—for example, radio, television, newspapers, magazines, Internet, or outdoor signs—to disseminate the advertising.

Promotion managers supervise staffs of promotion specialists. They direct promotion programs combining advertising with purchase incentives to increase sales. In an effort to establish closer contact with purchasers—dealers, distributors, or consumers—promotion programs may involve direct mail, telemarketing, television or radio advertising, catalogs, exhibits, inserts in newspapers, Internet advertisements or websites, in-store displays or product endorsements, and special events. Purchase incentives may include discounts, samples, gifts, rebates, coupons, sweepstakes, and contests.

Marketing managers develop the firm's detailed marketing strategy. With the help of subordinates, including *product development managers* and *market research managers,* they determine the demand for products and services offered by the firm and its competitors. In addition, they identify potential markets—for example, business firms, wholesalers, retailers, government, or the general public. Marketing managers develop pricing strategy with an eye towards maximizing the firm's share of the market and its profits while ensuring that the firm's customers are satisfied. In collaboration with sales, product development, and other managers, they monitor trends that indicate the need for new products and services and oversee product development. Marketing managers work with advertising and promotion managers to promote the firm's products and services and to attract potential users.

Public relations managers supervise public relations specialists (see the *Handbook* statement on public relations specialists). These managers direct publicity programs to a targeted public. They often specialize in a specific area, such as crisis management—or in a specific industry, such as healthcare. They use every available communication media in their effort to maintain the support of the specific group upon whom their organization's success depends, such as consumers, stockholders, or the general public. For example, public relations managers may clarify or justify the firm's point of view on health or environmental issues to community or special interest groups.

Public relations managers also evaluate advertising and promotion programs for compatibility with public relations efforts and serve as the eyes and ears of top management. They observe social, economic, and political trends that might ultimately have an effect upon the firm, and make recommendations to enhance the firm's image based on those trends.

Public relations managers may confer with labor relations managers to produce internal company communications—such as news about

Working under pressure is unavoidable when schedules change and problems arise, but deadlines and goals must still be met.

employee-management relations—and with financial managers to produce company reports. They assist company executives in drafting speeches, arranging interviews, and other forms of public contact; oversee company archives; and respond to information requests. In addition, some handle special events such as sponsorship of races, parties introducing new products, or other activities the firm supports in order to gain public attention through the press without advertising directly.

Sales managers direct the firm's sales program. They assign sales territories, set goals, and establish training programs for the sales representatives (see *Handbook* statements on services sales representatives). Managers advise the sales representatives on ways to improve their sales performance. In large, multiproduct firms, they oversee regional and local sales managers and their staffs. Sales managers maintain contact with dealers and distributors. They analyze sales statistics gathered by their staffs to determine sales potential and inventory requirements and monitor the preferences of customers. Such information is vital to develop products and maximize profits.

Working Conditions

Advertising, marketing, and public relations managers are provided with offices close to top managers. Long hours, including evenings and weekends, are common. Almost 40 percent of advertising, marketing, and public relations managers worked 50 hours or more a week, compared to 15 percent for all occupations. Working under pressure is unavoidable when schedules change and problems arise, but deadlines and goals must still be met.

Substantial travel may be involved. For example, attendance at meetings sponsored by associations or industries is often mandatory. Sales managers travel to national, regional, and local offices and to various dealers and distributors. Advertising and promotion managers may travel to meet with clients or representatives of communications media. At times, public relations managers travel to meet with special interest groups or government officials. Job transfers between headquarters and regional offices are common, particularly among sales managers.

Employment

Advertising, marketing, and public relations managers held about 485,000 jobs in 1998. They are found in virtually every industry. Industries employing them in significant numbers include wholesale trade, manufacturing firms, advertising, computer and data processing services, and management and public relations.

Training, Advancement, and Other Qualifications

A wide range of educational backgrounds are suitable for entry into advertising, marketing, and public relations managerial jobs, but many employers prefer a broad liberal arts background. A bachelor's degree in sociology, psychology, literature, or philosophy, among other subjects, is acceptable. However, requirements vary depending upon the particular job.

For marketing, sales, and promotion management positions, some employers prefer a bachelor's or master's degree in business administration with an emphasis on marketing. Courses in business law, economics, accounting, finance, mathematics, and statistics are advantageous. In highly technical industries, such as computer and electronics manufacturing, a bachelor's degree in engineering or science combined with a master's degree in business administration is preferred.

For advertising management positions, some employers prefer a bachelor's degree in advertising or journalism. A course of study should include marketing, consumer behavior, market research, sales, communication methods and technology, and visual arts—for example, art history and photography.

For public relations management positions, some employers prefer a bachelor's or master's degree in public relations or journalism. The individual's curriculum should include courses in advertising, business administration, public affairs, political science, and creative and technical writing.

For all these specialties, courses in management and completion of an internship while in school are highly recommended. Familiarity with word processing and data base applications also is important for many advertising, marketing, and public relations management positions. Today, interactive marketing, product promotion, and advertising are increasingly prevalent, and computer skills are vital.

Most advertising, marketing, and public relations management positions are filled by promoting experienced staff or related professional or technical personnel. For example, many managers are former sales representatives, purchasing agents, buyers, product or brand specialists, advertising specialists, promotion specialists, and public relations specialists. In small firms, where the number of positions is limited, advancement to a management position usually comes slowly. In large firms, promotion may occur more quickly.

Although experience, ability, and leadership are emphasized for promotion, advancement can be accelerated by participation in management training programs conducted by many large firms. Many firms also provide their employees with continuing education opportunities, either in-house or at local colleges and universities, and encourage employee participation in seminars and conferences, often provided by professional societies. In collaboration with colleges and universities, numerous marketing and related associations sponsor national or local management training programs. Courses include brand and product management, international marketing, sales management evaluation, telemarketing and direct sales, promotion, marketing communication, market research, organizational communication, and data processing systems procedures and management. Many firms pay all or part of the cost for those who successfully complete courses.

Some associations (listed under sources of additional information) offer certification programs for advertising, marketing, and public relations managers. Certification is a sign of competence and achievement in this field that is particularly important in a competitive job market. While relatively few advertising, marketing, and public relations managers currently are certified, the number of managers who seek certification is expected to grow. For example, Sales and Marketing Executives International offers a management certification program based on education and job performance. The Public Relations Society of America offers an accreditation program for public relations practitioners based on years of experience and an examination.

Persons interested in becoming advertising, marketing, and public relations managers should be mature, creative, highly motivated, resistant to stress, flexible, and decisive. The ability to communicate persuasively, both orally and in writing, with other managers, staff, and the public is vital. Advertising, marketing, and public relations managers also need tact, good judgment, and exceptional ability to establish and maintain effective personal relationships with supervisory and professional staff members and client firms.

Because of the importance and high visibility of their jobs, advertising, marketing, and public relations managers often are prime candidates for advancement to the highest ranks. Well-trained, experienced, successful managers may be promoted to higher positions in their own or other firms. Some become top executives. Managers with extensive experience and sufficient capital may open their own businesses.

Job Outlook

Advertising, marketing, and public relations manager jobs are highly coveted and will be sought by other managers or highly experienced professional and technical personnel, resulting in substantial competition. College graduates with extensive experience, a high level of creativity, and strong communication skills should have the best job opportunities. Those who have new media and interactive marketing skills will be particularly sought after.

Employment of advertising, marketing, and public relations managers is expected to increase faster than the average for all occupations through 2008. Increasingly intense domestic and global competition in products and services offered to consumers should require greater marketing, promotional, and public relations efforts by managers. Management and public relations firms may experience particularly rapid growth as businesses increasingly hire contractors for these services rather than support additional full-time staff.

Projected employment growth varies by industry. For example, employment of advertising, marketing, and public relations managers is expected to grow much faster than average in most business services industries, such as computer and data processing, and in management and public relations firms, while little or no change is projected in manufacturing industries.

Earnings

Median annual earnings of advertising, marketing, promotions, public relations, and sales managers in 1998 were $57,300. The middle 50 percent earned between $38,230 and $84,950 a year. The lowest 10 percent earned less than $28,190 and the highest 10 percent earned more than $116,160 a year. Median annual earnings in the industries employing the largest number of advertising, marketing, promotions, public relations, and sales managers in 1997 were as follows:

Professional and commercial equipment	$69,800
Telephone communications	64,100
Computer and data processing services	60,800
Advertising	54,300
Management and public relations	51,100

According to a National Association of Colleges and Employers survey, starting salaries for marketing majors graduating in 1999 averaged about $31,900; advertising majors, about $26,600.

Salary levels vary substantially depending upon the level of managerial responsibility, length of service, education, firm size, location, and industry. For example, manufacturing firms usually pay advertising, marketing, and public relations managers higher salaries than nonmanufacturing firms do. For sales managers, the size of their sales territory is another important determinant of salary. Many managers earn bonuses equal to 10 percent or more of their salaries.

Related Occupations

Advertising, marketing, and public relations managers direct the sale of products and services offered by their firms and the communication of information about their firms' activities. Other personnel involved with advertising, marketing, and public relations include art directors, artists and commercial artists, copy chiefs, copywriters, writers and editors, lobbyists, marketing research analysts, public relations specialists, promotion specialists, and sales representatives.

Sources of Additional Information

For information about careers and certification in sales and marketing, contact:

☛ Sales and Marketing Executives International, 5500 Interstate North Pkwy., No. 545, Atlanta, GA 30328-4662. Internet: **http://www.smei.org**

For information about careers in advertising management, contact:

☛ American Association of Advertising Agencies, 405 Lexington Ave., New York, NY 10174-1801. Internet: **http://www.aaaa.org**

☛ American Advertising Federation, Education Services Department, 1101 Vermont Ave. NW., Suite 500, Washington, DC 20005. Internet: **http://www.aaf.org**

Information about careers and certification in public relations management is available from:

☛ Public Relations Society of America, 33 Irving Place, New York, NY 10003-2376. Internet: **http://www.prsa.org**

Budget Analysts

(O*NET 21117)

Significant Points

- One out of 3 budget analysts work in Federal, State, and local governments.
- A bachelor's degree generally is the minimum educational requirement; however, some employers require a master's degree.
- Competition for jobs should remain keen due to the substantial number of qualified applicants; those with a master's degree should have the best job prospects.

Nature of the Work

Deciding how to distribute limited financial resources efficiently is an important challenge in all organizations. In most large and complex organizations, this task would be nearly impossible were it not for budget analysts. These professionals play the primary role in the development, analysis, and execution of budgets, which are used to allocate current resources and estimate future requirements. Without effective analysis and feedback about budgetary problems, many private and public organizations could become bankrupt.

Budget analysts can be found in private industry, nonprofit organizations, and the public sector. In private sector firms, a budget analyst examines, analyzes, and seeks new ways to improve efficiency and increase profits. Although analysts working in nonprofit and governmental organizations usually are not concerned with profits, they still try to find the most efficient distribution of funds and other resources among various departments and programs.

Budget analysts have many responsibilities in these organizations, but their primary task is providing advice and technical assistance in the preparation of annual budgets. At the beginning of each budget cycle, managers and department heads submit proposed operating and financial plans to budget analysts for review. These plans outline expected programs, including proposed program increases and new initiatives; estimated costs and expenses; and capital expenditures needed to finance these programs.

Analysts examine the budget estimates or proposals for completeness, accuracy, and conformance with established procedures, regulations, and organizational objectives. Sometimes, they employ cost-benefit analysis to review financial requests, assess program trade-offs, and explore alternative funding methods. They also examine past and current budgets and research economic and financial developments that affect the organization's spending. This process enables analysts to evaluate proposals in terms of the organization's priorities and financial resources.

After this initial review process, budget analysts consolidate the individual departmental budgets into operating and capital budget summaries. These summaries contain comments and supporting statements that support or argue against funding requests. Budget summaries are then submitted to senior management, or as is often the case in local and State governments, to appointed or elected officials. Budget analysts then help the chief operating officer, agency head, or other top managers analyze the proposed plan and devise possible alternatives if the projected results are unsatisfactory. The final decision to approve the budget, however, is usually made by the organization head in a private firm or elected officials in government, such as the State legislative body.

Throughout the remainder of the year, analysts periodically monitor the budget by reviewing reports and accounting records to determine if allocated funds have been spent as specified. If deviations appear between the approved budget and actual performance, budget analysts may write a report explaining the causes of the variations along with recommendations for new or revised budget procedures. In order to avoid or alleviate deficits, they may recommend program cuts or reallocation of excess funds. They also inform program managers and others within their organization of the status and availability of funds in different budget accounts. Before any changes are made to an existing program or a new one is implemented, a budget analyst assesses its efficiency and effectiveness. Analysts also may also be involved in long-range planning activities such as projecting future budget needs.

The budget analyst's role has broadened as limited funding has led to downsizing and restructuring throughout private industry

Budget analysts examine budget proposals for completeness, accuracy, and conformance with established procedures.

and government. Not only do they develop guidelines and policies governing the formulation and maintenance of the budget, but they also measure organizational performance, assess the effect of various programs and policies on the budget, and help draft budget-related legislation. In addition, budget analysts sometimes conduct training sessions for company or government agency personnel regarding new budget procedures.

Working Conditions

Budget analysts usually work in a comfortable office setting. Long hours are common among these workers, especially during the initial development and mid-year and final reviews of budgets. The pressure of deadlines and tight work schedules during these periods can be extremely stressful, and analysts are usually required to work more than the routine 40 hours a week.

Budget analysts spend the majority of their time working independently, compiling and analyzing data and preparing budget proposals. Nevertheless, their schedule is sometimes interrupted by special budget requests, meetings, and training sessions. Some budget analysts travel to obtain budget details and explanations of various programs from coworkers, or to personally observe funding allocation.

Employment

Budget analysts held about 59,000 jobs throughout private industry and government in 1998. Federal, State, and local governments are major employers, accounting for one-third of all budget analyst jobs. The Department of Defense employed 7 of every 10 budget analysts working for the Federal Government. Other major employers include schools, hospitals, and banks.

Training, Other Qualifications, and Advancement

Private firms and government agencies generally require candidates for budget analyst positions to have at least a bachelor's degree. Within the Federal Government, a bachelor's degree in any field is sufficient for an entry-level budget analyst position. State and local governments have varying requirements, but a bachelor's degree in one of many areas—accounting, finance, business or public administration, economics, political science, statistics, or a social science such as sociology—may qualify one for entry into the occupation. Sometimes, a field closely related to the employing industry or organization, such as engineering, may be preferred. An increasing number of States and other employers require a candidate to possess a master's degree to ensure adequate analytical and communication skills. Some firms prefer candidates with backgrounds in business because business courses emphasize quantitative and analytical skills. Occasionally, budget and financial experience can be substituted for formal education.

Because developing a budget involves manipulating numbers and requires strong analytical skills, courses in statistics or accounting are helpful, regardless of the prospective budget analyst's major field of study. Financial analysis is automated in almost every organization, and therefore familiarity with word processing and the financial software packages used in budget analysis is often required. Software packages commonly used by budget analysts include electronic spreadsheets and database and graphics software. Employers usually prefer job candidates who already possess these computer skills.

In addition to analytical and computer skills, those seeking a career as a budget analyst must also be able to work under strict time constraints. Strong oral and written communication skills are essential for analysts because they must prepare, present, and defend budget proposals to decision makers.

Entry-level budget analysts may receive some formal training when they begin their jobs, but most employers feel that the best training is obtained by working through one complete budget cycle. During the cycle, which is typically one year, analysts become familiar with the various steps involved in the budgeting process. The Federal Government, on the other hand, offers extensive on-the-job and classroom training for entry-level trainees. In addition to on-the-job training, budget analysts are encouraged to participate in the various classes offered throughout their careers.

Budget analysts start their careers with limited responsibilities. In the Federal Government, for example, beginning budget analysts compare projected costs with prior expenditures; consolidate and enter data prepared by others; and assist higher grade analysts by doing research. As analysts progress, they begin to develop and formulate budget estimates and justification statements; perform in-depth analyses of budget requests; write statements supporting funding requests; advise program managers and others on the status and availability of funds in different budget activities; and present and defend budget proposals to senior managers.

Beginning analysts usually work under close supervision. Capable entry-level analysts can be promoted into intermediate level positions within 1 to 2 years, and then into senior positions within a few more years. Progressing to a higher level means added budgetary responsibility and can lead to a supervisory role. Because of the importance and high visibility of their jobs, senior budget analysts are prime candidates for promotion to management positions in various parts of the organization.

Job Outlook

Employment of budget analysts is expected to grow about as fast as the average for all occupations through 2008. Employment growth will be driven by the continuing demand of the Nation's public and private sector organizations for sound financial analysis. In addition to employment growth, many job openings will result from the need to replace experienced budget analysts who transfer to other occupations or leave the labor force.

Despite the increase in demand for budget analysts, competition for jobs should remain keen due to the substantial number of qualified applicants. Candidates with a master's degree should have the best job opportunities. Familiarity with computer financial software packages should also enhance a jobseeker's employment prospects in this field.

Expanding automation is playing a complex role in the job outlook for budget analysts. Computers allow budget analysts to process more data in less time, enabling them to be more productive. However, because analysts now have a greater supply of data available to them, their jobs are becoming more complicated. In addition, as businesses become increasingly complex and specialization within organizations becomes more common, planning and financial control increasingly demand attention. These factors should offset any adverse computer-induced effects on employment of budget analysts.

In coming years, companies will continue to rely heavily on budget analysts to examine, analyze, and develop budgets. Because the financial analysis performed by budget analysts is an important function in every large organization, the employment of budget analysts has remained relatively unaffected by downsizing in the Nation's workplaces. In addition, because financial and budget reports must be completed during periods of economic growth and slowdowns, budget analysts usually are less subject to layoffs during economic downturns than many other workers.

Earnings

Salaries of budget analysts vary widely by experience, education, and employer. Median annual earnings of budget analysts in 1998 were $44,950. The middle 50 percent earned between $36,190 and $61,410. The lowest 10 percent earned less than $30,000 and the highest 10 percent earned more than $81,160.

According to a survey conducted by Robert Half International, a staffing services firm specializing in accounting and finance, starting salaries of budget and other financial analysts in small firms ranged from $27,000 to $30,500 in 1998; in large organizations, from $29,500 to $33,750. In small firms, analysts with 1 to 3 years of experience earned from $30,750 to $36,750; in large companies, from $34,000 to $44,750. Senior analysts in small firms earned from $36,500 to $42,000; in large firms, from $41,750 to $53,750. Earnings of managers in this field ranged from $42,750 to $54,750 a year in small firms, while managers in large organizations earned between $51,750 and $69,500.

In the Federal Government, budget analysts usually started as trainees earning $20,600 or $25,500 a year in 1999. Candidates with a master's degree might begin at $31,200. Beginning salaries were slightly higher in selected areas where the prevailing local pay level was higher. The average annual salary in 1999 for budget analysts employed by the Federal Government in nonsupervisory, supervisory, and managerial positions was $52,000.

Related Occupations

Budget analysts review, analyze, and interpret financial data; make recommendations for the future; and assist in the implementation of new ideas. Workers who use these skills in other occupations include accountants and auditors, economists, financial analysts, financial managers, and loan officers.

Sources of Additional Information

Information about career opportunities as a budget analyst may be available from your State or local employment service.

Information on acquiring a job as a budget analyst with the Federal Government may be obtained from the Office of Personnel Management through a telephone-based system. Consult your telephone directory under U.S. Government for a local number, or call (912) 757-3000; TDD (912) 744-2299. That number is not tollfree and charges may result. Information also is available from their Internet site: **http://www.usajobs.opm.gov**

Construction and Building Inspectors

(O*NET 21908A, 21908B, and 83005B)

Significant Points

- Local governments, primarily municipal or county building departments, employed nearly 60 percent of these workers.
- Construction and building inspectors tend to be older, more experienced workers who have spent years working in related occupations.

Nature of the Work

Construction and building inspectors examine the construction, alteration, or repair of buildings, highways and streets, sewer and water systems, dams, bridges, and other structures to ensure compliance with building codes and ordinances, zoning regulations, and contract specifications. Building codes and standards are the primary means by which building construction is regulated in the United States to assure the health and safety of the general public. Inspectors make an initial inspection during the first phase of construction, and follow-up inspections throughout the construction project to monitor compliance with regulations. However, no inspection is ever exactly the same. In areas where certain types of severe weather or natural disasters are more common, inspectors monitor compliance with additional safety regulations designed to protect structures and occupants in these events.

Building inspectors inspect the structural quality and general safety of buildings. Some specialize—for example, in structural steel or reinforced concrete structures. Before construction begins, *plan examiners* determine whether the plans for the building or other structure comply with building code regulations, and if they are suited to the engineering and environmental demands of the building site. Inspectors visit the work site before the foundation is poured to inspect the soil condition and positioning and depth of the footings. Later, they return to the site to inspect the foundation after it has been completed. The size and type of structure, as well as the rate of completion, determine the number of other site visits they must make. Upon completion of the project, they make a final comprehensive inspection.

In addition to structural characteristics, a primary concern of building inspectors is fire safety. They inspect structures' fire sprinklers, alarms, and smoke control systems, as well as fire exits. Inspectors assess the type of construction, building contents, adequacy of fire protection equipment, and risks posed by adjoining buildings.

There are many types of inspections and inspectors. *Electrical inspectors* examine the installation of electrical systems and equipment to ensure they function properly and comply with electrical codes and standards. They visit work sites to inspect new and existing sound and security systems, wiring, lighting, motors, and generating equipment. They also inspect the installation of the electrical wiring for heating and air-conditioning systems, appliances, and other components.

Elevator inspectors examine lifting and conveying devices such as elevators, escalators, moving sidewalks, lifts and hoists, inclined railways, ski lifts, and amusement rides.

Mechanical inspectors inspect the installation of the mechanical components of commercial kitchen appliances, heating and air-conditioning equipment, gasoline and butane tanks, gas and oil piping, and gas-fired and oil-fired appliances. Some specialize in boilers or ventilating equipment as well.

Plumbing inspectors examine plumbing systems, including private disposal systems, water supply and distribution systems, plumbing fixtures and traps, and drain, waste, and vent lines.

Public works inspectors ensure that Federal, State, and local government construction of water and sewer systems, highways, streets, bridges, and dams conforms to detailed contract specifications. They inspect excavation and fill operations, the placement of forms for concrete, concrete mixing and pouring, asphalt paving, and grading operations. They record the work and materials used so that contract payments can be calculated. Public works inspectors may specialize in highways, structural steel, reinforced concrete, or ditches. Others specialize in dredging operations required for bridges and dams or for harbors.

Home inspectors generally conduct inspections of newly built or previously owned homes. Increasingly, prospective home buyers hire home inspectors to inspect and report the condition of a home's major systems, components, and structure. They are typically hired either immediately prior to a purchase offer on a home, or as a contingency to a sales contract. In addition to structural quality, home inspectors must be able to inspect all home systems and features, from plumbing, electrical, and heating or cooling systems to roofing.

The owner of a building or structure under construction employs *specification inspectors* to ensure work is done according to design specifications. They represent the owners' interests, not the general public. Insurance companies and financial institutions also may use specification inspectors.

Details concerning construction projects, building and occupancy permits, and other documentation are generally stored on computers so they can easily be retrieved, kept accurate, and updated. For example, inspectors may use laptop computers to record their findings while inspecting a site. Most inspectors use computers to help them monitor the status of construction inspection activities and keep track of issued permits.

Construction inpsector confers with supervisor to ensure that construction conforms to approved plans.

Although inspections are primarily visual, most inspectors, except home inspectors, may use tape measures, survey instruments, metering devices, and test equipment such as concrete strength measurers. They keep a log of their work, take photographs, file reports, and, if necessary, act on their findings. For example, construction inspectors notify the construction contractor, superintendent, or supervisor when they discover a code or ordinance violation or something that does not comply with the contract specifications or approved plans. If the problem is not corrected within a reasonable or specified period of time, government inspectors have authority to issue a "stop-work" order.

Many inspectors also investigate construction or alterations being done without proper permits. Inspectors who are employees of municipalities enforce laws pertaining to the proper design, construction, and use of buildings. They direct violators of permit laws to obtain permits and submit to inspection.

Working Conditions

Construction and building inspectors usually work alone. However, several may be assigned to large, complex projects, particularly because inspectors tend to specialize in different areas of construction. Though they spend considerable time inspecting construction work sites, inspectors also spend time in a field office reviewing blueprints, answering letters or telephone calls, writing reports, and scheduling inspections.

Inspection sites are dirty and may be cluttered with tools, materials, or debris. Inspectors may have to climb ladders or many flights of stairs, or crawl around in tight spaces. Although their work is not generally considered hazardous, inspectors, like other construction workers, wear hard hats and adhere to other safety requirements while at a construction site.

Inspectors normally work regular hours. However, they may work additional hours during periods when a lot of construction is taking place. Also, if an accident occurs at a construction site, inspectors must respond immediately and may work additional hours to complete their report.

Employment

Construction and building inspectors held about 68,000 jobs in 1998. Local governments, primarily municipal or county building departments, employed nearly 60 percent. Employment of local government inspectors is concentrated in cities and in suburban areas undergoing rapid growth. Local governments employ large inspection staffs, including many plan examiners or inspectors who specialize in structural steel, reinforced concrete, boiler, electrical, and elevator inspection.

Another 17 percent of construction and building inspectors worked for engineering and architectural services firms, conducting inspections for a fee or on a contract basis. Most of the remaining inspectors were employed by the Federal and State governments. Many construction inspectors employed by the Federal Government work for the U.S. Army Corps of Engineers. Other Federal employers include the Tennessee Valley Authority and the Departments of Agriculture, Housing and Urban Development, and Interior.

Training, Other Qualifications, and Advancement

Although requirements vary considerably depending upon where one is employed, individuals who want to become construction and building inspectors should have a thorough knowledge of construction materials and practices in either a general area, such as structural or heavy construction, or in a specialized area, such as electrical or plumbing systems, reinforced concrete, or structural steel. Construction or building inspectors need several years of experience as a manager, supervisor, or craft worker before becoming inspectors. Many previously worked as carpenters, electricians, plumbers, or pipefitters.

Because inspectors need to possess the right mix of technical knowledge, experience and education, employers prefer to hire inspectors who have formal training, as well as experience. Most require at least a high school diploma or equivalent, even for those with considerable experience. More often, employers look for persons who have studied engineering or architecture, or who have a degree from a community or junior college, with courses in construction technology, drafting, mathematics, and building inspection. Many community colleges offer certificate or associate degree programs in building inspection technology. Courses in blueprint reading, algebra, geometry, and English are also useful.

Construction and building inspectors must be in good physical condition in order to walk and climb about construction sites. They must also have a driver's license. In addition, Federal, State, and many local governments may require that inspectors pass a civil service exam.

Construction and building inspectors usually receive much of their training on the job, although they must learn building codes and standards on their own. Working with an experienced inspector, they learn about inspection techniques; codes, ordinances, and regulations; contract specifications; and record-keeping and reporting duties. They may begin by inspecting less complex types of construction, such as residential buildings, and then progress to more difficult assignments. An engineering or architectural degree is often required for advancement to supervisory positions.

Because they advise builders and the general public on building codes, construction practices, and technical developments, construction and building inspectors must keep abreast of changes in these areas. Continuing education is imperative in this field. Many employers provide formal training programs to broaden inspectors' knowledge of construction materials, practices, and techniques. Inspectors who work for small agencies or firms that do not conduct training programs can expand their knowledge and upgrade their skills by attending State-sponsored training programs, by taking college or correspondence courses, or by attending seminars sponsored by various related organizations such as model code organizations.

Most States and cities require some type of certification for employment and, even if not required, certification can enhance an inspector's opportunities for employment and advancement to more responsible positions. To become certified, inspectors with substantial experience and education must pass stringent examinations on code requirements, construction techniques, and materials. The three major model code organizations offer voluntary certification as do other professional membership associations. In most cases, there are no education or experience prerequisites, and certification consists of passing an examination in a designated field. Many categories of certification are awarded for inspectors and plan examiners in a variety of disciplines, including the designation "CBO," Certified Building Official.

Job Outlook

Employment of construction and building inspectors is expected to grow as fast as the average for all occupations through 2008. Growing concern for public safety and improvements in the quality of construction should continue to stimulate demand for construction and building inspectors. Despite the expected employment growth, most job openings will arise from the need to replace inspectors who transfer to other occupations or leave the labor force. Construction and building inspectors tend to be older, more experienced workers who have spent years working in other occupations.

Opportunities should be best for highly experienced supervisors and craft workers who have some college education, engineering or architectural training, or who are certified as inspectors or plan examiners. Thorough knowledge of construction practices and skills in areas such as reading and evaluating blueprints and plans are essential. However, inspectors are involved in all phases of construction, including maintenance and repair work, and are therefore less likely to lose jobs during recessionary periods when new construction slows. As the population grows and the volume of real estate transactions increases, greater emphasis on home inspections should result in rapid growth in employment of home inspectors. In addition, there should be good opportunities in engineering, architectural, and management services firms due to the tendency of governments—particularly the Federal and State—to contract out inspection work, as well as expected growth in private inspection services.

Earnings

Median annual earnings of construction and building inspectors were $37,540 in 1998. The middle 50 percent earned between $29,540 and $47,040. The lowest 10 percent earned less than $22,770 and the highest 10 percent earned more than $61,820. Median annual earnings in the industries employing the largest numbers of construction and building inspectors in 1997 were:

Engineering and architectural services	$36,500
Local government, except education and hospitals	36,300
State government, except education and hospitals	32,700

Generally, building inspectors, including plan examiners, earn the highest salaries. Salaries in large metropolitan areas are substantially higher than those in small local jurisdictions.

Related Occupations

Construction and building inspectors combine knowledge of construction principles and law with an ability to coordinate data, diagnose problems, and communicate with people. Workers in other occupations using a similar combination of skills include engineers, drafters, estimators, industrial engineering technicians, surveyors, architects, and construction managers.

Sources of Additional Information

Information about certification and a career as a construction or building inspector is available from the following model code organizations:

☛ International Conference of Building Officials, 5360 Workman Mill Rd., Whittier, CA 90601-2298. Internet: **http://www.icbo.org**

☛ Building Officials and Code Administrators International, Inc., 4051 West Flossmoor Rd., Country Club Hills, IL 60478. Internet: **http://www.bocai.org**

☛ Southern Building Code Congress International, Inc., 900 Montclair Rd., Birmingham, AL 35213.

Information about a career as a home inspector is available from:

☛ American Society of Home Inspectors, Inc., 932 Lee St., Suite 101, Des Plaines, IL 60016. Internet: **http://www.ashi.com**

For information about a career as a State or local government construction or building inspector, contact your State or local employment service.

Construction Managers

(O*NET 15017B)

Significant Points

- Construction managers must be available, often 24 hours a day, to deal with delays, bad weather, or emergencies at the site.
- The increasing level and complexity of construction activity should spur demand for managers.
- Individuals who combine industry work experience with a bachelor's degree in construction or building science or construction management should have the best job prospects.

Nature of the Work

Construction managers plan and direct construction projects. They may have job titles, such as *constructor, construction superintendent, general superintendent, project engineer, project manager, general construction manager, or executive construction manager.* Construction managers may be owners or salaried employees of a construction management or contracting firm, or may work under contract or as a salaried employee of the owner, developer, contractor, or management firm overseeing the construction project. The *Handbook* uses the term "construction manager" to describe salaried or self-employed managers who oversee construction supervisors and workers.

In contrast with the *Handbook* definition, "construction manager" is defined more narrowly within the construction industry to denote a management firm, or an individual employed by such a firm, involved in management oversight of a construction project. Under this definition, construction managers usually represent the owner or developer with other participants throughout the project. Although they usually play no direct role in the actual construction of a structure, they typically schedule and coordinate all design and construction processes including the selection, hiring, and oversight of specialty trade contractors.

Managers and professionals who work in the construction industry, such as general managers, project engineers, cost estimators, and others, are increasingly called *constructors*. Through education and past work experience, this broad group of professionals manages, coordinates, and supervises the construction process from the conceptual development stage through final construction on a timely and economical basis. Given designs for buildings, roads, bridges, or other projects, constructors oversee the organization, scheduling, and implementation of the project to execute those designs. They are responsible for coordinating and managing people, materials, and equipment; budgets, schedules, and contracts; and the safety of employees and the general public.

On large projects, construction managers may work for a *general contractor*—the firm with overall responsibility for all activities. There they oversee the completion of all construction in accordance with the engineer or architect's drawings and specifications and prevailing building codes. They arrange for *trade contractors* to perform specialized craft work or other specified construction work. On small projects, such as remodeling a home, a self-employed construction manager or skilled trades worker who directs and oversees employees is often referred to as the construction "contractor."

Large construction projects, such as an office building or industrial complex, are too complicated for one person to manage. These projects are divided into many segments: Site preparation, including land clearing and earth moving; sewage systems; landscaping and road construction; building construction, including excavation and laying foundations, erection of structural framework, floors, walls, and roofs; and building systems, including fire protection, electrical, plumbing, air-conditioning, and heating. Construction managers may work as part of a team or be in charge of one or more of these activities.

Construction managers regularly review engineering and architectural drawings to monitor work progress and ensure compliance with specifications.

Construction managers evaluate various construction methods and determine the most cost-effective plan and schedule. They determine the appropriate construction methods and schedule all required construction site activities into logical, specific steps, budgeting the time required to meet established deadlines. This may require sophisticated estimating and scheduling techniques, and use of computers with specialized software. This also involves the selection and coordination of trade contractors hired to complete specific pieces of the project—which could include everything from structural metalworking and plumbing, to painting and carpet installation. Construction managers determine the labor requirements and, in some cases, supervise or monitor the hiring and dismissal of workers. They oversee the performance of all trade contractors and are responsible for ensuring all work is completed on schedule.

Construction managers direct and monitor the progress of construction activities, at times through other construction supervisors. This includes the delivery and use of materials, tools, and equipment; the quality of construction, worker productivity, and safety. They are responsible for obtaining all necessary permits and licenses and, depending upon the contractual arrangements, direct or monitor compliance with building and safety codes and other regulations. They may have several subordinates, such as assistant managers or superintendents, field engineers, or crew supervisors, reporting to them.

Construction managers regularly review engineering and architectural drawings and specifications to monitor progress and ensure compliance with plans and specifications. They track and control construction costs to avoid cost overruns. Based upon direct observation and reports by subordinate supervisors, managers may prepare daily reports of progress and requirements for labor, material, and machinery and equipment at the construction site. They meet regularly with owners, trade contractors, architects, and other design professionals to monitor and coordinate all phases of the construction project.

Working Conditions

Construction managers work out of a main office from which the overall construction project is monitored, or out of a field office at the construction site. Management decisions regarding daily construction activities are usually made at the job site. Managers usually travel when the construction site is in another State or when they are responsible for activities at two or more sites. Management of overseas construction projects usually entails temporary residence in another country.

Construction managers must be "on call," often 24 hours a day, to deal with delays, bad weather, or emergencies at the site. Most work more than a standard 40-hour week because construction may proceed around-the-clock. This type of work schedule can go on for days, even weeks, to meet special project deadlines, especially if there are delays.

Although the work usually is not considered inherently dangerous, construction managers must be careful while touring construction sites. Managers must establish priorities and assign duties. They need to observe job conditions and to be alert to changes and potential problems, particularly involving safety on the job site and adherence to regulations.

Employment

Construction managers held about 270,000 jobs in 1998. Around 45,000 were self-employed. About 85 percent of salaried construction managers were employed in the construction industry, about 36 percent by specialty trade contractors—for example, plumbing, heating and air-conditioning, and electrical contractors—and about 38 percent by general building contractors. Engineering, architectural, and construction management services firms, as well as local governments, educational institutions, and real estate developers employed others.

Training, Other Qualifications, and Advancement

Persons interested in becoming a construction manager need a solid background in building science, business, and management, as well as related work experience within the construction industry. They need to understand contracts, plans, and specifications, and to be knowledgeable about construction methods, materials, and regulations. Familiarity with computers and software programs for job costing, scheduling, and estimating is increasingly important.

Traditionally, persons advance to construction management positions after having substantial experience as construction craft workers—carpenters, masons, plumbers, or electricians, for example—or after having worked as construction supervisors or as owners of independent specialty contracting firms overseeing workers in one or more construction trades. However, more and more employers—particularly, large construction firms—hire individuals who combine industry work experience with a bachelor's degree in construction or building science or construction management. Practical industry experience is very important, whether through internships, cooperative education programs, or tenure in the industry.

Construction managers should be flexible and work effectively in a fast-paced environment. They should be decisive and work well under pressure, particularly when faced with unexpected occurrences or delays. The ability to coordinate several major activities at once, while analyzing and resolving specific problems, is essential, as is understanding engineering, architectural, and other construction drawings. Good oral and written communication skills are also important, as are leadership skills. Managers must be able to establish a good working relationship with many different people, including owners, other managers, design professionals, supervisors, and craft workers.

Advancement opportunities for construction managers vary depending upon an individual's performance, and the size and type of company for which they work. Within large firms, managers may eventually become top-level managers or executives. Highly experienced individuals may become independent consultants; some serve as expert witnesses in court or as arbitrators in disputes. Those with the required capital may establish their own construction management services, specialty contracting or general contracting firm.

In 1998, over 100 colleges and universities offered 4-year degree programs in construction management or construction science. These programs include courses in project control and development, site planning, design, construction methods, construction materials, value analysis, cost estimating, scheduling, contract administration, accounting, business and financial management, building codes and standards, inspection procedures, engineering and architectural sciences, mathematics, statistics, and information technology. Graduates from 4-year degree programs are usually hired as assistants to project managers, field engineers, schedulers, or cost estimators. An increasing number of graduates in related fields—engineering or architecture, for example—also enter construction management, often after having had substantial experience on construction projects or after completing graduate studies in construction management or building science.

Around 30 colleges and universities offer a master's degree program in construction management or construction science, and at least two offer a Ph.D. in the field. Master's degree recipients, especially those with work experience in construction, typically become construction managers in very large construction or construction management companies. Often, individuals who hold a bachelor's degree in an unrelated field seek a master's degree in order to work in the construction industry. Doctoral degree recipients usually become college professors or conduct research.

Many individuals also attend training and educational programs sponsored by industry associations, often in collaboration with postsecondary institutions. A number of 2-year colleges throughout the country offer construction management or construction technology programs.

Both the American Institute of Constructors (AIC) and the Construction Management Association of America (CMAA) have established voluntary certification programs for construction professionals. Requirements combine written examinations with verification of professional experience. AIC awards the designations Associate Constructor (AC) and Certified Professional Constructor (CPC) to candidates who meet the requirements and pass appropriate construction examinations. CMAA awards the designation Certified Construction Manager (CCM) to practitioners who meet the requirements in a construction management firm, complete a professional construction management "capstone" course, and pass a technical examination. Although certification is not required to work in the construction industry, voluntary certification can be valuable because it provides evidence of competence and experience.

Job Outlook

Employment of construction managers is expected to increase about as fast as the average for all occupations through 2008, as the level and complexity of construction activity continues to grow. Prospects in construction management, engineering and architectural services, and construction contracting firms should be best for persons who have a bachelor's or higher degree in construction science, construction management, or construction engineering as well as practical experience working in construction. Employers prefer applicants with previous construction work experience who can combine a strong background in building technology with proven supervisory or managerial skills. In addition to job growth, many openings should result annually from the need to replace workers who transfer to other occupations or leave the labor force.

The increasing complexity of construction projects should increase demand for management level personnel within the construction industry, as sophisticated technology and the proliferation of laws setting standards for buildings and construction materials, worker safety, energy efficiency, and environmental protection have further complicated the construction process. Advances in building materials and construction methods and the growing number of multipurpose buildings, electronically operated "smart" buildings, and energy-efficient structures will further add to the demand for more construction managers. However, employment of construction managers can be sensitive to the short-term nature of many construction projects and cyclical fluctuations in construction activity.

Earnings

Earnings of salaried construction managers and self-employed independent construction contractors vary depending upon the size and nature of the construction project, its geographic location, and economic conditions. In addition to typical benefits, many salaried construction managers receive benefits such as bonuses and use of company motor vehicles.

Median annual earnings of construction managers in 1998 were $47,610. The middle 50 percent earned between $36,360 and $70,910. The lowest 10 percent earned less than $28,970, and the highest 10 percent earned more than $89,480. Median annual earnings in the industries employing the largest numbers of managers in 1997 were:

Nonresidential building construction	$47,700
Plumbing, heating, and air conditioning	47,000
Heavy construction, except highway	45,700
Miscellaneous special trade contractors	44,200
Residential building construction	40,600

According to a 1999 salary survey by the National Association of Colleges and Employers, candidates with a bachelor's degree in construction management received offers averaging $34,300 a year. Bachelor's degree candidates with degrees in construction science received offers averaging $36,600.

Related Occupations

Construction managers participate in the conceptual development of a construction project and oversee its organization, scheduling, and implementation. Occupations in which similar functions are performed include architects, civil engineers, construction supervisors, cost engineers, cost estimators, real estate developers, electrical engineers, industrial engineers, landscape architects, and mechanical engineers.

Sources of Information

For information about career opportunities in the construction industry, contact:

☛ Associated Builders and Contractors, 1300 North 17th St., Rosslyn, VA 22209. Internet: **http://www.abc.org**

☛ Associated General Contractors of America, 1957 E St. NW, Washington, DC 20006-5199. Internet: **http://www.agc.org**

For information about constructor certification and professional career opportunities in the construction industry, contact:

☛ American Institute of Constructors, 466 94th Ave. North, St. Petersburg, FL 33702. Internet: **http://www.aicnet.org**

For information about construction management and construction manager certification, contact:

☛ Construction Management Association of America, 7918 Jones Branch Dr., Suite 540, McLean, VA 22102. Internet: **http://www.access.digex.net/~cmaa**

Information on accredited construction science and management programs and accreditation requirements is available from:

☛ American Council for Construction Education, 1300 Hudson Lane, Suite 3, Monroe, LA 71201-6054. Internet: **http://www.acce.org**

Cost Estimators

(O*NET 21902 and 85305D)

Significant Points

- Growth of the construction industry, where about 58 percent of all cost estimators are employed, will be the driving force behind the demand for these workers.
- Job prospects in construction should be best for those workers with a degree in construction management or construction science, engineering, or architecture, and who have practical experience in various phases of construction or in a specialty craft area.

Nature of the Work

Accurately forecasting the cost of future projects is vital to the survival of any business. Cost estimators develop cost information for owners or managers to use in determining resource and material quantities, making bids for contracts, determining if a new product will be profitable, or determining which products are making a profit for a firm.

Regardless of the industry in which they work, estimators compile and analyze data on all the factors that can influence costs—such as materials, labor, location, and special machinery requirements, including computer hardware and software. Job duties vary widely depending on the type and size of the project. *Costs engineers* usually have an engineering background and apply scientific principles and methods to undertake feasibility studies, value engineering, and life-cycle costing.

The methods of and motivations for estimating costs can vary greatly, depending on the industry. On a construction project, for example, the estimating process begins with the decision to submit a bid. After reviewing various drawings and specifications, the estimator visits the site of the proposed project. The estimator needs to gather information on access to the site and availability of electricity, water, and other services, as well as surface topography and drainage. The information developed during the site visit usually is recorded in a signed report that is made part of the final project estimate.

After the site visit is completed, the estimator determines the quantity of materials and labor the firm will have to furnish. This process, called the quantity survey or "takeoff," involves completing standard estimating forms, filling in dimensions, number of units, and other information. A cost estimator working for a general contractor, for example, will estimate the costs of all items the contractor must provide. Although subcontractors will estimate their costs as part of their own bidding process, the general contractor's cost estimator often analyzes bids made by subcontractors as well. Also during the takeoff process, the estimator must make decisions concerning equipment needs, sequence of operations, and crew size. Allowances for the waste of materials, inclement weather, shipping delays, and other factors that may increase costs must also be incorporated in the estimate.

On completion of the quantity surveys, the estimator prepares a total project cost summary, including the costs of labor, equipment, materials, subcontracts, overhead, taxes, insurance, markup, and any other costs that may affect the project. The chief estimator then prepares the bid proposal for submission to the owner.

Construction cost estimators may also be employed by the project's architect or owner to estimate costs or track actual costs relative to bid specifications as the project develops. In large construction companies employing more than one estimator, it is common practice for estimators to specialize. For instance, one may estimate only electrical work and another may concentrate on excavation, concrete, and forms.

In manufacturing and other firms, cost estimators usually are assigned to the engineering, cost, or pricing departments. The estimators' goal in manufacturing is to accurately estimate the costs associated with making products. The job may begin when management requests an estimate of the costs associated with a major redesign of an existing product or the development of a new product or production process. When estimating the cost of developing a new product, for example, the estimator works with engineers, first reviewing blueprints or conceptual drawings to determine the machining operations, tools, gauges, and materials that would be required for the job. The estimator then prepares a parts list and determines whether it is more efficient to produce or to purchase the parts. To do this, the estimator must initiate inquiries for price information from potential suppliers. The next step is to determine the cost of manufacturing each component of the product. Some high technology products require a tremendous amount of computer programming during the design phase. The cost of software development is one of the fastest growing and most difficult activities to estimate. Some cost estimators now specialize in only estimating computer software development and related costs.

The cost estimator then prepares time-phase charts and learning curves. Time-phase charts indicate the time required for tool design and fabrication, tool "debugging"—finding and correcting all problems—manufacturing of parts, assembly, and testing. Learning curves graphically represent the rate at which performance improves with practice. These curves are commonly called "cost reduction" curves because many problems—such as engineering changes, rework, parts shortages, and lack of operator skills—diminish as the number of parts produced increases, resulting in lower unit costs.

Cost estimators compile and analyze data on all factors that can influence costs, including materials, labor, location, and special machinery requirements.

Using all of this information, the estimator then calculates the standard labor hours necessary to produce a predetermined number of units. Standard labor hours are then converted to dollar values, to which are added factors for waste, overhead, and profit to yield the unit cost in dollars. The estimator then compares the cost of purchasing parts with the firm's cost of manufacturing them to determine which is cheaper.

Computers play an integral role in cost estimating today, because estimating may involve complex mathematical calculations and require advanced mathematical techniques. For example, to undertake a parametric analysis, a process used to estimate project costs on a per unit basis subject to the specific requirements of a project, cost estimators use a computer database containing information on costs and conditions of many other similar projects. Although computers cannot be used for the entire estimating process, they can relieve estimators of much of the drudgery associated with routine, repetitive, and time-consuming calculations. Computers are also used to produce all of the necessary documentation with the help of word-processing and spreadsheet software. This leaves estimators with more time to study and analyze projects and can lead to more accurate estimates.

Working Conditions

Although estimators spend most of their time in an office, construction estimators must make visits to project work sites that can be dusty, dirty, and occasionally hazardous environments. Likewise, estimators in manufacturing must spend time on the factory floor where it also can be noisy and dirty. In some industries, frequent travel between a firm's headquarters and its subsidiaries or subcontractors also may be required.

Although estimators normally work a 40-hour week, overtime is common. Cost estimators often work under pressure and stress, especially when facing bid deadlines. Inaccurate estimating can cause a firm to lose out on a bid or lose money on a job that was not accuraately estimated.

Employment

Cost estimators held about 152,000 jobs in 1998, about 58 percent of whom were in the construction industry. Another 26 percent of salaried cost estimators were employed in manufacturing industries. The remainder worked for engineering and architectural services firms, business services firms, and throughout a wide range of other industries. Operations research, production control, cost, and price analysts who work for government agencies may also do significant amounts of cost estimating in the course of their regular duties. In addition, the duties of construction managers may also include estimating costs. (For more information, see the statements on operations research analysts and construction managers elsewhere in the *Handbook*.)

Cost estimators work throughout the country, usually in or near major industrial, commercial, and government centers, and in cities and suburban areas undergoing rapid change or development.

Training, Other Qualifications, and Advancement

Entry requirements for cost estimators vary by industry. In the construction industry, employers increasingly prefer individuals with a degree in building construction, construction management, construction science, engineering, or architecture. However, most construction estimators also have considerable construction experience, gained through tenure in the industry, internships, or cooperative education programs. Applicants with a thorough knowledge of construction materials, costs, and procedures in areas ranging from heavy construction to electrical work, plumbing systems, or masonry work have a competitive edge.

In manufacturing industries, employers prefer to hire individuals with a degree in engineering, physical science, operations research, mathematics, or statistics, or in accounting, finance, business, economics, or a related subject. In most industries, great emphasis is placed on experience involving quantitative techniques.

Cost estimators should have an aptitude for mathematics, be able to quickly analyze, compare, and interpret detailed and sometimes poorly defined information, and be able to make sound and accurate judgments based on this knowledge. Assertiveness and self-confidence in presenting and supporting their conclusions are important, as are strong communications and interpersonal skills, because estimators may work as part of a project team alongside managers, owners, engineers, and design professionals. Cost estimators also need knowledge of computers, including word-processing and spreadsheet packages. In some instances, familiarity with special estimation software or programming skills may also be required.

Regardless of their background, estimators receive much training on the job; almost every company has its own way of handling estimates. Working with an experienced estimator, they become familiar with each step in the process. Those with no experience reading construction specifications or blueprints first learn that aspect of the work. They then may accompany an experienced estimator to the construction site or shop floor where they observe the work being done, take measurements, or perform other routine tasks. As they become more knowledgeable, estimators learn how to tabulate quantities and dimensions from drawings and how to select the appropriate material prices.

For most estimators, advancement takes the form of higher pay and prestige. Some move into management positions, such as project manager for a construction firm or manager of the industrial engineering department for a manufacturer. Others may go into business for themselves as consultants, providing estimating services for a fee to government or construction and manufacturing firms.

Many colleges and universities include cost estimating as part of bachelor's and associate degree curriculums in civil engineering, industrial engineering, and construction management or construction engineering technology. In addition, cost estimating is a significant part of many master's degree programs in construction science or construction management. Organizations representing cost estimators, such as American Association of Cost Engineers (AACE) International and the Society of Cost Estimating and Analysis, also sponsor educational and professional development programs. These programs help students, estimators-in-training, and experienced estimators stay abreast of changes affecting the profession. Specialized courses and programs in cost estimating techniques and procedures are also offered by many technical schools, community colleges, and universities.

Voluntary certification can be valuable to cost estimators, because it provides professional recognition of the estimator's competence and experience. In some instances, individual employers may even require professional certification for employment. Both AACE International and the Society of Cost Estimating and Analysis administer certification programs. To become certified, estimators usually must have between 3 and 7 years of estimating experience and must pass both a written and an oral examination. In addition, certification requirements may include publication of at least one article or paper in the field.

Job Outlook

Overall employment of cost estimators is expected to grow about as fast as average for all occupations through the year 2008. No new projects in construction, manufacturing, or other industries are undertaken without careful analysis and estimation of the costs involved. In addition to openings created by growth, some job openings will also arise from the need to replace workers who transfer to other occupations or leave the labor force.

Growth of the construction industry, where about 58 percent of all cost estimators are employed, will be the driving force behind the demand for these workers. The fastest growing sectors of the construction industry are expected to be special trade contractors and those associated with heavy construction and spending on the Nation's infrastructure. Construction and repair of highways and streets, bridges, and construction of more subway systems, airports, water and sewage systems, and electric power plants and transmission lines will stimulate demand for many more cost estimators. Job prospects in construction should be best for cost estimators with a degree in construction management or construction science, engineering, or architecture, who have practical experience in various phases of construction or in a specialty craft area.

Employment of cost estimators in manufacturing should remain relatively stable as firms continue to use their services to identify and control their operating costs. Experienced estimators with degrees in engineering, science, mathematics, business administration, or economics and who have computer expertise should have the best job prospects in manufacturing.

Earnings

Salaries of cost estimators vary widely by experience, education, size of firm, and industry. Median annual earnings of cost estimators in 1998 were $40,590. The middle 50 percent earned between $31,270 and $53,490. The lowest 10 percent earned less than $24,330, and the highest 10 percent earned more than $79,400. Median annual earnings in the industries employing the largest numbers of managers in 1997 were:

Industry	Earnings
Nonresidential building construction	$43,400
Electrical work	40,800
Plumbing, heating, and air conditioning	40,700
Miscellaneous special trade contractors	39,200
Residential building construction	35,300

College graduates with degrees in fields such as engineering or construction management that provide a strong background in cost estimating could start at a higher level. According to a 1999 salary survey by the National Association of Colleges and Employers, bachelor's degree candidates with degrees in construction science received offers averaging about $36,600 a year. Bachelor's degree candidates with degrees in construction management received offers averaging $34,300 a year.

Related Occupations

Other workers who quantitatively analyze information include appraisers, cost accountants, auditors, budget analysts, cost engineers, economists, financial analysts, loan officers, operations research analysts, underwriters, and value engineers. In addition, the duties of production managers and construction managers may also involve analyzing costs.

Sources of Additional Information

Information about career opportunities, certification, educational programs, and cost estimating techniques may be obtained from:

☛ AACE International, 209 Prairie Ave., Suite 100, Morgantown, WV 26505. Internet: **http://www.aacei.org**

☛ Professional Construction Estimators Association of America, P.O. Box 11626, Charlotte, NC 28220-1626. Internet: **http://www.pcea.org**

☛ Society of Cost Estimating and Analysis, 101 S. Whiting St., Suite 201, Alexandria, VA 22304. Internet: **http://www.erols.com/scea**

Education Administrators

(O*NET 15005A and 15005B)

Significant Points

- Most jobs require experience in a related occupation, such as teacher or admissions counselor, and a master's or doctoral degree.
- Many jobs offer high earnings, considerable community prestige, and the satisfaction of working with young people.
- Competition will be keen for jobs in higher education, but opportunities should be better at the elementary and secondary school level.

Nature of the Work

Smooth operation of an educational institution requires competent administrators. Education administrators provide direction, leadership, and day-to-day management of educational activities in schools, colleges and universities, businesses, correctional institutions, museums, and job training and community service organizations. (College presidents and school superintendents are covered in the *Handbook* statement on general managers and top executives.) *Education administrators* set educational standards and goals and establish the policies and procedures to carry them out. They develop academic programs; monitor students' educational progress; train and motivate teachers and other staff; manage guidance and other student services; administer recordkeeping; prepare budgets; handle relations with parents, prospective and current students, employers, and the community; and perform many other duties.

Education administrators also supervise managers, support staff, teachers, counselors, librarians, coaches, and others. In an organization such as a small daycare center, one administrator may handle all these functions. In universities or large school systems, responsibilities are divided among many administrators, each with a specific function.

Those who manage elementary and secondary schools are called *principals.* They set the academic tone and hire, evaluate, and help improve the skills of teachers and other staff. Principals confer with staff to advise, explain, or answer procedural questions. They visit classrooms, observe teaching methods, review instructional objectives, and examine learning materials. They actively work with teachers to develop and maintain high curriculum standards, develop mission statements, and set performance goals and objectives. Principals must use clear, objective guidelines for teacher appraisals, since pay is often based on performance ratings.

Principals also meet and interact with other administrators, students, parents, and representatives of community organizations. Decision-making authority has increasingly shifted from school district central offices to individual schools. Thus, parents, teachers, and other members of the community play an important role in setting school policies and goals. Principals must pay attention to the concerns of these groups when making administrative decisions.

Principals prepare budgets and reports on various subjects, including finances and attendance, and oversee the requisitioning and allocation of supplies. As school budgets become tighter, many principals are more involved in public relations and fund raising to secure financial support for their schools from local businesses and the community.

Principals must take an active role to ensure that students meet national academic standards. Many principals develop school/business partnerships and school-to-work transition programs for students. Increasingly, principals must be sensitive to the needs of the rising number of non-English speaking and culturally diverse students. Growing enrollments, which are leading to overcrowding at many existing schools, are also a cause for concern. When addressing problems of inadequate resources, administrators serve as advocates to build new schools or repair existing ones.

Schools continue to be involved with students' emotional welfare as well as their academic achievement. As a result, principals face responsibilities outside the academic realm. For example, in response to the growing number of dual-income and single-parent families and teenage parents, schools have established before- and after-school child-care programs or family resource centers, which also may offer parenting classes and social service referrals. With the help of community organizations, some principals have established programs to combat increases in crime, drug and alcohol abuse, and sexually transmitted disease among students.

Assistant principals aid the principal in the overall administration of the school. Some assistant principals hold this position for several years to prepare for advancement to principal; others are career assistant principals. They are responsible for scheduling student classes, ordering textbooks and supplies, and coordinating transportation, custodial, cafeteria, and other support services. They usually handle discipline, attendance, social and recreational programs, and health and safety. They also may counsel students on personal, educational, or vocational matters. With site-based management, assistant principals play a greater role in developing curriculum, evaluating teachers, and school-community relations—responsibilities previously assumed solely by the principal. The number of assistant principals a school employs may vary depending on the number of students.

Administrators in school district central offices manage public schools under their jurisdiction. This group includes those who direct subject area programs such as English, music, vocational education, special education, and mathematics. They plan, evaluate, standardize, and improve curriculums and teaching techniques, and help teachers improve their skills and learn about new methods and materials. They oversee career counseling programs, and testing which measures students' abilities and helps place them in appropriate classes. Central office administrators also include directors of programs such as guidance, school psychology, athletics, curriculum and instruction, and professional development. With site-based management, administrators have transferred primary responsibility for many of these programs to the principals, assistant principals, teachers, and other staff.

In colleges and universities, *academic deans, deans of faculty, provosts,* and *university deans* assist presidents and develop budgets and academic policies and programs. They also direct and coordinate the activities of deans of individual colleges and chairpersons of academic departments.

College or university department heads or *chairpersons* are in charge of departments such as English, biological science, or mathematics. In addition to teaching, they coordinate schedules of classes and teaching assignments; propose budgets; recruit, interview, and hire applicants for teaching positions; evaluate faculty members; encourage faculty development; and perform other administrative duties. In overseeing their departments, chairpersons must consider and balance the concerns of faculty, administrators, and students.

Education administrators provide leadership and day-to-day management of elementary and secondary schools and colleges and universities.

Higher education administrators provide student services. *Vice presidents of student affairs or student life, deans of students, and directors of student services* may direct and coordinate admissions, foreign student services, health and counseling services, career services, financial aid, and housing and residential life, as well as social, recreational, and related programs. In small colleges, they may counsel students. *Registrars* are custodians of students' records. They register students, prepare student transcripts, evaluate academic records, assess and collect tuition and fees, plan and implement commencement, oversee the preparation of college catalogs and schedules of classes, and analyze enrollment and demographic statistics. *Directors of admissions* manage the process of recruiting, evaluating, and admitting students, and work closely with financial aid directors, who oversee scholarship, fellowship, and loan programs. Registrars and admissions officers must adapt to technological innovations in student information systems. For example, for those whose institutions present information—such as college catalogs and schedules—on the Internet, knowledge of on-line resources, imaging, and other computer skills is important. *Directors of student activities* plan and arrange social, cultural, and recreational activities, assist student-run organizations, and may conduct new student orientation. *Athletic directors* plan and direct intramural and intercollegiate athletic activities, including publicity for athletic events, preparation of budgets, and supervision of coaches.

Working Conditions

Education administrators hold management positions with significant responsibility. Coordinating and interacting with faculty, parents, and students can be fast-paced and stimulating, but also stressful and demanding. Some jobs include travel. Principals and assistant principals whose main duty often is discipline may find working with difficult students challenging and frustrating. The number of school-age children is rising, and some school systems have hired assistant principals because a school's population increased significantly. However, in other school systems, principals may manage larger student bodies, which can be stressful.

Many education administrators work more than 40 hours a week, including some nights and weekends when they oversee school activities. Most administrators work 10 or 11 months a year, but some work year round.

Employment

Education administrators held about 447,000 jobs in 1998. About 9 out of 10 were in educational services, which includes elementary, secondary, and technical schools, and colleges and universities. The rest worked in child day care centers, religious organizations, job training centers, State departments of education, and businesses and other organizations that provided training for their employees.

Training, Other Qualifications, and Advancement

Most education administrators begin their careers in related occupations, and prepare for a job in education administration by completing a master's or doctoral degree. Because of the diversity of duties and levels of responsibility, their educational backgrounds and experience vary considerably. Principals, assistant principals, central office administrators, and academic deans usually have held teaching positions before moving into administration. Some teachers move directly into principal positions; others first become assistant principals, or gain experience in other central office administrative jobs at either the school or district level in positions such as department head, curriculum specialist, or subject matter advisor. In some cases, administrators move up from related staff jobs such as recruiter, guidance counselor, librarian, residence hall director, or financial aid or admissions counselor.

To be considered for education administrator positions, workers must first prove themselves in their current jobs. In evaluating candidates, supervisors look for determination, confidence, innovativeness, motivation, and leadership. The ability to make sound decisions and organize and coordinate work efficiently is essential. Since much of an administrator's job involves interacting with others—such as students, parents, and teachers—they must have strong interpersonal skills and be effective communicators and motivators. Knowledge of management principles and practices, gained through work experience and formal education, is important. A familiarity with computer technology is a plus for principals, who are becoming increasingly involved in gathering information and coordinating technical resources for their students and classrooms.

In most public schools, principals, assistant principals, and school administrators in central offices need a master's degree in education administration or educational supervision. Some principals and central office administrators have a doctorate or specialized degree in education administration. In private schools, which are not subject to State certification requirements, some principals and assistant principals hold only a bachelor's degree; however, the majority have a master's or doctoral degree. Most States require principals to be licensed as school administrators. License requirements vary by State. National standards for school leaders, including principals and supervisors, were recently developed by the Interstate School Leaders Licensure Consortium. Several States currently use these national standards as guidelines to assess beginning principals for licensure, and many more States are expected to adopt the standards for this purpose. Some States require administrators to take continuing education courses to keep their certification, thus ensuring that administrators have the most up-to-date skills. The number and type of courses required to maintain certification vary by State.

Academic deans and chairpersons usually have a doctorate in their specialty. Most have held a professorship in their department before advancing. Admissions, student affairs, and financial aid directors and registrars sometimes start in related staff jobs with bachelor's degrees—any field usually is acceptable—and obtain advanced degrees in college student affairs or higher education administration. A Ph.D. or Ed.D. usually is necessary for top student affairs positions. Computer literacy and a background in mathematics or statistics may be assets in admissions, records, and financial work.

Advanced degrees in higher education administration, educational supervision, and college student affairs are offered in many colleges and universities. The National Council for Accreditation of Teacher Education accredits these programs. Education administration degree programs include courses in school management, school law, school finance and budgeting, curriculum development and evaluation, research design and data analysis, community relations, politics in education, counseling, and leadership. Educational supervision degree programs include courses in supervision of instruction and curriculum, human relations, curriculum development, research, and advanced pedagogy courses.

Education administrators advance by moving up an administrative ladder or transferring to larger schools or systems. They also may become superintendent of a school system or president of an educational institution.

Job Outlook

Expect substantial competition for prestigious jobs as higher education administrators. Many faculty and other staff meet the education and experience requirements for these jobs, and seek promotion. However, the number of openings is relatively small; only the most highly qualified are selected. Candidates who have the most formal education and who are willing to relocate should have the best job prospects.

On the other hand, it is becoming more difficult to attract candidates for some principal, vice principal, and administration jobs at the elementary and secondary school level, particularly in districts where crowded conditions and smaller budgets make the work more stressful. Many teachers no longer have a strong incentive to move into these positions. The pay is not significantly higher and does not compensate for the added workload, responsibilities, and pressures of the position. Also, site-based management has given teachers more decision-making responsibility in recent years, possibly satisfying their desire to move into administration.

Employment of education administrators is expected to grow about as fast as the average for all occupations over the 1998-2008 period. Additional openings will result from the need to replace administrators who retire or transfer to other occupations.

School enrollments at the elementary, secondary, and postsecondary level are all expected to grow over the projection period. Rather than opening new schools, many schools will enlarge to accommodate more students, increasing the need for additional assistant principals to help with the larger workload. Employment of education administrators will also grow as more services are provided to students and as efforts to improve the quality of education continue.

However, budget constraints are expected to moderate growth in this profession. At the postsecondary level, some institutions have been reducing administrative staffs to contain costs. Some colleges are consolidating administrative jobs and contracting with other providers for some administrative functions.

Earnings

Salaries of education administrators depend on several factors, including the location and enrollment size of the school or school district. Median annual earnings of education administrators in 1998 were $60,400 a year. The middle 50 percent earned between $43,870 and $80,030 a year. The lowest 10 percent earned less than $30,480; the highest 10 percent earned more than $92,680. Median annual earnings in the industries employing the largest numbers of education administrators in 1997 were as follows:

Elementary and secondary schools	$61,800
Colleges and universities	60,000
Vocational schools	43,700
Miscellaneous schools and educational services	33,800
Child day care services	25,000

According to a survey of public schools, conducted by the Educational Research Service, average salaries for principals and assistant principals in the 1997-98 school year were as follows:

Directors, managers, coordinators, and supervisors of instructional services	$73,058
Principals:	
Elementary school	$64,653
Junior high/middle school	68,740
Senior high school	74,380
Assistant principals:	
Elementary school	$53,206
Junior high/middle school	57,768
Senior high school	60,999

In 1997-98, according to the College and University Personnel Association, median annual salaries for selected administrators in higher education were as follows:

Academic deans:	
Medicine	$235,000
Law	160,400
Engineering	121,841
Business	90,745
Arts and sciences	87,293
Education	85,013
Social sciences	64,022
Mathematics	60,626
Student services directors:	
Admissions and registrar	$52,500
Student financial aid	48,448
Student activities	36,050

Related Occupations

Education administrators apply organizational and leadership skills to provide services to individuals. Workers in related occupations include medical and health services managers, social service agency administrators, recreation and park managers, museum directors, library directors, and professional and membership organization executives. Since principals and assistant principals usually have extensive teaching experience, their backgrounds are similar to those of teachers and many school counselors.

Sources of Additional Information

For information on elementary and secondary school principals, assistant principals, and central office administrators, contact:

☛ American Federation of School Administrators, 1729 21st St. NW., Washington, DC 20009.

☛ American Association of School Administrators, 1801 North Moore St., Arlington, VA 22209.

For information on elementary school principals and assistant principals, contact:

☛ The National Association of Elementary School Principals, 1615 Duke St., Alexandria, VA 22314-3483.

For information on collegiate registrars and admissions officers, contact:

☛ American Association of Collegiate Registrars and Admissions Officers, One Dupont Circle NW., Suite 520, Washington, DC 20036-1171.

For information on college and university personnel, contact:

☛ The College and University Personnel Association, 1233 20th St. NW., Washington, DC 20036-1250.

For information on professional development and graduate programs for college student affairs administrators, visit the National Association of Student Personnel Administrators Internet site: **http://www.naspa.org**

Employment Interviewers, Private or Public Employment Service

(O*NET 21508)

Significant Points

- Although employers prefer applicants with a college degree, educational requirements range from a high school diploma to a master's or doctoral degree.
- Most new jobs will arise in personnel supply firms, especially those specializing in temporary help.

Nature of the Work

Whether you are looking for a job or trying to fill one, you might need the help of an employment interviewer. These workers, sometimes called personnel consultants, human resources coordinators, personnel development specialists, or employment brokers, help jobseekers find employment and employers find qualified employees. Employment interviewers obtain information from employers as well as jobseekers and put together the best combination of applicant and job.

The majority of employment interviewers are employed in private personnel supply firms or State employment security offices. Those in personnel supply firms who place permanent employees are usually called counselors. These workers offer tips on personal appearance, suggest ways to present a positive image, provide background information on the company with which an interview is scheduled, and recommend interviewing techniques. Employment interviewers in some firms specialize in placing applicants in particular kinds of jobs—for example, secretarial, word processing, computer programming and computer systems analysis, engineering, accounting, law, or health. Counselors in such firms usually have 3 to 5 years of work experience in their field.

Some employment interviewers work in temporary help services companies, placing the company's employees in firms that need temporary help. Employment interviewers take job orders from client firms and match their requests against a list of available workers. They select the most qualified workers available and assign them to the firms requiring assistance.

Regular evaluation of employee job skills is an important part of the job for interviewers working in temporary help services companies. Initially, interviewers evaluate or test new employees' skills to determine their abilities and weaknesses. The results are kept on file and referred to when filling job orders. In some cases, the company trains employees to improve their skills, so interviewers periodically reevaluate or retest employees to identify any new skills they may have developed.

Traditionally, firms that placed permanent employees dealt with highly skilled applicants, such as lawyers or accountants, and those placing temporary employees dealt with less skilled workers, such as secretaries or data entry operators. However, temporary help services increasingly place workers with a wide range of educational backgrounds and work experience. Businesses are now turning to temporary employees to fill all types of positions—from clerical to managerial, professional, and technical—to reduce the wage and benefit costs associated with hiring permanent employees.

The duties of employment interviewers in job service centers differ somewhat from those in personnel supply firms because applicants may lack marketable skills. In these centers, jobseekers present resumes and fill out forms regarding education, job history, skills, awards, certificates, and licenses. An employment interviewer reviews these forms and asks the applicant about the type of job sought and salary range desired.

Because an applicant in these centers may have unrealistic expectations, employment interviewers must be tactful, but persuasive. Some applicants are high school dropouts or have poor English skills, a history of drug or alcohol dependency, or a prison record. The amount and nature of special help for such applicants vary from State to State. In some States, it is the employment interviewer's responsibility to counsel hard-to-place applicants and refer them elsewhere for literacy or language instruction, vocational training, transportation assistance, child care, and other services. In other States, specially trained counselors perform this task.

Applicants may also need help identifying the kind of work for which they are best suited. The employment interviewer evaluates the applicant's qualifications and either chooses an appropriate occupation or class of occupations or refers the applicant for vocational testing. After identifying an appropriate job type, the employment interviewer searches the file of job orders seeking a possible job match and refers the applicant to the employer if a match is found. If no match is found, the interviewer shows the applicant how to use listings of available jobs.

Employment interviewers need good interpersonal skills.

Besides helping individuals find jobs, employment interviewers help firms fill job openings. The services they provide depend on the company or type of agency they work for and the clientele it serves. In most of these agencies, employers usually pay private agencies to recruit workers. The employer places a "job order" with the agency describing the opening and listing requirements including education, licenses or credentials, and experience. Employment interviewers often contact the employer to determine their exact personnel needs. The employment interviewer then reviews the job requirements and the jobseeker qualifications to determine the best possible match of position and applicant. Although computers are increasingly used to keep records and match employers with jobseekers, personal contact with an employment interviewer remains an essential part of an applicant's job search.

A private industry employment interviewer must also be a salesperson. Counselors pool together a group of qualified applicants and try to sell them to many different companies. Often a consultant will call a company that has never been a client with the aim of filling their employment needs. Maintaining good relations with employers is an important part of the employment interviewer's job because this helps assure a steady flow of job orders. Being prepared to fill an opening quickly with a qualified applicant impresses employers most and keeps them as clients.

Working Conditions

Employment interviewers usually work in comfortable, well-lit offices, often using a computer to match information about employers and jobseekers. Some interviewers, however, may spend much of their time out of the office conducting interviews. The work can be hectic, especially in temporary help service companies that supply clients with immediate help for short periods of time. The private placement industry is competitive and, some overtime may be required.

Employment

Employment interviewers held about 66,000 jobs in 1998. Over half worked in the private sector for personnel supply services, typically for employment placement firms or temporary help services companies. About 2 out of 10 worked for State or local government. Others were employed by organizations that provide various services, such as job training and vocational rehabilitation.

Employees of career consulting or outplacement firms are not included in these estimates. Workers in these firms help clients market themselves; they do not act as job brokers, nor do they match individuals with particular vacancies. (Employment counselors, who perform these functions, are discussed in the *Handbook* statement on counselors.)

Training, Other Qualifications, and Advancement

Although most public and private agencies prefer to hire college graduates for interviewer jobs, a degree is not always necessary. Hiring requirements in the private sector reflect a firm's management approach as well as the placements in which its interviewers specialize. Those who place highly-trained individuals such as accountants, lawyers, engineers, physicians, or managers usually have some training or experience in the field in which they are placing workers. Thus, a bachelor's, master's, or even a doctoral degree may be a prerequisite for some interviewers. Even with the right education, however, sales ability is still required to succeed in the private sector.

Educational requirements play a lesser role for interviewers placing clerks or laborers—a high school diploma may be sufficient. In these positions, qualities such as energy level, telephone voice, and sales ability take precedence over educational attainment. Other desirable qualifications for employment interviewers include good communications skills, a desire to help people, office skills, and adaptability. A friendly, confidence-winning manner is an asset because personal interaction plays a large role in this occupation. Increasingly, employment interviewers use computers as a tool; thus, basic knowledge of computers is helpful.

Entry-level employment interviewer positions in the public sector are usually filled by college graduates, even though the positions do not always require a bachelor's degree. Some States allow substitution of suitable work experience for college education. Suitable experience is usually defined as working in close contact with the public or spending time in other jobs, including clerical jobs, in a job service office. In States that permit employment interviewers to engage in counseling, course work in counseling may be required.

Most States and many large city and county governments use some form of merit system for hiring interviewers. Applicants may take a written exam, undergo a preliminary interview, or submit records of their education and experience for evaluation. Those who meet the standards are placed on a list from which the top-ranked candidates are selected for later interviews and possible hiring.

Advancement as an employment interviewer in the public sector is often based on a system providing regular promotions and salary increases for those meeting established standards. Advancement to supervisory positions is highly competitive. In personnel supply firms, advancement often depends on one's success in placing workers and usually takes the form of greater responsibility and higher income. Successful individuals occasionally establish their own businesses.

Job Outlook

Employment in this occupation is expected to grow about as fast as the average for all occupations through the year 2008. The majority of new jobs will arise in personnel supply firms, especially those specializing in temporary help. Job growth is not anticipated in State job service offices because of budgetary limitations, the growing use of computerized job matching and information systems, and increased contracting out of employment services to private firms. In addition to openings resulting from growth, a small number of openings will stem from the need to replace experienced interviewers who transfer to other occupations, retire, or stop working for other reasons.

Economic expansion and new business formation should mean growing demand for the services of personnel supply firms and employment interviewers. Firms that lack the time or resources to develop their own screening procedures will continue to turn to personnel firms. Rapid expansion of firms supplying temporary help in particular will be responsible for much of the growth in this occupation. Businesses of all types are turning to temporary help services companies for additional workers to handle short-term assignments, staff one-time projects, launch new programs, and reduce wage and benefit costs associated with hiring permanent employees.

Entry into this occupation is relatively easy for college graduates and for people who have had some college courses, except in those positions specializing in placement of workers with highly specialized training, such as lawyers, doctors, and engineers.

Employment interviewers who place permanent workers may lose their jobs during recessions because employers reduce or eliminate hiring for permanent positions during downturns in the economy. State job service employment interviewers are less susceptible to layoffs than those who place permanent or temporary personnel in the private sector.

Earnings

Median annual earnings of employment interviewers in 1998 were $29,800. The middle 50 percent earned between $23,520 and $39,600. The lowest 10 percent earned less than $18,420 and the highest 10 percent earned more than $73,180. Employment interviewers earn slightly more in urban areas.

Earnings in private firms vary, in part, because the basis for compensation varies. Workers in personnel supply firms tend to be paid on a commission basis; those in temporary help service companies receive a salary. When workers are paid on a commission basis, total earnings depend on the type and number of placements. In general, those who place more highly skilled or hard-to-find employees earn more. An interviewer or counselor working strictly on a commission basis often makes around 30 percent of what he or she bills the client, although this varies widely from firm to firm.

Some employment interviewers work on a salary-plus-commission basis because they fill difficult or highly specialized positions requiring long periods of search. The salary is usually small by normal standards; however, it guarantees these individuals security through slow times. The commission provides the incentive and opportunity for higher earnings.

Some personnel supply firms employ new workers for a 2- to 3-month probationary period during which they draw a regular salary. This gives new workers time to develop their skills and acquire clients while simultaneously giving employers an opportunity to evaluate them. If hired, their earnings are then usually based on commission.

Related Occupations

Employment interviewers serve as intermediaries for jobseekers and employers. Workers in several other occupations do similar jobs. Personnel officers, for example, screen and help hire new employees, but they concern themselves mainly with the hiring needs of the firm; they never represent individual jobseekers. Personnel officers may also have additional duties in areas such as payroll or benefits management.

Career counselors help students and alumni find jobs, but they primarily emphasize career counseling and decision making, not placement. Counselors in community organizations and vocational rehabilitation facilities help clients find jobs, but they also assist with drug or alcohol dependencies, housing, transportation, child care, and other problems that stand in the way of finding and keeping a job.

Sources of Additional Information

For information on a career as an employment interviewer/counselor, contact:

☛ National Association of Personnel Services, 3133 Mt. Vernon Ave., Alexandria, VA 22305. Internet: **http://www.napsweb.org**

☛ American Staffing Association, 277 South Washington St., Suite 200, Alexandria, VA 22314. Internet: **http://www.natss.org**

For information on a career as an employment interviewer in State employment security offices, contact:

☛ Interstate Conference of Employment Security Agencies, 444 North Capitol St. NW., Suite 142, Washington, DC 20001. Internet: **http://www.icesa.org**

Engineering, Natural Science, and Computer and Information Systems Managers

(O*NET 13017A, 13017B, and 13017C)

Significant Points

- Projected job growth stems primarily from rapid growth among computer-related occupations.
- Employers prefer managers with advanced technical knowledge and strong communication and administrative skills.

Nature of the Work

Engineering, natural science, and computer and information systems managers plan, coordinate, and direct research, design, production, and computer-related activities. They may supervise engineers, scientists, technicians, computer specialists, and information technology workers, along with support personnel.

These managers use advanced technical knowledge of engineering, science, and computer and information systems to oversee a variety of activities. They determine scientific and technical goals within broad outlines provided by top management. These goals may include the redesigning of an aircraft, improvements in manufacturing processes, the development of large computer networks, or advances in scientific research. Managers make detailed plans for the accomplishment of these goals—for example, working with their staff, they may develop the overall concepts of a new product or identify technical problems standing in the way of project completion.

Engineering managers direct the technical work of their staff.

To perform effectively, they must also possess knowledge of administrative procedures, such as budgeting, hiring, and supervision. These managers propose budgets for projects and programs, and make decisions on staff training and equipment purchases. They hire and assign scientists, engineers, computer specialists, information technology workers, and support personnel to carry out specific parts of the projects. They supervise the work of these employees, review their output, and establish administrative procedures and policies.

In addition, these managers use communication skills extensively. They spend a great deal of time coordinating the activities of their unit with other units or organizations. They confer with higher levels of management; with financial, production, marketing, and other managers; and with contractors and equipment and materials suppliers.

Engineering managers supervise people who design and develop machinery, products, systems, and processes; or direct and coordinate production, operations, quality assurance, testing, or maintenance in industrial plants. Many are plant engineers, who direct and coordinate the design, installation, operation, and maintenance of equipment and machinery in industrial plants. Others manage research and development teams that produce new products and processes or improve existing ones.

Natural science managers oversee the work of life and physical scientists, including agricultural scientists, chemists, biologists, geologists, medical scientists, and physicists. These managers direct research and development projects, and coordinate activities such as testing, quality control, and production. They may work on basic research projects or on commercial activities. Science managers sometimes conduct their own research in addition to managing the work of others.

Computer and information systems managers direct the work of systems analysts, computer programmers, and other computer-related workers. These managers plan and coordinate activities such as the installation and upgrading of hardware and software; programming and systems design; the development of computer networks; and the implementation of Internet and intranet sites. They analyze the computer and information needs of their organization and determine personnel and equipment requirements. They assign and review the work of their subordinates, and purchase necessary equipment.

Working Conditions

Engineering, natural science, and computer and information systems managers spend most of their time in an office. Some managers, however, may also work in laboratories or industrial plants, where they are normally exposed to the same conditions as research scientists and may occasionally be exposed to the same conditions as production workers. Most managers work at least 40 hours a week and may work much longer on occasion to meet project deadlines. Some may experience considerable pressure in meeting technical or scientific goals within short timeframes or tight budgets.

Employment

Engineering, natural science, and computer and information systems managers held about 326,000 jobs in 1998. About 1 in 3 works in services industries, primarily for firms providing computer and data processing, engineering and architectural, or research and testing services. Manufacturing industries employ another third. Manufacturing industries with the largest employment include industrial machinery and equipment, electronic and other electrical equipment, transportation equipment, instruments, and chemicals. Other large employers include government agencies, communications and utilities companies, and financial and insurance firms.

Training, Other Qualifications, and Advancement

Strong technical knowledge is essential for engineering, natural science, and computer and information systems managers, who must understand and guide the work of their subordinates and explain the work in non-technical terms to senior management and potential customers. Therefore, these management positions usually require work experience and formal education similar to that of engineers, mathematicians, scientists, or computer professionals.

Most engineering managers begin their careers as engineers, after completing a bachelor's degree in the field. To advance to higher level positions, engineers generally must assume management responsibility. To fill management positions, employers seek engineers who possess administrative and communications skills in addition to technical knowledge in their specialty. Many engineers gain these skills by obtaining master's degrees in engineering management or business administration. Employers often pay for such training; in large firms, some courses required in these degree programs may be offered on-site.

Many science managers begin their careers as chemists, biologists, geologists, or scientists in other disciplines. Most scientists engaged in basic research have a Ph.D.; some in applied research and other activities may have a bachelor's or master's degree. Science managers must be specialists in the work they supervise. In addition, employers prefer managers with communication and administrative skills and, increasingly, familiarity with computers. Graduate programs allow scientists to augment their undergraduate training with instruction in other fields, such as management or computer technology. Given the rapid pace of scientific developments, science managers must continuously upgrade their knowledge.

Many computer and information systems managers have experience as systems analysts; others may have experience as computer engineers, programmers, or operators, or in other computer occupations. A bachelor's degree is usually required for management positions and a graduate degree is often preferred by employers. However, a few computer and information systems managers may have only an associate degree. Employers seek managers who have experience with the specific software or technology to be used on the job. In addition to technical skills, employers also seek managers who have business and interpersonal skills.

Engineering, natural science, and computer and information systems managers may advance to progressively higher leadership positions within their discipline. Some may become managers in non-technical areas such as marketing, human resources, or sales. In high technology firms, managers in non-technical areas often must possess the same specialized knowledge as managers in technical areas. For example, employers in an engineering firm may prefer to hire experienced engineers as sales people because the complex services offered by the firm can only be marketed by someone with specialized engineering knowledge.

Job Outlook

Employment of engineering, natural science, and computer and information systems managers is expected to increase much faster than the average for all occupations through the year 2008. Technological advancements will increase the employment of engineers, scientists, and computer-related workers; as a result, the demand for managers to direct these workers will also increase. In addition, job openings will result from the need to replace managers who retire or move into other occupations. Opportunities for obtaining a management position will be best for workers with advanced technical knowledge and strong communication and administrative skills.

Underlying the growth of engineering and natural science managers are competitive pressures and advancing technologies which require companies to update and improve products and services more frequently. Investment in facilities and equipment to expand research and output should increase the need for engineering and science managers. Faster-than-average employment growth among electrical, electronics, and civil engineers will provide strong employment opportunities for engineering managers in these areas. Among scientists, faster-than-average growth in the employment of biologists and medical scientists will provide similar opportunities for natural science managers.

Employment of computer and information systems managers is expected to grow rapidly due to the increasing use of information technologies. In order to remain competitive, firms will continue to install sophisticated computer networks, set up Internet and intranet sites, and engage in electronic commerce. The fast-paced expansion of the computer and data processing services industry will contribute strongly to the increased demand for these managers. In addition, employment growth is expected across a variety of industries reflecting the widespread importance of information technology.

Opportunities for those who wish to become engineering, natural science, and computer and information systems managers should be closely related to the growth of the occupations they supervise and the industries in which they are found. (See the statements on engineers, life and physical scientists, computer programmers, and computer systems analysts, engineers, and scientists elsewhere in the *Handbook*.)

Earnings

Earnings for engineering, natural science, and computer and information systems managers vary by specialty and level of responsibility. Median annual earnings of these managers in 1998 were $75,330. The middle 50 percent earned between $57,610 and $94,450. The lowest 10 percent earned less than $44,580 and the highest 10 percent earned more than $119,900. Median annual earnings in the industries employing the largest numbers of these managers in 1997 were:

Computer and office equipment manufacturing	$87,500
Electronic components and accessories manufacturing	79,000
Research and testing services	77,700
Computer and data processing services	76,800
Engineering and architectural services	74,300
Federal Government	73,200
State government, except education and hospitals	63,500

According to RHI Consulting, average starting salaries in 1999 for information technology managers ranged from $50,500 to well over $100,000, depending on the area of specialization. A survey of manufacturing firms, conducted by Abbot, Langer & Associates, reported that in 1998, the median annual income of engineering department managers and superintendents was $85,600; the corresponding figure for research and development managers was about $75,400.

In addition, engineering, natural science, and computer and information systems managers, especially those at higher levels, often receive more benefits—such as expense accounts, stock option plans, and bonuses—than non-managerial workers in their organizations.

Related Occupations

The work of engineering, natural science, and computer and information systems managers is closely related to that of engineers, life scientists, physical scientists, computer professionals, and mathematicians. It is also related to the work of other managers, especially general managers and top executives.

Sources of Additional Information

For information about a career as an engineering, natural science, or computer and information systems manager, contact the sources of additional information for engineers, life scientists, physical scientists, and computer occupations that are listed in statements on these occupations elsewhere in the *Handbook.*

Farmers and Farm Managers

(O*NET 79999C, 79999D, 79999G, 79999J, 79999K, 79999L, and 79999M)

Significant Points

- Modern farming requires a combination of formal education and work experience, sometimes acquired through growing up on a farm or through internships now becoming available.
- Overall employment is projected to decline because of increasing productivity and consolidation.
- New developments in marketing and organic farming are making small-scale farming economically viable again.

Nature of the Work

American farmers and farm managers direct the activities of one of the world's largest and most productive agricultural sectors. They produce enough food and fiber to meet the needs of our Nation and for export.

Farmers may be owners or tenants who rent the use of land. The type of farm they operate determines their specific tasks. On crop farms—farms growing grain, cotton, and other fibers, fruit, and vegetables—farmers are responsible for planning, tilling, planting, fertilizing, cultivating, spraying, and harvesting. After the harvest, they make sure the crops are properly packaged, stored, or marketed. Livestock, dairy, and poultry farmers must feed, plan, and care for the animals and keep barns, pens, coops, and other farm buildings clean and in good condition. They also oversee breeding and marketing activities. Horticultural specialty farmers oversee the production of ornamental plants, nursery products—such as flowers, bulbs, shrubbery, and sod—and fruits and vegetables grown in greenhouses. Aquaculture farmers raise fish and shellfish in marine, brackish, or fresh water, usually in ponds, floating net pens, raceways, or recirculating systems. They stock, feed, protect, and otherwise manage aquatic life sold for consumption or used for recreational fishing.

Farmers make many managerial decisions. Their farm output is strongly influenced by the weather, disease, fluctuations in prices of domestic and foreign farm products, and Federal farm programs. In a crop operation, farmers usually determine the best time to plant seed, apply fertilizer and chemicals, harvest, and market. They use different strategies to protect themselves from unpredictable changes in the markets for agricultural products. Many farmers carefully

Farmer works with technician to test dairy herd for butterfat content of milk.

plan the combination of crops they grow so if the price of one crop drops, they will have sufficient income from another to make up for the loss. Others, particularly operators of smaller farms, may choose to sell their goods directly through farmers' markets, or use cooperatives to reduce their financial risk. For example, Community Supported Agriculture (CSA) is a cooperative where consumers buy shares of a harvest prior to the planting season, thus freeing the farmer from having to bear all the financial risks.

Farmers who plan ahead may be able to store their crops or keep their livestock to take advantage of better prices later in the year. Those who participate in the futures market—where contracts and options on futures contracts on commodities are traded through stock brokers—try to anticipate or track changes in the supply of and demand for agricultural commodities, and thus changes in the prices of farm products. By buying or selling futures contracts, or by pricing their products in advance of future sales, they attempt to either limit their risk or reap greater profits than would normally be realized. They may have to secure loans from credit agencies to finance the purchase of machinery, fertilizer, livestock, and feed. Farming operations have become more complex in recent years, so many farmers use computers to keep financial and inventory records. They also use computer databases and spreadsheets to manage breeding, dairy, and other farm operations.

Farmers' tasks range from caring for livestock, to operating machinery, and to maintaining equipment and facilities. The size of the farm often determines which of these tasks farmers will handle themselves. Operators of small farms usually perform all tasks, physical and administrative. They keep records for tax purposes, service machinery, maintain buildings, and grow vegetables and raise animals. Operators of large farms have employees who help with the physical work that small-farm operators do themselves. Although employment on most farms is limited to the farmer and one or two family workers or hired employees, some large farms have 100 or more full-time and seasonal workers. Some of these employees are in nonfarm occupations, working as truckdrivers, sales representatives, bookkeepers, and computer specialists.

Farm managers guide and assist farmers and ranchers in maximizing the financial returns to their land by managing the day-to-day activities. Their duties and responsibilities vary widely. For example, the owner of a very large livestock farm may employ a farm manager to oversee a single activity, such as feeding livestock. On the other hand, when managing a small crop farm for an absentee owner, a farm manager may assume responsibility for all functions, from selecting the crops to participating in planting and harvesting. Farm management firms and corporations involved in agriculture employ highly trained professional farm managers who may manage farm operations or oversee tenant operators of several farms. In these cases, farm managers may establish output goals; determine financial constraints; monitor production and marketing; hire, assign, and supervise workers; determine crop transportation and storage requirements; and oversee maintenance of the property and equipment.

Working Conditions

The work of farmers and farm managers is often strenuous, their work hours are frequently long, and their days off during the planting, growing, and harvesting seasons are rare. Nevertheless, for those who enter farming, these disadvantages are outweighed by the opportunities for living in a rural area, working outdoors, being self-employed, and making a living working the land. Farmers and farm managers on crop farms usually work from sunrise to sunset during the planting and harvesting seasons. During the rest of the year they plan next season's crops, market their output, and repair machinery; some may earn additional income by working a second job off the farm.

On livestock producing farms, work goes on throughout the year. Animals, unless they are grazing, must be fed and watered every day, and dairy cows must be milked two or three times a day. Many livestock and dairy farmers monitor and attend to the health of their herds, which may include assisting birthing animals. Such farmers rarely get the chance to get away unless they hire an assistant or arrange for a temporary substitute.

Farmers who grow produce and perishables have different demands on their time. For example, organic farmers must maintain cover crops during the cold months, which keeps them occupied with farming beyond the typical growing season.

Farm work also can be hazardous. Tractors and other farm machinery can cause serious injury and workers must be constantly alert on the job. The proper operation of equipment and handling of chemicals is necessary to avoid accidents and protect the environment.

On very large farms, farmers spend substantial time meeting with farm managers or farm supervisors in charge of various activities. Professional farm managers overseeing several farms may divide their time between traveling to meet farmers or landowners and planning the farm operations in their offices. As farming practices and agricultural technology become more sophisticated, farmers and farm managers are spending more time in offices and at computers, where they electronically manage many aspects of their businesses. Some farmers also spend time at conferences, particularly during the winter months, trading information.

Employment

Farmers and farm managers held nearly 1.5 million jobs in 1998. About 88 percent were self-employed farmers. Most farmers manage crop production activities while others manage livestock and dairy production. A relatively small number were involved in agricultural services, such as contract harvesting and farm labor contracting.

The soil, topography of the land, and the climate of an area generally determine the type of farming done. For example, wheat, corn, and other grains are most efficiently grown on large farms on level land where large, complex machinery can be used. Thus, these crops are prevalent on the prairies and plains of Iowa, Illinois, Indiana, Nebraska, Ohio, Kansas, and southern Minnesota and Wisconsin. Crops requiring longer growing seasons, such as cotton, tobacco, and peanuts, are grown chiefly in the South. Most of the country's fruits and vegetables come from California, Texas, and Florida. Many dairy herds are found in the areas with good pasture land, such as Wisconsin, New York, and Minnesota. However, in recent years dairy farming has expanded rapidly in California, Arizona, and Texas.

Training, Other Qualifications, and Advancement

Growing up on a family farm and participating in agricultural programs for young people (sponsored by the National Future Farmers of America Organization or the 4-H youth educational programs) are important sources of training for those interested in pursuing agriculture as a career. However, modern farming requires increasingly complex scientific, business, and financial decisions. Therefore, even people who were raised on farms must acquire the appropriate education.

Not all farm managers grew up on farms. For these people, a bachelor's degree in business with a concentration in agriculture is important. In addition to formal education, they need several years of work experience in the different aspects of farm operations in order to qualify for a farm manager position.

Students should select the college most appropriate to their specific interests and location. In the United States, all State university systems have one land-grant university with a school of agriculture. Common programs of study include agronomy, dairy science, agricultural economics and business, horticulture, crop and fruit science, and animal science. For students interested in aquaculture, formal programs are available, and include coursework in fisheries biology, fish culture, hatchery management and maintenance, and hydrology. Whatever one's interest, the college curriculum should include courses in agricultural production, marketing, and economics.

Professional status can be enhanced through voluntary certification as an Accredited Farm Manager (AFM) by the American Society of Farm Managers and Rural Appraisers. Certification requires several years of farm management experience, the appropriate academic background—a bachelor's degree or preferably a master's degree in a field of agricultural science—and passing courses and examinations relating to business, financial, and legal aspects of farm management.

Farmers and farm managers need to keep abreast of continuing advances in farming methods both in the United States and abroad. Besides print journals that inform the agricultural community, the spread of the Internet and the World Wide Web allows quick access to the latest developments in areas such as agricultural marketing, legal arrangements, or growing crops, vegetables and livestock. Electronic mail, on-line journals and newsletters from agricultural organizations also speed the exchange of information directly between farming associations and individual farmers.

Farmers must also have enough technical knowledge of crops, growing conditions, and plant diseases to make decisions ensuring the successful operation of their farms. A rudimentary knowledge of veterinary science, as well as animal husbandry, is important for livestock and dairy farmers. Knowledge of the relationship between farm operations—for example, the use of pesticides—and environmental conditions is essential. Mechanical aptitude and the ability to work with tools of all kinds are also valuable skills for the operator of a small farm, who often maintains and repairs machinery or farm structures.

Farmers and farm managers need the managerial skills necessary to organize and operate a business. A basic knowledge of accounting and bookkeeping is essential in keeping financial records, while a knowledge of credit sources is vital for buying seed, fertilizer, and other inputs necessary for planting. Farmers and farm managers must also be familiar with complex safety regulations and requirements of governmental agricultural support programs. Computer skills are increasingly important, especially on large farms, where computers are widely used for recordkeeping and business analysis. For example, some farmers use personal computers to access the Internet to get the latest information on prices of farm products and other agricultural news.

High school training should include courses in mathematics and biology and other life sciences. Completion of a 2-year and preferably a 4-year bachelor's degree program in a college of agriculture is becoming increasingly important. But even after obtaining formal education, novices may need to spend time working under an experienced farmer to learn how to put to practice the skills learned through academic training. A small number of farms offer, on a formal basis, apprenticeships to help young people acquire such practical skills.

Job Outlook

The expanding world population is increasing the demand for food and fiber. Demand for U.S. agricultural exports of beef, poultry, and feed grain is expected to grow in the long run as developing nations improve their economies and personal incomes. However, increasing productivity in the highly efficient U.S. agricultural production industry is expected to meet domestic consumption needs and export requirements with fewer workers. Employment of farmers and farm managers is expected to continue to decline through the year 2008. The overwhelming majority of job openings will result from the need to replace farmers who retire or leave the occupation for economic or other reasons.

Market pressures will continue the long-term trend toward consolidation into fewer and larger farms over the 1998-2008 period, further reducing the number of jobs for farmers and farm managers. Some farmers acquire farms by inheritance; however, purchasing a farm or additional land is expensive and requires substantial capital. In addition, sufficient funds are required to withstand the adverse effects of climate and price fluctuations upon farm output and income and to cover operating costs—livestock, feed, seed, and fuel. Also, the complexity of modern farming and keen competition among farmers leaves little room for the marginally successful farmer.

Despite the expected continued consolidation of farm land and the projected decline in overall employment of farmers and farm managers, an increasing number of small-scale farmers have developed successful market niches that involve personalized, direct contact with their customers. Many are finding opportunities in organic food production, as more consumers demand food grown without pesticides or chemicals. Others use farmers' markets that cater directly to urban and suburban consumers, allowing the farmers to capture a greater share of consumers' food dollar. Some small-scale farmers, such as some dairy farmers, belong to collectively owned marketing cooperatives that process and sell their product. Other farmers participate in Community Supported Agriculture cooperatives that allow consumers to directly buy a share of the farmer's harvest.

Aquaculture should also continue to provide some new employment opportunities over the 1998-2008 period. Overfishing has resulted in declining ocean catches, and the growing demand for certain seafood items—such as shrimp, salmon, and catfish—has spurred the growth of aquaculture farms. Aquaculture output increased strongly between 1983 and the mid-1990s. Efforts to produce more farm-raised fish and shellfish should continue to increase in response to demand growth.

Earnings

Farmers' incomes vary greatly from year to year because prices of farm products fluctuate depending upon weather conditions and other factors that influence the amount and quality of farm output and the demand for those products. A farm that shows a large profit in one year may show a loss in the following year. Under the 1996 Farm Act, Federal Government subsidy payments, which have traditionally shielded some grain producers from the ups and downs of the market, were set at fixed levels regardless of yields or prices. Consequently, these farmers may experience more income variability from year to year than in the past. The Act also phases out price supports for dairy farmers, and may result in lower incomes for dairy producers. Many farmers—primarily operators of small farms—have income from off-farm business activities, often greater than that of their farm income.

Full-time, salaried farm managers, with the exception of horticultural managers, had median weekly earnings of $447 in 1998. The middle half earned between $302 and $619. The highest paid 10 percent earned more than $852 and the lowest paid 10 percent earned less than $220. Horticultural specialty farm managers generally earn considerably more.

Farmers and self-employed farm managers make their own provisions for benefits. As members of farm organizations, they may derive benefits such as group discounts on health and life insurance premiums.

Related Occupations

Farmers and farm managers strive to improve the quality of agricultural products and the efficiency of farms. Workers with similar functions include agricultural engineers, animal breeders, animal scientists, county agricultural agents, dairy scientists, extension service specialists, feed and farm management advisors, horticulturists, plant breeders, and poultry scientists.

Sources of Additional Information

For general information about farming and agricultural occupations, contact:

☛ Center for Rural Affairs, P.O. Box 46, Walthill, NE 68067.

For information about certification as an accredited farm manager, contact:

☛ American Society of Farm Managers and Rural Appraisers, 950 Cherry St., Suite 508, Denver, CO 80222. Internet: **http://www.agri-associations.org**

For information on aquaculture, education, training, or Community Supported Agriculture, contact:

☛ Alternative Farming System Information Center (AFSIC), National Agricultural Library USDA, 10301 Baltimore Ave., Room 304, Beltsville, MD 20705-2351. Internet: **http://www.nal.usda.gov/afsic**

☛ Appropriate Technology Transfer for Rural Areas, P.O. Box 3657, Fayetteville, AR 72702. Internet: **http://www.attra.org/attra-pub/atmatlst.html#resource**

For general information about farm occupations, opportunities, and 4-H activities, contact your local county extension service office.

Financial Managers

(O*NET 13002A and 13002B)

Significant Points

- A bachelor's degree in finance, accounting, or related field is the minimum academic preparation, but many employers increasingly seek graduates with a master's degree and a strong analytical background.
- The continuing need for skilled financial managers will spur average employment growth.

Nature of the Work

Almost every firm, government agency, and organization has one or more financial managers who oversee the preparation of financial reports, direct investment activities, and implement cash management strategies. As computers are increasingly used to record and organize data, many financial managers are spending more time developing strategies and implementing the long-term goals of their organization.

The duties of financial managers vary with their specific titles, which include chief financial officer, vice president of finance, controller, treasurer, credit manager, and cash manager. *Chief financial officers* (CFOs), for example, are the top financial executives of an organization. They oversee all financial and accounting functions and formulate and administer the organization's overall financial plans and policies. In small firms, CFOs usually handle all financial management functions. In large firms, they direct these activities through other financial managers who head each financial department.

Controllers direct the preparation of financial reports that summarize and forecast the organization's financial position, such as income statements, balance sheets, and analysis of future earnings or expenses. Controllers are also in charge of preparing special reports required by regulatory authorities. Often, controllers oversee the accounting, audit, and budget departments. *Treasurers* and *finance officers* direct the organization's financial goals, objectives, and budgets. They oversee the investment of funds and manage associated risks, supervise cash management activities, execute capital-raising strategies to support a firm's expansion, and deal with mergers and acquisitions.

Cash managers monitor and control the flow of cash receipts and disbursements to meet the business and investment needs of the firm. For example, cash flow projections are needed to determine whether loans must be obtained to meet cash requirements or whether surplus cash should be invested in interest-bearing instruments. *Risk*

Financial managers must be familiar with the latest financial software.

and *insurance managers* oversee programs to minimize risks and losses that may arise from financial transactions and business operations undertaken by the institution. They also manage the organization's insurance budget. *Credit managers* oversee the firm's issuance of credit. They establish credit rating criteria, determine credit ceilings, and monitor the collections of past due accounts. Managers specializing in international finance develop financial and accounting systems for the banking transactions of multinational organizations.

Financial institutions, such as commercial banks, savings and loan associations, credit unions, and mortgage and finance companies, employ additional financial managers, often with the title Vice President. These executives oversee various functions, such as lending, trusts, mortgages, and investments, or programs, including sales, operations, or electronic financial services. They may be required to solicit business, authorize loans, and direct the investment of funds, always adhering to Federal and State laws and regulations.

Branch managers of financial institutions administer and manage all the functions of a branch office, which may include hiring personnel, approving loans and lines of credit, establishing a rapport with the community to attract business, and assisting customers with account problems. Financial managers who work for financial institutions must keep abreast of the rapidly growing array of financial services and products.

In addition to the general duties described above, all financial managers perform tasks unique to their organization or industry. For example, government financial managers must be experts on the government appropriations and budgeting processes, whereas health care financial managers must be knowledgeable about issues surrounding health care financing. Moreover, financial managers must be aware of special tax laws and regulations that affect their industry.

Areas in which financial managers are playing an increasingly important role involve mergers and consolidations and global expansion and financing. These developments require extensive specialized knowledge on the part of the financial manager to reduce risks and maximize profit. Financial managers are increasingly hired on a temporary basis to advise senior managers on these and other matters. In fact, some firms contract out all accounting and financial functions to companies that provide these services.

The role of financial manager, particularly in business, is changing in response to technological advances that have significantly reduced the amount of time it takes to produce financial reports. Financial managers now perform more data analysis and use it to offer ideas to senior managers on how to maximize profits. They often work on teams acting as business advisors to top management. Financial managers need to keep abreast of the latest computer technology in order to increase the efficiency of their firm's financial operations.

Working Conditions

Financial managers work in comfortable offices, often close to top managers and to departments that develop the financial data these managers need. They typically have direct access to state-of-the-art computer systems and information services. Financial managers commonly work long hours, often up to 50 or 60 per week. They are generally required to attend meetings of financial and economic associations and may travel to visit subsidiary firms or meet customers.

Employment

Financial managers held about 693,000 jobs in 1998. Although these managers are found in virtually every industry, more than a third were employed by services industries, including business, health, social, and management services. Nearly 3 out of 10 were employed by financial institutions, such as banks, savings institutions, finance companies, credit unions, insurance companies, securities dealers, and real estate firms.

Training, Other Qualifications, and Advancement

A bachelor's degree in finance, accounting, economics, or business administration is the minimum academic preparation for financial managers. However, many employers increasingly seek graduates with a master's degree, preferably in business administration, economics, finance, or risk management. These academic programs develop analytical skills and provide knowledge of the latest financial analysis methods and technology.

Experience may be more important than formal education for some financial manager positions—notably branch managers in banks. Banks typically fill branch manager positions by promoting experienced loan officers and other professionals who excel at their jobs. Other financial managers may enter the profession through formal management trainee programs offered by the company.

Continuing education is vital for financial managers, reflecting the growing complexity of global trade, shifting Federal and State laws and regulations, and a proliferation of new, complex financial instruments. Firms often provide opportunities for workers to broaden their knowledge and skills by encouraging employees to take graduate courses at colleges and universities or attending conferences related to their specialty. Financial management, banking, and credit union associations, often in cooperation with colleges and universities, sponsor numerous national and local training programs. Persons enrolled prepare extensively at home, then attend sessions on subjects such as accounting management, budget management, corporate cash management, financial analysis, international banking, and information systems. Many firms pay all or part of the costs for those who successfully complete courses. Although experience, ability, and leadership are emphasized for promotion, advancement may be accelerated by this type of special study.

In some cases, financial managers may also broaden their skills and exhibit their competency in specialized fields by attaining professional certification. For example, the Association for Investment Management and Research confers the Chartered Financial Analyst designation on investment professionals who have a bachelor's degree, pass three test levels, and meet work experience requirements. The National Association of Credit Management administers a three-part certification program for business credit professionals. Through a combination of experience and examinations, these financial managers pass through the level of Credit Business Associate, to Credit Business Fellow, and finally to Certified Credit Executive. The Treasury Management Association confers the Certified Cash Manager credential on those who have 2 years of relevant experience and pass an exam, and the Certified Treasury Executive designation on those who meet more extensive experience and continuing education requirements. More recently, the Association of Government Accountants has begun to offer the Certified Government Financial Manager certification to those who have the appropriate education and experience and who pass three examinations. Financial managers who specialize in accounting may earn the Certified Public Accountant (CPA) or Certified Management Accountant (CMA) designations. (See the *Handbook* statement on accountants and auditors.)

Candidates for financial management positions need a broad range of skills. Interpersonal skills are increasingly important because these jobs involve managing people and working as part of a team to solve problems. Financial managers must have excellent communication skills to explain complex financial data. Because financial managers work extensively with various departments in their firm, a broad overview of the business is essential.

Financial managers should be creative thinkers and problem solvers, applying their analytical skills to business. They must be comfortable with computer technology. As financial operations are increasingly affected by the global economy, they must have knowledge of international finance; even a foreign language may be important.

Because financial management is critical for efficient business operations, well-trained, experienced financial managers who display a strong grasp of the operations of various departments within their organization are prime candidates for promotion to top management positions. Some financial managers transfer to closely related positions in other industries. Those with extensive experience and access to sufficient capital may start their own consulting firms.

Job Outlook

The outlook for financial managers is good for those with the right skills. Expertise in accounting and finance is fundamental, and a master's degree enhances one's job prospects. Strong computer skills and knowledge of international finance are important, as are excellent communication skills as the job increasingly involves working on strategic planning teams. Mergers, acquisitions, and corporate downsizing will continue to adversely affect employment of financial managers, but growth of the economy and the need for financial expertise will keep the profession growing about as fast as the average for all occupations through 2008.

The banking industry, which employs the most financial managers, is expected to continue to consolidate and reduce the number of financial managers. Employment of bank branch managers, in particular, will grow very little or not at all as banks open fewer branches and promote electronic and Internet banking to cut costs. In contrast, the securities and commodities industry will hire more financial managers to handle increasingly complex financial transactions and manage investments. Financial managers are being hired throughout industry to manage assets and investments, handle mergers and acquisitions, raise capital, and assess global financial transactions. Risk managers, who assess risks for insurance and investment purposes, are in especially great demand.

Some financial managers may be hired on a temporary basis to see a company through a short-term crisis or to offer suggestions for boosting profits. Other companies may contract out all accounting and financial operations. Even in these cases, however, financial managers may be needed to oversee the contracts.

Computer technology has reduced the time and staff required to produce financial reports. As a result, forecasting earnings, profits, and costs, and generating ideas and creative ways to increase profitability will become the major role of corporate financial managers over the next decade. Financial managers who are familiar with computer software and applications that can assist them in this role will be needed.

Earnings

Median annual earnings of financial managers were $55,070 in 1998. The middle 50 percent earned between $38,240 and $83,800. The lowest 10 percent had earnings of less than $27,680, while the top 10 percent earned over $118,950. Median annual earnings in the industries employing the largest number of financial managers in 1997 are shown below.

Security brokers and dealers	$95,100
Computer and data processing	63,200
Management and public relations	62,800
Local government, excluding education and hospitals	48,700
Commercial banks	45,800
Savings institutions	41,800

According to a 1999 survey by Robert Half International, a staffing services firm specializing in accounting and finance, salaries of assistant controllers and treasurers varied from $42,700 in the smallest firms to $84,000 in the largest firms; corporate controllers earned between $47,500 and $141,000; and chief financial officers and treasurers earned from $65,000 to $319,200. Salaries are generally 10 percent higher for those with a graduate degree or Certified Public Accountant or Certified Management Accountant designation.

The results of the Treasury Management Association's 1999 compensation survey are presented in table 1. The earnings listed in the table represent total compensation, including bonuses and deferred compensation.

Table 1. Average earnings for selected financial managers, 1999

Vice president of finance	$165,400
Chief financial officer	150,100
Treasurer	129,800
Controller	109,700
Assistant treasurer	96,500
Director treasury/finance	93,200
Assistant controller	75,900
Senior analyst	63,000
Cash manager	56,600
Analyst	45,500

SOURCE: Treasury Management Association

Large organizations often pay more than small ones, and salary levels can also vary by the type of industry and location. Many financial managers in private industry receive additional compensation in the form of bonuses, which also vary substantially by size of firm. Deferred compensation in the form of stock options is also becoming more common.

Related Occupations

Financial managers combine formal education with experience in one or more areas of finance, such as asset management, lending, credit operations, securities investment, or insurance risk and loss control. Workers in other occupations requiring similar training and skills include accountants and auditors, budget officers, credit analysts, loan officers, insurance consultants, portfolio managers, pension consultants, real estate advisors, securities analysts, and underwriters.

Sources of Additional Information

For information about financial management careers, contact:

☛ American Bankers Association, 1120 Connecticut Ave. NW., Washington, DC 20036. Internet: **http://www.aba.com**

☛ Financial Management Association International, College of Business Administration, University of South Florida, Tampa, FL 33620-5500. Internet: **http://www.fma.org**

☛ Financial Executives Institute, 10 Madison Ave., P.O. Box 1938, Morristown, NJ 07962-1938. Internet: **http://www.fei.org**

For information about financial careers in business credit management; the Credit Business Associate, Credit Business Fellow, and Certified Credit Executive programs; and institutions offering graduate courses in credit and financial management, contact:

☛ National Association of Credit Management, Credit Research Foundation, 8840 Columbia 100 Parkway, Columbia, MD 21045-2158. Internet: **http://www.nacm.org**

For information about careers in treasury and financial management and the Certified Cash Manager and Certified Treasury Executive programs, contact:

☛ Treasury Management Association, 7315 Wisconsin Ave., Suite 600 West, Bethesda, MD 20814. Internet: **http://www.tma-net.org**

For information about the Chartered Financial Analyst program, contact:

☛ Association for Investment Management and Research, P.O. Box 3668, Charlottesville, VA 22903. Internet: **http://www.aimr.org**

For information about the Certified Government Financial Manager designation, contact:

☛ Association for Government Accountants, 2208 Mount Vernon Ave., Alexandria, VA 22301-1314. Internet: **http://www.agacgfm.org**

Funeral Directors and Morticians

(O*NET 39011 and 39014)

Significant Points

- Job opportunities should be good, but mortuary science graduates may have to relocate to find jobs as funeral directors.
- Funeral directors must be licensed by their State.

Nature of the Work

Funeral practices and rites vary greatly among various cultures and religions. Among the many diverse groups in the United States, funeral practices usually share some common elements: Removal of the deceased to a mortuary, preparation of the remains, performance of a ceremony that honors the deceased and addresses the spiritual needs of the family, and the burial or destruction of the remains. Funeral directors arrange and direct these tasks for grieving families.

Funeral directors also are called morticians or undertakers. This career may not appeal to everyone, but those who work as funeral directors take great pride in their ability to provide efficient and appropriate services. They also comfort the family and friends of the deceased.

Funeral directors arrange the details and handle the logistics of funerals. They interview the family to learn what they desire with regard to the nature of the funeral, the clergy members or other persons who will officiate, and the final disposition of the remains. Sometimes the deceased leaves detailed instructions for their own funerals. Together with the family, funeral directors establish the location, dates, and times of wakes, memorial services, and burials. They arrange for a hearse to carry the body to the funeral home or mortuary.

Funeral directors also prepare obituary notices and have them placed in newspapers, arrange for pallbearers and clergy, schedule the opening and closing of a grave with the cemetery, decorate and prepare the sites of all services, and provide transportation for the remains, mourners, and flowers between sites. They also direct preparation and shipment of remains for out-of-State burial.

Most funeral directors also are trained, licensed, and practicing *embalmers*. Embalming is a sanitary, cosmetic, and preservative process through which the body is prepared for interment. If more than 24 hours elapses between death and interment, State laws usually require that the remains be refrigerated or embalmed.

The embalmer washes the body with germicidal soap and replaces the blood with embalming fluid to preserve the body. Embalmers may reshape and reconstruct disfigured or maimed bodies using materials, such as clay, cotton, plaster of Paris, and wax. They also may apply cosmetics to provide a natural appearance, and then dress the body and place it in a casket. Embalmers maintain records such as embalming reports, and itemized lists of clothing or valuables delivered with the body. In large funeral homes, an embalming staff of two or more embalmers, plus several apprentices, may be employed.

Funeral services may take place in a home, house of worship, funeral home or at the gravesite or crematory. Services may be nonreligious, but often they reflect the religion of the family, so funeral directors must be familiar with the funeral and burial customs of many faiths, ethnic groups, and fraternal organizations. For example, members of some religions seldom have the bodies of the deceased embalmed or cremated.

Funeral directors explain burial options and arrange the details of funerals with clients.

Burial in a casket is the most common method of disposing of remains in this country, although entombment also occurs. Cremation, which is the burning of the body in a special furnace, is increasingly selected because it can be more convenient and less costly. Cremations are appealing because the remains can be shipped easily, kept at home, buried, or scattered. Memorial services can be held anywhere, and at any time, sometimes months later when all relatives and friends can get together. Even when the remains are cremated, many people still want a funeral service.

A funeral service followed by cremation need not be any different from a funeral service followed by a burial. Usually cremated remains are placed in some type of permanent receptacle, or urn, before being committed to a final resting place. The urn may be buried, placed in an indoor or outdoor mausoleum or columbarium, or interred in a special urn garden that many cemeteries provide for cremated remains.

Funeral directors handle the paper work involved with the person's death, such as submitting papers to State authorities so that a formal certificate of death may be issued and copies distributed to the heirs. They may help family members apply for veterans' burial benefits, and notify the Social Security Administration of the death. Also, funeral directors may apply for the transfer of any pensions, insurance policies, or annuities on behalf of survivors.

Funeral directors also prearrange funerals. Increasingly, they arrange funerals in advance of need to provide peace of mind by ensuring that the client's wishes will be taken care of in a way that is satisfying to the person and to those who will survive.

Most funeral homes are small, family-run businesses, and the funeral directors either are owner-operators or employees of the operation. Funeral directors, therefore, are responsible for the success and the profitability of their businesses. Directors keep records of expenses, purchases, and services rendered; prepare and send invoices for services; prepare and submit reports for unemployment insurance; prepare Federal, State, and local tax forms; and prepare itemized bills for customers. Funeral directors increasingly are using computers for billing, bookkeeping and marketing. Some are beginning to use the Internet to communicate with clients who are pre-planning their funerals, or to assist clients by developing electronic obituaries and guest books.Directors strive to foster a cooperative spirit and friendly attitude among employees and a compassionate demeanor towards the families. A growing number of funeral directors also are involved in helping individuals adapt to changes in their lives following a death through post-death support group activities.

Most funeral homes have a chapel, one or more viewing rooms, a casket-selection room, and a preparation room. An increasing number also have a crematory on the premises. Equipment may include a hearse, a flower car, limousines, and sometimes an ambulance. They usually stock a selection of caskets and urns for families to purchase or rent.

Working Conditions

Funeral directors often work long, irregular hours. Many work on an on-call basis, because they may be needed to remove remains in the middle of the night. Shift work sometimes is necessary because funeral home hours include evenings and weekends. In smaller funeral homes, working hours vary, but in larger homes employees usually work 8 hours a day, 5 or 6 days a week.

Funeral directors occasionally come into contact with the remains of persons who had contagious diseases, but the possibility of infection is remote if strict health regulations are followed.

To show proper respect and consideration for the families and the dead, funeral directors must dress appropriately. The profession usually requires short, neat haircuts and trim beards, if any, for men. Suits, ties, and dresses are customary for a conservative look.

Employment

Funeral directors held about 28,000 jobs in 1998. Almost 1 in 10 were self-employed. Nearly all worked in the funeral service and crematory industry.

Training, Other Qualifications, and Advancement

Funeral directors must be licensed in all but one State, Colorado. Licensing laws vary from State to State, but most require applicants to be 21 years old, have 2 years of formal education that includes studies in mortuary science, serve a 1-year apprenticeship, and pass a qualifying examination. After becoming licensed, new funeral directors may join the staff of a funeral home. Embalmers must be licensed in all States, and some States issue a single license for both funeral directors and embalmers. In States that have separate licensing requirements for the two positions, most people in the field obtain both licenses. Persons interested in a career as a funeral director should contact their State licensing board for specific requirements.

College programs in mortuary science usually last from 2 to 4 years; the American Board of Funeral Service Education accredits 49 mortuary science programs. Two-year programs are offered by a small number of community and junior colleges, and a few colleges and universities offer both 2- and 4-year programs. Mortuary science programs include courses in anatomy, physiology, pathology, embalming techniques, restorative art, business management, accounting and use of computers in funeral home management, and client services. They also include courses in the social sciences and legal, ethical, and regulatory subjects, such as psychology, grief counseling, oral and written communication, funeral service law, business law, and ethics.

The Funeral Service Educational Foundation and many State associations offer continuing education programs designed for licensed funeral directors. These programs address issues in communications, counseling, and management. Thirty-two States have requirements that funeral directors receive continuing education credits in order to maintain their licenses.

Apprenticeships must be completed under an experienced and licensed funeral director or embalmer. Depending on State regulations, apprenticeships last from 1 to 3 years and may be served before, during, or after mortuary school. Apprenticeships provide practical experience in all facets of the funeral service from embalming to transporting remains.

State board licensing examinations vary, but they usually consist of written and oral parts and include a demonstration of practical skills. Persons who want to work in another State may have to pass the examination for that State; however, some States have reciprocity arrangements and will grant licenses to funeral directors from another State without further examination.

High school students can start preparing for a career as a funeral director by taking courses in biology and chemistry and participating in public speaking or debate clubs. Part-time or summer jobs in funeral homes consist mostly of maintenance and clean-up tasks, such as washing and polishing limousines and hearses, but these tasks can help students become familiar with the operation of funeral homes.

Important personal traits for funeral directors are composure, tact, and the ability to communicate easily with the public. They also should have the desire and ability to comfort people in their time of sorrow.

Advancement opportunities are best in larger funeral homes—funeral directors may earn promotions to higher paying positions such as branch manager or general manager. Some directors eventually acquire enough money and experience to establish their own funeral home businesses.

Job Outlook

Employment of funeral directors is expected to increase about as fast as the average for all occupations through 2008. Not only is the population expanding, but also the proportion of people over the age of 55 is projected to grow during the coming decade. Consequently, the number of deaths is expected to increase, spurring demand for funeral services.

The need to replace funeral directors and morticians who retire or leave the occupation for other reasons will account for even more job openings than employment growth. Typically, a number of mortuary science graduates leave the profession shortly after becoming licensed funeral directors to pursue other career interests, and this trend is expected to continue. Also, more funeral directors are 55 years old and over compared to workers in other occupations, and will be retiring in greater numbers between 1998 and 2008. Although employment opportunities for funeral directors are expected to be good, mortuary science graduates may have to relocate to find jobs in funeral service.

Earnings

Median annual earnings for funeral directors were $35,040 in 1998. The middle 50 percent earned between $25,510 and $48,260. The lowest 10 percent earned less than $17,040 and the top 10 percent more than $78,550.

Salaries of funeral directors depend on the number of years of experience in funeral service, the number of services performed, the number of facilities operated, the area of the country, the size of the community, and the level of formal education. Funeral directors in large cities earned more than their counterparts in small towns and rural areas.

Related Occupations

The job of a funeral director requires tact, discretion, and compassion when dealing with grieving people. Others who need these qualities include members of the clergy, social workers, psychologists, psychiatrists, and other health care professionals.

Sources of Additional Information

For a list of accredited mortuary science programs and information on the funeral service profession, write to:

☛ The National Funeral Directors Association, 13625 Bishop's Drive, Brookfield, WI 53005.

For information about college programs in mortuary science, scholarships, and funeral service as a career, contact:

☛ The American Board of Funeral Service Education, 38 Florida Avenue, Portland, ME 04103.

For information on continuing education programs in funeral service, contact:

☛ The Funeral Service Educational Foundation, 13625 Bishop's Drive, Brookfield, WI 53005.

General Managers and Top Executives

(O*NET 19005B)

Significant Points

- General managers and top executives are among the highest paid workers; however, long hours and considerable travel are often required.
- Competition for top managerial jobs should remain intense due to the large number of qualified applicants and relatively low turnover.

Nature of the Work

All organizations have specific goals and objectives that they strive to meet. General managers and top executives devise strategies and formulate policies to ensure that these objectives are met. Although they have a wide range of titles—such as chief executive officer, president, executive vice president, owner, partner, brokerage office manager, school superintendent, and police chief—all formulate policies and direct the operations of businesses and corporations, nonprofit institutions, and other organizations. (Chief executives who formulate policy in government are discussed in detail in the *Handbook* statement on government chief executives and legislators.)

A corporation's goals and policies are established by the chief executive officer in collaboration with other top executives, who are overseen by a board of directors. In a large corporation, the chief executive officer meets frequently with subordinate executives to ensure that operations are implemented in accordance with these policies. The chief executive officer of a corporation retains overall accountability; however, a chief operating officer may be delegated several responsibilities, including the authority to oversee executives who direct the activities of various departments and implement the organization's policies on a day-to-day basis. In publicly-held and nonprofit corporations, the board of directors is ultimately accountable for the success or failure of the enterprise, and the chief executive officer reports to the board.

The nature of other high level executives' responsibilities depends upon the size of the organization. In large organizations, their duties are highly specialized. Managers of cost and profit centers, for instance, are responsible for the overall performance of one aspect of the organization, such as manufacturing, marketing, sales, purchasing, finance, personnel, training, administrative services, electronic data processing, property management, transportation, or the legal services department. (Some of these and other managerial occupations are discussed elsewhere in this section of the *Handbook*.)

General managers and top executives must communicate clearly and persuasively.

In smaller organizations, such as independent retail stores or small manufacturers, a partner, owner, or general manager is often also responsible for purchasing, hiring, training, quality control, and day-to-day supervisory duties. (See the *Handbook* statement on retail managers.)

Working Conditions

Top executives are usually provided with spacious offices and support staff. General managers in large firms or nonprofit organizations usually have comfortable offices close to the top executives to whom they report. Long hours, including evenings and weekends, are standard for most top executives and general managers, though their schedules may be flexible.

Substantial travel between international, national, regional, and local offices to monitor operations and meet with customers, staff, and other executives often is required of managers and executives. Many managers and executives also attend meetings and conferences sponsored by various associations. The conferences provide an opportunity to meet with prospective donors, customers, contractors, or government officials and allow managers and executives to keep abreast of technological and managerial innovations.

In large organizations, frequent job transfers between local offices or subsidiaries are common. General managers and top executives are under intense pressure to earn higher profits, provide better service, or attain fundraising and charitable goals. Executives in charge of poorly performing organizations or departments usually find their jobs in jeopardy.

Employment

General managers and top executives held over 3.3 million jobs in 1998. They are found in every industry, but wholesale, retail, and services industries employ over 6 out of 10.

Training, Other Qualifications, and Advancement

The educational background of managers and top executives varies as widely as the nature of their responsibilities. Many general managers and top executives have a bachelor's degree or higher in liberal arts or business administration. Their major often is related to the departments they direct—for example, a manager of finance may have a degree in accounting and a manager of information systems might have a degree in computer science. Graduate and professional degrees are common. Many managers in administrative, marketing, financial, and manufacturing activities have a master's degree in business administration. Managers in highly technical manufacturing and research activities often have a master's degree in engineering or a doctoral degree in a scientific discipline. A law degree is mandatory for managers of legal departments; hospital administrators generally have a master's degree in health services administration or business administration. (For additional information, see the *Handbook* statement on health services managers.)

In the public sector, many managers have liberal arts degrees in public administration or one of the social sciences. Park superintendents, for example, often have liberal arts degrees, whereas police chiefs are usually graduates of law enforcement academies and hold degrees in criminal justice or a related field. College presidents typically have a doctorate in the field they originally taught, and school superintendents often have a masters degree in education administration. (See the *Handbook* statement on education administrators.)

Since many general manager and top executive positions are filled by promoting experienced, lower level managers when an opening occurs, many are promoted from within the organization. In industries such as retail trade or transportation, for instance, it is possible for individuals without a college degree to work their way up within the company and become managers. Many companies prefer, however, that their top executives have specialized backgrounds and hire individuals who are managers in other organizations.

General managers and top executives must have highly developed personal skills. An analytical mind able to quickly assess large amounts of information and data is very important, as is the ability to consider and evaluate the interrelationships of numerous factors. General managers and top executives must also be able to communicate clearly and persuasively. Other qualities critical for managerial success include leadership, self-confidence, motivation, decisiveness, flexibility, sound business judgment, and determination.

Advancement may be accelerated by participation in company training programs that impart a broader knowledge of company policy and operations. Managers can also help their careers by becoming familiar with the latest developments in management techniques at national or local training programs sponsored by various industry and trade associations. Senior managers who often have experience in a particular field, such as accounting or engineering, also attend executive development programs to facilitate their promotion to general managers. Participation in conferences and seminars can expand knowledge of national and international issues influencing the organization and can help develop a network of useful contacts.

General managers may advance to top executive positions, such as executive vice president, in their own firm or they may take a corresponding position in another firm. They may even advance to peak corporate positions such as chief operating officer or chief executive officer. Chief executive officers often become members of the board of directors of one or more firms, typically as a director of their own firm and often as chair of its board of directors. Some general managers and top executives establish their own firms or become independent consultants.

Job Outlook

Employment of general managers and top executives is expected to grow about as fast as the average for all occupations through 2008. These high level managers are essential employees because they plan, organize, direct, control, and coordinate the operations of an organization and its major departments or programs. Therefore, top managers should be more immune to automation and corporate restructuring—factors which are expected to adversely affect employment of lower level managers. Because this is a large occupation, many openings will occur each year as executives transfer to other positions, start their own businesses, or retire. Because many executives who leave their jobs transfer to other executive or managerial positions, however, openings for new entrants are limited and intense competition is expected for top managerial jobs.

Projected employment growth of general managers and top executives varies widely among industries, largely reflecting overall industry growth. Overall employment growth is expected to be faster than average in services industries, but only about as fast as average in finance, insurance, and real estate industries. Employment of general managers and top executives is projected to decline along with overall employment in most manufacturing industries.

Experienced managers whose accomplishments reflect strong leadership qualities and the ability to improve the efficiency or competitive position of an organization will have the best opportunities. In an increasingly global economy, experience in international economics, marketing, information systems, and knowledge of several languages may also be beneficial.

Earnings

General managers and top executives are among the highest paid workers. However, salary levels vary substantially depending upon the level of managerial responsibility, length of service, and type, size, and location of the firm. For example, a top manager in a very large corporation can earn significantly more than a counterpart in a small firm.

Median annual earnings of general managers and top executives in 1998 were $55,890. The middle 50 percent earned between $34,970 and $94,650. Because the specific responsibilities of general managers vary significantly within industries, earnings also tend to vary considerably. Median annual earnings in the industries employing the largest numbers of general managers and top executives in 1997 were:

Management and public relations	$91,400
Computer and data processing services	90,600
Wholesale trade machinery, equipment, and supplies	65,900
Gasoline service stations	36,800
Eating and drinking places	33,000

Salaries vary substantially by type and level of responsibilities and by industry. According to a salary survey done by Executive Compensation Reports, a division of Harcourt Brace & Company, the median salary for CEOs of public companies from the fiscal year 1998 *Fortune 500* list was approximately $800,000. Three quarters of CEOs in the nonprofit sector made under $100,000 in 1998, according to a survey by Abbott, Langer, & Associates.

In addition to salaries, total compensation often includes stock options, dividends, and other performance bonuses. The use of executive dining rooms and company cars, expense allowances, and company-paid insurance premiums and physical examinations also are among benefits commonly enjoyed by general managers and top executives in private industry. A number of CEOs also are provided with company-paid club memberships, a limousine with driver, and other amenities.

Related Occupations

General managers and top executives plan, organize, direct, control, and coordinate the operations of an organization and its major departments or programs. The members of the board of directors and lower level managers are also involved in these activities. Other managerial occupations have similar responsibilities; however, they are concentrated in specific industries or are responsible for a specific department within an organization. They include administrative services managers, education administrators, financial managers, and restaurant and food service managers. Government occupations with similar functions are President, governor, mayor, commissioner, and legislator.

Sources of Additional Information

For a variety of information on general managers and top executives, including educational programs and job listings, contact:

☛ American Management Association, 1601 Broadway, New York, NY 10019-7420. Internet: **http://www.amanet.org**

☛ National Management Association, 2210 Arbor Blvd., Dayton, OH 45439. Internet: **http://www.nma1.org**

Government Chief Executives and Legislators

(O*NETet 19005A)

Significant Points

- Over 9 out of 10 government chief executives and legislators work in local government.
- Most government chief executives and legislators are elected; local government managers are appointed.
- Few long-term career opportunities are available.
- There is less competition for executive and legislative jobs in small communities that offer part-time positions with little or no compensation or staff support.

Nature of the Work

Chief executives and legislators at the Federal, State, and local levels direct government activities and pass laws that affect us daily. These

Government chief executives and legislators oversee budgets and ensure that resources are properly used.

officials consist of the President and Vice President of the United States, members of Congress, State governors and lieutenant governors, members of the State legislators, county chief executives and commissioners, city, town and township council members, mayors, and city, county, town, and township managers. (Many small communities have top government officials who are volunteers and receive no salary. These individuals are not included in the employment or salary numbers provided in this *Handbook* statement.)

Most chief executives are elected by their constituents, but many managers are hired by a local government executive, council, or commission, to whom they are directly responsible. These officials formulate and establish government policy and develop Federal, State, or local laws and regulations. (General administrators who do not have overall responsibility for the government entity are discussed in the *Handbook* statement on general managers and top executives.)

Government chief executives, like their counterparts in the private sector, have overall responsibility for the performance of their organizations. Working with legislators, they set goals and organize programs to attain them. These executives also appoint department heads, who oversee the civil servants who carry out programs enacted by legislative bodies. As in the private sector, government chief executives oversee budgets and insure that resources are used properly and programs are carried out as planned.

Chief executives carry out a number of other important functions, such as meeting with legislators and constituents to determine the level of support for proposed programs. In addition, they often nominate citizens to boards and commissions, encourage business investment, and promote economic development in their communities. To do all of these varied tasks effectively, chief executives of large governments rely on a staff of highly skilled aides and assistants to research issues that concern the public. Executives that control small governmental bodies, however, often do this work by themselves.

Legislators are elected officials who enact or amend laws. They include U.S. Senators and Representatives, State senators and representatives, and county, city, and town commissioners and council members. Legislators introduce, examine, and vote on bills to pass official legislation. In preparing such legislation, they study staff reports and hear testimony from constituents, representatives of interest groups, board and commission members, and others with an interest in the issue under consideration. They usually must approve budgets and the appointments of nominees for leadership posts who are submitted by the chief executive. In some bodies, the legislative council appoints the city, town, or county manager.

Working Conditions

The working conditions of chief executives and legislators vary with the size and budget of the governmental unit. Time spent at work ranges from a few hours a week for some local leaders to stressful weeks of 60 or more hours for members of the U.S. Congress. Similarly, some jobs require only occasional out-of-town travel, while others involve long periods away from home, such as when attending sessions of the legislature.

U.S. Senators and Representatives, governors and lieutenant governors, and chief executives and legislators in municipalities work full time, year-round, as do most county and city managers. Many State legislators work full time on government business while the legislature is in session (usually for 2 to 6 months a year or every other year) and work only part time when the legislature is not in session. Some local elected officials work a schedule that is officially designated as part time, but actually is the equivalent of a full-time schedule when unpaid duties are taken into account. In addition to their regular schedules, most chief executives are on call to handle emergencies.

Employment

Chief executives and legislators held about 80,000 jobs in 1998. About 9 out of 10 worked in local government. Chief executives and legislators in the Federal Government consist of the 100 Senators, 435 Representatives, and the President and Vice President. State governors, lieutenant governors, legislators, chief executives, professional managers, and council and commission members of local governments make up the remainder.

Government chief executives and legislators who do not hold full-time, year-round positions often continue to work in the occupation they held before being elected.

Training, Other Qualifications, and Advancement

Apart from meeting minimum age, residency, and citizenship requirements, candidates for public office have no established training or qualifications. Candidates come from a wide variety of occupations, but many do have some political experience as staffers or members of government bureaus, boards, or commissions. Successful candidates usually become well-known through their political campaigns and some have built voter name recognition through their work with community religious, fraternal, or social organizations.

Increasingly, candidates target information to voters through advertising paid for by their respective campaigns, so fund raising skills are essential for candidates. Management-level work experience and public service help develop the fund raising, budgeting, public speaking, and problem solving skills that are needed to run an effective political campaign. Candidates must make decisions quickly, sometimes on the basis of limited or contradictory information. They should also be able to inspire and motivate their constituents and staff. Additionally, they must know how to reach compromises and satisfy conflicting demands of constituents. National, State, and some local campaigns require massive amounts of energy and stamina, traits vital to successful candidates.

Virtually all town, city, and county managers have at least a bachelor's degree, and the majority hold a master's degree. A master's degree in public administration is recommended, including courses in public financial management and legal issues in public administration. Working in management support positions in government is a prime source of the experience and personal contacts required to eventually secure a manager position. For example, applicants often gain experience as management analysts or assistants in government departments working for committees, councils, or chief executives. In this capacity, they learn about planning, budgeting, civil engineering, and other aspects of running a government. With sufficient experience, they may be hired to manage a small government.

Generally, a town, city, or county manager is first hired by a smaller community. Advancement often takes the form of securing positions with progressively larger towns, cities, or counties. A broad knowledge of local issues, combined with communication skills and the ability to compromise, are essential for advancement in this field.

Advancement opportunities for elected officials are not clearly defined. Because elected positions normally require a period of residency and local public support is critical, officials usually advance to other offices only in the jurisdictions where they live. For example, council members may run for mayor or for a position in the State government, and State legislators may run for governor or for Congress. Many officials are not politically ambitious, however, and do not seek advancement. Others lose their bids for reelection or voluntarily leave the occupation. A lifetime career as a government chief executive or legislator is rare.

Job Outlook

Overall, little or no change in employment is expected among government chief executives and legislators through 2008. Few new governments at any level are likely to form, and the number of chief executives and legislators in existing governments rarely changes. However, some increase will occur at the local level as counties, cities, and towns take on professional managers or move from volunteer to paid, career executives to deal with population growth, Federal regulations, and long-range planning.

Elections give newcomers the chance to unseat incumbents or to fill vacated positions. The level of competition in elections varies from place to place. There tends to be less competition in small communities that offer part-time positions with low or no salaries and little or no staff compared to large municipalities with prestigious full-time positions offering high salaries, staff, and greater exposure.

Earnings

Median annual earnings of government chief executives and legislators were $19,130 in 1998. The middle 50 percent earned between $12,090 and $47,470. The lowest 10 percent earned less than $11,460, and the highest 10 percent earned more than $81,230.

Earnings of public administrators vary widely, depending on the size of the governmental unit and on whether the job is part time, full time and year round, or full time for only a few months a year. Salaries range from little or nothing for a small town council member to $200,000 a year for the President of the United States.

The International City/County Management Association reports the average annual salary of chief elected city officials was about $12,900, and the average salary for city managers was $70,500 in 1997. According to the International Personnel Management association, city managers earned an average of $101,800 and county managers $95,500 in 1999. Also, the National Conference of State Legislatures reports that the salary for legislators in the 40 States that paid an annual salary and the District of Columbia ranged from $3,700 in South Dakota on even years to $75,600 in California and $80,600 in the District of Columbia. In 8 States, legislators received a daily salary plus an additional allowance for living expenses while legislatures were in session. New Hampshire paid no expenses and $200 per 2-year term, while New Mexico paid no salary at all but did pay a daily expense allowance.

The Council of State Governments reports in their *Book of the States, 1998-99* that gubernatorial annual salaries ranged from a low of $60,000 in Arkansas to a high of $130,000 in New York. In addition to a salary, most governors received benefits such as transportation and an official residence. The governor of Florida has the largest staff with 264 while the governor of Wyoming has the smallest with 14.

In 1999, U.S. Senators and Representatives earned $136,700, the Senate and House Majority and Minority leaders earned $151,800, and the Vice President was paid $175,400.

Related Occupations

Related occupations include managerial positions that require a broad range of skills and administrative expertise, such as corporate chief executives and board members, as well as high ranking officers in the military.

Sources of Additional Information

Information on appointed officials in local government can be obtained from:

☛ The Council of State Governments, P.O. Box 11910, Iron Works Pike, Lexington, KY 40578-1910. Internet: **http://www.statesnews.org**

☛ International City Management Association (ICMA), 777 North Capital NE., Suite 500, Washington, DC 20002.
Internet: **http://www.icma.org**

☛ National Association of Counties, 440 First St. NW., Suite 800, Washington, DC 20001. Internet: **http://www.naco.org**

☛ National League of Cities, 1301 Pennsylvania Ave. NW., Washington, DC 20004. Internet: **http://www.nlc.org**

Health Services Managers

(O*NET 15008A and 15008B)

Significant Points

- Earnings of health services managers are high, but long work hours are common.
- Employment will grow fastest in home health agencies, residential care facilities, and practitioners' offices and clinics.

Nature of the Work

Health care is a business and like every other business, it needs good management to keep it running smoothly, especially during times of change. The term "health services manager" encompasses individuals who plan, direct, coordinate, and supervise the delivery of health care. Health services managers include generalists and specialists. Generalists manage or help to manage an entire facility or system, while specialists are in charge of specific clinical departments or services.

The structure and financing of health care is changing rapidly. Future health services managers must be prepared to deal with evolving integrated health care delivery systems, restructuring of work, technological innovations, and an increased focus on preventive care. They will be called upon to improve efficiency in health care facilities and the quality of the health care provided. Increasingly, health services managers work in organizations in which they must optimize efficiency of a variety of interrelated services, ranging from inpatient care to outpatient follow-up care, for example.

Large facilities usually have several assistant administrators to aid the top administrator and to handle daily decisions. They may direct

Health services managers must deal with evolving health care delivery systems.

activities in clinical areas such as nursing, surgery, therapy, medical records or health information; or in nonhealth areas such as finance, housekeeping, human resources, and information management. (Because the nonhealth departments are not directly related to health care, these managers are not included in this statement. For information about them, see the statements on managerial occupations elsewhere in the *Handbook*).

In smaller facilities, top administrators handle more of the details of daily operations. For example, many nursing home administrators manage personnel, finance, facility operations, and admissions, and have a larger role in resident care.

Clinical managers have more specific responsibilities than generalists, and have training and/or experience in a specific clinical area. For example, directors of physical therapy are experienced physical therapists, and most health information and medical record administrators have a bachelor's degree in health information or medical record administration. These managers establish and implement policies, objectives, and procedures for their departments; evaluate personnel and work; develop reports and budgets; and coordinate activities with other managers.

In group practices, managers work closely with physicians. Whereas an office manager may handle business affairs in small medical groups, leaving policy decisions to the physicians themselves, larger groups usually employ a full-time administrator to advise on business strategies and coordinate day-to-day business.

A small group of 10 or 15 physicians might employ one administrator to oversee personnel matters, billing and collection, budgeting, planning, equipment outlays, and patient flow. A large practice of 40 or 50 physicians may have a chief administrator and several assistants, each responsible for different areas.

Health services managers in health maintenance organizations (HMOs) and other managed care settings perform functions similar to those in large group practices, except their staffs may be larger. In addition, they may do more work in the areas of community outreach and preventive care than managers of a group practice. The size of the administrative staff in HMOs varies according to the size and type of HMO.

Some health services managers oversee the activities of a number of facilities in health systems. Such systems may contain both inpatient and outpatient facilities and offer a wide range of patient services.

Working Conditions

Most health services managers work long hours. Facilities such as nursing homes and hospitals operate around the clock, and administrators and managers may be called at all hours to deal with problems. They may also travel to attend meetings or inspect satellite facilities.

Employment

Health services managers held about 222,000 jobs in 1998. Almost one-half of all jobs were in hospitals. About 1 in 4 were in nursing and personal care facilities or offices and clinics of physicians. The remainder worked mostly in home health agencies, ambulatory facilities run by state and local governments, offices of dentists and other health practitioners, medical and dental laboratories, residential care facilities, and other social service agencies.

Training, Other Qualifications, and Advancement

Health services managers must be familiar with management principles and practices. A master's degree in health services administration, long-term care administration, health sciences, public health, public administration, or business administration is the standard credential for most generalist positions in this field. However, a bachelor's degree is adequate for some entry-level positions in smaller facilities and for some entry-level positions at the departmental level within health care organizations. Physicians' offices and some other facilities may substitute on-the-job experience for formal education.

For clinical department heads, a degree in the appropriate field and work experience may be sufficient for entry, but a master's degree in health services administration or a related field may be required to advance. For example, nursing service administrators are usually chosen from among supervisory registered nurses with administrative abilities and a graduate degree in nursing or health services administration.

Bachelor's, master's, and doctoral degree programs in health administration are offered by colleges, universities, and schools of public health, medicine, allied health, public administration, and business administration. In 1999, 67 schools had accredited programs leading to the master's degree in health services administration, according to the Accrediting Commission on Education for Health Services Administration.

Some graduate programs seek students with undergraduate degrees in business or health administration; however, many graduate programs prefer students with a liberal arts or health profession background. Candidates with previous work experience in health care may also have an advantage. Competition for entry to these programs is keen, and applicants need above-average grades to gain admission.

These programs usually last between 2 and 3 years. They may include up to 1 year of supervised administrative experience, and course work in areas such as hospital organization and management, marketing, accounting and budgeting, human resources administration, strategic planning, health economics, and health information systems. Some programs allow students to specialize in one type of facility—hospitals; nursing homes; mental health facilities; HMOs; or medical groups. Other programs encourage a generalist approach to health administration education.

New graduates with master's degrees in health services administration may start as department managers or in staff positions. The level of the starting position varies with the experience of the applicant and size of the organization. Hospitals and other health facilities offer postgraduate residencies and fellowships, which usually are staff positions. Graduates from master's degree programs also take jobs in HMOs, large group medical practices, clinics, mental health facilities, multifacility nursing home corporations, and consulting firms.

Graduates with bachelor's degrees in health administration usually begin as administrative assistants or assistant department heads in larger hospitals, or as department heads or assistant administrators in small hospitals or nursing homes.

All States and the District of Columbia require nursing home administrators to have a bachelor's degree, pass a licensing examination, complete a State-approved training program, and pursue continuing education. A license is not required in other areas of health services management.

Health services managers are often responsible for millions of dollars of facilities and equipment and hundreds of employees. To make effective decisions, they need to be open to different opinions and good at analyzing contradictory information. They must understand finance and information systems, and be able to interpret data. Motivating others to implement their decisions requires strong leadership abilities. Tact, diplomacy, flexibility, and communication skills are essential because health services managers spend most of their time interacting with others.

Health services managers advance by moving into more responsible and higher paying positions, such as assistant or associate administrator, or by moving to larger facilities.

Job Outlook

Employment of health services managers is expected to grow faster than the average for all occupations through 2008 as health services continue to expand and diversify. Opportunities for health services managers should be closely related to growth in the industry in which they are employed. Opportunities will be especially good in home health care, long-term care, and nontraditional health organizations, such as managed care operations and consulting firms—particularly for health services managers with work experience in the health care field and strong business and management skills.

Hospitals will continue to employ the most managers, although the number of jobs will grow slowly compared to other areas. As hospitals continue to consolidate, centralize, and diversify functions, competition will increase at all job levels.

Employment will grow the fastest in home health agencies, residential care facilities, and practitioners' offices and clinics. Many services previously provided in hospitals will be shifted to these sectors, especially as medical technologies improve. Demand in medical group practice management will grow as medical group practices become larger and more complex. Health services managers will need to deal with the pressures of cost containment and financial accountability, as well as the increased focus on preventive care. They will also become more involved in trying to improve the health of their communities.

Health services managers will also be employed by health care management companies who provide management services to hospitals and other organizations, as well as specific departments such as emergency, information management systems, managed care contract negotiations, and physician recruiting.

Earnings

Median annual earnings of medical and health service managers were $48,870 in 1998. The middle 50 percent earned between $37,900 and $71,580 a year. The lowest 10 percent earned less than $28,600 and the highest 10 percent earned more than $88,730 a year. Median annual earnings in the industries employing the largest number of medical and health service managers in 1997 were as follows:

Hospitals	$52,600
Home health care services	45,800
Health and allied services, not elsewhere classified	44,700
Nursing and personal care facilities	43,600
Offices and clinics of medical doctors	39,600

Earnings of health services managers vary by type and size of the facility, as well as by level of responsibility. For example, the Medical Group Management Association reported that the median salary in 1998 for administrators by group practice size was: fewer than 7 physicians, $60,000; 7 to 25 physicians, $76,700; and more than 26 physicians, $124,500.

According to a survey by *Modern Healthcare* magazine, median annual compensation in 1998 for managers of the following clinical departments was: Respiratory therapy, $57,700; home health care, $62,400; ambulatory and outpatient services, $66,200, radiology, $66,800; clinical laboratory, $66,900; physical therapy, $68,100; rehabilitation services, $73,400; and nursing services, $100,200. Salaries also varied according to size of facility and geographic region.

According to the Buck Survey conducted by the American Health Care Association in 1997, nursing home administrators' median annual earnings were $52,800. The middle 50 percent earned between $44,300 and $60,300 a year. Assistant administrators had median annual earnings of about $35,000, with the middle 50 percent earning between $28,700 and $41,200.

Related Occupations

Health services managers have training or experience in both health and management. Other occupations requiring knowledge of both fields are public health directors, social welfare administrators, directors of voluntary health agencies and health professional associations, and underwriters in health insurance companies.

Sources of Additional Information

General information about health administration is available from:

☛ American College of Healthcare Executives, One North Franklin St., Suite 1700, Chicago, IL 60606. Internet: **http://www.ache.org**

Information about undergraduate and graduate academic programs in this field is available from:

☛ Association of University Programs in Health Administration, 730 11th St., NW., Washington, DC 20001-4510.
Internet: **http://www.aupha.org**

For a list of accredited graduate programs in health services administration, contact:

☛ Accrediting Commission on Education for Health Services Administration, 730 11th St., NW., Washington, DC 20001-4510.

For information about career opportunities in long-term care administration, contact:

☛ American College of Health Care Administrators, 325 S. Patrick St., Alexandria, VA 22314.

For information about career opportunities in medical group practices and ambulatory care management, contact:

☛ Medical Group Management Association, 104 Inverness Terrace East, Englewood, CO 80112.

For information about health care office managers, contact:

☛ Professional Association of Health Care Office Managers, 461 East Ten Mile Rd., Pensacola, FL 32534-9712.
Internet: **http://www.pahcom.com**

Hotel Managers and Assistants

(O*NET 15026A)

Significant Points

- Long hours and the stress of dealing with hotel patrons result in high turnover among hotel managers.
- College graduates with degrees in hotel or restaurant management should have good job opportunities.

Nature of the Work

A comfortable room, good food, and a helpful hotel staff can make being away from home an enjoyable experience for both vacationing families and business travelers. Hotel managers and assistant managers help their guests have a pleasant stay by providing many of the comforts of home, including cable television, fitness equipment, and voice mail. Additionally, some hotels have health spas and other specialized services that the hotel manager and assistant help keep running smoothly. For business travelers, hotel managers often schedule available meeting rooms and electronic equipment, including slide projectors and fax machines.

Hotel managers are responsible for keeping the operation of their establishments efficient and profitable. In a small hotel, motel, or inn with a limited staff, the manager may oversee all aspects of operations. However, large hotels may employ hundreds of workers, and the general manager is usually aided by a number of assistant managers assigned to the various departments of the operation. In hotels of every size, managerial duties vary significantly by job title.

The *general manager*, for example, has overall responsibility for the operation of the hotel. Within guidelines established by the owners of the hotel or executives of the hotel chain, the general manager sets room rates, allocates funds to departments, approves expenditures, and establishes standards for service to guests, decor, housekeeping, food quality, and banquet operations. Managers who work for chains may also organize and staff a newly built hotel, refurbish an older hotel, or reorganize a hotel or motel that is not operating successfully. In order to fill some low-paying service and clerical jobs in hotels, some general managers attend career fairs. (For more information, see the statement on general managers and top executives elsewhere in the *Handbook*.)

Resident managers live in hotels and are on call 24 hours a day to resolve problems or emergencies. In general, though, they typically work an 8-hour day and oversee the day-to-day operations of the hotel. In many hotels, the general manager is also the resident manager.

Executive housekeepers ensure guest rooms, meeting and banquet rooms, and public areas are clean, orderly, and well maintained. They also train, schedule, and supervise the work of housekeepers, inspect rooms, and order cleaning supplies.

Front office managers coordinate reservations and room assignments as well as train and direct the hotel's front desk staff. They ensure that guests are treated courteously, complaints and problems are resolved,

Because hotels are open around the clock, night and weekend work is common.

and requests for special services are carried out. Front office managers often have authorization to adjust charges posted on a customer's bill.

Food and beverage managers direct the food service operations of hotels. They oversee the hotels' restaurants, cocktail lounges, and banquet facilities. These managers also supervise food and beverage preparation and service workers, plan menus, set schedules, estimate costs, and deal with food suppliers. (For more information on similar workers in other industries, see the statement on restaurant and food service managers elsewhere in the *Handbook*.)

Convention services managers coordinate the activities of large hotels' various departments for meetings, conventions, and special events. They meet with representatives of groups or organizations to plan the number of rooms to reserve, the desired configuration of hotel meeting space, and the banquet services. During the meeting or event, they resolve unexpected problems and monitor activities to ensure that hotel operations conform to the expectations of the group.

Assistant managers help run the day-to-day operations of the hotel. In large hotels they may be responsible for activities such as personnel, accounting, office administration, marketing and sales, purchasing, security, maintenance, and pool, spa, or recreational facilities. In smaller hotels, these duties may be combined into one position. Some hotels allow an assistant manager to make decisions regarding hotel guest charges when a manager is unavailable.

Computers are used extensively by hotel managers and their assistants to keep track of the guest's bill, reservations, room assignments, meetings, and special events. In addition, computers are used to order food, beverages, and supplies, as well as to prepare reports for hotel owners and top-level managers. Managers work with computer specialists to ensure that the hotel's computer system functions properly. Should the hotel's computer system fail, managers must continue to meet guests' needs.

Working Conditions

Because hotels are open around the clock, night and weekend work is common. Many hotel managers work more than 40 hours per week. Managers who live in the hotel usually have regular work schedules, but they may be called to work at any time. Some employees of resort hotels are managers during the busy season and have other duties during the rest of the year.

Hotel managers sometimes experience the pressures of coordinating a wide range of functions. Conventions and large groups of tourists may present unusual problems. Moreover, dealing with irate guests can be stressful. The job can be particularly hectic for front office managers during check-in and check-out time. Computer failures can further complicate an already busy time.

Employment

Hotel managers and assistant managers held about 76,000 jobs in 1998. Self-employed managers—primarily owners of small hotels and motels—held a significant number of these jobs. Companies that manage hotels and motels under contract employed some managers.

Training, Other Qualifications, and Advancement

Hotels increasingly emphasize specialized training. Postsecondary training in hotel or restaurant management is preferred for most hotel management positions, although a college liberal arts degree may be sufficient when coupled with related hotel experience. Internships or part-time or summer work is an asset to students seeking a career in hotel management. The experience gained and the contacts made with employers can greatly benefit them after graduation. Most bachelor's degree programs include work-study opportunities.

In the past, many managers were promoted from the ranks of front desk clerks, housekeepers, waiters and chefs, and hotel sales workers. Although some employees still advance to hotel management positions without education beyond high school, postsecondary education is preferred. Restaurant management training or experience is also a good background for entering hotel management because the success of a hotel's food service and beverage operations is often of great importance to the profitability of the entire establishment.

In 1998, nearly 200 community and junior colleges and some universities offered associate, bachelor's, and graduate degree programs in hotel or restaurant management. When combined with technical institutes, vocational and trade schools, and other academic institutions, over 800 educational facilities have programs leading to formal recognition in hotel or restaurant management. Hotel management programs include instruction in hotel administration, accounting, economics, marketing, housekeeping, food service management and catering, and hotel maintenance engineering. Computer training is also an integral part of hotel management training due to the widespread use of computers in reservations, billing, and housekeeping management.

Hotel managers must be able to get along with many different people, even in stressful situations. They must be able to solve problems and concentrate on details. Initiative, self-discipline, effective communication skills, and the ability to organize and direct the work of others are also essential for managers at all levels.

Most hotels promote employees who have proven their ability and completed formal education in hotel management. Graduates of hotel or restaurant management programs usually start as trainee assistant managers. Some large hotels sponsor specialized on-the-job management training programs allowing trainees to rotate among various departments and gain a thorough knowledge of the hotel's operation. Other hotels may help finance formal training in hotel management for outstanding employees. Newly built hotels, particularly those without well-established on-the-job training programs, often prefer experienced personnel for managerial positions.

Large hotel and motel chains may offer better opportunities for advancement than small, independently owned establishments, but relocation every several years often is necessary for advancement. The large chains have more extensive career ladder programs and offer managers the opportunity to transfer to another hotel or motel in the chain or to the central office. Career advancement can be accelerated by completion of certification programs offered by the associations listed below. These programs usually require a combination of course work, examinations, and experience.

Job Outlook

Employment of hotel managers and assistants is expected to grow more slowly than the average for all occupations through 2008. Long hours and stressful working conditions result in high turnover in this field, so additional job openings are expected to occur as experienced managers transfer to other occupations, retire, or stop working for other reasons. Job opportunities in hotel management are expected to be especially good for persons with college degrees in hotel or restaurant management.

Increasing business travel and domestic and foreign tourism will drive employment growth of hotel managers and assistants. Managerial jobs are not expected to grow as rapidly as the hotel industry overall, however. As the industry consolidates, many chains and franchises will acquire independently owned establishments and increase the number of economy-class rooms to accommodate bargain-conscious guests. Economy hotels offer clean, comfortable rooms and front desk services without costly extras like restaurants and room service. Because there are not as many departments in these hotels, fewer managers will be needed. In addition, front desk clerks are increasingly assuming some responsibilities previously reserved for managers, further limiting the growth of managers and their assistants.

Additional demand for managers, however, is expected in suite hotels as some guests, especially business customers, are willing to pay higher prices for rooms with kitchens and suites that provide the space needed to conduct meetings. In addition to job growth in suite hotels and economy-class hotels, large full-service hotels—offering restaurants, fitness centers, large meeting rooms, and play areas for children, among other amenities—will continue to offer many trainee and managerial opportunities.

Earnings

Median annual earnings of hotel managers and assistants were $26,700 in 1998. The middle 50 percent of these workers earned between $19,820 and $34,690. The lowest 10 percent had earnings of less than $14,430, while the top 10 percent earned over $45,520. In 1997, median annual earnings in the hotel and other lodging places industry, where nearly all of these workers are employed, were $28,600.

Salaries of hotel managers and assistants vary greatly according to their responsibilities and the segment of the hotel industry in which they are employed. Managers may earn bonuses up to 25 percent of their basic salary in some hotels and may also be furnished with lodging, meals, parking, laundry, and other services. In addition to typical benefits, some hotels offer profit-sharing plans and educational assistance to their employees.

Related Occupations

Other occupations concerned with organizing and directing a business where customer service is the cornerstone of their success include restaurant managers, apartment building managers, retail store managers, and office managers.

Sources of Additional Information

For information on careers and scholarships in hotel management, contact:

☛ The American Hotel and Motel Association (AH&MA), Information Center, 1201 New York Ave. NW., Washington, DC 20005-3931.

Information on careers in the lodging industry and professional development and training programs may be obtained from:

☛ The Educational Institute of the American Hotel and Motel Association, P.O. Box 531126 Orlando, FL 32853-1126.
Internet: **http://www.ei-ahma.org**

For information on educational programs, including correspondence courses, in hotel and restaurant management, write to:

☛ Council on Hotel, Restaurant, and Institutional Education, 1200 17th St. NW., Washington, DC 20036-3097.

Information on careers in housekeeping management may be obtained from:

☛ National Executive Housekeepers Association, Inc., 1001 Eastwind Dr., Suite 301, Westerville, OH 43081. Phone: (800) 200-6342.

Human Resources, Training, and Labor Relations Specialists and Managers

(O*NET 13005A, 13005B, 13005C, 13005E, 21511A, 21511B, 21511C, 21511D, 21511E, and 21511F)

Significant Points

- Employers usually seek college graduates for entry-level jobs.
- Depending on the job duties, a strong background in human resources, business, technical, or liberal arts subjects may be preferred.
- The job market is likely to remain competitive because of the abundant supply of qualified college graduates and experienced workers.

Nature of the Work

Attracting the most qualified employees and matching them to the jobs for which they are best suited is important for the success of any organization. However, many enterprises are too large to permit close contact between top management and employees. Human resources, training, and labor relations specialists and managers provide this link. These individuals recruit and interview employees, and advise on hiring decisions in accordance with policies and requirements that have been established in conjunction with top management. In an effort to improve morale and productivity and limit job turnover, they also help their firms effectively use employee skills, provide training opportunities to enhance those skills, and boost employee satisfaction with their jobs and working conditions. Although some jobs in the human resources field require only limited contact with people outside the office, dealing with people is an essential part of the job.

In a small organization, a *human resources generalist* may handle all aspects of human resources work, requiring a broad range of knowledge. The responsibilities of human resources generalists can vary widely, depending on their employer's needs. In a large corporation, the top human resources executive usually develops and coordinates personnel programs and policies. (Executives are included in the *Handbook* statement on general managers and top executives.) These policies are usually implemented by a director or manager of human resources and, in some cases, a director of industrial relations.

The *director of human resources* may oversee several departments, each headed by an experienced manager, who most likely specializes in one personnel activity such as employment, compensation, benefits, training and development, or employee relations.

Employment and placement managers oversee the hiring and separation of employees and supervise various workers, including equal employment opportunity specialists and recruitment specialists.

Recruiters maintain contacts within the community and may travel extensively, often to college campuses, to search for promising job applicants. Recruiters screen, interview, and in some cases, test applicants. They may also check references and extend job offers. These workers must be thoroughly familiar with the organization and its personnel policies to discuss wages, working conditions, and promotional opportunities with prospective employees. They must also keep informed about equal employment opportunity (EEO) and affirmative action guidelines and laws, such as the Americans With Disabilities Act.

EEO officers, representatives or *affirmative action coordinators* handle this area in large organizations. They investigate and resolve EEO grievances, examine corporate practices for possible violations, and compile and submit EEO statistical reports.

Employer relations representatives, who usually work in government agencies, maintain working relationships with local employers and promote the use of public employment programs and services. Similarly, *employment interviewers*—whose many job titles include *personnel consultants, personnel development specialists*, and *human resources coordinators*—help match job seekers with employers. (For more information on this occupation, see the statement on employment interviewers elsewhere in the *Handbook*.)

Job analysts, sometimes called *position classifiers*, perform very exacting work. They collect and examine detailed information about job duties to prepare job descriptions. These descriptions explain the duties, training, and skills each job requires. Whenever a large organization introduces a new job or reviews existing jobs, it calls upon the expert knowledge of the job analyst.

Occupational analysts conduct research, usually in large firms. They are concerned with occupational classification systems and study the effects of industry and occupational trends upon worker relationships. They may serve as technical liaison between the firm and industry, government, and labor unions.

Establishing and maintaining a firm's pay system is the principal job of the *compensation manager*. Assisted by staff specialists, compensation managers devise ways to ensure fair and equitable pay rates. They may conduct surveys to see how their rates compare with others and to see that the firm's pay scale complies with changing laws and regulations. In addition, compensation managers often oversee their firm's performance evaluation system, and they may design reward systems such as pay-for-performance plans.

Employee benefits managers handle the company's employee benefits program, notably its health insurance and pension plans. Expertise in designing and administering benefits programs continues to gain importance as employer-provided benefits account for a growing proportion of overall compensation costs, and as benefit plans increase in number and complexity. For example, pension benefits might include savings and thrift, profit sharing, and stock ownership plans; health benefits may include long-term catastrophic illness insurance and dental insurance. Familiarity with health benefits is a top priority, as more firms struggle to cope with the rising cost of health care for employees and retirees. In addition to health insurance and pension coverage, some firms offer employees life and accidental death and dismemberment insurance, disability insurance, and relatively new benefits designed to meet the needs of a changing work force, such as parental leave, child and elder care, long-term nursing home care insurance, employee assistance and wellness programs, and flexible benefits plans. Benefits managers must keep abreast of changing Federal and State regulations and legislation that may affect employee benefits.

Employee assistance plan managers, also called *employee welfare managers*, are responsible for a wide array of programs covering occupational safety and health standards and practices; health promotion and physical fitness, medical examinations, and minor health treatment, such as first aid; plant security; publications; food service and recreation activities; car pooling and transportation programs, such as transit subsidies; employee suggestion systems; child and elder care; and counseling services. Child care and elder care are increasingly important due to growth in the number of dual-income households and the elderly population. Counseling may help employees deal with emotional disorders, alcoholism, or marital, family, consumer, legal, and financial problems. Some employers offer career counseling as well. In large firms, certain programs, such as security and safety, may be in separate departments headed by other managers.

Training and development managers supervise training. Increasingly, management recognizes that training offers a way of developing skills, enhancing productivity and quality of work, and building loyalty to the firm. Training is widely accepted as a method of improving employee morale, but this is only one of the reasons for its growing importance. Other factors include the complexity of the work environment, the rapid pace of organizational and technological change, and the growing number of jobs in fields that constantly generate new knowledge. In addition, advances in learning theory have provided insights into how adults learn, and how training can be organized most effectively for them.

Training specialists plan, organize, and direct a wide range of training activities. Trainers conduct orientation sessions and arrange on-the-job training for new employees. They help rank-and-file workers maintain and improve their job skills, and possibly prepare for jobs requiring greater skill. They help supervisors improve their interpersonal skills in order to deal effectively with employees. They may set up individualized training plans to strengthen an employee's existing skills or teach new ones. Training specialists in some companies set up programs to develop executive potential among employees in lower-level positions. In government-supported training programs, training specialists function as case managers. They first assess the training needs of clients, then guide them through the most appropriate training method. After training, clients may either be referred to employer relations representatives or receive job placement assistance.

Planning and program development is an important part of the training specialist's job. In order to identify and assess training needs within the firm, trainers may confer with managers and supervisors or conduct surveys. They also periodically evaluate training effectiveness.

Depending on the size, goals, and nature of the organization, trainers may differ considerably in their responsibilities and in the methods they use. Training methods include on-the-job training; schools in

In addition to recruiting and interviewing, human resources, training, and labor relations specialists and managers provide training to enhance workers' skills and job satisfaction.

which shop conditions are duplicated for trainees prior to putting them on the shop floor; apprenticeship training; classroom training; programmed instruction, which may involve interactive videos and other computer-aided instructional technologies; simulators; conferences; and workshops.

The *director of industrial relations* forms labor policy, oversees industrial labor relations, negotiates collective bargaining agreements, and coordinates grievance procedures to handle complaints resulting from disputes with unionized employees. The director of industrial relations also advises and collaborates with the director of human resources, other managers, and members of their staff, because all aspects of personnel policy—such as wages, benefits, pensions, and work practices—may be involved in drawing up a new or revised contract.

Labor relations managers and their staff implement industrial labor relations programs. When a collective bargaining agreement is up for negotiation, labor relations specialists prepare information for management to use during negotiation, which requires familiarity with economic and wage data as well as extensive knowledge of labor law and collective bargaining trends. The labor relations staff interprets and administers the contract with respect to grievances, wages and salaries, employee welfare, health care, pensions, union and management practices, and other contractual stipulations. As union membership is continuing to decline in most industries, industrial relations personnel are working more with employees who are not members of a labor union.

Dispute resolution—attaining tacit or contractual agreements—has become increasingly important as parties to a dispute attempt to avoid costly litigation, strikes, or other disruptions. Dispute resolution also has become more complex, involving employees, management, unions, other firms, and government agencies. Specialists involved in dispute resolution must be highly knowledgeable and experienced, and often report to the director of industrial relations. *Conciliators*, or *mediators*, advise and counsel labor and management to prevent and, when necessary, resolve disputes over labor agreements or other labor relation's issues. *Arbitrators*, sometimes called umpires or referees, decide disputes that bind both labor and management to specific terms and conditions of labor contracts. Labor relations specialists who work for unions perform many of the same functions on behalf of the union and its members.

Other emerging specialists include *international human resources managers*, who handle human resources issues related to a company's foreign operations, and *human resources information system specialists*, who develop and apply computer programs to process personnel information, match job seekers with job openings and handle other personnel matters.

Working Conditions

Personnel work usually takes place in clean, pleasant, and comfortable office settings. Arbitrators and mediators may work out of their homes. Many human resources, training, and labor relations specialists and managers work a standard 35- to 40-hour week. However, longer hours might be necessary for some workers—for example, labor relations specialists and managers, arbitrators, and mediators—when contract agreements are being prepared and negotiated.

Although most human resources, training, and labor relations specialists and managers work in the office, some travel extensively. For example, recruiters regularly attend professional meetings and visit college campuses to interview prospective employees; arbitrators and mediators often must travel to the site chosen for negotiations.

Employment

Human resources, training, and labor relations specialists and managers held about 597,000 jobs in 1998. They were employed in virtually every industry. Specialists accounted for 3 out of 5 positions; managers, 2 out of 5. About 14,000 specialists were self-employed, working as consultants to public and private employers.

The private sector accounted for about 80 percent of salaried jobs. Among these salaried jobs, services industries—including business, health, social, management, and educational services—accounted for about 40 percent of jobs; labor organizations, the largest employer among specific services industries, accounted for over 20 percent of those. Manufacturing industries accounted for 17 percent of salaried jobs; while finance, insurance, and real estate firms accounted for about 11 percent of jobs.

Federal, State, and local governments employed about 14 percent of human resources specialists and managers. They handled the recruitment, interviewing, job classification, training, salary administration, benefits, employee relations, and related matters of the Nation's public employees.

Training, Other Qualifications, and Advancement

Because of the diversity of duties and level of responsibility, the educational backgrounds of human resources, training, and labor relations specialists and managers vary considerably. In filling entry-level jobs, employers usually seek college graduates. Many employers prefer applicants who have majored in human resources, personnel administration, or industrial and labor relations. Others look for college graduates with a technical or business background or a well-rounded liberal arts education.

Many colleges and universities have programs leading to a degree in personnel, human resources, or labor relations. Some offer degree programs in personnel administration or human resources management, training and development, or compensation and benefits. Depending on the school, courses leading to a career in human resources management may be found in departments of business administration, education, instructional technology, organizational development, human services, communication, or public administration, or within a separate human resources institution or department.

Because an interdisciplinary background is appropriate in this field, a combination of courses in the social sciences, business, and behavioral sciences is useful. Some jobs may require a more technical or specialized background in engineering, science, finance, or law, for example. Most prospective human resources specialists should take courses in compensation, recruitment, training and development, and performance appraisal, as well as courses in principles of management, organizational structure, and industrial psychology. Other relevant courses include business administration, public administration, psychology, sociology, political science, economics, and statistics. Courses in labor law, collective bargaining, labor economics, labor history, and industrial psychology also provide a valuable background for the prospective labor relations specialist. As in many other fields, knowledge of computers and information systems is also useful.

An advanced degree is increasingly important for some jobs. Many labor relations jobs require graduate study in industrial or labor relations. A strong background in industrial relations and law is highly desirable for contract negotiators, mediators, and arbitrators; in fact, many people in these specialties are lawyers. A background in law is also desirable for employee benefits managers and others who must interpret the growing number of laws and regulations. A master's degree in human resources, labor relations, or in business administration with a concentration in human resources management is highly recommended for those seeking general and top management positions.

For many specialized jobs in the human resources field, previous experience is an asset; for more advanced positions, including managers as well as arbitrators and mediators, it is essential. Many employers prefer entry-level workers who have gained some experience through an internship or work-study program while in school. Personnel administration and human resources development require the ability to work with individuals as well as a commitment to organizational goals. This field also demands other skills people may develop elsewhere—using computers, selling, teaching, supervising, and volunteering, among others. This field offers clerical workers opportunities for advancement to professional positions.

Responsible positions are sometimes filled by experienced individuals from other fields, including business, government, education., social services administration, and the military.

The human resources field demands a range of personal qualities and skills. Human resources, training, and labor relations specialists and managers must speak and write effectively. The growing diversity of the workforce requires that they work with or supervise people with various cultural backgrounds, levels of education, and experience. They must be able to cope with conflicting points of view, function under pressure, and demonstrate discretion, integrity, fair-mindedness, and a persuasive, congenial personality.

The duties given to entry-level workers will vary depending on whether they have a degree in human resource management, have completed an internship, or have some other type of human resources-related experience. Entry-level employees commonly learn the profession by performing administrative duties—helping to enter data into computer systems, compiling employee handbooks, researching information for a supervisor, or answering the phone and handling routine questions. Entry-level workers often enter formal or on-the-job training programs in which they learn how to classify jobs, interview applicants, or administer employee benefits. They then are assigned to specific areas in the personnel department to gain experience. Later, they may advance to a managerial position, overseeing a major element of the personnel program—compensation or training, for example.

Exceptional human resources workers may be promoted to director of personnel or industrial relations, which can eventually lead to a top managerial or executive position. Others may join a consulting firm or open their own business. A Ph.D. is an asset for teaching, writing, or consulting work.

Most organizations specializing in human resources offer classes intended to enhance the marketable skills of their members. Some organizations offer certification programs, which are signs of competence and can enhance one's advancement opportunities. For example, the International Foundation of Employee Benefit Plans confers the Certified Employee Benefit Specialist designation to persons who complete a series of college-level courses and pass exams covering employee benefit plans. The Society for Human Resources Management has two levels of certification—Professional in Human Resources, and Senior Professional in Human Resources; both require experience and a comprehensive exam.

Job Outlook

The job market for human resources, training, and labor relations specialists and managers is likely to remain competitive given the abundant supply of qualified college graduates and experienced workers. In addition to openings due to growth, many job openings will result from the need to replace workers who transfer to other occupations or leave the labor force.

Employment of human resources, training, and labor relations specialists and managers is expected to grow about as fast as the average for all occupations through 2008. New jobs will stem from increasing efforts throughout industry to recruit and retain quality employees. Employers are expected to devote greater resources to job-specific training programs in response to the increasing complexity of many jobs, the aging of the work force, and technological advances that can leave employees with obsolete skills. In addition, legislation and court rulings setting standards in various areas—occupational safety and health, equal employment opportunity, wages, health, pension, and family leave, among others—will increase demand for human resources, training, and labor relations experts. Rising health care costs, in particular, should spur demand for specialists to develop creative compensation and benefits packages that firms can offer prospective employees. Employment of labor relations staff, including arbitrators and mediators, should grow as firms become more involved in labor relations, and attempt to resolve potentially costly labor-management disputes out of court. Additional job growth may stem from increasing demand for specialists in international human resources management and human resources information systems.

Employment demand should be strong among firms involved in management, consulting, and personnel supply, as businesses increasingly contract out personnel functions or hire personnel specialists on a temporary basis to meet the increasing cost and complexity of training and development programs. Demand should also increase in firms that develop and administer complex employee benefits and compensation packages for other organizations.

Demand for human resources, training, and labor relations specialists and managers is also governed by the staffing needs of the firms for which they work. A rapidly expanding business is likely to hire additional human resources workers—either as permanent employees or consultants—while a business that has experienced a merger or a reduction in its work force will require fewer human resources workers. Also, as human resources management becomes increasingly important to the success of an organization, some small and medium-size businesses that do not have a human resources department may assign employees various human resources duties together with other unrelated responsibilities. In any particular firm, the size and the job duties of the human resources staff are determined by the firm's organizational philosophy and goals, skills of its work force, pace of technological change, government regulations, collective bargaining agreements, standards of professional practice, and labor market conditions.

Job growth could be limited by the widespread use of computerized human resources information systems that make workers more productive. Similar to other workers, employment of human resources, training, and labor relations specialists and managers, particularly in larger firms, may be adversely affected by corporate downsizing and restructuring.

Earnings

Median annual earnings of human resources managers were $49,010 in 1998. The middle 50 percent earned between $35,400 and $73,830. The lowest 10 percent earned less than $25,750 and the highest 10 percent earned more than $91,040. Median annual earnings in the industries employing the largest numbers of human resources managers in 1997 were:

Local government, except education and hospitals	$50,800
Hospitals	48,200
Management and public relations	44,800
Labor organizations	36,700
Personnel supply services	35,900

Median annual earnings of human resources, training, and labor relations specialists were $37,710 in 1998. The middle 50 percent earned between $28,200 and $50,160. The lowest 10 percent earned less than $20,310 and the highest 10 percent earned more than $75,440. Median annual earnings in the industries employing the largest numbers of human resources, training, and labor relations specialists in 1997 were:

Federal Government	$51,800
Local government, except education and hospitals	39,900
Hospitals	35,000
State government, except education and hospitals	34,100
Labor organizations	29,700

According to a 1999 salary survey conducted by the National Association of Colleges and Employers, bachelor's degree candidates majoring in human resources, including labor relations, received starting offers averaging $29,800 a year.

According to a November 1998 survey of compensation in the human resources field, conducted by Abbott, Langer, and Associates of Crete, Illinois, the median total cash compensation for selected personnel and labor relations occupations were:

Occupation	Compensation
Industrial and labor relations directors	$183,900
Compensation and benefits directors	88,000
Divisional human resources directors	84,100
Training directors	79,400
Recruitment and interviewing managers	75,100
Employee and community relations directors	73,500
Plant/location human resources managers	62,000
Compensation supervisors	53,300
Human resources information systems specialists	49,300
Employee assistance and employee counseling specialists	47,500
Employee services and employee recreation specialists	47,300
Employee and industrial plant nurses	46,000
EEO and affirmative action specialists	44,800
Safety specialists	43,700
Training material development specialists	43,500
Benefits specialists (managerial and professional jobs)	41,500
Training generalists (computer)	39,600
Classroom instructors	35,300
Employment interviewing specialists	35,100
Job evaluation specialists	34,100
Human resources records specialists	32,400

In the Federal Government, persons with a bachelor's degree or 3 years' general experience in the personnel field generally started at $23,300 a year in 1999. Those with a superior academic record or an additional year of specialized experience started at $28,000 a year. Those with a master's degree may start at $33,400, and those with a doctorate in a personnel field may start at $44,500. Beginning salaries were slightly higher in areas where the prevailing local pay level was higher. There are no formal entry-level requirements for managerial positions. Applicants must possess a suitable combination of educational attainment, experience, and record of accomplishment.

Related Occupations

All human resources occupations are closely related. Other workers with skills and expertise in interpersonal relations include counselors, lawyers, psychologists, sociologists, social workers, public relations specialists, and teachers. These occupations are described elsewhere in the *Handbook*.

Sources of Additional Information

For information about careers in employee training and development, contact:

☛ American Society for Training and Development, 1640 King St., Box 1443, Alexandria, VA 22313. Internet: **http://www.astd.org**

For information about careers and certification in employee compensation and benefits, contact:

☛ American Compensation Association, 14040 Northsight Blvd., Scottsdale, AZ 85260. Internet: **http://www.acaonline.org**

Information about careers and certification in employee benefits is available from:

☛ International Foundation of Employee Benefit Plans, 18700 W. Bluemound Rd., P.O. Box 69, Brookfield, WI 53008-0069. Internet: **http://www.ifebp.org**

For information about academic programs in industrial relations, write to:

☛ Industrial Relations Research Association, University of Wisconsin, 7226 Social Science Bldg., 1180 Observatory Dr., Madison, WI 53706. Internet: **http://www.irra.ssc.wisc.edu**

Information about personnel careers in the health care industry is available from:

☛ American Society for Healthcare Human Resources Administration, One North Franklin, 31st Floor, Chicago, IL 60606. Internet: **http://www.ashhra.org**

Industrial production managers plan the production schedule within budgetary limitations and time constraints.

Industrial Production Managers

(O*NET 15014)

Significant Points

- The projected decline in employment reflects increasing productivity and organizational restructuring.
- Applicants with college degrees in industrial engineering, management, or business administration, and particularly those with an undergraduate engineering degree and a master's degree in business administration, enjoy the best job prospects.

Nature of the Work

Industrial production managers coordinate the resources and activities required to produce millions of goods every year in the United States. Although their duties vary from plant to plant, industrial production managers share many of the same major responsibilities. These include production scheduling, staffing, equipment, quality control, inventory control, and the coordination of production activities with those of other departments.

The primary mission of industrial production managers is planning the production schedule within budgetary limitations and time constraints. This entails analyzing the plant's personnel and capital resources to select the best way of meeting the production quota. Industrial production managers determine which machines will be used, whether overtime or extra shifts are necessary, and the sequence of production. They also monitor the production run to make sure that it stays on schedule and correct any problems that may arise.

Industrial production managers must also monitor product standards. When quality drops below the established standard, they must determine why standards are not being maintained and how to improve the product. If the problem is poor work, the manager may implement better training programs, reorganize the manufacturing process, or institute employee suggestion or involvement programs. If the cause is substandard materials, the manager works with the purchasing department to improve the quality of the product's components.

Because the work of many departments is interrelated, managers work closely with heads of other departments such as sales, purchasing, and traffic to plan and implement company goals, policies, and procedures. For example, the production manager works with the purchasing department to ensure that plant inventories are maintained at their optimal level. This is vital to a firm's operation because maintaining the inventory of materials necessary for production ties up the firm's financial resources, yet insufficient quantities cause delays in production. A breakdown in communications between the production manager and the purchasing department can cause slowdowns and a failure to meet production schedules. Computers are important in this coordination, and also in providing up-to-date information on inventory, work-in-progress, and quality standards.

Production managers usually report to the plant manager or the vice president for manufacturing, and may act as liaison between executives and first-line supervisors. (Information about these workers can be found in the statements on general managers and top executives, and blue-collar worker supervisors, elsewhere in the *Handbook*). In many plants, one production manager is responsible for all aspects of production. In large plants with several operations—aircraft assembly, for example—there are managers in charge of each operation, such as machining, assembly, or finishing.

Working Conditions

Most industrial production managers divide their time between the shop floor and their offices. While on the floor, they must follow established health and safety practices and wear the required protective clothing and equipment. The time in the office, which is often located on or near the production floor, is usually spent meeting with subordinates or other department managers, analyzing production data, and writing and reviewing reports.

Most industrial production managers work more than 40 hours a week, especially when production deadlines must be met. In facilities that operate around the clock, managers often work late shifts and may be called at any hour to deal with emergencies. This could mean going to the plant to resolve the problem, regardless of the hour, and staying until the situation is under control. Dealing with production workers as well as superiors when working under the pressure of production deadlines or emergency situations can be stressful. Restructuring has eliminated levels of management and support staff, which shifts more responsibilities to production managers and compounds this stress.

Employment

Industrial production managers held about 208,000 jobs in 1998. Although employed throughout the manufacturing sector, about one half are employed in firms that produce industrial machinery and equipment, transportation equipment, electronic and electrical equipment, fabricated metal products, instruments and related products, and food products. Production managers work in all parts of the country, but jobs are most plentiful in areas where manufacturing is concentrated.

Training, Other Qualifications, and Advancement

Because of the diversity of manufacturing operations and job requirements, there is no standard preparation for this occupation. Many industrial production managers have a college degree in business administration, management, or industrial engineering. Others have a master's degree in business administration (MBA). Some are former production line supervisors who have been promoted. Although many employers prefer candidates with a business or engineering background, some companies hire well-rounded liberal arts graduates.

As production operations become more sophisticated, an increasing number of employers are looking for candidates with MBAs. Combined with an undergraduate degree in engineering, this is considered particularly good preparation. Companies also are placing greater importance on a candidate's personality. Because the job requires the ability to compromise, persuade, and negotiate, successful production managers must be well-rounded and have excellent communication skills.

Those who enter the field directly from college or graduate school often are unfamiliar with the firm's production process. As a result, they may spend their first few months on the job in the company's training program. These programs familiarize trainees with the production line, company policies, and the requirements of the job. In larger companies, they may also include assignments to other departments, such as purchasing and accounting. A number of companies hire college graduates as blue-collar worker supervisors and later promote them.

Some industrial production managers have worked their way up the ranks, perhaps after having worked as blue-collar worker supervisors. These workers already have an intimate knowledge of the production process and the firm's organization. To be selected for promotion, they must have demonstrated leadership qualities and usually have taken company-sponsored courses in management skills and communication techniques.

In addition to formal training, industrial production managers must keep informed of new production technologies and management practices. Many belong to professional organizations and attend trade shows where new equipment is displayed; they also attend industry conferences and conventions where changes in production methods and technological advances are discussed.

Industrial production managers with a proven record of superior performance may advance to plant manager or vice president for manufacturing. Others transfer to jobs at larger firms with more responsibilities. Opportunities also exist as consultants. (For more information, see the statement on management analysts elsewhere in the *Handbook*.)

Job Outlook

Employment of industrial production managers is expected to decline slightly through 2008. However, a number of job openings will stem from the need to replace workers who transfer to other occupations or leave the labor force. Applicants with a college degree in industrial engineering, management, or business administration, and particularly those with an undergraduate engineering degree and a master's degree in business administration, enjoy the best job prospects. Employers also are likely to seek candidates who have excellent communication skills, and who are personable, flexible, and eager to enhance their knowledge and skills through ongoing training.

Although manufacturing output is projected to rise, growing productivity among production managers and organizational restructuring will limit the demand for these workers. Productivity gains will result from the increasing use of computers for scheduling, planning, and coordination. Scheduling or planning has become less important as manufacturers have become more responsive to changing demand. In addition, a growing emphasis on quality in the production process has redistributed some of the production manager's oversight responsibilities to supervisors and workers on the production line. Because production managers are so essential to the efficient operation of a plant, they have not been greatly affected by recent efforts to flatten management structures. Nevertheless, this trend has led production managers to assume more responsibilities and has discouraged the creation of more employment opportunities.

Earnings

Median annual earnings for industrial production managers in 1998 were $56,320. The middle 50 percent earned between $41,300 and $79,830. The lowest 10 percent earned less than $31,790 and the highest 10 percent earned more than $97,310. Median annual earnings in the manufacturing industries employing the largest numbers of industrial production managers in 1997 were

Industry	Earnings
Motor vehicles	$68,700
Electronic components and accessories	59,700
Miscellaneous plastics products, not elsewhere classified	48,500
Fabricated structural metal products	46,400
Commercial printing	45,800

Salaries of industrial production managers vary significantly by industry and plant size. According to Abbott, Langer, and Associates, the average salary for all production managers was $50,400 in 1998. In addition to salary, industrial production managers may receive bonuses based on job performance.

Related Occupations

Industrial production managers oversee production staff and equipment, insure that production goals and quality standards are being met, and implement company policies. Individuals with similar functions include materials, operations, purchasing, and transportation managers. Other occupations requiring similar training and skills are sales engineer, manufacturer's sales representative, materials engineer, and industrial engineer.

Sources of Additional Information

Information on industrial production management can be obtained from:

☛ National Management Association, 2210 Arbor Blvd., Dayton, OH 45439. Internet: **http://www.nma1.org**

☛ American Management Association, 1601 Broadway, 10th Floor, New York, NY 10019. Internet: **http://www.amanet.org**

Inspectors and Compliance Officers, Except Construction

(O*NET 21911A, 21911B, 21911D, 21911E, 21911F, 21911H, 21911J, 21911L, 21911P, 21911R, and 21911T)

Significant Points

- About 4 out of 5 inspection and compliance jobs are in Federal, State, and local government agencies that enforce rules on health, safety, food quality, licensing, and finance.
- Because of the diversity of functions they perform, job qualifications vary widely.

Nature of the Work

Inspectors and compliance officers help to keep workplaces safe, food healthy, and the environment clean. They also ensure that workers' rights are recognized in a variety of settings. These workers enforce rules on matters as diverse as health, safety, food quality, licensing, and finance. As the following occupations demonstrate, their duties vary widely, depending on their area of responsibility and level of experience.

Aviation safety inspectors work for the Federal Aviation Administration (FAA) and oversee the avionics, maintenance, and operations of air carriers and similar establishments. They evaluate technicians, pilots, and other personnel; assess facilities and training programs; inspect aircraft and related equipment for airworthiness, and investigate and report on accidents and violations.

Bank examiners investigate financial institutions concerning compliance with Federal or State charters and regulations governing the institution's operations and solvency. Examiners schedule audits to protect the institution's shareholders and the interests of depositors. They recommend acceptance or rejection of applications for mergers and acquisitions, and testify as to the viability of chartering new institutions. They interview officials in the firm or other persons with knowledge of the bank's operations, review financial reports, and identify deficiencies and deviations from Federal and State laws.

Consumer safety inspectors and *officers* inspect food, feeds, pesticides, weights and measures, biological products, cosmetics, drugs, medical equipment, and radiation emitting products. Working individually or in teams under a senior inspector, they check on firms that use, produce, handle, store, or market products they regulate. They ensure that standards are maintained and respond to consumer complaints by questioning employees, vendors, and others to obtain evidence. Inspectors look for inaccurate product labeling, inaccurate scales, and for decomposition or chemical or bacteriological contamination that could result in a product becoming harmful to health. After completing their inspection, inspectors discuss their observations with plant managers or business owners to point out areas where corrective measures are needed. They write reports of their findings and compile evidence for use in court if legal action must be taken.

Environmental health inspectors work primarily for governments. They analyze substances in order to determine contamination or the presence of disease and investigate sources of contamination to try to ensure that food, water, and air meet government standards. They certify the purity of food and beverages produced in dairies and processing plants or served in restaurants, hospitals, and other institutions. Inspectors may find pollution sources through collection and analysis of air, water, or waste samples. When they determine the nature and cause of pollution, they initiate action to stop it and force the firm or individual who caused the pollutants to pay to clean it up.

Equal opportunity specialists enforce laws and regulations which prohibit discrimination on the basis of race, color, national origin, religion, sex, disability, and age in employment and the provision of services. They conduct on-site compliance reviews in accordance with agency and Department of Justice policy and regulations, gather facts related to allegations of discrimination, and make recommendations for resolving complaints. They then prepare statistical analysis and reports relative to implementation of civil rights and equal opportunity programs and refer cases to the legal system for adjudication when necessary.

Food Inspectors ensure that the product is fit for human consumption in compliance with Federal laws governing the wholesomeness and purity of meat and poultry products. This is accomplished through inspection involving a visual examination of the live animal or poultry prior to slaughter, and post-mortem inspection to determine that the product is not contaminated and that sanitation procedures are maintained. Processing food inspectors specialize in processed meat and poultry products, and all other ingredients contained in the final product, including frozen dinners, canned goods, and cured and smoked products. They have the authority to shut the plant down if there is a problem that they are unable to resolve.

Mine safety and health inspectors carry out the major operational mission of the Department of Labor's Mine Safety and Health Administration (MSHA). They primarily conduct on-site inspections or investigations of underground and surface mines, mills and quarries in search of conditions that are potentially hazardous to the safety and health of workers. They inspect to insure that equipment is properly maintained and used, and that mining practices are carried out in accordance with

Qualifications for inspectors and compliance officers vary widely.

safety and health laws and regulations. They also investigate accidents and disasters, and may help direct rescue and fire fighting operations when fires or explosions occur. MSHA's Inspectors work to identify the causes of accidents to determine how they might be prevented in the future, and they investigate complaints to determine whether laws and regulations have been violated. Inspectors discuss findings directly with mine management and issue citations describing violations and hazards that must be corrected. They have the authority to close a mining operation if they encounter a work situation that presents an imminent danger to workers. They may also be called upon by mine personnel to provide technical advice and assistance.

Occupational Safety and Health Administration (OSHA) inspectors serve the Department of Labor as expert consultants on the application of safety principles, practices, and techniques in the workplace. They conduct fact-finding investigations of workplaces to determine the existence of specific safety hazards. They may be assigned to conduct safety inspections and investigations and use technical equipment and sampling and measuring devices and supplies required in the field. These inspectors attempt to prevent accidents by using their knowledge of engineering safety codes and standards, and they may order suspension of activities that pose threats to workers.

Park rangers enforce laws and regulations in State and national parks. They protect natural, cultural, and human resources, and enforce criminal laws of the United States including the apprehension of violators. Rangers also implement wilderness and backcountry management plans; monitor grazing, mining, and concessions activities; and work closely with resource management specialists and employees to identify and communicate resource threats, perform resource inventories, implement resource projects, and monitor researchers. Other rangers give natural resources talks, lead guided walks, and conduct community outreach and environmental education programs.

Securities compliance examiners implement regulations concerning securities and real estate transactions. They investigate applications for registration of securities sales and complaints of irregular securities transactions and recommend legal action when necessary.

Other inspectors and compliance officers include attendance officers, logging operations inspectors, travel accommodations raters, coroners, code inspectors, mortician investigators, and dealer-compliance representatives. (Construction and building inspectors, who perform closely related work, are discussed elsewhere in the *Handbook*.)

Working Conditions

Inspectors and compliance officers work with many different people and in a variety of environments. Their jobs often involve considerable field work, and some inspectors travel frequently. When traveling, they are generally furnished with an automobile or are reimbursed for travel expenses.

Inspectors may experience unpleasant, stressful, and dangerous working conditions. For example, mine safety and health inspectors are exposed to many of the same physically strenuous conditions and hazards as miners, and the work may be performed in unpleasant, stressful, and dangerous working conditions. Federal food inspectors work in highly mechanized plant environments near operating machinery with moving parts or with poultry or livestock in confined areas in extreme temperatures and on slippery floors. The duties often require working with sharp knives, moderate lifting, and walking or standing for long periods of time. Park rangers often work outdoors in rugged terrain and in very hot or bitterly cold weather for extended periods.

Many inspectors work long and often irregular hours. Inspectors may find themselves in adversarial roles when the organization or individual being inspected objects to the process or its consequences.

Employment

Inspectors and compliance officers held about 176,000 jobs in 1998. State governments employed 30 percent, the Federal Government—chiefly the Departments of Defense, Labor, Treasury, and Agriculture—employed 31 percent, and local governments employed 19 percent. The remaining 20 percent were employed throughout the private sector in education, hospitals, insurance companies, and manufacturing firms.

Inspectors and compliance officers who work for the Federal Government are employed by a wide range of agencies. Some consumer safety inspectors, for example, work for the U.S. Food and Drug Administration, but the majority of these inspectors work for State governments. Most food inspectors and agricultural commodity graders are employed by the U.S. Department of Agriculture. Many health inspectors work for State and local governments. Compliance inspectors are employed primarily by the Departments of Treasury and Labor on the Federal level, as well as by State and local governments. The Department of Defense employs the most quality assurance inspectors. Aviation safety inspectors work for the Federal Aviation Administration. The Environmental Protection Agency employs inspectors to verify compliance with pollution control and other laws. The U.S. Department of Labor and many State governments employ safety and health inspectors, equal opportunity officers, and mine safety and health inspectors. The U.S. Department of Interior employs park rangers.

Training, Other Qualifications, and Advancement

Because of the diversity of the functions they perform, qualifications for inspector and compliance officer jobs vary widely. Requirements include a combination of education, experience, and passing scores on written examinations. Many employers, including the Federal Government, require college degrees for some positions. Experience in the area being investigated is also a prerequisite for many positions. Although not exhaustive, the following examples illustrate the range of qualifications for various inspector jobs.

Air carrier avionics inspector positions must possess aircraft electronics work experience involving the maintenance and repair of avionics systems in large aircraft, aircraft avionics experience in a repair station, air carrier repair facility, or military repair facility; 3 years of supervisory experience in aircraft avionics as a lead mechanic or repairer who supervises others; and aircraft avionics work experience within the last 3 years.

Air carrier maintenance inspectors must possess an FAA mechanic certificate with airframe and power plant ratings; aviation maintenance work experience involving the maintenance and repair of airframes, power plants, and systems of large aircraft under an airworthiness maintenance and inspection program; aircraft maintenance experience in a repair station, air carrier repair facility, or military repair facility; 3 years of supervisory experience in aviation maintenance as a lead mechanic or repairer who supervises others; and some aviation maintenance work experience within the last 3 years.

Air carrier operations inspectors must possess an airline transport pilot certificate or commercial pilot certificate with instrument airplane rating; pilot experience in large multiengine aircraft with a minimum of 1,500 total flight hours as a pilot or copilot; pilot-in-command experience in large aircraft within the last 3 years; a minimum of 100 flight hours within the last 3 years; 1,000 flight hours within the last 5 years; the successful completion of turbojet evaluation; and no more than 2 flying accidents in the last 5 years.

Applicants for positions as mine safety and health inspectors generally must have experience in mine safety, management, or supervision. Some may possess a skill such as that of an electrician (for mine electrical inspectors). Applicants must meet strict medical requirements and be physically able to perform arduous duties efficiently. Many mine safety inspectors are former miners.

Bank examiners need 5 or more years of experience in examining or auditing (internal or external) financial institutions. Candidates should have demonstrated a thorough understanding of a broad range of business risks as well as safety and soundness issues. Successful candidates typically have experience in evaluating computer risk management in financial institutions, including recovery planning, information security, and data integrity.

Environmental health inspectors, also called sanitarians in many States, may have completed a full 4-year course of study that meets all the requirements for a bachelor's degree, and that included or was supplemented by at least 30 semester hours in a science or any combination of sciences directly related to environmental health—for example, sanitary science, public health, chemistry, microbiology, or any appropriate agricultural, biological, or physical science. Alternately, they may have 4 years of specialized experience in inspectional, investigational, technical support, or other work that provided a fundamental understanding of environmental health principles, methods, and techniques equivalent to that which would have been gained through a 4-year college curriculum or some combination of education and experience as described above. In most States, they are licensed by examining boards.

All inspectors and compliance officers are trained in the applicable laws or inspection procedures through some combination of classroom and on-the-job training. In general, people who want to enter this occupation should be responsible and like detailed work. Inspectors and compliance officers should be able to communicate well.

Federal Government inspectors and compliance officers whose job performance is satisfactory advance through their career ladder to a specified full-performance level. For positions above this level, usually supervisory positions, advancement is competitive and based on agency needs and individual merit. Advancement opportunities in State and local governments and the private sector are often similar to those in the Federal Government.

Job Outlook

Average growth in employment of inspectors and compliance officers is expected through 2008, reflecting a balance of continuing public demand for a safe environment and quality products against the desire for smaller government and fewer regulations. Additional job openings will arise from the need to replace those who transfer to other occupations, retire, or leave the labor force for other reasons. In private industry, employment growth will reflect industry growth and the continuing self-enforcement of government and company regulations and policies, particularly among franchise operations in various industries.

Employment of inspectors and compliance officers is seldom affected by general economic fluctuations. Federal, State, and local governments, which employ four-fifths of all inspectors, provide considerable job security.

Earnings

The median annual salary of inspectors and compliance officers, except construction, was $36,820 in 1998. The middle half earned between $28,540 and $48,670. The lowest 10 percent earned less than $22,750, while the highest 10 percent earned over $72,280. Inspectors and compliance officers employed by local governments had earnings of $31,800 in 1997; those who worked for State governments earned a median annual salary of $33,700; and those in the Federal Government earned $39,900.

In the Federal Government, the annual starting salaries for inspectors varied from $25,500 to $31,200 in 1999, depending on the nature of the inspection or compliance activity. Beginning salaries were slightly higher in selected areas where the prevailing local pay level was higher. The following presents average salaries for selected inspectors and compliance officers in the Federal Government in nonsupervisory, supervisory, and managerial positions in early 1999.

Occupation	Salary
Air safety investigators	$68,900
Highway safety inspectors	68,100
Aviation safety inspectors	65,100
Railroad safety inspectors	60,500
Mine safety and health inspectors	58,000
Environmental protection specialists	58,000
Equal employment opportunity officials	57,900
Safety and occupational health managers	54,000
Public health quarantine inspectors	52,500
Quality assurance inspectors	50,600
Securities compliance examiners	43,300
Park ranger	42,100
Agricultural commodity graders	41,600
Consumer safety inspectors	37,300
Food inspectors	35,200
Environmental protection assistants	31,600

Most inspectors and compliance officers work for Federal, State, and local governments or in large private firms, most of which generally offer more generous benefits than do smaller firms.

Related Occupations

Inspectors and compliance officers ensure that laws and regulations are obeyed. Others who enforce laws and regulations include construction and building inspectors; fire marshals; Federal, State, and local law enforcement professionals; correctional officers; and fish and game wardens.

Sources of Additional Information

Information on obtaining a job with the Federal Government is available from the Office of Personnel Management through a telephone-based system. Consult a telephone directory under U.S. Government for a local number or call (912) 757-3000; TDD (912) 744-2299. The number is not tollfree and charges may result. Information also is available from their Internet site: **http://www.usajobs.opm.gov**

Information about jobs in Federal, State, and local government as well as in private industry is available from the State Employment Service.

Insurance Underwriters

(O*NET 21102)

Significant Points

- Employment is projected to grow more slowly than average as insurance companies increasingly use "smart" underwriting software systems that automatically analyze and rate insurance applications.
- Most large insurance companies prefer college graduates who have a degree in business administration, finance, or related fields and possess excellent communications and problem-solving skills.

Nature of the Work

Insurance companies protect individuals and organizations from financial loss by assuming billions of dollars in risks each year. Underwriters are needed to identify and calculate the risk of loss from policyholders, establish appropriate premium rates, and write policies that cover these risks. An insurance company may lose business to competitors if the underwriter appraises risks too conservatively, or it may have to pay more claims if the underwriting actions are too liberal.

Underwriters determine premium rates for insurance policies.

With the aid of computers, underwriters analyze information in insurance applications to determine if a risk is acceptable and will not result in a loss. Applications are often supplemented with reports from loss-control consultants, medical reports, and actuarial studies. Underwriters then must decide whether to issue the policy and the appropriate premium to charge. In making this determination, underwriters serve as the main link between the insurance carrier and the insurance agent. On occasion, they accompany sales agents to make presentations to prospective clients.

Technology plays an important role in an underwriter's job. Underwriters use computer applications called "smart systems" to manage risks more efficiently and accurately. These systems automatically analyze and rate insurance applications, recommending acceptance or denial of the risk, and adjusting the premium rate in accordance with the risk. With these systems, underwriters are better equipped to make sound decisions and avoid excessive losses.

Most underwriters specialize in one of three major categories of insurance—life, health, or property and casualty. Life and health insurance underwriters may further specialize in group or individual policies. The increased complexity of insurance plans and attention to the "bottom line" is changing the nature of underwriting. In the past, insurance agents acting as underwriters, particularly in the life and health fields, could accept or reject applications. Now this underwriting role is done mostly by full-time underwriters in the home or field office of the insurance company.

Property and casualty underwriters usually specialize in commercial or personal lines and then often by type of risk insured, such as fire, homeowners, automobile, marine, liability, or workers' compensation. In cases where casualty companies provide insurance through a single "package" policy, covering various types of risks, the underwriter must be familiar with different lines of insurance. For business insurance, the underwriter often must be able to evaluate the firm's entire operation in appraising its application for insurance.

An increasing proportion of insurance sales, particularly in life and health insurance, is being made through group contracts. A standard group policy insures everyone in a specified group through a single contract at a standard premium rate. The group underwriter analyzes the overall composition of the group to assure that the total risk is not excessive. Another type of group policy provides members of a group—a labor union, for example—with individual policies reflecting their needs. These usually are casualty policies, such as those covering automobiles. The casualty underwriter analyzes the application of each group member and makes individual appraisals. Some group underwriters meet with union or employer representatives to discuss the types of policies available to their group.

Working Conditions

Underwriters have desk jobs that require no unusual physical activity. Their offices usually are comfortable and pleasant. Although underwriters typically work a standard 40-hour week, more are working longer hours due to the downsizing of many insurance companies. Most underwriters are based in a home office, but they occasionally attend meetings away from home for several days. Construction and marine underwriters frequently travel to inspect work sites and assess risks.

Employment

Insurance underwriters held about 97,000 jobs in 1998. The following tabulation shows the percent distribution of employment by industry:

Industry	Percent
Property and casualty insurance carriers	34
Insurance agents, brokers, and services	31
Life insurance carriers	16
Medical service and health insurance carriers	6
Pension funds and miscellaneous insurance carriers	5
Other industries	8

The majority of underwriters work for insurance companies called "carriers." Of these underwriters, most work for property and casualty insurance carriers, and secondly for life insurance carriers. Most of the remaining underwriters work in insurance agencies or for organizations that offer insurance services to insurance companies and policyholders. A small number of underwriters work in agencies owned and operated by banks, mortgage companies, and real estate firms.

Most underwriters are based in the insurance company's home office, but some, mostly in the property and casualty area, work out of regional branch offices of the insurance company. These underwriters usually have the authority to underwrite risks and determine an appropriate rating without consulting the home office.

Training, Other Qualifications, and Advancement

For entry level underwriting jobs, most large insurance companies prefer college graduates who have a degree in business administration or finance, with courses or experience in accounting. However, a bachelor's degree in almost any field—plus courses in business law and accounting—provides a good general background and may be sufficient to qualify. Computer knowledge is essential.

New employees usually start as underwriter trainees or assistant underwriters. They may help collect information on applicants and evaluate routine applications under the supervision of an experienced risk analyst. Property and casualty trainees study claim files to become familiar with factors associated with certain types of losses. Many larger insurers offer work-study training programs, lasting from a few months to a year. As trainees gain experience, they are assigned policy applications that are more complex and cover greater risks. These require the use of computers for more efficient analysis and processing.

Continuing education is necessary for advancement. Insurance companies usually pay tuition for underwriting courses that their trainees successfully complete; some also offer salary incentives. Independent study programs for experienced property and casualty underwriters are also available. The Insurance Institute of America offers a program called "Introduction to Underwriting" for beginning underwriters, and the specialty designation, AU, or Associate in Underwriting, the second formal step in developing a career in underwriting. To earn the AU designation, underwriters complete a series of courses and examinations that generally last 2 years.

The American Institute for Chartered Property Casualty Underwriters awards the designation, CPCU, or Chartered Property and Casualty Underwriter, the third and final stage of development for an underwriter. Earning the more advanced CPCU designation takes about 5 years, and requires passing 10 examinations covering personal and commercial insurance, risk management, business and insurance law, accounting, finance, management, economics, and ethics. Although CPCU's may be underwriters, the CPCU is intended for everyone working in all aspects of property and casualty insurance. The American College offers the Chartered Life Underwriter (CLU) designation and the Registered Health Underwriter (RHU) designation for all professionals working in the fields of life and health insurance.

Underwriting can be a satisfying career for people who enjoy analyzing information and paying attention to detail. In addition, underwriters must possess good judgment in order to make sound decisions. Excellent communication and interpersonal skills are also essential, as much of their work involves dealing with agents and other insurance professionals.

Experienced underwriters who complete courses of study may advance to senior underwriter or underwriting manager positions. Some underwriting managers are promoted to senior managerial jobs. At some carriers, a master's degree is needed to achieve this level. Other underwriters are attracted to the earnings potential of sales and therefore obtain State licenses to sell insurance and insurance products as agents or brokers.

Job Outlook

Employment of underwriters is expected to increase more slowly than the average for all occupations through 2008. Computer-assisted software that helps underwriters analyze policy applications more quickly and accurately has made underwriters more productive and capable of taking on a greater workload. Mergers and acquisitions of insurance companies are also expected to continue to result in more downsizing of insurance carriers. Most job openings will result from the need to replace underwriters who transfer or leave the occupation, although several new job openings are being created for underwriters in the area of product development. These underwriters help set the premiums for new insurance products, such as in the growing field of long-term care insurance.

The best job prospects will be for underwriters with the right skills and credentials, such as excellent computer and communication skills, coupled with a background in finance. Job prospects may be better in health insurance than in property and casualty and life insurance. As Federal and State laws require health insurers to accept more applicants for insurance, the number of policies sold will increase. Also, as the population ages, there will be a greater need for health and long-term care insurance.

Because insurance is considered a necessity for people and businesses, there will always be a need for underwriters. It is a profession that is less subject to recession and layoffs than other fields. Underwriters who specialize, though, may have difficulty transferring to another underwriting specialty if downsizing were to occur.

Earnings

Median annual earnings of insurance underwriters were $38,710 in 1998. The middle 50 percent earned between $29,790 and $51,460 a year. The lowest 10 percent earned less than $23,750; while the top 10 percent earned over $77,430. Median annual earnings in the industries employing the largest number of insurance underwriters in 1997 were:

Industry	Earnings
Medical service and health insurance	$40,000
Life insurance	39,800
Fire, marine, and casualty insurance	39,100
Insurance agents, brokers, and service	32,200

Insurance companies usually provide better than average benefits, including employer-financed group life, health, and retirement plans.

Related Occupations

Underwriters make decisions on the basis of financial data. Other workers with the same type of responsibility include auditors, budget analysts, financial advisers, loan officers, credit managers, real estate appraisers, and risk managers.

Sources of Additional Information

Information about a career as an insurance underwriter is available from the home offices of many life insurance and property-liability insurance companies. Information about careers in the property-casualty insurance field can be obtained by contacting:

☛ The Insurance Information Institute, 110 William St., New York, NY 10038. Internet: **http://www.iii.org**

Information on the underwriting function, in particular, and the CPCU and AU designation can be obtained from:

☛ The American Institute for Chartered Property and Casualty Underwriters, and the Insurance Institute of America, 720 Providence Rd., P.O. Box 3016, Malvern, PA 19355-0716. Internet: **http://www.aicpcu.org**

Loan Officers and Counselors

(O*NET 21108)

Significant Points

- Loan officer positions generally require a bachelor's degree in finance, economics, or a related field; training or experience in banking, lending, or sales is advantageous.

Loan officers obtain financial information from clients.

- Low interest rates will keep demand for loans high, causing employment of loan officers to grow about as fast as average; growth will be tempered by technology that makes these employees more productive.

Nature of the Work

For many individuals, taking out a loan may be the only way to afford a house, car, or college education. Likewise for businesses, loans are essential to start many companies, purchase inventory, or invest in capital equipment. *Loan officers* facilitate this lending by seeking potential clients and assisting them in applying for loans. Loan officers also gather information about clients and businesses to ensure that an informed decision is made regarding the quality of the loan and the probability of repayment.

Loan officers usually specialize in commercial, consumer, or mortgage loans. Commercial or business loans help companies pay for new equipment or expand operations; consumer loans include home equity, automobile, and personal loans; and mortgage loans are made to purchase real estate or to refinance an existing mortgage. In addition, banks and other lenders are offering a growing variety of loans. Loan officers must keep abreast of new types of loans and other financial products and services, so they can meet their customers' needs.

In many instances, loan officers act as salespeople. Commercial loan officers, for example, contact firms to determine the firms' demand for loans. If the firm is seeking new funds, the loan officer will try to persuade the company to obtain the loan from their institution. Similarly, mortgage loan officers develop relationships with commercial and residential real estate agencies, so when an individual or firm buys a property, the real estate agent might recommend contacting that loan officer for financing.

Once this initial contact has been made, loan officers guide clients through the process of applying for a loan. This process begins with a formal meeting or telephone call with a prospective client, during which the loan officer obtains basic information about the purpose of the loan and explains the different types of loans and credit terms that are available to the applicant. Sometimes, the loan officer assists the client in filling out the application and answers questions about the process.

After completing the forms, the loan officer begins the process of analyzing and verifying the application to determine the client's creditworthiness. The loan officer may request a copy of the client's credit history from one of the major credit reporting agencies, or in the case of commercial loans, she or he may request copies of the company's financial statements. Loan officers include this information and their written comments in a loan file, used to analyze the viability of the loan vis-à-vis the lending institution's requirements. At this point, the loan officer, in consultation with her or his manager, decides whether to grant the loan. If approved, a repayment schedule is then arranged with the client.

A loan that would otherwise be denied may be approved, if the customer can provide the lender with appropriate collateral—property pledged as security for the payment of a loan. For example, when lending money for a college education, the bank may insist that the borrower offer her or his home as collateral. If the borrower were ever unable to repay the loan, the borrower would have to sell the home to raise the necessary money.

Once the loan has been granted, *loan counselors*, also called loan collection officers, may need to contact borrowers with delinquent accounts to help them find a method of repayment to avoid default on the loan. If a repayment plan cannot be developed, the loan counselor initiates collateral liquidation, in which case the collateral used to secure the loan—a home or car, for example—is seized by the lender and sold to repay the loan. A loan officer can also perform this function.

Working Conditions

Working as a loan officer usually involves considerable travel. For example, commercial and mortgage loan officers frequently work away from their offices and rely on laptop computers, cellular phones, and pagers to keep in contact with their offices and clients. Mortgage loan officers often work out of their home or car, visiting offices or homes of clients while completing loan applications. Commercial loan officers sometimes travel to other cities to prepare complex loan agreements. Consumer loan officers and loan counselors, however, are likely to spend most of their time in an office.

Most loan officers and counselors work a standard 40-hour week, but many work longer, depending on the number of clients and the demand for loans. Mortgage loan officers can work especially long hours, because they are free to take on as many customers as they choose. Loan officers usually carry a heavy caseload and sometimes cannot accept new clients until they complete current cases. They are especially busy when interest rates are low, triggering a surge in loan applications.

Employment

Loan officers and counselors held about 227,000 jobs in 1998. Approximately half were employed by commercial banks, savings institutions, and credit unions. Others were employed by nonbank financial institutions, such as mortgage banking and brokerage firms and personal credit firms.

Loan officers are employed throughout the Nation, but most work in urban and suburban areas. In rural areas, the branch or assistant manager often handles the loan application process.

Training, Other Qualifications, and Advancement

Loan officer positions generally require a bachelor's degree in finance, economics, or a related field. Most employers prefer applicants who are familiar with computers and their applications in banking. For commercial or mortgage loan officer jobs, training or experience in sales is highly valued by potential employers. Loan officers without college degrees usually have reached their positions by advancing through the ranks of an organization and acquiring several years of work experience in various other occupations, such as teller or customer service representative.

The American Institute of Banking, which is affiliated with the American Bankers Association, offers correspondence courses and college and university classes for students interested in lending as well as for experienced loan officers who want to keep their skills current. The Mortgage Bankers Association's School of Mortgage Banking also offers classes, both classroom and Internet-based, for people involved in real estate lending. Completion of these courses and programs enhances one's employment and advancement opportunities.

Persons planning a career as a loan officer or counselor should be capable of developing effective working relationships with others, confident in their abilities, and highly motivated. For public relations purposes, loan officers must be willing to attend community events as a representative of their employer.

Capable loan officers and counselors may advance to larger branches of the firm or to managerial positions, while less capable workers—and those having inadequate academic preparation—could be assigned to smaller branches and might find promotion difficult. Advancement beyond a loan officer position usually includes supervising other loan officers and clerical staff.

Job Outlook

Employment of loan officers and counselors is expected to grow faster than the average for all occupations through 2008. Job growth will be driven by an increasing population, expanding economy, and low interest rates, which will lead to more applications for commercial, consumer, and mortgage loans. Growth in the variety and complexity of loans, coupled with the importance of loan officers to the success of banks and other lending institutions, should also assure employment growth. Although increased demand will generate many new jobs, most openings will result from the need to replace workers who leave the occupation or retire.

Employment growth will be tempered by several factors. First, refinancing of mortgages, a major contributor to the recent growth in the number of loan officers, is expected to diminish, because people who needed to refinance have already done so. Also, computers, underwriting software, and communication technologies are making loan officers more productive. They can now spend more time in the field with prospective clients, while still keeping in touch with the office. Also, qualifying applicants for loans is being made easier with computers performing much of the analysis. The Internet is also expected to slightly dampen the demand for loan officers, as a growing number of people apply for loans online.

Employment of loan officers is subject to the upturns and downturns of the economy. When interest rates decline dramatically, there is a surge in real estate buying and refinancing that requires additional loan officers specializing in mortgage financing. When the real estate market returns to normal, loan officers can be subject to layoffs. The same applies to commercial loan officers whose workloads increase during good economic times, as companies seek to invest more in their businesses. In difficult economic conditions, loan counselors are likely to see an increase in the number of delinquent loans.

Even in economic downturns, however, loans remain the major source of revenue for banks, so the fundamental role of loan officers will contribute to job stability. Moreover, because loan officers are often paid by commission, the bank may retain them simply by paying less compensation. As in the past, college graduates and those with banking, lending, or sales experience should have the best job prospects.

Earnings

Median annual earnings of loan officers and counselors were $35,340 in 1998. The middle 50 percent earned between $26,380 and $50,240. The lowest 10 percent had earnings of less than $20,990, while the top 10 percent earned over $82,270. Median annual earnings in the industries employing the largest number of loan officers and counselors in 1997 were:

Industry	Earnings
Commercial banks	$36,400
Mortgage bankers and brokers	34,700
Savings institutions	34,700
Personal credit institutions	26,800
Credit unions	25,300

The form of compensation for loan officers varies. Most loan officers are paid a commission that is based on the number of loans they originate. In this way, commissions are used to motivate loan officers to bring in more loans. Some institutions pay only salaries, while others pay their loan officers a salary plus a commission or bonus, based on the number of loans originated. Banks and other lenders sometimes offer their loan officers free checking privileges and somewhat lower interest rates on personal loans.

According to a salary survey conducted by Robert Half International, a staffing services firm specializing in accounting and finance, residential real estate mortgage loan officers earned between $31,600 and $47,000 in 1998; commercial real estate mortgage loan officers, between $46,000 and $74,000; consumer loan officers, between $30,000 and $49,000; and commercial loan officers, between $38,400 and $85,000. Smaller banks ordinarily paid 15 percent less than larger banks. Loan officers who are paid on a commission basis usually earn more than those on salary only.

Related Occupations

Loan officers help the public manage financial assets and secure loans. Occupations that involve similar functions include securities and financial services sales representatives, financial aid officers, real estate agents and brokers, and insurance agents and brokers.

Sources of Additional Information

Information about a career as a loan officer or counselor can be obtained from:

☛ American Bankers Association, 1120 Connecticut Ave. NW., Washington, DC 20036. Internet: **http://www.aba.com**

☛ Mortgage Bankers Association of America, 1125 15th St. NW., Washington, DC 20005. Internet: **http://www.mbaa.org**

State bankers' associations can furnish specific information about job opportunities in their State. Also, individual banks can supply information about job openings and the activities, responsibilities, and preferred qualifications of their loan officers.

Management Analysts

(O*NET 21905)

Significant Points

- Almost 55 percent are self-employed, about four times the average for other executive, administrative, and managerial occupations.
- Most positions in the private sector require a master's degree and at least five years of specialized experience.
- Despite projected faster than average employment growth, intense competition is expected for jobs.

Nature of the Work

As the business environment becomes more complex, the Nation's firms are continually faced with new challenges. Firms increasingly rely on management analysts help them remain competitive amidst these changes. Management analysts, often referred to as management consultants in the private sector, analyze and propose ways to improve an organization's structure, efficiency, or profits. For example, a small but rapidly growing company that needs help improving the system of control over inventories and expenses may decide to employ a consultant who is an expert in just-in-time inventory management. In another case, a large company that has recently acquired a new division may hire management analysts to help reorganize their corporate structure and eliminate duplicate or non-essential jobs.

Firms providing management analysis range in size from a single practitioner to large international organizations employing thousands of consultants. Some analysts and consultants specialize in a specific industry while others specialize by type of business function, such as human resources or information systems. In government, management analysts tend to specialize by type of agency. The work of management analysts and consultants varies with each client or employer, and from project to project. Some projects require a team of consultants, each specializing in one area. In other projects, consultants work independently with the organization's managers. In all cases, analysts and consultants collect, review, and analyze information, in order to make recommendations to management.

Management analysts and consultants propose ways to improve organizations.

Both public and private organizations use consultants for a variety of reasons. Some lack the internal resources needed to handle a project, while others need a consultant's expertise to determine what resources will be required and what problems may be encountered, if they pursue a particular opportunity. To retain a consultant, a company first solicits proposals from a number of consulting firms specializing in the area in which it needs assistance. These proposals include the estimated cost and scope of the project, staffing requirements, references from a number of previous clients, and a completion deadline. The company then selects the proposal that best suits its needs.

After obtaining an assignment or contract, management analysts first define the nature and extent of the problem. During this phase, they analyze relevant data, which may include annual revenues, employment, or expenditures, and interview managers and employees while observing their operations. The analyst or consultant then develops solutions to the problem. In the course of preparing their recommendations, they take into account the nature of the organization, the relationship it has with others in that industry, and its internal organization and culture. Insight into the problem is often gained by building and solving mathematical models.

Once they have decided on a course of action, consultants report their findings and recommendations to the client. These suggestions are usually submitted in writing, but oral presentations regarding findings are also common. For some projects, management analysts are retained to help implement their suggestions.

Management analysts in government agencies use the same skills as their private-sector colleagues to advise managers on many types of issues, most of which are similar to the problems faced by private firms. For example, if an agency is planning to purchase personal computers, it must first determine which type to buy, given its budget and data processing needs. In this case, management analysts would assess the prices and characteristics of various machines and determine which best meets their department's needs.

Working Conditions

Management analysts usually divide their time between their offices and the client's site. In either situation, much of an analyst's time is spent indoors in clean, well-lit offices. Since they must spend a significant portion of their time with clients, analysts travel frequently.

Analysts and consultants generally work at least 40 hours a week. Uncompensated overtime is common, especially when approaching project deadlines. Analysts may experience a great deal of stress as a result of trying to meet a client's demands, often on a tight schedule.

Self-employed consultants can set their workload and hours and work at home. On the other hand, their livelihood depends on their ability to maintain and expand their client base. Salaried consultants also must impress potential clients to get and keep clients for their company.

Employment

Management analysts held about 344,000 jobs in 1998. They are found throughout the country, but employment is concentrated in large metropolitan areas. Almost 55 percent of these workers were self-employed. Most of the remainder worked in financial and management consulting firms and for Federal, State, and local governments. The majority of those working for the Federal Government are in the Department of Defense.

Training, Other Qualifications, and Advancement

Educational requirements for entry-level jobs in this field vary widely between private industry and government. Employers in private industry generally seek individuals with a master's degree in business administration or a related discipline and at least 5 years of experience in the field in which they plan to consult. Most government agencies hire people with a bachelor's degree and no pertinent work experience for entry-level management analyst positions.

Many fields of study provide a suitable educational background for this occupation because of the wide range of areas addressed by management analysts. These include most academic programs in business and management, as well as computer and information sciences and engineering. In addition to the appropriate formal education, most entrants to this occupation have years of experience in management, human resources, inventory control, or other specialties. Analysts also routinely attend conferences to keep abreast of current developments in their field.

Management analysts often work with minimal supervision, so they should be self-motivated and disciplined. Analytical skills, the ability to get along with a wide range of people, strong oral and written communication skills, good judgment, time management skills, and creativity are other desirable qualities. The ability to work in teams is also becoming a more important attribute in the field as consulting teams become more common.

As consultants gain experience, they often become solely responsible for a specific project full time, taking on more responsibility and managing their own hours. At the senior level, consultants may supervise lower-level workers and become more involved in seeking out new business. Those with exceptional skills may eventually become a partner or principal in the firm. Others with entrepreneurial ambition may open their own firm.

A high percentage of management consultants are self-employed, partly because business start-up costs are low. Self-employed consultants also can share office space, administrative help, and other resources with other self-employed consultants or small consulting firms—thus reducing overhead costs. Because many small consulting firms fail each year for lack of managerial expertise and clients, those interested in opening their own firm must have good organizational and marketing skills and several years of consulting experience.

The Institute of Management Consultants, a division of the Council of Consulting Organizations, Inc., offers the Certified Management Consultant (CMC) designation to those who pass an examination and meet minimum levels of education and experience. Certification is not mandatory for management consultants, but it may give a job seeker a competitive advantage.

Job Outlook

Despite projected rapid employment growth, keen competition is expected for jobs as management analysts. Because analysts can come from such diverse educational backgrounds, the pool of applicants from which employers can draw is quite large. Furthermore, the independent and challenging nature of the work, combined with high earnings potential, make this occupation attractive to many. Job opportunities are expected to be best for those with a graduate degree, industry expertise, and a talent for salesmanship and public relations.

Employment of management analysts is expected to grow faster than the average for all occupations through 2008, as industry and government increasingly rely on outside expertise to improve the performance of their organizations. Job growth is projected in very large consulting firms with international expertise and in smaller niche consulting firms that specialize in specific areas, such as biotechnology, health care, human resources, engineering, and telecommunications. Growth in the number of individual practitioners may be hindered, however, by clients' increasing demand for a team approach, which enables examination of a variety of different issues and problems within an organization.

Employment growth of management analysts and consultants has been driven by a number a changes in the business environment that have forced American firms to take a closer look at their operations. As international and domestic markets have become more competitive, firms have needed to use resources more efficiently. Management analysts are increasingly sought to help reduce costs, streamline operations, and develop marketing strategies. As this process continues and businesses downsize, even more opportunities will be created for analysts to perform duties that were previously handled internally.

In addition, many companies will rely on analysts to organize and evaluate their restructuring efforts. Businesses attempting to expand internationally will need the skills of management analysts to help with organizational, administrative, and other issues. Further, as businesses increasingly rely on technology, there will be more demand for analysts with a technical background, such as engineering or biotechnology, particularly when combined with a master's degree in business administration. Finally, management analysts will also be in greater demand in the public sector, as Federal, State, and local agencies are expected to seek ways to become more efficient.

Earnings

Salaries for management analysts vary widely by experience, education, and employer. Median annual earnings of management analysts in 1998 were $49,470. The middle 50 percent earned between $39,420 and $72,690. The lowest 10 percent earned less than $31,800, and the highest 10 percent earned more than $88,470. Median annual earnings in the industries employing the largest numbers of management analysts and consultants in 1997 were:

Industry	Earnings
Management and public relations	$57,200
Federal government	56,400
Local government, except education and hospitals	47,500
Computer and data processing services	47,500
State government, except education and hospitals	39,600

According to a 1998 survey by the Association of Management Consulting Firms, earnings—including bonuses and/or profit sharing—for research associates in member firms averaged $38,900; for entry level consultants, $50,500; for management consultants, $69,700; for senior consultants, $96,800; for junior partners, $151,100; and for senior partners, $266,700.

Salaried management analysts usually receive common benefits such as health and life insurance, a retirement plan, vacation and sick leave, as well as less common benefits such as profit sharing and bonuses for outstanding work. In addition, all travel expenses usually are reimbursed by the employer. Self-employed consultants have to maintain their own office and provide their own benefits.

Related Occupations

Management analysts collect, review, and analyze data; make recommendations; and implement their ideas. Others who use similar skills include managers, computer systems analysts, operations research analysts, economists, and financial analysts. Researchers prepare data and reports for analysts to use in their recommendations.

Sources of Additional Information

Information about career opportunities in management consulting is available from:

☛ The Association of Management Consulting Firms, 3580 Lexington Ave., Suite 1700, New York, NY 10168.
Internet: **http://www.amcf.org**

Information about the Certified Management Consultant designation can be obtained from:

☛ The Institute of Management Consultants, 1200 19th St. NW., Suite 300, Washington DC 20036. Internet: **http://www.imcusa.org**

For information about a career as a State or local government management analyst, contact your State or local employment service. Information on obtaining a management analyst position with the Federal Government may be obtained from the Office of Personnel Management through a telephone based system. Consult your telephone directory under U.S. Government for a local number or call (912) 757-3000; TDD (912) 744-2299. That number is not tollfree and charges may result. Information also is available from their Internet site: **http://www.usajobs.opm.gov**

Property, Real Estate, and Community Association Managers

(O*NET 15011B)

Significant Points

- Most enter the occupation as on-site managers of apartment complexes, condominiums, or community associations, or as assistant managers at large property management firms.
- Opportunities should be best for those with college degrees in business administration or related fields.
- Almost one half were self-employed, three times the average for all executive, administrative, and managerial occupations.

Property managers coordinate with maintenance staff to inspect the grounds, facilities, and equipment to determine if repairs or maintenance are needed.

Nature of the Work

Many people own some type of real estate, such as a house. To businesses and investors, however, properly managed real estate is a potential source of income and profits rather than a place of shelter. Property, real estate, and community association managers maintain and increase the value of real estate investments for investors. *Property and real estate managers* oversee the performance of income-producing commercial or residential properties; *community association managers* manage the communal property and services of condominium or community associations.

When owners of apartments, office buildings, retail, or industrial properties lack the time or expertise needed for day-to-day management of their real estate investments, they often hire a property or real estate manager. The manager is either directly employed by the owner or indirectly employed through a contract with a property management firm.

Property managers handle the financial operations of the property, insuring that mortgages, taxes, insurance premiums, payroll, and maintenance bills are paid on time. Some property managers, called *asset property managers*, supervise the preparation of financial statements and periodically report to the owners on the status of the property, occupancy rates, dates of lease expirations, and other matters.

If necessary, property managers negotiate contracts for janitorial, security, groundskeeping, trash removal, and other services. When contracts are awarded competitively, managers solicit bids from several contractors and recommend to the owners which bid to accept. They monitor the performance of contractors, and investigate and resolve complaints from residents and tenants when services are not properly provided. Managers also purchase supplies and equipment for the property, and make arrangements with specialists for repairs that cannot be handled by regular property maintenance staff.

In addition to these duties, property managers must understand and comply with provisions of legislation, such as the Americans with Disabilities Act and the Federal Fair Housing Amendment Act, as well as local fair housing laws. They must insure that their renting and advertising practices are not discriminatory and that the property itself complies with State and Federal regulations.

On-site property managers are responsible for day-to-day operations for one piece of property, such as an office building, shopping center, or apartment complex. To insure the property is safe and being maintained properly, on-site managers routinely inspect the grounds, facilities, and equipment to determine if repairs or maintenance are needed. They meet not only with current residents when handling requests for repairs or trying to resolve complaints, but also with prospective residents or tenants to show vacant apartments or office space. On-site managers are also responsible for enforcing the terms of rental or lease agreements, such as rent collection, parking and pet restrictions, and termination-of-lease procedures. Other important duties of on-site managers include keeping accurate, up-to-date records of income and expenditures from property operations and the submission of regular expense reports to the asset property manager or owners.

Property managers who do not work on-site act as a liaison between the on-site manager and the owner. They also market vacant space to prospective tenants through the use of a leasing agent, advertising, or by other means, and establish rental rates in accordance with prevailing local conditions.

Some property managers, often called *real estate asset managers*, act as the property owners' agent and adviser for the property. They plan and direct the purchase, development, and disposition of real estate on behalf of the business and investors. These managers focus on long-term strategic financial planning rather than day-to-day operations of the property.

When deciding to acquire property, real estate asset managers take several factors into consideration, such as property values, taxes, zoning, population growth, and traffic volume and patterns. Once a site is selected, they negotiate contracts for the purchase or lease of the property, securing the most beneficial terms. Real estate asset managers periodically review their company's real estate holdings and identify properties that are no longer financially attractive. They then negotiate the sale or termination of the lease of properties selected for disposal. For more information, see the statement on real estate agents and brokers, located elsewhere in the *Handbook*.

The work of community association managers differs from that of other residential property managers. Instead of renters, they interact on a daily basis with homeowners—members of the community association employing the manager. Hired by the volunteer board of directors of the association, the community association manager administers the daily affairs and oversees the maintenance of property and facilities that the homeowners own and use jointly through the association. Smaller community associations usually cannot afford professional management, but managers of larger condominiums or homeowner associations have many of the same responsibilities as the managers of large apartment complexes. Some homeowner associations encompass thousands of homes, and, in addition to administering the associations' financial records and budget, their managers are responsible for the operation of community pools, golf courses, community centers, and the maintenance of landscaping and parking areas. Community association managers may also meet with the elected boards of directors to discuss and resolve legal and environmental issues or disputes between neighbors.

Property managers who work for land development companies acquire land and plan construction of shopping centers, houses, apartments, office buildings, or industrial parks. They negotiate with representatives of local governments, other businesses, community and public interest groups, and public utilities to eliminate obstacles to the development of land and gain support for a planned project. It sometimes takes years to win approval for a project, and in the process managers may have to modify plans for the project many times. Once they are free to proceed with a project, managers negotiate short-term loans to finance the construction of the project, and later negotiate long-term permanent mortgage loans. They then contract with architectural firms to draw up detailed plans, and with construction companies to build the project.

Working Conditions

Offices of most property managers are clean, modern, and well-lighted. However, many spend a major portion of their time away from their desks. On-site managers in particular may spend a large portion of their workday away from their office visiting the building engineer, showing apartments, checking on the janitorial and maintenance staff, or investigating problems reported by tenants. Property managers frequently visit the properties they oversee, sometimes on a daily basis when contractors are doing major repair or renovation work. Real estate asset managers may spend time away from home while traveling to company real estate holdings or searching for properties that might be acquired.

Property managers often must attend meetings in the evening with residents, property owners, community association boards of directors, or civic groups. Not surprisingly, many property managers put in long work weeks, especially before financial and tax reports are due. Some apartment managers are required to live in apartment complexes where they work so they are available to handle any emergency that occurs when they are off duty. They usually receive compensatory time off for working nights or weekends. Many apartment managers receive time off during the week so that they are available on weekends to show apartments to prospective residents.

Employment

Property managers held about 315,000 jobs in 1998. Most worked for real estate operators and lessors or for property management firms. Others worked for real estate development companies, government agencies that manage public buildings, and corporations with extensive holdings of commercial properties. Almost one half of property managers were self-employed.

Training, Other Qualifications, and Advancement

Most employers prefer to hire college graduates for property management positions. Entrants with degrees in business administration, accounting, finance, real estate, public administration, or related fields are preferred, but those with degrees in the liberal arts may also qualify. Good speaking, writing, computer, and financial skills, as well as an ability to deal tactfully with people, are essential in all areas of property management.

Most people enter property management as an on-site manager of an apartment complex, condominium, or community association, or as an assistant manager at a large property management firm. As they acquire experience working under the direction of a property manager, they may advance to positions with greater responsibility at larger properties. Those who excel as on-site managers often transfer to assistant property manager positions where they can acquire experience handling a broad range of property management responsibilities.

Previous employment as a real estate agent may be an asset to on-site managers because it provides experience useful in showing apartments or office space. In the past, those with backgrounds in building maintenance have advanced to on-site manager positions on the strength of their knowledge of building mechanical systems, but this is becoming less common as employers are placing greater emphasis on administrative, financial, and communication abilities for managerial jobs.

Although most people entering jobs such as assistant property manager do so on the strength of on-site management experience, employers are increasingly hiring inexperienced college graduates with bachelor's or master's degrees in business administration, accounting, finance, or real estate for these positions. Assistants work closely with a property manager and learn how to prepare budgets, analyze insurance coverage and risk options, market property to prospective tenants, and collect overdue rent payments. In time, many assistants advance to property manager positions.

The responsibilities and compensation of property managers increase as they manage more and larger properties. Most property managers are responsible for several properties at a time, and as their careers advance they are gradually entrusted with larger properties whose management is more complex. Many specialize in the management of one type of property, such as apartments, office buildings, condominiums, cooperatives, homeowner associations, or retail properties. Managers who excel at marketing properties to tenants may specialize in managing new properties, while those who are particularly knowledgeable about buildings and their mechanical systems might specialize in the management of older properties requiring renovation or more frequent repairs. Some experienced property managers open their own property management firms.

Persons most commonly enter real estate asset manager jobs by transferring from positions as property managers or real estate brokers. Real estate asset managers must be good negotiators, adept at persuading and handling people, and good at analyzing data to assess the fair market value of property or its development potential. Resourcefulness and creativity in arranging financing are essential for managers who specialize in land development.

Many employers encourage attendance at short-term formal training programs conducted by various professional and trade associations active in the real estate field. Employers send managers to these programs to improve their management skills and expand their knowledge of specialized subjects, such as the operation and maintenance of building mechanical systems, enhancing property values, insurance and risk management, personnel management, business and real estate law, tenant relations, communications, and accounting and financial concepts. Managers also participate in these programs to prepare themselves for positions of greater responsibility in property management. Completion of these programs, together with related job experience and a satisfactory score on a written examination, leads to certification, or the formal award of a professional designation, by the sponsoring association. In addition to these qualifications, some associations require their members to adhere to a specific code of ethics. Some of the organizations offering such programs are listed at the end of this statement.

Managers of public housing subsidized by the Federal Government are required to be certified, but many property managers, who work with all types of property, choose to earn a professional designation voluntarily because it represents formal industry recognition of their achievements and status in the occupation. Real estate asset managers who buy or sell property are required to be licensed by the State in which they practice.

Job Outlook

Employment of property, real estate, and community association managers is projected to increase as fast as the average for all occupations through the year 2008. Many job openings are expected to occur as property managers transfer to other occupations or leave the labor force. Opportunities should be best for those with a college degree in business administration, real estate, or a related field; as well as those who attain a professional designation.

Growth in the demand for on-site property managers will be greatest in several areas. In commercial real estate, the demand for managers is expected to accompany the projected expansion in wholesale and retail trade; finance, insurance, and real estate; and services. Some additional employment growth will come from expansion of existing buildings.

An increase in the Nation's stock of apartments and houses also should require more property managers. Developments of new homes are increasingly being organized with community or homeowner associations that provide community services and oversee jointly owned common areas, requiring professional management. To help properties become more profitable, more commercial and multi-unit residential property owners are expected to place their investments in the hands of professional managers.

Growth in demand should also arise as a result of the changing demographic composition of the population. The number of older people will increase during the projection period, creating a need for various types of suitable housing, such as assisted living arrangements and retirement communities. Accordingly, there will be a need for property managers to operate these facilities, especially those who have a background in the operation and administrative aspects of running a health unit.

Earnings

Median annual earnings of salaried property, real estate, and community association managers were $29,930 in 1998. The middle 50 percent earned between $21,020 and $43,080 a year. The lowest 10 percent earned less than $14,570 and the highest 10 percent earned more than $74,500 a year. Median annual earnings of salaried property, real estate, and community association managers in 1997 were $29,700 in the real estate agents and managers industry and $26,900 in the real estate operators and lessors industry.

Many resident apartment managers receive the use of an apartment as part of their compensation package. Property managers often are given the use of a company automobile, and managers employed in land development often receive a small percentage of ownership in projects they develop.

Related Occupations

Property managers plan, organize, staff, and manage the real estate operations of businesses. Workers who perform similar functions in other fields include city managers, education administrators, facilities managers, health services managers, hotel managers and assistants, real estate agents and brokers, and restaurant and food service managers.

Sources of Additional Information

General information about education and careers in property management is available from:

☛ Institute of Real Estate Management, 430 N. Michigan Ave., Chicago, IL 60611. Internet: **http://www.irem.org**

☛ International Council of Shopping Centers, 665 5th Ave., New York, NY 10022. Internet: **http://www.icsc.org**

For information on careers and certification programs in commercial property management, contact:

☛ Building Owners and Managers Association International, 1201 New York Ave. NW., Suite 300, Washington, DC 20005. Internet: **http://www.boma.org**

☛ Building Owners and Managers Institute, 1521 Ritchie Hwy., Arnold, MD 21012. Internet: **http://www.bomi-edu.org**

For information on careers and certification programs in residential property management, contact:

☛ Community Associations Institute, 1630 Duke St., Alexandria, VA 22314. Internet: **http://www.caionline.org**

☛ National Apartment Association, 201 N. Union St., Suite 200, Alexandria, VA 22314. Internet: **http://www.naahq.org**

☛ National Association of Residential Property Managers, 6300 Dutchmans Pkwy., Louisville, KY 40205. Internet: **http://www.narpm.org**

Purchasing Managers, Buyers, and Purchasing Agents

(O*NET 13008, 21302, 21305A, 21308A)

Significant Points

- Computerization has reduced the demand for lower-level buyers.
- About one-half were employed in wholesale trade or manufacturing establishments.

Nature of the Work

Purchasing managers, buyers, and purchasing agents seek to obtain the highest quality merchandise at the lowest possible purchase cost for their employers. In general, *purchasers* buy goods and services for their company or organization, whereas some *buyers* buy items for resale. They determine which commodities or services are best, choose the suppliers of the product or service, negotiate the lowest price, and award contracts that ensure the correct amount of the product or service is received at the appropriate time. In order to accomplish these tasks successfully, purchasing managers, buyers, and purchasing agents study sales records and inventory levels of current stock, identify foreign and domestic suppliers, and keep abreast of changes affecting both the supply of and demand for products and materials for which they are responsible.

Purchasing managers, buyers, and purchasing agents evaluate suppliers based upon price, quality, service support, availability, reliability, and selection. To assist them in their search, they review catalogs, industry periodicals, directories, trade journals, and Internet sites. They research the reputation and history of the suppliers and may advertise anticipated purchase actions in order to solicit bids. At meetings, trade shows, conferences, and visits to suppliers' plants and distribution centers, they examine products and services, assess a supplier's production and distribution capabilities, and discuss other technical and business considerations that influence the purchasing decision. Once all the necessary information on suppliers is gathered, orders are placed and contracts are awarded to those suppliers who meet the purchasers' needs. Other specific job duties and responsibilities vary by employer and by the type of commodities or services to be purchased.

Purchasing professionals employed by government agencies or manufacturing firms are usually called purchasing directors, managers, or agents; buyers or industrial buyers; or contract specialists. These workers acquire product materials, intermediate goods, machines, supplies, services, and other materials used in the production of a final product. Some purchasing managers specialize in negotiating and supervising supply contracts and are called contract or supply managers. Purchasing agents and managers obtain items ranging from raw materials, fabricated parts, machinery, and office supplies to construction services and airline tickets. The flow of work—or even the entire production process—can be slowed or halted if the right materials, supplies, or equipment are not on hand when needed. To be effective, purchasing professionals must have a working technical knowledge of the goods or services to be purchased.

In large industrial organizations, a distinction often is drawn between the work of a buyer or purchasing agent and that of a purchasing manager. Purchasing agents and buyers commonly focus on routine purchasing tasks, often specializing in a commodity or group of related commodities—for example, steel, lumber, cotton, grains, fabricated metal products, or petroleum products. The purchaser usually tracks things such as market conditions, price trends, or futures markets. Purchasing managers usually handle the more complex or critical purchases and may supervise a group of purchasing agents handling other goods and services. Whether a person is titled purchasing manager, buyer, or purchasing agent depends more on specific industry and employer practices than on specific job duties.

Changing business practices have altered the traditional roles of purchasing professionals in many industries. For example, manufacturing companies increasingly involve purchasing professionals at most stages of product development because of their ability to forecast a part's or material's cost, availability, and suitability for its intended purpose. Furthermore, potential problems with the supply of materials may be avoided by consulting the purchasing department in the early stages of product design.

Businesses might also enter into integrated supply contracts. These contracts increase the importance of supplier selection because agreements are larger in scope and longer in duration. Integrated supply incorporates all members of the supply chain including the supplier, transportation companies, and the retailer. A major responsibility of most purchasers is to work out problems that may occur with a supplier because the success of the relationship affects the buying firm's performance.

Purchasing professionals often work closely with other employees in their own organization when deciding on purchases, an arrangement sometimes called team buying. For example, they may discuss the design of custom-made products with company design engineers, quality problems in purchased goods with quality assurance engineers and production supervisors, or shipment problems with managers in the receiving department before submitting an order.

Contract specialists and managers in various levels of government award contracts for an array of items, including office and building supplies, services for the public, and construction projects. They may use sealed bids, but usually use negotiated agreements for complex items. Increasingly, purchasing professionals in government are placing solicitations for and accepting bids and offers through the Internet. Government purchasing agents and managers must follow strict laws and regulations in their work. These legal requirements occasionally are changed, so agents and contract specialists must stay informed about the latest regulations.

Other professionals, who buy finished goods for resale, are employed by wholesale and retail establishments where they commonly are referred to as "buyers" or "merchandise managers." Wholesale and retail buyers are an integral part of a complex system of distribution and merchandising that caters to the vast array of consumer needs and desires. Wholesale buyers purchase goods directly from manufacturers or from other wholesale firms for resale to retail firms, commercial establishments, institutions, and other organizations. In retail firms, buyers purchase goods from wholesale firms or directly from manufacturers for resale to the public. Buyers largely determine which products their establishment will sell. Therefore, it is essential that they have the ability to accurately predict what will appeal to consumers. They must constantly stay informed of the latest trends because failure to do so could jeopardize profits and the reputation of their company. Buyers also follow ads in newspapers and other media to check competitors' sales activities and watch general economic conditions to anticipate consumer buying patterns. Buyers working for large and medium-sized firms usually specialize in acquiring one or two lines of merchandise, whereas buyers working for small stores may purchase their complete inventory.

Purchasing managers study various financial reports to determine the best price.

The use of private-label merchandise and the consolidation of buying departments have increased the responsibilities of retail buyers. Private-label merchandise, produced for a particular retailer, requires buyers to work closely with vendors to develop and obtain the desired product. The downsizing and consolidation of buying departments is also increasing the demands placed on buyers because, although the amount of work remains unchanged, there are fewer people to accomplish it. The result is an increase in the workloads and levels of responsibility.

Many merchandise managers assist in the planning and implementation of sales promotion programs. Working with merchandising executives, they determine the nature of the sale and purchase accordingly. They also work with advertising personnel to create the ad campaign. For example, they may determine the media in which the advertisement will be placed—newspapers, direct mail, television, or some combination of these. In addition, merchandising managers often visit the selling floor to ensure that the goods are properly displayed. Often, assistant buyers are responsible for placing orders and checking shipments.

Computers are having a major effect on the jobs of purchasing managers, buyers and purchasing agents. In manufacturing and service industries, computers handle most of the more routine tasks—enabling purchasing professionals to concentrate mainly on the analytical aspects of the job. Computers are used to obtain instant and accurate product and price listings, to track inventory levels, process routine orders, and help determine when to make purchases. Computers also maintain lists of bidders and offers, record the history of supplier performance, and issue purchase orders.

Computerized systems have dramatically simplified many of the routine acquisition functions and improved the efficiency of determining which products are selling. For example, cash registers connected to computers, known as point-of-sale terminals, allow organizations to maintain centralized, up-to-date sales and inventory records. This information can then be used to produce weekly sales reports that reflect the types of products in demand. Buyers also use computers to gain instant access to the specifications for thousands of commodities, inventory records, and their customers' purchase records. Some firms are linked with manufacturers or wholesalers by electronic purchasing systems, the Internet, or extranets. These systems improve the speed for selection and ordering and provide information on availability and shipment, allowing buyers to better concentrate on the selection of goods and suppliers.

Working Conditions

Most purchasing managers, buyers, and purchasing agents work in comfortable, well-lighted offices. They frequently work more than the standard 40-hour week because of special sales, conferences, or production deadlines. Evening and weekend work is also common. For those working in retail trade, this is especially true prior to holiday seasons. Consequently, many retail firms discourage the use of vacation time from late November until early January.

Buyers and merchandise managers often work under great pressure because wholesale and retail stores are so competitive; buyers need physical stamina to keep up with the fast-paced nature of their work.

Many purchasing managers, buyers, and purchasing agents travel at least several days a month. Purchasers for worldwide manufacturing companies and large retailers, and buyers of high fashion, may travel outside the United States.

Employment

Purchasing managers, buyers, and purchasing agents held about 547,000 jobs in 1998. About one-half worked in wholesale trade or manufacturing establishments such as distribution centers or factories, and another one-fifth worked in retail trade establishments such as grocery or department stores. The remainder worked mostly in service establishments or different levels of government. A small number were self-employed.

Training, Other Qualifications, and Advancement

Qualified persons usually begin as trainees, purchasing clerks, expediters, junior buyers, or assistant buyers. Retail and wholesale firms prefer to hire applicants who are familiar with the merchandise they sell as well as with wholesaling and retailing practices. Some retail firms promote qualified employees to assistant buyer positions; others recruit and train college graduates as assistant buyers. Most employers use a combination of methods.

Educational requirements tend to vary with the size of the organization. Large stores and distributors, especially those in wholesale and retail trade, prefer applicants who have completed a bachelor's degree program with a business emphasis. Many manufacturing firms tend to put a greater emphasis on formal training. They prefer applicants with a bachelor's or master's degree in business, economics, or technical training such as engineering or one of the applied sciences.

Regardless of academic preparation, new employees must learn the specifics of their employers' business. Training periods vary in length, with most lasting 1 to 5 years. In wholesale and retail establishments, most trainees begin by selling merchandise, supervising sales workers, checking invoices on material received, and keeping track of stock on hand, although widespread use of computers has simplified many of these tasks. As they progress, retail trainees are given increased buying-related responsibilities.

In manufacturing, new purchasing employees often are enrolled in company training programs and spend a considerable amount of time learning about company operations and purchasing practices. They work with experienced purchasers to learn about commodities, prices, suppliers, and markets. In addition, they may be assigned to the production planning department to learn about the material requirements system and the inventory system the company uses to keep production and replenishment functions working smoothly.

Purchasing managers, buyers, and purchasing agents must be computer literate, including knowing how to use word processing and spreadsheet software. Other important qualities include the ability to analyze technical data in suppliers' proposals; good communication, negotiation, and math skills; knowledge of supply chain management; and the ability to perform financial analyses.

Persons who wish to become wholesale or retail buyers should be good at planning and decision making and have an interest in merchandising. Anticipating consumer preferences and ensuring that goods are in stock when they are needed require resourcefulness, good judgment, and self-confidence. Buyers must be able to make decisions quickly and take risks. Marketing skills and the ability to identify products that will sell are also very important. Employers often look for leadership ability because buyers spend a large portion of their time supervising assistant buyers and dealing with manufacturers' representatives and store executives.

Experienced buyers may advance by moving to a department that manages a larger volume or by becoming a merchandise manager. Others may go to work in sales for a manufacturer or wholesaler.

An experienced purchasing agent or buyer may become an assistant purchasing manager in charge of a group of purchasing professionals before advancing to purchasing manager, supply manager, or director of materials management. At the top levels, duties may overlap with other management functions such as production, planning, or marketing.

Regardless of industry, continuing education is essential for advancement. Many purchasers participate in seminars offered by professional societies and take college courses in purchasing. Although no national standard exists, professional certification is becoming increasingly important.

In private industry, recognized marks of experience and professional competence are the designations Accredited Purchasing Practitioner (A.P.P.) and Certified Purchasing Manager (C.P.M.), conferred by the National Association of Purchasing Management, and Certified Purchasing Professional (C.P.P.), conferred by the American Purchasing Society. In Federal, State, and local government, the indications of professional competence are Certified Professional Public Buyer (C.P.P.B.) and Certified Public Purchasing Officer (C.P.P.O.), conferred by the National Institute of Governmental Purchasing.

Most of these are awarded only after work-related experience and education requirements are met, and written or oral exams are completed successfully.

Job Outlook

Employment of purchasing managers, buyers, and purchasing agents is expected to grow more slowly than average through the year 2008. Demand for these workers will not keep up with the rising level of economic activity because the increasing use of computers has allowed much of the paperwork typically involved in ordering and procuring supplies to be eliminated, reducing the demand for lower-level buyers who perform these duties. Also, limited sourcing and long-term contracting have allowed companies to negotiate with fewer suppliers less frequently. Consequently, most job openings will result from the need to replace workers who transfer to other occupations or leave the labor force.

In retail trade, mergers and acquisitions have forced the consolidation of buying departments, eliminating jobs. In addition, larger retail stores are removing their buying departments from geographic markets and centralizing them at their headquarters, eliminating more jobs.

The increased use of credit cards by some employees to purchase supplies without using the services of the procurement or purchasing office, combined with the growing number of buys being made electronically, will restrict demand for purchasing agents within governments and many manufacturing firms.

Persons who have a bachelor's degree in business should have the best chance of obtaining a buyer job in wholesale or retail trade or within government. A bachelor's degree, combined with industry experience and knowledge of a technical field, will be an advantage for those interested in working for a manufacturing or industrial company. Government agencies and larger companies usually require a master's degree in business or public administration for top-level purchasing positions.

Earnings

Median annual earnings of purchasing managers were $41,830 in 1998. The middle 50 percent earned between $29,930 and $63,520 a year. The lowest 10 percent earned less than $22,290 and the highest 10 percent earned more than $86,740 a year. Median annual earnings in the industries employing the largest number of purchasing managers in 1997 were as follows:

Electrical goods	$39,300
Professional and commercial equipment	37,700
Machinery, equipment, and supplies	36,400
Department stores	35,500
Grocery stores	25,900

Median annual earnings for purchasing agents, except wholesale, retail, and farm products were $38,040 in 1998. The middle 50 percent earned between $29,660 and $49,660 a year. The lowest 10 percent earned less than $23,960 and the highest 10 percent earned more than $74,050 a year. Median annual earnings in the industries employing the largest number of purchasing agents, except wholesale, retail, and farm products in 1997 were as follows:

Federal government	$47,200
Aircraft and parts	41,100
Electronic components and accessories	36,600
Local government, except education and hospitals	35,300
Hospitals	29,300

Median annual earnings for wholesale and retail buyers, except farm products were $31,560 in 1998. The middle 50 percent earned between $23,490 and $42,920 a year. The lowest 10 percent earned less than $17,730 and the highest 10 percent earned more than $66,480 a year. Median annual earnings in the industries employing the largest number of wholesale and retail buyers, except farm products in 1997 were as follows:

Groceries and related products	$36,200
Machinery, equipment, and supplies	29,300
Professional and commercial equipment	28,800
Grocery stores	25,100
Miscellaneous shopping goods stores	24,700

Purchasing managers, buyers, and purchasing agents receive the same benefits package as their coworkers, including vacations, sick leave, life and health insurance, and pension plans. In addition to standard benefits, retail buyers often earn cash bonuses based on their performance and may receive discounts on merchandise bought from the employer.

Related Occupations

Workers in other occupations who need a knowledge of marketing and the ability to assess demand are advertising, marketing, and public relations managers; insurance sales agents; manufacturers' and wholesale sales representatives; material recording, scheduling, dispatching, and distributing occupations; retail salespersons; sales engineers; and sales managers.

Sources of Additional Information

Further information about education, training, and/or certification for purchasing careers is available from:

☛ American Purchasing Society, 430 W. Downer Pl., Aurora, IL 60506. Internet: **http://www.american-purchasing.com**

☛ National Association of Purchasing Management, P.O. Box 22160, Tempe, AZ 85285-2169. Internet: **http://www.napm.org**

☛ National Institute of Governmental Purchasing, Inc., 151 Spring St., Herndon, VA 20170. Internet: **http://www.nigp.org**

☛ Federal Acquisition Institute (MVI), Office of Acquisition Policy, General Services Administration, 1800 F St. NW., Room 4017, Washington, DC 20405. Internet: **http://www.gsa.gov/staff/v/training.htm**

Restaurant and Food Service Managers

(O*NET 15026B)

Significant Points

- Although many experienced food and beverage preparation and service workers are promoted to fill jobs, job opportunities are expected to be best for those with bachelor's or associate degrees in restaurant and institutional food service management.
- Job opportunities should be better for salaried managers than for self-employed managers, as restaurants increasingly affiliate with national chains rather than being independently owned.

Nature of the Work

The daily responsibilities of many restaurant and food service managers can be as complicated as some meals prepared by a fine chef. In addition to the traditional duties of selecting and pricing menu items, using food and other supplies efficiently, and achieving quality in food preparation and service, managers are now responsible for a growing number of administrative and human resource tasks. For example, managers must carefully find and evaluate new ways of recruiting new employees in a tight job market. Once hired, managers must also find creative ways to retain experienced workers.

In most restaurants and institutional food service facilities, the manager is assisted in these duties by one or more assistant managers, depending on the size and operating hours of the establishment. In most large establishments, as well as in many smaller ones, the management team consists of a *general manager*, one or more *assistant managers*, and an *executive chef.* The executive chef is responsible for the operation of the kitchen, while the assistant managers oversee service in the dining room and other areas. In smaller restaurants, the executive chef also may be the general manager, and sometimes an owner. In fast-food restaurants and other food service facilities open for long hours, often 7 days a week, the manager is aided by several assistant managers, each of whom supervises a shift of workers. (For additional information on these other workers, see the *Handbook* statements on general managers and top executives and chefs, cooks, and other kitchen workers.)

One of the most important tasks of restaurant and food service managers is selecting successful menu items. This task varies by establishment because although many restaurants rarely change their menu, others make frequent alterations. Managers or executive chefs select menu items, taking into account the likely number of customers and the past popularity of dishes. Other issues taken into consideration when planning a menu include unserved food left over from prior meals that should not be wasted, the need for variety, and the availability of foods due to changing seasons. Managers or executive chefs analyze the recipes of the dishes to determine food, labor, overhead costs and to assign prices to various dishes. Menus must be developed far enough in advance that supplies can be ordered and received in time.

On a daily basis, managers estimate food consumption, place orders with suppliers, and schedule the delivery of fresh food and beverages. They receive and check the content of deliveries, evaluating the quality of meats, poultry, fish, fruits, vegetables, and baked goods. To ensure good service, managers meet with sales representatives from restaurant suppliers to place orders replenishing stocks of tableware, linens, paper, cleaning supplies, cooking utensils, and furniture and fixtures. They also arrange for equipment maintenance and repairs and coordinate a variety of services such as waste removal and pest control.

The quality of food and services in restaurants depends largely on a manager's ability to interview, hire, and, when necessary, fire employees. This is especially true in tight labor markets, when many managers report difficulty in hiring experienced food and beverage preparation and service workers. Managers may attend career fairs or arrange for newspaper advertising to expand their pool of applicants.

Restaurant and food service managers check for consistent quality in food preparation and service.

Once a new employee is hired, managers explain the establishment's policies and practices and oversee any necessary training. Managers also schedule the work hours of employees, making sure there are enough workers present to cover peak dining periods. If employees are unable to work, managers may have to fill in for them. Some managers regularly help with cooking, clearing of tables, or other tasks.

Another fundamental responsibility of restaurant and food service managers is supervising the kitchen and dining room. For example, managers often oversee all food preparation and cooking, examining the quality and portion sizes to ensure that dishes are prepared and garnished correctly and in a timely manner. They also investigate and resolve customers' complaints about food quality or service. To maintain company and government sanitation standards, they direct the cleaning of the kitchen and dining areas and washing of tableware, kitchen utensils, and equipment. Managers also monitor the actions of their employees and patrons on a continual basis to ensure that health and safety standards and local liquor regulations are obeyed.

In addition to their regular duties, restaurant and food service managers have a variety of administrative responsibilities. Although much of this work is delegated to a bookkeeper in a larger establishment, managers in most smaller establishments, such as fast-food restaurants, must keep records of the hours and wages of employees, prepare the payroll, and fill out paperwork in compliance with licensing laws and reporting requirements of tax, wage and hour, unemployment compensation, and Social Security laws. Managers also maintain records of supply and equipment purchases and ensure that accounts with suppliers are paid on a regular basis. In addition, managers in full-service restaurants record the number, type, and cost of items sold to evaluate and discontinue dishes that may be unpopular or less profitable.

Many managers are able to ease the burden of recordkeeping and paperwork through the use of computers. Point-of-service (POS) systems are used in many restaurants to increase employee productivity and allow managers to track the sales of specific menu items. Using a POS system, a server keys in the customer's order and the computer immediately sends the order to the kitchen so preparation can begin. The same system totals checks, acts as a cash register and credit card authorizer, and tracks daily sales. To minimize food costs and spoilage, many managers use inventory tracking software to compare the record of daily sales from the POS with a record of present inventory. In some establishments, when supplies needed for the preparation of popular menu items run low, additional inventory can be ordered directly from the supplier using the computer. Computers also allow restaurant and food service managers to more efficiently keep track of employee schedules and pay.

Managers are among the first to arrive in the morning, and the last to leave. At the conclusion of each day, or sometimes each shift, managers tally the cash and charge receipts received and balance them against the record of sales. In most cases, they are responsible for depositing the day's receipts at the bank or securing them in a safe place. Finally, managers are responsible for locking up, checking that ovens, grills, and lights are off, and switching on alarm systems.

Working Conditions

Evenings and weekends are popular dining periods, making night and weekend work common among managers. Many managers of institutional food service facilities work more conventional hours because factory and office cafeterias are usually open only on weekdays for breakfast and lunch. Hours for many managers are unpredictable, however, as managers may have to fill in for absent workers on short notice. It is common for restaurant and food service managers to work 50 to 60 hours or more per week.

Managers often experience the pressure of simultaneously coordinating a wide range of activities. When problems occur, it is the responsibility of the manager to resolve them with minimal disruption to customers. The job can be hectic during peak dining hours, and dealing with irate customers or uncooperative employees can be stressful.

Employment

Restaurant and food service managers held about 518,000 jobs in 1998. Most managers are salaried, but about 1 in 6 is self-employed. Most work in restaurants or for contract institutional food service companies, while a smaller number are employed by educational institutions, hospitals, nursing and personal care facilities, and civic, social, and fraternal organizations. Jobs are located throughout the country, with large cities and tourist areas providing more opportunities for full-service dining positions.

Training, Other Qualifications, and Advancement

Most food service management companies and national or regional restaurant chains recruit management trainees from 2- and 4-year college hospitality management programs. Food service and restaurant chains prefer to hire people with degrees in restaurant and institutional food service management, but they often hire graduates with degrees in other fields who have demonstrated interest and aptitude. Some restaurant and food service manager positions, particularly self-service and fast-food, are filled by promoting experienced food and beverage preparation and service workers. Waiters, waitresses, chefs, and fast-food workers demonstrating potential for handling increased responsibility sometimes advance to assistant manager or management trainee jobs. Executive chefs need extensive experience working as chefs, and general managers need experience as assistant managers.

A bachelor's degree in restaurant and food service management provides a particularly strong preparation for a career in this occupation. In 1998, more than 150 colleges and universities offered 4-year programs in restaurant and hotel management or institutional food service management. For those not interested in pursuing a 4-year degree, more than 800 community and junior colleges, technical institutes, and other institutions offer programs in these fields leading to an associate degree or other formal certification. Both 2- and 4-year programs provide instruction in subjects such as nutrition and food planning and preparation, as well as accounting, business law and management, and computer science. Some programs combine classroom and laboratory study with internships that provide on-the-job experience. In addition, many educational institutions offer culinary programs that provide food preparation training. This training can lead to a career as a cook or chef and provide a foundation for advancement to an executive chef position.

Most employers emphasize personal qualities when hiring managers. For example, self-discipline, initiative, and leadership ability are essential. Managers must be able to solve problems and concentrate on details. They need good communication skills to deal with customers and suppliers, as well as to motivate and direct their staff. A neat and clean appearance is a must because they often are in close personal contact with the public. Restaurant and food service management can be demanding, so good health and stamina also are important.

Most restaurant chains and food service management companies have rigorous training programs for management positions. Through a combination of classroom and on-the-job training, trainees receive instruction and gain work experience in all aspects of the operations of a restaurant or institutional food service facility. Topics include food preparation, nutrition, sanitation, security, company policies and procedures, personnel management, recordkeeping, and preparation of reports. Training on use of the restaurant's computer system is increasingly important as well. Usually after 6 months or a year, trainees receive their first permanent assignment as an assistant manager.

A measure of professional achievement for restaurant and food service managers is the designation of certified Foodservice Management Professional (FMP). Although not a requirement for employment or advancement in the occupation, voluntary certification provides recognition of professional competence, particularly for managers who acquired their skills largely on the job. The Educational Foundation of the National Restaurant Association awards the FMP designation to managers who achieve a qualifying score on a written examination, complete a series of courses that cover a range of food service management topics, and meet standards of work experience in the field.

Willingness to relocate often is essential for advancement to positions with greater responsibility. Managers typically advance to larger establishments or regional management positions within restaurant chains. Some eventually open their own eating and drinking establishments. Others transfer to hotel management positions because their restaurant management experience provides a good background for food and beverage manager jobs in hotels and resorts.

Job Outlook

Employment of restaurant and food service managers is expected to increase about as fast as the average for all occupations through 2008. In addition to employment growth, the need to replace managers who transfer to other occupations or stop working will create many job openings. Opportunities to fill these openings are expected to be best for those with a bachelor's or associate degree in restaurant and institutional food service management.

Projected employment growth varies by industry. Eating and drinking places will provide the most new jobs as the number of eating and drinking establishments increases along with the population, personal incomes, and leisure time. In addition, manager jobs will increase in eating and drinking places as schools, hospitals, and other businesses contract out more of their food services to institutional food service companies within the eating and drinking industry.

Food service manager jobs still are expected to increase in many of these other industries, but growth will be slowed as contracting out becomes more common. Growth in the elderly population should result in more food service manager jobs in nursing homes and other health-care institutions, and residential-care and assisted-living facilities.

Job opportunities should be better for salaried managers than for self-employed managers. New restaurants are increasingly affiliated with national chains rather than being independently owned and operated. As this trend continues, fewer owners will manage restaurants themselves, and more restaurant managers will be employed by larger companies to run establishments.

Employment in eating and drinking establishments is not very sensitive to changes in economic conditions, so restaurant and food service managers are rarely laid off during hard times. However, competition among restaurants is always intense, and many restaurants do not survive.

Earnings

Median earnings of food service and lodging managers were $26,700 in 1998. The middle 50 percent earned between $19,820 and $34,690. The lowest paid 10 percent earned $14,430 or less, while the highest paid 10 percent earned over $45,520. Median annual earnings in the industries employing the largest number of food service and lodging managers in 1997 are shown below.

Hotels and motels	$28,600
Eating and drinking places	25,000
Elementary and secondary schools	21,300

In addition to typical benefits, most salaried restaurant and food service managers receive free meals and the opportunity for additional training depending on their length of service.

Related Occupations

Restaurant and food service managers direct the activities of businesses, which provide a service to customers. Other managers in service-oriented businesses include hotel managers and assistants, health services admiistrators, retail store managers, and bank managers.

Sources of Additional Information

Information about a career as a restaurant and food service manager, 2- and 4-year college programs in restaurant and food service management and certification as a Foodservice Management Professional is available from:

☛ The Educational Foundation of the National Restaurant Association, Suite 1400, 250 South Wacker Dr., Chicago, IL 60606.

General information on hospitality careers may be obtained from:

☛ Council on Hotel, Restaurant, and Institutional Education, 1200 17th St. NW., Washington, DC 20036-3097.

Additional information about job opportunities in the field may be obtained from local employers and local offices of the State employment service.

Professional and Technical Occupations

Air Transportation-Related Occupations

Aircraft Pilots and Flight Engineers

(O*NET 97702B, 97702C, 97702D, 97702E, 97702H, and 97702J)

Significant Points

- Competition is expected for jobs because aircraft pilots have very high earnings, especially those employed by national airlines.
- Pilots usually start with smaller commuter and regional airlines to acquire the experience needed to qualify for higher paying jobs with national airlines.
- Most pilots have traditionally learned to fly in the military, but growing numbers are entering from civilian FAA certified pilot training schools.

Nature of the Work

Pilots are highly trained professionals who fly airplanes and helicopters to carry out a wide variety of tasks. Although most pilots transport passengers and cargo, others are involved in more unusual tasks, such as dusting crops, spreading seed for reforestation, testing aircraft, directing fire fighting efforts, tracking criminals, monitoring traffic, and rescuing and evacuating injured persons.

Except on small aircraft, two pilots usually make up the cockpit crew. Usually, the most experienced pilot, the *captain*, is in command and supervises all other crew members. The pilot and copilot share flying and other duties, such as communicating with air traffic controllers and monitoring the instruments. Some large aircraft have a third pilot—*the flight engineer*—who assists the other pilots by monitoring and operating many of the instruments and systems, making minor inflight repairs, and watching for other aircraft. New technology can perform many flight tasks, however, and virtually all new aircraft now fly with only two pilots, who rely more heavily on computerized controls. As older, less technologically sophisticated aircraft continue to retire from airline fleets, flight engineer jobs will diminish.

Before departure, pilots plan their flights carefully. They thoroughly check their aircraft to make sure that the engines, controls, instruments, and other systems are functioning properly. They also make sure that baggage or cargo has been loaded correctly. They confer with flight dispatchers and aviation weather forecasters to find out about weather conditions enroute and at their destination. Based on this information, they choose a route, altitude, and speed that will provide the fastest, safest, and smoothest flight. When flying under instrument flight rules—procedures governing the operation of the aircraft when there is poor visibility—the pilot in command, or the company dispatcher, normally files an instrument flight plan with air traffic control so that the flight can be coordinated with other air traffic.

Takeoff and landing are the most difficult parts of the flight and require close coordination between the pilot and first officer. For example, as the plane accelerates for takeoff, the pilot concentrates on the runway while the first officer scans the instrument panel. To calculate the speed they must attain to become airborne, pilots consider the altitude of the airport, outside temperature, weight of the plane, and the speed and direction of the wind. The moment the plane reaches takeoff speed, the first officer informs the pilot, who then pulls back on the controls to raise the nose of the plane.

Unless the weather is bad, the actual flight is relatively easy. Airplane pilots, with the assistance of autopilot and the flight management computer, steer the plane along their planned route and are monitored by the air traffic control stations they pass along the way. They regularly scan the instrument panel to check their fuel supply, the condition of their engines, and the air-conditioning, hydraulic, and other systems. Pilots may request a change in altitude or route if circumstances dictate. For example, if the ride is rougher than expected, they may ask air traffic control if pilots flying at other altitudes have reported better conditions. If so, they may request a change. This procedure also may be used to find a stronger tailwind or a weaker headwind to save fuel and increase speed.

In contrast, helicopters are used for short trips at relatively low altitude, so pilots must be constantly on the lookout for trees, bridges, power lines, transmission towers, and other dangerous obstacles. Regardless of the type of aircraft, all pilots must monitor warning devices designed to help detect sudden shifts in wind conditions that can cause crashes.

Pilots must rely completely on their instruments when visibility is poor. Using the altimeter readings, they know how high above ground they are and whether or not they can fly safely over mountains and other obstacles. Special navigation radios give pilots precise information which, with the help of special maps, tell them their exact position. Other very sophisticated equipment provides directions to a point just above the end of a runway and enables pilots to land completely "blind."

Once on the ground, pilots must complete records on their flight for their organization and the Federal Aviation Administration (FAA).

The number of nonflying duties that pilots have depends on the employment setting. Airline pilots have the services of large support staffs, and consequently, perform few nonflying duties. Pilots employed by other organizations such as charter operators or businesses have many other duties. They may load the aircraft, handle all passenger luggage to ensure a balanced load, and supervise refueling; other nonflying responsibilities include keeping records, scheduling flights, arranging for major maintenance, and performing minor aircraft maintenance and repair work.

Some pilots are instructors. They teach their students the principles of flight in ground-school classes and demonstrate how to operate aircraft in dual-controlled planes and helicopters. A few specially trained pilots are "examiners" or "check pilots." They periodically fly with other pilots or pilot's license applicants to make sure that they are proficient.

Working Conditions

By law, airline pilots cannot fly more than 100 hours a month or more than 1,000 hours a year. Most airline pilots fly an average of 75 hours a month and work an additional 75 hours a month performing nonflying duties. About one-fifth of all pilots work more than 40 hours a week. Most spend a considerable amount of time away from home because the majority of flights involve overnight layovers. When pilots are away from home, the airlines provide hotel accommodations, transportation between the hotel and airport, and an allowance for meals and other expenses. Airlines operate flights at all hours of the day and night, so work schedules often are irregular. Flight assignments are based on seniority.

Before departure, pilots plan their flights carefully.

Those pilots not employed by the airlines often have irregular schedules as well; they may fly 30 hours one month and 90 hours the next. Because these pilots frequently have many nonflying responsibilities, they have much less free time than airline pilots. Except for business pilots, most do not remain away from home overnight. They may work odd hours. Flight instructors may have irregular and seasonal work schedules depending on their students' available time and the weather. Instructors frequently work at night or on weekends.

Airline pilots, especially those on international routes, often suffer jet lag—fatigue caused by many hours of flying through different time zones. The work of test pilots, who check the flight performance of new and experimental planes, may be dangerous. Pilots who are crop dusters may be exposed to toxic chemicals and seldom have the benefit of a regular landing strip. Helicopter pilots involved in police work may be subject to personal injury.

Although flying does not involve much physical effort, the mental stress of being responsible for a safe flight, no matter what the weather, can be tiring. Pilots must be alert and quick to react if something goes wrong, particularly during takeoff and landing.

Employment

Civilian pilots held about 94,000 jobs in 1998. About 84 percent worked for airlines. Others worked as flight instructors at local airports or for large businesses that fly company cargo and executives in their own airplanes or helicopters. Some pilots flew small planes for air taxi companies, usually to or from lightly traveled airports not served by major airlines. Others worked for a variety of businesses performing tasks such as crop dusting, inspecting pipelines, or conducting sightseeing trips. Federal, State, and local governments also employed pilots. A few pilots were self-employed.

The employment of airplane pilots is not distributed like the population. Pilots are more concentrated in California, Texas, Georgia, Washington, Nevada, Hawaii, and Alaska, which have a high amount of flying activity relative to their population.

Training, Other Qualifications, and Advancement

All pilots who are paid to transport passengers or cargo must have a commercial pilot's license with an instrument rating issued by the FAA. Helicopter pilots must hold a commercial pilot's certificate with a helicopter rating. To qualify for these licenses, applicants must be at least 18 years old and have at least 250 hours of flight experience. The time can be reduced through participation in certain flight school curricula approved by the FAA. They also must pass a strict physical examination to make sure that they are in good health and have 20/20 vision with or without glasses, good hearing, and no physical handicaps that could impair their performance. Applicants must pass a written test that includes questions on the principles of safe flight, navigation techniques, and FAA regulations. They also must demonstrate their flying ability to FAA or designated examiners.

To fly in periods of low visibility, pilots must be rated by the FAA to fly by instruments. Pilots may qualify for this rating by having 105 hours of flight experience, including 40 hours of experience in flying by instruments; they also must pass a written examination on procedures and FAA regulations covering instrument flying and demonstrate to an examiner their ability to fly by instruments.

Airline pilots must fulfill additional requirements. Pilots must have an airline transport pilot's license. Applicants for this license must be at least 23 years old and have a minimum of 1,500 hours of flying experience, including night and instrument flying, and pass FAA written and flight examinations. Usually they also have one or more advanced ratings, such as multi-engine aircraft or aircraft type ratings dependent upon the requirements of their particular flying jobs. Because pilots must be able to make quick decisions and accurate judgments under pressure, many airline companies reject applicants who do not pass required psychological and aptitude tests.

All licenses are valid as long as a pilot can pass the periodic physical examinations and tests of flying skills required by Federal Government and company regulations.

The Armed Forces have always been an important source of trained pilots for civilian jobs. Military pilots gain valuable experience on jet aircraft and helicopters, and persons with this experience are usually preferred for civilian pilot jobs. This primarily reflects the extensive flying time military pilots receive. Persons without armed forces training also become pilots by attending flight schools. The FAA has certified about 600 civilian flying schools, including some colleges and universities that offer degree credit for pilot training. Over the projection period, Federal budget reductions are expected to reduce military pilot training. As a result, FAA certified schools will train a larger share of pilots than in the past. Prospective pilots may also learn to fly by taking lessons from individual FAA-certified flight instructors.

Although some small airlines will hire high school graduates, most airlines require at least 2 years of college and prefer to hire college graduates; about 90 percent of all pilots have completed some college. In fact, most entrants to this occupation have a college degree. If the number of college educated applicants continues to increase, employers may make a college degree an educational requirement.

Depending on the type of aircraft, new airline pilots start as first officers or flight engineers. Although some airlines favor applicants who already have a flight engineer's license, they may provide flight engineer training for those who have only the commercial license. Many pilots begin with smaller regional or commuter airlines where they obtain experience flying passengers on scheduled flights into busy airports in all weather conditions. These jobs often lead to higher paying jobs with bigger, national airlines.

Initial training for airline pilots includes a week of company indoctrination, 3 to 6 weeks of ground school and simulator training, and 25 hours of initial operating experience, including a check-ride with an FAA aviation safety inspector. Once trained and "on the line," pilots are required to attend recurrent training and simulator checks twice a year throughout their career.

Organizations other than airlines usually require less flying experience. However, a commercial pilot's license is a minimum requirement, and employers prefer applicants who have experience in the type of craft they will be flying. New employees usually start as first officers, or fly less sophisticated equipment. Test pilots often are required to have an engineering degree.

Advancement for all pilots usually is limited to other flying jobs. Many pilots start as flight instructors, building up their flying hours while they earn money teaching. As they become more experienced, these pilots occasionally fly charter planes or perhaps get jobs with small air transportation firms, such as air taxi companies. Some advance to business flying jobs. A small number get flight engineer jobs with the airlines.

In the airlines, advancement usually depends on seniority provisions of union contracts. After 1 to 5 years, flight engineers advance according to seniority to first officer and, after 5 to 15 years, to captain. Seniority also determines which pilots get the more desirable routes. In a nonairline job, a first officer may advance to pilot and, in large companies, to chief pilot or director of aviation in charge of aircraft scheduling, maintenance, and flight procedures.

Job Outlook

Pilots are expected to face considerable competition for jobs through the year 2008 because the number of applicants for new positions is expected to exceed the number of job openings. Competition will be especially keen early in the projection period due to a temporary increase in the pool of qualified pilots seeking jobs. Mergers and bankruptcies during the recent restructuring of the industry caused a large number of airline pilots to lose their jobs. Also, Federal budget reductions resulted in many pilots leaving the Armed Forces. These and other qualified pilots seek jobs in this occupation because it offers very high earnings, glamour, prestige, and free or low cost travel benefits. As time passes, some pilots will fail to maintain their qualifications and the number of applicants competing for each opening should decline. Factors affecting demand, however, are not expected to ease that competition.

Relatively few jobs will be created from rising demand for pilots as employment is expected to increase more slowly than the average for all occupations through 2008. The expected growth in airline passenger and cargo traffic will create a need for more airliners, pilots, and flight instructors. However, computerized flight management systems on new aircraft will eliminate the need for flight engineers on those planes, thus restricting the growth of pilot employment. In addition, the trend toward using larger planes in the airline industry will increase pilot productivity. Future business travel could also be adversely affected by the growing use of teleconferencing; facsimile mail; and electronic communications, such as e-mail; as well as the elimination of many middle management positions in corporate downsizing. Employment of business pilots is expected to grow slower than in the past as more businesses opt to fly with regional and smaller airlines serving their area rather than buy and operate their own aircraft. On the other hand, the number of helicopter pilots is expected to increase more rapidly as the demand expands for the type of services that helicopters can offer, such as police and rescue operations.

Job openings resulting from the need to replace pilots who retire or leave the occupation traditionally have been very low. Aircraft pilots usually have a strong attachment to their occupation because it requires a substantial investment in specialized training that is not transferable to other fields, and it commonly offers very high earnings. However, many of the pilots who were hired in the late 1960's are approaching the age for mandatory retirement, so retirements of pilots are expected to increase and generate several thousand job openings each year.

Pilots who have logged the greatest number of flying hours in the more sophisticated equipment typically have the best prospects. This is the reason military pilots usually have an advantage over other applicants. Job seekers with the most FAA licenses will also have a competitive advantage. Opportunities for pilots in the regional commuter airlines and international service are expected to be more favorable as these segments are expected to grow faster than other segments of the industry.

Employment of pilots is sensitive to cyclical swings in the economy. During recessions, when a decline in the demand for air travel forces airlines to curtail the number of flights, airlines may temporarily furlough some pilots. Commercial and corporate flying, flight instruction, and testing of new aircraft also decline during recessions, adversely affecting pilots in those areas.

Earnings

Earnings of airline pilots are among the highest in the Nation, and depend on factors such as the type, size, and maximum speed of the plane, and the number of hours and miles flown. For example, pilots who fly jet aircraft usually earn higher salaries than turbo-prop pilots do. In 1998, median annual earnings of aircraft pilots and flight engineers were $91,750. Pilots and flight engineers may earn extra pay for night and international flights.

Airline pilots usually are eligible for life and health insurance plans financed by the airlines. They also receive retirement benefits and if they fail the FAA physical examination at some point in their careers, they get disability payments. In addition, pilots receive an expense allowance, or "per diem," for every hour they are away from home. Per diem can represent up to $500 each month in addition to their salary. Some airlines also provide allowances to pilots for purchasing and cleaning their uniforms. As an additional benefit, pilots and their immediate families usually are entitled to free or reduced fare transportation on their own and other airlines.

More than one-half of all aircraft pilots are members of unions. Most of the pilots who fly for the major airlines are members of the Airline Pilots Association, International, but those employed by one major airline are members of the Allied Pilots Association. Some flight engineers are members of the Flight Engineers' International Association.

Related Occupations

Although they are not in the cockpit, air traffic controllers and flight dispatchers also play an important role in making sure flights are safe and on schedule, and participate in many of the decisions pilots must make.

Sources of Additional Information

Information about job opportunities, salaries for a particular airline and the qualifications required may be obtained by writing to the personnel manager of the airline.

For information on airline pilots, contact:

☛ Airline Pilots Association, 1625 Massachusetts Ave. NW., Washington, DC 20036.

☛ Air Transport Association of America, 1301 Pennsylvania Ave. NW., Suite 1110, Washington, DC 20006.

For information on helicopter pilots, contact:

☛ Helicopter Association International, 1619 Duke St., Alexandria, VA 22314.

For a copy of List of Certificated Pilot Schools, write to:

☛ Superintendent of Documents, U.S. Government Printing Office, Washington, DC 20402. There is a $2.75 charge for this publication.

For information about job opportunities in companies other than airlines, consult the classified section of aviation trade magazines and apply to companies that operate aircraft at local airports.

Air Traffic Controllers

(O*NET 39002)

Significant Points

- Nearly all air traffic controllers are employed and trained by the Federal Government.
- Keen competition is expected in this occupation.
- Aircraft controllers earn relatively high pay and have good benefits.

Nature of the Work

The air traffic control system is a vast network of people and equipment that ensures the safe operation of commercial and private aircraft. Air traffic controllers coordinate the movement of air traffic to make certain that planes stay a safe distance apart. Their immediate concern is safety, but controllers also must direct planes efficiently to minimize delays. Some regulate airport traffic; others regulate flights between airports.

Although *airport tower* or *terminal controllers* watch over all planes traveling through the airport's airspace, their main responsibility is to organize the flow of aircraft in and out of the airport. Relying on radar and visual observation, they closely monitor each plane to ensure a safe distance between all aircraft and to guide pilots between the hangar or ramp and the end of the airport's airspace. In addition, controllers keep pilots informed about changes in weather conditions such as wind shear—a sudden change in the velocity or direction of the wind that can cause the pilot to lose control of the aircraft.

During arrival or departure, several controllers direct each plane. As a plane approaches an airport, the pilot radios ahead to inform the terminal of its presence. The controller in the radar room, just beneath the control tower, has a copy of the plane's flight plan and already has observed the plane on radar. If the path is clear, the controller directs the pilot to a runway; if the airport is busy, the plane is fitted into a traffic pattern with other aircraft waiting to land. As the plane nears the runway, the pilot is asked to contact the tower. There, another controller, who also is watching the plane on radar, monitors the aircraft the last mile or so to the runway, delaying any departures that would interfere with the plane's landing. Once the plane has landed, a ground controller in the tower directs it along the taxiways to its assigned gate. The ground controller usually works entirely by sight, but may use radar if visibility is very poor.

The procedure is reversed for departures. The ground controller directs the plane to the proper runway. The local controller then informs the pilot about conditions at the airport, such as weather, speed and direction of wind, and visibility. The local controller also issues runway clearance for the pilot to take off. Once in the air, the plane is guided out of the airport's airspace by the departure controller.

After each plane departs, airport tower controllers notify *enroute controllers* who will next take charge. There are 21 enroute control centers located around the country, each employing 300 to 700 controllers, with more than 150 on duty during peak hours at the busier facilities. Airplanes usually fly along designated routes; each center is assigned a certain airspace containing many different routes. Enroute controllers work in teams of up to three members, depending on how heavy traffic is; each team is responsible for a section of the center's airspace. A team, for example, might be responsible for all planes that are between 30 to 100 miles north of an airport and flying at an altitude between 6,000 and 18,000 feet.

To prepare for planes about to enter the team's airspace, the radar associate controller organizes flight plans coming off a printer. If two planes are scheduled to enter the team's airspace at nearly the same time, location, and altitude, this controller may arrange with the preceding control unit for one plane to change its flight path. The previous unit may have been another team at the same or an adjacent center, or a departure controller at a neighboring terminal. As a plane approaches a team's airspace, the radar controller accepts responsibility for the plane from the previous controlling unit. The controller also delegates responsibility for the plane to the next controlling unit when the plane leaves the team's airspace.

The radar controller, who is the senior team member, observes the planes in the team's airspace on radar and communicates with the pilots when necessary. Radar controllers warn pilots about nearby planes, bad weather conditions, and other potential hazards. Two planes on a collision course will be directed around each other. If a pilot wants to change altitude in search of better flying conditions, the controller will check to determine that no other planes will be along the proposed path. As the flight progresses, the team responsible for the aircraft notifies the next team in charge. Through team coordination, the plane arrives safely at its destination.

Both airport tower and enroute controllers usually control several planes at a time; often, they have to make quick decisions about completely different activities. For example, a controller might direct a plane on its landing approach and at the same time provide pilots entering the airport's airspace with information about conditions at the airport. While instructing these pilots, the controller also would observe other planes in the vicinity, such as those in a holding pattern waiting for permission to land, to ensure that they remain well separated.

In addition to airport towers and enroute centers, air traffic controllers also work in flight service stations operated at over 100 locations. These *flight service specialists* provide pilots with information on the station's particular area, including terrain, preflight and inflight weather information, suggested routes, and other information important to the safety of a flight. Flight service station specialists help pilots in emergency situations and initiate and coordinate searches for missing or overdue aircraft. However, they are not involved in actively managing air traffic.

Some air traffic controllers work at the Federal Aviation Administration's (FAA) Air Traffic Control Systems Command Center in Herndon, Virginia, where they oversee the entire system. They look for situations that will create bottlenecks or other problems in the system, then respond with a management plan for traffic into and out of the troubled sector. The objective is to keep traffic levels in the trouble spots manageable for the controllers working at enroute centers.

Currently, the FAA is in the midst of developing and implementing a new automated air traffic control system. As a result, more powerful computers will help controllers deal with the demands of increased air traffic. Some traditional air traffic controller tasks—like determining how far apart planes should be kept—will be done by computer. Present separation standards call for a 2,000-foot vertical spacing between two aircraft operating above 29,000 feet and flying the same ground track. With the aid of new technologies, the FAA will be able to reduce this vertical separation standard to 1,000 feet. Improved communication between computers on airplanes and those on the ground also is making the controller's job a little easier.

At present controllers sit at consoles with green-glowing screens that display radar images generated by a computer. In the future, controllers will work at a modern workstation computer that depicts air routes in full-color on a 20- by 20-inch screen. The controllers will select radio channels simply by touching on-screen buttons instead of turning dials or switching switches. The new technology will also enable controllers to zoom in on selected corners of the air space that is their responsibility and get better images of moving traffic than is possible with today's machines. However, the new automated air traffic control system will not be fully operational until at least 2003.

The FAA is also considering implementing a system called "free flight" which would give pilots much more freedom in operating their aircraft. The change will require new concepts of shared responsibility between controllers and pilots. Air traffic controllers will still be central to the safe operation of the system, but their responsibilities will eventually shift from controlling to monitoring flights. At present, controllers assign routes, altitudes, and speeds. Under the new system, airlines and pilots would choose them. Controllers would intervene only to ensure that aircraft remained at safe distances from one another, to prevent congestion in terminal areas and entry into closed airspace, or to otherwise ensure safety. Today's practices often result in planes zigzagging from point to point along corridors rather than flying from city to city in a straight line. This results in lost time and fuel. However, it may be several years before a free flight system is implemented, despite its potential advantages. For the system to work, new equipment must be added for pilots and controllers, and new procedures developed to accommodate both the tightly controlled and flexible aspects of free flight. Budget constraints within the Federal Government may delay or slow implementation.

Working Conditions

Controllers work a basic 40-hour week; however, they may work additional hours for which they receive overtime pay or equal time off. Because most control towers and centers operate 24 hours a day, 7 days a week, controllers rotate night and weekend shifts.

During busy times, controllers must work rapidly and efficiently. This requires total concentration to keep track of several planes at the same time and make certain all pilots receive correct instructions. The mental stress of being responsible for the safety of several aircraft and their passengers can be exhausting for some persons.

Employment

Air traffic controllers held about 30,000 jobs in 1998. They were employed by the Federal Government at airports—in towers and flight service stations—and in enroute traffic control centers. The overwhelming majority worked for the FAA.. Some professional controllers conduct research at the FAA's national experimental center near Atlantic City, New Jersey. Others serve as instructors at the FAA Academy in Oklahoma City, Oklahoma. A small number of civilian controllers worked for the Department of Defense. In addition to controllers employed by the Federal Government, some worked for private air traffic control companies providing service to non-FAA towers.

Controllers are usually responsible for several planes at one time.

Training, Other Qualifications, and Advancement

Air traffic controller trainees are selected through the competitive Federal Civil Service system. Applicants must pass a written test that measures their ability to learn the controller's duties. Applicants with experience as a pilot, navigator, or military controller can improve their rating by scoring well on the occupational knowledge portion of the examination. Abstract reasoning and three-dimensional spatial visualization are among the aptitudes the exam measures. In addition, applicants usually must have 3 years of general work experience or 4 years of college, or a combination of both. Applicants also must survive a week of screening at the FAA Academy in Oklahoma City, which includes aptitude tests using computer simulators and physical and psychological examinations. Successful applicants receive drug screening tests. For airport tower and enroute center positions, applicants must be less than 31 years old. Those 31 years old and over are eligible for positions at flight service stations.

Controllers must be articulate, because pilots must be given directions quickly and clearly. Intelligence and a good memory also are important because controllers constantly receive information that they must immediately grasp, interpret, and remember. Decisiveness is also required because controllers often have to make quick decisions. The ability to concentrate is crucial because controllers must make these decisions in the midst of noise and other distractions.

Trainees learn their jobs through a combination of formal and on-the-job training. They receive 7 months of intensive training at the FAA academy, where they learn the fundamentals of the airway system, FAA regulations, controller equipment, aircraft performance characteristics, as well as more specialized tasks. To receive a job offer, trainees must successfully complete the training and pass a series of examinations, including a controller skills test that measures speed and accuracy in recognizing and correctly solving air traffic control problems. The test requires judgments on spatial relationships and requires application of the rules and procedures contained in the Air Traffic Control Handbook. Based on aptitude and test scores, trainees are selected to work at either an enroute center or a tower.

After graduation, it takes several years of progressively more responsible work experience, interspersed with considerable classroom instruction and independent study, to become a fully qualified controller. This training includes instruction in the operation of the new, more automated air traffic control system—including the automated Microwave Landing System that enables pilots to receive instructions over automated data links—that is being installed in control sites across the country.

Controllers who fail to complete either the academy or the on-the-job portion of the training are usually dismissed. Controllers must pass a physical examination each year and a job performance examination twice each year. Failure to become certified in any position at a facility within a specified time may also result in dismissal. Controllers also are subject to drug screening as a condition of continuing employment.

At airports, new controllers begin by supplying pilots with basic flight data and airport information. They then advance to ground controller, then local controller, departure controller, and finally, arrival controller. At an enroute traffic control center, new controllers first deliver printed flight plans to teams, gradually advancing to radar associate controller and then radar controller.

Controllers can transfer to jobs at different locations or advance to supervisory positions, including management or staff jobs in air traffic control and top administrative jobs in the FAA. However, there are only limited opportunities for a controller to switch from a position in an enroute center to a tower.

Job Outlook

Extremely keen competition is expected for air traffic controller jobs because the occupation attracts many more qualified applicants than the small number of job openings that result from replacement needs. Turnover is very low because of the relatively high pay and liberal retirement benefits, and controllers have a very strong attachment to the occupation. Most of the current work force was hired as a result of the controller's strike during the 1980's, so the average age of current controllers is fairly young. Relatively few controllers will be eligible to retire over the 1998-2008 period.

Employment of air traffic controllers is expected to show little or no change through the year 2008. Employment growth is not expected to keep pace with growth in the number of aircraft flying because of the implementation of a new air traffic control system over the next 10 years. This computerized system will assist the controller by automatically making many of the routine decisions. Automation will allow controllers to handle more traffic, thus increasing their productivity.

Air traffic controllers who continue to meet the proficiency and medical requirements enjoy more job security than most workers. The demand for air travel and the workloads of air traffic controllers decline during recessions, but controllers seldom are laid off.

Earnings

Median annual earnings of air traffic controllers in 1998 were $64,880. The middle 50 percent earned between $50,980 and $78,840. The lowest 10 percent earned less than $36,640 and the highest 10 percent earned more than $87,210.

The average annual salary for air traffic controllers in the Federal Government—which employs 86 percent of the total—in nonsupervisory, supervisory, and managerial positions was $48,300 in 1999. Both the worker's job responsibilities and the complexity of the particular facility determine a controller's pay. For example, controllers who work at the FAA's busiest air traffic control facilities earn higher pay.

Depending on length of service, air traffic controllers receive 13 to 26 days of paid vacation and 13 days of paid sick leave each year, life insurance, and health benefits. In addition, controllers can retire at an earlier age and with fewer years of service than other Federal employees. Air traffic controllers are eligible to retire at age 50 with 20 years of service as an active air traffic controller or after 25 years of active service at any age. There is a mandatory retirement age of 56 for controllers who manage air traffic.

Related Occupations

Other occupations that involve the direction and control of traffic in air transportation are airline-radio operator and airplane dispatcher.

Sources of Additional Information

Information on acquiring a job as an air traffic controller with the Federal Government may be obtained from the Office of Personnel Management (OPM) through a telephone-based system. Consult your telephone directory under U.S. Government for a local number or call (912) 757-3000; TDD (912) 744-2299. That number is not toll free and charges may result. Information also is available from their Internet site: **http://www.usajobs.opm.gov**

Engineers

Significant Points

- A bachelor's degree is required for entry-level jobs.
- Starting salaries are significantly higher than those of college graduates in other fields.
- Continuing education is critical to keep abreast of the latest technology.

Nature of the Work

Engineers apply the theories and principles of science and mathematics to research and develop economical solutions to technical problems. Their work is the link between scientific discoveries and commercial applications. Engineers design products, machinery to build those products, factories in which those products are made, and the systems that ensure the quality of the product and efficiency of the workforce and manufacturing process. Engineers design, plan, and supervise the construction of buildings, highways, and transit systems. They develop and implement improved ways to extract, process, and use raw materials, such as petroleum and natural gas. They develop new materials that both improve the performance of products and help implement advances in technology. They harness the power of the sun, the Earth, atoms, and electricity for use in supplying the Nation's power needs, and create millions of products using power. Engineering knowledge is applied to improving many things, including the quality of health care, the safety of food products, and the efficient operation of financial systems.

Engineers consider many factors when developing a new product. For example, in developing an industrial robot, engineers determine precisely what function the robot needs to perform; design and test the robot's components; fit the components together in an integrated plan; and evaluate the design's overall effectiveness, cost, reliability, and safety. This process applies to many different products, such as chemicals, computers, gas turbines, helicopters, and toys.

In addition to design and development, many engineers work in testing, production, or maintenance. These engineers supervise production in factories, determine the causes of breakdowns, and test manufactured products to maintain quality. They also estimate the time and cost to complete projects. Some work in engineering management or in sales, where an engineering background enables them to discuss technical aspects and assist in product planning, installation, and use. (See the statements on engineering, natural science, and computer and information systems managers, and manufacturers' and wholesale sales representatives, elsewhere in the *Handbook*.)

Most engineers specialize. More than 25 major specialties are recognized by professional societies, and the major branches have numerous subdivisions. Some examples include structural, environmental, and transportation engineering, which are subdivisions of civil engineering; and ceramic, metallurgical, and polymer engineering, which are subdivisions of materials engineering. Engineers may also specialize in one industry such as motor vehicles or in one field of technology, such as jet engines or semiconductor materials.

This section, which contains an overall discussion of engineering, is followed by separate sections on 10 engineering branches: Aerospace, chemical, civil, electrical and electronics, industrial, materials, mechanical, mining, nuclear, and petroleum engineering. (Computer engineers are discussed in the statement on computer systems analysts, engineers, and scientists elsewhere in the *Handbook*.) Some branches of engineering not covered in detail here, but for which there are established college programs, include architectural engineering—the design of a building's internal support structure; biomedical engineering—the application of engineering to medical and physiological problems; environmental engineering—a growing discipline involved with identifying, solving, and alleviating environmental problems; and marine engineering—the design and installation of ship machinery and propulsion systems.

Engineers in each branch have a base of knowledge and training that can be applied in many fields. Electrical and electronics engineers, for example, work in the medical, computer, missile guidance, and power distribution fields. Because there are many separate problems to solve in a large engineering project, engineers in one field often work closely with specialists in other scientific, engineering, and business occupations.

Engineers use computers to produce and analyze designs; to simulate and test how a machine, structure, or system operates; and to generate specifications for parts. Many engineers also use computers to monitor product quality and control process efficiency. They spend a great deal of time writing reports and consulting with other engineers, as complex projects often require an interdisciplinary team of engineers. Supervisory engineers are responsible for major components or entire projects.

Working Conditions

Most engineers work in office buildings, laboratories, or industrial plants. Others may spend time outdoors at construction sites, mines, and oil and gas exploration sites, where they monitor or direct operations or solve onsite problems. Some engineers travel extensively to plants or work sites.

Many engineers work a standard 40-hour week. At times, deadlines or design standards may bring extra pressure to a job. When this happens, engineers may work longer hours and experience considerable stress.

Employment

In 1998, engineers held 1.5 million jobs. The following tabulation shows the distribution of employment by engineering specialty.

Specialty	*Employment*	*Percent*
Total, all engineers	1,462,000	100.0
Electrical and electronics	357,000	24
Mechanical	220,000	15
Civil	195,000	13
Industrial	126,000	9
Aerospace	53,000	4
Chemical	48,000	3
Materials	20,000	1
Petroleum	12,000	<1
Nuclear	12,000	<1
Mining	4,000	<1
All other engineers	415,000	28

Almost half of all wage and salary engineering jobs were found in manufacturing industries, such as transportation equipment, electrical and electronic equipment, industrial machinery, and instruments and related products. In 1998, about 390,000 wage and salary jobs were in services industries, primarily in engineering and architectural services, research and testing services, and business services, where firms designed construction projects or did other engineering work on a contractual basis. Engineers also worked in the communications, utilities, and construction industries.

Federal, State and local governments employed about 166,000 wage and salary engineers in 1998. Over half of these were in the Federal Government, mainly in the Departments of Defense, Transportation, Agriculture, Interior, and Energy, and in the National Aeronautics and Space Administration. Most engineers in State and local government agencies worked in highway and public works departments. In 1998, about 50,000 engineers were self-employed, many as consultants.

Engineers are employed in every State, in small and large cities, and in rural areas. Some branches of engineering are concentrated in particular industries and geographic areas, as discussed in statements later in this chapter.

Training, Other Qualifications, and Advancement

A bachelor's degree in engineering is generally required for entry-level engineering jobs. College graduates with a degree in a physical science or mathematics may occasionally qualify for some engineering jobs, especially in specialties in high demand. Most engineering degrees are granted in electrical, mechanical, or civil engineering. However, engineers trained in one branch may work in related branches. For example, many aerospace engineers have training in mechanical engineering. This flexibility allows employers to meet staffing needs in new technologies and specialties in which engineers are in short supply. It also allows engineers to shift to fields with better employment prospects or to ones that match their interests more closely.

In addition to the standard engineering degree, many colleges offer degrees in engineering technology, which are offered as either 2- or 4-year programs. These programs prepare students for practical design and production work, rather than for jobs that require more theoretical and scientific knowledge. Graduates of 4-year technology programs may get jobs similar to those obtained by graduates with a bachelor's degree in engineering. Some employers regard technology program graduates as having skills between those of a technician and an engineer.

Graduate training is essential for engineering faculty positions, but is not required for the majority of entry-level engineering jobs. Many engineers obtain graduate degrees in engineering or business administration to learn new technology, broaden their education, and enhance their promotion opportunities. Many high-level executives in government and industry began their careers as engineers.

About 320 colleges and universities offer bachelor's degree programs in engineering that are accredited by the Accreditation Board for Engineering and Technology (ABET), and about 250 colleges offer accredited bachelor's degree programs in engineering technology. ABET accreditation is based on an examination of an engineering program's student achievement, program improvement, faculty, curricular content, facilities, and institutional commitment. Although most institutions offer programs in the major branches of engineering, only a few offer some of the smaller specialties. Also, programs of the same title may vary in content. For example, some programs emphasize industrial practices, preparing students for a job in industry, whereas others are more theoretical and are better for students preparing to take graduate work. Therefore, students should investigate curricula and check accreditations carefully before selecting a college. Admissions requirements for undergraduate engineering schools include a solid background in mathematics (algebra, geometry, trigonometry, and calculus), sciences (biology, chemistry, and physics), and courses in English, social studies, humanities, and computers.

Bachelor's degree programs in engineering are typically designed to last 4 years, but many students find that it takes between 4 and 5 years to complete their studies. In a typical 4-year college curriculum, the first 2 years are spent studying mathematics, basic sciences, introductory engineering, humanities, and social sciences. In the last 2 years, most courses are in engineering, usually with a concentration in one branch. For example, the last 2 years of an aerospace program might include courses such as fluid mechanics, heat transfer, applied aerodynamics, analytical mechanics, flight vehicle design, trajectory dynamics, and aerospace propulsion systems. Some programs offer a general engineering curriculum; students then specialize in graduate school or on the job.

Some engineering schools and 2-year colleges have agreements whereby the 2-year college provides the initial engineering education; and the engineering school automatically admits students for their last 2 years. In addition, a few engineering schools have arrangements, whereby a student spends 3 years in a liberal arts college studying pre-engineering subjects and 2 years in an engineering school studying core subjects, and then receives a bachelor's degree from each school. Some colleges and universities offer 5-year master's degree programs. Some 5- or even 6-year cooperative plans combine classroom study and practical work, permitting students to gain valuable experience and finance part of their education.

All 50 States and the District of Columbia require licensure for engineers whose work may affect life, health, or property, or who offer their services to the public. Engineers who are licensed are called Professional Engineers (PE). This licensure generally requires a degree from an ABET-accredited engineering program, 4 years of relevant work experience, and successful completion of a State examination. Recent graduates can start the licensing process by taking the examination in two stages. The initial examination can be taken upon graduation. Engineers who pass this examination are commonly called Engineers in Training (EIT). The EIT certification is usually valid for 10 years. After acquiring suitable work experience, EITs can take the second examination, the Principles and Practice of Engineering Exam. While Professional Engineers must be licensed in each State in which they practice, most states recognize licensure from other states. Many civil, electrical, mechanical, and chemical engineers are certified as PEs.

Engineers should be creative, inquisitive, analytical, and detail-oriented. They should be able to work as part of a team and beable to communicate well, both orally and in writing.

Beginning engineering graduates usually work under the supervision of experienced engineers and, in large companies, may also receive formal classroom or seminar-type training. As new engineers gain knowledge and experience, they are assigned more difficult projects with greater independence to develop designs, solve problems, and make decisions. Engineers may advance to become technical specialists or to supervise a staff or team of engineers and technicians. Some eventually become engineering managers or enter other managerial or sales jobs. (See the statements under executive, administrative, and managerial occupations, and under marketing and sales occupations, elsewhere in the *Handbook*.)

Job Outlook

Employment opportunities in engineering are expected to be good through 2008. Overall engineering employment is expected to increase about as fast as the average for all occupations, while the number of engineering degrees granted has remained fairly constant over the past several years. Projected growth varies by specialty, ranging from a decline among mining engineers to faster-than-average growth among electrical and electronics engineers. Competitive pressures and advancing technology will force companies to improve and update product designs increasingly more frequently, and to optimize their manufacturing processes. Employers will rely on engineers to further increase productivity, as investment in plant and equipment increases to expand output of goods and services. New computer systems have improved the design process, enabling engineers to produce and analyze various product designs much more rapidly than in the past. Despite these widespread applications, computer technology is not expected to limit employment opportunities. Finally, additional engineers will be needed to improve or build new roads, bridges, water and pollution control systems, and other public facilities.

Many engineering jobs are related to developing technologies used in national defense. Because defense expenditures—particularly expenditures for aircraft, missiles, and other weapons systems—are not expected to return to previously high levels, job outlook may not be as favorable for engineers working in defense-related fields.

The number of bachelor's degrees awarded in engineering has declined since 1986.

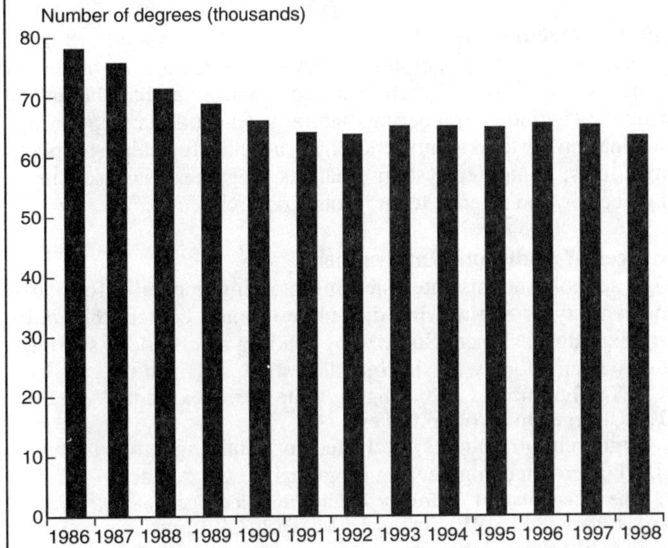

Source: Engineering Workforce Commission

The number of bachelor's degrees awarded in engineering began declining in 1987, as shown in the accompanying chart, and has continued to stay at about the same level through much of the 1990s. Although it is difficult to project engineering enrollments, the total number of graduates from engineering programs is not expected to increase significantly over the projection period. Some engineering schools have restricted enrollments, especially in defense-related fields, such as aerospace engineering, to accommodate reduced job opportunities.

Although only a relatively small proportion of engineers leaves the profession each year, many job openings will arise from replacement needs. A greater proportion of replacement openings is created by engineers who transfer to management, sales, or other professional specialty occupations than by those who leave the labor force.

Most industries are less likely to lay off engineers than other workers. Many engineers work on long-term research and development projects or in other activities that continue even during economic slowdowns. In industries such as electronics and aerospace, however, large cutbacks in defense expenditures and government research and development funds, as well as the trend toward contracting out engineering work to engineering services firms, have resulted in significant layoffs for engineers.

It is important for engineers, like those working in other technical occupations, to continue their education throughout their careers, because much of their value to their employer depends on their knowledge of the latest technology. Although the pace of technological change varies by engineering specialty and industry, advances in technology have affected every engineering discipline significantly. Engineers in high-technology areas, such as advanced electronics, may find that technical knowledge can become obsolete rapidly. Even those who continue their education are vulnerable if the particular technology or product in which they have specialized becomes obsolete. By keeping current in their field, engineers are able to deliver the best solutions and greatest value to their employers. Engineers who have not kept current in their field may find themselves passed over for promotions or vulnerable to layoffs, should they occur. On the other hand, it is often these high-technology areas that offer the greatest challenges, the most interesting work, and the highest salaries. Therefore, the choice of engineering specialty and employer involves an assessment not only of the potential rewards but also of the risk of technological obsolescence.

Related Occupations

Engineers apply the principles of physical science and mathematics in their work. Other workers who use scientific and mathematical principles include engineering, natural science, and computer and information systems managers; physical and life scientists; mathematicians; computer systems analysts, engineers, and scientists; engineering and science technicians; and architects.

Sources of Additional Information

High school students interested in obtaining general information on a variety of engineering disciplines should contact the Junior Engineering Technical Society, by sending a self-addressed business-size envelope with six first-class stamps affixed to:

☛ JETS-Guidance, at 1420 King St., Suite 405, Alexandria, VA 22314-2794. Internet: **http://www.jets.org**

High school students interested in obtaining information on ABET-accredited engineering programs should contact:

☛ The Accreditation Board for Engineering and Technology, Inc., 111 Market Place, Suite 1050, Baltimore, MD 21202-4012.
Internet: **http://www.abet.org**

College students interested in obtaining information on Professional Engineer licensure should contact:

☛ The National Society of Professional Engineers, 1420 King St., Alexandria, VA 22314-2794. Internet: **http://www.nspe.org**

Information on obtaining an engineering position with the Federal Government is available from the Office of Personnel Management through a telephone-based system. Consult your telephone directory under U.S. Government for a local number or call (912) 757-3000; TDD (912) 744-2299. That number is not toll free, and charges may result. Information is also available from the Internet site: **http://www.usajobs.opm.gov**

Non-high school students and those wanting more detailed information should contact societies representing the individual branches of engineering. Each can provide information about careers in the particular branch.

Aerospace Engineering

☛ Aerospace Industries Association, 1250 Eye St., NW., Washington, DC 20005. Internet: **http://www.aia-aerospace.org**

☛ American Institute of Aeronautics and Astronautics, Inc., Suite 500, 1801 Alexander Bell Dr., Reston, VA 20191-4344. Enclose $2 to receive guidance materials and information.
Internet: **http://www.aiaa.org**

Chemical Engineering

☛ American Institute of Chemical Engineers, Three Park Ave., New York, NY 10016-5901. Internet: **http://www.aiche.org**

☛ American Chemical Society, Department of Career Services, 1155 16th St. NW., Washington, DC 20036. Internet: **http://www.acs.org**

Civil Engineering

☛ American Society of Civil Engineers, 1801 Alexander Bell Dr., Reston, VA 20191-4400. Internet: **http://www.asce.org**

Electrical and Electronics Engineering

☛ Institute of Electrical and Electronics Engineers—United States of America, 1828 L St. NW., Suite 1202, Washington, DC 20036. Internet: **http://www.ieee-usa.org**

Industrial Engineering

☛ Institute of Industrial Engineers, Inc., 25 Technology Park/Atlanta, Norcross, GA 30092. Internet: **http://www.iienet.org**

Materials Engineering

☛ The Minerals, Metals, & Materials Society, 184 Thorn Hill Rd., Warrendale, PA 15086. Internet: **http://www.tms.org**

☛ ASM International Foundation, Materials Park, OH 44073-0002. Internet: **http://www.asm-intl.org**

Mechanical Engineering

☛ The American Society of Mechanical Engineers, Three Park Ave., New York, NY 10016. Internet: **http://www.asme.org**

☛ American Society of Heating, Refrigerating, and Air-Conditioning Engineers, Inc., 1791 Tullie Circle NE, Atlanta, GA 30329. Internet: **http://www.ashrae.org**

Mining Engineering

☛ The Society for Mining, Metallurgy, and Exploration, Inc., P.O. Box 625002, Littleton, CO 80162-5002. Internet: **http://www.smenet.org**

Nuclear Engineering

☛ American Nuclear Society, 555 North Kensington Ave., LaGrange Park, IL 60525. Internet: **http://www.ans.org**

Petroleum Engineering

☛ Society of Petroleum Engineers, P.O. Box 833836, Richardson, TX 75083-3836. Internet: **http://www.spe.org**

Aerospace Engineers

(O*NET 22102)

Nature of the Work

Aerospace engineers are responsible for developing extraordinary machines, from airplanes that weigh over a half a million pounds to spacecraft that travel over 17,000 miles an hour. They design, develop, and test aircraft, spacecraft, and missiles and supervise manufacturing of these products. Aerospace engineers who work with aircraft are considered *aeronautical engineers*, and those working specifically with spacecraft are considered *astronautical engineers*.

Aerospace engineers develop new technologies for use in aviation, defense systems, and space exploration, often specializing in areas like structural design, guidance, navigation and control, instrumentation and communication, or production methods. They also may specialize in a particular type of aerospace product, such as commercial transports, military fighter jets, helicopters, spacecraft, or missiles and rockets. Aerospace engineers may be experts in aerodynamics, thermodynamics, celestial mechanics, propulsion, acoustics, or guidance and control systems.

Employment

Aerospace engineers held about 53,000 jobs in 1998. Almost one-half worked in the aircraft and parts and guided missile and space vehicle manufacturing industries. Federal Government agencies, primarily the Department of Defense and the National Aeronautics and Space Administration, provided about 1 out of 7 jobs. Business services, engineering and architectural services, research and testing services, and electrical and electronics manufacturing firms accounted for most of the remaining jobs.

California, Washington, Texas, and Florida—States with large aerospace manufacturers—employ the most aerospace engineers.

Job Outlook

Those seeking employment as aerospace engineers are likely to face keen competition because the supply of graduates is expected to exceed the number of job openings. Employment of aerospace engineers is expected to grow more slowly than the average for all occupations through 2008. The decline in Defense Department expenditures for military aircraft, missiles, and other aerospace systems has caused mergers and acquisitions among defense contractors. In addition,

An aerospace engineer tests avionics equipment.

Federal Government funding for research and development of new systems has also declined. Offsetting these declines, however, is the projected growth in the civilian sector due to orders from domestic and foreign airlines that need to accommodate increasing passenger traffic and to replace the present fleet of airliners with quieter and more fuel-efficient aircraft. Most job openings will result from the need to replace aerospace engineers who transfer to other occupations or leave the labor force.

Earnings

Median annual earnings of aerospace engineers were $66,950 in 1998. The middle 50 percent earned between $51,170 and $82,620. The lowest 10 percent earned less than $42,650 and the highest 10 percent earned more than $93,880. Median annual earnings in the industries employing the largest numbers of aerospace engineers in 1997 were:

Aircraft and parts	$72,200
Federal Government	70,000
Guided missiles, space vehicles, and parts	58,200

According to a 1999 salary survey by the National Association of Colleges and Employers, bachelor's degree candidates in aerospace engineering received starting offers averaging about $40,700 a year; master's degree candidates, $54,200; and Ph.D. candidates, $64,400.

(See introduction to the section on engineers for information on working conditions, training requirements, and sources of additional information.)

Chemical Engineers

(O*NET 22114)

Nature of the Work

Chemical engineers apply the principles of chemistry and engineering to solve problems involving the production or use of chemicals. They design equipment and develop processes for large scale chemical manufacturing, plan and test methods of manufacturing the products and treating the by-products, and supervise production. Chemical engineers also work in a variety of maufacturing industries other than chemical manufacturing such as electronics, photographic equipment, and pulp and paper mills.

Because the knowledge and duties of chemical engineers cut across many fields, they apply principles of chemistry, physics, mathematics, and mechanical and electrical engineering. They frequently specialize in a particular operation such as oxidation or polymerization. Others specialize in a particular area such as pollution control or the production of specific products such as automotive plastics or chlorine bleach. Chemical engineers are increasingly using computer technology to optimize all phases of research and production; therefore they need to understand how to apply computer skills to process analysis, automated control systems, and statistical quality control.

Employment

Chemical engineers held about 48,000 jobs in 1998. Manufacturing industries employed over 70 percent of all employees, primarily in the

Although many chemical engineers are employed by manufacturers, much of the job growth is expected to occur in services industries.

electronics, petroleum refining, paper, chemical, and related industries. Most others worked for engineering services, research and testing services, or consulting firms that design chemical plants. Some also worked on a contract basis for government agencies or as independent consultants.

Job Outlook

Chemical engineering graduates may face keen competition for jobs as the number of openings is projected to be substantially lower than the number of graduates. Employment of chemical engineers is projected to grow as fast as the average for all occupations though 2008. Although overall employment in the chemical manufacturing industry is expected to decline, chemical companies will continue to research and develop new chemicals and more efficient processes to increase output of existing chemicals. Among manufacturing industries, specialty chemicals, plastics materials, pharmaceuticals, and electronics may provide the best opportunities. Much of the projected growth in employment of chemical engineers, however, will be in nonmanufacturing industries, especially services industries.

Earnings

Median annual earnings of chemical engineers were $64,760 in 1998. The middle 50 percent earned between $49,360 and $81,520. The lowest 10 percent earned less than $41,380 and the highest 10 percent earned more than $92,240.

According to a 1999 salary survey by the National Association of Colleges and Employers, bachelor's degree candidates in chemical engineering received starting offers averaging about $46,900 a year; master's degree candidates in chemical engineering, $52,100; and Ph.D. candidates in chemical engineering, $67,300.

(See introduction to the section on engineers for information on working conditions, training requirements, and sources of additional information.)

Civil Engineers

(O*NET 22121)

Nature of the Work

Civil engineers design and supervise the construction of roads, buildings, airports, tunnels, dams, bridges, and water supply and sewage systems. Major specialties within civil engineering are structural, water resources, environmental, construction, transportation, and geotechnical engineering.

Many civil engineers hold supervisory or administrative positions, from supervisor of a construction site to city engineer. Others may work in design, construction, research, and teaching.

Employment

Civil engineers held about 195,000 jobs in 1998. Almost half were employed by firms providing engineering consulting services, primarily developing designs for new construction projects. Another one third of the jobs were in Federal, State, and local government agencies. The construction industry, public utilities, transportation, and manufacturing industries accounted for most of the remaining employment. About 12,000 civil engineers were self-employed, many as consultants.

Civil engineers usually work near major industrial and commercial centers, often at construction sites. Some projects are situated in remote areas or in foreign countries. In some jobs, civil engineers move from place to place to work on different projects.

Job Outlook

Employment of civil engineers is expected to increase faster than the average for all occupations through 2008. Spurred by general

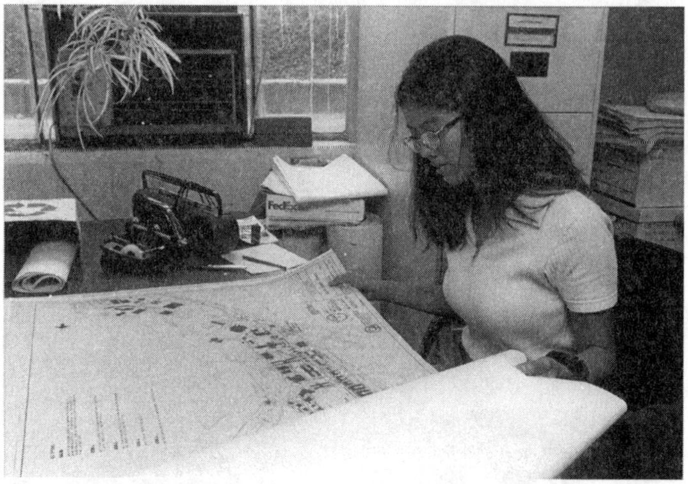

Civil engineers take safety and environmental concerns into account when designing construction projects.

population growth and an expanding economy, more civil engineers will be needed to design and construct higher capacity transportation, water supply, and pollution control systems; large buildings and building complexes; and to repair or replace existing roads, bridges, and other public structures. In addition to job growth, openings will result from the need to replace civil engineers who transfer to other occupations or leave the labor force.

Because construction and related industries—including those providing design services—employ many civil engineers, employment opportunities will vary by geographic area and may decrease during economic slowdowns, when construction is often curtailed.

Earnings

Median annual earnings of civil engineers were $53,450 in 1998. The middle 50 percent earned between $41,800 and $74,550. The lowest 10 percent earned less than $34,270 and the highest 10 percent earned more than $87,350. Median annual earnings in the industries employing the largest numbers of civil engineers in 1997 were:

Industry	Earnings
Federal government	$64,000
Heavy construction, except highway	61,300
Local government, except education and hospitals	52,100
Engineering and architectural services	49,300
State government, except education and hospitals	48,900

According to a 1999 salary survey by the National Association of Colleges and Employers, bachelor's degree candidates in civil engineering received starting offers averaging about $36,100 a year; master's degree candidates in civil engineering, $42,300; and Ph.D. candidates in civil engineering, $58,600.

(See introduction to the section on engineers for information on working conditions, training requirements, and sources of additional information.)

Electrical and Electronics Engineers

(O*NET 22126A and 22126B)

Nature of the Work

From computer chips that process millions of instructions every second to radar systems that detect weather patterns days in advance, electrical and electronics engineers are responsible for a wide range of technologies. Electrical and electronics engineers design, develop, test, and supervise the manufacture of electrical

Electrical and electronics engineers design and test equipment used by other scientists.

and electronic equipment. Some of this equipment includes power generating, controlling, and transmission devices used by electric utilities; electric motors, machinery controls, lighting, and wiring in buildings, automobiles, and aircraft; and in radar and navigation systems, computer and office equipment, and broadcast and communications systems.

Electrical and electronics engineers specialize in different areas such as power generation, transmission, and distribution; communications; computer electronics; and electrical equipment manufacturing—or a subdivision of these areas—industrial robot control systems or aviation electronics, for example. Electrical and electronics engineers design new products, write performance requirements, and develop maintenance schedules. They also test equipment, solve operating problems, and estimate the time and cost of engineering projects. (See the statement on computer systems analysts, engineers, and scientists elsewhere in the *Handbook.*)

Employment

Electrical and electronics engineers held about 357,000 jobs in 1998, making it the largest branch of engineering. Most jobs were in engineering and business consulting firms, government agencies, and manufacturers of electrical and electronic equipment, industrial machinery, and professional and scientific instruments. Communications and utilities firms, manufacturers of aircraft and guided missiles, and computer and data processing services firms accounted for most of the remaining jobs.

California, Texas, New York, and New Jersey—states with many large electronics firms—employ over one-third of all electrical and electronics engineers.

Job Outlook

Electrical and electronics engineering graduates should have favorable job opportunities. The number of job openings resulting from employment growth and the need to replace electrical engineers who transfer to other occupations or leave the labor force is expected to be in rough balance with the supply of graduates. Employment of electrical and electronics engineers is expected to grow faster than the average for all occupations through 2008.

Projected job growth stems largely from increased demand for electrical and electronic goods, including computers and communications equipment. The need for electronics manufacturers to invest heavily in research and development to remain competitive and have a scientific edge will provide openings for graduates who have learned the latest technologies. Opportunities for electronics engineers in defense-related firms should improve as aircraft and weapons systems are upgraded with improved navigation, control, guidance, and targeting systems. However, job growth is expected to be fastest in services industries—particularly consulting firms that provide electronic engineering expertise.

Continuing education is important for electrical and electronics engineers. Engineers who fail to keep up with the rapid changes in technology risk technological obsolescence, which makes them more susceptible to layoffs or, at a minimum, more likely to be passed over for advancement.

Earnings

Median annual earnings of electrical and electronics engineers were $62,660 in 1998. The middle 50 percent earned between $47,080 and $80,160. The lowest 10 percent earned less than $38,470 and the highest 10 percent earned more than $91,490. Median annual earnings in the industries employing the largest numbers of electrical and electronics engineers in 1997 were:

Federal government	$68,000
Computer and office equipment	67,100
Electronic components and accessories	59,900
Communications equipment	59,400
Engineering and architectural services	58,900

According to a 1999 salary survey by the National Association of Colleges and Employers, bachelor's degree candidates in electrical and electronics engineering received starting offers averaging about $45,200 a year; master's degree candidates, $57,200; and Ph.D. candidates, $70,800.

(See introduction to the section on engineers for information on working conditions, training requirements, and sources of additional information.)

Industrial Engineers, Except Safety Engineers

(O*NET 22128)

Nature of the Work

Industrial engineers determine the most effective ways for an organization to use the basic factors of production—people, machines, materials, information, and energy—to make a product or provide a service. They are the bridge between management goals and operational performance. They are more concerned with increasing productivity through the management of people, methods of business organization, and technology than are engineers in other specialties, who generally work more with products or processes.

To solve organizational, production, and related problems most efficiently, industrial engineers carefully study the product and its requirements, use mathematical methods such as operations research to meet those requirements, and design manufacturing and information systems. They develop management control systems to aid in financial planning and cost analysis, design production planning and control systems to coordinate activities and control product quality, and design or improve systems for the physical distribution of goods and services. Industrial engineers determine which plant location has the best combination of raw materials availability, transportation, and costs. They also develop wage and salary administration systems and job evaluation programs. Many industrial engineers move into management positions because the work is closely related.

Employment

Industrial engineers held about 126,000 jobs in 1998. Over 70 percent of these jobs were in manufacturing industries. Because their skills can be used in almost any type of organization, industrial engineers are more widely distributed among manufacturing industries than other engineers.

Industrial engineers often use computers to improve products and services.

Their skills can be readily applied outside manufacturing as well. Some work in engineering and management services, utilities, and business services; others work for government agencies or as independent consultants.

Job Outlook

Employment of industrial engineers is expected to grow about as fast as the average for all occupations through 2008, reflecting industrial growth, more complex business operations, and greater use of automation in factories and offices. Because the main function of an industrial engineer is to make a higher quality product as efficiently as possible, their services should be in demand in the manufacturing sector as firms seek to reduce costs and increase productivity through scientific management. In addition to job growth, openings will result from the need to replace industrial engineers who transfer to other occupations or leave the labor force.

Earnings

Median annual earnings of industrial engineers were $52,610 in 1998. The middle 50 percent earned between $42,690 and $73,870. The lowest 10 percent earned less than $35,250 and the highest 10 percent earned more than $87,010. Median annual earnings in the manufacturing industries employing the largest numbers of industrial engineers in 1997 were:

Motor vehicles and equipment	$58,900
Electronic components and accessories	48,800
Aircraft and parts	44,100

According to a 1999 salary survey by the National Association of Colleges and Employers, bachelor's degree candidates in industrial engineering received starting offers averaging about $43,100 a year; master's degree candidates, $49,900.

(See introduction to the section on engineers for information on working conditions, training requirements, and sources of additional information.)

Materials Engineers

(O*NET 22105A, 22105B, 22105C, and 22105D)

Nature of the Work

Materials engineers manipulate the atomic and molecular structure of substances to create products such as computer chips and television screens to golf clubs and snow skis. They work with metals, ceramics, plastics, semiconductors, and combinations of materials called composites to create new materials that meet certain mechanical, electrical, and chemical requirements. They also test and evaluate existing materials for new applications. Materials engineers specializing in metals can be considered *metallurgical engineers*, while those specializing in ceramics can be considered *ceramic engineers*.

Most metallurgical engineers work in one of the three main branches of metallurgy—extractive or chemical, physical, and mechanical or process. Extractive metallurgists are concerned with removing metals from ores and refining and alloying them to obtain useful metal. Physical metallurgists study the nature, structure, and physical properties of metals and their alloys, and methods of processing them into final products. Mechanical metallurgists develop and improve metalworking processes such as casting, forging, rolling, and drawing.

Ceramic engineers develop new ceramic materials and methods for making ceramic materials into useful products. Ceramics include all nonmetallic, inorganic materials that generally require high temperatures in their processing. Ceramic engineers work on products as diverse as glassware, automobile and aircraft engine components, fiber-optic communication lines, tile, and electric insulators.

Employment

Materials engineers held about 20,000 jobs in 1998. Because materials are building blocks for other goods, materials engineers are widely distributed among manufacturing industries. In fact, over half of materials engineers worked in metal-producing and processing; electronic and other electrical equipment; transportation equipment; industrial machinery and equipment; and stone, clay, and glass products manufacturing. They also worked in services industries such as engineering and management, business, and health services. Most remaining materials engineers worked for Federal and State governments.

Job Outlook

Employment of materials engineers is expected to grow more slowly than the average for all occupations through 2008. Many of the manufacturing industries in which materials engineers are concentrated—such as primary metals; industrial machinery and equipment; and stone, clay, and glass products—are expected to experience declines in employment. As firms outsource their materials engineering needs, however, employment growth is expected in many services industries including research and testing, personnel

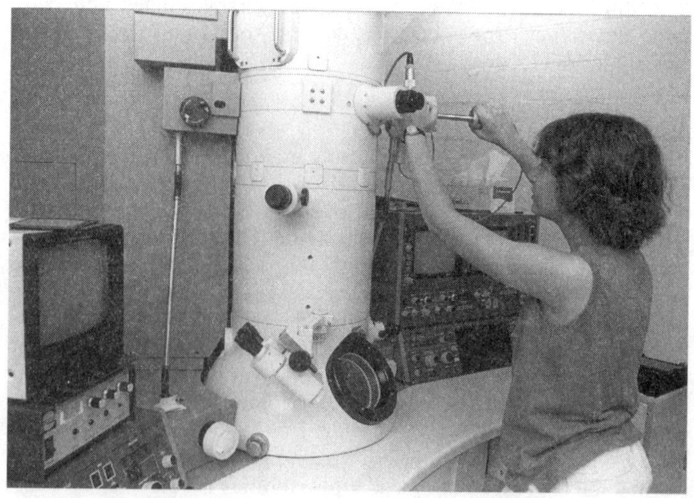

Materials engineers analyze the physical and chemical characteristics of substances.

supply, health, and engineering and architectural services. In addition to growth, job openings will result from the need to replace materials engineers who transfer to other occupations or leave the labor force.

Earnings

Median annual earnings of materials engineers were $57,970 in 1998. The middle 50 percent earned between $43,890 and $77,730. The lowest 10 percent earned less than $34,890 and the highest 10 percent earned more than $89,600. In the Federal Government, materials engineers in supervisory, nonsupervisory, and management positions averaged $68,000 a year in early 1999.

According to a 1999 salary survey by the National Association of Colleges and Employers, bachelor's degree candidates in materials engineering received starting offers averaging about $43,400 a year.

(See introduction to the section on engineers for information on working conditions, training requirements, and sources of additional information.)

Mechanical Engineers

(O*NET 22135)

Nature of the Work

Mechanical engineers research, develop, design, manufacture and test tools, engines, machines, and other mechanical devices. They work on power-producing machines such as electricity-producing generators, internal combustion engines, steam and gas turbines, and jet and rocket engines. They also develop power-using machines such as refrigeration and air-conditioning equipment, robots used in manufacturing, machine tools, materials handling systems, and industrial production equipment. Mechanical engineers also design tools needed by other engineers for their work.

Mechanical engineers work in many industries and their work varies by industry and function. Some specialties include applied mechanics; computer-aided design and manufacturing; energy systems; pressure vessels and piping; and heating, refrigeration, and air-conditioning systems. Mechanical engineering is the broadest engineering discipline, extending across many interdependent specialties. Mechanical engineers may work in production operations, maintenance, or technical sales; many are administrators or managers.

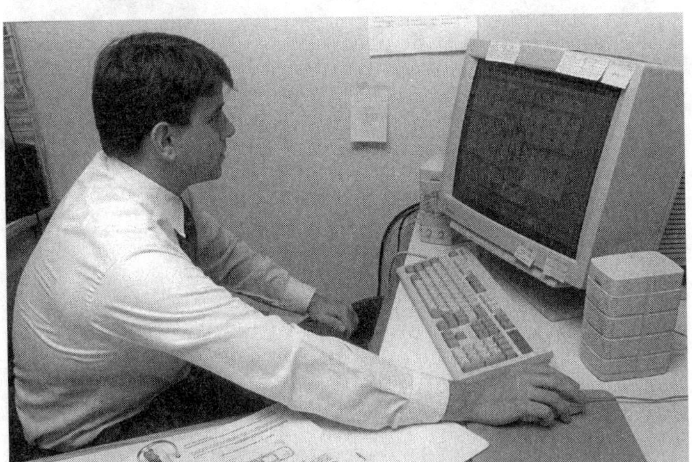

Mechanical engineers increasingly use computers to perform modeling and simulation.

Employment

Mechanical engineers held about 220,000 jobs in 1998. Almost 3 out of 5 jobs were in manufacturing—mostly in machinery, transportation equipment, electrical equipment, instruments, and fabricated metal products industries. Engineering and management services, business services, and the Federal Government provided most of the remaining jobs.

Job Outlook

Employment of mechanical engineers is projected to grow about as fast as the average for all occupations though 2008. Although overall manufacturing employment is expected to decline, employment of mechanical engineers in manufacturing should increase as the demand for improved machinery and machine tools grows and industrial machinery and processes become increasingly complex. Employment of mechanical engineers in business and engineering services firms is expected to grow faster than average as other industries in the economy increasingly contract out to these firms to solve engineering problems. In addition to job openings from growth, many openings should result from the need to replace workers who transfer to other occupations or leave the labor force.

Earnings

Median annual earnings of mechanical engineers were $53,290 in 1998. The middle 50 percent earned between $42,680 and $74,220. The lowest 10 percent earned less than $35,290 and the highest 10 percent earned more than $87,000. Median annual earnings in the industries employing the largest numbers of mechanical engineers in 1997 were:

Federal government	$66,800
Engineering and architectural services	55,800
Electronic components and accessories	52,900
Aircraft and parts	51,800
Motor vehicles and equipment	48,500

According to a 1999 salary survey by the National Association of Colleges and Employers, bachelor's degree candidates in mechanical engineering received starting offers averaging about $43,300 a year; master's degree candidates, $51,900; and Ph.D. candidates, $64,300.

(See introduction to the section on engineers for information on working conditions, training requirements, and sources of additional information.)

Mining Engineers, Including Mine Safety Engineers

(O*NET 22108)

Nature of the Work

Mining engineers find, extract, and prepare coal, metals, and minerals for use by manufacturing industries and utilities. They design open pit and underground mines, supervise the construction of mine shafts and tunnels in underground operations, and devise methods for transporting minerals to processing plants. Mining engineers are responsible for the safe, economical, and environmentally sound operation of mines. Some mining engineers work with geologists and metallurgical engineers to locate and appraise new ore deposits. Others develop new mining equipment or direct mineral processing operations to separate minerals from the dirt, rock, and other materials with which they are mixed. Mining engineers frequently specialize in the mining of one mineral or metal, such as coal or gold. With increased emphasis on protecting the environment, many mining engineers work to solve problems related to land reclamation and water and air pollution.

Mining engineers often spend time outdoors at work sites.

Employment

Mining engineers held about 4,400 jobs in 1998. While one-half worked in the mining industry, other mining engineers worked in government agencies, manufacturing industries, or engineering consulting firms.

Mining engineers are usually employed at the location of natural deposits, often near small communities, and sometimes outside the United States. About one-third of mining engineers employed in the U.S. work in Nevada, Colorado, Arizona, West Virginia, and Wyoming. Those in research and development, management, consulting, or sales, however, are often located in metropolitan areas.

Job Outlook

Employment of mining engineers is expected to decline through 2008. Most of the industries in which mining engineers are concentrated—such as coal, metal, and mineral mining, as well as stone, clay, and glass products manufacturing—are expected to experience declines in employment.

Although there are no job openings expected to result from employment growth, there should be openings resulting from the need to replace mining engineers who transfer to other occupations or leave the labor force. A large number of mining engineers currently employed are approaching retirement age. In addition, there are a relatively small number of schools offering mining engineering programs, and the small number of graduates is not expected to increase.

Mining operations around the world recruit graduates of U.S. mining engineering programs. Consequently, job opportunities may be better worldwide than within the United States. As a result, graduates should be prepared for the possibility of frequent travel or even living abroad.

Earnings

Median annual earnings of mining engineers were $56,090 in 1998. The middle 50 percent earned between $43,350 and $75,650. The lowest 10 percent earned less than $34,930 and the highest 10 percent earned more than $87,380. In the Federal Government, mining engineers in supervisory, nonsupervisory, and management positions averaged $62,300 a year in early 1999.

According to a 1999 salary survey by the National Association of Colleges and Employers, bachelor's degree candidates in mining engineering received starting offers averaging about $39,600 a year.

(See introduction to the section on engineers for information on working conditions, training requirements, and sources of additional information.)

Nuclear Engineers

(O*NET 22117)

Nature of the Work

Nuclear engineers research and develop the processes, instruments, and systems used to derive benefits from nuclear energy and radiation. They design, develop, monitor, and operate nuclear plants used to generate power. They may work on the nuclear fuel cycle—the production, handling, and use of nuclear fuel and the safe disposal of waste produced by nuclear energy—or on fusion energy. Some specialize in the development of nuclear power sources for spacecraft; others develop industrial and medical uses for radioactive materials, such as equipment to diagnose and treat medical problems.

Employment

Nuclear engineers held about 12,000 jobs in 1998. About 60 percent were in utilities, the Federal Government, and engineering consulting firms. More than half of all federally employed nuclear engineers were civilian employees of the Navy, and most of the rest worked for the Department of Energy or the Tennessee Valley Authority. Most nonfederally employed nuclear engineers worked for public utilities or engineering consulting companies. Some worked for defense manufacturers or manufacturers of nuclear power equipment.

Many nuclear engineers work for public utilities.

Job Outlook

Good opportunities should exist for nuclear engineers because the small number of nuclear engineering graduates is likely to be in rough balance with the number of job openings. Because this is a small occupation, projected job growth will generate few openings; consequently, most openings will result from the need to replace nuclear engineers who transfer to other occupations or leave the labor force.

Employment of nuclear engineers is expected to grow more slowly than the average for all occupations through 2008. Due to public concerns over the cost and safety of nuclear power, there are no commercial nuclear power plants under construction in the United States. Nevertheless, nuclear engineers will be needed to operate existing plants. In addition, nuclear engineers will be needed to work in defense-related areas, to develop nuclear medical technology, and to improve and enforce waste management and safety standards.

Earnings

Median annual earnings of nuclear engineers were $71,310 in 1998. The middle 50 percent earned between $57,160 and $85,460. The lowest 10 percent earned less than $48,830 and the highest 10 percent earned more than $106,400. In the Federal Government, nuclear engineers in supervisory, nonsupervisory, and management positions averaged $67,100 a year in early 1999.

(See introduction to the section on engineers for information on working conditions, training requirements, and sources of additional information.)

Petroleum Engineers

(O*NET 22111)

Nature of the Work

Petroleum engineers search the world for reservoirs containing oil or natural gas. Once discovered, petroleum engineers work with geologists and other specialists to understand the geologic formation and properties of the rock containing the reservoir, determine the drilling methods to be used, and monitor drilling and production operations. They design equipment and processes to achieve the maximum profitable recovery of oil and gas, often using computer models to simulate reservoir performance using different recovery techniques.

Because only a small proportion of oil and gas in a reservoir will flow out under natural forces, petroleum engineers develop and use various enhanced recovery methods. These include injecting water, chemicals, gases, or steam into an oil reservoir to force more of the oil out, and computer-controlled drilling or fracturing to connect a larger area of a reservoir to a single well. Since even the best techniques in use today recover only a portion of the oil and gas in a reservoir, petroleum engineers research and develop technology and methods to increase this proportion and lower the cost of drilling and production operations.

Employment

Petroleum engineers held about 12,000 jobs in 1998, mostly in the oil and gas extraction, petroleum refining, and related industries. Employers include major oil companies and hundreds of smaller, independent oil exploration, production, and service companies. Engineering consulting firms and government agencies also employ petroleum engineers. Others work as independent consultants.

Most petroleum engineers work where oil and gas are found. Large numbers are employed in Texas, Louisiana, Oklahoma,

Petroleum engineers are involved in many aspects of oil and gas extraction.

California, and Colorado, including offshore sites. Many American petroleum engineers also work overseas in oil-producing countries. Because petroleum engineers specialize in the discovery and production of oil and gas, relatively few are employed in the transportation and retail sectors of the oil and gas industry.

Job Outlook

Despite a projected decline in employment, opportunities for petroleum engineers should be favorable because the relatively small number of graduates is expected to be in rough balance with the number of job openings. Most opportunities will result from the need to replace petroleum engineers who transfer to other occupations or leave the labor force. Also, petroleum engineers work around the world, and many employers seek U.S.-trained petroleum engineers for jobs in other countries.

Employment of petroleum engineers is expected to decline through 2008 unless oil and gas prices unexpectedly rise enough to encourage increased exploration for oil in the United States. A high price of oil and gas makes it profitable for oil exploration and production firms to seek oil and gas reservoirs, and they will hire petroleum engineers to do so. Low oil prices, however, make it cheaper to purchase needed oil from other countries, such as Saudi Arabia, which have vast oil reserves. Also, the best exploration opportunities are in other countries because many of the most likely petroleum-producing areas in the United States have already been explored. However, the implementation of new technologies that expand drilling possibilities and improve the performance of reservoirs in the U.S. and the Gulf of Mexico may create new opportunities.

Earnings

Median annual earnings of petroleum engineers were $74,260 in 1998. The middle 50 percent earned between $56,020 and $93,280. The lowest 10 percent earned less than $42,870 and the highest 10 percent earned more than $115,820.

According to a 1999 salary survey by the National Association of Colleges and Employers, bachelor's degree candidates in petroleum engineering received starting offers averaging about $50,400.

(See introduction to the section on engineers for information on working conditions, training requirements, and sources of additional information.)

Engineering Technicians

(O*NET 22502, 22505A, 22505B, 22505C, 22508, 22511, 22599B, 22599C, 22599D, 22599E, 22599G, and 93111B)

Significant Points

- Electrical and electronic engineering technicians comprise about 43 percent of all engineering technicians.
- The type and quality of training programs vary considerably; prospective students should carefully select a program.
- Most employers prefer applicants with an associate degree in engineering technology.

Nature of the Work

Engineering technicians use the principles and theories of science, engineering, and mathematics to solve technical problems in research and development, manufacturing, sales, construction, inspection, and maintenance. Their work is more limited in scope and more practically oriented than that of scientists and engineers. Many engineering technicians assist engineers and scientists, especially in research and development. Others work in quality control—inspecting products and processes, conducting tests, or collecting data. In manufacturing, they may assist in product design, development, or production.

Engineering technicians, who work in research and development, build or set up equipment, prepare and conduct experiments, calculate or record the results, as well as help engineers in other ways. Some make prototype versions of newly designed equipment. They also assist in design work, often using computer-aided design equipment.

Engineering technicians, who work in manufacturing, support the work of engineers. They may prepare specifications for materials, devise and run tests to ensure product quality, or study ways to improve manufacturing efficiency. They may also supervise production workers to make sure they follow prescribed procedures.

Most engineering technicians specialize in certain areas, learning skills and working in the same disciplines as engineers. Occupational titles, therefore, tend to follow the same structure as engineers. *Chemical engineering technicians* are usually employed in industries producing pharmaceuticals, chemicals, and petroleum products, among others. They work in laboratories as well as processing plants. They help develop new chemical products and processes, test processing equipment and instrumentation, monitor quality, and operate chemical manufacturing facilities.

Civil engineering technicians help civil engineers plan and build highways, buildings, bridges, dams, wastewater treatment systems, and other structures, and perform related surveys and studies. Some inspect water and wastewater treatment systems to ensure pollution control requirements are met. Others estimate construction costs and specify materials to be used. Some may even prepare drawings or perform land-surveying duties. (Separate statements on cost estimators, drafters, and surveyors can be found elsewhere in the *Handbook*.)

Electrical and electronics engineering technicians help design, develop, test, and manufacture electrical and electronic equipment such as radios, radar, sonar, television, industrial and medical measuring or control devices, navigational equipment, and computers. They may work in product evaluation and testing, using measuring and diagnostic devices to adjust, test, and repair equipment. Workers who only repair electrical and electronic equipment are discussed in several other statements on mechanics, installers, and repairers found elsewhere in the *Handbook*. Many of these repairers are often referred to as electronics technicians.

Electrical and electronic engineering technology is also applied to a wide variety of systems such as communications and process controls. *Electromechanical engineering technicians* combine fundamental principles of mechanical engineering technology with knowledge of electrical and electronic circuits to design, develop, test, and manufacture electrical and computer controlled mechanical systems.

Industrial engineering technicians study the efficient use of personnel, materials, and machines in factories, stores, repair shops, and offices. They prepare layouts of machinery and equipment, plan the flow of work, make statistical studies, and analyze production costs.

Mechanical engineering technicians help engineers design, develop, test, and manufacture industrial machinery, mechanical parts, and other equipment. They may assist in testing a guided missile or planning and designing an electric power generation plant. They make sketches and rough layouts, record data, make computations, analyze results, and write reports. When planning production, mechanical engineering technicians prepare layouts and drawings of the assembly process and of parts to be manufactured. They estimate labor costs, equipment life, and plant space. Some test and inspect machines and equipment in manufacturing departments or work with engineers to eliminate production problems.

Working Conditions

Most engineering technicians work at least 40 hours a week in laboratories, offices, manufacturing or industrial plants, or on construction sites. Some may be exposed to hazards from equipment, chemicals, or toxic materials.

Employment

Engineering technicians held about 771,000 jobs in 1998. About 335,000 of these were electrical and electronics engineering technicians. About 30 percent of all engineering technicians worked in durable goods manufacturing, mainly in the electrical and electronic machinery and equipment, industrial machinery and equipment, instruments and related products, and transportation equipment industries. Another 30 percent worked in service industries, mostly in engineering or business services companies that do engineering work on contract for government, manufacturing, or other organizations.

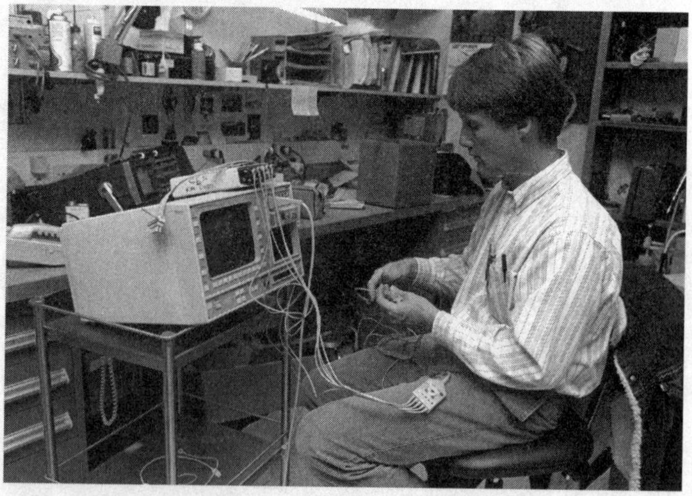

Engineering technicians use computer-aided equipment to devise and run tests to ensure product quality.

In 1998, the Federal Government employed about 39,000 engineering technicians. The major employer was the Department of Defense, followed by the Departments of Transportation, Agriculture, and Interior, the Tennessee Valley Authority, and the National Aeronautics and Space Administration. State governments employed about 30,000, and local governments about 26,000.

Training, Other Qualifications, and Advancement

Although it may be possible to qualify for a few engineering technician jobs without formal training, most employers prefer to hire someone with at least a 2-year associate degree in engineering technology. Training is available at technical institutes, community colleges, extension divisions of colleges and universities, public and private vocational-technical schools, and through some technical training programs in the Armed Forces. Persons with college courses in science, engineering, and mathematics may qualify for some positions but may need additional specialized training and experience. Although engineering technicians usually are not required to be certified by employers, such certification may provide jobseekers a competitive advantage.

Prospective engineering technicians should take as many high school science and math courses as possible to prepare for postsecondary programs in engineering technology. Most 2-year associate degree programs accredited by the Technology Accreditation Commission of the Accreditation Board for Engineering and Technology (TAC/ABET) require, at a minimum, college algebra and trigonometry, and one or two basic science courses. Depending on the specialty, more math or science may be required.

The type of technical courses required also depends on the specialty. For example, prospective mechanical engineering technicians may take courses in fluid mechanics, thermodynamics, and mechanical design; electrical engineering technicians may take classes in electric circuits, microprocessors, and digital electronics; and those preparing to work in environmental engineering technology need courses in environmental regulations and safe handling of hazardous materials.

Because many engineering technicians may assist in design work, creativity is desirable. Good communication skills and the ability to work well with others is also important since they are often part of a team of engineers and other technicians.

Engineering technicians usually begin by performing routine duties under the close supervision of an experienced technician, technologist, engineer, or scientist. As they gain experience, they are given more difficult assignments with only general supervision. Some engineering technicians eventually become supervisors.

Many publicly and privately operated schools provide technical training; the type and quality of programs vary considerably. Therefore, prospective students should be careful in selecting a program. They should contact prospective employers regarding their preferences and ask schools to provide information about the kinds of jobs obtained by graduates, instructional facilities and equipment, and faculty qualifications. Graduates of ABET-accredited programs are usually recognized to have achieved an acceptable level of competence in the mathematics, science, and technical courses required for this occupation.

Technical institutes offer intensive technical training, but less theory and general education than community colleges. Many offer 2-year associate degree programs, and are similar to or part of a community college or State university system. Other technical institutes are run by private, often for-profit, organizations, sometimes called proprietary schools. Their programs vary considerably in length and types of courses offered, although some are 2-year associate degree programs.

Community colleges offer curriculums similar to those in technical institutes but may include more theory and liberal arts. Often there may be little or no difference between technical institute and community college programs, as both offer associate degrees. After completing the 2-year program, some graduates get jobs as engineering technicians, while others continue their education at 4-year colleges. However, there is a difference between an associate degree in pre-engineering and one in engineering technology. Students who enroll in a 2-year pre-engineering program may find it very difficult to find work as an engineering technician should they decide not to enter a 4-year engineering program, because pre-engineering programs usually focus less on hands-on applications and more on academic preparatory work. Conversely, graduates of 2-year engineering technology programs may not receive credit for many of the courses they have taken if they choose to transfer to a 4-year engineering program. Colleges with these 4-year programs usually do not offer engineering technician training, but college courses in science, engineering, and mathematics are useful for obtaining a job as an engineering technician. Many 4-year colleges offer bachelor's degrees in engineering technology, but graduates of these programs are often hired to work as technologists or applied engineers, not technicians.

Area vocational-technical schools include postsecondary public institutions that serve local students and emphasize training needed by local employers. Most require a high school diploma or its equivalent for admission.

Other training in technical areas may be obtained in the Armed Forces. Many military technical training programs are highly regarded by employers. However, skills acquired in military programs often are narrowly focused, so they may not be useful in civilian industry, which often requires broader training. Therefore, some additional training may be needed, depending on the acquired skills and the kind of job.

The National Institute for Certification in Engineering Technologies (NICET) has established a voluntary certification program for engineering technicians. Certification is available at various levels, each level combining a written examination in one of over 30 specialties with a certain amount of job-related experience.

Job Outlook

Opportunities will be best for individuals with an associate degree in engineering technology. As technology becomes more sophisticated, employers continue to look for technicians who are skilled in new technology and require a minimum of additional job training.

Overall employment of engineering technicians is expected to increase about as fast as the average for all occupations through 2008. As production of technical products continues to grow, competitive pressures will force companies to improve and update manufacturing facilities and product designs more rapidly than in the past. However, the growing availability and use of advanced technologies, such as computer-aided design and drafting and computer simulation, will continue to increase productivity and limit job growth. In addition to growth, many job openings will be created to replace technicians who retire or leave the labor force.

Like engineers, employment of engineering technicians is influenced by local and national economic conditions. As a result, the employment outlook varies with industry and specialization. Employment of some types of engineering technicians, such as civil engineering and aeronautical engineering technicians, experience greater cyclical fluctuations than others. Increasing demand for more sophisticated electrical and electronic products, as well as the expansion of these products and systems into all areas of industry and manufacturing processes, will contribute to average growth in the largest specialty—electrical and electronics engineering technicians. At the same time, new specializations will contribute to growth among all other engineering technicians. Fire protection engineering technology, for example, is one of many new specialties for which demand is increasing.

Earnings

Median annual earnings of electrical and electronics engineering technicians were $35,970 in 1998. The middle 50 percent earned between $27,680 and $45,750. The lowest 10 percent earned less than $21,710 and the highest 10 percent earned more than $62,540. Median annual earnings in the industries employing the largest numbers of engineering technicians in 1997 are shown below:

Engineering and architectural services	$36,600
Computer and data processing services	33,600
Computer and office equipment	33,000
Electrical components and accessories	32,100
Personnel supply services	25,400

Median annual earnings of all other engineering technicians and technologists in 1998 were $37,310. The middle 50 percent earned between $28,510 and $47,610. The lowest 10 percent earned less than $22,230 and the highest 10 percent earned more than $68,720. Median annual earnings in the industries employing the largest numbers of other engineering technicians and technologists in 1997 are shown below:

Federal Government	$42,700
Electrical components and accessories	33,500
Engineering and architectural services	32,600
Local government	32,200
State government	27,500

In the Federal Government, engineering technicians started at about $18,600, $21,200, or $25,000 in early 1999, depending on their education and experience. Beginning salaries were slightly higher in selected areas of the country where the prevailing local pay level was higher.

Related Occupations

Engineering technicians apply scientific and engineering principles usually acquired in postsecondary programs below the baccalaureate level. Similar occupations include science technicians, drafters, surveyors, broadcast and sound technicians, and health technologists and technicians.

Sources of Additional Information

For a small fee, information on a variety of engineering technician and technology careers is available from:

☛ The Junior Engineering Technical Society (JETS), at 1420 King St., Suite 405, Alexandria, VA 22314-2794. Enclose $3.50 to obtain a full package of guidance materials and information. Brochures are available free on JETS Internet site: **http://www.jets.org**

Information on ABET-accredited engineering technology programs is available from:

☛ Accreditation Board for Engineering and Technology, Inc. 111 Market Place, Suite 1050, Baltimore, MD 21202. Internet: **http://www.abet. org**

Architects, Surveyors, and Drafters

Architects, Except Landscape and Naval

(O*NET 22302)

Significant Points

- About 30 percent were self-employed—over three times the proportion for all professionals.
- Licensing requirements include a professional degree in architecture, a period of practical training or internship, and passing all divisions of the Architect Registration Examination.
- Beginners may face competition, especially for jobs in the most prestigious firms; summer internship experience and knowledge of computer-aided design and drafting technology are advantages.

Nature of the Work

Architects design buildings and other structures. The design of a building involves far more than its appearance. Buildings must also be functional, safe, and economical, and must suit the needs of the people who use them. Architects take all these things into consideration when they design buildings and other structures.

Architects provide professional services to individuals and organizations planning a construction project. They may be involved in all phases of development, from the initial discussion with the client through the entire construction process. Their duties require specific skills—designing, engineering, managing, supervising, and communicating with clients and builders.

The architect and client discuss the objectives, requirements, and budget of a project. In some cases, architects provide various predesign services—conducting feasibility and environmental impact studies, selecting a site, or specifying the requirements the design must meet. For example, they may determine space requirements by researching the number and type of potential users of a building. The architect then prepares drawings and a report presenting ideas for the client to review.

After the initial proposals are discussed and accepted, architects develop final construction plans. These plans show the building's appearance and details for its construction. Accompanying these are drawings of the structural system; air-conditioning, heating, and ventilating systems; electrical systems; plumbing; and possibly site and landscape plans. They also specify the building materials and, in some cases, the interior furnishings. In developing designs, architects follow building codes, zoning laws, fire regulations, and other ordinances, such as those requiring easy access by disabled persons. Throughout the planning stage, they make necessary changes. Although they have traditionally used pencil and paper to produce design and construction drawings, architects are increasingly turning to computer-aided design and drafting (CADD) technology for these important tasks.

Architects may also assist the client in obtaining construction bids, selecting a contractor, and negotiating the construction contract. As construction proceeds, they may visit the building site to ensure the contractor is following the design, adhering to the schedule, using the specified materials, and meeting quality work standards. The job is not complete until all construction is finished, required tests are made, and construction costs are paid. Sometimes, architects also provide postconstruction services, such as facilities management. They advise on energy efficiency measures, evaluate how well the building design adapts to the needs of occupants, and make necessary improvements.

Architects design a wide variety of buildings, such as office and apartment buildings, schools, churches, factories, hospitals, houses, and airport terminals. They also design complexes such as urban centers, college campuses, industrial parks, and entire communities. They may also advise on the selection of building sites, prepare cost analysis and land-use studies, and do long-range planning for land development.

Architects sometimes specialize in one phase of work. Some specialize in the design of one type of building—for example, hospitals, schools, or housing. Others focus on planning and predesign

Architects spend much of their time updating plans after receiving feedback from other design professionals.

services or construction management, and do little design work. They often work with engineers, urban planners, interior designers, landscape architects, and others. In fact, architects spend a great deal of their time in coordinating information from, and the work of, other professionals engaged in the same project. Consequently, architects are now using the Internet to update designs and communicate changes for the sake of speed and cost savings.

During a training period leading up to licensing as architects, entry-level workers are called intern-architects. This training period, which generally lasts three years, gives them practical work experience while they prepare for the Architect Registration Examination (ARE). Typical duties may include preparing construction drawings on CADD, or assisting in the design of one part of a project.

Working Conditions

Architects usually work in a comfortable environment. Most of their time is spent in offices consulting with clients, developing reports and drawings, and working with other architects and engineers. However, they often visit construction sites to review the progress of projects.

Architects may occasionally be under stress, working nights and weekends to meet deadlines. In 1998, almost 2 out of 5 architects worked more than 40 hours a week, in contrast to 1 in 4 workers in all occupations combined.

Employment

Architects held about 99,000 jobs in 1998. The majority of jobs were in architectural firms—most of which employ fewer than 5 workers. A few worked for general building contractors, and for government agencies responsible for housing, planning, or community development, such as the U.S. Departments of Defense and Interior, and the General Services Administration. About 3 in 10 architects were self-employed.

Training, Other Qualifications, and Advancement

All States and the District of Columbia require individuals to be licensed (registered) before they may call themselves architects or contract to provide architectural services. Many architecture school graduates work in the field even though they are not licensed. However, a licensed architect is required to take legal responsibility for all work. Licensing requirements include a professional degree in architecture, a period of practical training or internship, and passage of all sections of the ARE.

In many States, the professional degree in architecture must be from one of the 105 schools of architecture with programs accredited by the National Architectural Accrediting Board (NAAB). However, State architectural registration boards set their own standards, so graduation from a non NAAB-accredited program may meet the educational requirement for licensing in some States. Several types of professional degrees in architecture are available through colleges and universities. The majority of all architectural degrees are from 5-year Bachelor of Architecture programs, intended for students entering from high school or with no previous architectural training. Some schools offer a 2-year Master of Architecture program for students with a preprofessional undergraduate degree in architecture or a related area, or a 3- or 4-year Master of Architecture program for students with a degree in another discipline. In addition, there are many combinations and variations of these programs.

The choice of degree type depends upon each individual's preference and educational background. Prospective architecture students should consider the available options before committing to a program. For example, although the 5-year Bachelor of Architecture program offers the fastest route to the professional degree, courses are specialized and, if the student does not complete the program, moving to a nonarchitectural program may be difficult. A typical program includes courses in architectural history and theory, building design, professional practice, math, physical sciences, and liberal arts. Central to most architectural programs is the design studio, where students put into practice the skills and concepts learned in the classroom. During the final semester of many programs, students devote their studio time to creating an architectural project from beginning to end, culminating in a 3-dimensional model of their design.

Many schools of architecture also offer graduate education for those who already have a bachelor's or master's degree in architecture or other areas. Although graduate education beyond the professional degree is not required for practicing architects, it is for research, teaching, and certain specialties.

Architects must be able to visually communicate their ideas to clients. Artistic and drawing ability is very helpful in doing this, but not essential. More important are a visual orientation and the ability to conceptualize and understand spatial relationships. Good communication skills, the ability to work independently or as part of a team, and creativity are important qualities for anyone interested in becoming an architect. Computer literacy is also required as most firms use computers for writing specifications, 2- and 3-dimensional drafting, and financial management. A knowledge of computer-aided design and drafting (CADD) is helpful and will become essential as architectural firms continue to adopt this technology. Recently, the profession recognized National CAD Standards (NCS); architecture students who master NCS will have an advantage in the job market.

All State architectural registration boards require a training period before candidates may sit for the ARE and become licensed. Many States have adopted the training standards established by the Intern Development Program, a branch of the American Institute of Architects and the National Council of Architectural Registration Boards. These standards stipulate broad and diversified training under the supervision of a licensed architect over a 3-year period. New graduates usually begin as intern-architects in architectural firms, where they assist in preparing architectural documents or drawings. They may also do research on building codes and materials, or write specifications for building materials, installation criteria, the quality of finishes, and other related details. Graduates with degrees in architecture also enter related fields such as graphic, interior, or industrial design; urban planning; real estate development; civil engineering; or construction management. In such cases, an architectural license (and thus the internship period) is not required.

After completing the internship period, intern-architects are eligible to sit for the ARE. The examination tests candidates on architectural knowledge, and is given in sections throughout the year. Candidates who pass the ARE and meet all standards established by their State board are licensed to practice in that State.

After becoming licensed and gaining experience, architects take on increasingly responsible duties, eventually managing entire projects. In large firms, architects may advance to supervisory or managerial positions. Some architects become partners in established firms; others set up their own practice.

Several States require continuing education to maintain a license, and many more States are expected to adopt mandatory continuing education. Requirements vary by State, but usually involve the completion of a certain number of credits every year or two through seminars, workshops, formal university classes, conferences, self-study courses, or other sources.

Job Outlook

Prospective architects may face competition for entry-level jobs, especially if the number of architectural degrees awarded remain at current levels or increases. Employment of architects is projected to grow about as fast as the average for all occupations through 2008 and additional job openings will stem from the need to replace architects who retire or leave the labor force for other reasons. However, many individuals are attracted to this occupation, and the number of applicants often exceeds the number of available jobs, especially in the most prestigious firms. Prospective architects who complete at least one summer internship—either paid or unpaid—while in school and who know CADD technology (especially that which conforms to the new national standards) will have a distinct advantage in obtaining an intern-architect position after graduation.

Employment of architects is strongly tied to the level of local construction, particularly nonresidential structures such as office buildings, shopping centers, schools, and healthcare facilities. After a boom in non-residential construction during the 1980s, building slowed significantly during the first half of the 1990s. Despite slower labor force growth and increases in telecommuting and flexiplace work, however, non-residential construction is expected to grow more quickly between 1998 and 2008 than during the previous decade, driving demand for more architects.

As the stock of buildings ages, demand for remodeling and repair work should grow considerably. The needed renovation and rehabilitation of old buildings, particularly in urban areas where space for new buildings is becoming limited, is expected to provide many job opportunities for architects. In addition, demographic trends and changes in health care delivery are influencing the demand for certain institutional structures, and should also provide more jobs for architects in the future. For example, increases in the school-age population have resulted in new school construction. Additions to existing schools (especially colleges and universities), as well as overall modernization, will continue to add to demand for architects through 2008. Growth is expected in the number of adult care centers, assisted-living facilities, and community health clinics, all of which are preferable, less costly alternatives to hospitals and nursing homes.

Because construction—particularly office and retail—is sensitive to cyclical changes in the economy, architects will face particularly strong competition for jobs or clients during recessions, and layoffs may occur. Those involved in the design of institutional buildings such as schools, hospitals, nursing homes, and correctional facilities, will be less affected by fluctuations in the economy.

Even in times of overall good job opportunities, however, there may be areas of the country with poor opportunities. Architects who are licensed to practice in one State must meet the licensing requirements of other States before practicing elsewhere. These requirements are becoming more standardized, however, facilitating movement to other States.

Earnings

Median annual earnings of architects were $47,710 in 1998. The middle 50 percent earned between $37,380 and $68,920. The lowest 10 percent earned less than $30,030 and the highest 10 percent earned more than $87,460.

According to the American Institute of Architects, the median compensation, including bonuses, for intern-architects in architectural firms was $35,200 in 1999. Licensed architects with 3 to 5 of years experience had median earnings of $41,100; licensed architects with 8 to 10 years of experience, but who were not managers or principals of a firm, earned $54,700. Principals or partners of firms had median earnings of $132,500 in 1999, although partners in some large practices earned considerably more. Similar to other industries, small architectural firms (fewer than 5 employees) are less likely than larger firms to provide employee benefits.

Earnings of partners in established architectural firms may fluctuate because of changing business conditions. Some architects may have difficulty establishing their own practices, and may go through a period when their expenses are greater than their income, requiring substantial financial resources.

Related Occupations

Architects design and construct buildings and related structures. Others who engage in similar work are landscape architects, building contractors, civil engineers, urban planners, interior designers, industrial designers, and graphic designers.

Sources of Additional Information

Information about education and careers in architecture can be obtained from:

☛ Careers in Architecture Program, The American Institute of Architects, 1735 New York Ave. NW., Washington, DC 20006.
Internet: **http://www.aiaonline.com**

Drafters

(O*NET 22514A, 22514B, 22514C, 22514D, and 22517)

Significant Points

- The type and quality of postsecondary drafting programs varies considerably; prospective students should be careful in selecting a program.
- Opportunities should be best for individuals who have at least 2 years of postsecondary training in drafting and considerable skill and experience using computer-aided drafting (CAD) systems.
- Demand for particular drafting specializations varies geographically, depending on the needs of local industry.

Nature of the Work

Drafters prepare technical drawings and plans used by production and construction workers to build everything from manufactured products such as spacecraft or industrial machinery to structures such as office buildings or oil and gas pipelines. Their drawings provide visual guidelines, showing the technical details of the products and structures, specifying dimensions, materials to be used, and procedures and processes to be followed. Drafters fill in technical details, using drawings, rough sketches, specifications, codes, and calculations previously made by engineers, surveyors, architects, or scientists. For example, they use their knowledge of standardized building techniques to draw in the details of a structure. Some drafters use their knowledge of engineering and manufacturing theory and standards to draw the parts of a machine in order to determine design elements such as the number and kind of fasteners needed to assemble it. They use technical handbooks, tables, calculators, and computers to do this.

Traditionally, drafters sat at drawing boards and used compasses, dividers, protractors, triangles, and other drafting devices to prepare a drawing manually. Most drafters now use computer-aided drafting (CAD) systems to prepare drawings. These systems employ computer work stations which create a drawing on a video screen. The drawings are stored electronically so that revisions or duplications can be made easily. These systems also permit drafters to easily and quickly prepare variations of a design. Although this equipment has become easier to operate, CAD is only a tool. Persons who produce technical drawings using CAD still function as a drafter, and need most of the knowledge of traditional drafters—relating to drafting skills and standards—as well as CAD skills.

As CAD technology advances and the cost of the systems continues to fall, it is likely that almost all drafters will use CAD systems regularly in the future. However, manual drafting may still be used in certain applications, especially in specialty firms that produce many one-of-a-kind drawings with little repetition.

Drafting work has many specializations and titles may denote a particular discipline of design or drafting. *Architectural drafters* draw architectural and structural features of buildings and other structures. They may specialize by the type of structure, such as residential or commercial, or by material used, such as reinforced concrete, masonry, steel, or timber.

Aeronautical drafters prepare engineering drawings detailing plans and specifications used for the manufacture of aircraft, missiles, and parts.

Electrical drafters prepare wiring and layout diagrams used by workers who erect, install, and repair electrical equipment and wiring in communication centers, powerplants, electrical distribution systems, and buildings.

Drafters use their knowledge of standardized building techniques to draw the details of a structure.

Electronic drafters draw wiring diagrams, circuit board assembly diagrams, schematics, and layout drawings used in the manufacture, installation, and repair of electronic devices and components.

Civil drafters prepare drawings and topographical and relief maps used in major construction or civil engineering projects such as highways, bridges, pipelines, flood control projects, and water and sewage systems.

Mechanical drafters prepare detail and assembly drawings of a wide variety of machinery and mechanical devices, indicating dimensions, fastening methods, and other requirements.

Process piping or *pipeline drafters* prepare drawings used for layout, construction, and operation of oil and gas fields, refineries, chemical plants, and process piping systems.

Working Conditions

Drafters usually work in comfortable offices furnished to accommodate their tasks. They may sit at adjustable drawing boards or drafting tables when doing manual drawings, although most drafters work at computer terminals much of the time. Because they spend long periods of time in front of computer terminals doing detailed work, drafters may be susceptible to eyestrain, back discomfort, and hand and wrist problems.

Employment

Drafters held about 283,000 jobs in 1998. Over 35 percent of all drafters worked in engineering and architectural services firms that design construction projects or do other engineering work on a contract basis for organizations in other industries. Another 29 percent worked in durable goods manufacturing industries, such as machinery, electrical equipment, and fabricated metals. The remainder were mostly employed in the construction, communications, utilities, and personnel supply services industries. About 17,600 were self-employed in 1998.

Training, Other Qualifications, and Advancement

Employers prefer applicants for drafting positions who have completed postsecondary school training in drafting, which is offered by technical institutes, community colleges, and some 4-year colleges and universities. Employers are most interested in applicants who have well-developed drafting and mechanical drawing skills; a knowledge of drafting standards, mathematics, science, and engineering technology; and a solid background in computer-aided drafting and design techniques. In addition, communication and problem-solving skills are important.

Individuals planning careers in drafting should take courses in math, science, computer technology, design or computer graphics, and any high school drafting courses available. Mechanical and visual aptitude are also important. Prospective drafters should be able to draw freehand, three-dimensional objects and do detailed work accurately and neatly. Artistic ability is helpful in some specialized fields, as is knowledge of manufacturing and construction methods. In addition, prospective drafters should have good interpersonal skills because they work closely with engineers, surveyors, architects, and other professionals.

Entry level or junior drafters usually do routine work under close supervision. After gaining experience, intermediate level drafters progress to more difficult work with less supervision. They may be required to exercise more judgment and perform calculations when preparing and modifying drawings. Drafters may eventually advance to senior drafter, designer, or supervisor. Many employers pay for continuing education, and with appropriate college degrees, drafters may go on to become engineering technicians, engineers, or architects.

Many types of publicly and privately operated schools provide some form of drafting training. The kind and quality of programs vary considerably. Therefore, prospective students should be careful in selecting a program. They should contact prospective employers regarding their preferences and ask schools to provide information about the kinds of jobs obtained by graduates, type and condition of instructional facilities and equipment, and faculty qualifications.

Technical institutes offer intensive technical training but less of the general education than do junior and community colleges. Certificates or diplomas based on completion of a certain number of course hours may be rewarded. Many offer 2-year associate degree programs, which are similar to or part of the programs offered by community colleges or State university systems. Other technical institutes are run by private, often for-profit, organizations, sometimes called proprietary schools. Their programs vary considerably in both length and type of courses offered.

Community colleges offer curriculums similar to those in technical institutes but include more courses on theory and liberal arts. Often there is little or no difference between technical institute and community college programs. However, courses taken at community colleges are more likely to be accepted for credit at 4-year colleges than those at technical institutes. After completing a 2-year associate degree program, graduates may obtain jobs as drafters or continue their education in a related field at 4-year colleges. Four-year colleges usually do not offer drafting training, but college courses in engineering, architecture, and mathematics are useful for obtaining a job as a drafter.

Area vocational-technical schools are postsecondary public institutions that serve local students and emphasize training needed by local employers. Many offer introductory drafting instruction. Most require a high school diploma or its equivalent for admission.

Technical training obtained in the Armed Forces can also be applied in civilian drafting jobs. Some additional training may be necessary, depending on the technical area or military specialty.

The American Design Drafting Association (ADDA) has established a certification program for drafters. Although drafters are not usually required to be certified by employers, certification demonstrates that nationally recognized standards have been met. Individuals who wish to become certified must pass the Drafter Certification Test, which is administered periodically at ADDA-authorized test sites. Applicants are tested on their knowledge and understanding of basic drafting concepts such as geometric construction, working drawings, and architectural terms and standards.

Job Outlook

Employment of drafters is expected to grow more slowly than the average for all occupations through 2008. Although industrial growth and increasingly complex design problems associated with new products and manufacturing will increase the demand for drafting services, greater use of CAD equipment by architects and engineers, as well as drafters, should offset this growth in demand. Many job openings, however, are expected to arise as drafters move to other occupations or leave the labor force.

Opportunities should be best for individuals who have at least 2 years of postsecondary training in a drafting program that provides strong technical skills, and who have considerable skill and experience using CAD systems. CAD has increased the complexity of drafting applications while enhancing the productivity of drafters. It has also enhanced the nature of drafting by creating more possibilities for design and drafting. As technology continues to advance, employers will look for drafters having a strong background in fundamental drafting principles with a higher level of technical sophistication and an ability to apply this knowledge to a broader range of responsibilities.

Demand for particular drafting specializations varies throughout the country because employment is usually contingent upon the needs of local industry. Employment of drafters remains highly concentrated in industries that are sensitive to cyclical changes in the economy, such as engineering and architectural services and durable goods manufacturing. During recessions, drafters may be laid off. However, a growing number of drafters should continue to be employed on a temporary or contract basis, as more companies turn to the personnel supply services industry to meet their changing needs.

Earnings

Median hourly earnings of drafters were $15.56 in 1998. The middle 50 percent earned between $12.29 and $19.73. The lowest 10 percent earned less than $10.19 and the highest 10 percent earned more than $24.84. Median hourly earnings in the industries employing the largest numbers of drafters in 1997 are shown below:

Industry	Earnings
Motor vehicles and equipment	$21.50
Personnel supply services	16.20
Miscellaneous business services	15.60
Fabricated structural metal products	14.30

Related Occupations

Other workers who prepare or analyze detailed drawings and make precise calculations and measurements include architects, landscape architects, designers, engineers, engineering technicians, science technicians, cartographers, and surveyors.

Sources of Additional Information

Information on schools offering programs in drafting and related fields is available from:

☛ Accrediting Commission of Career Schools and Colleges of Technology, 2101 Wilson Blvd., Suite 302, Arlington, VA 22201.

Information about certification is available from:

☛ American Design Drafting Association, P.O. Box 11937, Columbia, SC 29211. Internet: **http://www.adda.org**.

Landscape Architects

(O*NET 22308)

Significant Points

- Over 40 percent are self-employed—four times the proportion for all professionals.
- A bachelor's degree in landscape architecture is the minimum requirement for entry-level jobs; many employers prefer to hire landscape architects who have completed at least one internship.
- Because many landscape architects work for small firms or are self-employed, benefits tend to be less generous than those provided to workers in large organizations.

Nature of the Work

Everyone enjoys attractively designed residential areas, public parks and playgrounds, college campuses, shopping centers, golf courses, parkways, and industrial parks. Landscape architects design these areas so that they are not only functional but beautiful and compatible with the natural environment as well. They plan the location of buildings, roads, and walkways and the arrangement of flowers, shrubs, and trees. Historic preservation and natural resource conservation and reclamation are other important objectives to which landscape architects may apply their knowledge of the environment as well as their design and artistic talents.

Many types of organizations—from real estate development firms starting new projects to municipalities constructing airports or parks—hire landscape architects, who are often involved with the development of a site from its conception. Working with architects, surveyors, and engineers, landscape architects help determine the best arrangement of roads and buildings. They also collaborate with environmental scientists, foresters, and other professionals to find the best way to conserve or restore natural resources. Once these decisions are made, landscape architects create detailed plans indicating new topography, vegetation, walkways, and other landscaping details, such as fountains and decorative features.

In planning a site, landscape architects first consider the nature and purpose of the project and the funds available. They analyze the natural elements of the site, such as the climate, soil, slope of the land, drainage, and vegetation; observe where sunlight falls on the site at different times of the day and examine the site from various angles; and assess the effect of existing buildings, roads, walkways, and utilities on the project.

After studying and analyzing the site, they prepare a preliminary design. To account for the needs of the client as well as the conditions at the site, they frequently make changes before a final design is approved. They also take into account any local, State, or Federal regulations such as those protecting wetlands or historic resources. Computer-aided design (CAD) has become an essential tool for most landscape architects in preparing designs. Many landscape architects also use video simulation to help clients envision the proposed ideas and plans. For larger scale site planning, landscape architects also use geographic information systems technology, a computer mapping system.

Throughout all phases of the planning and design, landscape architects consult with other professionals involved in the project. Once the design is complete, they prepare a proposal for the client. They produce detailed plans of the site, including written reports, sketches, models, photographs, land-use studies, and cost estimates, and submit them for approval by the client and by regulatory agencies. When the plans are approved, landscape architects prepare working drawings showing all existing and proposed features. They also outline in detail the methods of construction and draw up a list of necessary materials.

Although many landscape architects supervise the installation of their design, some are involved in the construction of the site. However, the developer or landscape contractor usually does this.

Some landscape architects work on a variety of projects. Others specialize in a particular area, such as residential development, historic landscape restoration, waterfront improvement projects, parks and playgrounds, or shopping centers. Still others work in regional planning and resource management; feasibility, environmental impact, and cost studies; or site construction.

Most landscape architects do at least some residential work, but relatively few limit their practice to individual homeowners. Residential landscape design projects usually are too small to provide suitable income compared with larger commercial or multiunit residential projects. Some nurseries offer residential landscape design services, but these services often are performed by lesser qualified landscape designers or others with training and experience in related areas.

A landscape architect reviews plans for a project.

Landscape architects who work for government agencies do site and landscape design for government buildings, parks, and other public lands, as well as park and recreation planning in national parks and forests. In addition, they prepare environmental impact statements and studies on environmental issues such as public land-use planning. Some restore degraded land, such as mines or landfills.

Working Conditions

Landscape architects spend most of their time in offices creating plans and designs, preparing models and cost estimates, doing research, or attending meetings with clients and other professionals involved in a design or planning project. The remainder of their time is spent at the site. During the design and planning stage, landscape architects visit and analyze the site to verify that the design can be incorporated into the landscape. After the plans and specifications are completed, they may spend additional time at the site observing or supervising the construction. Those who work in large firms may spend considerably more time out of the office because of travel to sites outside the local area.

Salaried employees in both government and landscape architectural firms usually work regular hours; however, they may work overtime to meet a project deadline. Hours of self-employed landscape architects vary.

Employment

Landscape architects held about 22,000 jobs in 1998. About 1out of 2 salaried workers were employed in firms that provide landscape architecture services. Architectural and engineering firms employed most of the rest. The Federal Government also employs these workers, primarily in the U.S. Departments of Agriculture, Defense, and Interior. About 2 of every 5 landscape architects were self-employed.

Employment of landscape architects is concentrated in urban and suburban areas throughout the country. Some landscape architects work in rural areas, particularly those in the Federal Government who plan and design parks and recreation areas.

Training, Other Qualifications, and Advancement

A bachelor's or master's degree in landscape architecture is usually necessary for entry into the profession. The bachelor's degree in landscape architecture takes 4 or 5 years to complete. There are two types of accredited master's degree programs. The master's degree as a first professional degree is a 3-year program designed for students with an undergraduate degree in another discipline; this is the most common type. The master's degree as the second professional degree is a 2-year program for students who have a bachelor's degree in landscape architecture and wish to teach or specialize in some aspect of landscape architecture, such as regional planning or golf course design.

In 1999, 58 colleges and universities offered 75 undergraduate and graduate programs in landscape architecture that were accredited by the Landscape Architecture Accreditation Board of the American Society of Landscape Architects.

College courses required in this field usually include technical subjects such as surveying, landscape design and construction, landscape ecology, site design, and urban and regional planning. Other courses include history of landscape architecture, plant and soil science, geology, professional practice, and general management. Many landscape architecture programs are adding courses that address environmental issues. In addition, most students at the undergraduate level take a year of prerequisite courses such as English, mathematics, and social and physical science. The design studio is an important aspect of many landscape architecture curriculums. Whenever possible, students are assigned real projects, providing them with valuable hands-on experience. While working on these projects, students become more proficient in the use of computer-aided design, geographic information systems, and video simulation.

In 1999, 46 States required landscape architects to be licensed or registered. Licensing is based on the Landscape Architect Registration Examination (L.A.R.E.), sponsored by the Council of Landscape Architectural Registration Boards and administered over a 3-day period. Admission to the exam usually requires a degree from an accredited school plus 1 to 4 years of work experience, although standards vary from State to State. Currently, 17 States require the passage of a State examination in addition to the L.A.R.E. to satisfy registration requirements. State examinations, which are usually 1 hour in length and completed at the end of the L.A.R.E., focus on laws, environmental regulations, plants, soils, climate, and any other characteristics unique to the State.

Because State requirements for licensure are not uniform, landscape architects may not find it easy to transfer their registration from one State to another. However, those who meet the national standards of graduating from an accredited program, serving 3 years of internship under the supervision of a registered landscape architect, and passing the L.A.R.E. can satisfy requirements in most States. Through this means, a landscape architect can obtain certification from the Council of Landscape Architectural Registration Boards, and so gain reciprocity (the right to work) in other States.

In the Federal Government, candidates for entry positions should have a bachelor's or master's degree in landscape architecture. The Federal Government does not require its landscape architects to be licensed.

Persons planning a career in landscape architecture should appreciate nature, enjoy working with their hands, and possess strong analytical skills. Creative vision and artistic talent are also desirable qualities. Good oral communication skills are essential; landscape architects must be able to convey their ideas to other professionals and clients and to make presentations before large groups. Strong writing skills are also valuable, as is knowledge of computer applications of all kinds, including word processing, desktop publishing, and spreadsheets. Landscape architects use these tools to develop presentations, proposals, reports, and land impact studies for clients, colleagues, and superiors. The ability to draft and design using CAD software is essential. Many employers recommend that prospective landscape architects complete at least one summer internship with a landscape architecture firm in order to gain an understanding of the day-to-day operations of a small business, including how to win clients, generate fees, and work within a budget.

In States where licensure is required, new hires may be called "apprentices" or "intern landscape architects" until they become licensed. Their duties vary depending on the type and size of employing firm. They may do project research or prepare working drawings, construction documents, or base maps of the area to be landscaped. Some are allowed to participate in the actual design of a project. However, interns must perform all work under the supervision of a licensed landscape architect. Additionally, all drawings and specifications must be signed and sealed by the licensed landscape architect, who takes legal responsibility for the work. After gaining experience and becoming licensed, landscape architects usually can carry a design through all stages of development. After several years, they may become project managers, taking on the responsibility for meeting schedules and budgets, in addition to overseeing the project design; and later, associates or partners, with a proprietary interest in the business.

Many landscape architects are self-employed because start-up costs, after an initial investment in CAD software, are relatively low. Self-discipline, business acumen, and good marketing skills are important qualities for those who choose to open their own business. Even with these qualities, however, some may struggle while building a client base.

Those with landscape architecture training also qualify for jobs closely related to landscape architecture, and may, after gaining some experience, become construction supervisors, land or environmental planners, or landscape consultants.

Job Outlook

Employment of landscape architects is expected to increase as fast as the average for all occupations through the year 2008. The level of new construction plays an important role in determining demand for landscape architects. Overall, anticipated growth in construction is expected to increase demand for landscape architectural services over the long run.

Increased development of open space into recreation areas, wildlife refuges, and parks will also require the skills of landscape architects. The recent passage of the Transportation Equity Act for the Twenty-First Century is expected to spur employment for landscape architects, particularly in State and local governments. This Act, known as TEA-21, provides funds for surface transportation and transit programs, such as interstate highway maintenance and environment-friendly pedestrian and bicycle trails. However, opportunities will vary from year to year and by geographic region, depending on local economic conditions. During a recession, when real estate sales and construction slow down, landscape architects may face layoffs and greater competition for jobs. The need to replace landscape architects who retire or leave the labor force for other reasons is expected to produce nearly as many job openings as employment growth.

An increasing proportion of office and other commercial and industrial development will occur outside cities. These projects are typically located on larger sites with more surrounding land which needs to be designed by a landscape architect, in contrast to urban development, which often includes little or no surrounding land. Also, as the cost of land rises, the importance of good site planning and landscape design grows. Increasingly, new development is contingent upon compliance with environmental regulations and land use zoning, spurring demand for landscape architects to help plan sites and integrate man-made structures with the natural environment in the least disruptive way.

Budget tightening in the Federal Government might restrict hiring in the Forest Service and the National Park Service, agencies that traditionally employ the most landscape architects in the Federal government. Instead, such agencies may increasingly contract out for landscape architecture services, providing additional employment opportunities in private landscape architecture firms.

In addition to the work related to new development and construction, landscape architects are expected to be involved in historic preservation, land reclamation, and refurbishment of existing sites. Because landscape architects can work on many different types of projects, they may have an easier time than other design professionals finding employment when traditional construction slows down.

New graduates can expect to face competition for jobs in the largest and most prestigious landscape architecture firms. The number of professional degrees awarded in landscape architecture has remained steady over the years, even during times of fluctuating demand due to economic conditions. Opportunities will be best for landscape architects who develop strong technical and communication skills and a knowledge of environmental codes and regulations. Those with additional training or experience in urban planning increase their opportunities for employment in landscape architecture firms that specialize in site planning as well as landscape design. Many employers prefer to hire entry-level landscape architects who have internship experience, which significantly reduces the amount of on-the-job training required.

Earnings

In 1998, median annual earnings for landscape architects were $37,930. The middle 50 percent earned between $28,820 and

$50,550. The lowest 10 percent earned less than $22,800 and the highest 10 percent earned over $78,920. Most landscape architects worked in the landscape and horticultural services industry, where their median annual earnings were $33,600 in 1997.

In 1999, the average annual salary for all landscape architects in the Federal Government in nonsupervisory, supervisory, and managerial positions was about $57,500.

Because many landscape architects work for small firms or are self-employed, benefits tend to be less generous than those provided to workers in large organizations.

Related Occupations

Landscape architects use their knowledge of design, construction, land-use planning, and environmental issues to develop a landscape project. Others whose work requires similar skills are architects, surveyors, civil engineers, soil conservationists, and urban and regional planners. Landscape architects also know how to grow and use plants in the landscape. Botanists, who study plants in general, and horticulturists, who study ornamental plants as well as fruit, vegetable, greenhouse, and nursery crops, do similar work.

Sources of Additional Information

Additional information, including a list of colleges and universities offering accredited programs in landscape architecture, is available from:

☛ American Society of Landscape Architects, Career Information, 636 Eye Street, NW., Washington, DC 20001. Internet: **http://www.asla.org**

General information on registration or licensing requirements is available from:

☛ Council of Landscape Architectural Registration Boards, 12700 Fair Lakes Circle, Suite 110, Fairfax, VA 22033.

Surveyors, Cartographers, Photogrammetrists, and Surveying Technicians

(O*NET 22311A, 22311B, 22521A, 22521B, and 25103B)

Significant Points

- Over 8 out of 10 are employed in engineering services and government.
- Computer skills enhance employment opportunities.

Nature of the Work

Measuring and mapping the earth's surface is the responsibility of several different types of workers. Traditional *land surveyors* establish official land, air space, and water boundaries. They write descriptions of land for deeds, leases, and other legal documents; define air space for airports; and measure construction and mineral sites. Other surveyors provide data relevant to the shape, contour, location, elevation, or dimension of land or land features. *Surveying technicians* assist land surveyors by operating survey instruments and collecting information. *Cartographers* compile geographic, political, and cultural information and prepare maps of large areas.

Land surveyors manage survey parties that measure distances, directions, and angles between points and elevations of points, lines, and contours on the earth's surface. They plan the fieldwork, select known survey reference points, and determine the precise location of important features in the survey area. Surveyors research legal records and look for evidence of previous boundaries. They record the results of the survey, verify the accuracy of data, and prepare plots, maps, and reports. Surveyors who establish boundaries must be licensed by the State in which they work.

A survey party gathers the information needed by the land surveyor. A typical survey party consists of a party chief and several surveying technicians and helpers. The party chief, who may be either a land surveyor or a senior surveying technician, leads day-to-day work activities. Surveying technicians assist the party chief by adjusting and operating surveying instruments, such as the theodolite (used to measure horizontal and vertical angles) and electronic distance-measuring equipment. Surveying technicians or assistants position and hold the vertical rods, or targets, that the theodolite operator sights on to measure angles, distances, or elevations. They may also hold measuring tapes, if electronic distance-measuring equipment is not used. Surveying technicians compile notes, make sketches, and enter the data obtained from these instruments into computers. Survey parties may include laborers or helpers who perform less skilled duties, such as clearing brush from sight lines, driving stakes, or carrying equipment.

New technology is changing the nature of the work of surveyors and surveying technicians. For larger projects, surveyors are increasingly using the Global Positioning System (GPS), a satellite system that precisely locates points on the earth by using radio signals transmitted via satellites. To use this system, a surveyor places a satellite signal receiver—a small instrument mounted on a tripod—on a desired point. The receiver simultaneously collects information from several satellites to locate a precise position. The receiver can also be placed in a vehicle for tracing out road systems. Since receivers now come in different sizes and shapes and the cost of the receivers has fallen, much more surveying work is being done using GPS. Surveyors then must interpret and check the results produced by the new technology.

Cartographers measure, map, and chart the earth's surface, which involves everything from geographical research and data compilation to actual map production. They collect, analyze, and interpret both spatial data—such as latitude, longitude, elevation, and distance—and nonspatial data—such as population density, land use patterns, annual precipitation levels, and demographic characteristics. Cartographers prepare maps in either digital or graphic form, using information provided by geodetic surveys, aerial photographs, and satellite data. *Photogrammetrists* prepare detailed maps and drawings from aerial photographs, usually of areas that are inaccessible or difficult to survey by other methods. *Map editors* develop and verify map contents from aerial photographs and other reference sources.

Some surveyors perform specialized functions that are closer to those of a cartographer than to those of a traditional surveyor. For example, *geodetic surveyors* use high-accuracy techniques, including satellite observations, to measure large areas of the earth's surface. *Geophysical prospecting surveyors* mark sites for subsurface exploration, usually petroleum related. *Marine surveyors* survey harbors, rivers, and other bodies of water to determine shorelines, topography of the bottom, water depth, and other features.

The work of surveyors and cartographers is changing because of advancements in technology. These advancements include not only the GPS, but also new earth resources data satellites, improved aerial photography, and geographic information systems (GIS)—which are computerized data banks of spatial data. From the older specialties of photogrammetrist and cartographer, a new type of mapping scientist is emerging. The *geographic information specialist* combines the functions of mapping science and surveying into a broader field concerned with the collection and analysis of geographic information.

Working Conditions

Surveyors usually work an 8-hour day, 5 days a week, and may spend a lot of time outdoors. Sometimes they work longer hours during the summer, when weather and light conditions are most suitable for fieldwork.

A surveyor sets up equipment to measure and record recent changes to the topography.

Land surveyors and technicians engage in active, and sometimes strenuous, work. They often stand for long periods, walk considerable distances, and climb hills with heavy packs of instruments and other equipment. They can also be exposed to all types of weather. Traveling is often part of the job; they may commute long distances, stay overnight, or temporarily relocate near a survey site.

While surveyors can spend considerable time inside planning surveys, analyzing data, and preparing reports and maps, cartographers spend virtually all their time in offices and seldom visit the sites they are mapping.

Employment

Surveyors, cartographers, photogrammetrists, and surveying technicians held about 110,000 jobs in 1998. Engineering and architectural services firms employed about 64 percent of these workers. Federal, State, and local governmental agencies employed an additional 17 percent. Major Federal Governmental employers are the U.S. Geological Survey, the Bureau of Land Management, the Army Corps of Engineers, the Forest Service, the National Oceanic and Atmospheric Administration, and the National Imagery and Mapping Agency (NIMA). Most surveyors in State and local government work for highway departments and urban planning and redevelopment agencies. Construction firms, mining and oil and gas extraction companies, and public utilities also employ surveyors, cartographers, photogrammetrists, and surveying technicians. About 6,800 were self-employed in 1998.

Training, Other Qualifications, and Advancement

Most people prepare for a career as a licensed surveyor by combining postsecondary school courses in surveying with extensive on-the-job training. However, as technology advances, a 4-year degree is becoming more of a prerequisite. About 25 universities now offer 4-year programs leading to a B.S. degree in surveying. Junior and community colleges, technical institutes, and vocational schools offer 1-, 2-, and 3-year programs in both surveying and surveying technology.

All 50 States license land surveyors. For licensure, most State licensing boards require that individuals pass two written examinations, one prepared by the State and one given by the National Council of Examiners for Engineering and Surveying. In addition, they must meet varying standards of formal education and work experience in the field. In the past, many individuals started as members of survey crews and worked their way up to become licensed surveyors with little formal training in surveying. However, because of advancing technology and an increase in licensing standards, formal education requirements are increasing. At present, most States require some formal post-high school education coursework and 10 to 12 years of surveying experience to gain licensure. However, requirements vary among States. Generally, the quickest route to licensure is a combination of 4 years of college, 2 to 4 years of experience (a few States do not require any), and passing the licensing examinations. An increasing number of States require a bachelor's degree in surveying or in a closely related field, such as civil engineering or forestry (with courses in surveying), regardless of the number of years of experience.

High school students interested in surveying should take courses in algebra, geometry, trigonometry, drafting, mechanical drawing, and computer science. High school graduates with no formal training in surveying usually start as an apprentice. Beginners with postsecondary school training in surveying can usually start as technicians or assistants. With on-the-job experience and formal training in surveying—either in an institutional program or from a correspondence school—workers may advance to senior survey technician, then to party chief, and in some cases, to licensed surveyor (depending on State licensing requirements).

The American Congress on Surveying and Mapping has a voluntary certification program for surveying technicians. Technicians are certified at four levels requiring progressive amounts of experience, in addition to passing written examinations. Although not required for State licensure, many employers require certification for promotion to positions with greater responsibilities.

Surveyors should have the ability to visualize objects, distances, sizes, and abstract forms. They must work with precision and accuracy because mistakes can be costly. Members of a survey party must be in good physical condition, because they work outdoors and often carry equipment over difficult terrain. They need good eyesight, coordination, and hearing to communicate verbally and manually (using hand signals). Surveying is a cooperative process, so good interpersonal skills and the ability to work as part of a team are important. Leadership qualities are important for party chief and other supervisory positions.

Cartographers and photogrammetrists usually have a bachelor's degree in a field such as engineering, forestry, geography, or a physical science. Although it is possible to enter these positions through previous experience as a photogrammetric or cartographic technician, most cartographic and photogrammetric technicians now have had some specialized postsecondary school training. With the development of Geographic Information Systems, cartographers and photogrammetrists need additional education and stronger technical skills—including more experience with computers—than in the past.

The American Society for Photogrammetry and Remote Sensing has a voluntary certification program for photogrammetrists. To qualify for this professional distinction, individuals must meet work experience standards and pass an oral or written examination.

Job Outlook

Overall employment of surveyors, cartographers, photogrammetrists, and surveying technicians is expected to grow about as fast as the average through the year 2008. The widespread availability and use of advanced technologies, such as the Global Positioning System, Geographic Information Systems, and remote sensing, are increasing both the accuracy and productivity of survey and mapping work. Job openings, however, will continue to result from the need to replace workers who transfer to other occupations or leave the labor force altogether.

Prospects will be best for surveying technicians, whose growth is expected to be slightly faster than the average for all occupations through 2008. The short training period needed to learn to operate the equipment, the current lack of any formal testing or licensing, and the relatively lower wages all make for a healthy demand for these technicians, as well as for a readily available supply.

As technologies become more complex, opportunities will be best for surveyors, cartographers, and photogrammetrists who have at least a bachelor's degree and strong technical skills. Increasing demand for geographic data, as opposed to traditional surveying services, will mean better opportunities for cartographers and photogrammetrists involved in the development and use of geographic and land information systems. New technologies, such as GPS and GIS may also enhance employment opportunities for surveyors and surveying technicians who have the educational background enabling them to use these systems, but upgraded licensing requirements will continue to limit opportunities for those with less education.

Even as demand increases in nontraditional areas such as urban planning and natural resource exploration and mapping, opportunities for surveyors, cartographers, and photogrammetrists should remain concentrated in engineering, architectural, and surveying services firms. Growth in construction through 2008 should require surveyors to lay out streets, shopping centers, housing developments, factories, office buildings, and recreation areas. However, employment may fluctuate from year to year along with construction activity.

Earnings

Median annual earnings of surveyors, cartographers, and photogrammetrists were $37,640 in 1998. The middle 50 percent earned between $27,580 and $50,380. The lowest 10 percent earned less than $21,510 and the highest 10 percent earned more than $76,880.

Median hourly earnings of surveying technicians were $11.20 in 1997 for those employed in engineering and architectural services, while those employed by local governments received median hourly earnings of $13.50. The middle 50 percent of all surveying technicians earned between $9.86 and $16.54 in 1998. The lowest 10 percent earned less than $7.61 and the highest 10 percent earned more than $21.14.

In 1999, land surveyors in nonsupervisory, supervisory, and managerial positions in the Federal Government earned an average salary of $52,400; cartographers earned an average salary of $56,300. The average Federal salary for geodetic technicians is $48,800; for surveying technicians, about $31,300; and for cartographic technicians, about $37,200.

Related Occupations

Surveying is related to the work of civil engineers and architects, since an accurate survey is the first step in land development and construction projects. Cartography and geodetic surveying are related to the work of geologists and geophysicists, who study the earth's internal composition, surface, and atmosphere. Cartography is also related to the work of geographers and urban planners, who study and decide how the earth's surface is used.

Sources of Additional Information

Information about career opportunities, licensure requirements, and the surveying technician certification program is available from:

☛ American Congress on Surveying and Mapping, 5410 Grosvenor Lane, Suite 100, Bethesda, MD 20814-2122.

General information on careers in photogrammetry is available from:

☛ ASPRS: The Imaging and Geospacial Information Society, 5410 Grosvenor Lane, Suite 210, Bethesda, MD 20814.

General information on careers in cartography is available from:

☛ North American Cartographic Information Society, P.O. Box 399, Milwaukee, WI 53201-0399.

Computer, Mathematical, and Operations Research Occupations

Actuaries

(O*NET 25313)

Significant Points

- A strong background in mathematics is essential for an actuary.
- About 2 out of 3 actuaries are employed in the insurance industry.
- Employment opportunities will be good despite the limited number of openings in this small occupation as stringent qualifying requirements induced by the examination system limit the number of new entrants.

Nature of the Work

Actuaries are essential employees because they determine future risk, make price decisions, and formulate investment strategies. Some actuaries also design insurance, financial, and pension plans and ensure that these plans are maintained on a sound financial basis. Most actuaries specialize in life and health or property and casualty insurance; others work primarily in finance or employee benefits. Some use a broad knowledge of business and mathematics in investment, risk classification, or pension planning.

Regardless of specialty, actuaries assemble and analyze data to estimate probabilities of an event taking place, such as death, sickness, injury, disability, or property loss. They also address financial questions, including the level of pension contributions required to produce a certain retirement income level or the projected future return on investments. Moreover, actuaries may help determine company policy and sometimes explain complex technical matters to company executives, government officials, shareholders, policyholders, or the public in general. They may testify before public agencies on proposed legislation affecting their businesses or explain changes in contract provisions to customers. They also may help companies develop plans to enter new lines of business.

Most actuaries are employed in the insurance industry, in which they estimate the amount a company will pay in claims. For example, property/casualty actuaries calculate the expected amount of claims resulting from automobile accidents, which varies depending on the insured person's age, sex, driving history, type of car, and other factors. Actuaries ensure that the price, or premium, charged for such insurance will enable the company to cover claims and other expenses. This premium must be profitable and yet competitive with other insurance companies.

Actuaries employed in other industries perform several different functions. The small but growing group of actuaries in the financial services industry, for example, manages credit and helps price corporate security offerings. Because banks now offer their customers investment products such as annuities and asset management services, actuaries increasingly help financial institutions manage the substantial risks associated with these products. Actuaries employed as pension actuaries enrolled under the provisions of the Employee Retirement Income Security Act of 1974 (ERISA) evaluate pension plans covered by that act and report on their financial soundness to plan members, sponsors, and Federal regulators.

In addition to salaried actuaries, numerous consulting actuaries provide advice to clients on a contract basis. Their clients include insurance companies, corporations, health maintenance organizations, health care providers, government agencies, and attorneys. The duties of most consulting actuaries are similar to those of other actuaries. For example, some design pension plans through calculating the future value of current deductions from earnings and determining the amount of employer contributions. Others provide advice to health care plans or financial services firms. Consultants sometimes testify in court regarding the value of potential lifetime earnings of a person who is disabled or killed in an accident, the current value of future pension benefits in divorce cases, or other complex calculations. Many consulting actuaries work in reinsurance, where one insurance company arranges to share a large prospective liability policy with another insurance company in exchange for a percentage of the premium.

Working Conditions

Actuaries have desk jobs, and their offices are usually comfortable and pleasant. They often work at least 40 hours a week. Some actuaries, particularly consulting actuaries, may travel to meet with clients. Consulting actuaries may also experience more erratic employment and be expected to work more than 40 hours per week.

Employment

Actuaries held about 16,000 jobs in 1998. Almost one-half of the actuaries who were wage and salary workers were employed in the insurance industry. Some had jobs in life and health insurance companies, while property and casualty insurance companies, pension funds, or insurance agents and brokers employed others. Most of the remaining actuaries worked for firms providing services, especially management and public relations, or for actuarial consulting services. A relatively small number of actuaries were employed by security and commodity brokers or government agencies. Some developed computer software for actuarial calculations. In 1998, 2,300 actuaries were self-employed.

Using their broad knowledge of business and mathematics, actuaries work in investment, risk classification, and employee benefits.

Training, Other Qualifications, and Advancement

Applicants for beginning actuarial jobs usually have a bachelor's degree in mathematics, actuarial science, statistics, or a business-related discipline, such as economics, finance, or accounting. About 55 colleges and universities offer an actuarial science program, and most colleges and universities offer a degree in mathematics or statistics. Some companies hire applicants without specifying a major, provided that the applicant has a working knowledge of mathematics, including calculus, probability, and statistics, and has demonstrated this ability by passing at least the beginning few actuarial exams required for professional designation. Courses in economics, accounting, computer science, finance, and insurance are also useful. Companies increasingly prefer well-rounded individuals who, in addition to a strong technical background, have some training in liberal arts and business.

Two professional societies sponsor programs leading to full professional status in their specialty. The first, the Society of Actuaries (SOA), administers a series of actuarial examinations for the life and health insurance, pension, and finance and investment fields. The Casualty Actuarial Society (CAS), on the other hand, gives a series of examinations for the property and casualty field, which includes fire, accident, medical malpractice, workers compensation, and personal injury liability.

The first parts of the SOA and CAS examination series are jointly sponsored by the two societies and cover the same material. For this reason, students do not need to commit themselves to a specialty until they have taken the initial examinations. These examinations test an individual's competence in probability, calculus, statistics, and other branches of mathematics. The first few examinations help students evaluate their potential as actuaries. Those who pass one or more examinations have better opportunities for employment at higher starting salaries than those who do not.

Actuaries are encouraged to complete the entire series of examinations as soon as possible, advancing first to the Associate level, and then to the Fellowship level. Advanced casualty topics include investment and assets, dynamic financial analysis, and valuation of insurance topics. Completion of the examination process usually takes from 5 to 10 years. Examinations are given twice a year, in May and November. Although many companies allot time to their employees for study, extensive home study is required to pass the examinations, and many actuaries study for months to prepare for each examination. It is likewise common for employers to pay the hundreds of dollars for fees and study materials. Most reach the Associate level within 4 to 6 years and the Fellowship level a few years later.

Specific requirements apply for pension actuaries, who verify the financial status of defined benefit pension plans to the Federal Government. These actuaries must be enrolled by the Joint Board for the Enrollment of Actuaries. To qualify for enrollment, applicants must meet certain experience and examination requirements, as stipulated by the Joint Board.

To perform their duties effectively, actuaries must keep up with current economic and social trends and legislation, as well as developments in health, business, finance, and economics that could affect insurance or investment practices. Good communication and interpersonal skills are also important, particularly for prospective consulting actuaries.

Beginning actuaries often rotate among different jobs in an organization to learn various actuarial operations and phases of insurance work, such as marketing, underwriting, and product development. At first, they prepare data for actuarial projects or perform other simple tasks. As they gain experience, actuaries may supervise clerks, prepare correspondence, draft reports, and conduct research. They may move from one company to another early in their careers as they move up to higher positions.

Advancement depends largely on job performance and the number of actuarial examinations passed. Actuaries with a broad knowledge of the insurance, pension, investment, or employee benefits fields can advance to administrative and executive positions in their companies. Actuaries with supervisory ability may advance to management positions in other areas, such as underwriting, accounting, data processing, marketing, or advertising. Some actuaries assume faculty positions in the Nation's colleges and universities. (See the statement on college and university faculty elsewhere in the *Handbook*.)

Job Outlook

Employment of actuaries is expected to grow more slowly than the average for all occupations through 2008. Although expected growth in managed health plans in the health services industry should provide good prospects for actuaries, anticipated downsizing and merger activity in the insurance agent and broker industry will adversely affect the outlook for these workers. Prospective actuaries who pass several beginning actuarial exams will find relatively few job openings. The number of openings to replace those who leave the occupation each year is limited and new openings are restricted by the relatively small size of the occupation.

Actuarial employment is projected to grow in property and casualty insurance as this sector experiences growth in terms of employment and billing. Actuaries will continue to be involved in the development of product liability insurance, medical malpractice, and workers' compensation coverage. The development of new financial tools such as dynamic financial analysis has increased the demand for property and casualty actuaries. The growing need to evaluate catastrophic risks such as earthquakes and calculate prices for insuring facilities against such risks is another source of increasing demand for property and casualty actuaries. Planning for the systematic financing of environmental risks, such as toxic waste clean-up, will further lift demand for actuaries in this specialty.

Employment of consulting actuaries is expected to grow faster than employment of actuaries among life insurance carriers—traditionally the leading employer of actuaries. As many life insurance carriers seek to boost profitability by streamlining operations, actuarial employment may be cut back. Investment firms and large corporations may increasingly turn to consultants to provide actuarial services formerly performed in-house.

Earnings

Median annual earnings of actuaries were $65,560 in 1998. The middle 50 percent earned between $45,560 and $89,860. The lowest 10 percent had earnings of less than $36,000, while the top 10 percent earned over $123,810. The average salary for actuaries employed by the Federal government was $72,800 in early 1999. According to the National Association of Colleges and Employers, annual starting salaries for bachelor's degree graduates in mathematics/actuarial science averaged about $37,300 in 1999.

Insurance companies and consulting firms give merit increases to actuaries as they gain experience and pass examinations. Some companies also offer cash bonuses for each professional designation achieved. A 1998 salary survey of insurance and financial services companies, conducted by the Life Office Management Association, Inc., indicated that the average base salary for an entry-level actuary with the largest U. S. companies was about $41,500. Associate Actuaries with the largest U. S. companies, who direct and provide leadership in the design, pricing, and implementation of insurance products, received an average salary of $88,000. Actuaries at the highest technical level without managerial responsibilities in the same size companies earned an average of $101,600.

Related Occupations

Actuaries determine the probability of income or loss from various risk factors. Other workers whose jobs involve related skills include accountants, economists, financial analysts, mathematicians, and statisticians.

Sources of Additional Information

For facts about actuarial careers, contact:

☛ American Academy of Actuaries, 1100 17th St. NW., 7th Floor, Washington, DC 20036. Internet: **http://www.actuary.org/index.htm**

For information about actuarial careers in life and health insurance, employee benefits and pensions, and finance and investments, contact:

☛ Society of Actuaries, 475 N. Martingale Rd., Suite 800, Schaumburg, IL 60173-2226. Internet: **http://www.soa.org**

For information about actuarial careers in property and casualty insurance, contact:

☛ Casualty Actuarial Society, 1100 N. Glebe Rd., Suite 600, Arlington, VA 22201. Internet: **http://www.casact.org**

Career information on actuaries specializing in pensions is available from:

☛ American Society of Pension Actuaries, 4350 N. Fairfax Dr., Suite 820, Arlington, VA 22203. Internet: **http://www.aspa.org**

Computer Systems Analysts, Engineers, and Scientists

(O*NET 21114C, 22127, 25102, 25103A, 25104, and 25199A)

Significant Points

- As computer applications continue to expand, these occupations are projected to be the fastest growing and rank among the top 20 in the number of new jobs created over the 1998-2008 period.
- Relevant work experience and a bachelor's degree are prerequisites for many jobs; for more complex jobs, a graduate degree is preferred.

Nature of the Work

The rapid spread of computers and information technology has generated a need for highly trained workers to design and develop new hardware and software systems and to incorporate new technologies. These workers—computer systems analysts, engineers, and scientists—include a wide range of computer-related occupations. Job tasks and occupational titles used to describe this broad category of workers evolve rapidly, reflecting new areas of specialization or changes in technology, as well as the preferences and practices of employers.

Systems analysts solve computer problems and enable computer technology to meet individual needs of an organization. They help an organization realize the maximum benefit from its investment in equipment, personnel, and business processes. This process may include planning and developing new computer systems or devising ways to apply existing systems' resources to additional operations. Systems analysts may design new systems, including both hardware and software, or add a new software application to harness more of the computer's power. Most systems analysts work with a specific type of system that varies with the type of organization they work for—for example, business, accounting or financial systems, or scientific and engineering systems. Systems development workers are also referred to as a *systems developer* and *systems architect*.

Analysts begin an assignment by discussing the systems problem with managers and users to determine its exact nature. They define the goals of the system and divide the solutions into individual steps and separate procedures. Analysts use techniques such as structured analysis, data modeling, information engineering, mathematical model building, sampling, and cost accounting to plan the system. They specify the inputs to be accessed by the system, design the processing steps, and format the output to meet the users' needs. They also may prepare cost-benefit and return-on-investment analyses to help management decide whether implementing the proposed system will be financially feasible.

When a system is accepted, analysts determine what computer hardware and software will be needed to set it up. They coordinate tests and observe initial use of the system to ensure it performs as planned. They prepare specifications, work diagrams, and structure charts for computer programmers to follow and then work with them to "debug," or eliminate errors from the system. Analysts, who do more in-depth testing of products, may be referred to as *software quality assurance analysts.* In addition to running tests, these individuals diagnose problems, recommend solutions, and determine if program requirements have been met.

In some organizations, *programmer-analysts* design and update the software that runs a computer. Because they are responsible for both programming and systems analysis, these workers must be proficient in both areas. (A separate statement on computer programmers appears elsewhere in the *Handbook.*) As this becomes more commonplace, these analysts increasingly work with object-oriented programming languages, as well as client/server applications development, and multimedia and Internet technology.

One obstacle associated with expanding computer use is the need for different computer systems to communicate with each other. Because of the importance of maintaining up-to-date information—accounting records, sales figures, or budget projections, for example—systems analysts work on making the computer systems within an organization compatible so that information can be shared. Many systems analysts are involved with "networking," connecting all the computers internally—in an individual office, department, or establishment—or externally, since many organizations now rely on e-mail or the World Wide Web. A primary goal of networking is to allow users to retrieve data and information from a mainframe computer or a server and use it on their machine. Analysts must design the hardware and software to allow free exchange of data, custom applications, and the computer power to process it all.

Networks come in many variations and *network systems and data communications analysts* design, test, and evaluate systems such as Local Area Networks (LAN), Wide Area Networks (WAN), Internet, Intranet, and other data communications systems. These analysts perform network modeling, analysis and planning; they may also research related products and make necessary hardware and software recommendations. *Telecommunications specialists* focus on the interaction between computer and communications equipment.

Computer engineers also work with the hardware and software aspects of systems design and development. They usually apply the theories and principles of science and mathematics to design hardware, software, networks, and processes and to solve technical problems. Whereas their work emphasizes the application of theory, computer engineers are also involved in building prototypes. They often work as part of a team that designs new computing devices or computer-related equipment, systems, or software. *Computer hardware engineers* usually design, develop, test, and supervise the manufacture of computer hardware—such as chips or device controllers. *Software engineers*, on the other hand, can be involved in the design and development of software systems for control and automation of manufacturing, business, and management processes. They may research, design, and test operating system software, compilers—software that converts programs for faster processing—and network distribution software. Software engineers or *software developers* working in applications development analyze users' needs and design, create, and modify general computer applications software or specialized utility programs. These professionals also possess strong programming skills, but they are more concerned with analyzing and solving programming problems than with writing code for programs. Some software engineers develop both packaged and systems software or create customized software applications for clients.

The title *computer scientist* can be applied to a wide range of computer professionals who usually design computers and the software that runs them, develop information technologies, and develop and adapt principles for applying computers to new uses. Computer scientists perform many of the same duties as other computer professionals, but their jobs are distinguished by the higher level of theoretical expertise and innovation they apply to complex problems and the creation or application of new technology.

Computer scientists can work as theorists, researchers, or inventors. Those employed by academic institutions work in areas ranging from complexity theory, to hardware, to programming language design. Some work on multi-disciplinary projects, such as developing and advancing uses of virtual reality in robotics. Their counterparts in private industry work in areas such as applying theory, developing specialized languages or information technologies, or designing programming tools, knowledge-based systems, or even computer games.

Database administrators work with database management systems software and determine ways to organize and store data. They set up computer databases and test and coordinate changes to them. Since they also may design implementation and system security, database administrators often plan and coordinate security measures.

Computer support specialists provide technical assistance, support, and advice to customers and users. This group includes *technical support specialists*, *help-desk technicians*, and *customer service representatives.* These troubleshooters interpret problems and provide technical support for hardware, software, and systems. They answer phone calls, use automated diagnostic programs, and resolve recurrent problems. Support specialists may work within an organization or directly for a computer or software vendor. Increasingly, these technical professionals work for help-desk or support services firms, where they provide customer support on a contract basis to clients as more of this type of work is outsourced.

Other computer scientists include workers who are involved in analysis, application, or design of a particular system or piece of the system. *Network* or *computer systems administrators*, for example, design, install, and support an organization's LAN, WAN, network segment, Internet or Intranet system. They maintain network hardware and software, analyze problems, and monitor the network to ensure availability to system users. Administrators also may plan, coordinate, and implement network security measures. In some organizations, *computer security specialists* may plan, coordinate, and implement the organization's information security. These and other

Computer support specialists answer phone calls, use automated diagnostic programs, and resolve problems.

growing specialty occupations reflect the increasing emphasis on client-server applications, the growth of the Internet, the expansion of World Wide Web applications and Intranets, and the demand for more end-user support. In addition, growth of the Internet and expansion of the World Wide Web, the graphical portion of the Internet, have generated a variety of occupations relating to design, development, and maintenance of websites and their servers. For example, *webmasters* are responsible for all technical aspects of a website, including performance issues such as speed of access, and for approving site content. *Internet* or *web developers*, also called *web designers*, are responsible for day-to-day site design and creation.

Working Conditions

Computer systems analysts, engineers and other computer scientists normally work in offices or laboratories in comfortable surroundings. They usually work about 40 hours a week—the same as many other professional or office workers. However, evening or weekend work may be necessary to meet deadlines or solve specific problems. Given the technology available today, telecommuting is common for computer professionals. As networks expand, more work, including technical support, can be done from remote locations using modems, laptops, electronic mail, and the Internet. For example, it is possible for technical personnel, such as computer support specialists, to connect to a customer's computer remotely to identify and fix problems.

Like other workers who spend long periods of time in front of a computer terminal typing on a keyboard, they are susceptible to eye strain, back discomfort, and hand and wrist problems such as carpal tunnel syndrome or cumulative trauma disorder.

Employment

Computer systems analysts, engineers, and scientists held about 1.5 million jobs in 1998, including about 114,000 who were self-employed. Their employment was distributed among the following detailed occupations:

Occupation	Jobs
Computer systems analysts	617,000
Computer support specialists	429,000
Computer engineers	299,000
Database administrators	87,000
All other computer scientists	97,000

Although they are increasingly employed in every sector of the economy, the greatest concentration of these workers is in the computer and data processing services industry. Firms in this industry provide nearly every service related to commercial computer use on a contract basis. Services include customized computer programming services and applications and systems software design; the design, development, and production of prepackaged computer software; systems integration, networking, and reengineering services; data processing and preparation services; information retrieval services including on-line databases and Internet services; on-site computer facilities management; the development and management of databases; and a variety of specialized consulting services. Many work in other areas, such as for government agencies, manufacturers of computer and related electronic equipment, insurance companies, financial institutions, and universities.

A growing number of computer professionals are employed on a temporary or contract basis—many of whom are self-employed, working independently as contractors or self-employed consultants. For example, a company installing a new computer system may need the services of several systems analysts just to get the system running. Because not all of them would be needed once the system is functioning, the company might contract with systems analysts or a temporary help agency or consulting firm. Such jobs may last from several months up to 2 years or more. This growing practice enables companies to bring in people with the exact skills they need to complete a particular project, rather than having to spend time or money training or retraining existing workers. Often, experienced consultants then train a company's in-house staff as a project develops.

Training, Other Qualifications, and Advancement

Due to the wide range of skills required, there are many ways workers enter computer-related occupations. Someone staffing a help-desk, for example, needs skills and training that differ from those of a computer engineer designing chips or a Webmaster responsible for creating and maintaining a web page. While there is no universally accepted way to prepare for a job as a computer professional, most employers place a premium on some formal college education. A bachelor's degree is a prerequisite for many jobs; however, some jobs may require only a 2-year degree. Relevant work experience also is very important. For more complex jobs, persons with graduate degrees are preferred.

Computer hardware engineers usually need a bachelor's degree in computer engineering or electrical engineering, whereas software engineers are more likely to hold a degree in computer science or in software engineering. Computer engineering programs emphasize hardware and may be offered as a degree option or in conjunction with electrical and electronics engineering. As a result, graduates of a computer engineering program from a school or college of engineering often find jobs designing and developing computer hardware or related equipment, even though they also have the skills required for developing systems or software. For computer science, however, there is more variation in where the department falls within an institution. Some may be part of a school or college of liberal arts while others may be within colleges of natural or applied sciences. Unless the program is part of the engineering department, the focus is on software, and graduates may work in areas of software engineering. A Ph.D., or at least a master's degree, in computer science or engineering is usually required for jobs in research laboratories or academic institutions.

For systems analyst, programmer-analyst, or even database administrator positions, many employers seek applicants who have a bachelor's degree in computer science, information science, or management information systems (MIS). Management information systems programs are usually part of the business school or college. These programs differ considerably from computer science programs, emphasizing business and management oriented coursework and business computing courses.

Despite the preference towards technical degrees, persons with degrees in a variety of majors find employment in computer-related occupations. The level of education and type of training employers require depend on employers' needs. One factor affecting these needs is changes in technology. As demonstrated by the current demand for workers with skills related to the Internet or World Wide Web, employers often scramble to find workers capable of implementing "hot" new technologies. Another factor driving employers' needs is the time frame in which a project must be completed.

Most community colleges and many independent technical institutes and proprietary schools offer an associate degree in computer science or a related information technology field. Many of these programs may be more geared toward meeting the needs of local businesses and more occupation specific than those designed for a 4-year degree. Some jobs may be better suited to the level of training these programs offer. Computer support specialists, for example, usually need only an associate's degree in a computer-related field, as well as significant hands on experience with computers.

Employers usually look for people who have broad knowledge of and experience with computer systems and technologies, strong problem solving and analysis skills, and good interpersonal skills. Courses in computer programming or systems design offer good preparation for a job in this field. For jobs in a business environment, employers usually want systems analysts to have business management or closely related skills, while a background in the physical sciences, applied mathematics, or engineering is preferred for work in scientifically oriented organizations. Art or graphic design skills may be desirable for webmasters or web developers.

Jobseekers can enhance their employment opportunities by participating in internship or co-op programs offered through their schools. Because many people develop advanced computer skills in one occupation and then transfer those skills into a computer occupation, a related background in the industry in which the job is located, such as financial services, banking, or accounting, can be important. Others have taken computer programming courses to supplement their study in fields such as accounting, inventory control, or other business areas. For example, a financial analyst proficient in computers might become a systems analyst or computer support specialist in financial systems development, while a computer programmer might move into a systems analyst job.

Computer systems analysts, engineers, and scientists must be able to think logically and have good communication skills. They often deal with a number of tasks simultaneously; the ability to concentrate and pay close attention to detail is important. Although computer specialists sometimes work independently, they often work in teams on large projects. They must be able to communicate effectively with computer personnel, such as programmers and managers, as well as with users or other staff who may have no technical computer background.

Computer engineers and scientists employed in industry may advance into managerial or project leadership positions. Those employed in academic institutions can become heads of research departments or published authorities in their field. Systems analysts may be promoted to senior or lead systems analyst. Those who show leadership ability also can become project managers or advance into management positions such as manager of information systems or chief information officer. Technical support specialists may also advance by developing expertise in an area that leads to other opportunities. For example, those responsible for network support may advance into network administration or network security. Computer professionals with work experience and considerable expertise in a particular subject area or application may find lucrative opportunities as independent consultants or choose to start their own computer consulting firms.

Technological advances come so rapidly in the computer field that continuous study is necessary to keep skills up to date. Employers, hardware and software vendors, colleges and universities, and private training institutions offer continuing education. Additional training may come from professional development seminars offered by professional computing societies.

Technical or professional certification is a way to demonstrate a level of competency or quality in a particular field. Product vendors or software firms also offer certification and may require professionals who work with their products to be certified. Many are widely sought and considered industry standards. Voluntary certification is also available through other organizations. Professional certification may provide a job seeker a competitive advantage.

Job Outlook

Computer systems analysts, engineers, and scientists are expected to be the fastest growing occupations through 2008. Employment of computing professionals is expected to increase much faster than average as technology becomes more sophisticated and organizations continue to adopt and integrate these technologies. Growth will be driven by very rapid growth in computer and data processing services, which is projected to be the fastest growing industry in the U.S. economy. In addition, thousands of job openings will arise annually from the need to replace workers who move into managerial positions or other occupations or who leave the labor force.

The demand for networking to facilitate the sharing of information, the expansion of client/server environments, and the need for specialists to use their knowledge and skills in a problem solving capacity will be major factors in the rising demand for computer systems analysts, engineers, and scientists. Moreover, falling prices of computer hardware and software should continue to induce more businesses to expand computerized operations and integrate new technologies. In order to maintain a competitive edge and operate more cost effectively, firms will continue to demand computer professionals who are knowledgeable about the latest technologies and able to apply them to meet the needs of businesses.

Increasingly, more sophisticated and complex technology is being made available to individual users who can design and implement more of their own applications and programs. The result is a growing demand for computer support specialists, help-desk personnel, and technical consultants. Likewise, the explosive growth in electronic commerce—doing business on the World Wide Web—and the continuing need to build and maintain databases that store critical information on customers, inventory, and projects is fueling demand for database administrators current on the latest technology.

New growth areas usually arise from the development of new technologies. The expanding integration of Internet technologies by businesses, for example, has resulted in a rising demand for a variety of skilled professionals who can develop and support Internet, Intranet, and web applications. The growth of electronic commerce means more establishments use the Internet to conduct their business on line. This translates into a need for information technology professionals who can help organizations use technology to communicate with employees, clients, and consumers. Explosive growth in these areas is also expected to fuel demand for specialists knowledgeable about network, data, and communications security.

As technology becomes more sophisticated and complex, employers in all areas demand a higher level of skill and expertise. Individuals with an advanced degree in computer science, computer engineering, or an MBA with a concentration in information systems should enjoy very favorable employment prospects. College graduates with a bachelor's degree in computer science, computer engineering, information science, or management information systems should also enjoy favorable prospects for employment, particularly if they have supplemented their formal education with practical experience. Because employers continue to seek computer professionals who can combine strong technical skills with good interpersonal and business skills, graduates with non-computer science degrees, who have had courses in computer programming, systems analysis, and other information technology areas, should also continue to find jobs as computer professionals. In fact, individuals with the right experience and training can work in a computer-related occupation regardless of their major or level of formal education.

Earnings

Median annual earnings of computer systems analysts were $52,180 in 1998. The middle 50 percent earned between $40,570 and $74,180 a year. The lowest 10 percent earned less than $32,470 and the highest 10 percent earned more than $87,810. Median annual earnings in the industries employing the largest numbers of computer systems analysts in 1997 were:

Industry	Earnings
Telephone communications	$63,300
Federal Government	56,900
Computer and data processing services	51,000
State government, except education and hospitals	43,500
Colleges and universities	38,400

Median annual earnings of computer engineers were $61,910 in 1998. The middle 50 percent earned between $46,240 and $80,500. The lowest 10 percent earned less than $37,150 and the highest 10 percent earned more than $92,850. Median annual earnings in the industries employing the largest numbers of computer engineers in 1997 were:

Computer and office equipment	$63,700
Measuring and controlling devices	62,000
Management and public relations	59,000
Computer and data processing services	56,700
Guided missiles, space vehicles, and parts	49,500

Median annual earnings of computer support specialists were $37,120 in 1998. The middle 50 percent earned between $28,880 and $48,810. The lowest 10 percent earned less than $22,930 and the highest 10 percent earned more than $73,790. Median annual earnings in the industries employing the largest numbers of computer support specialists in 1997 were:

Management and public relations	$37,900
Computer and data processing services	36,300
Computer and office equipment	36,300
Professional and commercial equipment	35,700
Personnel supply services	35,200

Median annual earnings of database administrators were $47,980 in 1998. The middle 50 percent earned between $36,440 and $69,920. The lowest 10 percent earned less than $28,320 and the highest 10 percent earned more than $86,200. Median annual earnings of database administrators employed in computer and data processing services in 1997 were $49,000.

Median annual earnings of all other computer scientists were $46,670 in 1998. The middle 50 percent earned between $34,290 and $70,250. The lowest 10 percent earned less than $26,690 and the highest 10 percent earned more than $87,730. Median annual earnings of all other computer scientists employed in computer and data processing services were $46,500 and in personnel supply services, $33,600 in 1997.

Starting salaries for computer scientists or computer engineers with a bachelor's degree can be significantly higher than starting salaries of bachelor's degree graduates in many other fields. According to the National Association of Colleges and Employers, starting salary offers for graduates with a bachelor's degree in computer engineering averaged about $45,700 in 1999; those with a master's degree, $58,700. Starting offers for graduates with a bachelor's degree in computer science averaged about $44,600; in computer programming, about $40,800; in information sciences, about $38,900; and in management information systems, $41,800 in 1999. Offers for those with the bachelor's degree vary by functional area for all types of employers, as shown in the following tabulation.

Hardware design and development	$45,900
Software design and development	45,600
Information systems	41,600
Systems analysis and design	41,100

Offers for graduates with a master's degree in computer science in 1999 averaged $51,400.

According to Robert Half International, starting salaries in 1999 ranged from $61,300 to $88,000 for database administrators, from $42,800 to $59,800 for network administrators, and from $27,000 to $46,000 for help-desk support staff. Starting salaries in software development ranged from $55,000 to $80,000 for software engineers and from $50,000 to $65,000 for software installer/developers. Salaries for Internet-related occupations ranged from $50,000 to $73,800 for security administrators, $51,500 to $73,000 for webmasters, and from $47,000 to $65,500 for web developers.

Related Occupations

Other workers who use research, logic, and creativity to solve business problems are computer programmers, financial analysts, urban planners, engineers, mathematicians, statisticians, operations research analysts, management analysts, and actuaries.

Sources of Additional Information

Further information about computer careers is available from:

☛ Association for Computing Machinery (ACM), 1515 Broadway, New York, NY 10036. Internet: **http://www.acm.org**

☛ Institute of Electrical and Electronics Engineers—United States of America, 1828 L Street, NW., Suite 1202, Washington, DC 20036. Internet: **http://www.ieee.org**

Information about becoming a Certified Computing Professional is available from:

☛ Institute for Certification of Computing Professionals (ICCP), 2200 East Devon Ave., Suite 268, Des Plaines, IL 60018. Internet: **http://www.iccp.org**

Information about becoming a Certified Quality Analyst is available from:

☛ Quality Assurance Institute, 7575 Dr. Phillips Blvd., Suite 350, Orlando, FL 32819. Internet: **http://www.qai.org**

Computer Programmers

(O*NET 25105)

Significant Points

- The level of education and experience required by employers has been rising, due to the increasing complexity of programming.
- A growing number of computer programmers are employed on a temporary or contract basis.
- Job prospects should be best for college graduates who are up to date with the latest skills and technologies.

Nature of the Work

Computer programmers write, test, and maintain the detailed instructions, called programs or software, that computers must follow to perform their functions. They also conceive, design, and test logical structures for solving problems by computer. Many technical innovations in programming—advanced computing technologies and sophisticated new languages and programming tools—have redefined the role of a programmer and elevated much of the programming work done today. As a result, it is becoming more difficult to distinguish different computer specialists—including programmers—since job titles shift so rapidly, reflecting new areas of specialization or changes in technology. Job titles and descriptions also may vary, depending on the organization. In this occupational statement, computer programmer refers to individuals whose main job function is programming; this group has a wide range of responsibilities and educational backgrounds.

Computer programs tell the computer what to do, such as which information to identify and access, how to process it, and what equipment to use. Programs vary widely depending upon the type of information to be accessed or generated. For example, the instructions involved in updating financial records are very different from those required to duplicate conditions on board an aircraft for pilots training in a flight simulator. Although simple programs can be written in a few hours, programs that use complex mathematical formulas, whose solutions can only be approximated, or that draw data from many existing systems, may require more than a year of work. In most cases, several programmers work together as a team under a senior programmer's supervision.

Programmers write specific programs by breaking down each step into a logical series of instructions the computer can follow. They then code these instructions in a conventional programming language, such as COBOL; an artificial intelligence language, such as

Prolog; or one of the most advanced function-oriented or object-oriented languages, such as Java, C++, or Visual Basic. Programmers usually know more than one programming language; and since many languages are similar, they can often learn new languages relatively easily. In practice, programmers are often referred to by the language they know, such as Java programmers, or the type of function they perform or environment in which they work, such as database programmers, mainframe programmers, or Internet programmers. In many large organizations, programmers follow descriptions that have been prepared by software engineers or systems analysts. These descriptions list the input required, the steps the computer must follow to process data, and the desired arrangement of the output.

Many programmers are involved in updating, repairing, modifying and expanding existing programs. When making changes to a section of code, called a *routine*, programmers need to make other users aware of the task the routine is to perform. They do this by inserting comments in the coded instructions, so others can understand the program. Innovations such as computer-aided software engineering (CASE) tools enable a programmer to concentrate on writing the unique parts of the program, because the tools automate various pieces of the program being built. CASE tools generate whole sections of code automatically, rather than line by line. This also yields more reliable and consistent programs and increases programmers' productivity by eliminating some routine steps.

Programmers test a program by running it, to ensure the instructions are correct and it produces the desired information. If errors do occur, the programmer must make the appropriate change and recheck the program until it produces the correct results, a process called debugging. Programmers working in a mainframe environment may prepare instructions for a computer operator who will run the program. (A separate statement on computer operators appears elsewhere in the *Handbook.*) They may also contribute to a manual for users.

Programmers often are grouped into two broad types: applications programmers and systems programmers. *Applications programmers* usually focus on business, engineering, or science. They write software to handle a specific job, such as a program to track inventory, within an organization. They may also revise existing packaged software. *Systems programmers*, on the other hand, maintain and control computer systems software, such as operating systems, networked systems and database systems. These workers make changes in the sets of instructions that determine how the network, workstations, and central processing unit of the system handle the various jobs they have been given and how they communicate with peripheral equipment, such as terminals, printers, and disk drives. Because of their knowledge of the entire computer system, systems programmers often help applications programmers determine the source of problems that may occur with their programs.

Programmers in software development companies may work directly with experts from various fields to create software—either programs designed for specific clients or packaged software for general use—ranging from games and educational software to programs for desktop publishing, financial planning, and spreadsheets. Much of this type of programming is in the preparation of packaged software, which comprises one of the most rapidly growing segments of the computer services industry.

In some organizations, particularly small ones, workers commonly referred to as *programmer-analysts* are responsible for both the systems analysis and the actual programming work. (A more detailed description of the work of programmer-analysts is presented in the statement on computer systems analysts, engineers, and scientists elsewhere in the *Handbook.*) Advanced programming languages and new object-oriented programming capabilities are increasing the efficiency and productivity of both programmers and users. The transition from a mainframe environment to one that is primarily personal computer (PC) based has blurred the once rigid distinction between the programmer and the user. Increasingly, adept end-users are taking over many of the tasks previously performed by programmers. For example, the growing use of packaged software, like spreadsheet and database management software packages, allows users to write simple programs to access data and perform calculations.

Programmers must ensure that the program produces the correct results.

Working Conditions

Programmers generally work in offices in comfortable surroundings. Many programmers may work long hours or weekends, to meet deadlines or fix critical problems that occur during off hours. Given the technology available, telecommuting is becoming common for a wide range of computer professionals—including computer programmers. Programmers can access a system from remote locations, to make corrections or fix problems.

Like other workers who spend long periods of time in front of a computer terminal typing at a keyboard, programmers are susceptible to eyestrain, back discomfort, and hand and wrist problems, such as carpal tunnel syndrome.

Employment

Computer programmers held about 648,000 jobs in 1998. Programmers are employed in almost every industry, but the largest concentration is in the computer and data processing services industry, which includes firms that write and sell software. Large numbers of programmers can also be found working for firms that provide engineering and management services, telecommunications companies, manufacturers of computer and office equipment, financial institutions, insurance carriers, educational institutions, and government agencies.

A growing number of computer programmers are employed on a temporary or contract basis or work as independent consultants, as companies demand expertise with new programming languages or specialized areas of application. Rather than hiring programmers as permanent employees and then laying them off after a job is completed, employers can contract with temporary help agencies, consulting firms, or directly with programmers themselves. A marketing firm, for example, may only require the services of several programmers to write and debug the software necessary to get a new data base-management system running. This practice also enables companies to bring in people with a specific set of skills—usually in one of the latest technologies—as it applies to their business needs. Bringing in an independent contractor or consultant with a certain level of experience in a new or advanced programming language, for example, enables an establishment to complete a particular job without having to retrain existing workers. Such jobs may last anywhere from several weeks to a year or longer. There were 31,000 self-employed computer programmers in 1998, and this number is expected to increase.

Training, Other Qualifications, and Advancement

While there are many training paths available for programmers, mainly because employers' needs are so varied, the level of education and experience employers seek has been rising, due to the growing number of qualified applicants and the increasing complexity of some programming tasks. Bachelor's degrees are now commonly required, although some programmers may qualify for certain jobs with 2-year degrees or certificates. College graduates who are interested in changing careers or developing an area of expertise also may return to a 2-year community college or technical school for additional training. In the absence of a degree, substantial specialized experience or expertise may be needed. Even with a degree, employers appear to be placing more emphasis on previous experience, for all types of programmers.

Table 1. Highest level of school completed or degree received, computer programmers, 1998

	Percent
High school graduate or equivalent or less	10.6
Some college, no degree	20.5
Associate degree	10.2
Bachelor's degree	45.3
Graduate degree	13.4

About 3 out of 5 computer programmers had a bachelor's degree or higher in 1998 (see table 1). Of these, some hold a degree in computer science, mathematics, or information systems, whereas others have taken special courses in computer programming, to supplement their study in fields such as accounting, inventory control, or other areas of business. As the level of education and training required by employers continues to rise, this percentage should increase in the future.

Required skills vary from job to job, but the demand for various skills is generally driven by changes in technology. Employers using computers for scientific or engineering applications usually prefer college graduates who have degrees in computer or information science, mathematics, engineering, or the physical sciences. Graduate degrees in related fields are required for some jobs. Employers who use computers for business applications prefer to hire people who have had college courses in information systems (MIS) and business and who possess strong programming skills. Although knowledge of traditional languages is still important, increasing emphasis is placed on newer, object-oriented programming languages and tools, such as C++, Visual Basic, and Java. Additionally, employers are seeking persons familiar with fourth and fifth generation languages that involve graphic user interface (GUI) and systems programming. Employers also prefer applicants who have general business skills and experience related to the operations of the firm. Students can improve their employment prospects by participating in a college work-study program or by undertaking an internship.

Most systems programmers hold a 4-year degree in computer science. Extensive knowledge of a variety of operating systems is essential. This includes being able to configure an operating system to work with different types of hardware and adapting the operating system to best meet the needs of a particular organization. Programmers must also be able to work with database systems, such as DB2, Oracle, or Sybase, for example.

When hiring programmers, employers look for people with the necessary programming skills who can think logically and pay close attention to detail. The job calls for patience, persistence, and the ability to work on exacting analytical work, especially under pressure. Ingenuity and imagination are also particularly important, when programmers design solutions and test their work for potential failures. The ability to work with abstract concepts and to do technical analysis is especially important for systems programmers, because they work with the software that controls the computer's operation. Since programmers are expected to work in teams and interact directly with users, employers want programmers who are able to communicate with nontechnical personnel.

Entry-level or junior programmers may work alone on simple assignments after some initial instruction or on a team with more experienced programmers. Either way, beginning programmers generally must work under close supervision. Because technology changes so rapidly, programmers must continuously update their training, by taking courses sponsored by their employer or software vendors.

For skilled workers who keep up to date with the latest technology, the prospects for advancement are good. In large organizations, programmers may be promoted to lead programmer and be given supervisory responsibilities. Some applications programmers may move into systems programming after they gain experience and take courses in systems software. With general business experience, programmers may become programmer analysts or systems analysts or be promoted to a managerial position. Other programmers, with specialized knowledge and experience with a language or operating system, may work in research and development areas, such as multimedia or Internet technology. As employers increasingly contract out programming jobs, more opportunities should arise for experienced programmers with expertise in a specific area to work as consultants.

Technical or professional certification is a way to demonstrate a level of competency or quality. Product vendors or software firms also offer certification and may require professionals who work with their products to be certified. Many are widely sought and considered industry standards. Voluntary certification is also available through other organizations. Professional certification may provide a job seeker a competitive advantage.

Job Outlook

Employment of programmers is expected to grow faster than the average for all occupations through 2008. Jobs for both systems and applications programmers should be plentiful in data processing service firms, software houses, and computer consulting businesses. These types of establishments are part of computer and data processing services, which is projected to be the fastest growing industry in the economy. As organizations attempt to control costs and keep up with changing technology, they will maintain a need for programmers to assist in conversions to new computer languages and systems. In addition, numerous job openings will result from the need to replace programmers who leave the labor force or transfer to other occupations such as manager or systems analyst.

Despite numerous openings, a number of factors will continue to moderate employment growth. The consolidation and centralization of systems and applications, developments in packaged software, advanced programming languages and tools, and the growing ability of users to design, write, and implement more of their own programs means more of the programming functions can be transferred to other types of workers. Furthermore, completion of Year 2000 work will mean that many programmers will need to be retrained and redeployed in other areas. And, as the level of technological innovation and sophistication increases, programmers should continue to face increasing competition from programming businesses overseas where much routine work can be outsourced at a lower cost.

Nevertheless, employers will continue to need programmers with strong technical skills who understand an employer's business and its programming needs. Given the importance of networking and the expansion of client/server environments, organizations will look for programmers who can support data communications and help implement electronic commerce and intranet strategies. Demand for programmers with strong object-oriented programming capabilities and technical specialization in areas such as client/server programming, multimedia technology, and graphic user interface (GUI), should arise from the expansion of intranets, extranets, and World Wide Web applications. Programmers will also be needed to create and maintain expert systems and embed these technologies in more and more products.

As programming tasks become increasingly sophisticated and an additional level of skill and experience is demanded by employers, graduates of 2-year programs and people with less than a 2-year degree or its equivalent in work experience should face strong competition for programming jobs. Competition for entry-level positions, however, can also affect applicants with a bachelor's degree. Prospects should be best for college graduates with knowledge of, and experience working with, a variety of programming languages and tools—including C++ and other object-oriented languages like Visual Basic and Java, as well as newer, domain-specific languages that apply to computer networking, data base management, and Internet application development. Because demand fluctuates with employers' needs, job seekers should keep up to date with the latest skills and technologies. Individuals who want to become programmers can enhance their prospects by combining the appropriate formal training with practical work experience.

Earnings

Median annual earnings of computer programmers were $47,550 in 1998. The middle 50 percent earned between $36,020 and $70,610 a year. The lowest 10 percent earned less than $27,670; the highest 10 percent earned more than $88,730. Median annual earnings in the industries employing the largest numbers of computer programmers in 1997 were:

Industry	Earnings
Personnel supply services	$53,700
Computer and data processing services	48,900
Telephone communications	48,800
Professional and commercial equipment	47,700
Management and public relations	46,400

According to the National Association of Colleges and Employers, starting salary offers for graduates with a bachelor's degree in computer programming averaged about $40,800 a year in 1999.

Programmers working in the West or Northeast earned somewhat more than those working in the South or Midwest. On average, systems programmers earn more than applications programmers.

According to Robert Half International, average annual starting salaries in 1999 ranged from $38,000 to $50,500 for applications development programmers and from $49,000 to $63,000 for systems programmers. Average starting salaries for Internet programmers ranged from $48,800 to $68,300.

Related Occupations

Other professional workers who must be detail-oriented include computer scientists, computer engineers, systems analysts, database administrators, statisticians, mathematicians, engineers, financial analysts, accountants, actuaries, and operations research analysts.

Sources of Additional Information

State employment service offices can provide information about job openings for computer programmers. Also check with your city's chamber of commerce for information on the area's largest employers.

For information about certification as a computing professional, contact:

☛ Institute for Certification of Computing Professionals (ICCP), 2200 East Devon Ave., Suite 268, Des Plaines, IL 60018. Internet: **http://www.iccp.org**

Further information about computer careers is available from:

☛ The Association for Computing Machinery (ACM), 1515 Broadway, New York, NY 10036. Internet: **http://www.acm.org**

☛ Institute of Electrical and Electronics Engineers—United States of America, 1828 L St. NW., Suite 1202, Washington, DC 20036. Internet: **http://www.ieee.org**

Mathematicians

(O*NET 25319A, 25319B, and 25319C)

Significant Points

- Employment is expected to decline because few mathematics graduates get jobs that have the title mathematician.
- Bachelor's and master's degree holders with extensive training in mathematics and a related discipline, such as computer science, economics, engineering, or operations research, should have good employment opportunities in related occupations.

Nature of the Work

Mathematics is one of the oldest and most fundamental sciences. Mathematicians use mathematical theory, computational techniques, algorithms, and the latest computer technology to solve economic, scientific, engineering, physics, and business problems. The work of mathematicians falls into two broad classes—theoretical (pure) mathematics and applied mathematics. These classes, however, are not sharply defined and often overlap.

Theoretical mathematicians advance mathematical knowledge by developing new principles and recognizing previously unknown relationships between existing principles of mathematics. Although they seek to increase basic knowledge without necessarily considering its practical use, such pure and abstract knowledge has been instrumental in producing or furthering many scientific and engineering achievements.

Applied mathematicians, on the other hand, use theories and techniques, such as mathematical modeling and computational methods, to formulate and solve practical problems in business, government, engineering, and the physical, life, and social sciences. For example, they may analyze the most efficient way to schedule airline routes between cities, the effect and safety of new drugs, the aerodynamic characteristics of an experimental automobile, or the cost effectiveness of alternate manufacturing processes for a businesses. Applied mathematicians working in industrial research and development may develop or enhance mathematical methods when solving a difficult problem. Some mathematicians, called cryptanalysts, analyze and decipher encryption systems designed to transmit military, political, financial, or law enforcement-related information in code.

Mathematicians use computers extensively to analyze data and develop models.

Applied mathematicians start with a practical problem, envision the separate elements of the process under consideration, and then reduce the elements into mathematical variables. They often use computers to analyze relationships among the variables and solve complex problems through developing models with alternate solutions.

Much of the work in applied mathematics is done by individuals with titles other than mathematician. In fact, because mathematics is the foundation upon which so many other academic disciplines are built, the number of workers using mathematical techniques is much greater than the number formally designated as mathematicians. For example, engineers, computer scientists, physicists, and economists are among those who use mathematics extensively. Some professionals, including statisticians, actuaries, and operations research analysts, actually are specialists in a particular branch of mathematics. (For more information, see statements on actuaries, operations research analysts, and statisticians elsewhere in the *Handbook*.)

Working Conditions

Mathematicians usually work in comfortable offices. They are often part of an interdisciplinary team that may include economists, engineers, computer scientists, physicists, technicians, and others. Deadlines, overtime work, special requests for information or analysis, and prolonged travel to attend seminars or conferences may be part of their jobs. Mathematicians who work in academia usually have a mix of teaching and research responsibilities.

Employment

Mathematicians held about 14,000 jobs in 1998. In addition, about 20,000 persons held mathematics faculty positions in colleges and universities in 1998, according to the American Mathematical Society. (See the statement on college and university faculty elsewhere in the *Handbook.*)

Many nonfaculty mathematicians work for Federal or State governments. The Department of Defense is the primary Federal employer of mathematicians, accounting for almost three-fourths of the mathematicians employed by the Federal Government. In the private sector, major employers include research and testing services, educational services, security and commodity exchanges, and management and public relations services. Within manufacturing, the drug industry is the key employer. Some mathematicians also work for banks, insurance companies, and public utilities.

Training, Other Qualifications, and Advancement

A doctoral degree in mathematics is usually the minimum education needed for prospective mathematicians, with the exception of the Federal Government. In the Federal Government, entry-level job candidates usually must have a 4-year degree with a major in mathematics or a 4-year degree with the equivalent of a mathematics major—24 semester hours of mathematics courses.

In private industry, job candidates typically need a Ph.D. degree to obtain jobs as mathematicians. Most of the positions designated for mathematicians are in research and development laboratories as part of technical teams. These research scientists engage in either basic research on pure mathematical principles or in applied research on developing or improving specific products or processes. The majority of those with a bachelor's or master's degree in mathematics who work in private industry do so not as mathematicians, but in related fields such as computer science, where they have titles such as computer programmer, systems analyst, or systems engineer.

A bachelor's degree in mathematics is offered by most colleges and universities. Mathematics courses usually required for this degree are calculus, differential equations, and linear and abstract algebra. Additional courses might include probability theory and statistics, mathematical analysis, numerical analysis, topology, discrete mathematics, and mathematical logic. Many colleges and universities urge or require students majoring in mathematics to take courses in a field that is closely related to mathematics, such as computer science, engineering, life science, physical science, or economics. A double major in mathematics and another discipline such as computer science, economics, or one of the sciences is particularly desirable to many employers. A prospective college mathematics major should take as many mathematics courses as possible while in high school.

In 1998, about 240 colleges and universities offered a master's degree as the highest degree in either pure or applied mathematics; and about 200 offered a Ph.D. in pure or applied mathematics. In graduate school, students conduct research and take advanced courses, usually specializing in a subfield of mathematics.

For work in applied mathematics, training in the field in which the mathematics will be used is very important. Mathematics is used extensively in the fields of physics, actuarial science, statistics, engineering, and operations research. Computer science, business and industrial management, economics, chemistry, geology, life sciences, and behavioral sciences are likewise dependent on applied mathematics. Mathematicians also should have substantial knowledge of computer programming because most complex mathematical computation and much mathematical modeling is done on a computer.

Mathematicians need good reasoning ability and persistence in order to identify, analyze, and apply basic principles to technical problems. Communication skills are also important, as mathematicians must be able to interact and discuss proposed solutions with people who may not have an extensive knowledge of mathematics.

Job Outlook

Employment of mathematicians is expected to decrease through 2008. The number of jobs available for workers whose educational background is solely in mathematics is not expected to increase significantly. Those whose educational background includes the study of a related discipline such as statistics or computer science will have better job opportunities. Advancements in technology usually lead to expanding applications of mathematics, and more workers with knowledge of mathematics will be required in the future. Many of these workers have job titles that reflect their occupation rather than the discipline of mathematics used in their work.

Bachelor's degree holders in mathematics are usually not qualified for most jobs as mathematicians. However, those with a strong background in computer science, electrical or mechanical engineering, or operations research should have good opportunities. In addition, bachelor's degree holders who meet State certification requirements may become high school mathematics teachers. (For additional information, see the statement on kindergarten, elementary, and secondary school teachers elsewhere in the *Handbook*.)

Holders of a master's degree in mathematics will face very strong competition for jobs in theoretical research. Similar to bachelor's degree holders, however, job opportunities in applied mathematics and related areas, such as computer programming, operations research, and engineering design will be more numerous. Academia continues to produce more Ph.D.s than the number of university positions available, so many of these mathematicians will need to find employment in industry and government.

Earnings

Median annual earnings of mathematicians were $49,120 in 1998. The middle 50 percent earned between $33,420 and $77,300. The lowest 10 percent had earnings of less than $25,150, while the top 10 percent earned over $101,990.

According to a 1999 survey by the National Association of Colleges and Employers, starting salary offers for mathematics graduates with a bachelor's degree averaged about $37,300 a year and for those with a master's degree, $42,000. Doctoral degree candidates averaged $58,900. The average annual salary for mathematicians employed by the Federal Government in supervisory, nonsupervisory, and managerial positions was $69,000; for mathematical statisticians, $69,000; and for cryptanalysts, $61,100 in early 1999.

Related Occupations

Other occupations that require extensive knowledge of mathematics or, in some cases, a degree in mathematics include actuary, statistician, computer programmer, systems analyst, systems engineer, and operations research analyst. A strong background in mathematics also facilitates employment in engineering, economics, finance, and physics.

Sources of Additional Information

For more information about careers and training in mathematics, especially for doctoral level employment, contact:

☛ American Mathematical Society, Department of Professional Programs and Services, P.O. Box 6248, Providence, RI 02940-6248.
Internet: **http://www.ams.org**

For more information about careers and training in mathematics, contact:

☛ Mathematical Association of America, 1529 18th St. NW., Washington, DC 20036. Internet: **http://www.maa.org**

For a 1998 resource guide on careers in mathematical sciences, contact:

☛ Conference Board of the Mathematical Sciences, 1529 18th St. NW., Washington, DC 20036. Internet: **http://www.maa.org/cbms/cbms.html**

For specific information on careers in applied mathematics, contact:

☛ Society for Industrial and Applied Mathematics, 3600 University City Science Center, Philadelphia, PA 19104-2688.
Internet: **http://www.siam.org/alterindex.htm**

Information on obtaining a job as a mathematician with the Federal Government may be obtained from the Office of Personnel Management through a telephone-based system. Consult your telephone directory under U.S. Government for a local number or call (912) 757-3000; TDD (912) 744-2299. This number is not toll free and charges may result. Information may also be obtained through their Internet site: **http:// www.usajobs.opm.gov**

Operations Research Analysts

(O*NET 25302)

Significant Points

- Individuals with a master's or Ph.D. degree in management science, operations research, or a closely related field should have good job prospects.
- Employment growth is projected to be slower than average.

Nature of the Work

Operations research (OR) and management science are terms that are used interchangeably to describe the discipline of applying quantitative techniques to make decisions and solve problems. Many methods used in operations research were developed during World War II to help take the guesswork out of missions such as deploying radar, searching for enemy submarines, and getting supplies where they were most needed. Following the war, numerous peacetime applications emerged, leading to the use of OR and management science in many industries and occupations.

The prevalence of operations research in the Nation's economy reflects the growing complexity of managing large organizations that require the efficient use of materials, equipment, and people. OR analysts determine the optimal means of coordinating these elements to achieve specified goals by applying mathematical principles to organizational problems. They solve problems in different ways and propose alternative solutions to management, which then chooses the course of action that best meets their goals. In general, OR analysts are concerned with issues such as strategy, forecasting, resource allocation, facilities layout, inventory control, personnel schedules, and distribution systems.

The duties of the operations research analyst vary according to the structure and management philosophy of the employer or client. Some firms centralize operations research in one department; others use operations research in each division. Some organizations contract operations research services with a consulting firm. Economists, systems analysts, mathematicians, industrial engineers, and others may apply operations research techniques to address problems in their respective fields. Operations research analysts may also work closely with senior managers to identify and solve a variety of problems.

Regardless of the type or structure of the client organization, operations research in its classical role of carrying out analysis to support management's quest for performance improvement entails a similar set of procedures. Managers begin the process by describing the symptoms of a problem to the analyst, who then formally defines the problem. For example, an operations research analyst for an auto manufacturer may be asked to determine the best inventory level for each of the parts needed on a production line and to determine the number of windshields to be kept in inventory. Too many windshields would be wasteful and expensive, while too few could result in an unintended halt in production.

Operations research analysts study such problems, then break them into their component parts. Analysts then gather information about each of these parts from a variety of sources. To determine the most efficient amount of inventory to be kept on hand, for example, OR analysts might talk with engineers about production levels, discuss purchasing arrangements with buyers, and examine data on storage costs provided by the accounting department.

With this information in hand, the analyst is ready to select the most appropriate analytical technique. Analysts could use several techniques—including simulation, linear and non-linear optimization, networks, waiting lines, discrete and random variables methods, dynamic programming, queuing models and other stochastic-process models, Markov decision processes, econometric methods, data envelopment analysis, neural networks, genetic algorithms, decision analysis, and the analytic hierarchy process. All of these techniques, however, involve the construction of a mathematical model that attempts to describe the system in use. The use of models enables the analyst to assign values to the different components, and determine the relationships between them. These values can be altered to examine what will happen to the system under different circumstances.

In most cases, the computer program used to solve the model must be modified repeatedly to reflect these different solutions. A model for airline flight scheduling, for example, might include variables for the cities to be connected, amount of fuel required to fly the routes, projected levels of passenger demand, varying ticket and fuel prices, pilot scheduling, and maintenance costs. By choosing different variables for the model, the analyst is able to produce the best flight schedule consistent with various sets of assumptions.

Upon concluding the analysis, the operations research analyst presents management with recommendations based on the results of the analysis. Additional computer programming based on different assumptions may be needed to help select the best recommendation offered by the OR analyst. Once management reaches a decision, the analyst may work with others in the organization to ensure the plan's successful implementation.

Working Conditions

Operations research analysts generally work regular hours in an office environment. Because they work on projects that are of immediate interest to top management, OR analysts often are under pressure to meet deadlines and work more than a 40-hour week.

Employment

Operations research analysts held about 76,000 jobs in 1998. Major employers include telecommunication companies, air carriers, computer and data processing services, financial institutions, insurance carriers, engineering and management services firms, and the Federal Government. Most operations research analysts in the Federal Government work for the Armed Forces, and many OR analysts in private industry work directly or indirectly on national defense. About 1 out of 5 analysts work for management, research, public relations, and testing agencies that do operations research consulting.

Operations research analysts use mathematical models to break down problems into their components before finding a solution.

Training, Other Qualifications, and Advancement

Employers generally prefer applicants with at least a master's degree in operations research, engineering, business, mathematics, information systems, or management science, coupled with a bachelor's degree in computer science or a quantitative discipline such as economics, mathematics, or statistics. Dual graduate degrees in operations research and computer science are especially attractive to employers. Operations research analysts also must be able to think logically and work well with people, and employers prefer workers with good oral and written communication skills.

In addition to formal education, employers often sponsor training for experienced workers, helping them keep up with new developments in OR techniques and computer science. Some analysts attend advanced university classes on these subjects at their employer's expense.

Because computers are the most important tools for quantitative analysis, training and experience in programming are required. Operations research analysts typically need to be proficient in database collection and management, programming, and in the development and use of sophisticated software programs.

Beginning analysts usually perform routine work under the supervision of more experienced analysts. As they gain knowledge and experience, they are assigned more complex tasks and given greater autonomy to design models and solve problems. Operations research analysts advance by assuming positions as technical specialists or supervisors. The skills acquired by operations research analysts are useful for higher-level management jobs, and experienced analysts may leave the field to assume nontechnical managerial or administrative positions.

Job Outlook

Individuals who hold a master's or Ph.D. degree in operations research, management science, or a closely related field should find good job opportunities through 2008, as the number of openings generated by employment growth and the need to replace those leaving the occupation is expected to exceed the number of persons graduating with these credentials. In addition, graduates with bachelor's degrees in operations research or management science from the limited number of schools offering these degree programs should find opportunities in a variety of related fields that allow them to use their quantitative abilities.

The slower than average employment growth expected for OR analysts will be driven by the continuing use of operations research and management science techniques to improve productivity, ensure quality, and reduce costs in private industry and government. This should result in a steady demand for workers knowledgeable in operations research techniques in the years ahead. Nevertheless, this growth will be relatively slow because few job openings in this field are expected to have the title operations research analyst.

Earnings

Median annual earnings of OR analysts were $49,070 in 1998. The middle 50 percent earned between $36,890 and $72,090. The lowest 10 percent had earnings of less than $29,780, while the top 10 percent earned over $87,720. Median annual earnings in the industries employing the largest number of OR analysts in 1997 are shown below.

Research and testing services	$64,000
Computer and data processing services	45,400
Commercial banks	37,500

The average annual salary for operations research analysts in the Federal Government in nonsupervisory, supervisory, and managerial positions was $72,000 in early 1999.

Related Occupations

Operations research analysts apply mathematical principles to large, complicated problems. Workers in other occupations that stress quantitative analysis include computer scientists, systems analysts, modeling specialists, logistics consultants, engineers, mathematicians, statisticians, and economists. Because its goal is improved organizational effectiveness, operations research also is closely allied to managerial occupations.

Sources of Additional Information

Information on career opportunities for operations research analysts is available from:

☛ The Institute for Operations Research and the Management Sciences, 901 Elkridge Landing Rd., Suite 400, Linthicum, MD 21090. Internet: **http://www.informs.org**

For information on OR careers in the Armed Forces and Department of Defense, contact:

☛ Military Operations Research Society, 101 South Whiting St., Suite 202, Alexandria, VA 22304. Internet: **http://www.mors.org**

Statisticians

(O*NET 25312)

Significant Points

- Many individuals with degrees in statistics enter jobs that do not have the title statistician.
- Job prospects as a statistician in private industry and academia will be best for those with a graduate degree and some work experience in statistics.

Nature of the Work

Statistics is the scientific application of mathematical principles to the collection, analysis and presentation of numerical data. Statisticians contribute to scientific inquiry by applying their mathematical knowledge to the design of surveys and experiments; collection, processing, and analysis of data; and interpretation of the results. Statisticians often apply their knowledge of statistical methods to a variety of subject areas, such as biology, economics, engineering, medicine, public health, psychology, marketing, and education. Many applications cannot occur without use of statistical techniques, such as designing experiments to gain Federal approval of a newly manufactured drug.

One especially useful technique used by statisticians is sampling—obtaining information about a population of people or group of things by surveying a small portion of the total. For example, to determine the size of the audience for particular programs, television-rating services survey only a few thousand families, rather than all viewers. Statisticians decide where and how to gather the data, determine the type and size of the sample group, and develop the survey questionnaire or reporting form. They also prepare instructions for workers who will collect and tabulate the data. Finally, statisticians analyze, interpret, and summarize the data using computer software.

In manufacturing industries, statisticians play an important role in quality control and product improvement. In an automobile company, for example, statisticians might design experiments to determine the failure time of engines exposed to extreme weather conditions by running individual engines until failure and breakdown. Such destructive tests are conducted on a representative sample of

Statisticians need good communication skills to convey complex ideas to a nontechnical audience.

the engines, and the results enable the company to identify changes that can improve engine performance.

Because statistical specialists are used in so many work areas, specialists who use statistics often have different professional designations. For example, a person using statistical methods on economic data may have the title econometrician, while statisticians in public health and medicine may hold titles of biostatistician, biometrician, or epidemiologist. (See the statement on economists and marketing research analysts elsewhere in the *Handbook*).

Working Conditions

Statisticians usually work regular hours in comfortable offices. Some statisticians travel to provide advice on research projects, supervise and set up surveys, or gather statistical data. Some may have duties that vary widely, such as designing experiments or performing fieldwork in various communities. Statisticians who work in academia generally have a mix of teaching and research responsibilities.

Employment

Persons holding the title of statistician held about 17,000 jobs in 1998. Over one-fourth of these jobs were in the Federal Government, where statisticians were concentrated in the Departments of Commerce, Agriculture, and Health and Human Services. Most of the remaining jobs were in private industry, especially in the biopharmaceutical industry. In addition, many professionals with a background in statistics were among the 20,000 mathematics faculty in colleges and universities in 1998, according to the American Mathematical Society. (See the statement on college and university faculty elsewhere in the *Handbook.*)

Training, Other Qualifications, and Advancement

Although more employment opportunities are becoming available to well qualified statisticians with bachelor's degrees, a master's degree in statistics or mathematics is the minimum educational requirement for most jobs with job title statistician. Research positions in institutions of higher education, for example, require a graduate degree, usually a doctorate, in statistics. Beginning positions in industrial research often require a master's degree combined with several years of experience.

The training required for employment as an entry level statistician in the Federal Government, however, is a bachelor's degree, including at least 15 semester hours of statistics or a combination of 15 hours of mathematics and statistics, if at least 6 semester hours are in statistics. Qualifying as a mathematical statistician in the Federal Government requires 24 semester hours of mathematics and statistics with a minimum of 6 semester hours in statistics and 12 semester hours in an area of advanced mathematics, such as calculus, differential equations, or vector analysis.

About 80 colleges and universities offered bachelor's degrees in statistics in 1998. Many other schools also offered degrees in mathematics, operations research, and other fields, which included a sufficient number of courses in statistics to qualify graduates for some beginning positions in the Federal Government. Required subjects for statistics majors include differential and integral calculus, statistical methods, mathematical modeling, and probability theory. Additional courses that undergraduates should take include linear algebra, design and analysis of experiments, applied multivariate analysis, and mathematical statistics.

In 1998, approximately 110 universities offered a master's degree program in statistics, and about 60 offered a doctoral degree program. Many other schools also offered graduate-level courses in applied statistics for students majoring in biology, business, economics, education, engineering, psychology, and other fields. Acceptance into graduate statistics programs does not require an undergraduate degree in statistics, although good training in mathematics is essential.

Because computers are used extensively for statistical applications, a strong background in computer science is highly recommended. For positions involving quality and productivity improvement, training in engineering or physical science is useful. A background in biological, chemical, or health science is important for positions involving the preparation and testing of pharmaceutical or agricultural products. Courses in economics and business administration are helpful for many jobs in market research, business analysis, and forecasting.

Good communications skills are important for prospective statisticians, in order to qualify for many positions in industry, where the need to explain technical matters to laymen is common. A solid understanding of business and the economy is important for those who plan to work in private industry.

Beginning statisticians are assigned work supervised by an experienced statistician. With experience, they may advance to positions with ample technical and supervisory responsibility. However, opportunities for promotion increase with advanced degrees. Master's and Ph.D. degree holders usually enjoy independence in their work and become qualified to engage in research, develop statistical methods, or, after a number of years of experience in a particular area, become statistical consultants.

Job Outlook

Job opportunities should remain favorable for individuals with statistical degrees, although many of these positions will not carry an explicit job title of statistician. Employment of those with the title statistician is expected to grow little through the year 2008. Many individuals will find positions in which they do not have the title statistician. This is especially true for those involved in analyzing and interpreting data from other disciplines such as economics, biological science, psychology, or engineering. In addition to the limited number of jobs resulting from growth, a number of openings will become available as statisticians retire, transfer to other occupations, or leave the work force for other reasons.

Among graduates with a bachelor's degree in statistics, those with a strong background in an allied field, such as finance, engineering, or computer science, should have the best prospects of finding jobs related to their field of study. Federal agencies will hire statisticians in many fields, including demography, agriculture, consumer and producer surveys, Social Security, health care, and environmental quality. Competition for entry level positions in the Federal Government is expected to be strong for those just meeting the minimum qualification standards for statisticians, since this is one of the few employers that considers a bachelor's degree to be an adequate entry level qualification. Those who meet State certification requirements may become high school statistics teachers. (For additional information, see the statement on kindergarten, elementary, and secondary school teachers elsewhere in the *Handbook*.)

Manufacturing firms will hire statisticians at the master's and doctoral degree levels for quality control of various products, including pharmaceuticals, motor vehicles, chemicals, and food. For example, pharmaceutical firms employ statisticians to assess the safety and effectiveness of new drugs. To address global product competition, motor vehicle manufacturers will need statisticians to improve the quality of automobiles, trucks, and their components by developing and testing new designs. Statisticians with knowledge of engineering and the physical sciences will find jobs in research and development, working with teams of scientists and engineers to help improve design and production processes to ensure consistent quality of newly developed products. Business firms will rely heavily on workers with a background in statistics, to forecast sales, analyze business conditions, and help solve management problems in order to maximize profits. In addition, sophisticated statistical services will increasingly be offered to other businesses by consulting firms.

Earnings

Median annual earnings of statisticians were $48,540 in 1998. The middle 50 percent earned between $35,800 and $71,030. The lowest 10 percent had earnings of less than $28,240, while the top 10 percent earned over $87,180. The average annual salary for statisticians in the Federal Government in nonsupervisory, supervisory, and managerial positions was $62,800 in early 1999, while mathematical statisticians averaged $69,000. According to a 1999 survey by the National Association of Colleges and Employers, starting salary offers for mathematics/statistics graduates with a bachelor's degree averaged about $37,300 a year.

Related Occupations

People in numerous occupations work with statistics. Among these are actuaries; mathematicians; operations research analysts; computer systems analysts and programmers; engineers; economists; financial analysts; and information, life, physical, and social scientists.

Sources of Additional Information

For information about career opportunities in statistics, contact:

☛ American Statistical Association, 1429 Duke St., Alexandria, VA 22314. Internet: **http://amstat.org/index.html**

For more information on careers and training in mathematics (a field closely related to statistics), especially for doctoral level employment, contact:

☛ American Mathematical Society, Department of Professional Programs and Services, P.O. Box 6248, Providence, RI 02940-6248. Internet: **http://www.ams.org**

Information on obtaining a job as a statistician with the Federal Government may be obtained from the Office of Personnel Management through a telephone-based system. Consult your telephone directory under U.S. Government for a local number, or call (912) 757-3000; TDD (912) 744-2299. This number is not toll free, and charges may result. Information may also be obtained through the Internet site: **http:// www.usajobs.opm.gov**

Agricultural and Food Scientists

(O*NET 24305A, 24305B, 24305C, and 24305D)

Significant Points

- A large proportion, about 40 percent, of salaried agricultural and food scientists works for Federal, State, and local governments.
- A bachelor's degree in agricultural science is sufficient for some jobs in applied research; a master's or doctoral degree is required for basic research.
- Those with advanced degrees have the best prospects; however, competition may be keen for some basic research jobs if Federal and State funding for these positions is cut.

Nature of the Work

The work of agricultural and food scientists plays an important part in maintaining the Nation's food supply through ensuring agricultural productivity and the safety of the food supply. Agricultural scientists study farm crops and animals and develop ways of improving their quantity and quality. They look for ways to improve crop yield and quality with less labor, control pests and weeds more safely and effectively, and conserve soil and water. They research methods of converting raw agricultural commodities into attractive and healthy food products for consumers.

Agricultural science is closely related to biological science, and agricultural scientists use the principles of biology, chemistry, physics, mathematics, and other sciences to solve problems in agriculture. They often work with biological scientists on basic biological research and in applying to agriculture the advances in knowledge brought about by biotechnology.

Many agricultural scientists work in basic or applied research and development. Others manage or administer research and development programs or manage marketing or production operations in companies that produce food products or agricultural chemicals, supplies, and machinery. Some agricultural scientists are consultants to business firms, private clients, or to government.

Depending on the agricultural or food scientist's area of specialization, the nature of the work performed varies.

Food science. Food scientists and technologists usually work in the food processing industry, universities, or the Federal Government, and help meet consumer demand for food products that are healthful, safe, palatable, and convenient. To do this, they use their knowledge of chemistry, microbiology, and other sciences to develop new or better ways of preserving, processing, packaging, storing, and delivering foods. Some food scientists engage in basic research, discovering new food sources; analyzing food content to determine levels of vitamins, fat, sugar, or protein; or searching for substitutes for harmful or undesirable additives, such as nitrites. They also develop ways to process, preserve, package, or store food according to industry and government regulations. Others enforce government regulations, inspecting food processing areas and ensuring that sanitation, safety, quality, and waste management standards are met. Food technologists generally work in product development, applying the findings from food science research to the selection, preservation, processing, packaging, distribution, and use of safe, nutritious, and wholesome food.

Plant science. Agronomy, crop science, entomology, and plant breeding are included in plant science. Scientists in these disciplines study plants and their growth in soils, helping producers of food, feed, and fiber crops to continue to feed a growing population while conserving natural resources and maintaining the environment. Agronomists and crop scientists not only help increase productivity, but also study ways to improve the nutritional value of crops and the quality of seed. Some crop scientists study the breeding, physiology, and management of crops and use genetic engineering to develop crops resistant to pests and drought. Entomologists conduct research to develop new technologies to control or eliminate pests in infested areas and prevent the spread of harmful pests to new areas, as well as technologies that are compatible with the environment. They also conduct research or engage in oversight activities aimed at halting the spread of insect-borne disease.

Soil science. Soil scientists study the chemical, physical, biological, and mineralogical composition of soils as they relate to plant or crop growth. They also study the responses of various soil types to fertilizers, tillage practices, and crop rotation. Many soil scientists who work for the Federal Government conduct soil surveys, classifying and mapping soils. They provide information and recommendations to farmers and other landowners regarding the best use of land and plant growth, and how to avoid or correct problems such as erosion. They may also consult with engineers and other technical personnel working on construction projects about the effects of, and solutions to, soil problems. Since soil science is closely related to environmental science, persons trained in soil science also apply their knowledge to ensure environmental quality and effective land use.

Animal science. Animal scientists work to develop better, more efficient ways of producing and processing meat, poultry, eggs, and milk. Dairy scientists, poultry scientists, animal breeders, and other related scientists study the genetics, nutrition, reproduction, growth, and development of domestic farm animals. Some animal scientists inspect and grade livestock food products, purchase livestock, or work in technical sales or marketing. As extension agents or consultants, animal scientists advise agricultural producers on how to upgrade animal housing facilities properly, lower mortality rates, handle waste matter, or increase production of animal products, such as milk or eggs.

Agricultural scientists gather data and inpsect results of their work in the field.

Working Conditions

Agricultural scientists involved in management or basic research tend to work regular hours in offices and laboratories. The working environment for those engaged in applied research or product development varies, depending on the discipline of agricultural science and the type of employer. For example, food scientists in private industry may work in test kitchens while investigating new processing techniques. Animal scientists working for Federal, State, or university research stations may spend part of their time at dairies, farrowing houses, feedlots, farm animal facilities, or outdoors conducting research associated with livestock. Soil and crop scientists also spend time outdoors conducting research on farms and agricultural research stations. Entomologists work in laboratories, insectories, or agricultural research stations, and may also spend time outdoors studying or collecting insects in their natural habitat.

Employment

Agricultural scientists held about 21,000 jobs in 1998. In addition, several thousand persons held agricultural science faculty positions in colleges and universities. (See the statement on college and university faculty elsewhere in the *Handbook*.)

About 40 percent of all nonfaculty salaried agricultural and food scientists work for Federal, State, or local governments. Nearly 1 out of 4 worked for the Federal Government in 1998, mostly in the Department of Agriculture. In addition, large numbers worked for State governments at State agricultural colleges or agricultural research stations. Some worked for agricultural service companies; others worked for commercial research and development laboratories, seed companies, pharmaceutical companies, wholesale distributors, and food products companies. About 3,700 agricultural scientists were self-employed in 1998, mainly as consultants.

Training, Other Qualifications, and Advancement

Training requirements for agricultural scientists depend on their specialty and on the type of work they perform. A bachelor's degree in agricultural science is sufficient for working some jobs in applied research or for assisting in basic research, but a master's or doctoral degree is required for basic research. A Ph.D. in agricultural science is usually needed for college teaching and for advancement to administrative research positions. Degrees in related sciences such as biology, chemistry, or physics or in related engineering specialties also may qualify persons for some agricultural science jobs.

All States have a land-grant college that offers agricultural science degrees. Many other colleges and universities also offer agricultural science degrees or some agricultural science courses. However, not every school offers all specialties. A typical undergraduate agricultural science curriculum includes communications, economics, business, and physical and life sciences courses, in addition to a wide variety of technical agricultural science courses. For prospective animal scientists, these technical agricultural science courses might include animal breeding, reproductive physiology, nutrition, and meats and muscle biology.

Students preparing as food scientists take courses such as food chemistry, food analysis, food microbiology, and food processing operations. Those preparing as crop or soil scientists take courses in plant pathology, soil chemistry, entomology, plant physiology, and biochemistry, among others. Advanced degree programs include classroom and fieldwork, laboratory research, and a thesis or dissertation based on independent research.

Agricultural and food scientists should be able to work independently or as part of a team and be able to communicate clearly and concisely, both in speaking and in writing. Most agricultural scientists also need an understanding of basic business principles.

The American Society of Agronomy offers certification programs in crops, agronomy, crop advising, soils, horticulture, plant pathology, and weed science. To become certified, applicants must meet certain standards for examination, education, and professional work experience.

Agricultural scientists who have advanced degrees usually begin in research or teaching. With experience, they may advance to jobs such as supervisors of research programs or managers of other agriculture-related activities.

Job Outlook

Employment of agricultural scientists is expected to grow about as fast as the average for all occupations through 2008. Additionally, the need to replace agricultural and food scientists who retire or otherwise leave the occupation permanently will account for many more job openings than projected growth.

Past agricultural research has resulted in the development of higher-yielding crops, crops with better resistance to pests and plant pathogens, and chemically-based fertilizers and pesticides. Further research is necessary as insects and diseases continue to adapt to pesticides, and as soil fertility and water quality deteriorate. Agricultural scientists are using new avenues of research in biotechnology to develop plants and food crops that require less fertilizer, fewer pesticides and herbicides, and even less rain.

Agricultural scientists will be needed to balance increased agricultural output with protection and preservation of soil, water, and ecosystems. They will increasingly encourage the practice "sustainable agriculture" by developing and implementing plans to manage pests, crops, soil fertility and erosion, and animal waste in ways that reduce the use of harmful chemicals and do little damage to the natural environment. Also, an expanding population and an increasing public focus on diet, health, and food safety, will result in job opportunities for food scientists and technologists.

Graduates with advanced degrees will be in the best position to enter jobs as agricultural scientists. However, competition may be keen for teaching positions in colleges or universities and for some basic research jobs, even for doctoral holders. Federal and State budget cuts may limit funding for these positions through 2008.

Bachelor's degree holders can work in some applied research and product development positions, but usually only in certain subfields, such as food science and technology. Also, the Federal Government hires bachelor's degree holders to work as soil scientists. Despite the more limited opportunities for those with only a bachelor's degree to obtain jobs as agricultural scientists, a bachelor's degree in agricultural science is useful for managerial jobs in businesses that deal with ranchers and farmers, such as feed, fertilizer, seed, and farm equipment manufacturers; retailers or wholesalers; and farm credit institutions. Four-year degrees may also help persons enter occupations such as farmer or farm or ranch manager, cooperative extension service agent, agricultural products inspector, or purchasing or sales agent for agricultural commodity or farm supply companies.

Earnings

Median annual earnings of agricultural and food scientists were $42,340 in 1998. The middle 50 percent earned between $32,370 and $59,240. The lowest 10 percent earned less than $24,200 and the highest 10 percent earned more than $79,820.

Average Federal salaries for employees in nonsupervisory, supervisory, and managerial positions in certain agricultural science specialties in 1999 were as follows: Animal science, $69,400; agronomy, $57,200; soil science, $53,600; horticulture, $53,800; and entomology, $65,600.

According to the National Association of Colleges and Employers, beginning salary offers in 1999 for graduates with a bachelor's degree in animal science averaged about $27,600 a year.

Related Occupations

The work of agricultural scientists is closely related to that of biologists and other natural scientists such as chemists, foresters, and conservation scientists. It is also related to agricultural production occupations such as farmer and farm manager and cooperative extension service agent. Certain specialties of agricultural science are also related to other occupations. For example, the work of animal scientists is related to that of veterinarians; horticulturists, to landscape architects; and soil scientists, to soil conservationists.

Sources of Additional Information

Information on careers in agricultural science is available from:

☛ American Society of Agronomy, Crop Science Society of America, Soil Science Society of America, 677 S. Segoe Rd., Madison, WI 53711-1086.

☛ Food and Agricultural Careers for Tomorrow, Purdue University, 1140 Agricultural Administration Bldg., West Lafayette, IN 47907-1140.

For information on careers in food technology, write to:

☛ Institute of Food Technologists, Suite 300, 221 N. LaSalle St., Chicago IL 60601-1291.

For information on education in food safety, contact:

☛ National Alliance for Food Safety, Office of the Secretariat, 205 Agriculture Building, University of Arkansas, Fayetteville, AR 72701.

For information on careers in entomology, contact:

☛ Entomological Society of America, 9301 Annapolis Rd., Lanham, MD 20706, Attn: Public Relations Coordinator.

Information on acquiring a job as an agricultural scientist with the Federal Government may be obtained from the Office of Personnel Management through a telephone-based system. Consult your telephone directory under U.S. Government for a local number, or call (912) 757-3000 (TDD 912-744-2299). That number is not toll-free and charges may result. Information also is available from their Internet site: **http://www.usajobs.opm.gov**

Biological and Medical Scientists

(O*NET 24308A, 24308B, 24308C, 24308D, 24308E, 24308F, 24308G, 24308H, 24308J, and 24311)

Significant Points

- Biological scientists usually require a Ph.D. degree for independent research but a master's degree is sufficient for some jobs in applied research or product development; a bachelor's degree is adequate for some non-research jobs.
- Medical scientist jobs require a Ph.D. degree in a biological science, but some jobs need a medical degree.
- Doctoral degree holders face considerable competition for independent research positions; holders of bachelor's or master's degrees in biological science can expect better opportunities in non-research positions.

Nature of the Work

Biological and medical scientists study living organisms and their relationship to their environment. Most specialize in some area of biology such as zoology (the study of animals) or microbiology (the study of microscopic organisms).

Many biological scientists and virtually all medical scientists work in research and development. Some conduct basic research to advance knowledge of living organisms, including viruses, bacteria, and other infectious agents. Past research has resulted in the development of vaccines, medicines, and treatments for cancer and other diseases. Basic biological and medical research continues to provide the building blocks necessary to develop solutions to human health problems and to preserve and repair the natural environment. Many biological and medical scientists work independently in private industry, university, or government laboratories, often exploring new areas of research or expanding on specialized research started in graduate school. Those who are not wage and salary workers in private industry typically submit grant proposals to obtain funding for their projects. Colleges and universities, private industry, and Federal Government agencies, such as the National Institutes of Health and the National Science Foundation, contribute to the support of scientists whose research proposals are determined to be financially feasible and have the potential to advance new ideas or processes.

Biological and medical scientists who work in applied research or product development use knowledge provided by basic research to develop new drugs and medical treatments, increase crop yields, and protect and clean up the environment. They usually have less autonomy than basic researchers to choose the emphasis of their research, relying instead on market-driven directions based on the firm's products and goals. Biological and medical scientists doing applied research and product development in private industry may be required to express their research plans or results to nonscientists who are in a position to veto or approve their ideas, and they must understand the business impact of their work. Scientists are increasingly working as part of teams, interacting with engineers, scientists of other disciplines, business managers, and technicians. Some biological and medical scientists also work with customers or suppliers, and manage budgets.

Biological and medical scientists who conduct research usually work in laboratories and use electron microscopes, computers, thermal cyclers, or a wide variety of other equipment. Some conduct experiments using laboratory animals or greenhouse plants. For some biological scientists, a good deal of research is performed outside of laboratories. For example, a botanist may do research in tropical rain forests to see what plants grow there, or an ecologist may study how a forest area recovers after a fire.

Some biological and medical scientists work in managerial or administrative positions, usually after spending some time doing research and learning about the firm, agency, or project. They may plan and administer programs for testing foods and drugs, for example, or direct activities at zoos or botanical gardens. Some biological scientists work as consultants to business firms or to government, while others test and inspect foods, drugs, and other products.

In the 1980s, swift advances in basic biological knowledge related to genetics and molecules spurred growth in the field of biotechnology. Biological and medical scientists using this technology manipulate the genetic material of animals or plants, attempting to make organisms more productive or resistant to disease. Research using biotechnology techniques, such as recombining DNA, has led to the discovery of important drugs, including human insulin and growth hormone. Many other substances not previously available in large quantities are starting to be produced by biotechnological means; some may be useful in treating cancer and other diseases. Today, many biological and medical scientists are involved in biotechnology, including those who work on the Human Genome project, isolating, identifying, and sequencing human genes. This work continues to lead to the discovery of the genes associated with specific diseases and inherited traits, such as certain types of cancer or obesity. These advances in biotechnology have opened up research opportunities in almost all areas of biology, including commercial applications in agriculture, environmental remediation, and the food and chemical industries.

Most biological scientists who come under the category of *biologist* are further classified by the type of organism they study or by the specific activity they perform, although recent advances in the understanding of basic life processes at the molecular and cellular levels have blurred some traditional classifications.

Aquatic biologists study plants and animals living in water. *Marine biologists* study salt water organisms and *limnologists* study fresh water organisms. Marine biologists are sometimes mistakenly called oceanographers, but oceanography is the study of the physical characteristics of oceans and the ocean floor. (See the statement on geologists, geophysicists, and oceanographers elsewhere in the *Handbook*.)

Biochemists study the chemical composition of living things. They analyze the complex chemical combinations and reactions involved in metabolism, reproduction, growth, and heredity. Biochemists and molecular biologists do most of their work in biotechnology, which involves understanding the complex chemistry of life.

Botanists study plants and their environment. Some study all aspects of plant life; others specialize in areas such as identification and classification of plants, the structure and function of plant parts, the biochemistry of plant processes, the causes and cures of plant diseases, and the geological record of plants.

Microbiologists investigate the growth and characteristics of microscopic organisms such as bacteria, algae, or fungi. *Medical microbiologists* study the relationship between organisms and disease or the effect of antibiotics on microorganisms. Other microbiologists specialize in environmental, food, agricultural, or industrial microbiology, virology (the study of viruses), or immunology (the study of mechanisms that fight infections). Many microbiologists use biotechnology to advance knowledge of cell reproduction and human disease.

Physiologists study life functions of plants and animals, both in the whole organism and at the cellular or molecular level, under normal and abnormal conditions. Physiologists often specialize in functions such as growth, reproduction, photosynthesis, respiration, or movement, or in the physiology of a certain area or system of the organism.

Zoologists study animals—their origin, behavior, diseases, and life processes. Some experiment with live animals in controlled or natural surroundings while others dissect dead animals to study their structure. Zoologists are usually identified by the animal group studied—ornithologists (birds), mammalogists (mammals), herpetologists (reptiles), and ichthyologists (fish).

Ecologists study the relationship among organisms and between organisms and their environments and the effects of influences such as population size, pollutants, rainfall, temperature, and altitude.

Agricultural and food scientists, who are sometimes referred to as biological scientists, are included in a separate statement elsewhere in the *Handbook*.

Biological scientists who do biomedical research are usually called *medical scientists*. Medical scientists work on basic research into normal biological systems to understand the causes of and to discover treatment for disease and other health problems. Medical scientists try to identify changes in a cell, chromosome, or even gene that signal the development of medical problems, such as different types of cancer. After identifying structures of or changes in organisms that provide clues to health problems, medical scientists work on the treatment of problems. For example, a medical scientist involved in cancer research may formulate a combination of drugs that will lessen the effects of the disease. Medical scientists with a medical degree can administer these drugs to patients in clinical trials, monitor their reactions, and observe the results. (Medical scientists without a medical degree normally collaborate with a medical doctor who deals directly with patients.) The medical scientist will return to the laboratory to examine the results and, if necessary, adjust the dosage levels to reduce negative side effects or to try to induce even better results. In addition to using basic research to develop treatments for health problems, medical scientists attempt to discover ways to prevent health problems from developing, such as affirming the link between smoking and increased risk of lung cancer, or between alcoholism and liver disease.

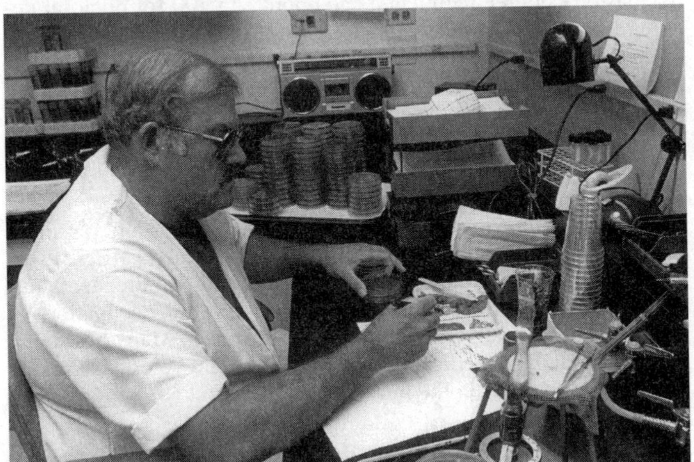

Biological and medical scientists who conduct research usually work in laboratories and use microscopes,computers, and other equipment.

Working Conditions

Biological and medical scientists usually work regular hours in offices or laboratories and usually are not exposed to unsafe or unhealthy conditions. Those who work with dangerous organisms or toxic substances in the laboratory must follow strict safety procedures to avoid contamination. Medical scientists also spend time working in clinics and hospitals administering drugs and treatments to patients in clinical trials. Many biological scientists such as botanists, ecologists, and zoologists take field trips that involve strenuous physical activity and primitive living conditions.

Some biological and medical scientists depend on grant money to support their research. They may be under pressure to meet deadlines and conform to rigid grant-writing specifications when preparing proposals to seek new or extended funding.

Employment

Biological and medical scientists held about 112,000 jobs in 1998. Almost 4 in 10 biological scientists were employed by Federal, State, and local governments. Federal biological scientists worked mainly in the U.S. Departments of Agriculture, the Interior, and Defense, and in the National Institutes of Health. Most of the rest worked in the drug industry, which includes pharmaceutical and biotechnology establishments; hospitals; or research and testing laboratories. About 2 in 10 medical scientists worked in State government, with most of the remainder found in research and testing laboratories, educational institutions, the drug industry, and hospitals.

In addition, many biological and medical scientists held biology faculty positions in colleges and universities. (See the statement on college and university faculty elsewhere in the *Handbook*.)

Training, Other Qualifications, and Advancement

For biological scientists, the Ph.D. degree usually is necessary for independent research and for advancement to administrative positions. A master's degree is sufficient for some jobs in applied research or product development and for jobs in management, inspection, sales, and service. The bachelor's degree is adequate for some non-research jobs. Some graduates with a bachelor's degree start as biological scientists in testing and inspection, or get jobs related to biological science such as technical sales or service representatives. In some cases, graduates with a bachelor's degree are able to work in a laboratory environment on their own projects, but this is unusual. Some may work as research assistants. Others become biological technicians, medical laboratory technologists or, with courses in education, high school biology teachers. (See the statements on clinical laboratory technologists and technicians; science technicians; and kindergarten, elementary, and secondary school teachers elsewhere in the *Handbook*.) Many with a bachelor's degree in biology enter medical, dental, veterinary, or other health profession schools.

Most colleges and universities offer bachelor's degrees in biological science and many offer advanced degrees. Curriculums for advanced degrees often emphasize a subfield such as microbiology or botany, but not all universities offer all curriculums. Advanced degree programs include classroom and field work, laboratory research, and a thesis or dissertation. Biological scientists who have advanced degrees often take temporary postdoctoral research positions that provide specialized research experience. In private industry, some may become managers or administrators within biology; others leave biology for nontechnical managerial, administrative, or sales jobs.

Biological scientists should be able to work independently or as part of a team and be able to communicate clearly and concisely, both orally and in writing. Those in private industry, especially those who aspire to management or administrative positions, should possess strong business and communication skills and be familiar with regulatory issues and marketing and management techniques. Those doing field research in remote areas must have physical stamina.

The Ph.D. degree in a biological science is the minimum education required for prospective medical scientists because the work of medical scientists is almost entirely research oriented. A Ph.D. degree qualifies one to do research on basic life processes or on particular medical problems or diseases, and to analyze and interpret the results of experiments on patients. Medical scientists who administer drug or gene therapy to human patients, or who otherwise interact medically with patients—such as drawing blood, excising tissue, or performing other invasive procedures—must have a medical degree. It is particularly helpful for medical scientists to earn both Ph.D. and medical degrees.

In addition to formal education, medical scientists usually spend several years in a postdoctoral position before they apply for permanent jobs. Postdoctoral work provides valuable laboratory experience, including experience in specific processes and techniques, such as gene splicing, which are transferable to other research projects. In some institutions, the postdoctoral position can lead to a permanent position.

Job Outlook

Despite prospects of faster-than-average job growth over the 1998-2008 period, biological and medical scientists can expect to face considerable competition for basic research positions. The Federal Government funds much basic research and development, including many areas of medical research. Recent budget tightening has led to smaller increases in Federal basic research and development expenditures, further limiting the dollar amount of each grant and slowing the growth of the number of grants awarded to researchers. At the same time, the number of newly trained scientists has continued to increase at a steady rate, so both new and established scientists have experienced greater difficulty winning and renewing research grants. If the number of advanced degrees awarded continues to grow unabated, this competitive scenario is likely to persist. Additionally, applied research positions in private industry may become more difficult to obtain if more scientists seek jobs in private industry than in the past due to the competitive job market for college and university faculty.

Opportunities for those with a bachelor's or master's degree in biological science are expected to be better. The number of science-related jobs in sales, marketing, and research management, for which non-Ph.D.'s usually qualify, are expected to be more plentiful than independent research positions. Non-Ph.D's may also fill positions as science or engineering technicians or health technologists and technicians. Some become high school biology teachers, while those with a doctorate in biological science may become college and university faculty. (See statements on science technicians, engineering technicians, health technologists and technicians, secondary school teachers, and college and university faculty elsewhere in the *Handbook*.)

Biological and medical scientists enjoyed very rapid gains in employment between the mid-1980s and mid-1990s, in part reflecting increased staffing requirements in new biotechnology companies. Employment growth should slow somewhat as increases in the number of new biotechnology firms slows and existing firms merge or are absorbed into larger ones. However, much of the basic biological research done in recent years has resulted in new knowledge, including the isolation and identification of new genes. Biological and medical scientists will be needed to take this knowledge to the next stage, which is the understanding of how certain genes function within an entire organism so that gene therapies can be developed to treat diseases. Even pharmaceutical and other firms not solely engaged in biotechnology are expected to increasingly use biotechnology techniques, spurring employment increases for biological and medical scientists. In addition, efforts to discover new and improved ways to clean up and preserve the environment will continue to add to growth. More biological scientists will be needed to determine the environmental impact of industry and government actions and to prevent or correct environmental problems. Expected expansion in research related to health issues, such as AIDS, cancer, and Alzheimer's disease, should also result in employment growth.

Biological and medical scientists are less likely to lose their jobs during recessions than those in many other occupations because many are employed on long-term research projects. However, a recession could further influence the amount of money allocated to new research and development efforts, particularly in areas of risky or innovative research. A recession could also limit the possibility of extension or renewal of existing projects.

Earnings

Median annual earnings of biological scientists were $46,140 in 1998. The middle 50 percent earned between $35,200 and $67,850. The lowest 10 percent earned less than $27,930 and the highest 10 percent earned more than $86,020. Median annual earnings in the industries employing the largest numbers of biological scientists in 1997 were:

Industry	Earnings
Federal Government	$48,600
Drugs	46,300
Research and testing services	40,800
State Government, except education and hospitals	38,000

Median annual earnings of medical scientists were $50,410 in 1998. The middle 50 percent earned between $37,740 and $79,370. The lowest 10 percent earned less than $29,550 and the highest 10 percent earned more than $109,050. Median annual earnings of medical scientists in 1997 were $52,200 in research and testing services.

According to the National Association of Colleges and Employers, beginning salary offers in 1999 averaged $29,000 a year for bachelor's degree recipients in biological science; about $34,450 for master's degree recipients; and about $45,700 for doctoral degree recipients.

In the Federal Government in 1999, general biological scientists in nonsupervisory, supervisory, and managerial positions earned an average salary of $56,000; microbiologists, $62,600; ecologists, $57,100; physiologists, $71,300; and geneticists, $68,200.

Related Occupations

Many other occupations deal with living organisms and require a level of training similar to that of biological and medical scientists. These include agricultural scientists, such as animal breeders, horticulturists, and entomologists, and the conservation occupations of forester, range manager, and soil conservationist. Many health occupations, such as medical doctors, dentists, and veterinarians, are also related to those in the biological sciences.

Sources of Additional Information

For information on careers in the biological sciences, contact:

☛ American Institute of Biological Sciences, Suite 200, 1444 I St. NW., Washington, DC 20005. Internet: **http://www.aibs.org**

For information on careers in physiology, contact:

☛ American Physiological Society, Education Office, 9650 Rockville Pike, Bethesda, MD 20814. Internet: **http://www.faseb.org/aps**

For information on careers in biotechnology, contact:

☛ Biotechnology Industry Organization, 1625 K St. NW., Suite 1100, Washington, DC 20006. Internet: **http://www.bio.org**

For information on careers in biochemistry, contact:

☛ American Society for Biochemistry and Molecular Biology, 9650 Rockville Pike, Bethesda, MD 20814.
Internet: **http://www.faseb.org/asbmb**

For a brochure titled, *Is a Career in the Pharmaceutical Sciences Right for Me?*, contact:

☛ American Association of Pharmaceutical Scientists, 1650 King Street, Suite 200, Alexandria, VA 22314 .
Internet: **http://www.aaps.org/sciaffairs/careerinps.htm**

For information on careers in botany, contact:

☛ Botanical Society of America, Business Office, 1735 Neil Ave., Columbus, OH 43210-1293. Internet: **http://www.botany.org**

For information on careers in microbiology, contact:

☛ American Society for Microbiology, Office of Education and Training—Career Information, 1325 Massachusetts Ave. NW., Washington, DC 20005. Internet: **http://www.asmusa.org**

For a free copy of "Sources of Career Information on Careers in Biology, Conservation, and Oceanography," visit the Smithsonian Institute website at **http://www.si.edu/resource/faq/nmnh/careers.htm** or call (202) 782-4612. That number is not toll-free and charges may result.

Information on acquiring a job as a biological or medical scientist with the Federal government may be obtained from the Office of Personnel Management through a telephone-based system. Consult your telephone directory under U.S. Government for a local number or call (912) 757-3000; TDD (912) 744-2299. That number is not toll-free and charges may result. Information also is available from their Internet site: **http://www.usajobs.opm.gov**

Conservation Scientists and Foresters

(O*NET 24302A, 24302B, 24302C, 24302D, and 24302E)

Significant Points

- About 2 out of 3 work for Federal, State, or local governments.
- A bachelor's degree in forestry, range management, or a related field is usually the minimum educational requirement.
- Projected average employment growth will stem from continuing emphasis on environmental protection and responsible land management.

Nature of the Work

Forests and rangelands supply wood products, livestock forage, minerals, and water; serve as sites for recreational activities; and provide habitats for wildlife. Conservation scientists and foresters manage, develop, use, and help protect these and other natural resources.

Foresters manage forested lands for a variety of purposes. Those working in private industry may procure timber from private landowners. To do this, foresters contact local forest owners and gain permission to take inventory of the type, amount, and location of all standing timber on the property, a process known as timber cruising. Foresters then appraise the timber's worth, negotiate the purchase of timber, and draw up a contract for procurement. Next, they subcontract with loggers or pulpwood cutters for tree removal, aid in road layout, and maintain close contact with the subcontractor's workers and the landowner to ensure that the work meets the landowner's requirements, as well as Federal, State, and local environmental specifications. Forestry consultants often act as agents for the forest owner, performing these duties and negotiating timber sales with industrial procurement foresters.

Throughout the process, foresters consider the economics of the purchase as well as the environmental impact on natural resources. To do this, they determine how best to conserve wildlife habitats, creek beds, water quality, and soil stability and how best to comply with environmental regulations. Foresters must balance the desire to conserve forested ecosystems for future generations with the need to use forest resources for recreational or economic purposes.

Through a process called regeneration, foresters also supervise the planting and growing of new trees. They choose and prepare the site, using controlled burning, bulldozers, or herbicides to clear weeds, brush, and logging debris. They advise on the type, number, and placement of trees to be planted. Foresters then monitor the seedlings to ensure healthy growth and to determine the best time for harvesting. If they detect signs of disease or harmful insects, they decide on the best course of treatment to prevent contamination or infestation of healthy trees.

Foresters who work for State and Federal governments manage public forests and parks and also work with private landowners to protect and manage forest land outside of the public domain. They may also design campgrounds and recreation areas.

Foresters use a number of tools to perform their jobs. Clinometers measure the heights, diameter tapes measure the diameter, and increment borers and bark gauges measure the growth of trees so that timber volumes can be computed and future growth estimated. Photogrammetry and remote sensing (aerial photographs and other imagery taken from airplanes and satellites) often are used for mapping large forest areas and for detecting widespread trends of forest and land use. Computers are used extensively, both in the office and in the field, for the storage, retrieval, and analysis of information required to manage the forest land and its resources.

Range managers, also called range *conservationists*, range *ecologists*, or range *scientists*, manage, improve, and protect rangelands to maximize their use without damaging the environment. Rangelands cover about 1 billion acres of the United States, mostly in the western States and Alaska. They contain many natural resources, including grass and shrubs for animal grazing, wildlife habitats, water from vast watersheds, recreation facilities, and valuable mineral and energy resources. Range managers help ranchers attain optimum livestock production by determining the number and kind of animals to graze, the grazing system to use, and the best season for grazing. At the same time, however, they maintain soil stability and vegetation for other uses such as wildlife habitats and outdoor recreation. They also plan and implement revegetation of disturbed sites.

Conservation scientists and foresters often use aerial photographs to map large forest areas.

Soil conservationists provide technical assistance to farmers, ranchers, State and local governments, and others concerned with the conservation of soil, water, and related natural resources. They develop programs designed to get the most productive use of land without damaging it. Conservationists visit areas with erosion problems, find the source of the problem, and help landowners and managers develop management practices to combat it.

Foresters and conservation scientists often specialize in one area such as forest resource management, urban forestry, wood technology, or forest economics.

Working Conditions

Working conditions vary considerably. Although some of the work is solitary, foresters and conservation scientists also deal regularly with landowners, loggers, forestry technicians and aides, farmers, ranchers, government officials, special interest groups, and the public in general. Some work regular hours in offices or labs. Others may split their time between field work and office work, while some—especially independent consultants or less experienced workers—spend the majority of their time outdoors overseeing or participating in hands-on work.

The work can be physically demanding. Some foresters and conservation scientists work outdoors in all types of weather, sometimes in isolated areas. Other foresters may need to walk long distances through densely wooded land to carry out their work. Foresters also may work long hours fighting fires. Conservation scientists often are called in to prevent erosion after a forest fire, and they provide emergency help after floods, mudslides, and tropical storms.

Employment

Conservation scientists and foresters held about 39,000 jobs in 1998. Nearly 3 out of 10 workers were in the Federal Government, mostly in the U.S. Department of Agriculture (USDA). Foresters were concentrated in the USDA's Forest Service; soil conservationists in the USDA's Natural Resource Conservation Service. Most range managers worked in the Department of the Interior's Bureau of Land Management or in the USDA's Natural Resource Conservation Service. Nearly another 3 out of 10 conservation scientists and foresters worked for State governments, and nearly 1 out of 10 worked for local governments. The remainder worked in private industry, mainly in research and testing services, the forestry industry, and logging and lumber companies and sawmills. Some were self-employed as consultants for private landowners, State and Federal governments, and forestry-related businesses.

Although conservation scientists and foresters work in every State, employment of foresters is concentrated in the western and southeastern States, where many national and private forests and parks, and most of the lumber and pulpwood-producing forests, are located. Range managers work almost entirely in the western States, where most of the rangeland is located. Soil conservationists, on the other hand, are employed in almost every county in the country.

Training, Other Qualifications, and Advancement

A bachelor's degree in forestry is the minimum educational requirement for professional careers in forestry. In the Federal Government, a combination of experience and appropriate education occasionally may substitute for a 4-year forestry degree, but job competition makes this difficult.

Fifteen States have mandatory licensing or voluntary registration requirements that a forester must meet in order to acquire the title "professional forester" and practice forestry in the State. Licensing or registration requirements vary by State, but usually entail completing a 4-year degree in forestry, a minimum period of training time, and passing an exam.

Foresters who wish to perform specialized research or teach should have an advanced degree, preferably a Ph.D.

Most land-grant colleges and universities offer bachelor's or higher degrees in forestry; 48 of these programs are accredited by the Society of American Foresters. Curriculums stress science, mathematics, communications skills, and computer science, as well as technical forestry subjects. Courses in forest economics and business administration supplement the student's scientific and technical knowledge. Forestry curricula increasingly include courses on best management practices, wetlands analysis, water and soil quality, and wildlife conservation, in response to the growing focus on protecting forested lands during timber harvesting operations. Prospective foresters should have a strong grasp on policy issues and on increasingly numerous and complex environmental regulations, which affect many forestry-related activities. Many colleges require students to complete a field session either in a camp operated by the college or in a cooperative work-study program with a Federal or State agency or private industry. All schools encourage students to take summer jobs that provide experience in forestry or conservation work.

A bachelor's degree in range management or range science is the usual minimum educational requirement for range managers; graduate degrees usually are required for teaching and research positions. In 1998, about 35 colleges and universities offered degrees in range management or range science or in a closely related discipline with a range management or range science option. A number of other schools offered some courses in range management or range science. Specialized range management courses combine plant, animal, and soil sciences with principles of ecology and resource management. Desirable electives include economics, forestry, hydrology, agronomy, wildlife, animal husbandry, computer science, and recreation.

Very few colleges and universities offer degrees in soil conservation. Most soil conservationists have degrees in environmental studies, agronomy, general agriculture, hydrology, or crop or soil science; a few have degrees in related fields such as wildlife biology, forestry, and range management. Programs of study usually include 30 semester hours in natural resources or agriculture, including at least 3 hours in soil science.

In addition to meeting the demands of forestry and conservation research and analysis, foresters and conservation scientists generally must enjoy working outdoors, be physically hardy, and be willing to move to where the jobs are. They must also work well with people and have good communications skills.

Recent forestry and range management graduates usually work under the supervision of experienced foresters or range managers. After gaining experience, they may advance to more responsible positions. In the Federal Government, most entry-level foresters work in forest resource management. An experienced Federal forester may supervise a ranger district, and may advance to forest supervisor, regional forester, or to a top administrative position in the national headquarters. In private industry, foresters start by learning the practical and administrative aspects of the business and acquiring comprehensive technical training. They are then introduced to contract writing, timber harvesting, and decision making. Some foresters work their way up to top managerial positions within their companies. Foresters in management usually leave the fieldwork behind, spending more of their time in an office, working with teams to develop management plans and supervising others. After gaining several years of experience, some foresters may become consulting foresters, working alone or with one or several partners. They contract with State or local governments, private landowners, private industry, or other forestry consulting groups.

Soil conservationists usually begin working within one county or conservation district and with experience may advance to the area, State, regional, or national level. Also, soil conservationists can transfer to related occupations such as farm or ranch management advisor or land appraiser.

Job Outlook

Employment of conservation scientists and foresters is expected to grow about as fast as the average for all occupations through

2008. Growth should be strongest in State and local governments and in research and testing services, where demand will be spurred by a continuing emphasis on environmental protection and responsible land management. Job opportunities are expected to be best for soil conservationists and other conservation scientists as government regulations, such as those regarding the management of stormwater and coastlines, has created demand for persons knowledgeable about erosion on farms and in cities and suburbs. Soil and water quality experts will also be needed as States attempt to improve water quality by preventing pollution by agricultural producers and industrial plants.

Fewer opportunities for conservation scientists and foresters are expected in the Federal Government, partly due to budgetary constraints. Also, Federal land management agencies, such as the Forest Service, have de-emphasized their timber programs and increasingly focused on wildlife, recreation, and sustaining ecosystems, thereby increasing demand for other life and social scientists relative to foresters. However, a large number of foresters are expected to retire or leave the Government for other reasons, resulting in some job openings between 1998 and 2008. In addition, a small number of new jobs will result from the need for range and soil conservationists to provide technical assistance to owners of grazing land through the Natural Resource Conservation Service.

The recent reductions in timber harvesting on public lands, most of which are located in the Northwest and California, also will dampen job growth for private industry foresters in these regions. Opportunities will be better for foresters in the Southeast, where much forested land is privately owned. Rising demand for timber on private lands will increase the need for forest management plans that maximize production while sustaining the environment for future growth. Salaried foresters working for private industry—such as paper companies, sawmills, and pulp wood mills—and consulting foresters will be needed to provide technical assistance and management plans to landowners.

Research and testing firms have increased their hiring of conservation scientists and foresters in recent years in response to demand for professionals to prepare environmental impact statements and erosion and sediment control plans, monitor water quality near logging sites, and advise on tree harvesting practices required by Federal, State, or local regulations. Hiring in these firms should continue during the 1998-2008 period, though at a slower rate than over the last ten years.

Earnings

Median annual earnings of conservation scientists and foresters in 1998 were $42,750. The middle 50 percent earned between $34,150 and $51,550. The lowest 10 percent earned less than $26,330 and the highest 10 percent earned more than $75,330. Median annual earnings of conservation scientists and foresters employed in State governments in 1997 were $37,400.

In 1999, most bachelor's degree graduates entering the Federal Government as foresters, range managers, or soil conservationists started at $20,600 or $25,500, depending on academic achievement. Those with a master's degree could start at $25,500 or $31,200. Holders of doctorates could start at $37,700 or, in research positions, at $45,200. Beginning salaries were slightly higher in selected areas where the prevailing local pay level was higher. In 1999, the average Federal salary for foresters in nonsupervisory, supervisory, and managerial positions was $51,000; for soil conservationists, $48,900; for rangeland managers, $46,300, and for forest products technologists, $68,300.

According to the National Association of Colleges and Employers, graduates with a bachelor's degree in natural resources received an average starting salary offer of $26,100 in 1999.

In private industry, starting salaries for students with a bachelor's degree were comparable to starting salaries in the Federal Government, but starting salaries in State and local governments were usually lower.

Conservation scientists and foresters who work for Federal, State, and local governments and large private firms generally receive more generous benefits than those working for smaller firms.

Related Occupations

Conservation scientists and foresters manage, develop, and protect natural resources. Other workers with similar responsibilities include agricultural scientists, agricultural engineers, biological scientists, environmental scientists and engineers, farm and ranch managers, and wildlife managers.

Sources of Additional Information

For information about the forestry profession and lists of schools offering education in forestry, send a self-addressed, stamped business envelope to:

☛ Society of American Foresters, 5400 Grosvenor Ln., Bethesda, MD 20814. Internet: **http://www.safnet.org**

For information about career opportunities in forestry in the Federal Government, contact:

☛ Chief, U.S. Forest Service, U.S. Department of Agriculture, P.O. Box 96090, SW., Washington, DC 20090-6090.

For information about a career in State forestry organizations, contact:

☛ National Association of State Foresters, 444 N. Capitol St. NW., Suite 540, Washington, DC 20001.

Information about a career as a range manager as well as a list of schools offering training is available from:

☛ Society for Range Management, 445 Union Blvd., Suite 230, Lakewood, CO 80228-1259. Internet: **http://srm.org**

Physical Scientists

Atmospheric Scientists

(O*NET 24108)

Significant Points

- The Federal Government employs more than 1 out of 3 meteorologists and is their largest employer.
- A bachelor's degree in meteorology, or in a closely related field with courses in meteorology, is the minimum educational requirement; a master's degree is necessary for some positions, and a Ph.D. is required for most research positions.
- Applicants may face competition if the number of degrees awarded in atmospheric science and meteorology remain near current levels.

Nature of the Work

Atmospheric science is the study of the atmosphere—the blanket of air covering the Earth. Atmospheric scientists, commonly called meteorologists, study the atmosphere's physical characteristics, motions, and processes, and the way it affects the rest of our environment. The best known application of this knowledge is in forecasting the weather. However, weather information and meteorological research are also applied in air-pollution control, agriculture, air and sea transportation, defense, and the study of trends in Earth's climate such as global warming, droughts, or ozone depletion.

Atmospheric scientists who forecast the weather, known professionally as *operational meteorologists*, is the largest group of specialists. They study information on air pressure, temperature, humidity, and wind velocity; and apply physical and mathematical relationships to make short- and long-range weather forecasts. Their data come from weather satellites, weather radars, and sensors and observers in many parts of the world. Meteorologists use sophisticated computer models of the world's atmosphere to make long-term, short-term, and local-area forecasts. These forecasts inform not only the general public, but also those who need accurate weather information for both economic and safety reasons, as in the shipping, air transportation, agriculture, fishing, and utilities industries.

The use of weather balloons, launched a few times a day to measure wind, temperature, and humidity in the upper atmosphere, is currently supplemented by sophisticated atmospheric monitoring equipment that transmits data as frequently as every few minutes. Doppler radar, for example, can detect airflow patterns in violent storm systems—allowing forecasters to better predict tornadoes and other hazardous winds, as well as to monitor the storm's direction and intensity. Combined radar and satellite observations allow meteorologists to predict flash floods.

Some atmospheric scientists work in research. *Physical meteorologists*, for example, study the atmosphere's chemical and physical properties; the transmission of light, sound, and radio waves; and the transfer of energy in the atmosphere. They also study factors affecting the formation of clouds, rain, snow, and other weather phenomena, such as severe storms. *Synoptic meteorologists* develop new tools for weather forecasting using computers and sophisticated mathematical models. *Climatologists* collect, analyze, and interpret past records of wind, rainfall, sunshine, and temperature in specific areas or regions. Their studies are used to design buildings, plan heating and cooling systems, and aid in effective land use and agricultural production. Other research meteorologists examine the most effective ways to control or diminish air pollution.

Working Conditions

Most weather stations operate around the clock 7 days a week. Jobs in such facilities usually involve night, weekend, and holiday work, often with rotating shifts. During weather emergencies, such as hurricanes, operational meteorologists may work overtime. Operational meteorologists are also often under pressure to meet forecast deadlines. Weather stations are found all over—at airports, in or near cities, and in isolated and remote areas. Some atmospheric scientists also spend time observing weather conditions and collecting data from aircraft. Weather forecasters who work for radio or television stations broadcast their reports from station studios, and may work evenings and weekends. Meteorologists in smaller weather offices often work alone; in larger ones, they work as part of a team. Meteorologists not involved in forecasting tasks work regular hours, usually in offices. Those who work for private consulting firms or for companies analyzing and monitoring emissions to improve air quality usually work with other scientists or engineers.

Atmospheric scientists who forecast the weather are known as operational meteorologists.

Employment

Atmospheric scientists held about 8,400 jobs in 1998. The Federal Government is the largest single employer of civilian meteorologists. The National Oceanic and Atmospheric Administration (NOAA) employed about 2,600 meteorologists; nearly 90 percent worked in the National Weather Service at stations throughout the Nation. The remainder of NOAA's meteorologists worked mainly in research and development or management. The Department of Defense employed about 280 civilian meteorologists. Others worked for research and testing services, private weather consulting services, and computer and data processing services.

Although several hundred people teach atmospheric science and related courses in college and university departments of meteorology or atmospheric science, physics, earth science, and geophysics, these individuals are classified as college or university faculty, rather than atmospheric scientists. (See the statement on college and university faculty elsewhere in the *Handbook*.)

In addition to civilian meteorologists, hundreds of Armed Forces members are involved in forecasting and other meteorological work. (See the statement on job opportunities in the Armed Forces elsewhere in the *Handbook*.)

Training, Other Qualifications, and Advancement

A bachelor's degree in meteorology or atmospheric science, or in a closely related field with courses in meteorology, is usually the minimum educational requirement for an entry-level position as an atmospheric scientist.

The preferred educational requirement for entry-level meteorologists in the Federal Government is a bachelor's degree—not necessarily in meteorology—but with at least 24 semester hours of meteorology courses, including 6 hours in the analysis and prediction of weather systems and 2 hours of remote sensing of the atmosphere or instrumentation. Other required courses include differential and integral calculus, differential equations, 6 hours of college physics, and at least 9 hours of courses appropriate for a physical science major—such as statistics, computer science, chemistry, physical oceanography, or physical climatology. Sometimes, a combination of experience and education may be substituted for a degree.

Although positions in operational meteorology are available for those with only a bachelor's degree, obtaining a master's degree enhances employment opportunities and advancement potential. A master's degree is usually necessary for conducting applied research and development, and a Ph.D. is required for most basic research positions. Students planning on a career in research and development need not necessarily major in atmospheric science or meteorology as an undergraduate. In fact, a bachelor's degree in mathematics, physics, or engineering provides excellent preparation for graduate study in atmospheric science.

Because atmospheric science is a small field, relatively few colleges and universities offer degrees in meteorology or atmospheric science, although many departments of physics, earth science, geography, and geophysics offer atmospheric science and related courses. Prospective students should make certain that courses required by the National Weather Service and other employers are offered at the college they are considering. Computer science courses, additional meteorology courses, a strong background in mathematics and physics, and good communication skills are important to prospective employers. Many programs combine the study of meteorology with another field, such as agriculture, oceanography, engineering, or physics. For example, hydrometeorology is the blending of hydrology (the science of Earth's water) and meteorology, and is the field concerned with the effect of precipitation on the hydrologic cycle and the environment. Students who wish to become broadcast meteorologists for radio or television stations should develop excellent communication skills through courses in speech, journalism, and related fields. Those interested in air quality work should take courses in chemistry and supplement their technical training with coursework in policy or government affairs.

Beginning atmospheric scientists often do routine data collection, computation, or analysis, and some basic forecasting. Entry-level operational meteorologists in the Federal Government are usually placed in intern positions for training and experience. During this period, they learn about the Weather Service's forecasting equipment and procedures, and rotate to different offices to learn about various weather systems. After completing the training period, they are assigned a permanent duty station. Experienced meteorologists may advance to supervisory or administrative jobs, or may handle more complex forecasting jobs. After several years of experience, some meteorologists establish their own weather consulting services.

The American Meteorological Society offers professional certification of consulting meteorologists, administered by a Board of Certified Consulting Meteorologists. Applicants must meet formal education requirements (though not necessarily have a college degree), pass an examination to demonstrate thorough meteorological knowledge, have a minimum of 5 years of experience or a combination of experience plus an advanced degree, and provide character references from fellow professionals.

Job Outlook

Employment of atmospheric scientists is projected to increase about as fast as the average for all occupations through 2008, and prospective atmospheric scientists may face competition if the number of degrees awarded in atmospheric science and meteorology remain near current levels. The National Weather Service (NWS) has completed an extensive modernization of its weather forecasting equipment and finished all hiring of meteorologists needed to staff the upgraded stations. The NWS has no plans to increase the number of weather stations or the number of meteorologists in existing stations for many years. Employment of meteorologists in other Federal agencies is expected to decline slightly as the Federal Government attempts to balance its budget.

On the other hand, job opportunities for atmospheric scientists in private industry are expected to be better than in the Federal Government over the 1998-2008 period. As research leads to continuing improvements in weather forecasting, demand should grow for private weather consulting firms to provide more detailed information than has formerly been available, especially to weather-sensitive industries. Farmers, commodity investors, radio and television stations, and utilities, transportation, and construction firms can greatly benefit from additional weather information more closely targeted to their needs than the general information provided by the National Weather Service. Additionally, research on seasonal and other long-range forecasting is yielding positive results, which should spur demand for more atmospheric scientists to interpret these forecasts and advise weather-sensitive industries. However, because many customers for private weather services are in industries sensitive to fluctuations in the economy, the sales and growth of private weather services depend on the health of the economy.

There will continue to be demand for atmospheric scientists to analyze and monitor the dispersion of pollutants into the air to ensure compliance with Federal environmental regulations outlined in the Clean Air Act of 1990, but employment increases are expected to be small.

Earnings

Median annual earnings of atmospheric scientists in 1998 were $54,430. The middle 50 percent earned between $38,570 and $75,260. The lowest 10 percent earned less than $27,250 and the highest 10 percent earned more than $87,760.

The average salary for meteorologists in nonsupervisory, supervisory, and managerial positions employed by the Federal Government was about $62,500 in 1999. Meteorologists in the Federal Government with a bachelor's degree and no experience received a starting salary of $20,600 or $25,500, depending on their college grades. Those with a master's degree could start at $25,500 or $31,200; those with the Ph.D., at $37,700 or $45,200. Beginning salaries for all degree levels are slightly higher in selected areas of the country where the prevailing local pay level is higher.

Related Occupations

Workers in other occupations concerned with the physical environment include oceanographers, geologists and geophysicists, hydrologists, physicists, mathematicians, and civil, chemical, and environmental engineers.

Sources of Additional Information

Information about careers in meteorology is available from:

☛ American Meteorological Society, 45 Beacon St., Boston, MA 02108. Internet: **http://www.ametsoc.org/AMS**

Information on acquiring a job as a meteorologist with the Federal Government may be obtained from the Office of Personnel Management through a telephone-based system. Consult your telephone directory under U.S. Government for a local number or call (912) 757-3000 (TDD 912 744-2299). That number is not toll-free and charges may result. Information also is available from their Internet site: **http://www.usajobs.opm.gov**

Chemists

(O*NET 24105)

Significant Points

- A bachelor's degree in chemistry or a related discipline is usually the minimum educational requirement; however, many research jobs require a Ph.D.
- Job growth will be concentrated in drug manufacturing and research and testing services firms.

Nature of the Work

Everything in the environment, whether naturally occurring or of human design, is composed of chemicals. Chemists search for and put to use new knowledge about chemicals. Chemical research has led to the discovery and development of new and improved synthetic fibers, paints, adhesives, drugs, cosmetics, electronic components, lubricants, and thousands of other products. Chemists also develop processes that save energy and reduce pollution, such as improved oil refining and petrochemical processing methods. Research on the chemistry of living things spurs advances in medicine, agriculture, food processing, and other fields.

Chemists apply their knowledge of chemistry in various ways. Many work in research and development (R&D). In basic research, chemists investigate properties, composition, and structure of matter and the laws that govern the combination of elements and reactions of substances. In applied research and development, they create new products and processes or improve existing ones, often using knowledge gained from basic research. For example, synthetic rubber and plastics resulted from research on small molecules uniting to form large ones, a process called polymerization. R&D chemists use computers and a wide variety of sophisticated laboratory instrumentation. The use of computers to analyze complex data allows chemists to practice combinatorial chemistry. This technique makes and tests large quantities of chemical compounds simultaneously in order to find compounds with desired properties. Combinatorial chemistry makes chemists more productive by saving time and materials and could result in more products being developed in the future. They also spend time documenting and analyzing the results of their work and writing formal reports.

Chemists also work in production and quality control in chemical manufacturing plants. They prepare instructions for plant workers that specify ingredients, mixing times, and temperatures for each stage in the process. They also monitor automated processes to ensure proper product yield, and they test samples of raw materials or finished products to ensure they meet industry and government standards, including the regulations governing pollution. Chemists record and report on test results, and improve existing or develop new test methods.

Chemists often specialize in a subfield. *Analytical chemists* determine the structure, composition, and nature of substances by examining and identifying the various elements or compounds that make up a substance. They study the relations and interactions of the parts and develop analytical techniques. They also identify the presence and concentration of chemical pollutants in air, water, and soil. *Organic chemists* study the chemistry of the vast number of carbon compounds that make up all living things. Organic chemists who synthesize elements or simple compounds to create new compounds or substances that have different properties and applications have developed many commercial products, such as drugs, plastics, and elastomers (elastic substances similar to rubber). *Inorganic chemists* study compounds consisting mainly of elements other than carbon, such as those in electronic components. *Physical chemists* study the physical characteristics of atoms and molecules and investigate how chemical reactions work. Their research may result in new and better energy sources.

Biochemists, whose work encompasses both biology and chemistry, are included in the statement on biological scientists elsewhere in the *Handbook*.

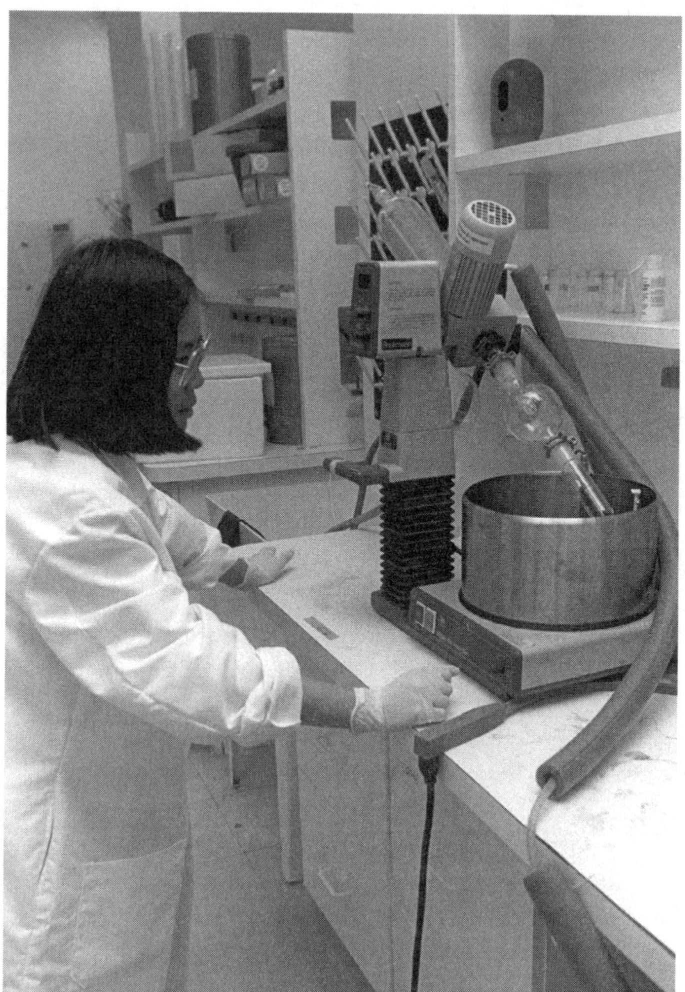

Chemists hold bachelor's, master's, and doctoral degrees.

Working Conditions

Chemists usually work regular hours in offices and laboratories. Research chemists spend much time in laboratories, but also work in offices when they do theoretical research or plan, record, and report on their lab research. Although some laboratories are small, others are large enough to incorporate prototype chemical manufacturing facilities as well as advanced equipment. Chemists do some of their work in a chemical plant or outdoors—while gathering water samples to test for pollutants, for example. Some chemists are exposed to health or safety hazards when handling certain chemicals, but there is little risk if proper procedures are followed.

Employment

Chemists held about 96,000 jobs in 1998. Nearly half of chemists are employed in manufacturing firms—mostly in the chemical manufacturing industry, which includes firms that produce plastics and synthetic materials, drugs, soaps and cleaners, paints, industrial organic chemicals, and other miscellaneous chemical products. Chemists also work for State and local governments, and for Federal agencies. Health and Human Services, which includes the Food and Drug Administration, the National Institutes of Health, and the Center for Disease Control, is the major Federal employer of chemists. The Departments of Defense and Agriculture, and the Environmental Protection Agency, also employ chemists. Other chemists work for research, development, and testing services. In addition, thousands of persons held chemistry faculty positions in colleges and universities. (See the statement on college and university faculty elsewhere in the *Handbook*.)

Chemists are employed in all parts of the country, but they are mainly concentrated in large industrial areas.

Training, Other Qualifications, and Advancement

A bachelor's degree in chemistry or a related discipline is usually the minimum educational requirement for entry-level chemist jobs. However, many research jobs require a Ph.D.

Many colleges and universities offer a bachelor's degree program in chemistry, about 620 of which are approved by the American Chemical Society (ACS). Several hundred colleges and universities also offer advanced degree programs in chemistry; around 320 master's programs, and about 190 doctoral programs are ACS-approved.

Students planning careers as chemists should take courses in science and mathematics, and should like working with their hands building scientific apparatus and performing experiments. Perseverance, curiosity, and the ability to concentrate on detail and to work independently are essential. In addition to required courses in analytical, inorganic, organic, and physical chemistry, undergraduate chemistry majors usually study biological sciences, mathematics, and physics. Those interested in the environmental field should also take courses in environmental studies and become familiar with current legislation and regulations. Computer courses are essential, as employers increasingly prefer job applicants who are able to apply computer skills to modeling and simulation tasks and operate computerized laboratory equipment.

Because research and development chemists are increasingly expected to work on interdisciplinary teams, some understanding of other disciplines, including business and marketing or economics, is desirable, along with leadership ability and good oral and written communication skills. Experience, either in academic laboratories or through internships or co-op programs in industry, also is useful. Some employers of research chemists, particularly in the pharmaceutical industry, prefer to hire individuals with several years of postdoctoral experience.

Graduate students typically specialize in a subfield of chemistry, such as analytical chemistry or polymer chemistry, depending on their interests and the kind of work they wish to do. For example, those interested in doing drug research in the pharmaceutical industry usually develop a strong background in synthetic organic chemistry. However, students normally need not specialize at the undergraduate level. In fact, undergraduates who are broadly trained have more flexibility when job hunting or changing jobs than if they narrowly define their interests. Most employers provide new graduates additional training or education.

In government or industry, beginning chemists with a bachelor's degree work in quality control, analytical testing, or assist senior chemists in research and development laboratories. Many employers prefer chemists with a Ph.D. or at least a master's degree to lead basic and applied research. A Ph.D. is also often preferred for advancement to many administrative positions.

Job Outlook

Employment of chemists is expected to grow about as fast as the average for all occupations through 2008. Job growth will be concentrated in drug manufacturing and research, development, and testing services firms. The chemical industry, the major employer of chemists, should face continued demand for goods such as new and better pharmaceuticals and personal care products, as well as more specialty chemicals designed to address specific problems or applications. To meet these demands, chemical firms will continue to devote money to research and development—through in-house teams or outside contractors—spurring employment growth of chemists.

Within the chemical industry, job opportunities are expected to be most plentiful in pharmaceutical and biotechnology firms. Stronger competition among drug companies and an aging population are contributing to the need for innovative and improved drugs discovered through scientific research. Chemical firms that develop and manufacture personal products such as toiletries and cosmetics must continually innovate and develop new and better products to remain competitive. Additionally, as the population grows and becomes better informed, the demand for different or improved grooming products—including vegetable-based products, products with milder formulas, treatments for aging skin, and products that have been developed using more benign chemical processes than in the past—will remain strong, spurring the need for chemists.

In most of the remaining segments of the chemical industry, employment growth is expected to decline as companies downsize and turn to outside contractors to provide specialized services. Nevertheless, some job openings will result from the need to replace chemists who retire or otherwise leave the labor force. Quality control will continue to be an important issue in the chemical and other industries that use chemicals in their manufacturing processes. Chemists will also be needed to develop and improve the technologies and processes used to produce chemicals for all purposes, and to monitor and measure air and water pollutants to ensure compliance with local, State, and Federal environmental regulations.

Outside the chemical industry, firms that provide research, development, and testing services are expected to be the source of numerous job opportunities between 1998 and 2008. Chemical companies, including drug manufacturers, are increasingly turning to these services to perform specialized research and other work formerly done by in-house chemists. Chemists will also be needed to work in research and testing firms that focus on environmental testing and cleanup.

During periods of economic recession, layoffs of chemists may occur—especially in the industrial chemicals industry. This industry provides many of the raw materials to the auto manufacturing and construction industries, both of which are vulnerable to temporary slowdowns during recessions.

Earnings

Median annual earnings of chemists in 1998 were $46,220. The middle 50 percent earned between $34,580 and $68,360. The lowest 10 percent earned less than $27,240 and the highest 10 percent earned more than $86,260. Median annual earnings in the industries employing the largest numbers of chemists in 1997 were:

Federal Government	$62,800
Drugs	43,300
Research and testing services	34,500

A survey by the American Chemical Society reports that the median salary of all their members with a bachelor's degree was $50,100 a year in 1999; with a master's degree, $61,000; and with a Ph.D., $76,000. Median salaries were highest for those working in private industry; those in academia earned the least. According to an ACS survey of recent graduates, inexperienced chemistry graduates with a bachelor's degree earned a median starting salary of $29,500 in 1998; with a master's degree, $38,500; and with a Ph.D., $59,300. Among bachelor's degree graduates, those who had completed internships or had other work experience while in school commanded the highest starting salaries.

In 1999, chemists in nonsupervisory, supervisory, and managerial positions in the Federal Government earned an average salary of $64,200.

Related Occupations

The work of chemical engineers, agricultural scientists, biological scientists, and chemical technicians is closely related to the work done by chemists. The work of other physical and life science occupations, such as physicists and medical scientists, may also be similar to that of chemists.

Sources of Additional Information

General information on career opportunities and earnings for chemists is available from:

☛ American Chemical Society, Education Division, 1155 16th St. NW., Washington, DC 20036. Internet: **http://www.acs.org**

Information on acquiring a job as a chemist with the Federal Government may be obtained from the Office of Personnel Management through a telephone-based system. Consult your telephone directory under U.S. Government for a local number or call (912) 757-3000; TDD (912) 744-2299. That number is not toll free and charges may result. Information also is available from their Internet site: **http://www.usajobs.opm.gov**

Geologists, Geophysicists, and Oceanographers

(O*NET 24111A and 24111B)

Significant Points

- Work at remote field sites is common.
- A bachelor's degree in geology or geophysics is adequate for entry-level jobs; better jobs with good advancement potential usually require at least a master's degree. A Ph.D. degree is required for most research positions in colleges and universities and in government.

Nature of the Work

Geologists, geophysicists, and oceanographers use their knowledge of the physical makeup and history of the Earth to locate water, mineral, and energy resources; protect the environment; predict future geologic hazards; and offer advice on construction and land use projects. By using sophisticated instruments and analyses of the Earth and water, geological scientists, also known as *geoscientists*, study the Earth's geologic past and present in order to make predictions about its future. For example, they may study the Earth's movements to try to predict when and where the next earthquake or volcano will occur and the probable impact on surrounding areas to minimize the damage.

Geology, geophysics, and oceanography are closely related fields; but there are major differences. *Geologists* study the composition, processes, and history of the Earth. They try to find out how rocks were formed and what has happened to them since formation. They also study the evolution of life by analyzing plant and animal fossils. *Geophysicists* use the principles of physics, mathematics, and chemistry to study not only the Earth's surface, but also its internal composition; ground and surface waters; atmosphere; oceans; and its magnetic, electrical, and gravitational forces. *Oceanographers* use their knowledge of geology and geophysics, in addition to biology and chemistry, to study the world's oceans and coastal waters. They study the motion and circulation of the ocean waters and their physical and chemical properties, and how these properties affect coastal areas, climate, and weather.

Many geologists, geophysicists and oceanographers are involved in the search for oil and gas, but other geological scientists play an important role in preserving and cleaning up the environment. Activities include designing and monitoring waste disposal sites, preserving water supplies, and reclaiming contaminated land and water to comply with Federal environmental regulations.

Geoscientists can spend a large part of their time in the field identifying and examining rocks, studying information collected by remote sensing instruments in satellites, conducting geological surveys, constructing field maps, and using instruments to measure the Earth's gravity and magnetic field. For example, they often perform seismic studies, which involve bouncing energy waves off buried rock layers, to search for oil and gas or understand the structure of subsurface rock layers. Seismic signals generated by earthquakes are used to determine the earthquake's location and intensity.

In laboratories, geologists and geophysicists examine the chemical and physical properties of specimens. They study fossil remains of animal and plant life or experiment with the flow of water and oil through rocks. Some geoscientists use two- or three-dimensional computer modeling to portray water layers and the flow of water or other fluids through rock cracks and porous materials. They use a variety of sophisticated laboratory instruments, including x-ray diffractometers, which determine the crystal structure of minerals, and petrographic microscopes, for the study of rock and sediment samples.

Geoscientists working in mining or the oil and gas industry sometimes process and interpret data produced by remote sensing satellites to help identify potential new mineral, oil, or gas deposits. Seismic technology is also an important exploration tool. Seismic waves are used to develop a three-dimensional picture of underground or underwater rock formations. Seismic reflection technology may also reveal unusual underground features that sometimes indicate accumulations of natural gas or petroleum, facilitating exploration and reducing the risks associated with drilling in previously unexplored areas.

Numerous subdisciplines or specialties fall under the two major disciplines of geology and geophysics that further differentiate the type of work geoscientists do. For example, *petroleum geologists* explore for oil and gas deposits by studying and mapping the subsurface of the ocean or land. They use sophisticated geophysical instrumentation, well log data, and computers to interpret geological information. *Engineering geologists* apply geologic principles to the fields of civil and environmental engineering, offering advice on major construction projects and assisting in environmental remediation and natural hazard reduction projects. *Mineralogists* analyze and classify minerals and precious stones according to composition and structure and study their environment in order to find new mineral resources. *Paleontologists* study fossils found in geological formations to trace the evolution of plant and animal life and the geologic history of the Earth. *Stratigraphers* study the formation and layering of rocks to understand the environment in which they were formed. *Volcanologists* investigate volcanoes and volcanic phenomena to try to predict the potential for future eruptions and possible hazards to human health and welfare.

Geophysicists may specialize in areas such as geodesy, seismology, or magnetic geophysics. *Geodesists* study the size and shape of the Earth, its gravitational field, tides, polar motion, and rotation. *Seismologists* interpret data from seismographs and other geophysical instruments to detect earthquakes and locate earthquake-related faults. *Geochemists* study the nature and distribution of chemical elements in ground water and Earth materials. *Geomagnetists* measure the Earth's magnetic field and use measurements taken over the past few centuries to devise theoretical models to explain the Earth's origin. *Paleomagnetists* interpret fossil magnetization in rocks and sediments from the continents and oceans, to record the spreading of the sea floor, the wandering of the continents, and the many reversals of polarity that the Earth's magnetic field has undergone through time. Other geophysicists study atmospheric sciences and space physics. (See the statements

Geoscientists use a variety of sophisticated equipment.

on atmospheric scientists and physicists and astronomers elsewhere in the *Handbook.*)

Hydrology is closely related to the disciplines of geology and geophysics. *Hydrologists* study the quantity, distribution, circulation, and physical properties of underground and surface waters. They study the form and intensity of precipitation, its rate of infiltration into the soil, its movement through the Earth, and its return to the ocean and atmosphere. The work they do is particularly important in environmental preservation, remediation, and flood control.

Oceanography also has several subdisciplines. *Physical oceanographers* study the ocean tides, waves, currents, temperatures, density, and salinity. They study the interaction of various forms of energy, such as light, radar, sound, heat, and wind with the sea, in addition to investigating the relationship between the sea, weather, and climate. Their studies provide the Maritime Fleet with up-to-date oceanic conditions. *Chemical oceanographers* study the distribution of chemical compounds and chemical interactions that occur in the ocean and sea floor. They may investigate how pollution affects the chemistry of the ocean. *Geological and geophysical oceanographers* study the topographic features and the physical makeup of the ocean floor. Their knowledge can help oil and gas producers find these minerals on the bottom of the ocean. *Biological oceanographers*, often called marine biologists, study the distribution and migration patterns of the many diverse forms of sea life in the ocean. (See the statement on biological and medical scientists elsewhere in the *Handbook.*)

Working Conditions

Some geoscientists spend the majority of their time in an office, but many others divide their time between fieldwork and office or laboratory work. Geologists often travel to remote field sites by helicopter or four-wheel drive vehicles and cover large areas on foot. An increasing number of exploration geologists and geophysicists work in foreign countries, sometimes in remote areas and under difficult conditions. Oceanographers may spend considerable time at sea on academic research ships. Fieldwork often requires working long hours, but workers are usually rewarded by longer than normal vacations. Geoscientists in research positions with the Federal Government or in colleges and universities often are required to design programs and write grant proposals in order to continue their data collection and research. Geoscientists in consulting jobs face similar pressures to market their skills and write proposals to maintain steady work. Travel is often required to meet with prospective clients or investors.

Employment

Geologists, geophysicists, and oceanographers held about 44,000 jobs in 1998. Many more individuals held geology, geophysics, and oceanography faculty positions in colleges and universities, but they are considered college and university faculty. (See the statement on college and university faculty elsewhere in the *Handbook.*)

Among salaried geologists and geophysicists, nearly 1 in 3 were employed in engineering and management services, and 1 in 6 worked for oil and gas extraction companies or metal mining companies. About 1 geoscientist in 8 was self-employed; most were consultants to industry or government.

The Federal Government employed about 5,800 geologists, geophysicists, oceanographers, and hydrologists in 1998. Over half worked for the Department of the Interior, mostly within the U.S. Geological Survey (USGS). Others worked for the Departments of Defense, Agriculture, Commerce, and Energy, and the Environmental Protection Agency. Over 3,000 worked for State agencies, such as State geological surveys and State departments of conservation.

Training, Other Qualifications, and Advancement

A bachelor's degree in geology or geophysics is adequate for some entry-level jobs, but more job opportunities and better jobs with good advancement potential usually require at least a master's degree in geology or geophysics. Persons with degrees in physics, chemistry, mathematics, or computer science may also qualify for some geophysics or geology jobs, if their coursework included study in geology. A Ph.D. degree is required for most research positions in colleges and universities, Federal agencies, and State geological surveys.

Hundreds of colleges and universities offer a bachelor's degree in geology; fewer schools offer programs in geophysics, oceanography, or other geosciences. Other programs offering related training for beginning geological scientists include geophysical technology, geophysical engineering, geophysical prospecting, engineering geology, petroleum geology, hydrology, and geochemistry. In addition, several hundred universities award advanced degrees in geology or geophysics.

Traditional geoscience courses emphasizing classical geologic methods and topics (such as mineralogy, paleontology, stratigraphy, and structural geology) are important for all geoscientists. Those students interested in working in the environmental or regulatory fields, either in environmental consulting firms or for Federal or State governments, should take courses in hydrology, hazardous waste management, environmental legislation, chemistry, fluid mechanics, and geologic logging. An understanding of environmental regulations and government permit issues is also valuable for those planning to work in mining and oil and gas extraction. Computer skills are essential for prospective geoscientists; students who have some experience with computer modeling, data analysis and integration, digital mapping, remote sensing, and geographic information systems (GIS) will be the most prepared entering the job market. A knowledge of the Global Positioning System (GPS)—a locator system that uses satellites—is also very helpful. Some employers seek applicants with field experience, so a summer internship may be beneficial to prospective geoscientists.

Geologists, geophysicists, and oceanographers must have good interpersonal skills, because they usually work as part of a team with other scientists, engineers, and technicians. Strong oral and written communication skills are also important, because writing technical reports and research proposals, as well as communicating research results to others, are important aspects of the work. Because many jobs require foreign travel, knowledge of a second language is becoming an important attribute to employers. Geoscientists must be inquisitive and able to think logically and have an open mind. Those involved in fieldwork must have physical stamina.

Geologists and geophysicists often begin their careers in field exploration or as research assistants or technicians in laboratories or offices. They are given more difficult assignments as they gain experience. Eventually, they may be promoted to project leader, program manager, or another management and research position.

Job Outlook

Employment of geologists, geophysicists, and oceanographers is expected to grow about as fast as the average through 2008. The need to replace geologists, geophysicists, and oceanographers who retire will result in many additional job openings over the next decade. Driving the growth will be the need for organizations to comply with an increasing number of environmental laws and regulations, particularly those regarding groundwater contamination and flood control. Increased construction and exploration for oil and natural gas abroad will require geoscientists to work overseas. In the short-run, however, low energy prices, oil company mergers, and stagnant or declining government funding for research may affect the hiring of petroleum geologists and geoscientists involved in research.

In the past, employment of geologists and some other geoscientists has been cyclical and largely affected by the price of oil and gas.

When prices were low, oil and gas producers curtailed exploration activities and laid off geologists. When prices were up, companies had the funds and incentive to renew exploration efforts and hire geoscientists in large numbers. In recent years, a growing worldwide demand for oil and gas and new exploration and recovery techniques—particularly in deep water and previously inaccessible sites—have returned some stability to the petroleum industry, with a few companies increasing their hiring of geoscientists. Growth in this area, though, will be limited due to increasing efficiencies in finding oil and gas. Geoscientists who speak a foreign language and who are willing to work abroad should enjoy the best opportunities.

In the environmental field, the need for companies to comply with an increasing number of laws and regulations will contribute to the demand for geoscientists, especially hydrologists and engineering geologists. As the population increases and moves to more environmentally sensitive locations, geoscientists will be needed to assess building sites for potential geologic hazards and to address issues of pollution control and waste disposal. An expected increase in highway building and other infrastructure projects will be an additional source of jobs for engineering geologists.

Jobs with the Federal and State governments and with organizations dependent on Federal funds for support will experience little growth over the next decade, unless budgets increase significantly. This lack of funding will affect mostly oceanographers and those geoscientists performing basic research.

Earnings

Median annual earnings of geologists, geophysicists, and oceanographers were $53,890 in 1998. The middle 50 percent earned between $39,830 and $79,630 a year. The lowest 10 percent earned less than $30,950 and the highest 10 percent earned more than $101,390. Median annual earnings in the industries employing the largest number of geoscientists in 1997 were as follows.

Industry	Earnings
Crude petroleum and natural gas	$81,900
Management and public relations	44,900
Engineering and architectural services	44,700

According to the National Association of Colleges and Employers, beginning salary offers in 1999 for graduates with bachelor's degrees in geology and the geological sciences averaged about $34,900 a year; graduates with a master's degree averaged $44,700.

In 1999, the Federal Government's average salary for geologists in managerial, supervisory, and nonsupervisory positions was $64,400; for geophysicists, $72,500; for hydrologists, $58,900; and for oceanographers, $66,000.

The petroleum, mineral, and mining industries offer higher salaries, but less job security, than other industries. These industries are vulnerable to recessions and changes in oil and gas prices, among other factors, and usually release workers when exploration and drilling slow down.

Related Occupations

Many geologists and geophysicists work in the petroleum and natural gas industry. This industry also employs many other workers in the scientific and technical aspects of petroleum and natural gas exploration and extraction, including engineering technicians, science technicians, petroleum engineers, and surveyors. Also, some life scientists, physicists, chemists, and atmospheric scientists—as well as mathematicians, computer scientists, soil scientists, and cartographers—perform related work in both petroleum and natural gas exploration and extraction and in environment-related activities.

Sources of Additional Information

Information on training and career opportunities for geologists is available from:

☛ American Geological Institute, 4220 King St., Alexandria, VA 22302-1502. Internet: **http://www.agiweb.org**

☛ Geological Society of America, P.O. Box 9140, Boulder, CO 80301-9140. Internet: **http://www.geosociety.org**

☛ American Association of Petroleum Geologists, P.O. Box 979, Tulsa, OK 74101. **Internet: http://www.aapg.org**

Information on training and career opportunities for geophysicists is available from:

☛ American Geophysical Union, 2000 Florida Ave. NW., Washington, DC 20009. Internet**: http://www.agu.org**

☛ Society of Exploration Geophysicists, 8801 South Yale, Tulsa, OK 74137. Internet: **http://www.seg.org**

A list of education and training programs in oceanography and related fields is available from:

☛ Marine Technology Society, 1828 L St. NW, Suite 906, Washington, DC 20036. Internet: **http://www.mtsociety.org**

Information on acquiring a job as a geologist, geophysicist, hydrologist, or oceanographer with the Federal Government may be obtained through a telephone-based system from the Office of Personnel Management. Consult your telephone directory under U.S. Government for a local number, or call (912) 757-3000 (TDD 912 744-2299). This number is not toll-free, and charges may result. Information also is available from the Internet site: **http://www.usajobs.opm.gov**

Physicists and Astronomers

(O*NET 24102A and 24102B)

Significant Points

- A doctoral degree is the usual educational requirement because most jobs are in basic research and development; a bachelor's or master's degree is sufficient for some jobs in applied research and development.
- As funding for research grows slowly or not at all, new Ph.D. graduates will face competition for basic research jobs.

Nature of the Work

Physicists explore and identify basic principles governing the structure and behavior of matter, the generation and transfer of energy, and the interaction of matter and energy. Some physicists use these principles in theoretical areas, such as the nature of time and the origin of the universe; others apply their physics knowledge to practical areas, such as the development of advanced materials, electronic and optical devices, and medical equipment.

Physicists design and perform experiments with lasers, cyclotrons, telescopes, mass spectrometers, and other equipment. Based on observations and analysis, they attempt to discover and explain laws describing the forces of nature, such as gravity, electromagnetism, and nuclear interactions. Physicists also find ways to apply physical laws and theories to problems in nuclear energy, electronics, optics, materials, communications, aerospace technology, navigation equipment, and medical instrumentation.

Astronomy is sometimes considered a subfield of physics. *Astronomers* use the principles of physics and mathematics to learn about the fundamental nature of the universe, including the sun, moon, planets, stars, and galaxies. They also apply their knowledge to solve problems in navigation, space flight, and satellite communications and to develop the instrumentation and techniques used to observe and collect astronomical data.

Most physicists work in research and development. Some do basic research to increase scientific knowledge. Physicists who conduct applied research build upon the discoveries made through basic research and work to develop new devices, products, and processes. For instance, basic research in solid-state physics led to the development of transistors and then to the integrated circuits used in computers.

Physicists also design research equipment. This equipment often has additional unanticipated uses. For example, lasers are used in surgery; microwave devices are used for ovens; and measuring instruments can analyze blood or the chemical content of foods. A small number of physicists work in inspection, testing, quality control, and other production-related jobs in industry.

Much physics research is done in small or medium-size laboratories. However, experiments in plasma, nuclear, high energy, and some other areas of physics require extremely large, expensive equipment, such as particle accelerators. Physicists in these subfields often work in large teams. Although physics research may require extensive experimentation in laboratories, research physicists still spend time in offices planning, recording, analyzing, and reporting on research.

Almost all astronomers do research. Some are theoreticians, working on the laws governing the structure and evolution of astronomical objects. Others analyze large quantities of data gathered by observatories and satellites and write scientific papers or reports on their findings. Some astronomers actually operate, usually as part of a team, large space- or ground-based telescopes. However, astronomers may spend only a few weeks each year making observations with optical telescopes, radio telescopes, and other instruments. For many years, satellites and other space-based instruments have provided tremendous amounts of astronomical data. New technology resulting in improvements in analytical techniques and instruments, such as computers and optical telescopes and mounts, is leading to a resurgence in ground-based research. A small number of astronomers work in museums housing planetariums. These astronomers develop and revise programs presented to the public and may direct planetarium operations.

Physicists generally specialize in one of many subfields—elementary particle physics, nuclear physics, atomic and molecular physics, physics of condensed matter (solid-state physics), optics, acoustics, space physics, plasma physics, or the physics of fluids. Some specialize in a subdivision of one of these subfields. For example, within condensed matter physics, specialties include superconductivity, crystallography, and semiconductors. However, all physics involves the same fundamental principles, so specialties may overlap, and physicists may switch from one subfield to another. Also, growing numbers of physicists work in combined fields, such as biophysics, chemical physics, and geophysics.

Working Conditions

Physicists often work regular hours in laboratories and offices. At times, however, those who are deeply involved in research may work long or irregular hours. Most do not encounter unusual hazards in their work. Some physicists temporarily work away from home at national or international facilities with unique equipment, such as particle accelerators. Astronomers who make observations using ground-based telescopes may spend long periods of time in observatories; this work usually involves travel to remote locations. Long hours, including routine night work, may create temporarily stressful conditions.

Physicists and astronomers need mathematical and computer skills.

Physicists and astronomers whose work is dependent on grant money are often under pressure to write grant proposals to keep their work funded.

Employment

Physicists and astronomers held nearly 18,000 jobs in 1998. About 2 in 10 nonfaculty physicists and astronomers worked for commercial or noncommercial research, development, and testing laboratories. The Federal Government employed almost 2 in 10, mostly in the Department of Defense, but also in the National Aeronautics and Space Administration (NASA), and the Departments of Commerce, Health and Human Services, and Energy. Other physicists and astronomers worked in colleges and universities in nonfaculty positions, or for State governments, drug companies, and electronic equipment manufacturers.

Besides the jobs described above, many physicists and astronomers held faculty positions in colleges and universities. (See the statement on college and university faculty elsewhere in the *Handbook*.)

Although physicists and astronomers are employed in all parts of the country, most work in areas in which universities, large research and development laboratories, or observatories are located.

Training, Other Qualifications, and Advancement

A doctoral degree is the usual educational requirement for physicists and astronomers, because most jobs are in basic research and development. Additional experience and training in a postdoctoral research appointment, although not required, is important for physicists and astronomers aspiring to permanent positions in basic research in universities and government laboratories. Many physics and astronomy Ph.D. holders ultimately teach at the college or university level.

Master's degree holders usually do not qualify for basic research positions but do qualify for many kinds of jobs requiring a physics background, including positions in manufacturing and applied research and development. Physics departments in some colleges and universities are creating professional master's degree programs to specifically prepare students for physics-related research and development in private industry that does not require a Ph.D. degree. A master's degree may suffice for teaching jobs in 2-year colleges. Those with bachelor's degrees in physics are rarely qualified to fill positions as research or teaching physicists. They are, however, usually qualified to work in an engineering-related area, software development and other scientific fields, to work as technicians, or to assist in setting up computer networks and sophisticated laboratory equipment. Some may qualify for applied research jobs in private industry or nonresearch positions in the Federal Government. Some become science teachers in secondary schools. Astronomy bachelor's or master's degree holders often enter a field unrelated to astronomy, and they are qualified to work in planetariums running science shows, to assist astronomers doing research, and to operate space- and ground-based telescopes and other astronomical instrumentation. (See the statements on engineers; geologists, geophysicists, and oceanographers; computer programmers; and computer systems analysts, engineers, and scientists elsewhere in the *Handbook*.)

About 760 colleges and universities offer a bachelor's degree in physics. Undergraduate programs provide a broad background in the natural sciences and mathematics. Typical physics courses include electromagnetism, optics, thermodynamics, atomic physics, and quantum mechanics.

In 1998, 183 colleges and universities had departments offering Ph.D. degrees in physics. Another 72 departments offered a master's as their highest degree. Graduate students usually concentrate in a subfield of physics, such as elementary particles or condensed matter. Many begin studying for their doctorate immediately after receiving their bachelor's degree.

About 70 universities grant degrees in astronomy, either through an astronomy, physics, or a combined physics/astronomy department. Applicants to astronomy doctoral programs face competition for available slots. Those planning a career in astronomy should have a very strong physics background. In fact, an undergraduate degree in either physics or astronomy is excellent preparation, followed by a Ph.D. in astronomy.

Mathematical ability, problem solving and analytical skills, an inquisitive mind, imagination, and initiative are important traits for anyone planning a career in physics or astronomy. Prospective physicists who hope to work in industrial laboratories applying physics knowledge to practical problems should broaden their educational background to include courses outside of physics, such as economics, computer technology, and business management. Good oral and written communication skills are also important because many physicists work as part of a team, write research papers or proposals, or have contact with clients or customers with non-physics backgrounds.

Many physics and astronomy Ph.D.'s begin their careers in a postdoctoral research position, where they may work with experienced physicists as they continue to learn about their specialty and develop ideas and results to be used in later work. Initial work may be under the close supervision of senior scientists. After some experience, physicists perform increasingly complex tasks and work more independently. Those who develop new products or processes sometimes form their own companies or join new firms to exploit their own ideas.

Job Outlook

Historically, many physicists and astronomers have been employed on research projects—often defense-related. Small or no increases in defense-related research and a continued slowdown in the growth of civilian physics-related basic research will result in little change in employment of physicists and astronomers through the year 2008. The need to replace physicists and astronomers who retire will account for almost all expected job openings. Budget tightening in the Federal Government may also affect employment of physicists, especially those dependent on Federal research grants. The Federal Government funds numerous noncommercial research facilities. The Federally Funded Research and Development Centers (FFRDCs) whose missions include a significant physics component are largely funded by the Department of Energy (DOE) or the Department of Defense (DOD), and their R&D budgets have not kept pace with inflation in recent years. Continuing budget tightening may limit funding and, consequently, the scope of physics-related research in these facilities.

In recent years, many persons with a physics background have found employment in private industry in the areas of information technology, semiconductor technology, and other applied sciences. This trend is expected to continue; however, many of these positions will be under job titles such as computer software engineer, computer programmer, engineer, and systems developer, rather than physicist.

For several years, the number of doctorates granted in physics has been much greater than the number of openings for physicists, resulting in keen competition, particularly for research positions in colleges and universities and research and development centers. Competitive conditions are beginning to ease, because the number of doctorate degrees awarded has begun dropping, following recent declines in enrollment in graduate physics programs. However, new doctoral graduates should still expect to face competition for research jobs, not only from fellow graduates, but also from an existing supply of postdoctoral workers seeking to leave low-paying, temporary positions and non-U.S. citizen applicants. Also, the competition for grant money for physics-related research projects is likely to remain intense during the projection period.

Although research and development budgets in private industry will continue to grow, many research laboratories in private industry are expected to reduce basic research, which includes much physics research, in favor of applied or manufacturing research and product and software development. Although many physicists and astronomers will be eligible for retirement over the next decade, it is probable not all of them will be replaced when they retire.

Opportunities may be more numerous for those with a master's degree, particularly graduates from programs preparing students for applied research and development, product design, and manufacturing positions in industry. Many of these positions, however, will have titles other than physicist, such as engineer or computer scientist.

Persons with only a bachelor's degree in physics or astronomy are not qualified to enter most physicist or astronomer research jobs but may qualify for a wide range of positions in engineering, technician, mathematics, and computer- and environment-related occupations. Those who meet State certification requirements can become high school physics teachers, an occupation reportedly in strong demand in many school districts. (See the statements on these occupations elsewhere in the *Handbook*.) Despite competition for traditional physics and astronomy research jobs, individuals with a physics degree at any level will find their skills useful for entry to many other occupations.

Earnings

Median annual earnings of physicists and astronomers in 1998 were \$73,240. The middle 50 percent earned between \$56,230 and \$90,440. The lowest 10 percent earned less than \$41,830 and the highest 10 percent earned more than \$113,800.

According to a 1999 National Association of Colleges and Employers survey, the average annual starting salary offer to physics doctoral degree candidates was \$60,300.

The American Institute of Physics reported a median annual salary of \$70,000 in 1998 for its members with Ph.D.'s; with master's degrees, \$57,000; and with bachelor's degrees, \$54,000. Those working in temporary postdoctoral positions earned significantly less.

The average annual salary for physicists employed by the Federal Government was \$79,400 in early 1999 and for astronomy and space scientists, \$81,300.

Related Occupations

The work of physicists and astronomers relates closely to that of engineers, chemists, atmospheric scientists, geophysicists, computer scientists, computer programmers, and mathematicians.

Sources of Additional Information

General information on career opportunities in physics is available from:

☛ American Institute of Physics, Career Services Division and Education and Employment Division, One Physics Ellipse, College Park, MD 20740-3843. Internet: **http://www.aip.org**

☛ The American Physical Society, One Physics Ellipse, College Park, MD 20740-3844. Internet: **http://www.aps.org**

For a brochure containing information on careers in astronomy, send your request to:

☛ American Astronomical Society, Education Office, University of Chicago, 5640 South Ellis Ave., Chicago IL 60637.
Internet: **http://www.aas.org**

Science Technicians

(O*NET 22599F, 24502A, 24502B, 24502C, 24502D, 24505A, 24505B, 24505C, 24505D, 24505E, 24508A, 24508B, 24511B, 24511E, 24599A, 24599B, 24599C, and 25323)

Significant Points

- Science technicians in production jobs often work in 8-hour shifts around the clock.
- Job opportunities are expected to be very good for qualified graduates of science technician training programs or applied science technology programs who are well trained on equipment used in laboratories and production facilities.

Nature of the Work

Science technicians use the principles and theories of science and mathematics to solve problems in research and development and to help invent and improve products and processes. However, their jobs are more practically oriented than those of scientists. Technicians set up, operate, and maintain laboratory instruments, monitor experiments, make observations, calculate and record results, and often develop conclusions. They must keep detailed logs of all their work-related activities. Those who work in production monitor manufacturing processes and may be involved in ensuring quality by testing products for proper proportions of ingredients, purity, or for strength and durability.

As laboratory instrumentation and procedures have become more complex in recent years, the role of science technicians in research and development has expanded. In addition to performing routine tasks, many technicians also develop and adapt laboratory procedures to achieve the best results, interpret data, and devise solutions to problems, under the direction of scientists. Moreover, technicians must master the laboratory equipment, so they can adjust settings when necessary, and recognize when equipment is malfunctioning.

The increasing use of robotics to perform many routine tasks has freed technicians to operate more sophisticated laboratory equipment. Science technicians make extensive use of computers, computer-interfaced equipment, robotics, and high-technology industrial applications, such as biological engineering.

Most science technicians specialize, learning skills and working in the same disciplines as scientists. Occupational titles, therefore, tend to follow the same structure as scientists. *Agricultural technicians* work with agricultural scientists in food, fiber, and animal research, production, and processing. Some conduct tests and experiments to improve the yield and quality of crops or to increase the resistance of plants and animals to disease, insects, or other hazards. Other agricultural technicians do animal breeding and nutrition work.

Biological technicians work with biologists studying living organisms. Many assist scientists who conduct medical research—helping to find a cure for cancer or AIDS, for example. Those who work in pharmaceutical companies help develop and manufacture medicinal and pharmaceutical preparations. Those working in the field of microbiology generally work as lab assistants, studying living organisms and infectious agents. Biological technicians also analyze organic substances, such as blood, food, and drugs, and some examine evidence in criminal investigations. Biological technicians working in biotechnology labs use the knowledge and techniques gained from basic research by scientists, including gene splicing and recombinant DNA, and apply these techniques in product development.

Chemical technicians work with chemists and chemical engineers, developing and using chemicals and related products and equipment. Most do research and development, testing, or other laboratory work. For example, they might test packaging for design, integrity of materials, and environmental acceptability; assemble and operate new equipment to develop new products; monitor product quality; or develop new production techniques. Some chemical technicians collect and analyze samples of air and water to monitor pollution levels. Those who focus on basic research might produce compounds through complex organic synthesis. Chemical technicians within chemical plants are also referred to as *process technicians*. They may operate equipment, monitor plant processes and analyze plant materials.

Environmental technicians perform laboratory and field tests to monitor environmental resources and determine the contaminants and sources of pollution. They may collect samples for testing or be involved in abating, controlling, or remediating sources of environmental pollutants. Some are responsible for waste management operations, control and management of hazardous materials inventory, or general activities involving regulatory compliance. There is a growing emphasis on pollution prevention activities.

Nuclear technicians operate nuclear test and research equipment, monitor radiation, and assist nuclear engineers and physicists in research. Some also operate remote control equipment to manipulate radioactive materials or materials to be exposed to radioactivity.

Petroleum technicians measure and record physical and geologic conditions in oil or gas wells, using instruments lowered into wells or by analysis of the mud from wells. In oil and gas exploration, these technicians collect and examine geological data or test geological samples to determine petroleum and mineral content. Some petroleum technicians, called *scouts*, collect information about oil and gas well drilling operations, geological and geophysical prospecting, and land or lease contracts.

Other science technicians collect weather information or assist oceanographers.

Working Conditions

Science technicians work under a wide variety of conditions. Most work indoors, usually in laboratories, and have regular hours. Some occasionally work irregular hours to monitor experiments that can't be completed during regular working hours. Production technicians often work in 8-hour shifts around the clock.

Science technicians put theory into practice.

Others, such as agricultural, petroleum, and environmental technicians, perform much of their work outdoors, sometimes in remote locations.

Some science technicians may be exposed to hazards from equipment, chemicals, or toxic materials. Chemical technicians sometimes work with toxic chemicals or radioactive isotopes, nuclear technicians may be exposed to radiation, and biological technicians sometimes work with disease-causing organisms or radioactive agents. However, these working conditions pose little risk, if proper safety procedures are followed.

Employment

Science technicians held about 227,000 jobs in 1998. Over 37 percent worked in manufacturing—mostly in the chemical industry—but also in the food processing industry. About 12 percent worked in education services, and another 15 percent worked in research and testing services. In 1998, the Federal Government employed about 14,000 science technicians, mostly in the Departments of Defense, Agriculture, and Interior.

Training, Other Qualifications, and Advancement

There are several ways to qualify for a job as a science technician. Many employers prefer applicants who have at least 2 years of specialized training or an associate degree in applied science or science-related technology. Because employers' preferences vary, however, some science technicians have a bachelor's degree in chemistry or biology or have taken several science and math courses at 4-year colleges.

Many technical and community colleges offer associate degrees in a specific technology or a more general education in science and mathematics. A number of 2-year associate degree programs are designed to provide easy transfer to a 4-year college or university, if desired. Technical institutes usually offer technician training, but provide less theory and general education than technical or community colleges. The length of programs at technical institutes varies, although 1-year certificate programs and 2-year associate degree programs are common. Some schools offer cooperative-education or internship programs, allowing students the opportunity to work at a local company or other workplace, while attending classes in alternate terms. Participation in such programs can significantly enhance a student's employment prospects.

Persons interested in careers as science technicians should take as many high school science and math courses as possible. Science courses taken beyond high school, in an associate's or bachelor's program, should be laboratory oriented, with an emphasis on bench skills. Because computers and computer-interfaced equipment are often used in research and development laboratories, technicians should have strong computer skills. Communication skills are also important; technicians are often required to report their findings both through speaking and in writing. Additionally, technicians should be able to work well with others, because teamwork is common.

Prospective science technicians can acquire good career preparation through 2-year formal training programs that combine the teaching of scientific principles and theory with practical hands-on application in a laboratory setting with up-to-date equipment. Graduates of 4-year bachelor's degree programs in science who have considerable experience in laboratory-based courses, have completed internships, or held summer jobs in laboratories, are also well-qualified for science technician positions and are preferred by some employers. However, those with a bachelor's degree who accept technician jobs generally cannot find employment that uses their advanced academic education.

Technicians usually begin work as trainees in routine positions, under the direct supervision of a scientist or a more experienced technician. Job candidates whose training or educational background encompasses extensive hands-on experience with a variety of laboratory equipment, including computers and related equipment, usually require a short period of on-the-job training. As they gain experience, technicians take on more responsibility and carry out assignments under only general supervision, and some eventually become supervisors. However, technicians employed at universities often have their fortunes tied to particular professors; when professors retire or leave, these technicians face uncertain employment prospects.

Job Outlook

Employment of science technicians is expected to increase more slowly than the average for all occupations through the year 2008. Continued growth of scientific and medical research, as well as the development and production of technical products, should stimulate demand for science technicians in all areas. In particular, the growing number of agricultural and medicinal products developed from using biotechnology techniques will increase the need for biological technicians. Employment growth will also be fueled by demand for technicians to help regulate waste products; to collect air, water, and soil samples for measuring levels of pollutants; to monitor compliance with environmental regulations; and to clean up contaminated sites. However, growth will be moderated somewhat by an expected slowdown in overall employment in the chemical industry.

Job opportunities are expected to be very good for qualified graduates of science technician training programs or applied science technology programs, who are well trained on equipment used in industrial and government laboratories and production facilities. As the instrumentation and techniques used in industrial research, development, and production become increasingly more complex, employers are seeking well trained individuals with highly developed technical and communication skills. In addition to opportunities created by growth, many job openings should arise from the need to replace technicians who retire or leave the labor force for other reasons.

Earnings

Median hourly earnings of science technicians were $14.92 in 1998. The middle 50 percent earned between $11.48 and $19.38. The lowest 10 percent earned less than $9.28 and the highest 10 percent earned more than $24.20. Median hourly earnings were $11.20 for chemical technicians and $11.80 for biological and agricultural technicians working in research and testing services in 1997. Chemical technicians working in drug manufacturing earned an hourly median of $15.30 in 1997. Median hourly earnings in the industries employing the largest number of all other science technicians in 1997 were as follows:

Federal Government	$16.50
State government, except education and hospitals	14.80
Local government, except education and hospitals	14.50
Research and testing services	14.40
Personnel supply services	11.30

In the Federal Government in 1999, science technicians started at $16,400, $18,400, or $20,600, depending on education and experience. Beginning salaries were slightly higher in selected areas of the country where the prevailing local pay level was higher. The average annual salary for biological science technicians in nonsupervisory, supervisory, and managerial positions employed by the Federal Government in early 1999 was $30,300; for mathematical technicians, $41,000; for physical science technicians, $38,200; for geodetic technicians, $48,800; for hydrologic technicians, $36,000; and for meteorologic technicians, $45,200.

Related Occupations

Other technicians who apply scientific principles at a level usually taught in 2-year associate degree programs include engineering technicians, broadcast technicians, drafters, and health technologists and technicians. Some of the work of agricultural and biological technicians is related to that in agriculture and forestry occupations.

Sources of Additional Information

For information about a career as a chemical technician, contact:

☛ American Chemical Society, Education Division, Career Publications, 1155 16th St. NW., Washington, DC 20036. Internet: **http://www.acs.org**

Legal Occupations

Lawyers and Judicial Workers

(O*NET 28102, 28105, and 28108)

Significant Points

- Formal educational requirements for lawyers include a 4-year college degree, 3 years in law school, and successful completion of a written bar examination.
- Competition for admission to most law schools is intense.
- Aspiring lawyers and judges should encounter significant competition for jobs.

Nature of the Work

The legal system affects nearly every aspect of our society, from buying a home to crossing the street. Lawyers and judicial workers form the backbone of this vital system, linking the legal system and society in myriad ways. For this reason, they hold positions of great responsibility and are obligated to adhere to a strict code of ethics.

Lawyers, also called *attorneys*, act both as advocates and advisors in our society. As advocates, they represent one of the parties in criminal and civil trials by presenting evidence and arguing in court to support their client. As advisors, lawyers counsel their clients concerning their legal rights and obligations and suggest particular courses of action in business and personal matters. Whether acting as advocate or advisor, all attorneys research the intent of laws and judicial decisions and apply the law to the specific circumstances faced by their client.

The more detailed aspects of a lawyer's job depend upon his or her field of specialization and position. While all lawyers are licensed to represent parties in court, some appear in court more frequently than others. Trial lawyers, who specialize in trial work, must be able to think quickly and speak with ease and authority. In addition, familiarity with courtroom rules and strategy are particularly important in trial work. Still, trial lawyers spend the majority of their time outside the courtroom conducting research, interviewing clients and witnesses, and handling other details in preparation for trial.

Lawyers may specialize in a number of different areas, such as bankruptcy, probate, international, or elder law. Those specializing in environmental law, for example, may represent public interest groups, waste disposal companies, or construction firms in their dealings with the Environmental Protection Agency (EPA) and other State and Federal agencies. They help clients prepare and file for licenses and applications for approval before certain activities may occur. In addition, they represent clients' interests in administrative adjudications.

Some lawyers concentrate in the growing field of intellectual property. These lawyers help protect clients' claims to copyrights, art work under contract, product designs, and computer programs. Still other lawyers advise insurance companies about the legality of insurance transactions. They write insurance policies to conform with the law and to protect companies from unwarranted claims. When claims are filed against insurance companies, they review the claims and represent the companies in court.

The majority of lawyers are found in private practice, where they concentrate on criminal or civil law. In criminal law, lawyers represent individuals who have been charged with crimes and argue their cases in courts of law. Attorneys dealing with civil law assist clients with litigation, wills, trusts, contracts, mortgages, titles, and leases. Other lawyers handle only public interest cases—civil or criminal—which may have an impact extending well beyond the individual client.

Lawyers are sometimes employed full time by a single client. If the client is a corporation, the lawyer is known as "house counsel," and usually advises the company concerning legal issues related to its business activities. These issues might involve patents, government regulations, contracts with other companies, property interests, or collective bargaining agreements with unions.

A significant number of attorneys are employed at the various levels of government. Lawyers who work for State attorneys general, prosecutors, public defenders, and courts play a key role in the criminal justice system. At the Federal level, attorneys investigate cases for the Department of Justice and other agencies. Government lawyers also help develop programs, draft and interpret laws and legislation, establish enforcement procedures, and argue civil and criminal cases on behalf of the government.

Other lawyers work for legal aid societies—private, nonprofit organizations established to serve disadvantaged people. These lawyers generally handle civil, rather than criminal cases. A relatively small number of trained attorneys work in law schools. Most are faculty members who specialize in one or more subjects; however, some serve as administrators. Others work full time in nonacademic settings and teach part time. (For additional information, see the *Handbook* section on college and university faculty.)

To perform the varied tasks described above more efficiently, lawyers increasingly utilize various forms of technology. While all lawyers continue to use law libraries to prepare cases, some supplement their search of conventional printed sources with computer sources, such as the Internet and legal databases. Software is used to search this legal literature automatically and to identify legal texts relevant to a specific case. In litigation involving many supporting documents, lawyers may use computers to organize and index material. Lawyers also use electronic filing, videoconferencing, and voice-recognition technology to more effectively share information with other parties involved in a case.

Many attorneys advance to become *judges* and other *judicial workers*. Judges apply the law and oversee the legal process in courts according to local, State, and Federal statutes. They preside over cases concerning every aspect of society, from traffic offenses to disputes over management of professional sports, or from the rights of huge corporations to questions of disconnecting life support equipment for terminally ill persons. They must ensure that trials and hearings are conducted fairly and that the court administers justice in a manner which safeguards the legal rights of all parties involved.

The most visible responsibility of judges is presiding over trials or hearings and listening as attorneys represent the parties present. Judges rule on the admissibility of evidence and the methods of conducting testimony, and they may be called upon to settle disputes between opposing attorneys. They ensure that rules and procedures are followed, and if unusual circumstances arise for which standard procedures have not been established, judges determine the manner in which the trial will proceed based on their interpretation of the law.

Judges often hold pretrial hearings for cases. They listen to allegations and determine whether the evidence presented merits a trial. In criminal cases, judges may decide that persons charged with crimes should be held in jail pending their trial, or they may set conditions for release. In civil cases, judges occasionally impose restrictions upon the parties until a trial is held.

In many trials, juries are selected to decide guilt or innocence in criminal cases or liability and compensation in civil cases. Judges instruct juries on applicable laws, direct them to deduce the facts from the evidence presented, and hear their verdict. When the law does not require a jury trial or when the parties waive their right to a jury, judges decide the cases. In such cases, the judge determines guilt and imposes sentences in a criminal case; in civil cases, the judge rewards relief—such as compensation for damages—to the parties in the lawsuit (also called litigants).

Judges also work outside the courtroom "in chambers." In their private offices, judges read documents on pleadings and motions, research legal issues, write opinions, and oversee the court's operations. In some jurisdictions, judges also manage the courts' administrative and clerical staff.

Judges' duties vary according to the extent of their jurisdictions and powers. *General trial court judges* of the Federal and State court systems have jurisdiction over any case in their system. They usually try civil cases transcending the jurisdiction of lower courts and all cases involving felony offenses. Federal and State *appellate court judges*, although few in number, have the power to overrule decisions made by trial court or administrative law judges if they determine that legal errors were made in a case or if legal precedent does not support the judgment of the lower court. They rule on a small number of cases and rarely have direct contacts with litigants. Instead, they usually base their decisions on lower court records and lawyers' written and oral arguments.

All lawyers use law libraries to prepare cases, and some supplement their research using computers.

Many State court judges preside in courts in which jurisdiction is limited by law to certain types of cases. A variety of titles are assigned to these judges, but among the most common are *municipal court judge*, *county court judge*, *magistrate*, or *justice of the peace*. Traffic violations, misdemeanors, small claims cases, and pretrial hearings constitute the bulk of the work of these judges, but some States allow them to handle cases involving domestic relations, probate, contracts, and other selected areas of the law.

Administrative law judges, sometimes called *hearing officers* or *adjudicators*, are employed by government agencies to make determinations for administrative agencies. They make decisions on a person's eligibility for various Social Security benefits or worker's compensation, protection of the environment, enforcement of health and safety regulations, employment discrimination, and compliance with economic regulatory requirements.

Working Conditions

Lawyers and judicial workers do most of their work in offices, law libraries, and courtrooms. Lawyers sometimes meet in clients' homes or places of business and, when necessary, in hospitals or prisons. They may travel to attend meetings, gather evidence, and appear before courts, legislative bodies, and other authorities.

Salaried lawyers usually have structured work schedules. Lawyers in private practice may work irregular hours while conducting research, conferring with clients, or preparing briefs during nonoffice hours. Lawyers often work long hours, and about half regularly work 50 hours or more per week. They may face particularly heavy pressure, especially when a case is being tried. Preparation for court includes keeping abreast of the latest laws and judicial decisions.

Although work is not generally seasonal, the work of tax lawyers and other specialists may be an exception. Because lawyers in private practice can often determine their own workload and when they will retire, many stay in practice well beyond the usual retirement age.

Many judges work a standard 40-hour week, but a third of all judges work over 50 hours per week. Some judges with limited jurisdiction are employed part time and divide their time between their judicial responsibilities and other careers.

Employment

Lawyers held about 681,000 jobs in 1998; judges, magistrates and other judicial workers about 71,000. About 7 out of 10 lawyers practiced privately, either in law firms or in solo practices. Most of the remaining lawyers held positions in government, the greatest number at the local level. In the Federal Government, lawyers work for many different agencies but are concentrated in the Departments of Justice, Treasury, and Defense. A small number of lawyers are employed as house counsel by public utilities, banks, insurance companies, real estate agencies, manufacturing firms, welfare and religious organizations, and other business firms and nonprofit organizations. Some salaried lawyers also have part-time independent practices; others work as lawyers part time while working full time in another occupation.

All judges, magistrates, and other judicial workers were employed by Federal, State, or local governments, with about 4 out of 10 holding positions in the Federal Government.

Training, Other Qualifications, and Advancement

To practice law in the courts of any State or other jurisdiction, a person must be licensed, or admitted to its bar, under rules established by the jurisdiction's highest court. All States require that applicants for admission to the bar pass a written bar examination; most jurisdictions also require applicants to pass a separate written ethics examination. Lawyers who have been admitted to the bar in one jurisdiction may occasionally be admitted to the bar in another without taking an examination, if they meet that jurisdiction's standards of good moral character and have a specified period of legal experience. Federal courts and agencies set their own qualifications for those practicing before them.

To qualify for the bar examination in most States, an applicant must usually obtain a college degree and graduate from a law school accredited by the American Bar Association (ABA) or the proper State authorities. ABA accreditation signifies that the law school—particularly its library and faculty—meets certain standards developed to promote quality legal education. ABA currently accredits 183 law schools; others are approved by State authorities only. With certain exceptions, graduates of schools not approved by the ABA are restricted to taking the bar examination and practicing in the State or other jurisdiction in which the school is located; most of these schools are in California. In 1997, seven States accepted the study of law in a law office or in combination with study in a law school; only California accepts the study of law by correspondence as qualifying for taking the bar examination. Several States require registration and approval of students by the State Board of Law Examiners, either before they enter law school or during the early years of legal study.

Although there is no nationwide bar examination, 47 States, the District of Columbia, Guam, the Northern Mariana Islands, Puerto Rico and the Virgin Islands require the 6-hour Multistate Bar Examination (MBE) as part of the bar examination; the MBE is not required in Indiana, Louisiana, and Washington. The MBE covers issues of broad interest and is sometimes given in addition to a locally prepared State bar examination. The 3-hour Multistate Essay Examination (MEE) is used as part of the State bar examination in several States. States vary in their use of MBE and MEE scores.

Many states have begun to require Multistate Performance Testing (MPT) to test the practical skills of beginning lawyers. This program has been well received and many more States are expected to require performance testing in the future. Requirements vary by State, although the test usually is taken at the same time as the bar exam and is a one-time requirement.

The required college and law school education usually takes 7 years of full-time study after high school—4 years of undergraduate study followed by 3 years in law school. Although some law schools accept a very small number of students after 3 years of college, most require applicants to have a bachelor's degree. To meet the needs of students who can attend only part time, a number of law schools have night or part-time divisions which usually require 4 years of study; about 1 in 10 graduates from ABA approved schools attends part time.

Although there is no recommended "prelaw" major, prospective lawyers should develop proficiency in writing and speaking, reading, researching, analyzing, and thinking logically—skills needed to succeed both in law school and in the profession. Regardless of major, a multidisciplinary background is recommended. Courses in English, foreign languages, public speaking, government, philosophy, history, economics, mathematics, and computer science, among others, are useful. Students interested in a particular aspect of law may find related courses helpful. For example, prospective patent lawyers need a strong background in engineering or science, and future tax lawyers must have extensive knowledge of accounting.

Acceptance by most law schools depends on the applicant's ability to demonstrate an aptitude for the study of law, usually through good undergraduate grades, the Law School Admission Test (LSAT), the quality of the applicant's undergraduate school, any prior work experience, and sometimes a personal interview. However, law schools vary in the weight they place on each of these and other factors.

All law schools approved by the ABA, except for those in Puerto Rico, require applicants to take the LSAT. Nearly all law schools require applicants to have certified transcripts sent to the Law School Data Assembly Service, which then sends applicants' LSAT scores and their standardized records of college grades to the law schools of their choice. Both this service and the LSAT are administered by the Law School Admission Council.

Competition for admission to many law schools is intense, especially for the most prestigious schools. Enrollments in these schools rose very rapidly during the 1970s, as applicants far outnumbered available seats. Although the number of applicants decreased markedly in the 1990s, the number of applicants to most law schools still greatly exceeds the number that can be admitted.

During the first year or year and a half of law school, students usually study core courses such as constitutional law, contracts, property law, torts, civil procedure, and legal writing. In the remaining time, they may elect specialized courses in fields such as tax, labor, or corporate law. Law students often acquire practical experience by participation in school sponsored legal clinic activities, in the school's moot court competitions in which students conduct appellate arguments, in practice trials under the supervision of experienced lawyers and judges, and through research and writing on legal issues for the school's law journal.

A number of law schools have clinical programs in which students gain legal experience through practice trials and law school projects under the supervision of practicing lawyers and law school faculty. Law school clinical programs might include work in legal aid clinics, for example, or on the staff of legislative committees. Part-time or summer clerkships in law firms, government agencies, and corporate legal departments also provide valuable experience. Such training can lead directly to a job after graduation and help students decide what kind of practice best suits them. Clerkships may also be an important source of financial aid.

In 1997, law students in 52 jurisdictions were required to pass the Multistate Professional Responsibility Examination (MPRE), which tests their knowledge of the ABA codes on professional responsibility and judicial conduct. In some States, the MPRE may be taken during law school, usually after completing a course on legal ethics.

Law school graduates receive the degree of *juris doctor* (J.D.) as the first professional degree. Advanced law degrees may be desirable for those planning to specialize, research, or teach. Some law students pursue joint degree programs, which usually require an additional semester or year. Joint degree programs are offered in a number of areas, including law and business administration or public administration.

After graduation, lawyers must keep informed about legal and nonlegal developments that affect their practice. Currently, 39 States and jurisdictions mandate Continuing Legal Education (CLE). Many law schools and State and local bar associations provide continuing education courses that help lawyers stay abreast of recent developments. Some States allow CLE credits to be obtained through participation in seminars on the Internet.

The practice of law involves a great deal of responsibility. Individuals planning careers in law should like to work with people and be able to win the respect and confidence of their clients, associates, and the public. Perseverance, creativity, and reasoning ability are also essential to lawyers, who often analyze complex cases and handle new and unique legal problems.

Most beginning lawyers start in salaried positions. Newly-hired, salaried attorneys usually start as associates and work with more experienced lawyers or judges. After several years of gaining more responsibilities, some lawyers are admitted to partnership in their firm or go into practice for themselves. Others become full-time law school faculty or administrators; a growing number of these lawyers have advanced degrees in other fields as well.

Some attorneys use their legal training in administrative or managerial positions in various departments of large corporations. A transfer from a corporation's legal department to another department often is viewed as a way to gain administrative experience and rise in the ranks of management.

A number of lawyers become judges, and most judges have first been lawyers. In fact, Federal and State judges are usually required to be lawyers. About 40 States allow nonlawyers to hold limited jurisdiction judgeships, but opportunities are better for those with law experience. Federal administrative law judges must be lawyers and pass a competitive examination administered by the U.S. Office of Personnel Management. Some State administrative law judges and other hearing officials are not required to be lawyers, but law degrees are preferred for most positions.

Federal judges are appointed for life by the President and are confirmed by the Senate. Federal administrative law judges are appointed by the various Federal agencies with virtually lifetime tenure. Some State judges are appointed, and the remainder are elected in partisan or nonpartisan State elections. Many State and local judges serve fixed renewable terms, which range from 4 or 6 years for some trial court judgeships to as long as 14 years or life for other trial or appellate court judges. Judicial nominating commissions, composed of members of the bar and the public, are used to screen candidates for judgeships in many States and for some Federal judgeships.

All States have some type of orientation for newly elected or appointed judges. The Federal Judicial Center, ABA, National Judicial College, and National Center for State Courts provide judicial education and training for judges and other judicial branch personnel. General and continuing education courses usually last from a couple of days to 3 weeks in length. Over half of all States and Puerto Rico require judges to enroll in continuing education courses while serving on the bench.

Job Outlook

Individuals interested in pursuing careers as lawyers or judicial workers should encounter stiff competition through 2008. The number of law school graduates is expected to continue to strain the economy's capacity to absorb them. As for judges, the prestige associated with serving on the bench should insure continued, intense competition for openings.

Employment of lawyers grew very rapidly from the early 1970s through the early 1990s, but has started to level off recently. Through 2008, employment is expected to grow about as fast as the average for all occupations. Continuing demand for lawyers will result primarily from growth in the population and the general level of business activities. Demand will also be spurred by growth of legal action in such areas as health care, intellectual property, international law, elder law, environmental law, and sexual harassment. In addition, the wider availability and affordability of legal clinics and prepaid legal service programs should result in increased use of legal services by middle-income people.

However, employment growth is expected to be slower than in the past. In an effort to reduce the money spent on legal fees, many businesses are increasingly utilizing large accounting firms and paralegals to perform some of the same functions similar as lawyers. For example, accounting firms may provide employee benefit counseling, process documents, or handle various other services previously performed by the law firm. Also, mediation and dispute resolution are increasingly used as alternatives to litigation.

Competition for job openings should continue to be keen because of the large numbers graduating from law school each year. During the 1970s, the annual number of law school graduates more than doubled, outpacing the rapid growth of jobs. Growth in the yearly number of law school graduates slowed during the early to mid-1980s, but increased again to current levels in the late 1980s to early 1990s. Although graduates with superior academic records from well-regarded law schools will have more job opportunities, most graduates should encounter stiff competition for jobs.

Perhaps as a result of this fierce competition, lawyers are increasingly finding work in nontraditional areas for which legal training is an asset, but not normally a requirement—for example, administrative, managerial, and business positions in banks, insurance firms, real estate companies, government agencies, and other organizations. Employment opportunities are expected to continue to arise in these organizations at a growing rate.

As in the past, some graduates may have to accept positions in areas outside their field of interest or for which they feel overqualified. Some recent law school graduates who are unable to find permanent positions are turning to the growing number of temporary staffing firms that place attorneys in short-term jobs until they are able to secure full-time positions. This service allows companies to hire lawyers on an "as needed" basis and allows beginning lawyers to develop practical skills while looking for permanent positions.

Due to the competition for jobs, a law graduate's geographic mobility and work experience assume greater importance. The willingness to relocate may be an advantage in getting a job, but to be licensed in another State, a lawyer may have to take an additional State bar examination. In addition, employers increasingly seek graduates who have advanced law degrees and experience in a specialty such as tax, patent, or admiralty law.

Employment growth for lawyers will continue to be concentrated in salaried jobs, as businesses and all levels of government employ a growing number of staff attorneys, and as employment in the legal services industry grows in larger law firms. Most salaried positions are in urban areas where government agencies, law firms, and big corporations are concentrated. The number of self-employed lawyers is expected to increase slowly, reflecting the difficulty of establishing a profitable new practice in the face of competition from larger, established law firms. Moreover, the growing complexity of law, which encourages specialization, along with the cost of maintaining up-to-date legal research materials, favors larger firms.

For lawyers who wish to work independently, establishing a new practice will probably be easiest in small towns and expanding suburban areas. In such communities, competition from larger established law firms is likely to be less than in big cities, and new lawyers may find it easier to become known to potential clients.

Some lawyers are adversely affected by cyclical swings in the economy. During recessions, the demand declines for some discretionary legal services, such as planning estates, drafting wills, and handling real estate transactions. Also, corporations are less likely to litigate cases when declining sales and profits result in budgetary restrictions. Some corporations and law firms will not hire new attorneys until business improves or may cut staff to contain costs. Several factors, however, mitigate the overall impact of recessions on lawyers. During recessions, for example, individuals and corporations face other legal problems, such as bankruptcies, foreclosures, and divorces requiring legal action.

Employment of judges is expected to grow more slowly than the average for all occupations. Contradictory social forces affect the demand for judges. Growing public concerns about crime, safety, and efficient administration of justice should spur demand, while public budgetary pressures will limit job growth.

Competition for judgeships should remain intense. As in the past, most job openings will arise as judges retire. Although judges traditionally have held their positions until late in life, early retirement is becoming more common, a factor which should increase job openings. Nevertheless, becoming a judge will still be difficult; not only must judicial candidates compete with other qualified people, they often must also gain political support in order to be elected or appointed.

Earnings

In 1998, the median annual earnings of all lawyers was $78,170. The middle half of the occupation earned between $51,450 and $114,520. The bottom decile earned less than $37,310. Median annual earnings in the industries employing the largest numbers of lawyers in 1997 are shown below.

Industry	Earnings
Legal services	$78,700
Federal government	78,200
Fire, marine, and casualty insurance	74,400
State government	59,400
Local government	49,200

Median salaries of lawyers 6 months after graduation from law school in 1998 varied by type of work, as indicated by table 1.

Table 1. Median salaries of lawyers 6 months after graduation, 1998

All graduates	$45,000
Type of work	
Private practice	60,000
Business/industry	50,000
Academe	38,000
Judicial clerkship	37,500
Government	36,000
Public interest	31,000

SOURCE: National Association for Law Placement

Salaries of experienced attorneys vary widely according to the type, size, and location of their employer. Lawyers who own their own practices usually earn less than those who are partners in law firms. Lawyers starting their own practice may need to work part time in other occupations to supplement their income until their practice is well established.

Earnings among judicial workers also vary significantly. According to the Administrative Office of the U.S. Courts, the Chief Justice of the United States Supreme Court earned $175,400, and the Associate Justices earned $167,900. Federal district court judges had salaries of $136,700 in 1998, as did judges in the Court of Federal Claims and the Court of International Trade; circuit court judges earned $145,000 a year. Federal judges with limited jurisdiction, such as magistrates and bankruptcy court judges, had salaries of $125,800.

According to a survey by the National Center for State Courts, annual salaries of associate justices of States' highest courts averaged $105,100 in 1997, and ranged from about $77,100 to $137,300. Salaries of State intermediate appellate court judges averaged $103,700, and ranged from $79,400 to $124,200. Salaries of State judges of general jurisdiction trial courts averaged $94,000, and ranged from $72,000 to $115,300.

Most salaried lawyers and judges are provided health and life insurance, and contributions are made on their behalf to retirement plans. Lawyers who practice independently are only covered if they arrange and pay for such benefits themselves.

Related Occupations

Legal training is useful in many other occupations. Some of these are arbitrator, mediator, journalist, patent agent, title examiner, legislative assistant, lobbyist, FBI special agent, political office holder, and corporate executive.

Sources of Additional Information

Information on law schools and a career in law may be obtained from:

☛ American Bar Association, 750 North Lake Shore Dr., Chicago, IL 60611. Internet: **http://www.abanet.org**

Information on the LSAT, the Law School Data Assembly Service, applying to law school, and financial aid for law students may be obtained from:

☛ Law School Admission Council, P.O. Box 40, Newtown, PA 18940. Internet: **http://www.lsac.org**

Information on acquiring a job as a lawyer with the Federal Government may be obtained from the Office of Personnel Management through a telephone-based system. Consult your telephone directory under U.S. Government for a local number or call (912) 757-3000; TDD (912) 744-2299. This number is not toll-free and charges may result. Information also is available from their Internet site: **http://www.usajobs.opm.gov**

The requirements for admission to the bar in a particular State or other jurisdiction may also be obtained at the State capital from the clerk of the Supreme Court or the administrator of the State Board of Bar Examiners.

Paralegals

(O*NET 28305)

Significant Points

- While some paralegals train on the job, employers increasingly prefer graduates of postsecondary paralegal training programs.
- Paralegals are projected to rank among the fastest growing occupations in the economy as they increasingly perform many legal tasks formerly carried out by lawyers.
- Stiff competition is expected as the number of graduates of paralegal training programs and others seeking to enter the profession outpaces job growth.

Nature of the Work

While lawyers assume ultimate responsibility for legal work, they often delegate many of their tasks to paralegals. In fact, paralegals continue to assume a growing range of tasks in the Nation's legal offices and perform many of the same tasks as lawyers. Nevertheless, they are still explicitly prohibited from carrying out duties which are considered to be the practice of law, such as setting legal fees, giving legal advice, and presenting cases in court.

One of a paralegal's most important tasks is helping lawyers prepare for closings, hearings, trials, and corporate meetings. Paralegals investigate the facts of cases and ensure all relevant information is considered. They also identify appropriate laws, judicial decisions, legal articles, and other materials that are relevant to assigned cases. After they analyze and organize the information, paralegals may prepare written reports that attorneys use in determining how cases should be handled. Should attorneys decide to file lawsuits on behalf of clients, paralegals may help prepare the legal arguments, draft pleadings and motions to be filed with the court, obtain affidavits, and assist attorneys during trials. Paralegals also organize and track files of all important case documents and make them available and easily accessible to attorneys.

In addition to this preparatory work, paralegals also perform a number of other vital functions. For example, they help draft contracts, mortgages, separation agreements, and trust instruments. They may also assist in preparing tax returns and planning estates. Some paralegals coordinate the activities of other law office employees and maintain financial records for the office. Various additional tasks may differ, depending on the employer.

Paralegals are found in all types of organizations, but most are employed by law firms, corporate legal departments, and various levels of government. In these organizations, they may work in all areas of the law, including litigation, personal injury, corporate law, criminal law, employee benefits, intellectual property, labor law, and real estate. Within specialties, functions often are broken down further so paralegals may deal with a specific area. For example, paralegals specializing in labor law may deal exclusively with employee benefits.

The duties of paralegals also differ widely based on the type of organization in which they are employed. Paralegals who work for corporations often assist attorneys with employee contracts, shareholder agreements, stock option plans, and employee benefit plans. They may also help prepare and file annual financial reports, maintain corporate minute books and resolutions, and secure loans for the corporation. Paralegals also occasionally review government regulations to ensure the corporation operates within the law.

The duties of paralegals who work in the public sector usually vary in each agency. In general, they analyze legal material for internal use, maintain reference files, conduct research for attorneys, and collect and analyze evidence for agency hearings. They may then prepare informative or explanatory material on laws, agency regulations, and agency policy for general use by the agency and the public. Paralegals employed in community legal service projects help the poor, the aged, and others in need of legal assistance. They file forms, conduct research, prepare documents, and when authorized by law, may represent clients at administrative hearings.

Paralegals in small and medium-sized law firms usually perform a variety of duties that require a general knowledge of the law. For example, they may research judicial decisions on improper police arrests or help prepare a mortgage contract. Paralegals employed by large law firms, government agencies, and corporations, however, are more likely to specialize in one aspect of the law.

A growing number of paralegals use computers in their work. Computer software packages and the Internet are increasingly used to search legal literature stored in computer databases and on CD-ROM. In litigation involving many supporting documents, paralegals may use computer databases to retrieve, organize, and index various materials. Imaging software allows paralegals to scan documents directly into a database, while billing programs help them to track hours billed to clients. Computer software packages may also be used to perform tax computations and explore the consequences of possible tax strategies for clients.

Working Conditions

Paralegals employed by corporations and government usually work a standard 40-hour week. Although most paralegals work year round, some are temporarily employed during busy times of the year, then released when the workload diminishes. Paralegals who work for law firms sometimes work very long hours when they are under pressure to meet deadlines. Some law firms reward such loyalty with bonuses and additional time off.

These workers handle many routine assignments, particularly when they are inexperienced. As they gain experience, Paralegals usually assume more varied tasks with additional responsibility. Paralegals do most of their work at desks in offices and law libraries. Occasionally, they travel to gather information and perform other duties.

Employment

Paralegals held about 136,000 jobs in 1998. Private law firms employed the vast majority; most of the remainder worked for corporate legal departments and the various levels of government. Within the Federal Government, the Department of Justice is the largest employer, followed by the Departments of Treasury and Defense, and the Federal Deposit Insurance Corporation. Other employers include State and local governments, publicly funded legal service centers, banks, real estate development companies, and insurance companies. A small number of paralegals own their own businesses and work as freelance legal assistants, contracting their services to attorneys or corporate legal departments.

Most paralegals are employed by law firms, corporate legal departments, and various levels of government.

Training, Other Qualifications, and Advancement

There are several ways to become a paralegal. Employers usually require formal paralegal training obtained through associate or bachelor's degree programs or through a certification program. Increasingly, employers prefer graduates of 4-year paralegal programs or college graduates who have completed paralegal certificate programs. Some employers prefer to train paralegals on the job, hiring college graduates with no legal experience or promoting experienced legal secretaries. Other entrants have experience in a technical field that is useful to law firms, such as a background in tax preparation for tax and estate practice or nursing or health administration for personal injury practice.

Over 800 formal paralegal training programs are offered by 4-year colleges and universities, law schools, community and junior colleges, business schools, and proprietary schools. There are currently 232 programs approved by the American Bar Association (ABA). Although this approval is neither required nor sought by many programs, graduation from an ABA-approved program can enhance one's employment opportunities. The requirements for admission to these programs vary. Some require certain college courses or a bachelor's degree; others accept high school graduates or those with legal experience; and a few schools require standardized tests and personal interviews.

Paralegal programs include 2-year associate's degree programs, 4-year bachelor's degree programs, and certificate programs that take only a few months to complete. Many certificate programs only require a high school diploma or GED for admission. Programs typically include courses on law and legal research techniques, in addition to courses covering specialized areas of law, such as real estate, estate planning and probate, litigation, family law, contracts, and criminal law. Many employers prefer applicants with specialized training.

The quality of paralegal training programs varies; the better programs usually include job placement. Programs increasingly include courses introducing students to the legal applications of computers. Many paralegal training programs include an internship in which students gain practical experience by working for several months in a law office, corporate legal department, or government agency. Experience gained in internships is an asset when seeking a job after graduation. Prospective students should examine the experiences of recent graduates before enrolling in those programs.

Although most employers do not require certification, earning a voluntary certificate from a professional society may offer advantages in the labor market. The National Association of Legal Assistants, for example, has established standards for certification requiring various combinations of education and experience. Paralegals who meet these standards are eligible to take a 2-day examination, given three times each year at several regional testing centers. Those who pass this examination may use the designation Certified Legal Assistant (CLA). In addition, the Paralegal Advanced Competency Exam, established in 1996 and administered through the National Federation of Paralegal Associations, offers professional recognition to paralegals with a bachelor's degree and at least 2 years of experience. Those who pass this examination may use the designation Registered Paralegal (RP).

Paralegals must be able to document and present their findings and opinions to their supervising attorney. They need to understand legal terminology and have good research and investigative skills.

Familiarity with the operation and applications of computers in legal research and litigation support is also increasingly important. Paralegals should stay informed of new developments in the laws that affect their area of practice. Participation in continuing legal education seminars allows paralegals to maintain and expand their legal knowledge.

Because paralegals frequently deal with the public, they should be courteous and uphold the ethical standards of the legal profession. The National Association of Legal Assistants, the National Federation of Paralegal Associations, and a few States have established ethical guidelines for paralegals to follow.

Paralegals are usually given more responsibilities and less supervision as they gain work experience. Experienced paralegals who work in large law firms, corporate legal departments, and government agencies may supervise and delegate assignments to other paralegals and clerical staff. Advancement opportunities also include promotion to managerial and other law-related positions within the firm or corporate legal department. However, some paralegals find it easier to move to another law firm when seeking increased responsibility or advancement.

Job Outlook

Paralegals are projected to rank among the fastest growing occupations in the economy through 2008. However, stiff competition for jobs should continue as the number of graduates of paralegal training programs and others seeking to enter the profession outpaces job growth. Employment growth stems from law firms and other employers with legal staffs increasingly hiring paralegals to lower the cost and increase the availability and efficiency of legal services. The majority of job openings for paralegals in the future will be new jobs created by rapid employment growth; other job openings will arise as people leave the occupation.

Private law firms will continue to be the largest employers of paralegals, but a growing array of other organizations, such as corporate legal departments, insurance companies, real estate and title insurance firms, and banks will also continue to hire paralegals. These organizations are expected to grow as an increasing population requires additional legal services, especially in areas such as intellectual property, health care, international, elder, sexual harassment, and environmental law. The growth of prepaid legal plans should also contribute to the demand for legal services. Paralegal employment in these organizations is expected to increase as paralegals are assigned a growing range of tasks and are increasingly employed in small and medium-sized establishments.

Job opportunities for paralegals will expand in the public sector as well. Community legal service programs, which provide assistance to the poor, aged, minorities, and middle-income families, will employ additional paralegals to minimize expenses and serve the most people. Federal, State, and local government agencies, consumer organizations, and the courts should also continue to hire paralegals in increasing numbers.

To a limited extent, paralegal jobs are affected by the business cycle. During recessions, demand declines for some discretionary legal services, such as planning estates, drafting wills, and handling real estate transactions. Corporations are less inclined to initiate litigation when falling sales and profits lead to fiscal belt tightening. As a result, full-time paralegals employed in offices adversely affected by a recession may be laid off or have their work hours reduced. On the other hand, during recessions, corporations and individuals are more likely to face other problems that require legal assistance, such as bankruptcies, foreclosures, and divorces. Paralegals, who provide many of the same legal services as lawyers at a lower cost, tend to fare relatively better in difficult economic conditions.

Earnings

Earnings of paralegals vary greatly. Salaries depend on education, training, experience, type and size of employer, and the geographic location of the job. In general, paralegals who work for large law firms or in large metropolitan areas earn more than those who work for smaller firms or in less populated regions. In 1998, full-time, wage and salary paralegals had median annual earnings of $32,760. The middle 50 percent earned between $26,240 and 40,960. The top 10 percent earned more than $50,290, while the bottom 10 percent earned less than $21,770. Median annual earnings in the industries employing the largest numbers of paralegals in 1997 are shown below:

Federal government	$43,900
Local government	32,200
Legal services	30,300

According to the National Association of Legal Assistants, paralegals had an average salary of $34,000 in 1997. In addition to a salary, many paralegals received a bonus, which averaged about $2,100. According to the National Federation of Paralegal Associations, starting salaries of paralegals with 1 year or less experience averaged $30,700 in 1997.

Related Occupations

Several other occupations call for a specialized understanding of the law and the legal system, but do not require the extensive training of a lawyer. These include abstractors, claim examiners, compliance and enforcement inspectors, occupational safety and health workers, patent agents, and title examiners.

Sources of Additional Information

General information on a career as a paralegal can be obtained from:

☛ Standing Committee on Legal Assistants, American Bar Association, 750 North Lake Shore Dr., Chicago, IL 60611. Internet: **http://www.abanet.org/legalassts**

For information on the Certified Legal Assistant exam, schools that offer training programs in a specific State, and standards and guidelines for paralegals, contact:

☛ National Association of Legal Assistants, Inc., 1516 South Boston St., Suite 200, Tulsa, OK 74119. Internet: **http://www.nala.org**

Information on a career as a paralegal, schools that offer training programs, job postings for paralegals, the Paralegal Advanced Competency Exam, and local paralegal associations can be obtained from:

☛ National Federation of Paralegal Associations, P.O. Box 33108, Kansas City, MO 64114. Internet: **http://www.paralegals.org**

Information on paralegal training programs, including the pamphlet "How to Choose a Paralegal Education Program," may be obtained from:

☛ American Association for Paralegal Education, P.O. Box 40244, Overland Park, KS 66204. Internet: **http://www.aafpe.org**

Information on acquiring a job as a paralegal specialist with the Federal Government may be obtained from the Office of Personnel Management through a telephone-based system. Consult your telephone directory under U.S. Government for a local number or call (912) 757-3000; TDD (912) 744-2299. This call is not toll-free, and charges may result. Information also is available from their Internet site: **http://www.usajobs.opm.gov**

Social Scientists

Economists and Marketing Research Analysts

(O*NET 27102A and 27102B)

Significant Points

- Demand for qualified marketing research analysts should be strong.
- Candidates who hold a master's degree in economics have much better employment prospects than bachelor's degree holders.

Nature of the Work

Economists. Economists study how society distributes scarce resources such as land, labor, raw materials, and machinery to produce goods and services. They conduct research, collect and analyze data, monitor economic trends, and develop forecasts. They research issues such as energy costs, inflation, interest rates, imports, or employment levels.

Most economists are concerned with practical applications of economic policy. They use their understanding of economic relationships to advise businesses and other organizations, including insurance companies, banks, securities firms, industry and trade associations, labor unions, and government agencies. Economists use mathematical models to develop programs predicting answers to questions such as the nature and length of business cycles, the effects of a specific rate of inflation on the economy, or the effects of tax legislation on unemployment levels.

Economists devise methods and procedures for obtaining the data they need. For example, sampling techniques may be used to conduct a survey, and various mathematical modeling techniques may be used to develop forecasts. Preparing reports on research results is an important part of an economist's job. Relevant data must be reviewed and analyzed, applicable tables and charts prepared, and the results presented in clear, concise language that can be understood by non-economists. Presenting economic and statistical concepts in a meaningful way is particularly important for economists whose research is directed toward making policies for an organization.

Economists who work for government agencies may assess economic conditions in the United States or abroad, in order to estimate the economic effects of specific changes in legislation or public policy. They may study areas such as how the dollar's fluctuation against foreign currencies affects import and export levels. The majority of government economists work in the area of agriculture, labor, or quantitative analysis; some economists work in almost every area of government. For example, economists in the U.S. Department of Commerce study production, distribution, and consumption of commodities produced overseas, while economists employed with the Bureau of Labor Statistics analyze data on the domestic economy such as prices, wages, employment, productivity, and safety and health. An economist working in State or local government might analyze data on the growth of school-aged populations, prison growth, and employment and unemployment rates, in order to project spending needs for future years.

Marketing Research Analysts. Marketing research analysts are concerned with the potential sales of a product or service. They analyze statistical data on past sales to predict future sales. They gather data on competitors and analyze prices, sales, and methods

Economists and marketing research analysts must effectively present research results.

of marketing and distribution. Like economists, marketing research analysts devise methods and procedures for obtaining the data they need. They often design telephone, personal, or mail interview surveys to assess consumer preferences. Trained interviewers, under the marketing research analyst's direction, usually conduct the surveys.

After compiling the data, marketing research analysts evaluate it and make recommendations to their client or employer based upon their findings. They provide a company's management with information needed to make decisions on the promotion, distribution, design, and pricing of company products or services. The information may also be used to determine the advisability of adding new lines of merchandise, opening new branches, or otherwise diversifying the company's operations. Analysts may conduct opinion research to determine public attitudes on various issues. This can help political or business leaders and others assess public support for their electoral prospects or advertising policies.

Working Conditions

Economists and marketing research analysts have structured work schedules. They often work alone, writing reports, preparing statistical charts, and using computers, but they may also be an integral part of a research team. Most work under pressure of deadlines and tight schedules, which may require overtime. Their routine may be interrupted by special requests for data, as well as by the need to attend meetings or conferences. Frequent travel may be necessary.

Employment

Economists and marketing research analysts held about 70,000 jobs in 1998. Private industry provided about 4 out of 5 jobs for salaried workers, particularly economic and marketing research firms, management consulting firms, banks, securities and commodities brokers, and computer and data processing companies. A wide range of government agencies provided the remaining jobs, primarily for economists. The Departments of Labor, Agriculture, and Commerce are the largest Federal employers of economists. A number of economists and marketing research analysts combine a full-time job in government, academia, or business with part-time or consulting work in another setting.

Employment of economists and marketing research analysts is concentrated in large cities. Some economists work abroad for companies with major international operations, for U.S. Government agencies, and for international organizations like the World Bank and the United Nations.

Besides the jobs described above, many economists and marketing research analysts held faculty positions in colleges and universities. Economics and marketing faculty have flexible work schedules, and may divide their time among teaching, research, consulting, and administration. (See the statement on college and university faculty elsewhere in the *Handbook*.)

Training, Other Qualifications, and Advancement

Graduate training is required for many private sector economist and marketing research analyst jobs, and for advancement to more responsible positions. Economics includes many specialties at the graduate level, such as advanced economic theory, econometrics, international economics, and labor economics. Students should select graduate schools strong in specialties in which they are interested. Marketing research analysts may earn advanced degrees in economics, business administration, marketing, statistics, or some closely related discipline. Some schools help graduate students find internships or part-time employment in government agencies, economic consulting firms, financial institutions, or marketing research firms prior to graduation.

Undergraduate economics majors can choose from a variety of courses, ranging from microeconomics, macroeconomics, and econometrics, to more philosophical courses, such as the history of economic thought.

In addition to courses in business, marketing, and consumer behavior, marketing majors should take other liberal arts and social science courses, including economics, psychology, English, and sociology. Because of the importance of quantitative skills to economists and marketing researchers, courses in mathematics, statistics, econometrics, sampling theory and survey design, and computer science are extremely helpful.

In the Federal Government, candidates for entry-level economist positions must have a bachelor's degree with a minimum of 21 semester hours of economics and 3 hours of statistics, accounting, or calculus. Competition is keen for positions requiring only a bachelor's degree, however, and additional education or superior academic performance is likely to be required to gain employment.

A master's degree is usually the minimum requirement for a job as an instructor in junior and community colleges. In most colleges and universities, however, a Ph.D. is necessary for appointment as an instructor. A Ph.D. and extensive publications in academic journals are required for a professorship, tenure, and promotion.

Whether working in government, industry, research organizations, marketing, or consulting firms, economists and marketing research analysts with graduate degrees usually qualify for more responsible research and administrative positions. Many businesses, research and consulting firms, and government agencies seek individuals who have strong computer and quantitative skills and can perform complex research. A Ph.D. is necessary for top economist or marketing positions in many organizations. Many corporation and government executives have a strong background in economics or marketing.

A bachelor's degree with a major in economics or marketing may not be sufficient to obtain some positions as an economist or marketing analyst, but is excellent preparation for many entry-level positions as a research assistant, administrative or management trainee, marketing interviewer, or any of a number of professional sales jobs.

Aspiring economists and marketing research analysts should gain experience gathering and analyzing data, conducting interviews or surveys, and writing reports on their findings while in college. This experience can prove invaluable later in obtaining a full-time position in the field, since much of their work, in the beginning, may center on these duties. With experience, economists and marketing research analysts eventually are assigned their own research projects.

Those considering careers as economists or marketing research analysts should be able to pay attention to details because much time is spent on precise data analysis. Patience and persistence are necessary qualities since economists and marketing research analysts must spend long hours on independent study and problem solving. At the same time, they must work well with others, especially marketing research analysts, who often oversee interviews for a wide variety of individuals. Economists and marketing research analysts must be able to present their findings, both orally and in writing, in a clear, meaningful way.

Job Outlook

Employment of economists and marketing research analysts is expected to grow about as fast as the average for all occupations through 2008. Many job openings are likely to result from the need to replace experienced workers who transfer to other occupations, retire, or leave the labor force for other reasons.

Opportunities for economists should be best in private industry, especially in research, testing, and consulting firms, as more companies contract out for economic research services. The growing complexity of the global economy, competition, and increased reliance on quantitative methods for analyzing the current value of future funds, business trends, sales, and purchasing should spur demand for economists. The growing need for economic analyses in virtually every industry should result in additional jobs for economists. Employment of economists in the Federal Government should decline more slowly than other occupations in the Federal workforce. Slow employment growth is expected among economists in State and local government.

An advanced degree coupled with a strong background in economic theory, mathematics, statistics, and econometrics provides the basis for acquiring any specialty within the field. Those skilled in quantitative techniques and their application to economic modeling and forecasting, coupled with good communications skills, should have the best job opportunities.

Bachelor degree holders in economics may face competition for the limited number of economist positions for which they qualify. They will qualify for a number of other positions, however, where they can take advantage of their economic knowledge in conducting research, developing surveys, or analyzing data. Many graduates with bachelor's degrees will find good jobs in industry and business as management or sales trainees, or administrative assistants. Economists with good quantitative skills are qualified for research assistant positions in a broad range of fields.

Candidates who meet State certification requirements may become high school economics teachers. The demand for secondary school economics teachers is expected to grow, as economics becomes an increasingly important and popular course. (See the statement on kindergarten, elementary, and secondary school teachers elsewhere in the *Handbook*.)

Ph.D. degree holders in economics and marketing are likely to face keen competition for teaching positions in colleges and universities. However, opportunities should be good in other areas such as industry and consulting firms.

Demand for qualified marketing research analysts should be strong due to an increasingly competitive economy. Marketing research provides organizations valuable feedback from purchasers, allowing companies to evaluate consumer satisfaction and more effectively plan for the future. As companies seek to expand their market and consumers become better informed, the need for marketing professionals will increase.

Opportunities for marketing research analysts with graduate degrees should be good in a wide range of employment settings, particularly in marketing research firms, as companies find it more profitable to contract out for marketing research services rather than support their own marketing department. Other organizations, including financial services organizations, health care institutions, advertising firms, manufacturing firms producing consumer goods, and insurance companies may offer job opportunities for marketing research analysts.

Those with a bachelor's degree, who have a strong background in mathematics, statistics, survey design, and computer science, may be hired by private firms as research assistants or interviewers.

Earnings

Median annual earnings of economists and marketing research analysts were $48,330 in 1998. The middle 50 percent earned between $34,650 and $74,500 a year. The lowest 10 percent earned less than $26,540 and the highest 10 percent earned more than $94,810 a year. Median annual earnings in the industries employing the largest number of economists and marketing research analysts in 1997 were as follows:

Federal Government	$65,300
Management and public relations	51,900
Research and testing services	47,500

The Federal Government recognizes education and experience in certifying applicants for entry-level positions. The entrance salary for economists having a bachelor's degree was about $20,600 a year in 1999; however, those with superior academic records could begin at $25,500. Those having a master's degree could qualify for positions at an annual salary of $31,200. Those with a Ph.D. could begin at $37,700, while some individuals with experience and an advanced degree could start at $45,200. Starting salaries were slightly higher in selected areas where the prevailing local pay was higher. The average annual salary for economists employed by the Federal Government was $67,800 a year in early 1999.

Related Occupations

Economists are concerned with understanding and interpreting financial matters, among other subjects. Other jobs in this area include financial managers, financial planners, insurance underwriters, actuaries, credit analysts, loan officers, and budget analysts.

Marketing research analysts do research to find out how well the market receives products or services. This may include planning, implementation, and analysis of surveys to determine people's needs and preferences. Other jobs using these skills include psychologists, sociologists, and urban and regional planners.

Sources of Additional Information

For information on careers in economics and business, contact:

☛ National Association for Business Economics, 1233 20th St. NW., Suite 505, Washington, DC 20036. Internet: **http://www.nabe.com**

For information about careers and salaries in marketing research, contact:

☛ Marketing Research Association, 1344 Silas Deane Hwy., Suite 306, Rocky Hill, CT 06067-0230. Internet: **http://www.mra-net.org**

☛ Council of American Survey Research Organizations, 3 Upper Devon, Port Jefferson, NY 11777. Internet: **http://www.casro.org/index.htm**

Information on acquiring a job as an economist with the Federal Government may be obtained from the Office of Personnel Management (OPM) through a telephone-based system. Consult your telephone directory under U.S. Government for a local number or call (912) 757-3000; TDD (912) 744-2299. This number is not tollfree and charges may result. Information also is available from the OPM Internet site: **http://www.usajobs.opm.gov**

Psychologists

(O*NET 27108A, 27108C, 27108D, 27108E, 27108G, 27108H, and 27108J)

Significant Points

- One half of psychologists are self-employed, about 5 times the average for professional workers.
- A doctoral degree is usually required for employment as a licensed clinical or counseling psychologist.
- Opportunities for employment in psychology for those with only a bachelor's degree are severely limited.

Nature of the Work

Psychologists study the human mind and human behavior. Research psychologists investigate the physical, cognitive, emotional, or social aspects of human behavior. Psychologists in applied fields provide mental health care in hospitals, clinics, schools, or private settings.

Like other social scientists, psychologists formulate hypotheses and collect data to test their validity. Research methods may vary depending on the topic under study. Psychologists sometimes gather information through controlled laboratory experiments or by administering personality, performance, aptitude, and intelligence tests. Other methods include observation, interviews, questionnaires, clinical studies, and surveys.

Psychologists apply their knowledge to a wide range of endeavors, including health and human services, management, education, law, and sports. In addition to a variety of work settings, psychologists usually specialize in one of a number of different areas. *Clinical psychologists*—who constitute the largest specialty—usually work in counseling centers, independent or group practices, hospitals, or clinics. They help mentally and emotionally disturbed clients adjust to life and may help medical and surgical patients deal with illnesses or injuries. Some work in physical rehabilitation settings, treating patients with spinal cord injuries, chronic pain or illness, stroke, arthritis, and neurologic conditions. Others help people deal with times of personal crisis, such as divorce or the death of a loved one.

Clinical psychologists often interview patients and give diagnostic tests. They may provide individual, family, or group psychotherapy, and design and implement behavior modification programs. Some clinical psychologists collaborate with physicians and other specialists to develop and implement treatment and intervention programs that patients can understand and comply with. Other clinical psychologists work in universities and medical schools, where they train graduate students in the delivery of mental health and behavioral medicine services. Some administer community mental health programs.

Areas of specialization within clinical psychology include health psychology, neuropsychology, and geropsychology. *Health psychologists* promote good health through health maintenance counseling programs designed to help people achieve goals such as to stop smoking or lose weight. *Neuropsychologists* study the relation between the brain and behavior. They often work in stroke and head injury programs. *Geropsychologists* deal with the special problems faced by the elderly. The emergence and growth of these specialties reflects the increasing participation of psychologists in providing direct services to special patient populations.

Counseling psychologists use various techniques, including interviewing and testing, to advise people on how to deal with problems of everyday living. They work in settings such as university counseling centers, hospitals, and individual or group practices. (Also see the statements on counselors and social workers elsewhere in the *Handbook*.)

School psychologists work in elementary and secondary schools or school district offices to resolve students' learning and behavior problems. They collaborate with teachers, parents, and school personnel to improve classroom management strategies or parenting skills, counter substance abuse, work with students with disabilities or gifted and talented students, and improve teaching and learning strategies. They may evaluate the effectiveness of academic programs, behavior management procedures, and other services provided in the school setting.

Industrial-organizational (I/O) psychologists apply psychological principles and research methods to the workplace in the interest of improving productivity and the quality of worklife. They also are involved in research on management and marketing problems. They conduct applicant screening, training and development, counseling, and organizational development and analysis. An industrial psychologist might work with management to reorganize the work setting to improve productivity or quality of life in the workplace. They frequently act as consultants, brought in by management in order to solve a particular problem.

Developmental psychologists study the physiological, cognitive, and social development that takes place throughout life. Some specialize in behavior during infancy, childhood, and adolescence, or changes that occur during maturity or old age. They may also study developmental disabilities and their effects. Increasingly, research is developing ways to help elderly people stay as independent as possible.

Social psychologists examine people's interactions with others and with the social environment. They work in organizational consultation, marketing research, systems design, or other applied psychology fields. Prominent areas of study include group behavior, leadership, attitudes, and perception.

Experimental or *research psychologists* work in university and private research centers and in business, nonprofit, and governmental organizations. They study behavior processes with human beings and animals such as rats, monkeys, and pigeons. Prominent areas of study in experimental research include motivation, thinking, attention, learning and memory, sensory and perceptual processes, effects of substance abuse, and genetic and neurological factors affecting behavior.

A psychologist's working conditions vary by specialty and place of employment.

Working Conditions

A psychologist's specialty and place of employment determine working conditions. Clinical, school, and counseling psychologists in private practice have their own offices and set their own hours. However, they often offer evening and weekend hours to accommodate their clients. Those employed in hospitals, nursing homes, and other health facilities may work shifts including evenings and weekends, while those who work in schools and clinics generally work regular hours.

Psychologists employed as faculty by colleges and universities divide their time between teaching and research and may also have administrative responsibilities. Many have part-time consulting practices. Most psychologists in government and industry have structured schedules.

Increasingly, many work as part of a team and consult with other psychologists and professionals. Many psychologists experience pressures due to deadlines, tight schedules, and overtime work. Their routine may be interrupted frequently. Travel is required to attend conferences or conduct research.

Employment

Psychologists held about 166,000 jobs in 1998. Educational institutions employed about 4 out of 10 salaried psychologists in positions other than teaching, such as counseling, testing, research, and administration. Three out of 10 were employed in health services, primarily in hospitals, mental health clinics, rehabilitation centers, nursing homes, and other health facilities. Government agencies at the Federal, State, and local levels employed about 17 percent. Governments employ psychologists in hospitals, clinics, correctional facilities, and other settings. The Department of Veterans Affairs and the Department of Defense employ a majority of the psychologists working for Federal agencies. Some psychologists work in social service organizations, research organizations, management consulting firms, marketing research firms, and other businesses.

After several years of experience, some psychologists—usually those with doctoral degrees—enter private practice or set up private research or consulting firms. About one half of psychologists are self-employed.

In addition to the jobs described above, many held positions as psychology faculty at colleges and universities, and as high school psychology teachers. (See the statements on college and university faculty and kindergarten, elementary, and secondary school teachers elsewhere in the *Handbook*.)

Training, Other Qualifications, and Advancement

A doctoral degree is usually required for employment as a licensed clinical or counseling psychologist. Psychologists with a Ph.D. qualify for a wide range of teaching, research, clinical, and counseling positions in universities, elementary and secondary schools, private industry, and government. Psychologists with a Doctor of Psychology (Psy.D.) degree usually work in clinical positions. An Educational Specialist (Ed.S.) degree will qualify an individual to work as a school psychologist. Persons with a master's degree in psychology may work as industrial-organizational psychologists. Others work as psychological assistants, under the supervision of doctoral-level psychologists, and conduct research or psychological evaluations.

A bachelor's degree in psychology qualifies a person to assist psychologists and other professionals in community mental health centers, vocational rehabilitation offices, and correctional programs. They may work as research or administrative assistants or become sales or management trainees in business. Some work as technicians in related fields such as marketing research. However, without additional academic training, their opportunities in psychology are severely limited.

In the Federal Government, candidates having at least 24 semester hours in psychology and one course in statistics qualify for entry-level positions. Because this is one of the few areas in which one can work as a psychologist without an advanced degree, competition for these jobs is keen.

Clinical psychologists usually must have completed the Ph.D. or Psy.D. requirements and served an internship. Vocational and guidance counselors usually need 2 years of graduate study in counseling and 1 year of counseling experience. School psychology requires a master's degree followed by a 1-year internship.

Most students need at least 2 years of full-time graduate study to earn a master's degree in psychology. Requirements usually include practical experience in an applied setting and a master's thesis based on an original research project.

A doctoral degree usually requires 5 to 7 years of graduate study. The Ph.D. degree culminates in a dissertation based on original research. Courses in quantitative research methods, which include the use of computer-based analysis, are an integral part of graduate study and are necessary to complete the dissertation. The Psy.D. may be based on practical work and examinations rather than a dissertation. In clinical or counseling psychology, the requirements for the doctoral degree usually include at least a 1-year internship.

Competition for admission into graduate programs is keen. Some universities require an undergraduate major in psychology. Others prefer only course work in basic psychology with courses in the biological, physical, and social sciences, statistics, and mathematics.

The American Psychological Association (APA) presently accredits doctoral training programs in clinical, counseling, and school psychology. The National Council for Accreditation of Teacher Education, with the assistance of the National Association of School Psychologists, also is involved in the accreditation of advanced degree programs in school psychology. The APA also accredits institutions that provide internships for doctoral students in school, clinical, and counseling psychology.

Psychologists in independent practice or those who offer any type of patient care, including clinical, counseling, and school psychologists, must meet certification or licensing requirements in all States and the District of Columbia. Licensing laws vary by State and by type of position. Clinical and counseling psychologists usually require a doctorate in psychology, completion of an approved internship, and 1 to 2 years of professional experience. In addition, all States require that applicants pass an examination. Most State boards administer a standardized test and many supplement that with additional oral or essay questions. Most States certify those with a master's degree as school psychologists after completion of an internship. Some States require continuing education for license renewal.

Most States require that licensed or certified psychologists limit their practice to areas in which they have developed professional competence through training and experience.

The American Board of Professional Psychology (ABPP) recognizes professional achievement by awarding certification, primarily in clinical psychology, clinical neuropsychology, counseling, forensic, industrial-organizational, and school psychology. Candidates for ABPP certification need a doctorate in psychology, 5 years of experience, professional endorsements, and a passing grade on an examination.

Aspiring psychologists who are interested in direct patient care must be emotionally stable, mature, and able to deal effectively with people. Sensitivity, compassion, and the ability to lead and inspire others are particularly important qualities for clinical work and counseling. Research psychologists should be able to do detailed work independently and as part of a team. Excellent communications skills are necessary to succeed in research. Patience and perseverance are vital qualities because results from psychological treatment of patients or from research usually take a long time.

Job Outlook

Employment of psychologists is expected to grow about as fast as the average for all occupations through 2008. Employment in health care will grow fastest in outpatient mental health and substance abuse treatment clinics. Numerous job opportunities will also arise in schools, public and private social service agencies, and management consulting services. Companies will use psychologists' expertise in survey design, analysis, and research to provide marketing evaluation and statistical analysis. The increase in employee assistance programs, which offer employees help with personal problems, should also spur job growth.

Opportunities for people holding doctorates from leading universities in areas with an applied emphasis, such as clinical, counseling, health, and educational psychology, should have particularly good prospects. Psychologists with extensive training in quantitative research methods and computer science may have a competitive edge over applicants without this background.

Graduates with a master's degree in psychology qualify for positions in school and industrial-organizational psychology. Graduates of master's degree programs in school psychology should have the best job prospects, as schools are expected to increase student counseling and mental health services. Masters' degree holders with several years of industrial experience can obtain jobs in consulting and marketing research. Other master's degree holders may find jobs as psychological assistants in the community mental health field, which often requires direct supervision by a licensed psychologist. Still others may find jobs involving research and data collection and analysis in universities, government, or private companies.

Very few opportunities directly related to psychology will exist for bachelor's degree holders. Some may find jobs as assistants in rehabilitation centers, or in other jobs involving data collection and analysis. Those who meet State certification requirements may become high school psychology teachers.

Earnings

Median annual earnings of salaried psychologists were $48,050 in 1998. The middle 50 percent earned between $36,570 and $70,870 a year. The lowest 10 percent earned less than $27,960 and the highest 10 percent earned more than $88,280 a year. Median annual earnings in the industries employing the largest number of psychologists in 1997 were as follows:

Industry	Earnings
Offices of other health care practitioners	$54,000
Hospitals	49,300
Elementary and secondary schools	47,400
State government, except education and hospitals	41,600
Health and allied services, not elsewhere classified	38,900

The Federal Government recognizes education and experience in certifying applicants for entry-level positions. In general, the starting salary for psychologists having a bachelor's degree was about $20,600 in 1999; those with superior academic records could begin at $25,500. Psychologists with a master's degree and 1 year of experience could start at $31,200. Psychologists having a Ph.D. or Psy.D. degree and 1 year of internship could start at $37,800, and some individuals with experience could start at $45,200. Beginning salaries were slightly higher in selected areas of the country where the prevailing local pay level was higher. The average annual salary for psychologists in the Federal Government was $66,800 in early 1999.

Related Occupations

Psychologists are trained to conduct research and teach, evaluate, counsel, and advise individuals and groups with special needs. Others who do this kind of work include marketing research analysts, advertising and public relations managers, clinical social workers, physicians, sociologists, clergy, special education teachers, and counselors.

Sources of Additional Information

For information on careers, educational requirements, financial assistance, and licensing in all fields of psychology, contact:

☛ American Psychological Association, Research Office and Education in Psychology and Accreditation Offices, 750 1st St. NE., Washington, DC 20002. Internet: **http://www.apa.org**

For information on careers, educational requirements, certification, and licensing of school psychologists, contact:

☛ National Association of School Psychologists, 4030 East West Hwy., Suite 402, Bethesda, MD 20814. Internet: **http://www.naspweb.org**

Information about State licensing requirements is available from:

☛ Association of State and Provincial Psychology Boards, P.O. Box 4389, Montgomery, AL 36103-4389. Internet: **http://www.asppb.org**

Information on obtaining a job with the Federal Government may be obtained from the Office of Personnel Management through a telephone-based system. Consult your telephone directory under U.S. Government for a local number or call (912) 757-3000 (TDD 912 744-2299). This number is not tollfree and charges may result. Information also is available from their Internet site: **http://www.usajobs.opm.gov**

Urban and Regional Planners

(O*NET 27105)

Significant Points

- Most entry-level jobs require a master's degree, although a bachelor's degree and related work experience is sufficient for some positions.
- Most new jobs will arise in more affluent, rapidly growing urban and suburban communities.

Nature of the Work

Planners develop long- and short-term land use plans to provide for growth and revitalization of urban, suburban, and rural communities, while helping local officials make decisions concerning social, economic, and environmental problems. Because local governments employ the majority of urban and regional planners, they are often referred to as community, regional, or city planners.

Planners promote the best use of a community's land and resources for residential, commercial, institutional, and recreational purposes. Planners may be involved in various other activities, including decisions on alternative public transportation system plans, resource development, and protection of ecologically sensitive regions. They address issues such as traffic congestion, air pollution, and the effect of growth and change on a community. They may formulate plans relating to the construction of new school buildings, public housing, or other infrastructure. Some planners are involved in environmental issues ranging from pollution control to wetland preservation, forest conservation, or the location of new landfills. Planners also may be involved with drafting legislation on environmental, social, and economic issues, such as sheltering the homeless, planning a new park, or meeting the demand for new correctional facilities.

Planners examine proposed community facilities such as schools to be sure these facilities will meet the changing demands placed upon them over time. They keep abreast of economic and legal issues involved in zoning codes, building codes, and environmental regulations. They ensure that builders and developers follow these codes and regulations. Planners also deal with land use issues created by population movements. For example, as suburban growth and economic development create more new jobs outside cities, the need for public transportation that enables workers to get to these jobs increases. In response, planners develop transportation models for possible implementation and explain their details to planning boards and the general public.

Before preparing plans for community development, planners report on the current use of land for residential, business, and community purposes. These reports include information on the location and capacity of streets, highways, water and sewer lines, schools, libraries, and cultural and recreational sites. They also provide data on the types of industries in the community, characteristics of the population, and employment and economic trends. With this information, along with input from citizens' advisory committees, planners design the layout of land uses for buildings and other facilities such as subway lines and stations, and prepare reports showing how their programs can be carried out and what they will cost.

Planners use computers to record and analyze information, and to prepare reports and recommendations for government executives and others. Computer databases, spreadsheets, and analytical techniques are widely used to project program costs and forecast future trends in employment, housing, transportation, or population. Computerized geographic information systems enable planners to map land areas and overlay maps with geographic variables, such as population density, as well as to combine and manipulate geographic information to produce alternative plans for land use or development.

Urban and regional planners often confer with land developers, civic leaders, and public officials. They may function as mediators in community disputes and present alternatives acceptable to opposing parties. Planners may prepare material for community relations programs, speak at civic meetings, and appear before legislative committees and elected officials to explain and defend their proposals.

In large organizations, planners usually specialize in a single area such as transportation, demography, housing, historic preservation, urban design, environmental and regulatory issues, or economic development. In small organizations, planners must be able to do various kinds of planning.

Working Conditions

Urban and regional planners are often required to travel to inspect the features of land under consideration for development or regulation, including its current use and the types of structures on it. Some local government planners involved in site development inspections spend most of their time in the field. Although most planners have a scheduled 40-hour workweek, they frequently attend evening or weekend meetings or public hearings with citizens'

Urban and regional planners often confer with land developers, civic leaders, and public officials.

groups. Planners may experience the pressure of deadlines and tight work schedules, as well as political pressure generated by interest groups affected by land use proposals.

Employment

Urban and regional planners held about 35,000 jobs in 1998, and about 6 out of 10 were employed by local governments. An increasing proportion of planners is employed in the private sector for companies involved with research and testing or management and public relations. Others are employed in State agencies dealing with housing, transportation, or environmental protection, and a small number work for the Federal Government.

Training, Other Qualifications, and Advancement

Employers prefer workers who have advanced training. Most entry-level jobs in Federal, State, and local government agencies require a master's degree in urban or regional planning, urban design, geography, or a similar course of study. For some positions, a bachelor's degree and related work experience is sufficient. A bachelor's degree from an accredited planning program, coupled with a master's degree in architecture, landscape architecture, or civil engineering, is good preparation for entry-level planning jobs in areas such as urban design, transportation, or the environment. A master's degree from an accredited planning program provides the best training for a number of planning fields. Although graduates from one of the limited number of accredited bachelor's degree programs qualify for many entry-level positions, their advancement opportunities are often limited unless they acquire an advanced degree.

Courses in related disciplines such as architecture, law, earth sciences, demography, economics, finance, health administration, geographic information systems, and management are highly recommended. In addition, familiarity with computer models and statistical techniques is necessary.

In 1999, about 80 colleges and universities offered an accredited master's degree program, and about 10 offered an accredited bachelor's degree program in urban or regional planning. These programs are accredited by the Planning Accreditation Board, which consists of representatives of the American Institute of Certified Planners, the American Planning Association, and the Association of Collegiate Schools of Planning. Most graduate programs in planning require a minimum of 2 years.

Specializations most commonly offered by planning schools are environmental planning, land use and comprehensive planning, economic development, housing, historic preservation, and social planning. Other popular offerings include community development, transportation, and urban design. Graduate students spend considerable time in studios, workshops, and laboratory courses learning to analyze and solve planning problems. They are often required to work in a planning office part time or during the summer. Local government planning offices frequently offer students internships, providing experience that proves invaluable in obtaining a full-time planning position after graduation.

The American Institute of Certified Planners (AICP), a professional institute within the American Planning Association (APA), grants certification to individuals who have the appropriate combination of education and professional experience and pass an examination. Certification may be helpful for promotion.

Planners must be able to think in terms of spatial relationships and visualize the effects of their plans and designs. Planners should be flexible and able to reconcile different viewpoints and to make constructive policy recommendations. The ability to communicate effectively, both orally and in writing, is necessary for anyone interested in this field.

After a few years of experience, planners may advance to assignments requiring a high degree of independent judgment, such as designing the physical layout of a large development or recommending policy and budget options. Some public sector planners are promoted to community planning director and spend a great deal of time meeting with officials, speaking to civic groups, and supervising a staff. Further advancement occurs through a transfer to a larger jurisdiction with more complex problems and greater responsibilities, or into related occupations, such as director of community or economic development.

Job Outlook

Employment of urban and regional planners is expected to grow about as fast as the average for all occupations through 2008, due to the need for State and local governments to provide public services such as regulation of commercial development, the environment, transportation, housing, and land use and development. Non-governmental initiatives dealing with historic preservation and redevelopment will provide additional openings. Some job openings will also arise from the need to replace experienced planners who transfer to other occupations, retire, or leave the labor force for other reasons.

Most planners work for local governments with limited resources and many demands for services. When communities need to cut expenditures, planning services may be cut before more basic services such as police or education. As a result, the number of openings in private industry for consulting positions is expected to grow more rapidly than the number of openings in government.

Most new jobs for urban and regional planners will arise in more affluent, rapidly expanding communities. Local governments need planners to address an array of problems associated with population growth. For example, new housing developments require roads, sewer systems, fire stations, schools, libraries, and recreation facilities that must be planned while considering budgetary constraints. Small town chambers of commerce, economic development authorities and tourism bureaus may hire planners, preferring candidates with some background in marketing and public relations.

Earnings

Median annual earnings of urban and regional planners were $42,860 in 1998. The middle 50 percent earned between $32,920 and $56,150 a year. The lowest 10 percent earned less than $26,020 and the highest 10 percent earned more than $80,090 a year. Median annual earnings for urban and regional planners in 1997 were $40,700 in local government and $38,900 in State government.

Related Occupations

Urban and regional planners develop plans for the growth of urban, suburban, and rural communities. Others whose work is similar include architects, landscape architects, city managers, civil engineers, environmental engineers, directors of community or economic development, and geographers.

Sources of Additional Information

Information on careers, salaries, and certification in urban and regional planning is available from:

☛ American Planning Association, Education Division, 122 South Michigan Ave., Suite 1600, Chicago, IL 60603.
Internet: **http://www.planning.org**

Social Scientists, Other

(O*NET 24199A, 27199A, 27199B, 27199C, 27199D, 27199E, 27199F, 27199G, and 27199H)

Significant Points

- Educational attainment of social scientists is among the highest of all occupations.
- Job opportunities are expected to be best in social service agencies, research and testing services, and management consulting firms.

Nature of the Work

The major social science occupations covered in this statement include anthropologists, geographers, historians, political scientists, and sociologists. (Economists, psychologists, and urban and regional planners are covered in the preceding *Handbook* statements.)

Social scientists study all aspects of society—from past events and achievements to human behavior and relationships between groups. Their research provides insights that help us understand different ways in which individuals and groups make decisions, exercise power, and respond to change. Through their studies and analyses, social scientists suggest solutions to social, business, personal, governmental, and environmental problems.

Research is a major activity for many social scientists. They use various methods to assemble facts and construct theories. Applied research usually is designed to produce information that will enable people to make better decisions or manage their affairs more effectively. Interviews and surveys are widely used to collect facts, opinions, or other information. Information collection takes many forms including living and working among the population being studied; field investigations, the analysis of historical records and documents; experiments with human or animal subjects in a laboratory; administration of standardized tests and questionnaires; and preparation and interpretation of maps and computer graphics. The work of the major specialties in social science—other than psychologists, economists, and urban and regional planners—varies greatly. Specialists in one field, however, often find that their research overlaps work being conducted in another discipline.

Anthropologists study the origin and the physical, social, and cultural development and behavior of humans. They may study the way of life, archaeological remains, language, or physical characteristics of people in various parts of the world. Some compare the customs, values, and social patterns of different cultures. Anthropologists usually concentrate in sociocultural anthropology, archaeology, linguistics, or biological-physical anthropology. Sociocultural anthropologists study customs, cultures, and social lives of groups in settings that vary from nonindustrialized societies to modern urban centers. Archaeologists recover and examine material evidence, such as ruins, tools, and pottery remaining from past human cultures in order to determine the history, customs, and living habits of earlier civilizations. Linguistic anthropologists study the role of language in various cultures. Biological-physical anthropologists study the evolution of the human body, look for the earliest evidences of human life, and analyze how culture and biology influence one another. Most anthropologists specialize in one particular region of the world.

Geographers analyze distributions of physical and cultural phenomena on local, regional, continental, and global scales. Economic geographers study the distribution of resources and economic activities. Political geographers are concerned with the relationship of geography to political phenomena, whereas cultural geographers study the geography of cultural phenomena. Physical geographers study variations in climate, vegetation, soil, and landforms, and their implications for human activity. Urban and transportation geographers study cities and metropolitan areas, while regional geographers study the physical, economic, political, and cultural characteristics of regions, ranging in size from a congressional district to entire continents. Medical geographers study health care delivery systems, epidemiology (the study of the causes and control of epidemics), and the effect of the environment on health. (Some occupational classification systems include geographers under physical scientists rather than social scientists.)

Historians research, analyze, and interpret the past. They use many sources of information in their research, including government and institutional records, newspapers and other periodicals, photographs, interviews, films, and unpublished manuscripts such as personal diaries and letters. Historians usually specialize in a country or region; a particular time period; or a particular field, such as social, intellectual, political, or diplomatic history. Biographers

Social scientists study all aspects of human society.

collect detailed information on individuals. Genealogists trace family histories. Other historians help study and preserve archival materials, artifacts, and historic buildings and sites.

Political scientists study the origin, development, and operation of political systems and public policy. They conduct research on a wide range of subjects such as relations between the United States and other countries, the institutions and political life of nations, the politics of small towns or a major metropolis, or the decisions of the U.S. Supreme Court. Studying topics such as public opinion, political decision-making, ideology, and public policy, they analyze the structure and operation of governments as well as various political entities. Depending on the topic, a political scientist might conduct a public opinion survey, analyze election results, analyze public documents, or interview public officials.

Sociologists study society and social behavior by examining the groups and social institutions people form, as well as various social, religious, political, and business organizations. They also study the behavior and interaction of groups, trace their origin and growth, and analyze the influence of group activities on individual members. They are concerned with the characteristics of social groups, organizations, and institutions; the ways individuals are affected by each other and by the groups to which they belong; and the effect of social traits such as sex, age, or race on a person's daily life. The results of sociological research aid educators, lawmakers, administrators, and others interested in resolving social problems and formulating public policy.

Most sociologists work in one or more specialties, such as social organization, stratification, and mobility; racial and ethnic relations; education; family; social psychology; urban, rural, political, and comparative sociology; sex roles and relations; demography; gerontology; criminology; or sociological practice.

Working Conditions

Most social scientists have regular hours. Generally working behind a desk, either alone or in collaboration with other social scientists, they read and write research reports. Many experience the pressures of writing and publishing articles, deadlines and tight schedules, and sometimes they must work overtime, for which they usually are not reimbursed. Social scientists often work as an integral part of a research team, where good communications skills are important.

Travel may be necessary to collect information or attend meetings. Social scientists on foreign assignment must adjust to unfamiliar cultures, climates, and languages.

Some social scientists do fieldwork. For example, anthropologists, archaeologists, and geographers often travel to remote areas, live among the people they study, learn their languages, and stay for long periods at the site of their investigations. They may work under rugged conditions, and their work may involve strenuous physical exertion.

Social scientists employed by colleges and universities usually have flexible work schedules, often dividing their time among teaching, research and writing, consulting, or administrative responsibilities.

Employment

Social scientists held about 50,000 jobs in 1998. Many worked as researchers, administrators, and counselors for a wide range of employers, including Federal, State, and local governments, educational institutions, social service agencies, research and testing services, and management consulting firms. Other employers include international organizations, associations, museums, and historical societies.

Many additional individuals with training in a social science discipline teach in colleges and universities, and in secondary and elementary schools. (For more information, see the *Handbook* statements on college and university faculty, and kindergarten, elementary, and secondary school teachers.) The proportion of social scientists that teach varies by specialty—for example, the academic world usually is a more important source of jobs for graduates in history than for graduates in the other fields of study.

Training, Other Qualifications, and Advancement

Educational attainment of social scientists is among the highest of all occupations. The Ph.D. or equivalent degree is a minimum requirement for most positions in colleges and universities and is important for advancement to many top level nonacademic research and administrative posts. Graduates with master's degrees in applied specialties usually have better professional opportunities outside of colleges and universities, although the situation varies by field. Graduates with a master's degree in a social science qualify for teaching positions in junior colleges. Bachelor's degree holders have limited opportunities and in most social science occupations do not qualify for "professional" positions. The bachelor's degree does, however, provide a suitable background for many different kinds of entry-level jobs, such as research assistant, administrative aide, or management or sales trainee. With the addition of sufficient education courses, social science graduates also can qualify for teaching positions in secondary and elementary schools.

Training in statistics and mathematics is essential for many social scientists. Mathematical and quantitative research methods are increasingly used in geography, political science, and other fields. The ability to use computers for research purposes is mandatory in most disciplines.

Depending on their jobs, social scientists may need a wide range of personal characteristics. Because they constantly seek new information about people, things, and ideas, intellectual curiosity and creativity are fundamental personal traits. The ability to think logically and methodically is important to a political scientist comparing, for example, the merits of various forms of government. Objectivity, open-mindedness, and systematic work habits are important in all kinds of social science research. Perseverance is essential for an anthropologist, who might spend years accumulating artifacts from an ancient civilization. Excellent written and oral communication skills are essential for all these professionals.

Job Outlook

Overall employment of social scientists is expected to grow about as fast as the average for all occupations through 2008. Prospects are best for those with advanced degrees, and usually are better in disciplines such as sociology and geography, which offer more opportunities in nonacademic settings.

Government agencies, social service organizations, marketing, research and consulting firms, and a wide range of businesses seek social science graduates, although often in jobs with titles unrelated to their academic discipline. Social scientists will face stiff competition for academic positions. However, the growing importance and popularity of social science subjects in secondary schools is strengthening the demand for social science teachers at that level.

Candidates seeking positions as social scientists can expect to encounter competition in many areas of social science. Some social science graduates, however, will find good employment opportunities in areas outside traditional social science, often in related jobs that require good research, communication, and quantitative skills.

Earnings

Median annual earnings of all other social scientists (excluding economists, psychologists, and urban and regional planners) were $38,990 in 1998. The middle 50 percent earned between $28,950 and $56,550 a year. The lowest 10 percent earned less than $21,530 and the highest 10 percent earned more than $80,640 a year. Median annual earnings of all other social scientists in 1997 were $53,700 in the Federal Government and $37,300 in State government, except education and hospitals.

In the Federal Government, social scientists with a bachelor's degree and no experience could start at $20,600 or $25,500 a year in 1999, depending on their college records. Those with a master's degree could start at $31,200, and those with a Ph.D. degree could begin at $37,700, while some individuals with experience and an advanced degree could start at $45,200. Beginning salaries were slightly higher in selected areas of the country where the prevailing local pay level was higher.

Related Occupations

A number of occupations requiring training and personal qualities similar to those of social scientists are covered elsewhere in the *Handbook*. These include lawyers, statisticians, mathematicians, computer programmers, computer scientists, computer engineers, computer systems analysts, reporters and correspondents, social workers, college and university faculty, and counselors.

Sources of Additional Information

Detailed information about economists and marketing research analysts, psychologists, and urban and regional planners is presented elsewhere in the *Handbook*.

For information about careers in anthropology, contact:

☛ The American Anthropological Association, 4350 N. Fairfax Dr., Suite 640, Arlington, VA 22203. Internet: **http://www.aaanet.org**

For information about careers in archaeology, contact:

☛ Society for American Archaeology, 900 2nd St. NE., Suite 12, Washington, DC 20002. Internet: **http://www.saa.org**

☛ Archaeological Institute of America, 656 Beacon St., Boston, MA 02215. Internet: **http://www.archaeological.org**

For information about careers in geography, contact:

☛ Association of American Geographers, 1710 16th St. NW, Washington, DC 20009. Internet: **http://www.aag.org**

Information on careers for historians is available from:

☛ American Historical Association, 400 A St. SE, Washington, DC 20003. Internet: **http://www.theaha.org**

☛ Organization of American Historians, 112 North Bryan St., Bloomington, IN 47408. Internet: **http://www.oah.org**

☛ American Association for State and Local History, 1717 Church St., Nashville, TN 37203-2991. Internet: **http://www.aaslh.org**

For information about careers in political science, contact:

☛ National Association of Schools of Public Affairs and Administration, 1120 G St. NW, Suite 730, Washington, DC 20005.
Internet: **http://www.naspaa.org**

Information about careers in sociology is available from:
☛ American Sociological Association, 1307 New York Ave. NW., Suite 700, Washington, DC 20005. Internet: **http://www.asanet.org**

For information about careers in demography, contact:
☛ Population Association of America, 721 Ellsworth Dr., Suite 303, Silver Spring, MD 20910. Internet: **http://www.popassoc.org**

Social and Recreation Workers

Human Service Workers and Assistants

(O*NET 27308)

Significant Points

- Human service worker and assistant occupations are projected to be among the fastest growing.
- Job opportunities should be excellent, particularly for applicants with appropriate postsecondary education, but pay is low.

Nature of the Work

Human service workers and assistants is a generic term for people with various job titles, including social service assistant, case management aide, social work assistant, community support worker, alcohol or drug abuse counselor, mental health aide, community outreach worker, life skill counselor, and gerontology aide. They usually work under the direction of professionals from a variety of fields, such as nursing, psychiatry, psychology, rehabilitative or physical therapy, or social work. The amount of responsibility and supervision they are given varies a great deal. Some have little direct supervision; others work under close direction.

Human service workers and assistants provide direct and indirect client services. They assess clients' needs, establish their eligibility for benefits and services, and help clients obtain them. They examine financial documents such as rent receipts and tax returns to determine whether the client is eligible for food stamps, Medicaid, welfare, and other human service programs. They also arrange for transportation and escorts, if necessary, and provide emotional support. Human service workers and assistants monitor and keep case records on clients and report progress to supervisors and case managers. Human service workers and assistants also may transport or accompany clients to group meal sites, adult daycare centers, or doctors' offices. They may telephone or visit clients' homes to make sure services are being received, or to help resolve disagreements, such as those between tenants and landlords. They also may help clients complete insurance or medical forms, as well as applications for financial assistance. Additionally, social and human service workers and assistants may assist others with daily living needs.

Human service workers and assistants play a variety of roles in a community. They may organize and lead group activities, assist clients in need of counseling or crisis intervention, or administer a food bank or emergency fuel program. In halfway houses, group homes, and government-supported housing programs, they assist adults who need supervision with personal hygiene and daily living skills. They review clients' records, ensure that they take correct doses of medication, talk with family members, and confer with medical personnel and other care givers to gain better insight into clients' backgrounds and needs. Human service workers and assistants also provide emotional support and help clients become involved in their own well being, in community recreation programs, and in other activities.

In psychiatric hospitals, rehabilitation programs, and outpatient clinics, human service workers and assistants work with professional care providers, such as psychiatrists, psychologists, and social workers to help clients master everyday living skills, to teach them how to communicate more effectively, and to get along better with others. They support the client's participation in a treatment plan, such as individual or group counseling or occupational therapy.

Working Conditions

Working conditions of human service workers and assistants vary. Some work in offices, clinics, and hospitals, while others work in group homes, shelters, sheltered workshops, and day programs. Many spend their time in the field visiting clients. Most work a 40-hour week, although some work in the evening and on weekends.

The work, while satisfying, can be emotionally draining. Understaffing and relatively low pay may add to the pressure. Turnover is reported to be high, especially among workers without academic preparation for this field.

Employment

Human service workers and assistants held about 268,000 jobs in 1998. Almost half worked in private social or human services agencies, offering a variety of services, including adult daycare, group meals, crisis intervention, counseling, and job training. Many human service workers and assistants supervised residents of group homes and halfway houses. About one-third were employed by State and local governments, primarily in public welfare agencies and facilities for mentally disabled and developmentally challenged individuals. Human service workers and assistants also held jobs in clinics, detoxification units, community mental health centers, psychiatric hospitals, day treatment programs, and sheltered workshops.

Human service workers and assistants assess clients' needs and help them obtain appropriate benefits and services.

Training, Other Qualifications, and Advancement

Although a bachelor's degree usually is not required for this occupation, employers increasingly are seeking individuals with relevant work experience or education beyond high school. Certificates or associate degrees in subjects such as social work, human services, or one of the social or behavioral sciences meet most employers' requirements.

Human services programs have a core curriculum that trains students to observe patients and record information, conduct patient interviews, implement treatment plans, employ problem-solving techniques, handle crisis intervention matters, and use proper case management and referral procedures. General education courses in liberal arts, sciences, and the humanities also are part of the curriculum. Many degree programs require completion of a supervised internship.

Educational attainment often influences the kind of work an employee may be assigned and the degree of responsibility that may be entrusted to them. For example, workers with no more than a high school education are likely to receive extensive on-the-job training to work in direct-care services, while employees with a college degree might be assigned to do supportive counseling, coordinate program activities, or manage a group home. Human service workers and assistants with proven leadership ability, either from previous experience or as a volunteer in the field, often receive greater autonomy in their work. Regardless of the academic or work background of employees, most employers provide some form of in-service training, such as seminars and workshops, to their employees.

Hiring requirements in group homes tend to be more stringent than in other settings. For example, employers may require employees to have a valid driver's license or to submit to a criminal background investigation.

Employers try to select applicants who have effective communication skills, a strong sense of responsibility, and the ability to manage time effectively. Many human services jobs involve direct contact with people who are vulnerable to exploitation or mistreatment; therefore, patience, understanding, and a strong desire to help others, are highly valued characteristics.

Formal education almost always is necessary for advancement. In general, advancement requires a bachelor's or master's degree in counseling, rehabilitation, social work, human services management, or a related field.

Job Outlook

Opportunities for human service workers and assistants are expected to be excellent, particularly for applicants with appropriate postsecondary education. The number of human service workers and assistants is projected to grow much faster than the average for all occupations between 1998 and 2008—ranking among the most rapidly growing occupations. The need to replace workers who move into new positions due to advancement, retirement, or for other reasons will create many additional job opportunities. This occupation, however, is not attractive to everyone. It can be draining emotionally and the pay is relatively low. Qualified applicants should have little difficulty finding employment.

Faced with rapid growth in the demand for social and human services, employers are developing new strategies for delivering and funding services. Many employers increasingly will rely on human service workers and assistants to undertake greater responsibility in delivering services to clients.

Opportunities are expected to be best in job training programs, residential care facilities, and private social service agencies, which include such services as adult daycare and meal delivery programs. Demand for these services will expand with the growing number of elderly, who are more likely to need services. In addition, social and human service workers and assistants will continue to be needed to provide services to pregnant teenagers, the homeless, the mentally disabled and developmentally challenged, and those with substance-abuse problems.

Job training programs are expected to require additional human service workers and assistants. As social welfare policies shift focus from benefit-based programs to work-based initiatives, there will be an increased demand for people to teach job skills to the people who are new to or re-entering the workforce. Additionally, streamlined and downsized businesses create increased demand for persons with job retraining expertise. Human service workers and assistants will help companies to cope with new modes of conducting business and employees to master new job skills.

Residential care establishments should face increased pressures to respond to the needs of the chronically and mentally ill. Many of these patients have been deinstitutionalized and lack the knowledge or the ability to care for themselves. Also, more community-based programs, supported independent living sites, and group residences are expected to be established to house and assist the homeless, and the chronically, and mentally, ill. As a result, demand for human service workers and assistants will increase.

The number of jobs for human service workers and assistants will grow more rapidly than overall employment in State and local governments. State and local governments employ many of their human service workers and assistants in corrections and public assistance departments. Although employment in corrections departments is growing, employment of social and human service workers and assistants is not expected to grow as rapidly as employment in other corrections jobs, such as guards or corrections officers. Public assistance programs have been employing more human service workers and assistants in an attempt to employ fewer social workers, who are more educated, thus more highly paid.

Earnings

Median annual earnings of human service workers and assistants were $21,360 in 1998. The middle 50 percent earned between $16,620 and $27,070. The top 10 percent earned more than $33,840, while the lowest 10 percent earned less than $13,540.

Median hourly earnings in the industries employing the largest numbers of human service workers and assistants in 1997 were:

Industry	Earnings
State government, except education and hospitals	$25,600
Local government, except education and hospitals	23,500
Hospitals	21,200
Health and allied services, not elsewhere classified	20,600
Social services, not elsewhere classified	20,200

Related Occupations

Workers in other occupations that require skills similar to those of human service workers and assistants include social workers, religious workers, residential counselors, child-care workers, occupational therapy assistants, physical therapy assistants, psychiatric aides, and activity leaders.

Sources of Additional Information

Information on academic programs in human services may be found in most directories of 2- and 4-year colleges, available at libraries or career counseling centers.

For information on programs and careers in human services, contact:

- National Organization for Human Service Education, Brookdale Community College, Lincroft, NJ 07738.
- Council for Standards in Human Services Education, Northern Essex Community College, Haverhill, MA 01830.

Information on job openings may be available from State employment service offices or directly from city, county, or State departments of health, mental health and mental retardation, and human resources.

Recreation Workers

(O*NET 27311)

Significant Points

- The recreation field has an unusually large number of part-time, seasonal, and volunteer jobs.
- Educational requirements range from a high school diploma to a graduate degree.
- Competition will remain keen for full-time career positions; persons with formal training and experience gained in part-time or seasonal recreation jobs should have the best opportunities.

Nature of the Work

People spend much of their leisure time participating in a wide variety of organized recreational activities, such as aerobics, arts and crafts, little league baseball, tennis, camping, and softball. Recreation workers plan, organize, and direct these activities in local playgrounds and recreation areas, parks, community centers, health clubs, religious organizations, camps, theme parks, and most tourist attractions. Increasingly, recreational workers are also found in workplaces, where they organize and direct leisure activities and athletic programs for employees of all ages.

Recreation workers plan, organize, and direct various athletic and leisure activities.

These workers hold a variety of positions at different levels of responsibility. *Recreation leaders*, who are responsible for a recreation program's daily operation, primarily organize and direct participants. They may lead and give instruction in dance, drama, crafts, games, and sports; schedule use of facilities and keep records of equipment use; and ensure recreation facilities and equipment are used properly. Workers who provide instruction and coach teams in specialties such as art, music, drama, swimming, or tennis may be called *activity specialists*.

Recreation supervisors oversee recreation leaders and also plan, organize, and manage recreational activities to meet the needs of a variety of populations. These workers often serve as liaisons between the director of the park or recreation center and the recreation leaders. Recreation supervisors with more specialized responsibilities may also direct special activities or events and oversee a major activity, such as aquatics, gymnastics, or performing arts.

Directors of recreation and parks develop and manage comprehensive recreation programs in parks, playgrounds, and other settings. Directors usually serve as technical advisors to State and local recreation and park commissions and may be responsible for recreation and park budgets.

Camp counselors lead and instruct children and teenagers in outdoor-oriented forms of recreation, such as swimming, hiking, horseback riding, and camping. In addition, counselors provide campers with specialized instruction in activities such as archery, boating, music, drama, gymnastics, tennis, and computers. In resident camps, counselors also provide guidance and supervise daily living and general socialization. (Workers in a related occupation, *recreational therapists,* help individuals recover or adjust to illness, disability, or specific social problems; this occupation is described elsewhere in the *Handbook*.)

Working Conditions

The work setting for recreation workers may vary from a cruise ship, to a woodland recreational park, to a playground in the center of a large urban community. Regardless of setting, most recreation workers spend much of their time outdoors and may work in a variety of weather conditions. Recreation directors and supervisors, however, typically spend most of their time in an office, planning programs and special events. Because full-time recreation workers spend more time acting as managers than as hands-on activities leaders, they engage in less physical activity. Nevertheless, recreation workers at all levels risk suffering an injury during physical activities.

Most recreation workers put in about 40 hours a week. People entering this field, especially camp counselors, should expect some night and weekend work and irregular hours. About 3 out of 10 work part time, and many jobs are seasonal.

Employment

Recreation workers held about 241,000 jobs in 1998, and many additional workers held summer jobs in this occupation. Of those with year-round jobs as recreation workers, about half worked in park and recreation departments of municipal and county governments. Nearly 1 in 4 worked in membership organizations, such as the Boy or Girl Scouts, the YMCA, and Red Cross, or worked for programs run by social service organizations, including senior centers, adult daycare programs, or residential care facilities like halfway houses, group homes, and institutions for delinquent youth. Another 1 out of 10 worked for nursing and other personal care facilities.

Other employers of recreation workers included commercial recreation establishments, amusement parks, sports and entertainment centers, wilderness and survival enterprises, tourist attractions, vacation excursion companies, hotels and resorts, summer camps, health and athletic clubs, and apartment complexes.

The recreation field has an unusually large number of part-time, seasonal, and volunteer jobs. These jobs include summer camp counselors, lifeguards, craft specialists, and after-school and weekend recreation program leaders. In addition, many teachers and college students accept jobs as recreation workers when school is not in session. The vast majority of volunteers serve as activity leaders at local day-camp programs, or in youth organizations, camps, nursing homes, hospitals, senior centers, YMCAs, and other settings. Some volunteers serve on local park and recreation boards and commissions. Volunteer experience, part-time work during school, or a summer job can lead to a full-time career as a recreation worker.

Training, Other Qualifications, and Advancement

Educational requirements for recreation workers range from a high school diploma, or sometimes less for many summer jobs, to graduate degrees for some administrative positions in large public recreation systems. Full-time career professional positions usually require a college degree with a major in parks and recreation or leisure studies, but a bachelor's degree in any liberal arts field may be sufficient for some jobs in the private sector. In industrial recreation, or "employee services" as it is more commonly called, companies prefer to hire those with a bachelor's degree in recreation or leisure studies and a background in business administration.

Specialized training or experience in a particular field, such as art, music, drama, or athletics, is an asset for many jobs. Some jobs also require certification. For example, when teaching or coaching water-related activities, a lifesaving certificate is a prerequisite. Graduates of associate degree programs in parks and recreation, social work, and other human services disciplines also enter some career recreation positions. High school graduates occasionally enter career positions, but this is not common. Some college students work part time as recreation workers while earning degrees.

A bachelor's degree and experience are preferred for most recreation supervisor jobs and required for most higher-level administrator jobs. However, increasing numbers of recreation workers who aspire to administrator positions obtain master's degrees in parks and recreation or related disciplines. Also, many persons in other disciplines, including social work, forestry, and resource management, pursue graduate degrees in recreation.

Programs leading to an associate or bachelor's degree in parks and recreation, leisure studies, or related fields are offered at several hundred colleges and universities. Many also offer master's or doctoral degrees in this field. In 1997, 93 bachelor's degree programs in parks and recreation were accredited by the National Recreation and Park Association (NRPA). Accredited programs provide broad exposure to the history, theory, and practice of park and recreation management. Courses offered include community organization, supervision and administration, recreational needs of special populations, such as older adults or the disabled, and supervised fieldwork. Students may specialize in areas such as therapeutic recreation, park management, outdoor recreation, industrial or commercial recreation, and camp management.

The American Camping Association offers workshops and courses for experienced camp directors at different times and locations throughout the year. Some national youth associations offer training courses for camp directors at the local and regional levels.

Persons planning recreation careers should be outgoing, good at motivating people, and sensitive to the needs of others. Good health and physical fitness are typically required, while activity planning calls for creativity and resourcefulness. Individuals contemplating careers in recreation at the supervisory or administrative level should develop managerial skills. College courses in management, business administration, accounting, and personnel management are likely to be useful.

Certification in the recreation field is offered by the NRPA National Certification Board. The NRPA, along with its State chapters, offers certification as a Certified Leisure Professional (CLP) for those with a college degree in recreation, and as a Certified Leisure Technician (CLT) for those with less than 4 years of college. Other NRPA certifications include Certified Leisure Provisional Professional (CLPP), Certified Playground Inspector (CPI), and Aquatic Facility Operations (AFO) Certification. Continuing education is necessary to remain certified.

Job Outlook

Competition will remain keen for career positions in recreation, as the number of jobseekers for full-time positions is expected to exceed the number of job openings. Opportunities for staff positions should be best for persons with formal training and experience gained in part-time or seasonal recreation jobs. Those with graduate degrees should have the best opportunities for supervisory or administrative positions.

Prospects are better for those seeking the large number of temporary, seasonal jobs. These positions, which are typically filled by high school or college students, do not generally have formal education requirements and are open to anyone with the desired personal qualities. Employers compete for a share of the vacationing student labor force, and although salaries in recreation are often lower than those in other fields, the nature of the work and the opportunity to work outdoors is attractive to many. Seasonal employment prospects as program directors should be good for applicants with specialized training and certification in an activity like swimming.

Employment of recreation workers is expected to grow about as fast as the average for all occupations through 2008, as growing numbers of people spend more time and money on leisure services. Growth in these jobs will also stem from increased interest in fitness and health and the rising demand for recreational opportunities for older adults in senior centers and retirement communities. In particular, jobs will increase in social services as more recreation workers are needed to develop and lead activity programs in senior centers, halfway houses, children's homes, and daycare programs for people with special needs.

Recreation worker jobs will also continue to increase as more businesses recognize the benefits of recreation programs and other services like wellness programs and elder care. Job growth will also occur in the commercial recreation industry—in amusement parks, athletic clubs, camps, sports clinics, and swimming pools.

Employment of recreation workers in local government—where nearly half of these workers are employed—is expected to grow more slowly than in other industries due to budget constraints. As a result, some local park and recreation departments are expected to do less hiring for permanent, full-time positions than in the past. Because resources and priorities for public services differ from one community to another, this sector's share of recreation worker employment will vary widely by region.

Earnings

Median hourly earnings of recreation workers who worked full time in 1998 were $7.93. The middle 50 percent earned between about $6.14 and $10.65, while the top 10 percent earned $14.74 or more. However, earnings of recreation directors and others in supervisory or managerial positions can be substantially higher. Hourly earnings in the industries employing the largest number of recreation workers in 1997 were:

Nursing and personal care facilities	$8.10
Local government, except education and hospitals	8.00
Individual and family services	7.30
Civic and social associations	6.80
Miscellaneous amusement and recreation services	6.20

Most public and private recreation agencies provide full-time recreation workers with typical benefits; part-time workers receive few, if any, benefits.

Related Occupations
Recreation workers must exhibit leadership and sensitivity in dealing with people. Other occupations that require similar personal qualities include recreational therapists, social workers, parole officers, human relations counselors, school counselors, clinical and counseling psychologists, and teachers.

Sources of Additional Information
For information on jobs in recreation, contact employers such as local government departments of parks and recreation, nursing and personal care facilities, and YMCAs.

Ordering information for materials describing careers and academic programs in recreation is available from:

☛ National Recreation and Park Association, Division of Professional Services, 22377 Belmont Ridge Road, Ashburn, VA 20148-4501. Internet: **http://www.nrpa.org**

For information on careers in employee services and corporate recreation, contact:

☛ National Employee Services and Recreation Association, 2211 York Rd., Suite 207, Oakbrook, IL 60521. Internet: **http://www.nesra.org**

Social Workers

(O*NET 27305A, 27305B, 27305C, and 27302)

Significant Points

- A bachelor's degree is the minimum requirement for many entry-level jobs, but a master's degree in social work (MSW)—required for clinical practice—or a related field is becoming the norm for many positions.
- Employment is projected to grow much faster than average.
- Competition for jobs is expected to be keen in cities but opportunities should be good in rural areas.

Nature of the Work
Social work is a profession for those with a strong desire to help people, to make things better, and to make a difference. Social workers help people function the best way they can in their environment, deal with their relationships with others, and solve personal and family problems.

Social workers often see clients who face a life-threatening disease or a social problem. These problems may include inadequate housing, unemployment, lack of job skills, financial distress, serious illness or disability, substance abuse, unwanted pregnancy, or antisocial behavior. Social workers also assist families that have serious domestic conflicts, including those involving child or spousal abuse.

Through direct counseling, social workers help clients identify their concerns, consider effective solutions, and find reliable resources. Social workers typically consult and counsel clients and arrange for services that can help them. Often, they refer clients to specialists in services such as debt counseling, childcare or elder care, public assistance, or alcohol or drug rehabilitation. Social workers then follow through with the client to assure that services are helpful and that clients make proper use of the services offered. Social workers may review eligibility requirements, help fill out forms and applications, visit clients on a regular basis, and provide support during crises.

Social workers practice in a variety of settings. In hospitals and psychiatric hospitals, they provide or arrange for a range of support services. In mental health and community centers, social workers provide counseling services on marriage, family, and adoption matters, and they help people through personal or community emergencies, such as dealing with loss or grief or arranging for disaster assistance. In schools, they help children, parents, and teachers cope with problems. In social service agencies, they help people locate basic benefits, such as income assistance, housing, and job training. Social workers also offer counseling to those receiving therapy for addictive or physical disorders in rehabilitation facilities, and to people in nursing homes in need of routine living care. In employment settings, they counsel people with personal, family, professional, or financial problems affecting their work performance. Social workers who work in courts and correction facilities evaluate and counsel individuals in the criminal justice system to cope better in society. In private practice, they provide clinical or diagnostic testing services covering a wide range of personal disorders.

Social workers often provide social services in health-related settings that now are governed by managed care organizations. To contain costs, these organizations are emphasizing short-term intervention, ambulatory and community-based care, and greater decentralization of services.

Most social workers specialize in an area of practice. Although some conduct research or are involved in planning or policy development, most social workers prefer an area of practice in which they interact with clients.

Clinical social workers offer psychotherapy or counseling and a range of diagnostic services in public agencies, clinics, and private practice.

Child welfare or family services social workers may counsel children and youths who have difficulty adjusting socially, advise parents on how to care for disabled children, or arrange for homemaker services during a parent's illness. If children have serious problems in school, child welfare workers may consult with parents, teachers, and counselors to identify underlying causes and develop plans for treatment. Some social workers assist single parents, arrange adoptions, and help find foster homes for neglected, abandoned, or abused children. Child welfare workers also work in residential institutions for children and adolescents.

Child or adult protective services social workers investigate reports of abuse and neglect and intervene if necessary. They may initiate legal action to remove children from homes and place them temporarily in an emergency shelter or with a foster family.

Mental health social workers provide services for persons with mental or emotional problems. Such services include individual and group therapy, outreach, crisis intervention, social rehabilitation, and training in skills of everyday living. They may also help plan for supportive services to ease patients' return to the community. (Counselors and psychologists, who may provide similar services, are discussed elsewhere in the *Handbook*.)

Health care social workers help patients and their families cope with chronic, acute, or terminal illnesses and handle problems that may stand in the way of recovery or rehabilitation. They may organize support groups for families of patients suffering from cancer, AIDS, Alzheimer's disease, or other illnesses. They also advise family caregivers, counsel patients, and help plan for their needs after discharge by arranging for at-home services—from meals-on-wheels to oxygen equipment. Some work on interdisciplinary teams that evaluate certain kinds of patients—geriatric or organ transplant patients, for example.

School social workers diagnose students' problems and arrange needed services, counsel children in trouble, and help integrate disabled students into the general school population. School social workers deal with problems such as student pregnancy, misbehavior in class, and excessive absences. They also advise teachers on how to cope with problem students.

Criminal justice social workers make recommendations to courts, prepare pre-sentencing assessments, and provide services to prison inmates and their families. Probation and parole officers provide similar services to individuals sentenced by a court to parole or probation.

Occupational social workers usually work in a corporation's personnel department or health unit. Through employee assistance programs, they help workers cope with job-related pressures or personal problems that affect the quality of their work. They often offer direct counseling to employees whose performance is hindered by emotional or family problems or substance abuse. They also develop education programs and refer workers to specialized community programs.

Gerontology social workers specialize in services to the aged. They run support groups for family caregivers or for the adult children of aging parents. Also, they advise elderly people or family members about the choices in such areas as housing, transportation, and long-term care; they also coordinate and monitor services.

Social work administrators perform overall management tasks in a hospital, clinic, or other setting that offers social worker services.

Social work planners and policy-makers develop programs to address such issues as child abuse, homelessness, substance abuse, poverty, and violence. These workers research and analyze policies, programs, and regulations. They identify social problems and suggest legislative and other solutions. They may help raise funds or write grants to support these programs.

Working Conditions

Full-time social workers usually work a standard 40-hour week; however, some occasionally work evenings and weekends to meet with clients, attend community meetings, and handle emergencies. Some, particularly in voluntary nonprofit agencies, work part time. Most social workers work in pleasant, clean offices that are well lit and well ventilated. Social workers usually spend most of their time in an office or residential facility, but also may travel locally to visit clients, to meet with service providers, or to attend meetings. Some may use one of several offices within a local area in which to meet with clients. The work, while satisfying, can be emotionally draining. Understaffing and large caseloads add to the pressure in some agencies.

Social workers consult and counsel clients and arrange for services that can help them.

Employment

Social workers held about 604,000 jobs in 1998. About 4 out of 10 jobs were in State, county, or municipal government agencies, primarily in departments of health and human services, mental health, social services, child welfare, housing, education, and corrections. Most private sector jobs were in social service agencies, hospitals, nursing homes, home health agencies, and other health centers or clinics.

Although most social workers are employed in cities or suburbs, some work in rural areas.

Training, Other Qualifications, and Advancement

A bachelor's in social work (BSW) degree is the most common minimum requirement to qualify for a job as a social worker; however, majors in psychology, sociology, and related fields may be sufficient to qualify for some entry-level jobs, especially in small community agencies. Although a bachelor's degree is required for entry into the field, an advanced degree has become the standard for many positions. A master's in social work (MSW) is necessary for positions in health and mental health settings and typically is required for certification for clinical work. Jobs in public agencies also may require an advanced degree, such as a master's in social service policy or administration. Supervisory, administrative, and staff training positions usually require at least an advanced degree. College and university teaching positions and most research appointments normally require a doctorate in social work (DSW or Ph.D).

As of 1999, the Council on Social Work Education accredited over 400 BSW programs and over 125 MSW programs. The Group for Advancement of Doctoral Education in Social Work listed 63 doctoral programs for Ph.D.'s in social work or DSW's (Doctor of Social Work). BSW programs prepare graduates for direct service positions such as case worker or group worker. They include courses in social work practice, social welfare policies, human behavior and the social environment, social research methods, social work values and ethics, dealing with a culturally diverse clientele, promotion of social and economic justice, and populations-at-risk. Accredited BSW programs require at least 400 hours of supervised field experience.

Master's degree programs prepare graduates for work in their chosen field of concentration and continue to develop their skills to perform clinical assessments, to manage large caseloads, and to explore new ways of drawing upon social services to meet the needs of clients. Master's programs last 2 years and include 900 hours of supervised field instruction, or internship. A part-time program may take 4 years. Entry into a master's program does not require a bachelor's in social work, but courses in psychology, biology, sociology, economics, political science, history, social anthropology, urban studies, and social work are recommended. In addition, a second language can be very helpful. Most master's programs offer advanced standing for those with a bachelor's degree from an accredited social work program.

All States and the District of Columbia have licensing, certification, or registration requirements regarding social work practice and the use of professional titles. Although standards for licensing vary by State, a growing number of States are placing greater emphasis on communications skills, professional ethics, and sensitivity for cultural diversity issues. Additionally, the National Association of Social Workers (NASW) offers voluntary credentials. The Academy of Certified Social Workers (ACSW) is granted to all social workers who have met established eligibility criteria. Social workers practicing in school settings may qualify for the School Social Work Specialist (SSWS) credential. Clinical social workers may earn either the Qualified Clinical Social Worker (QCSW) or the advanced credential—Diplomate in Clinical Social Work (DCSW). Social workers holding clinical credentials also may list themselves in the biannual publication of the *NASW Register of Clinical Social Workers*. Credentials are particularly important for those in private practice; some health insurance providers require them for reimbursement.

Social workers should be emotionally mature, objective, and sensitive to people and their problems. They must be able to handle responsibility, work independently, and maintain good working relationships with clients and coworkers. Volunteer or paid jobs as a social work aide offer ways of testing one's interest in this field.

Advancement to supervisor, program manager, assistant director, or executive director of a social service agency or department is possible, but usually requires an advanced degree and related work experience. Other career options for social workers include teaching, research, and consulting. Some also help formulate government policies by analyzing and advocating policy positions in government agencies, in research institutions, and on legislators' staffs.

Some social workers go into private practice. Most private practitioners are clinical social workers who provide psychotherapy, usually paid through health insurance. Private practitioners usually have at least a master's degree and a period of supervised work experience. A network of contacts for referrals also is essential.

Job Outlook

Employment of social workers is expected to increase much faster than the average for all occupations through 2008. The aged population is increasing rapidly, creating greater demand for health and other social services. Social workers also will be needed to help the sizable baby boom generation deal with depression and mental health concerns stemming from mid-life, career, or other personal and professional difficulties. In addition, continuing concern about crime, juvenile delinquency, and services for the mentally ill, the mentally retarded, AIDS patients, and individuals and families in crisis will spur demand for social workers in several areas of specialization. Many job openings will also stem from the need to replace social workers who leave the occupation.

The number of social workers in hospitals and many larger, long-term care facilities will increase in response to the need to ensure that the necessary medical and social services are in place when individuals leave the facility. However, this service need will be shared across several occupations. In an effort to control costs, these facilities increasingly emphasize discharging patients early, applying an interdisciplinary approach to patient care, and employing a broader mix of occupations—including clinical specialists, registered nurses, and health aides—to tend to patient care or client need.

Social worker employment in home health care services is growing, in part because hospitals are releasing patients earlier than in the past. However, the expanding senior population is an even larger factor. Social workers with backgrounds in gerontology are finding work in the growing numbers of assisted living and senior living communities.

Employment of social workers in private social service agencies will grow, but not as rapidly as demand for their services. Agencies increasingly will restructure services and hire more lower-paid human service workers and assistants instead of social workers. Employment in state and local government may grow somewhat in response to increasing needs for public welfare and family services; however, many of these services will be contracted out to private agencies. Additionally, employment levels may fluctuate depending on need and government funding for various social service programs.

Employment of school social workers is expected to grow, due to expanded efforts to respond to rising rates of teen pregnancy and to the adjustment problems of immigrants and children from single-parent families. Moreover, continued emphasis on integrating disabled children into the general school population will lead to more jobs. However, availability of State and local funding will dictate the actual job growth in schools.

Opportunities for social workers in private practice will expand because of the anticipated availability of funding from health insurance and public-sector contracts. Also, with increasing affluence, people will be better able to pay for professional help to deal with personal problems. The growing popularity of employee assistance programs also is expected to spur demand for private practitioners, some of whom provide social work services to corporations on a contractual basis.

Competition for social worker jobs is stronger in cities where demand for services often is highest, training programs for social workers are prevalent, and interest in available positions is strongest. However, opportunities should be good in rural areas, which often find it difficult to attract and retain qualified staff.

Earnings

Median annual earnings of social workers were $30,590 in 1998. The middle 50 percent earned between $24,160 and $39,240. The lowest 10 percent earned less than $19,250 and the top 10 percent earned more than $49,080. Median annual earnings in the industries employing the largest numbers of medical social workers in 1997 were:

Industry	Earnings
Home health care services	$35,800
Offices and clinics of medical doctors	33,700
Offices of other health care practitioners	32,900
State government, except education and hospitals	31,800
Hospitals	31,500

Median annual earnings in the industries employing the largest numbers of social workers, except medical, in 1997 were:

Industry	Earnings
Federal government	$45,300
Elementary and secondary schools	34,100
Local government, except education and hospitals	32,100
Hospitals	31,300
State government, except education and hospitals	30,800

Related Occupations

Through direct counseling or referral to other services, social workers help people solve a range of personal problems. Workers in occupations with similar duties include the clergy, mental health counselors, counseling psychologists, and human services workers and assistants.

Sources of Additional Information

For information about career opportunities in social work, contact:

☛ National Association of Social Workers, Career Information, 750 First St. NE., Suite 700, Washington, DC 20002-4241.

An annual *Directory of Accredited BSW and MSW Programs* is available for a nominal charge from:

☛ Council on Social Work Education, 1600 Duke St., Alexandria, VA 22314-3421. Internet: **http://www.cswe.org**

Information on licensing requirements and testing procedures for each State may be obtained from State licensing authorities, or from:

☛ American Association of State Social Work Boards, 400 South Ridge Parkway, Suite B, Culpeper, VA 22701. Internet: **http://www.aasswb.org**

Clergy

Nature of the Work

Religious beliefs—such as Buddhist, Christian, Jewish, or Moslem—are significant influences in the lives of millions of Americans, and prompt many believers to participate in organizations that reinforce their faith. Even within a religion many denominations may exist, with each group having unique traditions and responsibilities assigned to its clergy. For example, Christianity has over 70 denominations, while Judaism has 4 major branches, as well as groups within each branch, with diverse customs.

Clergy are religious and spiritual leaders, and teachers and interpreters of their traditions and faith. Most members of the clergy serve in a pulpit. They organize and lead regular religious services and officiate at special ceremonies, including confirmations, weddings, and funerals. They may lead worshipers in prayer, administer the sacraments, deliver sermons, and read from sacred texts such as the Bible, Torah, or Koran. When not conducting worship services, clergy organize, supervise, and lead religious education programs for their congregations. Clergy visit the sick or bereaved to provide comfort and they counsel persons who are seeking religious or moral guidance or who are troubled by family or personal problems. They also may work to expand the membership of their congregations and solicit donations to support their activities and facilities.

Clergy who serve large congregations often share their duties with associates or more junior clergy. Senior clergy may spend considerable time on administrative duties. They oversee the management of buildings, order supplies, contract for services and repairs, and supervise the work of staff and volunteers. Associate or assistant members of the clergy sometimes specialize in an area of religious service, such as music, education, or youth counseling. Clergy also work with committees and officials, elected by the congregation, who guide the management of the congregation's finances and real estate.

Some members of the clergy serve their religious communities in ways that do not call for them to hold positions in congregations. Some serve as chaplains in the Armed Forces and in hospitals, while others help to carry out the missions of religious community and social services agencies. A few members of the clergy serve in administrative or teaching posts in schools at all grade levels, including seminaries.

Working Conditions

Members of the clergy typically work long and irregular hours. Those who do not work in congregational settings may have more routine schedules. In 1998, almost one-fifth of full-time clergy worked 60 or more hours a week, 3 times that of all workers in professional specialty occupations. Although many of their activities are sedentary and intellectual in nature, clergy frequently are called upon on short notice to visit the sick, comfort the dying and their families, and provide counseling to those in need. Involvement in community, administrative, and educational activities sometimes require clergy to work evenings, early mornings, holidays, and weekends.

Because of their roles as leaders regarding spiritual and morality issues, some members of the clergy often feel obligated to address and resolve both societal problems and the personal problems of their congregants, which can lead to stress.

Training and Other Qualifications

Educational requirements for entry into the clergy vary greatly. Similar to other professional occupations, about 3 out of 4 members of the clergy have completed at least a bachelor's degree. Many denominations require that clergy complete a bachelor's degree and a graduate-level program of theological study; others will admit anyone who has been "called" to the vocation. Some faiths do not allow women to become clergy; however, those that do are experiencing increases in the numbers of women seeking ordination. Men and women considering careers in the clergy should consult their religious leaders to verify specific entrance requirements.

Individuals considering a career in the clergy should realize they are choosing not only a career but also a way of life. In fact, most members of the clergy remain in their chosen vocation throughout their lives; in 1998, 12 percent of clergy were 65 or older, compared to only 3 percent of workers in all professional specialty occupations.

Religious leaders must exude confidence and motivation, while remaining tolerant and able to listen to the needs of others. They should be capable of making difficult decisions, working under pressure, and living up to the moral standards set by their faith and community.

The following statements provide more detailed information on Protestant ministers, Rabbis, and Roman Catholic priests.

Protestant Ministers

(O*NET 27502)

Significant Points

- Entry requirements vary greatly; many denominations require a bachelor's degree followed by study at a theological seminary, whereas others have no formal educational requirements.
- Competition for positions is generally expected because of the large number of qualified candidates, but it will vary among denominations and geographic regions.

Nature of the Work

Protestant ministers lead their congregations in worship services and administer the various rites of the church, such as baptism, confirmation, and Holy Communion. The services that ministers conduct differ among the numerous Protestant denominations and even among congregations within a denomination. In many denominations, ministers follow a traditional order of worship; in others, they adapt the services to the needs of youth and other groups within the congregation. Most services include Bible readings, hymn singing, prayers, and a sermon. In some denominations, Bible readings by members of the congregation and individual testimonials constitute a large part of the service. In addition to these duties, ministers officiate at weddings, funerals, and other occasions.

Each Protestant denomination has its own hierarchical structure. Some ministers are responsible only to the congregation they serve, whereas others are assigned duties by elder ministers or by the bishops of the diocese they serve. In some denominations, ministers are reassigned to a new pastorate by a central governing body or diocese every few years.

Ministers who serve small congregations usually work personally with parishioners. Those who serve large congregations may share specific aspects of the ministry with one or more associates or assistants, such as a minister of education or a minister of music.

Employment

According to the National Council of Churches, there were over 400,000 Protestant ministers in 1998, including those who served without a regular congregation or those who worked in closely

Protestant ministers discuss religious and spiritual needs of parishioners with church members.

related fields, such as chaplains in hospitals, the Armed Forces, universities, and correctional institutions. Although there are many denominations, most ministers are employed by the five largest Protestant bodies—Baptist, Episcopalian, Lutheran, Methodist, and Presbyterian.

Although most ministers are located in urban areas, many serve two or more smaller congregations in less densely populated areas. Some small churches increasingly employ part-time ministers who are seminary students, retired ministers, or holders of secular jobs. Unpaid pastors serve other churches with meager funds. In addition, some churches employ specially trained members of the laity to conduct nonliturgical functions.

Training and Other Qualifications

Educational requirements for entry into the Protestant ministry vary greatly. Many denominations require, or at least strongly prefer, a bachelor's degree followed by study at a theological seminary. However, some denominations have no formal educational requirements, and others ordain persons having various types of training from Bible colleges or liberal arts colleges. Many denominations now allow women to be ordained, but others do not. Persons considering a career in the ministry should first verify the ministerial requirements with their particular denomination.

In general, each large denomination has its own schools of theology that reflect its particular doctrine, interests, and needs. However, many of these schools are open to students from other denominations. Several interdenominational schools associated with universities give both undergraduate and graduate training covering a wide range of theological points of view.

In 1998-99, the Association of Theological Schools in the United States and Canada accredited 135 Protestant denominational theological schools. These schools only admit students who have received a bachelor's degree or its equivalent from an accredited college. After college graduation, many denominations require a 3-year course of professional study in one of these accredited schools, or seminaries, for the degree of Master of Divinity.

The standard curriculum for accredited theological schools consists of four major categories: Biblical studies, history, theology, and practical theology. Courses of a practical nature include pastoral care, preaching, religious education, and administration. Many accredited schools require that students work under the supervision of a faculty member or experienced minister. Some institutions offer Doctor of Ministry degrees to students who have completed additional study—usually 2 or more years—and served at least 2 years as a minister. Scholarships and loans often are available for students of theological institutions.

Persons who have denominational qualifications for the ministry usually are ordained after graduation from a seminary or after serving a probationary pastoral period. Denominations that do not require seminary training ordain clergy at various appointed times. Some churches ordain ministers with only a high school education.

Women and men entering the clergy often begin their careers as pastors of small congregations or as assistant pastors in large churches. Pastor positions in large metropolitan areas or in large congregations often require many years of experience.

Job Outlook

Competition is expected to continue for paid Protestant ministers through the year 2008, reflecting slow growth of church membership and the large number of qualified candidates. Graduates of theological schools should have the best prospects. The degree of competition for paid positions will vary among denominations and geographic regions. For example, relatively favorable prospects are expected for ministers in evangelical churches. Competition, however, will be keen for responsible positions serving large, urban congregations. Ministers willing to work part time or for small, rural congregations should have better opportunities. Most job openings will stem from the need to replace ministers who retire, die, or leave the ministry.

For newly ordained Protestant ministers who are unable to find parish positions, employment alternatives include working in youth counseling, family relations, and social welfare organizations; teaching in religious educational institutions; or serving as chaplains in the Armed Forces, hospitals, universities, and correctional institutions.

Earnings

Salaries of Protestant clergy vary substantially, depending on experience, denomination, size and wealth of the congregation, and geographic location. For example, some denominations tie a minister's pay to the average pay of the congregation or the community. As a result, ministers serving larger, wealthier congregations often earned significantly higher salaries than those in smaller, less affluent areas or congregations. Ministers with modest salaries sometimes earn additional income from employment in secular occupations.

Sources of Additional Information

Persons who are interested in entering the Protestant ministry should seek the counsel of a minister or church guidance worker. Theological schools can supply information on admission requirements. Prospective ministers also should contact the ordination supervision body of their particular denomination, for information on special requirements for ordination.

Rabbis

(O*NET 27502)

Significant Points

- Ordination usually requires completion of a college degree followed by a 4- or 5-year program at a Jewish seminary.
- Graduates of Jewish seminaries have excellent job prospects, reflecting current unmet needs for rabbis and the need to replace the many rabbis approaching retirement age.

Nature of the Work

Rabbis serve Orthodox, Conservative, Reform, and Reconstructionist Jewish congregations. Regardless of the branch of Judaism they serve or their individual points of view, all rabbis preserve the substance of Jewish religious worship. Congregations differ in the extent to which they follow the traditional form of worship—for example, in the wearing of head coverings, in the use of Hebrew as the language of prayer, and in the use of instrumental music or a choir. Additionally, the format of the worship service and, therefore, the ritual that the rabbi uses may vary even among congregations belonging to the same branch of Judaism.

Rabbis have greater independence in religious expression than other clergy, because of the absence of a formal religious hierarchy in Judaism. Instead, rabbis are responsible directly to the board of trustees of the congregation they serve. Those serving large congregations may spend considerable time in administrative duties, working with their staffs and committees. Large congregations frequently have associate or assistant rabbis, who often serve as educational directors. All rabbis play a role in community relations. For example, many rabbis serve on committees, alongside business and civic leaders in their communities to help find solutions to local problems.

Rabbis also may write for religious and lay publications and teach in theological seminaries, colleges, and universities.

Employment

Based on information from organizations representing the 4 major branches of Judaism, there were approximately 1,800 Reform, 1,175 Conservative, 1,800 Orthodox, and 250 Reconstructionist rabbis in 1999. Although the majority served congregations, many rabbis functioned in other settings. Some taught in Jewish studies programs at colleges and universities, whereas others served as chaplains in hospitals, colleges, or the military. Additionally, some rabbis held positions in one of the many social service or Jewish community agencies.

Rabbis lead religious services by reading from the Torah, a sacred Jewish text.

Although rabbis serve Jewish communities throughout the Nation, they are concentrated in major metropolitan areas with large Jewish populations.

Training and Other Qualifications

To become eligible for ordination as a rabbi, a student must complete a course of study in a seminary. Entrance requirements and the curriculum depend upon the branch of Judaism with which the seminary is associated. Most seminaries require applicants to be college graduates.

Jewish seminaries typically take 5 years for completion of studies, with an additional preparatory year required for students without sufficient grounding in Hebrew and Jewish studies. In addition to the core academic program, training generally includes fieldwork and internships providing hands-on experience and, in some cases, study in Jerusalem. Seminary graduates are awarded the title Rabbi and earn the Master of Arts in Hebrew Letters degree. After more advanced study, some earn the Doctor of Hebrew Letters degree.

In general, the curricula of Jewish theological seminaries provide students with a comprehensive knowledge of the Bible, the Torah, rabbinic literature, Jewish history, Hebrew, theology, and courses in education, pastoral psychology, and public speaking. Students receive extensive practical training in dealing with social problems in the community. Training for alternatives to the pulpit, such as leadership in community services and religious education, is increasingly stressed. Some seminaries grant advanced academic degrees in such fields as biblical and Talmudic research. All Jewish theological seminaries make scholarships and loans available.

Major rabbinical seminaries include the Jewish Theological Seminary of America, which educates rabbis for the Conservative branch; the Hebrew Union College—Jewish Institute of Religion, which educates rabbis for the Reform branch; and the Reconstructionist Rabbinical College, which educates rabbis in the newest branch of Judaism. About 35 seminaries educate and ordain Orthodox rabbis. Although the number of Orthodox seminaries is relatively high, the number of students attending each seminary is low. The Orthodox movement, as a whole, constitutes only about 10 percent of the American Jewish community. The Rabbi Isaac Elchanan Theological Seminary and the Beth Medrash Govoha Seminary are representative Orthodox seminaries. In all cases, rabbinic training is rigorous. When students have become sufficiently learned in the Torah, the Bible, and other religious texts, they may be ordained with the approval of an authorized rabbi, acting either independently or as a representative of a rabbinical seminary.

Newly ordained rabbis usually begin as spiritual leaders of small congregations, assistants to experienced rabbis, directors of Hillel Foundations on college campuses, teachers in educational institutions, or chaplains in the Armed Forces. As a rule, experienced rabbis fill the pulpits of large, well-established Jewish congregations.

Job Outlook

Job opportunities for rabbis are expected to be excellent in all four of the major branches of Judaism through the year 2008, reflecting current unmet needs for rabbis, together with the need to replace the many rabbis approaching retirement age. Rabbis willing to work in small, underserved communities should have particularly good prospects.

Graduates of Orthodox seminaries who seek pulpits should have good opportunities as growth in enrollments slows and as many graduates seek alternatives to the pulpit. Reconstructionist rabbis are expected to have very good employment opportunities as membership expands rapidly. Conservative and Reform rabbis are expected to have excellent job opportunities serving congregations or in other settings because job prospects will be numerous in these two largest Jewish movements.

Earnings

Based on limited information, annual average earnings of rabbis generally ranged from $50,000 to $100,000 in 1998, including benefits. Benefits may include housing, health insurance, and a retirement plan. Income varies widely, depending on the size and financial status of the congregation, as well as denominational branch and geographic location. Rabbis may earn additional income from gifts or fees for officiating at ceremonies such as bar or bat mitzvahs and weddings.

Sources of Additional Information

Persons who are interested in becoming rabbis should discuss with a practicing rabbi their plans for this vocation. Information on the work of rabbis and allied occupations can be obtained from:

☛ Rabbinical Council of America, 305 7th Ave., New York, NY 10001. (Orthodox) Internet: **http://www.rabbis.org**

☛ The Jewish Theological Seminary of America, 3080 Broadway, New York, NY 10027. (Conservative) Internet: **http://www.jtsa.edu**

☛ Hebrew Union College-Jewish Institute of Religion, One West 4th St., New York, NY 10012. (Reform) Internet: **http://www.huc.edu**

☛ Reconstructionist Rabbinical College, 1299 Church Rd., Wyncote, PA 19095. (Reconstructionist) Internet: **http://www.rrc.edu**

Roman Catholic Priests

(O*NET 27502)

Significant Points

- Preparation generally requires 8 years of study beyond high school, usually including a college degree followed by 4 or more years of theology study at a seminary.
- The shortage of Roman Catholic priests is expected to continue, resulting in a very favorable outlook.

Nature of the Work

Priests in the Catholic Church belong to one of two groups—diocesan or religious. Both types of priests have the same powers, acquired through ordination by a bishop. Differences lie in their way of life, type of work, and the Church authority to which they are responsible. *Diocesan priests* commit their lives to serving the people of a diocese, a church administrative region, and generally work in parishes assigned by the bishop of their diocese. Diocesan priests take oaths of celibacy and obedience. *Religious priests* belong to a religious order, such as the Jesuits, Dominicans, or Franciscans. In addition to the vows taken by diocesan priests, religious priests take a vow of poverty.

Diocesan priests attend to the spiritual, pastoral, moral, and educational needs of the members of their church. A priest's day usually begins with morning meditation and mass and may end with an individual counseling session or an evening visit to a hospital or home. Many priests direct and serve on church committees, work in civic and charitable organizations, and assist in community projects. Some counsel parishioners preparing for marriage or the birth of a child.

Religious priests receive duty assignments from their superiors in their respective religious orders. Some religious priests specialize in teaching, whereas others serve as missionaries in foreign countries, where they may live under difficult and primitive conditions. Other religious priests live a communal life in monasteries, where they devote their lives to prayer, study, and assigned work.

Both religious and diocesan priests hold teaching and administrative posts in Catholic seminaries, colleges and universities, and

Roman Catholic priests attend to the spiritual, pastoral, moral, and educational needs of members of their church.

high schools. Priests attached to religious orders staff many of the Church's institutions of higher education and many high schools, whereas diocesan priests usually are concerned with the parochial schools attached to parish churches and with diocesan high schools. Members of religious orders do much of the missionary work conducted by the Catholic Church in this country and abroad.

Employment

According to *The Official Catholic Directory*, there were approximately 47,000 priests in 1998; about two-thirds were diocesan priests. There are priests in nearly every city and town and in many rural communities; however, the majority is in metropolitan areas, where most Catholics reside.

Training and Other Qualifications

Men exclusively are ordained as priests. Women may serve in church positions that do not require priestly ordination. Preparation for the priesthood generally requires 8 years of study beyond high school, usually including a college degree followed by 4 or more years of theology study at a seminary.

Preparatory study for the priesthood may begin in the first year of high school, at the college level, or in theological seminaries after college graduation. Nine high-school seminaries provided a college preparatory program in 1998. Programs emphasize English grammar, speech, literature, and social studies, as well as religious formation. Latin may be required, and modern languages are encouraged. In Hispanic communities, knowledge of Spanish is mandatory.

Those who begin training for the priesthood in college do so in one of 87 priesthood formation programs offered either through Catholic colleges or universities or in freestanding college seminaries. Preparatory studies usually include training in philosophy, religious studies, and prayer.

Today, most candidates for the priesthood have a 4-year degree from an accredited college or university, then attend one of 47 theological seminaries (also called theologates) and earn either the Master of Divinity or the Master of Arts degree. Thirty-five theologates primarily train diocesan priests, whereas 12 theologates mostly educate priests for religious orders. (Slight variations in training reflect the differences in their expected duties.) Theology coursework includes sacred scripture; dogmatic, moral, and pastoral theology; homiletics (art of preaching); Church history; liturgy (sacraments); and canon (church) law. Fieldwork experience usually is required.

Young men are never denied entry into seminaries because of lack of funds. In seminaries for diocesan priests, scholarships or loans are available, and contributions of benefactors and the

Catholic Church finance those in religious seminaries—who have taken a vow of poverty and are not expected to have personal resources.

Graduate work in theology beyond that required for ordination is also offered at a number of American Catholic universities or at ecclesiastical universities around the world, particularly in Rome. Also, many priests do graduate work in fields unrelated to theology. Priests are encouraged by the Catholic Church to continue their studies, at least informally, after ordination. In recent years, the Church has stressed continuing education for ordained priests in the social sciences, such as sociology and psychology.

A newly ordained diocesan priest usually works as an assistant pastor. Newly ordained priests of religious orders are assigned to the specialized duties for which they have been trained. Depending on the talents, interests, and experience of the individual, many opportunities for additional responsibility exist within the Church.

Job Outlook

The shortage of Roman Catholic priests is expected to continue, resulting in a very favorable job outlook through the year 2008. Many priests will be needed in the years ahead to provide for the spiritual, educational, and social needs of the increasing number of Catholics. In recent years, the number of ordained priests has been insufficient to fill the needs of newly established parishes and other Catholic institutions and to replace priests who retire, die, or leave the priesthood. This situation is likely to continue, as seminary enrollments remain below the levels needed to overcome the current shortfall of priests.

In response to the shortage of priests, permanent deacons and teams of clergy and laity increasingly are performing certain traditional functions within the Catholic Church. The number of ordained deacons has increased five-fold over the past 20 years, and this trend should continue. Throughout most of the country, permanent deacons have been ordained to preach and perform liturgical functions, such as baptisms, marriages, and funerals, and to provide service to the community. Deacons are not authorized to celebrate Mass, nor are they allowed to administer the Sacraments of Reconciliation and the Anointing of the Sick. Teams of clergy and laity undertake some liturgical and nonliturgical functions, such as hospital visits and religious teaching.

Earnings

Diocesan priests' salaries vary from diocese to diocese. According to the National Federation of Priests' Council, low-end cash only salaries averaged $12,936 per year in 1998; high-end salaries averaged $15,483 per year. Average salaries, including in-kind earnings, were $30,713 per year in 1998. In addition to a salary, diocesan priests receive a package of benefits that may include a car allowance, room and board in the parish rectory, health insurance, and a retirement plan.

Diocesan priests who do special work related to the church, such as teaching, usually receive a salary which is less than a lay person in the same position would receive. The difference between the usual salary for these jobs and the salary that the priest receives is called "contributed service." In some situations, housing and related expenses may be provided; in other cases, the priest must make his own arrangements. Some priests doing special work receive the same compensation that a lay person would receive.

Religious priests take a vow of poverty and are supported by their religious order. Any personal earnings are given to the order. Their vow of poverty is recognized by the Internal Revenue Service, which exempts them from paying Federal income tax.

Sources of Additional Information

Young men interested in entering the priesthood should seek the guidance and counsel of their parish priests and diocesan vocational office. For information regarding the different religious orders and the diocesan priesthood, as well as a list of the seminaries that prepare students for the priesthood, contact the diocesan director of vocations through the office of the local pastor or bishop.

Individuals seeking additional information about careers in the Catholic Ministry should contact their local diocese.

For information on training programs for the Catholic ministry, contact:

☛ Center for Applied Research in the Apostolate (CARA), Georgetown University, Washington, DC 20057.

Teachers and Instructors, Counselors, and Library Occupations

Adult and Vocational Education Teachers

(O*NET 31314 and 31317)

Significant Points

- More than one-third works part time; many also hold other jobs—often involving work related to the subject they teach.
- Practical experience is often all that is needed to teach vocational courses, but a graduate degree may be required to teach nonvocational courses.
- Opportunities should be best for part-time positions.

Nature of the Work

Adult and vocational education teachers work in four main areas—adult vocational-technical education, adult remedial education, adult continuing education, and prebaccalaureate training. *Adult vocational-technical education teachers* provide instruction for occupations that do not require a college degree, such as welder, dental hygienist, x-ray technician, auto mechanic, and cosmetologist. Other instructors help people update their job skills or adapt to technological advances. For example, an *adult education teacher* may train students how to use new computer software programs. *Adult remedial education teachers* provide instruction in basic education courses for school dropouts or others who need to upgrade their skills to find a job. *Adult continuing education teachers* teach courses that students take for personal enrichment, such as cooking, dancing, writing, exercise and physical fitness, photography, and personal finance.

Adult and vocational education teachers may lecture in classrooms or work in an industry or laboratory setting to give students hands-on experience. Increasingly, adult vocational-technical education teachers integrate academic and vocational curriculums so students obtain a variety of skills that can be applied to the "real world." For example, an electronics student may be required to take courses in principles of mathematics and science in conjunction with hands-on electronics skills. Generally, teachers demonstrate techniques, have students apply them, and critique the students' work. For example, welding instructors show students various welding techniques, watch them use tools and equipment, and have them repeat procedures until they meet the specific standards required by the trade.

Increasingly, minimum standards of proficiency are being established for students in various vocational-technical fields. Adult

Some adult education teachers help people update their job skills or adapt to technological changes.

and vocational education teachers must be aware of new standards and develop lesson plans to ensure that students meet basic criteria. Also, adult and vocational education teachers and community colleges are assuming a greater role in students' transition from school to work by helping establish internships and providing information about prospective employers.

Businesses also are increasingly providing their employees with work-related training to keep up with changing technology. Training is often provided through contractors, professional associations, or community colleges.

Adult education teachers who instruct in adult basic education programs may work with students who do not speak English; teach adults reading, writing, and mathematics up to the 8th-grade level; or teach adults through the 12th-grade level in preparation for the General Educational Development tests (GED). The GED offers the equivalent of a high school diploma. These teachers may refer students for counseling or job placement. Because many people who need adult basic education are reluctant to seek it, teachers also may recruit participants.

Adult and vocational education teachers also prepare lessons and assignments, grade papers and do related paperwork, attend faculty and professional meetings, and stay abreast of developments in their field. (For information on vocational education teachers in secondary schools, see the *Handbook* statement on kindergarten, elementary, and secondary school teachers.)

Working Conditions

Since adult and vocational education teachers work with adult students, they do not encounter some of the behavioral or social problems sometimes found with younger students. The adults attend by choice, are highly motivated, and bring years of experience to the classroom—attributes that can make teaching these students rewarding and satisfying. However, teachers in adult basic education deal with students at different levels of development who may lack effective study skills and self-confidence, and who may require more attention and patience than other students.

More than 1 in 3 adult and vocational education teachers work part time. To accommodate students who may have job or family responsibilities, many institutions offer courses at night or on weekends, which range from 2- to 4-hour workshops and 1-day minisessions to semester-long courses. Some adult and vocational education teachers have several part-time teaching assignments or work a full-time job in addition to their part-time teaching job, leading to long hours and a hectic schedule.

Although most adult and vocational education teachers work in classroom settings, some are consultants to businesses and teach classes at job sites.

Employment

Adult and vocational education teachers held about 588,000 jobs in 1998. About one-fifth were self-employed.

A variety of establishments employed adult and vocational education teachers in 1998: public school systems; community and junior colleges; universities; businesses that provide formal education and training for their employees; schools and institutes that teach automotive repair, bartending, business, computer skills, electronics, medical technology, and other subjects; dance studios; job training centers; community organizations; labor unions; and religious organizations.

Training, Other Qualifications, and Advancement

Training requirements vary by State and by subject. In general, teachers need work or other experiences in their field, and a license or certificate in fields where these usually are required for full professional status. In some cases, particularly at educational institutions, a master's or doctoral degree is required to teach nonvocational courses which can be applied towards a 4-year degree program. Many vocational teachers in junior or community colleges do not have a master's or doctoral degree but draw on their work experience and knowledge, bringing practical experience to the classroom. For general adult education classes, an acceptable portfolio of work is required. For example, to secure a job teaching a photography course, an applicant would need to show examples of previous work.

Most States and the District of Columbia require adult basic education teachers and adult literacy instructors to have a bachelor's degree from an approved teacher training program, and some States require teacher certification.

Adult and vocational education teachers update their skills through continuing education to maintain certification—requirements vary among institutions. Teachers may take part in seminars, conferences, or graduate courses in adult education or training and development, or may return to work in business or industry for a limited time. Businesses are playing a growing role in adult education, forming consortiums with training institutions and junior colleges and providing input to curriculum development. Adult and vocational education teachers maintain an ongoing dialogue with businesses to determine the most current skills needed in the workplace.

Adult and vocational education teachers should communicate and relate well with students, enjoy working with them, and be able to motivate them. Adult basic education instructors, in particular, must be patient, understanding, and supportive to make students comfortable, develop trust, and help them better understand concepts.

Some teachers advance to administrative positions in departments of education, colleges and universities, and corporate training departments. These positions often require advanced degrees, such as a doctorate in adult and continuing education. (See the statement on education administrators elsewhere in the *Handbook*.)

Job Outlook

Employment of adult and vocational education teachers is expected to grow about as fast as the average for all occupations through 2008 as the demand for adult education programs continues to rise. Opportunities should be best for part-time positions, especially in fields such as computer technology, automotive mechanics, and medical technology, which offer attractive—and often higher-paying—job opportunities outside of teaching.

According to the National Center for Education Statistics, an estimated 4 out of 10 adults participated in some form of adult education in 1997. Participation in continuing education grows as the educational attainment of the population increases. To keep abreast of changes in their fields and advances in technology, an increasing number of adults are taking courses—often subsidized or funded entirely by employers—for career advancement or to upgrade their skills. In addition, an increasing number of adults are participating in classes for personal enrichment and enjoyment. Enrollment in adult basic education and literacy programs is increasing because of changes in immigration policy that require basic competency in English and civics. And, more employers are demanding higher levels of basic academic skills—reading, writing, and arithmetic—which is increasing enrollment in remedial education and GED preparation classes.

Employment growth of adult vocational-technical education teachers will result from the need to train young adults for entry-level jobs. Experienced workers who want to switch fields or whose jobs have been eliminated due to changing technology or business reorganization also require training. Businesses are finding it essential to provide training to their workers to remain productive and globally competitive. Cooperation between businesses and educational institutions continues to increase to insure that students are taught the skills employers desire. This should result in greater demand for adult and vocational education teachers, particularly at community and junior colleges. Since adult education programs receive State and Federal funding, employment growth may be affected by government budgets.

Additional job openings for adult and vocational education teachers will stem from the need to replace persons who leave the occupation. Many teach part time and move into and out of the occupation for other jobs, family responsibilities, or retirement.

Earnings

Median annual earnings of adult education teachers were $24,800 in 1998. The middle 50 percent earned between $18,170 and $34,140. The lowest 10 percent earned less than $13,080 and the highest 10 percent earned more than $47,430. Median annual earnings in the industries employing the largest numbers of adult education teachers in 1997 were:

Industry	Earnings
Elementary and secondary schools	$29,900
Colleges and universities	25,900
Schools and educational services, not elsewhere classified	24,600
Dance studios, schools, and halls	23,600
Individual and family services	19,400

Median annual earnings of vocational education teachers were $34,430 in 1998. The middle 50 percent earned between $24,890 and $45,230. The lowest 10 percent earned less than $18,010 and the highest 10 percent earned more than $63,850. Median annual earnings in the industries employing the largest numbers of vocational education teachers in 1997 were:

Industry	Earnings
State government, except education and hospitals	$37,200
Elementary and secondary schools	37,000
Colleges and universities	34,800
Vocational schools	32,600
Schools and educational services, not elsewhere classified	24,700

Earnings varied widely by subject, academic credentials, experience, and region of the country. Part-time instructors usually are paid hourly wages and do not receive benefits or pay for preparation time outside of class.

Related Occupations

Adult and vocational education teaching requires a wide variety of skills and aptitudes, including the ability to influence, motivate, train, and teach; organizational, administrative, and communication skills; and creativity. Workers in other occupations that require these aptitudes include other teachers, counselors, school administrators, public relations specialists, employee development specialists, and social workers.

Sources of Additional Information

Information on adult basic education programs and teacher certification requirements is available from State departments of education and local school districts.

For information about adult vocational-technical education eaching positions, contact State departments of vocational-technical education.

For information on adult continuing education teaching positions, contact departments of local government, State adult education departments, schools, colleges and universities, religious organizations, and a wide range of businesses that provide formal training for their employees.

General information on adult and vocational education is available from:

☛ Association for Career and Technical Education, 1410 King St., Alexandria, VA 22314. Internet: **http://www.acteonline.org**

☛ ERIC Clearinghouse on Adult, Career, and Vocational Education, 1900 Kenny Rd., Columbus, OH 43210-1090. Internet: **http://www.ericacve.org**

Archivists, Curators, Museum Technicians, and Conservators

(O*NET 31511A, 31511B, 31511C, and 31511D)

Significant Points

- Employment usually requires graduate education and related work experience.
- Keen competition is expected because qualified applicants outnumber the most desirable job openings.

Nature of the Work

Archivists, curators, museum and archives technicians, and conservators search for, acquire, appraise, analyze, describe, arrange, catalogue, restore, preserve, exhibit, maintain, and store valuable items that can be used by researchers or for exhibitions, publications, broadcasting, and other educational programs. Depending on the occupation, these items include historical documents, audiovisual materials, institutional records, works of art, coins, stamps, minerals, clothing, maps, living and preserved plants and animals, buildings, computer records, or historic sites.

Archivists and curators plan and oversee the arrangement, cataloguing, and exhibition of collections and, along with technicians and conservators, maintain collections. Archivists and curators may coordinate educational and public outreach programs, such as tours, workshops, lectures, and classes, and may work with the boards of institutions to administer plans and policies. They also may research topics or items relevant to their collections. Although some duties of archivists and curators are similar, the types of items they deal with differ. Curators usually handle objects found in cultural, biological, or historical collections, such as sculptures, textiles, and paintings, while archivists mainly handle valuable records, documents, or objects that are retained because they originally accompanied and relate specifically to the document.

Archivists determine what portion of the vast amount of records maintained by various organizations, such as government agencies, corporations, or educational institutions, or by families and individuals, should be made part of permanent historical holdings, and which of these records should be put on exhibit. They maintain records in their original arrangement according to the creator's organizational scheme, and describe records to facilitate retrieval. Records may be saved on any medium, including paper, film, videotape, audiotape, electronic disk, or computer. They also may be copied onto some other format to protect the original, and to make them more accessible to researchers who use the records. As computers and various storage media evolve, archivists must keep abreast of technological advances in electronic information storage.

Archives may be part of a library, museum, or historical society, or may exist as a distinct unit within an organization or company. Archivists consider any medium containing recorded information as documents, including letters, books, and other paper documents, photographs, blueprints, audiovisual materials, and computer records. Any document that reflects organizational transactions, hierarchy, or procedures can be considered a record. Archivists often specialize in an area of history or technology so they can better determine what records in that area qualify for retention and should become part of the archives. Archivists also may work with specialized forms of records, such as manuscripts, electronic records, photographs, cartographic records, motion pictures, and sound recordings.

Computers are increasingly used to generate and maintain archival records. Professional standards for use of computers in handling archival records are still evolving. However, computers are expected to transform many aspects of archival collections as computer capabilities, including multimedia and worldwide web use, expand and allow more records to be stored and exhibited electronically.

Curators oversee collections in museums, zoos, aquariums, botanical gardens, nature centers, and historic sites. They acquire items through purchases, gifts, field exploration, inter-museum exchanges, or, in the case of some plants and animals, reproduction. Curators also plan and prepare exhibits. In natural history museums, curators collect and observe specimens in their natural habitat. Their work involves describing and classifying species, while specially trained collection managers and technicians provide hands-on care of natural history collections. Most curators use computer databases to catalogue and organize their collections. Many also use the Internet to make information available to other curators and the public. Increasingly, curators are expected to participate in grant writing and fund raising to support their projects.

Most curators specialize in a field, such as botany, art, paleontology, or history. Those working in large institutions may be highly specialized. A large natural history museum, for example, would employ specialists in birds, fishes, insects, and mollusks. Some curators maintain the collection, others do research, and others perform administrative tasks. Registrars, for example, keep track of and move objects in the collection. In small institutions, with only one or a few curators, one curator may be responsible for multiple tasks, from maintaining collections to directing the affairs of museums.

Conservators manage, care for, preserve, treat, and document works of art, artifacts, and specimens. This may require substantial historical, scientific, and archaeological research. They use X-rays, chemical testing, microscopes, special lights, and other laboratory equipment and techniques to examine objects and determine their condition, the need for treatment or restoration, and the appropriate method for preservation. They then document their findings and treat items to minimize deterioration or restore items to their original state. Conservators usually specialize in a particular material or group of objects, such as documents and books, paintings, decorative arts, textiles, metals, or architectural material.

Museum directors formulate policies, plan budgets, and raise funds for their museums. They coordinate activities of their staff to establish and maintain collections. As their role has evolved, museum directors increasingly need business backgrounds in addition to an understanding of the subject matter of their collections.

Museum technicians assist curators and conservators by performing various preparatory and maintenance tasks on museum items. Some museum technicians may also assist curators with research. Archives technicians help archivists organize, maintain, and provide access to historical documentary materials.

Archivists, curators, museum technicians, and conservators sometimes conduct research relevant to their collections.

Working Conditions

The working conditions of archivists and curators vary. Some spend most of their time working with the public, providing reference assistance and educational services. Others perform research or process records, which often means working alone or in offices with only a few people. Those who restore and install exhibits or work with bulky, heavy record containers may climb, stretch, or lift. Those in zoos, botanical gardens, and other outdoor museums or historic sites frequently walk great distances.

Curators who work in large institutions may travel extensively to evaluate potential additions to the collection, organize exhibitions, and conduct research in their area of expertise. However travel is rare for curators employed in small institutions.

Employment

Archivists, curators, museum technicians, and conservators held about 23,000 jobs in 1998. About a quarter were employed in museums, botanical gardens, and zoos, and approximately 2 in 10 worked in educational services, mainly in college and university libraries. Over one-third worked in Federal, State, and local government. Most Federal archivists work for the National Archives and Records Administration; others manage military archives in the Department of Defense. Most Federal Government curators work at the Smithsonian Institution, in the military museums of the Department of Defense, and in archaeological and other museums managed by the Department of Interior. All State governments have archival or historical records sections employing archivists. State and local governments have numerous historical museums, parks, libraries, and zoos employing curators.

Some large corporations have archives or records centers, employing archivists to manage the growing volume of records created or maintained as required by law or necessary to the firms' operations. Religious and fraternal organizations, professional associations, conservation organizations, major private collectors, and research firms also employ archivists and curators.

Conservators may work under contract to treat particular items, rather than as a regular employee of a museum or other institution. These conservators may work on their own as private contractors, or as an employee of a conservation laboratory or regional conservation center that contracts their services to museums.

Training, Other Qualifications, and Advancement

Employment as an archivist, conservator, or curator usually requires graduate education and related work experience. Many archivists and curators work in archives or museums while completing their formal education, to gain the "hands-on" experience that many employers seek when hiring.

Employers usually look for archivists with undergraduate and graduate degrees in history or library science, with courses in archival science. Some positions may require knowledge of the discipline related to the collection, such as business or medicine. An increasing number of archivists have a double master's degree in history and library science. There are currently no programs offering bachelor's or master's degrees in archival science. However, approximately 65 colleges and universities offer courses or practical training in archival science as part of history, library science, or another discipline. The Academy of Certified Archivists offers voluntary certification for archivists. Certification requires the applicant to have experience in the field and to pass an examination offered by the Academy.

Archivists need research and analytical ability to understand the content of documents and the context in which they were created, and to decipher deteriorated or poor quality printed matter, handwritten manuscripts, or photographs and films. A background in preservation management is often required of archivists since they are responsible for taking proper care of their records. Archivists also must be able to organize large amounts of information and write clear instructions for its retrieval and use. In addition, computer skills and the ability to work with electronic records and databases are increasingly important.

Many archives are very small, including one-person shops, with limited promotion opportunities. Archivists typically advance by transferring to a larger unit with supervisory positions. A doctorate in history, library science, or a related field may be needed for some advanced positions, such as director of a State archive.

For employment as a curator, most museums require a master's degree in an appropriate discipline of the museum's specialty—art, history, or archaeology—or museum studies. Many employers prefer a doctoral degree, particularly for curators in natural history or science museums. Earning two graduate degrees—in museum studies (museology) and a specialized subject—gives a candidate a distinct advantage in this competitive job market. In small museums, curatorial positions may be available to individuals with a bachelor's degree. For some positions, an internship of full-time museum work supplemented by courses in museum practices is needed.

Curatorial positions often require knowledge in a number of fields. For historic and artistic conservation, courses in chemistry, physics, and art are desirable. Since curators—particularly those in small museums—may have administrative and managerial responsibilities, courses in business administration, public relations, marketing, and fundraising also are recommended. Similar to archivists, curators need computer skills and the ability to work with electronic databases. Curators also need to be familiar with digital imaging, scanning technology, and copyright infringement, since many are responsible for posting information on the Internet.

Curators must be flexible because of their wide variety of duties. They need to design and present exhibits and, in small museums, manual dexterity to build exhibits or restore objects. Leadership ability and business skills are important for museum directors, while marketing skills are valuable for increasing museum attendance and fundraising.

In large museums, curators may advance through several levels of responsibility, eventually to museum director. Curators in smaller museums often advance to larger ones. Individual research and publications are important for advancement in larger institutions.

Museum technicians usually need a bachelor's degree in an appropriate discipline of the museum's specialty, museum studies training, or previous museum work experience, particularly in exhibit design. Similarly, archives technicians usually need a bachelor's degree in library science or history, or relevant work experience. Technician positions often serve as a stepping stone for individuals interested in archival and curatorial work. With the exception of small museums, a master's degree is needed for advancement.

When hiring conservators, employers look for a master's degree in conservation, or in a closely related field, and substantial experience. There are only a few graduate programs in museum conservation techniques in the United States. Competition for entry to these programs is keen; to qualify, a student must have a background in chemistry, archaeology or studio art, and art history, as well as work experience. For some programs, knowledge of a foreign language is also helpful. Conservation apprenticeships or internships as an undergraduate can also enhance one's admission prospects. Graduate programs last 2 to 4 years; the latter years include internship training. A few individuals enter conservation through apprenticeships with museums, nonprofit organizations, and conservators in private practice. Apprenticeships should be supplemented with courses in chemistry, studio art, and history. Apprenticeship training, although accepted, usually is a more difficult route into the conservation profession.

Relatively few schools grant a bachelor's degree in museum studies. More common are undergraduate minors or tracks of study that are part of an undergraduate degree in a related field, such as art history, history, or archaeology. Students interested in further study may obtain a master's degree in museum studies. Colleges and universities throughout the country offer master's degrees in museum studies. However, many employers feel that, while museum studies are helpful, a thorough knowledge of the museum's specialty and museum work experience are more important.

Continuing education, which enables archivists, curators, conservators, and museum technicians to keep up with developments in the field, is available through meetings, conferences, and workshops sponsored by archival, historical, and museum associations. Some larger organizations, such as the National Archives, offer such training in-house.

Job Outlook

Competition for jobs as archivists, curators, museum technicians, and conservators is expected to be keen as qualified applicants outnumber job openings. Graduates with highly specialized training, such as master's degrees in both library science and history, with a concentration in archives or records management, and extensive computer skills should have the best opportunities for jobs as archivists. A curator job is attractive to many people, and many applicants have the necessary training and subject knowledge; but there are only a few openings. Consequently, candidates may have to work part time, as an intern, or even as a volunteer assistant curator or research associate after completing their formal education. Substantial work experience in collection management, exhibit design, or restoration, as well as database management skills, will be necessary for permanent status. Job opportunities for curators should be best in art and history museums, since these are the largest employers in the museum industry.

The job outlook for conservators may be more favorable, particularly for graduates of conservation programs. However, competition is stiff for the limited number of openings in these programs, and applicants need a technical background. Students who qualify and successfully complete the program, have knowledge of a foreign language, and are willing to relocate, will have an advantage over less qualified candidates.

Employment of archivists, curators, museum technicians, and conservators is expected to increase about as fast as the average for all occupations through 2008. Jobs are expected to grow as public and private organizations emphasize establishing archives and organizing records and information, and as public interest in science, art, history, and technology increases. However, museums and other cultural institutions are often subject to funding cuts during recessions or periods of budget tightening, reducing demand for archivists and curators during these times. Although the rate of turnover among archivists and curators is relatively low, the need to replace workers who leave the occupation or stop working will create some additional job openings.

Earnings

Median annual earnings of archivists, curators, museum technicians, and conservators in 1998 were $31,750. The middle 50 percent earned between $23,090 and $43,840. The lowest 10 percent earned less than $16,340 and the highest 10 percent earned more than $63,580. Median annual earnings of archivists, curators, museum technicians, and conservators in 1997 were $28,400 in museums and art galleries.

Earnings of archivists and curators vary considerably by type and size of employer, and often by specialty. Average salaries in the Federal Government, for example, are usually higher than those in religious organizations. Salaries of curators in large, well-funded museums can be several times higher than those in small ones.

The average annual salary for all museum curators in the Federal Government in nonsupervisory, supervisory, and managerial positions was about $59,200 in 1999. Archivists averaged $57,500; museum specialists and technicians, $40,400; and archives technicians, $40,000.

Related Occupations

The skills that archivists, curators, museum technicians, and conservators use in preserving, organizing, and displaying objects or information of historical interest are shared by anthropologists, arborists, archaeologists, botanists, ethnologists, folklorists, genealogists, historians, horticulturists, information specialists, librarians, paintings restorers, records managers, and zoologists.

Sources of Additional Information

For information on archivists and on schools offering courses in archival studies, contact:

☛ Society of American Archivists, 527 South Wells St., 5th floor, Chicago, IL 60607-3922. Internet: **http://www.archivists.org**

For general information about careers as a curator and schools offering courses in museum studies, contact:

☛ American Association of Museums, 1575 I St. NW., Suite 400, Washington, DC 20005. Internet: **http://www.aam-us.org**

For information about conservation and preservation careers and education programs, contact:

☛ American Institute for Conservation of Historic and Artistic Works, 1717 K St. NW., Suite 301, Washington, DC 20006.
Internet: **http://palimpsest.stanford.edu/aic**

College and University Faculty

(O*NET 31202, 31204, 31206, 31209, 31210, 31212, 31114, 31216, 31218, 31222, 31224, 31226, and 31299)

Significant Points

- A Ph.D. is usually required for full-time, tenure-track positions in 4-year colleges and universities.
- Applicants for full-time college faculty positions should expect to face keen competition.
- Job prospects will continue to be better in certain fields—computer science, engineering, and business, for example—that offer attractive nonacademic job opportunities and attract fewer applicants for academic positions.

Nature of the Work

College and university faculty teach and advise nearly 15 million full- and part-time college students and perform a significant part of our Nation's research. Faculty also keep up with developments in their field and consult with government, business, nonprofit, and community organizations.

Faculty usually are organized into departments or divisions, based on subject or field. They usually teach several different courses—algebra, calculus, and statistics, for example. They may instruct undergraduate or graduate students, or both. College and university faculty may give lectures to several hundred students in large halls, lead small seminars, or supervise students in laboratories. They prepare lectures, exercises, and laboratory experiments; grade exams and papers; and advise and work with students individually. In universities, they also supervise graduate students' teaching and research. College faculty work with an increasingly varied student population made up of growing shares of part-time, older, and culturally and racially diverse students.

Faculty keep abreast of developments in their field by reading current literature, talking with colleagues, and participating in professional conferences. They also do their own research to expand knowledge in their field. They perform experiments; collect and analyze data; and examine original documents, literature, and other source material. From this process, they arrive at conclusions, and publish their findings in scholarly journals, books, and electronic media.

College and university faculty increasingly use technology in all areas of their work. In the classroom, they may use computers—including the Internet; electronic mail; software programs, such as statistical packages; and CD-ROMs—as teaching aids. Some faculty use closed-circuit and cable television, satellite broadcasts, and video, audio, and Internet teleconferencing to teach courses to students at remote sites. Faculty post course content, class notes, class schedules, and other information on the Internet. They also use computers to do research, participate in discussion groups, or publicize professional research papers. Faculty will use these technologies more as quality and affordability improve.

Most faculty members serve on academic or administrative committees that deal with the policies of their institution, departmental matters, academic issues, curricula, budgets, equipment purchases, and hiring. Some work with student and community organizations. Department chairpersons are faculty members who usually teach some courses but usually have heavier administrative responsibilities.

The proportion of time spent on research, teaching, administrative, and other duties varies by individual circumstance and type of institution. Faculty members at universities normally spend a significant part of their time doing research; those in 4-year colleges, somewhat less; and those in 2-year colleges, relatively little. The teaching load, however, often is heavier in 2-year colleges and somewhat lower at 4-year institutions. Full professors at all types of institutions usually spend a larger portion of their time conducting research than assistant professors, instructors, and lecturers.

College and university faculty teach, conduct research, and write scholarly papers.

Working Conditions

College faculty usually have flexible schedules. They must be present for classes, usually 12 to 16 hours per week, and for faculty and committee meetings. Most establish regular office hours for student consultations, usually 3 to 6 hours per week. Otherwise, faculty are free to decide when and where they will work, and how much time to devote to course preparation, grading, study, research, graduate student supervision, and other activities.

Initial adjustment to these responsibilities can be challenging as new faculty adapt to switching roles from student to teacher. This adjustment may be even more difficult should class sizes grow in response to faculty and budget cutbacks, increasing an instructor's workload. Also, many institutions are increasing their reliance on part-time faculty, who usually have limited administrative and student advising duties, which leaves the declining number of full-time faculty with a heavier workload. To ease the transition from student to teacher, some institutions offer career development programs.

Some faculty members work staggered hours and teach night and weekend classes. This is particularly true for faculty who teach at 2-year community colleges or institutions with large enrollments of older students with full-time jobs or family responsibilities. Most colleges and universities require faculty to work 9 months of the year, which allows them the time to teach additional courses, do research, travel, or pursue nonacademic interests during the summer and school holidays. Colleges and universities usually have funds to support faculty research or other professional development needs, including travel to conferences and research sites.

Faculty may experience a conflict between their responsibilities to teach students and the pressure to do research and to publish their findings. This may be a particular problem for young faculty seeking advancement in 4-year research universities. However, increasing emphasis on undergraduate teaching performance in tenure decisions may alleviate some of this pressure.

Part-time faculty usually spend little time on campus, because they do not have an office. In addition, they may teach at more than one college, requiring travel between places of employment, earning the name "gypsy faculty." Part-time faculty are usually not eligible for tenure. For those seeking full-time employment in academia, dealing with this lack of job security can be stressful.

Employment

College and university faculty held about 865,000 jobs in 1998, mostly in public institutions.

About 3 out of 10 college and university faculty worked part time in 1998. Some part-timers, known as "adjunct faculty," have primary jobs outside of academia—in government, private industry, or in nonprofit research—and teach "on the side." Others prefer to work part-time hours or seek full-time jobs but are unable to obtain them due to intense competition for available openings. Some work part time in more than one institution. Many adjunct faculty are not qualified for tenure-track positions because they lack a doctoral degree.

Training, Other Qualifications, and Advancement

Most college and university faculty are in four academic ranks: Professor, associate professor, assistant professor, and instructor. These positions are usually considered to be tenure-track positions. A small number of faculty, called lecturers, usually are not on the tenure track.

Most faculty members are hired as instructors or assistant professors. Four-year colleges and universities usually consider doctoral degree holders for full-time, tenure-track positions, but may hire master's degree holders or doctoral candidates for certain disciplines, such as the arts, or for part-time and temporary jobs. In 2-year colleges, master's degree holders fill most full-time positions. However, with increasing competition for available jobs, institutions can be more selective in their hiring practices. Master's degree holders may find it increasingly difficult to obtain employment as they are passed over in favor of candidates holding a Ph.D.

Doctoral programs, including time spent completing a master's degree and a dissertation, take an average of 6 to 8 years of full-time study beyond the bachelor's degree. Some programs, such as the humanities, take longer to complete; others, such as engineering, usually are shorter. Candidates specialize in a subfield of a discipline—for example, organic chemistry, counseling psychology, or European history—but also take courses covering the entire discipline. Programs include 20 or more increasingly specialized courses and seminars plus comprehensive examinations on all major areas of the field. Candidates also must complete a dissertation—a written report on original research in the candidate's major field of study. The dissertation sets forth an original hypothesis or proposes a model and tests it. Students in the natural sciences and engineering usually do laboratory work; in the humanities, they study original documents and other published material. The dissertation, done under the guidance of one or more faculty advisors, usually takes 1 or 2 years of full-time work.

In some fields, particularly the natural sciences, some students spend an additional 2 years on postdoctoral research and study before taking a faculty position. Some Ph.D.'s extend or take new postdoctoral appointments if they are unable to find a faculty job. Most of these appointments offer a nominal salary.

A major step in the traditional academic career is attaining tenure. New tenure-track faculty are usually hired as instructors or assistant professors, and must serve a certain period (usually 7 years) under term contracts. At the end of the contract period, their record of teaching, research, and overall contribution to the institution is reviewed; tenure is granted if the review is favorable. According to the American Association of University Professors, in 1998-99 about 65 percent of all full-time faculty held tenure, and about 86 percent were in tenure-track positions. Those denied tenure usually must leave the institution. Tenured professors cannot be fired without just cause and due process. Tenure protects the faculty's academic freedom—the ability to teach and conduct research without fear of being fired for advocating unpopular ideas. It also gives both faculty and institutions the stability needed for effective research and teaching, and provides financial security for faculty. Some institutions have adopted post-tenure review policies to encourage ongoing evaluation of tenured faculty.

The number of tenure-track positions is expected to decline as institutions seek flexibility in dealing with financial matters and changing student interests. Institutions will rely more heavily on limited term contracts and part-time faculty, shrinking the total pool of tenured faculty. Some institutions offer limited term contracts to prospective faculty—typically 2-, 3-, or 5-year, full-time contracts. These contracts may be terminated or extended at the end of the period. Institutions are not obligated to grant tenure to these contract holders. In addition, some institutions have limited the percentage of faculty who can be tenured.

Some faculty—based on teaching experience, research, publication, and service on campus committees and task forces—move into administrative and managerial positions, such as departmental chairperson, dean, and president. At 4-year institutions, such advancement requires a doctoral degree. At 2-year colleges, a doctorate is helpful but not usually required, except for advancement to some top administrative positions. (Deans and departmental chairpersons are covered in the *Handbook* statement on education administrators, while college presidents are included in the *Handbook* statement on general managers and top executives.)

College faculty should have inquiring and analytical minds, and a strong desire to pursue and disseminate knowledge. They must be able to communicate clearly and logically, both orally and in writing. They should be able to establish rapport with students and, as models for them, be dedicated to the principles of academic integrity and intellectual honesty. Additionally, they must be self-motivated and able to work in an environment where they receive little direct supervision.

Job Outlook

Employment of college and university faculty is expected to increase faster than the average for all occupations through 2008 as enrollments in higher education increase. Many additional openings will arise as faculty members retire. Nevertheless, prospective job applicants should expect to face competition, particularly for full-time, tenure-track positions at 4-year institutions.

Between 1998 and 2008, the traditional college-age (18-24) population will grow again after several years of decline. This population increase, along with a higher proportion of 18- to 24-year-olds attending college and a growing number of part-time, female, minority, and older students, will spur college enrollments. Enrollment is projected to rise from 14.6 million in 1998 to 16.1 million in 2008, an increase of about 10 percent (see the accompanying chart).

Growing numbers of students will necessitate hiring more faculty to teach. At the same time, many faculty will be retiring, opening up even more positions. Also, the number of doctor's degrees is expected to grow more slowly than in the past, somewhat easing the competition for some faculty positions.

Despite expected job growth and the need to replace retiring faculty, many in the academic community are concerned that institutions will increasingly favor the hiring of adjunct faculty over full-time, tenure-track faculty. For many years, keen competition for faculty jobs forced some applicants to accept part-time academic appointments that offered little hope of tenure, and others to seek nonacademic positions. Many colleges, faced with reduced State funding for higher education and growing numbers of part-time and older students, increased the hiring of part-time faculty to save money on pay and benefits and to accommodate the needs of nontraditional-age students. If funding remains tight over the projection period, this trend of hiring adjunct or part-time faculty is likely to continue. Because of uncertainty about future funding sources, some colleges and universities are also controlling costs by changing the mix of academic programs offered, eliminating some programs altogether, and increasing class size.

Even if the proportion of full-time positions does not shrink, job competition will remain keen for coveted tenure-track jobs. Some institutions are expected to increasingly hire full-time faculty on limited-term contracts, reducing the number of tenure-track positions available. Overall, job prospects will continue to be better in certain fields—business, engineering, health science, and computer science, for example—that offer attractive nonacademic job opportunities and attract fewer applicants for academic positions. Also, excellent job prospects in a field—for example, computer science—result in higher student enrollments, increasing faculty needs in that field. On the other hand, poor job prospects in a field, such as history in recent years, discourages students and reduces demand for faculty.

Enrollments in institutions of higher education are expected to continue increasing.

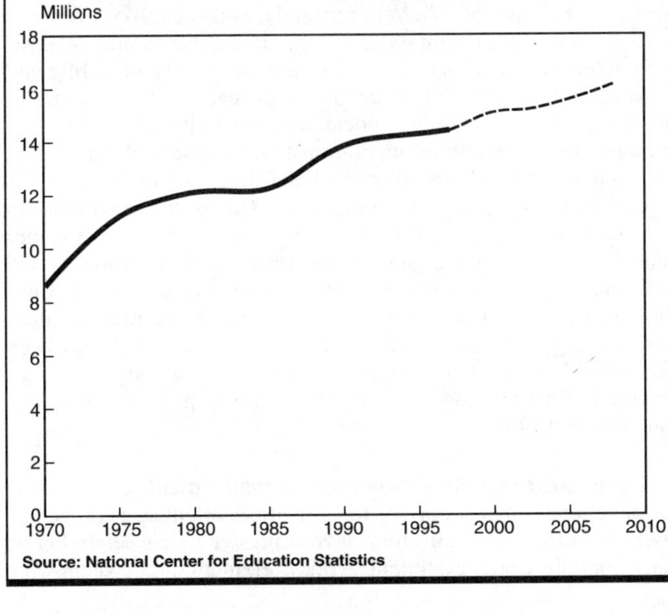

Source: National Center for Education Statistics

Earnings

Median annual earnings of college and university faculty in 1998 were $46,630. The middle 50 percent earned between $33,390 and $71,360. The lowest 10 percent earned less than $23,100; the highest 10 percent, more than $90,360.

Earnings vary according to faculty rank and type of institution, geographic area, and field. According to a 1998-99 survey by the American Association of University Professors, salaries for full-time faculty averaged $56,300. By rank, the average for professors was $72,700; associate professors, $53,200; assistant professors, $43,800; instructors, $33,400; and lecturers, $37,200. Faculty in 4-year institutions earn higher salaries, on the average, than those in 2-year schools. Average salaries for faculty in public institutions—$55,900—were lower in 1998-99 than those for private independent institutions—$63,500—but higher than those for religiously-affiliated private colleges and universities—$49,400. In fields with high-paying nonacademic alternatives—notably medicine and law but also engineering and business, among others—earnings exceed these averages. In others—such as the humanities and education—they are lower.

Most faculty members have significant earnings in addition to their base salary, from consulting, teaching additional courses, researching, writing for publication, or other employment.

Most college and university faculty enjoy some unique benefits, including access to campus facilities, tuition waivers for dependents, housing and travel allowances, and paid sabbatical leaves. Part-time faculty usually have fewer benefits, including health insurance, retirement benefits, and sabbatical leave, than full-time faculty.

Related Occupations

College and university faculty function both as teachers and as researchers. They communicate information and ideas. Related occupations include elementary and secondary school teachers, librarians, writers, consultants, lobbyists, trainers and employee development specialists, and policy analysts. Faculty research activities often are similar to those of scientists, as well as managers and administrators in industry, government, and nonprofit research organizations.

Sources of Additional Information

Professional societies generally provide information on academic and nonacademic employment opportunities in their fields. Names and addresses of these societies appear in statements elsewhere in the *Handbook*.

Special publications on higher education, available in libraries, such as *The Chronicle of Higher Education*, list specific employment opportunities for faculty.

Counselors

(O*NET 31514)

Significant Points

- About 6 out of 10 counselors have a master's degree.
- Most States require some form of counselor credentialing, licensure, certification, or registry for practice outside schools; all States require school counselors to hold a State school counseling certification.

Nature of the Work

Counselors assist people with personal, family, educational, mental health, and career decisions and problems. Their duties depend on the individuals they serve and the settings in which they work.

School and college counselors—in elementary, secondary, and postsecondary schools—help students evaluate their abilities, interests, talents, and personality characteristics to develop realistic academic and career goals. Counselors use interviews, counseling sessions, tests, or other methods when evaluating and advising students. They operate career information centers and career education programs. High school counselors advise on college majors, admission requirements, entrance exams, and financial aid and on trade, technical school, and apprenticeship programs. They help students develop job search skills such as resume writing and interviewing techniques. College career planning and placement counselors assist alumni or students with career development and job hunting techniques.

Elementary school counselors observe younger children during classroom and play activities and confer with their teachers and parents to evaluate their strengths, problems, or special needs. They also help students develop good study habits. They do less vocational and academic counseling than secondary school counselors.

School counselors at all levels help students understand and deal with their social, behavioral, and personal problems. They emphasize preventive and developmental counseling to provide students with the life skills needed to deal with problems before they occur, and to enhance personal, social, and academic growth. Counselors provide special services, including alcohol and drug prevention programs, and classes that teach students to handle conflicts without resorting to violence. Counselors also try to identify cases involving domestic abuse and other family problems that can affect a student's development. Counselors work with students individually, in small groups, or with entire classes. They consult and work with parents, teachers, school administrators, school psychologists, school nurses, and social workers.

Rehabilitation counselors help people deal with the personal, social, and vocational effects of disabilities. They counsel people with disabilities resulting from birth defects, illness or disease, accidents, or the stress of daily life. They evaluate the strengths and limitations of individuals, provide personal and vocational counseling, and arrange for medical care, vocational training, and job placement. Rehabilitation counselors interview individuals with disabilities and their families, evaluate school and medical reports, and confer and plan with physicians, psychologists, occupational therapists, and employers to determine the capabilities and skills of the individual. Conferring with the client, they develop a rehabilitation program, which often includes training to help the person develop job skills. They also work toward increasing the client's capacity to live independently.

Employment, or *vocational, counselors* help individuals make career decisions. They explore and evaluate the client's education, training, work history, interests, skills, and personal traits, and arrange for aptitude and achievement tests. They also work with individuals to develop job search skills and assist clients in locating and applying for jobs.

Mental health counselors emphasize prevention and work with individuals and groups to promote optimum mental health. They help individuals deal with addictions and substance abuse, suicide, stress management, problems with self-esteem, issues associated with aging, job and career concerns, educational decisions, issues of mental and emotional health, and family, parenting, and marital problems. Mental health counselors work closely with other mental health specialists, including psychiatrists, psychologists, clinical social workers, psychiatric nurses, and school counselors. (Information on other mental health specialists appears in the *Handbook* statements on physicians, psychologists, registered nurses, and social workers.)

Other counseling specialties include marriage and family, multicultural, or gerontological counseling. A gerontological counselor provides services to elderly persons who face changing lifestyles because of health problems, and helps families cope with these changes. A multicultural counselor helps employers adjust to an increasingly diverse workforce.

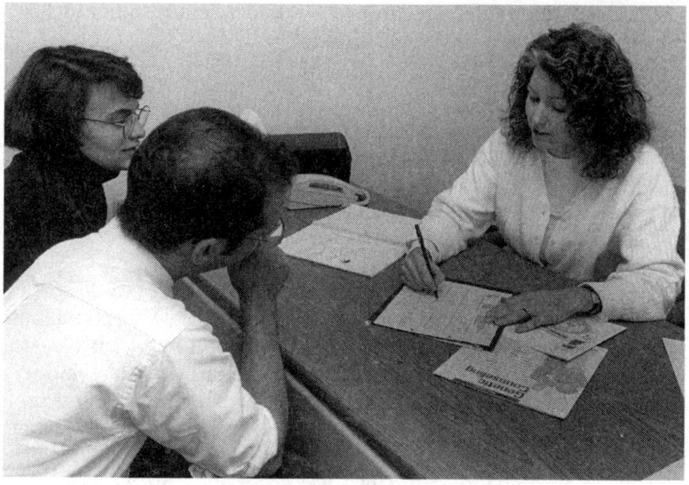

Counselors' duties depend on the individuals they serve and the settings in which they work.

Working Conditions

Most school counselors work the traditional 9- to 10-month school year with a 2- to 3-month vacation, although an increasing number are employed on 10 1/2- or 11-month contracts. They usually have the same hours as teachers. College career planning and placement counselors work long and irregular hours during recruiting periods.

Rehabilitation and employment counselors usually work a standard 40-hour week. Self-employed counselors and those working in mental health and community agencies often work evenings to counsel clients who work during the day.

Counselors must possess high physical and emotional energy to handle the array of problems they address. Dealing daily with these problems can cause stress.

Since privacy is essential for confidential and frank discussions with clients, counselors usually have private offices.

Employment

Counselors held about 182,000 jobs in 1998. (This employment estimate only includes vocational and educational counselors; employment data are not available for other counselors discussed in this statement, such as rehabilitation and mental health counselors.)

In addition to elementary and secondary schools and colleges and universities, counselors work in a wide variety of public and private establishments. These include health care facilities; job training, career development, and vocational rehabilitation centers; social agencies; correctional institutions; and residential care facilities, such as halfway houses for criminal offenders and group homes for children, the aged, and the disabled. Counselors also work in organizations engaged in community improvement and social change, as well as drug and alcohol rehabilitation programs and State and local government agencies. A growing number of counselors work in health maintenance organizations, insurance companies, group practice, and private practice. This growth has been spurred by laws allowing counselors to receive payments from insurance companies, and requiring employers to provide rehabilitation and counseling services to employees.

Training, Other Qualifications, and Advancement

Formal education is necessary to gain employment as a counselor. About 6 out of 10 counselors have a master's degree; fields of study include college student affairs, elementary or secondary school counseling, education, gerontological counseling, marriage and family counseling, substance abuse counseling, rehabilitation counseling, agency or community counseling, clinical mental health counseling, counseling psychology, career counseling, and related fields.

Graduate-level counselor education programs in colleges and universities usually are in departments of education or psychology. Courses are grouped into eight core areas: Human growth and development; social and cultural foundations; helping relationships; group work; career and lifestyle development; appraisal; research and program evaluation; and professional orientation. In an accredited program, 48 to 60 semester hours of graduate study, including a period of supervised clinical experience in counseling, are required for a master's degree. In 1999, 133 institutions offered programs in counselor education, including career, community, gerontological, mental health, school, student affairs, and marriage and family counseling that were accredited by the Council for Accreditation of Counseling and Related Educational Programs (CACREP). Another organization, the Council on Rehabilitation Education (CORE), accredits graduate programs in rehabilitation counseling. Accredited master's degree programs include a minimum of 2 years of full-time study, including 600 hours of supervised clinical internship experience.

In 1999, 45 States and the District of Columbia had some form of counselor credentialing, licensure, certification, or registry legislation governing practice outside schools. Requirements vary from State to State. In some States, credentialing is mandatory; in others, it is voluntary.

All States require school counselors to hold State school counseling certification; however, certification requirements vary from State to State. Some States require public school counselors to have both counseling and teaching certificates. Depending on the State, a master's degree in counseling and 2 to 5 years of teaching experience could be required for a school counseling certificate.

Counselors must be aware of educational and training requirements that are often very detailed and that vary by area and by counseling specialty. Prospective counselors should check with State and local governments, employers, and national voluntary certification organizations in order to determine which requirements apply.

Many counselors elect to be nationally certified by the National Board for Certified Counselors (NBCC), which grants the general practice credential, "National Certified Counselor." To be certified, a counselor must hold a graduate degree in counseling from a regionally accredited institution, have at least 2 years of supervised field experience in a counseling setting (graduates from counselor education programs accredited by the above mentioned CACREP are exempted), and pass NBCC's National Counselor Examination for Licensure and Certification (NCE). This national certification is voluntary and distinct from State certification. However, in some States those who pass the national exam are exempt from taking a State certification exam. NBCC also offers specialty certification in school, clinical mental health, and addictions counseling. To maintain their certification, counselors must take again and pass the NCE or complete 100 hours of acceptable continuing education credit every 5 years.

Another organization, the Commission on Rehabilitation Counselor Certification, offers voluntary national certification for rehabilitation counselors. Many employers require rehabilitation counselors to be nationally certified. To become certified, rehabilitation counselors usually must graduate from an accredited educational program, complete an internship, and pass a written examination. (Certification requirements vary according to an applicant's educational history. Employment experience, for instance, is required for those without a counseling degree other than the rehabilitation specialty.) They are then designated as "Certified Rehabilitation Counselors." To maintain their certification, counselors must re-take the certification exam or complete 100 hours of acceptable continuing education credit every 5 years.

Vocational and related rehabilitation agencies usually require a master's degree in rehabilitation counseling, counseling and guidance, or counseling psychology for rehabilitation counselor jobs. Some, however, accept applicants with a bachelor's degree in rehabilitation services, counseling, psychology, sociology, or related fields. A bachelor's degree often qualifies a person to work as a counseling aide, rehabilitation aide, or social service worker. Experience in employment counseling, job development, psychology, education, or social work is helpful.

Some States require counselors in public employment offices to have a master's degree; others accept a bachelor's degree with appropriate counseling courses.

Clinical mental health counselors usually have a master's degree in mental health counseling, another area of counseling, or in psychology or social work. Voluntary certification is available through the National Board for Certified Counselors, Inc. Generally, to receive certification as a clinical mental health counselor, a counselor must have a master's degree in counseling, 2 years of post-master's experience, a period of supervised clinical experience, a taped sample of clinical work, and a passing grade on a written examination.

Some employers provide training for newly hired counselors. Many have work-study programs so those employed counselors can earn graduate degrees. Counselors must participate in graduate studies, workshops, and personal studies to maintain their certificates and licenses.

Persons interested in counseling should have a strong interest in helping others and the ability to inspire repect, trust, and confidence. They should be able to work independently or as part of a team. Counselors follow the code of ethics associated with their respective certifications and licenses.

Prospects for advancement vary by counseling field. School counselors can move to a larger school; become directors or supervisors of counseling, guidance, or pupil personnel services; or, usually with further graduate education, become counselor educators, counseling psychologists, or school administrators. (See the statements on psychologists and education administrators elsewhere in the *Handbook*.) Some counselors choose to work at the State department of education.

Rehabilitation, mental health, and employment counselors can become supervisors or administrators in their agencies. Some counselors move into research, consulting, or college teaching, or go into private or group practice.

Job Outlook

Overall employment of counselors is expected to grow faster than the average for all occupations through 2008. In addition, numerous job openings will occur as many counselors reach retirement age. (This employment projection applies only to vocational and educational counselors. Future job market conditions for rehabilitation and mental health counselors are discussed later in this section.)

Employment of school and vocational counselors is expected to grow as a result of increasing enrollments, particularly in secondary and postsecondary schools, State legislation requiring counselors in elementary schools, and the expanded responsibilities of counselors. Counselors are becoming more involved in crisis and preventive counseling, helping students deal with issues ranging from drug and alcohol abuse to death and suicide. Also, the growing diversity of student populations is presenting challenges to counselors in dealing with multicultural issues. Budgetary constraints, however, can dampen job growth of school counselors. When funding is tight, schools usually prefer to hire new teachers before adding counselors in an effort to keep classroom sizes at acceptable levels. If this happens, student-to-counselor ratios in many schools could increase as student enrollments grow.

As with other government jobs, the number of employment counselors, who work primarily for State and local government, could be limited by budgetary constraints. However, demand for government employment counseling could grow as new welfare laws require welfare recipients to find jobs. Opportunities for employment counselors working in private job training services should grow as counselors provide training and other services to laid-off workers, experienced workers seeking a new or second career, full-time homemakers seeking to enter or reenter the work force, and workers who want to upgrade their skills.

Demand is expected to be strong for rehabilitation and mental health counselors. Under managed care systems, insurance companies increasingly provide for reimbursement of counselors, enabling many counselors to move from schools and government agencies to private practice. Counselors are also forming group practices to receive expanded insurance coverage. The number of people who need rehabilitation services will rise as advances in medical technology continue to save lives that only a few years ago would have been lost. In addition, legislation requiring equal employment rights for people with disabilities will spur demand for counselors. Counselors not only will help individuals with disabilities with their transition into the work force, but also will help companies comply with the law. Employers are also increasingly offering employee assistance programs that provide mental health and alcohol and drug abuse services. A growing number of people are expected to use these services as the elderly population grows, and as society focuses on ways of developing mental well-being, such as controlling stress associated with job and family responsibilities.

Earnings

Median annual earnings of vocational and educational counselors in 1998 were $38,650. The middle 50 percent earned between $28,400 and $49,960. The lowest 10 percent earned less than $21,230 and the highest 10 percent earned more than $73,920. Median annual earnings in the industries employing the largest numbers of vocational and educational counselors in 1997 are shown below:

Elementary and secondary schools	$42,100
State government, except education and hospitals	35,800
Colleges and universities	34,700
Job training and related services	24,100
Individual and family services	22,300

School counselors can earn additional income working summers in the school system or in other jobs.

Self-employed counselors who have well-established practices, as well as counselors employed in group practices, usually have the highest earnings, as do some counselors working for private firms, such as insurance companies and private rehabilitation companies.

Related Occupations

Counselors help people evaluate their interests, abilities, and disabilities, and deal with personal, social, academic, and career problems. Others who help people in similar ways include college and student affairs workers, teachers, personnel workers and managers, human services workers, social workers, psychologists, psychiatrists, psychiatric nurses, members of the clergy, occupational therapists, training and employee development specialists, and equal employment opportunity/affirmative action specialists.

Sources of Additional Information

For general information about counseling, as well as information on specialties such as school, college, mental health, rehabilitation, multicultural, career, marriage and family, and gerontological counseling, contact:

☛ American Counseling Association, 5999 Stevenson Ave., Alexandria, VA 22304-3300. Internet: **http://www.counseling.org**

For information on accredited counseling and related training programs, contact:

☛ Council for Accreditation of Counseling and Related Educational Programs, American Counseling Association, 5999 Stevenson Ave., 4th floor, Alexandria, VA 22304. Internet: **http://www.counseling.org/cacrep**

For information on national certification requirements for counselors, contact:

☛ National Board for Certified Counselors, Inc., 3 Terrace Way, Suite D, Greensboro, NC 27403-3660. Internet: **http://www.nbcc.org**

For information on certification requirements for rehabilitation counselors and a list of accredited rehabilitation education programs, contact:

☛ Commission on Rehabilitation Counselor Certification, 1835 Rohlwing Rd., Suite E, Rolling Meadows, IL 60008.

State departments of education can supply information on colleges and universities that offer approved guidance and counseling training for State certification and licensure requirements.

State employment service offices have information about job opportunities and entrance requirements for counselors.

Instructors and Coaches, Sports and Physical Training

(O*NET 31321)

Significant Points

- Work hours are often irregular.
- For many positions, certification is required.

Nature of the Work

An increasing value is being placed upon physical fitness within our society. Consequently, Americans are engaging in more physical fitness programs, joining athletic clubs, and being encouraged to participate in physical education and activity at all ages. Sports and physical training instructors and coaches help participants improve their physical fitness and athletic skills.

Sports instructors and coaches teach non-professional individual and team sports to students. (For information on physical education teachers see the section on school teachers elsewhere in the *Handbook*; coaches of professional athletes are classified with athletes, coaches, umpires, and related workers which are included in the section on Data for Occupations Not Studied in Detail elsewhere in the *Handbook*.) Sports instructors and coaches organize, lead, instruct, and referee outdoor and indoor games such as volleyball, football, and soccer. They instruct individuals or groups in beginning or advanced exercises. Using their knowledge of sports, physiology, and corrective techniques, they determine the type and level of difficulty of exercises, prescribe specific movements, and correct individuals' technique. Some instructors and coaches also teach and demonstrate use of training apparatus, such as trampolines or weights. Sports instructors and coaches may also select, store, issue, and inventory equipment, materials, and supplies.

Physical training instructors tend to focus more on physical fitness activities rather than organized sports. They teach and lead exercise activities to individuals or groups ranging from beginning to advanced levels. These activities take place in a gym, health club or other recreational facility. Because activities are as diverse as aerobics, calisthenics, weight lifting, gymnastics, scuba diving, yoga, and may include self-defense training such as karate, instructors tend to specialize in one or a few types of activities. *Personal trainers* work one-on-one in health clubs or clients' homes. They evaluate an individual's abilities, determine a suitable training program, demonstrate a variety of exercises, offer encouragement, and monitor their correct use of exercise equipment and other apparatus.

Sports instructors and coaches instruct and referee the outdoor and indoor games of people learning to play a sport.

Depending on the sport or physical activity involved, instructors and coaches use different kinds of equipment. Many work with children or young adults, helping them to learn new physical and social skills, while also improving their physical condition.

Working Conditions
Irregular work hours are common—many instructors and coaches work part-time, evenings, and weekends. Instructors and coaches in educational institutions may work additional hours during the sports season. Some coach more than one sport, and may work year round. Some work outdoors, depending on the sport or activity. Instructors and coaches may travel frequently to games and other sporting events. Their work is often strenuous and they must guard against injury when participating in activities or instructing others.

Employment
Sports and physical training instructors and coaches held about 359,000 jobs in 1998. About 1 out of 6 was self-employed. Almost half of salaried workers were in public or private educational institutions. Amusement and recreation services, including health clubs, gymnasiums, and sports and recreation clubs provided almost as many jobs. Most of the remaining jobs were found in civic and social associations.

Training, Other Qualifications, and Advancement
Education and training requirements for instructors and coaches vary greatly by type of employer, area of expertise, and level of responsibilities. Some entry-level positions only require experience derived as a participant in the sport or activity, while others require substantial education or experience. For example, aerobics instructor jobs are usually filled by persons who develop an avid interest in the activity by taking aerobics classes and then become certified. On the other hand, some coaches must have qualifying experience such as past participation in the sport, or must work their way up through the coaching ranks.

School coaches and sports instructors at all levels usually have a bachelor's degree. Employers within the education industry often draw first from teachers and faculty when seeking to fill a position. If no one suitable is found they hire someone from outside. Coaches may have to be certified, in accordance with the school district's policies. Some districts require recertification every 2 years. A master's degree may increase opportunities for employment and advancement. Degree programs are offered in exercise sports science, physiology, kinesiology, nutrition and fitness, physical education, and sports medicine.

Certification is highly desirable for those interested in becoming a fitness, aerobics, tennis, karate, golf, or any other kind of instructor. Often one must be at least 18 years old and CPR certified. There are many certifying organizations specific to the various types of sports or activities and their training requirements vary depending on their standards. Part-time workers and those in smaller facilities are less likely to need formal education or training.

Instructors and coaches must relate well to others. They also must be resourceful and flexible to successfully instruct and motivate individual students or groups. Good communication and leadership skills are essential.

Job Outlook
An increased need for instructors and coaches is expected to increase employment in this occupation faster than the average for all occupations through the year 2008. Additional job opportunities will be generated by the need to replace workers who leave the occupation. Job prospects should be best for those with bachelor's degrees and extensive experience within their specialization.

Demand for instructors and coaches will remain high as long as the public continues to participate in sports as a form of entertainment, recreation, and physical conditioning. Health and fitness clubs will continue to change to address the public's ever-changing tastes. In addition, as the more active baby-boomers replace their more sedentary parents in retirement, the demand for sports and recreation instructors and coaches will increase.

Earnings
Median hourly earnings of sports and physical training instructors and coaches were $10.69 in 1998. The middle 50 percent earned between $6.54 and $16.48 an hour. The lowest 10 percent earned less than $5.70 and the highest 10 percent earned more than $23.10 an hour. Median hourly earnings in the industries employing the largest number of sports and physical training instructors and coaches in 1997 were as follows:

Colleges and universities	$13.70
Elementary and secondary schools	11.00
Miscellaneous amusement and recreation services	9.70
Civic and social associations	7.80

Earnings vary by education level, certification, and geographic region. Some instructors and coaches are paid a salary, others may be paid by the hour, per session, or based on the number of participants.

Related Occupations
Coaches and instructors have extensive knowledge of physiology and sports, and instruct, inform, and encourage participants. Other workers with similar duties include athletic directors, athletic trainers, dietitians and nutritionists, physical therapists, recreational therapists, school teachers, and umpires.

Sources of Additional Information
Information about a career as a fitness professional is available from:
☛ American Council on Exercise, 5820 Oberlin Dr., Suite 102, San Diego, CA 92121-3787. Internet: **http://www.acefitness.org**

For information on a career as a coach, contact:
☛ National High School Athletic Coaches Association, P.O. Box 4342, Hamden, CT 06514. Internet: **http://www.hscoaches.org**

Librarians

(O*NET 31502A and 31502B)

Significant Points

- A master's degree in library science is usually required; special librarians often need an additional graduate or professional degree.

- Applicants for librarian jobs in large cities or suburban areas will face competition, while those willing to work in rural areas should have better job prospects.

Nature of the Work

The traditional concept of a library is being redefined, from a place to access paper records or books, to one which also houses the most advanced mediums, including CD-ROM, the Internet, virtual libraries, and remote access to a wide range of resources. Consequently, librarians are increasingly combining traditional duties with tasks involving quickly changing technology. Librarians assist people in finding information and using it effectively in their personal and professional lives. They must have knowledge of a wide variety of scholarly and public information sources, and follow trends related to publishing, computers, and the media to effectively oversee the selection and organization of library materials. Librarians manage staff and develop and direct information programs and systems for the public to ensure information is organized to meet users' needs.

Most librarian positions incorporate three aspects of library work—user services, technical services, and administrative services. Even librarians specializing in one of these areas perform other responsibilities. Librarians in user services, such as reference and children's librarians, work with the public to help them find the information they need. This involves analyzing users' needs to determine what information is appropriate, and searching for, acquiring, and providing information. It also includes an instructional role, such as showing users how to access information. For example, librarians commonly help users navigate the Internet, showing them how to most efficiently search for relevant information. Librarians in technical services, such as acquisitions and cataloguing, acquire and prepare materials for use and often do not deal directly with the public. Librarians in administrative services oversee the management and planning of libraries, negotiate contracts for services, materials, and equipment, supervise library employees, perform public relations and fundraising duties, prepare budgets, and direct activities to ensure that everything functions properly.

In small libraries or information centers, librarians usually handle all aspects of the work. They read book reviews, publishers' announcements, and catalogues to keep up with current literature and other available resources, and select and purchase materials from publishers, wholesalers, and distributors. Librarians prepare new materials by classifying them by subject matter, and describe books and other library materials so they are easy to find. They supervise assistants who prepare cards, computer records, or other access tools that direct users to resources. In large libraries, librarians often specialize in a single area, such as acquisitions, cataloguing, bibliography, reference, special collections, or administration. Teamwork is increasingly important to ensure quality service to the public.

Librarians also compile lists of books, periodicals, articles, and audiovisual materials on particular subjects, analyze collections, and recommend materials. They collect and organize books, pamphlets, manuscripts, and other materials in a specific field, such as rare books, genealogy, or music. In addition, they coordinate programs such as storytelling for children, and literacy skills and book talks for adults; conduct classes; publicize services; provide reference help; write grants; and oversee other administrative matters.

Librarians are classified according to the type of library in which they work—public libraries, school library media centers, academic libraries, and special libraries. Some librarians work with specific groups, such as children, young adults, adults, or the disadvantaged. In school library media centers, librarians help teachers develop curricula, acquire materials for classroom instruction, and sometimes team-teach.

Librarians also work in information centers or libraries maintained by government agencies, corporations, law firms, advertising agencies, museums, professional associations, medical centers, hospitals, religious organizations, and research laboratories. They build and arrange an organization's information resources, which are usually limited to subjects of special interest to the organization. These special librarians can provide vital information services by preparing abstracts and indexes of current periodicals, organizing bibliographies, or analyzing background information and preparing reports on areas of particular interest. For instance, a special librarian working for a corporation could provide the sales department with information on competitors or new developments affecting their field.

Many libraries have access to remote databases, and maintain their own computerized databases. The widespread use of automation in libraries makes database searching skills important to librarians. Librarians develop and index databases and help train users to develop searching skills for the information they need. Some libraries are forming consortiums with other libraries through electronic mail. This allows patrons to simultaneously submit information requests to several libraries. The Internet is also expanding the amount of available reference information. Librarians must be aware of how to use these resources in order to locate information.

Librarians with computer and information systems skills can work as automated systems librarians, planning and operating computer systems, and information science librarians, designing information storage and retrieval systems and developing procedures for collecting, organizing, interpreting, and classifying information. These librarians analyze and plan for future information needs. (See statements on computer engineers and scientists and computer systems analysts elsewhere in the *Handbook*.) The increased use of automated information systems enables librarians to focus on administrative and budgeting responsibilities, grant writing, and specialized research requests, while delegating more technical and user services responsibilities to technicians. (See statement on library technicians elsewhere in the *Handbook*.)

Increasingly, librarians apply their information management and research skills to arenas outside of libraries—for example, database development, reference tool development, information systems, publishing, Internet coordination, marketing, and training of database users. Entrepreneurial librarians sometimes start their own consulting practices, acting as free-lance librarians or information brokers and providing services to other libraries, businesses, or government agencies.

Working Conditions

Librarians spend a significant portion of time at their desks or in front of computer terminals; extended work at video display terminals can

Librarians in small libraries are more likely to have a wide range of duties.

cause eyestrain and headaches. Assisting users in obtaining information for their jobs, recreational purposes, and other uses can be challenging and satisfying; at the same time, working with users under deadlines can be demanding and stressful.

More than 2 out of 10 librarians work part time. Public and college librarians often work weekends and evenings, and have to work some holidays. School librarians usually have the same workday schedule as classroom teachers and similar vacation schedules. Special librarians usually work normal business hours, but in fast-paced industries, such as advertising or legal services, they can work longer hours during peak times.

Employment
Librarians held about 152,000 jobs in 1998. Most were in school and academic libraries; others were in public and special libraries. A small number of librarians worked for hospitals and religious organizations. Others worked for governments.

Training, Other Qualifications, and Advancement
A master's degree in library science (MLS) is necessary for librarian positions in most public, academic, and special libraries, and in some school libraries. The Federal Government requires an MLS or the equivalent in education and experience. Many colleges and universities offer MLS programs, but employers often prefer graduates of the approximately 50 schools accredited by the American Library Association. Most MLS programs require a bachelor's degree; any liberal arts major is appropriate.

Most MLS programs take 1 year to complete; others take 2. A typical graduate program includes courses in the foundations of library and information science, including the history of books and printing, intellectual freedom and censorship, and the role of libraries and information in society. Other basic courses cover material selection and processing, the organization of information, reference tools and strategies, and user services. Courses are adapted to educate librarians to use new resources brought about by advancing technology such as on-line reference systems, Internet search methods, and automated circulation systems. Course options can include resources for children or young adults; classification, cataloguing, indexing, and abstracting; library administration; and library automation. Computer related course work is an increasingly important part of an MLS degree.

An MLS provides general preparation for library work, but some individuals specialize in a particular area such as reference, technical services, or children's services. A Ph.D. degree in library and information science is advantageous for a college teaching position, or a top administrative job in a college or university library or large library system.

In special libraries, an MLS is also usually required. In addition, most special librarians supplement their education with knowledge of the subject specialization, sometimes earning a master's, doctoral, or professional degree in the subject. Subject specializations include medicine, law, business, engineering, and the natural and social sciences. For example, a librarian working for a law firm may also be a licensed attorney, holding both library science and law degrees. In some jobs, knowledge of a foreign language is needed.

State certification requirements for public school librarians vary widely. Most States require school librarians, often called library media specialists, to be certified as teachers and have courses in library science. In some cases, an MLS, perhaps with a library media specialization, or a master's in education with a specialty in school library media or educational media, is needed. Some States require certification of public librarians employed in municipal, county, or regional library systems.

Librarians participate in continuing training once they are on the job to keep abreast of new information systems brought about by changing technology.

Experienced librarians can advance to administrative positions, such as department head, library director, or chief information officer.

Job Outlook
Slower than average employment growth, coupled with an increasing number of MLS graduates, will result in more applicants competing for fewer jobs. However, because MLS programs increasingly focus on computer skills, graduates will be qualified for other, computer-related occupations. Applicants for librarian jobs in large metropolitan areas, where most graduates prefer to work, will face competition; those willing to work in rural areas should have better job prospects.

Some job openings for librarians will stem from projected slower-than-average employment growth through 2008. Replacement needs will account for more job openings over the next decade, as some librarians reach retirement age.

The increasing use of computerized information storage and retrieval systems could contribute to slow growth in the demand for librarians. Computerized systems make cataloguing easier, which library technicians now handle. In addition, many libraries are equipped for users to access library computers directly from their homes or offices. These systems allow users to bypass librarians and conduct research on their own. However, librarians are needed to manage staff, help users develop database searching techniques, address complicated reference requests, and define users' needs.

Opportunities will be best for librarians outside traditional settings. Nontraditional library settings include information brokers, private corporations, and consulting firms. Many companies are turning to librarians because of their research and organizational skills, and knowledge of computer databases and library automation systems. Librarians can review vast amounts of information and analyze, evaluate, and organize it according to a company's specific needs. Librarians are also hired by organizations to set up information on the Internet. Librarians working in these settings may be classified as systems analysts, database specialists and trainers, webmasters or web developers, or LAN (local area network) coordinators.

Earnings
Salaries of librarians vary according to the individual's qualifications and the type, size, and location of the library. Librarians with primarily administrative duties often have greater earnings. Median annual earnings of librarians in 1998 were $38,470. The middle 50 percent earned between $30,440 and $48,130. The lowest 10 percent earned less than $22,970 and the highest 10 percent earned more than $67,810. Median annual earnings in the industries employing the largest numbers of librarians in 1997 were as follows:

Elementary and secondary schools	$38,900
Colleges and universities	38,600
Local government, except education and hospitals	32,600

The average annual salary for all librarians in the Federal Government in nonsupervisory, supervisory, and managerial positions was $56,400 in 1999.

Related Occupations
Librarians play an important role in the transfer of knowledge and ideas by providing people with access to the information they need and want. Jobs requiring similar analytical, organizational, and communicative skills include archivists, information scientists, museum curators, publishers' representatives, research analysts, information brokers, and records managers. The management aspect of a librarian's work is similar to the work of managers in a variety of business and government settings. School librarians have many

duties similar to those of school teachers. Other jobs requiring the computer skills of some librarians include webmasters or web developers, database specialists, and systems analysts.

Sources of Additional Information

Information on librarianship, including information on scholarships or loans, is available from the American Library Association. For a listing of accredited library education programs, check their homepage:

☛ American Library Association, Office for Human Resource Development and Recruitment, 50 East Huron St., Chicago, IL 60611. Internet: **http://www.ala.org**

For information on a career as a special librarian, write to:

☛ Special Libraries Association, 1700 18th St. NW., Washington, DC 20009.

Information on graduate schools of library and information science can be obtained from:

☛ Association for Library and Information Science Education, P.O. Box 7640, Arlington, VA 22207. Internet: **http://www.sils.umich.edu/ALISE**

For information on a career as a law librarian, scholarship information, and a list of ALA-accredited schools offering programs in law librarianship, contact:

☛ American Association of Law Libraries, 53 West Jackson Blvd., Suite 940, Chicago, IL 60604. Internet: **http://www.ala.org**

For information on employment opportunities as a health sciences librarian, scholarship information, credentialing information, and a list of MLA-accredited schools offering programs in health sciences librarianship, contact:

☛ Medical Library Association, 6 N. Michigan Ave., Suite 300, Chicago, IL 60602. Internet: **http://www.mlanet.org**

Information on acquiring a job as a librarian with the Federal Government may be obtained from the Office of Personnel Management through a telephone-based system. Consult your telephone directory under U.S. Government for a local number or call (912) 757-3000; TDD (912) 744-2299. That number is not toll free and charges may result. Information also is available from their Internet site: **http://www.usajobs.opm.gov**

Information concerning requirements and application procedures for positions in the Library of Congress can be obtained directly from:

☛ Human Resources Office, Library of Congress, 101 Independence Ave. SE., Washington, DC 20540-2231.

State library agencies can furnish information on scholarships available through their offices, requirements for certification, and general information about career prospects in the State. Several of these agencies maintain job hotlines reporting openings for librarians.

State departments of education can furnish information on certification requirements and job opportunities for school librarians.

Many library science schools offer career placement services to their alumni and current students. Some allow non-affiliated students and jobseekers to use their services.

Library Technicians

(O*NET 31505)

Significant Points

- Training ranges from on-the-job to a bachelor's degree.
- Experienced library technicians can advance by obtaining a Master of Library Science degree.

Nature of the Work

Library technicians help librarians acquire, prepare, and organize material, and assist users in finding information. Technicians in small libraries handle a range of duties; those in large libraries usually specialize. As libraries increasingly use new technologies—such as CD-ROM, the Internet, virtual libraries, and automated databases—the duties of library technicians will expand and evolve accordingly. Library technicians are assuming greater responsibilities, in some cases taking on tasks previously performed by librarians. (See the statement on librarians elsewhere in the *Handbook.*)

Library technicians help librarians acquire, prepare, and organize material.

Depending on the employer, library technicians can have other titles, such as library technical assistants. Library technicians direct library users to standard references, organize and maintain periodicals, prepare volumes for binding, handle interlibrary loan requests, prepare invoices, perform routine cataloguing and coding of library materials, retrieve information from computer databases, and supervise support staff.

The widespread use of computerized information storage and retrieval systems has resulted in technicians handling more technical and user services, such as entering catalogue information into the library's computer, that were once performed by librarians. Technicians assist with customizing databases. In addition, technicians instruct patrons how to use computer systems to access data. The increased use of automation has reduced the amount of clerical work performed by library technicians. Many libraries now offer self-service registration and circulations with computers, decreasing the time library technicians spend manually recording and inputting records.

Some library technicians operate and maintain audiovisual equipment, such as projectors, tape recorders, and videocassette recorders, and assist users with microfilm or microfiche readers. They also design posters, bulletin boards, or displays.

Those in school libraries encourage and teach students to use the library and media center. They also help teachers obtain instructional materials and assist students with special assignments. Some work in special libraries maintained by government agencies, corporations, law firms, advertising agencies, museums, professional societies, medical centers, and research laboratories, where they conduct literature searches, compile bibliographies, and prepare abstracts, usually on subjects of particular interest to the organization.

Working Conditions

Technicians answer questions and provide assistance to library users. Those who prepare library materials sit at desks or computer terminals for long periods and can develop headaches or eyestrain from working with video display terminals. Some duties, like calculating circulation statistics, can be repetitive and boring. Others, such as performing computer searches using local and regional library networks and cooperatives, can be interesting and challenging.

Library technicians in school libraries work regular school hours. Those in public libraries and college and university (academic) libraries also work weekends, evenings and some holidays. Library technicians in special libraries usually work normal business hours, although they often work overtime as well.

Library technicians usually work under the supervision of a librarian, although they work independently in certain situations.

Employment
Library technicians held about 72,000 jobs in 1998. Most worked in school, academic, or public libraries. Some worked in hospitals and religious organizations. The Federal Government, primarily the Department of Defense and the Library of Congress, and State and local governments also employed library technicians.

Training, Other Qualifications, and Advancement
Training requirements for library technicians vary widely, ranging from a high school diploma to specialized postsecondary training. Some employers hire individuals with work experience or other training; others train inexperienced workers on the job. Other employers require that technicians have an associate or bachelor's degree. Given the rapid spread of automation in libraries, computer skills are needed for many jobs. Knowledge of databases, library automation systems, on-line library systems, on-line public access systems, and circulation systems is valuable.

Some 2-year colleges offer an associate of arts degree in library technology. Programs include both liberal arts and library-related study. Students learn about library and media organization and operation, and how to order, process, catalogue, locate, and circulate library materials and work with library automation. Libraries and associations offer continuing education courses to keep technicians abreast of new developments in the field.

Library technicians usually advance by assuming added responsibilities. For example, technicians often start at the circulation desk, checking books in and out. After gaining experience, they may become responsible for storing and verifying information. As they advance, they may become involved in budget and personnel matters in their department. Some library technicians advance to supervisory positions and are in charge of the day-to-day operation of their department.

Job Outlook
Employment of library technicians is expected to grow about as fast as the average for all occupations through 2008. Some job openings will result from the need to replace library technicians who transfer to other fields or leave the labor force. Similar to other fields, willingness to relocate enhances an aspiring library technician's job prospects.

The increasing use of library automation is expected to spur job growth among library technicians. Computerized information systems have simplified certain tasks, such as descriptive cataloguing, which can now be handled by technicians instead of librarians. For instance, technicians can now easily retrieve information from a central database and store it in the library's computer. Although budgetary constraints could dampen employment growth of library technicians in school, public, and college and university libraries, libraries sometimes use technicians to perform some librarian duties in an effort to stretch shrinking budgets. Growth in the number of professionals and other workers who use special libraries should result in relatively fast employment growth among library technicians in those settings.

Earnings
Median annual earnings of library technicians in 1998 were $21,730. The middle 50 percent earned between $16,500 and $27,340. The lowest 10 percent earned less than $12,610 and the highest 10 percent earned more than $33,370. Median annual earnings in the industries employing the largest numbers of library technicians in 1997 are shown below:

Local government, except education and hospitals	$22,200
Colleges and universities	21,400
Elementary and secondary schools	18,300

Salaries of library technicians in the Federal Government averaged $29,700 in 1999.

Related Occupations
Library technicians perform organizational and administrative duties. Workers in other occupations with similar duties include library assistants, information clerks, record clerks, medical record technicians, and title searchers.

Sources of Additional Information
Information about a career as a library technician can be obtained from:

☛ Council on Library/Media Technology, P.O. Box 951, Oxon Hill, MD 20750. Internet: **http://library.ucr.edu/COLT**

For information on training programs for library/media technical assistants, write to:

☛ American Library Association, Office for Human Resource Development and Recruitment, 50 East Huron St., Chicago, IL 60611. Internet: **http://www.ala.org**

Information on acquiring a job as a library technician with the Federal Government may be obtained from the Office of Personnel Management through a telephone-based system. Consult your telephone directory under U.S. Government for a local number or call (912) 757-3000; TDD (912) 744-2299. That number is not toll free and charges may result. Information also is available from their Internet site: **http://www.usajobs.opm.gov**

Information concerning requirements and application procedures for positions in the Library of Congress can be obtained directly from:

☛ Human Resources Office, Library of Congress, 101 Independence Ave. SE., Washington, DC 20540-2231.

State library agencies can furnish information on requirements for technicians, and general information about career prospects in the State. Several of these agencies maintain job hotlines reporting openings for library technicians.

State departments of education can furnish information on requirements and job opportunities for school library technicians.

School Teachers—Kindergarten, Elementary, and Secondary

(O*NET 31304, 31305, and 31308)

Significant Points

- Public school teachers must have at least a bachelor's degree, complete an approved teacher education program, and be licensed.
- Many States offer alternative licensing programs to attract people into teaching, especially for hard-to-fill positions.
- Employment growth for secondary school teachers will be more rapid than for kindergarten and elementary school teachers due to student enrollments, but job outlook will vary by geographic area and subject specialty.

Nature of the Work
Teachers act as facilitators or coaches, using interactive discussions and "hands-on" learning to help students learn and apply concepts

in subjects such as science, mathematics, or English. As teachers move away from the traditional repetitive drill approaches and rote memorization, they are using more "props" or "manipulatives" to help children understand abstract concepts, solve problems, and develop critical thought processes. For example, they teach the concepts of numbers or adding and subtracting by playing board games. As children get older, they use more sophisticated materials such as science apparatus, cameras, or computers.

Many classes are becoming less structured, with students working in groups to discuss and solve problems together. Preparing students for the future workforce is the major stimulus generating the changes in education. To be prepared, students must be able to interact with others, adapt to new technology, and logically think through problems. Teachers provide the tools and environment for their students to develop these skills.

Kindergarten and elementary school teachers play a vital role in the development of children. What children learn and experience during their early years can shape their views of themselves and the world, and affect later success or failure in school, work, and their personal lives. Kindergarten and elementary school teachers introduce children to numbers, language, science, and social studies. They use games, music, artwork, films, slides, computers, and other tools to teach basic skills.

Most elementary school teachers instruct one class of children in several subjects. In some schools, two or more teachers work as a team and are jointly responsible for a group of students in at least one subject. In other schools, a teacher may teach one special subject—usually music, art, reading, science, arithmetic, or physical education—to a number of classes. A small but growing number of teachers instruct multilevel classrooms, with students at several different learning levels.

Secondary school teachers help students delve more deeply into subjects introduced in elementary school and expose them to more information about the world. Secondary school teachers specialize in a specific subject, such as English, Spanish, mathematics, history, or biology. They teach a variety of related courses—for example, American history, contemporary American problems, and world geography.

Special education teachers—who instruct elementary and secondary school students who have a variety of disabilities—are discussed separately in this section of the *Handbook*.

Teachers may use films, slides, overhead projectors, and the latest technology in teaching, including computers, telecommunication systems, and video discs. Use of computer resources, such as educational software and the Internet, exposes students to a vast range of experiences and promotes interactive learning. Through the Internet, American students can communicate with students in other countries. Students also use the Internet for individual research projects and information gathering. Computers are used in other classroom activities as well, from helping students solve math problems to learning English as a second language. Teachers may also use computers to record grades and perform other administrative and clerical duties. They must continually update their skills so they can instruct and use the latest technology in the classroom.

Teachers often work with students from varied ethnic, racial, and religious backgrounds. With growing minority populations in many parts of the country, it is important for teachers to establish rapport with a diverse student population. Accordingly, some schools offer training to help teachers enhance their awareness and understanding of different cultures. Teachers may also include multicultural programming in their lesson plans to address the needs of all students, regardless of their cultural background.

Teachers design classroom presentations to meet student needs and abilities. They also work with students individually. Teachers plan, evaluate, and assign lessons; prepare, administer, and grade tests; listen to oral presentations; and maintain classroom discipline. They observe and evaluate a student's performance and potential,

School teachers make classroom presentations and provide individual instruction.

and increasingly are asked to use new assessment methods. For example, teachers may examine a portfolio of a student's artwork or writing to judge the student's overall progress. They then can provide additional assistance in areas where a student needs help. Teachers also grade papers, prepare report cards, and meet with parents and school staff to discuss a student's academic progress or personal problems.

In addition to classroom activities, teachers oversee study halls and homerooms and supervise extracurricular activities. They identify physical or mental problems and refer students to the proper resource or agency for diagnosis and treatment. Secondary school teachers occasionally assist students in choosing courses, colleges, and careers. Teachers also participate in education conferences and workshops.

In recent years, site-based management, which allows teachers and parents to participate actively in management decisions, has gained popularity. In many schools, teachers are increasingly involved in making decisions regarding the budget, personnel, textbook choices, curriculum design, and teaching methods.

Working Conditions

Seeing students develop new skills and gain an appreciation of knowledge and learning can be very rewarding. However, teaching may be frustrating when dealing with unmotivated and disrespectful students. Occasionally, teachers must cope with unruly behavior and violence in the schools. Teachers may experience stress when dealing with large classes, students from disadvantaged or multicultural backgrounds, and heavy workloads.

Teachers are sometimes isolated from their colleagues because they work alone in a classroom of students. However, some schools are allowing teachers to work in teams and with mentors to enhance their professional development.

Including school duties performed outside the classroom, many teachers work more than 40 hours a week. Most teachers work the traditional 10-month school year with a 2-month vacation during the summer. Those on the 10-month schedule may teach in summer sessions, take other jobs, travel, or pursue other personal interests. Many enroll in college courses or workshops to continue their education. Teachers in districts with a year-round schedule typically work 8 weeks, are on vacation for 1 week, and have a 5-week midwinter break.

Most States have tenure laws that prevent teachers from being fired without just cause and due process. Teachers may obtain tenure after they have satisfactorily completed a probationary period of teaching, normally 3 years. Tenure does not absolutely guarantee a job, but it does provide some security.

Employment

Teachers held about 3.4 million jobs in 1998. Of those, about 1.9 million were kindergarten and elementary school teachers, and 1.4 million were secondary school teachers. Employment is distributed geographically, much the same as the population.

Training, Other Qualifications, and Advancement

All 50 States and the District of Columbia require public school teachers to be licensed. Licensure is not required for teachers in private schools. Usually licensure is granted by the State board of education or a licensure advisory committee. Teachers may be licensed to teach the early childhood grades (usually nursery school through grade 3); the elementary grades (grades 1 through 6 or 8); the middle grades (grades 5 through 8); a secondary education subject area (usually grades 7 through 12); or a special subject, such as reading or music (usually grades K through 12).

Requirements for regular licenses vary by State. However, all States require a bachelor's degree and completion of an approved teacher training program with a prescribed number of subject and education credits as well as supervised practice teaching. About one-third of the States also require technology training as part of the teacher certification process. A number of States require specific minimum grade point averages for teacher licensure. Other States require teachers to obtain a master's degree in education, which involves at least 1 year of additional coursework beyond the bachelor's degree with a specialization in a particular subject.

Almost all States require applicants for teacher licensure to be tested for competency in basic skills such as reading, writing, teaching, and subject matter proficiency. Most States require continuing education for renewal of the teacher's license. Many States have reciprocity agreements that make it easier for teachers licensed in one State to become licensed in another.

Increasingly, many States are moving towards implementing performance-based standards for licensure, which require passing a rigorous comprehensive teaching examination to obtain a provisional license. Teachers must then demonstrate satisfactory teaching performance over an extended period of time to obtain a full license.

Many States offer alternative teacher licensure programs for people who have bachelor's degrees in the subject they will teach, but lack the necessary education courses required for a regular license. Alternative licensure programs were originally designed to ease teacher shortages in certain subjects, such as mathematics and science. The programs have expanded to attract other people into teaching, including recent college graduates and mid-career changers. In some programs, individuals begin teaching quickly under provisional licensure. After working under the close supervision of experienced educators for 1 or 2 years while taking education courses outside school hours, they receive regular licensure if they have progressed satisfactorily. Under other programs, college graduates who do not meet licensure requirements take only those courses that they lack, and then become licensed. This may take 1 or 2 semesters of full-time study. States may issue emergency licenses to individuals who do not meet requirements for a regular license when schools cannot attract enough qualified teachers to fill positions. Teachers who need licensure may enter programs that grant a master's degree in education, as well as a license.

For several years, the National Board for Professional Teaching Standards has offered voluntary national certification for teachers. To become nationally certified, teachers must prove their aptitude by compiling a portfolio showing their work in the classroom, and by passing a written assessment and evaluation of their teaching knowledge. Currently, teachers may become certified in one of seven areas. These areas are based on the age of the students and, in some cases, subject area. For example, teachers may obtain a certificate for teaching English Language Arts to early adolescents (ages 11-15), or they may become certified as early childhood generalists. All States recognize national certification, and many States and school districts provide special benefits to teachers holding national certification. Benefits typically include higher salaries and reimbursement for continuing education and certification fees. Additionally, many States allow nationally certified teachers to carry a license from one State to another.

The National Council for Accreditation of Teacher Education currently accredits over 500 teacher education programs across the United States. Generally, 4-year colleges require students to wait until their sophomore year before applying for admission to teacher education programs. Traditional education programs for kindergarten and elementary school teachers include courses—designed specifically for those preparing to teach—in mathematics, physical science, social science, music, art, and literature, as well as prescribed professional education courses such as philosophy of education, psychology of learning, and teaching methods. Aspiring secondary school teachers either major in the subject they plan to teach while also taking education courses, or major in education and take subject courses. Teacher education programs are now required to include classes in the use of computers and other technologies to maintain accreditation. Most programs require students to perform a student teaching internship.

Many States now offer professional development schools, which are partnerships between universities and elementary or secondary schools. Students enter these 1-year programs after completion of their bachelor's degree. Professional development schools merge theory with practice and allow the student to experience a year of teaching first-hand, with professional guidance.

In addition to being knowledgeable in their subject, the ability to communicate, inspire trust and confidence, and motivate students, as well as to understand their educational and emotional needs, is essential for teachers. Teachers must be able to recognize and respond to individual differences in students, and employ different teaching methods that will result in higher student achievement. They also should be organized, dependable, patient, and creative. Teachers must also be able to work cooperatively and communicate effectively with other teaching staff, support staff, parents, and other members of the community.

With additional preparation, teachers may move into positions as school librarians, reading specialists, curriculum specialists, or guidance counselors. Teachers may become administrators or supervisors, although the number of these positions is limited and competition can be intense. In some systems, highly qualified, experienced teachers can become senior or mentor teachers, with higher pay and additional responsibilities. They guide and assist less experienced teachers while keeping most of their own teaching responsibilities.

Job Outlook

The job market for teachers varies widely by geographic area and by subject specialty. Many inner cities—often characterized by overcrowded conditions and higher than average crime and poverty rates—and rural areas—characterized by their remote location and relatively low salaries—have difficulty attracting enough teachers, so job prospects should continue to be better in these areas than in suburban districts. Currently, many school districts have difficulty hiring qualified teachers in some subjects—mathematics, science (especially chemistry and physics), bilingual education, and computer science. Specialties that currently have an abundance of qualified teachers include general elementary education, physical education, and social studies. Teachers who are geographically mobile and who obtain licensure in more than one subject should have a distinct advantage in finding a job. With enrollments of minorities increasing, coupled with a shortage of minority teachers, efforts to recruit minority teachers should intensify. Also, the number of non-English speaking students has grown dramatically, especially in California and Florida which have large Spanish-speaking student populations, creating demand for bilingual teachers and those who teach English as a second language.

Overall employment of kindergarten, elementary, and secondary school teachers is expected to increase about as fast as the average for all occupations through the year 2008. The expected retirement of a large number of teachers currently in their 40s and 50s should open up many additional jobs. However, projected employment growth varies among individual teaching occupations.

Employment of secondary school teachers is expected to grow faster than the average for all occupations through the year 2008, while average employment growth is projected for kindergarten and elementary school teachers. Assuming relatively little change in average class size, employment growth of teachers depends on population growth rates and corresponding student enrollments. Enrollments of secondary school students are expected to grow throughout most of the projection period. (See chart 1.) On the other hand, elementary school enrollment is projected to increase until the year 2001, and then decline. (See chart 2.)

The number of teachers employed is also dependent on State and local expenditures for education. Pressures from taxpayers to limit spending could result in fewer teachers than projected; pressures to spend more to improve the quality of education could increase the teacher workforce.

In anticipation of growing student enrollments at the secondary school level, many States are implementing policies that will encourage more students to become teachers. Some are giving large signing bonuses that are distributed over the teacher's first few years of teaching. Some are expanding State scholarships; issuing loans for moving expenses; and implementing loan-forgiveness programs, allowing education majors with at least a B average to receive State-paid tuition as long as they agree to teach in the State for 4 years.

The supply of teachers also is expected to increase in response to reports of improved job prospects, more teacher involvement in school policy, and greater public interest in education. In recent years, the total number of bachelor's and master's degrees granted in education has steadily increased. In addition, more teachers will be drawn from a reserve pool of career changers, substitute teachers, and teachers completing alternative certification programs, relocating to different schools, and reentering the workforce.

Earnings

Median annual earnings of kindergarten, elementary, and secondary school teachers ranged from $33,590 to $37,890 in 1998; the lowest 10 percent, $19,710 to $24,390; the top 10 percent, $53,720 to $70,030.

According to the American Federation of Teachers, beginning teachers with a bachelor's degree earned an average of $25,700 in the 1997-98 school year. The estimated average salary of all public elementary and secondary school teachers in the 1997-98 school year was $39,300. Private school teachers generally earn less than public school teachers.

In 1998, over half of all public school teachers belonged to unions—mainly the American Federation of Teachers and the National Education Association—that bargain with school systems over wages, hours, and the terms and conditions of employment.

In some schools, teachers receive extra pay for coaching sports and working with students in extracurricular activities. Some teachers earn extra income during the summer working in the school system or in other jobs.

Chart 1. **Secondary school enrollments are expected to increase through the year 2007.**

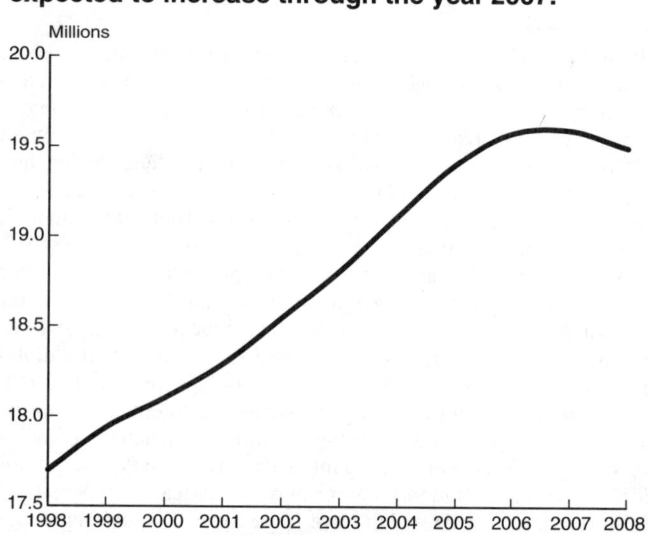

Source: National Center for Education Statistics

Chart 2. **Elementary school enrollments are expected to increase through the year 2001, then decrease.**

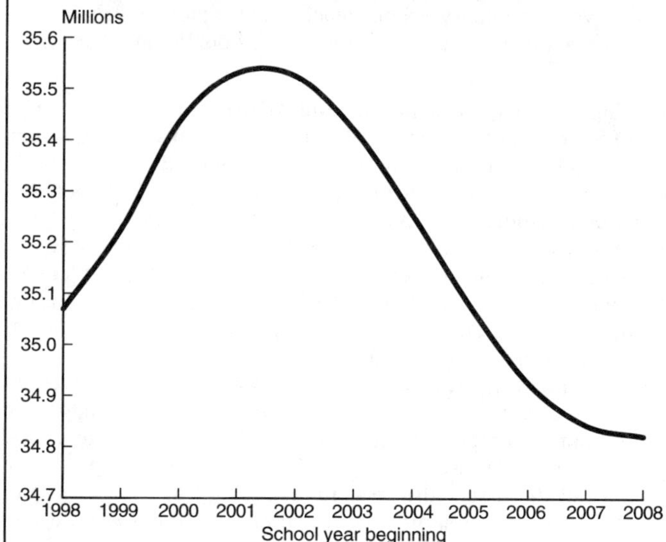

Source: National Center for Education Statistics

Related Occupations

Kindergarten, elementary, and secondary school teaching requires a variety of skills and aptitudes, including a talent for working with children; organizational, administrative, and recordkeeping abilities; research and communication skills; the power to influence, motivate, and train others; patience; and creativity. Workers in other occupations requiring some of these aptitudes include college and university faculty, counselors, education administrators, employment interviewers, librarians, preschool teachers and child-care workers, public relations specialists, sales representatives, social workers, and trainers and employee development specialists.

Sources of Additional Information

Information on licensure or certification requirements and approved teacher training institutions is available from local school systems and State departments of education.

Information on teachers' unions and education-related issues may be obtained from:

☛ American Federation of Teachers, 555 New Jersey Ave. NW, Washington, DC 20001.

☛ National Education Association, 1201 16th St. NW, Washington, DC 20036.

A list of institutions with accredited teacher education programs can be obtained from:

☛ National Council for Accreditation of Teacher Education, 2010 Massachusetts Ave. NW., Suite 500, Washington, DC 20036. Internet: **http://www.ncate.org**

For information on national teacher certification, contact:

☛ National Board for Professional Teaching Standards, 26555 Evergreen Rd., Suite 400, Southfield, MI 48076. Internet: **http://www.nbpts.org**

For information on alternative certification programs, contact:

☛ ERIC Clearinghouse on Teacher Education, 1307 New York Ave. NW., Washington, DC 20005-4701.

Special Education Teachers

(O*NET 31311A, 31311B, and 31311C)

Significant Points

- A bachelor's degree, completion of an approved teacher preparation program, and a license are required to qualify; many States require a master's degree.
- Many States offer alternative licensure programs to attract people into these jobs.
- Job openings arising from rapid employment growth and some job turnover mean excellent job prospects; many school districts report shortages of qualified teachers.

Special education teachers design and modify instruction to meet students' special needs.

Nature of the Work

Special education teachers work with children and youths who have a variety of disabilities. Most special education teachers instruct students at the elementary, middle, and secondary school level, although some teachers work with infants and toddlers. Special education teachers design and modify instruction to meet a student's special needs. Teachers also work with students who have other special instructional needs, including the gifted and talented.

The various types of disabilities delineated in Federal legislation concerning special education programs include specific learning disabilities, speech or language impairments, mental retardation, emotional disturbance, multiple disabilities, hearing impairments, orthopedic impairments, other health impairments, visual impairments, autism, deaf-blindness, and traumatic brain injury. Students are classified under one of the categories, and special education teachers are prepared to work with specific groups.

Special education teachers use various techniques to promote learning. Depending on the disability, teaching methods can include individualized instruction, problem-solving assignments, and group or individual work. Special education teachers are legally required to help develop an Individualized Education Program (IEP) for each special education student. The IEP sets personalized goals for each student and is tailored to a student's individual learning style and ability. This program includes a transition plan outlining specific steps to prepare special education students for middle school or high school, or in the case of older students, a job or postsecondary study. Teachers review the IEP with the student's parents, school administrators, and often the student's general education teacher. Teachers work closely with parents to inform them of their child's progress and suggest techniques to promote learning at home.

Teachers design curricula, assign work geared toward each student's ability, and grade papers and homework assignments. Special education teachers are involved in a student's behavioral as well as academic development. They help special education students develop emotionally, be comfortable in social situations, and be aware of socially acceptable behavior. Preparing special education students for daily life after graduation is an important aspect of the job. Teachers help students learn routine skills, such as balancing a checkbook, or provide them with career counseling.

As schools become more inclusive, special education teachers and general education teachers increasingly work together in general education classrooms. Special education teachers help general educators adapt curriculum materials and teaching techniques to meet the needs of disabled students. They coordinate the work of teachers, teacher assistants, and themselves to meet the requirements of inclusive special education programs, in addition to teaching special education students. A large part of a special education teacher's job involves interacting with others. They communicate frequently with parents, social workers, school psychologists, occupational and physical therapists, school administrators, and other teachers.

Special education teachers work in a variety of settings. Some have their own classrooms and teach only special education students; others work as special education resource teachers and offer individualized help to students in general education classrooms; and others teach with general education teachers in classes composed of both general and special education students. Some teachers work in a resource room, where special education students work several hours a day, separate from their general education classroom. A significantly smaller proportion of special education teachers works in residential facilities or tutor students in homebound or hospital environments.

Early identification of a child with special needs is another important part of a special education teacher's job. Early intervention is essential in educating these children. Special education teachers who work with infants usually travel to the child's home to work with the child and his or her parents.

Technology is playing an increasingly important role in special education. Special education teachers use specialized equipment such as computers with synthesized speech, interactive educational software programs, and audiotapes.

Working Conditions

Special education teachers enjoy the challenge of working with these students and the opportunity to establish meaningful relationships. Although helping students with disabilities can be highly rewarding, the work can also be emotionally and physically draining. Special education teachers are under considerable stress due to heavy workloads and tedious administrative tasks. They must produce a substantial amount of paperwork documenting each student's progress. Exacerbating this stress is the threat of litigation by students' parents if correct procedures are not followed, or if the parent feels their child is not receiving an adequate education. The physical and emotional demands of the job cause some special education teachers to leave the occupation.

Many schools offer year-round education for special education students, but most special education teachers work the traditional 10-month school year.

Employment

Special education teachers held about 406,000 jobs in 1998. The majority of special education teachers were employed in elementary, middle, and secondary public schools. The rest worked in separate educational facilities—public or private—residential facilities, or in homebound or hospital environments.

Training, Other Qualifications, and Advancement

All 50 States and the District of Columbia require special education teachers to be licensed. Special education licensure varies by State. In many States, special education teachers receive a general education credential to teach kindergarten through grade 12. These teachers train in a specialty, such as learning disabilities or behavioral disorders. Some States offer general special education licenses, others license several different specialties within special education, while others require teachers to first obtain a general education license and then an additional license in special education. State boards of education or a licensure advisory committee usually grant licenses.

All States require a bachelor's degree and completion of an approved teacher preparation program with a prescribed number of subject and education credits and supervised practice teaching. Many States require special education teachers to obtain a master's degree in special education, involving at least one year of additional coursework, including a specialization, beyond the bachelor's degree.

Some States have reciprocity agreements allowing special education teachers to transfer their license from one State to another, but many still require special education teachers to pass licensing requirements for that State. In the future, employers may recognize certification or standards offered by national organization.

Many colleges and universities across the United States offer programs in special education, including undergraduate, master's, and doctoral programs. Special education teachers usually undergo longer periods of training than general education teachers. Most bachelor's degree programs are 4-year programs including general and specialized courses in special education. However, an increasing number of institutions require a fifth year or other postbaccalaureate preparation. Courses include educational psychology, legal issues of special education, child growth and development, and knowledge and skills needed for teaching students with disabilities. Some programs require specialization. Others offer generalized special education degrees, or study in several specialized areas. The last year of the program is usually spent student teaching in a classroom supervised by a certified teacher.

Alternative and emergency licenses are available in many States, due to the need to fill special education teaching positions. Alternative licenses are designed to bring college graduates and those changing careers into teaching more quickly. Requirements for an alternative license may be less stringent than for a regular license and vary by State. In some programs, individuals begin teaching quickly under a provisional license. They can obtain a regular license by teaching under the supervision of licensed teachers for a period of 1 to 2 years while taking education courses. Emergency licenses are granted when States have difficulty finding licensed special education teachers to fill positions.

Special education teachers must be patient, able to motivate students, understanding of their students' special needs, and accepting of differences in others. Teachers must be creative and apply different types of teaching methods to reach students who are having difficulty. Communication and cooperation are essential traits because special education teachers spend a great deal of time interacting with others, including students, parents, and school faculty and administrators.

Special education teachers can advance to become supervisors or administrators. They may also earn advanced degrees and become instructors in colleges that prepare others for special education teaching. In some school systems, highly experienced teachers can become mentor teachers to less experienced ones; they provide guidance to these teachers while maintaining a light teaching load.

Job Outlook

Employment of special education teachers is expected to increase faster than the average for all occupations through 2008, spurred by continued growth in the number of special education students needing services, legislation emphasizing training and employment for individuals with disabilities, and educational reform. Turnover will lead to additional job openings as special education teachers switch to general education or change careers altogether. Rapid employment growth and job turnover should result in a very favorable job market.

Special education teachers have excellent job prospects, as many school districts report shortages of qualified teachers. Job outlook varies by geographic area and specialty. Positions in rural areas and inner cities are more plentiful than job openings in suburban or wealthy urban areas. In addition, job opportunities may be better in certain specialties—such as speech or language impairments, and learning disabilities—because of large enrollment increases of special education students classified under these disability categories. Legislation encouraging early intervention and special education for infants, toddlers, and preschoolers has created a need for early childhood special education teachers. Special education teachers who are bilingual or have multicultural experience are also needed to work with an increasingly diverse student population.

The number of students requiring special education services has been steadily increasing, as indicated by the accompanying chart. This trend is expected to continue because of legislation which expanded the age range of children receiving special education services to include those from birth to age 21; medical advances resulting in more survivors of accidents and illness; the postponement of childbirth by more women, resulting in a greater number of premature births and children born with birth defects; and growth in the general population.

Earnings

Median annual earnings of special education teachers in 1998 were $37,850. The middle 50 percent earned between $30,410 and $48,390. The lowest 10 percent earned less than $25,450; the highest 10 percent, more than $78,030.

The number of special education students, age 21 or younger served by federally supported programs, grew by 1.6 million between 1984 and 1996.

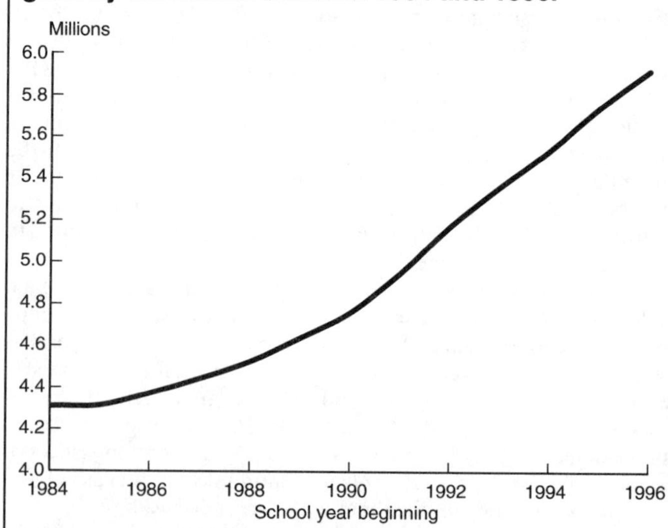

Source: National Center for Education Statistics

In 1998, about 58 percent of special education teachers belonged to unions—mainly the American Federation of Teachers and the National Education Association—that bargain with school systems over wages, hours, and the terms and conditions of employment.

In some schools, teachers receive extra pay for coaching sports and working with students in extracurricular activities. Some teachers earn extra income during the summer, working in the school system or in other jobs.

Related Occupations

Special education teachers work with students who have disabilities and special needs. Other occupations involved with the identification, evaluation, and development of students with disabilities include school psychologists, social workers, speech pathologists, rehabilitation counselors, adapted physical education teachers, special education technology specialists, and occupational, physical, creative arts, and recreational therapists.

Sources of Additional Information

For information on professions related to early intervention and education for children with disabilities, a list of accredited schools, teacher certification, financial aid information, and general information on related personnel issues—including recruitment, retention, and supply of and demand for special education professionals—contact:

☛ National Clearinghouse for Professions in Special Education, Council for Exceptional Children, 1920 Association Dr., Reston, VA 20191-1589. Internet: **http://www.special-ed-careers.org**

To learn more about the special education teacher certification and licensing requirements in your State, contact your State's department of education.

Health Diagnosticians

Chiropractors

(O*NET 32113)

Significant Points

- Employment of chiropractors is expected to increase rapidly and job prospects should be good.
- Chiropractic care of back, neck, extremities, and other joint damage has become more accepted as a result of recent research and changing attitudes.
- In chiropractic, as in other types of independent practice, earnings are relatively low in the beginning, but increase as the practice grows.

Nature of the Work

Chiropractors, also known as doctors of chiropractic or chiropractic physicians, diagnose and treat patients whose health problems are associated with the body's muscular, nervous, and skeletal systems, especially the spine. Chiropractors believe interference with these systems impairs normal functions and lowers resistance to disease. They also hold that spinal or vertebral dysfunction alters many important body functions by affecting the nervous system, and that skeletal imbalance through joint or articular dysfunction, especially in the spine, can cause pain.

The chiropractic approach to health care is holistic, stressing the patient's overall health and wellness. It recognizes that many factors affect health, including exercise, diet, rest, environment, and heredity. Chiropractors use natural, drugless, nonsurgical health treatments, and rely on the body's inherent recuperative abilities. They also recommend lifestyle changes—in eating, exercise, and sleeping habits, for example—to their patients. When appropriate, chiropractors consult with and refer patients to other health practitioners.

Like other health practitioners, chiropractors follow a standard routine to secure the information needed for diagnosis and treatment. They take the patient's medical history, conduct physical, neurological, and orthopedic examinations, and may order laboratory tests. X rays and other diagnostic images are important tools because of the emphasis on the spine and its proper function. Chiropractors also employ a postural and spinal analysis common to chiropractic diagnosis.

In cases in which difficulties can be traced to involvement of musculoskeletal structures, chiropractors manually adjust the spinal column. Many chiropractors use water, light, massage, ultrasound, electric, and heat therapy. They may also apply supports such as straps, tapes, and braces. Chiropractors counsel patients about wellness concepts such as nutrition, exercise, lifestyle changes, and stress management, but do not prescribe drugs or perform surgery.

Some chiropractors specialize in sports injuries, neurology, orthopedics, nutrition, internal disorders, or diagnostic imaging.

Many chiropractors are solo or group practitioners who also have the administrative responsibilities of running a practice. In larger offices, chiropractors delegate these tasks to office managers and chiropractic assistants. Chiropractors in private practice are responsible for developing a patient base, hiring employees, and keeping records.

Working Conditions

Chiropractors work in clean, comfortable offices. The average workweek is about 40 hours, although longer hours are not uncommon. Solo practitioners set their own hours, but may work evenings or weekends to accommodate patients.

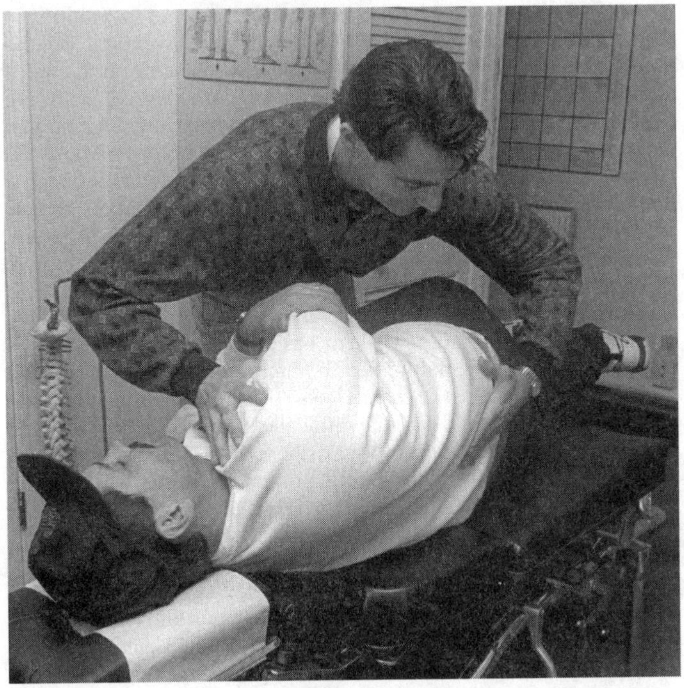

Most chiropractors are solo practitioners, treating patients and running the practice.

Chiropractors, like other health practitioners, are sometimes on their feet for long periods of time. Chiropractors who take x rays employ appropriate precautions against the dangers of repeated exposure to radiation.

Employment

Chiropractors held about 46,000 jobs in 1998. Most chiropractors are in solo practice, although some are in group practice or work for other chiropractors. A small number teach, conduct research at chiropractic institutions, or work in hospitals and clinics.

Many chiropractors are located in small communities. There are geographic imbalances in the distribution of chiropractors, in part because many establish practices close to chiropractic institutions.

Training, Other Qualifications, and Advancement

All States and the District of Columbia regulate the practice of chiropractic and grant licenses to chiropractors who meet educational and examination requirements established by the State. Chiropractors can only practice in States where they are licensed. Some States have agreements permitting chiropractors licensed in one State to obtain a license in another without further examination, provided that educational, examination, and practice credentials meet State specifications.

Most State boards require at least 2 years of undergraduate education, and an increasing number require a 4-year bachelor's degree. All boards require completion of a 4-year chiropractic college course at an accredited program leading to the Doctor of Chiropractic degree.

For licensure, most State boards recognize either all or part of the four-part test administered by the National Board of Chiropractic Examiners. State examinations may supplement the National Board tests, depending on State requirements.

To maintain licensure, almost all States require completion of a specified number of hours of continuing education each year. Continuing education programs are offered by accredited chiropractic programs and institutions, and chiropractic associations. Special councils within some chiropractic associations also offer programs leading to clinical specialty certification, called "diplomate" certification, in areas such as orthopedics, neurology, sports injuries, occupational and industrial health, nutrition, diagnostic imaging, thermography, and internal disorders.

In 1998, there were 16 chiropractic programs and institutions in the United States accredited by the Council on Chiropractic Education. All required applicants to have at least 60 semester hours of undergraduate study leading toward a bachelor's degree, including courses in English, the social sciences or humanities, organic and inorganic chemistry, biology, physics, and psychology. Many applicants have a bachelor's degree, which may eventually become the minimum entry requirement. Several chiropractic colleges offer prechiropractic study, as well as a bachelor's degree program. Recognition of prechiropractic education offered by chiropractic colleges varies among the State boards.

During the first 2 years, most chiropractic programs emphasize classroom and laboratory work in basic science subjects such as anatomy, physiology, public health, microbiology, pathology, and biochemistry. The last 2 years stress courses in manipulation and spinal adjustments, and provide clinical experience in physical and laboratory diagnosis, neurology, orthopedics, geriatrics, physiotherapy, and nutrition. Chiropractic programs and institutions grant the degree of Doctor of Chiropractic (D.C.).

Chiropractic requires keen observation to detect physical abnormalities. It also takes considerable hand dexterity to perform adjustments, but not unusual strength or endurance. Chiropractors should be able to work independently and handle responsibility. As in other health-related occupations, empathy, understanding, and the desire to help others are good qualities for dealing effectively with patients.

Newly licensed chiropractors can set up a new practice, purchase an established one, or enter into partnership with an established practitioner. They may also take a salaried position with an established chiropractor, a group practice, or a health care facility.

Job Outlook

Job prospects are expected to be good for persons who enter the practice of chiropractic. Employment of chiropractors is expected to grow faster than the average for all occupations through the year 2008 as consumer demand for alternative medicine grows. Chiropractors emphasize the importance of healthy lifestyles and do not prescribe drugs or perform surgery. As a result, chiropractic care is appealing to many health-conscious Americans. Chiropractic treatment of back, neck, extremities, and other joint damage has become more accepted as a result of recent research and changing attitudes about alternative health care practices. The rapidly expanding older population, with their increased likelihood of mechanical and structural problems, will also increase demand.

Demand for chiropractic treatment is also related to the ability of patients to pay, either directly or through health insurance. Although more insurance plans now cover chiropractic services, the extent of such coverage varies among plans. Increasingly, chiropractors must educate communities about the benefits of chiropractic care in order to establish a successful practice.

In this occupation, replacement needs arise almost entirely from retirements. Chiropractors usually remain in the occupation until they retire; few transfer to other occupations. Establishing a new practice will be easiest in areas with a low concentration of chiropractors.

Earnings

Median annual earnings of salaried chiropractors were $63,930 in 1998. The middle 50 percent earned between $36,820 and $110,820 a year.

Self-employed chiropractors usually earn more than salaried chiropractors. According to the American Chiropractic Association, average income for all chiropractors, including the self-employed, was about $86,500, after expenses, in 1997. In chiropractic, as in other types of independent practice, earnings are relatively low in the beginning, and increase as the practice grows. Earnings are also influenced by the characteristics and qualifications of the practitioner, and geographic location. Self-employed chiropractors must provide for their own health insurance and retirement.

Related Occupations

Chiropractors treat and work to prevent bodily disorders and injuries. So do physicians, dentists, optometrists, podiatrists, veterinarians, occupational therapists, and physical therapists.

Sources of Additional Information

General information on chiropractic as a career is available from:

☛ American Chiropractic Association, 1701 Clarendon Blvd., Arlington, VA 22209. Internet: **http://www.amerchiro.org**

☛ International Chiropractors Association, 1110 North Glebe Rd., Suite 1000, Arlington, VA 22201. Internet: **http://www.chiropractic.org**

☛ World Chiropractic Alliance, 2950 N. Dobson Rd., Suite 1, Chandler, AZ 85224-1802.

☛ Dynamic Chiropractic, P.O. Box 6100, Huntington, CA 92615. Internet: **http://www.chiroweb.com**

For a list of chiropractic programs and institutions, as well as general information on chiropractic education, contact:

☛ Council on Chiropractic Education, 7975 North Hayden Rd., Suite A-210, Scottsdale, AZ 85258.

For information on State education and licensure requirements, contact:

☛ Federation of Chiropractic Licensing Boards, 901 54th Ave., Suite 101, Greeley, CO 80634. Internet: **http://www.fclb.org/fclb**

For information on requirements for admission to a specific chiropractic college, as well as scholarship and loan information, contact the admissions office of the individual college.

Dentists

(O*NET 32105A, 32105B, 32105D, 32105F, and 32105G)

Significant Points

- Most dentists have at least 8 years of education beyond high school.
- Employment of dentists is expected to grow slower than the average as young people are troubled less by tooth decay.
- Dental care will focus more on prevention, including teaching people how to care better for their teeth.

Nature of the Work

Dentists diagnose, prevent, and treat teeth and tissue problems. They remove decay, fill cavities, examine x rays, place protective plastic sealants on children's teeth, straighten teeth, and repair fractured teeth. They also perform corrective surgery on gums and supporting bones to treat gum diseases. Dentists extract teeth and make models and measurements for dentures to replace missing teeth. They provide instruction on diet, brushing, flossing, the use of fluorides, and other aspects of dental care, as well. They also administer anesthetics and write prescriptions for antibiotics and other medications.

Dentists use a variety of equipment, including x-ray machines, drills, and instruments such as mouth mirrors, probes, forceps, brushes, and scalpels. They also wear masks, gloves, and safety glasses to protect themselves and their patients from infectious diseases.

Dentists in private practice oversee a variety of administrative tasks, including bookkeeping, and buying equipment and supplies. They may employ and supervise dental hygienists, dental assistants, dental laboratory technicians, and receptionists. (These occupations are described elsewhere in the *Handbook*.)

Most dentists are general practitioners, handling a variety of dental needs. Other dentists practice in one of eight specialty areas. *Orthodontists*, the largest group of specialists, straighten teeth. The next largest group, *oral and maxillofacial surgeons*, operate on the mouth and jaws. The remainder may specialize as *pediatric dentists* (dentistry for children); *periodontists* (treating gums and bone supporting the teeth); *prosthodontists* (making artificial teeth or dentures); *endodontists* (root canal therapy); *public health dentists*; and *oral pathologists* (studying oral diseases).

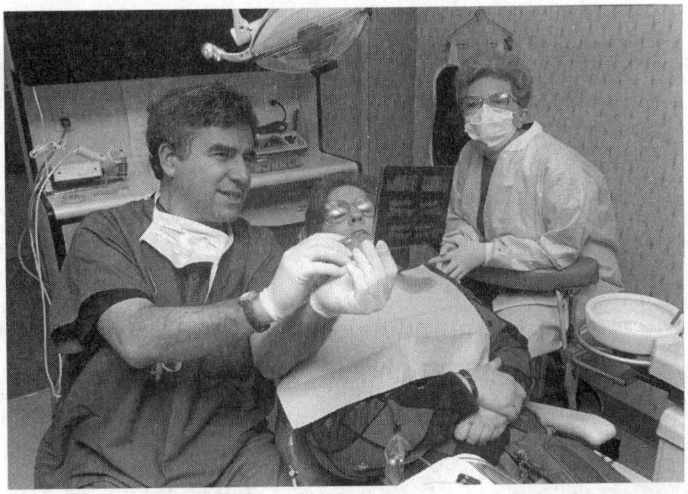

Dentists will focus on preventive care, teaching people how to better care for their teeth.

Working Conditions

Most dentists work 4 or 5 days a week. Some work evenings and weekends to meet their patients' needs. Most full-time dentists work about 40 hours a week, but others work more. Initially, dentists may work more hours as they establish their practice. Experienced dentists often work fewer hours. A considerable number continue in part-time practice well beyond the usual retirement age.

Most dentists are "solo practitioners," meaning they own their own businesses and work alone or with a small staff. Some dentists have partners, and a few work for other dentists as associate dentists.

Employment

Dentists held about 160,000 jobs in 1998. About 9 out of 10 dentists are in private practice. Others work in private and public hospitals and clinics, the Federal Government, and in dental research.

Training, Other Qualifications, and Advancement

All 50 States and the District of Columbia require dentists to be licensed. In most States, a candidate must graduate from a dental school accredited by the American Dental Association's Commission on Dental Accreditation, and pass written and practical examinations to qualify for a license. Candidates may fulfill the written part of the State licensing by passing the National Board Dental Examinations. Individual States or regional testing agencies give the written or practical examinations.

Currently, about 17 States require dentists to obtain a specialty license before practicing as a specialist. Requirements include 2 to 4 years of postgraduate education and, in some cases, completion of a special State examination. Most State licenses permit dentists to engage in both general and specialized practice. Dentists who want to teach or do research usually spend an additional 2 to 5 years in advanced dental training, in programs operated by dental schools or hospitals.

Dental schools require a minimum of 2 years of college-level predental education. However, most dental students have at least a bachelor's degree. Predental education emphasizes course work in the sciences.

All dental schools require applicants to take the Dental Admissions Test (DAT). When selecting students, schools consider scores earned on the DAT, the applicants' grade point average, and information gathered through recommendations and interviews.

Dental school usually lasts 4 academic years. Studies begin with classroom instruction and laboratory work in basic sciences including anatomy, microbiology, biochemistry, and physiology. Beginning courses in clinical sciences, including laboratory techniques, are also provided at this time. During the last 2 years, students treat patients, usually in dental clinics, under the supervision of licensed dentists.

Most dental schools award the degree of Doctor of Dental Surgery (D.D.S.). The rest award an equivalent degree, Doctor of Dental Medicine (D.M.D.).

Dentistry requires diagnostic ability and manual skills. Dentists should have good visual memory, excellent judgment of space and shape, a high degree of manual dexterity, and scientific ability. Good business sense, self-discipline, and communication skills are helpful for success in private practice. High school and college students who want to become dentists should take courses in biology, chemistry, physics, health, and mathematics.

Some dental school graduates work for established dentists as associates for a year or two in order to gain experience and save money to equip an office of their own. Most dental school graduates, however, purchase an established practice or open a new practice immediately after graduation. Each year about one-fourth to one-third of new graduates enroll in postgraduate training programs to prepare for a dental specialty.

Job Outlook

Employment of dentists is expected to grow slower than the average for all occupations through 2008. Although employment growth will provide some job opportunities, most jobs will result from the need to replace the large number of dentists projected to retire. Job prospects should be good if the number of dental school graduates does not grow significantly, thus keeping the supply of newly qualified dentists near current levels.

Demand for dental care should grow substantially through 2008. As members of the baby-boom generation advance into middle age, a large number will need maintenance on complicated dental work, such as bridges. In addition, elderly people are more likely to retain their teeth than were their predecessors, so they will require much more care than in the past. The younger generation will continue to need preventive check-ups despite treatments such as fluoridation of the water supply, which decreases the incidence of tooth decay.

Dental care will focus more on prevention, including teaching people how to care better for their teeth. Dentists will increasingly provide care that is aimed at preventing tooth loss—rather than just providing treatments, such as fillings. Improvements in dental technology will also allow dentists to provide more effective and less painful treatment to their patients.

However, the employment of dentists is not expected to grow as rapidly as the demand for dental services. As their practices expand, dentists are likely to hire more dental hygienists and dental assistants to handle routine services.

Earnings

Median annual earnings of salaried dentists were $110,160 in 1998. Earnings vary according to number of years in practice, location, hours worked, and specialty.

Self-employed dentists in private practice tend to earn more than salaried dentists. A relatively large proportion of dentists is self-employed. Like other business owners, these dentists must provide their own health insurance, life insurance, and retirement benefits.

Related Occupations

Dentists examine, diagnose, prevent, and treat diseases and abnormalities. So do clinical psychologists, optometrists, physicians, chiropractors, veterinarians, and podiatrists.

Sources of Additional Information

For information on dentistry as a career and a list of accredited dental schools, contact:

☛ American Dental Association, Commission on Dental Accreditation, 211 E. Chicago Ave., Chicago, IL 60611. Internet: **http://www.ada.org**

☛ American Association of Dental Schools, 1625 Massachusetts Ave. NW., Washington, DC 20036. Internet: **http://www.aads.jhu.edu**

The American Dental Association will also furnish a list of State boards of dental examiners. Persons interested in practicing dentistry should obtain the requirements for licensure from the board of dental examiners of the State in which they plan to work.

Prospective dental students should contact the office of student financial aid at the schools to which they apply, for information on scholarships, grants, and loans, including Federal financial aid.

Optometrists

(O*NET 32108)

Significant Points

- All States and the District of Columbia require that optometrists be licensed, which requires a Doctor of Optometry degree from an accredited optometry school and passing both a written and a clinical State board examination.
- Employment growth will be fastest in retail optical stores and outpatient clinics.
- Optometrists usually remain in practice until they retire, so job openings arising from replacement needs are low.

Nature of the Work

Over half of the people in the United States wear glasses or contact lenses. Optometrists (doctors of optometry, also known as O.D.'s) provide most primary vision care.

Optometrists examine people's eyes to diagnose vision problems and eye diseases. They use instruments and observation to examine eye health and to test patients' visual acuity, depth and color perception, and their ability to focus and coordinate the eyes. They analyze test results and develop a treatment plan. Optometrists prescribe eyeglasses and contact lenses, and provide vision therapy and low vision rehabilitation. They administer drugs to patients to aid in the diagnosis of eye vision problems and prescribe drugs to treat some eye diseases. Optometrists often provide pre- and post-operative care to cataract, laser vision correction, and other eye surgery patients. They also diagnose conditions due to systemic diseases such as diabetes and high blood pressure, and refer patients to other health practitioners as needed.

Optometrists should not be confused with ophthalmologists or dispensing opticians. Ophthalmologists are physicians who perform eye surgery, and diagnose and treat eye diseases and injuries. Like optometrists, they also examine eyes and prescribe eyeglasses and contact lenses. Dispensing opticians fit and adjust eyeglasses and in some States may fit contact lenses according to prescriptions written by ophthalmologists or optometrists. (See statements on physicians and dispensing opticians elsewhere in the *Handbook*.)

Most optometrists are in general practice. Some specialize in work with the elderly, children, or partially sighted persons who need specialized visual devices. Others develop and implement ways to protect workers' eyes from on-the-job strain or injury. Some specialize in contact lenses, sports vision, or vision therapy. A few teach optometry, perform research, or consult.

Most optometrists are private practitioners who also handle the business aspects of running an office, such as developing a patient base, hiring employees, keeping records, and ordering equipment and supplies. Optometrists who operate franchise optical stores may also have some of these duties.

Working Conditions

Optometrists work in places—usually their own offices—which are clean, well lighted, and comfortable. Most full-time optometrists work about 40 hours a week. Many work Saturdays and evenings

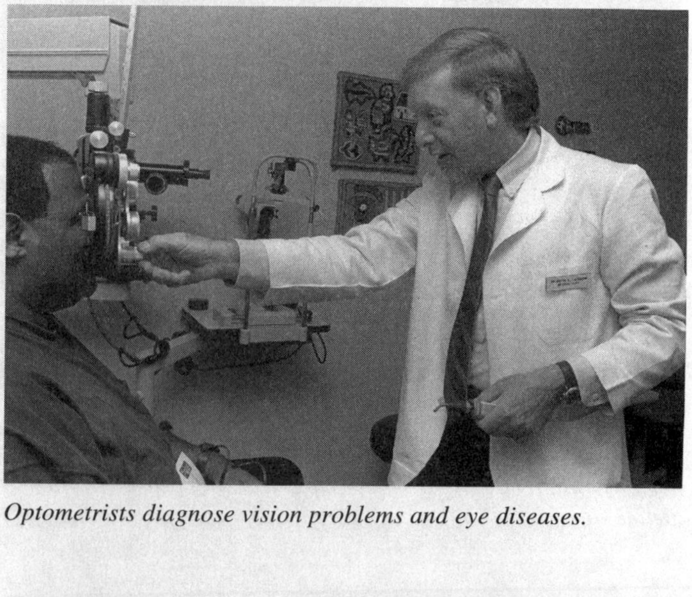

Optometrists diagnose vision problems and eye diseases.

to suit the needs of patients. Emergency calls, once uncommon, have increased with the passage of therapeutic drug laws expanding optometrists' ability to prescribe medications.

Employment

Optometrists held about 38,000 jobs in 1998. The number of jobs is greater than the number of practicing optometrists because some optometrists hold two or more jobs. For example, an optometrist may have a private practice, but also work in another practice, clinic, or vision care center. According to the American Optometric Association, about two-thirds of practicing optometrists are in private practice.

Although many optometrists practice alone, a growing number are in a partnership or group practice. Some optometrists work as salaried employees of other optometrists or of ophthalmologists, hospitals, health maintenance organizations (HMO's), or retail optical stores. A small number of optometrists are consultants for industrial safety programs, insurance companies, manufacturers of ophthalmic products, HMO's, and others.

Training, Other Qualifications, and Advancement

All States and the District of Columbia require that optometrists be licensed. Applicants for a license must have a Doctor of Optometry degree from an accredited optometry school and pass both a written and a clinical State board examination. In many States, applicants can substitute the examinations of the National Board of Examiners in Optometry, usually taken during the student's academic career, for part or all of the written examination. Licenses are renewed every 1 to 3 years and in all States, continuing education credits are needed for renewal.

The Doctor of Optometry degree requires completion of a 4-year program at an accredited optometry school preceded by at least 3 years of preoptometric study at an accredited college or university (most optometry students hold a bachelor's degree or higher). In 1999, 17 U.S. schools and colleges of optometry held an accredited status with the Council on Optometric Education of the American Optometric Association.

Requirements for admission to schools of optometry include courses in English, mathematics, physics, chemistry, and biology. A few schools require or recommend courses in psychology, history, sociology, speech, or business. Applicants must take the Optometry Admissions Test, which measures academic ability and scientific comprehension. Most applicants take the test after their sophomore or junior year. Competition for admission is keen.

Optometry programs include classroom and laboratory study of health and visual sciences, as well as clinical training in the diagnosis and treatment of eye disorders. Included are courses in pharmacology, optics, vision science, biochemistry, and systemic disease.

Business ability, self-discipline, and the ability to deal tactfully with patients are important for success. The work of optometrists requires attention to detail and good manual dexterity.

Optometrists wishing to teach or do research may study for a master's or Ph.D. degree in visual science, physiological optics, neurophysiology, public health, health administration, health information and communication, or health education. One-year postgraduate clinical residency programs are available for optometrists who wish to specialize in any of the following: family practice optometry, pediatric optometry, geriatric optometry, vision therapy, contact lenses, hospital based optometry, primary care optometry, or ocular disease.

Job Outlook

Employment of optometrists is expected to grow about as fast as the average for all occupations through 2008 in response to the vision care needs of a growing and aging population. As baby boomers age, they will be more likely to visit optometrists and ophthalmologists because of the onset of vision problems in middle age, including computer-related vision problems. The demand for optometric services will also increase because of growth in the oldest age group, with their increased likelihood of cataracts, glaucoma, diabetes, and hypertension. Employment of optometrists will also grow due to greater recognition of the importance of vision care, rising personal incomes, and growth in employee vision care plans. Employment growth will be fastest in retail optical stores and outpatient clinics.

Employment of optometrists would grow more rapidly were it not for anticipated productivity gains that will allow each optometrist to see more patients. These gains will result from greater use of optometric assistants and other support personnel, and the introduction of new equipment and procedures. New surgical procedures using lasers are available that can correct some vision problems, but they remain expensive.

In addition to growth, the need to replace optometrists who leave the occupation will create employment opportunities. Relatively few opportunities from this source are expected, however, because most optometrists continue to practice until they retire; few transfer to other occupations.

Earnings

Median annual earnings of salaried optometrists were $68,500 in 1998. The middle 50 percent earned between $43,750 and $93,700 a year. The lowest 10 percent earned less than $24,820 and the highest 10 percent earned more than $123,770 a year. Salaried optometrists tend to earn more initially than do optometrists who set up their own independent practice. In the long run, those in private practice usually earn more.

According to the American Optometric Association, new optometry graduates in their first year of practice earned median net incomes of $55,000 in 1998. Overall, optometrists earned median net incomes of $92,000.

Related Occupations

Workers in other occupations who apply scientific knowledge to prevent, diagnose, and treat disorders and injuries are chiropractors, dentists, physicians, podiatrists, veterinarians, speech-language pathologists, and audiologists.

Sources of Additional Information

For information on optometry as a career and a listing of accredited optometric educational institutions, as well as required preoptometry courses, contact:

☛ American Optometric Association, Educational Services, 243 North Lindbergh Blvd., St. Louis, MO 63141-7881. Internet: **http://www.aoanet.org**

☛ Association of Schools and Colleges of Optometry, 6110 Executive Blvd., Suite 510, Rockville, MD 20852. Internet: **http://www.opted.org**

The Board of Optometry in each State can supply information on licensing requirements.

For information on specific admission requirements and sources of financial aid, contact the admissions officer of individual optometry schools.

Physicians

(O*NET 32102A, 32102B, 32102E, 32102F, 32102J, and 32102U)

Significant Points

- Physicians are much more likely to work as salaried employees of group medical practices, clinics, or health care networks than in the past.
- Formal education and training requirements are among the longest of any occupation, but earnings are among the highest.

Nature of the Work

Physicians serve a fundamental role in our society and have an effect upon all our lives. They diagnose illnesses and prescribe and administer treatment for people suffering from injury or disease. Physicians examine patients, obtain medical histories, and order, perform, and interpret diagnostic tests. They counsel patients on diet, hygiene, and preventive health care.

There are two types of physicians: The M.D.—Doctor of Medicine—and the D.O.—Doctor of Osteopathic Medicine. M.D.s are also known as allopathic physicians. While both M.D.s and D.O.s may use all accepted methods of treatment, including drugs and surgery, D.O.s place special emphasis on the body's musculoskeletal system, preventive medicine, and holistic patient care.

About a third of M.D.s—and more than half of D.O.s—are primary care physicians. They practice general and family medicine, general internal medicine, or general pediatrics and are usually the first health professionals patients consult. Primary care physicians tend to see the same patients on a regular basis for preventive care and to treat a variety of ailments. General and family practitioners emphasize comprehensive health care for patients of all ages and for the family as a group. Those in general internal medicine provide care mainly for adults who may have problems associated with the body's organs. General pediatricians focus on the whole range of children's health issues. When appropriate, primary care physicians refer patients to specialists, who are experts in medical fields such as obstetrics and gynecology, cardiology, psychiatry, or surgery (table 1).

Table 1. Percent distribution of M.D.s by specialty, 1997

	Percent
Total	100.0
Primary care	
Internal medicine	17.0
General and family practice	10.7
Pediatrics	7.3
Medical specialties	
Allergy	.5
Cardiovascular diseases	2.5
Dermatology	1.2
Gastroenterology	1.3
Obstetrics and gynecology	5.2
Pediatric cardiology	.2
Pulmonary diseases	.9
Surgical specialties	
Colon and rectal surgery	.1
General surgery	5.4
Neurological surgery	.6
Ophthalmology	2.3
Orthopedic surgery	3.0
Otolaryngology	1.2
Plastic surgery	.8
Thoracic surgery	.3
Urological surgery	1.3
Other specialties	
Aerospace medicine	.1
Anesthesiology	4.4
Child psychiatry	.7
Diagnostic radiology	2.6
Emergency medicine	2.7
Forensic pathology	.1
General preventive medicine	.2
Neurology	1.6
Nuclear medicine	.2
Occupational medicine	.4
Pathology	2.4
Physical medicine and rehabilitation	.8
Psychiatry	5.2
Public health	.2
Radiology	1.1
Radiation oncology	.5
Other specialty	.8
Unspecified/unknown/inactive	14.1

SOURCE: American Medical Association

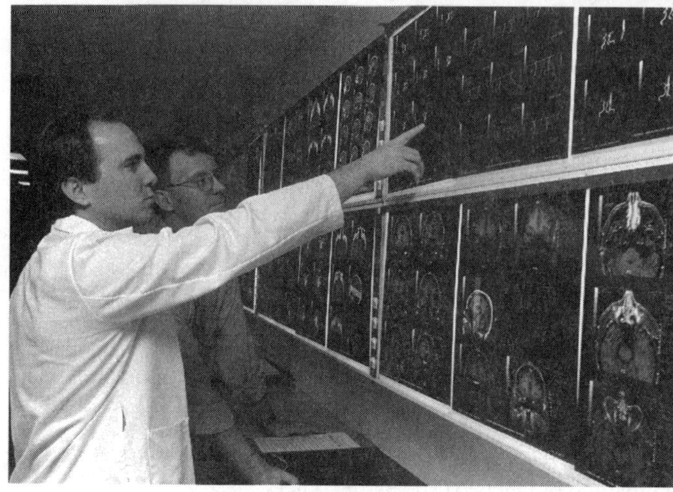

Many physicians work long, irregular hours.

D.O.s are more likely to be primary care providers than M.D.s, although they can be found in all specialties. Over half of D.O.s practice general or family medicine, general internal medicine, or general pediatrics. Common specialties for D.O.s include emergency medicine, anesthesiology, obstetrics and gynecology, psychiatry, and surgery.

Working Conditions

Many physicians work long, irregular hours. More than one-third of all full-time physicians worked 60 hours or more a week in 1998. They must travel frequently between office and hospital to care for their patients. Increasingly, physicians practice in groups or health care organizations that provide back-up coverage and allow for more time off. These physicians often work as part of a team coordinating care for a population of patients; they are less independent than solo practitioners of the past. Physicians who are on-call deal with many patients' concerns over the phone, and may make emergency visits to hospitals or nursing homes.

Employment

Physicians (M.D.s and D.O.s) held about 577,000 jobs in 1998. About 7 out of 10 were in office-based practice, including clinics and Health Maintenance Organizations (HMOs); about 2 out of 10 were employed by hospitals. Others practiced in the Federal Government, most in Department of Veterans Affairs hospitals and clinics or in the Public Health Service of the Department of Health and Human Services.

A growing number of physicians are partners or salaried employees of group practices. Organized as clinics or as groups of physicians, medical groups can afford expensive medical equipment and realize other business advantages. Also, hospitals are integrating physician practices into health care networks that provide a continuum of care both inside and outside the hospital setting.

The New England and Middle Atlantic States have the highest ratio of physicians to population; the South Central States, the lowest. D.O.s are more likely than M.D.s to practice in small cities and towns and in rural areas. M.D.s tend to locate in urban areas, close to hospital and educational centers.

Training and Other Qualifications

It takes many years of education and training to become a physician: 4 years of undergraduate school, 4 years of medical school, and 3 to 8 years of internship and residency, depending on the specialty selected. A few medical schools offer a combined undergraduate and medical school program that lasts 6 years instead of the customary 8 years.

Premedical students must complete undergraduate work in physics, biology, mathematics, English, and inorganic and organic chemistry. Students also take courses in the humanities and the social sciences. Some students also volunteer at local hospitals or clinics to gain practical experience in the health professions.

The minimum educational requirement for entry to a medical or osteopathic school is 3 years of college; most applicants, however, have at least a bachelor's degree, and many have advanced degrees. There are 144 medical schools in the United States—125 teach allopathic medicine and award a Doctor of Medicine (M.D.) degree; 19 teach osteopathic medicine and award the Doctor of Osteopathic Medicine (D.O.) degree. Acceptance to medical school is very competitive. Applicants must submit transcripts, scores from the Medical College Admission Test, and letters of recommendation. Schools also consider character, personality, leadership qualities, and participation in extracurricular activities. Most schools require an interview with members of the admissions committee.

Students spend most of the first 2 years of medical school in laboratories and classrooms taking courses such as anatomy, biochemistry, physiology, pharmacology, psychology, microbiology, pathology, medical ethics, and laws governing medicine. They also learn to take medical histories, examine patients, and diagnose illness. During the last 2 years, students work with patients under the supervision of experienced physicians in hospitals and clinics to learn acute, chronic, preventive, and rehabilitative care. Through rotations in internal medicine, family practice, obstetrics and gynecology, pediatrics, psychiatry, and surgery, they gain experience in the diagnosis and treatment of illness.

Following medical school, almost all M.D.s enter a residency—graduate medical education in a specialty that takes the form of paid on-the-job training, usually in a hospital. Most D.O.s serve a 12-month rotating internship after graduation before entering a residency which may last 2 to 6 years. Physicians may benefit from residencies in managed care settings by gaining experience with this increasingly common type of medical practice.

All States, the District of Columbia, and U.S. territories license physicians. To be licensed, physicians must graduate from an accredited medical school, pass a licensing examination, and complete 1 to 7 years of graduate medical education. Although physicians licensed in one State can usually get a license to practice in another without further examination, some States limit reciprocity. Graduates of foreign medical schools can usually qualify for licensure after passing an examination and completing a U.S. residency.

M.D.s and D.O.s seeking board certification in a specialty may spend up to 7 years—depending on the specialty—in residency training. A final examination immediately after residency, or after 1 or 2 years of practice, is also necessary for board certification by the American Board of Medical Specialists (ABMS) or the American Osteopathic Association (AOA). There are 24 specialty boards, ranging from allergy and immunology to urology. For certification in a subspecialty, physicians usually need another 1 to 2 years of residency.

A physician's training is costly, and whereas education costs have increased, student financial assistance has not. Over 80 percent of medical students borrow money to cover their expenses.

People who wish to become physicians must have a desire to serve patients, be self-motivated, and be able to survive the pressures and long hours of medical education and practice. Physicians must also have a good bedside manner, emotional stability, and the ability to make decisions in emergencies. Prospective physicians must be willing to study throughout their career to keep up with medical advances. They will also need to be flexible to respond to the changing demands of a rapidly evolving health care system.

Job Outlook

Employment of physicians will grow faster than the average for all occupations through the year 2008 due to continued expansion of the health care industries. The growing and aging population will drive overall growth in the demand for physician services. In addition, new technologies permit more intensive care: Physicians can do more tests, perform more procedures, and treat conditions previously regarded as untreatable.

Although job prospects may be better for primary care physicians such as general and family practitioners, general pediatricians, and general internists, a substantial number of jobs for specialists will also be created in response to patient demand for access to specialty care.

The number of physicians in training has leveled off and is likely to decrease over the next few years, alleviating the effects of any physician oversupply. However, future physicians may be more likely to work fewer hours, retire earlier, have lower earnings, or have to practice in underserved areas. Opportunities should be good in some rural and low income areas, because some physicians find these areas unattractive due to lower earnings potential, isolation from medical colleagues, or other reasons.

Unlike their predecessors, newly trained physicians face radically different choices of where and how to practice. New physicians are much less likely to enter solo practice and more likely to take salaried jobs in group medical practices, clinics, and health care networks.

Earnings

Physicians have among the highest earnings of any occupation. According to the American Medical Association, median income, after expenses, for allopathic physicians was about $164,000 in 1997. The middle 50 percent earned between $120,000 and $250,000 a year. Self-employed physicians—those who own or are part owners of their medical practice—had higher median incomes than salaried physicians. Earnings vary according to number of years in practice; geographic region; hours worked; and skill, personality, and professional reputation. As shown in table 2, median income of allopathic physicians, after expenses, also varies by specialty.

Table 2. Median net income of M.D.s after expenses, 1997

All physicians	$164,000
Radiology	260,000
Anesthesiology	220,000
Surgery	217,000
Obstetrics/gynecology	200,000
Emergency medicine	195,000
Pathology	175,000
General internal medicine	147,000
General/Family practice	132,000
Psychiatry	130,000
Pediatrics	120,000

SOURCE: American Medical Association

Average salaries of medical residents ranged from about $34,100 in 1998-99 for those in their first year of residency to about $42,100 for those in their sixth year, according to the Association of American Medical Colleges.

Related Occupations

Physicians work to prevent, diagnose, and treat diseases, disorders, and injuries. Professionals in other occupations requiring similar skills and critical judgment include acupuncturists, audiologists, chiropractors, dentists, nurse practitioners, optometrists, physician assistants, podiatrists, speech pathologists, and veterinarians.

Sources of Additional Information

For a list of allopathic medical schools and residency programs, as well as general information on premedical education, financial aid, and medicine as a career, contact:

☛ Association of American Medical Colleges, Section for Student Services, 2450 N St. NW., Washington, DC 20037-1131. Internet: **http://www.aamc.org**

For a list of osteopathic medical schools, as well as general information on premedical education, financial aid, and medicine as a career, contact:

☛ American Association of Colleges of Osteopathic Medicine, 5550 Friendship Blvd., Suite 310, Chevy Chase, MD 20815-7321. Internet: **http://www.aacom.org**

For general information on physicians, contact:

☛ American Medical Association, Department of Communications and Public Relations, 515 N. State St., Chicago, IL 60610. Internet: **http://www.ama-assn.org**

☛ American Osteopathic Association, Department of Public Relations, 142 East Ontario St., Chicago, IL 60611. Internet: **http://www.aoa-net.org**

Information on Federal scholarships and loans is available from the directors of student financial aid at schools of allopathic and osteopathic medicine.

Information on licensing is available from State boards of examiners.

Podiatrists

(O*NET 32111)

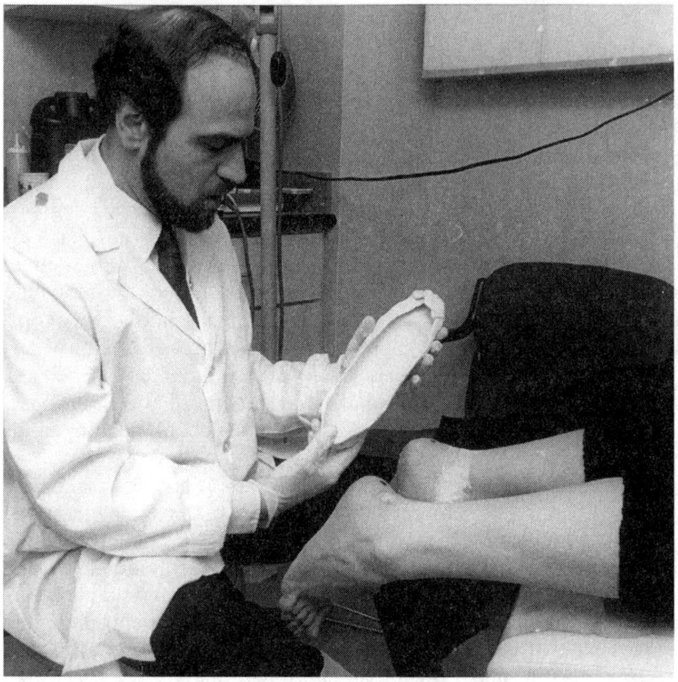

Podiatrists use plaster casts to aid in the design of corrective footwear for patients.

Significant Points

- A limited number of job openings for podiatrists is expected because the occupation is small and most podiatrists remain in the occupation until they retire.
- Most podiatrists are solo practitioners, although more are entering partnerships and multi-specialty group practices.
- Podiatrists enjoy very high earnings.

Nature of the Work

Americans spend a great deal of time on their feet. As the Nation becomes more active across all age groups, the need for foot care will become increasingly important to maintaining a healthy lifestyle.

The human foot is a complex structure. It contains 26 bones—plus muscles, nerves, ligaments, and blood vessels—and is designed for balance and mobility. The 52 bones in your feet make up about one fourth of all the bones in your body. Podiatrists, also known as doctors of podiatric medicine (DPMs), diagnose and treat disorders, diseases, and injuries of the foot and lower leg to keep this part of the body working properly.

Podiatrists treat corns, calluses, ingrown toenails, bunions, heel spurs, and arch problems; ankle and foot injuries, deformities and infections; and foot complaints associated with diseases such as diabetes. To treat these problems, podiatrists prescribe drugs, order physical therapy, set fractures, and perform surgery. They also fit corrective inserts called orthotics, design plaster casts and strappings to correct deformities, and design custom-made shoes. Podiatrists may use a force plate to help design the orthotics. Patients walk across a plate connected to a computer that "reads" the patients' feet, picking up pressure points and weight distribution. From the computer readout, podiatrists order the correct design or recommend treatment.

To diagnose a foot problem, podiatrists also order x rays and laboratory tests. The foot may be the first area to show signs of serious conditions such as arthritis, diabetes, and heart disease. For example, diabetics are prone to foot ulcers and infections due to poor circulation. Podiatrists consult with and refer patients to other health practitioners when they detect symptoms of these disorders.

Most podiatrists have a solo practice, although more are forming group practices with other podiatrists or health practitioners. Some specialize in surgery, orthopedics, primary care, or public health. Besides these board-certified specialties, podiatrists may practice a subspecialty such as sports medicine, pediatrics, dermatology, radiology, geriatrics, or diabetic foot care.

Podiatrists who are in private practice are responsible for running a small business. They may hire employees, order supplies, and keep records, among other tasks. In addition, some educate the community on the benefits of foot care through speaking engagements and advertising.

Working Conditions

Podiatrists usually work in their own offices. They may also spend time visiting patients in nursing homes or performing surgery at a hospital, but usually have fewer after-hours emergencies than other doctors. Those with private practices set their own hours, but may work evenings and weekends to meet the needs of their patients.

Employment

Podiatrists held about 14,000 jobs in 1998. Most podiatrists are solo practitioners, although more are entering partnerships and multi-specialty group practices. Others are employed in hospitals, nursing homes, the U.S. Public Health Service, and the Department of Veterans Affairs.

Training, Other Qualifications, and Advancement

All States and the District of Columbia require a license for the practice of podiatric medicine. Each defines its own licensing requirements. Generally, the applicant must be a graduate of an accredited college of podiatric medicine and pass written and oral examinations. Some States permit applicants to substitute the examination of the National Board of Podiatric Examiners, given in the second and fourth years of podiatric medical college, for part or all of the written State examination. Most States also require completion of a postdoctoral residency program. Many States grant reciprocity to podiatrists who are licensed in another State. Most States require continuing education for licensure renewal.

Prerequisites for admission to a college of podiatric medicine include the completion of at least 90 semester hours of undergraduate study, an acceptable grade point average, and suitable scores on the Medical College Admission Test (MCAT). All require 8 semester hours each of biology, inorganic chemistry, organic chemistry, and physics, and 6 hours of English. The science courses should be those designed for pre-medical students. Potential podiatric medical students may also be evaluated on the basis of extracurricular and community activities, personal interviews, and letters of recommendation. Over 90 percent of podiatric students have at least a bachelor's degree.

Colleges of podiatric medicine offer a 4-year program whose core curriculum is similar to that in other schools of medicine. During the first 2 years, students receive classroom instruction in basic sciences, including anatomy, chemistry, pathology, and pharmacology. Third- and fourth-year students have clinical rotations in private practices, hospitals, and clinics. During these rotations, they learn how to take general and podiatric histories, perform routine physical examinations, interpret tests and findings, make diagnoses, and perform therapeutic procedures. Graduates receive the doctor of podiatric medicine (DPM) degree.

Most graduates complete a hospital residency program after receiving a DPM. Residency programs last from 1 to 3 years. Residents receive advanced training in podiatric medicine and surgery and serve clinical rotations in anesthesiology, internal medicine, pathology, radiology, emergency medicine, and orthopedic and general surgery. Residencies lasting more than 1 year provide more extensive training in specialty areas.

There are a number of certifying boards for the podiatric specialties of orthopedics, primary medicine, or surgery. Certification means that the DPM meets higher standards than those required for licensure. Each board requires advanced training, completion of written and oral examinations, and experience as a practicing podiatrist. Most managed care organizations prefer board-certified podiatrists.

People planning a career in podiatry should have scientific aptitude, manual dexterity, interpersonal skills, and good business sense.

Podiatrists may advance to become professors at colleges of podiatric medicine, department chiefs of hospitals, or general health administrators.

Job Outlook

Employment of podiatrists is expected to grow about as fast as the average for all occupations through 2008. More people will turn to podiatrists for foot care as the elderly population grows. The elderly have more years of wear and tear on their feet and legs than most younger people, so they are more prone to foot ailments. Injuries sustained by an increasing number of men and women of all ages leading active lifestyles will also spur demand for podiatric care.

Medicare and most private health insurance programs cover acute medical and surgical foot services, as well as diagnostic x rays and leg braces. Details of such coverage vary among plans. However, routine foot care—including the removal of corns and calluses—is ordinarily not covered, unless the patient has a systemic condition that has resulted in severe circulatory problems or areas of desensitization in the legs or feet. Like dental services, podiatric care is more dependent on disposable income than other medical services.

Employment of podiatrists would grow even faster were it not for continued emphasis on controlling the costs of specialty health care. Insurers will balance the cost of sending patients to podiatrists against the cost and availability of substitute practitioners, such as physicians and physical therapists. Opportunities will be better for board-certified podiatrists, because many managed care organizations require board-certification. Opportunities for newly trained podiatrists will be better in group medical practices, clinics, and health networks than in a traditional solo practice. Establishing a practice will be most difficult in the areas surrounding colleges of podiatric medicine because podiatrists are concentrated in these locations.

Over the next 10 years, members of the "baby boom" generation will begin to retire, creating vacancies. Relatively few job openings from this source are expected, however, because the occupation is small.

Earnings

Median annual earnings of salaried podiatrists were $79,530 in 1998. However, only about one-half of podiatrists were salaried in 1998. Salaried podiatrists tend to earn less than self-employed podiatrists.

According to a survey by the American Podiatric Medical Association, average net income for podiatrists in private practice was about $116,000 in 1997. Those practicing for less than 2 years earned an average of about $61,000; those practicing 16 to 30 years earned an average of about $146,000.

Related Occupations

Workers in other occupations who apply scientific knowledge to prevent, diagnose, and treat disorders and injuries are chiropractors, dentists, optometrists, physicians, and veterinarians.

Sources of Additional Information

For information on podiatric medicine as a career, contact:

☛ American Podiatric Medical Association, 9312 Old Georgetown Rd., Bethesda, MD 20814-1621. Internet: **http://www.apma.org**

Information on colleges of podiatric medicine, entrance requirements, curriculums, and student financial aid is available from:

☛ American Association of Colleges of Podiatric Medicine, 1350 Piccard Dr., Suite 322, Rockville, MD 20850-4307.
Internet: **http://www.aacpm.org**

Veterinarians

(O*NET 32114A, 32114B, and 32114C)

Significant Points

- Graduation from an accredited college of veterinary medicine and a license to practice are required.
- Competition for admission to veterinary school is keen.

Nature of the Work

Veterinarians play a major role in the health care of pets, livestock, and zoo, sporting, and laboratory animals. Some veterinarians use their skills to protect humans against diseases carried by animals and conduct clinical research on human and animal health problems. Others work in basic research, broadening the scope of fundamental theoretical knowledge, and in applied research, developing new ways to use knowledge.

Most veterinarians perform clinical work in private practices. More than one-half of these veterinarians predominately, or exclusively, treat small animals. Small animal practitioners usually care for companion animals, such as dogs and cats, but also treat birds, reptiles, rabbits, and other animals that can be kept as pets. Some veterinarians work in mixed animal practices where they see pigs, goats, sheep, and some nondomestic animals, in addition to companion animals. Veterinarians in clinical practice diagnose animal health problems; vaccinate against diseases, such as distemper and rabies; medicate animals suffering from infections or illnesses; treat and dress wounds; set fractures; perform surgery; and advise owners about animal feeding, behavior, and breeding.

A small number of private practice veterinarians work exclusively with large animals, focusing mostly on horses or cows but may also care for various kinds of food animals. These veterinarians usually drive to farms or ranches to provide veterinary services for herds or individual animals. Much of this work involves preventive care to maintain the health of the food animals. These veterinarians test for and vaccinate against diseases and consult with farm or ranch owners and managers on animal production, feeding, and housing issues. They also treat and dress wounds, set fractures, and perform surgery—including cesarean sections on birthing animals. Veterinarians also euthanize animals when necessary. Other veterinarians care for zoo, aquarium, or laboratory animals.

Veterinarians who treat animals use medical equipment, such as stethoscopes; surgical instruments; and diagnostic equipment, such as radiographic and ultra-sound equipment. Veterinarians working in research use a full range of sophisticated laboratory equipment.

Veterinarians can contribute to human as well as animal health. A number of veterinarians work with physicians and scientists as they research ways to prevent and treat human health problems, such as cancer, AIDS, and alcohol or drug abuse. Some determine the effects of drug therapies, antibiotics, or new surgical techniques by testing them on animals.

Some veterinarians are involved in food safety at various levels. Veterinarians who are livestock inspectors check animals for transmissible diseases, advise owners on treatment, and may quarantine animals. Veterinarians who are meat, poultry, or egg product inspectors examine slaughtering and processing plants, check live animals and carcasses for disease, and enforce government regulations regarding food purity and sanitation.

Working Conditions

Veterinarians often work long hours, with one-third of full-time workers spending 50 or more hours on the job. Those in group practices may take turns being on call for evening, night, or weekend work; and solo practitioners can work extended and weekend hours, responding to emergencies or squeezing in unexpected appointments.

Veterinarians in large animal practice also spend time driving between their office and farms or ranches. They work outdoors in all kinds of weather, and have to treat animals or perform surgery under less-than-sanitary conditions. When working with animals that are frightened or in pain, veterinarians risk being bitten, kicked, or scratched.

Veterinarians working in non-clinical areas, such as public health and research, have working conditions similar to those of other professionals in those lines of work. In these cases, veterinarians enjoy clean, well-lit offices or laboratories and spend much of their time dealing with people rather than animals.

A veterinarian checks a pet's vision.

Employment

Veterinarians held about 57,000 jobs in 1998. About 30 percent were self-employed in solo or group practices. Most others were employees of another veterinary practice. The Federal Government employed about 1,900 civilian veterinarians, chiefly in the U.S. Department of Agriculture, and about 400 military veterinarians in the U.S. Army and U.S. Air Force. Other employers of veterinarians are State and local governments, colleges of veterinary medicine, medical schools, research laboratories, animal food companies, and pharmaceutical companies. A few veterinarians work for zoos; but most veterinarians caring for zoo animals are private practitioners who contract with zoos to provide services, usually on a part-time basis.

Training, Other Qualifications, and Advancement

Prospective veterinarians must graduate from a 4-year program at an accredited college of veterinary medicine with a Doctor of Veterinary Medicine (D.V.M. or V.M.D.) degree and obtain a license to practice. There are 27 colleges in 26 States that meet accreditation standards set by the Council on Education of the American Veterinary Medical Association. The prerequisites for admission vary by veterinary medical college. Many of these colleges do not require a bachelor's degree for entrance; but all require a significant number of credit hours—ranging from 45 to 90 semester hours—at the undergraduate level. However, most of the students admitted have completed an undergraduate program.

Preveterinary courses emphasize the sciences; and veterinary medical colleges typically require classes in organic and inorganic chemistry, physics, biochemistry, general biology, animal biology, animal nutrition, genetics, vertebrate embryology, cellular biology, microbiology, zoology, and systemic physiology. Some programs require calculus; some require only statistics, college algebra and trigonometry, or precalculus; and others require no math at all. Most veterinary medical colleges also require core courses, including some in English or literature, the social sciences, and the humanities.

Most veterinary medical colleges will only consider applicants who have a minimum grade point average (GPA). The required GPA varies by school, from a low of 2.5 to a high of 3.2, based on a maximum GPA of 4.0. However, the average GPA of candidates at most schools is higher than these minimums. Those who receive offers of admission usually have a GPA of 3.0 or better.

In addition to satisfying preveterinary course requirements, applicants must also submit test scores from the Graduate Record Examination (GRE), the Veterinary College Admission Test (VCAT), or the Medical College Admission Test (MCAT), depending on the preference of each college.

Additionally, in the admissions process, veterinary medical colleges weigh heavily a candidate's veterinary and animal experience. Formal experience, such as work with veterinarians or scientists in clinics, agribusiness, research, or in some area of health science, is particularly advantageous. Less formal experience, such as working with animals on a farm or ranch or at a stable or animal shelter, is also helpful. Students must demonstrate ambition and an eagerness to work with animals.

Competition for admission to veterinary school is keen. The number of accredited veterinary colleges has remained at 27 since 1983, whereas the number of applicants has risen. About 1 in 3 applicants was accepted in 1998. Most veterinary medical colleges are public, State-supported institutions and reserve the majority of their openings for in-state residents. Twenty-one States that do not have a veterinary medical college agree to pay a fee or subsidy to help cover the cost of veterinary education for a limited number of their residents at one or more out-of-state colleges. Nonresident students who are admitted under such a contract may have to pay out-of-state tuition, or they may have to repay their State of residency all, or part, of the subsidy provided to the contracting college. Residents of the remaining 3 States (Connecticut, Maine, and Vermont) and the District of Columbia may apply to any of the 27 veterinary medical colleges as an *at-large* applicant. The number of positions available to at-large applicants is very limited at most schools, making admission difficult.

While in veterinary medical college, students receive additional academic instruction in the basic sciences for the first 2 years. Later in the program, students are exposed to clinical procedures, such as diagnosing and treating animal diseases and performing surgery. They also do laboratory work in anatomy, biochemistry, medicine, and other scientific subjects. At most veterinary medical colleges, students who plan a career in research can earn both a D.V.M degree and a Doctor of Philosophy (Ph.D.) degree at the same time.

Veterinary graduates who plan to work with specific types of animals or specialize in a clinical area, such as pathology, surgery, radiology, or laboratory animal medicine, usually complete a 1-year internship. Interns receive a small salary but usually find that their internship experience leads to a higher beginning salary, relative to other starting veterinarians. Veterinarians who seek board certification in a specialty must also complete a 2- to 3-year residency program that provides intensive training in specialties, such as internal medicine, oncology, radiology, surgery, dermatology, anesthesiology, neurology, cardiology, ophthalmology, and exotic small animal medicine.

All States and the District of Columbia require that veterinarians be licensed before they can practice. The only exemptions are for veterinarians working for some Federal agencies and some State governments. Licensing is controlled by the States and is not strictly uniform, although all States require successful completion of the D.V.M. degree—or equivalent education—and passage of a national board examination. The Educational Commission for Foreign Veterinary Graduates (ECFVG) grants certification to individuals trained outside the U.S. who demonstrate that they meet specified requirements for the English language and clinical proficiency. ECFVG certification fulfills the educational requirement for licensure in all States except Nebraska. Applicants for licensure satisfy the examination requirement by passing the North American Veterinary Licensing Exam (NAVLE), which replaces the National Board Examination (NBE) and the Clinical Competency Test (CCT) as of April 2000. The new NAVLE, administered on computer, takes one day to complete and consists of 360 multiple-choice questions, covering all aspects of veterinary medicine. The NAVLE also includes visual materials designed to test diagnostic skills.

The majority of States also require candidates to pass a State jurisprudence examination covering State laws and regulations. Some States also do additional testing on clinical competency. There are few reciprocal agreements between States, making it difficult for a veterinarian to practice in a different State without first taking another State examination.

Thirty-nine States have continuing education requirements for licensed veterinarians. Requirements differ by State and may involve attending a class or otherwise demonstrating knowledge of recent medical and veterinary advances.

Most veterinarians begin as employees or partners in established practices. Despite the substantial financial investment in equipment, office space, and staff, many veterinarians with experience set up their own practice or purchase an established one.

Newly trained veterinarians can become U.S. Government meat and poultry inspectors, disease-control workers, epidemiologists, research assistants, or commissioned officers in the U.S. Public Health Service, U.S. Army, or U.S. Air Force. A State license may be required.

Prospective veterinarians must have good manual dexterity. They should have an affinity for animals and the ability to get along with animal owners. Additionally, they should be able to quickly make decisions in emergencies.

Job Outlook

Employment of veterinarians is expected to grow faster than the average for all occupations through the year 2008. Job openings stemming from the need to replace veterinarians who retire or otherwise leave the labor force will be almost as numerous as new jobs resulting from employment growth over the 1998-2008 period.

Most veterinarians practice in animal hospitals or clinics and care primarily for companion animals. The number of pets is expected to increase more slowly during the projection period than in the previous decade and may moderate growth in the demand for veterinarians who specialize in small animals. One reason for this is that the large baby-boom generation is aging and will probably acquire fewer dogs and cats than earlier. However, as non-necessity income generally increases with age, those who own pets may be more inclined to seek veterinary services. In addition, pet owners are becoming more aware of the availability of advanced care and may increasingly take advantage of nontraditional veterinary services, such as preventive dental care, and may more willingly pay for intensive care than in the past. Finally, new technologies and medical advancements should permit veterinarians to offer better care to animals. Veterinarians who enter small animal practice will probably face competition. Large numbers of new graduates continue to be attracted to small animal medicine because they prefer to deal with pets and to live and work near highly populated areas. However, an oversupply does not necessarily limit the ability of veterinarians to find employment or to set up and maintain a practice in a particular area. Such an oversupply could result in veterinarians taking positions requiring much evening or weekend work to accommodate the extended hours of operation that many practices are offering. Others could take salaried positions in retail stores offering limited veterinary services. Most self-employed veterinarians will probably have to work hard and long to build a sufficient clientele.

The number of jobs for large animal veterinarians is expected to grow slowly, because productivity gains in the agricultural production industry mean demand for fewer veterinarians than before to treat food animals. Nevertheless, job prospects may be better for veterinarians who specialize in farm animals than for small animal practitioners, because most veterinary medical college graduates do not have the desire to work in rural or isolated areas.

Continued support for public health and food safety, disease control programs, and biomedical research on human health problems will contribute to the demand for veterinarians, although such positions are few in number. Also, anticipated budget tightening in the Federal Government may lead to low funding levels for some programs, limiting job growth. Veterinarians with training in public health and epidemiology should have the best opportunities for a career in the Federal Government.

Earnings

Median annual earnings of veterinarians were \$50,950 in 1998. The middle 50 percent earned between \$39,580 and \$78,670. The lowest 10 percent earned less than \$31,320 and the highest 10 percent earned more than \$106,370.

Average starting salaries of 1998 veterinary medical college graduates varied by type of practice, as indicated by table 1.

Table 1. Average starting salaries of veterinary medical college graduates, 1998

Type of practice	
Large animal, exclusive	$37,200
Large animal, predominant	37,500
Mixed animal	35,900
Small animal, exclusive	37,600
Small animal, predominant	36,300
Equine	29,200

SOURCE: American Veterinary Medical Association

New veterinary medical college graduates who enter the Federal Government usually start at $37,700. Beginning salaries were slightly higher in selected areas where the prevailing local pay level was higher. The average annual salary for veterinarians in the Federal Government in nonsupervisory, supervisory, and managerial positions was $61,600 in 1999.

Related Occupations

Veterinarians prevent, diagnose, and treat diseases, disorders, and injuries in animals. Those who do similar work for humans include chiropractors, dentists, optometrists, physicians, and podiatrists. Veterinarians have extensive training in physical and life sciences, and some do scientific and medical research, closely paralleling occupations such as biological, medical, and animal scientists.

Animal trainers, animal breeders, and veterinary technicians work extensively with animals. Like veterinarians, they must have patience and feel comfortable with animals. However, the level of training required for these occupations is substantially less than that needed by veterinarians.

Sources of Additional Information

For more information on careers in veterinary medicine and a list of U.S. schools and colleges of veterinary medicine, send a letter-size, self-addressed, stamped envelope to:

☛ American Veterinary Medical Association, 1931 N. Meacham Rd., Suite 100, Schaumburg, IL 60173-4360.

For information on scholarships, grants, and loans, contact the financial aid officer at the veterinary schools to which you wish to apply.

For information on veterinary education, write to:

☛ Association of American Veterinary Medical Colleges, 1101 Vermont Ave. NW., Suite 710, Washington, DC 20005.

For information on the Federal agencies that employ veterinarians and a list of addresses for each agency, write to:

☛ National Association of Federal Veterinarians, 1101 Vermont Ave. NW., Suite 710, Washington, DC 20005.

Health Assessment and Treating Occupations

Dietitians and Nutritionists

(O*NET 32521)

Significant points

- Employment of dietitians is expected to grow about as fast as the average for all occupations through the year 2008 due to increased emphasis on disease prevention by improved health habits.
- Dietitians and nutritionists need at least a bachelor's degree in dietetics, foods and nutrition, food service systems management, or a related area.

Nature of the Work

Dietitians and nutritionists plan food and nutrition programs and supervise the preparation and serving of meals. They help prevent and treat illnesses by promoting healthy eating habits, scientifically evaluating clients' diets, and suggesting diet modifications, such as less salt for those with high blood pressure or reduced fat and sugar intake for those who are overweight.

Dietitians run food service systems for institutions such as hospitals and schools, promote sound eating habits through education, and conduct research. Major areas of practice are clinical, community, management, research, business and industry, and consultant dietetics.

Clinical dietitians provide nutritional services for patients in institutions such as hospitals and nursing homes. They assess patients' nutritional needs, develop and implement nutrition programs, and evaluate and report the results. They also confer with doctors and other health care professionals in order to coordinate medical and nutritional needs. Some clinical dietitians specialize in the management of overweight patients, care of the critically ill, or of renal (kidney) and diabetic patients. In addition, clinical dietitians in nursing homes, small hospitals, or correctional facilities may also manage the food service department.

Community dietitians counsel individuals and groups on nutritional practices designed to prevent disease and promote good health. Working in places such as public health clinics, home health agencies, and health maintenance organizations, they evaluate individual needs, develop nutritional care plans, and instruct individuals and their families. Dietitians working in home health agencies provide instruction on grocery shopping and food preparation to the elderly, individuals with special needs, and children.

Increased interest in nutrition has led to opportunities in food manufacturing, advertising, and marketing, in which dietitians analyze foods, prepare literature for distribution, or report on issues such as the nutritional content of recipes, dietary fiber, or vitamin supplements.

Management dietitians oversee large-scale meal planning and preparation in health care facilities, company cafeterias, prisons, and schools. They hire, train, and direct other dietitians and food service workers; budget for and purchase food, equipment, and supplies; enforce sanitary and safety regulations; and prepare records and reports.

Consultant dietitians work under contract with health care facilities or in their own private practice. They perform nutrition screenings for their clients, and offer advice on diet-related concerns such as weight loss or cholesterol reduction. Some work for wellness programs, sports teams, supermarkets, and other nutrition-related businesses. They may consult with food service managers, providing expertise in sanitation, safety procedures, menu development, budgeting, and planning.

Working Conditions

Most dietitians work a regular 40-hour week, although some work weekends. Many dietitians work part time.

Dietitians and nutritionists usually work in clean, well-lighted, and well-ventilated areas. However, some dietitians work in warm, congested kitchens. Many dietitians and nutritionists are on their feet for most of the workday.

Employment

Dietitians and nutritionists held about 54,000 jobs in 1998. Over half were in hospitals, nursing homes, or offices and clinics of physicians.

Dietitians and nutritionists plan food and nutrition programs and supervise food preparation and service.

State and local governments provided about 1 job in 6—mostly in health departments and other public health related areas. Other jobs were in restaurants, social service agencies, residential care facilities, diet workshops, physical fitness facilities, school systems, colleges and universities, and the Federal Government—mostly in the Department of Veterans Affairs. Some were employed by firms that provide food services on contract to such facilities as colleges and universities, airlines, correctional facilities, and company cafeterias.

Some dietitians were self-employed, working as consultants to facilities such as hospitals and nursing homes, and seeing individual clients.

Training, Other Qualifications, and Advancement

High school students interested in becoming a dietitian or nutritionist should take courses in biology, chemistry, mathematics, health, and communications. Dietitians and nutritionists need at least a bachelor's degree in dietetics, foods and nutrition, food service systems management, or a related area. College students in these majors take courses in foods, nutrition, institution management, chemistry, biochemistry, biology, microbiology, and physiology. Other suggested courses include business, mathematics, statistics, computer science, psychology, sociology, and economics.

Twenty-seven of the 41 States with laws governing dietetics require licensurc, 13 require certification, and 1 requires registration. The Commission on Dietetic Registration of the American Dietetic Association (ADA) awards the Registered Dietitian credential to those who pass a certification exam after completing their academic coursework and supervised experience. Since practice requirements vary by State, interested candidates should determine the requirements of the State in which they want to work before sitting for any exam.

As of 1999, there were 235 bachelor's and master's degree programs approved by the ADA's Commission on Accreditation/Approval for Dietetics Education (CAADE). Supervised practice experience can be acquired in two ways. There are 51 ADA-accredited coordinated programs combining academic and supervised practice experience in a 4- to5-year program. The second option requires completion of 900 hours of supervised practice experience, either in one of the 225 CAADE-accredited internships or in one of the 25 CAADE-approved preprofessional practice programs. Internships and preprofessional practice programs may be full-time programs lasting 9 to 12 months, or part-time programs lasting 2 years. Students interested in research, advanced clinical positions, or public health may need a graduate degree.

Experienced dietitians may advance to assistant, associate, or director of a dietetic department, or become self-employed. Some dietitians specialize in areas such as renal or pediatric dietetics. Others may leave the occupation to become sales representatives for equipment, pharmaceutical, or food manufacturers.

Job Outlook

Employment of dietitians is expected to grow about as fast as the average for all occupations through 2008 due to increased emphasis on disease prevention by improved dietary habits. A growing and aging population will increase the demand for meals and nutritional counseling in nursing homes, schools, prisons, community health programs, and home health care agencies. Public interest in nutrition and the emphasis on health education and prudent lifestyles will also spur demand, especially in management. Besides employment growth, job openings will also result from the need to replace experienced workers who leave the occupation.

The number of dietitian positions in hospitals is expected to grow slowly as hospitals continue to contract out food service operations. On the other hand, employment is expected to grow fast in contract providers of food services, social services agencies, and offices and clinics of physicians.

Employment growth for dietitians and nutritionists may be somewhat constrained by some employers substituting other workers such as health educators, food service managers, and dietetic technicians. Growth also is constrained by limitations on insurance reimbursement for dietetic services.

Earnings

Median annual earnings of dietitians and nutritionists were $35,020 in 1998. The middle 50 percent earned between $28,010 and $42,720 a year. The lowest 10 percent earned less than $20,350 and the highest 10 percent earned more than $51,320 a year. Median annual earnings in the industries employing the largest number of dietitians and nutritionists in 1997 were as follows:

Hospitals	$34,900
Local government, except education and hospitals	31,200
Nursing and personal care facilities	28,400

According to the American Dietetic Association, median annual income for registered dietitians in 1997 varied by practice area as follows: clinical nutrition, $35,500; food and nutrition management, $44,900; community nutrition, $34,900; consultation and business, $46,000; and education and research, $45,200. Salaries also vary by years in practice, educational level, geographic region, and size of community.

Related Occupations
Dietitians and nutritionists apply the principles of food and nutrition in a variety of situations. Jobs similar to management dietitians' include home economists and food service managers. Nurses and health educators often provide services related to those of community dietitians.

Sources of Additional Information
For a list of academic programs, scholarships, and other information about dietetics, contact:
☛ The American Dietetic Association, 216 West Jackson Blvd., Suite 800, Chicago, IL 60606-6995. Internet: **http://www.eatright.org**

Occupational Therapists

(O*NET 32305)

Significant Points

- Employment is projected to increase over the 1998-2008 period, but due to the effects of Federal limits on reimbursement for therapy services, the majority of expected employment growth is expected to occur during the second half of the projection period.
- Occupational therapists are increasingly taking on supervisory roles.
- More than one-fourth of occupational therapists work part time.

Nature of the Work
Occupational therapists help people improve their ability to perform tasks in their daily living and working environments. They work with individuals who have conditions that are mentally, physically, developmentally, or emotionally disabling. They also help them to develop, recover, or maintain daily living and work skills. Occupational therapists not only help clients improve basic motor functions and reasoning abilities, but also compensate for permanent loss of function. Their goal is to help clients have independent, productive, and satisfying lives.

Occupational therapists assist clients in performing activities of all types, ranging from using a computer, to caring for daily needs such as dressing, cooking, and eating. Physical exercises may be used to increase strength and dexterity, while paper and pencil exercises may be chosen to improve visual acuity and the ability to discern patterns. A client with short-term memory loss, for instance, might be encouraged to make lists to aid recall. A person with coordination problems might be assigned exercises to improve hand-eye coordination. Occupational therapists also use computer programs to help clients improve decision making, abstract reasoning, problem solving, and perceptual skills, as well as memory, sequencing, and coordination—all of which are important for independent living.

For those with permanent functional disabilities, such as spinal cord injuries, cerebral palsy, or muscular dystrophy, therapists instruct in the use of adaptive equipment such as wheelchairs, splints, and aids for eating and dressing. They also design or make special equipment needed at home or at work. Therapists develop computer-aided adaptive equipment and teach clients with severe limitations how to use it. This equipment enables clients to communicate better and to control other aspects of their environment.

Some occupational therapists, called industrial therapists, treat individuals whose ability to function in a work environment has been impaired. They arrange employment, plan work activities, and evaluate the client's progress.

Occupational therapists may work exclusively with individuals in a particular age group, or with particular disabilities. In schools, for example, they evaluate children's abilities, recommend and provide therapy, modify classroom equipment, and in general, help children participate as fully as possible in school programs and activities. Occupational therapy is also beneficial to the elderly population. Therapists help senior citizens lead more productive, active and independent lives through a variety of methods, including the use of adaptive equipment.

Occupational therapists in mental health settings treat individuals who are mentally ill, mentally retarded, or emotionally disturbed. To treat these problems, therapists choose activities that help people learn to cope with daily life. Activities include time management skills, budgeting, shopping, homemaking, and use of public transportation. They may also work with individuals who are dealing with alcoholism, drug abuse, depression, eating disorders, or stress related disorders.

Recording a client's activities and progress is an important part of an occupational therapist's job. Accurate records are essential for evaluating clients, billing, and reporting to physicians and others.

Working Conditions
Occupational therapists in hospitals and other health care and community settings usually work a 40-hour week. Those in schools may also participate in meetings and other activities, during and after the school day. More than one-fourth of occupational therapists work part-time.

An occupational therapist uses special activities to help a patient build strength in the lower arm and hand.

In large rehabilitation centers, therapists may work in spacious rooms equipped with machines, tools, and other devices generating noise. The job can be tiring, because therapists are on their feet much of the time. Those providing home health care may spend time driving from appointment to appointment. Therapists also face hazards such as back strain from lifting and moving clients and equipment.

Therapists are increasingly taking on supervisory roles. Due to rising health care costs, third party payers are beginning to encourage occupational therapy assistants and aides to take more hands-on responsibility. By having assistants and aides work more closely with clients under the guidance of a therapist, the cost of therapy should be more modest.

Employment

Occupational therapists held about 73,000 jobs in 1998; about 1 in 4 worked part time. About 1 in 10 occupational therapists held more than one job in 1998. The largest number of jobs was in hospitals, including many in rehabilitation and psychiatric hospitals. Other major employers include offices and clinics of occupational therapists and other health practitioners, school systems, home health agencies, nursing homes, community mental health centers, adult daycare programs, job training services, and residential care facilities.

Some occupational therapists are self-employed in private practice. They see clients referred by physicians or other health professionals, or provide contract or consulting services to nursing homes, schools, adult daycare programs, and home health agencies.

Training, Other Qualifications, and Advancement

A bachelor's degree in occupational therapy is the minimum requirement for entry into this field. All States, Puerto Rico, and the District of Columbia regulate occupational therapy. To obtain a license, applicants must graduate from an accredited educational program, and pass a national certification examination. Those who pass the test are awarded the title of registered occupational therapist.

In 1999, entry-level education was offered in 88 bachelor's degree programs; 11 post-bachelor's certificate programs for students with a degree other than occupational therapy; and 53 entry-level master's degree programs. Nineteen programs offered a combined bachelor's and master's degree and 2 offered an entry-level doctoral degree. Most schools have full-time programs, although a growing number also offer weekend or part-time programs.

Occupational therapy coursework includes physical, biological, and behavioral sciences, and the application of occupational therapy theory and skills. Completion of 6 months of supervised fieldwork is also required.

Persons considering this profession should take high school courses in biology, chemistry, physics, health, art, and the social sciences. College admissions offices also look favorably at paid or volunteer experience in the health care field.

Occupational therapists need patience and strong interpersonal skills to inspire trust and respect in their clients. Ingenuity and imagination in adapting activities to individual needs are assets. Those working in home health care must be able to successfully adapt to a variety of settings.

Job Outlook

Employment of occupational therapists is expected to increase faster than the average for all occupations through 2008. However, Federal legislation imposing limits on reimbursement for therapy services may continue to adversely affect the job market for occupational therapists in the near term. Because of the effects of these provisions, the majority of expected employment growth for occupational therapists is expected to occur in the second half of the projection period.

Over the long run, the demand for occupational therapists should continue to rise as a result of growth in the number of individuals with disabilities or limited function requiring therapy services. The baby-boom generation's movement into middle age, a period when the incidence of heart attack and stroke increases, will increase the demand for therapeutic services. The rapidly growing population 75 years of age and above (an age that suffers from a high incidence of disabling conditions), will also demand additional services. Medical advances now enable more patients with critical problems to survive. These patients may need extensive therapy.

Hospitals will continue to employ a large number of occupational therapists to provide therapy services to acutely ill inpatients. Hospitals will also need occupational therapists to staff their outpatient rehabilitation programs.

Employment growth in schools will result from expansion of the school-age population and extended services for disabled students. Therapists will be needed to help children with disabilities prepare to enter special education programs.

Earnings

Median annual earnings of occupational therapists were $48,230 in 1998. The middle 50 percent earned between $39,140 and $68,570 a year. The lowest 10 percent earned less than $30,850 and the highest 10 percent earned more than $86,540 a year. Median annual earnings in the industries employing the largest number of occupational therapists in 1997 were as follows:

Industry	Earnings
Nursing and personal care facilities	$57,000
Offices of other health care practitioners	51,800
Hospitals	46,200
Elementary and secondary schools	38,200

Related Occupations

Occupational therapists use specialized knowledge to help individuals perform daily living skills and achieve maximum independence. Other workers performing similar duties include orthotists, prosthetists, physical therapists, chiropractors, speech pathologists, audiologists, rehabilitation counselors, and recreational therapists.

Sources of Additional Information

For more information on occupational therapy as a career and a list of education programs, send a self-addressed label and $5.00 to:

- The American Occupational Therapy Association, 4720 Montgomery Ln., P.O. Box 31220, Bethesda, MD 20824-1220.
Internet: **http://www.aota.org**

Pharmacists

(O*NET 32517)

Significant Points

- Pharmacists are becoming more involved in drug therapy decision-making and patient counseling.
- Earnings are very high, but some pharmacists work long hours, nights, weekends, and holidays.

Nature of the Work

Pharmacists dispense drugs prescribed by physicians and other health practitioners and provide information to patients about medications and their use. They advise physicians and other health practitioners on the selection, dosages, interactions, and side effects of medications. Pharmacists must understand the use, composition, and clinical effects of drugs. Compounding—the actual mixing of ingredients to form powders, tablets, capsules, ointments, and solutions—is only a small part of a pharmacist's practice, because most medicines are produced by pharmaceutical companies in a standard dosage and drug delivery form.

Pharmacists in community or retail pharmacies counsel patients, as well as answer questions about prescription drugs, such as possible adverse reactions or interactions. They provide information about over-the-counter drugs and make recommendations after asking a series of health questions, such as whether the customer is taking any other medications. They also give advice about durable medical equipment and home health care supplies. Those who own or manage community pharmacies may sell nonhealth-related merchandise, hire and supervise personnel, and oversee the general operation of the pharmacy. Some community pharmacists provide specialized services to help patients manage conditions such as diabetes, asthma, smoking cessation, or high blood pressure.

Pharmacists in hospitals and clinics dispense medications and advise the medical staff on the selection and effects of drugs. They may make sterile solutions and buy medical supplies. They also assess, plan, and monitor drug regimens. They counsel patients on the use of drugs while in the hospital, and on their use at home when they are discharged. Pharmacists may also evaluate drug use patterns and outcomes for patients in hospitals or managed care organizations.

Pharmacists who work in home health care monitor drug therapy and prepare infusions—solutions that are injected into patients—and other medications for use in the home.

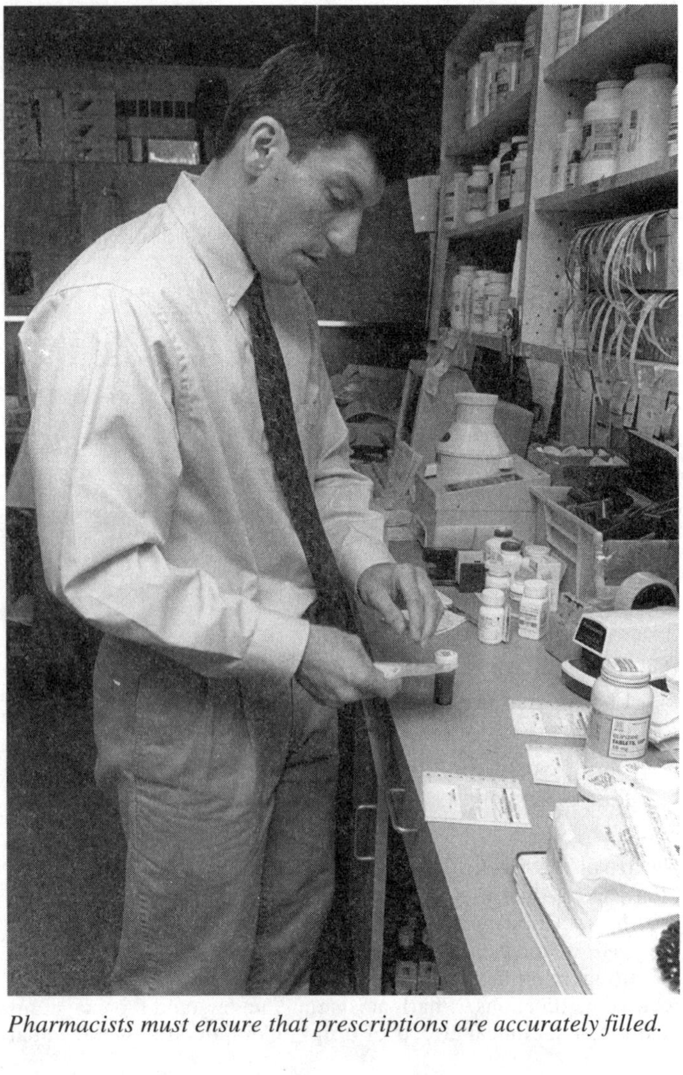

Pharmacists must ensure that prescriptions are accurately filled.

Most pharmacists keep confidential computerized records of patients' drug therapies to ensure that harmful drug interactions do not occur. They frequently teach pharmacy students serving as interns in preparation for graduation and licensure.

Some pharmacists specialize in specific drug therapy areas, such as psychiatric disorders, intravenous nutrition support, oncology, nuclear pharmacy, and pharmacotherapy.

Working Conditions

Pharmacists usually work in clean, well-lighted, and well-ventilated areas. Many pharmacists spend most of their workday on their feet. When working with sterile or potentially dangerous pharmaceutical products, pharmacists wear gloves and masks and work with other special protective equipment. Many community and hospital pharmacies are open for extended hours or around the clock, so pharmacists may work evenings, nights, weekends, and holidays. Consultant pharmacists may travel to nursing homes or other facilities to monitor people's drug therapy.

About 1 out of 7 pharmacists worked part time in 1998. Most full-time salaried pharmacists worked about 40 hours a week. Some, including most self-employed pharmacists, worked more than 50 hours a week.

Employment

Pharmacists held about 185,000 jobs in 1998. About 3 out of 5 worked in community pharmacies, either independently owned or part of a drug store chain, grocery store, department store, or mass merchandiser. Most community pharmacists were salaried employees, but some were self–employed owners. About one-quarter of salaried pharmacists worked in hospitals, and others worked in clinics, mail-order pharmacies, pharmaceutical wholesalers, home health care agencies, or the Federal Government.

Some pharmacists hold more than one job. They may work a standard week in their primary work setting, and also work part time elsewhere.

Training, Other Qualifications, and Advancement

A license to practice pharmacy is required in all States, the District of Columbia, and U.S. territories. To obtain a license, one must serve an internship under a licensed pharmacist, graduate from an accredited college of pharmacy, and pass a State examination. Most States grant a license without extensive reexamination to qualified pharmacists already licensed by another State—check with State boards of pharmacy for details. Many pharmacists are licensed to practice in more than one State. States may require continuing education for license renewal.

In 1998, 81 colleges of pharmacy were accredited to confer degrees by the American Council on Pharmaceutical Education. Nearly all pharmacy programs grant the degree of Doctor of Pharmacy (Pharm.D.) which requires at least 6 years of postsecondary study. A small number of pharmacy schools continue to award the 5-year Bachelor of Science (B.S.) in pharmacy degree. However, all accredited pharmacy schools are expected to graduate their last B.S. class by the year 2005. Either a Pharm.D. or B.S. degree currently fulfills the requirements to take the licensure examination of a state board of pharmacy.

Requirements for admission to colleges of pharmacy vary. A few colleges admit students directly from high school. Most colleges of pharmacy, however, require 1 or 2 years of college-level prepharmacy education. Entry requirements usually include mathematics and basic sciences, such as chemistry, biology, and physics, as well as courses in the humanities and social sciences. Some colleges require the applicant to take the Pharmacy College Admissions Test.

All colleges of pharmacy offer courses in pharmacy practice, designed to teach students to dispense prescriptions, communicate with patients and other health professionals, and to strengthen their understanding of professional ethics and practice management responsibilities. Pharmacists' training increasingly emphasizes direct patient care, as well as consultative services to other health professionals.

In the 1997-1998 academic year, 60 colleges of pharmacy awarded the Master of Science degree or the Ph.D. degree. Although a number of pharmacy graduates interested in further training pursue an advanced degree in pharmacy, there are other options. Some complete 1- or 2-year residency programs or fellowships. Pharmacy residencies are postgraduate training programs in pharmacy practice. Pharmacy fellowships are highly individualized programs designed to prepare participants to work in research laboratories.

Areas of graduate study include pharmaceutics and pharmaceutical chemistry (physical and chemical properties of drugs and dosage forms), pharmacology (effects of drugs on the body), and pharmacy administration, including pharmacoeconomics and social-behavioral aspects of patient care.

Prospective pharmacists should have scientific aptitude, good communication skills, and a desire to help others. They must also be conscientious and pay close attention to detail, because the decisions they make affect human lives.

In community pharmacies, pharmacists usually begin at the staff level. After they gain experience and secure the necessary capital, some become owners or part owners of pharmacies. Pharmacists in chain drug stores may be promoted to pharmacy supervisor or manager at the store level, then to the district or regional level, and later to an executive position within the chain's headquarters.

Hospital pharmacists may advance to supervisory or administrative positions. Pharmacists in the pharmaceutical industry may advance in marketing, sales, research, quality control, production, packaging, and other areas.

Job Outlook

Employment of pharmacists is expected to grow slower than the average for all occupations through the year 2008, despite the increased pharmaceutical needs of a larger and older population, and greater use of medication.

Retail pharmacies are taking steps to increase their prescription volume to make up for declining dispensing fees. Automation of drug dispensing and greater use of pharmacy technicians will help them to dispense more prescriptions. The number of community pharmacists needed in the future will depend on the expansion rate of chain drug stores and the willingness of insurers to reimburse pharmacists for providing clinical services to patients taking prescription medications. With its emphasis on cost control, managed care encourages growth of lower-cost prescription drug distributors such as mail-order firms for certain medications. Slower employment growth is expected in traditional chain and independent pharmacies.

Employment in hospitals is also expected to grow slowly, as hospitals reduce inpatient stays, downsize, and consolidate departments. Pharmacy services are shifting to long-term, ambulatory, and home care settings, where opportunities for pharmacists will be best. New opportunities for pharmacists are emerging in managed care organizations, where pharmacists analyze trends and patterns in medication use for their populations of patients. Fast growth is also expected for pharmacists trained in research, disease management, and pharmacoeconomics—determining the costs and benefits of different drug therapies.

Cost-conscious insurers and health systems may continue to emphasize the role of pharmacists in primary and preventive health services. They realize that the expense of using medication to treat diseases and conditions is often considerably less than the potential costs for patients whose conditions go untreated. Pharmacists can also reduce the expenses resulting from unexpected complications due to allergic reactions or medication interactions.

The increased number of middle aged and elderly people will spur demand for pharmacists in all practice settings. The number of prescriptions influences the demand for pharmacists, and the middle aged and elderly populations use more prescription drugs, on average, than younger people.

Other factors likely to increase the demand for pharmacists through the year 2008 include the likelihood of scientific advances that will make more drug products available, new developments in administering medication, and increasingly sophisticated consumers seeking more information about drugs.

Earnings

Median annual earnings of pharmacists in 1998 were $66,220. The middle 50 percent earned between $52,310 and $80,250 a year. The lowest 10 percent earned less than $42,550 and the highest 10 percent more than $88,670 a year. Median annual earnings in the industries employing the largest numbers of pharmacists in 1997 were as follows:

Grocery stores	$67,000
Drug stores and proprietary stores	63,400
Hospitals	62,600
Federal government	61,700

According to a survey by *Drug Topics* magazine, published by Medical Economics Co., average base salaries of full-time, salaried pharmacists were about $59,700 a year in 1998. Pharmacists working in chain drug stores had an average base salary of about $62,300 a year, while pharmacists working in independent drug stores averaged about $56,300, and hospital pharmacists averaged about $59,500 a year. Overall, salaries for pharmacists were highest on the West coast. Many pharmacists also receive compensation in the form of bonuses, overtime, and profit-sharing.

Related Occupations

Persons in other professions who may work with pharmaceutical compounds are biological technicians, medical scientists, pharmaceutical chemists, and pharmacologists.

Sources of Additional Information

For information on pharmacy as a career, preprofessional and professional requirements, programs offered by all the colleges of pharmacy, and student financial aid, contact:

☛ American Association of Colleges of Pharmacy, 1426 Prince St., Alexandria, VA 22314. Internet: **http://www.aacp.org**

General information on careers in pharmacy is available from:

☛ American Society of Health-System Pharmacists, 7272 Wisconsin Ave., Bethesda, MD 20814. Internet: **http://www.ashp.org**

☛ American Pharmaceutical Association, 2215 Constitution Ave. NW., Washington, DC 20037-2985. Internet: **http://www.aphanet.org**

☛ National Association of Chain Drug Stores, 413 N. Lee St., P.O. Box 1417-D49, Alexandria, VA 22313-1480. Internet: **www.nacds.org**

State licensure requirements are available from each State's Board of Pharmacy.

Information on specific college entrance requirements, curriculums, and financial aid is available from any college of pharmacy.

Physical Therapists

(O*NET 32308)

Significant Points

- Although the effects of Federal limits on reimbursement for therapy services will cause keen competition for jobs during the first half of the projection period, employment is expected to increase over the 1998-2008 period.

- Competition for entrance into physical therapist educational programs is very intense.
- By 2002, all physical therapist programs seeking accreditation will be required to offer master's degrees and above.

Nature of the Work

Physical therapists provide services that help restore function, improve mobility, relieve pain, and prevent or limit permanent physical disabilities of patients suffering from injuries or disease. They restore, maintain, and promote overall fitness and health. Their patients include accident victims and individuals with disabling conditions such as low back pain, arthritis, heart disease, fractures, head injuries, and cerebral palsy.

Therapists examine patients' medical histories, then test and measure their strength, range of motion, balance and coordination, posture, muscle performance, respiration, and motor function. They also determine patients' ability to be independent and reintegrate into the community or workplace after injury or illness. Next, they develop treatment plans describing a treatment strategy, the purpose, and anticipated outcome. Physical therapist assistants, under the direction and supervision of a physical therapist, may be involved in the implementation of the treatment plan. Physical therapist aides perform routine support tasks, as directed by the therapist. (Physical therapist assistants and aides are discussed elsewhere in the *Handbook.*)

Treatment often includes exercise for patients who have been immobilized and lack flexibility, strength, or endurance. They encourage patients to use their own muscles to further increase flexibility and range of motion before finally advancing to other exercises improving strength, balance, coordination, and endurance. Their goal is to improve how an individual functions at work and home.

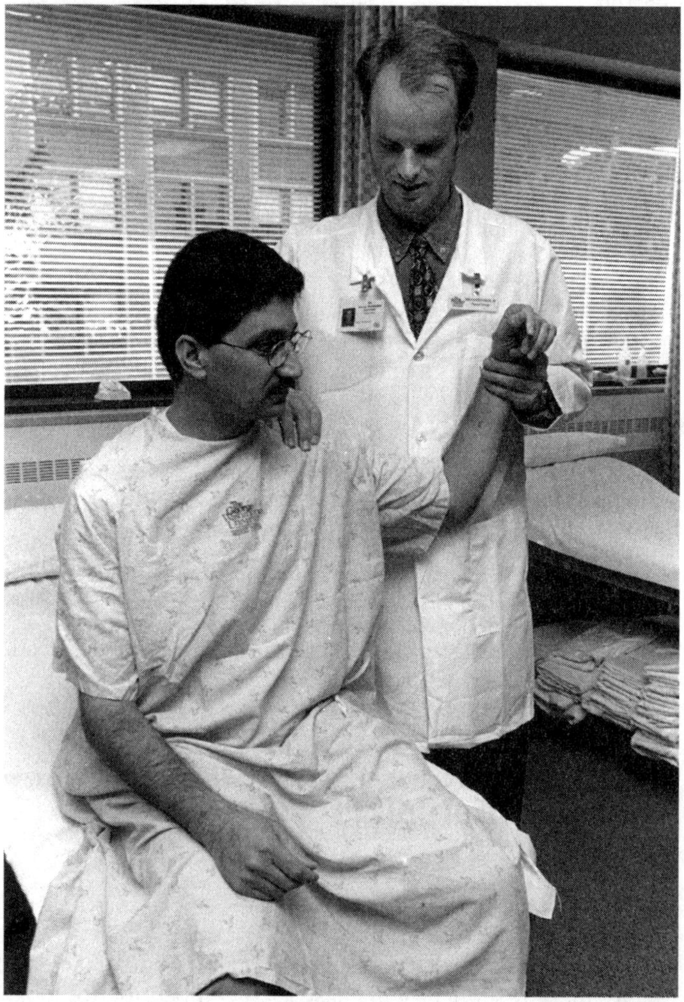

A physical therapist helps a patient increase range of motion after an injury.

Physical therapists also use electrical stimulation, hot packs or cold compresses, and ultrasound to relieve pain and reduce swelling. They may use traction or deep-tissue massage to relieve pain. Therapists also teach patients to use assistive and adaptive devices such as crutches, prostheses, and wheelchairs. They may also show patients exercises to do at home to expedite their recovery.

As treatment continues, physical therapists document progress, conduct periodic examinations, and modify treatments when necessary. Such documentation is used to track the patient's progress, and identify areas requiring more or less attention.

Physical therapists often consult and practice with a variety of other professionals, such as physicians, dentists, nurses, educators, social workers, occupational therapists, speech-language pathologists, and audiologists.

Some physical therapists treat a wide range of ailments; others specialize in areas such as pediatrics, geriatrics, orthopedics, sports medicine, neurology, and cardiopulmonary physical therapy.

Working Conditions

Physical therapists practice in hospitals, clinics, and private offices that have specially equipped facilities or they treat patients in hospital rooms, homes, or schools.

Most physical therapists work a 40-hour week, which may include some evenings and weekends. The job can be physically demanding because therapists often have to stoop, kneel, crouch, lift, and stand for long periods of time. In addition, physical therapists move heavy equipment and lift patients or help them turn, stand, or walk.

Employment

Physical therapists held about 120,000 jobs in 1998; about 1 in 4 worked part time. The number of jobs is greater than the number of practicing physical therapists because some physical therapists hold two or more jobs. For example, some may have a private practice, but also work part time in another health facility. About 1 in 10 physical therapists held more than one job in 1998.

Over two-thirds of physical therapists were employed in either hospitals or offices of physical therapists. Other jobs were in home health agencies, outpatient rehabilitation centers, offices and clinics of physicians, and nursing homes. Some physical therapists are self-employed in private practices. They may provide services to individual patients or contract to provide services in hospitals, rehabilitation centers, nursing homes, home health agencies, adult daycare programs, and schools. They may be in solo practice or be part of a consulting group. Physical therapists also teach in academic institutions and conduct research.

Training, Other Qualifications, and Advancement

All States require physical therapists to pass a licensure exam after graduating from an accredited physical therapist educational program before they can practice.

According to the American Physical Therapy Association, there were 189 accredited physical therapist programs in 1999. Of the accredited programs, 24 offered bachelor's degrees, 157 offered master's degrees, and 8 offered doctoral degrees. By 2002, all physical therapist programs seeking accreditation will be required to offer degrees at the master's degree level and above, in accordance with the Commission on Accreditation in Physical Therapy Education.

Physical therapist programs start with basic science courses such as biology, chemistry, and physics, and then introduce specialized courses such as biomechanics, neuroanatomy, human growth and development, manifestations of disease, examination techniques, and therapeutic procedures. Besides classroom and laboratory instruction, students receive supervised clinical experience. Individuals who have a 4-year degree in another field and want to be a physical therapist, should enroll in a master's or a doctoral level physical therapist educational program.

Competition for entrance into physical therapist educational programs is very intense, so interested students should attain superior grades in high school and college, especially in science courses. Courses useful when applying to physical therapist educational programs include anatomy, biology, chemistry, social science, mathematics, and physics. Before granting admission, many professional education programs require experience as a volunteer in a physical therapy department of a hospital or clinic.

Physical therapists should have strong interpersonal skills to successfully educate patients about their physical therapy treatments. They should also be compassionate and posses a desire to help patients. Similar traits are also needed to interact with the patient's family.

Physical therapists are expected to continue professional development by participating in continuing education courses and workshops. A number of States require continuing education to maintain licensure.

Job Outlook

Employment of physical therapists is expected to grow faster than the average for all occupations through 2008. However, Federal legislation imposing limits on reimbursement for therapy services may continue to adversely affect the job market for physical therapists in the near term. Because of the effects of these provisions, the majority of expected employment growth for physical therapists will occur in the second half of the projection period.

Over the long run, the demand for physical therapists should continue to rise as a result of growth in the number of individuals with disabilities or limited function requiring therapy services. The rapidly growing elderly population is particularly vulnerable to chronic and debilitating conditions that require therapeutic services. Also, the baby-boom generation is entering the prime age for heart attacks and strokes, increasing the demand for cardiac and physical rehabilitation. More young people will need physical therapy as technological advances save the lives of a larger proportion of newborns with severe birth defects.

Future medical developments should also permit a higher percentage of trauma victims to survive, creating additional demand for rehabilitative care. Growth may also result from advances in medical technology which permit treatment of more disabling conditions.

Widespread interest in health promotion should also increase demand for physical therapy services. A growing number of employers are using physical therapists to evaluate worksites, develop exercise programs, and teach safe work habits to employees in the hope of reducing injuries.

Earnings

Median annual earnings of physical therapists were $56,600 in 1998. The middle 50 percent earned between $44,460 and $77,810 a year. The lowest 10 percent earned less than $35,700 and the highest 10 percent earned more than $90,870 a year. Median annual earnings in the industries employing the largest number of physical therapists in 1997 were as follows:

Home health care services	$65,600
Nursing and personal care facilities	60,400
Offices of other health care practitioners	56,600
Offices and clinics of medical doctors	55,100
Hospitals	50,100

Related Occupations

Physical therapists rehabilitate persons with physical disabilities. Others who work in the rehabilitation field include occupational therapists, speech pathologists, audiologists, orthotists, prosthetists, and respiratory therapists.

Sources of Additional Information

Additional information on a career as a physical therapist and a list of accredited educational programs in physical therapy are available from:

☛ American Physical Therapy Association, 1111 North Fairfax St., Alexandria, VA 22314-1488. Internet: **http://www.apta.org**

Physician Assistants

(O*NET 32511)

Significant Points

- The typical physician assistant program lasts about 2 years and usually requires at least 2 years of college and some health care experience for admission.
- Earnings are high and job opportunities should be good.

Nature of the Work

Physician assistants (PAs) provide health care services with supervision by physicians. They should not be confused with medical assistants, who perform routine clinical and clerical tasks. (Medical assistants are discussed elsewhere in the *Handbook.*) PAs are formally trained to provide diagnostic, therapeutic, and preventive health care services, as delegated by a physician. Working as members of the health care team, they take medical histories, examine patients, order and interpret laboratory tests and x rays, and make diagnoses. They also treat minor injuries by suturing, splinting, and casting. PAs record progress notes, instruct and counsel patients, and order or carry out therapy. In 46 States and the District of Columbia, physician assistants may prescribe medications. PAs may also have managerial duties. Some order medical and laboratory supplies and equipment and may supervise technicians and assistants.

Physician assistants always work with the supervision of a physician. However, PAs may provide care in rural or inner city clinics

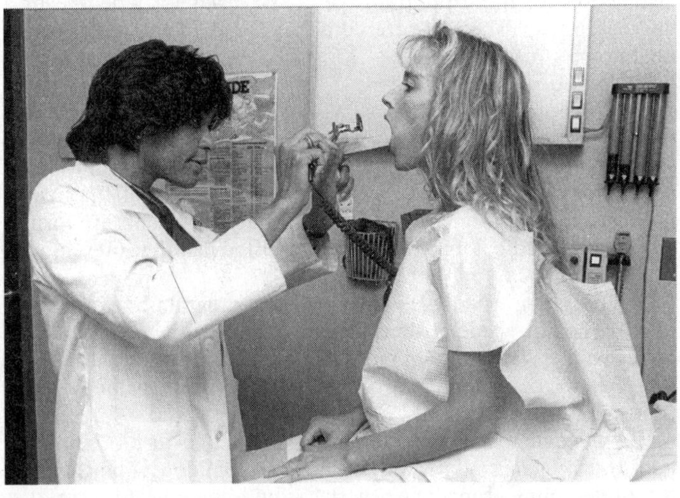

Physician assistants are projected to be among the fastest growing occupations.

where a physician is present for only 1 or 2 days each week, conferring with the supervising physician and other medical professionals as needed or required by law. PAs may also make house calls or go to hospitals and nursing homes to check on patients and report back to the physician.

The duties of physician assistants are determined by the supervising physician and by State law. Aspiring PAs should investigate the laws and regulations in the States where they wish to practice.

Many PAs work in primary care areas such as general internal medicine, pediatrics, and family medicine. Others work in specialty areas, such as general and thoracic surgery, emergency medicine, orthopedics, and geriatrics. PAs specializing in surgery provide pre- and post-operative care and may work as first or second assistants during major surgery.

Working Conditions

Although PAs usually work in a comfortable, well-lighted environment, those in surgery often stand for long periods, and others do considerable walking. Schedules vary according to practice setting and often depend on the hours of the supervising physician. The workweek of PAs in physicians' offices may include weekends, night hours, or early morning hospital rounds to visit patients. They may also be on-call. PAs in clinics usually work a 40-hour week.

Employment

Physician assistants held about 66,000 jobs in 1998. The number of jobs is greater than the number of practicing PAs because some hold two or more jobs. For example, some PAs work with a supervising physician, but also work in another practice, clinic, or hospital. According to the American Academy of Physician Assistants, there were about 34,200 certified PA's in clinical practice, as of January 1999.

Sixty-seven percent of jobs for PA's were in the offices and clinics of physicians, dentists, or other health practitioners. About 21 percent were in hospitals. The rest were mostly in public health clinics, nursing homes, prisons, home health care agencies, and the Department of Veterans Affairs.

According to the American Academy of Physician Assistants, about one-third of all PAs provide health care to communities having fewer than 50,000 residents where physicians may be in limited supply.

Training, Other Qualifications, and Advancement

All States require that new PAs complete an accredited, formal education program. As of July 1999, there were 116 accredited or provisionally accredited educational programs for physician assistants; 64 of these programs offered a bachelor's degree or a degree option. The rest offered either a certificate, an associate degree, or a master's degree. Most PA graduates have at least a bachelor's degree.

Admission requirements vary, but many programs require 2 years of college and some work experience in the health care field. Students should take courses in biology, English, chemistry, math, psychology, and social sciences. More than half of all applicants hold a bachelor's or master's degree. Many applicants are former emergency medical technicians, other allied health professionals, or nurses.

PA programs usually last 2 years. Most programs are in schools of allied health, academic health centers, medical schools, or 4-year colleges; a few are in community colleges, the military, or hospitals. Many accredited PA programs have clinical teaching affiliations with medical schools.

PA education includes classroom instruction in biochemistry, nutrition, human anatomy, physiology, microbiology, clinical pharmacology, clinical medicine, geriatric and home health care, disease prevention, and medical ethics. Students obtain supervised clinical training in several areas, including primary care medicine, inpatient medicine, surgery, obstetrics and gynecology, geriatrics, emergency medicine, psychiatry, and pediatrics. Sometimes, PA students serve one or more of these "rotations" under the supervision of a physician who is seeking to hire a PA. These rotations often lead to permanent employment.

As of 1999, 49 States and the District of Columbia had legislation governing the qualifications or practice of physician assistants; Mississippi did not. All jurisdictions required physician assistants to pass the Physician Assistants National Certifying Examination, administered by the National Commission on Certification of Physician Assistants (NCCPA)—open openly to graduates of accredited PA educational programs. Only those successfully completing the examination may use the credential "Physician Assistant-Certified (PA-C)." In order to remain certified, PAs must complete 100 hours of continuing medical education every 2 years. Every 6 years, they must pass a recertification examination or complete an alternate program combining learning experiences and a take-home examination.

Some PA's pursue additional education in order to practice in a specialty area such as surgery, neonatology, or emergency medicine. PA postgraduate residency training programs are available in areas such as internal medicine, rural primary care, emergency medicine, surgery, pediatrics, neonatology, and occupational medicine. Candidates must be graduates of an accredited program and be certified by the NCCPA.

Physician assistants need leadership skills, self-confidence, and emotional stability. They must be willing to continue studying throughout their career to keep up with medical advances.

As they attain greater clinical knowledge and experience, PAs can advance to added responsibilities and higher earnings. However, by the very nature of the profession, individual PAs are always supervised by physicians.

Job Outlook

Employment opportunities are expected to be good for physician assistants, particularly in areas or settings that have difficulty attracting physicians, such as rural and inner city clinics. Employment of PAs is expected to grow much faster than the average for all occupations through the year 2008 due to anticipated expansion of the health services industry and an emphasis on cost containment.

Physicians and institutions are expected to employ more PAs to provide primary care and assist with medical and surgical procedures because PAs are cost-effective and productive members of the health care team. Physician assistants can relieve physicians of routine duties and procedures. Telemedicine—using technology to facilitate interactive consultations between physicians and physician assistants—will also expand the use of physician assistants.

Besides the traditional office-based setting, PAs should find a growing number of jobs in institutional settings such as hospitals, academic medical centers, public clinics, and prisons. Additional PAs may be needed to augment medical staffing in inpatient teaching hospital settings if the number of physician residents is reduced. In addition, State-imposed legal limitations on the numbers of hours worked by physician residents are increasingly common and encourage hospitals to use PAs to supply some physician resident services. Opportunities will be best in States that allow PAs a wider scope of practice, such as the ability to prescribe medication.

Earnings

Median annual earnings of physician assistants were $47,090 in 1998. The middle 50 percent earned between $25,110 and $71,450 a year. The lowest 10 percent earned less than $18,600 and the highest 10 percent earned more than $86,760 a year.

Median annual earnings of physician assistants in 1997 were $41,100 in offices and clinics of medical doctors and $57,100 in hospitals.

According to the American Academy of Physician Assistants, median income for physician assistants in full-time clinical practice in 1998 was about $62,200; median income for first-year graduates was about $54,000. Income varies by specialty, practice setting, geographical location, and years of experience.

Related Occupations

Other health workers who provide direct patient care that requires a similar level of skill and training include nurse practitioners, physical therapists, occupational therapists, clinical psychologists, nurse anesthetists, nurse midwives, clinical nurse specialists, speech-language pathologists, and audiologists.

Sources of Additional Information

For information on a career as a physician assistant, contact:

☛ American Academy of Physician Assistants Information Center, 950 North Washington St., Alexandria, VA 22314-1552. Internet: **http://www.aapa.org**

For a list of accredited programs and a catalog of individual PA training programs, contact:

☛ Association of Physician Assistant Programs, 950 North Washington St., Alexandria, VA 22314-1552. Internet: **http://www.apap.org**

For eligibility requirements and a description of the Physician Assistant National Certifying Examination, write to:

☛ National Commission on Certification of Physician Assistants, Inc., 157 Technology Pkwy., Suite 800, Norcross, GA 30092-2913. Internet: **http://www.nccpa.net**

Recreational Therapists

(O*NET 32317)

Significant Points

- Employment of recreational therapists is expected to increase, due to expansion in long-term care, physical and psychiatric rehabilitation, and services for people with disabilities.
- Opportunities should generally be best for persons with a bachelor's degree in therapeutic recreation or in recreation with a concentration in therapeutic recreation.

Nature of the Work

Recreational therapists, also referred to as therapeutic recreation specialists, provide treatment services and recreation activities to individuals with disabilities, illnesses, or other disabling conditions. These therapists use a variety of techniques to treat or maintain the physical, mental, and emotional well-being of clients. Treatments may include the use of arts and crafts, animals, sports, games, dance and movement, drama, music, and community outings. Therapists help individuals reduce depression, stress, and anxiety. They also help individuals recover basic motor functioning and reasoning abilities, build confidence, and socialize effectively to enable greater independence, as well as to reduce or eliminate the effects of illness or disability. Additionally, they help integrate people with disabilities into the community, by helping them use community resources and recreational activities. Recreational therapists should not be confused with recreation workers, who organize recreational activities primarily for enjoyment. (Recreation workers are discussed elsewhere in the *Handbook.*)

Recreational therapists help people with disabling conditions live fuller lives through activities.

In acute health care settings, such as hospitals and rehabilitation centers, recreational therapists treat and rehabilitate individuals with specific health conditions, usually in conjunction or collaboration with physicians, nurses, psychologists, social workers, and physical and occupational therapists. In long-term care facilities and residential facilities, recreational therapists use leisure activities—especially structured group programs—to improve and maintain general health and well-being. They may also treat clients and provide interventions to prevent further medical problems and secondary complications related to illness and disabilities.

Recreational therapists assess clients, based on information from standardized assessments, observations, medical records, medical staff, family, and clients themselves. They then develop and carry out therapeutic interventions consistent with client needs and interests. For example, clients isolated from others, or with limited social skills, may be encouraged to play games with others, or right-handed persons with right-side paralysis may be instructed to adapt to using their non-affected left side to throw a ball or swing a racket. Recreational therapists may instruct patients in relaxation techniques to reduce stress and tension, stretching and limbering exercises, proper body mechanics for participation in recreation activities, pacing and energy conservation techniques, and individual as well as team activities. Additionally, therapists observe and document patients' participation, reactions, and progress.

Community based therapeutic recreation specialists may work in park and recreation departments, special education programs for school districts, or programs for older adults and people with disabilities. Included in the latter group are programs and facilities such as assisted living, adult day service centers and substance abuse rehabilitation centers. In these programs, therapists use interventions to develop specific skills while providing opportunities for exercise, mental stimulation, creativity, and fun. Although most therapists are employed in other areas, those who work in schools help counselors, teachers, and parents address the special needs of students—most importantly, easing the transition into adult life for disabled students.

Working Conditions

Recreational therapists provide services in special activity rooms but also plan activities and prepare documentation in offices. When working with clients during community integration programs, they may travel locally to instruct clients on the accessibility of public transportation and other public areas, such as parks, playgrounds, swimming pools, restaurants, and theaters.

Therapists often lift and carry equipment as well as lead recreational activities. Recreational therapists generally work a 40-hour week that may include some evenings, weekends, and holidays.

Employment

Recreational therapists held about 39,000 jobs in 1998. About 38 percent of salaried jobs for therapists were in hospitals, and 26 percent were in nursing and personal care facilities. Others worked in residential facilities, community mental health centers, adult day care programs, correctional facilities, community programs for people with disabilities, and substance abuse centers. About 1 out of 3 therapists was self-employed, generally contracting with long-term care facilities or community agencies to develop and oversee programs.

Training, Other Qualifications, and Advancement

A bachelor's degree in therapeutic recreation, or in recreation with a concentration in therapeutic recreation, is the usual requirement for entry-level positions. Persons may qualify for paraprofessional positions with an associate degree in therapeutic recreation or a health care related field. An associate degree in recreational therapy; training in art, drama, or music therapy; or qualifying work experience may be sufficient for activity director positions in nursing homes.

Most employers prefer to hire candidates who are certified therapeutic recreation specialists (CTRS). The National Council for Therapeutic Recreation Certification (NCTRC) certifies therapeutic recreation specialists. To become certified, specialists must have a bachelor's degree, pass a written certification examination, and complete an internship of at least 360 hours, under the supervision of a certified therapeutic recreation specialist. A few colleges or agencies may require 600 hours of internship.

There are approximately 150 programs that prepare recreational therapists. Most offer bachelors degrees, although some offer associate, master's, or doctoral degrees. As of 1998, there were 43 recreation programs with options in therapeutic recreation accredited by the National Council on Accreditation.

Recreational therapy programs include courses in assessment, treatment and program planning, intervention design, and evaluation. Students also study human anatomy, physiology, abnormal psychology, medical and psychiatric terminology, characteristics of illnesses and disabilities, professional ethics, and the use of assistive devices and technology.

Recreational therapists should be comfortable working with persons who are ill or have disabilities. Therapists must be patient, tactful, and persuasive when working with people who have a variety of special needs. Ingenuity, a sense of humor, and imagination are needed to adapt activities to individual needs; and good physical coordination is necessary to demonstrate or participate in recreational activities.

Therapists may advance to supervisory or administrative positions. Some teach, conduct research, or perform contract consulting work.

Job Outlook

Employment of recreational therapists is expected to grow as fast as the average for all occupations through the year 2008, because of anticipated expansion in long-term care, physical and psychiatric rehabilitation, and services for people with disabilities. However, the total number of job openings will be relatively low, because the occupation is small. Opportunities should be best for persons with a bachelor's degree in therapeutic recreation or in recreation with an option in therapeutic recreation.

Health care facilities will provide a growing number of jobs in hospital-based adult day care and outpatient programs and in units offering short-term mental health and alcohol or drug abuse services. Rehabilitation, home-health care, transitional programs, and psychiatric facilities will provide additional jobs.

The rapidly growing number of older adults is expected to spur job growth for therapeutic recreation specialists and recreational therapy paraprofessionals in assisted living facilities, adult day care programs, and social service agencies. Continued growth is also expected in community residential facilities, as well as day care programs for individuals with disabilities.

Earnings

Median annual earnings of recreational therapists were $27,760 in 1998. The middle 50 percent earned between $21,580 and $35,000 a year. The lowest 10 percent earned less than $16,380 and the highest 10 percent earned more than $42,440 a year. Median annual earnings for recreational therapists in 1997 were $29,700 in hospitals and $21,900 in nursing and personal care facilities.

Related Occupations

Recreational therapists primarily design activities to help people with disabilities lead more fulfilling and independent lives. Other workers who have similar jobs are recreational therapy paraprofessionals, orientation therapists for persons who are blind or have visual impairments, art therapists, drama therapists, dance therapists, music therapists, occupational therapists, physical therapists, and rehabilitation counselors.

Sources of Additional Information

For information on how to order materials describing careers and academic programs in recreational therapy, write to:

☛ American Therapeutic Recreation Association, P.O. Box 15215, Hattiesburg, MS 39402-5215. Internet: **http://www.atra-tr.org**

☛ National Therapeutic Recreation Society, 22377 Belmont Ridge Rd., Ashburn, VA 20148-4501.
Internet: **http://www.nrpa.org/branches/ntrs.htm**

Certification information may be obtained from:

☛ National Council for Therapeutic Recreation Certification, P.O. Box 479, Thiells, NY 10984-0479.

Registered Nurses

(O*NET 32502)

Significant Points

- The largest health care occupation, with over 2 million jobs.
- One of the 10 occupations projected to have the largest numbers of new jobs.
- Earnings are above average, particularly for advanced practice nurses who have additional education or training.

Nature of the Work

Registered nurses (R.N.s) work to promote health, prevent disease, and help patients cope with illness. They are advocates and health educators for patients, families, and communities. When providing direct patient care, they observe, assess, and record symptoms, reactions, and progress; assist physicians during treatments and examinations; administer medications; and assist in convalescence and rehabilitation. R.N.s also develop and manage nursing care plans; instruct patients and their families in proper care; and help individuals and groups take steps to improve or maintain their health. While State laws govern the tasks R.N.s may perform, it is usually the work setting, which determines their day-to-day job duties.

Hospital nurses form the largest group of nurses. Most are staff nurses, who provide bedside nursing care and carry out medical regimens. They may also supervise licensed practical nurses and aides. Hospital nurses usually are assigned to one area such as surgery, maternity, pediatrics, emergency room, intensive care, or treatment of cancer patients. Some may rotate among departments.

Office nurses care for outpatients in physicians' offices, clinics, surgicenters, and emergency medical centers. They prepare patients for and assist with examinations, administer injections and medications, dress wounds and incisions, assist with minor surgery, and maintain records. Some also perform routine laboratory and office work.

Nursing home nurses manage nursing care for residents with conditions ranging from a fracture to Alzheimer's disease. Although they usually spend most of their time on administrative and supervisory tasks, R.N.s also assess residents' medical condition, develop treatment plans, supervise licensed practical nurses and nursing aides, and perform difficult procedures such as starting intravenous fluids. They also work in specialty-care departments, such as long-term rehabilitation units for strokes and head-injuries.

Home health nurses provide periodic services, prescribed by a physician, to patients at home. After assessing patients' home environments, they care for and instruct patients and their families. Home health nurses care for a broad range of patients, such as those recovering from illnesses and accidents, cancer, and child birth. They must be able to work independently and may supervise home health aides.

Public health nurses work in government and private agencies and clinics, schools, retirement communities and other community settings. They focus on populations, working with individuals, groups, and families to improve the overall health of communities. They also work as partners with communities to plan and implement programs. Public health nurses instruct individuals, families, and other groups in health education, disease prevention, nutrition, and child care. They arrange for immunizations, blood pressure testing, and other health screening. These nurses also work with community leaders, teachers, parents, and physicians in community health education.

Occupational health or *industrial nurses* provide nursing care at worksites to employees, customers, and others with minor injuries and illnesses. They provide emergency care, prepare accident reports, and arrange for further care if necessary. They also offer health counseling, assist with health examinations and inoculations, and assess work environments to identify potential health or safety problems.

Head nurses or *nurse supervisors* direct nursing activities. They plan work schedules and assign duties to nurses and aides, provide or arrange for training, and visit patients to observe nurses and to insure that care is proper. They may also insure records are maintained and equipment and supplies are ordered.

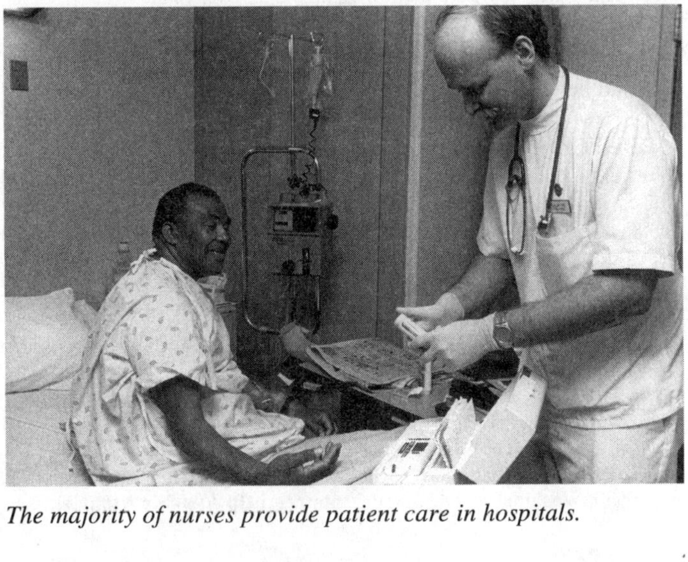

The majority of nurses provide patient care in hospitals.

At the advanced level, *nurse practitioners* provide basic primary health care. They diagnose and treat common acute illnesses and injuries. Nurse practitioners can prescribe medications in all States and the District of Columbia. Other advanced practice nurses include *clinical nurse specialists, certified registered nurse anesthetists,* and *certified nurse-midwives.* Advanced practice nurses have met higher educational and clinical practice requirements beyond the basic nursing education and licensing required of all R.N.s.

Working Conditions

Most nurses work in well-lighted, comfortable health care facilities. Home health and public health nurses travel to patients' homes and to schools, community centers, and other sites. Nurses may spend considerable time walking and standing. They need emotional stability to cope with human suffering, emergencies, and other stresses. Because patients in hospitals and nursing homes require 24-hour care, nurses in these institutions may work nights, weekends, and holidays. They may also be on-call; available to work on short notice. Office, occupational health, and public health nurses are more likely to work regular business hours. Almost 1 in 10 R.N.s held more than one job in 1998.

Nursing has its hazards, especially in hospitals, nursing homes, and clinics where nurses may care for individuals with infectious diseases such as hepatitis. Nurses must observe rigid guidelines to guard against these and other dangers such as radiation, chemicals used for sterilization of instruments, and anesthetics. In addition, they are vulnerable to back injury when moving patients, shocks from electrical equipment, and hazards posed by compressed gases.

Employment

As the largest health care occupation, registered nurses held about 2.1 million jobs in 1998. About 3 out of 5 jobs were in hospitals, in inpatient and outpatient departments. Others were mostly in offices and clinics of physicians and other health practitioners, home health care agencies, nursing homes, temporary help agencies, schools, and government agencies. The remainder worked in residential care facilities, social service agencies, religious organizations, research facilities, management and public relations firms, insurance agencies, and private households. About 1 out of 4 R.N.s worked part time.

Training, Other Qualifications, and Advancement

In all States, students must graduate from a nursing program and pass a national licensing examination to obtain a nursing license. Nurses may be licensed in more than one State, either by examination or endorsement of a license issued by another State. Licenses must be periodically renewed. Some States require continuing education for licensure renewal.

In 1998, there were over 2,200 entry level R.N. programs. There are three major educational paths to nursing: Associate degree in nursing (A.D.N.), bachelor of science degree in nursing (B.S.N.), and diploma. A.D.N. programs, offered by community and junior colleges, take about 2 years. About half of all R.N. programs in 1998 were at the A.D.N. level. B.S.N. programs, offered by colleges and universities, take 4 or 5 years. About one-fourth of all programs in 1998 offered degrees at the bachelor's level. Diploma programs, given in hospitals, last 2 to 3 years. Only a small number of programs, about 4 percent, offer diploma level degrees. Generally, licensed graduates of any of the three program types qualify for entry level positions as staff nurses.

There have been attempts to raise the educational requirements for an R.N. license to a bachelor's degree and, possibly, create new job titles. These changes, should they occur, will probably be made State by State, through legislation or regulation. Changes in licensure requirements would not affect currently licensed R.N.s, who would be "grandfathered" in, no matter what their educational preparation. However, individuals considering nursing should carefully weigh the pros and cons of enrolling in a B.S.N. program, since their advancement opportunities are broader. In fact, many career paths are open only to nurses with bachelor's or advanced degrees. A bachelor's degree is usually necessary for administrative positions and is a prerequisite for admission to graduate nursing programs in research, consulting, teaching, or a clinical specialization.

Many A.D.N. and diploma-trained nurses enter bachelor's programs to prepare for a broader scope of nursing practice. They can often find a hospital position and then take advantage of tuition reimbursement programs to work toward a B.S.N.

Nursing education includes classroom instruction and supervised clinical experience in hospitals and other health facilities. Students take courses in anatomy, physiology, microbiology, chemistry, nutrition, psychology and other behavioral sciences, and nursing. Coursework also includes liberal arts classes.

Supervised clinical experience is provided in hospital departments such as pediatrics, psychiatry, maternity, and surgery. A growing number of programs include clinical experience in nursing homes, public health departments, home health agencies, and ambulatory clinics.

Nurses should be caring and sympathetic. They must be able to accept responsibility, direct or supervise others, follow orders precisely, and determine when consultation is required.

Experience and good performance can lead to promotion to more responsible positions. Nurses can advance, in management, to assistant head nurse or head nurse. From there, they can advance to assistant director, director, and vice president. Increasingly, management level nursing positions require a graduate degree in nursing or health services administration. They also require leadership, negotiation skills, and good judgment. Graduate programs preparing executive level nurses usually last 1 to 2 years.

Within patient care, nurses can advance to clinical nurse specialist, nurse practitioner, certified nurse-midwife, or certified registered nurse anesthetist. These positions require 1 or 2 years of graduate education, leading in most instances to a master's degree, or to a certificate.

Some nurses move into the business side of health care. Their nursing expertise and experience on a health care team equip them to manage ambulatory, acute, home health, and chronic care services. Some are employed by health care corporations in health planning and development, marketing, and quality assurance. Other nurses work as college and university faculty or do research.

Job Outlook

Employment of registered nurses is expected to grow faster than the average for all occupations through 2008 and because the occupation is large, many new jobs will result. There will always be a need for traditional hospital nurses, but a large number of new nurses will be employed in home health, long-term, and ambulatory care.

Faster than average growth will be driven by technological advances in patient care, which permit a greater number of medical problems to be treated, and an increasing emphasis on primary care. In addition, the number of older people, who are much more likely than younger people to need medical care, is projected to grow very rapidly. Many job openings also will result from the need to replace experienced nurses who leave the occupation, especially as the median age of the registered nurse population continues to rise.

Employment in hospitals, the largest sector, is expected to grow more slowly than in other health-care sectors. While the intensity of nursing care is likely to increase, requiring more nurses per patient, the number of inpatients (those who remain overnight) is not likely to increase much. Patients are being released earlier and more procedures are being done on an outpatient basis, both in and outside hospitals. Most rapid growth is expected in hospitals' outpatient facilities, such as same-day surgery, rehabilitation, and chemotherapy.

Employment in home health care is expected to grow rapidly. This is in response to a growing number of older persons with functional disabilities, consumer preference for care in the home, and technological advances which make it possible to bring increasingly complex treatments into the home. The type of care demanded will require nurses who are able to perform complex procedures.

Employment in nursing homes is expected to grow much faster than average due to increases in the number of people in their eighties and nineties, many of whom will require long-term care. In addition, the financial pressure on hospitals to release patients as soon as possible should produce more nursing home admissions. Growth in units to provide specialized long-term rehabilitation for stroke and head injury patients or to treat Alzheimer's victims will also increase employment.

An increasing proportion of sophisticated procedures, which once were performed only in hospitals, are being performed in physicians' offices and clinics, including ambulatory surgicenters and emergency medical centers. Accordingly, employment is expected to grow faster than average in these places as health care in general expands.

In evolving integrated health care networks, nurses may rotate among employment settings. Since jobs in traditional hospital nursing positions are no longer the only option, R.N.s will need to be flexible. Opportunities will be good for nurses with advanced education and training, such as nurse practitioners.

Earnings

Median annual earnings of registered nurses were $40,690 in 1998. The middle 50 percent earned between $34,430 and $49,070 a year. The lowest 10 percent earned less than $29,480 and the highest 10 percent earned more than $69,300 a year. Median annual earnings in the industries employing the largest numbers of registered nurses in 1997 were as follows:

Personnel supply services	$43,000
Hospitals	39,900
Home health care services	39,200
Offices and clinics of medical doctors	36,500
Nursing and personal care facilities	36,300

Many employers offer flexible work schedules, child care, educational benefits, and bonuses.

Related Occupations

Workers in other health care occupations with responsibilities and duties related to those of registered nurses are occupational therapists, emergency medical technicians, physical therapists, physician assistants, and respiratory therapists.

Sources of Additional Information

For information on a career as a registered nurse and nursing education, contact:

☛ National League for Nursing, 61 Broadway, New York, NY 10006. Internet: **http://www.nln.org**

For a list of B.S.N. and graduate programs, write to:

☛ American Association of Colleges of Nursing, 1 Dupont Circle NW., Suite 530, Washington, DC 20036. Internet: **http://www.aacn.nche.edu**

Information on registered nurses is also available from:

☛ American Nurses Association, 600 Maryland Ave. SW., Washington, DC 20024-2571. Internet: **http://www.nursingworld.org**

Respiratory Therapists

(O*NET 32302)

Significant Points

- Hospitals will continue to employ more than 9 out of 10 respiratory therapists, but a growing number will work in home health agencies, respiratory therapy clinics, and nursing homes.
- Job opportunities will be best for therapists who work with newborns and infants.

Nature of the Work

Respiratory therapists evaluate, treat, and care for patients with breathing disorders. To evaluate patients, therapists test the capacity of the lungs and analyze oxygen and carbon dioxide concentration. They also measure the patient's potential of hydrogen (pH), which indicates the acidity or alkalinity level of the blood. To measure lung capacity, therapists have patients breathe into an instrument that measures the volume and flow of oxygen during inhalation and exhalation. By comparing the reading with the norm for the patient's age, height, weight, and sex, respiratory therapists can determine whether lung deficiencies exist. To analyze oxygen, carbon dioxide, and pH levels, therapists draw an arterial blood sample, place it in a blood gas analyzer, and relay the results to a physician.

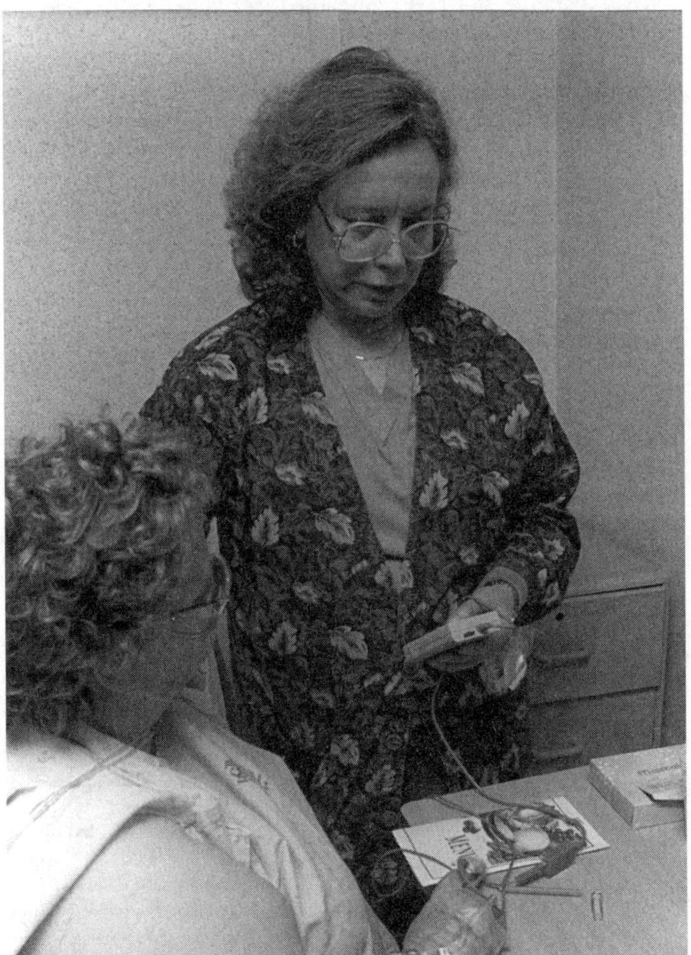

A respiratory therapist measures the oxygen in a patient's bloodstream.

Respiratory therapists treat all types of patients, ranging from premature infants whose lungs are not fully developed, to elderly people whose lungs are diseased. These workers provide temporary relief to patients with chronic asthma or emphysema and emergency care for patients who suffered heart failure or a stroke or are victims of drowning or shock. Respiratory therapists most commonly use oxygen or oxygen mixtures, chest physiotherapy, and aerosol medications. To increase a patient's concentration of oxygen, therapists place an oxygen mask or nasal cannula on a patient and set the oxygen flow at the level prescribed by a physician. Therapists also connect patients who cannot breathe on their own to ventilators that deliver pressurized oxygen into the lungs. They insert a tube into a patient's trachea, or windpipe; connect the tube to the ventilator; and set the rate, volume, and oxygen concentration of the oxygen mixture entering the patient's lungs.

Therapists regularly check on patients and equipment. If the patient appears to be having difficulty, or if the oxygen, carbon dioxide, or pH level of the blood is abnormal, they change the ventilator setting, according to the doctor's order or check equipment for mechanical problems. In home care, therapists teach patients and their families to use ventilators and other life support systems. Additionally, they visit several times a month to inspect and clean equipment and ensure its proper use and make emergency visits, if equipment problems arise.

Respiratory therapists perform chest physiotherapy on patients to remove mucus from their lungs and make it easier for them to breathe. For example, during surgery, anesthesia depresses respiration, so this treatment may be prescribed to help get the patient's lungs back to normal and to prevent congestion. Chest physiotherapy also helps patients suffering from lung diseases, such as cystic fibrosis, that cause mucus to collect in the lungs. In this procedure, therapists place patients in positions to help drain mucus, thump and vibrate patients' rib cages, and instruct them to cough.

Respiratory therapists also administer aerosols—generally liquid medications suspended in a gas that forms a mist which is inhaled—and teach patients how to inhale the aerosol properly to assure its effectiveness.

Therapists are increasingly asked to perform tasks that fall outside their traditional role. Tasks are expanding into cardiopulmonary procedures like electrocardiograms and stress testing, as well as other tasks like drawing blood samples from patients. Therapists also keep records of materials used and charges to patients. Additionally, some teach or supervise other respiratory therapy personnel.

Working Conditions

Respiratory therapists generally work between 35 and 40 hours a week. Because hospitals operate around the clock, therapists may work evenings, nights, or weekends. They spend long periods standing and walking between patients' rooms. In an emergency, therapists work under a great deal of stress.

Because gases used by respiratory therapists are stored under pressure, they are potentially hazardous. However, adherence to safety precautions and regular maintenance and testing of equipment minimize the risk of injury. As with many health occupations, respiratory therapists run a risk of catching infectious diseases, but carefully following proper procedures minimizes this risk, as well.

Employment

Respiratory therapists held about 86,000 jobs in 1998. About 9 out of 10 jobs were in hospital departments of respiratory care, anesthesiology, or pulmonary medicine. Home health agencies, respiratory therapy clinics, and nursing homes accounted for most of the remaining jobs.

Training, Other Qualifications, and Advancement

Formal training is necessary for entry to this field. Training is offered at the postsecondary level by hospitals, medical schools, colleges and universities, trade schools, vocational-technical institutes, and the Armed Forces. Some programs prepare graduates for jobs as registered respiratory therapists (RRT); other, shorter programs lead to jobs as certified respiratory therapists (CRT). According to the Committee on Accreditation for Respiratory Care (CoARC), there were 327 registered respiratory therapist programs and 134 certified respiratory therapist programs in the United States in 1999.

Formal training programs vary in length and in the credential or degree awarded. Most of the CoARC-accredited registered respiratory therapist programs last 2 years and lead to an associate degree. Some, however, are 4-year bachelor's degree programs. Areas of study for respiratory therapy programs include human anatomy and physiology, chemistry, physics, microbiology, and mathematics. Technical courses deal with procedures, equipment, and clinical tests.

More and more therapists receive on-the-job training, allowing them to administer electrocardiograms and stress tests, as well as draw blood samples from patients.

Therapists should be sensitive to patients' physical and psychological needs. Respiratory care workers must pay attention to detail, follow instructions, and work as part of a team. In addition, operating complicated respiratory therapy equipment requires mechanical ability and manual dexterity.

High school students interested in a career in respiratory care should take courses in health, biology, mathematics, chemistry, and physics. Respiratory care involves basic mathematical problem solving and an understanding of chemical and physical principles. For example, respiratory care workers must be able to compute medication dosages and calculate gas concentrations.

Over 40 States license respiratory care personnel. The National Board for Respiratory Care offers voluntary certification and registration to graduates of CoARC-accredited programs. Two credentials are awarded to respiratory therapists who satisfy the requirements: Registered Respiratory Therapist (RRT) and Certified Respiratory Therapist (CRT). All graduates—those from 2- and 4-year programs in respiratory therapy, as well as those from 1-year CRT programs—may take the CRT examination. CRTs who meet education and experience requirements can take a separate examination, leading to the award of the RRT.

Individuals who have completed a 4-year program in a nonrespiratory field but have college level courses in anatomy, physiology, chemistry, biology, microbiology, physics, and mathematics can become a CRT, after graduating from an accredited 1- or 2-year program. After they receive 2 years of clinical experience, they are eligible to take the registry exam to become an RRT.

Most employers require applicants for entry-level or generalist positions to hold the CRT or be eligible to take the certification examination. Supervisory positions and those in intensive care specialties usually require the RRT (or RRT eligibility).

Respiratory therapists advance in clinical practice by moving from care of general to critical patients who have significant problems in other organ systems, such as the heart or kidneys. Respiratory therapists, especially those with 4-year degrees, may also advance to supervisory or managerial positions in a respiratory therapy department. Respiratory therapists in home care and equipment rental firms may become branch managers.

Job Outlook

Job opportunities are expected to remain good. Employment of respiratory therapists is expected to increase much faster than the average for all occupations through the year 2008, because of substantial growth of the middle-aged and elderly population—a development that will heighten the incidence of cardiopulmonary disease.

Older Americans suffer most from respiratory ailments and cardiopulmonary diseases such as pneumonia, chronic bronchitis, emphysema, and heart disease. As their numbers increase, the need for respiratory therapists will increase, as well. In addition, advances in treating victims of heart attacks, accident victims, and premature infants (many of whom are dependent on a ventilator during part of their treatment) will increase the demand for the services of respiratory care practitioners.

Opportunities are expected to be highly favorable for respiratory therapists with cardiopulmonary care skills and experience working with infants.

Although hospitals will continue to employ the vast majority of therapists, a growing number of therapists can expect to work outside of hospitals in home health agencies, respiratory therapy clinics, or nursing homes.

Earnings

Median annual earnings for respiratory therapists were $34,830 in 1998. The middle 50 percent earned between $30,040 and $39,830 a year. The lowest 10 percent earned less than $25,910 and the highest 10 percent earned more than $46,760 a year.

Related Occupations

Respiratory therapists, under the supervision of a physician, administer respiratory care and life support to patients with heart and lung difficulties. Other workers who care for, treat, or train people to improve their physical condition include dialysis technicians, registered nurses, occupational therapists, physical therapists, and radiation therapists.

Sources of Additional Information

Information concerning a career in respiratory care is available from:

☛ American Association for Respiratory Care, 11030 Ables Ln., Dallas, TX 75229-4593. Internet: **http://www.aarc.org**

Information on gaining credentials as a respiratory therapy practitioner can be obtained from:

☛ The National Board for Respiratory Care, Inc., 8310 Nieman Rd., Lenexa, KS 66214-1579. Internet: **http://www.nbrc.org**

For the current list of CoARC-accredited educational programs for respiratory therapy occupations, write to:

☛ Committee on Accreditation for Respiratory Care, 1248 Harwood Rd., Bedford, TX 76021-4244. Internet: **http://www.coarc.com**

Speech-Language Pathologists and Audiologists

(O*NET 32314)

Significant Points

- About half work in schools, and most others are employed by healthcare facilities.
- A master's degree in speech-language pathology or audiology is the standard credential.

Nature of the Work

Speech-language pathologists assess, treat, and help to prevent speech, language, cognitive, communication, voice, swallowing, fluency, and other related disorders; audiologists identify, assess, and manage auditory, balance, and other neural systems.

Speech-language pathologists work with people who cannot make speech sounds, or cannot make them clearly; those with speech rhythm and fluency problems, such as stuttering; people with voice quality problems, such as inappropriate pitch or harsh voice; those with problems understanding and producing language; and those with cognitive communication impairments, such as attention, memory, and problem solving disorders. They may also work with people who have oral motor problems causing eating and swallowing difficulties.

Speech and language problems can result from hearing loss, brain injury or deterioration, cerebral palsy, stroke, cleft palate, voice pathology, mental retardation, or emotional problems. Problems can be congenital, developmental, or acquired. Speech-language pathologists use written and oral tests, as well as special instruments, to diagnose the nature and extent of impairment and to record and analyze speech, language, and swallowing irregularities. Speech-language pathologists develop an individualized plan of care, tailored to each patient's needs. For individuals with little or no speech capability, speech-language pathologists select augmentative alternative communication methods, including automated devices and sign language, and teach their use. They teach these individuals how to make sounds, improve their voices, or increase their language skills to communicate more effectively. Speech-language pathologists help patients develop, or recover, reliable communication skills so patients can fulfill their educational, vocational, and social roles.

Most speech-language pathologists provide direct clinical services to individuals with communication disorders. In speech and language clinics, they may independently develop and carry out treatment programs. In medical facilities, they may work with physicians, social workers, psychologists, and other therapists to develop and execute treatment plans. Speech-language pathologists in schools develop individual or group programs, counsel parents, and may assist teachers with classroom activities.

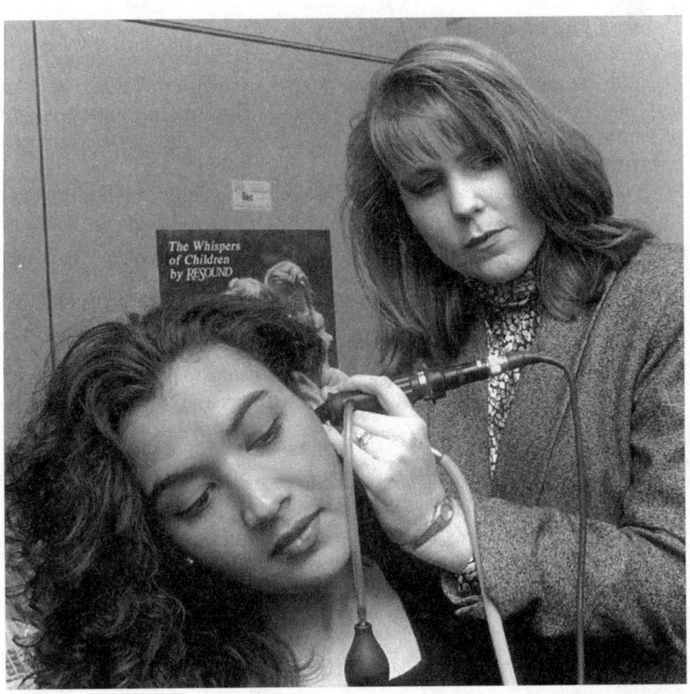

Using specialized video equipment, an audiologist examines a patient's ear canal.

Speech-language pathologists keep records on the initial evaluation, progress, and discharge of clients. This helps pinpoint problems, tracks client progress, and justifies the cost of treatment when applying for reimbursement. They counsel individuals and their families concerning communication disorders and how to cope with the stress and misunderstanding that often accompany them. They also work with family members to recognize and change behavior patterns that impede communication and treatment and show them communication-enhancing techniques to use at home.

Some speech-language pathologists conduct research on how people communicate. Others design and develop equipment or techniques for diagnosing and treating speech problems.

Audiologists work with people who have hearing, balance, and related problems. They use audiometers, computers, and other testing devices to measure the loudness at which a person begins to hear sounds, the ability to distinguish between sounds, and the nature and extent of hearing loss. Audiologists interpret these results and may coordinate them with medical, educational, and psychological information to make a diagnosis and determine a course of treatment.

Hearing disorders can result from a variety of causes including trauma at birth, viral infections, genetic disorders, exposure to loud noise, or aging. Treatment may include examining and cleaning the ear canal, fitting and dispensing hearing aids or other assistive devices, and audiologic rehabilitation (including auditory training or instruction in speech or lip reading). Audiologists may recommend, fit, and dispense personal or large area amplification systems, such as hearing aids and alerting devices. Audiologists provide fitting and tuning of cochlear implants and provide the necessary rehabilitation for adjustment to listening with implant amplification systems. They also measure noise levels in workplaces and conduct hearing protection programs in industry, as well as in schools and communities.

Audiologists provide direct clinical services to individuals with hearing or balance disorders. In audiology (hearing) clinics, they may independently develop and carry out treatment programs. Audiologists, in a variety of settings, work as members of interdisciplinary professional teams in planning and implementing service delivery for children and adults, from birth to old age. Similar to speech-language pathologists, audiologists keep records on the initial evaluation, progress, and discharge of clients. These records help pinpoint problems, track client progress, and justify the cost of treatment, when applying for reimbursement.

Audiologists may conduct research on types of, and treatment for, hearing, balance, and related disorders. Others design and develop equipment or techniques for diagnosing and treating these disorders.

Working Conditions

Speech-language pathologists and audiologists usually work at a desk or table in clean comfortable surroundings. The job is not physically demanding but does require attention to detail and intense concentration. The emotional needs of clients and their families may be demanding. Most full-time speech-language pathologists and audiologists work about 40 hours per week; some work part-time. Those who work on a contract basis may spend a substantial amount of time traveling between facilities.

Employment

Speech-language pathologists and audiologists held about 105,000 jobs in 1998. About one-half provided services in preschools, elementary and secondary schools, or colleges and universities. Others were in offices of speech-language pathologists and audiologists; hospitals; offices of physicians; speech, language, and hearing centers; home health agencies; or other facilities.

Some speech-language pathologists and audiologists are self-employed in private practice. They contract to provide services in schools, physician's offices, hospitals, or nursing homes, or work as consultants to industry. Audiologists are more likely to be employed in independent healthcare offices, while speech-language pathologists are more likely to work in school settings.

Training, Other Qualifications, and Advancement
Of the States that regulate licensing (44 for speech-language pathologists and 49 for audiologists), almost all require a master's degree or equivalent. Other requirements are 300 to 375 hours of supervised clinical experience, a passing score on a national examination, and 9 months of postgraduate professional clinical experience. Thirty-six States have continuing education requirements for licensure renewal. Medicaid, medicare, and private health insurers generally require a practitioner to be licensed to qualify for reimbursement.

About 235 colleges and universities offer graduate programs in speech-language pathology. Courses cover anatomy and physiology of the areas of the body involved in speech, language, and hearing; the development of normal speech, language, and hearing; the nature of disorders; acoustics; and psychological aspects of communication. Graduate students also learn to evaluate and treat speech, language, and hearing disorders and receive supervised clinical training in communication disorders.

About 115 colleges and universities offer graduate programs in audiology in the United States. Course work includes anatomy; physiology; basic science; math; physics; genetics; normal and abnormal communication development; auditory, balance and neural systems assessment and treatment; audiologic rehabilitation; and ethics.

Speech-language pathologists can acquire the Certificate of Clinical Competence in Speech-Language Pathology (CCC-SLP) offered by the American Speech-Language-Hearing Association, and audiologists can earn the Certificate of Clinical Competence in Audiology (CCC-A). To earn a CCC, a person must have a graduate degree and 375 hours of supervised clinical experience, complete a 36-week postgraduate clinical fellowship, and pass a written examination. According to the American Speech-Language Hearing Association, as of 2007, audiologists will need to have a bachelor's degree and complete 75 hours of credit toward a doctoral degree in order to seek certification. As of 2012, audiologists will have to earn a doctoral degree in order to be certified.

Speech-language pathologists and audiologists should be able to effectively communicate diagnostic test results, diagnoses, and proposed treatment in a manner easily understood by their clients. They must be able to approach problems objectively and provide support to clients and their families. Because a client's progress may be slow, patience, compassion, and good listening skills are necessary.

Job Outlook
Employment of speech-language pathologists and audiologists is expected to grow much faster than the average for all occupations through the year 2008. Because hearing loss is strongly associated with aging, rapid growth in the population age 55 and over will cause the number of persons with hearing impairment to increase markedly. In addition, baby boomers are now entering middle age, when the possibility of neurological disorders and associated speech, language, and hearing impairments increases. Medical advances are also improving the survival rate of premature infants and trauma and stroke victims, who then need assessment and possible treatment.

Employment growth in health services would be even faster except for Federal legislation imposing limits on reimbursement for therapy services that may continue to adversely affect the job market for therapy providers over the near term. Because of the effects of these provisions, the majority of expected employment growth in health services will occur in the second half of the projection period.

Employment in schools will increase along with growth in elementary and secondary school enrollments, including enrollment of special education students. Federal law guarantees special education and related services to all eligible children with disabilities. Greater awareness of the importance of early identification and diagnosis of speech, language, and hearing disorders will also increase employment.

The number of speech-language pathologists and audiologists in private practice will rise due to the increasing use of contract services by hospitals, schools, and nursing homes. In addition to job openings stemming from employment growth, some openings for speech-language pathologists and audiologists will arise from the need to replace those who leave the occupation.

Earnings
Median annual earnings of speech-language pathologists and audiologists were $43,080 in 1998. The middle 50 percent earned between $34,580 and $55,260 a year. The lowest 10 percent earned less than $27,460 and the highest 10 percent earned more than $80,720 a year. Median annual earnings in the industries employing the largest number of speech-language pathologists and audiologists in 1997 were as follows:

Hospitals	$44,800
Offices of other health care practitioners	44,500
Elementary and secondary schools	38,400

According to a 1999 survey by the American Speech-Language-Hearing Association, the median annual salary for full-time certified speech-language pathologists or audiologists who worked 11 or 12 months annually was $44,000. For those who worked 9 or 10 months annually, median annual salaries for speech-language pathologists were $40,000; for audiologists, $42,000.

Related Occupations
Speech-language pathologists specialize in the prevention, diagnosis, and treatment of speech and language problems. Workers in related occupations include occupational therapists, optometrists, physical therapists, psychologists, recreational therapists, and rehabilitation counselors.

Audiologists specialize in the prevention, diagnosis, and treatment of hearing problems. Workers in related occupations include neurologists, neonatologists, acoustical engineers, industrial hygienists, and other rehabilitation professionals.

Sources of Additional Information
State licensing boards can provide information on licensure requirements. State departments of education can supply information on certification requirements for those who wish to work in public schools.

General information on careers in speech-language pathology and audiology is available from:

☛ American Speech-Language-Hearing Association, 10801 Rockville Pike, Rockville, MD 20852. Internet: **http://www.asha.org**

Information on a career in audiology is also available from:

☛ American Academy of Audiology, 8201 Greensboro Dr., Suite 300, McLean, VA 22102.

Health Technologists and Technicians

Cardiovascular Technologists and Technicians

(O*NET 32925 and 32926)

Significant Points

- Employment will grow as fast as the average, but the number of job openings created will be low, because the occupation is small.
- About 8 out of 10 jobs are in hospitals, in both inpatient and outpatient settings.

Nature of the Work

Cardiovascular technologists and technicians assist physicians in diagnosing and treating cardiac (heart) and peripheral vascular (blood vessel) ailments.

Cardiovascular technologists specializing in cardiac catheterization procedures are called *cardiology technologists*. They assist physicians with invasive procedures in which a small tube, or catheter, is wound through a patient's blood vessel from a spot on the patient's leg into the heart. This is done to determine if a blockage exists and for other diagnostic purposes. In balloon angioplasty, a procedure used to treat blockages of blood vessels, technologists assist physicians who insert a catheter with a balloon on the end to the point of the obstruction.

Technologists prepare patients for these procedures by first positioning them on an examining table and then shaving, cleaning, and administering anesthesia to the top of the patient's leg near the groin. During the procedures, they monitor patients' blood pressure and heart rate using electrocardiogram (EKG) equipment and notify the physician, if something appears wrong. Technologists may also prepare and monitor patients during open-heart surgery and the implantation of pacemakers.

Cardiovascular technologists and technicians may specialize in noninvasive peripheral vascular tests. Those who assist physicians in the diagnosis of disorders affecting circulation are known as *vascular technologists.* Vascular technologists use ultrasound instrumentation, such as doppler ultrasound, to noninvasively record vascular information, such as blood pressure, limb volume changes, oxygen saturation, cerebral circulation, peripheral circulation, and abdominal circulation. Many of these tests are performed during or immediately after surgery. Technologists and technicians who use ultrasound on the heart are referred to as *echocardiographers*. They use ultrasound equipment that transmits sound waves and then collects the echoes to form an image on a screen.

Cardiovascular technicians who obtain electrocardiograms are known as *electrocardiograph* (abbreviated *EKG* or *ECG) technicians*. To take a basic EKG, which traces electrical impulses transmitted by the heart, technicians attach electrodes to the patient's chest, arms, and legs, and then manipulate switches on an electrocardiograph machine to obtain a reading. This test is done before most kinds of surgery and as part of a routine physical examination, especially for persons who have reached middle age or have a history of cardiovascular problems.

EKG technicians with advanced training perform Holter monitor and stress testing. For a Holter monitoring, technicians place electrodes on the patient's chest and attach a portable EKG monitor to the patient's belt. Following 24 to 48 hours of normal routine for the patient, the technician removes a cassette tape from the monitor and places it in a scanner. After checking the quality of the recorded impulses on an electronic screen, the technician prints the information from the tape, so a physician can interpret it later. The printed output from the scanner is eventually used by a physician to diagnose heart ailments.

For a treadmill stress test, EKG technicians document the patient's medical history, explain the procedure, connect the patient to an EKG monitor, and obtain a baseline reading and resting blood pressure. Next, they monitor the heart's performance, while the patient is walking on a treadmill, gradually increasing the treadmill's speed to observe the effect of increased exertion. Those cardiovascular technicians who perform EKG and stress tests are known as "noninvasive" technicians, because the techniques they use do not require the insertion of probes or other instruments into the patient's body.

Some cardiovascular technologists and technicians schedule appointments, type doctor interpretations, maintain patient files, and care for equipment.

Working Conditions

Technologists and technicians generally work a 5-day, 40-hour week that may include weekends. Those in catheterization labs tend to work longer hours and may work evenings. They may also be on call during the night and on weekends.

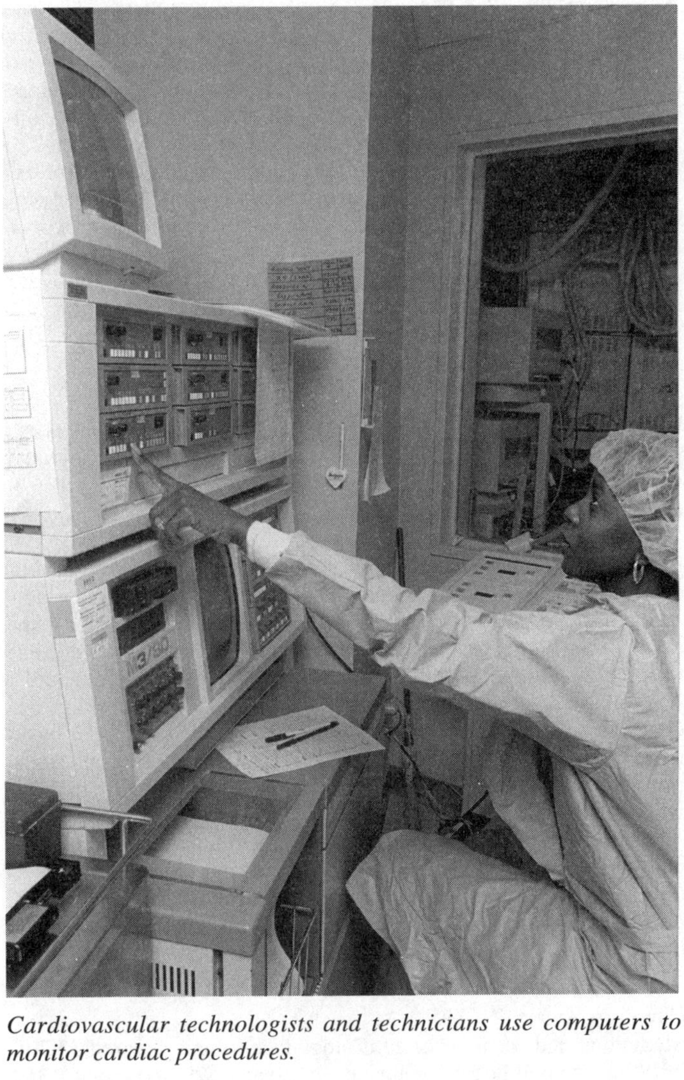

Cardiovascular technologists and technicians use computers to monitor cardiac procedures.

Cardiovascular technologists and technicians spend a lot of time walking and standing. Those who work in catheterization labs may face stressful working conditions, because they are in close contact with patients who have serious heart ailments. Some patients, for example, may encounter complications from time to time that have life or death implications.

Employment
Cardiovascular technologists and technicians held about 33,000 jobs in 1998. Most worked in hospital cardiology departments, whereas some worked in cardiologists' offices, cardiac rehabilitation centers, or ambulatory surgery centers. About one-third were EKG technicians.

Training, Other Qualifications, and Advancement
Although some cardiovascular technologists, vascular technologists, and echocardiographers are currently trained on the job, an increasing number receive training in 2- to 4-year programs. Cardiology technologists normally complete a 2-year junior or community college program. One year is dedicated to core courses followed by a year of specialized instruction in either invasive, noninvasive, or noninvasive peripheral cardiology. Those who are qualified in a related allied health profession only need to complete the year of specialized instruction. Graduates from programs accredited by the Joint Review Committee on Education in Cardiovascular Technology are eligible to register as professional technologists with the American Registry of Diagnostic Medical Sonographers or Cardiovascular Credentialing International.

For basic EKGs, Holter monitoring, and stress testing, 1-year certificate programs exist; but most EKG technicians are still trained on the job by an EKG supervisor or a cardiologist. On-the-job training usually lasts about 8 to 16 weeks. Most employers prefer to train people already in the health care field—nursing aides, for example. Some EKG technicians are students enrolled in 2-year programs to become technologists, working part-time to gain experience and make contact with employers.

Cardiovascular technologists and technicians must be reliable, have mechanical aptitude, and be able to follow detailed instructions. A pleasant, relaxed manner for putting patients at ease is an asset.

Job Outlook
Employment of cardiovascular technologists and technicians is expected to grow as fast as the average for all occupations through the year 2008, with technologists and technicians experiencing different patterns of employment change.

Employment of *cardiology technologists* is expected to grow much faster than the average for all occupations. Growth will occur as the population ages, because older people have a higher incidence of heart problems. Likewise, employment of vascular technologists will grow faster than the average, as advances in vascular technology reduce the need for more costly and invasive procedures.

In contrast, employment of *EKG technicians* is expected to decline, as hospitals train nursing aides and others to perform basic EKG procedures. Individuals trained in Holter monitoring and stress testing are expected to have more favorable job prospects than those who can only perform a basic EKG.

Some job openings for cardiovascular technologists and technicians will arise from replacement needs, as individuals transfer to other jobs or leave the labor force. Relatively few job openings, due to both growth and replacement needs are expected, however, because the occupation is small.

Earnings
Median annual earnings of cardiology technologists were $35,770 in 1998. The middle 50 percent earned between $29,060 and $42,350 a year. The lowest 10 percent earned less than $23,010 and the highest 10 percent earned more than $49,780 a year. Median annual earnings of cardiology technologists in 1997 were $34,500 in hospitals.

Median annual earnings of EKG technicians were $24,360 in 1998. The middle 50 percent earned between $19,660 and $30,860 a year. The lowest 10 percent earned less than $16,130 and the highest 10 percent earned more than $39,060 a year. Median annual earnings of EKG technicians in 1997 were $23,200 in hospitals.

Related Occupations
Cardiovascular technologists and technicians operate sophisticated equipment that helps physicians and other health practitioners diagnose and treat patients. So do nuclear medicine technologists, radiologic technologists, diagnostic medical sonographers, electroneurodiagnostic technologists, perfusionists, radiation therapists, and respiratory therapists.

Sources of Additional Information
For general information about a career in cardiovascular technology contact:

☛ Alliance of Cardiovascular Professionals, 910 Charles St., Fredericksburg, VA 22401.

For a list of accredited programs in cardiovascular technology, contact:

☛ Joint Review Committee on Education in Cardiovascular Technology, 3525 Ellicott Mills Dr., Suite N, Ellicott City, MD 21043-4547.

For information on vascular technology, contact:

☛ The Society of Vascular Technology, 4601 Presidents Dr., Suite 260, Lanham, MD 20706-4365.

For information on echocardiography, contact:

☛ American Society of Echocardiography, 4101 Lake Boone Trail, Suite 201, Raleigh, NC 27607.

For information regarding registration and certification contact:

☛ Cardiovascular Credentialing International, 4456 Corporation Lane, Suite 110, Virginia Beach, VA 23462.

☛ American Registry of Diagnostic Medical Sonographers, 600 Jefferson Plaza, Suite 360, Rockville, MD 20852-1150.

Clinical Laboratory Technologists and Technicians

(O*NET 32902, 32905, and 66099D)

Significant Points

- Medical and clinical laboratory technologists usually have a bachelor's degree with a major in medical technology or in one of the life sciences; medical and clinical laboratory technicians need either an associate's degree or a certificate.
- Competition for jobs has increased, and individuals may now have to spend more time seeking employment than in the past.

Nature of the Work
Clinical laboratory testing plays a crucial role in the detection, diagnosis, and treatment of disease. Clinical laboratory technologists and technicians, also known as medical technologists and technicians, perform most of these tests.

Clinical laboratory personnel examine and analyze body fluids, tissues, and cells. They look for bacteria, parasites, and other microorganisms; analyze the chemical content of fluids; match blood for transfusions, and test for drug levels in the blood to show how a patient is responding to treatment. These technologists also prepare specimens for examination, count cells, and look for abnormal cells. They use automated equipment and instruments capable of performing a number of tests simultaneously, as well as microscopes, cell counters, and other sophisticated laboratory equipment. Then they analyze the results and relay them to physicians. With increasing automation and the use of computer technology, the work of technologists and technicians has become less hands-on and more analytical.

The complexity of tests performed, the level of judgment needed, and the amount of responsibility workers assume depend largely on the amount of education and experience they have.

Medical and clinical laboratory technologists generally have a bachelor's degree in medical technology or in one of the life sciences, or they have a combination of formal training and work experience. They perform complex chemical, biological, hematological, immunologic, microscopic, and bacteriological tests. Technologists microscopically examine blood, tissue, and other body substances. They make cultures of body fluid and tissue samples, to determine the presence of bacteria, fungi, parasites, or other microorganisms. They analyze samples for chemical content or reaction and determine blood glucose and cholesterol levels. They also type and cross match blood samples for transfusions.

Medical and clinical laboratory technologists evaluate test results, develop and modify procedures, and establish and monitor programs, to insure the accuracy of tests. Some medical and clinical laboratory technologists supervise medical and clinical laboratory technicians.

Technologists in small laboratories perform many types of tests, whereas those in large laboratories generally specialize. Technologists who prepare specimens and analyze the chemical and hormonal contents of body fluids are *clinical chemistry technologists*. Those who examine and identify bacteria and other microorganisms are *microbiology technologists*. *Blood bank technologists* collect, type, and prepare blood and its components for transfusions. *Immunology technologists* examine elements and responses of the human immune system to foreign bodies. *Cytotechnologists* prepare slides of body cells and microscopically examine these cells for abnormalities that may signal the beginning of a cancerous growth.

Medical and clinical laboratory technicians perform less complex tests and laboratory procedures than technologists. Technicians may prepare specimens and operate automatic analyzers, for example, or they may perform manual tests following detailed instructions. Like technologists, they may work in several areas of the clinical laboratory or specialize in just one. *Histology technicians* cut and stain tissue specimens for microscopic examination by pathologists, and *phlebotomists* collect blood samples. They usually work under the supervision of medical and clinical laboratory technologists or laboratory managers.

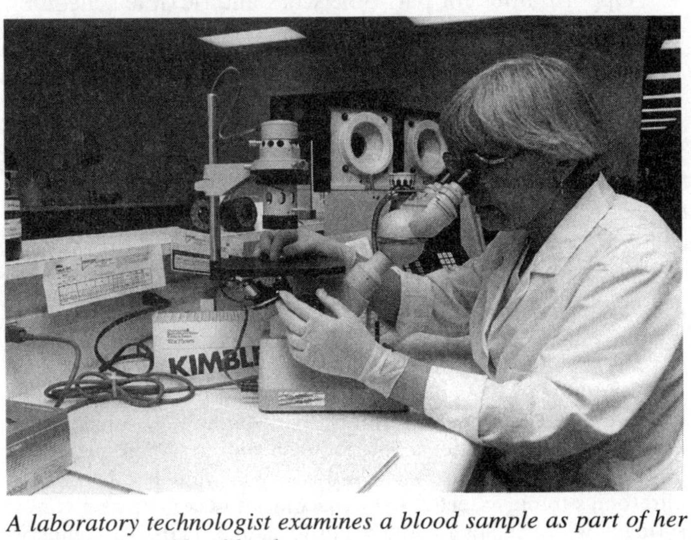

A laboratory technologist examines a blood sample as part of her evaluation at a blood bank.

Working Conditions

Hours and other working conditions vary, according to the size and type of employment setting. In large hospitals or in independent laboratories that operate continuously, personnel usually work the day, evening, or night shift and may work weekends and holidays. Laboratory personnel in small facilities may work on rotating shifts, rather than on a regular shift. In some facilities, laboratory personnel are on call several nights a week or on weekends, available in case of emergency.

Clinical laboratory personnel are trained to work with infectious specimens. When proper methods of infection control and sterilization are followed, few hazards exist.

Laboratories usually are well lighted and clean; however, specimens, solutions, and reagents used in the laboratory sometimes produce odors. Laboratory workers may spend a great deal of time on their feet.

Employment

Clinical laboratory technologists and technicians held about 313,000 jobs in 1998. About half worked in hospitals. Most of the remaining jobs were found in medical laboratories or offices and clinics of physicians. A small number were in blood banks, research and testing laboratories, and in the Federal Government—at Department of Veterans Affairs hospitals and U.S. Public Health Service facilities. About 1 laboratory worker in 5 worked part time.

Training, Other Qualifications, and Advancement

The usual requirement for an entry level position as a medical or clinical laboratory technologist is a bachelor's degree with a major in medical technology or in one of the life sciences. Universities and hospitals offer medical technology programs. It is also possible to qualify through a combination of on-the-job and specialized training.

Bachelor's degree programs in medical technology include courses in chemistry, biological sciences, microbiology, mathematics, and specialized courses devoted to knowledge and skills used in the clinical laboratory. Many programs also offer or require courses in management, business, and computer applications. The Clinical Laboratory Improvement Act (CLIA) requires technologists who perform certain highly complex tests to have at least an associate's degree.

Medical and clinical laboratory technicians generally have either an associate's degree from a community or junior college or a certificate from a hospital, vocational or technical school, or from one of the Armed Forces. A few technicians learn their skills on the job.

Nationally recognized accrediting agencies in clinical laboratory science include the National Accrediting Agency for Clinical Laboratory Sciences (NAACLS), the Commission on Accreditation of Allied Health Education Programs (CAAHEP), and the Accrediting Bureau of Health Education Schools (ABHES). The NAACLS fully accredits 288 and approves 249 programs providing education for medical and clinical laboratory technologists, histologic technicians, and medical and clinical laboratory technicians. ABHES accredits training programs for medical and clinical laboratory technicians.

Some States require laboratory personnel to be licensed or registered. Information on licensure is available from State departments of health or boards of occupational licensing. Certification is a voluntary process by which a nongovernmental organization, such as a professional society or certifying agency, grants recognition to an individual whose professional competence meets prescribed standards. Widely accepted by employers in the health industry, certification is a prerequisite for most jobs and often is necessary for advancement. Agencies certifying medical and clinical laboratory technologists and technicians include the Board of Registry of the American Society of Clinical Pathologists, the American Medical Technologists, and the Credentialing Commission of the International Society for Clinical

Laboratory Technology. These agencies have different requirements for certification and different organizational sponsors.

Clinical laboratory personnel need good analytical judgment and the ability to work under pressure. Close attention to detail is essential, because small differences or changes in test substances or numerical readouts can be crucial for patient care. Manual dexterity and normal color vision are highly desirable. With the widespread use of automated laboratory equipment, computer skills are important. In addition, technologists in particular are expected to be good at problem solving.

Technologists may advance to supervisory positions in laboratory work or become chief medical or clinical laboratory technologists or laboratory managers in hospitals. Manufacturers of home diagnostic testing kits and laboratory equipment and supplies seek experienced technologists to work in product development, marketing, and sales. Graduate education in medical technology, one of the biological sciences, chemistry, management, or education usually speeds advancement. A doctorate is needed to become a laboratory director. However, federal regulation allows directors of moderate complexity laboratories to have either a master's degree or a bachelor's degree combined with the appropriate amount of training and experience. Technicians can become technologists through additional education and experience.

Job Outlook

Employment of clinical laboratory workers is expected to grow about as fast as the average for all occupations through the year 2008, as the volume of laboratory tests increases with population growth and the development of new types of tests. Hospitals and independent laboratories have recently undergone considerable consolidation and restructuring, to boost productivity and allow the same number of personnel to perform more tests than previously possible. Consequently, competition for jobs has increased; and individuals may now have to spend more time seeking employment than in the past.

Technological advances will continue to have two opposing effects on employment through 2008. New, increasingly powerful diagnostic tests will encourage additional testing and spur employment. However, advances in laboratory automation and simple tests, which make it possible for each worker to perform more tests, should slow growth. Research and development efforts are targeted at simplifying routine testing procedures, so nonlaboratory personnel, physicians and patients, in particular, can perform tests now done in laboratories. In addition, automation may be used to prepare specimens, a job traditionally done by technologists and technicians.

Although significant, growth will not be the only source of opportunities. As in most occupations, many openings will result from the need to replace workers who transfer to other occupations, retire, or stop working for some other reason.

Earnings

Median annual earnings of clinical laboratory technologists and technicians were $32,440 in 1998. The middle 50 percent earned between $24,970 and $39,810 a year. The lowest 10 percent earned less than $19,380 and the highest 10 percent earned more than $48,290 a year. Median annual earnings in the industries employing the largest numbers of medical and clinical laboratory technologists in 1997 were:

Offices and clinics of medical doctors	$40,300
Federal Government	39,600
Hospitals	36,500
Medical and dental laboratories	35,600

Median annual earnings in the industries employing the largest numbers of medical and clinical laboratory technicians in 1997 were:

Hospitals	$26,600
Offices and clinics of medical doctors	25,500
Medical and dental laboratories	24,800
Health and allied services, not elsewhere classified	22,400

Related Occupations

Clinical laboratory technologists and technicians analyze body fluids, tissue, and other substances using a variety of tests. Similar or related procedures are performed by analytical, water purification, and other chemists; science technicians; crime laboratory analysts; food testers; and veterinary laboratory technicians.

Sources of Additional Information

Career and certification information is available from:

☛ American Society of Clinical Pathologists, Board of Registry, P.O. Box 12277, Chicago, IL 60612. Internet: **http://www.ascp.org/bor**

☛ American Medical Technologists, 710 Higgins Rd., Park Ridge, IL 60068. Internet: **http://www.amt1.com**

☛ American Society of Cytopathology, 400 West 9th St., Suite 201, Wilmington, DE 19801.

☛ International Society for Clinical Laboratory Technology, 917 Locust St., Suite 1100, St. Louis, MO 63101-1413.

For more career information, write to:

☛ American Society for Clinical Laboratory Science, 7910 Woodmont Ave., Suite 530, Bethesda, MD 20814.

☛ American Association of Blood Banks, 8101 Glenbrook Rd., Bethesda, MD 20814-2749.

For a list of accredited and approved educational programs for clinical laboratory personnel, write to:

☛ National Accrediting Agency for Clinical Laboratory Sciences, 8410 W. Bryn Mawr Ave., Suite 670, Chicago, IL 60631.

For a list of training programs for medical and clinical laboratory technicians accredited by the Accrediting Bureau of Health Education Schools, write to:

☛ Accrediting Bureau of Health Education Schools, 803 West Broad St., Suite 730, Falls Church, VA 22046. Internet: **http://www.abhes.org**

For information about a career as a medical and clinical laboratory technician and schools offering training, contact:

☛ National Association of Health Career Schools, 2301 Academy Dr., Harrisburg, PA 17112.

Dental Hygienists

(O*NET 32908)

Significant Points

- Dental hygienists are projected to be one of the 30 fastest growing occupations.
- Population growth and greater retention of natural teeth will stimulate demand for dental hygienists.
- Opportunities for part-time work and flexible schedules are common.

Nature of the Work

Dental hygienists clean teeth and provide other preventive dental care, as well as teach patients how to practice good oral hygiene. Hygienists examine patients' teeth and gums, recording the presence of diseases or abnormalities. They remove calculus, stains, and plaque from teeth; take and develop dental x rays; and apply cavity preventive agents such as fluorides and pit and fissure sealants. In some States, hygienists administer local anesthetics and anesthetic gas; place and carve filling materials, temporary fillings, and periodontal dressings; remove sutures; and smooth and polish metal restorations.

Dental hygienists also help patients develop and maintain good oral health. For example, they may explain the relationship between diet and oral health, inform patients how to select toothbrushes, and show patients how to brush and floss their teeth.

Dental hygienists use hand and rotary instruments, lasers, and ultrasonics to clean teeth; x-ray machines to take dental pictures; syringes with needles to administer local anesthetics; and models of teeth to explain oral hygiene.

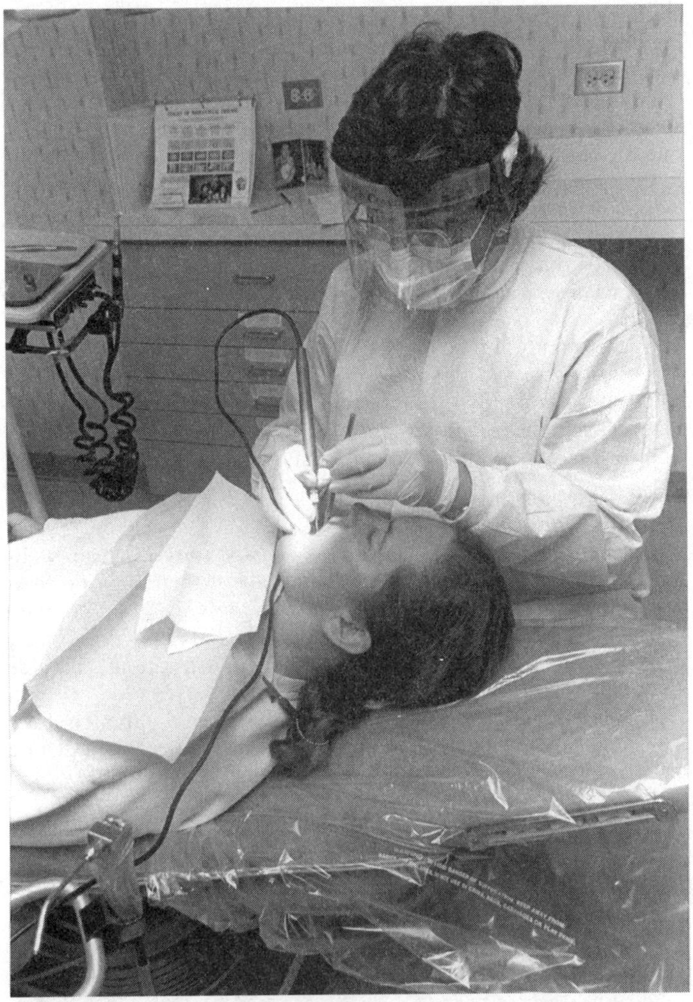

Dental hygienists clean and examine teeth and gums, noting the presence of diseases or abnormalities.

Working Conditions

Flexible scheduling is a distinctive feature of this job. Full-time, part-time, evening, and weekend work is widely available. Dentists frequently hire hygienists to work only 2 or 3 days a week, so hygienists may hold jobs in more than one dental office.

Dental hygienists work in clean, well-lighted offices. Important health safeguards include strict adherence to proper radiological procedures, and use of appropriate protective devices when administering anesthetic gas. Dental hygienists also wear safety glasses, surgical masks, and gloves to protect themselves from infectious diseases.

Employment

Dental hygienists held about 143,000 jobs in 1998. Because multiple job holding is common in this field, the number of jobs exceeds the number of hygienists. About 3 out of 5 dental hygienists worked part time—less than 35 hours a week.

Almost all dental hygienists work in private dental offices. Some work in public health agencies, hospitals, and clinics.

Training, Other Qualifications, and Advancement

Dental hygienists must be licensed by the State in which they practice. To qualify for licensure, a candidate must graduate from an accredited dental hygiene school and pass both a written and clinical examination. The American Dental Association Joint Commission on National Dental Examinations administers the written examination accepted by all States and the District of Columbia. State or regional testing agencies administer the clinical examination. In addition, most States require an examination on legal aspects of dental hygiene practice. Alabama allows candidates to take its examinations if they have been trained through a State-regulated on-the-job program in a dentist's office.

In 1999, the Commission on Dental Accreditation accredited about 250 programs in dental hygiene. Although some programs lead to a bachelor's degree, most grant an associate degree. Thirteen universities offer master's degree programs in dental hygiene or a related area.

An associate degree is sufficient for practice in a private dental office. A bachelor's or master's degree is usually required for research, teaching, or clinical practice in public or school health programs.

About half of the dental hygiene programs prefer applicants who have completed at least 1 year of college. However, requirements vary from school to school. Schools offer laboratory, clinical, and classroom instruction in subjects such as anatomy, physiology, chemistry, microbiology, pharmacology, nutrition, radiography, histology (the study of tissue structure), periodontology (the study of gum diseases), pathology, dental materials, clinical dental hygiene, and social and behavioral sciences.

Dental hygienists should work well with others and must have good manual dexterity because they use dental instruments within a patient's mouth with little room for error. High school students interested in becoming a dental hygienist should take courses in biology, chemistry, and mathematics.

Job Outlook

Employment of dental hygienists is expected to grow much faster than the average for all occupations through 2008, in response to increasing demand for dental care and the greater substitution of hygienists for services previously performed by dentists. Job prospects are expected to remain very good unless the number of dental hygienist program graduates grows much faster than during the last decade, and results in a much larger pool of qualified applicants.

Population growth and greater retention of natural teeth will stimulate demand for dental hygienists. Older dentists, who are less likely to employ dental hygienists, will leave and be replaced by recent graduates, who are more likely to do so. In addition, as dentists' workloads increase, they are expected to hire more hygienists to perform preventive dental care such as cleaning, so they may devote their own time to more profitable procedures.

Earnings

Median hourly earnings of dental hygienists were $22.06 in 1998. The middle 50 percent earned between $17.28 and $29.28 an hour. The lowest 10 percent earned less than $12.37 and the highest 10 percent earned more than $38.81 an hour.

Earnings vary by geographic location, employment setting, and years of experience. Dental hygienists who work in private dental offices may be paid on an hourly, daily, salary, or commission basis.

Benefits vary substantially by practice setting, and may be contingent upon full-time employment. Dental hygienists who work for school systems, public health agencies, the Federal Government, or State agencies usually have substantial benefits.

Related Occupations

Workers in other occupations supporting health practitioners in an office setting include dental assistants, ophthalmic medical assistants, podiatric medical assistants, office nurses, medical assistants, physician assistants, physical therapist assistants, and occupational therapy assistants.

Sources of Additional Information

For information on a career in dental hygiene and the educational requirements to enter this occupation, contact:

☛ Division of Professional Development, American Dental Hygienists' Association, 444 N. Michigan Ave., Suite 3400, Chicago, IL 60611. Internet: **http://www.adha.org**

For information about accredited programs and educational requirements, contact:

☛ Commission on Dental Accreditation, American Dental Association, 211 E. Chicago Ave., Suite 1814, Chicago, IL 60611.
Internet: **http://www.ada.org**

The State Board of Dental Examiners in each State can supply information on licensing requirements.

Electroneurodiagnostic Technologists

(O*NET 32923)

Significant Points

- The number of job openings created will be limited by slower than average employment growth and low replacement needs.
- Most technologists learn on the job, but opportunities should be best for technologists with formal postsecondary training.

Nature of the Work

Electroneurodiagnostic technologists use instruments such as an electroencephalograph (EEG) machine, to record electrical impulses transmitted by the brain and the nervous system. They help physicians diagnose brain tumors, strokes, epilepsy, and sleep disorders. They also measure the effects of infectious diseases on the brain, as well as determine whether individuals with mental or behavioral problems have an organic impairment, such as Alzheimer's disease. Furthermore, they determine *cerebral death*, the absence of brain activity, and assess the probability of recovery from a coma.

Electroneurodiagnostic technologists who specialize in basic or *resting* EEGs are called *EEG technologists*. The range of tests performed by electroneurodiagnostic technologists is broader than, but includes, those conducted by EEG technologists. Because it provides a more accurate description of work typically performed in the field, the title electroneurodiagnostic technologists generally has replaced that of EEG technologist.

Electroneurodiagnostic technologists take patients' medical histories, help patients relax, and then apply electrodes to designated spots on the patient's head. They must choose the most appropriate combination of instrument controls and electrodes, to correct for mechanical and electrical interference from somewhere other than the brain, such as eye movement or radiation from electrical sources.

Increasingly, technologists perform EEGs in the operating room, which requires that they understand anesthesia's effect on brain waves. For special procedure EEGs, technologists may secure electrodes to the chest, arm, leg, or spinal column, to record activity from both the central and peripheral nervous systems.

In ambulatory monitoring, technologists attach small recorders to patients to monitor the brain, and sometimes the heart, while patients carry out normal activities over a 24-hour period. They then remove the recorder and obtain a readout. Technologists review the readouts, selecting sections for the physician to examine.

Using *evoked potential* testing, technologists measure sensory and physical responses to specific stimuli. After attaching electrodes to the patient, they set the instrument for the type and intensity of the stimulus, increase the intensity until the patient reacts, and note the sensation level.

For nerve conduction tests, used to diagnose muscle and nerve problems, technologists place electrodes on the patient's skin over a nerve and over a muscle. Then they stimulate the nerve with an electrical current and record how long it takes the nerve impulse to reach the muscle.

Technologists who specialize in and administer sleep disorder studies are called *polysomnographic technologists*. Sleep disorder studies are usually conducted in a clinic called a sleep center. During the procedure, these technologists monitor the patient's respiration and heart and brain wave activity. These workers must know the dynamics of the cardiopulmonary systems during each stage of sleep. They coordinate readings from several organ systems, separate the readings according to the stages of sleep, and relay results to the physician. Polysomnographic technologists may also write technical reports summarizing test results.

Additionally, technologists look for changes in a patient's neurologic, cardiac, and respiratory status, which may indicate an emergency, such as a heart attack, and provide emergency care until help arrives.

Electroneurodiagnostic technologists may have supervisory or administrative responsibilities. They may manage an electroneurodiagnostic laboratory, arrange work schedules, keep records, schedule appointments, order supplies, provide instruction to less-experienced technologists, and maintain equipment.

Working Conditions

Electroneurodiagnostic technologists usually work in clean, well-lighted surroundings and spend about half of their time on their feet. They often work with patients who are very ill and require assistance. Technologists employed in hospitals may do all their work in a single room or may push equipment to a patient's bedside and obtain recordings there.

Most technologists work a standard workweek, although those in hospitals may be on call evenings, weekends, and holidays. Those performing sleep studies usually work evenings and nights.

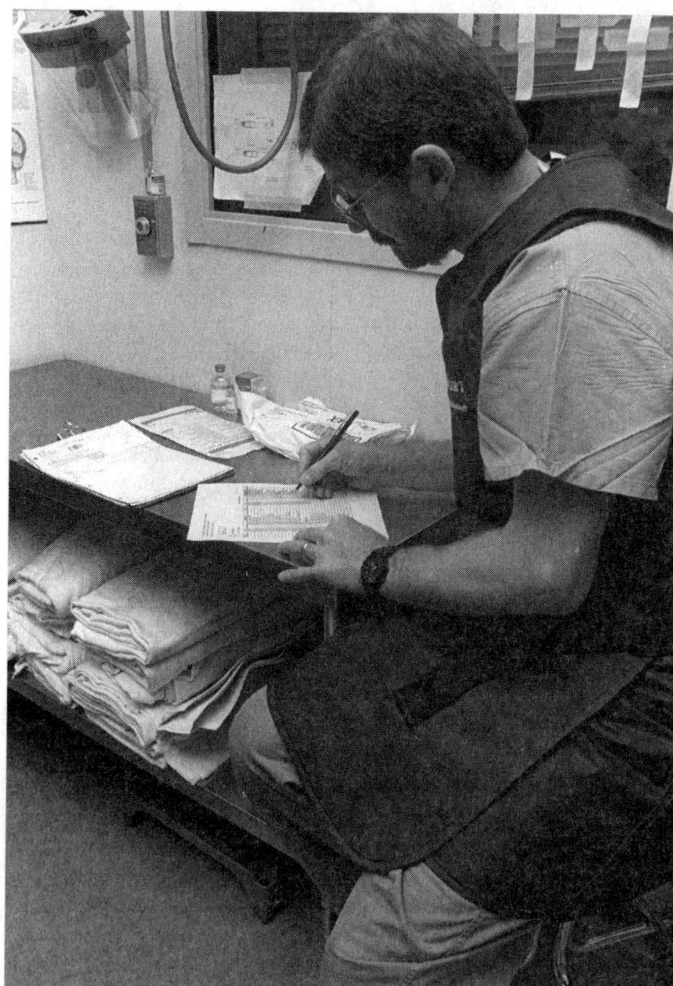

An electroneurodiagnostic technologist evaluates the results of an electroencephalograph (EEG).

Employment

Electroneurodiagnostic technologists held about 5,400 jobs in 1998. Most worked in neurology laboratories of hospitals, whereas others worked in offices and clinics of neurologists and neurosurgeons, sleep centers, or psychiatric facilities.

Training, Other Qualifications, and Advancement

Although most electroneurodiagnostic technologists currently employed learned their skills on the job, employers are beginning to favor those who have completed formal training. Some hospitals require applicants for trainee positions to have postsecondary training, whereas others only expect a high school diploma. Recommended high school and college subjects for prospective technologists include health, biology, anatomy, and mathematics. Often, on-the-job trainees are transfers from other hospital jobs, such as licensed practical nurses.

Formal postsecondary training is offered in hospitals and community colleges. In 1998, the Joint Review Committee on Education in Electroneurodiagnostic Technology approved 12 formal programs. Programs usually last from 1 to 2 years and include laboratory experience, as well as classroom instruction in human anatomy and physiology, neurology, neuroanatomy, neurophysiology, medical terminology, computer technology, electronics, and instrumentation. Graduates receive associate degrees or certificates.

The American Board of Registration of Electroencephalographic and Evoked Potential Technologists awards the credentials Registered EEG Technologist, Registered Evoked Potential Technologist, and Certificate in Neurophysiologic Intraoperative Monitoring to qualified applicants. The Association of Polysomnographic Technologists registers polysomnographic technologists. Applicants interested in taking the registration exam must have worked in a sleep center for at least 1 year. Although not generally required for staff level jobs, registration indicates professional competence, and is usually necessary for supervisory or teaching jobs. In addition, the American Association of Electrodiagnostic Technologists provides certification in the field of nerve conduction studies for electroneurodiagnostic technologists.

These technologists should have manual dexterity, good vision, good writing skills, an aptitude for working with electronic equipment, and the ability to work with patients as well as with other health personnel.

Experienced electroneurodiagnostic technologists can advance to chief or manager of an electroneurodiagnostic laboratory. Chief technologists are generally supervised by a physician—an electroencephalographer, neurologist, or neurosurgeon. Technologists may also teach or go into research.

Job Outlook

Employment of electroneurodiagnostic technologists is expected to grow more slowly than the average for all occupations through the year 2008. Although employment will increase as new procedures and technologies are developed and as the size of the population grows, productivity gains caused by increasingly sophisticated equipment and cross-trained employees will limit employment growth. Only a small number of openings are expected each year, due primarily to the need to replace technologists who transfer to other occupations or retire. Most jobs will be found in hospitals, but growth will be fastest in offices and clinics of neurologists.

Earnings

Median annual earnings of electroneurodiagnostic technologists were $32,070 in 1998. The middle 50 percent earned between $26,610 and $38,500 a year. The lowest 10 percent earned less than $22,200 and the highest 10 percent earned more than $46,620 a year.

Related Occupations

Other health personnel who operate medical equipment to diagnose and treat patients include radiologic technologists, nuclear medicine technologists, sonographers, perfusionists, and cardiovascular technologists.

Sources of Additional Information

For general information about a career in electroneurodiagnostics and a list of accredited training programs, contact:

☛ Executive Office, American Society of Electroneurodiagnostic Technologists, Inc., 204 W. 7th St., Carroll, IA 51401.
Internet: **http://www.aset.org**

For information on opportunities in sleep studies, contact:

☛ Association of Polysomnographic Technology, 2025 South Washington, Suite 300, Lansing, MI 48910-0817.

Information about specific accredited training programs is also available from:

☛ Joint Review Committee on Electroneurodiagnostic Technology, Route 1, Box 63A, Genoa, WI 54632.

Information on becoming a registered electroneurodiagnostic technologist is available from:

☛ American Board of Registration of Electroencephalgraphic and Evoked Potential Technologists, P.O. Box 916633, Longwood, FL 32791-6633.

Information on certification in the field of nerve conduction studies is available from:

☛ American Association of Electrodiagnostic Technologists, 35 Hallett Lane, Chatham, MA 02633-2408.

Emergency Medical Technicians and Paramedics

(O*NET 32508)

Significant Points

- Irregular hours and treating patients in life-or-death situations lead to job stress in this occupation.
- State requirements vary, but formal training and certification are required.
- Employment is projected to grow rapidly as paid emergency medical technician positions replace unpaid volunteers.

Nature of the Work

People's lives often depend on the quick reaction and competent care of emergency medical technicians (EMTs) and paramedics. Incidents as varied as automobile accidents, heart attacks, drownings, childbirth, and gunshot wounds all require immediate medical attention. EMTs and paramedics provide this vital attention as they care for and transport the sick or injured to a medical facility.

Depending on the nature of the emergency, EMTs and paramedics typically are dispatched to the scene by a 911 operator and often work with police and fire department personnel. Once they arrive, they determine the nature and extent of the patient's condition while trying to ascertain whether the patient has preexisting medical problems. Following strict procedures, they give appropriate emergency care and transport the patient. Some conditions can be handled following general rules and guidelines, while more complicated problems are carried out under the direction of medical doctors by radio.

EMTs and paramedics may use special equipment such as backboards to immobilize patients before placing them on stretchers and securing them in the ambulance for transport to a medical facility. Usually, one EMT or paramedic drives while the other monitors the patient's vital signs and gives additional care as needed. Some who work for hospital trauma centers, which use helicopters to transport critically ill or injured patients, are part of the flight crew.

At the medical facility, EMTs and paramedics help transfer patients to the emergency department, report their observations and actions to staff, and may provide additional emergency treatment. Some paramedics are trained to treat patients with minor injuries on the scene of an accident or at their home without transporting them to a medical facility. After each run, EMTs replace used supplies and check equipment. If a transported patient had a contagious disease, EMTs decontaminate the interior of the ambulance and report cases to the proper authorities.

Beyond these general duties, the specific responsibilities of EMTs and paramedics depend on their level of qualification and training. To determine this, the National Registry of Emergency Medical Technicians (NREMT) registers emergency medical service (EMS) providers at four levels: First Responder, EMT-Basic, EMT-Intermediate, and EMT-Paramedic. Some States, however, do their own certification and use numeric ratings from 1 to 4 to distinguish levels of proficiency.

The lowest level—First Responders—are trained to provide basic emergency medical care because they tend to be the first persons to arrive at the scene of an incident. Many firefighters, police officers, and other emergency workers have this level of training. The EMT-Basic, also known as EMT-1, represents the first component of the emergency medical technician system. An EMT-1 is trained to care for patients on accident scenes and on transport by ambulance to the hospital under medical direction. The EMT-1 has the emergency skills to assess a patient's condition and manage respiratory, cardiac, and trauma emergencies.

The EMT-Intermediate (EMT-2 and EMT-3) has more advanced training that allows administration of intravenous fluids, use of manual defibrillators to give lifesaving shocks to a stopped heart, and use of advanced airway techniques and equipment to assist patients experiencing respiratory emergencies. EMT-Paramedics (EMT-4) provide the most extensive pre-hospital care. In addition to the procedures already described, paramedics may administer drugs orally and intravenously, interpret electrocardiograms (EKGs), perform endotracheal intubations, and use monitors and other complex equipment.

Working Conditions

EMTs and paramedics work both indoors and outdoors, in all types of weather. They are required to do considerable kneeling, bending, and heavy lifting. These workers risk noise-induced hearing loss from sirens and back injuries from lifting patients. In addition, EMTs and paramedics may be exposed to diseases such as Hepatitis-B and AIDS, as well as violence from drug overdose victims or psychologically disturbed patients. The work is not only physically strenuous, but also stressful, involving life-or-death situations and suffering patients. Nonetheless, many people find the work exciting and challenging and enjoy the opportunity to help others.

EMTs are often the first to appear at the scene of injuries.

EMTs and paramedics employed by fire departments work about 50 hours a week. Those employed by hospitals frequently work between 45 and 60 hours a week, and those in private ambulance services, between 45 and 50 hours. Some of these workers, especially those in police and fire departments, are on call for extended periods. Because emergency services function 24 hours a day, EMTs and paramedics have irregular working hours that add to job stress.

Employment

EMTs and paramedics held about 150,000 jobs in 1998. In addition, there are many more volunteer EMTs, especially in smaller cities, towns, and rural areas, who work for departments where they may respond to only a few calls for service per month. Most career EMTs and paramedics work in metropolitan areas.

EMTs and paramedics are employed in a number of industries. Nearly half work in local and suburban transportation for private ambulance firms that transport and treat individuals on an emergency or non-emergency basis. About a third of EMTs and paramedics work in local government for fire departments and third service providers, in which emergency medical services are provided by an independent agency. Another fifth are found in hospitals, where they may work full-time within the medical facility or respond to calls in ambulances or helicopters to transport critically ill or injured patients.

Training, Other Qualifications, and Advancement

Formal training and certification is needed to become an EMT or paramedic. All 50 States possess a certification procedure. In 38 States and the District of Columbia, registration with the National Registry is required at some or all levels of certification. Other States administer their own certification examination or provide the option of taking the National Registry examination. To maintain certification, EMTs and paramedics must re-register, usually every 2 years. In order to re-register, an individual must be working as an EMT and meet a continuing education requirement.

Training is offered at progressive levels: EMT-Basic, also known as EMT-1; EMT-Intermediate, or EMT-2 and EMT-3; and EMT-paramedic, or EMT-4. The EMT-Basic represents the first level of skills required to work in the emergency medical system. Coursework typically emphasizes emergency skills such as managing respiratory, trauma, and cardiac emergencies and patient assessment. Formal courses are often combined with time in an emergency room or ambulance. The program also provides instruction and practice in dealing with bleeding, fractures, airway obstruction, cardiac arrest, and emergency childbirth. Students learn to use and maintain care for common emergency equipment, such as backboards, suction devices, splints, oxygen delivery systems, and stretchers. Graduates of approved EMT basic training programs who pass a written and practical examination administered by the State certifying agency or the National Registry of Emergency Medical Technicians earn the title of Registered EMT-Basic. The course is also a prerequisite for EMT-Intermediate and EMT-Paramedic training.

EMT-Intermediate training requirements vary from State to State. Applicants can opt to receive training in EMT-Shock Trauma, where the caregiver learns to start intravenous fluids and give certain medications, or in EMT-Cardiac, which includes learning heart rhythms and administering advanced medications. Training commonly includes 35-55 hours of additional instruction beyond EMT-Basic coursework and covers patient assessment as well as the use of advanced airway devices and intravenous fluids. Prerequisites for taking the EMT-Intermediate examination include registration as an

EMT-Basic, required classroom work, and a specified amount of clinical experience.

The most advanced level of training for this occupation is EMT-Paramedic. At this level, the caregiver receives additional training in body function and more advanced skills. The Paramedic Technology program usually lasts up to 2 years and results in an associate degree in applied science. Such education prepares the graduate to take the National Registry of Emergency Medical Technicians examination and become certified as an EMT-Paramedic. Extensive related coursework and clinical and field experience is required. Due to the longer training requirement, almost all EMT-Paramedics are in paid positions. Refresher courses and continuing education are available for EMTs and paramedics at all levels.

EMTs and paramedics should be emotionally stable, have good dexterity, agility, and physical coordination, and be able to lift and carry heavy loads. They also need good eyesight (corrective lenses may be used) with accurate color vision.

Advancement beyond the EMT-Paramedic level usually means leaving fieldwork. An EMT-Paramedic can become a supervisor, operations manager, administrative director, or executive director of emergency services. Some EMTs and paramedics become instructors, dispatchers, or physician assistants, while others move into sales or marketing of emergency medical equipment. A number of people become EMTs and paramedics to assess their interest in health care and then decide to return to school and become registered nurses, physicians, or other health workers.

Job Outlook

Employment of EMTs is expected to grow much faster than the average for all occupations through 2008. Much of this growth will occur as positions change from volunteer to paid and as the population grows, particularly older age groups that are the greatest users of emergency medical services. In addition to job growth, openings will occur because of replacement needs; some workers leave because of stressful working conditions, limited advancement potential, and the modest pay and benefits in the private sector.

Most opportunities for EMTs and paremedics are expected to arise in hospitals and private ambulance services. Competition will be greater for jobs in local government, including fire, police, and third service rescue squad departments, where job growth for these workers is expected to be slower.

Earnings

Earnings of EMTs depend on the employment setting and geographic location as well as the individual's training and experience. Median annual earnings of EMTs were $20,290 in 1998. The middle 50 percent earned between $15,660 and $26,240. The lowest 10 percent earned less than $12,700 and the highest 10 percent earned more than $34,480. In local and suburban transportation, where private ambulance firms are located, the median salary was $18,300 in 1997. In local government, except education and hospitals, the median salary was $21,900. In hospitals, the median salary was $19,900.

Those in emergency medical services who are part of fire or police departments receive the same benefits as firefighters or police officers. For example, many are covered by pension plans that provide retirement at half pay after 20 or 25 years of service or if disabled in the line of duty.

Related Occupations

Other workers in occupations that require quick and level-headed reactions to life-or-death situations are police officers, firefighters, air traffic controllers, and workers in other health occupations.

Sources of Additional Information

General information about EMTs and paramedics is available from:

☛ National Association of Emergency Medical Technicians, 408 Monroe St., Clinton, MS 39056. Internet: **http://www.naemt.org**

☛ National Registry of Emergency Medical Technicians, P.O. Box 29233, Columbus, OH 43229. Internet: **http://www.nremt.org**

☛ National Highway Transportation Safety Administration, EMS Divion, 400 7th St. SW., NTS-14, Washington DC.
Internet: **http://www.nhtsa.dot.gov/people/injury/ems/**

Health Information Technicians

(O*NET 32911)

Significant Points

- Health information technicians are projected to be one of the 20 fastest growing occupations.
- High school students can improve chances of acceptance into a health information education program by taking courses in biology, chemistry, health, and especially computer training.
- Most technicians will be employed by hospitals, but job growth will be faster in offices and clinics of physicians, nursing homes, and home health agencies.

Nature of the Work

Every time health care personnel treat a patient, they record what they observed, and how the patient was treated medically. This record includes information the patient provides concerning their symptoms and medical history, the results of examinations, reports of x-rays and laboratory tests, diagnoses, and treatment plans. Health information technicians organize and evaluate these records for completeness and accuracy.

Health information technicians, who may also be called medical record technicians, begin to assemble patients' health information by first making sure their initial medical charts are complete. They ensure all forms are completed and properly identified and signed, and all necessary information is in the computer. Sometimes, they talk to physicians or others to clarify diagnoses or get additional information.

Technicians assign a code to each diagnosis and procedure. They consult classification manuals and rely, also, on their knowledge of disease processes. Technicians then use a software program to assign the patient to one of several hundred "diagnosis-related groups," or DRG's. The DRG determines the amount the hospital will be reimbursed if the patient is covered by Medicare or other insurance programs using the DRG system. Technicians who specialize in coding are called health information coders, medical record coders, coder/abstractors, or coding specialists. In addition to the DRG system, coders use other coding systems, such as those geared towards ambulatory settings.

Technicians also use computer programs to tabulate and analyze data to help improve patient care or control costs, for use in legal actions, or in response to surveys. *Tumor registrars* compile and maintain records of patients who have cancer to provide information to physicians and for research studies.

Health information technicians' duties vary with the size of the facility. In large to medium facilities, technicians may specialize in one aspect of health information, or supervise health information clerks and transcribers while a *health information administrator* manages the department (see the statement on health services managers elsewhere in the *Handbook*). In small facilities, an accredited health information technician sometimes manages the department.

Working Conditions

Health information technicians usually work a 40-hour week. Some overtime may be required. In hospitals where health information departments are open 18-24 hours a day, 7 days a week, they may work day, evening, and night shifts.

Health information technicians organize and evaluate medical records for completeness and accuracy.

Health information technicians work in pleasant and comfortable offices. This is one of the few health occupations in which there is little or no physical contact with patients. Because accuracy is essential, technicians must pay close attention to detail. Health information technicians who work at computer monitors for prolonged periods must guard against eyestrain and muscle pain.

Employment

Health information technicians held about 92,000 jobs in 1998. About 2 out of 5 jobs were in hospitals. The rest were mostly in nursing homes, medical group practices, clinics, and home health agencies. Insurance firms that deal in health matters employ a small number of health information technicians to tabulate and analyze health information. Public health departments also hire technicians to supervise data collection from health care institutions and to assist in research.

Training, Other Qualifications, and Advancement

Health information technicians entering the field usually have an associate degree from a community or junior college. In addition to general education, coursework includes medical terminology, anatomy and physiology, legal aspects of health information, coding and abstraction of data, statistics, database management, quality improvement methods, and computer training. Applicants can improve their chances of admission into a program by taking biology, chemistry, health, and computer courses in high school.

Hospitals sometimes advance promising health information clerks to jobs as health information technicians, although this practice may be less common in the future. Advancement usually requires 2-4 years of job experience and completion of a hospital's in-house training program.

Most employers prefer to hire Accredited Record Technicians (ART), who must pass a written examination offered by AHIMA. To take the examination, a person must graduate from a 2-year associate degree program accredited by the Commission on Accreditation of Allied Health Education Programs (CAAHEP) of the American Medical Association. Technicians trained in non-CAAHEP accredited programs, or on the job, are not eligible to take the examination. In 1998, CAAHEP accredited 168 programs for health information technicians. Technicians who specialize in coding may also obtain voluntary certification.

Experienced health information technicians usually advance in one of two ways—by specializing or managing. Many senior health information technicians specialize in coding, particularly Medicare coding, or in tumor registry.

In large health information departments, experienced technicians may advance to section supervisor, overseeing the work of the coding, correspondence, or discharge sections, for example. Senior technicians with ART credentials may become director or assistant director of a health information department in a small facility. However, in larger institutions, the director is a health information administrator, with a bachelor's degree in health information administration. (See the statement on health services managers elsewhere in the *Handbook.*)

Job Outlook

Job prospects for formally trained technicians should be very good. Employment of health information technicians is expected to grow much faster than the average for all occupations through 2008, due to rapid growth in the number of medical tests, treatments, and procedures which will be increasingly scrutinized by third-party payers, regulators, courts, and consumers.

Hospitals will continue to employ a large percentage of health information technicians, but growth will not be as fast as in other areas. Increasing demand for detailed records in offices and clinics of physicians should result in fast employment growth, especially in large group practices. Rapid growth is also expected in nursing homes and home health agencies.

Earnings

Median annual earnings of health information technicians were $20,590 in 1998. The middle 50 percent earned between $16,670 and $25,440 a year. The lowest 10 percent earned less than $14,150 and the highest 10 percent earned more than $31,570 a year. Median annual earnings in the industries employing the largest number of health information technicians in 1997 were as follows:

Hospitals	$20,900
Nursing and personal care facilities	20,100
Offices and clinics of medical doctors	18,100

According to a 1997 survey by the American Health Information Management Association, the median annual salary for accredited health information technicians was $30,500. The average annual salary for health information technicians employed by the Federal Government was $27,500 in early 1999.

Related Occupations

Health information technicians need a strong clinical background to analyze the contents of medical records. Other occupations requiring knowledge of medical terminology, anatomy, and physiology without directly touching the patient, are medical secretaries, medical transcriptionists, medical writers, and medical illustrators.

Sources of Additional Information

Information on careers in health information technology, including a list of CAAHEP-accredited programs is available from:

☛ American Health Information Management Association, 233 N. Michigan Ave., Suite 2150, Chicago, IL 60601. Internet: **http://www.ahima.org**

Licensed Practical Nurses

(O*NET 32505)

Significant Points

- Training lasting about 1 year is available in about 1,100 State-approved programs, mostly in vocational or technical schools.
- Nursing homes will offer the most new jobs. Jobseekers in hospitals may face competition.

Nature of the Work

Licensed practical nurses (L.P.N.s), or licensed vocational nurses as they are called in Texas and California, care for the sick, injured, convalescent, and disabled under the direction of physicians and registered nurses. (The work of registered nurses is described elsewhere in the *Handbook*.)

Most L.P.N.s provide basic bedside care. They take vital signs such as temperature, blood pressure, pulse, and respiration. They also treat bedsores, prepare and give injections and enemas, apply dressings, give alcohol rubs and massages, apply ice packs and hot water bottles, and insert catheters. L.P.N's observe patients and report adverse reactions to medications or treatments. They collect samples from patients for testing, perform routine laboratory tests, feed them, and record food and liquid intake and output. They help patients with bathing, dressing, and personal hygiene, keep them comfortable, and care for their emotional needs. In States where the law allows, they may administer prescribed medicines or start intravenous fluids. Some L.P.N.s help deliver, care for, and feed infants. Some experienced L.P.N.s supervise nursing assistants and aides.

L.P.N.s in nursing homes, in addition to providing routine bedside care, may also help evaluate residents' needs, develop care plans, and supervise the care provided by nursing aides. In doctors' offices and clinics, they may also make appointments, keep records, and perform other clerical duties. L.P.N.s who work in private homes may also prepare meals and teach family members simple nursing tasks.

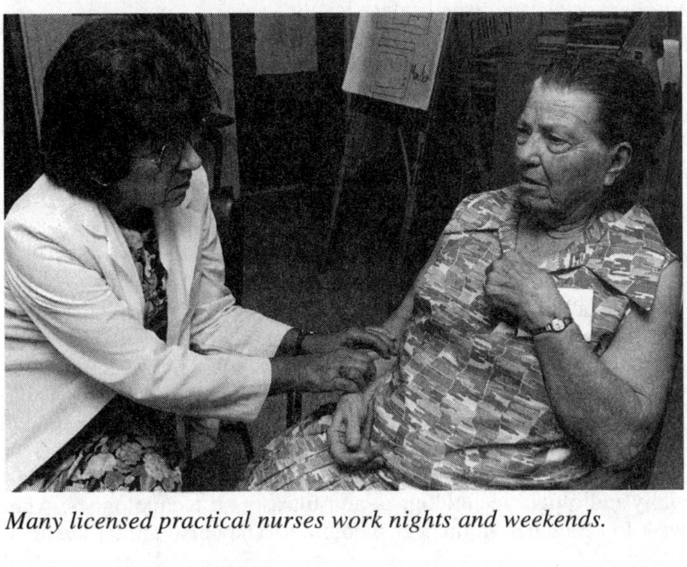

Many licensed practical nurses work nights and weekends.

Working Conditions

Most licensed practical nurses in hospitals and nursing homes work a 40-hour week, but because patients need round-the-clock care, some work nights, weekends, and holidays. They often stand for long periods and help patients move in bed, stand, or walk.

L.P.N.s may face hazards from caustic chemicals, radiation, and infectious diseases such as hepatitis. They are subject to back injuries when moving patients and shock from electrical equipment. They often must deal with the stress of heavy workloads. In addition, the patients they care for may be confused, irrational, agitated, or uncooperative.

Employment

Licensed practical nurses held about 692,000 jobs in 1998. Thirty-two percent of L.P.N.s worked in hospitals, 28 percent worked in nursing homes, and 14 percent in doctors' offices and clinics. Others worked for temporary help agencies, home health care services, residential care facilities, schools, or government agencies. About 1 in 4 worked part time.

Training, Other Qualifications, and Advancement

All States require L.P.N.s to pass a licensing examination after completing a State-approved practical nursing program. A high school diploma is usually required for entry, but some programs accept people without a diploma.

In 1998, approximately 1,100 State-approved programs provided practical nursing training. Almost 6 out of 10 students were enrolled in technical or vocational schools, while 3 out of 10 were in community and junior colleges. Others were in high schools, hospitals, and colleges and universities.

Most practical nursing programs last about 1 year and include both classroom study and supervised clinical practice (patient care). Classroom study covers basic nursing concepts and patient-care related subjects, including anatomy, physiology, medical-surgical nursing, pediatrics, obstetrics, psychiatric nursing, administration of drugs, nutrition, and first aid. Clinical practice is usually in a hospital, but sometimes includes other settings.

L.P.N.s should have a caring, sympathetic nature. They should be emotionally stable because work with the sick and injured can be stressful. As part of a health care team, they must be able to follow orders and work under close supervision.

Job Outlook

Employment of L.P.N.s is expected to grow as fast as the average for all occupations through 2008 in response to the long-term care needs of a rapidly growing population of very old people and to the general growth of health care. However, L.P.N.s seeking positions in hospitals may face competition, as the number of hospital jobs for L.P.N.s declines; the number of inpatients, with whom most L.P.N.s work, is not expected to increase much. As in most other occupations, replacement needs will be a major source of job openings.

Employment in nursing homes is expected to grow faster than the average. Nursing homes will offer the most new jobs for L.P.N.s as the number of aged and disabled persons in need of long-term care rises. In addition to caring for the aged, nursing homes will be called on to care for the increasing number of patients who have been released from the hospital and have not recovered enough to return home.

Much faster than average growth is expected in home health care services. This is in response to a growing number of older persons with functional disabilities, consumer preference for care in the home, and technological advances, which make it possible to bring increasingly complex treatments into the home.

An increasing proportion of sophisticated procedures, which once were performed only in hospitals, are being performed in physicians' offices and clinics, including ambulatory surgicenters and emergency medical centers, thanks largely to advances in technology. As a result, employment is projected to grow much faster than average in these places as health care in general expands.

Earnings

Median annual earnings of licensed practical nurses were $26,940 in 1998. The middle 50 percent earned between $23,160 and $31,870 a year. The lowest 10 percent earned less than $20,210 and the highest 10 percent earned more than $37,540 a year. Median annual earnings in the industries employing the largest numbers of licensed practical nurses in 1997 were as follows:

Personnel supply services	$30,200
Home health care services	27,600
Hospitals	25,300
Nursing and personal care facilities	26,200
Offices and clinics of medical doctors	24,500

Related Occupations

L.P.N.s work closely with people while helping them. So do emergency medical technicians, social and human service assistants, surgical technologists, and teacher assistants.

Sources of Additional Information

For information about practical nursing, contact:

☛ National League for Nursing, 61 Broadway, New York, NY 10006. Internet: **http://www.nln.org**

☛ National Association for Practical Nurse Education and Service, Inc., 1400 Spring St., Suite 330, Silver Spring, MD 20910.

Nuclear Medicine Technologists

(O*NET 32914)

Significant Points

- Relatively few job openings will occur because the occupation is small.
- Technologists trained in both nuclear medicine and radiologic technology or other modalities will have the best prospects.

Nature of the Work

In nuclear medicine, radionuclides—unstable atoms that emit radiation spontaneously—are used to diagnose and treat disease. Radionuclides are purified and compounded like other drugs to form radiopharmaceuticals. Nuclear medicine technologists administer these radiopharmaceuticals to patients, then monitor the characteristics and functions of tissues or organs in which they localize. Abnormal areas show higher or lower concentrations of radioactivity than normal.

Nuclear medicine technologists operate cameras that detect and map the radioactive drug in the patient's body to create an image on photographic film or a computer monitor. Radiologic technologists also operate diagnostic imaging equipment, but their equipment creates an image by projecting an x ray through the patient. (See the statement on radiologic technologists elsewhere in the *Handbook*.)

Nuclear medicine technologists explain test procedures to patients. They prepare a dosage of the radiopharmaceutical and administer it by mouth, injection, or other means. When preparing radiopharmaceuticals, technologists adhere to safety standards that keep the radiation dose to workers and patients as low as possible.

Technologists position patients and start a gamma scintillation camera, or "scanner," which creates images of the distribution of a

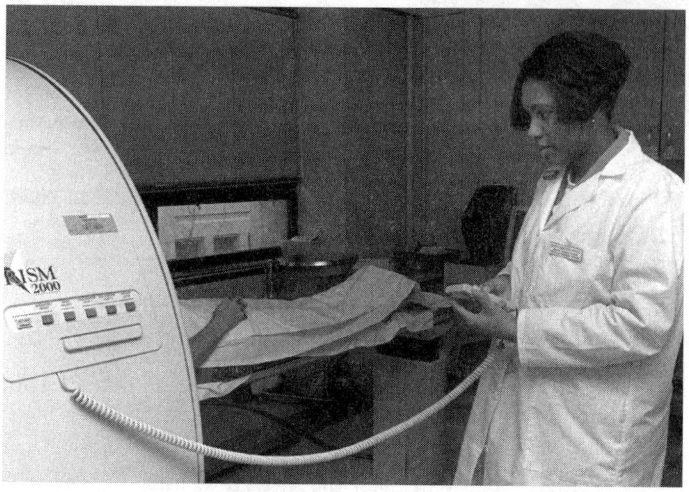

A nuclear medicine technologist prepares equipment for a full-body scan of a patient.

radiopharmaceutical as it localizes in and emits signals from the patient's body. Technologists produce the images on a computer screen or on film for a physician to interpret. Some nuclear medicine studies, such as cardiac function studies, are processed with the aid of a computer.

Nuclear medicine technologists also perform radioimmunoassay studies that assess the behavior of a radioactive substance inside the body. For example, technologists may add radioactive substances to blood or serum to determine levels of hormones or therapeutic drug content.

Technologists keep patient records and record the amount and type of radionuclides received, used, and disposed of.

Working Conditions

Nuclear medicine technologists generally work a 40-hour week. This may include evening or weekend hours in departments that operate on an extended schedule. Opportunities for part-time and shift work are also available. In addition, technologists in hospitals may have on-call duty on a rotational basis.

Because technologists are on their feet much of the day, and may lift or turn disabled patients, physical stamina is important.

Although there is potential for radiation exposure in this field, it is kept to a minimum by the use of shielded syringes, gloves, and other protective devices and adherence to strict radiation safety guidelines. Technologists also wear badges that measure radiation levels. Because of safety programs, however, badge measurements rarely exceed established safety levels.

Employment

Nuclear medicine technologists held about 14,000 jobs in 1998. About 8 out of 10 jobs were in hospitals. The rest were in physicians' offices and clinics, including imaging centers.

Training, Other Qualifications, and Advancement

Nuclear medicine technology programs range in length from 1 to 4 years and lead to a certificate, associate's degree, or bachelor's degree. Generally, certificate programs are offered in hospitals, associate programs in community colleges, and bachelor's programs in 4-year colleges and in universities. Courses cover physical sciences, the biological effects of radiation exposure, radiation protection and procedures, the use of radiopharmaceuticals, imaging techniques, and computer applications.

One-year certificate programs are for health professionals, especially radiologic technologists and ultrasound technologists, who wish to specialize in nuclear medicine. They also attract medical technologists, registered nurses, and others who wish to change fields or specialize. Others interested in the nuclear medicine technology field have three options: A 2-year certificate program, a 2-year associate program, or a 4-year bachelor's program.

The Joint Review Committee on Education Programs in Nuclear Medicine Technology accredits most formal training programs in nuclear medicine technology. In 1999, there were 96 accredited programs.

All nuclear medicine technologists must meet the minimum Federal standards on the administration of radioactive drugs and the operation of radiation detection equipment. In addition, about half of all States require technologists to be licensed. Technologists also may obtain voluntary professional certification or registration. Registration or certification is available from the American Registry of Radiologic Technologists and from the Nuclear Medicine Technology Certification Board. Most employers prefer to hire certified or registered technologists.

Technologists may advance to supervisor, then to chief technologist, and to department administrator or director. Some technologists specialize in a clinical area such as nuclear cardiology or computer analysis or leave patient care to take positions in research laboratories. Some become instructors or directors in nuclear medicine technology programs, a step that usually requires a bachelor's degree or a master's in nuclear medicine technology. Others leave the occupation to work as sales or training representatives for medical equipment and radiopharmaceutical manufacturing firms, or as radiation safety officers in regulatory agencies or hospitals.

Job Outlook

Employment of nuclear medicine technologists is expected to grow about as fast as the average for all occupations through the year 2008. The number of openings each year will be very low because the occupation is small. Growth will arise from an increase in the number of middle-aged and older persons who are the primary users of diagnostic procedures, including nuclear medicine tests. Nonetheless, job seekers will face more competition for jobs than in the recent past. In an attempt to employ fewer technologists and lower labor costs, hospitals continue to merge nuclear medicine and radiologic technology departments. Consequently, opportunities will be best for technologists who can perform both nuclear medicine and radiologic procedures.

Technological innovations may increase the diagnostic uses of nuclear medicine. One example is the use of radiopharmaceuticals in combination with monoclonal antibodies to detect cancer at far earlier stages than is customary today, and without resorting to surgery. Another is the use of radionuclides to examine the heart's ability to pump blood. Wider use of nuclear medical imaging to observe metabolic and biochemical changes for neurology, cardiology, and oncology procedures, will also spur some demand for nuclear medicine technologists.

On the other hand, cost considerations will affect the speed with which new applications of nuclear medicine grow. Some promising nuclear medicine procedures, such as positron emission tomography, are extremely costly, and hospitals contemplating them will have to consider equipment costs, reimbursement policies, and the number of potential users.

Earnings

Median annual earnings of nuclear medicine technologists were $39,610 in 1998. The middle 50 percent earned between $34,910 and $46,570 a year. The lowest 10 percent earned less than $30,590 and the highest 10 percent earned more than $52,770 a year.

Related Occupations

Nuclear medical technologists operate sophisticated equipment to help physicians and other health practitioners diagnose and treat patients. Radiologic technologists, diagnostic medical sonographers, cardiovascular technologists, electroneurodiagnostic technologists, clinical laboratory technologists, perfusionists, radiation therapists, and respiratory therapists also perform similar functions.

Sources of Additional Information

Additional information on a career as a nuclear medicine technologist is available from:

☛ The Society of Nuclear Medicine-Technologist Section, 1850 Samuel Morse Dr., Reston, VA 22090.

For information on a career as a nuclear medicine technologist, enclose a stamped, self-addressed business size envelope with your request to:

☛ American Society of Radiologic Technologists, Customer Service Department, 15000 Central Ave. SE., Albuquerque, NM 87123-3917, or call (800) 444-2778.

For a list of accredited programs in nuclear medicine technology, write to:

☛ Joint Review Committee on Educational Programs in Nuclear Medicine Technology, PMB 418, 1 2nd Avenue East, Suite C, Polson, MT 59860-2107.

Information on certification is available from:

☛ Nuclear Medicine Technology Certification Board, 2970 Clairmont Rd., Suite 610, Atlanta, GA 30329.

Opticians, Dispensing

(O*NET 32514)

Significant Points

- Although training requirements vary by State, most dispensing opticians receive training on-the-job or through apprenticeships lasting 2 to 4 years.
- Employment of dispensing opticians is expected to increase as fast as the average for all occupations through 2008 as demand grows for corrective lenses.

Nature of Work

Dispensing opticians fit eyeglasses and contact lenses, following prescriptions written by ophthalmologists or optometrists. (The work of optometrists is described in a statement elsewhere in the *Handbook*. See the statement on physicians for information about ophthalmologists.)

Dispensing opticians examine written prescriptions to determine lens specifications. They recommend eyeglass frames, lenses, and lens coatings after considering the prescription and the customer's occupation, habits, and facial features. Dispensing opticians measure clients' eyes, including the distance between the centers of the pupils and the distance between the eye surface and the lens. For customers without prescriptions, dispensing opticians may use a lensometer to record the present eyeglass prescription. They also may obtain a customer's previous record, or verify a prescription with the examining optometrist or ophthalmologist.

Dispensing opticians prepare work orders that give ophthalmic laboratory technicians information needed to grind and insert lenses into a frame. The work order includes lens prescriptions and information on lens size, material, color, and style. Some dispensing opticians grind and insert lenses themselves. After the glasses are made, dispensing opticians verify that the lenses have been ground to specifications. Then they may reshape or bend the frame, by hand or using pliers, so that the eyeglasses fit the customer properly and comfortably. Some also fix, adjust, and refit broken frames. They instruct clients about adapting to, wearing, or caring for eyeglasses.

Some dispensing opticians specialize in fitting contacts, artificial eyes, or cosmetic shells to cover blemished eyes. To fit contact

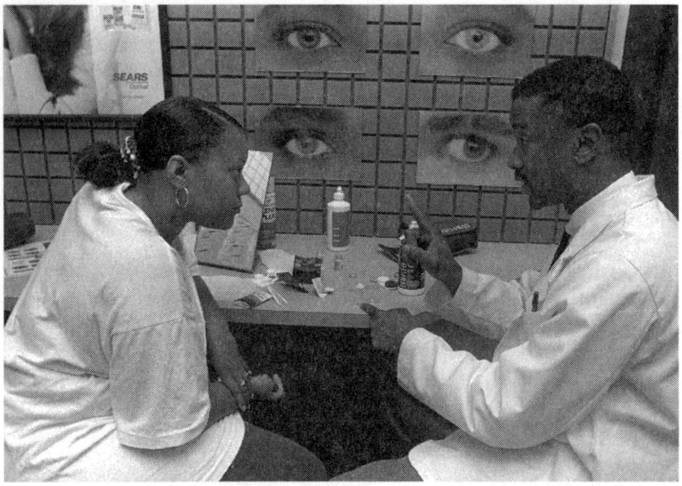

Dispensing opticians ensure that contacts fit properly and show customers how to insert, remove, and care for them.

lenses, dispensing opticians measure eye shape and size, select the type of contact lens material, and prepare work orders specifying the prescription and lens size. Fitting contact lenses requires considerable skill, care, and patience. Dispensing opticians observe customers' eyes, corneas, lids, and contact lenses with special instruments and microscopes. During several visits, opticians show customers how to insert, remove, and care for their contacts, and ensure the fit is correct.

Dispensing opticians keep records on customer prescriptions, work orders, and payments; track inventory and sales; and perform other administrative duties.

Working Conditions

Dispensing opticians work indoors in attractive, well-lighted, and well-ventilated surroundings. They may work in medical offices or small stores where customers are served one at a time, or in large stores where several dispensing opticians serve a number of customers at once. Opticians spend a lot of time on their feet. If they prepare lenses, they need to take precautions against the hazards associated with glass cutting, chemicals, and machinery.

Most dispensing opticians work a 40-hour week, although some work longer hours. Those in retail stores may work evenings and weekends. Some work part time.

Employment

Dispensing opticians held about 71,000 jobs in 1998. About 50 percent worked for ophthalmologists or optometrists who sell glasses directly to patients. Many also work in retail optical stores that offer one-stop shopping. Customers may have their eyes examined, choose frames, and have glasses made on the spot. Some work in optical departments of drug and department stores.

Training, Other Qualifications, and Advancement

Employers usually hire individuals with no background in opticianry or those who have worked as ophthalmic laboratory technicians and then provide the required training. (See the statement on ophthalmic laboratory technicians elsewhere in the *Handbook.*) Training may be informal, on-the-job or formal apprenticeship. Some employers, however, seek people with postsecondary training in opticianry.

Knowledge of physics, basic anatomy, algebra, geometry, and mechanical drawing is particularly valuable because training usually includes instruction in optical mathematics, optical physics, and the use of precision measuring instruments and other machinery and tools. Dispensing opticians deal directly with the public so they should be tactful, pleasant, and communicate well. Manual dexterity and the ability to do precision work are essential.

Large employers usually offer structured apprenticeship programs, and small employers provide more informal on-the-job training. In the 21 States that offer a license to dispensing opticians, individuals without postsecondary training work from 2 to 4 years as apprentices. Apprenticeship or formal training is offered in most States as well.

Apprentices receive technical training and learn office management and sales. Under the supervision of an experienced optician, optometrist, or ophthalmologist, apprentices work directly with patients, fitting eyeglasses and contact lenses. In the 21 States requiring licensure, information about apprenticeships and licensing procedures is available from the State board of occupational licensing.

Formal opticianry training is offered in community colleges and a few colleges and universities. In 1999, there were 25 programs accredited by the Commission on Opticianry Accreditation that awarded 2-year associate degrees in ophthalmic dispensing or optometric technology. There are also shorter programs of one year or less. Some States that offer a license to dispensing opticians allow graduates to take the licensure exam immediately upon graduation; others require a few months to a year of experience.

Dispensing opticians may apply to the American Board of Opticianry and the National Contact Lens Examiners for certification of their skills. Certification must be renewed every 3 years through continuing education.

Many experienced dispensing opticians open their own optical stores. Others become managers of optical stores or sales representatives for wholesalers or manufacturers of eyeglasses or lenses.

Job Outlook

Employment in this occupation is expected to increase as fast as the average for all occupations through 2008 as demand grows for corrective lenses. The number of middle-aged and elderly persons is projected to increase rapidly. Middle age is a time when many individuals use corrective lenses for the first time, and elderly persons require more vision care, on the whole, than others.

Fashion, too, influences demand. Frames come in a growing variety of styles and colors—encouraging people to buy more than one pair. Demand is also expected to grow in response to the availability of new technologies that improve the quality and look of corrective lenses, such as anti-reflective coatings and bifocal lenses without the line visible in old-style bifocals. Improvements in bifocal, extended wear, and disposable contact lenses will also spur demand.

The need to replace those who leave the occupation will result in job openings. Nevertheless, the total number of job openings will be relatively small because the occupation is small. This occupation is vulnerable to changes in the business cycle because eyewear purchases can often be deferred for a time. Employment of opticians can fall somewhat during economic downturns.

Earnings

Median annual earnings of dispensing opticians were $22,440 in 1998. The middle 50 percent earned between $17,680 and $28,560 a year. The lowest 10 percent earned less than $14,240 and the highest 10 percent earned more than $37,080 a year. Median annual earnings in the industries employing the largest number of dispensing opticians in 1997 were as follows:

Industry	Earnings
Offices and clinics of medical doctors	$25,900
Retail stores, not elsewhere classified	21,500
Offices of other health care practitioners	20,100

Related Occupations

Other workers who deal with customers and perform delicate work include jewelers, locksmiths, ophthalmic laboratory technicians, orthodontic technicians, dental laboratory technicians, prosthetics technicians, camera repairers, and watch repairers.

Sources of Additional Information

For general information about a career as a dispensing optician, contact:

☛ Opticians Association of America, 10341 Democracy Lane, Fairfax, VA 22030-2521. Internet: **http://www.opticians.org**

For general information about a career as a dispensing optician and a list of accredited training programs, contact:

☛ Commission on Opticianry Accreditation, 10341 Democracy Lane, Fairfax, VA 22030-2521. Internet: **http://www.coaccreditation.com**

For general information on opticianry and a list of home-study programs, seminars, and review materials, contact:

☛ National Academy of Opticianry, 8401 Corporate Drive, Suite 605, Landover, MD 20785. Internet: **http://www.nao.org**

Pharmacy Technicians and Assistants

(O*NET 32518)

Significant Points

- Opportunities for pharmacy technicians and assistants are expected to be good, especially for those with formal training or previous work experience.
- Many technicians and assistants work evenings, weekends, and some holidays.
- Seven out of 10 jobs were in retail pharmacies, either independently owned or part of a drug store chain, grocery store, department store, or mass merchandiser.

Nature of the Work

Pharmacy technicians and assistants help licensed pharmacists provide medication and other health care products to patients. *Pharmacy technicians* usually perform more complex tasks than assistants do, although in some States their duties and job titles overlap. Technicians usually perform routine tasks to help prepare prescribed medication for patients, such as counting and labeling. A pharmacist must check every prescription before it can be given to a patient. Technicians refer any questions regarding prescriptions, drug information, or health matters to a pharmacist (see the statement on pharmacists, located elsewhere in the *Handbook*). *Pharmacy assistants* usually have fewer, less complex responsibilities than technicians. Assistants are often clerks or cashiers who primarily answer telephones, handle money, stock shelves, and perform other clerical duties.

Pharmacy technicians who work in retail pharmacies have varying responsibilities depending on State rules and regulations. Technicians receive written prescriptions or requests for a prescription refill from patients or representatives. They must verify that the information on the prescription is complete and accurate. To prepare the prescription the technician must retrieve, count, pour, weigh, measure, and sometimes mix the medication. Then, they prepare the prescription labels, select the type of prescription container, and affix the prescription and auxiliary labels to the container. Once the prescription is filled, technicians price and file the prescription, which must be checked by a pharmacist before it is given to a patient. Technicians may establish and maintain patient profiles, prepare insurance claim forms, and stock and take inventory of prescription and over-the-counter medications. Some also clean the pharmacy equipment, help with the maintenance of equipment and supplies, and manage the cash register.

In hospitals, technicians have added responsibilities. They read patient charts and prepare and deliver the medicine to patients. The pharmacist must check the order before it is delivered to the patient. The technician then copies the information about the prescribed medication onto the patient's profile. Technicians may also assemble a 24-hour supply of medicine for every patient. They package and label each dose separately. The package is then placed in the medicine cabinet of each patient, until the supervising pharmacist checks it. It is then given to the patient. Technicians are responsible for keeping a running inventory of medicines, chemicals, and other supplies used.

Working Conditions

Pharmacy technicians and assistants work in clean, organized, well-lighted, and well-ventilated areas. Most of their workday is spent on their feet. They may be required to lift heavy boxes or to use stepladders to retrieve supplies from high shelves.

Technicians and assistants work the same hours as pharmacists. This includes evenings, nights, weekends, and some holidays. Most technicians work 35-45 hours a week. Since some hospital and retail pharmacies are open 24 hours a day, technicians and assistants may work varying shifts. There are many opportunities for part-time work in both retail and hospital settings.

Employment

Pharmacy technicians and assistants held about 170,000 jobs in 1998. Seven out of 10 jobs were in retail pharmacies, either independently owned or part of a drug store chain, grocery store, department store, or mass merchandiser. Two out of 10 jobs were in hospitals and a small number were in mail-order pharmacies, clinics, pharmaceutical wholesalers, and the Federal Government.

A pharmacy technician establishes and maintains patient profiles.

Training, Other Qualifications, and Advancement

Although most pharmacy technicians receive informal on-the-job training, employers are beginning to favor those who have completed formal training. However, there are currently few State and no Federal requirements for formal training or education of pharmacy technicians. Employers who can neither afford, nor have the time to give on-the-job training, often seek formally educated pharmacy technicians. Formal education programs emphasize the technicians' interest and dedication to the work to potential employers. Some hospitals, proprietary schools, vocational or technical colleges, and community colleges offer formal education programs.

Formal pharmacy technician education programs require classroom and laboratory work in a variety of areas, including medical and pharmaceutical terminology, pharmaceutical calculations, pharmacy record keeping, pharmaceutical techniques, and pharmacy law and ethics. Technicians are also required to learn medication names, actions, uses, and doses. Many training programs include clerkship or internships, where students gain hands-on experience in actual pharmacies. Students receive a diploma, certificate, or an associate degree, depending on the program.

Prospective pharmacy technicians with experience working as an assistant in a community pharmacy or volunteering in a hospital may have an advantage. Employers also prefer applicants with strong customer service and communication skills and experience managing inventories, counting, measuring, and using a computer. Technicians entering the field need strong spelling and reading skills. A background in mathematics, chemistry, English, and health education may also be beneficial.

The Pharmacy Technician Certification Board administers the National Pharmacy Technician Certification Examination. This exam is voluntary and displays the competency of the individual to act as a pharmacy technician. Eligible exam candidates must have a high school diploma or GED and those who pass the exam earn the title of Certified Pharmacy Technician. Certification helps technicians formalize their career and feel like part of a health care team. Employers know that individuals who pass the exam have a standardized body of knowledge and skills.

Certified technicians must be recertified every 2 years. Technicians must complete 20 contact hours of pharmacy related topics within the 2-year certification period to become eligible for recertification. At least 1 contact hour must be in the area of pharmacy law. Contact hours can be earned from several different sources including pharmacy associations, pharmacy colleges, and pharmacy technician training programs. Up to 10 contact hours can be earned when the technician is employed under the direct supervision and instruction of the pharmacist.

Successful pharmacy technicians are alert, observant, organized, dedicated, and responsible. They should be willing and able to take directions. They must enjoy precise work—details are sometimes a matter of life and death. Although a pharmacist must check and approve all their work, they should be able to work on their own without constant instruction from the pharmacist. Candidates interested in becoming pharmacy technicians cannot have prior records of drug or substance abuse.

Strong interpersonal and communication skills are needed because there is a lot of interaction with patients, coworkers, and health care professionals. Teamwork is very important because technicians are often required to work with other technicians.

Pharmacy assistants are almost always trained on-the-job. They may begin by observing a more experienced worker. After they become familiar with the store's equipment, policies, and procedures, they begin to work on their own. Once they become experienced workers, they are not likely to receive training, except when new equipment is introduced or when policies or procedures change. When necessary, on-the-job training is usually provided.

To become a pharmacy assistant, one should be able to perform repetitious work accurately. Assistants need good basic mathematics skills and good manual dexterity. Because they deal constantly with the public, pharmacy assistants should be neat in appearance, and able to deal pleasantly and tactfully with customers. Some employers may prefer people with experience typing, handling money, or operating specialized equipment, including computers.

Advancement is usually limited, although some technicians enroll in pharmacy school and become pharmacists.

Job Outlook

Employment of pharmacy technicians and assistants is expected to grow as fast as average for all occupations through 2008 due to the increased pharmaceutical needs of a larger and older population, and greater use of medication. The increased number of middle aged and elderly people will spur demand for technicians and assistants in all practice settings. The middle aged and elderly populations use more prescription drugs, on average, than younger people.

Job opportunities are expected to be good, especially for technicians and assistants with formal training or previous experience. Many jobs for pharmacy technicians and assistants will result from the need to replace workers who transfer to other occupations or leave the labor force. Opportunities for part-time work are also expected to be good.

Cost-conscious insurers, pharmacies, and health systems will continue to emphasize the role of technicians and assistants. As a result, pharmacy technicians and assistants will assume responsibility for more routine tasks previously performed by pharmacists. Pharmacy technicians will also need to learn and master new pharmacy technology as it surfaces. For example, robotic machines are used to dispense medicine into containers. Technicians oversee the machine, stock the bins, and label the containers. Although automation is becoming increasingly incorporated into the job, it will not necessarily reduce the need for technicians.

Many States have legislated the maximum number of technicians who can work under a pharmacist. In some States, increased demand for technicians has encouraged an expanded ratio of technicians to pharmacists.

Earnings

Median hourly earnings of pharmacy technicians in 1998 were $8.54. The middle 50 percent earned between $7.11 and $10.64; the lowest 10 percent, less than $6.08 and the highest 10 percent, more than $12.73. Median hourly earnings of pharmacy technicians were $8.00 in drug stores, $8.40 in grocery stores, and $8.50 in department stores in 1997.

Median hourly earnings of pharmacy aides, also called pharmacy technicians, were $8.88 in 1998. The middle 50 percent earned between $7.02 and $10.75; the lowest 10 percent, less than $5.94 and the highest 10 percent, more than $12.64. Median hourly earnings of pharmacy aides were $7.10 in drug stores and $9.60 in hospitals in 1997.

Certified technicians may earn more. Shift differentials for working evenings or weekends can also increase earnings. Some technicians belong to unions representing hospital or grocery store workers.

Related occupations

Workers in other medical support occupations include dental assistants, health information technicians, licensed practical nurses, medical secretaries, medical transcriptionists, occupational therapy assistants and aides, physical therapist assistants and aides, and surgical technologists.

Sources of Additional Information

For information on certification and a National Pharmacy Technician Certification Examination Candidate Handbook contact:

☛ Pharmacy Technician Certification Board, 2215 Constitution Ave. NW., Washington DC 20037. Internet: **http://www.ptcb.org**

For information on a career as a pharmacy technician, contact:

☛ American Society of Health System Pharmacists, 7272 Wisconsin Ave., Bethesda, MD 20814. Internet: **http://www.ashp.org**

☛ National Association of Chain Drug Stores, 413 N. Lee St., P.O. Box 1417-D49, Alexandria, VA 22313-1480. Internet: **www.nacds.org**

Radiologic Technologists

(O*NET 32919 and 32921)

Significant Points

- Radiologic technologists with cross training in nuclear medicine technology or other modalities will have the best prospects.
- Sonographers should experience somewhat better job opportunities than other radiologic technologists, as ultrasound becomes an increasingly attractive alternative to radiologic procedures.

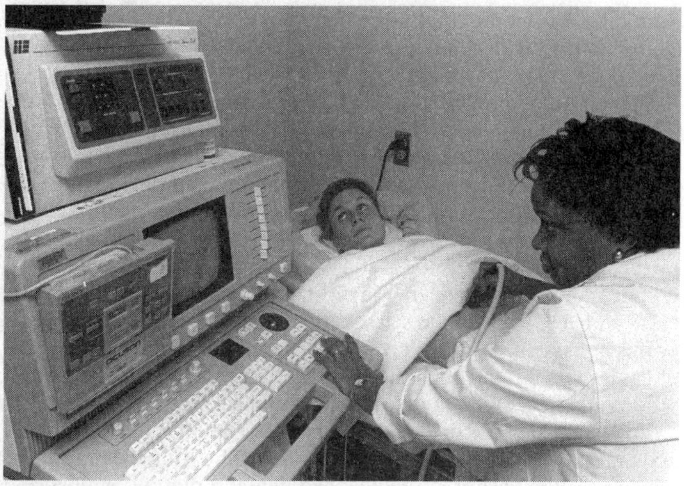

A diagnostic medical sonographer performs an abdominal ultrasound.

Nature of the Work

Perhaps the most familiar use of the x ray is the diagnosis of broken bones. However, medical uses of radiation go far beyond that. Radiation is used not only to produce images of the interior of the body, but to treat cancer as well. At the same time, the use of imaging techniques that do not involve x rays, such as ultrasound and magnetic resonance imaging (MRI), is growing rapidly. The term "diagnostic imaging" embraces these procedures as well as the familiar x ray.

Radiographers produce x-ray films (radiographs) of parts of the human body for use in diagnosing medical problems. They prepare patients for radiologic examinations by explaining the procedure, removing articles such as jewelry, through which x rays cannot pass, and positioning patients so that the parts of the body can be appropriately radiographed. To prevent unnecessary radiation exposure, technologists surround the exposed area with radiation protection devices, such as lead shields, or limit the size of the x-ray beam. Radiographers position radiographic equipment at the correct angle and height over the appropriate area of a patient's body. Using instruments similar to a measuring tape, technologists may measure the thickness of the section to be radiographed and set controls on the machine to produce radiographs of the appropriate density, detail, and contrast. They place the x-ray film under the part of the patient's body to be examined and make the exposure. They then remove the film and develop it.

Experienced radiographers may perform more complex imaging tests. For fluoroscopies, radiographers prepare a solution of contrast medium for the patient to drink, allowing the radiologist, a physician who interprets radiographs, to see soft tissues in the body. Some radiographers, called *CT technologists,* operate computerized tomography scanners to produce cross sectional views of patients. Others operate machines using giant magnets and radio waves rather than radiation to create an image and are called *magnetic resonance imaging (MRI) technologists*.

Sonographers, also known as ultrasonographers, direct nonionizing, high frequency sound waves into areas of the patient's body; the equipment then collects reflected echoes to form an image. The image is viewed on a screen and may be recorded on videotape or photographed for interpretation and diagnosis by physicians. Sonographers explain the procedure, record additional medical history, select appropriate equipment settings and use various patient positions as necessary. Viewing the screen as the scan takes place, sonographers look for subtle differences between healthy and pathological areas, decide which images to include, and judge if the images are satisfactory for diagnostic purposes. Sonographers may specialize in neurosonography (the brain), vascular (blood flows), echocardiography (the heart), abdominal (the liver, kidneys, spleen, and pancreas), obstetrics/gynecology (the female reproductive system), and ophthalmology (the eye).

Radiologic technologists must follow physicians' orders precisely and conform to regulations concerning use of radiation to protect themselves, their patients, and coworkers from unnecessary exposure.

In addition to preparing patients and operating equipment, radiologic technologists keep patient records and adjust and maintain equipment. They may also prepare work schedules, evaluate equipment purchases, or manage a radiology department.

Working Conditions

Most full-time radiologic technologists work about 40 hours a week; they may have evening, weekend, or on-call hours.

Technologists are on their feet for long periods and may lift or turn disabled patients. They work at diagnostic machines but may also do some procedures at patients' bedsides. Some radiologic technologists travel to patients in large vans equipped with sophisticated diagnostic equipment.

Although potential radiation hazards exist in this occupation, they are minimized by the use of lead aprons, gloves, and other shielding devices, as well as by instruments monitoring radiation exposure. Technologists wear badges measuring radiation levels in the radiation area, and detailed records are kept on their cumulative lifetime dose.

Employment

Radiologic technologists held about 162,000 jobs in 1998. Most technologists were radiographers, while the rest worked as sonographers. About 1 radiologic technologist in 5 worked part time. More than half of jobs for technologists are in hospitals. Most of the rest are in physicians' offices and clinics, including diagnostic imaging centers.

Training, Other Qualifications, and Advancement

Preparation for this profession is offered in hospitals, colleges and universities, vocational-technical institutes, and the Armed Forces. Hospitals, which employ most radiologic technologists, prefer to hire those with formal training.

Formal training is offered in radiography and diagnostic medical sonography (ultrasound). Programs range in length from 1 to 4 years and lead to a certificate, associate's degree, or bachelor's degree. Two-year associate's degree programs are most prevalent.

Some 1-year certificate programs are available for experienced radiographers or individuals from other health occupations, such as medical technologists and registered nurses, who want to change fields or specialize in sonography. A bachelor's or master's degree in one of the radiologic technologies is desirable for supervisory, administrative, or teaching positions.

The Joint Review Committee on Education in Radiologic Technology accredits most formal training programs for this field. They accredited 602 radiography programs in 1999. The Joint Review Committee on Education in Diagnostic Medical Sonography accredited 77 programs in sonography in 1998.

Radiography programs require, at a minimum, a high school diploma or the equivalent. High school courses in mathematics, physics, chemistry, and biology are helpful. The programs provide both classroom and clinical instruction in anatomy and physiology, patient care procedures, radiation physics, radiation protection, principles of imaging, medical terminology, positioning of patients, medical ethics, radiobiology, and pathology.

For training programs in diagnostic medical sonography, applicants with a background in science, or experience in one of the health professions, generally are preferred. Some programs consider applicants with liberal arts backgrounds, however, as well as high school graduates with courses in math and science.

In 1981, Congress passed the Consumer-Patient Radiation Health and Safety Act, which aims to protect the public from the hazards of unnecessary exposure to medical and dental radiation by ensuring operators of radiologic equipment are properly trained. Under the act, the Federal Government sets voluntary standards that the States, in turn, may use for accrediting training programs and certifying individuals who engage in medical or dental radiography. Because ultrasound does not use ionizing radiation, sonographers are excluded from this act.

In 1999, 35 States and Puerto Rico licensed radiologic technologists. No State requires sonographers to be licensed. Voluntary registration is offered by the American Registry of Radiologic Technologists (ARRT) in radiography. The American Registry of Diagnostic Medical Sonographers (ARDMS) certifies the competence of sonographers. To be eligible for registration, technologists generally must graduate from an accredited program and pass an examination. Many employers prefer to hire registered radiographers and sonographers.

With experience and additional training, staff technologists may become specialists, performing CT scanning, angiography, and magnetic resonance imaging. Experienced technologists may also be promoted to supervisor, chief radiologic technologist, and—ultimately—department administrator or director. Depending on the institution, courses or a master's degree in business or health administration may be necessary for the director's position. Some technologists progress by becoming instructors or directors in radiologic technology programs; others take jobs as sales representatives or instructors with equipment manufacturers.

Radiographers must complete 24 hours of continuing education every other year and provide documentation to prove they have complied with these requirements. Sonographers must complete 30 hours of continuing education every 3 years.

Job Outlook

Employment of radiologic technologists is expected to grow as fast as the average for all occupations through 2008, as the population grows and ages, increasing the demand for diagnostic imaging and therapeutic technology. Although physicians are enthusiastic about the clinical benefits of new technologies, the extent to which they are adopted depends largely on cost and reimbursement considerations. Some promising new technologies may not come into widespread use because they are too expensive and third-party payers may not be willing to pay for their use.

Sonographers should experience somewhat better job opportunities than radiographers. Ultrasound is becoming an increasingly attractive alternative to radiologic procedures. Ultrasound technology is expected to continue to evolve rapidly and spawn many new ultrasound procedures. Furthermore, because ultrasound does not use radiation for imaging, there are few possible side effects.

Radiologic technologists who are educated and credentialed in more than one type of imaging technology, such as radiography and ultrasonography or nuclear medicine, will have better employment opportunities as employers look for new ways to control costs. In hospitals, multi-skilled employees will be the most sought after, as hospitals respond to cost pressures by continuing to merge departments.

Hospitals will remain the principal employer of radiologic technologists. However, employment is expected to grow most rapidly in offices and clinics of physicians, including diagnostic imaging centers. Health facilities such as these are expected to grow very rapidly through 2008 due to the strong shift toward outpatient care, encouraged by third-party payers and made possible by technological advances that permit more procedures to be performed outside the hospital. Some job openings will also arise from the need to replace technologists who leave the occupation.

Earnings

Median annual earnings of radiologic technologists and technicians were $32,880 in 1998. The middle 50 percent earned between $27,560 and $39,420 a year. The lowest 10 percent earned less than $23,650 and the highest 10 percent earned more than $47,610 a year. Median annual earnings in the industries employing the largest number of radiologic technologists and technicians in 1997 were:

Industry	Earnings
Medical and dental laboratories	$34,400
Hospitals	31,600
Offices and clinics of medical doctors	30,800

Related Occupations

Radiologic technologists operate sophisticated equipment to help physicians, dentists, and other health practitioners diagnose and treat patients. Workers in related occupations include radiation dosimetrists, nuclear medicine technologists, cardiovascular technologists and technicians, radiation therapists, perfusionists, respiratory therapists, clinical laboratory technologists, and electroneurodiagnostic technologists.

Sources of Additional Information

For career information, enclose a stamped, self-addressed business size envelope with your request to:

☛ American Society of Radiologic Technologists, 15000 Central Ave. SE., Albuquerque, NM 87123-3917.

☛ Society of Diagnostic Medical Sonographers, 12770 Coit Rd., Suite 708, Dallas, TX 75251.

☛ American Healthcare Radiology Administrators, 111 Boston Post Rd., Suite 105, P.O. Box 334, Sudbury, MA 01776.

For the current list of accredited education programs in radiography, write to:

☛ Joint Review Committee on Education in Radiologic Technology, 20 N. Wacker Dr., Suite 600, Chicago, IL 60606-2901.

For a current list of accredited education programs in diagnostic medical sonography, write to:

☛ The Joint Review Committee on Education in Diagnostic Medical Sonography, 7108 S. Alton Way, Building C., Englewood, CO 80112. Internet: **http://www.caahep.org/programs/dms-prog.htm**

Surgical Technologists

(O*NET 32928)

Significant Points

- Most educational programs for surgical technologists last approximately 1 year and result in a certificate.
- Increased demand for surgical technologists is expected as the number of surgical procedures grows.

Nature of the Work

Surgical technologists, also called surgical or operating room technicians, assist in operations under the supervision of surgeons, registered nurses, or other surgical personnel. Before an operation, surgical technologists help set up the operating room with surgical instruments and equipment, sterile linens, and sterile solutions. They assemble, adjust, and check nonsterile equipment to ensure it is working properly. Technologists also prepare patients for surgery by washing, shaving, and disinfecting incision sites. They transport patients to the operating room, help position them on the operating table, and cover them with sterile surgical "drapes." Technologists also observe patients' vital signs, check charts, and help the surgical team scrub and put on gloves, gowns, and masks.

During surgery, technologists pass instruments and other sterile supplies to surgeons and surgeon assistants. They may hold retractors, cut sutures, and help count sponges, needles, supplies, and instruments. Surgical technologists help prepare, care for, and dispose of specimens taken for laboratory analysis and may help apply dressings. Some operate sterilizers, lights, or suction machines, and help operate diagnostic equipment. Technologists may also maintain supplies of fluids, such as plasma and blood.

After an operation, surgical technologists may help transfer patients to the recovery room and clean and restock the operating room.

Working Conditions

Surgical technologists work in clean, well-lighted, cool environments. They must stand for long periods and remain alert during operations. At times they may be exposed to communicable diseases and unpleasant sights, odors, and materials.

Most surgical technologists work a regular 40-hour week, although they may be on call or work nights, weekends and holidays on a rotating basis.

Employment

Surgical technologists held about 54,000 jobs in 1998. Most are employed by hospitals, mainly in operating and delivery rooms. Others are employed in clinics and surgical centers, and in the offices of physicians and dentists who perform outpatient surgery. A few, known as private scrubs, are employed directly by surgeons who have special surgical teams like those for liver transplants.

Training, Other Qualifications, and Advancement

Surgical technologists receive their training in formal programs offered by community and junior colleges, vocational schools, universities, hospitals, and the military. In 1998, the Commission on Accreditation of Allied Health Education Programs (CAAHEP) recognized 165 accredited programs. High school graduation normally is required for admission. Programs last 9 to 24 months and lead to a certificate, diploma, or associate degree. Shorter programs are designed for students who are already licensed practical nurses or military personnel with the appropriate training.

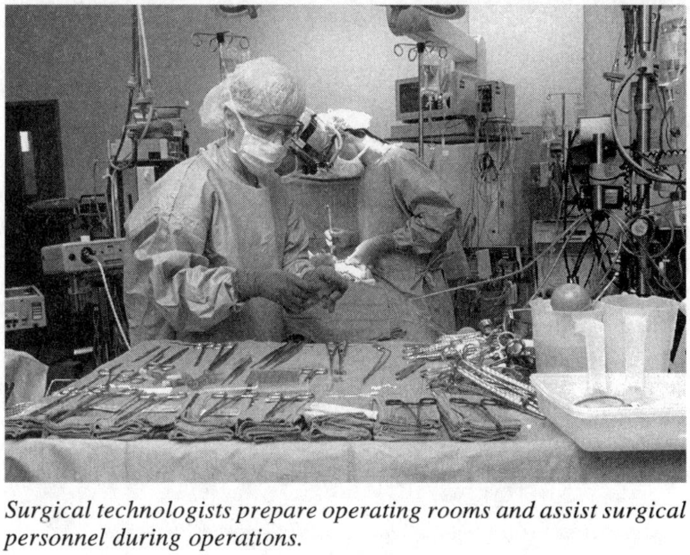

Surgical technologists prepare operating rooms and assist surgical personnel during operations.

Programs provide classroom education and supervised clinical experience. Students take courses in anatomy, physiology, microbiology, pharmacology, professional ethics, and medical terminology. Other studies cover the care and safety of patients during surgery, aseptic techniques, and surgical procedures. Students also learn to sterilize instruments; prevent and control infection; and handle special drugs, solutions, supplies, and equipment.

Technologists may obtain voluntary professional certification from the Liaison Council on Certification for the Surgical Technologist by graduating from a formal program and passing a national certification examination. They may then use the designation Certified Surgical Technologist, or CST. Continuing education or reexamination is required to maintain certification, which must be renewed every 6 years. Graduation from a CAAHEP-accredited program will be a prerequisite for certification by March 2000. Most employers prefer to hire certified technologists.

Surgical technologists need manual dexterity to handle instruments quickly. They also must be conscientious, orderly, and emotionally stable to handle the demands of the operating room environment. Technologists must respond quickly and know procedures well to have instruments ready for surgeons without having to be told. They are expected to keep abreast of new developments in the field. Recommended high school courses include health, biology, chemistry, and mathematics.

Technologists advance by specializing in a particular area of surgery, such as neurosurgery or open heart surgery. They may also work as circulating technologists. A circulating technologist is the "unsterile" member of the surgical team who prepares patients; helps with anesthesia; gets, opens, and holds packages for the "sterile" persons during the procedure; interviews the patient before surgery; keeps a written account of the surgical procedure; and answers the surgeon's questions about the patient during the surgery. With additional training, some technologists advance to first assistants, who help with retracting, sponging, suturing, cauterizing bleeders, and closing and treating wounds. Some surgical technologists manage central supply departments in hospitals, or take positions with insurance companies, sterile supply services, and operating equipment firms.

Job Outlook

Employment of surgical technologists is expected to grow much faster than the average for all occupations through the year 2008 as the volume of surgery increases. The number of surgical procedures is expected to rise as the population grows and ages. As the "baby boom" generation enters retirement age, the over 50 population will account for a larger portion of the general population. Older people require more surgical procedures. Technological advances, such as fiber optics and laser technology, will also permit new surgical procedures to be performed.

Hospitals will continue to be the primary employer of surgical technologists, although much faster employment growth is expected in offices and clinics of physicians, including ambulatory surgical centers.

Earnings

Median annual earnings of surgical technologists were $25,780 in 1998. The middle 50 percent earned between $22,040 and $30,230 a year. The lowest 10 percent earned less than $18,930 and the highest 10 percent earned more than $35,020 a year.

Related Occupations

Other health occupations requiring approximately 1 year of training after high school include licensed practical nurses, certified respiratory therapists, medical laboratory assistants, medical assistants, dental assistants, optometric assistants, and physical therapy aides.

Sources of Additional Information

For additional information on a career as a surgical technologist and a list of CAAHEP-accredited programs, contact:

☛ Association of Surgical Technologists, 7108-C South Alton Way, Englewood, CO 80112. Internet: **http://www.ast.org**

For information on certification, contact:

☛ Liaison Council on Certification for the Surgical Technologist, 7790 East Arapahoe Rd., Suite 240, Englewood, CO 80112-1274.

Communications-Related Occupations

Announcers

(O*NET 34017 and 34021)

Significant Points

- Competition for announcer jobs will continue to be keen.
- Jobs at small stations usually have low pay, but offer the best opportunities for beginners.
- Related work experience at a campus radio station or as an intern at a commercial station can be helpful in breaking into the occupation.

Nature of the Work

Announcers in radio and television perform a variety of tasks on and off the air. They announce station program information such as program schedules and station breaks for commercials or public service information, and they introduce and close programs. Announcers read prepared scripts or ad-lib commentary on the air when presenting news, sports, weather, time, and commercials. If a written script is required, they may do the research and writing. Announcers also interview guests and moderate panels or discussions. Some provide commentary for the audience during sporting events, parades, and other events. Announcers are often well known to radio and television audiences and may make promotional appearances and remote broadcasts for their stations.

Radio announcers are often called *disc jockeys*. Some disc jockeys specialize in one kind of music. They announce music selections and may decide what music to play. While on the air, they comment on the music, weather, and traffic. They may take requests from listeners, interview guests, and manage listener contests.

Newscasters or *anchors* work at large stations and specialize in news, sports, or weather. (See the related statement on news analysts, reporters, and correspondents elsewhere in the *Handbook*.) *Show hosts* may specialize in a certain area of interest such as politics, personal finance, sports, or health. They contribute to the preparation of the program content; interview guests; and discuss issues with viewers, listeners, or an in-studio audience.

Announcers at smaller stations may cover all of these areas and tend to have more off-air duties as well. They may operate the control board, monitor the transmitter, sell commercial time to advertisers, keep a log of the station's daily programming, and do production work. Consolidation and automation make it possible for announcers to do some work previously performed by broadcast technicians. (See the statement on broadcast and sound technicians elsewhere in the *Handbook*.) Announcers use the control board to broadcast programming, commercials, and public service announcements according to schedule. Public radio and television announcers are involved with station fundraising efforts.

Announcers frequently participate in community activities. Sports announcers, for example, may serve as masters of ceremonies at sports club banquets or may greet customers at openings of sporting goods stores.

Although most announcers are employed in radio and television broadcasting, some are employed in the cable television or motion picture production industries. Other announcers may use a public address system to provide information to the audience at sporting and other events. Some disc jockeys announce and play music at clubs, dances, restaurants, and weddings.

Working Conditions

Announcers usually work in well-lighted, air-conditioned, soundproof studios.

The broadcast day is long for radio and TV stations—some are on the air 24 hours a day—so announcers can expect to work unusual hours. Many present early morning shows, when most people are getting ready for work or commuting, while others do late night programs.

Competition for announcer jobs will be keen in large markets.

Announcers often work within tight schedule constraints, which can be physically and mentally stressful. For many announcers, the intangible rewards—creative work, many personal contacts, and the satisfaction of becoming widely known—far outweigh the disadvantages of irregular and often unpredictable hours, work pressures, and disrupted personal lives.

Employment

Announcers held about 60,000 jobs in 1998. Nearly all were staff announcers employed in radio and television broadcasting, but some were freelance announcers who sold their services for individual assignments to networks and stations, or to advertising agencies and other independent producers. Many announcing jobs are part time.

Training, Other Qualifications, and Advancement

Entry to this occupation is highly competitive. Formal training in broadcasting from a college or technical school (private broadcasting school) is valuable. Station officials pay particular attention to taped auditions that show an applicant's delivery and—in television—appearance and style on commercials, news, and interviews. Those hired by television stations usually start out as production assistants, researchers, or reporters and are given a chance to move into announcing if they show an aptitude for "on-air" work. Newcomers to TV broadcasting also may begin as news camera operators. (See the statement on photographers and camera operators elsewhere in the *Handbook.*) A beginner's chance of landing an on-air job is remote, except possibly for a small radio station. In radio, newcomers usually start out taping interviews and operating equipment.

Announcers usually begin at a station in a small community and, if qualified, may move to a better paying job in a large city. They also may advance by hosting a regular program as a disc jockey, sportscaster, or other specialist. Competition is particularly intense for employment by networks, and employers look for college graduates with at least several years of successful announcing experience.

Announcers must have a pleasant and well-controlled voice, good timing, excellent pronunciation, and must know correct grammar usage. Television announcers need a neat, pleasing appearance as well. Knowledge of theater, sports, music, business, politics, and other subjects likely to be covered in broadcasts improves chances for success. Announcers also must be computer-literate because programming is created and edited by computer. In addition, they should be able to ad-lib all or part of a show and to work under tight deadlines. The most successful announcers attract a large audience by combining a pleasing personality and voice with an appealing style.

High school and college courses in English, public speaking, drama, foreign languages, and computer science are valuable, and hobbies such as sports and music are additional assets. Students may gain valuable experience at campus radio or TV facilities and at commercial stations while serving as interns. Paid or unpaid internships provide students with hands-on training and the chance to establish contacts in the industry. Unpaid interns often receive college credit and are allowed to observe and assist station employees. Although the Fair Labor Standards Act limits the work unpaid interns may perform in a station, unpaid internships are the rule; sometimes they lead to paid internships. Paid internships are valuable because interns do work ordinarily done by regular employees and may even go on the air.

Persons considering enrolling in a broadcasting school should contact personnel managers of radio and television stations as well as broadcasting trade organizations to determine the school's reputation for producing suitably trained candidates.

Job Outlook

Competition for jobs as announcers will be keen because the broadcasting field attracts many more jobseekers than there are jobs. Small radio stations are more inclined to hire beginners, but the pay is low. Interns usually receive preference for available positions. Because competition for ratings is so intense in major metropolitan areas, large stations will continue to seek announcers who have proven that they can attract and retain a large audience.

Announcers who are knowledgeable in business, consumer, and health news may have an advantage over others. While specialization is more common at large stations and the networks, many small stations also encourage it.

Employment of announcers is expected to decline slightly through 2008 due to the lack of growth of new radio and television stations. Openings in this relatively small field will arise from the need to replace those who transfer to other kinds of work or leave the labor force. Job openings also arise because of high turnover within the occupation. Changes in station ownership, format, and ratings frequently cause periods of unemployment for many announcers. Many announcers leave the field because they cannot advance to better paying jobs.

Increasing consolidation of radio and television stations, new technology, and the growth of alternative media sources will contribute to the expected decline in employment of announcers. Consolidation in broadcasting may lead to increased use of syndicated programming and programs originating outside a station's viewing or listening area. Digital technology will increase the productivity of announcers, reducing the time spent on off-air technical and production work. In addition, all traditional media, including radio and television, may suffer losses in audience as the American public increases its use of personal computers.

Employment in this occupation is not significantly affected by downturns in the economy. If recessions cause advertising revenues to fall, stations tend to cut "behind-the-scenes" workers rather than announcers and broadcasters.

Earnings

Salaries in broadcasting vary widely but in general are relatively low except for announcers in large stations in major markets or who work for a network. They are higher in television than in radio and higher in commercial than in public broadcasting.

Median hourly earnings of announcers in 1998 were $8.62. The middle 50 percent earned between $6.17 and $12.76. The lowest 10 percent earned less than $5.63 and the highest 10 percent earned more than $21.28. Median hourly earnings of announcers in 1997 were $8.20 in the radio and television broadcasting industry.

Related Occupations

The success of announcers depends upon how well they communicate. Others who must be skilled at oral communication include interpreters, sales workers, public relations specialists, and teachers. Many announcers also must entertain their audience, so their work is similar to other entertainment-related occupations such as actors, directors and producers, dancers, and musicians.

Sources of Additional Information

General information on the broadcasting industry is available from:

☛ National Association of Broadcasters, 1771 N St. NW., Washington, DC 20036. Internet: **http://www.nab.org**

Broadcast and Sound Technicians

(O*NET 22599A, 34028B, and 34028C)

Significant Points

- Job applicants will face strong competition for the better paying jobs at radio and television stations serving large cities.

- Beginners need formal training in broadcast technology to obtain their first job at a smaller station.
- Evening, weekend, and holiday work is common.

Nature of the Work

Broadcast and sound technicians install, test, repair, set up, and operate the electronic equipment used to record and transmit radio and television programs, cable programs, and motion pictures. They work with television cameras, microphones, tape recorders, lighting, sound effects, transmitters, antennas, and other equipment. Some broadcast and sound technicians produce movie sound tracks in motion picture production studios, control the sound of live events, such as concerts, or record music in a recording studio.

In the control room of a radio or television broadcasting studio, these technicians operate equipment that regulates the signal strength, clarity, and range of sounds and colors of recordings or broadcasts. They also operate control panels to select the source of the material. Technicians may switch from one camera or studio to another, from film to live programming, or from network to local programming. By means of hand signals and, in television, telephone headsets, they give technical directions to other studio personnel.

Broadcast and sound technicians in small stations perform a variety of duties. In large stations and at the networks, technicians are more specialized, although job assignments may change from day to day. The terms "operator," "engineer," and "technician" often are used interchangeably to describe these jobs. *Transmitter operators* monitor and log outgoing signals and operate transmitters. *Maintenance technicians* set up, adjust, service, and repair electronic broadcasting equipment. *Audio control engineers* regulate volume and sound quality of television broadcasts, while *video control engineers* regulate their fidelity, brightness, and contrast. *Recording engineers* operate and maintain video and sound recording equipment. They may operate equipment designed to produce special effects, such as the illusions of a bolt of lightning or a police siren. *Sound mixers* or *rerecording mixers* produce the sound track of a movie, television, or radio program. After filming or recording, they may use a process called dubbing to insert sounds. *Field technicians* set up and operate broadcasting portable field transmission equipment outside the studio. Television news coverage requires so much electronic equipment, and the technology is changing so rapidly, that many stations assign technicians exclusively to news.

Chief engineers, *transmission engineers*, and *broadcast field supervisors* supervise the technicians who operate and maintain broadcasting equipment.

Broadcast and sound technicians install, operate, and maintain a variety of sophisticated equipment.

Working Conditions

Broadcast and sound technicians generally work indoors in pleasant surroundings. However, those who broadcast news and other programs from locations outside the studio may work outdoors in all types of weather. Technicians doing maintenance may climb poles or antenna towers, while those setting up equipment do heavy lifting.

Technicians in large stations and the networks usually work a 40-hour week under great pressure to meet broadcast deadlines, but may occasionally work overtime. Technicians in small stations routinely work more than 40 hours a week. Evening, weekend, and holiday work is usual, because most stations are on the air 18 to 24 hours a day, 7 days a week.

Those who work on motion pictures may be on a tight schedule to finish according to contract agreements.

Employment

Broadcast and sound technicians held about 37,000 jobs in 1998. About 2 out of 3 worked in radio and television broadcasting. Almost 10 percent worked in the motion picture industry. About 10 percent worked for cable and other pay television services. A few were self-employed. Television stations employ, on average, many more technicians than do radio stations. Some technicians are employed in other industries, producing employee communications, sales, and training programs. Technician jobs in television are located in virtually all cities, whereas jobs in radio are also found in many small towns. The highest paying and most specialized jobs are concentrated in New York City, Los Angeles, Chicago, and Washington, DC—the originating centers for most network programs. Motion picture production jobs are concentrated in Los Angeles and New York City.

Training, Other Qualifications, and Advancement

The best way to prepare for a broadcast and sound technician job is to obtain technical school, community college, or college training in broadcast technology or in engineering or electronics. This is particularly true for those who hope to advance to supervisory positions or jobs at large stations or the networks. In the motion picture industry people are hired as apprentice editorial assistants and work their way up to more skilled jobs. Employers in the motion picture industry usually hire experienced freelance technicians on a picture-by-picture basis. Reputation and determination are important in getting jobs.

Beginners learn skills on the job from experienced technicians and supervisors. They often begin their careers in small stations and, once experienced, move on to larger ones. Large stations usually only hire technicians with experience. Many employers pay tuition and expenses for courses or seminars to help technicians keep abreast of developments in the field.

The Federal Communications Commission no longer requires the licensing of broadcast technicians, as the Telecommunications Act of 1996 eliminated this licensing requirement. Certification by the Society of Broadcast Engineers is a mark of competence and experience. The certificate is issued to experienced technicians who pass an examination. By offering the Radio Operator and the Television Operator levels of certification, the Society of Broadcast Engineers has filled the void left by the elimination of the FCC license.

Prospective technicians should take high school courses in math, physics, and electronics. Building electronic equipment from hobby kits and operating a "ham," or amateur radio, are good experience, as is work in college radio and television stations.

Broadcast and sound technicians must have manual dexterity and an aptitude for working with electrical, electronic, and mechanical systems and equipment.

Experienced technicians can become supervisory technicians or chief engineers. A college degree in engineering is needed to become chief engineer at a large TV station.

Job Outlook

People seeking beginning jobs as radio and television broadcast technicians are expected to face strong competition in major metropolitan areas, where the number of qualified job seekers exceeds the number of openings. There, stations seek highly experienced personnel. Prospects for entry-level positions generally are better in small cities and towns for beginners with appropriate training.

The overall employment of broadcast and sound technicians is expected to grow slowly through the year 2008. An increase in the number of programming hours should require additional technicians. However, employment growth in radio and television broadcasting may be tempered somewhat because of slow growth in the number of new radio and television stations and laborsaving technical advances, such as computer-controlled programming and remote control of transmitters. Technicians who know how to install transmitters will be in demand as television stations replace existing analog transmitters with digital transmitters. Stations will begin broadcasting in both analog and digital formats, eventually switching entirely to digital.

Employment in the cable industry should grow because of new products coming to market, such as cable modems, which deliver high speed Internet access to personal computers, and digital set-top boxes, which transmit better sound and pictures, allowing cable operators to offer many more channels than in the past. These new products should cause traditional cable subscribers to sign up for additional services.

Employment in the motion picture industry will grow as fast as the average for all occupations. Job prospects are expected to remain competitive, because of the large number of people attracted to this relatively small field.

Virtually all job openings will result from the need to replace experienced technicians who leave the occupation. Turnover is relatively high for broadcast and sound technicians. Many leave the occupation for electronic jobs in other areas, such as computer technology or commercial and industrial repair.

Earnings

Television stations usually pay higher salaries than radio stations; commercial broadcasting usually pays more than public broadcasting; and stations in large markets pay more than those in small ones.

Median annual earnings of broadcast and sound technicians in 1998 were $25,270. The middle 50 percent earned between $16,940 and $40,310. The lowest 10 percent earned less than $12,620 and the highest 10 percent earned more than $67,020. Median annual earnings of broadcast and sound technicians in 1997 were $21,700 in the radio and television broadcasting industry.

Related Occupations

Broadcast and sound technicians need the electronics training and hand coordination necessary to operate technical equipment, and they generally complete specialized postsecondary programs. Similar occupations include engineering technicians, science technicians, health technologists and technicians, and electronic equipment repairers.

Sources of Additional Information

For information on careers for broadcast and sound technicians, write to:

☛ National Association of Broadcasters Employment Clearinghouse, 1771 N St. NW., Washington, DC 20036. Internet: **http://www.nab.org**

For information on certification, contact:

☛ Society of Broadcast Engineers, 8445 Keystone Crossing, Suite 140, Indianapolis, IN 46240. Internet: **http://www.sbe.org**

For information on careers in the motion picture and television industry, contact:

☛ Society of Motion Picture and Television Engineers (SMPTE), 595 West Hartsdale Ave., White Plains, NY 10607.

News Analysts, Reporters, and Correspondents

(O*NET 34002A, 34011, and 34014)

Significant Points

- Employment is expected to grow little and there should be keen competition for job openings.
- Less competition is expected for jobs with suburban and weekly newspapers and small radio and television stations.
- Jobs are often stressful because of irregular hours, frequent night and weekend work, and pressure to meet deadlines.

Nature of the Work

News analysts, reporters, and correspondents play a key role in our society. They gather information, prepare stories, and make broadcasts that inform us about local, State, national, and international events; present points of view on current issues; and report on the actions of public officials, corporate executives, special interest groups, and others who exercise power.

News analysts examine, interpret, and broadcast news received from various sources, and are also called *newscasters* or *news anchors.* News anchors present news stories and introduce videotaped news or live transmissions from on-the-scene reporters. Some newscasters at large stations and networks usually specialize in a particular type of news, such as sports or weather. *Weathercasters,* also called weather reporters, report current and forecasted weather conditions. They gather information from national satellite weather services, wire services, and local and regional weather bureaus. Some weathercasters are trained *meteorologists* and can develop their own weather forecasts. (See the statement on meteorologists elsewhere in the *Handbook.*) *Sportscasters* select, write, and deliver sports news. This may include interviews with sports personalities and coverage of games and other sporting events.

In covering a story, *reporters* investigate leads and news tips, look at documents, observe events at the scene, and interview people. Reporters take notes and may also take photographs or shoot videos. At their office, they organize the material, determine the focus or emphasis, write their stories, and can edit accompanying video material. Many reporters enter information or write stories on laptop computers, and electronically submit them to their offices from remote locations. In some cases, *newswriters* write a story from information collected and submitted by reporters. Radio and television reporters often compose stories and report "live" from the scene. At times, they later tape an introduction or commentary to their story in the studio. Some journalists also interpret the news or offer opinions to readers, viewers, or listeners. In this role, they are called *commentators* or *columnists.*

General assignment reporters write news, such as an accident, a political rally, the visit of a celebrity, or a company going out of business, as assigned. Large newspapers and radio and television stations assign reporters to gather news about specific categories or beats, such as crime or education. Some reporters specialize in fields such as health, politics, foreign affairs, sports, theater, consumer affairs, social events, science, business, and religion. Investigative reporters cover stories that take many days or weeks of information gathering. Some publications use teams of reporters instead of assigning specific beats, allowing reporters to cover a greater variety of stories. News teams may include reporters, editors, graphic artists, and photographers, working together to complete a story.

News analysts analyze, interpret, and broadcast news received from various sources.

News *correspondents* report on news occurring in the large U.S. and foreign cities where they are stationed. Reporters on small publications cover all aspects of the news: They take photographs, write headlines, lay out pages, edit wire service copy, and write editorials. Some also solicit advertisements, sell subscriptions, and perform general office work.

Working Conditions

The work of news analysts, reporters, and correspondents is usually hectic. They are under great pressure to meet deadlines and broadcasts are sometimes made with little time for preparation. Some work in comfortable, private offices; others work in large rooms filled with the sound of keyboards and computer printers, as well as the voices of other reporters. Curious onlookers, police, or other emergency workers can distract those reporting from the scene for radio and television. Covering wars, political uprisings, fires, floods, and similar events is often dangerous.

Working hours vary. Reporters on morning papers often work from late afternoon until midnight. Those on afternoon or evening papers generally work from early morning until early afternoon or mid afternoon. Radio and television reporters are usually assigned to a day or evening shift. Magazine reporters usually work during the day.

Reporters sometimes have to change their work hours to meet a deadline, or to follow late-breaking developments. Their work demands long hours, irregular schedules, and some travel. Many stations and networks are on the air 24 hours a day, so newscasters can expect to work unusual hours.

Employment

News analysts, reporters, and correspondents held about 67,000 jobs in 1998. About 6 of every 10 worked for newspapers—either large city dailies or suburban and small town dailies or weeklies. About 3 in 10 worked in radio and television broadcasting, and others worked for magazines and wire services.

Training, Other Qualifications, and Advancement

Most employers prefer individuals with a bachelor's degree in journalism, but some hire graduates with other majors. They look for experience on school newspapers or broadcasting stations and internships with news organizations. Large city newspapers and stations can also prefer candidates with a degree in a subject-matter specialty such as economics, political science, or business. Large newspapers and broadcasters also require a minimum of 3 to 5 years of experience as a reporter.

Bachelor's degree programs in journalism are available in over 400 colleges or universities. About three-fourths of the courses in a typical curriculum are in liberal arts; the remainder are in journalism. Journalism courses include introductory mass media, basic reporting and copy editing, history of journalism, and press law and ethics. Students planning a career in broadcasting take courses in radio and television newscasting and production. Those planning newspaper or magazine careers usually specialize in news-editorial journalism. Those planning careers in new media, such as online newspapers or magazines, require a merging of traditional and new journalism skills. To create a story for online presentation, they need to know how to use computer software to combine online story text with audio and video elements and graphics.

Many community and junior colleges offer journalism courses or programs; credits may be transferable to 4-year journalism programs.

Over 157 schools offered a master's degree in journalism in 1998; about 32 schools offered a Ph.D. degree. Some graduate programs are intended primarily as preparation for news careers, while others prepare journalism teachers, researchers and theorists, and advertising and public relations workers.

High school courses in English, journalism, and social studies provide a good foundation for college programs. Useful college liberal arts courses include English with an emphasis on writing, sociology, political science, economics, history, and psychology. Courses in computer science, business, and speech are useful, as well. Fluency in a foreign language is necessary in some jobs.

Although reporters need good word-processing skills, computer graphics and desktop publishing skills are also useful. Computer-assisted reporting involves the use of computers to analyze data in search of a story. This technique and the interpretation of the results require strong math skills and familiarity with databases. Knowledge of news photography also is valuable for entry-level positions, which sometimes combine reporter/camera operator or reporter/photographer responsibilities.

Experience in a part-time or summer job or an internship with a news organization is very important. (Most newspapers, magazines, and broadcast news organizations offer reporting and editing internships.) Work on high school and college newspapers, at broadcasting stations, or on community papers or Armed Forces publications also helps. In addition, journalism scholarships, fellowships, and assistantships awarded to college journalism students by universities, newspapers, foundations, and professional organizations are helpful. Experience as a stringer or freelancer, a part-time reporter, who is paid only for stories printed, is also advantageous.

Reporters should be dedicated to providing accurate and impartial news. Accuracy is important, both to serve the public and because untrue or libelous statements can lead to costly lawsuits. A nose for news, persistence, initiative, poise, resourcefulness, a good memory, and physical stamina are important, as well as the emotional stability to deal with pressing deadlines, irregular hours, and dangerous assignments. Broadcast reporters and news analysts must be comfortable on camera. All reporters must be at ease in unfamiliar places and with a variety of people. Positions involving on-air work require a pleasant voice and appearance.

Most reporters start at small publications or broadcast stations as general assignment reporters or copy editors. Large publications and stations hire few recent graduates; as a rule, they require new reporters to have several years of experience.

Beginning reporters cover court proceedings and civic and club meetings, summarize speeches, and write obituaries. With experience, they report more difficult assignments, cover an assigned beat, or specialize in a particular field.

Some news analysts and reporters can advance by moving to large newspapers or stations. A few experienced reporters become columnists, correspondents, writers, announcers, or public relations specialists. Others become editors in print journalism or program managers in broadcast journalism, who supervise reporters. Some eventually become broadcasting or publications industry managers.

Job Outlook

Overall employment of news analysts, reporters, and correspondents is expected to grow little through the year 2008—the result of mergers, consolidations, and closures of newspapers; decreased circulation; increased expenses; and a decline in advertising profits. In spite of little change in overall employment, some job growth is expected in radio and television stations, whereas more rapid growth is expected in new media areas, such as online newspapers and magazines.

Competition will continue to be keen for jobs on large metropolitan newspapers and broadcast stations and on national magazines. Talented writers who can handle highly specialized scientific or technical subjects have an advantage. Also, more newspapers than before are hiring stringers and freelancers.

Most entry-level openings arise on small publications, as reporters and correspondents become editors or reporters on larger publications or leave the field. Small town and suburban newspapers will continue to offer most opportunities for persons seeking to enter this field.

Turnover is relatively high in this occupation. Some find the work too stressful and hectic, or do not like the lifestyle and transfer to other occupations. Journalism graduates have the background for work in closely-related fields such as advertising and public relations, and many take jobs in these fields. Other graduates accept sales, managerial, or other non-media positions, because of the difficulty in finding media jobs.

The newspaper and broadcasting industries are sensitive to economic ups and downs, because these industries depend on advertising revenue. During recessions, few new reporters are hired; and some reporters lose their jobs.

Earnings

Salaries for news analysts, reporters, and correspondents vary widely but, in general, are relatively high, except at small stations and small publications, where salaries are often very low. Median annual earnings of news analysts were $26,470 in 1998. The middle 50 percent earned between $19,210 and $40,930. The lowest 10 percent earned less than $14,100 and the highest 10 percent earned more than $70,140. Median annual earnings of news analysts in radio and television broadcasting were $28,500 in 1997.

Median annual earnings of reporters and correspondents were $23,400 in 1997. The middle 50 percent earned between $17,500 and $35,600. The lowest 10 percent earned less than $12,900 and the highest 10 percent earned more than $55,100. Median annual earnings of reporters and correspondents in 1997 were $23,300 in radio and television broadcasting and $22,600 in newspapers.

According to a survey conducted by the National Association of Broadcasters and the Broadcast Cable Financial Management Association in 1997 and 1998, the annual average salary, including bonuses, for television news reporters was $33,200 and $32,300 for radio news reporters. Sportscasters averaged $52,600 in television broadcasting and $57,600 in radio broadcasting. Weathercasters earned an average of $55,000.

Related Occupations

News analysts, reporters, and correspondents must write clearly and effectively to succeed in their profession. Others for whom good writing ability is essential include technical writers, advertising copy writers, public relations workers, educational writers, fiction writers, biographers, screen writers, and editors. Many news analysts, reporters, and correspondents must also communicate information orally. Others for whom oral communication skills are vital are announcers, interpreters, sales workers, and teachers.

Sources of Additional Information

For information on careers in broadcast news and related scholarships and internships, contact:

☛ Radio and Television News Directors Foundation, 1000 Connecticut Ave. NW., Washington, DC 20036. Internet: **http://www.rtndf.org**

General information on the broadcasting industry is available from:

☛ National Association of Broadcasters, 1771 N St. NW., Washington, DC 20036. Internet: **http://www.nab.org**

Career information, including pamphlets entitled *Newspaper Career Guide*, and *Newspaper: What's In It For Me*? is available from:

☛ Newspaper Association of America, 1921 Gallows Rd., Suite 600, Vienna, VA 22182.

Information on careers in journalism, colleges and universities offering degree programs in journalism or communications, and journalism scholarships and internships may be obtained from:

☛ The Dow Jones Newspaper Fund, Inc., PO Box 300, Princeton, NJ 08543-0300. Internet: **http://www.dowjones.com**

Information on union wage rates for newspaper and magazine reporters is available from:

☛ The Newspaper Guild, Research and Information Department, 501 3rd St. NW., Suite 250, Washington, DC 20001.
Internet: **http://www.newsguild.org**

For a list of schools with accredited programs in journalism, send a stamped, self-addressed envelope to:

☛ The Accrediting Council on Education in Journalism and Mass Communications, University of Kansas School of Journalism, Stauffer-Flint Hall, Lawrence, KS 66045. Internet: **http://www.ukans.edu/~acejmc**

A pamphlet entitled *Newspaper Careers and Challenges for the Next Century*, can be obtained from:

☛ National Newspaper Association, 1525 Wilson Blvd., Suite 550, Arlington, VA 22209. Internet: **http://www.oweb.com/nna/home2.html**

Names and locations of newspapers and a list of schools and departments of journalism are published in the *Editor and Publisher International Year Book*, available in most public libraries and newspaper offices.

Public Relations Specialists

(O*NET 34008)

Significant Points

- Employment of public relations specialists is expected to increase faster than average, while keen competition is expected for entry-level jobs.
- Opportunities should be best for college graduates who combine a degree in journalism, public relations, advertising, or other communications-related fields with public relations work experience.

Nature of the Work

An organization's reputation, profitability, and even its continued existence can depend on the degree to which its targeted "publics" support its goals and policies. Public relations specialists serve as advocates for businesses, governments, universities, hospitals, schools, and other organizations, and build and maintain positive relationships with the public. As managers recognize the growing importance of good public relations to the success of their organizations, they increasingly rely on public relations specialists for advice on strategy and policy of such programs.

Public relations specialists handle organizational functions such as media, community, consumer, and governmental relations; political campaigns; interest-group representation; conflict mediation; or employee and investor relations. However, public relations is not only "telling the organization's story." Understanding the attitudes and concerns of consumers, employees, and various other groups is also a vital part of the job. To improve communications, public relations specialists establish and maintain cooperative relationships with representatives of community, consumer, employee, and public interest groups and those in print and broadcast journalism.

Informing the general public, interest groups, and stockholders of an organization's policies, activities, and accomplishments is an important part of a public relations specialist's job. Their work keeps management aware of public attitudes and concerns of the many groups and organizations with which they must deal.

Public relations specialists prepare press releases and contact people in the media who might print or broadcast their material. Many radio or television special reports, newspaper stories, and magazine articles start at the desks of public relations specialists. Sometimes the subject is an organization and its policies towards its employees or its role in the community. Often the subject is a public issue, such as health, nutrition, energy, or the environment.

Public relations specialists also arrange and conduct programs for contact between organization representatives and the public. For example, they set up speaking engagements and often prepare speeches for company officials. These specialists represent employers at community projects; make film, slide, or other visual presentations at meetings and school assemblies; and plan conventions. In addition, they are responsible for preparing annual reports and writing proposals for various projects.

In government, public relations specialists—who may be called press secretaries, information officers, public affairs specialists, or communications specialists—keep the public informed about the activities of government agencies and officials. For example, public affairs specialists in the Department of Energy keep the public informed about the proposed lease of offshore land for oil exploration. A press secretary for a member of Congress keeps constituents aware of their elected representative's accomplishments.

In large organizations, the key public relations executive, who is often a vice president, may develop overall plans and policies with other executives. In addition, public relations departments employ public relations specialists to write, do research, prepare materials, maintain contacts, and respond to inquiries.

People who handle publicity for an individual or who direct public relations for a small organization may deal with all aspects of the job. They contact people, plan and do research, and prepare material for distribution. They may also handle advertising or sales promotion work to support marketing.

Working Conditions

Some public relations specialists work a standard 35- to 40-hour week, but unpaid overtime is common. Occasionally they have to be at the job or on call around the clock, especially if there is an emergency or crisis. Public relations offices are busy places; work schedules can be irregular and frequently interrupted. Schedules often have to be rearranged to meet deadlines, deliver speeches, attend meetings and community activities, and travel out of town.

Public relations specialists put together information on an organization's policies, activities, and accomplishments.

Employment

Public relations specialists held about 122,000 jobs in 1998. Almost two-thirds of salaried public relations specialists worked in services industries—management and public relations firms, educational institutions, membership organizations, health care organizations, social service agencies, and advertising agencies, for example. Others worked for manufacturing firms, financial institutions, and government agencies. About 13,000 public relations specialists were self-employed.

Public relations specialists are concentrated in large cities where press services and other communications facilities are readily available, and many businesses and trade associations have their headquarters. Many public relations consulting firms, for example, are in New York, Los Angeles, Chicago, and Washington, DC. There is a trend, however, for public relations jobs to be dispersed throughout the Nation.

Training, Other Qualifications, and Advancement

Although there are no defined standards for entry into a public relations career, a college degree combined with public relations experience, usually gained through an internship, is considered excellent preparation for public relations work. The ability to write and speak well is essential. Many entry-level public relations specialists have a college major in public relations, journalism, advertising, or communications. Some firms seek college graduates who have worked in electronic or print journalism. Other employers seek applicants with demonstrated communications skills and training or experience in a field related to the firm's business—science, engineering, sales, or finance, for example.

In 1998, well over 200 colleges and about 100 graduate schools offered degree programs or special curricula in public relations, usually in a journalism or communications department. In addition, many other colleges offered at least one course in this field. The Accrediting Council on Education in Journalism and Mass Communications is the only agency authorized to accredit schools or departments of public relations. A common public relations sequence includes courses in public relations principles and techniques; public relations management and administration, including organizational development; writing, emphasizing news releases, proposals, annual reports, scripts, speeches, and related items; visual communications, including desktop publishing and computer graphics; and research, emphasizing social science research and survey design and implementation. Courses in advertising, journalism, business administration, political science, psychology, sociology, and creative writing also are helpful, as is familiarity with word processing and other computer applications. Specialties are offered in public relations for business, government, and nonprofit organizations.

Many colleges help students gain part-time internships in public relations that provide valuable experience and training. The Armed Forces can also be an excellent place to gain training and experience. Membership in local chapters of the Public Relations Student Society of America or the International Association of Business Communicators provides an opportunity for students to exchange views with public relations specialists and to make professional contacts that may help them find a job in the field. A portfolio of published articles, television or radio programs, slide presentations, and other work is an asset in finding a job. Writing for a school publication or television or radio station provides valuable experience and material for one's portfolio.

Creativity, initiative, good judgment, and the ability to express thoughts clearly and simply are essential. Decision making, problem solving, and research skills are also important.

People who choose public relations as a career need an outgoing personality, self-confidence, an understanding of human psychology, and an enthusiasm for motivating people. They should be competitive, yet flexible, and able to function as part of a team.

Some organizations, particularly those with large public relations staffs, have formal training programs for new employees. In smaller organizations, new employees work under the guidance of experienced staff members. Beginners often maintain files of material about company activities, scan newspapers and magazines for appropriate articles to clip, and assemble information for speeches and pamphlets. They may also answer calls from the press and public, work on invitation lists and details for press conferences, or escort visitors and clients. After gaining experience, they write news releases, speeches, and articles for publication or design and carry out public relations programs. Public relations specialists in smaller firms usually get all-around experience, whereas those in larger firms tend to be more specialized.

The Public Relations Society of America accredits public relations specialists who have at least 5 years of experience in the field and have passed a comprehensive 6-hour examination (5 hours written, 1 hour oral). The International Association of Business Communicators also has an accreditation program for professionals in the communications field, including public relations specialists. Those who meet all the requirements of the program earn the Accredited Business Communicator designation. Candidates must have at least 5 years of experience in a communication field and pass a written and oral examination. They also must submit a portfolio of work samples demonstrating involvement in a range of communication projects and a thorough understanding of communication planning. Employers consider professional recognition through accreditation a sign of competence in this field, and it may be especially helpful in a competitive job market.

Promotion to supervisory jobs may come as public relations specialists show they can handle more demanding assignments. In public relations firms, a beginner may be hired as a research assistant or account assistant and be promoted to account executive, account supervisor, vice president, and eventually senior vice president. A similar career path is followed in corporate public relations, although the titles may differ. Some experienced public relations specialists start their own consulting firms. (For more information on public relations managers, see the *Handbook* statement on advertising, marketing, and public relations managers.)

Job Outlook

Keen competition will likely continue for entry-level public relations jobs as the number of qualified applicants is expected to exceed the number of job openings. Opportunities should be best for individuals who combine a college degree in journalism, public relations, advertising, or another communications-related field with relevant work experience. Public relations work experience as an intern is an asset in competing for entry-level jobs. Applicants without the appropriate educational background or work experience will face the toughest obstacles.

Employment of public relations specialists is expected to increase faster than the average for all occupations through 2008. The need for good public relations in an increasingly competitive business environment should spur demand for public relations specialists in organizations of all sizes. Employment in public relations firms should grow as firms hire contractors to provide public relations services rather than support full-time staff. In addition to growth, numerous job opportunities should result from the need to replace public relations specialists who take other jobs or who leave the occupation altogether.

Earnings

Median annual earnings for salaried public relations specialists were $34,550 in 1998. The middle 50 percent earned between $26,430 and $46,330; the lowest 10 percent earned less than $21,050, and the top 10 percent earned more than $71,360. Median annual earnings in the industries employing the largest numbers of public relations specialists in 1997 were:

Industry	Earnings
Management and public relations	$35,100
State government, except education and hospitals	32,100
Colleges and universities	30,600

According to a salary survey conducted for the Public Relations Society of America, the overall median salary in public relations was about $49,100. Salaries in public relations ranged from less than $22,800 to more than $141,400. There was little difference between the median salaries for account executives in public relations firms, corporations, government, health care, or nonprofit organizations—all ranged from over $32,000 to nearly $34,000.

Public relations specialists in the Federal Government in nonsupervisory, supervisory, and managerial positions averaged about $56,700 a year in 1999.

Related Occupations

Public relations specialists create favorable attitudes among various organizations, special interest groups, and the public through effective communication. Other workers with similar jobs include fund raisers; lobbyists; advertising, marketing, and promotion managers; and police officers involved in community relations.

Sources of Additional Information

A comprehensive directory of schools offering degree programs or a sequence of study in public relations, a brochure on careers in public relations, and a $5 brochure entitled *Where Shall I go to Study Advertising and Public Relations* are available from:

☛ Public Relations Society of America, Inc., 33 Irving Place, New York, NY 10003-2376. Internet: **http://www.prsa.org**

Career information on public relations in hospitals and other health care settings is available from:

☛ The Society for Health Care Strategy and Market Development, One North Franklin St., 27th Floor, Chicago, IL 60606.
Internet: **http://www.shsmd.org**

For a list of schools with accredited programs in public relations in their journalism departments, send a stamped self-addressed envelope to:

☛ The Accrediting Council on Education in Journalism and Mass Communications, University of Kansas School of Journalism, Stauffer Flint Hall, Lawrence, KS 66045. Internet: **http://www.ukans.edu/~acejmc**

For information on accreditation for public relations specialists, contact:

☛ International Association of Business Communicators, One Hallidie Plaza, Suite 600, San Francisco, CA 94102. Internet: **http://www.iabc.com**

Writers and Editors, Including Technical Writers

(O*NET 34002B, 34002C, 34002D, 34002E, 34002F, 34002G, 34002J, 34002L, 34002M, and 34005)

Significant Points

- Most jobs require a college degree in the liberal arts—communications, journalism, and English are preferred—or a technical subject for technical writing positions.
- Competition is expected to be less for lower paying, entry-level jobs at small daily and weekly newspapers, trade publications, and radio and television broadcasting stations in small markets.

- Persons who fail to gain better paying jobs or earn enough as independent writers usually are able to transfer readily to communications-related jobs in other occupations.

Nature of the Work

Writers and editors communicate through the written word. *Writers* develop original fiction and nonfiction for books, magazines and trade journals, newspapers, technical reports, online distribution, company newsletters, radio and television broadcasts, movies, and advertisements. *Editors* select and prepare material for publication or broadcast and review and edit a writer's work.

Writers either select a topic or are assigned one by an editor. Then they gather information through personal observation, library and Internet research, and interviews. Writers select the material they want to use, organize it into a meaningful format, and use the written word to express ideas and convey information to readers. Often, writers revise or rewrite sections, searching for the best organization or the right phrasing.

Newswriters prepare news items for newspapers or news broadcasts, based on information supplied by reporters or wire services. Columnists analyze and interpret the news and write commentaries, based on reliable sources, personal knowledge, and experience. Editorial writers express opinions in accordance with their publication's viewpoint to stimulate public debate on current affairs. Columnists and editorial writers are able to take sides on issues and express their opinions, while other newswriters must be objective and neutral in their coverage. Reporters and correspondents, who also may write articles or copy for print or broadcast, are described elsewhere in this section of the *Handbook*.

Technical writers put scientific and technical information into easily understandable language. They prepare operating and maintenance manuals, catalogs, parts lists, assembly instructions, sales promotion materials, and project proposals. They also plan and edit technical reports and oversee preparation of illustrations, photographs, diagrams, and charts.

Copywriters prepare advertising copy for use by publication or broadcast media, to promote the sale of goods and services.

Established writers may work on a freelance basis. They sell their work to publishers, publication enterprises, manufacturing firms, public relations departments, or advertising agencies. Sometimes, they contract with publishers to write a book or article, or to complete specific assignments such as writing about a new product or technique.

Editors frequently write and almost always review, rewrite, and edit the work of writers. An editor's responsibilities vary depending on the employer and editorial position held. In the publishing industry, an editor's primary duties are to plan the contents of books, technical journals, trade magazines, and other general interest publications. Editors decide what material will appeal to readers, review and edit drafts of books and articles, offer comments to improve the work, and suggest possible titles. Additionally, they oversee the production of the publications.

Major newspapers and newsmagazines usually employ several types of editors. The *executive editor* oversees *assistant editors* who have responsibility for particular subjects, such as local news, international news, feature stories, or sports. Executive editors generally have the final say about what stories get published and how they should be covered. The *managing editor* usually is responsible for the daily operation of the news department. *Assignment editors* determine which reporters will cover a given story. *Copy editors* mostly review and edit a reporter's copy for accuracy, content, grammar, and style.

In smaller organizations, like small daily or weekly newspapers or membership newsletter departments, a single editor may do everything or share responsibility with only a few other people. Executive and managing editors typically hire writers, reporters, or other employees. They also plan budgets and negotiate contracts with freelance writers, sometimes called "stringers" in the news industry. In broadcasting companies, *program directors* have similar responsibilities.

Editors and program directors often have assistants. Many assistants, such as copy editors or *production assistants*, hold entry-level jobs. They review copy for errors in grammar, punctuation, and spelling, and check copy for readability, style, and agreement with editorial policy. They add and rearrange sentences to improve clarity or delete incorrect and unnecessary material. They also do research for writers and verify facts, dates, and statistics. Production assistants arrange page layouts of articles, photographs, and advertising; compose headlines; and prepare copy for printing. *Publication assistants* who work for publishing houses may read and evaluate manuscripts submitted by freelance writers, proofread printers' galleys, or answer letters about published material. Production assistants on small papers or in radio stations clip stories that come over the wire services' printers, answer phones, and make photocopies.

Most writers and editors use personal computers or word processors. Many use desktop or electronic publishing systems, scanners, and other electronic communications equipment.

Working Conditions

Some writers and editors work in comfortable, private offices; others work in noisy rooms filled with the sound of keyboards and computer printers as well as the voices of other writers tracking down information over the telephone. The search for information sometimes requires travel and visits to diverse workplaces, such as factories, offices, laboratories, the ballpark, or the theater, but many have to be content with telephone interviews and the library.

The workweek usually runs 35 to 40 hours. Those who prepare morning or weekend publications and broadcasts work some nights and weekends. Writers, especially newswriters, occasionally work overtime to meet deadlines or to cover late-developing stories. Deadlines and erratic work hours, often part of the daily routine for these jobs, may cause stress, fatigue, or burnout.

Employment

Writers and editors held about 341,000 jobs in 1998. Nearly one-third of salaried writers and editors works for newspapers, magazines,

Writers and editors may work in noisy rooms and under extreme pressure to meet deadlines.

and book publishers. Substantial numbers, mostly technical writers, work for computer software firms. Other writers and editors work in educational facilities, in advertising agencies, in radio and television broadcasting, in public relations firms, and on journals and newsletters published by business and nonprofit organizations, such as professional associations, labor unions, and religious organizations. Some develop publications and technical materials for government agencies or write for motion picture companies.

Jobs with major book publishers, magazines, broadcasting companies, advertising agencies and public relations firms, and the Federal Government are concentrated in New York, Chicago, Los Angeles, Boston, Philadelphia, San Francisco, and Washington, DC. Jobs with newspapers, business and professional journals, and technical and trade magazines are more widely dispersed throughout the country. Technical writers are employed throughout the country, but the largest concentrations are in the Northeast, Texas, and California.

Thousands of other individuals work as freelance writers, earning some income from their articles, books, and less commonly, television and movie scripts. Most support themselves with income derived from other sources.

Training, Other Qualifications, and Advancement

A college degree generally is required for a position as a writer or editor. Although some employers look for a broad liberal arts background, most prefer to hire people with degrees in communications, journalism, or English. For those who specialize in a particular area, such as science, fashion, or legal issues, additional background in the chosen field is helpful.

Technical writing requires a degree in, or some knowledge about, a specialized field—engineering, business, or one of the sciences, for example. In many cases, people with good writing skills can learn specialized knowledge on the job. Some transfer from jobs as technicians, scientists, or engineers. Others begin as research assistants, or trainees in a technical information department, develop technical communication skills, and then assume writing duties.

Writers and editors must be able to express ideas clearly and logically and should love to write. Creativity, curiosity, a broad range of knowledge, self-motivation, and perseverance also are valuable. Writers and editors must demonstrate good judgment and a strong sense of ethics in deciding what material to publish. Editors also need tact and the ability to guide and encourage others in their work.

For some jobs, the ability to concentrate amid confusion and to work under pressure is essential. Familiarity with electronic publishing, graphics, and video production equipment increasingly is needed. Online newspapers and magazines require knowledge of computer software used to combine online text with graphics, audio, video, and 3-D animation.

High school and college newspapers, literary magazines, community newspapers, and radio and television stations all provide valuable, but sometimes unpaid, practical writing experience. Many magazines, newspapers, and broadcast stations have internships for students. Interns write short pieces, conduct research and interviews, and learn about the publishing or broadcasting business.

In small firms, beginning writers and editors hired as assistants may actually begin writing or editing material right away. Opportunities for advancement can be limited, however. In larger businesses, jobs usually are more formally structured. Beginners generally do research, fact checking, or copy editing. They take on full-scale writing or editing duties less rapidly than do the employees of small companies. Advancement often is more predictable, though, coming with the assignment of more important articles.

Job Outlook

Employment of writers and editors is expected to increase faster than the average for all occupations through the year 2008. Employment of salaried writers and editors for newspapers, periodicals, book publishers, and nonprofit organizations is expected to increase as demand grows for their publications. Magazines and other periodicals increasingly are developing market niches, appealing to readers with special interests. Also, online publications and services are growing in number and sophistication, spurring the demand for writers and editors. Businesses and organizations are developing Internet websites and more companies are experimenting with publishing materials directly for the Internet. Advertising and public relations agencies, which also are growing, should be another source of new jobs.

Demand for technical writers is expected to increase because of the continuing expansion of scientific and technical information and the need to communicate it to others. In addition to job openings created by employment growth, many openings will occur as experienced workers transfer to other occupations or leave the labor force. Turnover is relatively high in this occupation; many freelancers leave because they cannot earn enough money.

Despite projections of fast employment growth and high turnover, the outlook for most writing and editing jobs is expected to be competitive. Many people with writing or journalism training are attracted to the occupation. Opportunities should be best for technical writers because of the growth in the high technology and electronics industries and the resulting need for people to write users' guides, instruction manuals, and training materials. This work requires people who are not only technically skilled as writers but are able to keep pace with changing technology. Also, individuals with the technical skills for working on the Internet may have an advantage finding a job as a writer or editor.

Opportunities for newswriting and editing positions on small daily and weekly newspapers and in small radio and television stations, where the pay is low, should be better than those in larger media markets. Some small publications hire freelance copy editors as backup for staff editors or as additional help with special projects. Persons preparing to be writers and editors benefit from academic preparation in another discipline as well, either to qualify them as writers specializing in that discipline or as a career alternative if they are unable to get a job in writing.

Earnings

Median annual earnings for writers and editors, including technical writers, were $36,480 in 1998. The middle 50 percent earned between $27,030 and $49,380 a year. The lowest 10 percent earned less than $20,920 and the highest 10 percent earned over $76,660. Median annual earnings in the industries employing the largest numbers of writers and editors of nontechnical material in 1997 were as follows:

Advertising	$38,100
Periodicals	$35,900
Books	$35,200
Newspapers	$28,500
Radio and television broadcasting	$26,300

Median annual earnings of technical writers and editors in computer data and processing services were $39,200 in 1997.

Related Occupations

Writers and editors communicate ideas and information. Other communications occupations include news analysts, reporters, and correspondents; radio and television announcers; advertising and public relations workers; and teachers.

Sources of Additional Information

For information on careers in technical writing, contact:

☛ Society for Technical Communication, Inc., 901 N. Stuart St., Suite 904, Arlington, VA 22203. Internet: **http://www.stc-va.org**

For information on union wage rates for newspaper and magazine editors, contact:

☛ The Newspaper Guild, Research and Information Department, 501 Third Street NW., Suite 250, Washington, DC 20001.

Visual Arts and Design Occupations

Designers

(O*NET 34038A, 34038B, 34038C, 34038D, 34038F, 34041, 34044, and 39999H)

Significant Points

- Four out of 10 designers are self-employed—almost four times the proportion for all professional specialty occupations.
- Creativity is crucial in all design occupations; formal education requirements range from a high school diploma for floral designers to a bachelor's degree for industrial designers.
- Despite projected faster-than-average employment growth, keen competition is expected for most jobs, because many talented individuals are attracted to careers as designers.

Nature of the Work

Designers are people with a desire to create. They combine practical knowledge with artistic ability to turn abstract ideas into formal designs for the clothes that we wear, the living and office space that we inhabit, and the merchandise that we buy. Designers usually specialize in a particular area of design, such as automobiles, clothing, furniture, home appliances, industrial equipment, interiors of homes or office buildings, movie and theater sets, packaging, or floral arrangements.

The first step in developing a new design or altering an existing one is to determine the needs of the client and the ultimate function for which the design is intended. When creating a design, the designer considers size, shape, weight, color, materials used, cost, ease of use, and safety.

The designer then prepares sketches—by hand or with the aid of a computer—to illustrate the vision for the design. After consulting with the client, an art or design director, or a product development team, the designer creates a detailed design using drawings, a structural model, computer simulations, or a full-scale prototype. Many designers are increasingly using computer-aided design (CAD) tools to create and better visualize the final product. Computer models allow greater ease and flexibility in making changes to a design, thus reducing design costs and cutting the time it takes to deliver a product to market. Industrial designers use computer-aided industrial design (CAID) to create designs and to communicate them to automated production tools.

Designers sometimes supervise assistants who carry out their creations. Designers who run their own businesses also may devote a considerable amount of time to developing new business contacts and to performing administrative tasks, such as reviewing catalogues and ordering samples.

Design encompasses a number of different fields. Many designers specialize in a particular area of design, whereas others work in more than one. *Industrial designers* develop countless manufactured products, including airplanes; cars; home appliances; children's toys; computer equipment; and medical, office, and recreational equipment. They combine artistic talent with research on product use, marketing, materials, and production methods to create the most functional and appealing design and to make the product competitive with others in the marketplace. Most industrial designers concentrate in an area of sub-specialization, such as kitchen appliances.

Furniture designers design furniture for manufacture. These designers use their knowledge of design trends, competitors' products, production costs, production capability, and characteristics of a company's market to create home and office furniture that is both functional and attractive. They also may prepare detailed drawings of fixtures, forms, or tools required in the production of furniture. Some furniture designers fashion custom pieces or styles according to a specific period or country. Furniture designers must be strongly involved with the fashion industry and aware of current trends and styles.

Interior designers plan the space and furnish the interiors of private homes, public buildings, and commercial or institutional establishments, such as offices, restaurants, hospitals, hotels, and theaters. They also plan the interiors for additions to and renovations of existing structures. Most interior designers specialize, and some further specialize in a related line of work. For example, some may concentrate in residential design, and others may further specialize by focusing on a particular room, such as kitchens or baths. With a client's tastes, needs, and budget in mind, interior designers prepare drawings and specifications for interior construction, furnishings, lighting, and finishes. Increasingly, designers use computers to plan layouts that can be changed easily to include ideas received from the client. Interior designers also design lighting and archi-

Designers combine practical knowledge with artistic ability to turn abstract ideas into formal designs.

tectural details, such as crown molding, coordinate colors and select furniture, floor coverings, and curtains. Interior designers must design space to conform to Federal, State, and local laws, including building codes. Design plans for public areas also must meet accessibility standards for the disabled and elderly.

Set, lighting, and costume designers create set, lighting, and costume designs for movie, television, and theater productions. They study scripts, confer with directors and other designers, and conduct research to determine the appropriate historical period, fashion and architectural styles.

Fashion designers design clothing and accessories. Some high-fashion designers are self-employed and design for individual clients. Other high-fashion designers cater to specialty stores or high fashion department stores. These designers create original garments, as well as follow established fashion trends. Most fashion designers, however, work for apparel manufacturers, adapting designs of men's, women's, and children's fashions for the mass market.

Textile designers, using their knowledge of textile materials and fashion trends, design fabric for garments, upholstery, rugs, and other products. Computers are widely used in pattern design and grading; intelligent pattern engineering (IPE) systems enable great automation in generating patterns.

Floral designers cut and arrange live, dried, or artificial flowers and foliage into designs, according to the customer's order. They trim flowers and arrange bouquets, sprays, wreaths, dish gardens, and terrariums. They usually work from a written order indicating the occasion, customer preference for color and type of flower, price, and the date, time, and place the floral arrangement or plant is to be ready to be delivered. The variety of duties performed by a floral designer depends on the size of the shop and the number of designers employed. In a small operation, the floral designer may own the shop and do almost everything, from growing and purchasing flowers to keeping financial records.

Merchandise displayers and window dressers plan and erect commercial displays, such as those in windows and interiors of retail stores and at trade exhibitions.

Working Conditions

Working conditions and places of employment vary. Designers employed by manufacturing establishments or design firms generally work regular hours in well-lighted and comfortable settings. Self-employed designers tend to work longer hours.

Designers frequently adjust their workday to suit their clients' schedules, meeting with them during evening or weekend hours, when necessary. Designers may transact business in their own offices, clients' homes or offices, or they may travel to other locations, such as showrooms, design centers, and manufacturing facilities.

Industrial designers usually work regular hours but occasionally work overtime to meet deadlines. In contrast, set, lighting, and costume designers work long and irregular hours, and they often are under pressure to make rapid changes. Fashion designers may work long hours, particularly during production deadlines or before fashion shows, when overtime usually is necessary. In addition, fashion designers may be required to travel to production sites across the United States and overseas. Interior designers generally work under deadlines and may work overtime to finish a job. They regularly carry heavy and bulky sample books to meetings with clients. Floral designers usually work regular hours in a pleasant work environment, except during holidays when overtime usually is required.

All designers face frustration at times, when their designs are rejected or when they cannot be as creative as they wish. Independent consultants, who are paid by the assignment, are under pressure to please clients and to find new ones to maintain an income.

Employment

Designers held about 423,000 jobs in 1998. Four out of 10 were self-employed.

Designers work in a number of different industries, depending on their design specialty. Most industrial designers, for example, work for engineering or architectural consulting firms or for large corporations. Interior designers usually work for furniture and home furnishings stores, interior designing services, and architectural firms. Many interior designers do freelance work—full time, part time, or in addition to a salaried job in another occupation.

Set, lighting, and costume designers work for theater companies and film and television production companies. Fashion designers generally work for textile, apparel, and pattern manufacturers, or for fashion salons, high-fashion department stores, and specialty shops. Most floral designers work for retail flower shops or in floral departments located inside grocery and department stores.

Training, Other Qualifications, and Advancement

Creativity is crucial in all design occupations. People in this field must have a strong sense of the aesthetic—an eye for color and detail, a sense of balance and proportion, and an appreciation for beauty. Sketching ability is helpful for most designers, but it is especially important for fashion designers. A good portfolio—a collection of examples of a person's best work—is often the deciding factor in getting a job. Except for floral design, formal preparation in design is necessary.

Educational requirements for entry-level positions vary. Some design occupations, notably industrial design, require a bachelor's degree. Interior designers normally need a college education, in part because few clients—especially commercial clients—are willing to entrust responsibility for designing living and working space to a designer with no formal credentials.

Interior design is the only design field subject to government regulation. According to the American Society for Interior Designers, 21 States and the District of Columbia require interior designers to be licensed. Because licensing is not mandatory in all States, an interior designer's professional standing is important. Membership in a professional association usually requires the completion of 3 or 4 years of postsecondary education in design, at least 2 years of practical experience in the field, and passage of the National Council for Interior Design qualification examination.

In fashion design, employers seek individuals with a 2- or 4-year degree who are knowledgeable in the areas of textiles, fabrics, and ornamentation, as well as trends in the fashion world. Similarly, furniture designers must keep abreast of trends in fashion and style, in addition to methods and tools used in furniture production. Several universities and schools of design offer degrees in furniture design.

Set, lighting, and costume designers typically have college degrees in their particular area of design. A Master of Fine Arts (MFA) degree from an accredited university program further establishes one's design credentials. Membership in the United Scenic Artists, Local 829, is a nationally recognized standard of achievement for scenic designers.

In contrast to the other design occupations, a high school diploma ordinarily suffices for floral design jobs. Most floral designers learn their skills on the job. When employers hire trainees, they generally look for high school graduates who have a flair for color and a desire to learn. Completion of formal training, however, is an asset for floral designers, particularly for advancement to the chief floral designer level. Vocational and technical schools offer programs in floral design, usually lasting less than a year, while 2- and 4-year programs in floriculture, horticulture, floral design, or ornamental horticulture are offered by community and junior colleges, and colleges and universities.

Formal training for some design professions also is available in 2- and 3-year professional schools that award certificates or associate degrees in design. Graduates of 2-year programs normally qualify as assistants to designers. The Bachelor of Fine Arts degree is granted at 4-year colleges and universities. The curriculum in these schools includes art and art history, principles of design, designing and sketching, and specialized studies for each of the individual design disciplines, such as garment construction, textiles, mechanical and architectural drawing, computerized design, sculpture, architecture, and basic engineering. A liberal arts education, with courses in merchandising, business administration, marketing, and psychology, along with training in art, also is a good background for most design fields. Additionally, persons with training or experience in architecture qualify for some design occupations, particularly interior design.

Computer-aided design (CAD) increasingly is used in all areas of design, except floral design, so many employers expect new designers to be familiar with the use of the computer as a design tool. For example, industrial designers extensively use computers in the aerospace, automotive, and electronics industries. Interior designers use computers to create numerous versions of interior space designs—making it possible for a client to see and choose among several designs; images can be inserted, edited, and replaced easily and without added cost. In furniture design, a chair's basic shape and structure may be duplicated and updated, by applying new upholstery styles and fabrics with the use of computers.

The National Association of Schools of Art and Design currently accredits about 200 postsecondary institutions with programs in art and design; most of these schools award a degree in art. Some award degrees in industrial, interior, textile, graphic, or fashion design. Many schools do not allow formal entry into a bachelor's degree program, until a student has finished a year of basic art and design courses successfully. Applicants may be required to submit sketches and other examples of their artistic ability.

The Foundation for Interior Design Education Research also accredits interior design programs and schools. Currently, there are more than 120 accredited programs in the United States and Canada, located in schools of art, architecture, and home economics.

Individuals in the design field must be creative, imaginative, persistent, and able to communicate their ideas in writing, visually, or verbally. Because tastes in style and fashion can change quickly, designers need to be well read, open to new ideas and influences, and quick to react to changing trends. Problem-solving skills and the ability to work independently and under pressure are important traits. People in this field need self-discipline to start projects on their own, to budget their time, and to meet deadlines and production schedules. Good business sense and sales ability also are important, especially for those who freelance or run their own business.

Beginning designers usually receive on-the-job training, and normally need 1 to 3 years of training before they advance to higher-level positions. Experienced designers in large firms may advance to chief designer, design department head, or other supervisory positions. Some designers become teachers in design schools and colleges and universities. Some experienced designers open their own firms.

Job Outlook

Despite projected faster-than-average employment growth, designers in most fields—with the exception of floral and furniture design—are expected to face keen competition for available positions. Many talented individuals are attracted to careers as designers. Individuals with little or no formal education in design, as well as those who lack creativity and perseverance, will find it very difficult to establish and maintain a career in design. Floral design should be the least competitive of all design fields because of the relatively low pay and limited opportunities for advancement, as well as the relatively high job turnover of floral designers in retail flower shops.

Overall, the employment of designers is expected to grow faster than the average for all occupations through the year 2008. In addition to employment growth, many job openings will result from the need to replace designers who leave the field. Increased demand for industrial designers will stem from the continued emphasis on product quality and safety; the demand for new products that are easy and comfortable to use; the development of high-technology products in medicine, transportation, and other fields; and growing global competition among businesses. Rising demand for professional design of private homes, offices, restaurants and other retail establishments, and institutions that care for the rapidly growing elderly population should spur employment growth of interior designers. Demand for fashion, textile, and furniture designers should remain strong, because many consumers are concerned with fashion and style.

Earnings

Median annual earnings for designers in all specialties except interior design were $29,200 in 1998. The middle 50 percent earned between $18,420 and $43,940. The lowest 10 percent earned less than $13,780 and the highest 10 percent earned over $68,310. Median annual earnings in the industries employing the largest numbers of designers, except interior designers, in 1997 were as follows:

Industry	Earnings
Engineering and architectural services	$41,300
Apparel, piece goods, and notions	38,400
Mailing, reproduction, and stenographic services	36,000
Retail stores, not elsewhere classified	16,500

Median annual earnings for interior designers were $31,760 in 1998. The middle 50 percent earned between $23,580 and $42,570. The lowest 10 percent earned less than $18,360 and the highest 10 percent earned over $65,810. Median annual earnings in the industries employing the largest numbers of interior designers in 1997 were as follows:

Industry	Earnings
Engineering and architectural services	$33,000
Furniture and home furnishings stores	27,800
Miscellaneous business services	26,800

Median annual earnings of merchandise displayers and window dressers were $18,180 in 1998. The lowest 10 percent earned less than $12,680; the highest 10 percent, over $28,910.

According to the Industrial Designers Society of America, the average base salary for an industrial designer with 1 to 2 years of experience was about $31,000 in 1998. Staff designers with 5 years of experience earned $39,000 whereas senior designers with 8 years of experience earned $51,000. Industrial designers in managerial or executive positions earned substantially more—up to $500,000 annually; however, $75,000 to $100,000 was more representative.

Related Occupations

Workers in other occupations who design or arrange objects, materials, or interiors to enhance their appearance and function include visual artists, architects, landscape architects, engineers, photographers, and interior decorators. Some computer-related occupations, including Internet page designers and webmasters, require design skills.

Sources of Additional Information

For an order form for a directory of accredited college-level programs in art and design (available for $15.00) or career information in design occupations, contact:

- National Association of Schools of Art and Design, 11250 Roger Bacon Dr., Suite 21, Reston, VA 20190.

For information on careers and a list of academic programs in industrial design, write to:

- Industrial Designers Society of America, 1142-E Walker Rd., Great Falls, VA 22066. Internet: **http://www.idsa.org**

For information on degree, continuing education, and licensure programs in interior design, contact:

- American Society for Interior Designers, 608 Massachusetts Ave. NE., Washington, DC 20002-6006.

For a list of schools with accredited programs in interior design, contact:

☛ Foundation for Interior Design Education Research, 60 Monroe Center NW., Grand Rapids, MI 49503. Internet: **http://www.fider.org**

For information about careers in floral design, contact:

☛ Society of American Florists, 1601 Duke St., Alexandria, VA 22314.

Photographers and Camera Operators

(O*NET 34023A, 34023B, and 34026)

Significant Points

- A "good eye" with imagination and creativity are essential.
- Only the most skilled and talented who have good business sense maintain a long-term career.
- More than one-half of all photographers and camera operators is self-employed.

Nature of the Work

Photographers and camera operators produce images that paint a picture, tell a story, or record an event that will be remembered long after the event. Making commercial quality photographs and movies requires technical expertise and creativity. Producing a successful picture includes choosing and presenting a subject to achieve a particular effect and selecting equipment to accomplish the desired goal. For example, photographers and camera operators may enhance the subject's appearance with lighting or draw attention to a particular aspect of the subject by blurring the background.

Today, many cameras adjust settings like shutter speed and aperture automatically. They also let the photographer adjust these settings manually, thus allowing greater creative and technical control over the picture-taking process. In addition to automatic and manual cameras, photographers and camera operators use an array of film, lenses, and equipment—from filters, tripods, and flash attachments to specially constructed motorized vehicles and lighting equipment.

Photographers use either a traditional camera or a newer digital camera that electronically records images. A traditional camera records images on silver halide film that is developed into prints. Some photographers send their film to laboratories for processing. Color film requires expensive equipment and exacting conditions for correct processing and printing. (See the statement on photographic process workers elsewhere in the *Handbook*.) Other photographers, especially those who use black and white film or require special effects, prefer to develop and print their own photographs. Photographers who do their own film developing must have the technical skill to operate a fully equipped darkroom or the appropriate computer software to be able process prints digitally.

Recent advances in electronic technology now make it possible for the professional photographer to develop standard 35mm or other types of film, and use flatbed scanners and photofinishing laboratories to produce computer-readable, digital images from film. Once the film has been converted to a digital image, a photographer then can edit and electronically transmit the images, making it easier and faster to shoot, develop, and transmit regular film pictures from remote locations.

Although most photographers still use silver-halide film cameras, more are using digital cameras that use electronic memory rather than a film negative to record an image. The electronic image can be transmitted instantly via a computer modem and telephone line or otherwise downloaded onto a personal computer. Then, using the computer and specialized software, the photographer can manipulate and enhance the scanned or digital image to create a desired effect. The images can be stored on compact disk (CD) the same way as music. Digital technology also allows the production of larger, more colorful, and more accurate prints or images for use in advertising, photographic art, and scientific research. Some photographers use this technology to create electronic portfolios, as well. Because much photography now involves the use of computer technology, photographers must have hands-on knowledge of computer editing software.

Most photographers specialize in portrait, commercial, or news photography. Others specialize in areas such as aerial, police, medical, or scientific photography, which typically requires additional knowledge in areas such as engineering, medicine, biology, or chemistry. A growing group of photographers are providing digital images directly for use on the Internet. Photography is also a fine art medium, and a small portion of photographers sell their photographs as artwork. In addition to technical proficiency, photographic art requires great emphasis on self-expression and creativity.

Portrait photographers take pictures of individuals or groups of people and often work in their own studios. Some specialize in weddings or school photographs. Portrait photographers who are business owners arrange for advertising, schedule appointments, set and adjust equipment, develop and retouch negatives, and mount and frame pictures. They also purchase supplies, keep records, bill customers, and may hire and train employees.

Commercial and industrial photographers take pictures of various subjects, such as buildings, models, merchandise, artifacts, and landscapes. These photographs are used in a variety of mediums, including books, reports, advertisements, and catalogs. Industrial photographers often take pictures of equipment, machinery, products, workers, and company officials. The pictures then are used for analyzing engineering projects, publicity, or as records of equipment development or deployment, such as placement of an offshore rig. Companies also use these photographs in publications, in reports to stockholders, or to advertise company products or services. This photography frequently is done on location.

News photographers, also called photojournalists, photograph newsworthy people; places; and sporting, political, and community events for newspapers, journals, magazines, or television. Some photojournalists are salaried staff; others work independently and are known as freelance photographers.

Self-employed photographers may license the use of their photographs through stock photo agencies. These agencies grant magazines and other customers the right to purchase the use of a photograph, and, in turn, pay the photographer on a commission basis. Stock photo agencies require an application from the photographer and a sizable portfolio. Once accepted, a large number of new submissions usually are required from a photographer each year. Photographers frequently have their photos placed on CD's for this purpose.

Camera operators use motion picture, television, or video cameras to film a wide range of subjects, including commercial motion pictures, documentaries, music videos, news events, and training sessions. Some film private ceremonies and special events. Like photographers, camera operators work in a variety of settings. Many video camera operators are employed by independent television stations, local affiliates, large cable and television networks, or smaller, independent production companies. *Studio camera operators* work in a broadcast studio and usually film their subjects from a fixed position. *News camera operators*, also called *electronic news gathering (ENG) operators*, work as part of a reporting team, following newsworthy events as they unfold. ENG operators may need to edit raw footage on the spot for relay to a television affiliate for broadcast.

Camera operators employed in the entertainment field use motion picture cameras to film movies, television programs, and commercials. Some specialize in filming cartoons or special effects for television and movies. *Television and movie studio camera operators* may be an integral part of the action, using cameras in any of

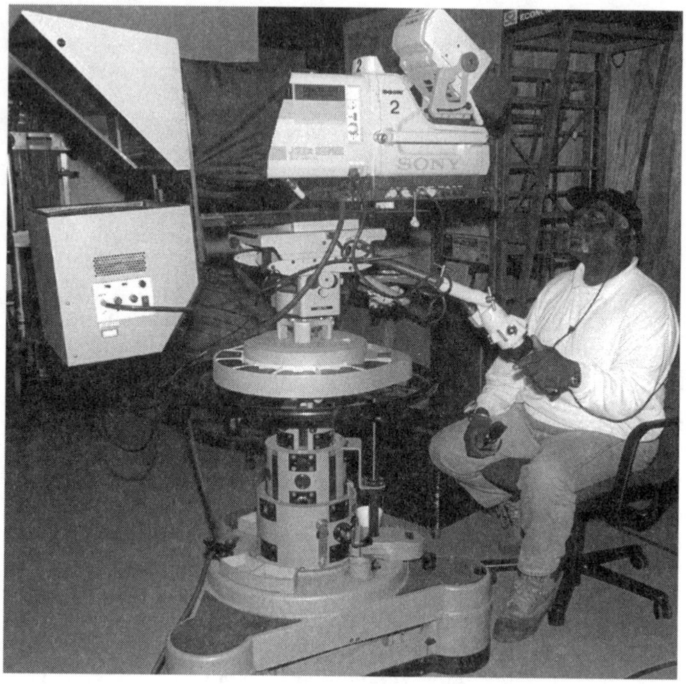

Photographers and camera operators produce images of an event that will be remembered long after the event itself.

several different camera mounts. For example, the camera operator can be stationary and shoot whatever passes in front of the lens, or the camera can be mounted on a track, with the camera operator responsible for shooting the scene from different angles or directions. Other camera operators sit on cranes and follow the action, while crane operators move them into position. *Steadicam operators* mount a harness and carry the camera on their shoulders to provide a more solid picture while they move about the action. Camera operators who work in the entertainment field often meet with directors, actors, and camera assistants to discuss ways of filming and improving scenes.

Working Conditions

Working conditions for photographers and camera operators vary considerably. Photographers and camera operators employed in government, television and commercial studios, and advertising agencies usually work a 5-day, 40-hour week. On the other hand, news photographers and ENG operators often work long, irregular hours and must be available to work on short notice. Camera operators working on a motion picture production also may work long, irregular hours.

Portrait photographers usually work in their own studios but also may travel to take photographs at the client's location, such as a school, a company office, or a private home. News and commercial photographers and ENG operators frequently travel locally, can stay overnight on assignments, or may travel to distant places for long periods of time. Camera operators filming television programs or motion pictures may travel to film on location.

Some photographers and camera operators work in uncomfortable, or even dangerous surroundings. This is especially true for photojournalists and ENG operators covering accidents, natural disasters, civil unrest, or military conflicts. Many photographers and camera operators must wait long hours in all kinds of weather for an event to take place and stand or walk for long periods while carrying heavy equipment. News photographers and ENG operators often work under severe time restrictions to meet deadlines.

Self-employment allows for greater autonomy, freedom of expression, and flexible scheduling. However, income can be uncertain and necessitates a continuous, time-consuming, and sometimes stressful search for new clients. Some self-employed photographers hire an assistant solely for the purpose of seeking additional business.

Employment

Photographers and camera operators held about 161,000 jobs in 1998. More than one-half was self-employed, a much higher proportion than the average for all occupations. Some self-employed photographers contracted with advertising agencies, magazines, or others to do individual projects at a predetermined fee, while others operated portrait studios or provided photographs to stock photo agencies.

Most salaried photographers worked in portrait or commercial photography studios. Newspapers, magazines, advertising agencies, and government agencies employed most of the others. Most camera operators were employed in television broadcasting or at motion picture studios; relatively few were self-employed. Most photographers and camera operators worked in metropolitan areas.

Training, Other Qualifications, and Advancement

Employers usually seek applicants with a "good eye," imagination, and creativity, as well as a good technical understanding of photography or camera operation. Formal education may be a requirement for many positions. Entry-level positions in photojournalism, or in industrial, scientific, or technical photography, for example, are likely to require a college degree in journalism or photography, with additional courses in the specific field being photographed. Camera operators usually acquire their skills through formal post-secondary training at vocational schools, colleges, universities, photographic institutes, or through on-the-job training.

Both photographers and camera operators need good eyesight, artistic ability, and hand-eye coordination. They should be patient, accurate, and enjoy working with details. Photographers should be able to work alone or with others, as they frequently deal with clients, graphic designers, and advertising and publishing specialists. Camera operators also should have communication skills, and, if needed, the ability to hold a camera by hand for extended periods of time.

Commercial photographers must be imaginative and original. Portrait photographers need the ability to help people relax in front of the camera. Photojournalists not only must be good with a camera, but also must understand the story behind an event so their pictures match the story. They must be decisive in recognizing a potentially good photograph and act quickly to capture it.

Individuals interested in photography should subscribe to photographic newsletters and magazines, join camera clubs, and seek employment in camera stores or photo studios. Individuals also should decide on an area of interest and specialize in it. Summer or part-time work for a photographic studio, cable or television network, newspaper, or magazine is an excellent way to gain experience and eventual entry into this field. Some photographers enhance their technical expertise by attending seminars. Many universities, community and junior colleges, vocational-technical institutes, and private trade and technical schools offer photography courses. Basic courses in photography cover equipment, processes, and techniques. Bachelors degree programs, especially those including business courses, provide a well-rounded education. Art schools offer useful training in design and composition.

Photographers may start out as assistants to experienced photographers. Assistants learn to mix chemicals, develop film, print photographs, and the other skills necessary to run a portrait or commercial photography business. After several years of experience, magazine and news photographers may advance to photography or picture editor positions. Some photographers and camera operators become teachers and provide instruction in their own particular area of expertise at technical schools, film schools, or universities.

Camera operators in entry-level jobs, including cinematography assistants, learn to set up lights, cameras, and other equipment. They may receive routine assignments requiring camera adjustments or decisions on what subject matter to capture. With increased experience, they may advance to more demanding assignments. Camera operators in the film and television industries usually are hired for a project based on recommendations from individuals such as producers, directors of photography, and camera assistants from previous projects, or through interviews with the producer. ENG and studio camera operators who work for television affiliates usually start in small markets to gain experience. Advancement for them means moving to larger media markets. Other camera operators may become directors of photography for movie studios, advertising agencies, or television programs.

Photographers and camera operators who wish to operate their own businesses, or freelance, need business skills as well as talent. These individuals must know how to submit bids; write contracts; hire models, if needed; get permission to shoot on locations that normally are not open to the public; obtain releases to use photographs of people; price photographs; know about copyright protection for their work; and keep financial records. Freelance photographers also should develop an individual style of photography in order to differentiate themselves from the competition. Some photographers enter the field by submitting unsolicited photographs to magazines and art directors at advertising agencies.

Job Outlook

Keen competition is expected for photographer and camera operator job openings because they attract so many people. The number of individuals interested in positions such as commercial photographer, photojournalist, and movie camera operator, is usually much greater than the number of openings. Those who succeed in landing a salaried job or attracting enough work to earn a living by freelancing are likely to be the most creative, able to adapt to rapidly changing technologies, and adept at operating a business. Related work experience, job-related training, or some unique skill or talent—such as a background in computers or electronics—also are beneficial to prospective photographers or camera operators. Often, new job entry requirements emerge, because employers can pick and choose among the most qualified and the most experienced applicants. For example, most photojournalists enter the field with a degree in journalism and are held to the same ethical standards as reporters and journalists.

Employment of photographers is expected to increase more slowly than the average for all occupations through 2008. Declines in the newspaper industry over the next decade should reduce demand for photographers to provide still images for print. Demand for photographers in radio and television broadcasting is expected to increase relative to other occupations in the industry because digital photography allows photographers to cover events more quickly and from remote locations. However, the industry is growing very little, so employment gains for photographers will be modest. On the other hand, demand for photographers is growing in news and wire services operations, where photographers using digital equipment will be needed to transmit digital images interactively. Demand for portrait photographers also should increase as the population grows. And, as the number of electronic versions of magazines, journals, and newspapers grows on the Internet, photographers will be needed to provide digital images.

Employment of camera operators is expected to increase faster than the average for all occupations through 2008. The rapid expansion of the entertainment market, especially the cable and other pay television services, will spur the growth of camera operators. Modest growth also is expected in the motion picture production and distribution industry resulting, in part, from the increase in the number of feature films that will be produced over the next decade, but also because computer and Internet services provide new outlets for interactive productions. Made-for-the-Internet broadcasts include live music videos, digital movies, sports, and general information or entertainment programming. These images can be delivered directly into the home either on compact discs or over the Internet through telephone lines.

Earnings

Median annual earnings of photographers in 1998 were $20,940. The middle 50 percent earned between $15,250 and $30,820. The lowest 10 percent earned less than $12,490 and the highest 10 percent earned more than $43,860. Median annual earnings in the industries employing the largest number of photographers in 1997 were:

Radio and television broadcasting	$27,400
Newspapers	24,100
Photographic studios, portrait	16,800

Median annual earnings for television, motion picture, and video camera operators were $21,530 in 1998. The middle 50 percent earned between $15,330 and $34,200. The lowest 10 percent earned less than $27,790 and the highest 10 percent earned more than $53,470. Median annual earnings of television, motion picture, and video camera operators in the radio and television broadcasting industry in 1997 were $17,000.

Most salaried photographers work full time and earn more than the majority of self-employed photographers, many of whom work part time, but some self-employed photographers also have high earnings. Many camera operators who work in film or video are freelancers; their earnings tend to fluctuate each year.

Unlike photojournalists and commercial photographers, few fine arts photographers are successful enough to support themselves solely through their art.

Related Occupations

Other jobs requiring visual arts talents include illustrators, designers, painters, sculptors, and photo editors.

Sources of Additional Information

Career information on photography is available from:

☛ Professional Photographers of America, Inc., 229 Peachtree St., NE, Suite 2200, Atlanta, GA 30303.

☛ Advertising Photographers of America, 7201 Melrose Ave., Los Angeles, CA 90046.

Visual Artists

(O*NET 34035A, 34035B, 34035C, 34035D, 34035E, 34038E, 39999E, and 39999H)

Significant Points

- Nearly 60 percent are self-employed—about six times the proportion in all professional occupations.
- Visual artists usually develop their skills through a bachelor's degree program or other postsecondary training in art or design.
- Keen competition is expected for both salaried jobs and freelance work, because many talented people are attracted to the glamorous and exciting image of the graphic and fine arts fields.

Nature of the Work

Visual artists create art to communicate ideas, thoughts, or feelings. They use a variety of methods—painting, sculpting, or illustration—

and an assortment of materials, including oils, watercolors, acrylics, pastels, pencils, pen and ink, plaster, clay, and computers. Visual artists' works may be realistic, stylized, or abstract and may depict objects, people, nature, or events.

Visual artists generally fall into one of three categories. Fine artists create art to satisfy their own need for self-expression. Illustrators and graphic designers, on the other hand, put their artistic skills at the service of commercial clients, such as major corporations; retail stores; and advertising, design, and publishing firms. (Designers other than graphic designers are discussed in a separate *Handbook* statement.)

Fine artists display their work in museums, commercial art galleries, corporate collections, and private homes. Some of their artwork may be commissioned (done on request from clients), but mostly it is sold on consignment through private art galleries or dealers. The gallery and artist predetermine how much each will earn from a consignment sale. Only the most successful fine artists are able to support themselves solely through the sale of their works. Most fine artists also hold other jobs. Those with teaching certificates may teach art in elementary or secondary schools, whereas those with a master's or doctorate degree may teach art in colleges or universities. Some fine artists work in arts administration in local, State, or Federal government arts programs. Others work in museums or art galleries as fine arts directors or as curators, who plan and set up art exhibits. Some of these artists work as art critics for newspapers or magazines, and some work as consultants to foundations or institutional collectors. Fine artists also give private art lessons. Sometimes fine artists must work in an unrelated field to support their art careers.

Fine artists work independently. Usually, fine artists specialize in one or two art forms, such as painting, sculpting, printmaking, and restoring. *Painters* work with two-dimensional art forms. These artists use shading, perspective, and color to produce works that depict realistic scenes or abstract expressions to evoke different moods and emotions.

Sculptors design three-dimensional art works—either by molding and joining materials such as clay, glass, wire, plastic, fabric, or metal or by cutting and carving forms from a block of plaster, wood, or stone. Some sculptors combine various materials to create mixed-media works. In recent years, some sculptors have incorporated light, sound, and motion into their works.

Printmakers create printed images from designs cut or etched into wood, stone, or metal. After cutting the design, the artist inks the surface of the woodblock or stone and rolls or stamps it onto paper to make an impression. Some printmakers make prints by graphically encoding data and processing it, using a computer. The computer-enhanced images are printed using printers with specially loaded software or are transmitted electronically to be viewed on the Internet.

Painting restorers preserve and restore damaged and faded paintings. They apply solvents and cleaning agents to clean the surfaces, reconstruct or retouch damaged areas, and apply preservatives to protect the paintings. This is very detailed work and usually is reserved for experts in the field.

Illustrators paint or draw pictures for books, magazines, and other publications; films; and paper products, including wrapping paper, stationery, greeting cards and calendars. Some work may be done using computers, which allow ideas to be mailed electronically between clients or presented on the Internet. Many of these artists do a variety of illustrations, whereas others specialize in a particular style, such as medical illustration, fashion illustration, cartoons, or animation.

Some illustrators draw storyboards for television commercials, movies, and animated features. Storyboards present television commercials in a series of scenes similar to a comic strip and allow an advertising agency to evaluate proposed commercials with the company doing the advertising. Storyboards also serve as guides to placing actors and cameras and to other details during the production of commercials.

Medical and *scientific illustrators* combine artistic skills with knowledge of the biological sciences. Medical illustrators draw illustrations of human anatomy and surgical procedures. Scientific illustrators draw illustrations of animals and plants. These illustrations are used in medical and scientific publications and in audiovisual presentations for teaching purposes. Medical illustrators also work for lawyers, producing exhibits for court cases and doctors.

Fashion artists draw illustrations of women's, men's, and children's clothing and accessories for newspapers, magazines, and other media.

Cartoonists draw political, advertising, social, and sports cartoons. Some cartoonists work with others who create the idea or story and write the captions. Most cartoonists, however, have humorous, critical, or dramatic talents, in addition to drawing skills.

Animators work in the motion picture and television industries. They draw by hand and use computers to create the large series of pictures which, when transferred to film or tape, form the animated cartoons seen in movies and on television.

Graphic designers use a variety of print, electronic, and film media to create designs that meet client needs. Most graphic designers use computer software to generate new images. They design promotional displays and marketing brochures for products and services, develop distinctive company logos for products and businesses, and create visual designs of annual reports and other corporate literature. Additionally, graphic designers, usually under the supervision of a design or art director, develop the overall layout and design of magazines, newspapers, journals, corporate reports, and other publications. Many graphic designers develop the graphics and layout of Internet websites. Graphic designers also produce the credits that appear before and after television programs and movies.

Freelance graphic designers put their artistic skills and vision to work on a project-by-project arrangement while working on a contract basis with other companies.

Art directors develop design concepts and review the material that is to appear in periodicals, newspapers, and other printed or visual media. They decide how best to present the information visually, so it is eye-catching, appealing, and organized. They make decisions about which photographs or artwork to use and oversee the layout design and production of the printed material. Art directors also may review graphics that appear on the Internet.

Working Conditions

Most visual artists work in art and design studios located in office buildings, or they work in their own homes. Some fine artists share studio space, where they also may exhibit their work. Studio surroundings usually are well lighted and ventilated; however, fine

Most visual artists are self-employed.

artists may be exposed to fumes from glue, paint, ink, and other materials. Graphic designers or illustrators who sit at drafting tables or use computers for extended periods of time may experience back pain, eye strain, or carpal tunnel syndrome.

Graphic designers and illustrators employed by publishing companies, art and design studios, and graphic design firms generally work a standard 40-hour week. During busy periods, they may work overtime to meet deadlines. Fine artists and self-employed graphic designers and illustrators can set their own hours, but may spend much time and effort selling their services to potential customers or clients and building a reputation.

Employment

Visual artists held about 308,000 jobs in 1998. Nearly 6 out of 10 were self-employed. Self-employed visual artists either are graphic designers who freelance, offering their services to advertising agencies, publishing houses, and other businesses, or fine artists who earn income when they sell a painting or other work of art.

Of the visual artists who were not self-employed, many were graphic designers who worked for advertising agencies, design firms, commercial art and reproduction firms, or printing and publishing companies. Other visual artists were employed by the motion picture and television industries, wholesale and retail trade establishments, and public relations firms.

Training, Other Qualifications, and Advancement

Training requirements for visual artists vary, depending upon the specialty. Although formal training is not strictly necessary for fine artists, it is very difficult to become skilled enough to make a living without some training. Many colleges and universities offer degree programs leading to the bachelor in fine arts (BFA) and master in fine arts (MFA) degrees. Coursework usually includes core subjects, such as English, social science, and natural science, in addition to art history and studio art. Art schools also offer postsecondary studio training in the fine arts. Typically, these programs focus more intensively on studio work than the academic programs in a university setting. Those who want to teach fine arts at the elementary or secondary levels must have a teaching certificate in addition to a bachelor's degree. An advanced degree in fine arts or arts administration is necessary for management or administrative positions in government or in foundations or for teaching in colleges and universities. (See the statements for college and university faculty; and kindergarten, elementary, and secondary school teachers elsewhere in the *Handbook*.)

Graphic designers must demonstrate artistic ability and creative thinking. Academic training leading to a bachelor's degree in art or design has almost become a necessity.

Illustrators learn drawing and sketching skills through training in art programs and extensive practice. Most employers prefer candidates with a bachelor's degree; however, some illustrators may be contracted based on past work.

The appropriate training and education for prospective medical illustrators is more specific. Medical illustrators must have both a demonstrated artistic ability and a detailed knowledge of living organisms, surgical and medical procedures, and human and animal anatomy. A 4-year bachelor's degree combining art and pre-medical courses usually is necessary, followed by a master's degree in medical illustration. This degree is offered in only five accredited schools in the United States.

Evidence of appropriate talent and skill, displayed in an artist's portfolio, is an important factor used by art and design directors, clients, and others in deciding whether to hire or contract out work. The portfolio is a collection of hand-made, computer-generated, photographic, or printed samples of the artist's best work. Assembling a successful portfolio requires skills usually developed in a bachelor's degree program or other postsecondary training in art, design, or visual communications. Internships also provide excellent opportunities for visual artists to develop and enhance their portfolios. Formal educational programs in art and design also provide training in computer techniques. Computers are used widely in the visual arts, and knowledge and training in them are critical for many jobs in these fields. Graphic designers, especially those who are new to the field or who work on a freelance basis, need good communication skills to convey their ideas to clients and to contract for services.

Visual artists hired by advertising agencies or graphic design studios often start with relatively routine work. While doing this work, however, they may observe and practice their skills on the side. Many visual artists freelance on a part-time basis while continuing to hold a full-time job until they are established. Others freelance part-time while still in school, to develop experience and to build a portfolio of published work.

Freelance visual artists try to develop a set of clients who regularly contract for work. Some freelance artists are widely recognized for their skill in specialties such as magazine or children's book illustration. These artists may earn high incomes and can pick and choose the type of work they do.

Fine artists and illustrators advance professionally as their work circulates and as they establish a reputation for a particular style. Many of the most successful artists and illustrators continually develop new ideas, and their work often evolves over time. Graphic designers may advance to assistant art director, art director, design director, and in some companies, creative director of an art or design department. Some artists prosper enough to succeed as freelance designers or to specialize in a particular area. Some graphic designers design web pages for their company's Internet site. Others open their own businesses.

Job Outlook

Employment of visual artists is expected to grow faster than the average for all occupations through the year 2008. Because the visual arts attract many talented people with creative ability, the number of aspiring visual artists continues to grow. Consequently, competition for both salaried jobs and freelance work in some, but not all, areas of visual arts is expected to be keen.

Fine artists mostly work on a freelance, or commission, basis and may find it difficult to earn a living solely by selling their artwork. Only the most successful fine artists receive major commissions for their work. Competition among artists for the privilege of being shown in galleries is expected to remain acute. And grants from sponsors such as private foundations, State and local arts councils, and the National Endowment for the Arts, should remain competitive. Nonetheless, studios, galleries, and individual clients are always on the lookout for artists who display outstanding talent, creativity, and style. Population growth, rising incomes, and growth in the number of people who appreciate fine arts will contribute to the demand for fine artists. Talented fine artists who have developed a mastery of artistic techniques and skills, including computer skills, will have the best job prospects.

The need for visual artists to illustrate and animate materials for magazines, journals, and other printed or electronic media will spur demand for illustrators of all types. Growth in the entertainment industry, including cable and other pay television broadcasting and motion picture production and distribution, will provide new job opportunities for cartoonists and animators. Competition for most illustration jobs, however, will be strong, because job opportunities are relatively few and the number of people interested in these positions usually exceeds the number of available openings. Employers should be able to choose among the most qualified candidates.

Very good opportunities for graphic designers are expected. Continuing growth of the Internet should provide many job opportunities, largely due to the demand for graphic designers to design and develop the layout of web pages. Additionally, businesses will continue to put emphasis on visually appealing concepts for use in communications, package design, publications, advertising, marketing, and television and video production, all of which require the skills of graphic designers. Despite strong demand for both freelance and salaried graphic designers, competition will be stiff for the best jobs because employers are willing to make attractive offers to the most talented and creative candidates.

Earnings

Median annual earnings of visual artists were about $31,690 a year in 1998. The middle 50 percent earned between $23,790 and $41,980 a year. The lowest 10 percent earned less than $17,910 and the highest 10 percent earned more than $64,580. Median annual earnings in the industries employing the largest number of visual artists in 1997 were as follows:

Industry	Earnings
Advertising	$34,800
Periodicals	33,000
Mailing, reproduction, stenographic services	32,700
Commercial printing	24,700
Newspapers	24,100

Earnings for self-employed visual artists vary widely. Some charge only a nominal fee while they gain experience and build a reputation for their work. Others, such as well-established freelance graphic designers and fine artists, can earn much more than salaried artists do. Like other self-employed workers, freelance artists must provide their own benefits.

Related Occupations

Many occupations in the advertising industry, such as account executive and creative director, are related to the fine arts and graphic design. Other workers who apply visual art skills include architects; landscape architects; photographers; and floral, industrial, and interior designers. Various printing occupations also are related to visual art, as is the work of art and design teachers. In addition, several occupational options associated with the Internet have emerged—for example, webmaster and Internet page designer. These jobs often require artistic talent, as well as computer skills.

Sources of Additional Information

For an order form for a directory of accredited college-level programs in art and design (available for $15.00) or career information in visual arts occupations, contact:

☛ The National Association of Schools of Art and Design, 11250 Roger Bacon Dr., Suite 21, Reston, VA 20190.

For information on careers in medical illustration, contact:

☛ The Association of Medical Illustrators, 2965 Flowers Road South, Suite 105, Atlanta, GA 30341.

For a list of schools offering degree programs in graphic design, contact:

☛ The American Institute of Graphic Arts, 164 Fifth Ave., New York, NY 10010.

Performing Arts Occupations

Actors, Directors, and Producers

(O*NET 34047F, 34056A, 34056B, 34056D, 34056E, 34056F, 34056G, 34056H, 34056J, and 34056K)

Significant Points

- Aspiring actors face frequent rejections in auditions and long periods of unemployment; competition for roles is often intense.
- While formal training is helpful, experience and talent are more important for success in this field.
- Because of erratic employment, earnings for actors are relatively low.

Nature of the Work

Although most people associate actors, directors, and producers with the screens of Hollywood or stages of Broadway, these workers are more likely to be found in a local theatre, television studio, circus, or comedy club. Actors, directors, and producers include workers as diverse as narrators; clowns; comedians; acrobats; jugglers; stunt, rodeo, and aquatic performers; casting, stage, news, sports, and public service directors; production, stage, and artist and repertoire managers; and producers and their assistants. In essence, actors, directors, and producers express ideas and create images in theaters, film, radio, television, and a variety of other media. They "make the words come alive" for their audiences.

Actors entertain and communicate with people through their interpretation of dramatic roles. However, only a few actors ever achieve recognition as stars—whether on stage, in motion pictures, or on television. A few others are well-known, experienced performers, who frequently are cast in supporting roles. Most actors struggle for a toehold in the profession and pick up parts wherever they can. Although actors often prefer a certain type of role, experience is so important to success in this field that even established actors continue to accept small roles, including commercials and product endorsements. Other actors work as background performers, or "extras," with small parts and no lines to deliver; still others work for theater companies, teaching acting courses to the public.

Directors interpret plays or scripts. In addition, they audition and select cast members, conduct rehearsals, and direct the work of the cast and crew. Directors use their knowledge of acting, voice, and movement to achieve the best possible performance, and they usually approve the scenery, costumes, choreography, and music.

Producers are entrepreneurs. They select plays or scripts, arrange financing, and decide on the size, cost, and content of a production. They hire directors, principal members of the cast, and key production staff members. Producers also negotiate contracts with artistic personnel, often in accordance with collective bargaining agreements. Producers work on a project from beginning to end, coordinating the activities of writers, directors, managers, and other personnel. Increasingly, producers who work on motion pictures must have a working knowledge of the new technology needed to create special effects.

Working Conditions

Acting demands patience and total commitment, because actors are often rejected in auditions and must endure long periods of unemployment between jobs. Actors typically work long, irregular hours, sometimes under adverse weather conditions that may exist "on location." They also must travel when shows are "on the road." Coupled with the heat of stage or studio lights and heavy costumes, these factors require stamina. Actors working on Broadway productions often work long hours during rehearsals, but generally work about 30 hours a week once the show opens. Evening work is a regular part of a stage actor's life, as several performances are often held on one day. Flawless performances require

Aspiring actors gain experience in a variety of media.

tedious memorization of lines and repetitive rehearsals. On television, actors must deliver a good performance with very little preparation.

Directors and producers often work under stress as they try to meet schedules, stay within budgets, and resolve personnel problems while putting together a production. Directors must be aware of union rules and how they affect production schedules. For example, actors must be paid a minimum salary and can work no more than a set number of hours, depending on their contract. Additional restrictions are placed on productions using child actors and animals.

Employment

In 1998, actors, directors, and producers held about 160,000 jobs in motion pictures, stage plays, television, and radio. Many others were between jobs, so the total number of actors, directors, and producers employed at some time during the year was higher. In winter, most employment opportunities on stage are in New York and other large cities, many of which have established professional regional theaters. In summer, stock companies in suburban and resort areas also provide employment. Actors, directors, and producers also find work on cruise lines and in amusement parks. In addition, many cities have small nonprofit professional companies such as "little theaters," repertory companies, and dinner theaters, which provide opportunities for local amateur talent as well as for professional entertainers. Normally, casts are selected in New York City for shows that go on the road.

Employment in motion pictures and films for television is centered in Hollywood and New York City. However, small studios are located throughout the country. In addition, many films are shot on location and may employ local professional and nonprofessional day players and extras. In television, opportunities are concentrated in the network centers of New York, Los Angeles, and Atlanta, but local television stations around the country also employ a substantial number of these workers.

Training, Other Qualifications, and Advancement

Although many people have the technical skills to enter this industry, few receive the opportunity to display their talent. To gain experience, most aspiring actors and directors take part in high school and college plays, or they work with little theaters and other acting groups. The best way to start is to use local opportunities and build on them. Local and regional theater experience may help in obtaining work in New York or Los Angeles. Actors and directors try to work their way up to major productions. Intense competition, however, ensures that few succeed.

Formal dramatic training or acting experience is generally necessary, although some people enter the field without it. Most people take college courses in theater, arts, drama, and dramatic literature. Many experienced actors pursue additional formal training to learn new skills and improve old ones. Actors often research their character's lifestyle and history, as well as information about the location of the story. Sometimes actors learn a foreign language or develop an accent to make their character more realistic.

Training can be obtained at dramatic arts schools in New York and Los Angeles, and at colleges and universities throughout the country that offer bachelor or higher degrees in dramatic and theater arts. College drama curriculums usually include courses in liberal arts, stage speech and movement, directing, playwriting, play production, design, and the history of the drama, as well as practical courses in acting.

Actors need talent, creative ability, and training that will enable them to portray different characters. Training in singing and dancing is especially useful for stage work. Actors must have poise, stage presence, the capability to affect an audience, and the ability to follow directions. Modeling experience may also be helpful. Physical appearance is often a deciding factor in being selected for particular roles.

Many professional actors rely on agents or managers to find work, negotiate contracts, and plan their careers. Agents generally earn a percentage of an actor's contract. Other actors rely solely on attending open auditions for parts. Trade publications list the time, date, and location of these auditions. Many of these auditions are only open to union members and union membership requires work experience.

To become a movie extra, one must usually be listed by a casting agency, such as Central Casting, a no-fee agency that supplies extras to the major movie studios in Hollywood. Applicants are accepted only when the number of persons of a particular type on the list—for example, athletic young women, old men, or small children—is below the foreseeable need. In recent years, only a very small proportion of applicants has succeeded in being listed.

There are no specific training requirements for directors and producers, so they come from many different backgrounds. Talent, experience, and business acumen are very important determinants of success for directors and producers. Actors, writers, film editors, and business managers commonly enter these fields. Producers often start in the industry working behind the scenes with successful directors. Additionally, formal training in directing and producing is available at a number of colleges and universities.

As the reputations of actors, directors, and producers grow, they are able to work on larger productions or in more prestigious theaters. Actors may also advance to lead or specialized roles. A few actors move into acting-related jobs, as drama coaches or directors of stage, television, radio, or motion picture productions. Some teach drama in colleges and universities.

The length of a performer's working life depends largely on training, skill, versatility, and perseverance. Although some actors, directors, and producers continue working throughout their lives, many leave the occupation after a short time because they cannot find enough work to make a living. In fact, many who stay with the occupation must take a second job to support themselves.

Job Outlook

Employment of actors, directors, and producers is expected to grow faster than the average for all occupations through 2008. In addition, an even greater number of job openings is expected to arise from the need to replace workers who leave the field. Nevertheless, competition for these jobs will be stiff, as the glamour of actor, director, and producer jobs, coupled with the lack of formal entry requirements, will attract many people to these occupations. As in the past, only the most talented will find regular employment.

Rising foreign demand for American productions, combined with a growing domestic market, should stimulate demand for actors and other production personnel. An increasing population, a greater desire to attend live performances, and the growth of cable and satellite television, television syndication, home movie rentals, and music videos will fuel this demand. In addition to the increasing demand for these media, attendance at stage productions is expected to grow, and touring productions of Broadway plays and other large shows are providing new opportunities for actors and directors. However, employment may be affected by government funding for the arts—a decline in funding could dampen future employment growth.

Earnings

Median annual earnings of actors, directors, and producers were $27,400 in 1998. Minimum salaries, hours of work, and other conditions of employment are covered in collective bargaining agreements between producers of shows and unions representing workers in this field. The Actors' Equity Association represents stage actors; Screen Actors Guild covers actors in motion pictures, including television, commercials, and films; and the American Federation of Television and Radio Artists (AFTRA) represents television and radio performers. Most stage directors belong to the Society of Stage Directors and Choreographers, and film and television directors belong to the Directors Guild of America. While these unions generally determine minimum salaries, any actor or director may negotiate for a salary higher than the minimum.

On July 1, 1998, the members of Screen Actors Guild and AFTRA approved a new joint contract covering all unionized employment. Under the contract, motion picture and television actors with speaking parts earned a minimum daily rate of $576, or $2,000 for a 5-day week, in 1998. Actors also receive contributions to their health and pension plans and additional compensation for reruns and foreign telecasts.

According to Actors Equity Association, the minimum weekly salary for actors in Broadway stage productions was $1,135 per week in 1998. Those in small "off-Broadway" theaters received minimums ranging from $450 to $600 a week, depending on the seating capacity of the theater. Smaller regional theaters pay $400-$600 per week. For shows on the road, actors receive about an additional $100 per day for living expenses. However, less than 15 percent of dues-paying members work during any given week. In 1998, less than half worked on a stage production. Average earnings for those able to find employment was less than $10,000 in 1998.

Some well-known actors have salary rates well above the minimums, and the salaries of the few top stars are many times the figures cited, creating the false impression that all actors are highly paid. In reality, earnings for most actors are low because employment is so erratic. Screen Actors Guild reports that the average income its members earn from acting is less than $5,000 a year. Therefore, most actors must supplement their incomes by holding jobs in other fields.

Many actors who work more than a set number of weeks per year are covered by a union health, welfare, and pension fund, including hospitalization insurance, to which employers contribute. Under some employment conditions, Actors' Equity and AFTRA members have paid vacations and sick leave.

Earnings of stage directors vary greatly. According to the Society of Stage Directors and Choreographers, summer theaters offer compensation, including "royalties" (based on the number of performances), usually ranging from $2,500 to $8,000 for a 3- to 4-week run of a production. Directing a production at a dinner theater will usually pay less than a summer theater but has more potential for royalties. Regional theaters may hire directors for longer periods of time, increasing compensation accordingly. The highest paid directors work on Broadway productions, commonly earning $100,000 plus royalties per show.

Producers seldom get a set fee; instead, they get a percentage of a show's earnings or ticket sales.

Related Occupations

People who work in occupations requiring acting skills include dancers, choreographers, disc jockeys, drama teachers or coaches, and radio and television announcers. Others working in occupations related to acting are playwrights, scriptwriters, stage managers, costume designers, makeup artists, hair stylists, lighting designers, and set designers. Workers in occupations involved with the business aspects of theater productions include managing directors, company managers, booking managers, publicists, and agents for actors, directors, and playwrights.

Sources of Additional Information

Information about opportunities in regional theaters may be obtained from:

☛ Theatre Communications Group, Inc., 355 Lexington Ave., New York, NY 10017.

A directory of theatrical programs may be purchased from:

☛ National Association of Schools of Theater, 11250 Roger Bacon Dr., Suite 21, Reston, VA 22090.

For general information on actors, directors, and producers, contact:

☛ Screen Actors Guild, 5757 Wilshire Blvd., Los Angeles, CA 90036-3600.

☛ Association of Independent Video and Filmmakers, 304 Hudson St., 6th Floor, New York, NY 10013.

☛ American Federation of Television and Radio Artists—Screen Actors Guild, 4340 East-West Hwy., Suite 204, Bethesda, MD 20814-4411.

Dancers and Choreographers

(O*NET 34053A and 34053B)

Significant Points

- Although most dancers stop performing by their late thirties, some remain in the field as choreographers, dance teachers, or artistic directors.
- Most dancers begin their formal training between the ages of 5 to 15 and have their professional auditions by age 17 or 18.
- Dancers and choreographers face intense competition for jobs; only the most talented find regular employment.

Nature of the Work

From ancient times to the present, dancers have expressed ideas, stories, rhythm, and sound with their bodies. They do this by using

Most dancers have rigorous practice schedules.

a variety of dance forms, including classical ballet and modern dance styles that allow free movement and self-expression. Many dancers combine stage work with teaching or choreography.

Dancers perform in a variety of settings, such as musical productions, and in folk, ethnic, tap, jazz, and other popular kinds of dancing. They also perform in opera, musical comedy, television, movies, music videos, and commercials, in which they may sing and act as well. Dancers most often perform as part of a group, although a few top artists perform solo.

Many dancers take their cues from choreographers, who create original dances and develop new interpretations of traditional dances. Because few dance routines are written down, choreographers instruct performers at rehearsals to achieve the desired effect. In addition, choreographers are also involved in auditioning performers.

Working Conditions

Dancing is strenuous. Due to the physical demands, most dancers stop performing by their late thirties, but they may continue to work in the field as choreographers, dance teachers and coaches, or artistic directors. Some celebrated dancers, however, continue performing beyond the age of 50.

Daily rehearsals require very long hours and for shows on the road, weekend travel often is required. Most performances are in the evening, while rehearsals and practice usually are scheduled during the day. As a result, dancers must often work late hours. The work environment ranges from modern, temperature-controlled facilities to older, uncomfortable surroundings.

Employment

Professional dancers and choreographers held an average of about 29,000 jobs at any one time in 1998. Many others were between engagements so that the total number of people employed as dancers over the course of the year was greater. Dancers and choreographers work in a variety of settings, including eating and drinking establishments, theatrical and television productions, dance studios and schools, dance companies and bands, concert halls, and amusement parks. Dancers who give lessons worked in secondary schools, colleges and universities, and private studios.

New York City is home to many major dance companies. Other cities with full-time professional dance companies include Atlanta, Boston, Chicago, Cincinnati, Cleveland, Columbus, Dallas, Houston, Miami, Milwaukee, Philadelphia, Pittsburgh, Salt Lake City, San Francisco, Seattle, and Washington, D.C.

Training, Other Qualifications, and Advancement

Training characteristics depends upon the type of dance. Early ballet training for women usually begins at 5 to 8 years of age and is often given by private teachers and independent ballet schools. Serious training traditionally begins between the ages of 10 and 12. Men often begin their training between the ages of 10 and 15. Students who demonstrate potential in the early teens receive more intensive and advanced professional training at regional ballet schools or schools conducted under the auspices of major ballet companies. Leading dance school companies often have summer training programs from which they select candidates for admission to their regular full-time training program. Early and intensive training also is important for modern dancers, but modern dance usually does not require as many years of training as ballet.

Most dancers have their professional auditions by age 17 or 18. Training beyond this age is an important component of the careers of professional dancers, who normally have 1 to 1 1/2 hours of lessons every day and spend many additional hours practicing and rehearsing.

Because of the strenuous and time-consuming training required, a dancer's formal academic instruction may be minimal. However, a broad, general education including music, literature, history, and the visual arts is helpful in the interpretation of dramatic episodes, ideas, and feelings. Dancers sometimes conduct research to learn more about the part they are playing.

Many colleges and universities confer bachelor's or higher degrees in dance, usually through the departments of music, theater, or fine arts. Most programs concentrate on modern dance, but many also offer courses in ballet and classical techniques, dance composition, dance history, dance criticism, and movement analysis.

A college education is not essential to obtain employment as a professional dancer. In fact, ballet dancers who postpone their first audition until graduation may have a disadvantage when competing with younger dancers. However, a college degree can help dancers who retire at an early age to enter another field of work.

Completion of a college program in dance and education is essential to qualify for employment as a college, elementary school, or high school dance teacher. Colleges, as well as conservatories, usually require graduate degrees, but performance experience often may be substituted. A college background is not necessary, however, for teaching dance or choreography in local recreational programs. Studio schools usually require teachers to have experience as performers.

Because of the rigorous practice schedules of most dancers, self-discipline, patience, perseverance, and a devotion to dance are essential to succeed in the field. Good health and physical stamina also are necessary attributes. Above all, dancers must have flexibility, agility, coordination, grace, a sense of rhythm, a feeling for music, and a creative ability to express oneself through movement.

Dancers seldom perform unaccompanied, so they must be able to function as part of a team. They should also be highly motivated and prepared to face the anxiety of intermittent employment and rejections when auditioning for work. For dancers, advancement takes the form of a growing reputation, more frequent work, bigger and better roles, and higher pay.

Choreographers typically are older dancers with years of experience in the theater. Through their performance as dancers, they develop reputations as skilled artists. Their reputation often leads to opportunities to choreograph productions.

Job Outlook

Dancers and choreographers face intense competition for jobs. The number of applicants will continue to exceed the number of job openings, and only the most talented will find regular employment.

Employment of dancers and choreographers is expected to grow about as fast as the average for all occupations through 2008, reflecting the public's continued interest in this form of artistic expression. However, cuts in funding for the National Endowment for the Arts and related organizations could adversely affect employment in this field. In addition to job openings that will arise each year due to increased demand, openings will occur as dancers and choreographers retire or leave the occupation for other reasons.

National dance companies should continue to provide most jobs in this field. Opera companies and dance groups affiliated with colleges and universities and television and motion pictures will also offer some opportunities. Moreover, the growing popularity of dance in recent years has resulted in increased employment opportunities in teaching dance. Additionally, music video channels will provide some opportunities for both dancers and choreographers.

Earnings

Median annual earnings of dancers and choreographers were $21,430 in 1998. Those working with producers, orchestras, or entertainers earned $25,000 in 1997. Dancers on tour received an additional allowance for room and board and extra compensation for overtime. Earnings from dancing are usually low because dancers' employment is irregular. They often must supplement their income by teaching dance or taking temporary jobs unrelated to the field.

Earnings of many professional dancers are governed by union contracts. Dancers in the major opera ballet, classical ballet, and modern dance corps belong to the American Guild of Musical Artists, Inc., AFL-CIO; those on live or videotaped television belong to the American Federation of Television and Radio Artists; those who perform in films and on TV belong to the Screen Actors Guild; and those in musical comedies are members of the Actors' Equity Association. The unions and producers sign basic agreements specifying minimum salary rates, hours of work, benefits, and other conditions of employment. However, the contract each dancer signs with the producer of the show may be more favorable than the basic agreement.

Dancers covered by union contracts are entitled to some paid sick leave, paid vacations, and various health and pension benefits, including extended sick pay and family leave provisions provided by their unions. Employers contribute toward these benefits. Dancers not covered by union contracts usually do not enjoy such benefits.

Related Occupations

Other workers who convey ideas through physical motion include ice skaters, dance critics, dance instructors, and dance therapists. Athletes in most sports also need the same strength, flexibility, agility, and body control as dancers.

Sources of Additional Information

Directories of dance study and degree programs may be purchased from:

☛ National Association of Schools of Dance, 11250 Roger Bacon Dr., Suite 21, Reston, VA 20190.

☛ The National Dance Association, 1900 Association Dr., Reston, VA 20191.

Musicians, Singers, and Related Workers

(O*NET 34047A, 34047B, 34047C, 34047E, and 34051)

Significant Points

- Part-time schedules and intermittent unemployment are common, and many musicians supplement their income with earnings from other sources.
- Aspiring musicians begin studying an instrument or training their voices at an early age; a bachelor's or higher degree in music or music education is required to teach at all educational levels.
- Competition for jobs is keen because the glamour and potentially high earnings attract many talented individuals; those who can play several instruments and types of music should enjoy the best job prospects.

Nature of the Work

Musicians, singers, and related workers play musical instruments, sing, compose, arrange, or conduct groups in instrumental or vocal performances. They may perform alone or as part of a group, before live audiences or in recording studios, television, radio, or movie productions. Although most of these entertainers play for live audiences, some prepare music exclusively for studios or computers. Regardless of the setting, musicians, singers, and related workers spend considerable time practicing, alone and with their band, orchestra, or other musical group.

Musicians often specialize in a particular kind of music or performance. Instrumental musicians, for example, play a musical instrument in an orchestra, band, rock group, or jazz group. Some play a variety of string, brass, woodwind, or percussion instruments or electronic synthesizers. Those who learn several related instruments, such as the flute and clarinet, have better employment opportunities.

Singers interpret music using their knowledge of voice production, melody, and harmony. They sing character parts or perform in their own individual style. Singers are often classified according to their voice range—soprano, contralto, tenor, baritone, or bass—or by the type of music they sing, such as opera, rock, reggae, folk, rap, or country and western.

Composers create original music such as symphonies, operas, sonatas, or popular songs. They transcribe ideas into musical notation using harmony, rhythm, melody, and tonal structure. Although most songwriters still practice their craft on instruments or with pen and paper, many songwriters now compose and edit music using computers.

Arrangers transcribe and adapt musical composition to a particular style for orchestras, bands, choral groups, or individuals. Components of music—including tempo, volume, and the mix of instruments needed—are arranged to express the composer's message. While some arrangers write directly into a musical composition, others use computer software to make changes.

Conductors lead instrumental music groups, such as orchestras, dance bands, and various popular ensembles. These leaders audition and select musicians, choose the music most appropriate for the talents and abilities of the musicians, and direct rehearsals and performances.

Musicians often specialize in a particular kind of music or performance.

Choral directors lead choirs and glee clubs, sometimes working with a band or orchestra conductor. Directors audition and select singers and lead them at rehearsals and performances to achieve harmony, rhythm, tempo, shading, and other desired musical effects.

Working Conditions
Musicians often perform at night and on weekends and spend much time in practice and rehearsal. Also, they frequently travel to perform in a variety of settings. Because many musicians find only part-time work and experience unemployment between engagements, they often supplement their income with other types of jobs. In fact, the stress of constantly looking for work leads many musicians to accept permanent, full-time jobs in other occupations, while working only part time as musicians.

Most instrumental musicians work closely with a variety of other people, including their colleagues, agents, employers, sponsors, and audiences. Although they usually work indoors, some perform outdoors for parades, concerts, and dances. In some taverns and restaurants, smoke and odors may be present, and lighting and ventilation may be inadequate.

Employment
Musicians, singers, and related workers held about 273,000 jobs in 1998. About three-quarters of these workers had part-time schedules. In addition, slightly over 2 in 5 were self-employed. Many jobs were found in cities in which entertainment and recording activities are concentrated, such as New York, Los Angeles, and Nashville.

Musicians, singers, and related workers are employed in a variety of settings. About 2 out of every 3 who earn a wage or salary are employed by religious organizations. Classical musicians may perform with professional orchestras or in small chamber music groups like quartets or trios. Musicians may work in opera, musical comedy, and ballet productions. They also perform in clubs and restaurants, and for weddings and other events. Well-known musicians and groups give their own concerts, appear "live" on radio and television, make recordings and music videos, or go on concert tours. The Armed Forces also offer careers in their bands and smaller musical groups.

Training, Other Qualifications, and Advancement
Aspiring musicians begin studying an instrument at an early age. They may gain valuable experience playing in a school or community band or orchestra or with a group of friends. Singers usually start training when their voices mature. Participation in school musicals or in a choir often provides good early training and experience.

Musicians need extensive and prolonged training to acquire the necessary skill, knowledge, and ability to interpret music. This training may be obtained through private study with an accomplished musician, in a college or university music program, in a music conservatory, or through practice with a group. For study in an institution, an audition frequently is necessary. Courses typically include musical theory, music interpretation, composition, conducting, and instrumental and voice instruction. Composers, conductors, and arrangers need advanced training in these subjects as well.

Many colleges, universities, and music conservatories grant bachelor's or higher degrees in music. A master's or doctoral degree is usually required to teach advanced music courses in colleges and universities; a bachelor's degree may be sufficient to teach basic courses. A degree in music education qualifies graduates for a State certificate to teach music in an elementary or secondary school.

Those who perform popular music must be knowledgeable about the style of music that interests them. In addition, classical training can expand their employment opportunities and musical abilities. Although voice training is an asset for singers of popular music, many with untrained voices have successful careers. As a rule, musicians take lessons with private teachers when young and seize every opportunity to make amateur or professional appearances.

Young persons who are considering careers in music should have musical talent, versatility, creativity, poise, and a good stage presence. Because quality performance requires constant study and practice, self-discipline is vital. Moreover, musicians who play concert and nightclub engagements must have physical stamina to endure frequent travel and night performances. They must also be prepared to face the anxiety of intermittent employment and rejections when auditioning for work.

Advancement for musicians usually means becoming better known and performing for increased earnings. Successful musicians often rely on agents or managers to find them performing engagements, negotiate contracts, and develop their careers.

Job Outlook
Competition for musician, singer, and related jobs is keen because the glamour and potentially high earnings in this occupation attract many talented individuals. Talent alone is no guarantee of success, however; most musicians have difficulty finding work and must endure periods of intermittent unemployment. Those who can play several instruments and types of music should enjoy the best job prospects.

Overall employment of musicians is expected to grow about as fast as the average for all occupations through 2008. Most new wage and salary jobs for musicians will arise in religious organizations, where the majority of these workers are employed. Average growth is also expected for self-employed musicians as people continue to attend concerts, shows, recitals, and other performances in coming years. Although demand for musicians will generate a number of job opportunities, most openings will arise from the need to replace those who leave the field each year because they are unable to make a living solely as musicians.

Earnings
Median annual earnings of musicians, singers, and related workers were $30,020 in 1998. Earnings often depend on a performer's professional reputation, place of employment, and on the number of hours worked. The most successful musicians can earn far more than the median earnings indicated above.

According to the American Federation of Musicians, minimum salaries in major orchestras ranged from about $21,000 to $95,000 per year during the 1998-99 performing season. Each orchestra works out a separate contract with its local union. Top orchestras have a season ranging from 24 to 52 weeks, with most major orchestras working 52 weeks. In regional orchestras, minimum salaries are often less because fewer performances are scheduled. Community orchestras often have more limited levels of funding and offer salaries that are much lower for seasons of shorter duration.

Although musicians employed by some symphony orchestras work under master wage agreements, which guarantee a season's work up to 52 weeks, many other musicians face relatively long periods of unemployment between jobs. Even when employed, however, many work part time in unrelated occupations. Thus, their earnings usually are lower than those in many other occupations. Moreover, because they may not work steadily for one employer, some performers cannot qualify for unemployment compensation, and few have typical benefits such as sick leave or vacations with pay. For these reasons, many musicians give private lessons or take jobs unrelated to music to supplement their earnings as performers.

Many musicians belong to a local of the American Federation of Musicians. Professional singers usually belong to a branch of the American Guild of Musical Artists.

Related Occupations

Music-related occupations include music writers and composers and music therapists. A large number of music teachers work in elementary and secondary schools, music conservatories, and colleges and universities, or are self-employed. Many who teach music also perform.

Instrument repairers, tuners, and copyists require technical knowledge of musical instruments. In addition, there are a number of occupations on the business side of music such as booking agents, concert managers, music publishers, and music store owners and managers, as well as salespersons of records, sheet music, and musical instruments. Others whose work involves music include disc jockeys, music critics, sound and audio technicians, music librarians, and radio and television announcers.

Sources of Additional Information

For a directory of schools, colleges, and universities that offer accredited programs in music and music teacher education, contact:

☛ National Association of Schools of Music, 11250 Roger Bacon Dr., Suite 21, Reston, VA 22091. Internet: **http://www.arts-accredit.org**

For information on careers for bluegrass musicians, contact:

☛ International Bluegrass Music Association, 207 East 2nd St., Owensboro, KY 42303.

Marketing and Sales Occupations

Cashiers

(O*NET 49023A)

Significant Points

- Good employment opportunities are expected due to the large number of workers who leave this occupation each year.
- The occupation offers plentiful opportunities for part-time work.

Nature of the Work

Supermarkets, department stores, gasoline service stations, movie theaters, restaurants, and many other businesses employ cashiers to register the sale of their merchandise. Most cashiers total bills, receive money, make change, fill out charge forms, and give receipts. Bank tellers, who perform similar duties but work in financial institutions, are discussed elsewhere in the *Handbook*.

Although specific job duties vary by employer, cashiers are usually assigned to a register at the beginning of their shifts and given drawers containing "banks" of money. They must count their banks to ensure they contain the correct amount of money and adequate supplies of change. At the end of their shifts, they once again count the drawers' contents and compare the totals with sales data. An occasional shortage of small amounts may be overlooked, but in many establishments, repeated shortages are grounds for dismissal.

In addition to counting the contents of their drawers at the end of their shifts, cashiers usually separate and total charge forms, return slips, coupons, and any other noncash items. Cashiers also handle returns and exchanges. They must ensure that merchandise is in good condition and determine where and when it was purchased and what type of payment was used.

After entering charges for all items and subtracting the value of any coupons or special discounts, cashiers total the bill and take payment. Acceptable forms of payment include cash, personal check, charge, and debit cards. Cashiers must know the store's policies and procedures for each type of payment the store accepts. For checks and charges, they may request additional identification from the customer or call in for an authorization. They must verify the age of customers purchasing alcohol or tobacco. When the sale is complete, cashiers issue a receipt to the customer and return the appropriate change. They may also wrap or bag the purchase.

Cashiers traditionally have totaled customers' purchases using cash registers—manually entering the price of each product bought. However, most establishments are now using more sophisticated equipment, such as scanners and computers. In a store with scanners, a cashier passes a product's Universal Product Code over the scanning device, which transmits the code number to a computer. The computer identifies the item and its price. In other establishments, cashiers manually enter codes into computers, and descriptions of the items and their prices appear on the screen.

Depending on the type of establishment, cashiers may have other duties as well. In many supermarkets, for example, cashiers weigh produce and bulk food as well as return unwanted items to the shelves. In convenience stores, cashiers may be required to know how to use a variety of machines, other than cash registers, and how to furnish money orders. Operating ticket-dispensing machines and answering customers' questions are common duties for cashiers who work at movie theaters and ticket agencies. Counter and rental clerks, who perform many similar duties, are discussed elsewhere in the *Handbook*.

Working Conditions

About one half of all cashiers work part time. Hours of work often vary depending on the needs of the employer. Generally, cashiers are expected to work weekends, evenings, and holidays to accommodate customers' needs. However, many employers offer flexible schedules. For example, full-time workers who work on weekends may receive time off during the week. Because the holiday season is the busiest time for most retailers, many employers restrict the use of vacation time from Thanksgiving through the beginning of January.

Most cashiers work indoors, usually standing in booths or behind counters. In addition, they are often unable to leave their workstations without supervisory approval because they are responsible for large sums of money. The work of cashiers can be very repetitious but improvements in workstation design are being made to combat problems caused by repetitive motion. In addition, the work can sometimes be dangerous. In 1998, cashiers were victims of 6.5 percent of all workplace homicides, although they made up less than 2.5 percent of the total workforce.

Employment

Cashiers held about 3.2 million jobs in 1998. Although employed in almost every industry, nearly one third of all jobs were in supermarkets and other food stores. Restaurants, department stores, gasoline service stations, drug stores, and other retail establishments also employed large

Cashiers try to provide customers friendly and efficient service.

numbers of these workers. Outside of retail establishments, many cashiers worked in hotels, schools, and motion picture theaters. Because cashiers are needed in businesses and organizations of all types and sizes, job opportunities are found throughout the country.

Training, Other Qualifications, and Advancement
Cashier jobs tend to be entry-level positions requiring little or no previous work experience. Although there are no specific educational requirements, employers filling full-time jobs often prefer applicants with high school diplomas.

Nearly all cashiers are trained on the job. In small businesses, an experienced worker often trains beginners. The first day is usually spent observing the operation and becoming familiar with the store's equipment, policies, and procedures. After this, trainees are assigned to a register—frequently under the supervision of a more experienced worker. In larger businesses, before being placed at cash registers, trainees spend several days in classes. Topics typically covered include a description of the industry and the company, store policies and procedures, equipment operation, and security.

Training for experienced workers is not common, except when new equipment is introduced or when procedures change. In these cases, the employer or a representative of the equipment manufacturer trains workers on the job.

Persons who want to become cashiers should be able to do repetitious work accurately. They also need basic mathematics skills and good manual dexterity. Because cashiers deal constantly with the public, they should be neat in appearance and able to deal tactfully and pleasantly with customers. In addition, some businesses prefer to hire persons who can operate specialized equipment or who have business experience, such as typing, selling, or handling money.

Advancement opportunities for cashiers vary. For those working part time, promotion may be to a full-time position. Others advance to head cashier or cash office clerk. In addition, this job offers a good opportunity to learn about an employer's business and can serve as a steppingstone to a more responsible position.

Job Outlook
As in the past, opportunities for cashiers are expected to continue to be good, due to rapid employment growth and the need to replace the large number of workers who transfer to other occupations or leave the labor force.

Cashier employment is expected to increase as fast as the average for all occupations through the year 2008 due to expanding demand for goods and services by a growing population. Traditionally, workers under the age of 25 have filled many of the openings in this occupation—in 1998, about half of all cashiers were 24 years of age or younger. Some establishments have begun hiring elderly and disabled persons as well to fill some of their job openings. Opportunities for part-time work are expected to continue to be excellent.

Earnings
The starting wage for many cashiers is the Federal minimum wage, which was $5.15 an hour in 1999. In some States, State law sets the minimum wage higher and establishments must pay at least that amount. Wages tend to be higher in areas where there is intense competition for workers.

Median hourly earnings of cashiers in 1998 were $6.58. The middle 50 percent earned between $5.95 and $8.22 an hour. The lowest 10 percent earned less than $5.66 and the highest 10 percent earned more than $9.82 an hour. Median hourly earnings in the industries employing the largest number of cashiers in 1997 were as follows:

Industry	Earnings
Department stores	$6.70
Grocery stores	6.30
Gasoline service stations	6.10
Drug stores and proprietary stores	5.80
Eating and drinking places	5.70

Benefits for full-time cashiers tend to be better than for those working part time. Cashiers often receive health and life insurance and paid vacations. In addition, those working in retail establishments often receive discounts on purchases, and cashiers in restaurants may receive free or low-cost meals. Some employers also offer employee stock option plans and education reimbursement plans.

Related Occupations
Cashiers accept payment for the purchase of goods and services. Other workers with similar duties include food and beverage service workers, bank tellers, counter and rental clerks, postal clerks and mail carriers, and retail salespersons, all of whom are discussed elsewhere in the *Handbook.*

Sources of Additional Information
General information on retailing is available from:

☛ National Retail Federation, 325 7th St. NW., Suite 1100, Washington, DC 20004. Internet: **http://www.nrf.com**

For information about employment opportunities as a cashier, contact:

☛ National Association of Convenience Stores, 1605 King St., Alexandria, VA 22314-2792.

☛ United Food and Commercial Workers International Union, Education Office, 1775 K St. NW., Washington, DC 20006-1502.

☛ Retail, Wholesale, and Department Store Union, 30 East 29th St., 4th Floor, New York, NY 10016.

Counter and Rental Clerks

(O*NET 49017)

Significant Points

- Jobs are primarily entry level and require little or no experience and little formal education.
- Part-time employment opportunities are expected to be plentiful.

Nature of the Work
Whether renting video tapes or air compressors, dropping off clothes to be dry-cleaned or appliances to be serviced, we rely on counter and rental clerks to handle these transactions efficiently. Although specific duties vary by establishment, counter and rental clerks answer questions involving product availability, cost, and rental provisions. Counter and rental clerks also take orders, calculate fees, receive payments, and accept returns. (Cashiers and retail salespersons, occupations with similar duties, are discussed elsewhere in the *Handbook.*)

Regardless of where they work, counter and rental clerks must be knowledgeable about the company's services, policies, and procedures. Depending on the type of establishment, counter and rental clerks use their special knowledge to give advice on a wide variety of products and services, which may range from hydraulic tools to shoe repair. For example, in the car rental industry, they inform customers about the features of different types of automobiles as well as daily and weekly rental costs. They also insure that customers meet age and other requirements for rental cars, and indicate when and in what condition cars must be returned. Those in the equipment rental industry have similar duties, but must also know how to operate and care for the machinery rented. In dry-cleaning establishments, counter clerks inform customers when items will be ready. In video rental stores, they advise customers about the length of rental, scan returned movies, restock the shelves, handle money, and log daily reports.

When taking orders, counter and rental clerks use various types of equipment. In some establishments, they write out tickets and order forms, although most use computers or bar code scanners. Most of these computer systems are user friendly, require very little data entry, and are customized for the firm. Scanners "read" the product code and display a description of the item on a computer screen. However, clerks must insure that the data on the screen accurately matches the product.

Working Conditions

Firms employing counter and rental clerks usually operate nights and weekends for the convenience of their customers. However, many employers offer flexible schedules. Some counter and rental clerks work 40-hour weeks, but about one-half are on part-time schedules—usually during rush periods, such as weekends, evenings, and holidays.

Working conditions are usually pleasant; most stores and service establishments are clean, well-lighted, and temperature controlled. However, clerks are on their feet much of the time and may be confined behind a small counter area. This job requires constant interaction with the public and can be taxing—especially during busy periods.

Employment

Counter and rental clerks held 469,000 jobs in 1998. About 1 of every 4 clerks worked for a video tape rental store. Other large employers included dry cleaners, automobile rental firms, equipment rental firms, and miscellaneous amusement and recreation establishments.

Counter and rental clerks are employed throughout the country but are concentrated in metropolitan areas, where personal services and renting and leasing services are in greater demand.

Counter and rental clerks are familiar with the company's products and rental terms and conditions.

Training, Other Qualifications, and Advancement

Counter and rental clerk jobs are primarily entry level and require little or no experience and little formal education. However, many employers prefer those with at least a high school diploma.

In most companies, counter and rental clerks are trained on the job, sometimes through the use of video tapes, brochures, and pamphlets. Clerks usually learn how to operate the equipment and become familiar with the establishment's policies and procedures under the observation of a more experienced worker. However, some employers have formal classroom training programs lasting from a few hours to a few weeks. Topics covered in this training include a description of the industry, the company and its policies and procedures, equipment operation, sales techniques, and customer service. Counter and rental clerks must also become familiar with the different products and services rented or provided by their company in order to give customers the best possible service.

Counter and rental clerks should enjoy working with people and have the ability to deal tactfully with difficult customers. They should be able to handle several tasks at once, while continuing to provide friendly service. In addition, good oral and written communication skills are essential.

Advancement opportunities depend on the size and type of company. Many establishments that employ counter or rental clerks tend to be small businesses, making advancement difficult. But in larger establishments with a corporate structure, jobs as counter and rental clerks offer good opportunities for workers to learn about their company's products and business practices. These jobs can be stepping stones to more responsible positions, because it is common in many establishments to promote counter and rental clerks into assistant manager positions.

In certain industries, such as equipment repair, counter and rental jobs may be an additional or alternate source of income for workers who are unemployed or entering semi-retirement. For example, retired mechanics could prove invaluable at tool rental centers because of their relevant knowledge.

Job Outlook

Employment in this occupation is expected to increase faster than the average for all occupations through the year 2008 due to businesses' desire to improve customer service. Industries employing counter and rental clerks that are expected to grow rapidly include equipment rental and leasing, automotive rentals, and amusement and recreation services. The number of new jobs created in other industries, such as video tape rental stores, will also be significant. Nevertheless, most job openings will arise from the need to replace experienced workers who transfer to other occupations or leave the labor force. Part-time employment opportunities are expected to be plentiful.

Earnings

Counter and rental clerks typically start at the minimum wage, which, in establishments covered by Federal law, was $5.15 an hour in 1999. In some States, State law sets the minimum wage higher and establishments must pay at least that amount. Wages also tend to be higher in areas where there is intense competition for workers. In addition to wages, some counter and rental clerks receive commissions, based on the number of contracts they complete or services they sell.

Median hourly earnings of counter and rental clerks in 1998 were $6.97. The middle 50 percent earned between $6.03 and $8.79 an hour. The lowest 10 percent earned less than $5.70 and the highest 10 percent earned more than $11.12 an hour. Median hourly earnings in the industries employing the largest number of counter and rental clerks in 1997 were as follows:

Industry	Earnings
Miscellaneous equipment rental and leasing	$8.20
Automotive rentals, no drivers	8.10
Miscellaneous amusement and recreation services	6.30
Laundry, cleaning, and garment services	6.20
Video tape rental	5.70

Full-time workers typically receive health and life insurance, paid vacation, and sick leave. Benefits for counter and rental clerks who work part-time tend to be significantly less than for those who work full-time. Many companies offer discounts to both full- and part-time employees on the services they provide.

Related Occupations

Counter and rental clerks take orders and receive payment for services rendered. Other workers with similar duties include bank tellers, cashiers, food and beverage service occupations, postal clerks, and retail salespersons.

Sources of Additional Information

For general information on employment in the equipment rental industry contact:

☛ American Rental Association, 1900 19th St., Moline, IL 61265. Internet: **http://www.ararental.org**

For more information about the work of counter clerks in dry cleaning and laundry establishments, contact:

☛ International Fabricare Institute, 12251 Tech Rd., Silver Spring, MD 20904. Internet: **http://www.ifi.org**

Demonstrators, Product Promoters, and Models

(O*NET 49032A and 49032B)

Significant Points

- Opportunities for demonstrators and product promoters should be plentiful but keen competition is expected for modeling jobs.
- Most jobs are part time.
- Many jobs require frequent employer paid travel.

Nature of the Work

Demonstrators, product promoters, and models create public interest in buying products such as clothing, cosmetics, food items, and housewares. The information they provide helps consumers make educated choices among the wide variety of products and services available.

Demonstrators and product promoters create public interest in buying a product by demonstrating it to prospective customers and answering their questions. They may also sell the demonstrated merchandise or gather names of prospects to contact at a later date or to pass on to a sales staff. *Demonstrators* promote sales of a product to consumers, while *product promoters* try to induce retail stores to sell particular products and market them effectively. Product demonstration is an effective technique used by both to introduce new products or promote sales of old products because it allows face to face interaction with potential customers.

Demonstrators and product promoters build current and future sales of both sophisticated and simple products, ranging from computer software to mops. They attract an audience by offering samples, administering contests, distributing prizes, and using direct mail advertising. They must greet and catch the attention of possible customers and quickly identify those who are interested and qualified. They inform and educate customers about the features of products and demonstrate their use with apparent ease to inspire confidence in the product and its manufacturer. They also distribute information such as brochures and applications. Some demonstrations are intended to generate immediate sales through impulse buying, while others are considered an investment to generate future sales and increase brand awareness. Many do both.

Demonstrations and product promotions are conducted in retail and grocery stores, shopping malls, trade shows, and outdoor fairs. Locations are selected based on both the nature of the product and the type of audience. Demonstrations at large events may require teams of demonstrators to handle large crowds efficiently. Some demonstrators promote products on videotape or on television programs, such as "infomercials" or home shopping programs.

Demonstrators and product promoters may prepare the content of a presentation and alter it to target a specific audience or to keep it current. They may participate in the design of an exhibit or customize exhibits for particular audiences. Results obtained by demonstrators and product promoters are analyzed, and presentations are adjusted to make them more effective. Demonstrators and product promoters also may be involved in transporting, assembling, and disassembling materials used in demonstrations.

A demonstrator's presentation may include visuals, models, case studies, testimonials, test results, and surveys. The equipment used for a demonstration varies with the product being demonstrated. A food product demonstration may require the use of cooking utensils, while a software demonstration may require the use of a multi-media computer. Demonstrators must be familiar with the product to be able to relate detailed information to customers and to answer any questions that arise before, during, or after a demonstration. Therefore, they may research the product to be presented, the products of competitors, and the interests and concerns of the target audience before conducting a demonstration. Demonstrations of complex products may require practice.

Models pose for photos or as subjects for paintings or sculptures. They display clothing such as dresses, coats, underclothing, swimwear, and suits for a variety of audiences and in different types of media. They model accessories, such as handbags, shoes, and jewelry, and promote beauty products, including fragrances and cosmetics. The most successful models, called "supermodels," hold celebrity status and often use their image to sell products such as books, calendars, and fitness videos. In addition to modeling, they may appear in movies and television shows.

Models' clients use printed publications, live modeling, and television to advertise and promote products and services. There are different categories of modeling jobs within these media, and the nature of a model's work may vary with each. Most modeling jobs are for printed publications and models usually do a combination of editorial, commercial, and catalog work. Editorial print modeling uses still photographs of models for fashion magazine covers and to accompany feature articles, but does not include modeling for advertisements. Commercial print modeling includes work for advertisements in magazines and newspapers, and outdoor advertisements such as billboards. Catalog models appear in department store and mail order catalogs.

During a photo shoot, a model poses to demonstrate the features of clothing and products. Models make small changes in posture and facial expression to capture the look desired by the client. As they shoot film, photographers instruct models to pose in certain positions and to interact with the physical surroundings. Models work closely with photographers, hair and clothing stylists, make-up artists, and clients to produce the desired look and to finish the photo shoot on schedule. Stylists and make-up artists prepare the model for the photo shoot, provide touch-ups, and change the look of models throughout the day. If stylists are not provided, models must apply their own make-up and bring their own clothing. Because the client spends time and money planning for and preparing an advertising campaign, the client is usually present to insure that the work is satisfactory. The client may also offer suggestions.

Editorial print work generally does not pay as well as other types of modeling, but provides exposure to a model and leads to commercial modeling opportunities. Most beginning fashion models work in foreign countries, where fashion magazines are more plentiful.

Live modeling is done in a variety of locations and live models stand, turn, and walk to demonstrate clothing to a variety of audiences. At fashion shows and in showrooms, garment buyers are the primary audience. Runway models display clothes that either are intended for direct sale to consumers or are the artistic expressions of the designer. High fashion, or haute couture, runway models confidently walk a narrow runway before an audience of photographers, journalists, designers, and garment buyers. Live modeling is also done in apparel marts, department stores, and fitting rooms of clothing designers. In retail establishments, models display clothing directly for shoppers and may be required to describe the features and price of the clothing. Other models pose for sketching artists, painters, and sculptors.

Models may also compete with actors and actresses for work in television and may even receive speaking parts. Television work includes commercials, cable television programs, and even game shows. However, television work is difficult to get because it pays well and provides a lot of exposure.

Because advertisers need to target very specific segments of the population, models may specialize in a certain area. Petite and plus size fashions are modeled by women whose dress size is smaller or larger than the typical model. Models who are disabled may be used to model fashions or products for disabled consumers. "Parts" models have a body part, such as a hand or foot, which is particularly well suited to model products such as fingernail polish or shoes.

Almost all models work through agents. Agents provide a link between models and clients. An agency receives a portion of the model's earnings in return for the agency's services. Agents scout for new faces, advise and train new models, and promote them to clients. A typical modeling job lasts only 1 day, so modeling agencies differ from other employment agencies by maintaining an ongoing relationship with the model. Agents find and maintain relationships with clients, arrange auditions called "go-sees," and book shoots if a model is hired. They also provide bookkeeping and billing services and may offer financial planning services. Relatively short careers and high incomes make financial planning an important issue for successful models. Because models are self-employed, detailed records of income and tax-deductible expenses must be kept.

Demonstrators, product promoters, and models often work before large crowds.

With the help of agents, models spend a considerable amount of time promoting and developing themselves. They assemble and maintain portfolios, print composite cards, and travel to go-sees. A portfolio is a collection of model's previous work that is carried to all go-sees and bookings. A composite card, or comp card, contains the best photographs from a model's portfolio along with his or her measurements.

Models must gather information before a job. From an agent, they learn the pay, date, time, and length of the shoot. Also, models must ask agents if hair, make-up, and clothing stylists will be provided. It is helpful to know what product is being promoted and what image they should project. Some models research the client and the product being modeled to prepare for a shoot. Models use a document called a "voucher" to record the rate of pay and the actual duration of the job. The voucher is used for billing purposes after both the client and model sign it. Once a job is completed, models must check in with their agency and plan for the next appointment.

Working Conditions

The majority of all demonstrators, product promoters, and models work part-time. Many positions are short term and last 6 months or less. Almost one quarter have variable work schedules.

Demonstrators and product promoters may work long hours while standing or walking, with little opportunity to rest. Some demonstrators and product promoters travel frequently. Night and weekend work is often required. The atmosphere of a crowded trade show or state fair is often hectic and demonstrators and product promoters may feel pressure to influence the greatest number of consumers possible in a very limited amount of time. However, many enjoy the opportunity to interact with a variety of people.

The work of a model is both glamorous and difficult and they may work under a variety of conditions. The coming season's fashions may be modeled in a comfortable, climate-controlled studio or in a cold, damp outdoor location. Schedules can be demanding and models must keep in constant touch with an agent so they do not miss an opportunity for work. Being away from friends and family and needing to focus on the photographer's instructions despite constant interruption for touch-ups, clothing, and set changes, can be stressful. Yet, successful models interact with a variety of people and enjoy frequent travel. They may meet potential clients at several go-sees in 1 day and often travel to work in distant cities, foreign countries, and exotic locations.

Employment

Demonstrators, product promoters, and models held about 92,000 jobs in 1998; about 9 out of 10 were demonstrator and product promoter jobs. About 46 percent of salaried jobs were in miscellaneous business services—which includes trade shows and demonstration services—and about 12 percent were in personnel supply services, which includes modeling agencies. Others worked in advertising, department stores, drug stores, grocery and related products wholesalers, grocery stores, management and public relations, and computer and data processing services. Less than 1 out of 20 was self-employed.

Demonstrator and product promoter jobs may be found in communities throughout the Nation, but modeling jobs are concentrated in New York, Los Angeles, and Miami.

Training, Other Qualifications, and Advancement

Formal training and education requirements are relatively few for demonstrators, product promoters, and models. Training is usually short-term, occurring over a period of days or weeks. Post-secondary education, while helpful, is usually not required. About 54 percent of these workers have no more than a high school diploma.

Demonstrators and product promoters usually receive on-the-job training. Training is primarily product-oriented since a demonstrator must be familiar with the product to demonstrate it properly. The length of training varies with the complexity of the product. Experience with the product or familiarity with similar products may be required for demonstration of complex products such as computers. During the training process, demonstrators may be familiarized with the manufacturer's corporate philosophy and preferred methods for dealing with customers.

Employers look for demonstrators and product promoters with good communication skills and a pleasant appearance and personality because dealing directly with the public can be challenging and difficult. Demonstrators and product promoters must be comfortable with public speaking. They should be able to entertain an audience and use humor, spontaneity, and personal interest in the product. Foreign language skills are helpful in many areas of the country.

While no formal training is required to begin a modeling career, models should be photogenic and have a basic knowledge of hair styling, make-up, and clothing. Some local governments require models under the age of 18 to hold a work permit. An attractive physical appearance is necessary to become a successful model. A model should also have flawless skin, healthy hair, and attractive facial features. Models must be within certain ranges for height, weight, and dress or coat size in order to meet the practical needs of fashion designers, photographers, and advertisers. Requirements may change slightly from time to time as our society's perceptions about physical beauty change; however, most fashion designers feel their clothing looks its best on tall, thin models. Although physical requirements may be relaxed for some types of modeling jobs, opportunities for those who do not meet these basic requirements are limited.

Because a model's career depends on preservation of his or her physical characteristics, models must control their diet, exercise regularly, and get enough sleep in order to stay healthy. Haircuts, pedicures, and manicures are necessary work-related expenses for models.

In addition to possessing physical beauty, models must be photogenic. The ability to relate to the camera in order to capture the desired look on film is essential and agents test prospective models using snapshots or professional photographs. For photographic and runway work, models must be able to move gracefully and confidently. Training in acting, voice, and dance is useful and allows a model to be considered for television work. Foreign language skills are useful because successful models travel frequently to foreign countries.

Since models must interact with a large number of people, personality plays an important role in success. Models must be professional, polite, and prompt; every contact could lead to future employment. Organizational skills are necessary to manage personal lives, financial matters, and busy work and travel schedules. Because competition for jobs is high and clients' needs are very specific, patience and persistence are essential.

Modeling schools provide training in posing, walking, make-up application, and other basic tasks, but do not necessarily lead to job opportunities. In fact, many agents prefer beginning models with little or no previous experience and discourage models from attending modeling schools and purchasing professional photographs. A model's selection of an agency is an important factor for advancement in the occupation. The better the reputation and skill of the agency, the more assignments a model is likely to get. Most clients prefer to work with agents so it is very difficult for a model to pursue a freelance career.

Agents continually scout for new faces and many of the top models are discovered in this way. Most agencies review snapshots or have open calls, where models are seen in person; this service is usually provided free of charge. Some agencies sponsor modeling contests and searches. Very few people who send in snapshots or attend open calls are offered contracts.

Agencies advise models on how to dress, wear make-up, and conduct themselves properly during go-sees and bookings. Because models' advancement depends on their previous work, development of a good portfolio is key to getting assignments. Models accumulate and display current tear sheets—examples of a model's editorial print work—and testing photographs in the portfolio. The higher the quality and currency of the photos in the portfolio, the more likely the model will find work.

Demonstrators and product promoters who perform well and show leadership ability may advance to other marketing and sales occupations or open their own businesses. Because modeling careers are relatively short, most eventually transfer to other occupations.

Job Outlook

The overall employment of demonstrators, product promoters, and models is expected to grow faster than the average through the year 2008. Job growth should be driven by growth in the number and size of trade shows and growth in the personnel supply services industry, which is among the fastest growing industries in the Nation. Additional job openings will arise from the need to replace demonstrators, product promoters, and models who transfer to other occupations, retire, or stop working for other reasons.

Job openings should be plentiful for demonstrators and product promoters through the year 2008. Employers may have difficulty finding qualified demonstrators who are willing to fill part-time, short term positions. In addition, product demonstration is considered a very effective marketing tool. Job growth should occur as firms devote a greater percentage of marketing budgets to product demonstration.

Because modeling is considered a glamorous occupation and there is a lack of formal entry requirements, those who wish to pursue a modeling career can expect keen competition for jobs. The modeling profession typically attracts many more job seekers than there are job openings available. Only models that closely meet the unique requirements of the occupation will achieve regular employment. The increasing diversification of the general population should require models representative of more diverse racial and ethnic groups. Work for male models should also increase as society becomes more receptive to the marketing of men's fashions. Because fashions change frequently, demand for a model's "look" may fluctuate; most models experience periods of unemployment.

Employment of demonstrators, product promoters, and models is affected by downturns in the business cycle. Many firms tend to reduce advertising budgets during recessions.

Earnings

Median hourly earnings of demonstrators and product promoters were $8.14 in 1998. The middle 50 percent earned between $6.95 and $9.71. The lowest 10 percent earned less than $6.17 and the highest 10 percent earned more than $13.16.

Employers of demonstrators, product promoters, and models generally pay for job-related travel expenses.

Earnings vary for different types of modeling and depend on the experience and reputation of the model. Female models typically earn more than male models for similar work. Models' hourly earnings can be relatively high, particularly for supermodels and others in high demand, but models may not have work every day, and jobs may last only a few hours. Models occasionally receive clothing or clothing discounts instead of or in addition to regular earnings. Almost all models work with agents and pay 15 to 20 percent of their earnings to receive an agent's services. Models who do not find immediate work may receive payments, called advances, from agents to cover promotional and living expenses. Models, like other self-employed workers, must provide their own health and retirement benefits.

Related Occupations

Demonstrators, product promoters, and models create public interest in buying clothing and products. Related marketing and sales occupations include retail sales workers, sales representatives, travel agents, insurance agents and brokers, and real estate agents and brokers.

Sources of Additional Information

For information about careers in modeling contact:

☛ The Models Guild, Office and Professional Employees International Union, AFL-CIO, CLC, 265 W. 14th Street, Suite 203, New York, NY 10011. Internet: **http://www.opeiu.org/models/tmg/main.htm**

For information about modeling schools and agencies in your area, contact a local consumer affairs organization such as the Better Business Bureau.

Insurance Sales Agents

(O*NET 43002)

Significant Points

- In spite of little or no employment growth, job opportunities should be good for people with the right skills.
- Employers prefer to hire college graduates and persons with proven sales ability or success in other occupations.
- Many beginners find it difficult to establish a sufficiently large clientele in this highly competitive business; consequently, some eventually leave for other jobs.

Nature of the Work

Most people have their first contact with an insurance company through an insurance sales agent or broker. These professionals help individuals, families, and businesses select insurance policies that provide the best protection for their lives, health, and property. *Insurance sales agents* may work exclusively for one insurance company or as "independent agents" selling for several companies. *Insurance brokers* represent several companies and place insurance policies for their clients with the company that offers the best rate and coverage. In either case, agents and brokers prepare reports, maintain records, seek out new clients, and, in the event of a loss, help policyholders settle insurance claims. Increasingly, some may also offer their clients financial analysis or advice on ways they can minimize risk.

Technology has greatly impacted the insurance agency, making it much more efficient and giving the agent the ability to take on more clients. Computers are now linked directly to the insurance companies, making the task of obtaining price quotes, and processing applications and service requests, much easier and faster. Computers also allow the agent to be better informed about new products that the insurance carriers may be offering.

Insurance sales agents may work evenings and weekends to accommodate clients.

Insurance sales agents sell one or more types of insurance, such as life, property damage and liability, health, disability, and long-term care. Life insurance agents specialize in selling policies that pay beneficiaries when a policyholder dies. Depending on the policyholder's circumstances, a cash-value policy can be designed to provide retirement income, funds for the education of children, or other benefits. Life insurance agents also sell annuities that promise a retirement income. Health insurance agents sell health insurance policies that cover the costs of medical care and loss of income due to illness or injury. They may also sell dental insurance and short and long-term disability insurance policies.

Property and casualty insurance agents and brokers sell policies that protect individuals and businesses from financial loss resulting from automobile accidents, fire, theft, storms, and other events that can damage property. For businesses, property and casualty insurance can also cover injured workers' compensation, product liability claims, or medical malpractice claims.

An increasing number of insurance agents and brokers offer comprehensive financial planning services to their clients, such as retirement planning, estate planning, or assistance in setting up pension plans for businesses. As a result, many insurance agents and brokers are involved in "cross-selling" or "total account development." Besides insurance, these agents may become licensed to sell mutual funds, variable annuities, and other securities. (See the statement on securities, commodities, and financial services sales representatives elsewhere in the *Handbook*.)

Because insurance sales agents obtain many new accounts through referrals, it is important that agents maintain regular contact with their clients to ensure their financial needs are being met. Developing a satisfied clientele that will recommend an agent's services to other potential customers is a key to success in this field. It is also becoming increasingly necessary for agents to develop new ways of marketing to compete with the insurance companies who sell directly to clients. Therefore, familiarity with the Internet may become important for obtaining future sales.

Working Conditions

Most insurance agents and brokers are based in small offices, from which they contact clients and provide insurance policy information. However, most of their time may be spent outside their offices, traveling locally to meet with clients, close sales, or investigate claims. Agents usually determine their own hours of work and often schedule evening and weekend appointments for the convenience of clients. Although most agents and brokers work a 40-hour week, some work 60 hours a week or longer. Commercial sales agents and brokers in particular may meet with clients during business hours and then spend evenings doing paperwork and preparing presentations to prospective clients.

Employment

Insurance agents and brokers held about 387,000 jobs in 1998. The following tabulation shows the percent distribution of wage and salary jobs by industry:

Industry	Percent
Insurance agents, brokers, and services	48
Life insurance carriers	26
Property and casualty insurance carriers	13
Medical service and health insurance carriers	6
Pension funds and miscellaneous insurance carriers	2
Other industries	5

While most insurance agents employed in wage and salary positions work for insurance agencies, nearly an equal number work directly for insurance carriers. Most of these agents are employed by life insurance companies, and a smaller number work for property, casualty, and medical and health insurance companies. Although most insurance agents specialize in life and health or property and casualty insurance, a growing number of "multiline agents" sell all lines of insurance. Approximately 3 out of 10 agents and brokers are self-employed.

Agents and brokers are employed throughout the country, but most work in or near large urban centers. Some insurance agents and brokers are employed in the headquarters of insurance companies, but the majority work out of local offices or independent agencies.

Training, Other Qualifications, and Advancement

For insurance agency jobs, most companies and independent agencies prefer to hire college graduates—particularly those who have majored in business or economics. A few hire high school graduates with proven sales ability or who have been successful in other types of work. In fact, most entrants to agent and broker jobs transfer from other occupations. In selling commercial insurance, technical experience in a field can be very beneficial in helping to sell policies to those in the same profession. As a result, new agents and brokers tend to be older than entrants in many other occupations.

College training may help agents or brokers grasp the technical aspects of insurance policies and the fundamentals and procedures of selling insurance. Many colleges and universities offer courses in insurance, and a few schools offer a bachelor's degree in insurance. College courses in finance, mathematics, accounting, economics, business law, marketing, and business administration enable insurance agents or brokers to understand how social and economic conditions relate to the insurance industry. Courses in psychology, sociology, and public speaking can prove useful in improving sales techniques. In addition, familiarity with computers and popular software packages has become very important, as computers provide instantaneous information on a wide variety of financial products and greatly improve agents' and brokers' efficiency.

Insurance agents and brokers must obtain a license in the States where they plan to sell insurance. Separate licenses are required for agents to sell life and health insurance and property and casualty insurance. In most States, licenses are issued only to applicants who complete specified pre-licensing courses and pass State examinations covering insurance fundamentals and State insurance laws. Agents and brokers who plan to sell mutual funds and other securities must also obtain a separate securities license from the National Association of Securities Dealers.

A number of organizations offer professional designation programs, which certify expertise in specialties such as life, health, property and casualty insurance, or financial consulting. Although these are voluntary, such programs assure clients and employers that an agent has a thorough understanding of the relevant specialty. Many professional societies now require agents to commit to continuing education in order to retain their designation.

Indeed, as the diversity of financial products sold by insurance agents and brokers increases, employers are placing greater emphasis on continuing professional education. It is important for insurance agents and brokers to keep up to date with issues concerning clients. Changes in tax laws, government benefit programs, and other State and Federal regulations can affect the insurance needs of clients and how agents conduct business. Agents and brokers can enhance their selling skills and broaden their knowledge of insurance and other financial services by taking courses at colleges and universities and by attending institutes, conferences, and seminars sponsored by insurance organizations. Most States have mandatory continuing education requirements focusing on insurance laws, consumer protection, and the technical details of various insurance policies.

Insurance agents and brokers should be enthusiastic, confident, disciplined, hard working, willing to solve problems, and able to communicate effectively. They should be able to inspire customer confidence. Because they usually work without supervision, agents and brokers must be able to plan their time well and have the initiative to locate new clients.

An insurance agent who shows sales ability and leadership may become a sales manager in a local office. A few advance to agency superintendent or executive positions. However, many who have built up a good clientele prefer to remain in sales work. Some, particularly in the property/casualty field, establish their own independent agencies or brokerage firms.

Job Outlook

Although employment of insurance agents and brokers is expected to show little growth through 2008, opportunities for agents will be favorable for persons with the right skills. This includes ambitious people who enjoy competitive sales work, have excellent interpersonal skills, and have developed expertise in a wide range of insurance and financial services. Because many beginners find it difficult to establish a suffi ciently large clientele in this commission-based occupation, some eventually leave for other jobs. Most job openings are likely to result from the need to replace agents who leave the occupation and the large number of agents expected to retire in the coming years.

Future demand for agents and brokers largely depends on the volume of sales of insurance and other financial products. While sales of life insurance are down, rising incomes and a concern for financial security during retirement are lifting sales of annuities, mutual funds, and other financial products sold by insurance agents. Sales of health and long-term care insurance are also expected to rise sharply as the population ages and as the law provides more people access to health insurance. In addition, a growing population will increase the demand for insurance for automobiles, homes, and high-priced valuables and equipment. As new businesses emerge and existing firms expand coverage, sales of commercial insurance should also increase, including coverage such as product liability, workers' compensation, employee benefits, and pollution liability insurance.

Employment of agents and brokers will not keep up with the rising level of insurance sales, however. One of the major reasons for this is rising productivity resulting from the growing application of computers to recordkeeping and cost calculations in insurance. Also, as competition grows and insurance companies attempt to find ways to reduce costs, many are seeking alternative, cheaper ways to distribute their products. For example, an increasing number of insurance companies are hiring their own sales staff to sell personal lines policies directly to the consumer over the phone and through the mail, thereby reducing the need for independent sales agents. In addition, sales of insurance products over the Internet are expected to increase.

A major source of growing competition over the next 10 years is the prospect of banks entering into this market. Currently, only a small number of banks sell insurance directly to consumers due to regulations that prohibit most banks from selling insurance and securities. These barriers are expected to fall in the near future and banks are anticipated to enter the broader financial services market. This will hurt the demand for agents in the long run as bank employees sell more insurance policies. In the short run, however, it may open up new opportunities for agents as banks hire licensed, experienced agents to sell insurance for them.

In spite of these trends, insurance and investments are becoming more complex, and many people and businesses lack the time and expertise to buy insurance without the advice of an agent. Insurance agents who are knowledgeable about their products and sell multiple lines of insurance and other financial products will remain in demand. Additionally, agents who take advantage of direct mail and Internet resources to advertise and promote their products can reduce the time it takes to develop sales leads, allowing them to concentrate on following up on potential clients. Most individuals and businesses consider insurance a necessity, regardless of economic conditions. Therefore, agents are not likely to face unemployment because of a recession.

Earnings

The median annual earnings of wage and salary insurance sales workers were $34,370 in 1998. The middle 50 percent earned between $24,650 and $52,020. The lowest 10 percent had earnings of $17,870 or less, while the top 10 percent earned over $91,890. Median annual earnings in the industries employing the largest number of insurance sales workers in 1997 were:

Fire, marine, and casualty insurance	$34,100
Insurance agents, brokers, and services	33,200
Medical service and health insurance	31,600
Life insurance	31,500

Many independent agents are paid by commission only, whereas sales workers who are employees of an agency or an insurance carrier may be paid in one of three ways—salary only, salary plus commission, or salary plus bonus. In general, commissions are the most common form of compensation, especially for experienced agents. The amount of commission depends on the type and amount of insurance sold, and whether the transaction is a new policy or a renewal. Bonuses are usually awarded when agents meet their sales goals or when an agency's profit goals are met. Some agents involved with financial planning receive a fee for their services rather than a commission.

Company-paid benefits to sales agents usually include continuing education, paid licensing training, group insurance plans, and office space and clerical support services. Some may pay for automobile and transportation expenses, attendance at conventions and meetings, promotion and marketing expenses, and retirement plans. Independent agents working for insurance agencies receive fewer benefits, but their commissions may be higher to help them pay for marketing and other expenses.

Related Occupations

Other workers who sell financial products or services include real estate agents and brokers, securities and financial services sales representatives, financial advisors, estate planning specialists, and manufacturers' sales workers.

Sources of Additional Information

Occupational information about insurance agents and brokers is available from the home office of many life and casualty insurance companies. Information on State licensing requirements may be obtained from the department of insurance at any State capital.

For information about insurance sales careers and training, contact:

☛ Independent Insurance Agents of America, 127 S. Peyton St., Alexandria, VA 22314. Internet: **http://www.iiaa.org**

☛ Insurance Vocational Education Student Training (InVEST), 127 S. Peyton St., Alexandria, VA 22314. Internet: **http://www.investprogram.org**

☛ National Association of Professional Insurance Agents, 400 N. Washington St., Alexandria, VA 22314. Internet: **http://www.pianet.com**

For information about health insurance sales careers, contact:

☛ National Association of Health Underwriters, 2000 N. 14th St., Ste. 450, Arlington, VA 22201. Internet: **http://www.nahu.org**

For information about insurance careers in the property and casualty field, contact:

☛ Insurance Information Institute, 110 William Street, New York, NY 10038.

For information regarding training for life insurance sales careers, contact:

☛ Life Underwriting Training Council, 7625 Wisconsin Ave., Bethesda, MD 20814.

For information about professional designation programs, contact:

☛ The American College, 270 Bryn Mawr Ave., Bryn Mawr, PA 19010-2195. Internet: **http://www.amercoll.edu**

☛ Society of Certified Insurance Counselors, 3630 North Hills Dr., Austin, TX 78731. Internet: **http://www.scic.com/alliance**

☛ The American Institute for Chartered Property and Casualty Underwriters, and the Insurance Institute of America, 720 Providence Rd., P.O. Box 3016, Malvern, PA 19355. Internet: **http://www.aicpcu.org**

Manufacturers' and Wholesale Sales Representatives

(O*NET 49002, 49005B, 49005C, 49005D, 49005F, 49005G, 49008)

Significant Points

- Many are self-employed manufacturers' agents who work for a commission.
- Although employers place an emphasis on a strong educational background, many individuals with previous sales experience still enter the occupation without a college degree.
- Many jobs require a great deal of travel.

Nature of the Work

Sales representatives are an important part of manufacturers' and wholesalers' success. Regardless of the type of product they sell, their primary duties are to interest wholesale and retail buyers and purchasing agents in their merchandise and to address any of the client's questions or concerns. They also advise clients on methods to reduce costs, use their products, and increase sales. Sales representatives market their company's products to manufacturers, wholesale and retail establishments, government agencies, and other institutions. (Retail salespersons, who sell directly to consumers, are discussed elsewhere in the *Handbook.*)

Depending on where they work, sales representatives have different job titles. Those employed directly by a manufacturer or wholesaler usually are called *sales representatives. Manufacturers' agents* are self-employed sales workers who contract their services to all types of manufacturing companies. Those selling technical products, for both manufacturers and wholesalers, are usually called *industrial sales workers* or *sales engineers.* However, many of these titles are used interchangeably.

Manufacturers' and wholesale sales representatives spend much of their time traveling to and visiting with prospective buyers and current clients. During a sales call, they discuss the customers' needs and suggest how their merchandise or services can meet those needs. They may show samples or catalogs that describe items their company stocks and inform customers about prices, availability, and how their products can save money and improve productivity. A vast number of manufacturers and wholesalers sell similar products, thus sales representatives must emphasize any unique qualities of their products and services. As independent agents, they might sell several complementary products made by different manufacturers and thus take an overall systems approach to their customer's business. Sales representatives may help install new equipment and train employees. They also take orders and resolve any problems or complaints with the merchandise.

Sales engineers are among the most highly trained sales workers. They usually sell products whose installation and optimal use requires a great deal of technical expertise and support—products such as material handling equipment, numerical-control machinery, and computer systems. Additionally, they provide information on their firm's products, help prospective and current buyers with technical problems, recommend improved materials and machinery for a firm's manufacturing process, design plans of proposed machinery layouts, estimate cost savings, and suggest training schedules for employees. In a process that may take several months, they present this information and negotiate the sale. Aided by a laptop computer connected to the Internet, they can often answer technical and nontechnical questions immediately.

Frequently, sales representatives who lack technical expertise work as a team with a technical expert. In this arrangement, the technical expert will attend the sales presentation to explain the product and answer questions or concerns. The sales representative makes the preliminary contact with customers, introduces the company's product, and closes the sale. The representative is then able to spend more time maintaining and soliciting accounts and less time acquiring technical knowledge. After the sale, representatives may make follow-up visits to ensure the equipment is functioning properly and may even help train customers' employees to operate and maintain new equipment.

Those selling consumer goods often suggest how and where merchandise should be displayed. Working with retailers, they may help arrange promotional programs, store displays, and advertising.

Obtaining new accounts is an important part of the job. Sales representatives follow leads from other clients, track advertisements in trade journals, participate in trade shows and conferences, and may visit potential clients unannounced. In addition, they may spend time meeting with and entertaining prospective clients during evenings and weekends.

Sales representatives have several duties beyond selling products. They also analyze sales statistics; prepare reports; and handle administrative duties, such as filing their expense account reports, scheduling appointments, and making travel plans. They study literature about new and existing products and monitor the sales, prices, and products of their competitors.

Manufacturers' agents who operate a sales agency must also manage their business. This requires organizational skills as well as knowledge of accounting, marketing, and administration.

A sales representative discusses the advantages of a product with a potential customer.

Working Conditions

Some manufacturers' and wholesale sales representatives have large territories and travel considerably. A sales region may cover several States, and so they may be away from home for several days or weeks at a time. Others work near their "home base" and travel mostly by automobile. Due to the nature of the work and the amount of travel, sales representatives typically work more than 40 hours per week.

Although the hours are long and often irregular, most sales representatives have the freedom to determine their own schedule. Consequently, they can arrange their appointments so they can have time off when they want it.

Dealing with different types of people can be demanding but stimulating. Sales representatives often face competition from representatives of other companies as well as from fellow workers. Companies usually set goals or quotas that representatives are expected to meet. Since their earnings depend on commissions, manufacturers' agents are also under the added pressure to maintain and expand their clientele.

Employment

Manufacturers' and wholesale sales representatives held about 1.5 million jobs in 1998. Three of every 4 salaried representatives worked in wholesale trade—mostly for distributors of machinery and equipment, groceries and related products, and motor vehicles and parts. Others were employed in manufacturing and mining. Due to the diversity of products and services sold, employment opportunities are available in every part of the country in all kinds of industries.

In addition to those working directly for a firm, many sales representatives are self-employed manufacturers' agents. They often form small sales firms and work for a straight commission based on the value of their own sales. However, manufacturers' agents usually gain experience and recognition with a manufacturer or wholesaler before becoming self-employed.

Training, Other Qualifications, and Advancement

The background needed for sales jobs varies by product line and market. The number of college graduates has increased and the job requirements have become more technical and analytical. Most firms now emphasize a strong educational background. Nevertheless, many employers still hire individuals with previous sales experience who do not have a college degree. For some consumer products, other factors such as sales ability, personality, and familiarity with brands are as important as a degree. On the other hand, firms selling industrial products often require a degree in science or engineering in addition to some sales experience. In general, companies are looking for the best and brightest individuals who have the personality and desire to sell.

Many companies have formal training programs for beginning sales representatives lasting up to two years. However, most businesses are accelerating these programs to reduce costs and expedite the returns from training. In some programs, trainees rotate among jobs in plants and offices to learn all phases of production, installation, and distribution of the product. In others, trainees take formal classroom instruction at the plant, followed by on-the-job training under the supervision of a field sales manager. Some sales representatives complete certification courses to become Certified Professional Manufacturers' Representatives (CPMRs).

New workers may be trained by accompanying experienced workers on their sales calls. As they gain familiarity with the firm's products and clients, these workers are given increasing responsibility until they are eventually assigned their own territory. As businesses experience greater competition, increased pressure is placed upon sales representatives to produce faster.

These workers stay abreast of new merchandise and the changing needs of their customers in a variety of ways. They attend trade shows where new products and technologies are showcased. They also attend conferences and conventions to meet other sales representatives and clients and discuss new product developments. In addition, the entire sales force may participate in company-sponsored meetings to review sales performance, product development, sales goals, and profitability.

Those who want to become manufacturers' and wholesale sales representatives should be goal-oriented, persuasive, and work well both independently and as part of a team. A pleasant personality and appearance, the ability to communicate well with people and problem-solving skills are highly valued. Furthermore, completing a sale can take several months and thus requires patience and perseverance. These workers are on their feet for long periods and may carry heavy sample cases, which necessitates some physical stamina. They should also enjoy traveling. Sales representatives spend much of their time visiting current and prospective clients.

Frequently, promotion takes the form of an assignment to a larger account or territory where commissions are likely to be greater. Experienced sales representatives may move into jobs as sales trainers, who instruct new employees on selling techniques and company policies and procedures. Those who have good sales records and leadership ability may advance to sales supervisor or district manager.

In addition to advancement opportunities within a firm, some manufacturers' agents go into business for themselves. Others find opportunities in purchasing, advertising, or marketing research.

Job Outlook

Overall, employment of manufacturers' and wholesale sales representatives is expected to grow more slowly than the average for all occupations through the year 2008. Continued growth due to the increasing variety and number of goods to be sold will be tempered by the increased effectiveness and efficiency of sales workers. Many job openings will result from the need to replace workers who transfer to other occupations or leave the labor force.

Prospective customers will still require sales workers to demonstrate or illustrate the particulars about the good or service. However, technology is expected to make them more effective and productive, for example, by providing accurate and current information to customers during sales presentations.

Within manufacturing, job opportunities for manufacturers' agents should be somewhat better than those for sales representatives. Manufacturers are expected to continue outsourcing sales duties to manufacturers' agents rather than using in-house or direct selling personnel. To their advantage, these agents are more likely to work in a sales area or territory longer than representatives, creating a better working relationship and understanding how customers operate their businesses. Also, by using agents who usually lend their services to more than one company, companies can share costs with the other companies involved with that agent.

Those interested in this occupation should keep in mind that direct selling opportunities in manufacturing are likely to be best for products with strong demand. Furthermore, jobs will be most plentiful in small wholesale and manufacturing firms because a growing number of these companies will rely on wholesalers' and manufacturers' agents to market their products as a way to control their costs and expand their customer base.

Employment opportunities and earnings may fluctuate from year to year because sales are affected by changing economic conditions, legislative issues, and consumer preferences. Prospects will be best for those with the appropriate knowledge or technical expertise as well as the personal traits necessary for successful selling.

Earnings

Compensation methods vary significantly by the type of firm and product sold. Most employers use a combination of salary and commission or salary plus bonus. Commissions are usually based on the amount of sales, whereas bonuses may depend on individual performance, on the performance of all sales workers in the group or district, or on the company's performance.

Median annual earnings of sales representatives, except retail, were $36,540, including commission, in 1998. The middle 50 percent earned between $26,350 and $51,580 a year. The lowest 10 percent earned less than $19,220 and the highest 10 percent earned more than $83,000 a year. Median annual earnings in the industries employing the largest number of sales representatives, except retail, in 1997 were as follows:

Industry	Earnings
Electrical goods	$36,700
Paper and paper products	36,700
Machinery, equipment, and supplies	36,400
Professional and commercial equipment	35,300
Groceries and related products	31,900

Median annual earnings of sales engineers, including commission, in 1998 were $54,600. The middle 50 percent earned between $41,240 and $79,480 a year. The lowest 10 percent earned less than $30,560 and the highest 10 percent earned more than $97,700 a year. Median annual earnings in the industries employing the largest number of sales engineers in 1997 were as follows:

Industry	Earnings
Computer and data processing services	$62,800
Electrical goods	56,600
Professional and commercial equipment	51,700
Machinery, equipment, and supplies	48,900

In addition to their earnings, sales representatives and engineers are usually reimbursed for expenses such as transportation costs, meals, hotels, and entertaining customers. They often receive benefits such as health and life insurance, pension plan, vacation and sick leave, personal use of a company car, and frequent flyer mileage. Some companies offer incentives such as free vacation trips or gifts for outstanding sales workers.

Unlike those working directly for a manufacturer or wholesaler, manufacturers' agents are paid strictly on commission. Depending on the type of product or products they are selling, their experience in the field, and the number of clients, their earnings can be significantly higher or lower than those working in direct sales. In addition, self-employed manufacturers' agents must pay their own travel, entertainment, and benefit expenses.

Related Occupations

Manufacturers' and wholesale sales representatives must have sales ability and knowledge of the products they sell. Other occupations that require similar skills are: advertising, marketing, and public relations managers; insurance sales agents; purchasing managers, buyers, and purchasing agents; real estate agents and brokers; securities, commodities, and financial services sales representatives; and services sales representatives.

Sources of Additional Information

Information on manufacturers' agents is available from:

☛ Manufacturers' Agents National Association, P.O. Box 3467, Laguna Hills, CA 92654-3467. Internet: **http://www.manaonline.org**

Career and certification information is available from:

☛ Sales and Marketing Executives International, 5500 Interstate North Pkwy., No. 545, Atlanta, GA 30328. Internet: **http://www.smei.org**

☛ Manufacturers' Representatives Educational Research Foundation, P.O. Box 247, Geneva, IL 60134. Internet: **http://www.mrerf.org**

Real Estate Agents and Brokers

(O*NET 43008)

Significant Points

- Real estate sales positions should continue to be relatively easy to obtain due to the large number of people who leave this occupation each year.

- Real estate agents and brokers must be licensed in every State and in the District of Columbia.

Nature of the Work

The purchase or sale of a home or investment property is not only one of the most important financial events in peoples' lives, but also one of the most complex transactions. As a result, people usually seek the help of real estate agents and brokers when buying or selling real estate.

Real estate agents and brokers have a thorough knowledge of the real estate market in their community. They know which neighborhoods will best fit clients' needs and budgets. They are familiar with local zoning and tax laws, and know where to obtain financing. Agents and brokers also act as an intermediary in price negotiations between buyers and sellers. Real estate agents are usually independent sales workers who provide their services to a licensed broker on a contract basis. In return, the broker pays the agent a portion of the commission earned from the agent's sale of the property.

Brokers are independent business people who, for a fee, sell real estate owned by others; they also may rent and manage properties for a fee. When selling real estate, brokers arrange for title searches and for meetings between buyers and sellers where details of the transactions are agreed upon and the new owners take possession. A broker's knowledge, resourcefulness, and creativity in arranging favorable financing for the prospective buyer often mean the difference between success and failure in closing a sale. In some cases, brokers and agents assume primary responsibility for closing sales; in others, lawyers or lenders do this. Brokers supervise agents who may have many of the same job duties. Brokers also manage their own offices, advertise properties, and handle other business matters. Some combine other types of work, such as selling insurance or practicing law, with their real estate business.

There is more to an agent or broker's job than just making sales. They must have properties to sell. Consequently, they spend a significant amount of time obtaining listings—owner agreements to place properties for sale with the firm. When listing a property for sale, agents and brokers compare the listed property with similar properties that have recently sold to determine its competitive market price. Once the property is sold, the agent who sold the property and the agent who obtained the listing both receive a portion of the commission. Thus, agents who sell a property they also listed can increase their commission.

Most real estate agents and brokers sell residential property. A small number, usually employed in large or specialized firms, sell commercial, industrial, agricultural, or other types of real estate. Every specialty requires knowledge of that particular type of property and clientele. Selling or leasing business property requires an understanding of leasing practices, business trends, and location needs. Agents who sell or lease industrial properties must know about the region's transportation, utilities, and labor supply. Whatever the type of property, the agent or broker must know how to meet the client's particular requirements.

Before showing residential properties to potential buyers, agents meet with buyers to get a feeling for the type of home the buyers would like. In this prequalifying phase, the agent determines how much buyers can afford to spend. In addition, they usually sign a loyalty contract which states the agent will be the only one to show them houses. An agent or broker uses a computer to generate lists of properties for sale, their location and description, and available sources of financing. In some cases, agents and brokers use computers to give buyers a virtual tour of properties in which they are interested. Buyers can view interior and exterior images or floor plans without leaving the real estate office.

Agents may meet several times with prospective buyers to discuss and visit available properties. Agents identify and emphasize the most pertinent selling points. To a young family looking for a house, they may emphasize the convenient floor plan, the area's low crime rate, and the proximity to schools and shopping centers. To a potential investor, they may point out the tax advantages of owning a rental property and the ease of finding a renter. If bargaining over price becomes necessary, agents must carefully follow their client's instructions and may have to present counteroffers in order to get the best possible price.

Once both parties have signed the contract, the real estate broker or agent must see to it that all special terms of the contract are met before the closing date. For example, if the seller agrees to a home inspection or a termite and radon inspection, the agent must make sure this is done. Also, if the seller agrees to any repairs, the broker or agent must see they are made. Increasingly, brokers and agents handle environmental problems by making sure the properties they sell meet environmental regulations. For example, they may be responsible for dealing with problems such as lead paint on the walls. While loan officers, attorneys, or other persons handle many details, the agent must check to make sure that they are completed.

Working Conditions

Increasingly, real estate agents and brokers work out of their homes instead of real estate offices because of advances in telecommunications and the ability to retrieve data on properties over the Internet. Even with this convenience, much of their time is spent away from their desk—showing properties to customers, analyzing properties for sale, meeting with prospective clients, or researching the state of the market.

Agents and brokers often work more than a standard 40-hour week; nearly 1 out of every 4 worked 50 hours or more a week in 1998. They often work evenings and weekends, and are always on call to suit the needs of clients. Business is usually slower during the winter season. Although the hours are long and often irregular, most agents and brokers also have the freedom to determine their own schedule. Consequently, they can arrange their work so they can have time off when they want it.

Employment

Real estate agents and brokers held about 347,000 jobs in 1998. Many worked part time, combining their real estate activities with other careers. More than two-thirds of real estate agents and brokers were self-employed. Real estate is sold in all areas, but employment is concentrated in large urban areas and in smaller, but rapidly growing communities.

Most real estate firms are relatively small; indeed, some are a one-person business. Some large real estate firms have several hundred agents operating out of many branch offices. Many brokers have franchise agreements with national or regional real estate organizations. Under this type of arrangement, the broker pays a fee in exchange for the privilege of using the more widely known name of the parent organization. Although franchised brokers often receive help training salespeople and running their offices, they bear the ultimate responsibility for the success or failure of their firm.

A real estate agent prints information on available properties for a client.

Real estate agents and brokers are older, on average, than most other workers. Historically, many homemakers and retired persons were attracted to real estate sales by the flexible and part time work schedules characteristic of this field. They could enter, leave, and later reenter the occupation, depending on the strength of the real estate market, family responsibilities, or other personal circumstances. Recently, however, the attractiveness of part time work has declined, as increasingly complex legal and technological requirements raise startup costs associated with becoming an agent.

Training, Other Qualifications, and Advancement

In every State and in the District of Columbia, real estate agents and brokers must be licensed. Prospective agents must be a high school graduate, at least 18 years old, and pass a written test. The examination—more comprehensive for brokers than for agents—includes questions on basic real estate transactions and laws affecting the sale of property. Most States require candidates for the general sales license to complete between 30 and 90 hours of classroom instruction. Those seeking a broker's license need between 60 and 90 hours of formal training and a specific amount of experience selling real estate, usually one to three years. Some States waive the experience requirements for the broker's license for applicants who have a bachelor's degree in real estate.

State licenses typically must be renewed every one or two years, usually without reexamination. However, many States require continuing education for license renewal. Prospective agents and brokers should contact the real estate licensing commission of the State in which they wish to work to verify exact licensing requirements.

As real estate transactions have become more legally complex, many firms have turned to college graduates to fill positions. A large number of agents and brokers have some college training. College courses in real estate, finance, business administration, statistics, economics, law, and English are helpful. For those who intend to start their own company, business courses such as marketing and accounting are as important as those in real estate or finance.

Personality traits are equally as important as academic background. Brokers look for applicants who possess a pleasant personality, honesty, and a neat appearance. Maturity, tact, trust-worthiness, and enthusiasm for the job are required in order to motivate prospective customers in this highly competitive field. Agents should also be well organized, detail oriented, and have a good memory for names, faces, and business details.

Those interested in jobs as real estate agents often begin in their own communities. Their knowledge of local neighborhoods is a clear advantage. Under the direction of an experienced agent, beginners learn the practical aspects of the job, including the use of computers to locate or list available properties and identify sources of financing.

Many firms offer formal training programs for both beginners and experienced agents. Larger firms usually offer more extensive programs for both beginners and experienced agents. Larger firms usually offer more extensive programs than smaller firms do. Over 1,000 universities, colleges, and junior colleges offer courses in real estate. At some, a student can earn an associate or bachelor's degree with a major in real estate; several offer advanced degrees. Many local real estate associations that are members of the National Association of Realtors sponsor courses covering the fundamentals and legal aspects of the field. Advanced courses in mortgage financing, property development and management, and other subjects are also available through various affiliates of the National Association of Realtors.

Advancement opportunities for agents may take the form of higher commission rates. As agents gain knowledge and expertise, they become more efficient in closing a greater number of transactions and increase their earnings. Experienced agents can advance in many large firms to sales or general manager. Persons who have received their broker's license may open their own offices. Others with experience and training in estimating property value may become real estate appraisers, and people familiar with operating and maintaining rental properties may become property managers. (See the statement on property, real estate, and community association managers elsewhere in the *Handbook*). Experienced agents and brokers with a thorough knowledge of business conditions and property values in their localities may enter mortgage financing or real estate investment counseling.

Job Outlook

Employment of real estate agents and brokers is expected to grow about as fast as the average for all occupations through the year 2008. However, a large number of job openings will arise due to replacement needs. Each year, thousands of jobs will become available as workers transfer to other occupations or leave the labor force. Not everyone is successful in this highly competitive field; many beginners become discouraged by their inability to get listings and to close a sufficient number of sales. Well-trained, ambitious people who enjoy selling should have the best chance for success.

Increasing use of electronic information technology will increase the productivity of agents and brokers as computers, faxes, modems, and databases become commonplace. Some real estate companies use computer-generated images to show houses to customers without leaving the office. Internet sites contain information on vast numbers of homes for sale, available to anyone. These devices enable an agent to serve a greater number of customers. Use of this technology may eliminate some marginal agents such as those practicing real estate part time or between jobs. These workers will not be able to compete as easily with full time agents who have invested in this technology. Changing legal requirements, like disclosure laws, may also dissuade some that are not serious about practicing full time from continuing to work part time.

Another factor expected to impact the need for agents and brokers is the ability of prospective customers to conduct their own searches for properties that meet their criteria by accessing real estate information on the Internet. While they won't be able to conduct the entire real estate transaction on-line, it does allow the prospective buyer the convenience of making a more informed choice of properties to visit, as well as the ability to find out about financing, inspections, and appraisals.

Employment growth in this field will stem primarily from increased demand for home purchases and rental units. Shifts in the age distribution of the population over the next decade will result in a growing number of persons in the prime working ages with careers and family responsibilities. This is the most geographically mobile group in our society, and the one that traditionally makes most of the home purchases. As their incomes rise, they also may be expected to invest in additional real estate.

Employment of real estate agents and brokers is very sensitive to swings in the economy. During periods of declining economic activity and tight credit, the volume of sales and the resulting demand for sales workers falls. During these periods, the earnings of agents and brokers decline, and many work fewer hours or leave the occupation altogether.

Earnings

The median annual earnings of salaried real estate agents, including commission, in 1998 were $28,020. The middle 50 percent earned between $19,060 and $46,360 a year. The lowest 10 percent earned less than $13,800 and the highest 10 percent earned more than $83,330 a year. Median annual earnings in the industries employing the largest number of salaried real estate agents in 1997 were as follows:

Residential building construction	$32,300
Real estate agents and managers	25,500
Real estate operators and lessors	19,100

Median annual earnings of salaried real estate brokers, including commission, in 1998 were $45,640. The middle 50 percent earned between $28,680 and $80,070 a year.

Commissions on sales are the main source of earnings of real estate agents and brokers. The rate of commission varies according to agent and broker agreement, the type of property, and its value.

The percentage paid on the sale of farm and commercial properties or unimproved land is usually higher than the percentage paid for selling a home.

Commissions may be divided among several agents and brokers. The broker and the agent in the firm who obtained the listing usually share their commission when the property is sold; the broker and the agent in the firm who made the sale also usually share their part of the commission. Although an agent's share varies greatly from one firm to another, often it is about half of the total amount received by the firm. Agents who both list and sell a property maximize their commission.

Income usually increases as an agent gains experience, but individual ability, economic conditions, and the type and location of the property also affect earnings. Sales workers who are active in community organizations and local real estate associations can broaden their contacts and increase their earnings. A beginner's earnings are often irregular because a few weeks or even months may go by without a sale. Although some brokers allow an agent a drawing account against future earnings, this practice is not usual with new employees. The beginner, therefore, should have enough money to live on for about six months or until commissions increase.

Related Occupations

Selling expensive items such as homes requires maturity, tact, and a sense of responsibility. Other sales workers who find these character traits important in their work include motor vehicle sales workers; securities, commodities, and financial services sales representatives; insurance sales agents; and manufacturers' and wholesale sales representatives.

Sources of Additional Information

Information on license requirements for real estate agents and brokers is available from most local real estate organizations or from the State real estate commission or board.

For more information about opportunities in real estate, contact:

☛ National Association of Realtors, Realtor Information Center, 430 North Michigan Ave., Chicago, IL 60611.

Retail Salespersons

(O*NET 49011 and 49999C)

Significant Points

- Good employment opportunities are expected due to the need to replace the large number of workers who leave the occupation each year.
- Most salespersons work evening and weekend hours, and long hours during Christmas and other peak retail periods.
- Opportunities for part-time work are plentiful.

Nature of the Work

Whether selling shoes, computer equipment, or automobiles, retail salespersons assist customers in finding what they are looking for and try to interest them in buying the merchandise. They describe a product's features, demonstrate its use, or show various models and colors. For some sales jobs, particularly those selling expensive and complex items, retail salespersons need special knowledge or skills. For example, salespersons who sell automobiles must be able to explain to customers the features of various models, the meaning of manufacturers' specifications, and the types of options and financing available.

Consumers spend millions of dollars every day on merchandise and often form their impressions of a store by evaluating its sales force. Therefore, retailers are increasingly stressing the importance of providing courteous and efficient service in order to remain competitive. When a customer wants an item that is not on the sales floor, for example, the salesperson may check the stockroom, place a special order, or call another store to locate the item.

In addition to selling, most retail salespersons, especially those who work in department and apparel stores, make out sales checks; receive cash, check, and charge payments; bag or package purchases; and give change and receipts. Depending on the hours they work, retail salespersons may have to open or close cash registers. This may include counting the money; separating charge slips, coupons, and exchange vouchers; and making deposits at the cash office. Salespersons are often held responsible for the contents of their registers, and repeated shortages are cause for dismissal in many organizations. (Cashiers, who have similar job duties, are discussed elsewhere in the *Handbook.*)

Salespersons may also handle returns and exchanges of merchandise, wrap gifts, and keep their work areas neat. In addition, they may help stock shelves or racks, arrange for mailing or delivery of purchases, mark price tags, take inventory, and prepare displays.

Frequently, salespersons must be aware of special sales and promotions. They must also recognize possible security risks and thefts and know how to handle or prevent such situations.

Working Conditions

Most salespersons in retail trade work in clean, comfortable, well-lighted stores. However, they often stand for long periods and may need supervisory approval to leave the sales floor.

The Monday through Friday, 9 to 5 work week is the exception, rather than the rule, in retail trade. Most salespersons work some evening and weekend hours, and long hours during Christmas and other peak retail periods. In addition, most retailers restrict the use of vacation time from Thanksgiving until early January.

This job can be rewarding for those who enjoy working with people. Patience and courtesy are required, especially when the work is repetitious and the customers demanding.

Employment

Retail salespersons held about 4.6 million jobs in 1998. They worked in stores ranging from small specialty shops employing a few workers, to giant department stores with hundreds of salespersons. In addition, some were self-employed representatives of direct sales companies and mail-order houses. The largest employers of retail salespersons are department stores, clothing and accessories stores, furniture and home furnishing stores, and motor vehicle dealers.

This occupation offers many opportunities for part-time work and is especially appealing to students, retirees, and others looking to supplement their income. However, most of those selling "big ticket"

Retail salespersons have a thorough knowledge of the products they sell.

items, such as cars, furniture, and electronic equipment, work full time and have substantial experience.

Because retail stores are found in every city and town, employment is distributed geographically in much the same way as the population.

Training, Other Qualifications, and Advancement

There usually are no formal education requirements for this type of work, although a high school diploma or equivalent is increasingly preferred. Employers look for people who enjoy working with others and have the tact and patience to deal with difficult customers. Among other desirable characteristics are an interest in sales work, a neat appearance, and the ability to communicate clearly and effectively. The ability to speak more than one language may be helpful for employment in stores in communities where people from various cultures tend to live and shop. Before hiring a salesperson, some employers may conduct a background check, especially for a job selling high-priced items.

In most small stores, an experienced employee, or the proprietor, instructs newly-hired sales personnel in making out sales checks and operating cash registers. In large stores, training programs are more formal and usually conducted over several days. Topics usually discussed are customer service, security, the store's policies and procedures, and how to work a cash register. Depending on the type of product they are selling, they may be given additional specialized training by manufacturers' representatives. For example, those working in cosmetics receive instruction on the types of products available and for whom the cosmetics would be most beneficial. Likewise, salespersons employed by motor vehicle dealers may be required to participate in training programs designed to provide information on the technical details of standard and optional equipment available on new models. Because providing the best service to customers is a high priority for many employers, employees are often given periodic training to update and refine their skills.

As salespersons gain experience and seniority, they usually move to positions of greater responsibility and may be given their choice of departments. This often means moving to areas with potentially higher earnings and commissions. The highest earnings potential is usually found in selling big-ticket items. This type of position often requires the most knowledge of the product and the greatest talent for persuasion.

Opportunities for advancement vary in small stores. In some establishments, advancement is limited, because one person, often the owner, does most of the managerial work. In others, however, some salespersons are promoted to assistant managers.

Traditionally, capable salespersons without college degrees could advance to management positions. However today, large retail businesses usually prefer to hire college graduates as management trainees, making a college education increasingly important. Despite this trend, motivated and capable employees without college degrees should still be able to advance to administrative or supervisory positions in large establishments.

Retail selling experience may be an asset when applying for sales positions with larger retailers or in other industries, such as financial services, wholesale trade, or manufacturing.

Job Outlook

As in the past, employment opportunities for retail salespersons are expected to continue to be good because of the many job openings created each year due to the need to replace the large number of workers who transfer to other occupations or leave the labor force. Additional openings will be created by growth in employment of retail salespersons. Employment is expected to increase about as fast as the average for all occupations through the year 2008 due to anticipated growth in retail sales created by a growing population. There will continue to be many opportunities for part-time workers, and demand will be strong for temporary workers during peak selling periods, such as the Christmas season.

During economic downturns, sales volumes and the resulting demand for sales workers usually decline. Purchases of costly items, such as cars, appliances, and furniture, tend to be postponed during difficult economic times. In areas of high unemployment, sales of many types of goods decline. However, because turnover of sales workers is usually very high, employers often can adjust employment levels simply by not replacing all those who leave.

Earnings

The starting wage for many retail sales positions is the Federal minimum wage, which was $5.15 an hour in 1999. In areas where employers have difficulty attracting and retaining workers, wages tend to be higher than the established minimum.

Median hourly earnings of retail salespersons, including commission, in 1998 were $7.61. The middle 50 percent earned between $6.18 and $9.84 an hour. The lowest 10 percent earned less than $5.76 and the highest 10 percent earned more than $14.53 an hour. Median hourly earnings in the industries employing the largest number of retail salespersons in 1997 were as follows:

Industry	Earnings
New and used car dealers	$15.10
Department stores	6.90
Miscellaneous shopping goods stores	6.70
Family clothing stores	6.40
Women's clothing stores	6.20

Compensation systems vary by type of establishment and merchandise sold. Salespersons receive hourly wages, commissions, or a combination of wages and commissions. Under a commission system, salespersons receive a percentage of the sales that they make. This system offers sales workers the opportunity to significantly increase their earnings, but they may find their earnings strongly depend on their ability to sell their product and the ups and downs of the economy. Employers may use incentive programs such as awards, banquets, bonuses, and profit-sharing plans to promote teamwork among the sales staff.

Benefits may be limited in smaller stores, but in large establishments benefits are usually comparable to those offered by other employers. In addition, nearly all salespersons are able to buy their store's merchandise at a discount, with the savings depending upon on the type of merchandise.

Related Occupations

Salespersons use sales techniques, coupled with their knowledge of merchandise, to assist customers and encourage purchases. Workers in a number of other occupations use these skills, including manufacturers' and wholesale sales representatives; services sales representatives; securities, commodities, and financial services sales representatives; counter and rental clerks; real estate agents and brokers; purchasing managers, buyers, and purchasing agents; insurance sales agents; and cashiers.

Sources of Additional Information

Information on careers in retail sales may be obtained from the personnel offices of local stores, or from State merchants' associations.

General information about retailing is available from:

☛ National Retail Federation, 325 7th St. NW., Suite 1100, Washington, DC 20004. Internet: **http://www.nrf.com**

Information about retail sales employment opportunities is available from:

☛ United Food and Commercial Workers International Union, Education Office, 1775 K St. NW., Washington, DC 20006-1502.

☛ Retail, Wholesale, and Department Store Union, 30 East 29th St., 4th Floor, New York, NY 10016.

Information about training for a career in automobile sales is available from:

☛ National Automobile Dealers Association, Public Relations Dept., 8400 Westpark Dr., McLean, VA 22102-3591.

Retail Sales Worker Supervisors and Managers

(O*NET 41002)

Significant Points

- Opportunities will be best for candidates with experience as a retail salesperson, cashier, or customer service worker.
- Work schedules may be irregular and often include evenings and weekends.
- Increasingly, a post-secondary degree is needed for advancement into upper management.

Nature of the Work

In every one of the thousands of retail stores across the country, there is at least one retail sales worker supervisor or manager. Because the retail trade industry provides goods and services directly to customers, the retail supervisor or manager is responsible for ensuring that customers receive satisfactory service and quality goods. They also answer customers' inquiries and handle complaints.

Retail supervisors and managers oversee the work of retail salespersons, cashiers, customer service representatives, stock clerks, and grocery clerks. (Some of these occupations are discussed elsewhere in the *Handbook*.) They are responsible for interviewing, hiring, and training employees, as well as preparing work schedules and assigning workers to specific duties. (Managers in eating and drinking places are discussed in the *Handbook* statement on restaurant and food service managers.)

The responsibilities of retail sales worker supervisors and managers vary, depending on the size and type of establishment, as well as the level of management. As the size of retail stores and the types of goods and services increase, these workers increasingly specialize in one department or one aspect of merchandising. Larger organizations tend to have many layers of management. As in other industries, supervisory-level retail managers usually report to their mid-level counterparts who, in turn, report to top-level managers. Small stores, and stores that carry specialized merchandise, usually have fewer levels of management.

Supervisory-level retail managers, often referred to as department managers, provide day-to-day oversight of individual departments, such as shoes, cosmetics, or housewares in large department stores; produce and meat in grocery stores; and sales in automotive dealerships.

Retail sales worker supervisors and managers resolve customers' complaints and respond to inquiries.

Department managers commonly are found in large retail stores. These managers establish and implement policies, goals, objectives, and procedures for their specific departments; coordinate activities with other department heads; and strive for smooth operations within their departments. They supervise employees who price and ticket goods and place them on display; clean and organize shelves, displays, and inventory in stockrooms; and inspect merchandise to ensure that none is outdated. Department managers also review inventory and sales records, develop merchandising techniques, coordinate sales promotions, and may greet and assist customers and promote sales and good public relations.

In small or independent retail stores, retail sales worker supervisors and managers not only directly supervise sales associates, but are also responsible for the operation of the entire store. In these instances, they may be called store managers. Some are also self-employed store owners.

Working Conditions

Most retail sales worker supervisors and managers have offices within the stores. Although some time is spent in the office completing merchandise orders or arranging work schedules, a large portion of their workday is spent on the sales floor.

Work hours of supervisors and managers vary greatly among retail establishments, because work schedules usually depend on customers' needs. Most managers and supervisors work 40 hours or more a week; long hours are not uncommon. This is particularly true during sales, holidays, busy shopping hours, and when inventory is taken. They are expected to work evenings and weekends but usually are compensated by getting a weekday off. Hours can change weekly, and managers sometimes must report to work on short notice, especially when employees are absent. Independent owners can often set their own schedules, but hours must be convenient to customers.

Employment

Retail sales worker supervisors and managers held about 1.7 million jobs in 1998. About 2 out of 5 were self-employed retail sales managers, mainly store owners. Although managers work throughout the retail trade industry, most are found in grocery and department stores, motor vehicle dealers, and clothing and accessory stores.

Training, Other Qualifications, and Advancement

Retail sales worker supervisors and managers usually acquire knowledge of management principles and practices—an essential requirement for a management position in retail trade—through work experience. Many supervisors and managers begin their careers on the sales floor as salespersons, cashiers, or customer service workers. In these positions, they learn merchandising, customer service, and the basic policies and procedures of the store.

The educational background of retail sales worker supervisors and managers varies widely. Regardless of the education received, business courses, including accounting; administration; marketing; management; and sales; as well as courses in psychology; sociology; and communication, are helpful. Supervisors and managers must be computer literate because almost all cash registers and inventory control systems are now computerized.

Most supervisors and managers who have post-secondary education hold associate or bachelor's degrees in liberal arts, social science, business, or management. To gain experience, many post-secondary students participate in internship programs that are usually developed jointly by individual schools and retail firms.

Once on the job, the type and amount of training available for supervisors and managers varies from store to store. Many national chains have formal training programs for management trainees that include both classroom and in-store training. Training may last from 1 week to 1 year or more, because many retail organizations require their trainees to gain experience during all shopping seasons. Other retail organizations may not have formal training programs.

Ordinarily, classroom training includes such topics as interviewing and customer service skills, employee and inventory management, and scheduling. Management trainees may work in one specific department while training on the job, or they may rotate through several departments to gain a well-rounded knowledge of the store's operation. Training programs for franchises are generally extensive, covering all func tions of the company's operation, including promotion, marketing, management, finance, purchasing, product preparation, human resource management, and compensation. College graduates can usually enter management training programs directly.

Retail sales worker supervisors and managers must get along with all types of people. They need initiative, self-discipline, good judgment, and decisiveness. Patience and a mild temperament are necessary when dealing with demanding customers. They must also be able to motivate, organize, and direct the work of subordinates and communicate clearly and persuasively with customers and other managers.

Individuals who display leadership and team building skills, self-confidence, motivation, and decisiveness become candidates for promotion to assistant store manager or store manager. A post-secondary degree may speed advancement, because it is viewed by employers as a sign of motivation and maturity—qualities deemed important for promotion to more responsible positions. In many retail establishments, managers are promoted from within the company. In small retail establishments, where the number of positions is limited, advancement to a higher management position may come slowly. Large establishments most often have extensive career ladder programs and may offer managers the opportunity to transfer to another store in the chain or to the central office if an opening occurs. Although promotions may occur more quickly in large establishments, some managers must relocate every several years in order to advance. Within a central office, retail sales supervisors and managers can become advertising, marketing, and public relations managers. These managers coordinate marketing plans, monitor sales, and propose advertisements and promotions. Supervisors and managers can also become purchasing managers, buyers, and purchasing agents who purchase goods and supplies for their organization or for resale. (These occupations are covered in other *Handbook* statements.)

Some supervisors and managers, who have worked in the retail industry for a long time, open their own stores. However, retail trade is highly competitive, and although many independent retail owners succeed, some fail to cover expenses and eventually go out of business. To prosper, retail owners usually need good business sense and strong customer service and public relations skills.

Job Outlook

Because most jobs for retail sales worker supervisors and managers do not require post-secondary education, competition is expected for jobs with the most attractive earnings and working conditions. Candidates who have retail experience will have the best opportunities.

Employment of retail sales worker supervisors and managers is expected to grow more slowly than average for all occupations through the year 2008. Growth in this occupation will be restrained somewhat as retail companies place more emphasis on sales staff employment levels and increase the number of responsibilities their retail sales worker supervisors and managers have. Some companies may require their sales staff to report directly to upper management personnel, bypassing the department-level manager. However, many job openings are expected to occur as experienced supervisors and managers move into higher levels of management, transfer to other occupations, or leave the labor force.

Projected employment growth of retail managers will mirror, in part, the patterns of employment growth in the industries in which they are concentrated. For example, average growth is expected in grocery stores as they expand their selection of merchandise to accommodate customers' desires for one-stop shopping. The number of self-employed retail sales worker supervisors and managers is expected to decline as independent retailers face increasing competition from national chains.

Unlike middle- and upper-level management positions, store-level retail supervisors and managers generally will not be affected by the restructuring and consolidation taking place at the corporate and headquarters level of many retail chain companies.

Earnings

Salaries of retail managers vary substantially, depending upon the level of responsibility; length of service; and type, size, and location of the firm.

Median annual earnings of salaried marketing and sales worker supervisors, including commission, in 1998 were $29,570. The middle 50 percent earned between $21,850 and $42,640 a year. The lowest 10 percent earned less than $16,700 and the highest 10 percent earned more than $71,910 a year. Median annual earnings in the industries employing the largest number of salaried marketing and sales worker supervisors in 1997 were as follows:

New and used car dealers	$50,100
Grocery stores	24,900
Miscellaneous shopping goods stores	22,400
Department stores	21,900
Gasoline service stations	21,000

Compensation systems vary by type of establishment and merchandise sold. Many managers receive a commission, or a combination of salary and commission. Under a commission system, retail managers receive a percentage of department or store sales. These systems offer managers the opportunity to significantly increase their earnings, but they may find that their earnings depend on their ability to sell their product and the condition of the economy. Managers who sell large amounts of merchandise often receive bonuses or other awards.

Retail managers receive typical benefits and, in some cases, stock options. In addition, retail managers generally are able to buy their store's merchandise at a discount.

Related Occupations

Retail supervisors and managers serve customers, supervise workers, and direct and coordinate the operations of an establishment. Others with similar responsibilities include managers in restaurants, wholesale trade, hotels, banks, and hospitals.

Sources of Additional Information

Information on employment opportunities for retail managers may be obtained from the employment offices of various retail establishments or State employment service offices.

General information on management careers in retail establishments is available from:

☛ National Retail Federation, 325 7th St. NW., Suite 1100, Washington, DC 20004. Internet: **http://www.nrf.com**

Information on management careers in grocery stores, and schools offering related programs, is available from:

☛ Food Marketing Institute, 800 Connecticut Ave. NW., Publications Dept., Washington, DC 20006-2701.

Information about management careers and training programs in the motor vehicle dealers industry is available from:

☛ National Automobile Dealers Association, Public Relations Dept., 8400 Westpark Dr., McLean, VA 22102-3591.

Information about management careers in convenience stores is available from:

☛ National Association of Convenience Stores, 1605 King St., Alexandria, VA 22314-2792.

Securities, Commodities, and Financial Services Sales Representatives

(O*NET 43014A and 43014B)

Significant Points

- A college degree and good sales ability are among the most important qualifications for this profession.
- Employment is expected to grow much faster than average due to increasing investment in securities and other financial products.
- Many beginning securities and commodities sales representatives leave the occupation because they are unable to establish a sufficient clientele; once established, however, these workers have a very strong attachment to their occupation because of high earnings and the considerable investment in training.

Nature of the Work

Most investors, whether they are individuals with a few hundred dollars to invest or large institutions with millions, use *securities, commodities, and financial services sales representatives* when buying or selling stocks, bonds, shares in mutual funds, insurance annuities, or other financial products. In addition, many clients use them for advice on investments and other financial matters.

Securities and commodities sales representatives, also called brokers, stockbrokers, registered representatives, account executives, or financial consultants, perform a variety of tasks depending on their specific job duties. When an investor wishes to buy or sell a security, for example, sales representatives may relay the order through their firms' computers to the floor of a securities exchange, such as the New York Stock Exchange. There, securities and commodities sales representatives known as *floor brokers* negotiate the price with other floor brokers, make the sale, and forward the purchase price to the sales representatives. If a security is not traded on an exchange, such as in the case of bonds and over-the-counter stocks, the broker sends the order to the firm's trading department. Here, other securities and commodities sales representatives, known as *dealers*, buy and sell securities directly from other dealers using their own funds or those of the firm, with the intention of reselling the security to customers at a profit. After the transaction has been completed, the broker notifies the customer of the final price.

Securities and commodities sales representatives also provide many related services for their customers. They may explain stock market terms and trading practices; offer financial counseling or advice on the purchase or sale of particular securities; and devise an individual client financial portfolio, which could include securities, life insurance, corporate and municipal bonds, mutual funds, certificates of deposit, annuities, and other investments.

Not all customers have the same investment goals. Some individuals prefer long-term investments for capital growth or to provide income over a number of years; others might want to invest in speculative securities that they hope will rise in price quickly. Securities and commodities sales representatives furnish information about advantages and disadvantages of an investment based on each person's objectives. They also supply the latest price quotes on any security, as well as information on the activities and financial positions of the corporations issuing these securities.

Most securities and commodities sales representatives serve individual investors, but others specialize in institutional investors. In institutional investing, sales representatives usually concentrate on a specific financial product, such as stocks, bonds, options, annuities, or commodity futures. At other times, they may also handle the sale of new issues, such as corporate securities issued to finance plant expansion.

The most important part of a sales representative's job is finding clients and building a customer base. Thus, beginning securities and commodities sales representatives spend much of their time searching for customers—relying heavily on telephone solicitation. They may also meet clients through business and social contacts. Many sales representatives find it useful to contact potential clients by teaching adult education investment courses or by giving lectures at libraries or social clubs. Brokerage firms may give sales representatives lists of people with whom the firm has done business in the past. Some brokers inherit the clients of representatives who have retired.

Financial services sales representatives sell banking and related services. They contact potential customers to explain their services and to ascertain customers' banking and other financial needs. In doing so, they discuss services such as deposit accounts, lines of credit, sales or inventory financing, certificates of deposit, cash management, or investment services. They may also solicit businesses to participate in consumer credit card programs. As banks offer more and increasingly complex financial services—for example, securities brokerage and financial planning—financial services sales representatives assume greater importance.

Also included in this occupation are *financial planners*, who use their knowledge of tax and investment strategies, securities, insurance, pension plans, and real estate to develop and implement financial plans for individuals and businesses. Planners interview clients to determine their assets, liabilities, cash flow, insurance coverage, tax status, and financial objectives. They then analyze this information and develop a financial plan tailored to each client's needs. Planners may also sell financial products, such as stocks, bonds, mutual funds, and insurance, or refer clients to other resources.

Working Conditions

Most securities and commodities sales representatives work in offices under fairly stressful conditions. They have access to "quote boards" or computer terminals that continually provide information on the prices of securities. When sales activity increases, due perhaps to unanticipated changes in the economy, the pace can become very hectic.

Established securities and commodities sales representatives usually work a standard 40 hour week. Beginners who are seeking customers may work longer hours. New brokers spend a great deal of time learning the firm's products and services and studying for exams to qualify them to sell other products, such as insurance and commodities. Most securities and commodities sales representatives accommodate customers by meeting with them in the evenings or on weekends.

A growing number of securities and commodities sales representatives, employed mostly by discount brokerage firms, work in call center environments. In these centers, hundreds of representatives spend much of the day on the telephone taking orders from clients or

Securities sales representatives offer investment advice to clients.

offering advice and information on different securities. Often these call centers operate 24 hours a day, requiring representatives to work in shifts.

Financial services sales representatives normally work 40 hours a week in a comfortable, less stressful office environment. They may spend considerable time outside the office meeting with present and prospective clients, attending civic functions, and participating in trade association meetings. Some financial services sales representatives work exclusively inside banks, providing service to "walk-in" customers.

Financial planners work in offices or out of their homes. They usually work standard business hours, but they often have to visit clients in the evenings or on weekends. Many teach evening classes or put on seminars in order to bring in more clients.

Employment

Securities, commodities, and financial services sales representatives held 303,000 jobs in 1998; securities and commodities sales representatives accounted for 8 out of 10. Although securities and commodities sales representatives are employed by brokerage and investment firms in all parts of the country, most sales representatives work for a small number of large firms with main offices in cities, especially New York.

Financial services sales representatives are employed by banks, savings and loan associations, and other credit institutions. Financial planners can work for credit unions, credit counseling firms, banks, and companies that specialize in offering financial advice. Other planners are self-employed workers, many of whom contract out their services with these firms.

Training, Other Qualifications, and Advancement

Because securities and commodities sales representatives must be knowledgeable about economic conditions and trends, a college education is important, especially in larger securities firms. In fact, the overwhelming majority of workers in this occupation are college graduates. Although employers seldom require specialized academic training, courses in business administration, economics, and finance are helpful.

Many employers consider personal qualities and skills more important than academic training. Employers seek applicants who have considerable sales ability, good interpersonal and communication skills, and a strong desire to succeed. Some employers also make sure that applicants have a good credit history and a clean record. Self-confidence and an ability to handle frequent rejections are also important ingredients for success.

Because maturity and the ability to work independently are important, many employers prefer to hire those who have achieved success in other jobs. Some firms prefer candidates with sales experience, particularly those who have worked on commission in areas such as real estate or insurance. Therefore, most entrants to this occupation transfer from other jobs. Some begin working as securities and commodities sales representatives following retirement from other fields.

Securities and commodities sales representatives must meet State licensing requirements, which usually include passing an examination and, in some cases, furnishing a personal bond. In addition, sales representatives must register as representatives of their firm with the National Association of Securities Dealers, Inc. (NASD). Before beginners can qualify as registered representatives, they must pass the General Securities Registered Representative Examination (Series 7 exam), administered by the NASD, and be an employee of a registered firm for at least 4 months. Most States require a second examination—the Uniform Securities Agents State Law Examination. These tests measure the prospective representative's knowledge of the securities business, customer protection requirements, and recordkeeping procedures. Many take correspondence courses in preparation for the securities examinations. Within two years, brokers are encouraged to take additional licensing exams in order to sell insurance and commodities.

Most employers provide on-the-job training to help securities and commodities sales representatives meet the registration requirements for certification. In most firms, this training period takes about 4 months. Trainees in large firms may receive classroom instruction in securities analysis, effective speaking, and the finer points of selling; take courses offered by business schools and associations; and undergo a period of on-the-job training lasting up to 2 years. Many firms like to rotate their trainees among various departments in the firm to give trainees a broad perspective of the securities business. In small firms, sales representatives often receive training in outside institutions and on the job.

Securities and commodities sales representatives must understand the basic characteristics of the wide variety of financial products offered by brokerage firms. Brokers periodically take training through their firms or outside institutions to keep abreast of new financial products and improve their sales techniques. Computer training is also important, as the securities sales business is highly automated. Since 1995, it has also become mandatory for all registered securities and commodities sales representatives to attend periodic continuing education classes to maintain their licenses. Courses consist of computer-based training in regulatory matters and company training on new products and services.

The principal form of advancement for securities and commodities sales representatives is an increase in the number and size of the accounts they handle. Although beginners usually service the accounts of individual investors, they may eventually handle very large institutional accounts, such as those of banks and pension funds. After taking a series of tests, some brokers become portfolio managers and have greater authority to make investment decisions over an account. Some experienced sales representatives become branch office managers and supervise other sales representatives while continuing to provide services for their own customers. A few representatives advance to top management positions or become partners in their firms.

Banks and other credit institutions prefer to hire college graduates for financial services sales jobs. A business administration degree with a specialization in finance or a liberal arts degree including courses in accounting, economics, and marketing serves as excellent preparation for this job.

In contrast to securities brokers, financial services sales representatives primarily learn their jobs through on-the-job training under the supervision of bank officers. Outstanding performance can lead to promotion to managerial positions.

There are no formal educational or licensure requirements for becoming a financial planner, but a license is required to offer advice or sell specific securities, mutual funds, or insurance products. And although a college education is not necessary to become a financial planner, the vast majority of planners have a bachelor's or master's degree. Courses in accounting, business administration, economics, and finance are particularly helpful.

Many planners also find it worthwhile to obtain a Certified Financial Planner (CFP) or Chartered Financial Consultant (ChFC) designation. These designations demonstrate to potential customers that a planner has extensive training and competency in the area of financial planning. The CFP designation is issued by the CFP Board of Standards in Denver, Colorado and requires relevant experience, completion of education requirements, passing an extensive examination, and adherence to an enforceable Code of Ethics. The ChFC designation is issued by the American College in Bryn Mawr, Pennsylvania, and requires experience and completion of a ten-course study program. Both programs have a continuing education requirement.

Job Outlook

Barring a significant decline in the stock market, the number of securities, commodities, and financial services sales representatives should grow much faster than the average for all occupations through 2008. As people's incomes continue to climb and they seek better returns on their investments, they will increasingly need the advice and services of a securities and commodities sales representative to realize their financial goals. Growth in the buying and selling of stocks over the Internet will reduce the need for brokers for many transactions.

Nevertheless, the rapid overall increase in investment is expected to spur rapid employment growth among these workers, as a majority of transactions will still require the advice and services of securities, commodities, and financial services sales representatives.

Baby boomers in their peak savings years will fuel much of the investment boom. Saving for retirement is being made much easier by the government, which continues to offer a number of tax-favorable pension plans, such as the 401(k) and the Roth IRA. More women in the workforce also means higher incomes and more women qualifying for pensions. And many of these pensions are self-directed—meaning that the recipient has the responsibility for investing the money. With such large amounts of money to invest, brokers and financial planners will be in demand to provide investment advice.

Other factors that will impact the demand for brokers are the increasing number and complexity of investment products as well as the effects of globalization. As the public and businesses become more sophisticated about investing, they are venturing into the options and futures markets. Brokers are needed to buy or sell these products, which are not available for trading online. Also, markets for investment are expanding with the increase in global trading of stocks and bonds. Further, the New York Stock Exchange has announced its intention to extend its trading hours to accommodate trading in foreign stocks and compete with foreign exchanges. If this takes place, it will vastly increase the demand for brokers, both on the floor of the exchange and in brokerage firms to handle the larger volume of trades.

Employment of brokers, however, will be adversely affected if the stock market or the economy suddenly declines. Even in good times, turnover is relatively high for beginning brokers who are unable to establish a sizable clientele. Once established, though, securities and commodities sales representatives have a very strong attachment to their occupation because of high earnings and the considerable investment in training. Competition is usually intense, especially in larger companies, with more applicants than jobs. Opportunities for beginning brokers should be better in smaller firms.

The number of financial services sales representatives in banks will increase faster than average as banks attempt to become a "one-stop-shop" for investing. Deregulation will allow banks to offer an increasing array of services, such as stocks and insurance, that they have been prevented from offering in the past. Financial planners can also be expected to grow faster than average as an increasingly wealthy population seeks advice on tax and estate planning, retirement planning, and investing.

Earnings

Median annual earnings of securities, commodities, and financial services sales representatives were $48,090 in 1998. The middle half earned between $31,400 and $103,040. The lowest 10 percent earned less than $22,660; the top 10 percent, more than $124,800.

Median annual earnings in the industries employing the largest number of securities and financial services sales representatives in 1997 were:

Industry	Earnings
Securities brokers and dealers	$53,700
Security and commodity services	46,900
Mortgage bankers and brokers	36,300
Commercial banks	33,000

Stockbrokers, who provide personalized service and more guidance over a client's investments, usually are paid a commission based on the amount of stocks, bonds, mutual funds, insurance, and other products they sell. Commission earnings are likely to be high when there is much buying and selling and low when there is a slump in market activity. Most firms provide sales representatives with a steady income by paying a "draw against commission"—a minimum salary based on commissions they can be expected to earn. Securities and commodities sales representatives who can provide their clients with the most complete financial services should enjoy the greatest income stability. Trainee brokers are usually paid a salary until they develop a client base. The salary gradually decreases in favor of commissions as the broker gains clients. A small but increasing number of full-service brokers are paid a percentage of the assets they oversee. This fee often includes a certain number of trades done for free.

Brokers who work for discount brokerage firms that promote the use of telephone and online trading services are usually paid a salary. Sometimes this salary is boosted by bonuses that reflect the profitability of the office.

Financial services sales representatives usually are paid a salary; some receive a bonus if they meet certain established goals. Earnings of financial planners can be wholly fee-based, which means they do not receive any commissions for selling a product they recommend. They simply charge by the hour or by the complexity of the financial plan. The majority of financial planners, though, receive commissions on the sale of insurance products or securities, in addition to charging a fee.

Related Occupations

Similar sales jobs requiring specialized knowledge include insurance sales agents and real estate agents.

Sources of Additional Information

For general information on the securities industry, contact:

☛ The Securities Industry Association, 120 Broadway, New York, NY 10271. Internet: **http://www.sia.com**

For information about the Certified Financial Planner designation, contact:

☛ The Certified Financial Planner Board of Standards, 1700 Broadway, Suite 2100, Denver, CO 80290-2101.
Internet: **http://www.cfp-board.org**

For information about job opportunities for financial services sales representatives in various States, contact State bankers' associations or write directly to a particular bank.

Services Sales Representatives

(O*NET 43017, 43023A, 43023B, 43099A, 43099B, and 49026)

Significant Points

- A significant part of earnings may be in the form of commissions, which can vary considerably depending on performance.
- Considerable travel may be required.

Nature of the Work

Services sales representatives, unlike sales representatives who sell manufactured products, sell an intangible product, a service. For example, services sales representatives for computer and data processing firms sell complex services such as inventory control, payroll processing, sales analysis, and financial reporting systems. Hotel services sales representatives contact associations, businesses, and social groups to solicit convention and conference business. Services sales representatives for personnel supply services firms locate clients and persuade them to hire their firm's employees. Those in the motion picture industry sell the rights for movie theaters to show their films. Other representatives sell automotive leasing, burial, shipping, protective, and management consulting services. Service sales representatives are also commonly known as "sales reps." (Information on other sales workers, including insurance sales agents; manufacturers' and wholesale sales representatives; real estate agents and brokers; retail salespersons; securities, commodities, and financial services sales representatives; and travel agents, appears elsewhere in the *Handbook.*)

Services sales representatives act as industry experts, consultants, and problem solvers. In some cases, they create demand for the firm's services. To do so, they must thoroughly understand a client's specific needs and objectives. Successful representatives relate their knowledge and understanding of the client's business to the services they offer to meet their objectives. For example, they might persuade a business to start advertising its products in ways it had not considered before.

There are several different categories of services sales jobs. *Outside services sales representatives* call on clients and prospects at their homes or offices. They may have an appointment, or they may practice "cold calling," arriving without an appointment. *Inside services sales representatives* work on their employer's premises, assisting individuals interested in the company's services. *Telemarketing sales representatives* sell over the telephone. They make large numbers of calls to prospects, attempting to sell the company's service themselves, or to arrange an appointment between the prospect and an outside sales representative. Some services sales representatives deal exclusively with one, or just a few, major clients.

Despite the diversity of services sold, the jobs of all services sales representatives have much in common. All sales representatives follow similar procedures to acquire new clients and must fully understand and be able to discuss the services their company offers. Many sales representatives develop lists of prospective clients through telephone and business directories, asking business associates and customers for leads, and calling on new businesses as they cover their assigned territory. Some services sales representatives acquire clients through inquiries about their company's services. The Internet now allows all sales reps to better target their clients, display information, research industry trends, and track competitors' offers.

Services sales representatives obtain many of their new accounts through referrals. Thus, their success hinges on developing a satisfied clientele who will continue to use their services and recommend them

Services sales representatives maintain customer relations on the phone and in person.

to other potential customers. Like other types of sales jobs, a respected reputation is crucial to success.

Regardless of how they first meet the client, all services sales representatives must explain how the offered service meet the client's needs. While demonstrating the company's service, they may answer questions about the nature and cost of the service. In addition, they might have to overcome objections in order to persuade potential customers to purchase the service. If they fail to make a sale on the first visit, they may follow up with more visits, letters, or phone calls. After closing a sale, services sales representatives generally follow up to see that the purchase meets the customer's needs, and to determine if additional services can be sold. Good customer service is an important factor in developing a satisfied clientele and can give a company an advantage in competing for future business.

Services sales work varies with the kind of service sold. Selling highly technical services, such as communications systems or computer consulting services, involves complex and lengthy sales negotiations. In addition, sales of such complex services may require extensive after-sale support. In these situations, sales reps may operate as part of a team of sales representatives and experts from other departments. Sales representatives can receive valuable technical assistance from their other team members. For example, those who sell computer and data processing services might work with a systems engineer. Teams enhance customer service and build strong long-term relationships with customers, resulting in increased sales.

The entire sales process can be lengthy. Sometimes a sales rep may periodically contact a potential customer for years before they make a sale. Because of the amount of time between the initial contact with a customer and the actual sale, representatives are in contact with numerous existing and potential clients at the same time. Sales representatives must be well organized and efficient in managing their work. When customers express a interest in the service, sales reps who sell complex technical services may have to develop detailed proposals for presentation to the customer outlining the detailed services to be provided and their cost. Sometimes proposals must be revised several times before a client is willing to accept it. Selling less complex services, such as linen supply, cleaning, or pest control services, generally involves simpler and shorter sales negotiations.

Sales representative jobs may also vary with the size of the employer. Those working for large companies may be assigned a specific territory, a specific line of services, or specific types of clients. In smaller companies, sales representatives may have broader responsibilities—administrative, marketing, or public relations, for example—in addition to their sales duties.

Sales representatives often service a specific territory. Representatives of companies offering services widely used by the public, such as Internet service providers, generally have numerous clients in a relatively small territory. On the other hand, sales representatives for firms that offer more specialized services, such as interpretation and translation, might need to service several States to acquire an adequate customer base.

Working Conditions

Many services sales workers frequently work more than 40 hours per week. Selling can be stressful work because their income and job security directly depends on their success in winning business for their employers. Companies generally set sales quotas and have contests with prizes for those with the most sales. Considerable pressure is placed on the sales representative to meet monthly sales quotas.

Working conditions for sales representatives vary. Outside sales representatives responsible for a large territory might spend a great deal of time traveling, sometimes for weeks at a time. Representatives with smaller territories might never travel overnight. Outside sales representatives usually spend part of their time in an office keeping records, setting up appointments with customers, and searching for new customers. Increasingly, outside sales representatives work out of home of fices or share office space with others rather than have their own permanently assigned space. Inside sales representatives and telemarketers spend all their time in their offices, which can range from bright and cheerful customer showrooms to cramped and noisy rooms.

Representatives often have the flexibility to set their own schedules as long as they meet their company's goals. The Internet allows representatives to do more work from home or while on the road, enabling them to send messages and documents to clients and coworkers, keep up with industry news, and access databases that help them to better target potential customers. Although they may accomplish more in less time, many work more hours than in the past, spending additional time on follow up and service calls.

Employment

Services sales representatives held over 841,000 jobs in 1998. Firms providing business services such as computer and data processing, contract telemarketing, personnel supply, and advertising provided two-thirds of all wage and salary jobs. The remainder of services sales representatives' jobs were in other service industries, including hotels and motels, motion pictures, education, and engineering and management services.

Training, Other Qualifications, and Advancement

Some employers require services sales representatives to have a college degree, but requirements vary depending on the industry a company represents. Employers who market advertising services seek individuals with a college degree in advertising, marketing, or business administration. Companies marketing educational services prefer individuals with a degree in education, marketing, or a related field. Many hotels seek graduates of hotel or tourism administration programs. Companies selling computer, engineering, health or other highly technical services generally require a bachelor's degree appropriate to their field. Certification and licensing is also becoming more common for sales and marketing representatives.

Employers may hire sales reps with only a high school diploma, if they have a proven sales record. This is particularly true for those who sell non-technical services, such as amusement and recreation services, cleaning services, Employers may hire sales reps with only a high school diploma, if they have a proven sales record. This is particularly true for those who sell non-technical services, such as amusement and recreation services, cleaning services, or photographic studios. Applicants enhance their chances of being hired into these positions if they have taken some relevant college courses. In general, smaller companies are more willing to hire unproven individuals.

Many firms conduct intensive training programs to acquaint new services sales representatives with the services and products of the firm, the history of the business, effective selling techniques, and administrative duties and policies. Sales representatives also attend seminars on a wide range of subjects given by outside or in-house trainers. These sessions acquaint them with new services and products or update their sales techniques or procedures and might include training to make them more effective in dealing with prospective customers.

To succeed, sales representatives should be persuasive and have a pleasant, outgoing, and enthusiastic disposition. Sales representatives must be highly motivated, energetic, well organized, and efficient. Good grooming and a neat appearance are essential, as are self-confidence, reliability, and the ability to communicate effectively. Sales representatives should be self-starters who have the ability to thrive under pressure to meet sales goals. They must also develop a thorough knowledge of the service they are selling, and anticipate and respond to their clients' questions and objections in a professional manner. In addition, they must be flexible to adjust to delays, problems, and the schedules of others.

Sales representatives with leadership ability and good sales records may advance to supervisory and managerial positions. Frequent contact with people in other firms provides sales reps with leads about job openings, enhancing advancement opportunities.

Job Outlook

Employment of services sales representatives, as a group, is expected to grow much faster than the average for all occupations through the year 2008 in response to growth of the services industries employing them. However, projected employment growth of services sales representatives varies by industry. For example, continued growth in factory and office automation should lead to much faster than average employment growth for computer and data processing services sales representatives. Employment in personnel supply services will grow as companies continue to outsource and use temporary employees. Growth will be tempered in some industries by the expanded use of various technologies, such as voice and electronic mail, portable phones, and laptop computers that all increase sales workers' productivity—especially while out of the office.

In addition to the job openings generated by employment growth, openings will occur each year because of the need to replace sales workers who transfer to other occupations or leave the labor force. Each year, many sales representatives discover they are unable to earn enough money and leave the occupation. Turnover is generally higher among representatives who sell non-technical services. As a result of this turnover, job opportunities should be good, especially for those with a college degree or a proven sales record.

With improved technology, some companies are cutting back on the expense of travel and on-site presentations and putting more emphasis on in-house sales via the Internet, direct calling, and teleconferencing. In addition, temporary or contract sales people may be used more frequently for outside sales.

Earnings

Median annual earnings of services sales representatives in selected business services were $34,910, including commission, in 1998. The middle 50 percent earned between $24,700 and $49,030 a year. The lowest 10 percent earned less than $17,640 and the highest 10 percent earned more than $79,790 a year. Median annual earnings in the service industries employing the largest numbers of sales agents in selected business services in 1997 were as follows:

Computer and data processing services	$41,200
Management and public relations	34,000
Mailing, reproduction, and stenographic services	33,100
Miscellaneous business services	29,500
Personnel supply services	28,500

Median annual earnings of advertising sales agents, including commission, were $31,850 in 1998. The middle 50 percent earned between $22,600 and $47,660 a year. The lowest 10 percent earned less than $16,210 and the highest 10 percent earned more than $83,080 a year.

Median annual earnings of telemarketers and other related workers, including commission, were $17,090 in 1998. The middle 50 percent earned between $14,080 and $21,830 a year. The lowest 10 percent earned less than $12,350 and the highest 10 percent earned more than $30,290 a year.

Services sales representatives are paid under various systems. Some receive a straight salary; others are paid solely on a commission basis—a percentage of the dollar value of their sales. Most firms use a combination of salary and commissions. Some services sales representatives receive a base salary, plus incentive pay that can add from 25 to 75 percent to their base salary. Many employers offer bonuses, including vacation trips and prizes for sales that exceed company quotas. Sales are affected by changing economic conditions and consumer and business expectations and so earnings may vary greatly from year to year. In addition to the same benefits package provided to other employees of the firm, employers may provide outside sales representatives expense accounts to cover meals and travel, computer and office equipment for use while traveling or at home, and sometimes a company car.

Related Occupations
Services sales representatives must have sales ability and knowledge of the service they sell. Workers in other occupations requiring these skills include: Advertising, marketing, and public relations managers; insurance sales agents; manufacturers' and wholesale sales representatives; purchasing managers, buyers, and purchasing agents; real estate agents and brokers; sales engineers; securities, commodities, and financial services sales representatives; and travel agents.

Sources of Additional Information
For details about career and certification information for services sales and marketing representatives, contact:
☛ Sales and Marketing Executives International, 5500 Interstate North Pkwy., Suite 545, Atlanta, GA 30328-4662.
Internet: **http://www.smei.org**

Travel Agents

(O*NET 43021)

Significant Points

- Training at a postsecondary vocational school or college or university is increasingly important for getting a job.
- Travel benefits, such as reduced rates for transportation and accommodations, attract many people to this occupation.
- Projected average employment growth reflects increases in spending on pleasure and business travel.

Nature of the Work
Constantly changing air fares and schedules, thousands of available vacation packages, and a vast amount of travel information on the Internet can make travel planning frustrating and time-consuming. To sort out the many travel options, tourists and businesspeople often turn to travel agents, who assess their needs and help them make the best possible travel arrangements. Also, many major cruise lines, resorts, and specialty travel groups use travel agents to promote travel packages to the millions of people who travel every year.

In general, travel agents give advice on destinations and make arrangements for transportation, hotel accommodations, car rentals, tours, and recreation. They may also advise on weather conditions, restaurants, and tourist attractions, and recreation. For international travel, agents also provide information on customs regulations, required papers (passports, visas, and certificates of vaccination), and currency exchange rates.

Travel agents consult a variety of published and computer-based sources for information on departure and arrival times, fares, and hotel ratings and accommodations. They may visit hotels, resorts, and restaurants to evaluate their comfort, cleanliness, and the quality of food and service so they can base recommendations on their own travel experiences or those of colleagues or clients.

Travel agents also promote their services, using telemarketing, direct mail, and the Internet. They make presentations to social and special interest groups, arrange advertising displays, and suggest company-sponsored trips to business managers. Depending on the size of the travel agency, an agent may specialize by type of travel, such as leisure or business, or destination, such as Europe or Africa.

Working Conditions
Travel agents spend most of their time behind a desk conferring with clients, completing paperwork, contacting airlines and hotels for travel arrangements, and promoting group tours. During vacation seasons and holiday periods they may be under a great deal of pressure. Many agents, especially those who are self-employed, frequently work long hours. With advanced computer systems and telecommunication networks, some travel agents are able to work at home.

Employment
Travel agents held about 138,000 jobs in 1998 and are found in every part of the country. More than 9 out of 10 salaried agents worked for travel agencies. Many of the remainder worked for membership organizations.

Training, Other Qualifications, and Advancement
The minimum requirement for those interested in becoming a travel agent is a high school diploma or equivalent. Technology and computerization are having a profound effect on the work of travel agents, however, and formal or specialized training is The minimum requirement for those interested in becoming a travel agent is a high school diploma or equivalent. Technology and computerization are having a profound effect on the work of travel agents, however, and formal or specialized training is becoming increasingly important. Many vocational schools offer 6- to 12-week full-time travel agent programs, as well as evening and weekend programs. Travel agent courses are also offered in public adult education programs and in community and 4-year colleges. A few colleges offer bachelor's or master's degrees in travel and tourism. Although few college courses relate directly to the travel industry, a college education is sometimes desired by employers to establish a background in fields such as computer science, geography, communication, foreign languages, and world history. Courses in accounting and business management

Travel agents compile information from various sources in order to plan their clients' travel itineraries.

also are important, especially for those who expect to manage or start their own travel agencies.

The American Society of Travel Agents (ASTA) offers a correspondence course that provides a basic understanding of the travel industry. Travel agencies also provide on-the-job training for their employees, a significant part of which consists of computer instruction. Computer skills are required by all employers to operate airline and centralized reservation systems.

Experienced travel agents can take advanced self or group study courses from the Institute of Certified Travel Agents (ICTA) that lead to the designation of Certified Travel Counselor (CTC). The ICTA also offers marketing and sales skills development programs and destination specialist programs, which provide a detailed knowledge of regions such as North America, Western Europe, the Caribbean, and the Pacific Rim.

Travel experience is an asset since personal knowledge about a city or foreign country often helps to influence clients' travel plans, as is experience as an airline reservation agent. Patience and the ability to gain the confidence of clients are also useful qualities. Travel agents must be well-organized, accurate, and meticulous to compile information from various sources and plan and organize their clients' travel itineraries. Other desirable qualifications include good writing, computer, and sales skills.

Some employees start as reservation clerks or receptionists in travel agencies. With experience and some formal training, they can take on greater responsibilities and eventually assume travel agent duties. In agencies with many offices, travel agents may advance to office manager or to other managerial positions.

Those who start their own agencies generally have had experience in an established agency. Before they can receive commissions, these agents usually must gain formal approval from suppliers or corporations, such as airlines, ship lines, or rail lines. The Airlines Reporting Corporation and the International Airlines Travel Agency Network, for example, are the approving bodies for airlines. To gain approval, an agency must be financially sound and employ at least one experienced manager or travel agent.

There are no Federal licensing requirements for travel agents. However, nine States—California, Florida, Hawaii, Illinois, Iowa, Ohio, Oregon, Rhode Island, and Washington—require some form of registration or certification of retail sellers of travel services. More information may be obtained by contacting the Office of the Attorney General or Department of Commerce for each State.

Job Outlook

Employment of travel agents is expected to grow about as fast as the average for all occupations through 2008. Many job openings will arise as new agencies open and existing agencies expand, but most openings will occur as experienced agents transfer to other occupations or leave the labor force.

Projected employment growth stems from increased spending on tourism and business travel over the next decade. With rising household incomes, smaller families, and an increasing number of older people who are more likely to travel, more people are expected to travel on vacation—and to do so more frequently—than in the past. Business travel should also grow as business activity expands. Further, managerial, professional, and sales occupations are projected to be among the fastest growing, and people in these occupations do the most business travel.

A variety of other factors will also lead to greater business for travel agents. For example, charter flights and larger, more efficient planes have brought air transportation within the budgets of more people, and the easing of Federal regulation of air fares and routes has fostered greater competition among airlines, resulting in more affordable service. In addition, American travel agents now organize more tours for the growing number of foreign visitors. Also, travel agents are often able to offer various travel packages at a substantial discount. Although most travel agencies now have automated reservation systems, this has not weakened demand for travel agents.

Some developments, however, may reduce job opportunities for travel agents in the future. The Internet increasingly will allow people to access travel information from their personal computers and make their own travel arrangements. Further, suppliers of travel services are increasingly able to make their services available through other means, such as electronic ticketing machines and remote ticket printers. Also, airline companies have put a cap on the amount of commissions they will pay to travel agencies. The full effect of these practices, though, have yet to be determined, and many consumers will still prefer to use a professional travel agent to ensure reliability and to save time and, in some cases, money.

The travel industry is sensitive to economic downturns and international political crises, when travel plans are likely to be deferred. Therefore, the number of job opportunities fluctuates.

Earnings

Experience, sales ability, and the size and location of the agency determine the salary of a travel agent. Median annual earnings of travel agents overall and in the passenger transportation arrangement industry, where most worked, were $23,010 in 1998. Most travel agents earned between $17,960 and $28,430. The bottom 10 percent of travel agents earned less than $13,770, while the top 10 percent earned over 34,670.

Salaried agents usually enjoy standard benefits that self-employed agents must provide for themselves. Among agencies, those focusing on corporate sales pay higher salaries and provide more extensive benefits, on average, than those who focus on leisure sales. When they travel for personal reasons, agents usually get reduced rates for transportation and accommodations. In addition, agents sometimes take "familiarization" trips, at no cost to themselves, to learn about various vacation sites. These benefits attract many people to this occupation.

Earnings of travel agents who own their agencies depend mainly on commissions from airlines and other carriers, cruise lines, tour operators, and lodging places. Commissions for domestic travel arrangements, cruises, hotels, sightseeing tours, and car rentals are about 7-10 percent of the total sale, and for international travel, about 10 percent. Travel agents may also charge clients a service fee for the time and expense involved in planning a trip.

During the first year of business or while awaiting corporation approval, self-employed travel agents often have low earnings. Their income usually is limited to commissions from hotels, cruises, and tour operators and to nominal fees for making complicated arrangements. Established agents may have lower earnings during economic downturns.

Related Occupations

Travel agents organize and schedule business, educational, or recreational travel or activities. Other workers with similar responsibilities include tour guides, meeting planners, airline reservation agents, rental car agents, and travel counselors.

Sources of Additional Information

For further information on training opportunities, contact:

☛ American Society of Travel Agents, Education Department, 1101 King St., Alexandria, VA 22314. Internet: **http://www.astanet.com/www/asta/pub/car/becomingagent.htmlx**

For information on certification qualifications, contact:

☛ The Institute of Certified Travel Agents, 148 Linden St., P.O. Box 812059, Wellesley, MA 02181-0012.

Administrative Support Occupations, Including Clerical

Adjusters, Investigators, and Collectors

(O*NET 21921, 53123, 53302, 533113, 53314, 53502, and 53508)

Significant Points

- A high school education is sufficient to qualify for most positions, but employers prefer to hire college graduates as claim representatives.
- Projected employment change varies by occupation—the number of adjustment clerks is expected to grow faster than average as businesses emphasize good customer relations, whereas welfare eligibility clerks will likely decline in number because of welfare reform legislation.

Nature of the Work

Adjusters, investigators, and collectors perform a wide range of functions, but their most important role is acting as intermediaries with the public. Insurance companies, department stores, banks, and social services agencies employ adjusters, investigators, and collectors to deal with the challenges they face such as handling complaints, interpreting and explaining policies or regulations, resolving billing disputes, collecting delinquent accounts, and determining eligibility for governmental assistance. The variety of titles and responsibilities in this grouping of occupations can be categorized into claim representatives, insurance processing clerks, adjustment clerks, bill and account collectors, and welfare eligibility workers and interviewers.

Claim Representatives. Insurance companies investigate claims, negotiate settlements, and authorize payments to claimants. *Claim representatives* do this work. When a policyholder files a claim for property damage or a hospital stay, for example, the claim representative must initially determine whether the customer's insurance policy covers the loss and the amount of the loss covered. They then must determine the amount to pay the claimant.

In life and health insurance companies, claim representatives are typically called *claim examiners*. Claim examiners usually specialize in group or individual insurance plans and in hospital, dental, or prescription drug claims. Examiners review health-related claims to see if the costs are reasonable based on the diagnosis. They check with guides that provide information on the average period of disability for various causes, expected treatments, and average hospital stay. Examiners will then either authorize the appropriate payment or refer the claim to an investigator for a more thorough review. Claim investigators look into any contestable claims.

Claim representatives working in life insurance review the causes of death, particularly in the case of an accident, as most life insurance companies pay additional benefits if the death is due to an accident. They may also review new applications for life insurance to make sure applicants have no serious illnesses that would prevent them from qualifying for insurance.

In the property and casualty insurance area, claim representatives handle minor claims filed by automobile or homeowner policyholders. These workers (also called "inside adjusters" or "telephone adjusters") contact claimants by telephone or mail to obtain information on repair costs, medical expenses, or other details the company requires. Many companies centralize this operation through a drive-in claims center, where the cost of repair is determined and a check is issued immediately. More complex cases, usually involving bodily injury, are referred to senior representatives, adjusters, or claim examiners. Cases may also be referred to "independent adjusters" who work for independent adjusting firms not affiliated with a particular insurance company. Some adjusters work with multiple types of insurance. Others specialize in homeowner claims, business losses, automotive damage, product liability, or workers' compensation. Material damage adjusters inspect automobile damage and use the latest computerized estimating equipment to prepare estimates of the damage.

In all of these specialties, claim adjusters primarily plan and schedule the work required to process a claim. They investigate claims by interviewing the claimant and witnesses, consulting police and hospital records, and inspecting property damage to determine the extent of the company's liability. The information from this work, including photographs and written or taped statements, is included in a report that is used to evaluate a claim. When the policyholder's claim is legitimate, the claim adjuster negotiates with the claimant and settles the claim. When claims are contested, adjusters may testify in court.

Claim representatives, adjusters, and examiners are making more use of computers to keep records of clients and actions taken in various claims. Most work on desktop computers, and many use portable laptop computers to enter or access information when they are on assignment away from their offices.

Insurance Processing Clerks. Processing new insurance policies, modifying existing policies, and recording claims is the work of *policy processing clerks*. Using computers, they process new policies by first reviewing the insurance application to ensure that all the questions have been answered. After underwriters have reviewed an application and the company determines that it will issue a policy, a policy processing clerk prepares the necessary forms and informs the insurance sales agent of the application's status. Policy processing clerks also update existing policies—such as a change in beneficiary, amount of coverage, or type of insurance—and recalculate premiums. They then mail correspondence notices regarding changes to the sales agent and policyholder. Policy processing clerks maintain computer files for each policyholder, including policies that are to be reinstated or canceled.

The majority of policy processing clerks work for insurance agencies, where they are usually referred to as customer service representatives. In this capacity, they perform a number of duties in addition to processing policies for customers. Customer service representatives also take calls from clients, answer questions, process changes to the policies, submit applications to the insurance carriers, and obtain information on claims.

Most of the remaining policy processing clerks work for large insurance companies. For many of them, the job is becoming more customer service related as more carriers deal directly with the public. These clerks usually work in call centers, in which they take policy information from current customers and enter it directly into the computer. Other policy processors handle policy changes initiated primarily by the insurance company.

Another type of insurance processing clerk is the *claims clerk*, also called *claims interviewer* or *claims processor*. These clerks obtain information from policyholders regarding claims from fire damage, personal injury or illness, or an automobile accident, for example. They are primarily responsible for getting the necessary information on a claim, such as specific details of an accident. This is usually done over the telephone while the claims clerk simultaneously enters the information into a computer. If information regarding the claim is missing, a claims clerk will call or write the insured or other party for the missing information. Once the information is entered, the claims clerk forwards the claim for payment or to a claim representative, who will further examine the claim. In addition to taking information, some claims clerks can pay small claims, direct insureds to auto repair facilities or local contractors to make home repairs, and may give limited direction to insureds on how to proceed with the claim in emergencies.

Adjustment Clerks. Investigating and resolving customers' complaints about merchandise, service, billing, or credit rating is done by *adjustment clerks*. They may work for banks, department stores, insurance companies, and other large organizations that sell products and services to the public. They are more commonly referred to as customer service representatives or customer complaint clerks.

Adjustment clerks examine all pertinent information to determine if a customer's complaint is valid. In department stores, this may mean checking sales slips, warranties, or the merchandise in question. In banks, these clerks might review records and videotapes of automated teller machine transactions. For insurance carriers, they may review the terms of the policies to see if a particular loss is covered. Regardless of the setting, these clerks get information—in person, by telephone, or through written correspondence—from all parties involved.

After evaluating the facts, adjustment clerks attempt to remedy the situation by exchanging merchandise, refunding money, crediting customers' accounts, or adjusting customers' bills. Adjustment clerks ensure that the appropriate changes are set in motion and follow up on the recommendations to ensure customer satisfaction. To prevent similar complaints in the future, they may recommend improvements in product, packaging, shipping, service, or billing methods and procedures. Adjustment clerks keep records of all relevant matters, using them to prepare reports for their supervisors.

In many organizations, adjustment clerks investigate billing errors and other customer complaints. They also respond to many types of inquiries from customers, including taking orders, canceling accounts, or simply providing information on the company's products and services. These requests may be handled immediately over the phone or may require the adjustment clerk to send a letter to the customer.

Bill and Account Collectors. Sometimes called collection agents, *bill and account collectors* ensure that customers pay their overdue accounts. Some are employed by third-party collection agencies, while others, known as "in-house collectors," work directly for the original creditors, such as department stores, hospitals, or banks.

The duties of bill and account collectors are similar in the many different organizations in which they are employed. First, collectors attempt to locate and notify customers of delinquent accounts, usually over the telephone, but sometimes by letter. When customers move without leaving a forwarding address, collectors may check with the post office, telephone companies, credit bureaus, or former neighbors to obtain their new address. This is called "skiptracing."

Once collectors find the debtor, they inform them of the overdue account and solicit payment. If necessary, they review the terms of the sale, service, or credit contract with the customer. Collectors also may attempt to learn the cause of the delay in payment. Where feasible, they offer the customer advice on how to pay off the debts, such as by taking out a bill consolidation loan. However, the collector's objective is always to ensure that the customer first pays the debt in question.

If a customer agrees to pay, collectors record this commitment and check later to verify that the payment was indeed made. Collectors may have authority to grant an extension of time if customers ask for one. If a customer fails to respond, collectors prepare a statement indicating this for the credit department of the establishment. In more extreme cases, collectors may initiate repossession proceedings, service disconnections, or hand the account over to an attorney for legal action. Most collectors handle other administrative functions for the accounts assigned to them. This may include recording changes of addresses, and purging the records of the deceased.

Collectors use computers and a variety of automated systems to keep track of overdue accounts. Collectors usually work at video display terminals that are linked to computers. In sophisticated predicted dialer systems, a computer dials the telephone automatically and the collector speaks only when a connection has been made. Such systems eliminate time spent calling busy or non-answering numbers. Many collectors use regular telephones, but others wear headsets like those used by telephone operators.

Welfare Eligibility Workers and Interviewers. *Welfare eligibility workers and interviewers*—sometimes referred to as intake workers, eligibility specialists, family investment counselors, or income maintenance specialists—determine who may receive welfare and other types of social assistance. Welfare eligibility workers and interviewers work with various public assistance programs. The best known are Aid to Families with Dependent Children, Medicaid, and Food Stamps. Depending on local circumstances, they may also work with other programs, such as those for public housing, refugee assistance, and fuel assistance. Although the majority work for State and local governments, a number of eligibility workers work in hospitals and physician offices where they interview patients regarding their eligibility for government assistance.

Many welfare eligibility workers and interviewers specialize in an area such as housing, but most are responsible for several areas. They also may assist social workers by informing them of pertinent information they have gathered during their interviews with applicants.

The primary task of these workers is interviewing and investigating applicants and recipients of public assistance. Based on the personal and financial information they obtain and the rules and regulations of each program, they initiate procedures to grant, modify, deny, or terminate individuals' eligibility for various aid programs. This information is recorded and evaluated to determine the amounts of the grants.

These workers often provide information to applicants and current recipients. For example, they may explain and interpret eligibility rules and regulations or identify other resources available in the community for financial or social welfare assistance. Eligibility workers also keep track of those on welfare, making sure recipients attend job training classes and seek employment. More experienced eligibility workers may help train new workers. In addition, they may be assigned to special fraud-detection units.

The authority of welfare eligibility workers and interviewers varies from one jurisdiction to another. In some places, senior workers are authorized to decide on an applicant's eligibility, subject to review by their supervisor. In other places, they can only make recommendations to their supervisors, who in turn make the ultimate decision.

Insurance adjusters review claims and determine an appropriate settlement.

An increasing number of jurisdictions are using computers to improve worker productivity and to reduce the incidence of welfare fraud. In these settings, welfare eligibility workers enter information into a computer as they interview applicants and recipients. In the most advanced systems, the computer terminal prompts them with a variety of questions to ask during an interview.

Although these workers usually interview applicants and recipients who visit their offices, they may make occasional home visits, especially if the applicant or recipient is elderly or disabled. They may also check with employers or other references to verify answers and get further information.

Working Conditions

Although adjusters, investigators, and collectors share many working conditions, differences exist in the various segments of this grouping of workers. Most claim representatives work a standard 5-day, 40-hour week and work in a typical office environment. However, many others work evening shifts and on weekends. As insurance companies place more emphasis on customer service, they are providing more claim services around the clock. This means that a growing number of claim representatives may work evenings and weekends staffing claims centers, many of which are open 24 hours a day, 7 days a week. Many claim adjusters, on the other hand, work outside the office, inspecting damaged buildings and automobiles. Occasionally, experienced adjusters are away from home for days when they travel to the scene of a disaster—such as a tornado, hurricane, or flood—to work with local adjusters and government officials. Some adjusters are on emergency call in the case of such incidents. Material damage adjusters can work at local claim centers where policyholders take their cars for estimates of damage. In general, adjusters are able to arrange their work schedule to accommodate evening and weekend appointments with clients. This accommodation may result in adjusters working 50 or 60 hours a week. Some report to the office every morning to get their assignments while others simply call from home and spend their days traveling to claim sites. This enables some adjusters to work independently.

Most insurance processing clerks work 40 hours a week in an office. Many of these workers sit at video display terminals and enter or access information while the customer is on the telephone. Because most companies provide 24-hour claim service to their policyholders, some claim clerks work evenings and weekends. Many claim clerks work part time.

Adjustment clerks or customer service representatives are increasingly available in the evenings and on weekends, particularly the growing number of clerks who work for catalog and Internet retailers. These clerks usually work in call-center environments, taking calls from customers 24 hours a day, 7 days a week. Other adjustment clerks work in the offices of businesses and work standard business hours.

Bill and account collectors, and welfare eligibility workers and interviewers work in offices, usually during regular business hours. However, some collectors work evenings and weekends when clients can be more easily reached. Some bill and account collectors work part time, while others can work as temporaries for collection agencies. Dealing with upset or angry clients is often part of the daily routine in these jobs, making the work stressful at times.

Employment

Adjusters, investigators, and collectors held about 1.5 million jobs in 1998. The following tabulation shows the percent distribution of employment by detailed occupation:

Occupation	Percent
Adjustment clerks	33
Bill and account collectors	21
Insurance policy processing clerks	12
Insurance adjusters, examiners, and investigators	12
Insurance claim clerks	11
Welfare eligibility workers and interviewers	7
Claims examiners, property and casualty insurance	3
All other adjusters and investigators	1

Insurance companies employ the vast majority of claim adjusters, examiners, investigators, policy processing clerks, and claim clerks. Hospitals and physician offices and independent adjusting and claims processing firms employ the remainder.

Adjustment clerks are found throughout the economy; however, they are concentrated in the wholesale and retail sectors. Wholesalers, department stores, or catalog and Internet retailers employ nearly 1 out of 4 adjustment clerks. Insurance companies, airlines, hospitals, and telephone companies are other major employers of these workers.

About 1 in 5 bill and account collectors works for a collection agency. Many others work in banks, department stores, governments, and other institutions that lend money and extend credit.

Around 3 of every 4 welfare eligibility workers and interviewers work for Federal, State or local government agencies. Most of those not employed by government work for private social service agencies and medical facilities.

Training, Other Qualifications, and Advancement

Training and entry requirements vary widely for adjuster, investigator, and collector jobs. A high school education is sufficient to qualify for most insurance processing clerk, adjustment clerk, and bill and account collector positions, while a bachelor's degree is preferred for most claim representative positions. While some college education is preferred for adjuster or welfare eligibility worker or interviewer positions, many people qualify for these positions on the strength of related prior work experience. Because a significant and growing proportion of adjusters, investigators, and collectors use computers, word processing and other computer skills are helpful.

Claim Representatives. Most companies prefer to hire college graduates for claim representative positions. Entry level workers may be hired without college coursework, however, if they have specialized experience. For example, people with knowledge of automobile mechanics or body repair may qualify as material damage adjusters and those with extensive clerical experience might be hired as inside adjusters. Both adjusters and examiners should be problem solvers and enjoy working with details.

No specific college major is recommended for these occupations. An adjuster, though, who has a business or an accounting background might specialize in claims of financial loss due to strikes, breakdowns in equipment, or damage to merchandise. College training in engineering is helpful in adjusting industrial claims, such as damage from fires and other accidents. A legal background is helpful in handling workers' compensation and product liability cases. Knowledge of computer applications is also extremely important for all claim representatives.

Six States require independent or public adjusters to be licensed. Applicants in these States usually must comply with one or more of the following: Pass a licensing examination covering the fundamentals of adjusting; complete an approved course in insurance or loss adjusting; furnish character references; be at least 20 or 21 years of age and a resident of the State; and file a surety bond.

Because they often work closely with claimants, witnesses, and other insurance professionals, claim representatives must be able to communicate effectively with others. Some companies require applicants to pass a series of written aptitude tests designed to measure communication, analytical, and general mathematical skills. They must also understand Federal and State insurance laws and regulations.

Most large insurance companies provide classroom training for entry level claim adjusters and examiners. For example, material damage adjusters may be offered classes about automobile body construction, analysis of collision data, repair cost estimation, and computerized estimating equipment.

Workers also may receive training through courses offered by the Insurance Institute of America, a nonprofit organization offering educational programs and professional certification to persons in the property-liability insurance industry. The Insurance Institute of America offers an Associate in Claims designation upon successful completion of four essay examinations. Adjusters can prepare for the examination through independent home study or company and public classes. The Institute also offers a certificate upon successful completion of the Introduction to Claims program and an examination. In addition, the International Claim Association offers a program on life and health insurance claim administration. Completion of the 6-examination program leads to the professional Associate, Life, and Health Claims designation.

Beginning adjusters and examiners work on small claims under the supervision of an experienced worker. As they learn more about claim investigation and settlement, they are assigned larger, more complex claims. Trainees are promoted as they demonstrate competence in handling assignments and as they progress in their coursework. Employees who demonstrate competence in claim work or administrative skills may be promoted to claims approver or claims manager. Other claim representatives are promoted to claim investigators.

Insurance Processing Clerks. A high school education is sufficient for most policy processing and customer service positions. For customer service jobs, applicants must possess excellent communication and customer service skills. All candidates should be familiar with computers and be able to type well. Previous office or customer service experience is also an asset.

A few experienced insurance processing clerks may be promoted to a clerical supervisor position. Advancement to a claim representative or an underwriting technician position is possible for clerks who demonstrate potential, have college coursework, or have taken specialized courses in insurance. Many companies offer training for their employees so they can acquire the knowledge necessary to advance.

Policy processing clerks working in customer service jobs can advance their career by obtaining the Certified Insurance Service Representative (CISR) designation administered by the Society of Certified Insurance Service Representatives. To earn the designation, applicants must attend five one-day classes and pass an examination at the end of each class.

Adjustment Clerks. Many employers do not require any formal education for adjustment clerk positions. Instead, they look for people who can read and write well and who possess good communication and interpersonal skills. Computer skills are also important. Foreign language skills are an asset for those adjustment clerks working in call centers handling a variety of callers from throughout the country.

Adjustment clerk is an entry level position in some, but not all, organizations. Depending on their assignment, new adjustment clerks may receive training on the job from a supervisor or an experienced coworker, or they may enter a formal training course offered by the organization. As companies strive for better customer service, training is becoming more important, covering such topics as how to use the company's computers, what standard forms to use, whom to contact in other departments of the organization, and how to deal with customers.

Bill and Account Collectors. While a high school diploma is sometimes required for bill and account collector positions, formal education beyond high school is not stressed. Prior experience in the field of telemarketing or as a telephone operator is helpful, as is knowledge of the billing process. Employers seek individuals who speak clearly and who are persistent and detail-oriented.

Employers normally provide training to new bill and account collectors. This training, which may last up to a couple of months, is usually conducted in a classroom or on the job. Although not required by law, many employers also require their collectors to get certified through the American Collectors Association (ACA). ACA seminars concentrate on current State and Federal compliance laws. Since most States recognize these credentials, ACA-certified collectors have greater career mobility. In training seminars, employers use videotapes, computer programs, role-playing, and hands-on experience. New collectors learn about locating customers, billing procedures, and most importantly, communications and negotiation. Learning to use the firm's computer and telephone systems is also an integral part of their training. Successful bill and account collectors may become supervisors. Some even start their own collection agencies.

Welfare Eligibility Workers and Interviewers. Hiring requirements for welfare eligibility workers and interviewers vary widely. Depending on the jurisdiction, applicants may need a high school diploma, associate degree, or bachelor's degree. Work experience in a closely related field—such as employment interviewing, social work, or insurance claims—may also qualify one for this job. In parts of the country with a high concentration of non-English speaking people, fluency in a foreign language may be an advantage.

Because they deal with people who are in difficult economic circumstances, welfare eligibility workers and interviewers should be compassionate and empathetic. They must be detail-oriented and able to follow the numerous procedures and regulations regarding eligibility. Welfare eligibility workers also must be very organized because they work under tight deadlines and often have large caseloads.

After they are hired, eligibility workers are given training, sometimes in a formal classroom setting, other times in a more informal manner. They are taught the policies, procedures, and program regulations that they are expected to use to determine eligibility. If a formal training program is selected, a supervisor or senior eligibility worker usually provides follow-up on-the-job training.

In some jurisdictions, advancement can result in being given the authority to determine eligibility or additional responsibilities. Senior eligibility workers may train new personnel and can advance to a supervisory position. Some workers can advance to the job of social worker, although additional formal education, such as a bachelor's or master's degree, usually is needed.

Job Outlook

Overall employment of adjusters, investigators, and collectors is expected to grow faster than the average for all occupations over the 1998-2008 period. Most job openings, however, will result from the need to replace workers who transfer to other occupations or leave the labor force.

Projected growth rates vary considerably by occupation. Employment of insurance claim representatives is expected to grow about as fast as average as an increasing volume of insurance will result in more insurance claims. The need for life, health, home, and automobile insurance will increase as the population expands and people accumulate assets and take on family responsibilities. Also, new or expanding businesses will need protection for new plants and equipment and for insurance covering their employees' health and safety. Growth in the insurance industry will translate into job growth because many of the duties of claim representatives are not easily automated. Opportunities should be particularly good for claim representatives who specialize in complex business insurance such as marine cargo, workers' compensation, and product liability. Also, representatives with some medical knowledge will be in demand by health insurers and health maintenance organizations as these companies seek additional claim examiners to improve public relations.

Insurance processing occupations are expected to grow about as fast as average, with claim clerks growing faster than policy processing clerks. Unlike other clerical jobs that are declining in number, many policy processors have transformed into customer service representatives with a wider range of responsibilities. Because policy changes can now be entered directly into the computer as the policy change is being requested, the customer service representative is the best person to perform this service. Agencies, in particular, are hiring more customer service representatives to essentially run the office while the agents spend more time soliciting clients. Also, the growing number of insurance companies that sell policies directly to the public are hiring more customer service representatives to handle policy changes directly from clients. Although the job has become highly automated and the changes can be made more easily, a person is still required to enter the data. However, policy processors who perform mostly clerical duties and have no customer service role will decline as their job becomes increasingly automated and the industry strives for paperless transactions.

Medical facilities and independent claims processing companies are increasingly hiring claims clerks to handle routine medical claims. This will keep the number of claims clerks growing at an average rate through 2008. However, claims clerks working for insurance companies—particularly health insurance—will grow more slowly as their job becomes increasingly automated through the implementation of electronic claims processing software that minimizes claims handling. However, in property and casualty insurance, the job still requires contact with policyholders and is less subject to automation than other clerical positions.

Employment of adjustment clerks is expected to grow faster than average as business establishments place an increased emphasis on maintaining good customer relations. An important aspect of good customer service is resolving customers' complaints and inquiries in a friendly and timely fashion. Because much of their work involves direct communication with customers, demand for adjustment clerks is expected to keep pace with growth in the number of customers. In particular, catalog and Internet retailers, whose growth is expected to skyrocket over the next 10 years, will demand more adjustment clerks acting as customer service representatives to handle an increasing number of requests.

Bill and account collector jobs also are expected to grow much faster than average as the level of consumer debt rises and as more companies seek to improve their debt collection by contracting with third party collection agencies. Government agencies are increasingly using third party collection agencies to collect on everything from parking tickets to child support payments and overdue taxes. Contrary to the pattern in most occupations, employment of bill and account collectors tends to rise during recessions, reflecting the difficulty that many people have in meeting their financial obligations.

Employment of welfare eligibility workers and interviewers is expected to decline as many people move from welfare to work, and as State and local governments attempt to curb growth in their expenditures for public assistance. The need to replace workers who leave this occupation will be large, however, as this job has a high turnover rate.

Earnings

Earnings of adjusters, investigators, and collectors vary significantly. The median annual earnings for selected occupations in 1998 were as follows:

Insurance adjusters, examiners, and investigators	$38,290
Welfare eligibility workers and interviewers	33,100
Insurance claims clerks	24,010
Insurance policy processing clerks	23,960
Bill and account collectors	22,540
Adjustment clerks	22,040

Workers in some occupations receive additional bonuses or benefits as part of their job. Adjusters are often furnished a cellular telephone and a company car or are reimbursed for use of their own vehicle for business purposes. Although many receive only a salary, some bill and account collectors receive commissions or bonuses in addition to salary, depending on how many cases they close.

Welfare eligibility workers and interviewers are twice as likely to belong to unions than workers in all occupations. In 1997, about 23 percent of all welfare eligibility workers and interviewers were union members, compared to 13 percent for all occupations. The two principal unions representing these workers are the American Federation of State, County, and Municipal Employees, and the Service Employees International Union.

Related Occupations

Insurance adjusters and examiners investigate, analyze, and determine the validity of their firm's liability concerning disability, illness, casualty, or property loss or damages. Workers in other occupations that require similar skills include cost estimators, budget analysts, and private investigators.

The work of bill and account collectors, adjustment clerks, and insurance processing clerks is similar to that of customer service representatives, telemarketers, telephone interviewers, and other workers who deal with the public over the telephone.

The work of welfare eligibility workers is similar to that of social and human service assistants, financial aid counselors, loan and credit counselors, probation officers, and other workers who interview customers or clients.

Sources of Additional Information

General information about a career as a claim representative or an insurance processing clerk is available from the home offices of many life and property and liability insurance companies. Information about career opportunities in these occupations also may be obtained from:

☛ Insurance Information Institute, 110 William St., New York, NY 10038. Internet: **http://www.iii.org**

Information about licensing requirements for claim adjusters may be obtained from the department of insurance in each State.

For information about the Associate in Claims (AIC) designation, or the Introduction to Claims program, contact:

☛ Insurance Institute of America, 720 Providence Rd., P.O. Box 3016, Malvern, PA 19355-0716. Internet: **http://www.aicpcu.org**

Information on the Associate, Life and Health Claims designation can be obtained from:

☛ Life Office Management Association, 2300 Windy Ridge Pkwy., Atlanta, GA 30327-4308. Internet: **http://www.loma.org**

Information on the Certified Insurance Service Representative designation can be obtained from:

☛ The Society of Certified Insurance Service Representatives, P.O. Box 27028, Austin, TX 78755. Internet: **http://www.scic.com**

Career information on bill and account collectors is available from:

☛ American Collectors Association, Inc., P.O. Box 39106, Minneapolis, MN 55439-0106. Internet: **http://www.collector.com**

Employment information on welfare eligibility workers and interviewers is available at social service offices of municipal, county, and State governments.

Bank Tellers

(O*NET 53102)

Significant Points

- The projected decline in employment of tellers reflects cost cutting by banks and the growing use of banking technology to perform routine banking services.
- Many job openings will arise from replacement needs in this large occupation because turnover is high, little formal education is required, and the position offers relatively low pay.
- Applicants trained to provide a variety of financial services, along with those seeking part-time work, should have the best job prospects.

Nature of the Work

The bank teller is the person most people associate with a bank. Tellers make up 28 percent of bank employees, and conduct most of a bank's routine transactions. Among their responsibilities are cashing checks, accepting deposits and loan payments, and processing withdrawals. They may also sell savings bonds, accept payment for customers' utility bills and charge cards, process necessary paperwork for certificates of deposit, and sell travelers' checks. Some tellers specialize in handling foreign currencies or commercial or business accounts.

Being a teller requires a great deal of attention to detail. Before cashing a check, a teller must verify the date, bank name, identification of the person to receive payment, and legality of the document. They must also make sure that written and numerical amounts agree and that the account has sufficient funds to cover the check. The teller then must carefully count cash to avoid errors. Sometimes a customer withdraws money in the form of a cashier's check, which the teller prepares and verifies. When accepting a deposit, tellers must check the accuracy of the deposit slip before processing the transaction.

Prior to starting their shift, tellers receive and count an amount of working cash for their drawer. A supervisor, usually the head teller, verifies this amount. Tellers use this cash for payments during the day and are responsible for its safe and accurate handling. Before leaving, tellers count cash on hand, list the currency-received tickets on a balance sheet, make sure the accounts balance, and sort checks and deposit slips. Over the course of a workday, tellers may also process numerous mail transactions. Some tellers replenish cash drawers and corroborate deposits and payments to automated teller machines (ATMs).

In most banks, head tellers are responsible for the teller line. In addition to the typical duties of a teller, a head teller's responsibilities include preparing work schedules, accessing the vault, ensuring the correct cash balance in the vault, and overseeing shipments of cash to and from the Federal Reserve.

Technology continues to play a large role in the job duties of all tellers. In most banks, for example, tellers use computer terminals to record deposits and withdrawals. These terminals often give tellers quick access to detailed information on customer accounts. Tellers can use this information to tailor services to fit a customer's needs or to recommend an appropriate bank product or service.

Because banks offer more and increasingly complex financial services, tellers in many banks are being trained to perform some functions of customer service representatives, in addition to their other duties. These tellers are required to learn about the various financial products and services the bank offers, so they can briefly explain them to customers and refer interested customers to appropriate specialized sales personnel. (Customer service representatives are discussed in the *Handbook* statement on interviewing and new accounts clerks.)

Working Conditions

Tellers generally work weekdays, although some evening and weekend work may be required. The job offers ample opportunity to work part time with flexible hours; in some banks, 90 percent of tellers work part time. Banks often hire part-time, or "peak-time," tellers for busy banking periods, such as lunch hours and Saturday mornings. An increasing number of tellers work outside a traditional bank setting, as more branches are established in shopping malls and grocery stores. These tellers usually work more evening and weekend hours and have more varied responsibilities than other tellers.

Tellers use computer terminals to record deposits and withdrawals.

Continual communication with customers, repetitive tasks, long periods of standing within a small area, and a high level of attention to security characterize the job. Tellers wishing to provide more personalized service in a less hectic environment often choose to work for a small bank. Full-time employment and a full range of benefits are also more common in smallbanks, leading to lower turnover rates.

Employment

Bank tellers held about 560,000 jobs in 1998; about 1 out of 3 worked part time. The overwhelming majority worked in commercial banks, savings institutions, or credit unions. The remaining were employed in a variety of other financial service companies.

Training, Other Qualifications, and Advancement

When hiring tellers, banks seek applicants who have excellent communication skills, enjoy working with the public, and possess a strong math aptitude. Tellers must feel comfortable handling large amounts of cash and working with computers and video terminals. In general, banks prefer applicants with some sales and cash handling experience. In some metropolitan areas, employers seek multilingual tellers.

Although tellers work independently, their recordkeeping is closely supervised. Accuracy and attention to detail are vital. Tellers should be courteous, attentive, and patient in dealing with the public, because customers often judge a bank by the way they are treated at the teller window. Maturity, tact, and the ability to quickly explain bank procedures and services are important in helping customers complete transactions or make financial decisions.

Many new tellers transfer from other occupations, and virtually all tellers have at least a high school education. Usually, new tellers in large banks receive at least one week of formal classroom training. Classes are followed by several weeks of on-the-job training, in which tellers observe experienced workers before doing the work themselves. Smaller banks rely primarily upon on-the-job training. In addition to instruction in basic duties, many banks now include extensive training in the bank's products and services, communication and sales skills, and instruction on equipment, such as ATMs and on-line video terminals.

In large banks, beginners usually start for a few days as limited-transaction tellers, cashing checks and processing simple transactions, before becoming full-service tellers. Often, banks simultaneously train tellers for other clerical duties as well.

Advancement opportunities are good for well-trained, motivated employees. Experienced tellers may advance to head teller, customer service representative, or new accounts clerk. Outstanding tellers who have had some college or specialized training offered by the banking industry may be promoted to a managerial position. Banks encourage this upward mobility by providing access to education and other sources of additional training.

Tellers can prepare for better jobs by taking courses offered or accredited by the American Institute of Banking (an educational affiliate of the American Bankers Association) or the Institute of Financial Education. These organizations have several hundred chapters in cities across the country and numerous study groups in small communities. They also offer correspondence courses and work closely with local colleges and universities in preparing courses of study. Most banks use the facilities of these organizations to conduct cooperative training programs or develop independent training programs. In addition, many banks refund employees' college tuition fees, upon successful completion of courses. Although most courses are meant for employed tellers, some community colleges offer preemployment training programs. These programs can help prepare applicants for a job in banking and can give them an advantage over other jobseekers.

Tellers who are trained to sell insurance products must receive a State license to sell insurance. This requires passing an examination, usually after taking a prelicensing course. (See the statement on insurance sales agents elsewhere in the *Handbook*.)

Job Outlook

Employment of bank tellers is expected to decline through 2008. Nevertheless, many job openings will arise from replacement needs, because turnover is high—a characteristic typical of large occupations that normally require little formal education and offer relatively low pay. Applicants for part-time jobs should fare better than applicants for full-time positions.

The banking industry will continue to undergo many changes that will impact employment of traditional tellers, who perform only routine transactions. Principal among these are technology, bank mergers, and changing employment needs. For example, ATMs and the increased use of direct deposit of paychecks and benefit checks have reduced the need for bank customers to interact with tellers for routine transactions. In addition, electronic banking is spreading rapidly throughout the banking industry. This type of banking, conducted over the telephone or through computer networks, will also reduce the number of tellers over the long run.

Bank mergers, particularly those involving competing banks, have reduced the number of branches as the newly formed banks cut costs and eliminate duplicate services. This has adversely affected employment of tellers who work primarily in branch offices. Bank mergers are expected to continue as banks seek to further reduce costs and offer more services that only large banks can provide, such as numerous ATM locations, more types of loans, and securities brokerage and insurance services.

Teller employment is also being impacted by the increasing use of 24-hour phone centers by many large banks. These telephone centers allow a customer to interact with a bank representative at a distant location, either by telephone or video terminal. Customer service representatives, who can handle a wider variety of transactions than tellers, including loan applications and credit card issuance, usually staff such centers.

Even though some banks have streamlined their branches, the total number of bank branches is expected to increase to meet the needs of a growing population. Branches are being added in nontraditional locations, such as grocery stores, malls, and mobile trailers designed to reach people who do not have easy access to banks. Often, these branches are open longer hours and offer greater customer convenience. Many of these nontraditional branch offices are small and are staffed by tellers who are trained as customer service representatives. As a result, tellers who can provide a variety of financial services will be in greater demand in the future.

Earnings

Median annual earnings of full-time bank tellers were $17,200 in 1998. The middle 50 percent earned between $14,660 and $20,180. The lowest 10 percent earned less than $12,970, while the top 10 percent earned more than $23,000. Some banks offer incentives that reward tellers for inducing customers to use other financial products and services offered by the bank. In general, greater responsibilities result in a higher salary. Experience, length of service, and, especially, the location and size of the bank also are important. Full-time tellers generally receive a full range of benefits, from life and health insurance to pension benefits, whereas part-time tellers often do not.

Median annual earnings in the industries employing the largest number of bank tellers in 1997 were:

Savings institutions	$16,800
Commercial banks	16,600
Credit unions	16,500

Related Occupations

Tellers combine customer service and knowledge of bank procedures with quickness and accuracy to process money, checks, and other financial items for customers. Other workers with similar duties include new accounts clerks, cashiers, toll collectors, post office clerks, auction clerks, and ticket sellers.

Sources of Additional Information

General information about tellers and other banking occupations, training opportunities, and the banking industry is available from:

☛ American Bankers Association, 1120 Connecticut Ave. NW, Washington, DC 20036. Internet: **http://www.aba.com**

State bankers' associations can furnish specific information about job opportunities in their State. Individual banks can provide detailed information about job openings and the activities, responsibilities, and preferred qualifications of tellers.

Communications Equipment Operators

(57102, 57105, 57108, 57111, and 57199)

Significant Points

- About 9 out of 10 communications equipment operators work as telephone operators.
- Workers are trained on the job.
- Employment is expected to decline due to new laborsaving communications technologies and consolidations in the telecommunications industry.

Nature of the Work

Most communications equipment operators work as telephone operators, assisting customers making telephone calls. Although most calls are connected automatically, callers sometimes require the assistance of an operator. *Central office operators* help customers complete local and long distance calls. *Directory assistance operators* provide customers with information such as phone numbers or area codes. *Switchboard operators* usually provide telephone assistance for a single organization; they relay incoming, outgoing, and interoffice calls.

When callers dial "0", they usually reach a central office operator, also known as a *local*, *long distance*, or *call completion operator*. Most of these operators work for telephone companies and many of their responsibilities have been automated. For example, callers can make international, collect, and credit card calls without the assistance of a central office operator. Other tasks previously handled by these operators, such as billing calls to third parties or monitoring the cost of a call, have also been automated.

Callers still need a central office operator for a limited number of tasks. These include placing person-to-person calls or interrupting busy lines if an emergency warrants the disruption. When natural disasters occur, such as storms or earthquakes, central office operators provide callers with emergency phone contacts. They also assist callers having difficulty with automated phone systems. An operator monitoring an automated system for placing collect calls, for example, may intervene if a caller needs assistance with the system.

Directory assistance operators provide callers with information such as telephone numbers or area codes. Most directory assistance operators work for telephone companies; increasingly they also work for companies that provide business services. Automated systems now handle many of the responsibilities once performed by directory assistance operators. The systems prompt callers for a listing, and may even connect the call after providing the phone number. However, directory assistance operators monitor many of the calls received by automated systems. The operators listen to recordings of the customer's request, and then key information into electronic directories to access the correct phone numbers. Directory assistance operators also provide personal assistance to customers having difficulty using the automated system.

Switchboard operators work for a wide variety of organizations, such as hospitals, hotels, and other businesses. They often operate private branch exchange (PBX) switchboards to relay incoming, outgoing, and interoffice calls. Switchboard operators may also handle other clerical duties, such as supplying information, taking messages, and announcing visitors. Technological improvements have automated many of the tasks handled by switchboard operators. New systems automatically connect outside calls to the correct destination, and voice mail systems take messages without the assistance of an operator.

Other communications equipment operators include workers who operate telegraphic typewriter, telegraph key, facsimile machine, and related equipment to transmit and receive signals and messages. They prepare messages according to prescribed formats, and verify and correct errors in messages. As part of their job, they may also adjust equipment for proper operation.

Working Conditions

Most communications equipment operators work in pleasant, well-lighted surroundings. Because telephone operators spend much time seated at keyboards and video monitors, employers often provide workstations designed to decrease glare and other physical discomforts. Such improvements reduce the incidence of eyestrain, back discomfort, and injury due to repetitive motion.

Central office and directory assistance operators must be accessible to customers 24 hours a day, and therefore work a variety of shifts. Some operators work split shifts, that is, they are on duty during peak calling periods in the late morning and early evening and off duty during the intervening hours. Telephone companies normally assign shifts by seniority, allowing the most experienced operators first choice of schedules. As a result, entry level operators may have less desirable schedules, including late evening, split shift, and weekend work. Telephone company operators may work overtime during emergencies.

Switchboard operators generally work the same hours as other clerical employees at their company. In most organizations, full-time operators work regular business hours over a 5-day workweek. Work schedules are more irregular in hotels, hospitals, and other organizations that require round-the-clock operator services. In these companies, switchboard operators may work in the evenings and on holidays and weekends.

Approximately 1 in 5 communications equipment operator works part-time. Because of the irregular nature of telephone operator schedules, many employers seek part-time workers for those shifts that are difficult to fill.

An operator's work may be quite repetitive and the pace hectic during peak calling periods. To maintain operator efficiency, supervisors at telephone companies often monitor operator performance including the amount of time spent on each call. The rapid pace of the job and frequent monitoring may cause stress. To reduce job-related stress, some workplaces attempt to create a more stimulating and less rigid working environment.

Switchboard operators may perform clerical work when not assisting callers.

Employment

Communications equipment operators held about 297,000 jobs in 1998. About 9 out of 10 worked as telephone operators. Employment was distributed as follows:

Occupation	Jobs
Switchboard operators	214,000
Directory assistance operators	23,000
Central office operators	23,000
All other communications equipment operators	36,000

Most switchboard operators worked for services establishments, such as personnel supply services, hospitals, and hotels and motels. The majority of central office and directory assistance operators worked in telephone companies.

Training, Other Qualifications, and Advancement

Communications equipment operators receive their training on the job. At large telephone companies, entry level central office and directory assistance operators may receive both classroom and on-the-job instruction that can last several weeks. At small telephone companies, operators usually receive shorter, less formal training. These operators may be paired with experienced personnel who provide hands-on instruction. Switchboard operators may also receive short-term, informal training, sometimes provided by the manufacturer of their switchboard equipment.

New employees receive training on equipment operation and procedures for maximizing efficiency. They are familiarized with company policies, including the level of customer service performance they are expected to deliver. Instructors monitor both the time and quality of trainees' responses to customer requests. Supervisors may continue to closely monitor new employees after their initial training session is complete.

Employers generally require a high school diploma for operator positions, and applicants should have strong reading, spelling, and numerical skills. Operators must have clear speech and good hearing. Computer literacy and typing skills are also important, and familiarity with a foreign language is helpful. Most companies place an emphasis on customer service skills; employers seek operators who will remain courteous to customers while working in a fast-paced environment.

After 1 or 2 years on the job, telephone operators may advance to other positions within a company. Many enter clerical occupations where their operator experience is valuable; these include positions as customer service agents, dispatchers, and receptionists. Operators with a more technical background and an interest in telecommunications may advance into positions installing and repairing equipment. Promotion to supervisory positions is also possible.

Job Outlook

Employment of communications equipment operators is projected to decline through 2008, largely due to new laborsaving communications technologies and consolidations in the telecommunications industry. Virtually all job openings will result from the need to replace communications equipment operators who transfer to other occupations or leave the labor force.

Developments in communications technologies, specifically the ease and accessibility of voice recognition systems, will continue to have a significant impact on the demand for telephone operators. The decline in employment will be sharpest among directory assistance operators; smaller decreases will occur for central office and switchboard operators. Voice recognition technology allows automated phone systems to recognize human speech. Callers speak directly to the system, which interprets the speech and then connects the call. Because voice recognition systems do not require callers to input data on a telephone keypad, they are easier to use than touch tone systems, and are accessible to rotary phone customers. The systems are also increasingly sophisticated in terms of the vocabulary and grammatical structures they can understand. However, many companies will continue to employ operators so those callers having problems can access a "live" employee if desired.

Electronic communications, such as the Internet and e-mail, provide alternatives to telephone communications and require no operators. Internet directory assistance services are expected to reduce the need for directory assistance operators. Local phone companies currently have the most reliable phone directory data; however, Internet services provide information such as addresses and maps, in addition to phone numbers. As telephones and computers converge, the convenience of Internet directory assistance is expected to attract many customers, eliminating the need for telephone operators to provide this service.

Consolidations among telephone companies also will reduce the need for operators. As communications technologies improve and long distance prices fall, telephone companies will consolidate their operator functions. Operators will be employed at fewer locations and will serve larger customer populations.

Earnings

Median hourly earnings of switchboard operators in 1998 were $8.76. The middle 50 percent earned between $7.20 and $10.63. The lowest 10 percent earned less than $6.21 and the highest 10 percent earned more than $12.86. Median hourly earnings in the industries employing the largest numbers of switchboard operators in 1997 are shown below:

Industry	Earnings
Telephone communications	$10.90
Offices and clinics of medical doctors	8.60
Hospitals	8.40
Hotels and motels	8.30
Personnel supply services	8.30
Miscellaneous business services	7.40

Median hourly earnings of central office operators in 1998 were $12.61. The middle 50 percent earned between $8.73 and $15.97. The lowest 10 percent earned less than $7.12 and the highest 10 percent earned more than $18.33.

Median hourly earnings of directory assistance operators in 1998 were $14.68. The middle 50 percent earned between $9.94 and $16.32. The lowest 10 percent earned less than $7.61 and the highest 10 percent earned more than $18.42.

Many central office and directory assistance operators working at telephone companies are members of the Communications Workers of America (CWA), or the International Brotherhood of Electrical Workers (IBEW). According to the CWA, telephone operators started at an average of $235 a week in 1998, and after 4 years on the job averaged $654 a week. According to the IBEW, hourly wages for most telephone operators ranged from a minimum of about $10.50 to a maximum of about $17.30 in 1999. For these operators, union contracts govern wage rates, wage increases, and the time required to advance from one pay step to the next (it normally takes 4 years to rise from the lowest paying, nonsupervisory operator position to the highest). Contracts also call for extra pay for work beyond the normal 6 1/2 to 7 1/2 hours a day or 5 days a week, for Sunday and holiday work, and for a pay differential for night work and split shifts. Many contracts provide for a 1-week vacation with 6 months of service; 2 weeks for 1 to 6 years; 3 weeks for 7 to 14 years; 4 weeks for 15 to 24 years; and 5 weeks for 25 years and over. Holidays range from 9 to 11 days a year.

Related Occupations

Other workers who provide information to the general public include dispatchers; hotel, motel, and resort desk clerks; information clerks; receptionists; reservation and transportation ticket agents; and travel clerks.

Sources of Additional Information

For more details about employment opportunities, contact your telephone company or write to:

☛ Communications Workers of America, 501 3rd St. NW., Washington, DC 20001. Internet: **http://www.cwa-union.org**

☛ International Brotherhood of Electrical Workers, Telecommunications Department, 1125 15th. St. NW., Room 807, Washington, DC 20005.

For more information on the telephone industry, contact:

☛ United States Telephone Association, 1401 H St. NW., Suite 600, Washington, DC 20005-2164. Internet: **http://www.usta.org**

Computer Operators

(O*NET 56011 and 56014)

Significant Points

- Employment is expected to decline sharply, due to advances in technology.
- Opportunities will be best for operators who are familiar with a variety of operating systems and who keep up to date with the latest technology.

Nature of the Work

Computer operators oversee the operation of computer hardware systems, ensuring that these machines are used as efficiently as possible. They may work with mainframes, minicomputers, or networks of personal computers. Computer operators must anticipate problems and take preventive action, as well as solve problems that occur during operations.

The duties of computer operators vary with the size of the installation, the type of equipment used, and the policies of the employer. Generally, operators control the console of either a mainframe digital computer or a group of minicomputers. Working from operating instructions prepared by programmers, users, or operations managers, computer operators set controls on the computer and on peripheral devices required to run a particular job.

Computer operators load equipment with tapes, disks, and paper, as needed. While the computer is running—which may be 24 hours a day for large computers—computer operators monitor the control console and respond to operating and computer messages. Messages indicate the individual specifications of each job being run. If an error message occurs, operators must locate and solve the problem or terminate the program. Operators also maintain logbooks or operating records, listing each job that is run and events such as machine malfunctions that occur during their shift. In addition, computer operators may help programmers and systems analysts test and debug new programs. (See the statements on computer programmers and computer systems analysts, engineers, and scientists elsewhere in the *Handbook*.)

As the trend toward networking computers accelerates, a growing number of computer operators are working on personal computers (PCs) and minicomputers. In many offices, factories, and other work settings, PCs and minicomputers are connected in networks, often referred to as local area networks (LANs) or multi-user systems. Whereas users in the area operate some of these computers, many require the services of full-time operators. The tasks performed are very similar to those performed on large computers.

As organizations continue to look for opportunities to increase productivity, automation is expanding into additional areas of computer operations. Sophisticated software coupled with robotics, enable a computer to perform many routine tasks formerly done by computer operators. Scheduling, loading and downloading programs, mounting tapes, rerouting messages, and running periodic reports can be done without the intervention of an operator. Consequently, these improvements will change what computer operators do in the future. As technology advances, the responsibilities of many computer operators are shifting to areas such as network operations, user support, and database maintenance.

Working Conditions

Computer operating personnel generally work in well-lighted, well-ventilated, comfortable rooms. Because many organizations use their computers 24 hours a day, 7 days a week, computer operators may be required to work evening or night shifts and weekends. Shift assignments usually are made based on seniority. However, increasingly automated operations will lessen the need for shift work, because many companies let the computer take over operations during less desirable working hours. In addition, advances in telecommuting technologies—such as faxes, modems, and e-mail—and data center automation, such as automated tape libraries, enable some operators to monitor batch processes, check systems performance, and record problems for the next shift.

Since computer operators generally spend a lot of time in front of a computer monitor, as well as performing repetitive tasks such as loading and unloading printers, they may be susceptible to eyestrain, back discomfort, and hand and wrist problems.

Computer operators load equipment with tapes, disks, and paper as needed.

Employment

In 1998, computer operators held about 251,000 jobs. The majority of jobs for computer operators are found in organizations such as wholesale trade establishments, manufacturing companies, data processing service firms, financial institutions, and government agencies that have data processing needs requiring large computer installations. A large number of computer operators are employed by service firms in the computer and data processing services industry, as more companies contract out the operation of their data processing centers.

Training, Other Qualifications, and Advancement

Workers usually receive on-the-job training in order to become acquainted with their employer's equipment and routines. The length of training varies with the job and the experience of the worker. However, previous work experience is the key to obtaining an operator job in many large establishments. Employers generally look for specific, hands-on experience with the type of equipment and related operating systems they use. Additionally, formal computer-related training, perhaps through a community college or technical school, is recommended. Related training can also be obtained through the Armed Forces and from some computer manufacturers. As computer technology changes and data processing centers become more automated, increasingly more employers will require candidates to have formal training and experience for operator jobs.

Because computer technology changes so rapidly, operators must be adaptable and willing to learn. Analytical and technical expertise are also needed, particularly by operators who work in automated data centers, to deal with the unique or high-level problems a computer is not programmed to handle. Operators must be able to communicate well, to work effectively with programmers or users, as well as with other operators. Additionally, computer operators must be able to work independently, because they may have little or no direct supervision.

A few computer operators may advance to supervisory jobs, although most management positions within data processing or computer operations centers require advanced formal education, such as a bachelor's (or higher) degree. Through on-the-job experience and additional formal education, some computer operators may advance to jobs in areas such as network operations or support. As they gain experience in programming, some operators may advance to jobs as programmers or analysts. A move into these types of jobs is becoming much more difficult, as employers increasingly require candidates for more skilled computer jobs to possess at least a bachelor's degree.

Job Outlook

Employment of computer operators is expected to decline sharply through the year 2008. Experienced operators are expected to compete for the small number of openings that will arise each year to replace workers who transfer to other occupations or leave the labor force. Opportunities will be best for operators who are familiar with a variety of operating systems and who keep up to date with the latest technology.

Advances in technology have reduced both the size and cost of computer equipment, while increasing the capacity for data storage and processing automation. These improvements in technology have fueled an expansion in the use of sophisticated computer hardware and software in practically every industry in such areas as factory and office automation, telecommunications, medicine, education, and administration. The expanding use of software that automates computer operations gives companies the option of making systems user-friendly, greatly reducing the need for operators. These new technologies will require operators to monitor a greater number of operations at the same time and be capable of solving a broader range of problems that may arise. The result is that fewer and fewer operators will be needed to perform more highly skilled work.

Computer operators who are displaced by automation may be reassigned to support staffs that maintain personal computer networks or assist other members of the organization. Operators who keep up with changing technology, by updating their skills and enhancing their training, should have the best prospects of moving into other areas such as network administration and technical support. Others may be retrained to perform different job duties, such as supervising an operations center, maintaining automation packages, or analyzing computer operations to recommend ways to increase productivity. In the future, operators who wish to work in the computer field will need to know more about programming, automation software, graphics interface, client/server environments, and open systems, in order to take advantage of changing opportunities.

Earnings

Median annual earnings of computer operators, except peripheral equipment operators were $25,030 in 1998. The middle 50 percent earned between about $20,410 and $31,610 a year. The lowest 10 percent earned less than $16,260; the highest 10 percent earned more than $39,130. Median annual earnings in the industries employing the largest numbers of computer operators, except peripheral equipment operators in 1997 are shown below:

Computer and data processing services	$24,300
Hospitals	23,600
Personnel supply services	22,600
Federal government	22,500
Commercial banks	20,200

In the Federal Government, computer operators with a high school diploma started at about $21,600 a year in 1999; those with 1 year of college started at $23,000. Applicants with operations experience started at higher salaries.

Median annual earnings of peripheral equipment operators were $22,860 in 1998. The middle 50 percent earned between $18,240 and $29,370 a year. The lowest 10 percent earned less than $14,870; the highest 10 percent earned more than $37,220.

According to Robert Half International, the average starting salaries for console operators ranged from $26,000 to $35,500 in 1999. Salaries generally are higher in large organizations than in small ones.

Related Occupations

Other occupations involving work with computers include computer scientists, engineers, and systems analysts; computer programmers, and computer service technicians. Other occupations in which workers operate electronic office equipment include data entry keyers, secretaries, typists and word processors, and typesetters and compositors.

Sources of Additional Information

For information about work opportunities in computer operations, contact firms that use computers such as banks, manufacturing and insurance firms, colleges and universities, and data processing service organizations. The local office of the State employment service can supply information about employment and training opportunities.

Court Reporters, Medical Transcriptionists, and Stenographers

(O*NET 55302A and 55302B)

Significant Points

- A high school diploma is sufficient for stenographers; employers prefer medical transcriptionists who have completed a vocational school or community college program; and court reporters usually need a 2- or 4-year postsecondary school degree.
- Overall employment is projected to grow about as fast as the average, as rapid growth among medical transcriptionists is offset by the decline among stenographers.
- Because of their relatively high salaries, keen competition should exist for court reporter positions; certified court reporters and medical transcriptionists should enjoy the best job prospects.

Nature of the Work

Although court reporters, medical transcriptionists, and stenographers all transcribe spoken words, the specific responsibilities of each of these workers differ markedly. Court reporters and stenographers typically take verbatim reports of speeches, conversations, legal proceedings, meetings, and other events when written accounts of spoken words are necessary for correspondence, records, or legal proof. Medical transcriptionists, on the other hand, translate and edit recorded dictation by physicians and other healthcare providers regarding patient assessment and treatment.

Court reporters document all statements made in official proceedings using a stenotype machine, which allows them to press multiple keys at a time to record combinations of letters representing sounds, words, or phrases. These symbols are then recorded on computer disks or CD-ROM, which are then translated and displayed as text in a process called computer-aided transcription. Stenotype machines used for real-time captioning are linked directly to the computer. As the reporter keys in the symbols, they instantly appear as text on the screen. This is used for closed captioning for the hearing-impaired on television, or in courts, classrooms, or meetings. In all of these cases, accuracy is crucial because there is only one person creating an official transcript.

Although many court reporters record official proceedings in the courtroom, the majority of court reporters work outside the courtroom. Freelance reporters, for example, take depositions for attorneys in offices and document proceedings of meetings, conventions, and other private activities. Others capture the proceedings in government agencies of all levels, from the U.S. Congress to State and local governing bodies. Court reporters who specialize in captioning live television programming, commonly known as *stenocaptioners*, work for television networks or cable stations captioning news, emergency broadcasts, sporting events, and other programming.

Medical transcriptionists use headsets and transcribing machines to listen to recordings by physicians and other healthcare professionals. These workers transcribe a variety of medical reports about emergency room visits, diagnostic imaging studies, operations, chart reviews, and final summaries. To understand and accurately transcribe dictated reports into a format that is clear and comprehensible for the reader, the medical transcriptionist must understand the language of medicine, anatomy and physiology, diagnostic procedures, and treatment. They also must be able to translate medical jargon and abbreviations into their expanded forms. After reviewing and editing for grammar and clarity, the medical transcriptionist transcribes the dictated reports and returns them in either printed or electronic form to the dictator for review and signature, or correction. These reports eventually become a part of the patient's permanent file. (Medical secretaries, who are discussed in the *Handbook* statement on secretaries, may also transcribe as part of their jobs.)

Stenographers take dictation and then transcribe their notes on a word processor or onto a computer diskette. They may take dictation using either shorthand or a stenotype machine, which prints shorthand symbols. General stenographers, including most beginners, take routine dictation and perform other office tasks such as typing, filing, answering telephones, and operating office machines. Experienced and highly skilled stenographers often supervise other stenographers, typists, and clerical workers and take more difficult dictation. For example, skilled stenographers may attend staff meetings and provide word-for-word records or summary reports of the proceedings to the participants. Some experienced stenographers take dictation in foreign languages; others work as public stenographers serving traveling business people and others. Technical stenographers must know the medical, legal, engineering, or scientific terminology used in a particular profession.

Medical transcriptionists use headsets to listen to recordings of physicians and other healthcare professionals.

Working Conditions

The majority of these workers are employed in comfortable settings. Court reporters, for example, work in the offices of attorneys, courtrooms, legislatures, and conventions. Medical transcriptionists are found in hospitals, doctors' offices, or medical transcription services. Stenographers usually work in clean, well-lighted offices. An increasing number of court reporters and medical transcriptionists work from home-based offices as subcontractors for law firms, hospitals, and transcription services.

Work in these occupations presents few hazards, although sitting in the same position for long periods can be tiring, and workers can suffer wrist, back, neck, or eye problems due to strain and risk repetitive motion injuries such as carpal tunnel syndrome. Also, the pressure to be accurate and fast can also be stressful.

Many court reporters, medical transcriptionists, and stenographers work a standard 40-hour week, although about 1 in 4 works part time. A substantial number of court reporters and medical transcriptionists are self-employed, which may result in irregular working hours.

Employment

Court reporters, medical transcriptionists, and stenographers held about 110,000 jobs in 1998. More than 1 in 4 were self-employed. Of those who worked for a wage or salary, about one-third worked for State and local governments, a reflection of the large number of court reporters working in courts, legislatures, and various agencies. About 1 in 4 worked for hospitals and physicians' offices, reflecting the concentration of medical transcriptionists in health services. Other transcriptionists, stenographers, and court reporters worked for colleges and universities, secretarial and court reporting services, temporary help supply services, and law firms.

Training, Other Qualifications, and Advancement

The training for each of the three occupations varies significantly. Court reporters usually complete a 2- or 4-year training program, offered by about 300 postsecondary vocational and technical schools and colleges. Currently, the National Court Reporters Association (NCRA) has approved about 110 programs, all of which offer courses in computer-aided transcription and real-time reporting. NCRA-approved programs require students to capture 225 words per minute. Court reporters in the Federal Government usually must capture at least 205 words a minute.

Some States require court reporters to be Notary Publics, or to be a Certified Court Reporter (CCR); reporters must pass a State certification test administered by a board of examiners to earn this designation. The National Court Reporters Association confers the designation, Registered Professional Reporter (RPR), upon those who pass a two-part examination and participate in continuing education programs. Although voluntary, the RPR designation is recognized as a mark of distinction in this field.

For medical transcriptionist positions, understanding medical terminology is essential. Good English grammar and punctuation skills are required, as well as familiarity with personal computers and word processing software. Good listening skills are also necessary, because some doctors and health care professionals speak English as a second language.

Employers prefer to hire transcriptionists who have completed postsecondary training in medical transcription, offered by many vocational schools and community colleges. Completion of a 2-year associate degree program—including coursework in anatomy, medical terminology, medicolegal issues, and English grammar and punctuation—is highly recommended. Many of these programs include supervised on-the-job experience. The American Association for Medical Transcription awards the voluntary designation, Certified Medical Transcriptionist (CMT), to those who earn passing scores on written and practical examinations. As in many other fields, certification is recognized as a sign of competence in medical transcription.

Stenographic skills are taught in high schools, vocational schools, community colleges, and proprietary business schools. For stenographer jobs, employers prefer to hire high school graduates and seldom have a preference among the many different shorthand methods. Although requirements vary in private firms, applicants with the best speed and accuracy usually receive first consideration in hiring. To qualify for jobs in the Federal Government, stenographers must be able to take dictation at a minimum of 80 words per minute and type at least 40 words per minute. Workers must achieve higher rates to advance to more responsible positions.

Stenographers, especially those with strong interpersonal and communication skills may advance to secretarial positions with more responsibilities. In addition, some stenographers complete the necessary education to become court reporters or medical transcriptionists.

Job Outlook

Overall employment of court reporters, medical transcriptionists, and stenographers is projected to grow about as fast as the average for all occupations through 2008. Employment growth among medical transcriptionists should be offset by the decline among stenographers, while the number of court reporters should remain fairly constant.

Demand for medical transcriptionists is expected to increase due to rapid growth in health care industries spurred by a growing and aging population. Advancements in voice recognition technology are not projected to reduce the need for medical transcriptionists because these workers will continue to be needed to review and edit drafts for accuracy. Moreover, growing numbers of medical transcriptionists will be needed to amend patients' records, edit for grammar, and discover discrepancies in medical records. Job opportunities should be the best for those who earn an associate degree or certification from the American Association for Medical Transcription.

There should be little or no change in employment of court reporters. Despite increasing numbers of civil and criminal cases, budget constraints limit the ability of Federal, State, and local courts to expand. The growing number of conventions, conferences, depositions, seminars, and similar meetings in which proceedings are recorded should create limited demand for court reporters. Although many of these events are videotaped, a written transcript must still be created for legal purposes or if the proceedings are to be published. In addition, the trend to provide instantaneous written captions for the deaf and hearing-impaired should strengthen demand for stenocaptioners. Because of their relatively high salaries, keen competition should exist for court reporter positions; those with certification should enjoy the best job prospects.

The widespread use of dictation machines has greatly reduced the need for office stenographers. Audio recording equipment and the use of personal computers by managers and other professionals should continue to further decrease the demand for these workers.

Earnings

Court reporters, medical transcriptionists, and stenographers had median annual earnings of $25,430 in 1998. The middle 50 percent earned between $21,060 and $31,470; the lowest paid 10 percent earned less than $17,060; and the highest paid 10 percent earned over $39,070. Median 1997 annual salaries in the industries employing the largest number of these workers were:

Industry	Salary
Local government, except education and hospitals	$29,300
State government, except education and hospitals	29,000
Mailing, reproduction, and stenographic services	28,600
Hospitals	23,500
Offices and clinics of medical doctors	22,600

Court reporters usually earn higher salaries than stenographers or medical transcriptionists, and many supplement their income by doing additional freelance work. According to a National Court Reporters Association survey of its members, average annual earnings for court reporters were about $54,000 in 1999. According to the 1999 HayGroup survey about three-quarters of healthcare institutions paid their medical transcriptionists for time worked, with average salaries ranging from $20,000 to $30,000 annually. About a fifth of those respondents used a combination of payment methods (time worked plus incentive for production), with average salaries ranging from $28,000 to $36,000 annually. Regardless of specialty, earnings depend on education, experience, and geographic location.

Related Occupations

A number of other workers type, record information, and process paperwork. Among these are administrative assistants, bookkeepers, receptionists, secretaries, and human resource clerks. Other workers who provide medical and legal support include paralegals, medical assistants, and medical record technicians.

Sources of Additional Information

For information about careers, training, and certification in court reporting, contact:

☛ National Court Reporters Association, 8224 Old Courthouse Rd., Vienna, VA 22182. Internet: **http://www.verbatimreporters.com**

For information on a career as a medical transcriptionist, contact:

☛ American Association for Medical Transcription, P.O. Box 576187, Modesto, CA 95357. Internet: **http://www.aamt.org/aamt**

For information on a career as a federal court reporter, contact:

☛ United States Court Reporters Association, 1904 Marvel Lane, Liberty, MO 64068. Internet: **http://www.uscra.org**

State employment service offices can provide information about job openings for court reporters, medical transcriptionists, and stenographers.

Information Clerks

Significant Points

- Numerous job openings should arise for most types of information clerks due to employment growth and high turnover.
- A high school diploma or its equivalent is the most common educational requirement.
- Because many information clerks deal directly with the public, a professional appearance and pleasant personality are imperative.

Nature of the Work

Information clerks are found in nearly every industry in the Nation, gathering data and providing information to the public. The specific duties of these clerks vary as widely as the job titles they hold. *Hotel, motel, and resort desk clerks,* for example, are a guest's first contact for check-in, check-out, and other services within hotels, motels, and resorts. *Interviewing and new account clerks,* found most often in medical facilities, research firms, and financial institutions, assist the public in completing forms, applications or questionnaires. *Receptionists* are often a visitor's or caller's first contact within an organization, providing information and routing calls. *Reservation and transportation ticket agents and travel clerks* assist the public in making travel plans, reservations, and purchasing tickets for a variety of transportation services.

Although their day-to-day duties vary widely, most information clerks greet customers, guests, or other visitors. Many also answer telephones and either obtain information from or provide information to the public. Most information clerks use multiline telephones, fax machines, and personal computers. This section, which contains an overall discussion of information clerks, is followed by separate sections providing additional information on the four types of clerks identified above.

Working Conditions

Working conditions vary for different types of information clerks, but most clerks work in areas that are clean, well lit, and relatively quiet. This is especially true for information clerks who greet customers and visitors and usually work in highly visible areas that are furnished to make a good impression. Reservation agents and interviewing clerks who spend much of their day talking on the telephone, however, commonly work away from the public, often in large centralized reservation or phone centers. Because a number of agents or clerks may share the same work space, it may be crowded and noisy. Interviewing clerks may conduct surveys on the street, in shopping malls, or go door to door.

Although most information clerks work a standard 40-hour week, about 3 out of 10 work part time. Some high school and college students work part time as information clerks, after school or during vacations. Some jobs—such as those in the transportation industry, hospitals, and hotels, in particular—may require working evenings, late night shifts, weekends, and holidays. This is also the case for a growing number of new accounts clerks who work for large banks with call centers that are staffed around the clock. Interviewing clerks conducting surveys or other research may mainly work evenings or weekends. In general, employees with the least seniority tend to be assigned the less desirable shifts.

The work performed by information clerks may be repetitious and stressful. For example, many receptionists spend all day answering telephones while performing additional clerical or secretarial tasks. Reservation agents and travel clerks work under stringent time constraints or have quotas on the number of calls answered or reservations made. Additional stress is caused by technology that enables management to electronically monitor use of computer systems, tape record telephone calls, or limit the time spent on each call.

The work of hotel, motel, and resort desk clerks and transportation ticket agents also can be stressful when trying to serve the needs of difficult or angry customers. When flights are canceled, reservations mishandled, or guests are dissatisfied, these clerks must bear the brunt of the customers' anger. Hotel desk clerks and ticket agents may be on their feet most of the time, and ticket agents may have to lift heavy baggage. In addition, prolonged exposure to a video display terminal may lead to eye strain for the many information clerks who work with computers.

Employment

Information clerks held over 1.9 million jobs in 1998. The following tabulation shows employment for the individual occupations.

Occupation	Employment
Receptionists	1,293,000
Interviewing and new account clerks	239,000
Reservation and transportation ticket agents and travel clerks	218,000
Hotel, motel, and resort desk clerks	159,000

Although information clerks are found in a variety of industries, employment is concentrated in hotels and motels, health services, banks and savings institutions, transportation, and firms providing business or real estate services.

Training, Other Qualifications, and Advancement

Although hiring requirements for information clerk jobs vary from industry to industry, a high school diploma or its equivalent is the most common educational requirement. Increasingly, familiarity or experience with computers and good interpersonal skills are often equally important to employers. For new account clerk and airline reservation and ticket agent jobs, some college education may be preferred.

Many information clerks deal directly with the public, so a professional appearance and pleasant personality are important. A clear speaking voice and fluency in the English language also are essential because these employees frequently use the telephone or public address systems. Good spelling and computer literacy are often needed, particularly because most work involves considerable computer use. It also is increasingly helpful for those wishing to enter the lodging or travel industries to speak a foreign language fluently.

With the exception of airline reservation and transportation ticket agents, orientation and training for information clerks usually takes place on the job. For example, orientation for hotel and motel desk clerks usually includes an explanation of the job duties and information about the establishment, such as room locations and available services. New employees learn job tasks through on-the-job training under the guidance of a supervisor or an experienced clerk. They often need additional training in how to use the computerized reservation, room assignment, and billing systems and equipment. Most information clerks continue to receive instruction on new procedures and company policies after their initial training ends.

Receptionists usually receive on-the-job training which may include procedures for greeting visitors, operating telephone and computer systems, and distributing mail, fax, and parcel deliveries. Some employers look for applicants who already possess certain skills, such as prior computer and word processing experience, or previous formal education.

Most airline reservation and ticket agents learn their skills through formal company training programs. In a classroom setting, they learn company and industry policies, computer systems, and ticketing procedures. They also learn to use the airline's computer system to obtain information on schedules, seat availability, and fares; to reserve space for passengers; and to plan passenger itineraries. They must also become familiar with airport and airline code designations, regulations, and safety procedures, and may be tested on this knowledge. After completing classroom instruction, new agents work on the job with supervisors or experienced agents for a period of time. During this period, supervisors may monitor telephone conversations to improve the quality of customer service. Agents are expected to provide good service while limiting the time spent on each call without being discourteous to customers. In contrast to the airlines, automobile clubs, bus lines, and railroads tend to train their ticket agents or travel clerks on the job through short in-house classes that last several days.

Most banks prefer to hire college graduates for new account clerk positions. Nevertheless, many new accounts clerks without college degrees start out as bank tellers and are promoted by demonstrating excellent communication skills and motivation to learn new skills. If a new accounts clerk has not been a teller before, he or she will often receive such training and work for several months as a teller. In both cases, new accounts clerks undergo formal training regarding the bank's procedures, products, and services.

Advancement for information clerks usually comes about either by transfer to a position with more responsibilities or by promotion to a supervisory position. Most companies fill office and administrative support supervisory and managerial positions by promoting individuals within their organization, so information clerks who acquire additional skills, experience, and training improve their advancement opportunities. Receptionists, interviewers, and new accounts clerks with word processing or other clerical skills may advance to a better paying job as a secretary or administrative assistant. Within the airline industry, a ticket agent may advance to lead worker on the shift.

Additional training is helpful in preparing information clerks for promotion. In the lodging industry, clerks can improve their chances for advancement by taking home or group study courses in lodging management, such as those sponsored by the Educational Institute of the American Hotel and Motel Association. In some industries—such as lodging, banking, or the airlines—workers commonly are promoted through the ranks. Positions such as airline reservation agent or hotel and motel desk clerk offer good opportunities for qualified workers to get started in the business. In a number of industries, a college degree may be required for advancement to management ranks.

Job Outlook

Overall employment of information clerks is expected grow about as fast as average for all occupations through 2008. In addition to many openings occurring as businesses and organizations expand, numerous job openings for information clerks will result from the need to replace experienced workers who transfer to other occupations or leave the labor force. Replacement needs are expected to be especially large in this occupation due to high turnover, as many young people work as information clerks for a few years before switching to other, higher paying jobs. The occupation is well suited to flexible work schedules, and many opportunities for part-time work will continue to be available, particularly as organizations attempt to cut labor costs by hiring more part-time or temporary workers.

The outlook for different types of information clerks is expected to vary in the coming decade. Economic growth and general business expansion are expected to stimulate faster than average growth among receptionists. Hotel, motel, and resort desk clerks are expected to grow faster than the average, as the composition of the lodging industry changes and services provided by these workers expand. Employment of interviewing clerks will also grow faster than average as these workers benefit from rapid growth in the health services industry, while average growth is expected among new accounts clerks as more of their functions are provided electronically. Much of this growth, however, will be due to an increase in part-time and temporary jobs. Reservation and transportation ticket agents and travel clerks are expected to grow more slowly than average due to productivity gains brought by technology and the increasing use of the Internet for travel services.

Earnings

Earnings vary widely by occupation and experience. Annual earnings ranged from less than $11,750 for the lowest paid 10 percent of hotel clerks to over $39,540 for the top 10 percent of reservation agents in 1998. Salaries of reservation and transportation ticket agents and travel clerks tend to be significantly higher than for other information clerks, while hotel, motel, and resort desk clerks tend to earn quite a bit less, as the following tabulation of median annual earnings shows.

Reservation and transportation ticket agents and travel clerks	$22,120
New accounts clerks	21,340
Receptionists	18,620
Interviewing clerks	18,540
Hotel, motel, and resort desk clerks	15,160

Earnings of hotel and motel desk clerks also vary considerably depending on the location, size, and type of establishment in which they work. For example, clerks at large luxury hotels and those located in metropolitan and resort areas generally pay clerks more than less exclusive or "budget" establishments and those located in less populated areas.

In early 1999, the Federal Government typically paid salaries ranging from $16,400 to $18,100 a year to beginning receptionists with a high school diploma or 6 months of experience. The average annual salary for all receptionists employed by the Federal Government was about $22,700 in 1999.

In addition to their hourly wage, full-time information clerks who work evenings, nights, weekends, or holidays may receive shift differential pay. Some employers offer educational assistance to their employees. Reservation and transportation ticket agents and travel clerks receive free or reduced rate travel on their company's carriers for themselves and their immediate family and, in some companies, for friends.

Related Occupations

A number of other workers deal with the public, receive and provide information, or direct people to others who can assist them. Among these are dispatchers, security guards, bank tellers, guides, telephone operators, records processing clerks, counter and rental clerks, survey workers, and ushers and lobby attendants.

Hotel, Motel, and Resort Desk Clerks

(O*NET 53808)

Nature of the Work

Hotel, motel, and resort desk clerks perform a variety of services for guests of hotels, motels, and other lodging establishments. Regardless of the type of accommodation, most desk clerks have similar responsibilities. Primarily, they register arriving guests, assign rooms, and check guests out at the end of their stay. They also keep records of room assignments and other registration information on computers. When guests check out, they prepare and explain the charges, as well as process payments.

Front desk clerks are always in the public eye and, through their attitude and behavior, greatly influence the public's impressions of the establishment. When answering questions about services, checkout times, the local community, or other matters of public interest, clerks must be courteous and helpful. Should guests report problems with their rooms, clerks contact members of the housekeeping or maintenance staff to correct them.

In some smaller hotels and motels, clerks may have a variety of additional responsibilities usually performed by specialized employees in larger establishments. In these places, the desk clerk is often responsible for all front office operations, information, and services. These clerks, for example, may perform the work of a bookkeeper, advance reservation agent, cashier, laundry attendant, and telephone switchboard operator.

Employment

Hotel, motel, and resort desk clerks held about 159,000 jobs in 1998. This occupation is well suited to flexible work schedules, as over 1 in 4 desk clerks works part time. Because hotels and motels need to be staffed 24 hours a day, evening and weekend work is common.

Hotel and motel clerks register arriving guests.

Job Outlook

Employment of hotel, motel, and resort desk clerks is expected to grow about as fast as the average for all occupations through 2008, as more hotels, motels, and other lodging establishments are built and occupancy rates rise. Job opportunities for hotel and motel desk clerks will result from an unusually high turnover rate. These openings occur each year as thousands of workers transfer to other occupations that offer better pay and advancement opportunities or simply leave the work force altogether. Opportunities for part-time work should continue to be plentiful, as nearly all front desks are staffed 24 hours a day, 7 days a week.

Employment of hotel and motel desk clerks should be favorably affected by an increase in business and leisure travel. Shifts in travel preference away from long vacations and toward long weekends and other, more frequent, shorter trips also should increase demand as this trend increases the total number of nights spent in hotels. The expansion of smaller, budget hotels relative to larger, luxury establishments reflects a change in the composition of the hotel and motel industry. As employment shifts from luxury hotels to more "no-frills" operations, the proportion of hotel desk clerks should increase in relation to staff such as waiters and waitresses and recreation workers.

However, the growing effort to cut labor costs while moving towards more efficient service is expected to slow the growth of desk clerk employment. The role of the front desk is changing as some of the more traditional duties are automated. New technologies automating check-in and check-out procedures now allow guests to bypass the front desk in many larger establishments, reducing staffing needs. The expansion of other technologies, such as interactive television and computer systems to dispense information, should further impact employment in the future as such services become more widespread.

Employment of desk clerks is sensitive to cyclical swings in the economy. During recessions, vacation and business travel declines and hotels and motels need fewer clerks. Similarly, desk clerk employment is affected by seasonal fluctuations in travel during high and low tourist seasons.

Sources of Additional Information

Information on working conditions, training requirements, and earnings appears in the *information clerks* introduction to this section.

Information on careers in the lodging industry, as well as information about professional development and training programs, may be obtained from:

☛ The Educational Institute of the American Hotel and Motel Association, P.O. Box 531126 Orlando, FL 32853-1126.
Internet: **http://www.ei-ahma.org**

Interviewing and New Accounts Clerks

(O*NET 53105 and 55332)

Nature of the Work

Interviewing and new accounts clerks obtain information from individuals and business representatives who are opening bank accounts, gaining admission to medical facilities, participating in consumer surveys, and completing various other forms. By mail, telephone, or in person, these workers solicit and verify information, create files, and perform a number of other related tasks.

The specific duties and job titles of interviewing and new accounts clerks depend upon the type of employer. In doctors' offices and other health care facilities, for example, *interviewing clerks* are also known as *admitting interviewers* or *patient representatives.* These workers obtain all preliminary information required for admission, such as the patient's name, address, age, medical history, present medications, previous hospitalizations, religion, persons to notify in case of emergency, attending physician, and the party responsible for payment. In some cases, interviewing clerks may be required to verify benefits with the person's insurance provider or work out financing options for those who might need it.

Other duties of interviewers in health care include assigning patients to rooms and summoning escorts to take patients to their rooms; sometimes these workers may escort patients themselves. Using the facility's computer system, they schedule lab work, x-rays, and surgeries and prepare admitting and discharge records and route them to appropriate departments. They may also bill patients, receive payments, and answer the telephone. In an outpatient or office setting, they also schedule appointments, keep track of cancellations, and provide general information about care. In addition, the role of the admissions staff, particularly in hospitals, is expanding to include a wide range of patient services from assisting patients with financial and medical questions to helping family members find hotel rooms.

Interviewing clerks who conduct market research surveys and polls for research firms have somewhat different responsibilities. These interviewers ask a series of prepared questions, record the responses, and forward the results to management. They may ask individuals questions about their occupation and earnings, political preferences, buying habits, or customer satisfaction. Although most interviews are conducted over the telephone, some are conducted in focus groups or by randomly polling people at a shopping mall. More recently, the Internet is being used to elicit people's opinions. Almost all interviewers use computers or similar devices to enter the responses to questions.

New accounts clerks, more commonly referred to as *customer service representatives*, handle a wide variety of operations in banks, credit unions, and other financial institutions. Their principal tasks are to handle customer inquiries, explain the institution's products and services to people, and refer customers to the appropriate sales personnel. If a person wants to open a checking or savings account, or an IRA, the customer service representative will interview the customer and enter the required information into a computer for processing. They will also assist people in applying for other services, such as ATM cards, direct deposit, and certificates of deposit. Some customer service representatives also sell traveler's checks, handle savings bonds, perform foreign currency transactions, and perform teller duties, as required. Although the majority of customer service representatives work in branch offices and deal directly with customers, a growing number are being hired by banks to work in central call centers, taking questions from customers 24 hours a day, entering appropriate information into customer records, and, if necessary, referring customers to other specialists in the financial institution.

Employment

Interviewing and new accounts clerks held about 239,000 jobs in 1998. More than half were employed by commercial banks and other depository institutions. The remainder worked mostly in hospitals and other health care facilities and for research and testing firms. Around 3 out of every 10 clerks worked part time.

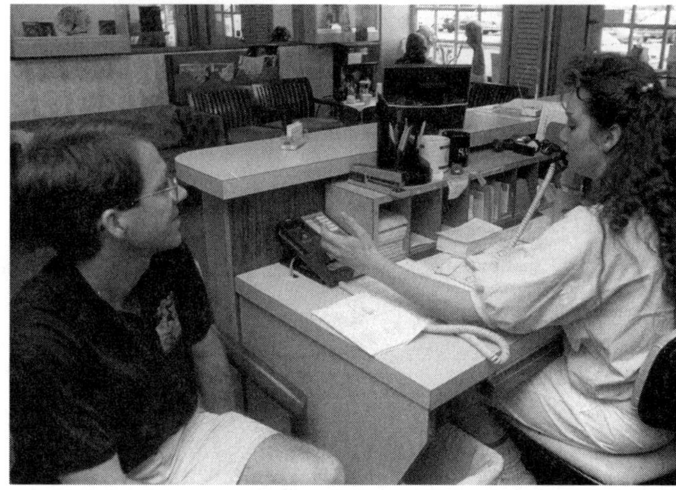

Jobs should be plentiful for medical facility admitting clerks.

Job Outlook

Overall employment of interviewing and new accounts clerks is expected to increase about as fast as the average for all occupations through 2008. Much of this growth will stem from an increase in part-time and temporary jobs. In addition to growth, a larger number of job openings is expected to arise from the need to replace the thousands of interviewing and new accounts clerks who leave the occupation or the work force each year. Job prospects to fill these openings will be best for applicants with a broad range of job skills, such as the good customer service, math, and telephone skills.

The number of interviewing clerks is projected to grow faster than average, reflecting growth in the health services industry. This industry will hire more admissions interviewers as health care facilities consolidate staff and expand the role of the admissions staff, and as an aging and growing population requires more visits to health care practitioners. In addition, increasing use of market research will create more jobs for interviewers to collect data. In the future, though, more market research is expected to be conducted over the Internet, thus reducing the need for telephone interviewers to make individual calls.

Employment of new accounts clerks, on the other hand, is expected to grow only as fast as average as bank employment slows and more services are provided electronically. However, these changes will favor employment of new accounts clerks over other workers in banks, particularly tellers, because of their ability to provide a wide range of services. Also, new accounts clerks will be hired in increasing numbers by banks to handle customer inquiries at their call centers.

Sources of Additional Information

Information on working conditions, training requirements, and earnings appears in the *Information clerks* introduction to this section.

State employment service offices can provide information about employment opportunities.

Receptionists

(O*NET 55305)

Nature of the Work

Receptionists are charged with a responsibility that may have a lasting impact on the success of an organization—making a good first impression. These workers are often the first representatives of an organization a visitor encounters, so they need to be courteous, professional, and helpful. Receptionists answer telephones, route calls, greet visitors, respond to inquiries from the public and provide information about the organization. In addition, receptionists contribute to the security of an organization by helping to monitor the access of visitors.

Whereas some tasks are common to most receptionists, the specific responsibilities of receptionists vary depending upon the type of establishment in which they work. For example, receptionists in hospitals and doctors' offices may gather personal and financial information and direct patients to the proper waiting rooms. In beauty or hair salons, however, they arrange appointments, direct customers to the hairstylist, and may serve as cashier. In factories, large corporations, and government offices, they may provide identification cards and arrange for escorts to take visitors to the proper office. Those working for bus and train companies respond to inquiries about departures, arrivals, stops, and other related matters.

Increasingly, receptionists use multiline telephone systems, personal computers, and fax machines. Despite the widespread use of automated answering systems or voice mail, many receptionists still take messages and inform other employees of visitors' arrivals or cancellation of an appointment. When they are not busy with callers, most receptionists are expected to perform a variety of office duties including opening and sorting mail, collecting and distributing parcels, making fax transmittals and deliveries, updating appointment calendars, preparing travel vouchers, and performing basic bookkeeping, word processing, and filing.

Receptionists answer telephones, route calls, greet visitors, and respond to inquiries from the public.

Employment

Receptionists held about 1.3 million jobs in 1998, accounting for over two-thirds of all information clerk jobs. More than two-thirds of all receptionists worked in services industries, and almost half of these were employed in the health services industry in doctors' and dentists' offices, hospitals, nursing homes, urgent care centers, surgical centers, and clinics. Manufacturing, wholesale and retail trade, government, and real estate industries also employed large numbers of receptionists. About 3 of every 10 receptionists worked part time.

Job Outlook

Employment of receptionists is expected to grow faster than the average for all occupations through 2008. This increase will result from rapid growth in services industries—including physician's offices, law firms, temporary help agencies, and consulting firms—where most receptionists are employed. In addition, high turnover in this large occupation will create numerous openings as receptionists transfer to other occupations or leave the labor force altogether. Opportunities should be best for persons with a wide range of clerical skills and experience.

Technology should have conflicting effects on the demand for receptionists. The increasing use of voice mail and other telephone automation reduces the need for receptionists by allowing one receptionist to perform work that formerly required several receptionists. However, increasing use of technology also has caused a consolidation of clerical responsibilities and growing demand for workers with diverse clerical skills. Because receptionists may perform a wide variety of clerical tasks, they should continue to be in demand. Further, receptionists perform many tasks that are of an interpersonal nature and are not easily automated, ensuring continued demand for their services in a variety of establishments. Receptionists tend to be less subject to layoffs during recessions than other clerical workers because establishments need someone to perform their duties even during economic downturns.

Sources of Additional Information

Information on working conditions, training requirements, and earnings appears in the *Information Clerks* introduction to this section. State employment offices can provide information on job openings for receptionists.

Reservation and Transportation Ticket Agents and Travel Clerks

(O*NET 53802 and 53805)

Nature of the Work

Each year, millions of Americans travel by plane, train, ship, bus, and automobile. Many of these travelers rely on the services of reservation and transportation ticket agents and travel clerks. These ticket agents and clerks perform functions as varied as selling tickets, confirming reservations, checking baggage, and providing tourists with useful travel information.

Most *reservation agents* work for large hotel chains or airlines, helping people plan trips and make reservations. They usually work in large reservation centers answering telephone inquiries and offering suggestions on travel arrangements, such as routes, time schedules, rates, and types of accommodation. Reservation agents quote fares and room rates, provide travel information, and make and confirm transportation and hotel reservations. Most agents use proprietary networks to quickly obtain information needed to make, change, or cancel reservations for customers.

Transportation ticket agents are sometimes known as passenger service agents, passenger-booking clerks, reservation clerks, airport service agents, ticket clerks, or ticket sellers. They work in airports, train, and bus stations selling tickets, assigning seats to passengers, and checking baggage. In addition, they may answer inquiries and give directions, examine passports and visas, or check in pets. Other ticket agents, more commonly known as *gate* or *station agents*, work in airport terminals assisting passengers boarding airplanes. These workers direct passengers to the correct boarding area, check tickets and seat assignments, make boarding announcements, and provide special assistance to young, elderly, or disabled passengers when they board or disembark.

Most *travel clerks* are employed by membership organizations, such as automobile clubs. These workers, sometimes called *member services counselors* or *travel counselors*, plan trips, calculate mileage, and offer travel suggestions, such as the best route from the point of origin to the destination, for club members. Travel clerks also may prepare an itinerary indicating points of interest, restaurants, overnight accommodations, and availability of emergency services during the trip. In some cases, they make rental car, hotel, and restaurant reservations for club members.

Passenger rate clerks generally work for bus companies. They sell tickets for regular bus routes and arrange nonscheduled or chartered trips. They plan travel routes, compute rates, and keep customers informed of appropriate details. They also may arrange travel accommodations.

Employment

Reservation and transportation ticket agents and travel clerks held about 219,000 jobs in 1998. About 7 of every 10 are employed by airlines. Others work for membership organizations, such as automobile clubs; hotels and other lodging places; railroad companies; bus lines; and other companies that provide transportation services.

Although agents and clerks are found throughout the country, most work in large metropolitan airports, downtown ticket offices, large reservation centers, and train or bus stations. The remainder work in small communities served only by inter-city bus or railroad lines.

Job Outlook

Applicants for reservation and transportation ticket agent jobs are likely to encounter considerable competition, because the supply of qualified applicants exceeds the expected number of job openings. Entry requirements for these jobs are minimal, and many people seeking to get into the airline industry or travel business often start out in these types of positions. These jobs provide excellent travel benefits, and many people view airline and other travel-related jobs as glamorous.

Employment of reservation and transportation ticket agents and travel clerks is expected to grow more slowly than the average for all occupations through 2008. Although a growing population will demand additional travel services, employment of these workers will grow more slowly than this demand, because of the significant impact of technology on productivity. Automated reservations and ticketing, as well as "ticket-less" travel, for example, are reducing the need for some workers. Most train stations and airports now have satellite ticket printer locations, or "kiosks," that enable passengers to make reservations and purchase tickets themselves. Many passengers also are able to check flight times and fares, make reservations, and purchase tickets on the Internet. Nevertheless, all travel-related passenger services can never be fully automated, primarily for safety and security reasons. As a result, job openings will continue to become available as the occupation grows and as workers transfer to other occupations, retire, or leave the labor force altogether.

Airlines employ 7 of every 10 reservation and transportation ticket agents and travel clerks.

Employment of reservation and transportation ticket agents and travel clerks is sensitive to cyclical swings in the economy. During recessions, discretionary passenger travel declines, and transportation service companies are less likely to hire new workers and even may resort to layoffs.

Sources of Additional Information

Information on working conditions, training requirements, and earnings appears in the *Information Clerks* introduction to this section.

For information about job opportunities as reservation and transportation ticket agents and travel clerks, write the personnel manager of individual transportation companies. Addresses of airlines are available from:

☛ Air Transport Association of America, 1301 Pennsylvania Ave. NW., Suite 1100, Washington, DC 20004-1707.

Loan Clerks and Credit Authorizers, Checkers, and Clerks

(O*NET 53114, 53117, and 53121)

Significant Points

- A high school education is the minimum requirement; telephone, typing, and computer skills are also helpful.
- Increasing automation will result in slower than average employment growth despite an increase in loans and credit applications.

Nature of the Work

Loan clerks and credit authorizers, checkers, and clerks review credit history and obtain the information needed to determine the creditworthiness of loan and credit card applicants. They spend much of their day on the phone obtaining credit information from credit bureaus, employers, banks, credit institutions, and other sources to determine the applicant's credit history and ability to pay back the loan or charge.

Loan clerks, also called *loan processing clerks*, *loan closers*, or *loan service clerks*, assemble loan documents, process the paperwork associated with the loan, and assure that all information is complete and verified. Mortgage loans are the primary type of loan handled by loan clerks, who may also have to order appraisals on the property, set up escrow accounts, and secure any additional information required to transfer the property.

The specific duties of loan clerks vary by specialty. *Loan closers*, for example, complete the loan process by gathering the proper documents for signature at the closing, including deeds of trust, property insurance papers, and title commitments. They set the time and place for the closing, make sure all parties are present, and ensure that all conditions for settlement have been met. After settlement, the loan closer records all documents and submits the final loan package to the owner of the loan. *Loan service clerks* maintain the payment records once the loan is issued. These clerical workers process the paperwork for payment of fees to insurance companies and tax authorities and may also record changes to client addresses and loan ownership. When necessary, they answer calls from customers with routine inquiries.

The duties of *loan interviewers* are similar to those of loan clerks. They interview potential borrowers and help them fill out loan applications. Interviewers may then investigate the applicant's background and references, verify information on the application, and forward any findings, reports, or documents to the appraisal department. Finally, interviewers inform the applicant whether the loan has been accepted or denied.

Credit authorizers, checkers, and *clerks* process and authorize applications for credit, including credit cards. Although the distinctions between the three are becoming less, some generalities can still be made. *Credit clerks* typically handle the processing of the credit applications by verifying the information on the application, calling applicants if they need additional data, contacting credit bureaus for a credit rating, and obtaining any other information necessary to determine the applicant's creditworthiness. If the clerk works in a department store or other establishment that offers instant credit, the clerk enters applicant information into a computer at the point-of-sale. A credit rating will then be transmitted from a central office within seconds to determine whether the application should be rejected or approved.

Some organizations have *credit checkers,* who investigate a person's or business's credit history and current credit standing prior to issuing a loan or line of credit. They may also telephone or write to credit departments of businesses and service companies to obtain information about an applicant's credit standing. Credit reporting agencies and bureaus hire a number of checkers to secure, update, and verify information for credit reports. These workers are often called credit investigators or reporters.

Credit authorizers approve charges against customers' existing accounts. Most charges are approved automatically by computer. When accounts are past due, overextended, invalid, or show a change of address, however, sales persons refer transactions to credit authorizers located in a central office. These authorizers evaluate the customers' computerized credit records and payment histories to quickly decide whether or not to approve new charges.

Working Conditions

Loan clerks and credit authorizers, checkers, and clerks usually work a standard 35- to 40-hour week. However, they may work overtime during particularly busy periods. Loan clerks handling residential real estate experience busy periods during spring and summer and at the end of each month. For credit authorizers, busy periods are during the holiday shopping seasons and store sales. In retail establishments, authorizers may work nights and weekends during store hours. Authorizers and checkers may also work in call centers if they are employed by companies that have centralized this function at one location. Part-time work is available for a number of these occupations.

Credit clerks verify information on credit applications.

Employment

Loan clerks and credit authorizers, checkers, and clerks held about 254,000 jobs in 1998. About 8 out of 10 were employed by commercial and savings banks, credit unions, mortgage banks, and personal and business credit institutions. Credit reporting and collection agencies, and wholesale and retail trade establishments also employ these clerks.

Training, Other Qualifications, and Advancement

A high school education or equivalent is usually the minimum requirement for these entry level positions. Other requirements of the job include good telephone and organizational skills as well as the ability to pay close attention to details and meet tight deadlines. To enter and retrieve data quickly, computer skills are also important.

Most new employees are trained on the job, working under close supervision of more experienced employees. Some firms offer formal training that may include courses in telephone etiquette, computer use, and customer service skills. A number of credit workers also take courses in credit offered by banking and credit associations, public and private vocational schools, and colleges and universities. Workers in these positions can typically advance to loan or credit department supervisor, underwriter, loan officer, or team leader of a small group of clerks.

Job Outlook

Slower than average employment growth for loan clerks and credit authorizers, checkers, and clerks is expected through 2008. Despite a projected increase in the number of loans and credit applications, automation will allow fewer workers to process, check, and authorize applications than in the past. The effects of automation on employment will be moderated, however, by the many interpersonal aspects of the job. Mortgage loans, for example, require loan processors to personally verify financial data on the application, and loan closers are needed to assemble documents and prepare them for settlement.

Employment will also be adversely affected by changes in the financial services industry. For example, significant consolidation has occurred among mortgage loan servicing companies. As a result, fewer mortgage banking companies are involved in loan servicing, making the function more efficient and reducing the need for loan servicing clerks.

Credit scoring is another major development that has improved the productivity of these workers, further limiting employment growth. Companies and credit bureaus can now purchase software that quickly analyzes a person's creditworthiness and summarizes it into a "score." Credit issuers can then easily decide whether or not to accept or reject the application depending on the score, speeding up the authorization of loans or credit. Obtaining credit ratings is also much easier for credit checkers and authorizers, as businesses now have computer terminals that are directly linked to credit bureaus that provide immediate access to a person's credit history.

The job outlook for loan clerks and credit authorizers, checkers, and clerks is sensitive to overall economic activity. A downturn in the economy and a rise in interest rates usually lead to a decline in demand for credit and loans, particularly mortgage loans, possibly causing layoffs. Even in slow economic times, however, job openings will arise from the need to replace those who leave the occupation for various reasons.

Earnings

Median annual earnings of loan and credit clerks, the largest occupation among loan clerks and credit authorizers, checkers, and clerks, were about $22,580 in 1998. The middle 50 percent earned between $18,620 and $27,740. The lowest 10 percent had earnings of less than

$14,820, while the top 10 percent earned over $33,870. Median annual earnings in the industries employing the largest number of loan and credit clerks in 1997 were:

Mortgage bankers and brokers	$24,300
Savings institutions	22,100
Commercial banks	20,300
Credit unions	20,200
Personal credit intitutions	19,300

Among other workers in this occupational grouping, median annual earnings of credit checkers were $21,550 in 1998; credit authorizers earned $22,990; and loan interviewers made $23,190.

In addition to standard benefits, workers in retail establishments usually receive a discount on store purchases.

Related Occupations

Occupations with duties similar to those of loan clerks and credit authorizers, checkers, and clerks include claim clerks, customer complaint clerks, procurement clerks, probate clerks, and collection clerks.

Sources of Additional Information

General information about local job opportunities for loan clerks and credit authorizers, checkers, and clerks may be obtained from banks and credit institutions, retail stores, and credit reporting agencies.

For specific information on a career as a loan processor or loan closer, contact:

☛ Mortgage Bankers Association of America, 1125 15th St. NW., Washington, DC 20005. Internet: **http://www.mbaa.org**

Mail Clerks and Messengers

(O*NET 57302 and 57311A)

Significant Points

- This is a first job for many because there are no formal qualifications or training requirements.
- Automated mail systems and other computerized innovations are expected to limit employment growth; nevertheless, favorable job opportunities are expected due to the need to replace the large number of mail clerks and messengers who leave the occupation each year.

Nature of the Work

Mail clerks and messengers move and distribute information, documents, and small packages for businesses, institutions, and government agencies. *Mail clerks* handle the internal mail for most large organizations. Internal mail goes back and forth among people, offices, or departments within a firm or institution. It ranges from memos to key personnel to bulletins on job issues to all employees. Mail clerks sort internal mail and deliver it to their fellow employees, often using carts to carry the mail.

Mail clerks also handle external mail, serving as a link between the U.S. Postal Service and individual offices and workers. They sort incoming mail and deliver mail within large office buildings. They also prepare outgoing mail—which may range from advertising flyers, to customers' orders, to legal documents—for delivery to the post office. To facilitate delivery of outgoing mail, mail clerks often determine if the mail is to be sent registered, certified, special delivery, or first, second, third, or fourth class, and may group mailings by ZIP code. When necessary, they contact delivery services to send important letters or parcels. In larger organizations, or organizations with a large volume of outgoing mail, mail clerks operate machines that collate, fold, and insert material to be mailed into envelopes. They also operate machines that affix postage. In addition, mail clerks increasingly use computers to keep records of incoming and outgoing items.

Messengers, also called couriers, pick up and deliver letters, important business documents, or packages, which need to be sent or received in a hurry from within a local area. By sending an item by messenger, the sender ensures that it reaches its destination the same day or even within the hour. Messengers also deliver items, which the sender is unwilling to entrust to other means of delivery, such as important legal or financial documents. Some messengers pick up and deliver important packages, such as medical samples to be tested.

Messengers receive their instructions either by reporting to their office in person, by telephone, or by two-way radio. They then pick up the item and carry it to its destination. After a delivery, they check with their office and receive instructions about the next delivery. Consequently, most messengers spend much of their time outdoors or in their vehicle. Messengers usually maintain records of deliveries and often obtain signatures from the persons receiving the items.

Most messengers deliver items within a limited geographic area, such as a city or metropolitan area. Items, which need to go longer distances, usually are sent by mail or by an overnight delivery service. Some messengers carry items only for their employer, which typically might be a law firm, bank, or financial institution. Other messengers may act as part of an organization's internal mail system and mainly carry items between an organization's buildings or entirely within one building. Many messengers work for messenger or courier services; for a fee they pick up items from anyone and deliver them to specified destinations within a local area.

Messengers reach their destination by several methods. Many drive vans or cars or ride motorcycles. A few travel by foot, especially in urban areas or when making deliveries nearby. In congested urban areas, messengers often use bicycles to make deliveries. Bicycle messengers usually are employed by messenger or courier services. Although fax machines and computerized electronic mail can deliver information faster than messengers, an electronic copy cannot substitute for the original document for many types of business transactions.

Working Conditions

Working conditions for mail clerks are much different from the working conditions for most messengers. Most mail clerks work regular hours, spending much of their time in mailrooms, which are usually located in office buildings. They spend the remaining time making mail deliveries throughout the office building. Although mailrooms are usually clean and well lighted, there may be noise from mail-handling machines. Mail clerks spend most of their time on their

Mail clerks sort incoming mail and prepare outgoing mail for delivery to the post office.

feet, which can be tiring and physically demanding. They are sometimes required to lift heavy objects or operate a motor vehicle to make deliveries and pick-ups.

Messengers work in a less structured environment than mail clerks because they spend most of their time alone making deliveries and usually are not closely supervised. Although many messengers work full time during regular business hours, some messengers work nights and weekends.

Messengers, who deliver by bicycle, must be physically fit and are exposed to all weather conditions as well as the many hazards connected with heavy traffic. The pressure of making as many deliveries as possible to increase earnings can be stressful and may lead to unsafe driving or bicycling practices.

Employment

Mail clerks and messengers together held about 247,000 jobs in 1998; about 120,000 were messengers and about 128,000 were mail clerks.

About 14 percent of messengers worked for law firms, another 13 percent worked for hospitals and medical and dental laboratories, and 13 percent for local and long distance trucking establishments. Financial institutions, such as commercial banks, saving institutions, and credit unions, employed 7 percent. The rest were employed in a variety of other industries. Technically, many messengers are self-employed independent contractors because they provide their vehicles and, to a certain extent, set their own schedules, but in many respects they are like employees because they usually work for one company. Almost 1 of every 3 worked part time.

In 1998, about 12 percent of all mail clerks worked in Federal, State, and local governments, and both the insurance industry and personnel supply services industry employed 27 percent. Others were employed in a wide range of industries.

Training, Other Qualifications, and Advancement

There are no formal qualifications or training required to be a mail clerk or messenger, although some employers prefer high school graduates. This is a first job for many.

Mail clerks must be careful and dependable workers. They must be able to do routine work and work well with their hands. They are usually trained on the job. If they operate computers and mail-handling machinery to help prepare mailings, training may be provided by another employee or by a representative of the machinery manufacturer. Mail clerks are sometimes required to have a driver's license if they make deliveries to other buildings.

Messengers who work as independent contractors for a messenger or delivery service may be required to have a valid driver's license, a registered and inspected vehicle, a good driving record, and insurance coverage. Many messengers who are employees, rather than independent contractors, are also required to provide and maintain their own vehicle. A good knowledge of the geographic area in which they travel, as well as a good sense of direction, are also important.

Some mail clerks, depending on the size of the operation, advance to positions as clerical staff supervisors or office managers. Other mail clerks transfer to related jobs with the U.S. Postal Service, if they pass the competitive entrance examination. (The statement on postal clerks and mail carriers appears elsewhere in the *Handbook*.) Messengers, especially those who work for messenger or courier services, have limited advancement opportunities.

Job Outlook

Favorable employment opportunities are expected for mail clerks and messengers due to the need to replace the large number of workers who leave the occupation each year. Mail clerk and messenger jobs are attractive to many persons seeking their first job or a short-term source of income because the limited formal education and training requirements allow easy entry. This is especially true for messengers, many of whom work in this occupation a relatively short time.

Employment of mail clerks and messengers is expected to grow more slowly than average through 2008 despite an increasing volume of internal mail, parcels, business documents, promotional materials, and other written information that must be handled and delivered as the economy expands. Businesses' growing reliance on direct mail advertising and promotional materials to prospective customers will result in increasing amounts of mail to be handled. However, increasing automation of mail handling will enable mail clerks to handle a growing volume of mail.

Employment of messengers will continue to be adversely impacted by the more widespread use of electronic information-handling technology. For example, fax machines that allow copies of documents to be immediately sent across town or around the world have become standard office equipment. The transmission of information using electronic mail has also become commonplace and will continue to reduce the demand for messengers as more computers are networked or gain access to the Internet. However, messengers will still be needed to transport materials that cannot be sent electronically—such as legal documents, blueprints and other over-sized materials, large multipage documents, and securities. Also, messengers will still be required by medical and dental laboratories to pick up and deliver medical samples, specimens, and other materials.

Earnings

Median hourly earnings of mail clerks, except mail machine operators or postal service, were $8.49 in 1998. The middle 50 percent earned between $7.03 and $10.44. The lowest 10 percent earned less than $6.00 and the highest 10 percent earned more than $12.61. Median hourly earnings in the industries employing the largest numbers of mail clerks in 1997 were:

Federal Government	$10.00
Colleges and universities	8.90
Newspapers	7.30
Personnel supply services	7.20
Mailing, reproduction, stenographic services	7.10

Median hourly earnings of couriers and messengers were $8.02 in 1998. The middle 50 percent of messengers earned between $6.43 and $10.04. The lowest 10 percent earned less than $5.73 and the highest 10 percent earned more than $12.54. Messengers occasionally receive tips from clients, but this is not a significant part of their earnings. Median hourly earnings in the industries employing the largest numbers of couriers and messengers in 1997 were:

Hospitals	$8.00
Medical and dental laboratories	7.90
Commercial banks	7.80
Legal services	7.40
Trucking and courier services, except air	6.80

Messengers are compensated by salary, commission, or a combination of both. The commission usually is based on the fee charged to the customer and is usually considerably higher for those who strictly work by commission than for those messengers whose earnings are based on a combination of salary and commission. Other factors like the number of deliveries made and the distance traveled may also be taken into consideration when determining earnings. The more deliveries they make and the faster they travel, the more they earn. Some messengers work as independent contractors and therefore seldom receive paid vacations, sick leave, health insurance, or other typical benefits from the messenger or delivery company. They must provide their own transportation and must pay fuel and maintenance costs. Messengers working for employers other than messenger and courier services usually are paid by the hour and receive the benefits offered to all employees.

Related Occupations

Messengers and mail clerks sort and deliver letters, parcels, and other items. They also keep accurate records of their work. Others who do similar work are postal clerks and mail carriers; route drivers; traffic, shipping, and receiving clerks; and parcel post clerks.

Sources of Additional Information

Information about job opportunities may be obtained from local employers and local offices of the State employment service. Persons interested in mail clerk and messenger jobs may also contact messenger and courier services, mail order firms, banks, printing and publishing firms, utility companies, retail stores, or other large firms.

For information on training and certification programs in mail systems management, contact:

☛ Mail Systems Management Association, J.A.F. Building, P.O. Box 2155, New York, NY 10116-2155. Internet: **http://www.msma.com**

Material Recording, Scheduling, Dispatching, and Distributing Occupations

Significant Points

- Slower than average job growth is expected as additional automation increases worker productivity.
- Many of these occupations are entry level and do not require more than a high school diploma.

Nature of the Work

Workers in this group are responsible for a variety of communications, recordkeeping, and scheduling operations. Typically, they coordinate, expedite, and track orders for personnel, materials, and equipment.

Dispatchers receive requests for service and initiate action to provide that service. Duties vary, depending on the needs of the employer. Police, fire, and ambulance dispatchers, also called public safety dispatchers, handle calls from people reporting crimes, fires, and medical emergencies. Truck, bus, and train dispatchers schedule and coordinate the movement of these vehicles to ensure they arrive on schedule. Taxicab dispatchers relay requests for cabs to individual drivers, tow truck dispatchers take calls for emergency road service, and utility company dispatchers handle calls related to utility and telephone service.

Shipping, receiving, and traffic clerks track all incoming and outgoing shipments of goods transferred between businesses, suppliers, and customers. These clerks may be required to lift cartons of various sizes. Shipping clerks assemble, address, stamp, and ship merchandise or materials. Receiving clerks unpack, verify, and record incoming merchandise. In a small company, one clerk may perform all of these tasks. Traffic clerks record destination, weight, and charge of all incoming and outgoing shipments.

Stock clerks receive, unpack, and store materials and equipment, and maintain and distribute inventories. Inventories may be merchandise in wholesale and retail establishments, or equipment, supplies, or materials in other kinds of organizations. In small firms, stock clerks may perform all of the above tasks, as well as those usually handled by shipping and receiving clerks. In large establishments, they may be responsible only for one task.

(This introductory statement is followed by statements that provide more detail on dispatchers; shipping, receiving, and traffic clerks; and stock clerks.)

Other administrative support occupations in this group include *production, planning, and expediting clerks*—who coordinate and expedite the flow of work and material according to production schedules; *procurement clerks*—who draw up purchase orders to obtain merchandise or material; *weighers, measurers, checkers, and samplers*—who weigh, measure, and check materials; and *utility meter readers*—who read electric, gas, water, or steam meters and record the quantity used.

Working Conditions

Working conditions vary considerably by occupation and employment setting. Meter readers, for example, spend a good portion of their workday traveling around communities and neighborhoods taking readings, either directly or with remote reading equipment. The work of dispatchers can be very hectic when many calls come in at the same time. The job of public safety dispatcher is particularly stressful, because slow or improper response to a call can result in serious injury or further harm. Also, callers who are anxious or afraid may become excited and be unable to provide needed information; some may become abusive. Despite provocations, dispatchers must remain calm, objective, and in control of the situation.

Dispatchers sit for long periods, using telephones, computers, and two-way radios. Much of their time is spent at video display terminals, viewing monitors and observing traffic patterns. As a result of working for long stretches with computers and other electronic equipment, dispatchers can experience significant eyestrain and back discomfort. Generally, dispatchers work a 40-hour week; however, rotating shifts and compressed work schedules are common. Alternative work schedules are necessary to accommodate evening, weekend, and holiday work, as well as 24-hours-per-day, seven-days-per-week operations.

Shipping, receiving, traffic, and stock clerks work in a wide variety of businesses, institutions, and industries. Some work in warehouses, stock rooms, or in shipping and receiving rooms that may not be temperature controlled. Others may spend time in cold storage rooms or outside on loading platforms, where they are exposed to the weather. Most jobs involve frequent standing, bending, walking, and stretching. Some lifting and carrying of smaller items may also be involved. Although automation, robotics, and pneumatic devices have lessened the physical demands in this occupation, their use remains somewhat limited. Work still can be strenuous, even though mechanical material handling equipment is employed to move heavy items. The typical workweek is Monday through Friday; however, evening and weekend hours are standard for some jobs, such as stock clerks who work in retail trade, and may be required in others when large shipments are involved or when inventory is taken.

Employment

In 1998, material recording, scheduling, dispatching, and distributing workers held about 4 million jobs. Employment was distributed among the detailed occupations as follows:

Occupation	Jobs
Stock clerks	2,300,000
Shipping, receiving, and traffic clerks	774,000
Production, planning, and expediting clerks	248,000
Dispatchers	248,000
Procurement clerks	58,000
Weighers, measurers, checkers, and samplers	51,000
Meter readers, utilities	50,000
All other material recording, scheduling, dispatching, and distributing workers	196,000

About 7 out of 10 material recording, scheduling, dispatching, and distributing jobs were in services or wholesale and retail trade. Although these workers are found throughout the country, most work near population centers where retail stores, warehouses, factories, and large communications centers are concentrated.

Training, Other Qualifications, and Advancement

Many material recording, scheduling, dispatching, and distributing occupations are entry level and do not require more than a high school diploma. Employers, however, increasingly prefer to hire those familiar with computers and other electronic office and business equipment. Those who have taken business courses or have previous business, dispatching, or specific job-related experience may be preferred. Because the nature of the work is to communicate effectively with other people, good oral and written communications skills are essential. Typing, filing, recordkeeping, and other clerical skills are also important.

State or local government civil service regulations usually govern police, fire, emergency medical, and ambulance dispatching jobs. Candidates for these positions may have to pass written, oral, and performance tests. Also, they may be asked to attend training classes and attain the proper certification in order to qualify for advancement.

Trainees usually develop the necessary skills on the job. This informal training lasts from several days to a few months, depending on the complexity of the job. Dispatchers usually require the most extensive training. Working with an experienced dispatcher, they monitor calls and learn how to operate a variety of communications equipment, including telephones, radios, and wireless appliances. As trainees gain confidence, they begin to handle calls themselves. Many public safety dispatchers also participate in structured training programs sponsored by their employer. Some employers offer a course designed by the Association of Public Safety Communications Officials. This course covers topics such as interpersonal communications; overview of the police, fire, and rescue functions; modern public safety telecommunications systems; basic radio broadcasting; local, State, and national crime information computer systems; and telephone complaint/report processing procedures. Other employers develop in-house programs based on their own needs. Emergency medical dispatchers often receive special training or have special skills. Increasingly, public safety dispatchers receive training in stress and crisis management, as well as family counseling. Employers are recognizing the toll this work has on daily living and the potential impact stress has on the job, on the work environment, and in the home.

Communications skills and the ability to work under pressure are important personal qualities for dispatchers. Residency in the city or county of employment frequently is required for public safety dispatchers. Dispatchers in transportation industries must be able to deal with sudden influxes of shipments and disruptions of shipping schedules caused by bad weather, road construction, or accidents.

Although there are no mandatory licensing or certification requirements, some States require that public safety dispatchers possess a certificate to work on a State network, such as the Police Information Network. The Association of Public Safety Communications Officials, the National Academy of Emergency Medical Dispatch, and the International Municipal Signal Association all offer certification programs. Many dispatchers participate in these programs in order to improve their prospects for career advancement.

Stock clerks and shipping, receiving, and traffic clerks usually learn the job by doing routine tasks under close supervision. They learn how to count and mark stock, and then start keeping records and taking inventory. Strength, stamina, good eyesight, and an ability to work at repetitive tasks, sometimes under pressure, are important characteristics. Stock clerks, whose sole responsibility is to bring merchandise to the sales floor, stock shelves and racks, need little or no training. Shipping, receiving, and traffic clerks and stock clerks who handle jewelry, liquor, or drugs may be bonded.

Shipping, receiving, and traffic clerks start out by checking items to be shipped and then attaching labels and making sure the addresses are correct. Training in the use of automated equipment is usually done informally, on the job. As these occupations become more automated, however, workers in these jobs may need longer training in order to master the use of the equipment.

Advancement opportunities for material recording, scheduling, dispatching, and distributing workers vary with the place of employment. Dispatchers who work for private firms, which are usually small, will find few opportunities for advancement. Public safety dispatchers, on the other hand, may become a shift or divisional supervisor or chief of communications, or move to higher paying administrative jobs. Some go on to become police officers or firefighters. In large firms, stock clerks can advance to invoice clerk, stock control clerk, or procurement clerk. Shipping, receiving, and traffic clerks are promoted to head clerk and those with a broad understanding of shipping and receiving may enter a related field such as industrial traffic management. With additional training, some stock clerks and shipping, receiving, and traffic clerks advance to jobs as warehouse manager or purchasing agent.

Job Outlook

Overall employment of material recording, scheduling, dispatching, and distributing workers is expected to grow more slowly than the average for all occupations through 2008. However, projected employment growth varies by detailed occupation. Employment of stock clerks, for example, will be affected by increased automation. New technologies will enable clerks to handle more stock, thus holding down employment growth. The effect of automation also will tend to restrict potential employment growth among shipping, receiving, and traffic clerks. Automation in warehouses and stockrooms plus other productivity improvements will enable these clerks to handle materials more efficiently and more accurately than before. Overall employment of dispatchers, on the other hand, is projected to grow about as fast as the average for all occupations. While employment of public safety dispatchers is expected to grow more slowly than average as governments endeavor to combine dispatching services across governmental units and across governmental jurisdictions, average growth is expected among dispatchers not involved in public safety.

Because employment in material recording, scheduling, dispatching, and distributing occupations is substantial, workers who leave the labor force or transfer to other occupations are expected to create many job openings each year.

Earnings

Earnings of material recording, scheduling, dispatching, and distributing occupations vary somewhat by occupation and industry. The range of median hourly earnings in 1998 are shown in the following tabulation.

Occupation	Earnings
Production, planning, and expediting clerks	$14.07
Dispatchers, except police, fire, and ambulance	12.68
Meter readers, utilities	12.20
Dispatchers, police, fire, and ambulance	11.38
Procurement clerks	10.88
Shipping, receiving, and traffic clerks	10.82
Weighers, measurers, checkers, and samplers, recordkeeping	10.72
Stock clerks and order fillers	7.94
All other material recording, scheduling, and distribution workers	10.13

Workers in material recording, scheduling, dispatching, and distributing occupations usually receive the same benefits as most other workers. If uniforms are required, employers usually either provide the uniforms, or an allowance to purchase them.

Dispatchers

(O*NET 58002 and 58005)

Nature of the Work

The work of dispatchers varies greatly depending on the industry. Dispatchers keep records, logs, and schedules of the calls they receive, transportation vehicles they monitor and control, and actions they take. They maintain information on each call and then prepare a detailed report on all activities occurring during the shift. Many dispatchers employ computer-aided dispatch systems to accomplish these tasks.

Regardless of where they work, all dispatchers are assigned a specific territory and have responsibility for all communications within this area. Many work in teams, especially in large communications centers or companies. One person usually handles all dispatching calls to the response units or company's drivers, while the other members of the team usually receive the incoming calls and deal with the public.

Police, fire, and ambulance dispatchers, also called public safety dispatchers, monitor the location of emergency services personnel from any one or all of the jurisdiction's emergency services departments. They dispatch the appropriate type and number of units in response to calls for assistance. Dispatchers, or call takers, often are the first people the public contacts when they call for emergency assistance. If certified for emergency medical services, the dispatcher may provide medical instruction to those on the scene until the medical staff arrives.

Usually, dispatchers constitute the communications workforce on a shift. A dispatcher is responsible for communication within an assignment area, while the call takers receive calls and transfer information to the dispatchers. During the course of the shift, personnel will rotate such that the assignment responsibility of the dispatcher will be shared with those in the call taker role.

Police, fire, and ambulance dispatchers work in a variety of settings; they may work in a police station, a fire station, a hospital, or a centralized city communications center. In many cities, the police department serves as the communications center. In these situations, all 911 emergency calls go to the police department, where a dispatcher handles the police calls and screens the others before transferring them to the appropriate service.

When handling calls, dispatchers carefully question each caller to determine the type, seriousness, and location of the emergency. This information is posted either electronically by computer or, with decreasing frequency, by hand, and communicated immediately to uniformed or supervisory personnel. They quickly decide on the priority of the incident, the kind and number of units needed, and the location of the closest and most suitable ones available. Typically, there is a team of call takers who answer calls and relay the information to the dispatchers. Responsibility then shifts to the dispatchers who send response units to the scene and monitor the activity of the public safety personnel answering the dispatch.

When appropriate, dispatchers stay in close contact with other service providers—for example, a police dispatcher would monitor the response of the fire department when there is a major fire. In a medical emergency, dispatchers not only keep in close touch with the dispatched units, but also with the caller. They may give extensive pre-arrival first aid instructions while the caller is waiting for the ambulance. They continuously give updates on the patient's condition to the ambulance personnel, and often serve as a link between the medical staff in a hospital and the emergency medical technicians in the ambulance. (A separate statement on emergency medical technicians and paramedics appears elsewhere in the *Handbook*.)

Dispatchers send response units to the scene and monitor the activity of the public safety personnel answering the call.

Other dispatchers coordinate deliveries, service calls, and related activities for a variety of firms. *Truck dispatchers,* who work for local and long distance trucking companies, coordinate the movement of trucks and freight between cities. They direct the pickup and delivery activities of drivers. They receive customers' requests for pickup and delivery of freight; consolidate freight orders into truckloads for specific destinations; assign drivers and trucks; and draw up routes and pickup and delivery schedules. *Bus dispatchers* make sure local and long distance buses stay on schedule. They handle all problems that may disrupt service and dispatch other buses, or arrange for repairs to restore service and schedules. *Train dispatchers* ensure the timely and efficient movement of trains according to train orders and schedules. They must be aware of track switch positions, track maintenance areas, and the location of other trains running on the track. *Taxicab dispatchers*, or starters, dispatch taxis in response to requests for service and keep logs on all road service calls. *Tow truck dispatchers* take calls for emergency road service. They relay the problem to a nearby service station or a tow truck service and see to it that the emergency road service is completed. *Gas and water service dispatchers* monitor gas lines and water mains and send out service trucks and crews to take care of emergencies.

Employment

Dispatchers held 248,000 jobs in 1998. About one-third were police, fire, and ambulance dispatchers, almost all of whom worked for State and local governments—primarily for local police and fire departments. Most of the remaining dispatchers worked for local and long distance trucking companies and bus lines; telephone, electric, and gas utility companies; wholesale and retail establishments; railroads; and companies providing business services.

Although dispatching jobs are found throughout the country, most dispatchers work in urban areas where large communications centers and businesses are located.

Job Outlook

Overall employment of dispatchers is expected to grow about as fast as the average for all occupations through 2008. In addition to job growth, job openings will result from the need to replace those who transfer to other occupations or leave the labor force.

Employment of police, fire, and ambulance dispatchers is expected to grow more slowly than the average for all occupations. Intense competition for available resources among governmental units should limit the ability of many growing communities to keep pace with rapidly growing emergency services needs. To balance the increased demand for emergency services, many districts are seeking to consolidate their communications centers into a shared, areawide facility, thus further restricting opportunities in this industry. Individuals with computer skills and experience will have a greater opportunity for employment as public safety dispatchers.

Population growth and economic expansion are expected to lead to average employment growth for dispatchers not involved in public safety. Although the overall increase will be about average, not all specialties will be affected in the same way. For example, employment of taxicab, train, and truck dispatchers is sensitive to economic conditions. When economic activity falls, demand for transportation services declines. They may experience layoffs or a shortened workweek, and jobseekers may have some difficulty finding entry-level jobs. Employment of tow truck dispatchers, on the other hand, is seldom affected by general economic conditions because of the emergency nature of their business.

Related Occupations

Other occupations that involve directing and controlling the movement of vehicles, freight, and personnel, as well as information and message distribution, are airline dispatchers, air traffic controllers, radio and television transmitter operators, telephone operators, customer service representatives, and transportation agents.

Sources of Additional Information

For further information on training and certification for police, fire, and emergency dispatchers, contact:

☛ National Academy of Emergency Medical Dispatch, 139 East South Temple, Suite 530, Salt Lake City, UT 84111.
Internet: **http://www.naemd.org**

☛ Association of Public Safety Communications Officials, 2040 S. Ridgewood, South Daytona, FL 32119-2257.
Internet: **http://www.apcointl.org**

☛ International Municipal Signal Association, 165 East Union St., P.O. Box 539, Newark, NY 14513-1526.
Internet: **http://www.imsafety.org**

For general information on dispatchers, contact:

☛ Service Employees International Union, AFL-CIO, CLC, 1313 L St. NW., Washington, DC 20005-4100. Internet: **http://www.seiu.org**

☛ American Train Dispatchers Association, 1370 Ontario St., Cleveland, OH 44113. Internet: **http://www.ble.org/atdd/dwv.html**

Information on job opportunities for police, fire, and emergency dispatchers is available from personnel offices of State and local governments or police departments. Information about work opportunities for other types of dispatchers is available from local employers and State employment service offices.

(See introduction to the section on material recording, scheduling, dispatching, and distributing occupations for information on working conditions, training requirements, and earnings.)

Shipping, Receiving, and Traffic Clerks

(O*NET 58028)

Nature of the Work

Shipping, receiving, and traffic clerks keep records of all goods shipped and received. Their duties depend on the size of the establishment and the level of automation employed. Larger companies typically are better able to finance the purchase of computers and other equipment to handle some or all of a clerk's responsibilities. In smaller companies, a clerk maintains records, prepares shipments, and accepts deliveries. Working in both environments, shipping, receiving, and traffic clerks may lift cartons of various sizes.

Shipping clerks are record keepers responsible for all outgoing shipments. They prepare shipping documents and mailing labels, and make sure orders have been filled correctly. Also, they record items taken from inventory and note when orders were filled. Sometimes they fill the order themselves, obtaining merchandise from the stockroom, noting when inventories run low, and wrapping it or packing it in shipping containers. They also address and label packages, look up and compute freight or postal rates, and record the weight and cost of each shipment. Shipping clerks also may prepare invoices and furnish information about shipments to other parts of the company, such as the accounting department. Once a shipment is checked and ready to go, shipping clerks may move the goods from the plant—sometimes by forklift truck—to the shipping dock and direct its loading.

Receiving clerks perform tasks similar to those of shipping clerks. They determine whether orders have been filled correctly by verifying incoming shipments against the original order and the accompanying bill of lading or invoice. They make a record of the shipment and the condition of its contents. In many firms, receiving clerks use hand-held scanners to record bar codes on incoming products or by entering it into a computer. These data then can be transferred to the appropriate departments. The shipment is checked for any discrepancies in quantity, price, and discounts. Receiving clerks may route or move shipments to the proper department, warehouse section, or stockroom. They may also arrange for adjustments with shippers whenever merchandise is lost or damaged. Receiving clerks in small businesses also may perform duties similar to those of stock clerks. In larger establishments, receiving clerks may control all receiving-platform operations, such as truck scheduling, recording of shipments, and handling of damaged goods.

Shipping, receiving, and traffic clerks are responsible for tracking all outgoing and incoming shipments of goods transferred between businesses, suppliers, and customers.

Traffic clerks maintain records on the destination, weight, and charges on all incoming and outgoing freight. They verify rate charges by comparing the classification of materials with rate charts. In many companies, this work may be automated. Information either is scanned, or is hand-entered into a computer for use by accounting or other departments within the company. Also, they keep a file of claims for overcharges and for damage to goods in transit.

Employment

Shipping, receiving, and traffic clerks held about 774,000 jobs in 1998. Nearly 2 out of 3 were employed in manufacturing or by wholesale and retail establishments. Although jobs for shipping, receiving, and traffic clerks are found throughout the country, most clerks work in urban areas, where shipping depots in factories and wholesale establishments usually are located. (For information shipping, receiving, and traffic clerks working for the U.S. Postal Service, see the statement on postal clerks and mail carriers elsewhere in the *Handbook*).

Job Outlook

Employment of shipping, receiving, and traffic clerks is expected to grow more slowly than the average for all occupations through 2008. Employment growth will continue to be affected by automation, as all but the smallest firms move to hold down labor costs by using computers to store and retrieve shipping and receiving records.

Methods of material handling have changed significantly in recent years. Large warehouses are increasingly automated, using equipment such as computerized conveyor systems, robots, computer-directed trucks, and automatic data storage and retrieval systems. Automation, coupled with the growing use of hand-held scanners and personal computers in shipping and receiving departments, has increased the productivity of these workers.

Despite technology, job openings will continue to arise due to increasing economic and trade activity, and because certain tasks cannot be automated. For example, someone needs to check shipments before they go out and when they arrive to ensure everything is in order. In addition to job growth, openings will occur because of the need to replace shipping, receiving, and traffic clerks who leave the occupation. Because this is an entry-level occupation, many vacancies are created by normal career progression.

Related Occupations

Shipping, receiving, and traffic clerks record, check, and often store materials that a company receives. They also process and pack goods for shipment. Other workers who perform similar duties are stock clerks, material clerks, distributing clerks, routing clerks, express clerks, expediters, and order fillers.

Sources of Additional Information

General information about shipping, receiving, and traffic clerks can be obtained from:

☛ National Retail Federation, 325 Seventh St. NW., Suite 1000, Washington, DC 20004. Internet: **http://www.nrf.com/nri/**

(See introduction to the section on material recording, scheduling, dispatching, and distributing occupations for information on working conditions, training requirements, and earnings.)

Stock Clerks

(O*NET 49021, 58023, and 58026)

Nature of the Work

Stock clerks receive, unpack, check, store, and track merchandise or materials. They keep records of items entering or leaving the stock room and inspect damaged or spoiled goods. They sort, organize, and mark items with identifying codes, such as prices or stock or inventory control codes, so that inventories can be located quickly and easily. In larger establishments, where they may be responsible for only one task, they are called *inventory clerk, stock-control clerk, merchandise distributor, order filler, property custodian*, or *storekeeper*. In smaller firms, they may also perform tasks usually handled by shipping and receiving clerks. (A separate statement on shipping, receiving, and traffic clerks appears elsewhere in this section of the *Handbook*.)

Stock clerks are responsible for sorting, organizing, and marking items with identifying codes so that inventories can be located quickly and easily in warehouses and stores.

In many firms, stock clerks use hand-held scanners connected to computers to keep inventories up to date. In retail stores, stock clerks bring merchandise to the sales floor and stock shelves and racks. In stockrooms and warehouses, they store materials in bins, on floors, or on shelves. They may also be required to lift cartons of various sizes.

Employment

Stock clerks held about 2.3 million jobs in 1998, with about 80 percent working in wholesale and retail trade. The greatest numbers were employed in grocery and department stores, respectively. Jobs for stock clerks are found in all parts of the country, but most work in large urban areas that have many large suburban shopping centers, warehouses, and factories.

Job Outlook

Job prospects for stock clerks should be favorable even though employment is expected to grow more slowly than the average for all occupations through 2008. Because this occupation is very large and many jobs are entry level, numerous job openings will occur each year to replace those who transfer to other jobs or leave the labor force.

The growing use of computers for inventory control and the installation of new, automated equipment are expected to slow growth in demand for stock clerks. This is especially true in manufacturing and wholesale trade, industries whose operations are automated most easily. In addition to computerized inventory control systems, firms in these industries rely more on sophisticated conveyor belts and automatic high stackers to store and retrieve goods. Also, expanded use of battery-powered, driverless, automatically guided vehicles can be expected.

Employment of stock clerks who work in grocery, general merchandise, department, apparel, and accessories stores is expected to be somewhat less affected by automation because much of their work is done manually on the sales floor and is difficult to automate. In addition, the increasing role of large retail outlets and warehouses, as well as catalogue, mail, telephone, and Internet shopping services should bolster employment of stock clerks and order fillers in these sectors of retail trade.

Related Occupations

Workers who also handle, move, organize, and store materials include shipping and receiving clerks, distributing clerks, routing clerks, stock supervisors, and cargo checkers.

Sources of Additional Information

State employment service offices can provide information about job openings for stock clerks. Also, see clerical and sales occupations elsewhere in the *Handbook* for sources of additional information.

General information about stock clerks can be obtained from:

☛ National Retail Federation, 325 Seventh Street NW., Suite 1000, Washington, DC 20004. Internet: **http://www.nrf.com/nri/**

(See introduction to the section on material recording, scheduling, dispatching, and distributing occupations for information on working conditions, training requirements, and earnings.)

Office and Administrative Support Supervisors and Managers

(O*NET 51002A and 51002B)

Significant Points

- Most jobs are filled by promoting individuals from within the organization, very often from the ranks of clerks they subsequently supervise.

- Office automation will cause employment in some office and administrative support occupations to slow or even decline, but supervisors are more likely to retain their jobs because of their relatively higher skills and longer tenure.
- Applicants for office and administrative support supervisor or manager jobs are likely to encounter keen competition because their number should greatly exceed the number of job openings.

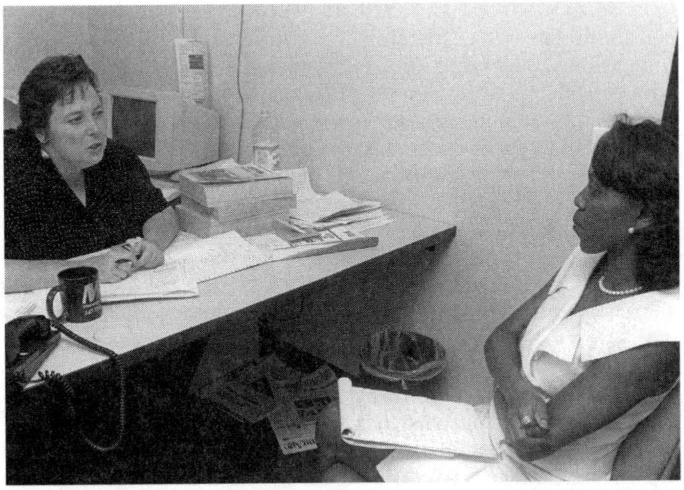

Office and administrative support supervisors and managers train new employees in office procedures.

Nature of the Work

All organizations need timely and effective office and administrative support to operate efficiently. Office and administrative support supervisors and managers coordinate this support. These workers are employed in virtually every sector of the economy, working in positions as varied as customer services manager, chief telephone operator, and shipping-and-receiving supervisor.

Although specific functions of office and administrative support supervisors and managers vary considerably, they share many common duties. For example, supervisors perform administrative tasks to ensure that their staffs can work efficiently. Equipment and machinery used in their departments must be in good working order. If the computer system goes down or a facsimile machine malfunctions, they must try to correct the problem or alert repair personnel. They also request new equipment or supplies for their department when necessary.

Planning the work of their staff and supervising them is a key function of this job. To do this effectively, the supervisor must know the strengths and weaknesses of each member of the staff, as well as the required level of quality and time allotted to each job. They must make allowances for unexpected absences and other disruptions by adjusting assignments or performing the work themselves if the situation requires it.

After allocating work assignments and issuing deadlines, office and administrative support supervisors oversee the work to ensure that it is proceeding on schedule and meets established quality standards. This may involve reviewing each person's work on a computer, as in the case of accounting clerks, or, in the case of customer services representatives, listening to how they deal with customers. When supervising long-term projects, the supervisor may meet regularly with staff members to discuss their progress.

Office and administrative support supervisors also evaluate each worker's performance. If a worker has done a good job, the supervisor records it in the employee's personnel file and may recommend a promotion or other award. Alternatively, if a worker is performing poorly, the supervisor discusses the problem with the employee to determine the cause and helps the worker improve his or her performance. This might require sending the employee to a training course or arranging personal counseling. If the situation does not improve, the supervisor may recommend a transfer, demotion, or dismissal.

Office and administrative support supervisors usually interview and evaluate prospective clerical employees. When new workers arrive on the job, supervisors greet them and provide orientation to acquaint them with the organization and its operating routines. Some supervisors may be actively involved in recruiting new workers, for example, by making presentations at high schools and business colleges. They may also serve as the primary liaisons between their offices and the general public through direct contact and by preparing promotional information.

Supervisors also help train new employees in organization and office procedures. They may teach new employees how to use the telephone system and operate office equipment. Because much clerical work is computerized, they must also teach new employees to use the organization's computer system. When new office equipment or updated computer software is introduced, supervisors retrain experienced employees in using it efficiently. If this is not possible, they may arrange for special outside training for their employees.

Office and administrative support supervisors often act as liaisons between the clerical staff and the professional, technical, and managerial staff. This may involve implementing new company policies or restructuring the workflow in their departments. They must also keep their superiors informed of their progress and abreast of any potential problems. Often this communication takes the form of research projects and progress reports. Because they have access to information such as their department's performance records, they may compile and present these data for use in planning or designing new policies.

Office and administrative support supervisors also may have to resolve interpersonal conflicts among the staff. In organizations covered by union contracts, supervisors must know the provisions of labor-management agreements and run their departments accordingly. They may meet with union representatives to discuss work problems or grievances.

Working Conditions

Office and administrative support supervisors and managers are employed in a wide variety of work settings, but most work in clean, well-lit, and usually comfortable offices.

Most work a standard 40-hour week. Because some organizations operate around the clock, office and administrative support supervisors may have to work nights, weekends, and holidays. Sometimes supervisors rotate among the three shifts; in other cases, shifts are assigned on the basis of seniority.

Employment

Office and administrative support supervisors and managers held over 1.6 million jobs in 1998. Although jobs for office and administrative support supervisors are found in practically every industry, the largest number are found in organizations with a large clerical work force such as banks, wholesalers, government agencies, retail establishments, business service firms, and insurance companies. Due to the need in most organizations for continuity of supervision, few office and administrative support supervisors and managers work on a temporary or part-time basis.

Training, Other Qualifications, and Advancement

Most firms fill administrative and office support supervisory and managerial positions by promoting clerical or administrative support workers within their organization. To become eligible for promotion to a supervisory position, clerical or administrative support workers must prove they are capable of handling additional responsibilities. When evaluating candidates, superiors look for strong teamwork, problem solving, leadership, and communication skills, as well as determination, loyalty, poise, and confidence. They also look for more specific supervisory attributes, such as the ability to organize and coordinate work efficiently, set priorities, and motivate others. Increasingly, supervisors need a broad base of office skills coupled with personal flexibility to adapt to changes in organizational structure and move among departments when necessary.

In addition, supervisors must pay close attention to detail in order to identify and correct errors made by the staff they oversee. Good working knowledge of the organization's computer system is also an advantage. Many employers require postsecondary training—in some cases, an associate's or even a bachelor's degree.

A clerk with potential supervisory abilities may be given occasional supervisory assignments. To prepare for full-time supervisory duties, he or she may attend in-house training or take courses in time management or interpersonal relations.

Some office and administrative support supervisor positions are filled with people from outside the organization. These positions may serve as entry-level training for potential higher-level managers. New college graduates may rotate through departments of an organization at this level to learn the work of the organization.

Job Outlook

Like other supervisory occupations, applicants for office and administrative support supervisor or manager jobs are likely to encounter keen competition because the number of applicants should greatly exceed the number of job openings. Employment of office and administrative support supervisors and managers is expected to grow about as fast as the average for all occupations through 2008. In addition to the job openings arising from growth, a larger number of openings will stem from the need to replace workers who transfer to other occupations or leave this large occupation for other reasons.

Employment of office and administrative support supervisors is primarily affected by the demand for clerical workers. Despite an increasing amount of clerical work, the spread of office automation should allow a wider variety of tasks to be performed by fewer office and administrative support workers. This will cause employment in some clerical occupations to slow or even decline, leading supervisors to have smaller staffs and perform more professional tasks. However, office and administrative support managers still will be needed to coordinate the increasing amount of clerical work and make sure the technology is applied and running properly. In addition, organizational restructuring continues to reduce some middle management positions, distributing more responsibility to office and administrative support supervisors. This added responsibility combined with relatively higher skills and longer tenure will place office and administrative support supervisors and managers among the clerical workers most likely to retain their jobs.

Earnings

Median annual earnings of full-time office and administrative support supervisors were $31,090 in 1998; the middle 50 percent earned between $23,950 and $40,250. The lowest paid 10 percent earned less than $19,060, while the highest paid 10 percent earned more than $52,570. In 1997, median earnings in the industries employing the largest numbers of office and administrative support supervisors were:

Federal government	$49,200
Local government, except education and hospitals	30,600
Hospitals	29,700
Offices and clinics of medical doctors	29,200
Commercial banks	27,400

In addition to typical benefits, some office and administrative support supervisors in the private sector may receive additional compensation in the form of bonuses and stock options.

Related Occupations

Office and administrative support supervisors and managers must understand and sometimes perform the work of the people whom they oversee, including accounting clerks, cashiers, bank tellers, and telephone operators. Their supervisory and administrative duties are similar to those of other supervisors and managers.

Sources of Additional Information

For a wide variety of information related to management occupations, including educational programs, contact:

☛ American Management Association, 1601 Broadway, New York, NY 10019-7420. Internet: **http://www.amanet.org**

☛ National Management Association, 2210 Arbor Blvd., Dayton, OH 45439. Internet: **http://www.nma1.org**

Office Clerks, General

(O*NET 55347)

Significant Points

- Although most jobs are entry level, previous office or business experience may be required for some positions.
- Plentiful job opportunities should stem from employment growth, the large size of the occupation, and turnover.

Nature of the Work

Rather than performing a single specialized task, the daily responsibilities of a general office clerk change with the needs of the specific jobs and the employer. Whereas some clerks spend their days filing or typing, others enter data at a computer terminal. They can also be called upon to operate photocopiers, fax machines, and other office equipment; prepare mailings; proofread copies; and answer telephones and deliver messages.

The specific duties assigned to a clerk vary significantly, depending upon the type of office in which a clerk works. An office clerk in a doctor's office, for example, would not perform the same tasks as a clerk in a large financial institution or in the office of an auto parts wholesaler. Although they may sort checks, keep payroll records, take inventory, and access information, clerks also perform duties unique to their employer, such as organizing medications, making transparencies for a presentation, or filling orders received by fax machine.

The specific duties assigned to a clerk also vary by level of experience. Whereas inexperienced employees make photocopies, stuff envelopes, or record inquiries, experienced clerks are usually given additional responsibilities. For example, they may maintain financial or

General office clerks hold over 3 million jobs.

other records, verify statistical reports for accuracy and completeness, handle and adjust customer complaints, make travel arrangements, take inventory of equipment and supplies, answer questions on departmental services and functions, or help prepare invoices or budgetary requests. Senior office clerks may be expected to monitor and direct the work of lower level clerks.

Working Conditions

For the most part, working conditions for office clerks are the same as those for other office employees within the same company. Those on a full-time schedule usually work a standard 40-hour week; however, some work shifts or overtime during busy periods. About 1 in 3 works part-time, whereas many other office clerks work as temporary workers.

Employment

Office clerks held about 3,021,000 jobs in 1998. Most are employed in relatively small businesses. Although they work in every sector of the economy, almost 60 percent worked in the services or wholesale and retail trade industries.

Training, Other Qualifications, and Advancement

Although most office clerk jobs are entry level administrative support positions, some previous office or business experience may be needed. Employers usually require a high school diploma, and some require typing, basic computer skills, and other general office skills. Familiarity with computer word processing software and applications is becoming increasingly important.

Training for this occupation is available through business education programs offered in high schools, community and junior colleges, and postsecondary vocational schools. Courses in word processing, other computer applications, and office practices are particularly helpful.

Because office clerks usually work with other office staff, they should be cooperative and able to work as part of a team. In addition, they should have good communication skills, be detail-oriented, and adaptable.

General office clerks who exhibit strong communication, interpersonal, and analytical skills may be promoted to supervisory positions. Others may move into different, more senior clerical or administrative jobs, such as receptionist, secretary, and administrative assistant. After gaining some work experience or specialized skills, many workers transfer to jobs with higher pay or greater advancement potential. Advancement to professional occupations within an establishment normally requires additional formal education, such as a college degree.

Job Outlook

Plentiful job opportunities are expected for general office clerks due to employment growth, the large size of the occupation, and turnover. Furthermore, growth in part-time and temporary clerical positions will lead to a large number of job openings. Prospects should be brightest for those who have knowledge of basic computer applications and office machinery, such as fax machines and copiers.

Employment of general office clerks is expected to grow about as fast as the average for all occupations through 2008. The employment outlook for office clerks will be affected by the increasing use of computers, expanding office automation, and the consolidation of clerical tasks. Automation has led to productivity gains, allowing a wide variety of duties to be performed by few office workers. However, automation also has led to a consolidation of clerical staffs and a diversification of job responsibilities. This consolidation increases the demand for general office clerks, because they perform a variety of clerical tasks. It will become increasingly common within small businesses to find a single general office clerk in charge of all clerical work.

Earnings

Median annual earnings of full-time office clerks were $19,580 in 1998; the middle 50 percent earned between $15,210 and $24,370 annually. Ten percent earned less than $12,570, and 10 percent more than $30,740. Median annual salaries in the industries employing the largest number of office clerks in 1997 are shown below:

Local government, except education and hospitals	$20,300
State government, except education and hospitals	20,100
Hospitals	19,400
Colleges and universities	18,600
Personnel supply services	16,700

In early 1999, the Federal Government paid office clerks a starting salary of between $13,400 and $18,400 a year, depending on education and experience. Office clerks employed by the Federal Government earned an average annual salary of about $28,100 in 1999.

Related Occupations

The duties of office clerks can include a combination of bookkeeping, typing, office machine operation, and filing; other administrative support workers who perform similar duties include information clerks and records processing clerks. Nonclerical entry-level jobs include cashier, medical assistant, teacher aide, and food and beverage service worker.

Sources of Additional Information

State employment service offices and agencies can provide information about job openings for general office clerks.

Postal Clerks and Mail Carriers

(O*NET 57305, 57308, and 58028)

Significant Points

- Relatively few people become postal clerks or mail carriers as their first jobs.
- Qualification is based on an examination.
- Because of the large number of qualified applicants, keen competition is expected.

Nature of the Work

Each week, the U.S. Postal Service delivers billions of pieces of mail, including letters, bills, advertisements, and packages. To do this in an efficient and timely manner, the Postal Service employs about 900,000 individuals, almost two-thirds of whom are postal clerks or mail carriers. Postal clerks wait on customers and ensure that mail is properly collected, sorted, and paid for, whereas mail carriers deliver mail to urban and rural residences and businesses throughout the United States.

Postal clerks, who are typically classified by job duties, perform a variety of functions in the Nation's post offices. Those who work as window or counter clerks, for example, sell stamps, money orders, postal stationary, and mailing envelopes and boxes. They also weigh packages to determine postage and check that packages are in satisfactory condition for mailing. These clerks register, certify, and insure mail and answer questions about postage rates, post office boxes, mailing restrictions, and other postal matters. Window and counter clerks also help customers file claims for damaged packages.

Postal clerks known as distribution clerks sort local mail for delivery to individual customers. A growing proportion of distribution clerks are known as mail processors and operate optical character readers (OCRs) and bar code sorters to arrange mail according to destination. OCRs "read" the ZIP code and spray a bar code onto the mail. Bar code sorters then scan the code and sort the mail. Because this is significantly faster than older sorting methods, it is becoming the standard sorting technology in mail processing centers.

Nevertheless, a number of distribution clerks still operate old electronic letter-sorting machines in some locations. These clerks push keys corresponding to the ZIP code of the local post office to

Despite increasing automation, some postal clerks still spend considerable time sorting mail by hand.

which each letter will be delivered. The machine then drops the letter into the proper slot. Still other clerks sort odd-sized letters, magazines, and newspapers by hand. In small post offices, some clerks perform all of the functions listed above.

Once clerks have processed and sorted the mail, it is ready to be delivered by mail carriers. Although carriers are classified by their type of route—either city or rural—duties of city and rural carriers are similar. Most travel established routes, delivering and collecting mail. Mail carriers start work at the post office early in the morning, where they arrange the mail in delivery sequence. Recently, automated equipment has reduced the time carriers need to sort the mail, allowing them to spend more time delivering mail.

Mail carriers cover their routes on foot, by vehicle, or a combination of both. On foot, they carry a heavy load of mail in a satchel or push it on a cart. In some urban and most rural areas, they use a car or small truck. Although the Postal Service provides vehicles to city carriers, most rural carriers have to use their own automobiles. Deliveries are made house-to-house, to roadside mailboxes, and to large buildings, such as offices or apartments, which generally have all the mailboxes at one location.

Besides delivering and collecting mail, carriers collect money for postage-due and COD (cash on delivery) fees and obtain signed receipts for registered, certified, and insured mail. If a customer is not home, the carrier leaves a notice that tells where special mail is being held. After completing their routes, carriers return to the post office with mail gathered from street collection boxes, homes, and businesses and turn in the mail, receipts, and money collected during the day.

The duties of some city carriers can be specialized, with some delivering only parcel post, whereas others pick up mail from mail collection boxes. In contrast to city carriers, rural carriers provide a wider range of postal services, in addition to delivering and picking up mail. For example, rural carriers may sell stamps and money orders and register, certify, and insure parcels and letters. All carriers, however, must be able to answer customers' questions about postal regulations and services and provide change-of-address cards and other postal forms when requested.

Working Conditions

Window clerks usually work in the public portion of clean, well-ventilated, and well-lit buildings. They have a variety of duties and frequent contact with the public, but they rarely work at night. However, they may have to deal with upset customers, stand for long periods, and are held accountable for an assigned stock of stamps and funds. Depending on the size of the post office in which they work, they may be required to perform sorting, as well.

The working conditions of other postal clerks can vary. In small post offices, clerks may sort mail by hand. In large post offices and mail processing centers, chutes and conveyors move the mail, and machines do much of the sorting. Despite the use of automated equipment, the work of postal clerks can be physically demanding. These workers are usually on their feet, reaching for sacks and trays of mail or placing packages and bundles into sacks and trays.

Mail distribution clerks can become tired and bored with the endless routine of moving and sorting mail. Many work at night or on weekends, because most large post offices process mail around the clock, and the largest volume of mail is sorted during the evening and night shifts. Workers can experience stress, as they process ever-larger quantities of mail under tight production deadlines and quotas.

Most carriers begin work early in the morning—those with routes in a business district can start as early as 4 a.m. Overtime hours are frequently required for urban carriers during peak delivery times, such as before the winter holidays. A carrier's schedule has its advantages, however. Carriers who begin work early in the morning are through by early afternoon and spend most of the day on their own, relatively free from direct supervision. Carriers spend most of their time outdoors, delivering mail in all kinds of weather. Even those who drive often must walk periodically when making deliveries and must lift heavy sacks of parcel post items when loading their vehicles. In addition, carriers must be cautious of potential hazards on their routes. Wet and icy roads and sidewalks can be treacherous, and each year numerous carriers are attacked by dogs.

Employment

The U.S. Postal Service employed 299,000 clerks and 332,000 mail carriers in 1998. About 95 percent of them worked full time. Most postal clerks provided window service and sorted mail at major metropolitan post offices, whereas some postal clerks worked at mail processing centers in mail distribution. Although the majority of mail carriers worked in cities and suburbs, about 53,000 were career rural carriers.

Postal clerks and mail carriers are classified as casual, part-time flexible, part-time regular, or full time. Casuals are hired for 90 days at a time to help process and deliver mail, during peak mailing or vacation periods. Part-time flexible workers do not have a regular work schedule or weekly guarantee of hours but are called in as the need arises. Part-time regulars have a set work schedule of fewer than 40 hours per week, often replacing regular full-time workers on their scheduled day off. Full-time postal employees work a 40-hour week over a 5-day period.

Training, Other Qualifications, and Advancement

Postal clerks and mail carriers must be at least 18 years old and U.S. citizens or have been granted permanent resident-alien status in the

United States. Qualification is based on a written examination that measures speed and accuracy at checking names and numbers and the ability to memorize mail distribution procedures. Applicants must pass a physical examination and drug test, as well, and may be asked to show that they can lift and handle mail sacks weighing 70 pounds. Applicants for mail carrier positions must have a driver's license, a good driving record, and receive a passing grade on a road test.

Jobseekers should contact the post office or mail processing center where they wish to work to determine when an exam will be given. Applicants' names are listed in order of their examination scores. Five points are added to the score of an honorably discharged veteran and 10 points to the score of a veteran who was wounded in combat or is disabled. When a vacancy occurs, the appointing officer chooses one of the top three applicants; the rest of the names remain on the list to be considered for future openings until their eligibility expires—usually 2 years after the examination date.

Relatively few people become postal clerks or mail carriers as their first job, because of keen competition and the customary waiting period of 1-2 years or more after passing the examination. It is not surprising, therefore, that most entrants transfer from other occupations.

New postal clerks are trained on the job by experienced workers. Many post offices offer classroom instruction on safety and defensive driving. Workers receive additional instruction, when new equipment or procedures are introduced. In these cases, workers usually are trained by another postal employee or a training specialist.

Window clerks and mail carriers should be courteous and tactful when dealing with the public, especially when answering questions or receiving complaints. A good memory and the ability to read rapidly and accurately are important. Good interpersonal skills are also vital, because mail distribution clerks work closely with other clerks, frequently under the tension and strain of meeting dispatch or transportation deadlines and quotas.

Postal clerks and mail carriers often begin on a part-time, flexible basis and become regular or full time, in order of seniority as vacancies occur. Full-time clerks may bid for preferred assignments, such as the day shift or a high level nonsupervisory position. Carriers can look forward to obtaining preferred routes, as their seniority increases or to getting high level jobs, such as carrier technician. Both clerks and carriers can advance to supervisory positions on a competitive basis.

Job Outlook

Those seeking jobs as postal clerks and mail carriers can expect to encounter keen competition, because the number of applicants will continue to exceed the number of openings. Employment of postal clerks and mail carriers is expected to increase more slowly than the average for all occupations through 2008. However, some jobs will become available because of the need to replace those who retire or stop working for other reasons.

Although efforts by the U.S. Postal Service to provide better service will increase the number of window clerks, the demand for window clerks will be offset by the use of electronic communications technologies and private delivery companies. Employment growth among distribution clerks will be slowed by the increasing use of automated materials handling equipment and optical character readers, bar code sorters, and other automated sorting equipment. However, despite greater use of productivity-increasing machinery, the expected increase in mail volume will require additional clerks.

Other conflicting factors are expected to influence demand for mail carriers. The competition from alternative delivery systems and new forms of electronic communication will not affect the volume of mail handled by the U.S. Postal Service. In fact, mail volume is expected to continue to increase, as population growth and partnerships with express delivery companies stimulate demand for mail delivery. However, increased use of the "delivery point sequencing" system, which allows machines to sort mail directly to the order of delivery, should decrease the amount of time carriers spend sorting their mail, allowing them more time to handle long routes. In addition, the Postal Service is moving toward more centralized mail delivery, such as the increased use of cluster boxes, to cut down on the number of door-to-door deliveries. These trends are expected to increase carrier productivity and lead to slower-than-average growth for these workers.

Employment and schedules in the Postal Service fluctuate with the demand for its services. When mail volume is high, full-time clerks and carriers work overtime, part-time clerks and carriers work additional hours, and casual clerks and carriers may be hired. When mail volume is low, overtime is curtailed, part-timers work fewer hours, and casual workers are discharged.

Earnings

Median annual earnings of postal mail carriers were $34,840 in 1998. The middle 50 percent earned between $30,430 and $37,950. The lowest 10 percent had earnings of less than $26,040, while the top 10 percent earned over $39,820. Median annual earnings of postal service clerks were $35,100 in 1998. The middle 50 percent earned between $32,140 and $37,580. The lowest 10 percent had earnings of less than $25,350, while the top 10 percent earned more than $39,070.

Postal workers enjoy a variety of employer-provided benefits similar to those enjoyed by Federal Government workers. The American Postal Workers Union or the National Association of Letter Carriers, both of which are affiliated with the AFL-CIO, represent most of these workers.

Related Occupations

Other workers whose duties are related to those of postal clerks include mail handlers, who unload the sacks of incoming mail and separate letters, parcel post, magazines, and newspapers. In addition, file clerks, routing clerks, sorters, material moving equipment operators, clerk typists, cashiers, and data entry operators do similar work. Others with duties related to those of mail carriers include messengers, merchandise deliverers, and delivery-route truckdrivers.

Sources of Additional Information

Local post offices and State employment service offices can supply details about entrance examinations and specific employment opportunities for postal clerks and mail carriers.

Records Processing Occupations

Significant Points

- Most jobs require only a high school diploma.
- Numerous job opportunities should arise due to high turnover in this occupation.
- Little or no change is expected in overall employment, reflecting the spread of computers and other office automation as well as organizational restructuring.

Nature of the Work

Without the assistance of workers in records processing occupations, many organizations would be lost. These workers maintain, update, and process a variety of records, ranging from payrolls to information on the shipment of goods or bank statements. They ensure that other workers get paid on time, customers' questions are answered, and records are kept of all transactions. (Additional information about specific records processing occupations appears in separate statements that follow this introductory statement.)

Depending on their specific titles, these workers perform a wide variety of recordkeeping duties. *Billing clerks and billing machine operators*, for example, prepare bills and invoices. *Bookkeeping, accounting, and auditing clerks* maintain financial data in computer and paper files. *Brokerage clerks* prepare and maintain the records generated when stocks, bonds, and other types of investments are traded. *File clerks* store and retrieve various kinds of office information for use by staff members. *Human resources clerks* maintain employee records. *Library assistants and bookmobile drivers* assist library patrons. *Order clerks* process incoming orders for goods and services. *Payroll and timekeeping clerks* compute wages for payroll records and review employee timecards. *Statement clerks* prepare monthly statements for bank customers. Other records processing clerks include *advertising clerks*—who receive orders for classified advertising for newspapers or magazines, prepare copy according to customer specifications, and verify conformance of published ads to specifications for billing purposes; and *correspondence clerks*—who reply to customers regarding damage claims, delinquent accounts, incorrect billings, complaints of unsatisfactory service, and requests for merchandise exchanges or returns.

The duties of records processing clerks vary with the size of the firm. In a small business, a bookkeeping clerk may handle all financial records and transactions, as well as payroll and personnel duties. A large firm, on the other hand, may employ specialized accounting, payroll, and human resources clerks. In general, however, clerical staffs in firms of all sizes increasingly perform a broader variety of tasks than in the past. This is especially true for clerical occupations involving accounting work. As the growing use of computers enables bookkeeping, accounting, and auditing clerks to become more productive, these workers may assume billing, payroll, and timekeeping duties.

Another change in these occupations is the growing use of financial software to enter and manipulate data. Computer programs automatically perform calculations on data that were previously calculated manually. Computers also enable clerks to access data within files more quickly than the former method of reviewing stacks of paper. Nevertheless, most workers still keep backup paper records for research, auditing, and reference purposes.

Despite the growing use of automation, interaction with the public and coworkers remains a basic part of the job for many records processing clerks. Payroll clerks, for example, answer questions concerning employee benefits; bookmobile drivers help patients in nursing homes and hospitals select books; and order clerks call customers to verify special mailing instructions.

Working Conditions

With the exception of library assistants and bookmobile drivers, records processing clerks typically are employed in an office environment. Most work alongside other clerical workers, but some records processing clerks work in centralized units away from the front office.

Because the majority of records processing clerks use computers on a daily basis, these workers may experience eye and muscle strain, backaches, headaches, and repetitive motion injuries. Also, clerks who review detailed data may have to sit for extended periods of time. Although the work does not require heavy lifting, file clerks and library assistants spend a lot of time on their feet and frequently stoop, bend, and reach. Finally, bookmobile drivers must maneuver large vehicles in all kinds of traffic and weather conditions, and may also be responsible for the maintenance of the bookmobile.

Most records processing clerks work regular business hours. Library assistants may work evenings and weekends, but those employed in school libraries usually work only during the school year. Accounting clerks may work longer hours to meet deadlines at the end of the fiscal year, during tax time, or when monthly and yearly accounting audits are performed. Billing, bookkeeping, and accounting clerks in hotels, restaurants, and stores may work overtime during peak holiday and vacation seasons. Similarly, order clerks in retail establishments typically work overtime during these seasons. Brokerage clerks may also have to work overtime if there is a high volume of activity in the stock or bond markets.

Employment

Records processing clerks held over 3.7 million jobs in 1998. The following tabulation shows employment in individual clerical occupations:

Occupation	Employment
Bookkeeping, accounting, and auditing clerks	2,078,000
Billing clerks and billing machine operators	449,000
Order clerks	362,000
File clerks	272,000
Payroll and timekeeping clerks	172,000
Library assistants and bookmobile drivers	127,000
Human resources clerks	142,000
Brokerage and statement clerks	92,000
Correspondence clerks	25,000
Advertising clerks	14,000

These workers are employed in virtually every industry. The largest number of records processing clerks work for firms providing health, business, and other types of services. Many also work in trade; finance, insurance, and real estate; manufacturing; and government.

Training, Other Qualifications, and Advancement

Employers typically require applicants to have at least a high school diploma or its equivalent. Although many employers prefer to hire record clerks with a higher level of education, it is only required in a few records processing occupations. For example, brokerage firms usually seek college graduates for brokerage clerk jobs, and order clerks in high-technology firms often need to understand scientific and mechanical processes, which may require some college education. Regardless of the type of work, most employers prefer workers who are computer-literate. Knowledge of word processing and spreadsheet software is especially valuable, as are experience working in an office and good interpersonal skills.

Records processing clerks often learn the skills they need in high schools, business schools, and community colleges. Business education programs offered by these institutions typically include courses in typing, word processing, shorthand, business communications, records management, and office systems and procedures. Specialized order clerks in technical positions obtain their training from technical institutes and 2- and 4-year colleges.

Some entrants into records processing occupations are college graduates with degrees in business, finance, or liberal arts. Although a degree is rarely required, many graduates accept entry-level clerical positions to get into a particular company or to enter the finance or accounting field with the hope of being promoted to professional or managerial positions. Some companies, such as brokerage and accounting firms, have a set plan of advancement that tracks college graduates from entry-level clerical jobs into managerial positions. Workers with college degrees are likely to start at higher salaries and advance more easily than those without degrees.

Once hired, records processing clerks usually receive on-the-job training. Under the guidance of a supervisor or other senior worker, new employees learn company procedures. Some formal classroom training may also be necessary, such as training in specific computer software.

Records processing clerks must be careful, orderly, and detail-oriented in order to avoid making errors and recognize errors made by others. These workers should also be discreet and trustworthy, because they frequently come in contact with confidential material. Additionally, payroll clerks, billing clerks, and bookkeeping, accounting, and auditing clerks should have a strong aptitude for numbers. Because statement clerks have access to confidential financial information, these workers must be bonded. Many bookmobile drivers are now required to have a commercial driver's license.

Records processing clerks usually advance by taking on more duties in the same occupation for higher pay or transferring to a closely related occupation. For example, some order clerks use their experience to move into sales positions. Most companies fill office and administrative support supervisory and managerial positions by promoting individuals from within their organization, so information clerks who acquire additional skills, experience, and training improve their advancement opportunities. With appropriate experience and education, some clerks may become accountants; personnel specialists; securities, commodities, and financial services sales representatives; or librarians.

Job Outlook
Little or no change is expected in employment of records processing clerks through 2008. Despite continued growth in the volume of business transactions, rising productivity stemming from the spread of office automation, as well as organizational restructuring, will adversely affect demand for records processing clerks. Turnover in this very large occupation, however, places it among those occupations providing the most job openings. As a result, opportunities should be plentiful for full-time, part-time, and seasonal employment, as records processing clerks transfer to other occupations or leave the labor force.

Many record clerk jobs have already become heavily automated. Productivity has increased significantly, as workers use personal computers instead of more time-consuming equipment such as typewriters, adding machines, and calculators. The growing use of bar code readers, point-of-sale terminals, and optical scanners also reduces much of the data entry handled by records processing clerks. Additionally, managers and professionals now do much of their own clerical work, using computers to access, create, and store data directly in their computer systems. The growing use of local area networks is also facilitating electronic data interchange—the sending of data from computer to computer—abolishing the need for clerks to reenter the data. To further eliminate duplicate functions, many large companies are consolidating their clerical operations in a central office where accounting, billing, personnel, and payroll functions are performed for all offices—main and satellite—within the organization.

Despite the spread of automation and organizational restructuring, average or faster-than-average job growth is projected for some records processing clerks, including billing clerks, brokerage clerks, and library assistants and bookmobile drivers.

Earnings
Salaries of records processing clerks vary considerably. The region of the country, size of city, and type and size of establishment all influence salary levels. The level of industry or technical expertise required and the complexity and uniqueness of a clerk's responsibilities may also affect earnings. Median annual earnings of full-time records processing clerks in 1998 are shown in the following tabulation:

Brokerage clerks	$27,920
Payroll and timekeeping clerks	24,560
Human resources clerks	24,360
Bookkeeping, accounting, and auditing clerks	23,190
Billing clerks	22,670
Correspondence clerks	22,270
Order clerks	21,550
Billing machine operators	20,560
Advertising clerks	20,550
Statement clerks	18,640
Library assistants and bookmobile drivers	16,980
File clerks	16,830

In the Federal Government, records processing clerks with a high school diploma or clerical experience typically started at $18,400 a year in 1999. Beginning salaries were slightly higher in areas where the prevailing local pay level was higher. The average salary for all human resources clerks employed by the Federal Government was $29,500 in 1999.

Related Occupations
Today, most records processing clerks enter data into a computer system and perform basic analysis of the data. Other clerical workers who enter and manipulate data include bank tellers, statistical clerks, receiving clerks, medical record clerks, hotel and motel clerks, credit clerks, and reservation and transportation ticket agents.

Sources of Additional Information
State employment service offices can provide information about job openings for records processing occupations.

Billing Clerks and Billing Machine Operators

(O*NET 55344 and 56002)

Nature of the Work
Billing clerks keep records, calculate charges, and maintain files of payments made for goods or services. Billing machine operators run machines that generate bills, statements, and invoices.

Billing clerks review purchase orders, bills of lading, sales tickets, hospital records, or charge slips to calculate the total amount due from a customer. Calculating the charges for an individual's hospital stay may require a letter to an insurance company; a clerk computing trucking rates for machine parts may consult a rate book. In accounting, law, consulting, and similar firms, billing clerks calculate client fees based on the actual time required to perform the task. They keep track of the accumulated hours and dollar amounts to charge to each job, the type of job performed for a customer, and the percentage of work completed.

After billing clerks review all necessary information, they compute the charges using calculators or computers. They then prepare itemized

A billing clerk reviews a bill for accuracy before sending it to the customer.

statements, bills, or invoices used for billing and recordkeeping purposes, depending on the organization's needs. In one organization, the clerk might prepare a bill containing the amount due and date and type of service; in another, the clerk would produce a detailed invoice with codes for all goods and services provided. This latter form might list items sold, credit terms, date of shipment or dates services were provided, a salesperson's or doctor's identification, if necessary, and the sales total.

After entering all information, *billing machine operators* then run off the bill to send to the customer. Computers and specialized billing software allow many clerks to calculate charges and prepare bills in one step. Computer packages prompt clerks to enter data from handwritten forms and manipulate the necessary entries of quantities, labor, and rates to be charged. Billing clerks verify the entry of information and check for errors before the computer prints the bill. After the bills are printed, billing clerks check them again for accuracy.

Employment

In 1998, billing clerks held about 342,000 jobs, and billing machine operators held about 107,000 jobs. One third of the billing clerks' jobs were in health services, mostly in physicians' offices. Transportation and wholesale trade industries each accounted for 1 out of 10 jobs. Most of the remaining jobs were found in manufacturing or retail trade.

Wholesale and retail trade establishments provided about one third of all billing machine operator jobs; service establishments, including health services, provided another third. Of the remaining jobs, most were found in banks and other financial institutions.

Job Outlook

Job openings for those seeking work as billing clerks or billing machine operators are expected to be numerous through the year 2008. Despite the lack of rapid employment growth, many job openings will occur as workers transfer to other occupations or leave the labor force. Turnover in this occupation is relatively high, which is characteristic of an entry-level occupation requiring only a high school diploma.

Employment of billing clerks is expected to grow about as fast as the average for all occupations through the year 2008. A growing economy and increased demand for billing services will result in more business transactions. Rising worker productivity as computers manage more account information will not keep employment from rising. More complex billing applications will increasingly require workers with greater technical expertise.

Employment of billing machine operators, on the other hand, is expected to decline through the year 2008. More advanced machines and computers will continue to replace billing machines, enabling billing clerks to perform the jobs formerly done by billing machine operators. In some organizations, productivity gains from billing software will increasingly allow accounting clerks to take over the responsibilities of billing clerks and billing machine operators.

(See the introductory statement on records processing occupations for information on working conditions, training requirements, and earnings.)

Bookkeeping, Accounting, and Auditing Clerks

(O*NET 49023B, 55338A, and 55338B)

Nature of the Work

Bookkeeping, accounting, and auditing clerks are an organization's financial recordkeepers. They compute, classify, record, and verify numerical data, to develop and maintain financial records.

In small establishments, *bookkeeping clerks* handle all aspects of financial transactions. They record debits and credits, compare current and past balance sheets, summarize details of separate ledgers, and prepare reports for supervisors and managers. They may also prepare bank deposits by compiling data from cashiers, verifying and balancing receipts, and sending cash, checks, or other forms of payment to the bank.

In large offices and accounting departments, *accounting clerks* have more specialized tasks. Their titles often reflect the type of accounting they do, such as accounts payable clerk or accounts receivable clerk. In addition, responsibilities vary by level of experience. Entry-level accounting clerks post details of transactions, total accounts, and compute interest charges. They may also monitor loans and accounts, to ensure that payments are up to date.

More advanced accounting clerks may total, balance, and reconcile billing vouchers; ensure completeness and accuracy of data on accounts; and code documents, according to company procedures. They post transactions in journals and on computer files and update these files when needed. Senior clerks also review computer printouts against manually maintained journals and make necessary corrections. They may also review invoices and statements, to ensure that all information is accurate and complete, and reconcile computer reports with operating reports.

Auditing clerks verify records of transactions posted by other workers. They check figures, postings, and documents for correct entry, mathematical accuracy, and proper codes. They also correct or note errors for accountants or other workers to adjust.

As organizations continue to computerize their financial records, many bookkeeping, accounting, and auditing clerks use specialized accounting software on personal computers. They increasingly post charges to accounts on computer spreadsheets and databases, as manual posting to general ledgers is becoming obsolete. These workers now enter information from receipts or bills into computers, which is then stored either electronically, as computer printouts, or both. Widespread use of computers has also enabled bookkeeping, accounting, and auditing clerks to take on additional responsibilities, such as payroll, timekeeping, and billing.

Employment

Bookkeeping, accounting, and auditing clerks held about 2.1 million jobs in 1998. About 25 percent worked in wholesale and retail trade, and 16 percent were in organizations providing business, health, and social services. Approximately 1 out of 3 of bookkeeping, accounting, and auditing clerks worked part time in 1998.

Job Outlook

Virtually all job openings for bookkeeping, accounting, and auditing clerks through 2008 will stem from replacement needs. Each year, numerous jobs will become available, as these clerks transfer to other occupations or leave the labor force. Although turnover is lower than among other record clerks, the large size of the occupation ensures

Bookkeeping, accounting, and auditing clerks develop and maintain financial records.

plentiful job openings, including many opportunities for temporary and part-time work.

Employment of bookkeeping, accounting, and auditing clerks is expected to decline through 2008. Although a growing economy will result in more financial transactions and other activities that require these clerical workers, the continuing spread of office automation will lift worker productivity and contribute to employment decline. In addition, organizations of all sizes will continue to consolidate various recordkeeping functions, thus reducing the demand for these clerks.

Information on working conditions, training requirements, and earnings appears in the introduction to records processing occupations.

Brokerage Clerks and Statement Clerks

(O*NET 53126 and 53128)

Nature of the Work

Brokerage clerks perform a number of different jobs with wide ranging responsibilities, but all involve computing and recording data on securities transactions. Brokerage clerks may also contact customers, take orders, and inform clients of changes to their accounts. Some of these jobs are more clerical and require only a high school diploma, while others are considered entry-level positions for which a bachelor's degree is needed. Brokerage clerks, who work in the operations departments of securities firms, on trading floors, and in branch offices, are also called margin clerks, dividend clerks, transfer clerks, and broker's assistants.

The broker's assistant, also called sales assistant, is the most common type of brokerage clerk. These workers typically assist two brokers, for whom they take calls from clients, write up order tickets, process the paperwork for opening and closing accounts, record a client's purchases and sales, and inform clients of changes in their accounts. All brokers' assistants must be knowledgeable about investment products so they can clearly communicate with clients. Those with a "Series 7" license can make recommendations to clients at the instruction of the broker. The Series 7 license is issued to securities and commodities sales representatives by the National Association of Securities Dealers and allows them to provide advice on securities to the public.

Brokerage clerks in the operations areas of securities firms perform many duties to facilitate the sale and purchase of stocks, bonds, commodities, and other kinds of investments. These clerks produce the necessary records of all transactions that occur in their area of the business. Job titles for many of these clerks depend upon the type of work they perform. Purchase-and-sale clerks, for example, match orders to buy with orders to sell. They balance and verify stock trades by comparing the records of the selling firm to those of the buying firm. Dividend clerks ensure timely payments of stock or cash dividends to clients of a particular brokerage firm. Transfer clerks execute customer requests for changes to security registration and examine stock certificates for adherence to banking regulations. Receive-and-deliver clerks facilitate the receipt and delivery of securities among firms and institutions. Margin clerks post accounts and monitor activity in customers' accounts to ensure that clients make payments and stay within legal boundaries concerning stock purchases.

Brokerage clerks record data on securities transactions.

Technology is changing the nature of many of these workers' jobs. A significant and growing number of brokerage clerks use custom-designed software programs to process transactions more quickly. Only a few customized accounts are still handled manually.

Statement clerks assemble, verify, and send bank statements every month. In many banks, statement clerks are called statement operators because they spend much of their workday running sophisticated, high-speed machines. These machines fold computer-printed statements, collate those longer than one page, insert statements and canceled checks into envelopes, and seal and weigh them for postage. Statement clerks load the machine with statements, canceled checks, and envelopes. They then monitor the equipment and correct minor problems. For more serious problems, they call repair personnel.

In banks that do not have such machines, statement clerks perform all operations manually. They may also be responsible for verifying signatures and checking for missing information on checks, placing canceled checks into trays, and retrieving them to send with the statements. In a growing number of banks, only the statement is printed and sent to the account holder. The canceled checks are not returned; this is known as check truncation.

Statement clerks are employed primarily by large banks. In smaller banks, a teller or bookkeeping clerk, who performs other duties during the rest of the month, usually handles the statement clerks' function. Some small banks send their statement information to larger banks for processing, printing, and mailing.

Employment

Brokerage clerks held about 77,000 jobs in 1998, and statement clerks held about 16,000 jobs. Brokerage clerks work in firms that sell securities and commodities. Banking institutions employed almost all statement clerks.

Job Outlook

Employment of brokerage clerks is expected to increase faster than the average for all occupations, while employment of statement clerks should decline. With people increasingly investing in securities, demand for brokerage clerks will climb to meet the needs of processing larger volumes of transactions. Because most back office operations are now computerized, employment growth among brokerage clerks is not expected to keep pace with overall employment growth in the securities and commodities industry; however, brokerage clerks will still be needed to update records, enter changes to customer's accounts, and verify securities transfers.

Broker's assistants will also increase in number along with the number of full-service brokers. Because these clerks spend much of their day answering telephone calls, placing orders, and often running the office, their jobs are not readily subject to automation.

The number of statement clerks is declining rapidly due to increasing technology in the Nation's banks. With the job of producing statements almost completely automated, the mailing of checks and statements is now done mostly by machine. In addition, the further spread of check truncation and the increased use of automated teller machines and other electronic money transfers should result in significantly fewer checks being written and processed.

(See introductory statement on records clerks for information on working conditions, training requirements, and earnings.)

File Clerks

(O*NET 55321)

Nature of the Work

The amount of information generated by organizations continues to grow rapidly. File clerks classify, store, retrieve, and update this information. In many small offices, they often have additional responsibilities, such as data entry, word processing, sorting mail, and operating copying or fax machines. They are employed across the Nation by organizations of all types.

File clerks, also called records, information, or record center clerks, examine incoming material and code it numerically, alphabetically, or by subject matter. They then store forms, letters, receipts, or reports in paper form or enter necessary information into other storage devices. Some clerks operate mechanized files that rotate to bring the needed records to them; others convert documents to films that are then stored on microforms, such as microfilm or microfiche. A growing number of file clerks use imaging systems that scan paper files or film and store the material on optical disks.

In order for records to be useful they must be up-to-date and accurate. File clerks ensure that new information is added to the files in a timely manner and may get rid of outdated file materials or transfer them to inactive storage. They also check files at regular intervals to make sure that all items are correctly sequenced and placed. Whenever records cannot be found, the file clerk attempts to locate the missing material. As an organization's needs for information change, file clerks also implement changes to the filing system established by supervisory personnel.

Many file clerks are employed by temporary help firms.

When records are requested, file clerks locate them and give them to the borrower. The record may be a sheet of paper stored in a file cabinet or an image on microform. In the first example, the clerk manually retrieves the document and hands or forwards it to the borrower. In the latter example, the clerk retrieves the microform and displays it on a microform reader. If necessary, file clerks make copies of records and distribute them. In addition, they keep track of materials removed from the files to ensure that borrowed files are returned.

Increasingly, file clerks use computerized filing and retrieval systems. These systems use a variety of storage devices, such as a mainframe computer, magnetic tape, CD-ROM, or floppy disk. To retrieve a document in these systems, the clerk enters the document's identification code, obtains the location, and pulls the document. Accessing files in a computer database is much quicker than locating and physically retrieving paper files. Even when files are stored electronically, however, backup paper or electronic copies usually are also kept.

Employment

File clerks held about 272,000 jobs in 1998. Although file clerk jobs are found in nearly every sector of the economy, about 90 percent of these workers are employed in services, government, finance, insurance, and real estate. More than 1 out of every 4 is employed in temporary services firms, and about 1 out of 3 worked part time in 1998.

Job Outlook

Employment of file clerks is expected to grow about as fast as the average for all occupations through 2008. Projected job growth stems from rising demand for file clerks to record and retrieve information in organizations across the economy. This growth will be moderated, however, by productivity gains stemming from office automation and the consolidation of clerical jobs. Nonetheless, job opportunities for file clerks should be plentiful because a large number of workers will be needed to replace workers who leave the occupation each year. High turnover among file clerks reflects the lack of formal training requirements, limited advancement potential, and relatively low pay.

Jobseekers who have typing and other secretarial skills and are familiar with a wide range of office machines, especially personal computers, should have the best job opportunities. File clerks should find many opportunities for temporary or part-time work, especially during peak business periods.

Information on working conditions, training requirements, and earnings appears in the introduction to records processing occupations.

Human Resources Clerks, Except Payroll and Timekeeping

(O*NET 55314)

Nature of the Work

Human resources clerks maintain the personnel records of an organization's employees. These records include information such as name, address, job title, and earnings, benefits such as health and life insurance, and tax withholding. On a daily basis, these clerks record and answer questions about employee absences and supervisory reports on job performance. When an employee receives a promotion or switches health insurance plans, the human resources clerk updates the appropriate form. Human resources clerks may also prepare reports for managers elsewhere within the organization. For example, they might compile a list of employees eligible for an award.

Human resources clerks often screen applications for employment.

In smaller organizations, some human resources clerks perform a variety of other clerical duties. They answer telephone or letter inquiries from the public, send out announcements of job openings or job examinations, and issue application forms. When credit bureaus and finance companies request confirmation of a person's employment, the human resources clerk provides authorized information from the employee's personnel records. Payroll departments and insurance companies may also be contacted to verify changes to records.

Some human resources clerks are also involved in hiring. They screen job applicants to obtain information such as education and work experience; administer aptitude, personality, and interest tests; explain the organization's employment policies and refer qualified applicants to the employing official; and request references from present or past employers. Also, human resources clerks inform job applicants, by telephone or letter, of their acceptance or rejection for employment.

Other human resources clerks are known as assignment clerks. Their role is to notify a firm's existing employees of position vacancies and to identify and assign qualified applicants. They keep track of vacancies throughout the organization and complete and distribute vacancy advertisement forms. These clerks review applications in response to advertisements and verify information, using personnel records. After a selection is made, they notify all the applicants of their acceptance or rejection.

In some job settings, human resources clerks have specific job titles. Identification clerks are responsible for security matters at defense installations. They compile and record personal data about vendors, contractors, and civilian and military personnel and their dependents. Job duties include interviewing applicants; corresponding with law enforcement authorities; and preparing badges, passes, and identification cards.

Employment

Human resources clerks held about 142,000 jobs in 1998. Although these workers are found in most industries, about 1 in every 5 works for a government agency. Colleges and universities, hospitals, department stores, and banks also employ large numbers of human resources clerks.

Job Outlook

Replacement needs will account for most job openings for human resources clerks. Jobs will open up, as clerks advance within the personnel department, take jobs unrelated to personnel administration, or leave the labor force.

Little or no change is expected in employment of human resources clerks through the year 2008, largely due to the increased use of computers. The growing use of computers in personnel or human resource departments means that a lot of data entry done by human resources clerks can be eliminated, as employees themselves enter the data and send it to the personnel office. This is most feasible in large organizations with multiple personnel offices. The increasing use of computers and other automated office equipment by managers and professionals in personnel offices also could mean less work for human resources clerks.

(See introductory statement on records processing occupations for information on working conditions, training requirements, and earnings.)

Library Assistants and Bookmobile Drivers

(O*NET 53902)

Nature of the Work

Library assistants and bookmobile drivers organize library resources and make them available to users. They assist librarians, and in some cases, library technicians.

Library assistants—sometimes referred to as library media assistants, library aides, or circulation assistants—register patrons so they can borrow materials from the library. They record the borrower's name and address from an application and then issue a library card. Most library assistants enter and update patrons' records using computer databases.

At the circulation desk, assistants lend and collect books, periodicals, video tapes, and other materials. When an item is borrowed, assistants stamp the due date on the material and record the patron's identification from his or her library card. They inspect returned materials for damage, check due dates, and compute fines for overdue material. They review records to compile a list of overdue materials and send out notices. They also answer patrons' questions and refer those they cannot answer to a librarian.

Throughout the library, assistants sort returned books, periodicals, and other items and return them to their designated shelves, files, or storage areas. They locate materials to be loaned, either for a patron or another library. Many card catalogues are computerized, so library assistants must be familiar with the computer system. If any materials have been damaged, these workers try to repair them. For example, they use tape or paste to repair torn pages or book covers and other specialized processes to repair more valuable materials.

Some library assistants specialize in helping patrons who have vision problems. Sometimes referred to as library, talking-books, or braille-and-talking-books clerks, they review the borrower's list of

Library assistants sort returned books, periodicals, and other items and shelve them in the proper place.

desired reading material. They locate those materials or closely related substitutes from the library collection of large type or braille volumes, tape cassettes, and open-reel talking books. They complete the paperwork and give or mail them to the borrower.

To extend library services to more patrons, many libraries operate bookmobiles. Bookmobile drivers take trucks stocked with books to designated sites on a regular schedule. Bookmobiles serve community organizations such as shopping centers, apartment complexes, schools, and nursing homes. They may also be used to extend library service to patrons living in remote areas. Depending on local conditions, drivers may operate a bookmobile alone or may be accompanied by a library technician.

When working alone, the drivers perform many of the same functions as a library assistant in a main or branch library. They answer patrons' questions, receive and check out books, collect fines, maintain the book collection, shelve materials, and occasionally operate audiovisual equipment to show slides or films. They participate and may assist in planning programs sponsored by the library such as reader advisory programs, used book sales, or outreach programs. Bookmobile drivers keep track of their mileage, the materials lent out, and the amount of fines collected. In some areas, they are responsible for maintenance of the vehicle and any photocopiers or other equipment in it. They record statistics on circulation and the number of people visiting the bookmobile. Drivers may also record requests for special items from the main library and arrange for the materials to be mailed or delivered to a patron during the next scheduled visit. Many bookmobiles are equipped with personal computers and CD-ROM systems linked to the main library system; this allows bookmobile drivers to reserve or locate books immediately. Some bookmobiles now offer Internet access to users.

Because bookmobile drivers may be the only link some people have to the library, much of their work is helping the public. They may assist handicapped or elderly patrons to the bookmobile, or shovel snow to assure their safety. They may enter hospitals or nursing homes to deliver books to patrons who are bedridden.

The schedules of bookmobile drivers depend on the size of the area being served. Some of these workers go out on their routes every day, while others go only on certain days. On these other days, they work at the library. Some also work evenings and weekends to give patrons as much access to the library as possible.

Employment

Library assistants and bookmobile drivers held about 127,000 jobs in 1998. Over one-half of these workers were employed by local government in public libraries; most of the remaining worked in school libraries. Opportunities for flexible schedules are abundant; over one-half of these workers were on part-time schedules.

Job Outlook

Opportunities should be good for persons interested in jobs as library assistants or bookmobile drivers through 2008. Turnover of these workers is quite high, reflecting the limited investment in training and subsequent weak attachment to this occupation. This work is attractive to retirees, students, and others who want a part-time schedule, and there is a lot of movement into and out of the occupation. Many openings will become available each year to replace workers who transfer to another occupation or leave the labor force. Some positions become available as library assistants move within the organization. Library assistants can be promoted to library technicians, and eventually supervisory positions in public service or technical service areas. Advancement opportunities are greater in larger libraries and may be more limited in smaller ones.

Employment is expected to grow about as fast as the average for all occupations through 2008. The vast majority of library assistants and bookmobile drivers work in public or school libraries. Efforts to contain costs in local governments and academic institutions of all types may result in more hiring of library support staff than librarians. Because most are employed by public institutions, library assistants and bookmobile drivers are not directly affected by the ups and downs of the business cycle. Some of these workers may lose their jobs, however, if there are cuts in government budgets.

Sources of Additional Information

Information about a career as a library assistant can be obtained from:

☛ Council on Library/Media Technology, P.O. Box 951, Oxon Hill, MD 20750. Internet: **http://library.ucr.edu/COLT**

Public libraries and libraries in academic institutions can provide information about job openings for library assistants and bookmobile drivers.

(See the introductory part of this section for information on working conditions, training requirements, and earnings.)

Order Clerks

(O*NET 55323)

Nature of the Work

Order clerks receive and process incoming orders for a wide variety of goods or services, such as spare parts for machines, consumer appliances, gas and electric power connections, film rentals, and articles of clothing. They are sometimes called order-entry clerks, customer service representatives, sales representatives, order processors, or order takers.

Orders for materials, merchandise, or services can come from inside or from outside of an organization. In large companies with many work sites, such as automobile manufacturers, clerks order parts and

A clerk takes an order for advertising space in a newspaper.

equipment from the company's warehouses. Inside order clerks receive orders from other workers employed by the same company or from salespersons in the field.

Many other order clerks, however, receive orders from outside companies or individuals. Order clerks in wholesale businesses, for instance, receive orders for merchandise from retail establishments that the retailer, in turn, sells to the public. An increasing number of order clerks work for catalogue companies and online retailers, receiving orders from individual customers by either phone, fax, regular mail, or e-mail. Order clerks dealing primarily with the public sometimes are referred to as outside order clerks.

Computers provide order clerks with ready access to information such as stock numbers, prices, and inventory. Orders frequently depend on which products are in stock and which products are most appropriate for the customer's needs. Some order clerks, especially those in industrial settings, must be able to give price estimates for entire jobs, not just single parts. Others must be able to take special orders, give expected arrival dates, prepare contracts, and handle complaints.

Many order clerks receive orders directly by telephone, entering the required information as the customer places the order. However, a rapidly increasing number of orders are now received through computer systems, the Internet, faxes, and e-mail. In some cases, these orders are sent directly from the customer's terminal to the order clerk's terminal. Orders received by regular mail are sometimes scanned into a database instantly accessible to clerks.

Clerks review orders for completeness and clarity. They may complete missing information or contact the customer for the information. Similarly, clerks contact customers, if customers need additional information, such as prices or shipping dates, or if delays in filling the order are anticipated. For orders received by regular mail, clerks extract checks or money orders, sort them, and send them for processing.

After an order has been verified and entered, the customer's final cost is calculated. The clerk then routes the order to the proper department—such as the warehouse—that actually sends out or delivers the item in question.

In organizations with sophisticated computer systems, inventory records are adjusted automatically, as sales are made. In less automated organizations, order clerks may adjust inventory records. Clerks may also notify other departments when inventories are low or when orders would deplete supplies.

Some order clerks must establish priorities in filling orders. For example, an order clerk in a blood bank may receive a request from a hospital for a certain type of blood. The clerk must first find out if the request is routine or an emergency and then take appropriate action.

Employment

Order clerks held about 362,000 jobs in 1998. About one half were in wholesale and retail establishments and about one quarter in manufacturing firms. Most of the remaining jobs for order clerks were in business services.

Job Outlook

Job openings for order clerks should be plentiful through the year 2008, due to sizable replacement needs. Numerous jobs will become available each year, to replace order clerks who transfer to other occupations or leave the labor force completely. Many of these openings will be for seasonal work, especially in catalogue companies or online retailers catering to holiday gift buyers.

Employment of order clerks is expected to grow more slowly than the average through the year 2008, as office automation continues to increase worker productivity. As the economy grows, increasingly more orders for goods and services will be placed. Demand for outside order clerks who deal mainly with the public or other businesses should remain fairly strong. The increasing use of online retailing and toll-free numbers that make placing orders easy and convenient will stimulate demand for these workers. However, productivity gains from increased automation will offset some of the growth in demand for outside order clerks, as each clerk is able to handle an increasingly higher volume of orders. In addition, orders placed over the Internet and other computer systems are often entered directly into the computer by the customer; thus, the order clerk is not involved at all in placing the order.

Employment growth of inside clerks will also be constrained by productivity gains due to automation. The spread of electronic data interchange, a system enabling computers to communicate directly with each other, allows orders within establishments to be placed with little human intervention. Besides electronic data interchange, *extranets* and other systems allowing a firm's employees to place orders directly are increasingly common.

Other types of automation will also limit the demand for order clerks. Sophisticated inventory control and automatic billing systems allow companies to track inventory and accounts with much less help from order clerks than in the past. Some companies use automated phone menus accessible with a touch-tone phone to receive orders, and others use answering machines. Developments in voice recognition technology may also further reduce the demand for order clerks.

(See the introductory statement on record clerks for information on working conditions, training requirements, and earnings.)

Payroll and Timekeeping Clerks

(O*NET 55341)

Nature of the Work

Payroll and timekeeping clerks perform a vital function—ensuring that employees are paid on time and that their paychecks are accurate. If inaccuracies arise, such as monetary errors or incorrect amounts of vacation time, these workers research and correct the records. In addition, they may also perform various other clerical tasks.

The fundamental task of *timekeeping clerks* is distributing and collecting timecards each pay period. They review employee workcharts, timesheets, and timecards, to ensure that information is properly recorded and that records have the signatures of authorizing officials. In companies that bill for the time spent by staff, such as law or accounting firms, timekeeping clerks make sure the hours recorded are charged to the correct job, so clients can be properly billed. These clerks also review computer reports listing timecards that cannot be processed because of errors, and they contact the employee or the employee's supervisor to resolve the problem. In addition, timekeeping clerks are responsible for informing managers and other employees of procedural changes in payroll policies.

Payroll and timekeeping clerks ensure that employees are paid on time and that their paychecks are accurate.

Payroll clerks, also called payroll technicians, screen timecards for calculating, coding, or other errors. They compute pay by subtracting allotments, including Federal and State taxes, retirement, insurance, and savings, from gross earnings. Increasingly, computers perform these calculations and alert payroll clerks to problems or errors in the data. In small organizations, or for new employees whose records are not yet entered into a computer system, clerks may perform the necessary calculations manually. In some small offices, clerks or other employees in the accounting department process payroll.

Payroll clerks also maintain paper backup files for research and reference. They record changes in employee addresses; close out files when workers retire, resign, or transfer; and advise employees on income tax withholding and other mandatory deductions. They also issue and record adjustments to pay because of previous errors or retroactive increases. Payroll clerks need to follow changes in tax and deduction laws, so they are aware of the most recent revisions. Finally, they prepare and mail earnings and tax withholding statements for employees' use in preparing income tax returns.

In small offices, payroll and timekeeping duties are likely to be included in the duties of a general office clerk, secretary, or accounting clerk. However, large organizations employ specialized payroll and timekeeping clerks to perform these functions.

Employment

Payroll and timekeeping clerks held about 172,000 jobs in 1998. About 35 percent of all payroll and timekeeping clerks worked in business, health, education, and social services; another 25 percent worked in manufacturing; and more than 10 percent were in wholesale and retail trade or in government. About 11 percent of all payroll and timekeeping clerks worked part time in 1998.

Job Outlook

Employment of payroll and timekeeping clerks is expected to decline through 2008, due to the continuing automation of payroll and timekeeping functions and the consolidation of clerical jobs. Nevertheless, a number of job openings should arise in coming years, as payroll and timekeeping clerks leave the labor force or transfer to other occupations. Many payroll clerks use this position as a steppingstone to higher-level accounting jobs.

As in many other clerical occupations, new technology will continue to allow many of the tasks formerly handled by payroll and timekeeping clerks to be partially or completely automated. For example, automated timeclocks, which calculate employee hours, allow large organizations to centralize their timekeeping duties in one location. At individual sites, employee hours are increasingly tracked by computer and verified by managers. This information is then compiled and sent to a central office to be processed by payroll clerks, eliminating the need to have payroll clerks at every site. In addition, the growing use of direct deposit eliminates the need to draft paychecks, because these funds are automatically transferred each pay period. Furthermore, timekeeping duties are increasingly being distributed to secretaries, general office clerks, or accounting clerks or are being contracted out to organizations that specialize in these services.

Information on working conditions, training requirements, and earnings appears in the introduction to records processing occupations.

Secretaries

(O*NET 21999C, 55102, 55105, and 55108)

Significant Points

- Increasing office automation and organizational restructuring will lead to little or no change in overall employment of secretaries.
- Employers increasingly require knowledge of software applications, such as word processing, spreadsheets, and database management.
- Job openings should be plentiful, especially for well-qualified and experienced secretaries, primarily due to the need to replace workers who leave this very large occupation.

Nature of the Work

As technology continues to expand in offices across the Nation, the role of the secretary has greatly evolved. Office automation and organizational restructuring have led secretaries to assume a wide range of new responsibilities once reserved for managerial and professional staff. Many secretaries now provide training and orientation to new staff, conduct research on the Internet, and learn to operate new office technologies. In the midst of these changes, however, their core responsibilities have remained much the same—performing and coordinating an office's administrative activities and ensuring that information is disseminated to staff and clients.

Secretaries are responsible for a variety of administrative and clerical duties necessary to run an organization efficiently. They serve as an information clearinghouse for an office, schedule appointments, provide information to callers, organize and maintain paper and electronic files, manage projects, and produce correspondence. They may also prepare correspondence, handle travel arrangements, and contact clients.

Secretaries are aided in these tasks by a variety of office equipment, such as facsimile machines, photocopiers, and telephone systems. In addition, secretaries increasingly use personal computers to run spreadsheet, word processing, database management, desktop publishing, and graphics programs—tasks previously handled by managers and other professionals. At the same time, these other workers have assumed many tasks traditionally assigned to secretaries, such as word processing and answering the telephone. Because secretaries are often relieved from dictation and typing, they can support several members of the professional staff. In a number of organizations, secretaries work in teams in order to work flexibly and share their expertise.

Specific job duties vary with experience and titles. Executive secretaries and administrative assistants, for example, perform fewer clerical tasks than lower-level secretaries. In addition to greeting visitors, arranging conference calls, and scheduling meetings, they may handle more complex responsibilities such as conducting research, preparing statistical reports, training employees, and supervising other clerical staff.

Secretaries are responsible for a variety of administrative and clerical duties.

Some secretaries, such as legal and medical secretaries, perform highly specialized work requiring knowledge of technical terminology and procedures. For instance, legal secretaries prepare correspondence and legal papers such as summonses, complaints, motions, responses, and subpoenas under the supervision of an attorney. They also may review legal journals and assist in other ways with legal research, such as verifying quotes and citations in legal briefs. Medical secretaries transcribe dictation, prepare correspondence, and assist physicians or medical scientists with reports, speeches, articles, and conference proceedings. They also record simple medical histories, arrange for patients to be hospitalized, and order supplies. Most medical secretaries need to be familiar with insurance rules, billing practices, and hospital or laboratory procedures. Other technical secretaries who assist engineers or scientists may prepare correspondence, maintain the technical library, and gather and edit materials for scientific papers.

Working Conditions

Secretaries usually work in offices with other professionals in schools, hospitals, or in legal and medical offices. Their jobs often involve sitting for long periods. If they spend a lot of time typing, particularly at a video display terminal, they may encounter problems of eyestrain, stress, and repetitive motion, such as carpal tunnel syndrome.

Office work can lend itself to alternative or flexible working arrangements, such as part time work. In fact, 1 secretary in 5 works part time and many others work in temporary positions. A few participate in job sharing arrangements in which two people divide responsibility for a single job. The majority of secretaries, however, are full-time employees who work a standard 40-hour week.

Employment

Secretaries held about 3.2 million jobs in 1998, ranking among the largest occupations in the U.S. economy. The following tabulation shows the distribution of employment by secretarial specialty.

Secretaries, total	3,195,000
Legal secretaries	285,000
Medical secretaries	219,000
Secretaries, except legal and medical	2,691,000

Secretaries are employed in organizations of every type. About 6 out of 10 secretaries are employed in firms providing services, ranging from education and health to legal and business services. Others work for firms engaged in manufacturing, construction, wholesale and retail trade, transportation, and communications. Banks, insurance companies, investment firms, and real estate firms are also important employers, as are Federal, State, and local government agencies.

Training, Other Qualifications, and Advancement

High school graduates who have basic office skills may qualify for entry-level secretarial positions. However, employers increasingly require knowledge of software applications, such as word processing, spreadsheets, and database management. Secretaries should be proficient in keyboarding and good at spelling, punctuation, grammar, and oral communication. Shorthand is necessary for some positions. Because secretaries must be tactful in their dealings with people, employers also look for good interpersonal skills. Discretion, good judgment, organizational ability, and initiative are especially important for higher-level secretarial positions.

As office automation continues to evolve, retraining and continuing education will remain an integral part of secretarial jobs. Changes in the office environment have increased the demand for secretaries who are adaptable and versatile. Secretaries may have to attend classes to learn how to operate new office technologies, such as information storage systems, scanners, the Internet, or new updated software packages.

Secretaries acquire skills in various ways. Training ranges from high school vocational education programs that teach office skills and keyboarding to 1- to 2-year programs in office administration offered by business schools, vocational-technical institutes, and community colleges. Many temporary help agencies also provide formal training in computer and office skills. These skills are most often acquired, however, through on-the-job instruction by other employees or by equipment and software vendors. Specialized training programs are available for students planning to become medical or legal secretaries or administrative technology specialists.

Testing and certification for entry-level office skills is available through the Office Proficiency Assessment and Certification program offered by the International Association of Administrative Professionals. As secretaries gain experience, they can earn the Certified Professional Secretary (CPS) designation by meeting certain experience requirements and passing an examination. Similarly, those without experience who want to be certified as a legal support professional may be certified as an Accredited Legal Secretary (ALS) by the Certifying Board of the National Association of Legal Secretaries. This organization also administers an examination to certify a legal secretary with 3 years of experience as a Professional Legal Secretary (PLS). Legal Secretaries International confers the designation Board Certified Civil Trial Legal Secretary in specialized areas such as litigation, real estate, probate, and corporate law, to those who have 5 years of law-related experience and pass an examination.

Secretaries generally advance by being promoted to other secretarial positions with more responsibilities. Qualified secretaries who broaden their knowledge of a company's operations and enhance their skills may be promoted to other positions such as senior or executive secretary, clerical supervisor, or office manager. Secretaries with word processing experience can advance to jobs as word processing trainers, supervisors, or managers within their own firms or in a secretarial or word processing service bureau. Secretarial experience can also lead to jobs such as instructor or sales representative with manufacturers of software or computer equipment. With additional training, many legal secretaries become paralegals.

Job Outlook

Job openings should be plentiful, particularly for well-qualified and experienced secretaries, stemming from the need to replace workers who transfer to other occupations or leave this very large occupation for other reasons each year. Overall, however, little or no change is expected in employment of secretaries over the 1998-2008 period.

Projected employment of secretaries will vary by occupational specialty. Rapid growth in the health and legal services industries should lead to average growth for medical and legal secretaries. However, employment of secretaries who do not specialize in legal or medical work—about 7 out of 8—is expected to remain flat. Rapidly growing industries—such as personnel supply, computer and data processing, and management and public relations—will generate new job opportunities.

Growing levels of office automation and organizational restructuring will continue to make secretaries more productive in coming years. Personal computers, electronic mail, scanners, facsimile machines, and voice message systems will allow secretaries to accomplish more in the same amount of time. The use of automated equipment is also changing the distribution of work in many offices. In some cases, such traditional secretarial duties as typing or keyboarding, filing, copying, and bookkeeping are being assigned to workers in other units or departments. Professionals and managers increasingly do their own word processing and much of their own correspondence rather than submit the work to secretaries and other support staff. Also, in some law offices and physicians' offices, paralegals and medical assistants are assuming some tasks formerly done by secretaries. As other workers assume more of these duties, there is a trend in many offices for professionals and managers to "share" secretaries. The traditional arrangement of one secretary per manager is becoming less prevalent; instead, secretaries increasingly support systems or units. This approach often means secretaries assume added responsibilities and are seen as valuable members of a team, but it also contributes to the decline in employment projected for most secretaries.

Developments in office technology are certain to continue, and they will bring about further changes in the secretary's work environment. However, many secretarial duties are of a personal, interactive nature and, therefore, not easily automated. Responsibilities such as planning conferences, working with clients, and transmitting staff instructions require tact and communication skills. Because technology cannot substitute for these personal skills, secretaries will continue to play a key role in most organizations.

Earnings

Median annual earnings of secretaries, excluding legal and medical secretaries, were $23,560 in 1998. The middle 50 percent earned between $18,770 and $29,400. The lowest 10 percent earned less than $14,410, and the highest 10 percent earned more than $36,050. Secretaries earn slightly more in urban areas. In 1997, median annual earnings in the industries employing the largest numbers of secretaries, excluding legal and medical secretaries, were:

Local government	$23,900
Hospitals	23,000
Colleges and universities	22,600
Elementary and secondary schools	22,300
Personnel supply services	21,500

In 1998, median annual earnings of legal secretaries were $30,050. Median annual earnings of medical secretaries were $22,390 in 1998; in offices and clinics of medical doctors they earned approximately $22,000 in 1997, and in hospitals, $21,400.

According to the International Association of Administrative Professionals, secretaries averaged $25,500 a year in 1998. Salaries vary a great deal, however, reflecting differences in skill, experience, and level of responsibility. Salaries also vary in different parts of the country; earnings are usually lowest in southern cities, and highest in northern and western cities. In addition, salaries vary by industry; salaries of secretaries tend to be highest in transportation, legal services, and public utilities, and lowest in retail trade and finance, insurance, and real estate. Certification in this field usually is rewarded by a higher salary.

The starting salary for inexperienced secretaries in the Federal Government was $18,400 a year in 1999. Beginning salaries were slightly higher in selected areas where the prevailing local pay level was higher. All secretaries employed by the Federal Government averaged about $30,200 a year in 1999.

Related Occupations

A number of other workers type, record information, and process paperwork. Among them are bookkeepers, receptionists, stenographers, personnel clerks, typists and word processors, paralegals, medical assistants, and medical record technicians. A growing number of secretaries share in managerial and human resource responsibilities. Occupations requiring these skills include office and administrative support supervisor, systems manager, office manager, and human resource specialist.

Sources of Additional Information

For information on the Certified Professional Secretary designation, contact:

☛ International Association of Administrative Professionals, 10502 NW Ambassador Dr., P.O. Box 20404, Kansas City, MO 64195-0404. Internet: **http://www.iaap-hq.org**

Information on the Board Certified Civil Trial Legal Secretary designation can be obtained from:

☛ Legal Secretaries International Inc., 8902 Sunnywood Dr., Houston, TX 77088-3729. Internet: **http://www.compassnet.com/legalsec**

Information on the Accredited Legal Secretary and Certified Professional Legal Secretary designations is available from:

☛ National Association of Legal Secretaries, 2448 East 81st St., Suite 3400, Tulsa, OK 74137-4238. Internet: **http://www.nals.org**

State employment offices provide information about job openings for secretaries.

Teacher Assistants

(O*NET 31521 and 53905)

Significant Points

- Almost half of all teacher assistants work part time.
- Educational requirements range from a high school diploma to some college training.
- Employment is expected to grow faster than average due to the need to assist and monitor students, to provide teachers with clerical assistance, and to help teachers meet the education needs of a growing special education population.

Nature of the Work

Teacher assistants, also called teacher aides or instructional aides, provide instructional and clerical support for classroom teachers, allowing teachers more time for lesson planning and teaching. Teacher assistants tutor and assist children in learning class material using the teacher's lesson plans, providing students with individualized attention. Teacher assistants also supervise students in the cafeteria, schoolyard, school discipline center, or on field trips. They record grades, set up equipment, and help prepare materials for instruction.

Large school districts hire some teacher assistants to perform exclusively non-instructional or clerical tasks, such as monitoring

Teacher aides instruct and assist students.

nonacademic settings. Playground and lunchroom attendants are examples of such assistants. Most teacher assistants, however, perform a combination of instructional and clerical duties. They generally instruct children, under the direction and guidance of teachers. They work with students individually or in small groups—listening while students read, reviewing or reinforcing class work, or helping them find information for reports. At the secondary school level, teacher assistants often specialize in a certain subject, such as math or science. Teacher assistants often take charge of special projects and prepare equipment or exhibits, such as for a science demonstration. Some assistants work in computer laboratories, helping students using computers and educational software programs.

In addition to instructing, assisting, and supervising students, teacher assistants grade tests and papers, check homework, keep health and attendance records, type, file, and duplicate materials. They also stock supplies, operate audiovisual equipment, and keep classroom equipment in order.

Many teacher assistants work extensively with special education students. Schools are becoming more inclusive, integrating special education students into general education classrooms. As a result, teacher assistants in general education and special education classrooms increasingly assist students with disabilities. Teacher assistants attend to a disabled student's physical needs, including feeding, teaching good grooming habits, or assisting students riding the school bus. They also provide personal attention to students with other special needs, such as those whose families live in poverty, or students who speak English as a second language, or who need remedial education. Teacher assistants help assess a student's progress by observing performance and recording relevant data.

Working Conditions

Almost half of all teacher assistants work part time. Most assistants who provide educational instruction work the traditional 9- to 10-month school year, usually in a classroom setting. Teacher assistants work outdoors supervising recess when weather allows, and spend much of their time standing, walking, or kneeling.

Seeing students develop and gain appreciation of the joy of learning can be very rewarding. However, working closely with students can be both physically and emotionally tiring. Teacher assistants who work with special education students often perform more strenuous tasks, including lifting, as they help students with their daily routine. Those who perform clerical work may tire of administrative duties, such as copying materials or typing.

Employment

Teacher assistants held about 1.2 million jobs in 1998. About 86 percent worked in public and private education, mostly in the elementary grades. A significant number assisted special education teachers in working with disabled children. Most of the others worked in child day care centers and religious organizations.

Training, Other Qualifications, and Advancement

Educational requirements for teacher assistants range from a high school diploma to some college training. Teacher assistants with instructional responsibilities usually require more training than those who do not perform teaching tasks. Increasingly, employers prefer teacher assistants who have some college training. Some teacher assistants are aspiring teachers who are working towards their degree while gaining experience. Many schools require previous experience in working with children. Schools often require a valid driver's license and perform a background check on applicants.

A number of 2-year and community colleges offer associate degree programs that prepare graduates to work as teacher assistants. However, most teacher assistants receive on-the-job training. Those who tutor and review lessons with students must have a thorough understanding of class materials and instructional methods, and should be familiar with the organization and operation of a school. Teacher assistants also must know how to operate audiovisual equipment, keep records, and prepare instructional materials, as well as have adequate computer skills.

Teacher assistants should enjoy working with children from a wide range of cultural backgrounds, and be able to handle classroom situations with fairness and patience. Teacher assistants also must demonstrate initiative and a willingness to follow a teacher's directions. They must have good writing skills and be able to communicate effectively with students and teachers. Teacher assistants who speak a second language, especially Spanish, are in great demand to communicate with growing numbers of students and parents whose primary language is not English.

About half of all States have established guidelines or minimum educational standards for the hiring and training of teacher assistants, and an increasing number of States are in the process of implementing them. Although requirements vary by State, most require an individual to have at least a high school diploma or general equivalency degree (G.E.D.), or some college training. In States that have not established guidelines or minimum educational standards, local school districts determine hiring requirements.

Advancement for teacher assistants, usually in the form of higher earnings or increased responsibility, comes primarily with experience or additional education. Some school districts provide time away from the job or tuition reimbursement so that teacher assistants can earn their bachelor's degrees and pursue licensed teaching positions. In return for tuition reimbursement, assistants are often required to teach a certain length of time for the school district.

Job Outlook

Employment of teacher assistants is expected to grow faster than the average for all occupations through 2008. Student enrollments are expected to rise, spurring demand for teacher assistants to assist and monitor students and provide teachers with clerical assistance. Teacher assistants will also be required to help teachers meet the educational needs of a growing special education population, particularly as these students are increasingly assimilated into general education classrooms. Education reform and the rising number of students who speak English as a second language will continue to contribute to the demand for teacher assistants. In addition to jobs stemming from employment growth, numerous job openings will arise as workers transfer to other occupations, leave the labor force to assume family responsibilities, return to school, or leave for other reasons—characteristic of occupations that require limited formal education and offer relatively low pay.

The number and size of special education programs are growing in response to increasing enrollments of students with disabilities. Federal legislation mandates appropriate education for all children, and emphasizes placing disabled children into regular school settings, when possible. Children with special needs require much personal attention, and special education teachers, as well as general education teachers with special education students, rely heavily on teacher assistants. At the secondary school level, teacher assistants work with special education students as job coaches, and help students make the transition from school to work.

School reforms that call for more individual instruction should further enhance employment opportunities for teacher assistants. Schools are hiring more teacher assistants to provide students with the personal instruction and remedial education they need.

Teacher assistant employment is sensitive to changes in State and local expenditures for education. Pressures on education budgets are greater in some States and localities than in others. A number of teacher assistant positions, such as those in Head Start classrooms, are financed through Federal Government programs, which are affected by budget constraints.

Earnings

Median hourly earnings of teacher assistants in 1998 were $7.61. The middle 50 percent earned between $6.08 and $9.51. The lowest 10 percent earned less than $5.61 and the highest 10 percent earned more than $11.27. Median hourly earnings in the industries employing the largest numbers of teacher assistants in 1997 were as follows:

Elementary and secondary schools	$7.30
Colleges and universities	7.10
Individual and family services	7.10
Child day care services	6.50
Local government, except education and hospitals	6.00

About 3 out of 10 teacher aides belonged to unions in 1998—mainly the American Federation of Teachers and the National Education Association—which bargain with school systems over wages, hours, and the terms and conditions of employment.

Related Occupations

Teacher assistants who instruct children have duties similar to those of preschool, elementary, and secondary school teachers and school librarians. However, teacher assistants do not have the same level of responsibility or training. The support activities of teacher assistants and their educational backgrounds are similar to those of child-care workers, family day care providers, library technicians, and library assistants.

Sources of Additional Information

For information on teacher assistants, including training and certification, contact:

☛ American Federation of Teachers, Paraprofessional and School Related Personnel Division, 555 New Jersey Ave. NW., Washington, DC 20001. Internet: **http://www.aft.org/psrp**

For information on a career as a teacher assistant, contact:

☛ National Resource Center for Paraprofessionals in Education and Related Services, 365 5th Ave., New York, NY 10016.
Internet: **http://web.gc.cuny.edu/dept/case/nrcp**

School superintendents and State departments of education can provide details about employment requirements.

Word Processors, Typists, and Data Entry Keyers

(O*NET 55307, 56017, and 56021)

Significant Points

- Workers can acquire their skills through high schools, community colleges, business schools, or self-teaching aids such as books or tapes.
- Overall employment is projected to decline due to the proliferation of personal computers and other technologies; however, the occupation's large size and high turnover should produce many job openings each year.
- Those with expertise in appropriate computer software applications should have the best job prospects.

Nature of the Work

Organizations need to process a rapidly growing amount of information. Word processors, typists, and data entry keyers help ensure this work is handled smoothly and efficiently. By typing texts, entering data into a computer, operating a variety of office machines, and performing other clerical duties, these workers help organizations keep up with the rapid changes of the "Information Age."

Word processors and typists usually set up and prepare reports, letters, mailing labels, and other text material. *Typists* make neat, typed copies of materials written by other clerical, professional, or managerial workers. They may begin as entry-level workers by typing headings on form letters, addressing envelopes, or preparing standard forms on typewriters or computers. As they gain experience, they are often assigned tasks requiring a higher degree of accuracy and independent judgment. Senior typists may work with highly technical material, plan and type complicated statistical tables, combine and rearrange materials from different sources, or prepare master copies.

Most keyboarding is now done on word processing equipment—usually a personal computer or part of a larger computer system—which normally includes a keyboard, video display terminal, and printer, and may have "add-on" capabilities such as optical character recognition readers. *Word processors* use this equipment to record, edit, store, and revise letters, memos, reports, statistical tables, forms, and other printed materials. Although it is becoming less common, some word processing workers are employed in centralized word processing teams that handle the transcription and typing for several departments.

In addition to the duties mentioned above, word processors and typists often perform other office tasks, such as answering telephones, filing, and operating copiers or other office machines. Job titles of these workers often vary to reflect these duties. Clerk typists, for example, combine typing with filing, sorting mail, answering telephones, and other general office work. Notereaders transcribe stenotyped notes of court proceedings into standard formats.

Data entry keyers usually input lists of items, numbers, or other data into computers or complete forms that appear on a computer screen. They may also manipulate existing data, edit current information, or proofread new entries to a database for accuracy. Some examples of data sources include customers' personal information, medical records, and membership lists. Usually this information is used internally by a company and may be reformatted before use by other departments or by customers.

Keyers use various types of equipment to enter data. Many keyers use a machine that converts the information they type to magnetic impulses on tapes or disks for entry into a computer system. Others prepare materials for printing or publication by using data entry composing machines. Some keyers operate on-line terminals or personal computers. Data entry keyers increasingly also work with non-keyboard forms of data entry such as scanners and electronically transmitted files. When using these new character recognition systems, data entry keyers often enter only those data which cannot be recognized by machines. In some offices, keyers also operate computer peripheral equipment such as printers and tape readers, act as tape librarians, and perform other clerical duties.

A job as a word processor, typist, or data entry keyer frequently serves as a steppingstone to higher paying jobs with increased responsibilities.

Working Conditions

Word processors, typists, and data entry keyers usually work a standard 40-hour week in clean offices. They sit for long periods and sometimes must contend with high noise levels caused by various office machines. These workers are susceptible to repetitive strain injuries, such as carpal tunnel syndrome and neck, back, and eye strain. To help prevent these from occurring, many offices have scheduled exercise breaks, ergonomically designed keyboards, and workstations that allow workers to stand or sit as they wish.

Employment

Word processors, typists, and data entry keyers held about 894,000 in 1998 and were employed in every sector of the economy. Some workers telecommute by working from their homes on personal computers linked by telephone lines to those in the main office. This enables them to type material at home while still being able to produce printed copy in their offices.

About 3 out of 10 word processors, typists, and data entry keyers held jobs in firms providing business services, including temporary help, word processing, and computer and data processing. Nearly 2 out of 10 worked in Federal, State, and local government agencies.

Training, Other Qualifications, and Advancement

Employers generally hire high school graduates who meet their requirements for keyboarding speed. Increasingly, employers also expect applicants to have word processing or data entry training or experience. Spelling, punctuation, and grammar skills are important, as is familiarity with standard office equipment and procedures.

Students acquire skills in keyboarding and in the use of word processing, spreadsheet, and database management computer software packages through high schools, community colleges, business schools, temporary help agencies, or self-teaching aids such as books or tapes.

For many people, a job as a word processor, typist, or data entry keyer is their first job after graduating from high school or after a period of full-time family responsibilities. This work frequently serves as a steppingstone to higher paying jobs with increased responsibilities. Large companies and government agencies usually have training programs to help clerical employees upgrade their skills and advance to other positions. It is common for word processors, typists, and data entry keyers to transfer to other clerical jobs, such as secretary or statistical clerk, or to be promoted to a supervisory job in a word processing or data entry center.

Job Outlook

Despite the projected decline in employment of word processors and typists and relatively slow growth of data entry keyers, the need to replace those who transfer to other occupations or leave this large occupation for other reasons will produce numerous job openings each year. Job prospects will be most favorable for those with the best technical skills—in particular, expertise in appropriate computer software applications. Word processors, typists, and data entry keyers must be willing to continuously upgrade their skills with new technologies.

In spite of rapid increases in the volume of information and business transactions, overall employment of word processors, typists, and data entry keyers is projected to decline through 2008. Although word processors, typists, and data entry keyers are all affected by productivity gains stemming from organizational restructuring and the implementation of new technologies, projected growth differs among these workers. Employment of word processors and typists is expected to decline due to the proliferation of personal computers which allow other workers to perform duties formerly assigned to word processors and typists. Most professionals and managers, for example, now use desktop personal computers to do their own word processing. Because technologies affecting data entry keyers tend to be costlier to implement, however, these workers will be less affected by technology and should experience slower than average growth.

Employment growth of data entry keyers still will be dampened by productivity gains, as various data capturing technologies, such as bar code scanners, voice recognition technologies and sophisticated character recognition readers, become more prevalent. These technologies can be applied to a variety of business transactions, such as inventory tracking, invoicing, and order placement. Moreover, as telecommunications technology improves, many organizations will increasingly take advantage of computer networks that allow data to be transmitted electronically, thereby avoiding the reentry of data. These technologies will allow more data to be entered automatically into computers, reducing the demand for data entry keyers.

In addition to technology, employment of word processors, typists, and data entry keyers will be adversely affected by domestic and international outsourcing. Many organizations have reduced or even eliminated permanent in-house staff, for example, in favor of temporary help and staffing services firms. Some large data entry and processing firms increasingly employ workers in nations with low wages to enter data. As international trade barriers continue to fall and telecommunications technology improves, this transfer will mean reduced demand for data entry keyers in the United States.

Earnings

Median annual earnings of word processors and typists in 1998 were $22,590. The middle 50 percent earned between $18,490 and $27,320. The lowest 10 percent earned less than $14,480, while the highest 10 percent earned more than $32,550. The salaries of these workers vary by industry and by region. In 1997, median annual earnings in the industries employing the largest numbers of word processors and typists were:

Elementary and secondary schools	$23,200
State government, except education and hospitals	22,500
Local government, except education and hospitals	22,400
Offices and clinics of medical doctors	21,800
Personnel supply services	20,200

Median annual earnings of data entry keyers in 1998 were $19,190. The middle 50 percent earned between $15,810 and $22,910. The lowest 10 percent earned less than $13,660, and the highest 10 percent earned more than $27,840. In 1997, median annual earnings in the industries employing the largest numbers of data entry keyers were:

State government, except education and hospitals	$21,300
Accounting, auditing, and bookkeeping	19,600
Computer and data processing services	17,500
Commercial banks	17,400
Personnel supply services	16,900

In the Federal Government, clerk-typists and data entry keyers without work experience started at about $16,400 a year in 1999. Beginning salaries were slightly higher in selected areas where the prevailing local pay level was higher. The average annual salary for all clerk-typists in the Federal Government was about $22,900 in 1999.

Related Occupations

Word processors, typists, and data entry keyers must transcribe information quickly. Other workers who deliver information in a timely manner are stenographers, dispatchers, and telephone operators. Word processors, typists, and data entry keyers also must be comfortable working with office automation, and in this regard they are similar to court reporters, medical transcriptionists, secretaries, and computer and peripheral equipment operators.

Sources of Additional Information

For information about job opportunities for word processors, typists, and data entry keyers, contact the nearest office of the State employment service.

Service Occupations

Cleaning, Buildings, and Grounds Service Occupations

Janitors and Cleaners and Institutional Cleaning Supervisors

(O*NET 61008, 67002, and 67005)

Significant Points

- Plentiful job openings should arise primarily from the need to replace those who leave this very large occupation each year; limited training requirements, low pay, and numerous part-time and temporary jobs should contribute to these replacement needs.
- Businesses providing janitorial and cleaning services on a contract basis are expected to be one of the fastest growing employers of these workers.

Nature of the Work

Janitors and cleaners—also called building custodians, executive housekeepers, or maids—keep office buildings, hospitals, stores, apartment houses, hotels, and other types of buildings clean and in good condition. Some only do cleaning, while others have a wide range of duties. They may fix leaky faucets, empty trashcans, do painting and carpentry, replenish bathroom supplies, mow lawns, and see that heating and air-conditioning equipment works properly. On a typical day, janitors may wet- or dry-mop floors, clean bathrooms, vacuum carpets, dust furniture, make minor repairs, and exterminate insects and rodents. In hospitals, where they are mostly known as maids or housekeepers, they may also wash bed frames, brush mattresses, make beds, and disinfect and sterilize equipment and supplies using germicides and sterilizing equipment. In hotels, aside from cleaning and maintaining the premises, they may deliver ironing boards, cribs, and rollaway beds to guests' rooms.

Janitors and cleaners use various equipment, tools, and cleaning materials. For one job, they may need a mop and bucket; for another, an electric polishing machine and a special cleaning solution. Improved building materials, chemical cleaners, and power equipment have made many tasks easier and less time-consuming, but janitors must learn proper use of equipment and cleaners to avoid harming floors, fixtures, and themselves.

Cleaning supervisors coordinate, schedule, and supervise the activities of janitors and cleaners. They assign tasks and inspect building areas to see that work has been done properly, issue supplies and equipment, inventory stocks to ensure an adequate amount of supplies are present, screen and hire job applicants, and recommend promotions, transfers, or dismissals. They also train new and experienced employees. Supervisors may prepare reports concerning room occupancy, hours worked, and department expenses. Some also perform cleaning duties.

Working Conditions

Because most office buildings are cleaned while they are empty, many cleaners work evening hours. Some, however, such as school and hospital custodians, work in the daytime. When there is a need for 24-hour maintenance, janitors may be assigned to shifts. Most full-time janitors, cleaners, and cleaning supervisors work about 40 hours a week. Part-time cleaners usually work in the evenings and on weekends.

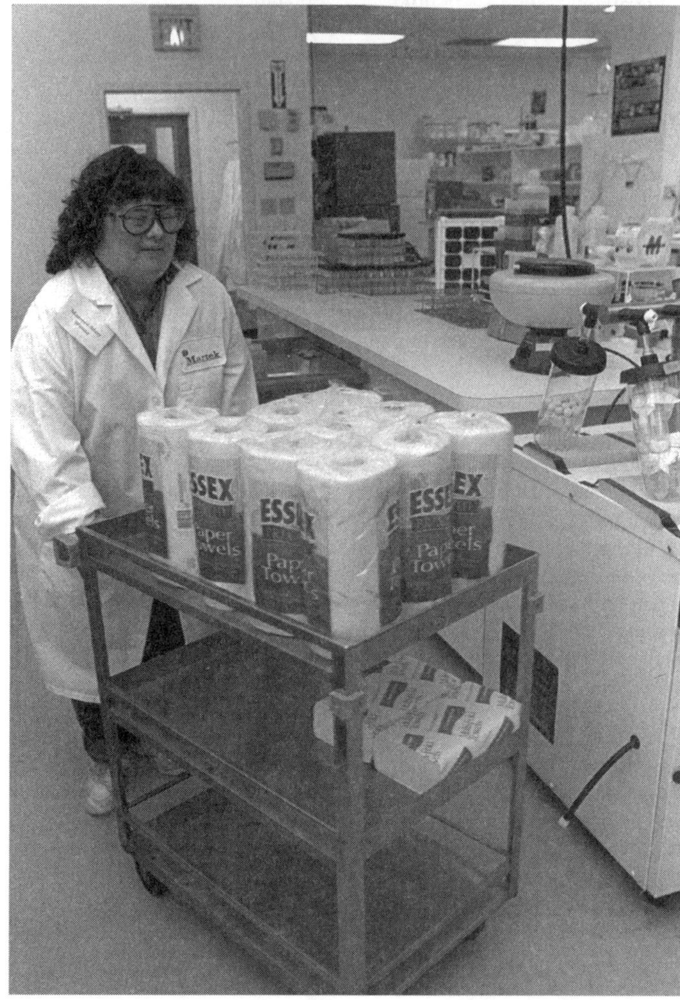

Janitors and cleaners use a variety of cleaning materials.

Janitors and cleaners and institutional cleaning supervisors in large office and residential buildings often work in teams. These teams consist of workers who specialize in vacuuming, trash pickup, and restroom cleaning, among other things. Supervisors conduct inspections to ensure the building is cleaned properly and the team is functioning efficiently.

Janitors and cleaners usually work inside heated, well-lighted buildings. However, they sometimes work outdoors sweeping walkways, mowing lawns, or shoveling snow. Working with machines can be noisy, and some tasks, such as cleaning bathrooms and trash rooms, can be dirty and unpleasant. Janitors may suffer cuts, bruises, and burns from machines, handtools, and chemicals. They spend most of their time on their feet, sometimes lifting or pushing heavy furniture or equipment. Many tasks, such as dusting or sweeping, require constant bending, stooping, and stretching. As a result, janitors may also suffer back injuries and sprains.

Employment

Janitors and cleaners and institutional cleaning supervisors held nearly 3.3 million jobs in 1998. Less than 5 percent were self employed.

Janitors and cleaners work in nearly every type of establishment and held about 97 percent of all jobs. About 23 percent worked for firms supplying building maintenance services on a contract basis; 16 percent in educational institutions; and 14 percent in hotels. Other employers included hospitals, restaurants, religious institutions, manufacturing firms, government agencies, and operators of apartment buildings, office buildings, and other types of real estate.

Institutional cleaning supervisors held about 87,000 jobs. About 37 percent were employed in hotels; 23 percent in firms supplying building maintenance services on a contract basis; 12 percent in hospitals; and 12 percent in nursing and personal care facilities. Other employers included educational institutions, residential care establishments, and amusement and recreation facilities.

Although cleaning jobs can be found in all cities and towns, most are located in highly populated areas where there are many office buildings, schools, apartment houses, and hospitals.

Training, Other Qualifications, and Advancement

No special education is required for most janitorial or cleaning jobs, but beginners should know simple arithmetic and be able to follow instructions. High school shop courses are helpful for jobs involving repair work.

Most janitors and cleaners learn their skills on the job. Usually, beginners work with an experienced cleaner, doing routine cleaning. As they gain more experience, they are assigned more complicated tasks.

In some cities, programs run by unions, government agencies, or employers teach janitorial skills. Students learn how to clean buildings thoroughly and efficiently, how to select and safely use various cleansing agents, and how to operate and maintain machines, such as wet and dry vacuums, buffers, and polishers. Students learn to plan their work, to follow safety and health regulations, to interact positively with people in the buildings they clean, and to work without supervision. Instruction in minor electrical, plumbing, and other repairs may also be given. Those who come in contact with the public should have good communication skills. Employers usually look for dependable, hard-working individuals who are in good health, follow directions well, and get along with other people.

Janitors and cleaners usually find work by answering newspaper advertisements, applying directly to organizations where they would like to work, contacting local labor unions, or contacting State employment service offices.

Advancement opportunities for janitorial workers are usually limited in organizations where they are the only maintenance worker. Where there is a large maintenance staff, however, janitors can be promoted to supervisor and to area supervisor or manager. A high school diploma improves the chances for advancement. Some janitors set up their own maintenance business.

Supervisors usually move up through the ranks. In many establishments, they are required to take some in-service training to improve their housekeeping techniques and procedures, and to enhance their supervisory skills.

A small number of cleaning supervisors and managers are members of the International Executive Housekeepers Association (IEHA). IEHA offers two kinds of certification programs to cleaning supervisors and managers—Certified Executive Housekeeper (CEH) and Registered Executive Housekeeper (REH). The CEH designation is offered to those with a high school education, while the REH designation is offered to those who have a 4-year college degree. Both designations are earned by attending courses and passing exams, and must be renewed every 2 years to ensure that workers keep abreast of new cleaning methods. Those with the REH designation usually oversee the cleaning services of hotels, hospitals, casinos, and other large institutions that rely on well-trained experts for their cleaning needs.

Job Outlook

Job openings should be plentiful for janitors and cleaners primarily because of the need to replace those who leave this very large occupation each year. Limited formal education and training requirements, low pay, and numerous part-time and temporary jobs should contribute to these replacement needs.

Many job opportunities will stem from job growth in addition to the need to replace workers who transfer to other occupations or leave the labor force. Employment of janitors and cleaners and institutional cleaning supervisors is expected to grow about as fast as average for all occupations through the year 2008. To clean the increasing number of office complexes, apartment houses, schools, factories, hospitals, and other buildings, more workers will be assigned to teams with more efficient cleaning equipment and supplies. As many firms reduce costs by hiring independent contractors, businesses providing janitorial and cleaning services on a contract basis are expected to be one of the faster growing employers of these workers.

Earnings

Median annual earnings of janitors and cleaners, including maids and housekeeping cleaners, were $15,340 in 1998. The middle 50 percent earned between $12,560 and $19,110. The lowest 10 percent earned less than $11,620 and the highest 10 percent earned more than $25,060. Median annual earnings in the industries employing the largest numbers of janitors and cleaners, including maids and housekeeping cleaners, in 1997 are shown below:

Industry	Earnings
Federal Government	$27,900
Hospitals	16,800
Hotels and motels	15,400
Nursing and personal care facilities	15,200
Services to buildings	13,900

Median annual earnings of institutional cleaning supervisors were $19,600 in 1998. The middle 50 percent earned between $15,580 and $24,850. The lowest 10 percent earned less than $13,150 and the highest 10 percent earned more than $31,930. Median annual earnings in the industries employing the largest numbers of institutional cleaning supervisors in 1997 are shown below:

Industry	Earnings
Hospitals	$22,400
Nursing and personal care facilities	20,200
Services to buildings	18,500
Hotels and motels	17,200

Related Occupations

Workers who specialize in one of the many job functions of janitors and cleaners include refuse collectors, floor waxers, street sweepers, window cleaners, gardeners, boiler tenders, pest controllers, and general maintenance repairers. Private household workers also have job duties similar to janitors and cleaners.

Sources of Additional Information

Information about janitorial jobs may be obtained from State employment service offices.

For information on certification in executive housekeeping, contact:

☛ International Executive Housekeepers Association, Inc., 1001 Eastwind Dr., Suite 301, Westerville, OH 43081-3361.
Internet: **http://www.ieha.org**

Landscaping, Groundskeeping, Nursery, Greenhouse, and Lawn Service Occupations

(O*NET 15017A, 15031, 15032, 72002D, 72002E, 79005, 79030B, 79033, 79036, and 79041)

Significant Points

- There are seldom minimum educational requirements for entry-level jobs and most workers learn through short-term on-the-job training.

- Opportunities should be excellent due to significant job turnover; but earnings for laborer jobs are low.

Nature of the Work

Attractively designed, healthy, and well-maintained lawns, gardens, and grounds create a positive first impression, establish a peaceful mood, and increase property values. Workers in landscaping, groundskeeping, nursery, greenhouse, and lawn service occupations are responsible for the variety of tasks necessary to achieve a pleasant and functional outdoor environment. They also care for indoor gardens and plantings in commercial and public facilities, such as malls, hotels, and botanical gardens.

Nursery and greenhouse workers help to cultivate the plants used to beautify landscapes. They prepare nursery acreage or greenhouse beds for planting; water, weed, and spray trees, shrubs, and plants; cut, roll, and stack sod; stake trees; tie, wrap, and pack flowers, plants, shrubs, and trees to fill orders; and dig up or move field-grown and containerized shrubs and trees. *Nursery and greenhouse managers* make decisions about the type and quantity of horticultural plants to be grown; select and purchase seed, fertilizers, and disease control chemicals; hire laborers and direct and coordinate their activities; manage recordkeeping, accounting, and marketing activities; and generally oversee operations.

Landscape contractors usually follow the designs developed by a landscape architect. They coordinate and oversee the installation of trees, flowers, shrubs, sod, benches, and other ornamental features. They also implement construction plans at the site, which may involve grading the property, installing lighting or sprinkler systems, and building walkways, terraces, patios, decks, and fountains. They must determine the type and amount of labor, equipment, and materials needed to complete a project, and inspect work at various stages of completion. Some work exclusively on large properties, such as office buildings and shopping malls, whereas others also provide these services to residential customers.

Landscaping laborers physically install and maintain landscaped areas. In addition to initially transporting and planting new vegetation, they also transplant, mulch, fertilize, water, and prune flowering plants, trees, and shrubs, and mow and water lawns. *Supervisors* generally perform the same work but are also responsible for directing the landscaping crew's activities, adhering to schedules, and keeping track of labor costs. Some landscaping laborers, called *pruners*, specialize in pruning, trimming, and shaping ornamental trees and shrubs. Others, called *lawn service workers*, specialize in maintaining lawns and shrubs for a fee. A growing number of residential and commercial clients, such as managers of office buildings, shopping malls, multi-unit residential buildings, and hotels and motels favor this full-service landscape maintenance. These workers perform a range of duties on a regular basis during the growing season, including mowing, edging, trimming, fertilizing, dethatching, and mulching. Those working for chemical lawn service firms are more specialized. They inspect lawns for problems and apply fertilizers, herbicides, pesticides, and other chemicals to stimulate growth and prevent or control weed, disease, or insect infestation, as well as practice integrated pest management techniques. *Lawn service managers* oversee operations, negotiate fees, schedule jobs, and hire and train new workers.

Groundskeeping laborers, also called groundskeepers or grounds maintenance personnel, maintain a variety of facilities including athletic fields, golf courses, cemeteries, university campuses, and parks. Many of their duties are similar to those of landscaping laborers. But, they also rake and mulch leaves, clear snow from walkways and parking lots, employ irrigation methods to adjust the amount of water consumption and prevent waste, and apply pesticides. They see to the proper upkeep and repair of sidewalks, parking lots, groundskeeping equipment, pools, fountains, fences, planters, and benches. *Grounds managers* may participate in many of the same tasks as maintenance personnel but typically have more extensive knowledge in horticulture, turf management, ornamental plants, landscape design and construction, pest management, irrigation, and erosion control. In addition, grounds managers have supervisory responsibilities and must manage and train personnel, draw up work contracts, efficiently allocate labor and financial resources, and engage in public relations activities.

Groundskeepers who care for athletic fields keep natural and artificial turf fields in top condition and mark out boundaries and paint turf with team logos and names before events. Groundskeepers must make sure the underlying soil on natural turf fields has the required composition to allow proper drainage and to support the appropriate grasses used on the field. They regularly mow, water, fertilize, and aerate the fields. In addition, groundskeepers apply chemicals and fungicides to control weeds, kill pests, and prevent diseases. Groundskeepers also vacuum and disinfect synthetic turf after use in order to prevent growth of harmful bacteria. They periodically remove the turf and replace the cushioning pad.

Workers who maintain golf courses work under the direction of *golf course superintendents* and are called *greenskeepers*. Greenskeepers do many of the same things other groundskeepers do. In addition, greenskeepers periodically relocate the holes on putting greens to eliminate uneven wear of the turf and add interest and challenge to the game. Greenskeepers also keep canopies, benches, ball washers, and tee markers repaired and freshly painted.

Some groundskeepers specialize in caring for cemeteries and memorial gardens. They dig graves to specified depth, generally using a backhoe. They may place concrete slabs on the bottom and around the sides of the grave to line it for greater support. When readying a site for the burial ceremony, they position the casket-lowering device over the grave, cover the immediate area with an artificial grass carpet, erect a canopy, and arrange folding chairs to accommodate mourners. They regularly mow grass, apply fertilizers and other chemicals, prune shrubs and trees, plant flowers, and remove debris from graves. They also must periodically build the ground up around new gravesites to compensate for settling.

Groundskeepers in parks and recreation facilities care for lawns, trees, and shrubs, maintain athletic fields and playgrounds, clean buildings, and keep parking lots, picnic areas, and other public spaces free of litter. They may also remove snow and ice from roads and walkways, erect and dismantle snow fences, and maintain swimming pools. These workers inspect buildings and equipment, make needed repairs, and keep everything freshly painted.

Landscaping, groundskeeping, and lawn service workers use handtools such as shovels, rakes, pruning saws, saws, hedge and brush trimmers, and axes, as well as power lawnmowers, chain saws, snow blowers, and electric clippers. Some use equipment such as tractors and twin-axle vehicles. Park, school, cemetery, and golf course groundskeepers may use sod cutters to harvest sod that will be replanted elsewhere. Athletic

Nursery workers must keep track of all plants on the premises.

turf groundskeepers use vacuums and other devices to remove water from athletic fields. In addition, some workers in large operations use spraying and dusting equipment. Landscape contractors and those in managerial positions increasingly use computers to develop plans and blueprints, to estimate and track project costs, and to maintain payroll and personnel information.

Working Conditions

Many of the jobs for landscaping, groundskeeping, and nursery workers are seasonal, mainly in the spring, summer, and fall when most planting, mowing and trimming, and cleanup are necessary. The work, most of which is performed outdoors in all kinds of weather, can be physically demanding and repetitive, involving much bending, lifting, and shoveling. Landscaping and groundskeeping workers may be under pressure to get the job completed, especially when preparing for scheduled events, such as athletic competitions or burials.

Those who work with pesticides, fertilizers, and other chemicals, as well as potentially dangerous equipment and tools such as power lawnmowers, chain saws, and power clippers, must exercise safety precautions. Workers who use motorized equipment must take care to protect against hearing damage.

Employment

Landscaping, groundskeeping, nursery, greenhouse, and lawn service workers held about 1,285,000 jobs in 1998. Employment was distributed as follows:

Landscaping and groundskeeping laborers	1,130,000
Lawn service managers	86,000
Pruners	45,000
Sprayers and applicators	19,000
Nursery and greenhouse managers	5,000

About one-third of wage and salaried workers were employed in companies providing landscape and horticultural services. Others worked for firms operating and building real estate, amusement and recreation facilities such as golf courses and race tracks, and retail nurseries and garden stores. Some were employed by local governments, installing and maintaining landscaping for parks, schools, hospitals, and other public facilities.

Almost 2 out of every 10 landscaping, groundskeeping, nursery, greenhouse, and lawn service workers were self-employed, providing landscape maintenance directly to customers on a contract basis. About 1 of every 6 worked part time, many of whom were school age.

Training, Other Qualifications, and Advancement

There usually are no minimum educational requirements for entry-level laborer positions in landscaping, groundskeeping, nursery, greenhouse, and lawn service occupations. In 1998, more than 4 in 10 workers did not have a high school diploma, although this diploma is necessary for some jobs. Short-term on-the-job training usually is sufficient to teach new hires how to operate equipment such as mowers, trimmers, leaf blowers, and small tractors, and follow correct safety procedures. Entry-level workers must be able to follow directions and learn proper planting procedures. If driving is an essential part of a job, employers look for applicants with a good driving record and some experience driving a truck. Workers who deal directly with customers must get along well with people. Employers also look for responsible, self-motivated individuals, because many gardeners and groundskeepers work with little supervision.

Laborers who demonstrate a willingness to work hard and quickly, have good communication skills, and take an interest in the business may advance to crew leader or other supervisory positions. Advancement or entry into positions as grounds manager or landscape contractor usually requires some formal education beyond high school, and several years of progressively responsible experience.

Prospective grounds managers or landscape contractors should be knowledgeable about turf care, horticulture, ornamental plants, soils, and erosion prevention and irrigation techniques. They must be familiar with all landscaping and grounds maintenance equipment, and know how and when to mix and apply fertilizers and pesticides. Some are responsible for designing and developing installation and maintenance plans for landscapes and proper grounds management. They also estimate and track project costs, and handle personnel issues. Those in managerial positions must also be aware of local or Federal environmental regulations and building codes. Several years of hands-on experience plus a 4-year bachelor's degree, a 2-year associate's degree, or a 1-year vocational-technical degree in grounds management or landscape design or a closely related "green" discipline, usually provide a good background for those who wish to deal with the full range of landscaping responsibilities. Some schools offer cooperative education programs in which students work alternate semesters or quarters for a lawn care or landscape contractor.

Most States require certification for workers who apply pesticides. Certification requirements vary, but usually include passing a test on the proper and safe use and disposal of insecticides, herbicides, and fungicides. Some States require that landscape contractors be licensed.

The Professional Grounds Management Society (PGMS) offers certification to grounds managers who have a combination of 8 years of experience and formal education beyond high school, and pass an examination covering subjects such as equipment management, personnel management, environmental issues, turf care, ornamentals, and circulatory systems. The PGMS also offers certification to groundskeepers who have a high school diploma or equivalent, plus 2 years of experience in the grounds maintenance field.

The Associated Landscape Contractors of America (ALCA) offers the designations, Certified Landscape Professional or Certified Landscape Technician, to those who meet established education and experience standards and pass an ALCA examination. The hands-on test for technicians covers areas such as maintenance equipment operation and the installation of plants by reading a plan. A written safety test is also administered.

Some workers in landscaping, groundskeeping, nursery, greenhouse, and lawn service occupations open their own business after several years of experience.

Job Outlook

Those interested in landscaping, groundskeeping, nursery, greenhouse, and lawn service occupations should find excellent job opportunities in the future. Because of high turnover, a large number of job openings is expected to result from the need to replace workers who transfer to other occupations or leave the labor force. These occupations attract many part-time workers. Some take landscaping, groundskeeping, or nursery jobs to earn money for school or only until they find a better-paying job. Because wages for beginners are low and the work is physically demanding, many employers have difficulty attracting enough workers to fill all openings.

Employment of landscaping, groundskeeping, nursery, greenhouse, and lawn service workers is expected to grow about as fast as the average for all occupations through the year 2008 in response to increasing demand for landscaping, groundskeeping, and related services. Expected growth in the construction of commercial and industrial buildings, shopping malls, homes, highways, and recreational facilities should contribute to demand for these workers. Developers will continue to use landscaping services, both interior and exterior, to attract prospective buyers and tenants.

The upkeep and renovation of existing landscaping and grounds are growing sources of demand for landscaping, groundskeeping, and lawn service workers. Owners of many existing buildings and facilities, including colleges and universities, recognize the importance of curb appeal and are expected to use these services more extensively to maintain and upgrade their properties. In recent years, the large number of baby boomers, wishing to conserve leisure time by contracting out for basic yard services, spurred employment growth in landscaping and lawn service occupations. Homeowners are expected to continue using such services to maintain the beauty and value of their property. As the "echo" boom generation (children of baby boomers) comes of age, the demand for parks, athletic fields, and recreational facilities also can be expected to add to the demand for landscaping, groundskeeping, and lawn service workers. The need for nursery and greenhouse laborers and managers will grow because of the continued popularity of home gardening, as well as the need to cultivate and provide the vegetation used by landscaping services.

Job opportunities for nonseasonal work are more numerous in regions with temperate climates where landscaping and lawn services are required all year. However, opportunities may vary depending on local economic conditions.

Earnings

Earnings vary widely depending on the particular landscaping position and experience, ranging from the minimum wage in some beginning laborer positions to more than $20.00 an hour in some manager jobs. The following tabulation presents 1998 median hourly earnings for landscaping, groundskeeping, nursery, greenhouse, and lawn service occupations:

Occupation	Earnings
Lawn service managers	$12.22
Nursery and greenhouse managers	12.19
Pruners	10.61
Sprayers and applicators	10.41
Landscaping and groundskeeping laborers	8.24

Median hourly earnings in the industries employing the largest numbers of landscaping and groundskeeping laborers in 1997 are shown below:

Industry	Earnings
Concrete work	$10.40
Local government, except education and hospitals	10.00
Real estate operators and lessors	7.70
Landscape and horticultural services	7.70
Miscellaneous amusement and recreation services	7.50

Related Occupations

Landscaping, groundskeeping, nursery, greenhouse, and lawn service workers perform most of their work outdoors and have some knowledge of plants and soils. Others whose jobs may be performed outdoors and are otherwise related are botanists, construction workers, landscape architects, farmers, horticultural workers, tree surgeon helpers, forest conservation workers, and soil conservation technicians.

Sources of Additional Information

For career and certification information, contact:

☛ Associated Landscape Contractors of America, Inc., 150 Elden Street, Suite 270, Herndon, VA 20170.

☛ Professional Grounds Management Society, 120 Cockeysville Rd., Suite 104, Hunt Valley, MD 21030.

Pest Controllers

(O*NET 67008)

Significant Points

- Federal and State laws require licensure through training and examination.
- Because many people do not find pest control work appealing, those with the necessary skills and interests should have favorable job prospects.

Nature of the Work

Roaches, rats, mice, spiders, termites, fleas, ants, and bees—few people welcome them into their homes or offices. Unwanted creatures that infest households, buildings, or surrounding areas are pests that can pose serious risk to human health and safety. It is a pest controller's job to control them.

Pest controllers locate, identify, destroy, and repel pests. They use their knowledge of pests' lifestyles and habits, along with an arsenal of pest management techniques—applying chemicals, setting traps, operating equipment, and even modifying structures—to alleviate pest problems.

The best known method of pest control is pesticide application. Pest controllers use two different types of pesticides—general use and restricted use. General use pesticides are the most widely used and are readily available; in diluted concentrations, they are available to the public. Restricted use pesticides are available only to certified professionals for controlling the most severe infestations. Their registration, labeling, and application are regulated by Federal law, interpreted by the Environmental Protection Agency (EPA), because of their potential harm to pest controllers, customers, and the environment.

Pesticides are not pest controllers' only tool, however. Pest controllers increasingly use a combination of pest management techniques, known as integrated pest management. One method involves using proper sanitation and creating physical barriers, for pests cannot survive without food and will not infest a building if they cannot enter it. Another method involves using baits, some of which destroy the pests and others that prevent them from reproducing. Yet another method involves using mechanical devices, such as traps and tools, that electrocute, freeze, or burn pests.

Integrated pest management is becoming popular for several reasons. First, pesticides can pose environmental and health risks. Second, some pests are becoming more resistant to pesticides in certain situations. Finally, an integrated pest management plan is more effective in the long term than use of a pesticide alone.

Most pest controllers perform duties for one of three positions—pest control technician, applicator, or supervisor. Position titles vary by State, but the hierarchy—based on training and responsibility required—remains consistent.

Pest control service technicians identify problem areas and operate and maintain traps. They assist applicators by carrying supplies, organizing materials, and preparing equipment. In addition, they may make sales presentations on pest control products or services.. Technicians are licensed to apply pesticides only under an applicator's supervision.

Certified pest control applicators, sometimes called exterminators, perform the same tasks technicians do. But they are also certified to apply all pesticides, both general and restricted use, without supervision and are licensed to supervise and train technicians in pesticide use. Within this group of workers are several subspecialties, including termite exterminators and fumigators.

Termite exterminators are applicators who specialize in controlling termites. They use chemicals and modify structures to eliminate and prevent termites. To treat infested areas, termite exterminators drill holes and cut openings into buildings to access infestations. To prevent further infestation, they modify foundations and dig holes and trenches around buildings. Some termite exterminators even repair structural damage caused by termites.

Fumigators are applicators who control pests using poisonous gasses called fumigants. Fumigators pretreat infested buildings by examining, measuring, and sealing the buildings. Then, using cylinders, hoses, and valves, they fill structures with the proper amount and concentration of fumigant. They also monitor the premises during treatment for leaking gas. To prevent accidental fumigant exposure, fumigators padlock doors and post warning signs.

Pest control supervisors, also known as operators, direct service technicians and certified applicators. Supervisors are licensed to apply pesticides, but they usually are more involved in running the business. Supervisors are responsible for ensuring employee adherence to rules and must resolve problems with regulatory officials. Most States

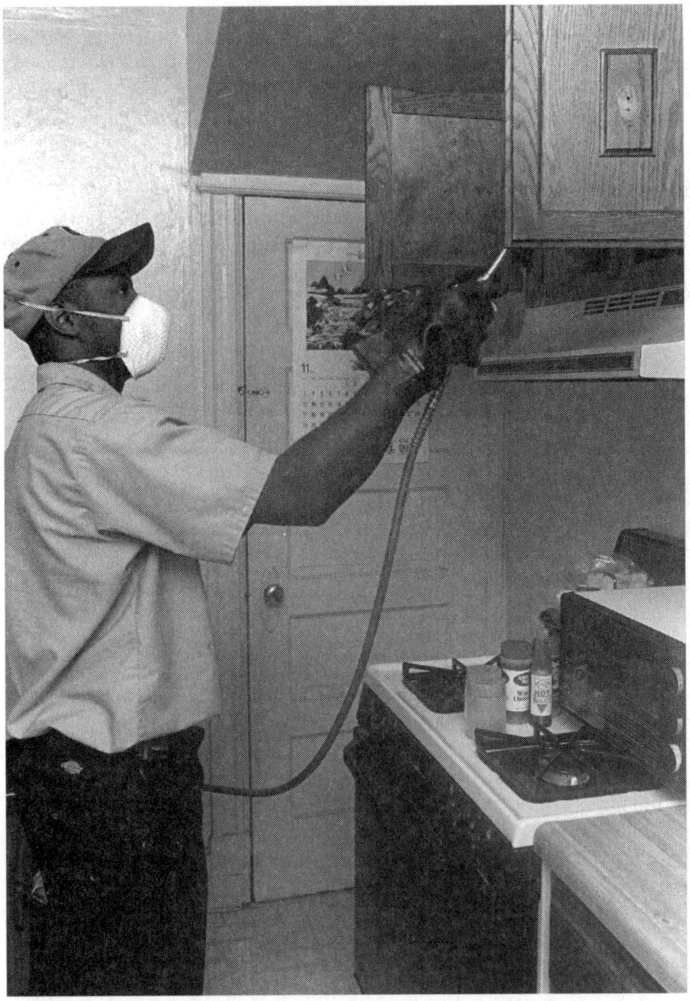

Pest controllers follow strict safety guidelines when working with pesticides.

require each pest control establishment to have a supervisor; self-employed business owners are usually supervisors.

Working Conditions

Pest controllers must kneel, bend, reach, and crawl to inspect, modify, and treat structures. They work both indoors and out, in all weather conditions. During warm weather, applicators may be uncomfortable wearing the heavy protective gear—such as respirators, gloves, and goggles—required for working with pesticides.

Almost half of all pest controllers work 40-hour weeks, but about a quarter work more hours. Pest controllers often work evenings and weekends, but about 90 percent of them work consistent shifts.

There are health risks associated with pesticide use. Various pest control chemicals are toxic and could pose health risks if not used properly. Extensive training required for certification and the use of recommended protective equipment minimizes these health risks, resulting in fewer reported cases of lost work. Because pest controllers travel to visit clients, the potential risk of motor vehicle accidents is another occupational hazard.

Employment

Pest controllers held about 52,000 jobs in 1998; over 90 percent of salaried workers were employed in the services to buildings industry. They are concentrated in States with warmer climates. In 1997, more than half of all pest controllers worked in California, Florida, Georgia, North Carolina, Tennessee, and Texas. About 14 percent were self-employed.

Training, Other Qualifications, and Advancement

A high school diploma or equivalent is the minimum qualification for most pest controller jobs. Although a college degree is not required, almost one-third of all pest controllers have either attended college or earned a degree.

Pest controllers must have basic skills in math, chemistry, and writing. Because of the extensive interaction pest controllers have with their customers, employers prefer to hire people who have good communication and interpersonal skills. In addition, most pest control companies require their employees to have a good driving record. Pest controllers must be in good health because of the physical demands of the job, and they also must be able to withstand extreme conditions—such as the heat of climbing into an attic in the summertime or the chill of sliding into a crawlspace during winter.

Both Federal and State laws regulate pest controllers. These laws require them to be certified through training and examination, for which most pest control firms help their employees prepare. Workers may receive both formal classroom and on-the-job training, but they must also study on their own. Because the pest control industry is constantly changing, workers must attend continuing education classes to maintain their certification.

Requirements for pest controllers vary by State. Pest controllers usually begin their careers as apprentice technicians. Before performing any pest control services, apprentices must attend general training in pesticide safety and use. In addition, they must train in each pest control category in which they wish to practice. Categories may include general pest control, rodent control, termite control, fumigation, and ornamental and turf control.

Training usually involves spending 10 hours in the classroom and 60 hours on the job for each category. After completing the required training, apprentices can provide supervised pest control services. Apprentices have up to 1 year to prepare for and pass the written examinations. Upon successful completion of the exams, the apprentice becomes licensed as a technician.

To be eligible to become applicators, technicians need 1 year of experience, 6 months of which must be as a licensed technician. This requirement is sometimes waived for individuals who have either a college degree in biological sciences or extensive related work experience. To become certified as applicators, technicians must pass an additional set of category exams. Depending on the State, applicators must attend additional classes every 1 to 6 years to be recertified.

Applicators with several years of experience often become supervisors. To qualify as a pest control supervisor, applicators must pass State-administered exams and have experience in the industry, usually a minimum of 2 years. Many supervisors are self-employed, reflecting the relative ease of entry into the field and the growing need for pest control. Therefore, the pest control industry provides a good opportunity for people interested in operating their own business.

Job Outlook

Many people do not find pest control work appealing, so those with the necessary skills and interests should have favorable prospects. Employment of pest controllers is expected to grow faster than the average for all occupations through 2008. In addition to job openings arising from employment growth, opportunities will arise when controllers transfer to other occupations or leave the labor force.

Demand for pest controllers is projected to increase for a number of reasons. An expanding client base will develop as environmental and health concerns, greater numbers of dual-income households, and improvements in the standard of living convince more people to hire professionals rather than attempt pest control work themselves. In addition, tougher regulations limiting pesticide use will demand more complex integrated pest management strategies. Furthermore, some of the newer materials used for insulation around foundations have made many homes more susceptible to pest infestation. Finally, continuing population shifts to the more pest-prone sunbelt States should increase the number of households in need of pest control.

Earnings

The hierarchy of pest controller positions also applies to earnings. Pest control supervisors usually earn the most and technicians the least, with earnings of certified applicators falling somewhere in between. Earnings data do not distinguish among job titles, however.

Median hourly earnings of full-time wage and salary pest controllers in 1998 were $10.81. The middle 50 percent earned between $8.80 and $13.02. The lowest 10 percent earned less than $6.68, and the top 10 percent earned over $15.67.

Many pest controllers work under a wage-plus commission system, which rewards workers who do their job well. Some firms offer bonuses to workers who exceed their performance goals.

Related Occupations

Pest controllers visit homes and places of business to provide building services. Other building services workers include construction equipment and materials salespeople, building cleaning personnel, electricians, carpenters, and heating, air-conditioning, and refrigeration technicians.

Sources of Additional Information

Private employment agencies and State employment services offices have information about available job opportunities for pest controllers.

For information about the training and certification required in your State, contact your local office of the U.S. Department of Agriculture or your State's Environmental Protection Agency.

For general information about a career in pest control, contact:

☛ National Pest Control Association, 8100 Oak St., Dunn Loring, VA 22027. Internet: **http://www.pestworld.org**

Food Preparation and Beverage Service Occupations

Chefs, Cooks, and Other Kitchen Workers

(O*NET 65021, 65026, 65028, 65032, 65035, 65038A, 65038B, and 69999E)

Significant Points

- Many young people work as chefs, cooks, and other kitchen workers—over 20 percent are between 16 and 19 years old.
- About 35 percent work part-time.
- Job openings are expected to be plentiful through 2008, reflecting average growth and substantial turnover in this large occupation.

Nature of the Work

A reputation for serving good food is essential to the success of any restaurant or hotel, whether it offers exotic cuisine or hamburgers. Chefs, cooks, and other kitchen workers are largely responsible for establishing and maintaining this reputation. Chefs and cooks do this by preparing meals, while other kitchen workers assist them by cleaning surfaces, peeling vegetable, and performing other duties.

In general, *chefs* and *cooks* measure, mix, and cook ingredients according to recipes. In the course of their work they use a variety of pots, pans, cutlery, and other equipment, including ovens, broilers, grills, slicers, grinders, and blenders. Chefs and cooks are often responsible for directing the work of other kitchen workers, estimating food requirements, and ordering food supplies. Some chefs and cooks also help plan meals and develop menus. Although the terms chef and cook are still used interchangeably, chefs tend to be more highly skilled and better trained than most cooks. Due to their skillful preparation of traditional dishes and refreshing twists in creating new ones, many chefs have earned fame for both themselves and the establishments where they work.

The specific responsibilities of chefs and cooks are determined by a number of factors, including the type of restaurant in which they work. *Institutional chefs* and *cooks*, for example, work in the kitchens of schools, cafeterias, businesses, hospitals, and other institutions. For each meal, they prepare a large quantity of a limited number of entrees, vegetables, and desserts. *Restaurant chefs* and *cooks* usually prepare a wider selection of dishes, cooking most orders individually. *Short-order cooks* prepare foods in restaurants and coffee shops that emphasize fast service. They grill and garnish hamburgers, prepare sandwiches, fry eggs, and cook french fries, often working on several orders at the same time. *Specialty fast-food cooks* prepare a limited selection of menu items in fast-food restaurants. They cook and package batches of food, such as hamburgers and fried chicken, which are prepared to order or kept warm until sold.

Bread and *pastry bakers*, called pastry chefs in some kitchens, produce baked goods for restaurants, institutions, and retail bakery shops. Unlike bakers who work in large, automated industrial bakeries, bread and pastry bakers need only to supply the customers who visit their establishment. They bake small quantities of breads, rolls, pastries, pies, and cakes, doing most of the work by hand. These bakers measure and mix ingredients, shape and bake the dough, and apply fillings and decorations. Some related workers are employed in coffee houses, which may also serve pastries or other snacks. These workers operate specialized equipment such as cappuccino and espresso machines. Some food products are made on the premises, while others are delivered daily.

Other kitchen workers, under the direction of chefs and cooks, perform tasks requiring less skill. They weigh and measure ingredients, go after pots and pans, and stir and strain soups and sauces. These workers also clean, peel, and slice vegetables and fruits and make salads. They may cut and grind meats, poultry, and seafood in preparation for cooking. Their responsibilities also include cleaning work areas, equipment, utensils, dishes, and silverware.

The number and types of workers employed in kitchens depends on the type of establishment. For example, fast-food outlets offer only a few items, which are prepared by fast-food cooks. Small, full-service restaurants offering casual dining often feature a limited number of easy-to-prepare items supplemented by short-order specialties and ready-made desserts. Typically, one cook prepares all the food with the help of a short-order cook and one or two other kitchen workers.

Large eating places tend to have varied menus and employ kitchen workers who prepare much more of the food they serve from scratch. Kitchen staffs often include several chefs and cooks, sometimes called assistant or apprentice chefs and cooks; a bread and pastry baker; and many less-skilled kitchen workers. Each chef or cook usually has a special assignment and often a special job title—vegetable, fry, or sauce cook, for example. Executive chefs coordinate the work of the kitchen staff and often direct the preparation of certain foods. They decide the size of servings, plan menus, and buy food supplies.

Working Conditions

Many restaurant and institutional kitchens have modern equipment, convenient work areas, and air-conditioning, but many kitchens in older and smaller eating places are not as well equipped. Working conditions depend on the type and quantity of food being prepared and the local laws governing food service operations. Workers usually must withstand the pressure and strain of working in close quarters, standing for hours at a time, lifting heavy pots and kettles, and working

Job openings are expected to be plentiful for chefs, cooks, and other kitchen workers.

near hot ovens and grills. Job hazards include slips and falls, cuts, and burns, but injuries are seldom serious.

Work hours in restaurants may include early mornings, late evenings, holidays, and weekends. Work schedules of chefs, cooks and other kitchen workers in factory and school cafeterias may be more regular. Nearly 1 in 3 cooks and 2 out of 5 other kitchen and food preparation workers work part time, compared to 1 out of 6 workers throughout the economy.

The wide range in dining hours creates work opportunities attractive to homemakers, students, and other individuals seeking supplemental income. For example, over 20 percent of kitchen and food preparation workers are 16-19 years old. Kitchen workers employed by public and private schools may work during the school year only, usually for 9 or 10 months. Similarly, establishments at vacation resorts usually only offer seasonal employment.

Employment

Chefs, cooks, and other kitchen workers held more than 3.3 million jobs in 1998. Restaurant cooks held 783,000 of these jobs; short-order and fast-food cooks, 677,000; institutional cooks, 418,000; bread and pastry bakers, 171,000; and other kitchen workers, 1,256,000.

About three-fifths of all chefs, cooks, and other kitchen workers were employed in restaurants and other retail eating and drinking places. One-fifth worked in institutions such as schools, universities, hospitals, and nursing homes. Grocery stores, hotels, and other organizations employed the remainder.

Training, Other Qualifications, and Advancement

Most chefs, cooks, and other kitchen workers start as fast-food or short-order cooks or in another lower-skilled kitchen position. These positions require little education or training, and most skills are learned on the job. After acquiring some basic food handling, preparation, and cooking skills, these workers may be able to advance to an assistant cook or short-order cook position.

Although a high school diploma is not required for beginning jobs, it is recommended for those planning a career as a cook or chef. High school or vocational school courses in business arithmetic and business administration are particularly helpful. Many school districts, in cooperation with State departments of education, provide on-the-job training and summer workshops for cafeteria kitchen workers with aspirations of becoming cooks. Large corporations in the food service and entertainment industries also offer paid internships and summer jobs, which can provide valuable experience.

To achieve the level of skill required of an executive chef or cook in a fine restaurant, many years of training and experience are necessary. An increasing number of chefs and cooks obtain their training through high school, post-high school vocational programs, or 2- or 4-year colleges. Chefs and cooks also may be trained in apprenticeship programs offered by professional culinary institutes, industry associations, and trade unions. An example is the 3-year apprenticeship program administered by local chapters of the American Culinary Federation in cooperation with local employers and junior colleges or vocational education institutions. In addition, some large hotels and restaurants operate their own training programs for cooks and chefs.

People who have had courses in commercial food preparation may be able to start in a cook or chef job without having to spend time in a lower-skilled kitchen job. Their education may give them an advantage when looking for jobs in better restaurants and hotels, where hiring standards often are high. Although some vocational programs in high schools offer training, employers usually prefer training given by trade schools, vocational centers, colleges, professional associations, or trade unions. Postsecondary courses range from a few months to 2 years or more and are open in some cases only to high school graduates. The Armed Forces are also a good source of training and experience.

Although curricula may vary, students in these programs usually spend most of their time learning to prepare food through actual practice. They learn to bake, broil, and otherwise prepare food, and to use and care for kitchen equipment. Training programs often include courses in menu planning, determination of portion size, food cost control, purchasing food supplies in quantity, selection and storage of food, and use of leftover food to minimize waste. Students also learn hotel and restaurant sanitation and public health rules for handling food. Training in supervisory and management skills sometimes is emphasized in courses offered by private vocational schools, professional associations, and university programs.

About 700 schools offer culinary courses across the Nation. The American Culinary Federation accredited about 100 training programs and a number of apprenticeship programs in 1998. Typical apprenticeships last three years and combine classroom and work experience. Accreditation is an indication that a culinary program meets recognized standards regarding course content, facilities, and quality of instruction. The American Culinary Federation also certifies pastry professionals, culinary educators, and chefs and cooks at the levels of cook, working chef, executive chef, and master chef. Certification standards are based primarily on experience and formal training.

Important characteristics for chefs, cooks, and other kitchen workers include the ability to work as part of a team, a keen sense of taste and smell, and personal cleanliness. Most States require health certificates indicating workers are free from communicable diseases.

Advancement opportunities for chefs and cooks are better than for most other food and beverage preparation and service occupations. Many chefs and cooks acquire high-paying positions and new cooking skills by moving from one job to another. Besides culinary skills, advancement also depends on ability to supervise less-skilled workers and limit food costs by minimizing waste and accurately anticipating the amount of perishable supplies needed. Some chefs and cooks go into business as caterers or restaurant owners, while others become instructors in vocational programs in high schools, community colleges, or other academic institutions. A number of cooks and chefs advance to executive chef positions or supervisory or management positions, particularly in hotels, clubs, and larger, more elegant restaurants. (For information on *executive chefs*, see the *Handbook* statement on restaurant and food service managers.)

Job Outlook

Job openings for chefs, cooks, and other kitchen workers are expected to be plentiful through 2008. While job growth will create new positions, the overwhelming majority of job openings will stem from the need to replace workers who leave their jobs. Minimal educational and training requirements, combined with a large number of part-time positions, make employment as chefs, cooks, and other kitchen workers attractive to people seeking a short-term source of income and a flexible schedule. In coming years, these workers will continue to transfer to other occupations or stop working to assume household responsibilities or to attend school full time, creating numerous openings for those entering the field.

These openings will be supplemented by new openings resulting from employment growth, as overall employment of chefs, cooks, and other kitchen workers is expected to increase about as fast as the average for all occupations through 2008. Employment growth will be spurred by increases in population, household income, and leisure time that will allow people to dine out and take vacations more often. In addition, growth in the number of two-income households will lead more families to opt for the convenience of dining out.

Projected employment growth varies by specialty. Increases in the number of families and the more affluent, 55-and-older population will lead to a growing number of restaurants that offer table service and more varied menus—requiring higher-skilled cooks and chefs. Also, the popularity of fresh baked breads and pastries should ensure continued rapid growth in the employment of bakers. Employment of short-order and specialty fast-food cooks, most of whom work in fast-food restaurants, also is expected to increase in response to growth of the 16-24 year-old population and the continuing fast-paced lifestyle of many Americans.

Employment of institutional and cafeteria chefs and cooks, on the other hand, will grow more slowly than other types of cooks. Their employment will not keep pace with the rapid growth in the educational and health services industries—where their employment is concentrated. As many high schools and hospitals try to make "institutional food" more attractive to students, staff, visitors, and patients, they increasingly contract out their food services. Many of the contracted companies emphasize fast food and employ short-order and fast-food cooks, instead of institutional and cafeteria cooks, reducing the demand for these workers.

Earnings

Wages of chefs, cooks, and other kitchen workers depend greatly on the part of the country and the type of establishment in which they are employed. Wages usually are highest in elegant restaurants and hotels, where many executive chefs are employed.

Median hourly earnings of restaurant cooks were $7.81 in 1998, with most earning between $6.38 and $9.53. Cooks in fast-food restaurants and short order cooks had median hourly earnings of $6.12, with most earning between $5.69 and $7.38. Median hourly earnings of bread and pastry bakers were $8.17; most earned between $6.57 and $10.36. Median hourly earnings in the industries employing the largest number of food preparation workers in 1997 were:

Hospitals	$7.55
Grocery stores	7.21
Elementary and secondary schools	7.16
Nursing and personal care facilities	6.92
Eating and drinking places	5.87

Some employers provide employees with uniforms and free meals, but Federal law permits employers to deduct from their employees' wages the cost or fair value of any meals or lodging provided, and some employers do so. Chefs, cooks, and other kitchen workers who work full time often receive typical benefits, but part-time workers usually do not.

In some large hotels and restaurants, kitchen workers belong to unions. The principal unions are the Hotel Employees and Restaurant Employees International Union and the Service Employees International Union.

Related Occupations

Workers who perform tasks similar to those of chefs, cooks, and other kitchen workers include butchers and meat cutters, cannery workers, and industrial bakers.

Sources of Additional Information

Information about job opportunities may be obtained from local employers and local offices of the State employment service.

Career information about chefs, cooks, and other kitchen workers, as well as a directory of 2- and 4-year colleges that offer courses or programs that prepare persons for food service careers, is available from:

☛ The National Restaurant Association, 1200 17th St. NW., Washington, DC 20036-3097.

For information on the American Culinary Federation's apprenticeship and certification programs for cooks, as well as a list of accredited culinary programs, send a self addressed, stamped envelope to:

☛ American Culinary Federation, P.O. Box 3466, St. Augustine, FL 32085.

For general information on hospitality careers, write to:

☛ Council on Hotel, Restaurant, and Institutional Education, 1200 17th St. NW., Washington, DC 20036-3097.

Food and Beverage Service Occupations

(O*NET 65002, 65005, 65008A, 65008B, 65011, 65014, 65017, 65041, 65099A, and 65099B)

Significant Points

- Most jobs are part time and many opportunities exist for young people—nearly 2 out of 3 food counter and fountain workers are 16-19 years old.
- Job openings are expected to be abundant through 2008, reflecting substantial turnover.
- Tips comprise a major portion of earnings; consequently, keen competition is expected for bartender, waiter and waitress, and other jobs in popular restaurants and fine dining establishments where potential earnings from tips are greatest.

Nature of the Work

Whether they work in small, informal diners or large, elegant restaurants, all food and beverage service workers aim to help customers have a positive dining experience in their establishments. These workers are responsible for greeting customers, taking food and drink orders, serving food, cleaning up after patrons, and preparing tables and dining areas. All of these duties require a high quality of services customers will return.

The largest group of these workers, *waiters* and *waitresses,* take customers' orders, serve food and beverages, prepare itemized checks, and sometimes accept payments. Their specific duties vary considerably, depending on the establishment where they work. In coffee shops, they are expected to provide fast and efficient, yet courteous service. In fine restaurants, where gourmet meals are accompanied by attentive formal service, waiters and waitresses serve meals at a more leisurely pace and offer more personal service to patrons. For example, servers may recommend a certain wine as a complement to a particular entree, explain how various items on the menu are prepared, or complete preparations on a salad or other special dishes at table side. Additionally, waiters and waitresses may check the identification of patrons to ensure they meet the minimum age requirement for the purchase of alcohol and tobacco products.

Depending on the type of restaurant, waiters and waitresses may perform additional duties usually associated with other food and beverage service occupations. These tasks may include escorting guests to tables, serving customers seated at counters, setting up and clearing tables, or operating a cash register. However, formal restaurants frequently hire other staff to perform these duties, allowing their waiters and waitresses to concentrate on customer service.

Bartenders fill drink orders that waiters and waitresses take from customers. They prepare standard mixed drinks and, occasionally, are asked to mix drinks to suit a customer's taste. Most bartenders know dozens of drink recipes and are able to mix drinks accurately, quickly, and without waste, even during the busiest periods. Besides mixing and serving drinks, bartenders collect payment, operate the cash register, clean up after customers leave, and often serve food to customers seated at the bar. Bartenders also check identification of customers seated at the bar, to ensure they meet the minimum age requirement for the purchase of alcohol and tobacco products. Bartenders usually are responsible for ordering and maintaining an inventory of liquor, mixes, and other bar supplies. They often form attractive displays out of bottles and glassware and wash the glassware and utensils after each use.

The majority of bartenders who work in eating and drinking establishments directly serve and interact with patrons. Because customers typically frequent drinking establishments for the friendly atmosphere, most bartenders must be friendly and helpful with customers. Bartenders at service bars, on the other hand, have little contact with customers because they work in small bars in restaurants, hotels, and clubs where only waiters and waitresses serve drinks. Some establishments, especially larger ones, use automatic equipment to mix drinks of varying complexity at the push of a button. Even in these establishments, however, bartenders still must be efficient and knowledgeable in case the device malfunctions or a customer requests a drink not handled by the equipment.

Hosts and *hostesses* try to create a good impression of a restaurant by warmly welcoming guests. Because hosts and hostesses are restaurants' personal representatives, they try to insure that service is prompt and courteous and that the meal meets expectations. They may courteously direct patrons to where coats and other personal items may be left and indicate where patrons can wait until their table is ready. Hosts and hostesses assign guests to tables suitable for the size of their group, escort patrons to their seats, and provide menus. They also schedule dining reservations, arrange parties, and organize any special services that are required. In some restaurants, they also act as cashiers.

Dining room attendants and *bartender helpers* assist waiters, waitresses, and bartenders by cleaning tables, removing dirty dishes, and keeping serving areas stocked with supplies. They replenish the supply of clean linens, dishes, silverware, and glasses in the dining room and keep the bar stocked with glasses, liquor, ice, and drink garnishes. Bartender helpers also keep bar equipment clean and wash glasses. Dining room attendants set tables with clean tablecloths, napkins, silverware, glasses, and dishes and serve ice water, rolls, and butter. At the conclusion of meals, they remove dirty dishes and soiled linens from tables. Cafeteria attendants stock serving tables with food, trays, dishes, and silverware and may carry trays to dining tables for patrons.

Counter attendants take orders and serve food at counters. In cafeterias, they serve food displayed on counters and steam tables, carve meat, dish out vegetables, ladle sauces and soups, and fill beverage glasses. In lunchrooms and coffee shops, counter attendants take orders from customers seated at the counter, transmit orders to the kitchen, and pick up and serve food. They also fill cups with coffee, soda, and other beverages and prepare fountain specialties, such as milkshakes and ice cream sundaes. Counter attendants prepare some short-order items, such as sandwiches and salads, and wrap or place orders in containers for carry out. They also clean counters, write itemized checks, and sometimes accept payment.

Fast-food workers take orders from customers at counters or drive-through windows at fast-food restaurants. They pick up the ordered beverage and food items, serve them to a customer, and accept payment. Many fast-food workers also cook and package food, make coffee, and fill beverage cups using drink-dispensing machines.

Working Conditions

Food and beverage service workers are on their feet most of the time and often carry heavy trays of food, dishes, and glassware. During busy dining periods, they are under pressure to serve customers quickly and efficiently. The work is relatively safe, but care must be taken to avoid slips, falls, and burns.

Part-time work is more common among food and beverage service workers than among workers in almost any other occupation. Those on part-time schedules include half of all waiters and waitresses, and 6 out of 10 food counter and fountain workers, compared to 1 out of 6 workers throughout the economy. Slightly more than half of all bartenders work full-time with 35 percent working part-time and the remainder working a variable schedule.

Part-time work is more common among food and beverage service workers than among workers in almost any other occupation.

The wide range in dining hours creates work opportunities attractive to homemakers, students, and other individuals seeking supplemental income. In fact, nearly 2 out of 3 food counter and fountain workers are between 16 and 19 years old. Many food and beverage service workers work evenings, weekends, and holidays. Some work split shifts—that is, they work for several hours during the middle of the day, take a few hours off in the afternoon, and then return to their jobs for evening hours.

Employment

Food and beverage service workers held over 5.4 million jobs in 1998. Waiters and waitresses held about 2,019,000 of these jobs; counter attendants and fast-food workers, 2,025,000; dining room and cafeteria attendants and bartender helpers, 405,000; bartenders, 404,000; hosts and hostesses, 297,000; and all other food preparation and service workers, 280,000.

Restaurants, coffee shops, bars, and other retail eating and drinking places employed the overwhelming majority of food and beverage service workers. Others worked in hotels and other lodging places, bowling alleys, casinos, country clubs, and other membership organizations.

Jobs are located throughout the country but are typically plentiful in large cities and tourist areas. Vacation resorts offer seasonal employment, and some workers alternate between summer and winter resorts, instead of remaining in one area the entire year.

Training, Other Qualifications, and Advancement

There are no specific educational requirements for food and beverage service jobs. Although many employers prefer to hire high school graduates for waiter and waitress, bartender, and host and hostess positions, completion of high school is usually not required for fast-food workers, counter attendants, and dining room attendants and bartender helpers. For many people, a job as a food and beverage service worker serves as a source of immediate income, rather than a career. Many entrants to these jobs are in their late teens or early twenties and have a high school education or less. Usually, they have little or no work experience. Many are full-time students or homemakers. Food and beverage service jobs are a major source of part-time employment for high school and college students.

Because maintaining a restaurant's image is important to its success, employers emphasize personal qualities. Food and beverage service workers are in close contact with the public, so these workers should be well-spoken and have a neat, clean appearance. They should enjoy dealing with all kinds of people and possess a pleasant disposition.

Waiters and waitresses need a good memory to avoid confusing customers' orders and to recall faces, names, and preferences of frequent patrons. These workers should also be good at arithmetic so they can total bills without the assistance of a calculator or cash register if necessary. In restaurants specializing in foreign foods, knowledge of a foreign language is helpful. Prior experience waiting on tables is preferred by restaurants and hotels that have rigid table service standards. Jobs at these establishments often have higher earnings, but they may also have higher educational requirements than less demanding establishments.

Usually, bartenders must be at least 21 years of age, but employers prefer to hire people who are 25 or older. Bartenders should be familiar with State and local laws concerning the sale of alcoholic beverages.

Most food and beverage service workers pick up their skills on the job by observing and working with more experienced workers. Some employers, particularly those in fast-food restaurants, use self-instruction programs with audiovisual presentations and instructional booklets to teach new employees food preparation and service skills. Some public and private vocational schools, restaurant associations, and large restaurant chains provide classroom training in a generalized food service curriculum.

Some bartenders acquire their skills by attending a bartending or vocational and technical school. These programs often include instruction on State and local laws and regulations, cocktail recipes, attire and conduct, and stocking a bar. Some of these schools help their graduates find jobs.

Due to the relatively small size of most food-serving establishments, opportunities for promotion are limited. After gaining some experience, some dining room and cafeteria attendants and bartender helpers are able to advance to waiter, waitress, or bartender jobs. For waiters, waitresses, and bartenders, advancement usually is limited to finding a job in a more expensive restaurant or bar where prospects for tip earnings are better. A few bartenders open their own businesses. Some hosts and hostesses and waiters and waitresses advance to supervisory jobs, such as maitre d'hotel, dining room supervisor, or restaurant manager. In larger restaurant chains, food and beverage service workers who excel at their work are often invited to enter the company's formal management training program. (For more information, see the *Handbook* statement on restaurant and food service managers.)

Job Outlook

Job openings are expected to be abundant for food and beverage service workers. Employment of food and beverage service occupations is expected to grow about as fast as the average for all occupations through 2008, stemming from increases in population, personal incomes, and leisure time. While employment growth will produce many new jobs, the overwhelming majority of openings will arise from the need to replace the high proportion of workers who leave this occupation each year. There is substantial movement into and out of the occupation because education and training requirements are minimal, and the predominance of part-time jobs is attractive to people seeking a short-term source of income rather than a career. However, keen competition is expected for bartender, waiter and waitress, and other food and beverage service jobs in popular restaurants and fine dining establishments, where potential earnings from tips are greatest.

Projected employment growth will vary by type of food and beverage service job. Growth in the number of families and the more affluent, 55-and-older population will result in more restaurants that offer table service and more varied menus—requiring waiters and waitresses and hosts and hostesses. Employment of fast-food workers also is expected to increase in response to the continuing fast-paced lifestyle of many Americans and the addition of healthier foods at many of these restaurants. However, little change is expected in the employment of dining room attendants, as waiters and waitresses increasingly assume their duties. Employment of bartenders is expected to decline as drinking of alcoholic beverages outside the home—particularly cocktails—continues to drop.

Earnings

Food and beverage service workers derive their earnings from a combination of hourly wages and customer tips. Earnings vary greatly, depending on the type of job and establishment. For example, fast-food workers and hosts and hostesses usually do not receive tips, so their wage rates may be higher than those of waiters and waitresses and bartenders, who may earn more from tips than from wages. In some restaurants, these workers contribute a portion of their tips to a tip pool, which is distributed among the establishment's other food and beverage service workers and kitchen staff. Tip pools allow workers who normally do not receive tips, such as dining room attendants, to share in the rewards of a well-served meal.

In 1998, median hourly earnings (not including tips) of full-time waiters and waitresses were $5.85. The middle 50 percent earned between $5.58 and $6.32; the top 10 percent earned at least $7.83. For most waiters and waitresses, higher earnings are primarily the result of receiving more in tips rather than higher hourly wages. Tips usually average between 10 and 20 percent of guests' checks, so waiters and waitresses working in busy, expensive restaurants earn the most.

Full-time bartenders had median hourly earnings (not including tips) of $6.25 in 1998. The middle 50 percent earned from $5.72 and $7.71; the top 10 percent earned at least $9.19 an hour. Like waiters and waitresses, bartenders employed in public bars may receive more than half of their earnings as tips. Service bartenders are often paid higher hourly wages to offset their lower tip earnings.

Median weekly hourly earnings (not including tips) of full-time dining room attendants and bartender helpers were $6.03 in 1998. The middle 50 percent earned between $5.67 and $7.11; the top 10 percent earned over $8.49 an hour. Most received over half of their earnings as wages; the rest of their income was a share of the proceeds from tip pools.

Full-time counter attendants and fast-food workers, except cooks, had median hourly earnings (not including tips) of $6.06 in 1998. The middle 50 percent earned between $5.67 and $7.14, while the highest 10 percent earned over $8.45 a hour. Although some counter attendants receive part of their earnings as tips, fast-food workers usually do not.

In establishments covered by Federal law, most workers beginning at the minimum wage earned $5.15 an hour in 1998. However, various minimum wage exceptions apply under specific circumstances to disabled workers, full-time students, youth under age 20 in their first 90 days of employment, tipped employees, and student-learners. Employers are also permitted to deduct from wages the cost, or fair value, of any meals or lodging provided. However, many employers provide free meals and furnish uniforms. Food and beverage service workers who work full time often receive typical benefits, while part-time workers usually do not.

In some large restaurants and hotels, food and beverage service workers belong to unions—principally the Hotel Employees and Restaurant Employees International Union and the Service Employees International Union.

Related Occupations

Other workers whose jobs involve serving customers and helping them enjoy themselves include flight attendants, butlers, and tour bus drivers.

Sources of Additional Information

Information about job opportunities may be obtained from local employers and local offices of the State employment service.

A guide to careers in restaurants, a list of 2- and 4-year colleges that have food service programs, and information on scholarships to those programs is available from:

☛ National Restaurant Association, 1200 17th St. NW., Washington, DC 20036-3097.

For general information on hospitality careers, write to:

☛ Council on Hotel, Restaurant, and Institutional Education, 1200 17th St. NW., Washington, DC 20036-3097.

Health Service Occupations

Dental Assistants

(O*NET 66002)

Significant Points

- Rapid employment growth and above average job turnover should result in good job opportunities.
- Population growth and greater retention of natural teeth by middle-aged and older people will fuel demand for dental services, and create opportunities for dental assistants.
- Dentists are expected to hire more assistants to perform routine tasks, so they may devote their own time to more profitable procedures.

Nature of the Work

Dental assistants perform a variety of patient care, office, and laboratory duties. They work at chair-side as dentists examine and treat patients. They make patients as comfortable as possible in the dental chair, prepare them for treatment, and obtain dental records. Assistants hand instruments and materials to dentists, and keep patients' mouths dry and clear by using suction or other devices. Assistants also sterilize and disinfect instruments and equipment, prepare tray setups for dental procedures, and instruct patients on postoperative and general oral health care.

Some dental assistants prepare materials for making impressions and restorations, expose radiographs, and process dental x-ray film as directed by a dentist. They may also remove sutures, apply anesthetics and cavity preventive agents to teeth and gums, remove excess cement used in the filling process, and place rubber dams on the teeth to isolate them for individual treatment.

Those with laboratory duties make casts of the teeth and mouth from impressions taken by dentists, clean and polish removable appliances, and make temporary crowns. Dental assistants with office duties schedule and confirm appointments, receive patients, keep treatment records, send bills, receive payments, and order dental supplies and materials.

Dental assistants should not be confused with dental hygienists, who are licensed to perform different clinical tasks. (See the statement on dental hygienists elsewhere in the *Handbook*.)

Dental assistants hand instruments and materials to dentists and keep patients' mouths dry and clear.

Working Conditions

Dental assistants work in a well-lighted, clean environment. Their work area is usually near the dental chair, so they can arrange instruments, materials, and medication, and hand them to the dentist when needed. Dental assistants wear gloves and masks to protect themselves from infectious diseases. Following safety procedures minimizes the risks of handling radiographic equipment.

Most dental assistants have a 32- to 40-hour workweek, which may include work on Saturdays or evenings.

Employment

Dental assistants held about 229,000 jobs in 1998. More than 3 out of 10 worked part time, sometimes in more than one dental office.

Virtually all dental assistants work in a private dental office. A small number work in dental schools, private and government hospitals, State and local public health departments, or in clinics.

Training, Other Qualifications, and Advancement

Most assistants learn their skills on the job, though some are trained in dental assisting programs offered by community and junior colleges, trade schools, technical institutes, or the Armed Forces. Assistants must be a dentist's "third hand"; therefore, dentists look for people who are reliable, can work well with others, and have good manual dexterity. High school students interested in a career as a dental assistant should take courses in biology, chemistry, health, and office practices.

The American Dental Association's Commission on Dental Accreditation approved 251 dental assisting training programs in 1999. Programs include classroom, laboratory, and preclinical instruction in dental assisting skills and related theory. In addition, students gain practical experience in dental schools, clinics, or dental offices. Most programs take 1 year or less to complete and lead to a certificate or diploma. Two-year programs offered in community and junior colleges lead to an associate degree. All programs require a high school diploma or its equivalent, and some require a typing or science course for admission. Some private vocational schools offer 4- to 6-month courses in dental assisting, but the Commission on Dental Accreditation does not accredit these.

Certification is available through the Dental Assisting National Board. Certification is an acknowledgment of an assistant's qualifications and professional competence, and may be an asset when seeking employment. In several States that have adopted standards for dental assistants who perform radiological procedures, completion of the certification examination meets those standards. Candidates may qualify to take the certification examination by graduating from an accredited training program, or by having 2 years of full-time experience as a dental assistant. In addition, applicants must have current certification in cardiopulmonary resuscitation.

Without further education, advancement opportunities are limited. Some dental assistants working the front office become office managers. Others, working chair-side, go back to school to become dental hygienists.

Job Outlook

Job prospects for dental assistants should be good. Employment is expected to grow much faster than the average for all occupations through the year 2008. Also, the proportion of workers leaving the occupation and who must be replaced is above average. Many opportunities are for entry-level positions offering on-the-job training.

Population growth and greater retention of natural teeth by middle-aged and older people will fuel demand for dental services. Older dentists, who are less likely to employ assistants, will leave and be replaced by recent graduates, who are more likely to use one, or even two. In addition, as dentists' workloads increase, they are expected to hire more assistants to perform routine tasks, so they may devote their own time to more profitable procedures.

Numerous job openings for dental assistants will arise from the need to replace assistants who leave the occupation. For many, this entry-level occupation provides basic training and experience and serves as a stepping-stone to more highly skilled and higher paying jobs. Other assistants leave the job to take on family responsibilities, return to school, retire, or for other reasons.

Earnings

Median hourly earnings of dental assistants were $10.88 in 1998. The middle 50 percent earned between $8.94 and $13.11 an hour. The lowest 10 percent earned less than $7.06 and the highest 10 percent earned more than $15.71 an hour.

Related Occupations

Workers in other occupations supporting health practitioners include medical assistants, physical therapist assistants, occupational therapy assistants, pharmacy technicians and assistants, and veterinary assistants.

Sources of Additional Information

Information about career opportunities, scholarships, accredited dental assistant programs, and requirements for certification is available from:

☛ Commission on Dental Accreditation, American Dental Association, 211 E. Chicago Ave., Suite 1814, Chicago, IL 60611. Internet: **http://www.ada.org**

☛ Dental Assisting National Board, Inc., 676 North Saint Clair, Suite 1880, Chicago, IL 60611. Internet: **http://www.dentalassisting.com**

For general information about a career as a dental assistant, including training and continuing education, contact:

☛ American Dental Assistants Association, 203 North LaSalle St., Suite 1320, Chicago, IL 60601.

For information about a career as a dental assistant and schools offering training, contact:

☛ National Association of Health Career Schools, 2301 Academy Dr., Harrisburg, PA 17112.

Information about certification as a dental assistant is available from:

☛ American Medical Technologists, 710 Higgins Rd., Park Ridge, IL 60068-5765. Internet: **http://www.amt1.com**

Medical Assistants

(O*NET 66005 and 66099A)

Significant Points

- Medical assistants is expected to be one of the 10 fastest growing occupations through the year 2008.
- Job prospects should be best for medical assistants with formal training or experience.

Nature of the Work

Medical assistants perform routine administrative and clinical tasks to keep the offices and clinics of physicians, podiatrists, chiropractors, and optometrists running smoothly. They should not be confused with physician assistants who examine, diagnose, and treat patients under the direct supervision of a physician. (Physician assistants are discussed elsewhere in the *Handbook*.)

The duties of medical assistants vary from office to office, depending on office location, size, and specialty. In small practices, medical assistants are usually "generalists," handling both administrative and clinical duties and reporting directly to an office manager, physician, or other health practitioner. Those in large practices tend to specialize in a particular area under the supervision of department administrators.

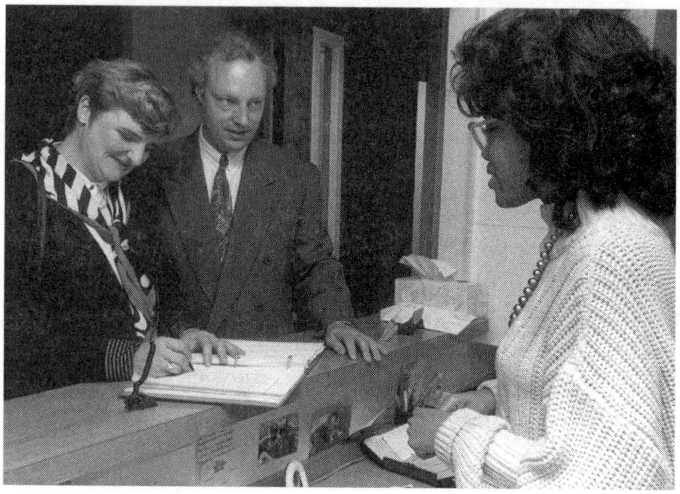

Medical assistants perform many administrative duties.

Medical assistants perform many administrative duties. They answer telephones, greet patients, update and file patient medical records, fill out insurance forms, handle correspondence, schedule appointments, arrange for hospital admission and laboratory services, and handle billing and bookkeeping.

Clinical duties vary according to State law and include taking medical histories and recording vital signs, explaining treatment procedures to patients, preparing patients for examination, and assisting the physician during the examination. Medical assistants collect and prepare laboratory specimens or perform basic laboratory tests on the premises, dispose of contaminated supplies, and sterilize medical instruments. They instruct patients about medication and special diets, prepare and administer medications as directed by a physician, authorize drug refills as directed, telephone prescriptions to a pharmacy, draw blood, prepare patients for x rays, take electrocardiograms, remove sutures, and change dressings.

Medical assistants may also arrange examining room instruments and equipment, purchase and maintain supplies and equipment, and keep waiting and examining rooms neat and clean.

Assistants who specialize have additional duties. *Podiatric medical assistants* make castings of feet, expose and develop x rays, and assist podiatrists in surgery. *Ophthalmic medical assistants* help ophthalmologists provide medical eye care. They administer diagnostic tests, measure and record vision, and test the functioning of eyes and eye muscles. They also show patients how to use eye dressings, protective shields, and safety glasses, and how to insert, remove, and care for contact lenses. Under the direction of the physician, they may administer medications, including eye drops. They also maintain optical and surgical instruments and assist the ophthalmologist in surgery.

Working Conditions

Medical assistants work in well-lighted, clean environments. They constantly interact with other people, and may have to handle several responsibilities at once.

Most full-time medical assistants work a regular 40-hour week. Some work part-time, evenings, or weekends.

Employment

Medical assistants held about 252,000 jobs in 1998. Sixty-five percent were in physicians' offices, and 14 percent were in offices of other health practitioners such as chiropractors, optometrists, and podiatrists. The rest were in hospitals, nursing homes, and other health care facilities.

Training, Other Qualifications, and Advancement

Most employers prefer to hire graduates of formal programs in medical assisting. Such programs are offered in vocational-technical high schools, postsecondary vocational schools, community and junior colleges, and in colleges and universities. Postsecondary programs usually last either 1 year, resulting in a certificate or diploma, or 2 years, resulting in an associate degree. Courses cover anatomy, physiology, and medical terminology as well as typing, transcription, recordkeeping, accounting, and insurance processing. Students learn laboratory techniques, clinical and diagnostic procedures, pharmaceutical principles, medication administration, and first aid. They study office practices, patient relations, medical law, and ethics. Accredited programs include an internship that provides practical experience in physicians' offices, hospitals, or other health care facilities.

Although formal training in medical assisting is available, such training—while generally preferred—is not always required. Some medical assistants are trained on the job, although this is less common than in the past. Applicants usually need a high school diploma or the equivalent. Recommended high school courses include mathematics, health, biology, typing, bookkeeping, computers, and office skills. Volunteer experience in the health care field is also helpful.

Two agencies recognized by the U.S. Department of Education accredit programs in medical assisting: the Commission on Accreditation of Allied Health Education Programs (CAAHEP) and the Accrediting Bureau of Health Education Schools (ABHES). In 1999, there were about 450 medical assisting programs accredited by CAAHEP and over 140 accredited by ABHES. The Committee on Accreditation for Ophthalmic Medical Personnel accredited 14 programs in ophthalmic medical assisting.

Although there is no licensing for medical assistants, some States require them to take a test or a short course before they can take x rays or perform other specific clinical tasks. Employers prefer to hire experienced workers or certified applicants who have passed a national examination, indicating that the medical assistant meets certain standards of competence. The American Association of Medical Assistants awards the Certified Medical Assistant credential; the American Medical Technologists awards the Registered Medical Assistant credential; the American Society of Podiatric Medical Assistants awards the Podiatric Medical Assistant Certified credential; and the Joint Commission on Allied Health Personnel in Ophthalmology awards the Ophthalmic Medical Assistant credential at three levels: Certified Ophthalmic Assistant, Certified Ophthalmic Technician, and Certified Ophthalmic Medical Technologist.

Because medical assistants deal with the public, they must be neat and well-groomed and have a courteous, pleasant manner. Medical assistants must be able to put patients at ease and explain physicians' instructions. They must respect the confidential nature of medical information. Clinical duties require a reasonable level of manual dexterity and visual acuity.

Medical assistants may be able to advance to office manager. They may qualify for a variety of administrative support occupations, or may teach medical assisting. Some, with additional education, enter other health occupations such as nursing and medical technology.

Job Outlook

Employment of medical assistants is expected to grow much faster than the average for all occupations through the year 2008 as the health services industry expands due to technological advances in medicine, and a growing and aging population. It is one of the fastest growing occupations.

Employment growth will be driven by the increase in the number of group practices, clinics, and other health care facilities that need a high proportion of support personnel, particularly the flexible medical assistant who can handle both administrative and clinical duties. Medical assistants primarily work in outpatient settings, where much faster than average growth is expected.

In view of the preference of many health care employers for trained personnel, job prospects should be best for medical assistants with formal training or experience, particularly those with certification.

Earnings

The earnings of medical assistants vary, depending on experience, skill level, and location. Median annual earnings of medical assistants were $20,680 in 1998. The middle 50 percent earned between $17,020 and $24,340 a year. The lowest 10 percent earned less than $14,020 and the highest 10 percent earned more than $28,640 a year. Median annual earnings in the industries employing the largest number of medical assistants in 1997 were as follows:

Offices and clinics of medical doctors	$20,800
Hospitals	20,400
Offices of osteopathic physicians	19,600
Health and allied services, nec	19,300
Offices of other health practitioners	18,500

Related Occupations

Workers in other medical support occupations include medical secretaries, hospital admitting clerks, pharmacy helpers, medical record clerks, dental assistants, occupational therapy aides, and physical therapy aides.

Sources of Additional Information

Information about career opportunities, CAAHEP-accredited educational programs in medical assisting, and the Certified Medical Assistant exam is available from:

☛ The American Association of Medical Assistants, 20 North Wacker Dr., Suite 1575, Chicago, IL 60606-2903.
Internet: **http://www.aama-ntl.org**

Information about career opportunities and the Registered Medical Assistant certification exam is available from:

☛ Registered Medical Assistants of American Medical Technologists, 710 Higgins Rd., Park Ridge, IL 60068-5765.
Internet: **http://www.amt1.com**

For a list of ABHES-accredited educational programs in medical assisting, write:

☛ Accrediting Bureau of Health Education Schools, 803 West Broad St., Suite 730, Falls Church, VA 22046. Internet: **http://www.abhes.org**

For information about a career as a medical assistant and schools offering training, contact:

☛ National Association of Health Career Schools, 2301 Academy Dr., Harrisburg, PA 17112.

Information about career opportunities, training programs, and the Certified Ophthalmic Assistant exam is available from:

☛ Joint Commission on Allied Health Personnel in Ophthalmology, 2025 Woodlane Dr., St. Paul, MN 55125-2995.
Internet: **http://www.jcahpo.org**

Information about careers for podiatric assistants is available from:

☛ American Society of Podiatric Medical Assistants, 2124 S. Austin Blvd., Cicero, IL 60650.

Nursing and Psychiatric Aides

(O*NET 66008 and 66014)

Significant Points

- Job prospects for nursing aides will be good because of fast growth and high turnover in this large occupation.
- Minimum education or training is generally required for entry level jobs, but earnings are low.

Nature of the Work

Nursing and psychiatric aides help care for physically or mentally ill, injured, disabled, or infirm individuals confined to hospitals, nursing or residential care facilities, and mental health settings. (Home health and personal care aides, whose duties are similar but who work in clients' homes, are discussed elsewhere in the *Handbook*.)

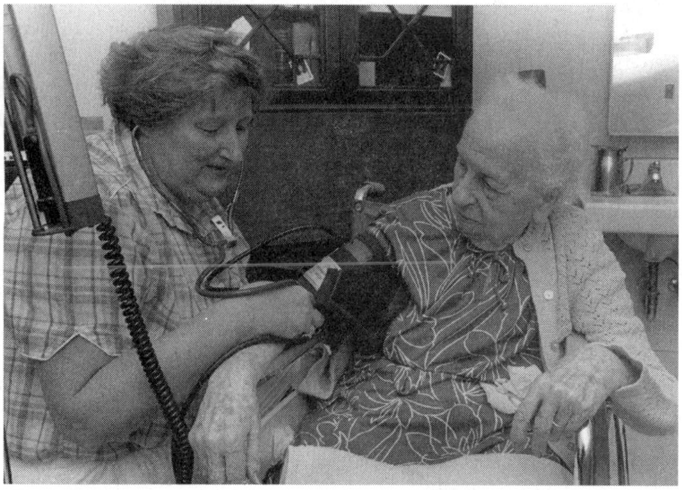

Nursing aides assist nurses in caring for the elderly, usually in nursing homes.

Nursing aides, also known as nursing assistants, geriatric aides, unlicensed assistive personnel, or hospital attendants, perform routine tasks under the supervision of nursing and medical staff. They answer patients' call bells, deliver messages, serve meals, make beds, and help patients eat, dress, and bathe. Aides may also provide skin care to patients; take temperatures, pulse, respiration, and blood pressure; and help patients get in and out of bed and walk. They may also escort patients to operating and examining rooms, keep patients' rooms neat, set up equipment, or store and move supplies. Aides observe patients' physical, mental, and emotional conditions and report any change to the nursing or medical staff.

Nursing aides employed in nursing homes are often the principal caregivers, having far more contact with residents than other members of the staff. Since some residents may stay in a nursing home for months or even years, aides develop ongoing relationships with them and interact with them in a positive, caring way.

Psychiatric aides are also known as mental health assistants and psychiatric nursing assistants. They care for mentally impaired or emotionally disturbed individuals. They work under a team that may include psychiatrists, psychologists, psychiatric nurses, social workers, and therapists. In addition to helping patients dress, bathe, groom, and eat, psychiatric aides socialize with them and lead them in educational and recreational activities. Psychiatric aides may play games such as cards with the patients, watch television with them, or participate in group activities such as sports or field trips. They observe patients and report any physical or behavioral signs which might be important for the professional staff to know. They accompany patients to and from wards for examination and treatment. Because they have the closest contact with patients, psychiatric aides have a great deal of influence on their outlook and treatment.

Working Conditions

Most full-time aides work about 40 hours a week, but because patients need care 24 hours a day, some aides work evenings, nights, weekends, and holidays. Many work part-time. Aides spend many hours standing and walking, and they often face heavy workloads. Because they may have to move patients in and out of bed or help them stand or walk, aides must guard against back injury. Nursing aides may also face hazards from minor infections and major diseases such as hepatitis, but can avoid infections by following proper procedures.

Nursing aides often have unpleasant duties; they empty bed pans and change soiled bed linens. The patients they care for may be disoriented, irritable, or uncooperative. Psychiatric aides must be prepared to care for patients whose illness may cause violent behavior. While their work can be emotionally demanding, many aides gain satisfaction from assisting those in need.

Employment

Nursing aides held about 1.4 million jobs in 1998, and psychiatric aides held about 95,000 jobs. About one-half of all nursing aides worked in nursing homes, and about one-fourth worked in hospitals. Others worked in residential care facilities, such as halfway houses and homes for the aged or disabled, or in private households. Most psychiatric aides worked in psychiatric units of general hospitals, psychiatric hospitals, State and county mental institutions, homes for mentally retarded and psychiatric patients, and community mental health centers.

Training, Other Qualifications, and Advancement

In many cases, neither a high school diploma nor previous work experience is necessary for a job as a nursing or psychiatric aide. A few employers, however, require some training or experience. Hospitals may require experience as a nursing aide or home health aide. Nursing homes often hire inexperienced workers who must complete a minimum of 75 hours of mandatory training and pass a competency evaluation program within 4 months of employment. Aides who complete the program are placed on the State registry of nursing aides. Some States require psychiatric aides to complete a formal training program.

These occupations can offer individuals an entry into the world of work. The flexibility of night and weekend hours also provides high school and college students a chance to work during the school year.

Nursing aide training is offered in high schools, vocational-technical centers, some nursing homes, and community colleges. Courses cover body mechanics, nutrition, anatomy and physiology, infection control, communication skills, and resident rights. Personal care skills such as how to help patients bathe, eat, and groom are also taught.

Some facilities, other than nursing homes, provide classroom instruction for newly hired aides, while others rely exclusively on informal on-the-job instruction from a licensed nurse or an experienced aide. Such training may last several days to a few months. From time to time, aides may also attend lectures, workshops, and in-service training.

Applicants should be healthy, tactful, patient, understanding, emotionally stable, dependable, and have a desire to help people. They should also be able to work as part of a team, have good communication skills, and be willing to perform repetitive, routine tasks.

Opportunities for advancement within these occupations are limited. To enter other health occupations, aides generally need additional formal training. Some employers and unions provide opportunities by simplifying the educational paths to advancement. Experience as an aide can also help individuals decide whether to pursue a career in the health care field.

Job Outlook

Job prospects for nursing aides should be good through the year 2008. Numerous openings will arise from a combination of fast growth and high turnover for this large occupation. Employment of nursing aides is expected to grow faster than the average for all occupations in response to an emphasis on rehabilitation and the long-term care needs of a rapidly growing elderly population. Employment will increase as a result of the expansion of nursing homes and other long-term care facilities for people with chronic illnesses and disabling conditions, many of whom are elderly. Financial pressure on hospitals to release patients as soon as possible should produce more nursing home admissions. Modern medical technology will also increase the employment of nursing aides. This technology, while saving and extending more lives, increases the need for long-term care provided by aides. As a result, nursing and personal care facilities are expected to grow rapidly and to provide most of the new jobs for nursing aides.

Employment of psychiatric aides is expected to grow slower than the average for all occupations. Employment will rise in response to the sharp increase in the number of older persons—many of whom will require mental health services. Employment of aides in outpatient community mental health centers is likely to grow because of increasing public acceptance of formal treatment for drug abuse and alcoholism, and a lessening of the stigma attached to those receiving mental health care. However, employment in hospitals—where one-half of psychiatric aides work—is likely to decline due to attempts to contain costs by limiting inpatient psychiatric treatment.

Replacement needs will constitute the major source of openings for aides. Turnover is high, a reflection of modest entry requirements, low pay, and lack of advancement opportunities.

Earnings

Median hourly earnings of nursing aides, orderlies, and attendants were $7.99 in 1998. The middle 50 percent earned between $6.72 and $9.54 an hour. The lowest 10 percent earned less than $5.87 and the highest 10 percent earned more than $11.33 an hour. Median hourly earnings in the industries employing the largest number of nursing aides, orderlies, and attendants in 1997 were as follows:

Local government, except education and hospitals	$9.20
Hospitals	8.10
Personnel supply services	8.10
Nursing and personal care facilities	7.50
Residential care	7.20

Median hourly earnings of psychiatric aides were $10.66 in 1998. The middle 50 percent earned between $8.33 and $13.36 an hour. The lowest 10 percent earned less than $6.87 and the highest 10 percent earned more than $15.28 an hour. Median hourly earnings of psychiatric aides in 1997 were $11.20 in State government and $9.80 in hospitals.

Aides in hospitals generally receive at least 1 week's paid vacation after 1 year of service. Paid holidays and sick leave, hospital and medical benefits, extra pay for late-shift work, and pension plans also are available to many hospital and some nursing home employees.

Related Occupations

Nursing and psychiatric aides help people who need routine care or treatment. So do home health and personal care aides, child-care workers, companions, occupational therapy aides, and physical therapy aides.

Sources of Additional Information

Information about employment opportunities may be obtained from local hospitals, nursing homes, psychiatric facilities, State boards of nursing and local offices of the State employment service.

For information about a career as a nursing aide and schools offering training, contact:

☛ National Association of Health Career Schools, 2301 Academy Dr., Harrisburg, PA 17112.

Occupational Therapy Assistants and Aides

(O*NET 66021)

Significant Points

- Qualifications of occupational therapy assistants are regulated by the States and these workers must complete an associate's degree or certificate program. In contrast, occupational therapy aides usually receive most of their training on the job.
- Aides are not licensed, so by law they are not allowed to perform as wide a range of tasks as occupational therapy assistants do.

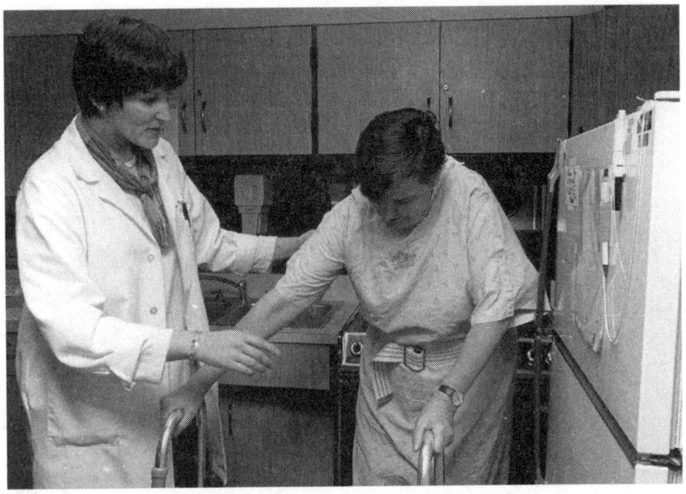

Occupational therapy assistants and aides help disabled patients function in home settings.

- Employment is projected to increase over the 1998-2008 period, but due to the effects of Federal limits on reimbursement for therapy services, the majority of expected employment growth is expected to occur during the second half of the projection period.

Nature of the Work

Occupational therapy assistants and aides work under the direction of occupational therapists to provide rehabilitative services to persons with mental, physical, emotional, or developmental impairments. The ultimate goal is to improve clients' quality of life by helping them compensate for limitations. For example, occupational therapy assistants help injured workers re-enter the labor force by helping them improve their motor skills or help persons with learning disabilities increase their independence, by teaching them to prepare meals or use public transportation.

Occupational therapy assistants help clients with rehabilitative activities and exercises outlined in a treatment plan developed in collaboration with an occupational therapist. Activities range from teaching the proper method of moving from a bed into a wheelchair, to the best way to stretch and limber the muscles of the hand. Assistants monitor an individual's activities to make sure they are performed correctly and to provide encouragement. They also record their client's progress for use by the occupational therapist. If the treatment is not having the intended effect, or the client is not improving as expected, the therapist may alter the treatment program in hopes of obtaining better results. In addition, occupational therapy assistants document billing of the client's health insurance provider.

Occupational therapy aides typically prepare materials and assemble equipment used during treatment and are responsible for a range of clerical tasks. Duties can include scheduling appointments, answering the telephone, restocking or ordering depleted supplies, and filling out insurance forms or other paperwork. Aides are not licensed, so by law they are not allowed to perform as wide a range of tasks as occupational therapy assistants do.

Working Conditions

Occupational therapy assistants and aides usually work during the day, but may occasionally work evenings or weekends, to accommodate a client's schedule. These workers should be in good physical condition, because they are on their feet for long periods of time and may be asked to help lift and move clients or equipment.

Employment
Occupational therapy assistants and aides held 19,000 jobs in 1998. About 4 out of 10 assistants and aides worked in offices of occupational therapists; and about 3 out of 10 worked in hospitals. The remainder worked primarily in nursing and personal care facilities, offices and clinics of physicians, social services agencies, outpatient rehabilitation centers, and home health agencies.

Training, Other Qualifications, and Advancement
Persons must complete an associate's degree or certificate program from an accredited community college or technical school to qualify for occupational therapy assistant jobs. In contrast, occupational therapy aides usually receive most of their training on the job.

There were 165 accredited occupational therapy assistant programs in the United States in 1999. The first year of study typically involves an introduction to healthcare, basic medical terminology, anatomy, and physiology. In the second year, courses are more rigorous and usually include occupational therapy courses in areas such as mental health, gerontology, and pediatrics. Students must also complete supervised fieldwork in a clinic or community setting. Applicants to occupational therapy assistant programs can improve their chances of admission by taking high school courses in biology and health and by performing volunteer work in nursing homes, occupational or physical therapist's offices, or elsewhere in the healthcare field.

Occupational therapy assistants are regulated in most States, and must pass a national certification examination after they graduate. Those who pass the test are awarded the title of certified occupational therapy assistant.

Occupational therapy aides usually receive most of their training on the job. Qualified applicants must have a high school diploma, strong interpersonal skills, and a desire to help people in need. Applicants may increase their chances of getting a job by volunteering their services, thus displaying initiative and aptitude to the employer.

Assistants and aides must be responsible, patient, and willing to take directions and work as part of a team. Furthermore, they should be caring and want to help people who are not able to help themselves.

Job Outlook
Employment of occupational therapy assistants and aides is expected to grow much faster than the average for all occupations through 2008. Growth will result from an aging population, including the baby-boom cohort, which will probably need substantial occupational therapy services. Demand will also result from advances in medicine that allow more people with critical problems to survive and then need rehabilitative therapy.

Employment growth would be even faster, except for Federal legislation imposing limits on reimbursement for therapy services. However, at the same time, third-party payers, concerned with rising health care costs are beginning to encourage occupational therapists to delegate more of the hands-on therapy work to occupational therapy assistants and aides. By having assistants and aides work more closely with clients under the guidance of a therapist, the cost of therapy should be more modest than otherwise.

Earnings
Median annual earnings of occupational therapy assistants and aides were $28,690 in 1998. The middle 50 percent earned between $20,050 and $36,900 a year. The lowest 10 percent earned less than $15,000 and the highest 10 percent earned more than $45,740 a year. Median annual earnings of occupational therapy assistants and aides in 1997 were $32,200 in offices of other health care practitioners and $27,000 in hospitals.

Related Occupations
Occupational therapy assistants and aides work under the direction of occupational therapists. Other occupations in the healthcare field that work under the supervision of professionals include dental assistants, medical assistants, optometric assistants, pharmacy assistants, and physical therapy assistants and aides.

Sources of Additional Information
Information on a career as an occupational therapy assistant and a list of accredited programs can be obtained by sending a self-addressed label and $5.00 to:

☛ The American Occupational Therapy Association, 4720 Montgomery Ln., P.O. Box 31220, Bethesda, MD 20824-1220. Internet: **http://www.aota.org**

Physical Therapist Assistants and Aides

(O*NET 66017)

Significant Points

- Employment is projected to increase over the 1998-2008 period, but due to the effects of Federal limits on reimbursement for therapy services, the majority of expected employment growth is expected to occur during the second half of the projection period.
- Most licensed physical therapist assistants have an associate's degree, but physical therapist aides usually learn skills on the job.
- Two-thirds of jobs for physical therapist assistants and aides were in hospitals or offices of physical therapists.

Nature of the Work
Physical therapist assistants and aides perform components of physical therapy procedures and related tasks selected and delegated by a supervising physical therapist. These workers assist physical therapists in providing services that help improve mobility, relieve pain, and prevent or limit permanent physical disabilities of patients suffering from injuries or disease. Patients include accident victims and individuals with disabling conditions, such as low back pain, arthritis, heart disease, fractures, head injuries, and cerebral palsy.

Physical therapist assistants perform a variety of tasks. Treatment procedures delegated to these workers, under the direction of therapists, involve exercises, massages, electrical stimulation, paraffin baths, hot and cold packs, traction, and ultrasound. Physical therapist assistants record the patient's responses to treatment and report to the physical therapist the outcome of each treatment.

Physical therapist aides help make therapy sessions productive, under the direct supervision of a physical therapist or physical therapist assistant. They are usually responsible for keeping the treatment area clean and organized and preparing for each patient's therapy. When patients need assistance moving to or from a treatment area, aides push them in a wheelchair, or provide them with a shoulder to lean on. Because they are not licensed, aides perform a more limited range of tasks than physical therapist assistants do.

The duties of aides include some clerical tasks, such as ordering depleted supplies, answering the phone, and filling out insurance forms and other paperwork. The extent to which an aide or an assistant performs clerical tasks depends on the size and location of the facility.

Working Conditions
The hours and days that physical therapist assistants and aides work vary, depending on the facility and whether they are full or part-time employees. Many outpatient physical therapy offices and clinics have evening and weekend hours, to help coincide with patients' personal schedules.

Physical therapist assistants and aides need to have a moderate degree of strength, due to the physical exertion required in assisting patients with their treatment. For example, in some cases, assistants and aides need to help lift patients. Additionally, constant kneeling, stooping, and standing for long periods are all part of the job.

Employment

Physical therapist assistants and aides held 82,000 jobs in 1998. They work alongside physical therapists in a variety of settings. Over two-thirds of all assistants and aides work in hospitals or offices of physical therapists. Others work in nursing and personal care facilities, outpatient rehabilitation centers, offices and clinics of physicians, and home health agencies.

Training, Other Qualifications, and Advancement

Physical therapist aides are trained on the job, but physical therapist assistants typically have earned an associate's degree from an accredited physical therapist assistant program. As of January 1997, 44 States and Puerto Rico regulated assistants. Additional requirements include certification in CPR and other first aid and a minimum number of hours of clinical experience.

According to the American Physical Therapy Association, there were 274 accredited physical therapist assistant programs in the United States as of 1999. Accredited physical therapist assistant programs are designed to last 2 years, or four semesters, and culminate in an associate's degree. Admission into physical therapist assistant programs is competitive, and it is not unusual for colleges to have long waiting lists of prospective candidates. Programs are divided into academic study and hands on clinical experience. Academic coursework includes algebra, anatomy and physiology, biology, chemistry, and psychology. Before students begin their clinical field experience, many programs require that they complete a semester of anatomy and physiology and have certifications in CPR and other first aid. Both educators and prospective employers view clinical experience as an integral part of ensuring that students understand the responsibilities of a physical therapist assistant.

A physical therapy aide prepares a pack for moist heat therapy.

Employers typically require physical therapist aides to have a high school diploma, strong interpersonal skills, and a desire to assist people in need. Most employers provide clinical on-the-job training.

Job Outlook

Employment of physical therapist assistants and aides is expected to grow much faster than the average through the year 2008. However, Federal legislation imposing limits on reimbursement for therapy services may continue to adversely affect the job market for physical therapist assistants and aides in the near term. Because of the effects of these provisions, the majority of expected employment growth for physical therapist assistants and aides is expected to occur in the second half of the projection period.

Over the long run, demand for physical therapist assistants and aides will continue to rise, with growth in the number of individuals with disabilities or limited function. The rapidly growing elderly population is particularly vulnerable to chronic and debilitating conditions that require therapeutic services. These patients often need additional assistance in their treatment, making the roles of assistants and aides vital. The large baby-boom generation is entering the prime age for heart attacks and strokes, further increasing the demand for cardiac and physical rehabilitation. Additionally, future medical developments should permit an increased percentage of trauma victims to survive, creating added demand for therapy services.

Licensed physical therapist assistants can enhance the cost-effective provision of physical therapy services. Once a patient is evaluated, and a treatment plan is designed by the physical therapist, the physical therapist assistant can provide many aspects of treatment, as prescribed by the therapist.

Earnings

Median annual earnings of physical therapist assistants and aides were \$21,870 in 1998. The middle 50 percent earned between \$16,700 and \$31,260 a year. The lowest 10 percent earned less than \$13,760 and the highest 10 percent earned more than \$39,730 a year. Median annual earnings in the industries employing the largest number of physical therapist assistants and aides in 1997 were as follows:

Industry	Earnings
Hospitals	\$21,200
Offices of other health care practitioners	20,700
Nursing and personal care facilities	19,200

Related Occupations

Physical therapist assistants and aides work under the supervision of physical therapists. Other assistants and aides in the health care field that work under the supervision of professionals include dental, medical, occupational therapy, optometric, podiatric, recreational therapy, and pharmacy assistants.

Sources of Additional Information

Information on a career as a physical therapist assistant and a list of schools offering accredited programs can be obtained from:

☛ The American Physical Therapy Association, 1111 North Fairfax Street, Alexandria, VA 22314-1488. Internet: **http://www.apta.org**

Personal Service Occupations

Barbers, Cosmetologists, and Related Workers

(O*NET 68002, 68005A, 68005B, 68005C, and 68008)

Significant Points

- Job opportunities for cosmetologists should be excellent, as employers report difficulties finding qualified workers to meet the growing demand for cosmetology services.
- All barbers and cosmetologists must be licensed.
- Very high proportions of these workers are self-employed or work flexible schedules.

Nature of the Work

Looking your best has never been easy. It requires the perfect hairstyle, exquisite nails, a neatly trimmed beard, or the proper make-up to accent your coloring. More and more, it also requires the services of barbers and cosmetologists. As people increasingly demand styles that are better suited to their individual characteristics, they must choose from a vast array of cosmetic products and rely on these professionals to help them make sense of the different options. Although tastes and fashions change from year to year, the basic task of barbers and cosmetologists has remained the same—helping people to look their best.

Barbers cut, trim, shampoo, and style hair. Many people still go to a barber for a haircut, but an increasing number seek more personalized hairstyling services, such as perms or coloring. In addition to these services, barbers may fit hairpieces, provide hair and scalp treatments, shave male customers, or give facial massages. Barbers in most States are licensed to perform all the duties of cosmetologists except skin care and nail treatment, but a growing number of barbers are trained to perform these services as well.

Cosmetologists primarily shampoo, cut, and style hair, but they also perform a number of other services. These workers, who are often called hairstylists, may advise patrons on how to care for their hair, straighten or permanent wave a customer's hair, or lighten or darken hair color. In addition, most cosmetologists are trained to give manicures, pedicures, and scalp and facial treatments; provide makeup analysis for women; and clean and style wigs and hairpieces. Cosmetologists are licensed to provide all the services of barbers except shaving men.

A growing number of workers in cosmetology offer specialized services. The largest and fastest growing of these is manicurists, who work exclusively on nails and provide manicures, pedicures, and nail extensions to clients. Another group of specialists is estheticians, who cleanse and beautify the skin by giving facials, full-body treatments, head and neck massages, and offer hair-removal through waxing. Electrologists use an electrolysis machine to remove hair. Finally, shampooers specialize in shampooing and conditioning patrons' hair in some larger salons.

In addition to their work with customers, barbers and cosmetologists are expected to keep their work area clean and their hairdressing implements sanitized. They may make appointments and keep records of hair color and permanent wave formulas used by their regular patrons. A growing number also actively sell hair products and other cosmetic supplies. Barbers and cosmetologists who operate their own salons have managerial duties that include hiring, supervising, and firing workers, as well as keeping records and ordering supplies.

Working Conditions

Barbers and cosmetologists work in clean, pleasant surroundings with good lighting and ventilation. Good health and stamina are important because these workers are on their feet for most of their shift. Prolonged exposure to some hair and nail chemicals may be hazardous and cause irritation, so special care must be taken.

Most full-time barbers and cosmetologists work 40 hours a week, but longer hours are common in this occupation, especially among self-employed workers. Work schedules may include evenings and weekends, when beauty and barber shops and salons are busiest. Although weekends and lunch periods are usually very busy, barbers and cosmetologists are able to take breaks during less popular times. Nearly half of all cosmetologists work part time or have variable schedules, double the rate for barbers and for all other workers in the economy.

Employment

Barbers and cosmetologists held 723,000 jobs in 1998. Employment in these occupations is distributed as follows:

Hairdressers, hairstylists, and cosmetologists	605,000
Barbers	54,000
Manicurists	49,000
Shampooers	15,000

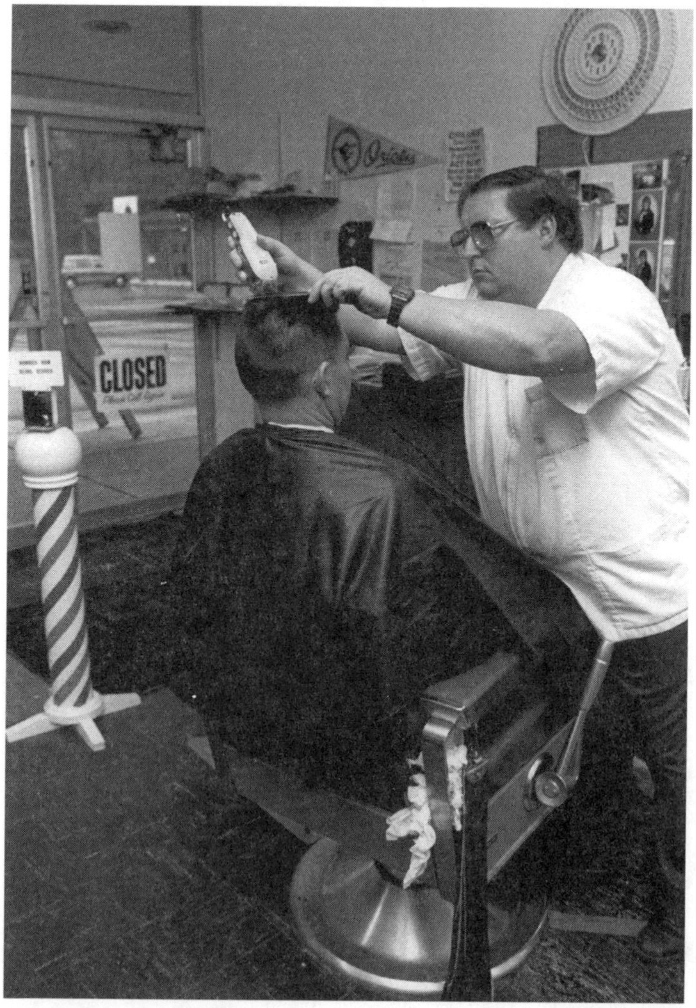

Barbers and cosmetologists should enjoy working with the public.

Most of these workers are employed in beauty salons, barber shops, or department stores, but they are also found in nursing and other residential care homes, drug and cosmetics stores, and photographic studios. Nearly every town has a barber shop or beauty salon, but employment in this occupation is concentrated in the most populous cities and States. Hairstylists usually work in cities and suburbs, where the greatest demand for their services exists.

Approximately 3 of every 4 barbers and 2 in 5 cosmetologists are self-employed. Many self-employed barbers and cosmetologists own the salon in which they work, but a growing share of these workers lease the booth or chair where they work from the salon's owner.

Training, Other Qualifications, and Advancement
Although all States require barbers and cosmetologists to be licensed, the qualifications for a license vary. Generally, a person must have graduated from a State-licensed barber or a cosmetology school and be at least 16 years old. A few States require applicants to pass a physical examination. Some States require graduation from high school while others require as little as an eighth grade education. In a few States, completion of an apprenticeship can substitute for graduation from a school, but very few barbers or cosmetologists learn their skills in this way. Applicants for a license usually are required to pass a written test and demonstrate an ability to perform basic barbering or cosmetology services.

Some States have reciprocity agreements that allow licensed barbers and cosmetologists to practice in a different State without additional formal training. Other States do not recognize training or licenses obtained in another State; consequently, persons who wish to become a barber or a cosmetologist should review the laws of the State in which they want to work before entering a training program.

Public and private vocational schools offer daytime or evening classes in barbering and cosmetology. Full-time programs in barbering and cosmetology usually last 10 to 24 months, but training for manicurists, estheticians, and electrologists requires significantly less time. An apprenticeship program can last from 1 to 3 years. Formal training programs include classroom study, demonstrations, and practical work. Students study the basic services—haircutting, shaving, facial massaging, and hair and scalp treatments—and, under supervision, practice on customers in school "clinics." Most schools also teach unisex hairstyling and chemical styling. Students attend lectures on the use and care of instruments, sanitation and hygiene, chemistry, basic anatomy and physiology, and recognition of certain skin ailments. Instruction also is provided in communication, sales, and general business practices. There are advanced courses for experienced barbers and cosmetologists in hairstyling, coloring, and the sale and service of hairpieces. Most schools teach hairstyling of men's as well as women's hair.

After graduating from a training program, students can take the State licensing examination. The examination consists of a written test and, in some cases, a practical test of cosmetology skills based on established performance criteria. A few States include an oral examination in which the applicant is asked to explain the procedures he or she is following while taking the practical test. In many States, cosmetology training may be credited towards a barbering license, and vice versa. A few States have even combined the two licenses into one hair styling license. In most States, a separate examination is given for people who want only a manicurist, esthetician, or electrolysis license.

For many barbers and cosmetologists, formal training and a license are only the first steps in a career that requires years of continuing education. Because hairstyles are constantly changing, barbers and cosmetologists must keep abreast of the latest fashions and beauty techniques. They do this by attending training in salons, at cosmetology schools, or at product shows. These shows offer workshops and demonstrations of the latest techniques and expose cosmetologists to a wide range of products that they can recommend to clients—an important skill as retail sales become a more important part of the salon industry.

Successful barbers or cosmetologists should have an understanding of fashion, art, and technical design. They should enjoy dealing with the public and be willing and able to follow patrons' instructions. Communication, image, and attitude also play an important role in career success. In fact, some cosmetology schools consider "people" skills to be such an integral part of the job that they require coursework in this area. Business skills are important for those who plan to operate their own salons, and the ability to be an effective salesperson is becoming vital for nearly all barbers and cosmetologists.

During their first months on the job, new workers are given relatively simple tasks or are assigned the simpler hairstyling patterns. Once they have demonstrated their skills, they are gradually permitted to perform the more complicated tasks such as giving shaves, coloring hair, or applying a permanent. As they continue to work in the field, more training is usually required to learn the techniques used in each salon and to build on the basics learned in cosmetology school.

Advancement usually takes the form of higher earnings as barbers and cosmetologists gain experience and build a steady clientele. Some barbers and cosmetologists manage large salons or open their own after several years of experience. Others teach in barber or cosmetology schools. Other options include becoming sales representatives for cosmetics firms, opening businesses as beauty or fashion consultants, or working as examiners for State licensing boards.

Job Outlook
Overall employment of barbers and cosmetologists is projected to grow about as fast as the average for all occupations through 2008, stemming from increasing population, incomes, and demand for cosmetology services. Job opportunities should be excellent as a growing number of employers report difficulties finding qualified applicants. In addition, numerous job openings will arise from turnover in this large occupation. Competition is expected for jobs and customers at the higher paying, prestigious salons, as applicants vie with a large pool of licensed and experienced cosmetologists. The number of self-employed, booth-renting cosmetologists should continue to grow, and opportunities will be better for those licensed to provide a broad range of cosmetology services.

Different employment trends are expected among the various specialties within this occupational grouping. Although employment of barbers is expected to decline, those entering the occupation should have good job prospects due to a large number of retirements, the return of men to barber shops, and the relatively small number of beauty school graduates opting to obtain barbering licenses. Within cosmetology, a surge in the demand for coloring services by teenagers and aging baby boomers, including men, will create many job openings for cosmetologists. Also, the rapid growth in the number of spa salons that provide a full range of services, including beauty wraps, pedicures, and massages, will generate numerous job openings for estheticians and cosmetologists trained to provide skin care services. In addition, jobs for manicurists will continue to climb.

Earnings
Barbers and cosmetologists receive income from a variety of sources. They may receive commissions based on the price of the service or a salary based on number of hours worked. All receive tips and many receive commissions on the products they sell. In addition, some salons pay bonuses to employees who bring in new business.

Median annual earnings in 1998 for full-time cosmetologists, the largest occupation in this category, were $15,150, excluding tips. The middle 50 percent earned between $12,270 and $20,540. The lowest 10 percent had earnings of less than $11,510, while the top 10 percent earned over $27,270. Median annual earnings, excluding tips, in the industries employing the largest number of hairdressers, hair stylists, and cosmetologists in 1997 were:

Beauty shops	$15,800
Drug and proprietary stores	12,500
Department stores	11,600

Among others in this occupational grouping, median annual earnings in 1998 for those working full time were $18,470 for barbers; $13,490 for manicurists; and $12,570 for shampooers. These numbers exclude tips.

A number of factors determine the total income for barbers and cosmetologists, including the size and location of the salon, the number of hours worked, customers' tipping habits, and the competition from other barber shops and salons. A cosmetologist's or barber's initiative and ability to attract and hold regular customers also are key factors in determining their earnings. Earnings for entry-level workers are usually low; however, for those who stay in the profession, earnings can be considerably higher.

Although some salons offer paid vacations and medical benefits, many self-employed and part-time workers in this occupation do not enjoy such common benefits.

Related Occupations

Other workers whose main activity consists of improving a patron's personal appearance include beauty consultants and make-up and wig specialists. Other related workers are employed in the beauty salon industry as instructors, beauty supply distributors, and salon managers.

Sources of Additional Information

A list of licensed training schools and licensing requirements for cosmetologists can be obtained from:

☛ National Accrediting Commission of Cosmetology Arts and Sciences, 901 North Stuart St., Suite 900, Arlington, VA 22203-1816. Internet: **http://www.naccas.org**

Information about a career in cosmetology is available from:

☛ National Cosmetology Association, 401 N. Michigan Ave., 22nd floor, Chicago, IL 60611. Internet: **http://www.nca-now.com**

For details on State licensing requirements and approved barber or cosmetology schools, contact the State board of barber examiners or the State board of cosmetology in your State capital.

Flight Attendants

(O*NET 68026)

Significant Points

- Job duties are learned through intensive formal training after being hired.
- The opportunity for travel attracts many to this career, but the job requires working nights, weekends, and holidays and frequently being away from home.

Nature of the Work

Major airlines are required by law to provide flight attendants for the safety of the flying public. Although the primary job of the flight attendants is to ensure that safety regulations are adhered to, they also try to make flights comfortable and enjoyable for passengers.

At least 1 hour before each flight, flight attendants are briefed by the captain, the pilot in command, on such things as emergency evacuation procedures, crew coordination, length of flights, expected weather conditions, and special passenger problems. Flight attendants make sure that first aid kits and other emergency equipment are aboard and in working order and that the passenger cabin is in order, with adequate supplies of food, beverages, and blankets. As passengers board the plane, flight attendants greet them, check their tickets, and instruct them on where to store coats and carry-on items.

Before the plane takes off, flight attendants instruct all passengers in the use of emergency equipment and check to see that seat belts are fastened, seat backs are in upright positions, and all carry-on items are properly stowed. In the air, helping passengers in the event of an emergency is the most important responsibility of a flight attendant. Safety-related actions may range from reassuring passengers during occasional encounters with strong turbulence to directing passengers who must evacuate a plane following an emergency landing. Flight attendants also answer questions about the flight; distribute reading material, pillows, and blankets; and help small children, elderly or disabled persons, and any others needing assistance. They may administer first aid to passengers who become ill. Flight attendants generally serve beverages and other refreshments and, on many flights, heat and distribute precooked meals or snacks. After the plane has landed, flight attendants take inventory of headsets, alcoholic beverages, and moneys collected. They also report any medical problems passengers may have had, and the condition of cabin equipment.

Lead or first flight attendants, sometimes known as pursers, oversee the work of the other attendants aboard the aircraft, while performing most of the same duties.

Working Conditions

Since airlines operate around the clock year round, flight attendants may work nights, holidays, and weekends. They usually fly 75 to 85 hours a month and, in addition generally spend about 75 to 85 hours a month on the ground preparing planes for flights, writing reports following completed flights, and waiting for planes to arrive. Because of variations in scheduling and limitations on flying time, many flight attendants have 11 or more days off each month. They may be away from their home base at least one-third of the time. During this period, the airlines provide hotel accommodations and an allowance for meal expenses.

The combination of free time and discount air fares provides flight attendants the opportunity to travel and see new places. However, the work can be strenuous and trying. Short flights require speedy service if meals are served and turbulent flights can make serving drinks and meals difficult. Flight attendants stand during much of the flight and must remain pleasant and efficient regardless of how tired they are or how demanding passengers may be. Occasionally, flight attendants must deal with disruptive passengers.

Flight attendants are susceptible to injuries because of the job demands in a moving aircraft. Back injuries and mishaps opening overhead compartments are common. In addition, medical problems can occur from irregular sleeping and eating patterns, dealing with stressful passengers, working in a pressurized environment, and breathing recycled air.

Employment

Flight attendants held about 99,000 jobs in 1998. Commercial airlines employed the vast majority of all flight attendants, most of whom live in the major city that is the airlines' home base. A small number of flight attendants worked for large companies that operated company aircraft for business purposes.

Flight attendants serve beverages and meals.

Training, Other Qualifications, and Advancement
Airlines prefer to hire poised, tactful, and resourceful people who can interact comfortably with strangers and remain calm under duress. Applicants usually must be at least 18 to 21 years old. Flight attendants must have excellent health and the ability to speak clearly. In addition, there generally are height requirements and most airlines want candidates with weight proportionate to height.

Prospective flight attendants usually must be willing to relocate, although some flight attendants are able to commute to and from their home base. Applicants must be high school graduates. Those having several years of college or experience in dealing with the public are preferred. More and more flight attendants being hired are college graduates. Highly desirable areas of concentration include such people oriented disciplines as psychology and education. Flight attendants for international airlines generally must speak an appropriate foreign language fluently. Some of the major airlines prefer candidates who can speak two major foreign languages for their international flights.

Once hired, candidates must undergo a period of training. The length of training depends on the size and type of carrier, ranging from 4 to 7 weeks, and takes place in the airline's flight training center. Airlines that do not operate training centers generally send new employees to the center of another airline. Airlines may provide transportation to the training centers and an allowance for board, room, and school supplies. However, new trainees are not considered employees of the airline until they successfully complete the training program. Some airlines may actually charge individuals for training. Trainees learn emergency procedures such as evacuating an airplane, operating emergency systems and equipment, administering first aid, and water survival tactics. In addition, trainees are taught how to deal with disruptive passengers and hijacking and terrorist situations. New hires learn flight regulations and duties, company operations and policies, and receive instruction on personal grooming and weight control. Trainees for the international routes get additional instruction in passport and customs regulations. Towards the end of their training, students go on practice flights. Additionally, flight attendants must receive 12 to 14 hours of annual training in emergency procedures and passenger relations.

After completing initial training, flight attendants are assigned to one of their airline's bases. New flight attendants are placed on "reserve status" and are called on either to staff extra flights or fill in for crew members who are sick or on vacation or rerouted. When not on duty, reserve flight attendants must be available to report for flights on short notice. They usually remain on reserve for at least 1 year, but in some cities it may take 5 to 10 years or longer to advance from reserve status. Flight attendants who no longer are on reserve bid monthly for regular assignments. Because assignments are based on seniority, usually only the most experienced attendants get their choice of assignments. Advancement takes longer today than in the past because experienced flight attendants are remaining in this career longer than they used to.

Some flight attendants become supervisors, or take on additional duties such as recruiting and instructing.

Job Outlook
Opportunities should be favorable for persons seeking flight attendant jobs because the number of applicants is expected to be roughly the same as the number of job openings. Those with at least 2 years of college and experience in dealing with the public should have the best chance of being hired.

As airline restrictions on employment have been abolished, turnover—which traditionally was very high—has declined. Nevertheless, the majority of job openings through the year 2008 should be due to the need to replace flight attendants who transfer to other occupations or who leave the labor force. Many flight attendants are attracted to the occupation by the glamour of the airline industry and the opportunity to travel, but some eventually leave in search of jobs that offer higher earnings and require fewer nights away from their families.

Employment of flight attendants is expected to grow faster than the average for all occupations through the year 2008. Growth in population and income is expected to increase the number of airline passengers. Airlines enlarge their capacity by increasing the number and size of planes in operation. Since Federal Aviation Administration safety rules require one attendant for every 50 seats, more flight attendants will be needed.

Employment of flight attendants is sensitive to cyclical swings in the economy. During recessions, when the demand for air travel declines, many flight attendants are put on part-time status or laid off. Until demand increases, few new flight attendants are hired.

Earnings
According to data from the Association of Flight Attendants, beginning flight attendants had median earnings of about $13,700 a year in 1998. Flight attendants with 6 years of experience had median annual earnings of about $20,000, while some senior flight attendants earned as much as $50,000 a year.

Beginning pay scales for flight attendants vary by carrier. New hires usually begin at the same pay scale regardless of experience, and all flight attendants receive the same future pay increases. Flight attendants receive extra compensation for night and international flights and for increased hours. In addition, some airlines offer incentive pay for working holidays or taking positions that require additional responsibility or paper work. Most airlines guarantee a minimum of 65 to 75 flight hours per month, with the option to work additional hours. Flight attendants also receive a "per diem" allowance for meal expenses while on duty away from home. In addition, flight attendants and their immediate families are entitled to free fares on their own airline and reduced fares on most other airlines.

Flight attendants are required to purchase uniforms and wear them while on duty. The airlines usually pay for uniform replacement items, and may provide a small allowance to cover cleaning and upkeep of the uniforms.

The majority of flight attendants hold union membership, primarily with the Association of Flight Attendants. Others may be members of the Transport Workers Union of America, the International Brotherhood of Teamsters, or other unions.

Related Occupations
Other jobs that involve helping people as a safety professional while requiring the ability to be calm even under trying circumstances include emergency medical technician, firefighter, maritime crew, and camp counselor.

Sources of Additional Information
Information about job opportunities and the qualifications required for a particular airline may be obtained by writing to the airline's personnel office.

Home Health and Personal Care Aides

(O*NET 66011 and 68035)

Significant Points

- Numerous job openings will result due to very fast employment growth and very high turnover.
- Education required for entry-level jobs is generally minimal, but earnings are low.

Nature of the Work
Home health and personal care aides help elderly, disabled, and ill persons live in their own homes instead of in a health facility. Most

work with elderly or disabled clients who need more extensive care than family or friends can provide. Some home health and personal care aides work with families in which a parent is incapacitated and small children need care. Others help discharged hospital patients who have relatively short-term needs.

In general, *home health aides* provide health-related services, such as administering oral medications under physicians' orders or direction of a nurse. In contrast, *personal care* and *home care aides* provide mainly housekeeping and routine personal care services. However, there can be substantial variation in job titles and overlap of duties.

Most home health and personal care aides provide some housekeeping services, as well as personal care to their clients. They clean clients' houses, do laundry, and change bed linens. Some aides plan meals (including special diets), shop for food, and cook. Home health and personal care aides may also help clients move from bed, bathe, dress, and groom. Some accompany clients outside the home, serving as guide, companion, and aide.

Home health and personal care aides also provide instruction and psychological support. For example, they may assist in toilet training a severely mentally handicapped child, or just listen to clients talk about their problems.

Home health aides may check pulse, temperature, and respiration; help with simple prescribed exercises; and assist with medication routines. Occasionally, they change nonsterile dressings, use special equipment such as a hydraulic lift, give massages and alcohol rubs, or assist with braces and artificial limbs.

In home care agencies, it is usually a registered nurse, a physical therapist, or a social worker who assigns specific duties and supervises home health and personal care aides. Aides keep records of services performed and of clients' condition and progress. They report changes in the client's condition to the supervisor or case manager. Home health and personal care aides also participate in case reviews, consulting with the team caring for the client—registered nurses, therapists, and other health professionals.

Working Conditions

The home health and personal care aide's daily routine may vary. Aides may go to the same home every day for months or even years. However, most aides work with a number of different clients, each job lasting a few hours, days, or weeks. Aides often visit four or five clients on the same day.

Home health and personal care aides provide housekeeping services, personal care, and emotional support for their clients.

Surroundings differ from case to case. Some homes are neat and pleasant, while others are untidy or depressing. Some clients are angry, abusive, depressed, or otherwise difficult; others are pleasant and cooperative.

Home health and personal care aides generally work on their own, with periodic visits by their supervisor. They receive detailed instructions explaining when to visit clients and what services to perform. Many aides work part time, and weekend hours are common.

Aides are individually responsible for getting to the client's home. They may spend a good portion of the working day traveling from one client to another; motor vehicle accidents are always a danger. They are particularly susceptible to injuries resulting from all types of overexertion when assisting patients, and falls inside and outside their homes. Mechanical lifting devices that are available in institutional settings are seldom available in patients' homes.

Employment

Home health and personal care aides held about 746,000 jobs in 1998. Most aides are employed by home health and personal care agencies, visiting nurse associations, residential care facilities with home health departments, hospitals, public health and welfare departments, community volunteer agencies, nursing and personal care facilities, and temporary help firms. Self-employed aides have no agency affiliation or supervision, and accept clients, set fees, and arrange work schedules on their own.

Training, Other Qualifications, and Advancement

In some States, this occupation is open to individuals with no formal training. On-the-job training is generally provided. Other States may require formal training, depending on Federal or State law.

The Federal Government has enacted guidelines for home health aides whose employers receive reimbursement from Medicare. Federal law requires home health aides to pass a competency test covering 12 areas: Communication skills; observation, reporting, and documentation of patient status and the care or services furnished; reading and recording vital signs; basic infection control procedures; basic elements of body function and changes; maintenance of a clean, safe, and healthy environment; recognition of, and procedures for, emergencies; the physical, emotional, and developmental characteristics of the patients served; personal hygiene and grooming; safe transfer techniques; normal range of motion and positioning; and basic nutrition.

A home health aide may take training before taking the competency test. Federal law suggests at least 75 hours of classroom and practical training supervised by a registered nurse. Training and testing programs may be offered by the employing agency, but must meet the standards of the Health Care Financing Administration. Training programs vary depending upon State regulations.

The National Association for Home Care offers national certification for home health and personal care aides. The certification is a voluntary demonstration that the individual has met industry standards.

Successful home health and personal care aides like to help people and do not mind hard work. They should be responsible, compassionate, emotionally stable, and cheerful. Aides should also be tactful, honest, and discreet because they work in private homes.

Home health and personal care aides must be in good health. A physical examination including State regulated tests such as those for tuberculosis may be required.

Advancement is limited. In some agencies, workers start out performing homemaker duties, such as cleaning. With experience and training, they may take on personal care duties. The most experienced home health aides assist with medical equipment such as ventilators, which help patients breathe.

Job Outlook

A large number of job openings are expected for home health and personal care aides, due to substantial growth and very high turnover.

Home health and personal care aides is expected to be one of the fastest growing occupations through the year 2008.

The number of people in their seventies and older is projected to rise substantially. This age group is characterized by mounting health problems requiring some assistance. Also, there will be an increasing reliance on home care for patients of all ages. This trend reflects several developments: Efforts to contain costs by moving patients out of hospitals and nursing facilities as quickly as possible, the realization that treatment can be more effective in familiar surroundings rather than clinical surroundings, and the development and improvement of medical technologies for in-home treatment.

In addition to jobs created by the increase in demand for these workers, replacement needs are expected to produce numerous openings. Turnover is high, a reflection of the relatively low skill requirements, low pay, and high emotional demands of the work. For these same reasons, many people are unwilling to perform this kind of work. Therefore, persons who are interested in this work and suited for it should have excellent job opportunities, particularly those with experience or training as home health, personal care, or nursing aides.

Earnings

Median hourly earnings of home health and personal care aides were $7.58 in 1998. The middle 50 percent earned between $6.41 and $8.81 an hour. The lowest 10 percent earned less than $5.73 and the highest 10 percent earned more than $10.51 an hour. Median hourly earnings in the industries employing the largest number of home health aides in 1997 were as follows:

Industry	Earnings
Home health care services	$8.00
Hospitals	7.90
Personnel supply services	7.70
Residential care	7.20
Individual and family services	7.20

Median hourly earnings in the industries employing the largest number of personal and home care aides in 1997 are shown below:

Industry	Earnings
Local government, except education and hospitals	$8.00
Job training and related services	7.30
Residential care	7.20
Individual and family services	7.00
Home health care services	6.00

Most employers give slight pay increases with experience and added responsibility. Aides are usually paid only for the time worked in the home. They normally are not paid for travel time between jobs. Most employers hire only "on-call" hourly workers and provide no benefits.

Related Occupations

Home health and personal care aide is a service occupation combining duties of health workers and social service workers. Workers in related occupations that involve personal contact to help or instruct others include attendants in children's institutions, childcare attendants in schools, child monitors, companions, nursing aides, nursery school attendants, occupational therapy aides, nursing aides, physical therapy aides, playroom attendants, and psychiatric aides.

Sources of Additional Information

General information about training and referrals to State and local agencies about opportunities for home health and personal care aides, a list of relevant publications, and information on national certification are available from:

☛ National Association for Home Care, 228 7th St. SE., Washington, DC 20003. Internet: **http://www.nahc.org**

For information about a career as a home health aide and schools offering training, contact:

☛ National Association of Health Career Schools, 2301 Academy Dr., Harrisburg, PA 17112.

Preschool Teachers and Child-Care Workers

(O*NET 31303 and 68038)

Significant Points

- About 40 percent of preschool teachers and child-care workers—more than 4 times the proportion for all workers—are self-employed; most of these are family child-care providers.
- A high school diploma and little or no experience are adequate for many jobs, but training requirements vary from a high school diploma to a college degree.
- Employment growth, high turnover, and relatively low training requirements will make it easy to enter this occupation.

Nature of the Work

Preschool teachers and child-care workers nurture and teach preschool children—age 5 or younger—in child-care centers, nursery schools, preschools, public schools, and family child-care homes. These workers play an important role in a child's development by caring for the child when parents are at work or away for other reasons. Some parents enroll their children in nursery schools or child-care centers primarily to provide them with the opportunity to interact with other children. In addition to attending to children's basic needs, these workers organize activities that stimulate the children's physical, emotional, intellectual, and social growth. They help children explore their interests, develop their talents and independence, build self-esteem, and learn how to behave with others.

Preschool teachers and child-care workers spend most of their day working with children. However, they do maintain contact with parents or guardians, through informal meetings or scheduled conferences, to discuss each child's progress and needs. Many preschool teachers and child-care workers keep records of each child's progress and suggest ways that parents can increase their child's learning and development at home. Some preschools and child-care centers actively recruit parent volunteers to work with the children and participate in administrative decisions and program planning.

Most preschool teachers and child-care workers perform a combination of basic care and teaching duties. Through many basic care activities, preschool teachers and child-care workers provide opportunities for children to learn. For example, a worker who shows a child how to

Preschool teachers and child-care workers use playful activities to teach young children.

tie a shoe teaches the child and also provides for that child's basic care needs. Preschool and child-care programs help children learn about trust and gain a sense of security.

Children at this age learn mainly through play. Recognizing the importance of play, preschool teachers and child-care workers build their program around it. They capitalize on children's play to further language development (storytelling and acting games), improve social skills (working together to build a neighborhood in a sandbox), and introduce scientific and mathematical concepts (balancing and counting blocks when building a bridge or mixing colors when painting). Thus, a less structured approach is used to teach preschool children, including small group lessons, one-on-one instruction, and learning through creative activities, such as art, dance, and music.

Interaction with peers is an important part of a child's early development. Preschool children are given an opportunity to engage in conversation and discussions, and learn to play and work cooperatively with their classmates. Preschool teachers and child-care workers play a vital role in preparing children to build the skills they will need in elementary school. (A statement on teacher assistants—who aid classroom teachers—appears elsewhere in the *Handbook*.)

Preschool teachers and child-care workers greet children as they arrive, help them remove outer garments, and select an activity of interest. When caring for infants, they feed and change them. To ensure a well-balanced program, preschool teachers and child-care workers prepare daily and long-term schedules of activities. Each day's activities balance individual and group play and quiet and active time. Children are given some freedom to participate in activities in which they are interested.

Helping to keep children healthy is an important part of the job. Preschool teachers and child-care workers serve nutritious meals and snacks and teach good eating habits and personal hygiene. They ensure that children have proper rest periods. They spot children who may not feel well or show signs of emotional or developmental problems and discuss these matters with their supervisor and the child's parents. In some cases, preschool teachers and child-care workers help parents identify programs that will provide basic health services.

Early identification of children with special needs, such as those with behavioral, emotional, physical, or learning disabilities, is important to improve their future learning ability. Special education teachers often work with these preschool children to provide the individual attention they need. (Special education teachers are covered in a separate statement in the *Handbook*.)

Working Conditions

Preschool facilities include private homes, schools, religious institutions, workplaces where employers provide care for employees' children, and private buildings. Individuals who provide care in their own homes are generally called family child-care providers. (Child-care workers who work in the child's home are covered in the statement on private household workers found elsewhere in the *Handbook*.)

Watching children grow, enjoy learning, and gain new skills can be very rewarding. While working with children, preschool teachers and child-care workers often improve the child's communication, learning, and other personal skills. The work is never routine; new activities and challenges mark each day. However, child care can be physically and emotionally taxing, as workers constantly stand, walk, bend, stoop, and lift to attend to each child's interests and problems.

To ensure that children receive proper supervision, State or local regulations may require certain ratios of workers to children. The ratio varies with the age of the children. Child development experts generally recommend that a single caregiver be responsible for no more than 3 or 4 infants (less than 1 year old), 5 or 6 toddlers (1 to 2 years old), or 10 preschool-age children (between 2 and 5 years old).

The working hours of preschool teachers and child-care workers vary widely. Child care centers are usually open year round with long hours so that parents can drop off and pick up their children before and after work. Some centers employ full-time and part-time staff with staggered shifts to cover the entire day. Some workers are unable to take regular breaks during the day due to limited staffing. Public and many private preschool programs operate during the typical 9- or 10-month school year, employing both full-time and part-time workers. Preschool teachers may work extra unpaid hours each week on curriculum planning, parent meetings, and occasional fundraising activities. Family child-care providers have flexible hours and daily routines, but may work long or unusual hours to fit parents' work schedules.

Turnover in this occupation is high. Many preschool teachers and child-care workers leave the occupation temporarily to fulfill family responsibilities, study, or for other reasons. Some workers leave permanently because they are interested in pursuing another occupation or because of dissatisfaction with long hours, low pay and benefits, and stressful conditions.

Employment

Preschool teachers and child-care workers held about 1.3 million jobs in 1998. Many worked part time. About 4 out of 10 preschool teachers and child-care workers are self-employed, most of whom are family child-care providers.

Over 60 percent of all salaried preschool teachers and child-care workers are found in child-care centers and preschools, and about 14 percent work for religious institutions. The remainder work in other community organizations and in State and local government. Some child-care programs are for-profit centers; some of these are affiliated with a local or national chain. Religious institutions, community agencies, school systems, and State and local governments operate nonprofit programs. About 2 percent of private industry establishments operate on-site child-care centers for the children of their employees.

Training, Other Qualifications, and Advancement

The training and qualifications required of preschool teachers and child-care workers vary widely. Each State has its own licensing requirements that regulate caregiver training, ranging from a high school diploma, to community college courses, to a college degree in child development or early childhood education. Some States require continuing education for workers in this field. However, State requirements are often minimal. Often, child-care workers can obtain employment with a high school diploma and little or no experience. Local governments, private firms, and publicly funded programs may have more demanding training and education requirements.

Some employers prefer to hire preschool teachers and child-care workers with a nationally recognized child-care development credential, secondary or postsecondary courses in child development and early childhood education, or work experience in a child-care setting. Other schools require their own specialized training. Public schools typically require a bachelor's degree and State teacher certification. Teacher training programs include a variety of liberal arts courses, courses in child development, student teaching, and prescribed professional courses, including instruction in teaching gifted, disadvantaged, and other children with special needs.

Preschool teachers and child-care workers must be enthusiastic and constantly alert, anticipate and prevent problems, deal with disruptive children, and provide fair but firm discipline. They must communicate effectively with the children and their parents, as well as other teachers and child-care workers. Workers should be mature, patient, understanding, and articulate, and have energy and physical stamina. Skills in music, art, drama, and storytelling are also important. Those who work for themselves must have business sense and management abilities.

Opportunities for advancement are limited in this occupation. However, as preschool teachers and child-care workers gain experience, some may advance to supervisory or administrative positions in large child-care centers or preschools. Often these positions require additional training, such as a bachelor's or master's degree. Other workers move on to work in resource and referral agencies, consulting with parents on available child services. A few workers become involved in policy or advocacy work related to child care and early childhood education. With a bachelor's degree, preschool teachers may become certified to teach in public schools at the kindergarten, elementary, and secondary school levels. Some workers set up their own child-care businesses.

Job Outlook

Employment of preschool teachers and child-care workers is projected to increase faster than the average for all occupations through the year 2008. In addition, many preschool teachers and child-care workers leave the occupation each year for other jobs, family responsibilities, or other reasons. High turnover, combined with job growth, is expected to create many openings for preschool teachers and child-care workers. Qualified persons who are interested in this work should have little trouble finding and keeping a job.

Future employment growth of preschool teachers and child-care workers will be rapid, but nevertheless considerably slower than in the last two decades because demographic changes that fueled much of the past enrollment growth are projected to slow. Labor force participation of women of childbearing age will increase very little and this group of women will decline as a percentage of the total labor force. Also, the number of children under 5 years of age is expected to rise very little by the year 2008. Nevertheless, the proportion of youngsters enrolled full- or part-time in child-care and preschool programs is likely to continue to increase, spurring demand for preschool teachers and child-care workers. Changes in perceptions of preprimary education may lead to increased public and private spending on child care. If more parents believe that some experience in center based care and preschool is beneficial to children, enrollment will increase. Government policy often favors increased funding of early childhood education programs and that trend should continue. The growing availability of government-funded programs may induce some parents to enroll their children in center-based care and preschool who otherwise would not. Some States also are increasing subsidization of the child-care services industry in response to welfare reform legislation. This reform may cause some mothers to enter the work force during the projection period as their welfare benefits are reduced or eliminated.

Earnings

Pay depends on the educational attainment of the worker and establishment type. Although the pay is generally very low, more education means higher earnings in some cases. Median annual earnings of preschool teachers were $17,310 in 1998. The middle 50 percent earned between $13,760 and $22,370. The lowest 10 percent earned less than $12,000 and the highest 10 percent earned more than $30,310. Median annual earnings in the industries employing the largest numbers of preschool teachers in 1997 were as follows:

Elementary and secondary schools	$23,300
Individual and family services	18,800
Social services, not elsewhere classified	17,900
Civic and social associations	17,300
Child day care services	15,700

Median hourly earnings of child-care workers were $6.61 in 1998. The middle 50 percent earned between $5.82 and $8.13. The lowest 10 percent earned less than $5.49 and the highest 10 percent earned more than $9.65. Median hourly earnings in the industries employing the largest numbers of child-care workers in 1997 were as follows:

Residential care	$7.60
Elementary and secondary schools	7.30
Civic and social associations	6.30
Child day care services	6.00
Miscellaneous amusement and recreation services	5.90

Earnings of self-employed child-care workers vary depending on the hours worked, number and ages of the children, and the location.

Benefits vary, but are minimal for most preschool and child-care workers. Many employers offer free or discounted child care to employees. Some offer a full benefits package, including health insurance and paid vacations, but others offer no benefits at all. Some employers offer seminars and workshops to help workers improve upon or learn new skills. A few are willing to cover the cost of courses taken at community colleges or technical schools.

Related Occupations

Child-care work requires patience; creativity; an ability to nurture, motivate, teach, and influence children; and leadership, organizational, and administrative skills. Others who work with children and need these aptitudes include teacher assistants, children's tutors, kindergarten and elementary school teachers, early childhood program directors, and child psychologists.

Sources of Additional Information

For information on careers in educating children and issues affecting preschool teachers and child-care workers, contact:

☛ National Association for the Education of Young Children, 1509 16th St. NW., Washington, DC 20036. Internet: **http://www.naeyc.org**

☛ Association for Childhood Education International, 17904 Georgia Ave., Suite 215, Olney, MD 20832-2277.

For eligibility requirements and a description of the Child Development Associate credential, contact:

☛ Council for Early Childhood Professional Recognition, 2460 16th St. NW., Washington, DC 20009. Internet: **http://www.cdacouncil.org**

For information about family child care and accreditation, contact:

☛ National Association for Family Child Care, 525 SW 5th St., Suite A, Des Moines, Iowa 50309-4501. Internet: **http://www.nafcc.org**

For information on salaries and efforts to improve compensation in child care, contact:

☛ Center for the Child Care Workforce, 733 15th St. NW., Suite 1037, Washington, DC 20005. Internet: **http://www.ccw.org**

State Departments of Human Services or Social Services can supply State regulations and training requirements for child-care workers.

Private Household Workers

(O*NET 62031, 62041, 62061, 69999E, and 79999N)

Significant Points

- Demand will far outstrip the supply of workers willing to provide private household services because the work is hard, earnings are low, and benefits and advancement opportunities are few.
- Persons who are interested in and suited for this work should have no trouble finding and keeping jobs.

Nature of the Work

Private household workers clean homes, care for children, plan and cook meals, do laundry, administer the household, and perform numerous other duties. Many types of households of various income levels employ these workers. Although wealthy families may employ a large staff, it is much more common for one worker to be employed in a household where both parents work. Many workers are employed in households having one parent. A number of household workers work part time for two or more employers.

Most household workers are *general house workers* and usually the only worker employed in the home. They dust and polish furniture; sweep, mop, and wax floors; vacuum; and clean ovens, refrigerators, and bathrooms. They may also wash dishes, polish silver, and change and make beds. Some wash, fold, and iron clothes; a few wash windows. Other duties may include looking after a child or an elderly person, cooking, feeding pets, answering the telephone and doorbell, and calling and waiting for repair workers. General house workers may also take clothes and laundry to the cleaners, buy groceries, and do many other errands.

Household workers whose primary responsibility is taking care of children are called *child-care workers*. Those employed on an hourly basis are usually called *baby-sitters*. Child-care workers bathe, dress, and feed children; supervise their play; wash their clothes; and clean their rooms. They may also put them to sleep and waken them, read to them, involve them in educational games, take them for doctors' visits, and discipline them. Those who are in charge of infants, sometimes called *infant nurses*, also prepare bottles and change diapers.

Nannies generally take care of children from birth to age 10 or 12, tending to the child's early education, nutrition, health, and other needs. They may also perform the duties of a general housekeeper, including general cleaning and laundry duties. *Governesses* look after children in addition to other household duties. They may help them with schoolwork, teach them a foreign language, and guide them in their general upbringing. (Child-care workers who work outside the child's home are covered in the statement on child-care workers elsewhere in the *Handbook*.)

Companions or *personal attendants* assist elderly, handicapped, or convalescent people. Depending on the employer's needs, a companion or attendant might help with bathing and dressing, preparing and serving meals, and keeping the house tidy. They also may read to their employers, write letters for them, play cards or games, and go with them on walks and outings. Companions may also accompany their employers to medical appointments and handle their social and business affairs.

Households with a large staff may include a household manager, housekeeper, or butler, as well as a cook, caretaker, and launderer. *Household managers, housekeepers,* and *butlers* hire, supervise, and coordinate the household staff to keep the household running smoothly. Butlers also receive and announce guests, answer telephones, deliver messages, serve food and drinks, chauffeur, or act as a personal attendant. *Cooks* plan and prepare meals, clean the kitchen, order groceries and supplies, and may also serve meals. *Caretakers* do heavy housework and general home maintenance. They wash windows, wax floors, and hang draperies. They maintain heating and other equipment and do light carpentry, painting, and odd jobs. They may also mow the lawn and do some gardening if the household does not have a gardener.

Working Conditions

Private household workers usually work in pleasant and comfortable homes or apartments. Most are day workers who live in their own homes and travel to work. Some live in the home of their employer, generally with their own room and bath. Live-ins usually work longer hours. However, if they work evenings or weekends, they may get other time off. Live-ins may feel isolated from family and friends. On the other hand, they often become part of their employer's family, and may derive satisfaction from caring for them. Being a general house worker can also be isolating, since work is usually done alone.

Many private household workers supervise children.

Housekeeping is hard work. Both day workers and live-ins are on their feet most of the day and do much walking, lifting, bending, stooping, and reaching. In addition, some employers may be very demanding.

Employment

Private household workers held about 928,000 jobs in 1998. About 65 percent were cleaners and servants, mostly day workers; about 33 percent were child-care workers, including baby sitters; and less than 3 percent were housekeepers, butlers, cooks, and launderers. Most jobs are in big cities and their affluent suburbs. Some are on large estates or in resorts away from cities.

Training, Other Qualifications, and Advancement

Private household workers generally do not need any special training. Individuals who cannot find other work because of limited language or other skills often turn to this work. Most jobs require the ability to clean, cook, or take care of children. These skills are generally learned by young people while helping with housework at home. Some training takes place on the job. Employers show the household workers what they want done and how. For child-care workers and companions, general education and the ability to get along with the person they will care for are most important.

Home economics courses in high schools and vocational and adult education schools offer training in cooking and child care. Courses in child development, first aid, and nursing in postsecondary schools are highly recommended.

Schools for butlers, nannies, and governesses teach household administration, early childhood education, nutrition, child care, and bookkeeping. These schools may offer certifications in household management—for example, Certified Household Manager, Certified Professional Nanny, or Certified Professional Governess—and assist in job placement. However, most private household workers get jobs through employment agencies and recommendations from previous employers.

Private household workers should work well with others and be honest, discreet, dependable, courteous, and neat. They also need physical stamina.

There are very few opportunities for advancement within this occupation. Few large households exist with big staffs where general house workers can advance to cook, executive housekeeper, butler, or governess, and these jobs may require specialized training. Advancement usually consists of better pay and working conditions. Workers may move to similar jobs in hotels, hospitals, and restaurants, where the pay and benefits are usually better. A few workers start companies that provide household services for a fee. Others transfer into better-paying, unrelated jobs.

Job Outlook

Job opportunities for people wishing to become private household workers are expected to be excellent through 2008, as the demand for these services continues to far outpace the supply of workers willing to provide them. Those with formal training or excellent recommendations from previous employers should be particularly sought after.

For many years, demand for household help has outstripped the supply of workers willing to take domestic jobs. The imbalance is expected to persist, and possibly worsen. Demand is expected to grow as more women join the labor force and need help running their households. Demand for companions and personal attendants is also expected to rise due to projected rapid growth in the elderly population.

The supply situation is not likely to improve. The physical demands of the work, low status, low pay, few benefits, and limited advancement potential deter many prospective household workers. Due to the limited supply of household workers, many employers have turned to domestic cleaning firms, child-care centers, and temporary help firms to meet their needs for household help. This trend is expected to continue. (See the statements on janitors and cleaners, preschool teachers and child-care workers, and home health and personal care aides elsewhere in the *Handbook*.)

Employment of private household workers is expected to decline through 2008. However, job openings will be numerous because of the need to replace workers who change jobs within the occupation and the large number of workers who leave these occupations every year. Persons who are interested in and suited for this work should have no trouble finding and keeping jobs.

Earnings

Earnings of private household workers depend on the type of work, the number of hours, household and staff size, geographic location, training, and experience.

Most private household workers are employed part time, or less than 35 hours a week. Some work only 2 or 3 days a week while others may work half a day 4 or 5 days a week. Earnings vary from about $10 an hour or more in a big city to less than the Federal minimum wage—$5.15 an hour in 1998. (Minimum wage laws may not cover private household workers who work just a few hours per week or have very low annual earnings.) In addition, day workers often get carfare and a free meal. Live-in domestics usually earn more than day workers and also get free room and board. However, they often work longer hours. Baby-sitters usually have the lowest earnings.

Usual median weekly earnings of all private household workers in 1998 were $223. Cleaners and servants earned $235 per week, cooks earned $380 per week, child-care workers earned $204 per week, and housekeepers and butlers earned $206 per week. Some full-time live-in housekeepers, cooks, butlers, nannies, and governesses earned considerably more. Based on limited information, experienced and highly recommended workers employed by wealthy families in major metropolitan areas may earn $800 to $1,200 a week.

Private household workers who live with their employers may be given room and board, medical benefits, a car, vacation days, and education benefits. However, most private household workers receive very limited or no benefits.

Related Occupations

Other workers with similar duties are building custodians, hotel and restaurant cleaners, child-care workers, home health and personal care aides, cooks, kitchen workers, waiters and waitresses, and bartenders.

Sources of Additional Information

Information about job opportunities for private household workers is available from local private employment agencies and State employment service offices.

For information about careers and schools offering training for nannies, contact:

☛ American Council of Nanny Schools, Delta College, University Center, MI 48710.

Veterinary Assistants and Nonfarm Animal Caretakers

(O*NET 34058G, 79017A, 79017B, 79017C, 79017D, and 79806)

Significant Points

- Animal lovers get satisfaction in this occupation, but aspects of the work can be unpleasant and physically and emotionally demanding.
- Most animal caretakers are trained on the job, but advancement depends on experience, formal training, and continuing education.

Nature of the Work

Many people like animals. But, as pet owners can attest, taking care of them is hard work. Animal caretakers, sometimes called animal attendants or animal keepers, feed, water, groom, bathe, and exercise animals and clean, disinfect, and repair their cages. They also play with the animals, provide companionship, and observe behavioral changes that could indicate illness or injury.

Boarding kennels, animal shelters, veterinary hospitals and clinics, stables, laboratories, aquariums, and zoological parks all house animals and employ caretakers. Job titles and duties vary by employment setting.

Kennel staff usually care for small companion animals like dogs and cats while their owners are working or traveling out of town. Beginning attendants perform basic tasks, such as cleaning cages and dog runs, filling food and water dishes, and exercising animals. Experienced attendants may provide basic animal health care, as well as bathe animals, trim nails, and attend to other grooming needs. Caretakers who work in kennels may also sell pet food and supplies, assist in obedience training, help with breeding, or prepare animals for shipping.

Animal caretakers who specialize in grooming, or maintaining a pet's—usually a dog's or cat's—appearance are called *groomers*. Some groomers work in kennels, veterinary clinics, animal shelters, or pet supply stores. Others operate their own grooming business. Groomers answer telephones, schedule appointments, discuss with clients their pets' grooming needs, and collect information on the pet's disposition and its veterinarian. Groomers are often the first to notice a medical problem, such as an ear or skin infection, that requires veterinary care.

Grooming the pet involves several steps: An initial brush-out is followed by a first clipping of hair or fur using electric clippers, combs, and grooming shears; the groomer then cuts the nails, cleans the ears,

An animal caretaker enjoys feeding a seal.

bathes, and blow-dries the animal, and ends with a final clipping and styling.

Animal caretakers in animal shelters perform a variety of duties and work with a wide variety of animals. In addition to attending to the basic needs of the animals, caretakers must also keep records of the animals received and discharged and any tests or treatments done. Some vaccinate newly admitted animals under the direction of a veterinarian or veterinary technician, and euthanize (painlessly put to death) seriously ill, severely injured, or unwanted animals. Caretakers in animal shelters also interact with the public, answering telephone inquiries, screening applicants for animal adoption, or educating visitors on neutering and other animal health issues.

Animal caretakers in stables are called *grooms*. They saddle and unsaddle horses, give them rubdowns, and walk them through a cool-off after a ride. They also feed, groom, and exercise the horses, clean out stalls and replenish bedding, polish saddles, clean and organize the tack (harness, saddle, and bridle) room, and store supplies and feed. Experienced grooms may help train horses.

Animal caretakers in animal hospitals or clinics are called *veterinary assistants*. Veterinarians rely on caretakers to keep a constant eye on the condition of animals under their charge. Caretakers watch as animals recover from surgery, check whether dressings are still on correctly, observe the animals' overall attitude, and notify a doctor if anything seems out of the ordinary. Caretakers clean constantly to maintain sanitary conditions in the hospital.

Laboratory animal caretakers work in research facilities and assist with the care of a wide variety of animals, including mice, rats, sheep, pigs, cattle, dogs, cats, monkeys, birds, fish, and frogs. They feed and water the animals, clean cages and change bedding, and observe the animals for signs of illness, disease, or injury. They may administer medications orally or topically according to instructions, prepare samples for laboratory examination, sterilize laboratory equipment, and record information regarding genealogy, diet, weight, medications, food intake, and clinical signs of pain and distress. They work with scientists, physicians, veterinary technicians, veterinarians, and laboratory technicians.

In zoos, caretakers called *keepers* prepare the diets and clean the enclosures of animals, and sometimes assist in raising them when they are very young. They watch for any signs of illness or injury, monitor eating patterns or any changes in behavior, and record their observations. Keepers also may answer questions and ensure that the visiting public behaves responsibly toward the exhibited animals. Depending on the zoo, keepers may be assigned to work with a broad group of animals such as mammals, birds, or reptiles, or they may work with a limited collection of animals such as primates, large cats, or small mammals.

Working Conditions

People who love animals get satisfaction from working with and helping them. However, some of the work may be unpleasant, as well as physically and emotionally demanding, and sometimes dangerous. Caretakers have to clean animal cages and lift, hold, or restrain animals, risking exposure to bites or scratches. Their work often involves kneeling, crawling, repeated bending, and lifting heavy supplies like bales of hay or bags of feed. Animal caretakers must take precautions when treating animals with germicides or insecticides. The work setting can be noisy.

Animal caretakers who witness abused animals or who assist in the euthanizing of unwanted, aged, or hopelessly injured animals may experience emotional stress. Those working for private humane societies and municipal animal shelters often deal with the public, some of whom might react with hostility to any implication that the owners are neglecting or abusing their pets. Such workers must maintain a calm and professional demeanor while they enforce the laws regarding animal care.

Caretakers may work outdoors in all kinds of weather. Hours are irregular: Animals have to be fed every day, so caretakers often work weekend and holiday shifts. In some animal hospitals, research facilities, and animal shelters an attendant is on duty 24 hours a day, which means night shifts. Most full-time caretakers work about 40 hours a week; some work 50 hours a week or more. Caretakers of show and sports animals travel to competitions.

Employment

Animal caretakers and veterinary assistants held about 181,000 jobs in 1998. About 45,000 of the total worked as veterinary assistants in veterinary services. The remainder worked primarily in boarding kennels, but also in animal shelters, stables, grooming shops, zoos, and local, State, and Federal agencies. In 1998, more than 1 out of every 4 animal caretakers was self-employed, and more than 1 in 3 worked part time.

Training, Other Qualifications, and Advancement

Most animal caretakers are trained on the job. Employers generally prefer to hire people with some experience with animals. Some training programs are available for specific types of animal caretakers, but formal training is usually not necessary for entry-level positions.

Most pet groomers learn their trade by completing an informal apprenticeship, usually lasting 6 to 10 weeks, under the guidance of an experienced groomer. Prospective groomers may also attend one of the 50 State-licensed grooming schools throughout the country, with programs varying in length from 4 to 18 weeks. The National Dog Groomers Association of America certifies groomers who pass a written examination, with a separate part testing practical skills. Beginning groomers often start by taking on one duty, such as bathing and drying the pet. They eventually assume responsibility for the entire grooming process, from the initial brush-out to the final clipping. Groomers who work in large retail establishments or kennels may, with experience, move into supervisory or managerial positions. Experienced groomers often choose to open their own shops.

Beginning animal caretakers in kennels learn on the job, and usually start by cleaning cages and feeding and watering animals. Kennel caretakers may be promoted to kennel supervisor, assistant manager, and manager, and those with enough capital and experience may open up their own kennels. The American Boarding Kennels Association (ABKA) offers a 3-stage, home-study program for individuals interested in pet care. The first two study programs address basic and advanced principles of animal care, while the third program focuses on in-depth animal care and good business procedures. Those who complete the third program and pass oral and written examinations administered by the ABKA become Certified Kennel Operators (CKO).

There are no formal educational requirements for animal caretakers in veterinary facilities. They are trained on the job, usually under the guidance of a veterinarian or veterinary technician. They start by performing tasks related to basic animal health care, such as keeping cages and examination areas sanitary. They also help veterinarians prepare for surgery, sterilize surgical equipment, observe recovering animals, and give medications and basic medical treatment under the directions of a veterinarian or veterinary technician. Highly motivated veterinary assistants may become veterinary technicians, with additional training from one of approximately 70 accredited veterinary technology programs.

Employers of entry-level laboratory animal caretakers generally require a high school diploma or General Educational Development (GED) test. A few colleges and vocational schools offer programs in laboratory animal science which provide training for technician positions, but such training is not strictly necessary. New animal caretakers working in laboratories begin by providing basic care to laboratory animals. With additional training, experience, and certification, they may advance to more technical positions in laboratory animal care, such as research assistant, mid-level technician, or senior-level technologist.

The American Association for Laboratory Animal Science (AALAS) offers certification for three levels of technician competence. Those who wish to become certified as Assistant Laboratory Animal Technicians (ALAT) must satisfy education and experience requirements before taking an examination administered by AALAS. Laboratory Animal Technician and Laboratory Animal Technologist are the second and third levels of certification of the AALAS.

Some zoological parks may require their caretakers to have a bachelor's degree in biology, animal science, or a related field. Most require experience with animals, preferably as a volunteer or paid keeper in a zoo. Zoo keepers may advance to senior keeper, assistant head keeper, head keeper, and assistant curator, but few openings occur, especially for the higher-level positions.

Animal caretakers in animal shelters are not required to have any specialized training, but training programs and workshops are increasingly available through the Humane Society of the United States, the American Humane Association, and the National Animal Control Association. Workshop topics include cruelty investigations, appropriate methods of euthanasia for shelter animals, and techniques for preventing problems with wildlife. With experience and additional training, caretakers in animal shelters may become adoption coordinators, animal control officers, emergency rescue drivers, assistant shelter managers, or shelter directors.

Job Outlook

Employment opportunities for animal caretakers and veterinary assistants generally are expected to be good. The outlook for caretakers in zoos, however, is not favorable; jobseekers will face keen competition because of expected slow growth in zoo capacity, low turnover, and the fact that the occupation attracts many candidates.

Employment is expected to grow faster than the average through 2008. The growth of the pet population, which drives employment of animal caretakers in kennels, grooming shops, animal shelters, and veterinary clinics and hospitals, is expected to slow. Nevertheless, pets remain popular and pet owners—including a large number of baby boomers whose disposable income is expected to increase as they age—may increasingly take advantage of grooming services, daily and overnight boarding services, and veterinary services, spurring employment growth for animal caretakers and veterinary assistants. Demand for animal caretakers in animal shelters is expected to remain steady. Communities are increasingly recognizing the connection between animal abuse and abuse toward humans, and should continue to commit funds to animal shelters, many of which are working hand-in-hand with social service agencies and law enforcement teams.

Despite growth in demand for animal caretakers, the overwhelming majority of jobs will result from the need to replace workers leaving the field. Many animal caretaker jobs that require little or no training have work schedules that tend to be flexible; therefore, it is ideal for people seeking their first job and for students and others looking for temporary or part-time work. Because turnover is quite high, largely due to the hard physical labor, the overall availability of jobs should be very good. Much of the work of animal caretakers is seasonal, particularly during vacation periods.

Earnings

Median hourly earnings of nonfarm animal caretakers were $7.12 in 1998. The middle 50 percent earned between $5.92 and $8.82. The bottom 10 percent earned less than $5.54 and the top 10 percent earned more than $11.39. Median hourly earnings in the industries employing the largest numbers of nonfarm animal caretakers in 1997 are shown below:

Industry	Earnings
Local government, except education and hospitals	$10.40
Commercial sports	7.60
Animal services, except veterinary	7.10
Membership organizations, not elsewhere classified	6.60
Veterinary services	6.20

Median hourly earnings of veterinary assistants were $7.79 in 1998. The middle 50 percent earned between $6.55 and $9.23. The lowest 10 percent earned less than $5.79 and the top 10 percent earned more than $10.80.

Related Occupations

Others who work extensively with animals include animal breeders, animal trainers, livestock farm workers, ranchers, veterinarians, veterinary technicians and technologists, and wildlife biologists and zoologists.

Sources of Additional Information

For more information on jobs in animal caretaking and control, and the animal shelter and control personnel training program, write to:

☛ The Humane Society of the United States, 2100 L St. NW., Washington, DC 20037-1598. Internet: **http://www.hsus.org**

☛ National Animal Control Association, P.O. Box 480851, Kansas City, MO 64148-0851.

To obtain a listing of State-licensed grooming schools, send a stamped, self-addressed envelope to:

☛ National Dog Groomers Association of America, Box 101, Clark, PA 16113.

For information on training and certification of kennel staff and owners, contact:

☛ American Boarding Kennels Association, 4575 Galley Rd., Suite 400A, Colorado Springs, CO 80915. Internet: **http://www.abka.com**

For information on laboratory animal technicians and certification, contact:

☛ American Association for Laboratory Animal Science, 9190 Crestwyn Hills Drive, Memphis, TN 38125.

Protective Service Occupations

Correctional Officers

(O*NET 61099E and 63017)

Significant Points

- The work can be stressful because of concern for personal safety.
- Job opportunities are expected to be very favorable due to much faster than average employment growth coupled with high turnover.
- Most jobs are in large regional jails or in prisons in rural areas.

Nature of the Work

Correctional officers are responsible for overseeing individuals who have been arrested and are awaiting trial or who have been convicted of a crime and sentenced to serve time in a jail, reformatory, or penitentiary. They maintain security and inmate accountability in order to prevent disturbances, assaults, or escapes. Officers have no law enforcement responsibilities outside the institution where they work. (For more information on related occupations, see the statement on police and detectives elsewhere in the *Handbook.*)

Police and sheriffs' departments in county and municipal jails or precinct station houses employ many correctional officers, also known as detention officers. Most of the approximately 3,300 jails in the United States are operated by county governments, with about three-quarters of all jails under the jurisdiction of an elected sheriff. Individuals in the jail population change constantly as some are released, some are convicted and transferred to prison, and new offenders are arrested and enter the system. Correctional officers in the American jail system hold and process more than 22 million people a year, with about half a million offenders in jail at any given time. When individuals are first arrested, the jail staff may not know their true identity or criminal record, and violent detainees may be placed in the general population. This is the most dangerous phase of the incarceration process for correctional officers.

Most correctional officers are employed in large regional jails or State and Federal prisons, watching over the approximately one million offenders who are incarcerated in Federal and State prisons at any given time. In addition to jails and prisons, a relatively small number of correctional officers oversee individuals being held by the Immigration and Naturalization Service before they are released or deported, or they work for correctional institutions that are run by private for-profit organizations. While both jails and prisons can be dangerous places to work, prison populations are more stable than jail populations, and correctional officers in prisons know the security and custodial requirements of the prisoners with whom they are dealing.

Regardless of the setting, correctional officers maintain order within the institution, and enforce rules and regulations. To help ensure that inmates are orderly and obey rules, correctional officers monitor the activities and supervise the work assignments of inmates. Sometimes, it is necessary for officers to search inmates and their living quarters for contraband like weapons or drugs, settle disputes between inmates, and enforce discipline. Correctional officers periodically inspect the facilities, checking cells and other areas of the institution for unsanitary conditions, contraband, fire hazards, and any evidence of infractions of rules. In addition, they routinely inspect locks, window bars, grilles, doors, and gates for signs of tampering. Finally, officers inspect mail and visitors for prohibited items.

Correctional officers report orally and in writing on inmate conduct and on the quality and quantity of work done by inmates. Officers also report security breaches, disturbances, violations of rules, and any unusual occurrences. They usually keep a daily log or record of their activities. Correctional officers cannot show favoritism and must report any inmate who violates the rules. Should the situation arise, they help the responsible law enforcement authorities investigate crimes committed within their institution or search for escaped inmates.

In jail and prison facilities with direct supervision cellblocks, officers work unarmed. They are equipped with communications devices so that they can summon help if necessary. These officers often work in a cell block alone, or with another officer, among the 50 to 100 inmates who reside there. The officers enforce regulations primarily through their interpersonal communications skills and the use of progressive sanctions, such as loss of some privileges.

More correctional officers are needed to oversee the growing number of inmates held in jails and prisons.

In the highest security facilities where the most dangerous inmates are housed, correctional officers often monitor the activities of prisoners from a centralized control center with the aid of closed circuit television cameras and a computer tracking system. In such an environment, the inmates may not see anyone but officers for days or weeks at a time and only leave their cells for showers, solitary exercise time, or visitors. Depending on the offender's security classification within the institution, correctional officers may have to restrain inmates in handcuffs and leg irons in order to safely escort them to and from cells and other areas to see authorized visitors. Officers also escort prisoners between the institution and courtrooms, medical facilities, and other destinations outside the institution.

Working Conditions

Working in a correctional institution can be stressful and hazardous. Every year, a number of correctional officers are injured in confrontations with inmates in the process of carrying out their daily duties. Correctional officers may work indoors or outdoors, depending on their specific duties. Some correctional institutions are well lit, temperature controlled, and ventilated, while others are old, overcrowded, hot, and noisy. Correctional officers usually work an 8-hour day, 5 days a week, on rotating shifts. Prison and jail security must be provided around the clock, which often means that officers work all hours of the day and night, weekends, and holidays. In addition, officers may be required to work paid overtime.

Employment

Correctional officers held about 383,000 jobs in 1998. Almost six of every 10 worked at State correctional institutions such as prisons, prison camps, and youth correctional facilities. Most of the remainder worked at city and county jails or other institutions run by local governments. About 12,000 correctional officers worked in Federal correctional institutions, and about 10,400 worked in privately owned and managed prisons.

Most correctional officers work in large institutions located in rural areas, although a significant number work in jails and other facilities located in law enforcement agencies throughout the country.

Training, Other Qualifications, and Advancement

Most institutions require that correctional officers be at least 18 to 21 years of age, have a high school education or its equivalent, have no felony convictions, and be a United States citizen. Promotion prospects may be enhanced through obtaining a postsecondary education.

Correctional officers must be in good health. Candidates for employment are generally required to meet formal standards of physical fitness, eyesight, and hearing. In addition, many jurisdictions use standard tests to determine applicant suitability to work in a correctional environment. Good judgment and the ability to think and act quickly are indispensable. Applicants are typically screened for drug abuse, subject to background checks, and required to pass a written examination.

Federal, State, and some local departments of corrections provide training for correctional officers based on guidelines established by the American Correctional Association and the American Jail Association. Some States have regional training academies which are available to local agencies. All States and local correctional agencies provide on-the-job training at the conclusion of formal instruction, including legal restrictions and interpersonal relations. Many systems require firearms proficiency and self-defense skills. Officer trainees typically receive several weeks or months of training in an actual job setting under the supervision of an experienced officer. Nevertheless, specific entry requirements and on-the-job training vary widely from agency to agency.

Academy trainees generally receive instruction on a number of subjects, including institutional policies, regulations, and operations, as well as custody and security procedures. As a condition of employment, new Federal correctional officers must undergo 200 hours of formal training within the first year of employment. They also must complete 120 hours of specialized training at the Federal Bureau of Prisons residential training center at Glynco, Georgia within the first 60 days after appointment. Experienced officers receive annual in-service training to keep abreast of new developments and procedures.

Some correctional officers are members of prison tactical response teams, which are trained to respond to disturbances, riots, hostage situations, forced cell moves, and other potentially dangerous confrontations. Team members receive training and practice with weapons, chemical agents, forced entry methods, crisis management, and other tactics.

With education, experience, and training, qualified officers may advance to correctional sergeant. Correctional sergeants supervise correctional officers and usually are responsible for maintaining security and directing the activities of other officers during an assigned shift or in an assigned area. Ambitious and qualified correctional officers can be promoted to supervisory or administrative positions all the way up to warden. Officers sometimes transfer to related areas, such as probation or parole officer.

Job Outlook

Job opportunities for correctional officers are expected to be very favorable through 2008. The need to replace correctional officers who transfer to other occupations or leave the labor force, coupled with rising employment demand, will generate thousands of job openings each year. In the past, some local and State corrections agencies have experienced difficulty in attracting and keeping qualified applicants, largely due to relatively low salaries and the concentration of jobs in rural locations. This situation is expected to continue.

Employment of correctional officers is expected to increase much faster than the average for all occupations through 2008, as additional officers are hired to supervise and control a growing inmate population. Increasing public concern about the spread of crime and illegal drugs—resulting in more arrests and convictions—and the adoption of mandatory sentencing guidelines calling for longer sentences and reduced parole for inmates will spur demand for correctional officers. Moreover, expansion and new construction of corrections facilities also are expected to create many new jobs for correctional officers, although State and local government budgetary constraints could affect the rate at which new facilities are built and staffed. Some employment opportunities will also arise in the private sector as public authorities contract with private companies to provide and staff corrections facilities.

Layoffs of correctional officers are rare because of increasing offender populations. While officers are allowed to join bargaining units, they are not allowed to strike.

Earnings

Median annual earnings of correctional officers were $28,540 in 1998. The middle 50 percent earned between $22,930 and $37,550. The lowest 10 percent had earnings of less than $18,810, while the top 10 percent earned over $46,320. Median annual earnings in the industries employing the largest numbers of correctional officers in 1997 in the public sector were $32,600 in the Federal Government, $29,700 in local government, and $27,300 in State government. In the management and public relations industry, where officers employed by privately operated prisons are classified, median annual earnings were $18,500.

According to a 1999 survey in *Corrections Compendium,* a national journal for corrections professionals, there is no common pattern or trend in correctional salaries around the United States. The variance between the low and high starting salaries exists for all positions and personnel of all experience levels. Beginning salaries for State correctional officers ranged from $14,600 in California to $34,100 in New Jersey. The median salary for correctional officers with more than one year of experience ranged from $18,000 in Mississippi to $44,800 in New Jersey.

At the Federal level, the starting salary was about $20,600 to $23,000 a year in 1999. Correctional officers rated Senior Officer Specialist, who are required to be able to work any correctional post within an institution, started at about $28,200 a year. Starting salaries were slightly higher in selected areas where prevailing local pay levels were higher. The annual average salary for correctional officers employed by the Federal Government was $36,500 in early 1999.

In addition to typical benefits, correctional officers employed in the public sector usually are provided with uniforms or a clothing allowance to purchase their own uniforms. Civil service systems or merit boards cover officers employed by the Federal Government and most State governments. Their retirement coverage entitles them to retire at age 50 after 20 years of service or at any age with 25 years of service.

Related Occupations

A number of options are available to those interested in careers in protective services and security. House or store detectives patrol business establishments to protect against theft and vandalism and to enforce standards of good behavior. Security guards protect people and property against theft, vandalism, illegal entry, and fire. Police officers and deputy sheriffs maintain law and order, prevent crime, and arrest offenders. Probation and parole officers monitor and counsel offenders in the community and evaluate their progress in becoming productive members of society. Some of these related occupations are discussed elsewhere in the *Handbook*.

Sources of Additional Information

Information about correctional jobs in a jail setting is available from:

☛ The American Jail Association, 2053 Day Rd., Suite 100, Hagerstown, MD 21740. Internet: **http://www.corrections.com/aja/index.html**

For information about careers as a correctional officer in jails and prisons, contact:

☛ The International Association of Correctional Officers (IACO), P.O. Box 81826, Lincoln, NE 68501.
Internet: **http://www.acsp.uic.edu/iaco**

Information on entrance requirements, training, and career opportunities for correctional officers on the Federal level may be obtained by calling the Federal Bureau of Prisons at (800) 347-7744.
Internet: **http://www.bop.gov**

Information on obtaining a job with the Federal Government is available from the Office of Personnel Management through a telephone-based system. Consult your telephone directory under U.S. Government for a local number or call (912) 757-3000; TDD (912) 744-2299. The number is not toll free and charges may result.
Internet: **http://www.usajobs.opm.gov**

Fire Fighting Occupations

(O*NET 61002A, 61002B, 63002A, 63002B, 63005, 63008A, and 63008B)

Significant Points

- Fire fighting involves hazardous conditions and long, irregular hours.
- Keen competition for jobs is expected; many people are attracted to the occupation because it provides considerable job security and the opportunity to perform an essential public service.

Nature of the Work

Every year, fires and other emergencies take thousands of lives and destroy property worth billions of dollars. Firefighters help protect the public against these dangers by rapidly responding to a variety of emergency situations. They are frequently the first emergency personnel at the scene of an accident or medical emergency and may be called upon to put out a fire, treat injuries, or perform other vital functions.

During duty hours, firefighters must be prepared to respond immediately to a fire or any other emergency that arises. Because fighting fires is dangerous and complex, it requires organization and teamwork. At every emergency scene, firefighters perform specific duties assigned by a superior officer. At fires, they connect hose lines to hydrants, operate a pump to high pressure hoses, and position ladders to deliver water to the fire. They also rescue victims and administer emergency medical aid as needed, ventilate smoke-filled areas, and attempt to salvage the contents of buildings. Their duties may change several times while the company is in action. Sometimes they remain at the site of a disaster for days at a time, rescuing trapped survivors and assisting with medical treatment.

Firefighters have assumed a range of responsibilities, including emergency medical services. In fact, most calls to which firefighters respond involve medical emergencies, and about half of all fire departments provide ambulance service for victims. Firefighters receive training in emergency medical procedures, and many fire departments require them to be certified as emergency medical technicians. (For more information, see the *Handbook* statement on emergency medical technicians and paramedics.)

Firefighters work in a variety of settings, including urban and suburban areas, airports, chemical plants, other industrial sites, and rural areas like grasslands and forests. In addition, some firefighters work in hazardous materials units that are trained for the control, prevention, and cleanup of oil spills and other hazardous materials incidents. Workers in urban and suburban areas, airports and industrial sites typically use conventional fire fighting equipment and tactics, while forest fires and major spills call for different methods.

In national forests and parks, rangers spot fires from watchtowers and report their findings to headquarters by telephone or radio. Forest rangers patrol to ensure travelers and campers comply with fire regulations. When fires break out, crews of firefighters are brought in to suppress the blaze using heavy equipment, handtools, and water hoses. One of the most effective means of battling the blaze is by creating fire lines through cutting down trees and digging out grass and other vegetation, creating bare land in the path of the fire that deprives it of fuel. Elite firefighters, called smoke jumpers, parachute from airplanes to reach inaccessible areas. This can be extremely hazardous because the crews have no way to escape if the wind shifts and causes the fire to burn toward them.

Between alarms, firefighters clean and maintain equipment, conduct practice drills and fire inspections, and participate in physical fitness activities. They also prepare written reports on fire incidents and review fire science literature to keep abreast of technological developments and changing administrative practices and policies.

Most fire departments have a fire prevention division, usually headed by a fire marshall and staffed by fire inspectors. Workers in this division conduct inspections of structures to prevent fires and ensure fire code compliance. These firefighters also work with developers and planners to check and approve plans for new buildings. Fire prevention personnel often speak on these subjects before public assemblies and civic organizations.

Some firefighters become fire investigators, who determine the origin and causes of fires. They collect evidence, interview witnesses, and prepare reports on fires in cases where the cause may be arson or criminal negligence. They are often called upon to testify in court.

Working Conditions

Firefighters spend much of their time at fire stations, which usually have features common to a residential facility like a dorm. When an alarm sounds, firefighters respond rapidly, regardless of the weather or hour. Fire fighting involves risk of death or injury from sudden cave-ins of floors, toppling walls, traffic accidents when responding to calls,

Fire fighting occupations offer the opportunity for public service and the satisfaction of helping others in need.

and exposure to flames and smoke. Firefighters may also come in contact with poisonous, flammable, or explosive gases and chemicals, as well as radioactive or other hazardous materials that may have immediate or long-term effects on their health. For these reasons, they must wear protective gear that can be very heavy and hot.

Work hours of firefighters are longer and vary more widely than hours of most other workers. Many work more than 50 hours a week, and sometimes they may work even longer. In some agencies, they are on duty for 24 hours, then off for 48 hours, and receive an extra day off at intervals. In others, they work a day shift of 10 hours for 3 or 4 days, a night shift of 14 hours for 3 or 4 nights, have 3 or 4 days off, and then repeat the cycle. In addition, firefighters often work extra hours at fires and other emergencies and are regularly assigned to work on holidays. Fire lieutenants and fire captains often work the same hours as the firefighters they supervise. Duty hours include time when firefighters study, train, and perform fire prevention duties.

Employment

Employment figures in this *Handbook* statement include only paid career firefighters—they do not cover volunteer firefighters, who perform the same duties and may comprise the majority of firefighters in a residential area. Paid career firefighters held about 314,000 jobs in 1998. More than 9 of every 10 worked in municipal or county fire departments. Some large cities have thousands of career firefighters, while many small towns have only a few. Most of the remainder worked in fire departments on Federal and State installations, including airports. Private fire fighting companies employ a small number of firefighters and usually operate on a subscription basis.

In response to the expanding role of firefighters, some municipalities have combined fire prevention, public fire education, safety, and emergency medical services into a single organization commonly referred to as a public safety organization. Some local and regional fire departments are being consolidated into county-wide establishments in order to reduce administrative staffs and cut costs, and to establish consistent training standards and work procedures.

Training, Other Qualifications, and Advancement

Applicants for municipal fire fighting jobs generally must pass a written exam; tests of strength, physical stamina, coordination, and agility; and a medical examination that includes drug screening. Workers may be monitored on a random basis for drug use after accepting employment. Examinations are generally open to persons who are at least 18 years of age and have a high school education or the equivalent. Those who receive the highest scores in all phases of testing have the best chances for appointment. The completion of community college courses in fire science may improve an applicant's chances for appointment. In recent years, an increasing proportion of entrants to this occupation has had some postsecondary education.

As a rule, entry-level workers in large fire departments are trained for several weeks at the department's training center or academy. Through classroom instruction and practical training, the recruits study fire fighting techniques, fire prevention, hazardous materials control, local building codes, and emergency medical procedures, including first aid and cardiopulmonary resuscitation. They also learn how to use axes, chain saws, fire extinguishers, ladders, and other fire fighting and rescue equipment. After successfully completing this training, they are assigned to a fire company, where they undergo a period of probation.

A number of fire departments have accredited apprenticeship programs lasting up to 5 years. These programs combine formal, technical instruction with on-the-job training under the supervision of experienced firefighters. Technical instruction covers subjects such as fire fighting techniques and equipment, chemical hazards associated with various combustible building materials, emergency medical procedures, and fire prevention and safety. Fire departments frequently conduct training programs, and some firefighters attend training sessions sponsored by the National Fire Academy. These training sessions cover topics including executive development, anti-arson techniques, disaster preparedness, hazardous materials control, and public fire safety and education. Some States also have extensive firefighter training and certification programs. In addition, a number of colleges and universities offer courses leading to 2- or 4-year degrees in fire engineering or fire science. Many fire departments offer firefighters incentives such as tuition reimbursement or higher pay for completing advanced training.

Among the personal qualities firefighters need are mental alertness, self-discipline, courage, mechanical aptitude, endurance, strength, and a sense of public service. Initiative and good judgment are also extremely important because firefighters make quick decisions in emergencies. Because members of a crew live and work closely together under conditions of stress and danger for extended periods, they must be dependable and able to get along well with others. Leadership qualities are necessary for officers, who must establish and maintain discipline and efficiency, as well as direct the activities of firefighters in their companies.

Most experienced firefighters continue studying to improve their job performance and prepare for promotion examinations. To progress to higher-level positions, they acquire expertise in advanced fire fighting equipment and techniques, building construction, emergency medical technology, writing, public speaking, management and budgeting procedures, and public relations.

Opportunities for promotion depend upon written examination results, job performance, interviews, and seniority. Increasingly, fire departments use assessment centers, which simulate a variety of actual job performance tasks, to screen for the best candidates for promotion. The line of promotion is usually to engineer, lieutenant, captain, battalion chief, assistant chief, deputy chief, and finally to chief. Many fire departments now require a bachelor's degree, preferably in fire science, public administration, or a related field, for promotion to positions higher than battalion chief. There are requirements for a master's degree for executive fire officer certification from the National Fire Academy and for State chief officer certification.

Job Outlook

Prospective firefighters are expected to face keen competition for available job openings. Many people are attracted to fire fighting because it is challenging and provides the opportunity to perform an essential public service, a high school education is usually sufficient, and a pension is guaranteed upon retirement after 20 years. Consequently, the number of qualified applicants in most areas exceeds the number of job openings, even though the written examination and physical requirements eliminate many applicants. This situation is expected to persist in coming years.

Employment of firefighters is expected to increase more slowly than the average for all occupations through 2008 as fire departments continue to compete with other public safety providers for funding. Most job growth will occur as volunteer fire fighting positions are converted to paid positions.

Turnover of firefighter jobs is unusually low, particularly for a hazardous occupation that requires a relatively limited investment in formal education. In addition to job growth, openings are expected to result from the need to replace those who retire, stop working for other reasons, or transfer to other occupations.

Layoffs of firefighters are uncommon. Fire protection is an essential service, and citizens are likely to exert considerable pressure on local officials to expand or at least preserve the level of fire protection. Even when budget cuts do occur, local fire departments usually cut expenses by postponing equipment purchases or not hiring new firefighters, rather than by laying off staff.

Earnings

Median annual earnings of firefighters were $31,170 in 1998. The middle 50 percent earned between $22,370 and $40,840. The lowest 10 percent earned less than $14,310, and the highest 10 percent earned more than $50,930. Firefighters employed in local government, except education and hospitals, had median earnings of $31,400 in 1997; those employed by State government, except education and hospitals, had median earnings of $29,400; and firefighters in the Federal government had median earnings of $26,900.

Median annual earnings of fire fighting and prevention supervisors were $44,830 in 1998. The middle 50 percent earned between $34,020 and $59,610. The lowest 10 percent earned less than $23,050, and the highest 10 percent earned more than $81,570. Fire fighting and prevention supervisors employed in local government, except education and hospitals, earned about $45,200 in 1997.

Median annual earnings of fire inspection occupations were $40,040 in 1998. The middle 50 percent earned between $30,500 and $50,610. The lowest 10 percent earned less than $22,150, and the highest 10 percent earned more than $73,570.

The International City-County Management Association's annual Police and Fire Personnel, Salaries, and Expenditures Survey revealed that 89 percent of the municipalities surveyed provided fire protection services in 1997. The following 1997 salaries pertain to sworn full-time positions.

	Minimum annual base salary	*Maximum annual base salary*
Firefighters	$26,900	$35,200
Engineer	32,200	39,800
Fire Lieutenant	35,100	41,100
Fire Captain	37,500	44,700
Assistant Fire Chief	43,900	53,200
Battalion Chief	45,300	56,000
Deputy Chief	45,900	56,900
Fire Chief	52,700	66,000

Firefighters who average more than a certain number of hours a week are required to be paid overtime. The hours threshold is determined by the department during the firefighter's work period, which ranges from 7 to 28 days. Firefighters often earn overtime for working extra shifts to maintain minimum staffing levels or for special emergencies.

Firefighters receive benefits usually including medical and liability insurance, vacation and sick leave, and some paid holidays. Almost all fire departments provide protective clothing (helmets, boots, and coats) and breathing apparatus, and many also provide dress uniforms. Firefighters are generally covered by pension plans, often providing retirement at half pay after 25 years of service or if disabled in the line of duty.

Many career firefighters are represented by the International Association of Firefighters, while many chief officers belong to the International Association of Fire Chiefs.

Related Occupations

Fire-protection engineers identify fire hazards in homes and workplaces and design prevention programs and automatic fire detection and extinguishing systems. Like firefighters, police officers and emergency medical technicians respond to emergencies and save lives.

Sources of Additional Information

Information about a career as a firefighter may be obtained from local fire departments and from:

☛ International Association of Firefighters, 1750 New York Ave. NW., Washington, DC 20006.
Internet: **http://www.iaff.org/iaff/index.html**

☛ U.S. Fire Administration, 16825 South Seton Ave., Emmitsburg, MD 21727.

Information about firefighter professional qualifications and a list of colleges and universities offering 2- or 4-year degree programs in fire science or fire prevention may be obtained from:

☛ National Fire Academy, Degrees at a Distance Program, 16825 South Seton Ave., Emmitsburg, MD 21727.
Internet: **http://www.usfa.fema.gov/nfa/index.htm**

Guards

(O*Net 63047)

Significant Points

- Favorable opportunities are expected for lower paying jobs, but stiff competition is likely for higher-paying positions at facilities requiring a high level of security, such as nuclear plants and government installations.
- Some positions, such as those of armored car guards, are hazardous.
- Because of limited formal training requirements and flexible hours, this occupation attracts many individuals seeking a second or part-time job.

Nature of the Work

Guards, who are also called security officers, patrol and inspect property to protect against fire, theft, vandalism, and illegal activity. These workers protect their employer's investment, enforce laws on the property, and deter criminal activity or other problems. They use radio and telephone communications to call for assistance from an ambulance, wrecker, or the police or fire departments as the situation dictates. Security guards write comprehensive reports outlining their observations and activities during their assigned shift. They may also interview witnesses or victims, prepare case reports, and testify in court.

Although all security guards perform many of the same duties, specific duties vary based on whether the guard works in a "static" security position or on a mobile patrol. Guards assigned to static security positions usually serve the client at one location for a specific length of time. These guards must become closely acquainted with the property and people associated with it, complete all tasks assigned them, and often monitor alarms and closed circuit TV cameras. In contrast, guards assigned to mobile patrol duty drive or walk from location to location and conduct security checks within an assigned geographical zone. They may detain or arrest criminal violators, answer service calls concerning criminal activity or problems, and issue traffic violation warnings.

Specific job responsibilities also vary with the size, type, and location of the employer. In department stores, guards protect people, records, merchandise, money, and equipment. They often work with undercover store detectives to prevent theft by customers or store employees and help in the apprehension of shoplifting suspects prior to arrival by police. In office buildings, banks, and hospitals, guards maintain order and protect the institutions' property, staff, and customers. At air, sea, and rail terminals and other transportation facilities, guards protect people, freight, property, and equipment. They may screen passengers and visitors for weapons and explosives using metal detectors and high-tech equipment, ensure nothing is stolen while being loaded or unloaded, and watch for fires and criminals.

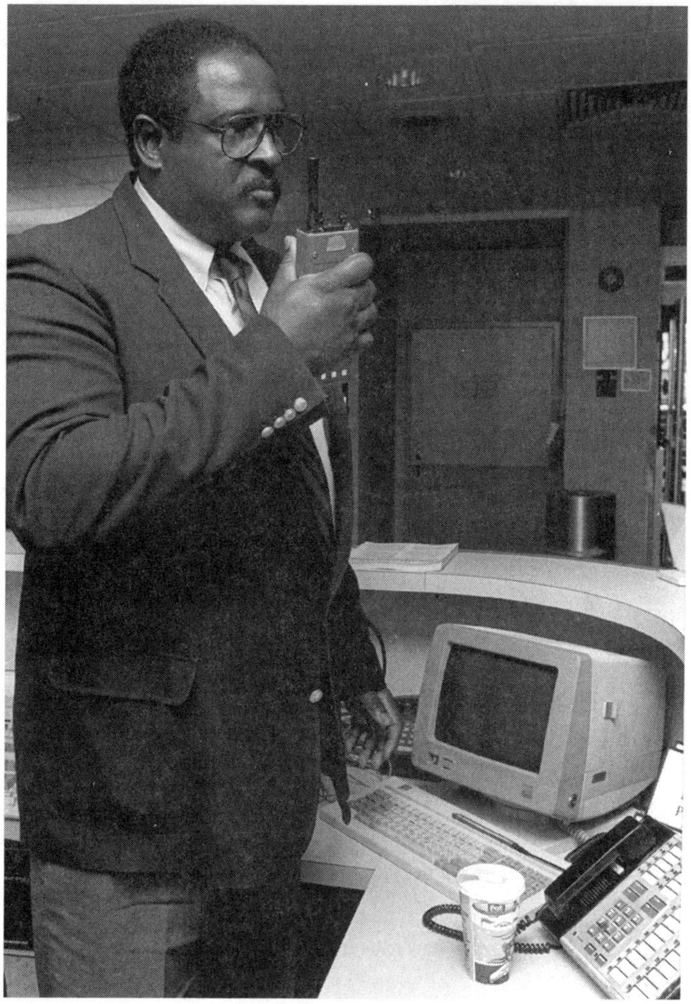

Guard positions are frequently filled through contracts with industrial security firms and commercial guard agencies.

Guards who work in public buildings such as museums or art galleries protect paintings and exhibits by inspecting people and packages entering and leaving the building. In factories, laboratories, government buildings, data processing centers, and military bases, security officers protect information, products, computer codes, and defense secrets. They check the credentials of people and vehicles entering and leaving the premises. Guards working at universities, parks, and sports stadiums perform crowd control, supervise parking and seating, and direct traffic. Security guards stationed at the entrance to bars and places of adult entertainment, such as nightclubs, prevent access by minors, collect cover charges at the door, maintain order among customers, and protect property and patrons.

Armored car guards protect money and valuables during transit. In addition, they protect individuals responsible for making commercial bank deposits from theft or bodily injury. When the armored car arrives at the door of a business, an armed guard enters, signs for the money, and returns to the truck with the valuables in hand. The return to the truck with the money and taking the deposits into the bank can be extremely hazardous for the guard, and a number of them have been robbed and shot in recent years, so armored car guards usually wear bullet-proof vests.

All security officers must show good judgment and common sense, follow directions and directives from supervisors, accurately testify in court, and follow company policy and guidelines. Guards should have a professional appearance and attitude and be able to interact with the public. They also must be able to take charge and direct others in emergencies or other dangerous incidents. In a large organization, the security manager is often in charge of a trained guard force divided into shifts; whereas in a small organization, a single worker may be responsible for all security.

Working Conditions
Most guards spend considerable time on their feet, either assigned to a specific post or patrolling buildings and grounds. Guards may be stationed at a guard desk inside a building to monitor electronic security and surveillance devices or to check the credentials of persons entering or leaving the premises. They also may be stationed outside at a guardhouse of the sort found at gated communities and use a portable radio or telephone that allows them to be in constant contact with a central station outside the guarded area. Guard work is usually routine, but guards must be constantly alert for threats to themselves and the property they are protecting. Guards who work during the day may have a great deal of contact with other employees and members of the public.

Guards usually work at least 8-hour shifts for 40 hours per week and are often on call in case an emergency arises. Some employers have three shifts, and guards rotate to equally divide daytime, weekend, and holiday work. Guards usually eat on the job instead of taking a regular break away from the site.

Employment
Guards held over 1 million jobs in 1998. Industrial security firms and guard agencies employed 60 percent of all wage and salary guards. These organizations provide security services on a contract basis, assigning their guards to buildings and other sites as needed. Most other security officers were employed by the organization they are responsible for guarding, such as banks, building management companies, hotels, hospitals, retail stores, restaurants, bars, schools, and government. Guard jobs are found throughout the country, most commonly in metropolitan areas. Over 1 in 4 guards worked part time, and many individuals held a second job as a guard to supplement their primary earnings.

A significant number of law-enforcement officers work as security guards when off-duty to supplement their incomes. Often working in uniform and with the official cars assigned to them, they add a high profile security presence to the establishment with which they have contracted. At construction sites and apartment complexes, for example, their presence often prevents trouble before it starts. Some shopping centers and theaters have officers mounted on horses or bicycles continuously ride around their parking lots to deter car theft and robberies. (Police and detectives are discussed separately in this section of the *Handbook*.)

Training, Other Qualifications, and Advancement
Most States require that guards be licensed. To be licensed as a guard, individuals must usually be at least 18 years old, pass a background check, and complete classroom training in such subjects as property rights, emergency procedures, and detention of suspected criminals. Drug testing is often required, and may be random and ongoing.

Many employers of unarmed guards do not have any specific educational requirements. For armed guards, employers usually prefer individuals who are high school graduates or hold an equivalent certification. Many jobs require a driver's license. For positions as armed guards, employers often seek people who have had responsible experience in other occupations.

Guards who carry weapons must be licensed by the appropriate government authority, and some receive further certification as special police officers, which allows them to make limited types of arrests while on duty. Armed guard positions have more stringent background checks and entry requirements than those of unarmed guards because of greater insurance liability risks. Compared to unarmed security guards, armed guards and special police typically enjoy higher earnings and benefits, greater job security, more advancement potential, and are usually given more training and responsibility.

Rigorous hiring and screening programs consisting of background checks and criminal record file and fingerprint checks are becoming the norm in the occupation. Applicants are expected to have good character references, no serious police record, and good health. They should be mentally alert, emotionally stable, and physically fit in order to cope with emergencies. Guards who have frequent contact with the public should communicate well.

Candidates for guard jobs in the Federal Government must have some experience in the occupation and pass a written examination in order to be certified by the General Services Administration. Armed Forces experience is an asset. For Federal guard positions, applicants must also qualify in the use of firearms and pass a test on first aid.

The amount of training guards receive varies. Training requirements are higher for armed guards because their employers are legally responsible for any use of force. Armed guards receive formal training in areas such as weapons retention and laws covering the use of force.

Many employers give newly hired guards instruction before they start the job and also provide on-the-job training. An increasing number of States are making ongoing training a legal requirement for retention of certification. Guards may receive training in protection, public relations, report writing, crisis deterrence, first aid, as well as specialized training relevant to their particular assignment.

Guards employed at establishments placing a heavy emphasis on security usually receive extensive formal training. For example, guards at nuclear power plants undergo several months of training before being placed on duty under close supervision. They are taught to use firearms, administer first aid, operate alarm systems and electronic security equipment, and spot and deal with security problems. Guards authorized to carry firearms may be periodically tested in their use.

Although guards in small companies may receive periodic salary increases, advancement opportunities are limited. Most large organizations use a military type of ranking that offers the possibility of advancement in position and salary. Some guards may advance to supervisor or security manager positions. Guards with management skills may open their own contract security guard agencies.

Job Outlook
Opportunities for most jobs as guards should be very favorable through the year 2008. Numerous job openings will stem from employment growth attributable to the desire for increased security, and from the need to replace those who leave this large occupation each year. Many opportunities are expected for persons seeking full-time employment, as well as for those seeking part-time or second jobs. However, competition is expected for higher-paying positions that require longer periods of training; these positions are usually found at facilities that require a high level of security, such as nuclear power plants or weapons installations.

Employment of guards is expected to grow faster than the average for all occupations through 2008, as increased concern about crime, vandalism, and terrorism will heighten the need for security. Demand for guards will also grow as private security firms increasingly perform duties, such as monitoring crowds at airports and providing security in courts, which were formerly handled by government police officers and marshals. Because enlisting the services of a security guard firm is easier and less costly than assuming direct responsibility for hiring, training, and managing a security guard force, job growth is expected to be concentrated among contract security guard agencies.

Earnings
Median annual earnings of guards were $16,240 in 1998. The middle 50 percent earned between $13,430 and $20,110. The lowest 10 percent had earnings of less than $11,970, while the top 10 percent earned

over $26,640. Median annual earnings in the industries employing the largest numbers of guards in 1997 are shown below.

Real estate operators and lessors	$20,300
Hospitals	19,500
Hotels and motels	18,000
Miscellaneous amusement and recreation services	15,800
Miscellaneous business services	14,800

Depending on their experience, newly hired guards in the Federal Government earned $16,400 or $18,400 a year in 1999. Beginning salaries were slightly higher in selected areas where the prevailing local pay level was higher. Guards employed by the Federal Government averaged about $26,300 a year in early 1999. These workers usually receive overtime pay as well as a wage differential for the second and third shifts.

Related Occupations

Guards protect property, maintain security, and enforce regulations and standards of conduct in the establishments at which they work. Related security and protective service occupations include law enforcement officers, bailiffs, correctional officers, house or store detectives, and private investigators.

Sources of Additional Information

Further information about work opportunities for guards is available from local security and guard firms and State employment service offices. Information about licensing requirements for guards may be obtained from the State licensing commission or the State police department. In States where local jurisdictions establish licensing requirements, contact a local government authority such as the sheriff, county executive, or city manager.

Police and Detectives

(O*Net 21911C, 61005, 63011A, 63011B, 63014A, 63014B, 63021, 63023, 63026, 63028A, 63028B, 63032, 63038, and 63041)

Significant Points

- Police work can be dangerous and stressful.
- The number of qualified candidates exceeds the number of job openings in Federal and State law enforcement agencies but is inadequate to meet growth and replacement needs in many local and special police departments.
- The largest number of employment opportunities will arise in urban communities with relatively low salaries and high crime rates.

Nature of the Work

People depend on police officers and detectives to protect their lives and property. Law enforcement officers, some of whom are State or Federal special agents or inspectors, perform these duties in a variety of ways, depending on the size and type of their organization. In most jurisdictions, they are expected to exercise authority when necessary, whether on or off duty.

According to the Bureau of Justice Statistics, about 65 percent of State and local law enforcement officers are uniformed personnel, who regularly patrol and respond to calls for service. Police officers who work in small communities and rural areas have general law enforcement duties. They may direct traffic at the scene of a fire, investigate a burglary, or give first aid to an accident victim. In large police departments, officers usually are assigned to a specific type of duty. Many urban police agencies are becoming more involved in community policing—a practice in which an officer builds relationships with the citizens of local neighborhoods and mobilizes the public to help fight crime.

Police agencies are usually organized into geographic districts, with uniformed officers assigned to patrol a specific area, such as part of the business district or outlying residential neighborhoods. Officers may work alone, but in large agencies they often patrol with a partner. While on patrol, officers attempt to become thoroughly familiar with their patrol area and remain alert for anything unusual. Suspicious circumstances and hazards to public safety are investigated or noted, and officers are dispatched to individual calls for assistance within their district. During their shift, they may identify, pursue, and arrest suspected criminals, resolve problems within the community, and enforce traffic laws.

Some police officers specialize in such diverse fields as chemical and microscopic analysis, training and firearms instruction, or handwriting and fingerprint identification. Others work with special units such as horseback, bicycle, motorcycle or harbor patrol, canine corps, or special weapons and tactics (SWAT) or emergency response teams. About 1 in 10 local and special law enforcement officers perform jail-related duties, and around 4 percent work in courts. Regardless of job duties or location, police officers and detectives at all levels must write reports and maintain meticulous records that will be needed if they testify in court.

Detectives are plainclothes investigators who gather facts and collect evidence for criminal cases. Some are assigned to interagency task forces to combat specific types of crime. They conduct interviews, examine records, observe the activities of suspects, and participate in raids or arrests. Detectives and State and Federal agents and inspectors usually specialize in one of a wide variety of violations such as homicide or fraud. They are assigned cases on a rotating basis and work on them until an arrest and conviction occurs or until the case is dropped.

Sheriffs and deputy sheriffs enforce the law on the county level. Sheriffs are usually elected to their posts and perform duties similar to those of a local or county police chief. Sheriffs' departments tend to be relatively small, most having fewer than 25 sworn officers. A deputy sheriff in a large agency will have similar specialized law enforcement duties as an officer in an urban police department. Nationwide, about 40 percent of full-time sworn deputies are uniformed officers assigned to patrol and respond to calls, 12 percent are investigators, 30 percent are assigned to jail-related duties, and 11 percent perform court-related duties, with the balance in administration. Police and sheriffs' deputies who provide security in city and county courts are sometimes called bailiffs.

State police officers (sometimes called State troopers or highway patrol officers) arrest criminals Statewide and patrol highways to enforce motor vehicle laws and regulations. Uniformed officers are best known for issuing traffic citations to motorists who violate the law. At the scene of accidents, they may direct traffic, give first aid, and call for emergency equipment. They also write reports used to determine the cause of the accident. State police officers are frequently called upon to render assistance to other law enforcement agencies.

State law enforcement agencies operate in every State except Hawaii. Seventy percent of the full-time sworn personnel in the 49 State police agencies are uniformed officers who regularly patrol and respond to calls for service. Fifteen percent are investigators; 2 percent are assigned to court-related duties; and the remaining 13 percent work in administrative or other assignments.

Public college and university police forces, public school district police, and agencies serving transportation systems and facilities are examples of special police agencies. There are more than 1,300 of these agencies with special geographic jurisdictions or enforcement responsibilities in the United States. More than three-fourths of the sworn personnel in special agencies are uniformed officers, and about 15 percent are investigators.

The Federal Government maintains a high profile in many areas of law enforcement. The Department of Justice is the largest employer of sworn Federal officers. *Federal Bureau of Investigation (FBI)* agents are the Government's principal investigators, responsible for investigating violations of more than 260 statutes and conducting sensitive national security investigations. Agents may conduct surveillance, monitor court-authorized wiretaps, examine business records, investigate white-collar crime, track the interstate movement of stolen property, collect evidence of espionage activities, or participate in sensitive undercover assignments. The FBI investigates organized crime, public corruption, financial crime, fraud against the government, bribery, copyright infringement, civil rights violations, bank robbery, extortion, kidnapping, air piracy, terrorism, foreign counterintelligence, interstate criminal activity, drug trafficking, and other violations of Federal statutes.

Drug Enforcement Administration (DEA) agents enforce laws and regulations relating to illegal drugs. Not only is the DEA the lead agency for domestic enforcement of Federal drug laws, but it also has sole responsibility for coordinating and pursuing U.S. drug investigations abroad. Agents may conduct complex criminal investigations, carry out surveillance of criminals, and infiltrate illicit drug organizations using undercover techniques.

U.S. marshals and deputy marshals protect the Federal courts and ensure the effective operation of the judicial system. They provide protection for the Federal judiciary, transport Federal prisoners, protect Federal witnesses, and manage assets seized from criminal enterprises. In addition, the Marshals Service pursues and arrests 55 percent of all Federal fugitives, more than all other Federal agencies combined.

Immigration and Naturalization Service (INS) agents and inspectors facilitate the entry of legal visitors and immigrants to the United States and detain and deport those arriving illegally. They consist of border patrol agents, immigration inspectors, criminal investigators and immigration agents, and detention and deportation officers. Nearly half of sworn INS officers are border patrol agents. *U.S. Border Patrol agents* protect more than 8,000 miles of international land and water boundaries. Their missions are to detect and prevent the smuggling and unlawful entry of undocumented aliens into the United States, apprehend those persons found in violation of the immigration laws, and interdict contraband, such as narcotics. *Immigration inspectors* interview and examine people seeking entrance to the United States and its territories. They inspect passports to determine whether people are legally eligible to enter the United States. Immigration inspectors also prepare reports, maintain records, and process applications and petitions for immigration or temporary residence in the United States.

Police officers often specialize in a particular field of law enforcement.

Special agents and inspectors employed by the U.S. Department of the Treasury work for the Bureau of Alcohol, Tobacco, and Firearms, the Customs Service, and the Secret Service. *Bureau of Alcohol, Tobacco, and Firearms* (ATF) agents regulate and investigate violations of Federal firearms and explosives laws, as well as Federal alcohol and tobacco tax regulations. *Customs agents* investigate violations of narcotics smuggling, money laundering, child pornography, customs fraud, and enforcement of the Arms Export Control Act. Domestic and foreign investigations involve the development and use of informants, physical and electronic surveillance, and examination of records from importers/exporters, banks, couriers, and manufacturers. They conduct interviews, serve on joint task forces with other agencies, and get and execute search warrants.

Customs inspectors inspect cargo, baggage, and articles worn or carried by people and carriers including vessels, vehicles, trains and aircraft entering or leaving the U.S. to enforce laws governing imports and exports. These inspectors examine, count, weigh, gauge, measure, and sample commercial and noncommercial cargoes entering and leaving the United States. Customs inspectors seize prohibited or smuggled articles, intercept contraband, and apprehend, search, detain, and arrest violators of U.S. laws. *U.S. Secret Service* special agents protect the President, Vice President, and their immediate families, Presidential candidates, ex-Presidents, and foreign dignitaries visiting the United States. Secret Service agents also investigate counterfeiting, forgery of Government checks or bonds, and fraudulent use of credit cards.

The U.S. Department of State *Bureau of Diplomatic Security* special agents are engaged in the battle against terrorism and their numbers are expected to grow rapidly as the threat of terrorism increases. Overseas, they advise ambassadors on all security matters and manage a complex range of security programs designed to protect personnel, facilities, and information. In the United States, they investigate passport and visa fraud, conduct personnel security investigations, issue security clearances, and protect the Secretary of State and a number of foreign dignitaries. They also train foreign civilian police and administer counter-terrorism and counter-narcotics reward programs.

Other Federal agencies employ police and special agents with sworn arrest powers and the authority to carry firearms. These agencies include the U.S. Postal Service, the Bureau of Indian Affairs Office of Law Enforcement under the Department of the Interior, the U.S. Forest Service under the Department of Agriculture, the National Park Service under the Department of the Interior, and Federal Air Marshals under the Department of Transportation. Other police agencies have evolved from the need for security for the agency's property and personnel. The largest such agency is the General Services Administration's Federal Protective Service, which provides security for Federal workers, buildings, and property.

Working Conditions

Police work can be very dangerous and stressful. In addition to the obvious dangers of confrontations with criminals, officers need to be constantly alert and ready to deal appropriately with a number of other threatening situations. Many law enforcement officers witness death and suffering resulting from accidents and criminal behavior. A career in law enforcement may take a toll on officers' private lives.

Uniformed officers, detectives, agents, and inspectors are usually scheduled to work 40-hour weeks, but paid overtime is common. Shift work is necessary because protection must be provided around the clock. Junior officers frequently work weekends, holidays, and nights. Police officers and detectives are required to work at any time their services are needed and may work long hours during investigations. In most jurisdictions, whether on or off duty, officers are expected to be armed and to exercise their arrest authority whenever necessary.

The jobs of some Federal agents such as U.S. Secret Service and DEA special agents require extensive travel, often on very short notice. They may relocate a number of times over the course of their careers. Some special agents in agencies such as the U.S. Border Patrol work outdoors in rugged terrain for long periods and in all kinds of weather.

Employment

Police and detectives held about 764,000 jobs in 1998. About 64 percent of police detectives and investigators were employed by local governments, primarily in cities with more than 25,000 inhabitants. Some cities have very large police forces, while hundreds of small communities employ fewer than 25 officers each. State police agencies employed about 11 percent of all police, detectives, and investigators; and various Federal agencies employed the other 25 percent. Seventy local, special, and State agencies employed 1,000 or more full-time sworn officers, including 41 local police agencies, 15 State police agencies, 12 sheriffs' departments, and two special police agencies—the New York City public school system and the Port Authority of New York/New Jersey.

Training, Other Qualifications, and Advancement

Civil service regulations govern the appointment of police and detectives in practically all States, large municipalities, and special police agencies, as well as in many smaller ones. Candidates must be U.S. citizens, usually at least 20 years of age, and must meet rigorous physical and personal qualifications. Physical examinations for entrance into law enforcement often include tests of vision, hearing, strength, and agility. Eligibility for appointment usually depends on performance in competitive written examinations and previous education and experience. In larger departments, where the majority of law enforcement jobs are found, applicants usually must have at least a high school education. Federal and State agencies typically require a college degree.

Because personal characteristics such as honesty, judgment, integrity, and a sense of responsibility are especially important in law enforcement, candidates are interviewed by senior officers, and their character traits and backgrounds are investigated. In some agencies, candidates are interviewed by a psychiatrist or a psychologist, or given a personality test. Most applicants are subjected to lie detector examinations or drug testing. Some agencies subject sworn personnel to random drug testing as a condition of continuing employment. Candidates for these positions should enjoy working with people and meeting the public.

The FBI has the largest number of special agents. To be considered for appointment as an FBI agent, an applicant either must be a graduate of an accredited law school or a college graduate with a major in accounting, fluency in a foreign language, or 3 years of full-time work experience. All new agents undergo 16 weeks of training at the FBI academy on the U.S. Marine Corps base in Quantico, Virginia.

Applicants for special agent jobs with the U.S. Department of Treasury's Secret Service and the Bureau of Alcohol, Tobacco, and Firearms must have a bachelor's degree or a minimum of 3 years' work experience. Prospective special agents undergo 10 weeks of initial criminal investigation training at the Federal Law Enforcement Training Center in Glynco, Georgia and another 17 weeks of specialized training with their particular agencies.

Applicants for special agent jobs with the U.S. Drug Enforcement Administration (DEA) must have a college degree and either 1 year of experience conducting criminal investigations, 1 year of graduate school, or have achieved at least a 2.95 grade point average while in college. DEA special agents undergo 14 weeks of specialized training at the FBI Academy in Quantico, Virginia.

Postal inspectors must have a bachelor's degree and 1 year of work experience. It is desirable that they have one of several professional certifications, such as that of certified public accountant. They also must pass a background suitability investigation, meet certain health requirements, undergo a drug screening test, possess a valid State driver's license, and be a U.S. citizen between 21 and 36 years of age when hired.

Law enforcement agencies are encouraging applicants to take postsecondary school training in law enforcement-related subjects. Many entry-level applicants for police jobs have completed some formal postsecondary education and a significant number are college graduates. Many junior colleges, colleges, and universities offer programs in law enforcement or administration of justice. Other courses helpful in preparing for a career in law enforcement include accounting, finance, electrical engineering, computer science, and foreign languages. Physical education and sports are helpful in developing the competitiveness, stamina, and agility needed for many law enforcement positions. Knowledge of a foreign language is an asset in many Federal agencies and urban departments.

Before their first assignments, officers usually go through a period of training. In State and large local departments, recruits get training in their agency's police academy, often for 12 to 14 weeks. In small agencies, recruits often attend a regional or State academy. Training includes classroom instruction in constitutional law and civil rights, State laws and local ordinances, and accident investigation. Recruits also receive training and supervised experience in patrol, traffic control, use of firearms, self-defense, first aid, and emergency response. Police departments in some large cities hire high school graduates who are still in their teens as police cadets or trainees. They do clerical work and attend classes for usually 1 to 2 years, at which point they reach the minimum age requirement and may be appointed to the regular force.

Police officers usually become eligible for promotion after a probationary period ranging from 6 months to 3 years. In a large department, promotion may enable an officer to become a detective or specialize in one type of police work, such as working with juveniles. Promotions to corporal, sergeant, lieutenant, and captain usually are made according to a candidate's position on a promotion list, as determined by scores on a written examination and on-the-job performance.

Continuing training helps police officers, detectives, and special agents improve their job performance. Through police department academies, regional centers for public safety employees established by the States, and Federal agency training centers, instructors provide annual training in self-defense tactics, firearms, use-of-force policies, sensitivity and communications skills, crowd-control techniques, relevant legal developments, and advances in law enforcement equipment. Many agencies pay all or part of the tuition for officers to work toward degrees in criminal justice, police science, administration of justice, or public administration, and pay higher salaries to those who earn such a degree.

Job Outlook

The opportunity for public service through law enforcement work is attractive to many because the job is challenging and involves much personal responsibility. Furthermore, law enforcement officers in many agencies may retire with a pension after 20 or 25 years of service, allowing them to pursue a second career while still in their 40s. Because of relatively attractive salaries and benefits, the number of qualified candidates exceeds the number of job openings in Federal law enforcement agencies and in most State, local, and special police departments—resulting in increased hiring standards and selectivity by employers. Competition is expected to remain keen for the higher paying jobs with State and Federal agencies and police departments in more affluent areas. Applicants with college training in police science, military police experience, or both should have the best opportunities. Opportunities will be best in urban communities whose departments offer relatively low salaries and where the crime rate is relatively high.

Employment of police officers and detectives is expected to increase faster than the average for all occupations through 2008. A more security-conscious society and concern about drug-related crimes should contribute to the increasing demand for police services. At the local and State levels, growth is likely to continue as long as crime remains a serious concern. However, employment growth at the Federal level will be tempered by continuing budgetary constraints faced by law enforcement agencies. Turnover in police and detective positions is among the lowest of all occupations. Even so, the need to replace workers who retire, transfer to other occupations, or stop working for other reasons will be the source of many job openings.

The level of government spending determines the level of employment for police officers, detectives, and special agents. The number of job opportunities, therefore, can vary from year to year and from place to place. Layoffs, on the other hand, are rare because retirements enable most staffing cuts to be handled through attrition. Trained law enforcement officers who lose their jobs because of budget cuts usually have little difficulty finding jobs with other agencies.

Earnings

In 1998, the median salary of police and detective supervisors was $48,700 a year. The middle 50 percent earned between $37,130 and $69,440; the lowest 10 percent were paid less than $28,780, while the highest 10 percent earned over $84,710 a year.

In 1998, the median salary of detectives and criminal investigators was $46,180 a year. The middle 50 percent earned between $35,540 and $62,520; the lowest 10 percent were paid less than $27,950, and the highest 10 percent earned over $80,120 a year.

Police patrol officers had a median salary of $37,710 in 1998. The middle 50 percent earned between $28,840 and $47,890; the lowest 10 percent were paid less than $22,270, while the highest 10 percent earned over $63,530 annually.

Sheriffs and deputy sheriffs had a median annual salary of $28,270 in 1998. The middle 50 percent earned between $23,310 and $36,090; the lowest 10 percent were paid less than $19,070, and the highest 10 percent earned over $44,420.

Federal law provides special salary rates to Federal employees who serve in law enforcement. Additionally, Federal special agents and inspectors receive law enforcement availability pay (LEAP) or administratively uncontrolled overtime (AUO)—equal to 25 percent of the agent's grade and step—awarded because of the large amount of overtime that these agents are expected to work. For example, in 1999 FBI agents enter service as GS 10 employees on the government pay scale at a base salary of $34,400, yet earned about $43,000 a year with availability pay. They can advance to the GS 13 grade level in field non-supervisory assignments at a base salary of $53,800 which is worth almost $67,300 with availability pay. Promotions to supervisory, management, and executive positions are available in grades GS 14 and GS 15, which pay a base salary of about $63,600 or $74,800 a year, respectively, and equaled $79,500 or $93,500 per year, including availability pay. Salaries were slightly higher in selected areas where the prevailing local pay level was higher. Because Federal agents may be eligible for a special law enforcement benefits package, applicants should ask their recruiter for more information.

The International City-County Management Association's annual Police and Fire Personnel, Salaries, and Expenditures Survey revealed that 84 percent of the municipalities surveyed provided police services in 1997. The following pertains to sworn full-time positions in 1997.

Title	*Minimum annual base salary*	*Maximum annual base salary*
Police officer	$28,200	$38,500
Police Corporal	31,900	39,000
Police Sergeant	38,200	45,100
Police Lieutenant	42,900	51,200
Police Captain	46,500	56,600
Deputy Chief	48,400	59,800
Police Chief	56,300	69,600

Total earnings for local, State, and special police and detectives frequently exceed the stated salary because of payments for overtime, which can be significant. In addition to the common benefits—paid vacation, sick leave, and medical and life insurance—most police and sheriffs' departments provide officers with special allowances for uniforms. Because police officers usually are covered by liberal pension plans, many retire at half-pay after 20 or 25 years of service.

Related Occupations

Police and detectives maintain law and order. Workers in related occupations include correctional officers, guards, and fire marshals.

Sources of Additional Information

Information about entrance requirements may be obtained from Federal, State, and local law enforcement agencies.

Further information about qualifications for employment as an FBI Special Agent is available from the nearest State FBI office. The address and phone number are listed in the local telephone directory. Internet: **http://www.fbi.gov**

Information about qualifications for employment as a DEA Special Agent is available from the nearest DEA office, or call (800) DEA-4288. Internet: **http://www.usdoj.gov/dea**

Information about career opportunities, qualifications, and training to become a deputy marshal is available from:

☛ United States Marshals Service, Employment and Compensation Division, Field Staffing Branch, 600 Army Navy Dr., Arlington, VA 2220. Internet: **http://www.usdoj.gov/marshals**

Career opportunities, qualifications, and training for U.S. Secret Service Special Agents is available from:

☛ U.S. Secret Service, Personnel Division, Room 912, 1800 G St. NW., Washington, DC 20223. Internet: **http://www.ustreas.gov/usss**

Information on career opportunities and Bureau of Alcohol, Tobacco and Firearms operations by writing to:

☛ U.S. Bureau of Alcohol, Tobacco and Firearms, Personnel Division, 650 Massachusetts Avenue NW., Room 4170, Washington, DC 20226. Internet: **http://www.atf.treas.gov**

Information about careers in the United States Border Patrol is available from:

☛ U.S. Border Patrol, Chester A. Arthur Building, 425 I St. NW, Washington DC 20536.
Internet: **http://www.ins.usdoj.gov/bpmain/index.htm**

Private Detectives and Investigators

(O*Net 63035)

Significant Points

- Work hours are often irregular for beginning detectives and investigators, many of whom work part time.
- Most applicants have related experience in other areas, such as law enforcement, insurance, or the military.
- Stiff competition is expected for better paying jobs because of the large number of qualified people who are attracted to this occupation.

Nature of the Work

Private detectives and investigators use many means to determine the facts in a variety of matters. To carry out investigations, they may use various types of surveillance or searches. To verify facts, such as an individual's place of employment or income, they may make phone calls or visit a subject's workplace. In other cases, especially those involving missing persons and background checks, investigators often interview people to gather as much information as possible about an individual. In all cases, private detectives and investigators assist attorneys, businesses, and the public with a variety of legal, financial, and personal problems.

Private detectives and investigators offer many services, including executive, corporate, and celebrity protection; pre-employment verification; and individual background profiles. They also provide assistance in civil liability and personal injury cases, insurance claims and fraud, child custody and protection cases, and pre-marital screening. Increasingly, they are hired to investigate individuals to prove or disprove infidelity.

Most detectives and investigators are trained to perform physical surveillance, often for long periods of time, in a car or van. They may observe a site, such as the home of a subject, from an inconspicuous location. The surveillance continues using still and video cameras, binoculars, and a cell or car phone, until the desired evidence is obtained. They also perform computer database searches, or work with someone who does. Computers allow detectives and investigators to quickly obtain massive amounts of information on probate records, telephone numbers, motor vehicle registrations, association membership lists, registered sex offenders, and other matters.

The duties of private detectives and investigators depend on the needs of their client. In a case involving fraudulent workers' compensation claims for an employer, for instance, investigators carry out long-term covert observation of the subject. If the investigator observes the subject performing an activity that contradicts injuries stated in a workers' compensation claim, the investigator would take video or still photographs to document the activity and report it to the client.

Private detectives and investigators often specialize. Those who focus on intellectual property theft, for example, investigate and document acts of piracy, help clients stop the illegal activity, and provide intelligence for prosecution and civil action. Other investigators specialize in financial profiles and asset searches. Their reports reflect information gathered through interviews, investigation and surveillance, and research, including review of public documents.

Legal investigators specialize in cases involving the courts and are normally employed by law firms or lawyers. They frequently assist in preparing criminal defenses, locate witnesses, serve legal documents, interview police and prospective witnesses, and gather and review evidence. Legal investigators may also collect information on the parties to the litigation, take photographs, testify in court, and assemble evidence and reports for trials.

Corporate investigators work for corporations other than investigative firms, in which they conduct internal and external investigations. In internal investigations, they may investigate drug use in the workplace, insure that expense accounts are not abused, or determine if employees are stealing merchandise or information. External investigations typically prevent criminal schemes originating outside the corporation, such as theft of company assets through fraudulent billing of products by suppliers.

Detectives and investigators who specialize in finance may be hired to develop confidential financial profiles of individuals or companies who are prospective parties to large financial transactions. These individuals are often Certified Public Accountants (CPAs) and work closely with investment bankers and accountants. They search for assets in order to recover damages awarded by a court in fraud or theft cases.

Detectives who work for retail stores or hotels are responsible for loss control and asset protection. Store detectives, also known as loss prevention agents, safeguard the assets of retail stores by apprehending anyone attempting to steal merchandise or destroy store property. They prevent theft by shoplifters, vendor representatives, delivery personnel, and even store employees. Store detectives also conduct periodic inspections of stock areas, dressing rooms, and rest rooms, and sometimes assist in opening and closing the store. They may prepare loss prevention and security reports for management and testify in court against persons they apprehend. Hotel detectives protect guests of the establishment from theft of their belongings and preserve order in the restaurants and bars in the building. They also may keep undesirable individuals such as known thieves off the premises.

Legal investigators are involved with courts, law firms, and lawyers.

Working Conditions

Private detectives and investigators often work irregular hours because of the need to conduct surveillance and contact people who are not available during normal working hours. Early morning, evening, weekend, and holiday work is common.

Many detectives and investigators spend time away from their offices conducting interviews or doing surveillance, but some work in their office most of the day conducting computer searches and making phone calls. Those who have their own agencies and employ other investigators may work primarily in an office and have normal business hours.

When working on a case away from the office, the environment might range from plush boardrooms to seedy bars. Store and hotel detectives work in the businesses that they protect. Investigators generally work alone, but they sometimes work with others during surveillance or when following a subject in order to avoid detection by the subject.

Some of the work involves confrontation, so the job can be stressful and dangerous. Detectives and investigators who carry handguns must be licensed by the appropriate authority. Some situations call for the investigator to be armed, such as certain bodyguard assignments for corporate or celebrity clients. In most cases, however, a weapon is not necessary because the purpose of their work is gathering information and not law enforcement or criminal apprehension. Owners of investigative agencies have the added stress of having to deal with demanding and sometimes distraught clients.

Employment

Private detectives and investigators held about 61,000 jobs in 1998. About 1 out of 4 was self-employed. Approximately a third of salaried private detectives and investigators worked for detective agencies, while another third were employed as store detectives in department or clothing and accessories stores. The remainder worked for hotels and other lodging places, legal services firms, and in other industries.

Training, Other Qualifications, and Advancement

There are no formal education requirements for most private detective and investigator jobs, although many private detectives have college degrees. Almost all private detectives and investigators have previous experience in other occupations. Some work initially for insurance or collections companies or in the private security industry. Many investigators enter the field after serving in military, government intelligence, or law enforcement jobs.

Former law enforcement officers, military investigators, and government agents often become private detectives or investigators as a second career because they are frequently able to retire after 20 years of service. Others enter from such diverse fields as finance, accounting, commercial credit, investigative reporting, insurance, and law. These individuals often can apply their prior work experience in a related investigative specialty. A few enter the occupation directly after graduation from college, generally with associate or bachelor of criminal justice or police science degrees.

The majority of the States and the District of Colombia require private detectives and investigators to be licensed by the State or local authorities. Licensing requirements vary widely. Some States have few requirements, and 5 States—Alaska, Colorado, Idaho, Mississippi, and South Dakota—have no Statewide licensing requirements, while others have stringent regulations. For example, the California Department of Consumer Affairs, Bureau of Security and Investigative Services, requires private investigators to be 18 years of age or older; have a combination of education in police science, criminal law, or justice, and experience equaling 3 years (6,000 hours) of investigative experience; pass an evaluation by the Department of Justice and a criminal history background check; and receive a qualifying score on a 2-hour written examination covering laws and regulations. There are additional requirements for a firearms permit. A growing number of States are enacting mandatory training programs for private detectives and investigators. In most States, convicted felons cannot receive a license.

For private detective and investigator jobs, most employers look for individuals with ingenuity who are persistent and assertive. A candidate must not be afraid of confrontation, should communicate well, and should be able to think on his or her feet. Good interviewing and interrogation skills also are important and are usually acquired in earlier careers in law enforcement or other fields. Because the courts are often the ultimate judge of a properly conducted investigation, the investigator must be able to present the facts in a manner a jury will believe.

Training in subjects such as criminal justice are helpful to aspiring private detectives and investigators. Most corporate investigators must have a bachelor's degree, preferably in a business-related field. Some corporate investigators have master's degrees in business administration or law, while others are certified public accountants. Corporate investigators hired by large companies may receive formal training from their employers on business practices, management structure, and various finance-related topics. The screening process for potential employees typically includes a background check of a candidate's criminal history.

Some investigators receive certification from a professional organization to demonstrate competency in a field. For example, the National Association of Legal Investigators (NALI) confers the designation Certified Legal Investigator on licensed investigators who devote a majority of their practice to negligence or criminal defense investigations. To receive the designation, applicants must satisfy experience, educational, and continuing training requirements, and must pass written and oral exams administered by the NALI.

Most private detective agencies are small, with little room for advancement. Usually there are no defined ranks or steps, so advancement takes the form of increases in salary and assignment status. Many detectives and investigators work for detective agencies at the beginning of their careers and after a few years start their own firms. Corporate and legal investigators may rise to supervisor or manager of the security or investigations department.

Job Outlook

Stiff competition is expected because private detective and investigator careers attract many qualified people, including relatively young retirees from law enforcement and military careers. Opportunities will be best for entry-level jobs with detective agencies or as store detectives on a part-time basis. Those seeking store detective jobs have the best prospects with large chains and discount stores.

Employment of private detectives and investigators is expected to grow faster than the average for all occupations through 2008. In addition to growth, replacement of those who retire or leave the occupation for other reasons should create many additional job openings, particularly among salaried workers. Increased demand for private detectives and investigators will result from fear of crime, increased litigation, and the need to protect confidential information and property of all kinds. More private investigators also will be needed to assist attorneys working on criminal defense and civil litigation. Growing financial activity worldwide will increase the demand for investigators to control internal and external financial losses, and to monitor competitors and prevent industrial spying.

Earnings

Median annual earnings of private detectives and investigators were $21,020 in 1998. The middle 50 percent earned between $16,340 and $31,520. The lowest 10 percent had earnings of less than $14,050, while the top 10 percent earned over $42,560. Department stores, where store detectives work, paid an average of $17,600 per year, while miscellaneous business services, where private investigators firms are found, paid an average of about $29,200 annually in 1997.

Earnings of private detectives and investigators vary greatly depending on their employer, specialty, and the geographic area in which they work. According to a study by Abbott, Langer & Associates, security/loss prevention directors and vice presidents averaged $65,500 a year in 1998; investigators, $49,300; and store detectives, $17,700. In addition to typical benefits, most corporate investigators received profit-sharing plans.

Related Occupations

Private detectives and investigators often collect information and protect the property and other assets of companies. Others with related duties include security guards, insurance claims examiners, inspectors, bill collectors, and law enforcement officers. Investigators who specialize in conducting financial profiles and asset searches perform work closely related to that of accountants and financial analysts.

Sources of Additional Information

For information on local licensing requirements, contact your State Department of Public Safety, State Division of Licensing, or your local or State police headquarters.

For information on a career as a legal investigator, contact:

☛ The National Association of Legal Investigators, P.O. Box 905, Grand Blanc, MI 48439. Internet: **http://www.nali.com/index.htm**

Mechanics, Installers, and Repairers

Electrical and Electronic Equipment Mechanics, Installers, and Repairers

Computer, Automated Teller, and Office Machine Repairers

(O*NET 85705 and 85926)

Significant Points

- Job opportunities will be best for applicants with knowledge of electronics, as well as repair experience.
- Employers prefer workers who have training in electronics from associate degree programs, vocational schools, or equipment manufacturers; for computer repair jobs, certification provides applicants with a competitive advantage.
- Faster than average job growth will be driven by the increasing dependence of business and residential customers on computers and sophisticated office machines.

Nature of the Work

Computer and automated teller machine repairers, also known as data processing equipment repairers, maintain mainframe and personal computers; printers and other peripheral equipment; and automated teller machines (ATMs). Declining equipment prices and the increasing popularity of the Internet have added to the widespread use of computers. ATMs are also widespread, allowing customers to carry out bank transactions without the assistance of a teller. ATMs now provide a growing variety of other services, including stamp, phone card, and ticket sales. Computer repairers primarily provide hands-on repair service. Workers who provide technical assistance, in person or via telephone, to computer system users are known as computer support specialists. (See the statement on computer systems analysts, engineers, and scientists elsewhere in the *Handbook.*)

Office machine repairers, also known as office machine and cash register servicers, work on photocopiers, cash registers, mail processing equipment, fax machines, and typewriters. Newer models of office machinery increasingly include computerized components that allow them to function more effectively than earlier models.

To install large equipment, such as mainframe computers and automated teller machines, repairers connect the equipment to power sources and communication lines. These lines allow the transmission of information over computer networks. For example, when an ATM dispenses cash, it also transmits the withdrawal information to the customer's bank. Workers may also install operating software and peripheral equipment, checking that all components are configured to correctly function together. The installation of personal computers and other small office machines is less complex and may be handled by the purchaser.

When equipment breaks down, many repairers travel to customers' workplaces or other locations to make the necessary repairs. These workers, known as field technicians, often have assigned areas where they perform preventive maintenance on a regular basis. Bench technicians work in repair shops located in stores, factories, or service centers. In small companies, repairers may work in both repair shops and at customer locations.

Computer repairers usually replace defective components, instead of repairing them. Replacement is common because components are inexpensive, and businesses are reluctant to shut down their computers for time-consuming repairs. Components commonly replaced by computer repairers include video cards, which transmit signals from the computer to the monitor; hard drives, which store data; and network cards, which allow communication over the network. Defective components may be given to bench technicians, who use software programs to diagnose the problem and who may repair the components, if possible.

When ATMs malfunction, computer networks recognize the problem and alert repairers. Common problems include worn magnetic heads on card readers, preventing the equipment from recognizing customer bankcards; and "pick failures," preventing the equipment from dispensing the correct amount of cash. Field technicians travel to the locations of ATMs and usually repair equipment by replacing defective components. Components that cannot be replaced are brought to a repair shop where bench technicians perform the necessary repairs. Field technicians perform routine maintenance on a regular basis, replacing worn parts and running diagnostic tests to insure that the equipment functions properly.

Office machine repairers usually work on machinery at the customer's workplace; customers may also bring small equipment to a repair shop for maintenance. Common malfunctions include paper misfeeds, due to worn or dirty parts, and poor copy quality, due to problems with lamps, lenses, or mirrors. These malfunctions can usually be resolved by simply cleaning components. Breakdowns may also result from failure of commonly used parts. For example, heavy usage of a photocopier may wear down the printhead, which applies ink to the final copy. In such cases, the repairer usually replaces the part, instead of repairing it.

Workers use a variety of tools for diagnostic tests and repair. To diagnose malfunctions, they use multimeters to measure voltage, current, and resistance; signal generators to provide test signals; and oscilloscopes to monitor equipment signals. When diagnosing computerized equipment, repairers also use software programs. To repair or

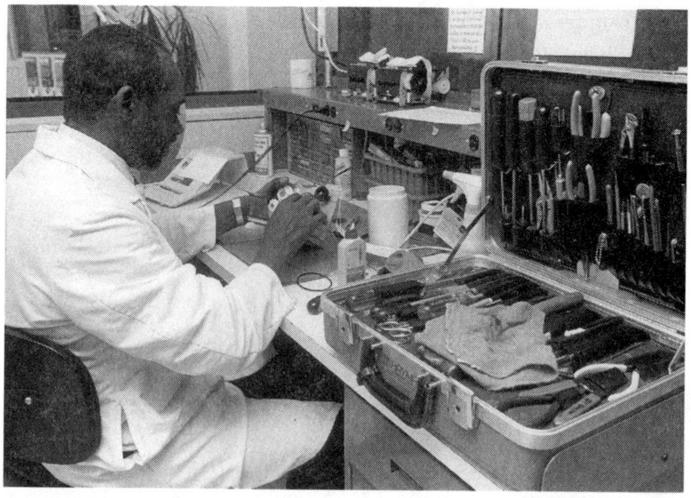

Computer, automated teller, and office machine repairers use specialized repair tools.

adjust equipment, workers use hand tools, such as pliers, screwdrivers, soldering irons, and wrenches.

Working Conditions

Repairers usually work in clean, well-lighted surroundings. Because computers and office machines are sensitive to extreme temperatures and to humidity, repair shops are usually air-conditioned and well ventilated. Field repairers must travel frequently to various locations to install, maintain, or repair customer equipment. ATM repairers may have to perform their jobs in small, confined spaces, which house the equipment.

Because computers and ATMs are critical for many organizations to function efficiently, data processing repairers often work around the clock. Their schedules may include evening, weekend, and holiday shifts; shifts may be assigned on the basis of seniority. Office machine repairers usually work regular business hours, because the equipment they repair is not as critical.

Although their job is not strenuous, repairers must lift equipment and work in a variety of postures. Repairers of computer monitors need to discharge voltage from the equipment to avoid electrocution. Workers may have to wear protective goggles.

Employment

Computer, automated teller, and office machine repairers held about 138,000 jobs in 1998. About 3 out of 5 repaired computer and automated teller equipment, and the remainder repaired office machines. Wholesale trade establishments employed about one half of the workers in this occupation; most of these establishments were wholesalers of professional and commercial equipment. Many workers were employed in computer and data processing services, as well as radio, television, and computer stores. About 1 in 8 computer, automated teller, and office machine repairers was self-employed.

Training, Other Qualifications, and Advancement

Knowledge of electronics is necessary for employment as a computer, automated teller, or office machine repairer. For positions repairing computers and automated teller machines, employers prefer workers who are certified as repairers or who have training in electronics from associate degree programs, vocational schools, or equipment manufacturers. Employers generally provide some training to new repairers; however, workers are expected to arrive on the job with a basic understanding of equipment repair. Employers may send experienced workers to training sessions to keep up with changes in technology and service procedures.

For positions repairing office machines, a basic understanding of electronics is important. Employers prefer applicants with training from vocational schools or equipment manufacturers or who have some work experience. Entry level employees at large companies normally receive on-the-job training lasting several months. This may include a week of classroom instruction followed by several months of hands-on training.

Field technicians work closely with customers and must have good communications skills and a neat appearance. Employers may also require that field technicians have a driver's license.

Several organizations administer certification programs for electronic or computer equipment repairers. A+ Certification is available through the Computing Technology Industry Association (CompTIA). Candidates must pass two tests to receive the certification, which assesses basic computer repair skills. The International Society of Certified Electronics Technicians (ISCET) and the Electronics Technicians Association (ETA) also administer certification programs. Repairers may specialize in a variety of skills, including computer repair. To receive certification, repairers must pass qualifying exams corresponding to their level of training and experience. Both programs offer associate certifications to entry level repairers.

Newly hired computer repairers may work on personal computers or peripheral equipment. With experience, they can advance to positions maintaining more sophisticated equipment, such as mainframe computers. Field repairers of automated teller machines may advance to bench technician positions responsible for more complex repairs. Experienced workers may become specialists who help other repairers diagnose difficult problems or work with engineers in designing equipment and developing maintenance procedures. Experienced workers may also move into management positions responsible for supervising other repairers.

Because of their familiarity with equipment, experienced repairers may also move into customer service or sales positions. Some experienced workers open their own repair shops or become wholesalers or retailers of electronic equipment.

Job Outlook

Employment of computer, automated teller, and office machine repairers is expected to grow faster than the average for all occupations through 2008. Growth will be driven by the increasing dependence of business and residential customers on computers and other sophisticated office machines. The need to maintain this equipment in working order will create many new jobs for repairers. In addition, openings will result from the need to replace repairers who retire or move into new occupations.

Employment growth will vary by occupation. Employment of computer and automated teller machine repairers is expected to grow much faster than the average, as reliance on computers and ATMs continues to increase. Although computer equipment continues to become less expensive and more reliable, malfunctions still occur and can cause severe problems for users, most of whom lack the knowledge to make repairs. Computers are critical to most businesses today and will become even more so to companies that do business on the Internet and households that make purchases on-line. In addition, people are becoming increasingly reliant on ATMs. Besides bank and retail transactions, ATMs provide an increasing number of other services, such as employee information processing and the distribution of government payments.

Conventional office machines, such as calculators, are inexpensive and often replaced instead of repaired. However, digital copiers and other newer office machines are more costly and complex. This equipment is often computerized, designed to work on a network, and can perform multiple functions. The growing need for repairers to service such sophisticated equipment should result in average employment growth among office machine repairers.

Earnings

Median hourly earnings of data processing equipment repairers, which includes repairers of computers and automated teller equipment, were $14.11 in 1998. The middle 50 percent earned between $10.72 and $18.55. The lowest 10 percent earned less than $8.09 and the highest 10 percent earned more than $23.27. Median hourly earnings in the industries employing the largest number of data processing equipment repairers in 1997 are shown below:

Computer and data processing services	$14.50
Professional and commercial equipment	13.40
Radio, television, and computer stores	10.90

Median hourly earnings of office machine and cash register servicers were $13.38 in 1998. The middle 50 percent earned between $10.68 and $17.48. The lowest 10 percent earned less than $8.46 and the highest 10 percent earned more than $21.92. Median hourly earnings of office machine and cash register servicers working for wholesalers of professional and commercial equipment were $12.80 in 1997.

Related Occupations

Workers in other occupations who repair and maintain electronic equipment include broadcast and sound technicians; electronic home entertainment equipment repairers; electronics repairers, commercial and industrial equipment; and telecommunications equipment mechanics, installers, and repairers.

Sources of Additional Information

For information on certification programs, contact:

☛ Computing Technology Industry Association, 450 East 22nd St., Suite 230, Lombard, IL 60148-6158.
Internet: **http://www.comptia.org**

☛ The International Society of Certified Electronics Technicians, 2708 West Berry St., Fort Worth, TX 76109. Internet: **http://www.iscet.org**

☛ Electronics Technicians Association, 602 North Jackson, Greencastle, IN 46135. Internet: **http://www.eta-sda.com**

Electronic Home Entertainment Equipment Repairers

(O*NET 85708)

Significant Points

- Job opportunities will be best for applicants with a basic knowledge of electronics, as well as repair experience.
- Employment of repairers is expected to decline because it is often cheaper to replace equipment rather than pay for repairs.

Nature of the Work

Electronic home entertainment equipment repairers, also called *service technicians*, repair a variety of equipment, including televisions and radios; stereo components; video and audio disc players; video cameras; and videocassette recorders. They also repair home security systems, intercom equipment, and home theater equipment, consisting of large-screen televisions and sophisticated, surround-sound systems.

Customers usually bring small, portable equipment to repair shops for servicing. Repairers at these locations, known as *bench technicians*, are equipped with a full array of electronic tools and parts. When larger, less mobile equipment breaks down, customers may pay repairers to come to their homes. These repairers, known as *field technicians*, travel with a limited set of tools and parts, and attempt to complete the repair at the customer's location. If the repair is complex, technicians may bring defective components back to the repair shop for a thorough diagnosis and repair.

When equipment breaks down, repairers check for common causes of trouble, such as dirty or defective components. Many repairs consist of simply cleaning and lubricating equipment. For example, cleaning the tape heads on a videocassette recorder will prevent tapes from sticking to the equipment. If routine checks do not locate the trouble, repairers may refer to schematics and manufacturers' specifications that provide instruction on how to locate problems. Repairers use a variety of test equipment to diagnose and identify malfunctions. Multimeters measure the voltage and resistance of the power supply; color bar and dot generators provide on-screen test patterns; signal generators provide test signals; and oscilloscopes measure complex waveforms produced by electronic equipment. Repairers use handtools such as pliers, screwdrivers, soldering irons, and wrenches to replace faulty parts. They also make adjustments to equipment, such as focusing and converging the picture of a television set or balancing the audio on a surround-sound system.

Most electronic home entertainment equipment repairers work in retail stores or repair shops.

Improved technologies have decreased the price of electronic home entertainment equipment. As a result, customers often replace broken equipment instead of repairing it.

Working Conditions

Most repairers work in well-lighted electrical repair shops. Field technicians, however, spend much time traveling in service vehicles and working in customers' residences.

Repairers may have to work in a variety of positions and carry heavy equipment. Although the work of repairers is comparatively safe, they must take precautions against minor burns and electric shock. As television monitors carry high voltage even when turned off, repairers need to discharge the voltage, before servicing such equipment.

Employment

Electronic home entertainment equipment repairers held about 36,000 jobs in 1998. Most repairers work in stores that sell and service electronic home entertainment products, or in electrical repair shops and service centers. About 1 in 5 electronic home entertainment equipment repairers was self-employed.

Training, Other Qualifications, and Advancement

Employers prefer applicants who have basic knowledge and skill in electronics. Applicants should be familiar with schematics and have some hands-on experience repairing electronic equipment. Many applicants gain these skills at vocational training programs and community colleges. Some learn from working with electronic equipment as a hobby. Entry level repairers may work closely with more experienced technicians who provide technical guidance.

Field technicians work closely with customers and must have good communications skills and a neat appearance. Employers may also require that field technicians have a driver's license.

The International Society of Certified Electronics Technicians (ISCET) and the Electronics Technicians Association (ETA) administer certification programs for electronics technicians. Repairers may specialize in a variety of skill areas, including consumer electronics. To receive certification, repairers must pass qualifying exams corresponding to their level of training and experience. Both programs offer associate certifications to entry level repairers.

Experienced repairers with advanced training may become specialists or troubleshooters, who help other repairers diagnose difficult problems. Workers with leadership ability may become supervisors of other repairers. Some experienced workers open their own repair shops.

Job Outlook

Employment of electronic home entertainment equipment repairers is expected to decline through 2008, due to decreased demand for repair work. Some job openings will occur, however, as repairers retire or gain higher paying jobs in other occupations requiring electronics experience. Opportunities will be best for applicants with hands-on experience and knowledge of electronics.

The need for repairers is declining because home entertainment equipment is less expensive than in the past. As technological developments have lowered equipment prices, the demand for repair services has decreased. When malfunctions do occur, it is often cheaper for consumers to replace equipment, rather than to pay for repairs.

Employment of repairers will continue to decline, despite the introduction of sophisticated equipment, such as digital televisions. As long as the price of such equipment remains high, purchasers will be willing to hire repairers when malfunctions occur. However, the need for repairers to maintain this costly equipment will not be great enough to offset the overall decline in demand.

Earnings

Median hourly earnings of electronic home entertainment equipment repairers were $11.32 in 1998. The middle 50 percent earned between $8.90 and $14.59. The lowest 10 percent earned less than $6.82 and the highest 10 percent earned more than $18.59. Median hourly earnings in the industries employing the largest number of electronic home entertainment equipment repairers in 1997 are shown below:

Electrical repair shops	$11.40
Radio, television, and computer stores	11.00

Related Occupations

Other workers who repair and maintain electronic equipment include broadcast and sound technicians; computer, automated teller, and office machine repairers; electronics repairers, commercial and industrial equipment; and telecommunications equipment mechanics, installers, and repairers.

Sources of Additional Information

For information on careers and certification, contact:

☛ The International Society of Certified Electronics Technicians, 2708 West Berry St., Fort Worth, TX 76109. Internet: **http://www.iscet.org**

☛ Electronics Technicians Association, 602 North Jackson, Greencastle, IN 46135. Internet: **http://www.eta-sda.com**

Electronics Repairers, Commercial and Industrial Equipment

(O*NET 85717A and 85717B)

Significant Points

- Job opportunities will be best for applicants with a thorough knowledge of electronics, as well as repair experience.
- Growth will result from the increasing use of commercial and industrial electronic equipment as businesses strive to lower costs by implementing automation.

Nature of the Work

Businesses and other organizations depend on complex electronic equipment for a variety of functions. Industrial controls automatically monitor and direct production processes on the factory floor. Transmitters and antennae provide communications links for many organizations. The Federal Government uses radar and missile control systems to provide for the national defense. These complex pieces of electronic equipment are installed, maintained, and repaired by electronics repairers of commercial and industrial equipment.

Many repairers, known as *field technicians*, travel to factories or other locations to repair equipment. These workers often have assigned areas where they perform preventive maintenance on a regular basis. When equipment breaks down, field technicians go to a customer's site to repair the equipment. *Bench technicians* work in repair shops located in factories and service centers. They work on components that cannot be repaired on the factory floor.

Some industrial electronic equipment is self-monitoring and alerts repairers to malfunctions. When equipment breaks down, repairers first check for common causes of trouble, such as loose connections or obviously defective components. If routine checks do not locate the trouble, repairers may refer to schematics and manufacturers' specifications that show connections and provide instructions on how to locate problems. Repairers use software programs and testing equipment to diagnose malfunctions. Multimeters measure voltage, current, and resistance; signal generators provide test signals; and oscilloscopes graphically display signals. Repairers also use handtools such as pliers, screwdrivers, soldering irons, and wrenches, to replace faulty parts and to adjust equipment.

Repairers of electronic commercial and industrial equipment adjust and calibrate equipment.

Because component repair is complex, and factories cannot allow production equipment to stand idle, repairers on the factory floor usually replace defective units, such as circuit boards, instead of fixing them. Defective units are usually sent back to the manufacturer or to a specialized repair shop for repair. Bench technicians at these locations have the training, tools, and parts to thoroughly diagnose and repair components. These workers also locate and repair circuit defects, such as poorly soldered joints on circuit boards. Electronics repairers of commercial and industrial equipment often coordinate their efforts with other workers installing and maintaining equipment. (See the statements on industrial machinery repairers and millwrights elsewhere in the *Handbook.*)

Working Conditions

Many repairers work on factory floors where they are subject to noise, dirt, vibration, and heat. Bench technicians work primarily in repair shops where the surroundings are relatively quiet, comfortable, and well lighted. Field technicians spend much time on the road, traveling to different customer locations.

Because electronic equipment is critical to industries and other organizations, repairers work around the clock. Their schedules may include evening, weekend, and holiday shifts; shifts may be assigned on the basis of seniority.

Repairers may have to do heavy lifting and work in a variety of postures. They must follow safety guidelines and often wear protective goggles and hardhats. When working on ladders or on elevated equipment, repairers must wear harnesses to prevent falls. Before repairing a piece of machinery, these workers must follow procedures to insure that others cannot start the equipment during the repair process. They must also take precautions against electric shock by locking off power to the unit under repair.

Employment

Electronics repairers of commercial and industrial equipment held about 72,000 jobs in 1998. About 1 out of 5 salaried repairers was employed by the Federal Government—almost all by the Department of Defense at military installations around the country. Many repairers also worked for wholesale trade companies, electrical repair shops, manufacturers of electronic components, and the telecommunications industry. About 1 in 10 repairers was self-employed.

Training, Other Qualifications, and Advancement

Knowledge of electronics is necessary for employment as an electronics repairer of commercial and industrial equipment. Many applicants gain this training through programs lasting 1 to 2 years at vocational schools and community colleges. Entry level repairers may work closely with more experienced technicians who provide technical guidance.

Repairers should have good eyesight and color perception in order to work with the intricate components used in electronic equipment. Field technicians work closely with customers and should have good communications skills and a neat appearance. Employers may also require that field technicians have a driver's license.

The International Society of Certified Electronics Technicians (ISCET) and the Electronics Technicians Association (ETA) administer certification programs for electronics technicians. Repairers may specialize—in industrial electronics, for example. To receive certification, repairers must pass qualifying exams corresponding to their level of training and experience. Both programs offer associate certifications to entry level repairers.

Experienced repairers with advanced training may become specialists or troubleshooters who help other repairers diagnose difficult problems. Others may move into higher paying jobs, such as skilled craft positions. Workers with leadership ability may become supervisors of other repairers. Some experienced workers open their own repair shops.

Job Outlook

Job opportunities should be best for applicants with a thorough knowledge of electronics, as well as electronics repair experience. Employment of electronics repairers of commercial and industrial equipment is expected to grow about as fast as the average for all occupations through 2008. Growth will be concentrated in private industry, where the increasing use of equipment will create new jobs for repairers. Employment of repairers in the Federal government will decline, however, as the Defense Department increases its use of outside contractors to provide repair services. In addition to employment growth, many job openings should result from the need to replace workers who transfer to other occupations or leave the labor force.

The use of commercial and industrial electronic equipment will become more widespread, as businesses strive to lower costs by increasing automation. Companies will install electronic controls, robots, sensors, and other equipment, to automate processes such as assembly and testing. As prices decline, applications will be found across a number of industries, including services, utilities, and construction, as well as manufacturing. Improved equipment reliability should not constrain employment growth; companies will increasingly rely on repairers, because any malfunction that idles commercial and industrial equipment is costly.

Earnings

Median hourly earnings of electronics repairers of commercial and industrial equipment were $17.11 in 1998. The middle 50 percent earned between $13.37 and $20.93. The lowest 10 percent earned less than $10.22 and the highest 10 percent earned more than $23.81. Median hourly earnings in the industries employing the largest numbers of electronics repairers of commercial and industrial equipment in 1997 are shown below:

Federal Government	$18.00
Professional and commercial equipment	15.60
Electrical repair shops	12.10

Related Occupations

Workers in other occupations who repair and maintain electronic equipment include broadcast and sound technicians; computer, automated teller, and office machine repairers; electronic home entertainment equipment repairers; and telecommunications equipment mechanics, installers, and repairers. Industrial machinery repairers and millwrights also install, maintain, and repair industrial machinery.

Sources of Additional Information

For information on careers and certification, contact:

☛ The International Society of Certified Electronics Technicians, 2708 West Berry St., Fort Worth, TX 76109. Internet: **http://www.iscet.org**

☛ Electronics Technicians Association, 602 North Jackson, Greencastle, IN 46135. Internet: **http://www.eta-sda.com**

Telecommunications Equipment Mechanics, Installers, and Repairers

(O*NET 85502, 85505, 85508, 85514, 85599A, 85599B, 85599C, and 85726)

Significant Points

- Growing demand for sophisticated telecommunications equipment will be offset by improved equipment reliability, resulting in average employment growth.
- Opportunities should be best for applicants with electronics training and computer skills.
- Weekend and holiday hours are common; repairers may be on call around the clock, in case of emergencies.

Nature of the Work

Telephones and radios depend on a variety of equipment to transmit communications signals. Electronic switches route telephone signals to their destinations. Switchboards direct telephone calls within a single location or organization. Radio transmitters and receivers relay signals from wireless phones and radios to their destinations. Newer telecommunications equipment is computerized and can communicate a variety of information, including data, graphics, and video. The workers who set up and maintain this sophisticated equipment are telecommunications equipment mechanics, installers, and repairers.

Central office installers set up switches, cables, and other equipment in telephone central offices. These locations are the hubs of a telephone network—they contain the switches that route telephone calls to their destinations. *PBX installers* set up private branch exchange (PBX) switchboards. This equipment relays incoming, outgoing, and interoffice calls for a single location or organization. To install switches and switchboards, installers first connect the equipment to power lines and communications cables and install frames and supports. They test the connections to insure that adequate power is available and that the communication links function. They also install equipment such as power systems, alarms, and telephone sets. New switches and switchboards are computerized; workers install software or may program the equipment to provide specific features. For example, as a cost-cutting feature, an installer may program a PBX switchboard to route calls over different lines at different times of the day. However, other workers, such as *network technicians* or *telecommunications specialists*, rather than installers generally handle complex programming. (The work of other computer specialists is described in the *Handbook* statement on computer systems analysts, engineers and scientists.) Finally, the installer performs tests to verify that the newly installed equipment functions properly.

The increasing reliability of telephone switches and switchboards has simplified maintenance. New telephone switches are self-monitoring and alert repairers to malfunctions. Some switches allow repairers to diagnose and correct problems from remote locations. When faced with a malfunction, the repairer may refer to manufacturers' manuals that provide maintenance instructions. PBX repairers determine if the problem is located within the PBX system, or if it originates in the telephone lines maintained by the local phone company. To fix the equipment, repairers may use small hand tools, including pliers and screwdrivers to replace defective components, such as circuit boards, fuses, or wiring. They may also install updated software or programs that maintain existing software.

Radio mechanics install and maintain radio transmitting and receiving equipment. This includes stationary equipment mounted on transmission towers and mobile equipment, such as radio communications systems in service and emergency vehicles. Newer radio equipment is also self-monitoring and may alert mechanics to potential malfunctions. When malfunctions occur, these mechanics examine equipment for damaged components and loose or broken wires. They use electrical measuring instruments to monitor signal strength, transmission capacity, interference, and signal delay. Additionally, they use hand tools to replace defective components and parts and adjust equipment, so it performs within required specifications.

Station installers and repairers—known commonly as *telephone installers and repairers*—install and repair telephone wiring and equipment on customers' premises. They install telephone service by connecting customers' telephone wires to outside service lines. These lines run on telephone poles or in underground conduits; the installer may climb poles or ladders, to make the connections. Once the telephone is connected, the line is tested, to insure that it receives a dial tone. When a maintenance problem occurs, repairers test the customers' lines, to determine if the problem is located in the customers' premises or in the outside service lines. When on-site procedures fail to resolve installation or maintenance problems, repairers may request support from their technical service center.

Other telecommunications equipment mechanics, installers, and repairers include workers who install and maintain telegraphic equipment and workers who connect wires from telephone lines to distributing frames in telephone company central offices.

Working Conditions

Telecommunications equipment mechanics, installers, and repairers generally work in clean, well-lighted, air-conditioned surroundings, such as a telephone company's central office, a customer's PBX location, or an electronic repair shop or service center. Telephone installers and repairers work on rooftops, ladders, and telephone poles. Radio mechanics may maintain equipment located on the tops of transmissions towers. While working outdoors, these workers are subject to a variety of weather conditions.

Nearly all telecommunications equipment mechanics, installers, and repairers work full time. Many work regular business hours, to meet the demand for repair services during the workday. Schedules are more irregular at companies that need repair services 24 hours a day or where installation and maintenance must take place after business hours. At these locations, mechanics work a variety of shifts including weekend and holiday hours. Repairers may be on call around the clock, in case of emergencies and may have to work overtime.

The work of most repairers involves lifting, reaching, stooping, crouching, and crawling. Adherence to safety precautions is important to guard against work hazards. These hazards include falls, minor burns, electrical shock, and contact with hazardous materials.

Telecommunications equipment mechanics, installers, and repairers may work outdoors.

Employment

Telecommunications equipment mechanics, installers, and repairers held about 125,000 jobs in 1998. Most worked for telephone communications companies. Many radio mechanics worked in electrical repair shops. The distribution of employment by occupation was as follows.

Occupation	Jobs
Central office and PBX installers and repairers	44,000
Station installers and repairers, telephone	24,000
Radio mechanics	7,000
All other telecommunications equipment mechanics, installers, and repairers	49,000

Training, Other Qualifications, and Advancement

Most employers seek applicants with post secondary training in electronics; familiarity with computers is also important. Training sources include 2- and 4-year college programs in electronics or communications, trade schools, and training provided by equipment and software manufacturers. Military experience with communications equipment is highly valued by many employers.

Newly hired mechanics usually receive some training from their employers. This may include formal classroom training in electronics, communications systems, or software and informal, hands-on training with communications equipment. Large companies may send mechanics to outside training sessions, to keep these employees informed of new equipment and service procedures. As networks have become more sophisticated—often including equipment from a variety of companies—the knowledge needed for installation and maintenance also has increased.

Mechanics must be able to distinguish colors, because wires are color-coded; they must also be able to hear distinctions in the various tones on a telephone system. For positions that require climbing poles and towers, workers must be in good physical shape. Repairers who handle assignments alone at a customer site must be able to work without close supervision. For workers who frequently contact customers, a pleasant personality, neat appearance, and good communications skills are also important.

Experienced mechanics with advanced training may become specialists or troubleshooters who help other repairers diagnose difficult problems, or work with engineers in designing equipment and developing maintenance procedures. Because of their familiarity with equipment, repairers are particularly well qualified to become manufacturers' sales workers. Workers with leadership ability also may become maintenance supervisors or service managers. Some experienced workers open their own repair services or shops or become wholesalers or retailers of electronic equipment.

Job Outlook

Employment of telecommunications equipment mechanics, installers, and repairers is expected to grow about as fast as the average for all occupations through 2008. Growth will be driven by the increasing demand for sophisticated telecommunications equipment. Although the need for installation work will grow as companies seek to upgrade their telecommunications networks, the need for maintenance work should decline, because of increasingly reliable self-monitoring and self-diagnosing equipment. Opportunities should be best for applicants with electronics training and computer skills.

Projected employment growth varies by occupation. Employment of central office and PBX installers and repairers is expected to grow faster than average, as the growing popularity of the Internet continues to place new demand on telecommunications networks. Conventional switches designed to handle voice communications will need to be replaced and upgraded with equipment that can communicate more complex information, such as data, videos, and graphics. Switches that can quickly relay both voice and data communications will become a necessity. Whereas increased reliability and automation of switching equipment will constrain employment growth, these effects will be offset by the strong demand for installation and upgrading of switching equipment.

Despite some demand for mechanics in the rapidly growing wireless telecommunication sector to build networks of receivers, transmitters, and other equipment, the employment of radio mechanics is projected to decline. The replacement of two-way radio systems by wireless systems, especially in service vehicles, has eliminated the need in many companies for on-site radio mechanics. The increased reliability of wireless equipment and the use of self-monitoring systems will continue to lessen this need.

Employment of station installers and repairers is also expected to decline. Pre-wired buildings and the increasing reliability of telephone equipment will decrease the need for installation and maintenance of customers' telephones. The popularity of the Internet may increase employment over the next few years, as additional households request the installation of second telephone lines. However, this should be offset by the deployment of new technologies, such as digital subscriber lines, which allow simultaneous voice and data communications, and wireless telecommunications services, which do not require installation.

Earnings

In 1998, median hourly earnings of central office and PBX installers and repairers were $21.00. The middle 50 percent earned between $18.09 and $23.52. The bottom 10 percent earned less than $13.92, whereas the top 10 percent earned more than $25.79. Median hourly earnings in the telephone communications industry were $20.40 in 1997.

Median hourly earnings of radio mechanics in 1998 were $14.71. The middle 50 percent earned between $11.21 and $18.73. The bottom 10 percent earned less than $9.09, whereas the top 10 percent earned more than $23.21.

Median hourly earnings of station installers and repairers in 1998 were $19.06. The middle 50 percent earned between $15.80 and $22.17. The bottom 10 percent earned less than $11.55, whereas the top 10 percent earned more than $24.07. Median hourly earnings were $18.90 in the telephone communications industry in 1997.

Central office installers, central office technicians, PBX installers, and telephone installers and repairers represented by the Communications Workers of America earned between $283 and $996 a week in 1998.

Telephone installers and repairers, represented by the International Brotherhood of Electrical Workers, earned between $12.60 and $22.50 an hour in 1999. Equipment installer technicians represented by the same union earned between $16.70 and $24.80 an hour in 1999.

Related Occupations

Related occupations that work with electronic equipment include broadcast and sound technicians; computer, automated teller, and office machine repairers; electronic home entertainment equipment repairers; and electronics repairers, commercial and industrial equipment. Electronics engineering technicians may also repair electronic equipment, as part of their duties.

Sources of Additional Information

For information on career opportunities, contact:

☛ International Brotherhood of Electrical Workers, Telecommunications Department, 1125 15th St. NW., Room 807, Washington, DC 20005.

☛ Communications Workers of America, 501 3rd St. NW., Washington, DC 20001. Internet: **http://www.cwa-union.org**

For information on the telephone communications industry, contact:

☛ United States Telephone Association, 1401 H St. NW., Suite 600, Washington, DC 20005-2164. Internet: **http://www.usta.org**

Other Mechanics, Installers, and Repairers

Aircraft Mechanics and Service Technicians

(O*NET 85323A, 85323B, 85326, and 85728A)

Significant Points

- The vast majority learn their job in 1 of about 200 trade schools certified by the Federal Aviation Administration.
- On the whole, opportunities should be favorable, but keen competition is likely for the best paying jobs with airlines.

Nature of the Work

To keep aircraft in peak operating condition, aircraft mechanics and service technicians perform scheduled maintenance, make repairs, and complete inspections required by the Federal Aviation Administration (FAA).

Many aircraft mechanics specialize in preventive maintenance. They inspect engines, landing gear, instruments, pressurized sections, accessories—brakes, valves, pumps, and air-conditioning systems, for example—and other parts of the aircraft and do the necessary maintenance and replacement of parts. Inspections take place following a schedule based on the number of hours the aircraft has flown, calendar days, cycles of operation, or a combination of these factors. To examine an engine, aircraft mechanics work through specially designed openings while standing on ladders or scaffolds, or use hoists or lifts to remove the entire engine from the craft. After taking an engine apart, mechanics use precision instruments to measure parts for wear and use x-ray and magnetic inspection equipment to check for invisible cracks. Worn or defective parts are repaired or replaced. They may also repair sheet metal or composite surfaces, measure the tension of control cables, and check for corrosion, distortion, and cracks in the fuselage, wings, and tail. After completing all repairs, mechanics must test the equipment to ensure that it works properly.

Mechanics specializing in repair work rely on the pilot's description of a problem to find and fix faulty equipment. For example, during a preflight check, a pilot may discover that the aircraft's fuel gauge does not work. To solve the problem, mechanics may troubleshoot the electrical system, using electrical test equipment to make sure no wires are broken or shorted out and replace any defective electrical or electronic components. Mechanics work as fast as safety permits, so the aircraft can be put back into service quickly.

Large, sophisticated planes are equipped with aircraft monitoring systems, consisting of electronic boxes and consoles that monitor the aircraft's basic operations and provide valuable diagnostic information to the mechanic.

Some mechanics work on one or many different types of aircraft, such as jets, propeller-driven airplanes, and helicopters. Others specialize in one section of a particular type of aircraft, such as the engine, hydraulics, or electrical system. *Powerplant mechanics* are

Aircraft mechanics inspect aircraft on a scheduled basis.

authorized to work on engines and do limited work on propellers. *Airframe mechanics* are authorized to work on any part of the aircraft except the instruments, powerplants, and propellers. *Combination airframe-and-powerplant mechanics*—called A & P mechanics—work on all parts of the plane, except instruments. The majority of mechanics working on civilian aircraft today are A & P mechanics. In small, independent repair shops, mechanics usually inspect and repair many different types of aircraft.

Avionics systems are now an integral part of aircraft design and have vastly increased aircraft capability. *Avionics technicians* repair and maintain components used for aircraft navigation and radio communications, weather radar systems, and other instruments and computers that control flight, engine, and other primary functions. These duties may require additional licenses, such as an FCC radiotelephone license. Because of technological advances, an increasing amount of time is spent repairing electronic systems, such as computerized controls. Technicians may also be required to analyze and develop solutions to complex electronic problems.

Working Conditions

Mechanics usually work in hangars or in other indoor areas, although they can work outdoors—sometimes in unpleasant weather—when hangars are full or when repairs must be made quickly. Mechanics often work under time pressure to maintain flight schedules or, in general aviation, to keep from inconveniencing customers. At the same time, mechanics have a tremendous responsibility to maintain safety standards, and this can cause the job to be stressful.

Frequently, mechanics must lift or pull objects weighing as much as 70 pounds. They often stand, lie, or kneel in awkward positions and occasionally must work in precarious positions on scaffolds or ladders. Also, noise and vibration are common when testing engines. Aircraft mechanics usually work 40 hours a week on 8-hour shifts around the clock. Overtime work is frequent.

Employment

Aircraft mechanics and service technicians held about 133,000 jobs in 1998. About two-thirds of all salaried mechanics worked for airlines or airports and flying fields, about 1 out of 8 worked for the Federal Government, and about 1 out of 7 worked for aircraft assembly firms. Most of the rest were general aviation mechanics, the majority of whom worked for independent repair shops or companies that operate their own planes to transport executives and cargo. Few mechanics were self-employed.

Most airline mechanics work at major airports near large cities. Civilian mechanics employed by the Armed Forces work at military installations. Large proportions of mechanics who work for aircraft assembly firms are located in California or Washington State. Others work for the FAA, many at the facilities in Oklahoma City, Atlantic City, or Washington, DC. Mechanics for independent repair shops work at airports in every part of the country.

Training, Other Qualifications, and Advancement

The majority of mechanics who work on civilian aircraft are certificated by the FAA as "airframe mechanic," "powerplant mechanic," or "avionics repair specialist." Mechanics who also have an inspector's authorization can certify work completed by other mechanics and perform required inspections. Uncertificated mechanics are supervised by those with certificates.

The FAA requires at least 18 months of work experience for an airframe, powerplant, or avionics repairer's certificate. For a combined A & P certificate, at least 30 months of experience working with both engines and airframes is required. Completion of a program at an FAA certificated mechanic school can substitute for the work experience requirement. Applicants for all certificates also must pass written and oral tests and demonstrate that they can do the work authorized by the certificate. To obtain an inspector's authorization, a mechanic must have held an A & P certificate for at least 3 years. Most airlines require that mechanics have a high school diploma and an A & P certificate.

Although a few people become mechanics through on-the-job training, most learn their job in one of about 200 trade schools certified by the FAA. About one-third of these schools award 2- and 4-year degrees in avionics, aviation technology, or aviation maintenance management.

FAA standards established by law require that certificated mechanic schools offer students a minimum of 1,900 actual class hours. Courses in these trade schools normally last from 24 to 30 months and provide training with the tools and equipment used on the job. Aircraft trade schools are placing more emphasis on technologies such as turbine engines, composite materials—including graphite, fiberglass, and boron—and aviation electronics, which are increasingly being used in the construction of new aircraft. Less emphasis is being placed on old technologies, such as woodworking and welding. Additionally, employers prefer mechanics who can perform a variety of tasks.

Some aircraft mechanics in the Armed Forces acquire enough general experience to satisfy the work experience requirements for the FAA certificate. With additional study, they may pass the certifying exam. In general, however, jobs in the military services are too specialized to provide the broad experience required by the FAA. Most Armed Forces mechanics have to complete the entire training program at a trade school, although a few receive some credit for the material they learned in the service. In any case, military experience is a great advantage when seeking employment; employers consider trade school graduates who have this experience to be the most desirable applicants.

Courses in mathematics, physics, chemistry, electronics, computer science, and mechanical drawing are helpful, because many of their principles are involved in the operation of aircraft and knowledge of these principles is often necessary to make repairs. Courses that develop writing skills are also important, because mechanics are often required to submit reports.

FAA regulations require current experience to keep the A & P certificate valid. Applicants must have at least 1,000 hours work experience in the previous 24 months or take a refresher course. As new and more complex aircraft are designed, more employers are requiring mechanics to take on-going training, to update their skills. Recent technological advances in aircraft maintenance necessitate a strong background in electronics—both for acquiring and retaining jobs in this field. FAA certification standards also make ongoing training mandatory. Every 24 months, mechanics are required to take at least 16 hours of training to keep their certificate. Many mechanics take courses offered by manufacturers or employers, usually through outside contractors.

Aircraft mechanics must do careful and thorough work that requires a high degree of mechanical aptitude. Employers seek applicants who are self-motivated, hard-working, enthusiastic, and able to diagnose and solve complex mechanical problems. Agility is important for the reaching and climbing necessary for the job. Because they may work on the top of wings and fuselages on large jet planes, aircraft mechanics must not be afraid of heights.

As aircraft mechanics gain experience, they may advance to lead mechanic (or crew chief), inspector, lead inspector, or shop supervisor positions. Opportunities are best for those who have an aircraft inspector's authorization. In the airlines, where promotion is often determined by examination, supervisors sometimes advance to executive positions. Those with broad experience in maintenance and overhaul might become inspectors with the FAA. With additional business and management training, some open their own aircraft maintenance facilities. Mechanics learn many different skills in their training that can be applied to other jobs, and some transfer to other skilled repairer occupations or electronics technician jobs.

Job Outlook

The outlook for aircraft mechanics should be favorable over the next 10 years. The small numbers of young workers in the labor force, coupled with few entrants from the military, and a large number of retirements point to good employment conditions for students just beginning training.

Job opportunities are likely to be the best at small commuter and regional airlines, FAA repair stations, and in general aviation. Because wages in these companies tend to be relatively low, there are fewer applicants for these jobs than for jobs with the major airlines. Also, some jobs will become available as experienced mechanics leave for higher paying jobs with airlines or transfer to another occupation. Mechanics will face competition for large airline jobs, because the high wages and travel benefits for these jobs attract more qualified applicants than there are openings. Prospects will be best for applicants with significant experience. Mechanics who keep abreast of technological advances in electronics, composite materials, and other areas will be in greatest demand. The number of job openings for aircraft mechanics in the Federal Government should decline, as the size of the Armed Forces is reduced.

Employment of aircraft mechanics is expected to increase about as fast as the average for all occupations through the year 2008. A growing population and rising incomes are expected to stimulate the demand for airline transportation, and the number of aircraft is expected to grow. However, employment growth will be restricted somewhat by increases in productivity, resulting from greater use of automated inventory control and modular systems that speed repairs and parts replacement.

Most job openings for aircraft mechanics through the year 2008 will stem from replacement needs. Each year, as mechanics transfer to other occupations or retire, several thousand job openings will arise. Aircraft mechanics have a comparatively strong attachment to the occupation, reflecting their significant investment in training and a love for aviation. However, because aircraft mechanics' skills are transferable to other occupations, some mechanics leave for work in related fields.

During recessions, declines in air travel force airlines to curtail the number of flights, which result in less aircraft maintenance and, consequently, layoffs for aircraft mechanics.

Earnings

Median hourly earnings of aircraft mechanics and service technicians were about $18.30 in 1998. The middle 50 percent earned between $14.91 and $22.12. The lowest 10 percent earned less than $11.92 and the highest 10 percent earned more than $24.40. Median hourly earnings in the industries employing the largest number of aircraft mechanics and service technicians in 1997 were:

Industry	Earnings
Air transportation, scheduled	$20.80
Federal government	17.40
Air transportation, nonscheduled	15.40
Aircraft and parts	15.20
Airports, flying fields, and services	14.60

Mechanics who work on jets for the major airlines generally earn more than those working on other aircraft. Airline mechanics and their immediate families receive reduced fare transportation on their own and most other airlines.

Almost one-half of all aircraft mechanics, including those employed by some major airlines, are covered by union agreements. The principal unions are the International Association of Machinists and Aerospace Workers and the Transport Workers Union of America. Some mechanics are represented by the International Brotherhood of Teamsters.

Related Occupations

Workers in some other occupations that involve similar mechanical and electrical work are electricians, electronic equipment repairers, and elevator repairers.

Sources of Additional Information

Information about jobs in a particular airline can be obtained by writing to the personnel manager of the company. For general information about aircraft mechanics, write to:

☛ Professional Aviation Maintenance Association, 636 I St. NW., Suite 300, Washington, DC 20001.

For information on jobs in a particular area, contact employers at local airports or local offices of the State employment service.

Automotive Body Repairers

(O*NET 85305A, 85305B, and 85305C)

Significant Points

- Many still learn this trade on the job as helpers, although employers prefer to hire persons with automotive body repair training.
- Good reading and basic mathematics skills are needed to follow instructions and diagrams in technical manuals.

Nature of the Work

Thousands of motor vehicles are damaged in traffic accidents every day. Although some of these vehicles are sold for salvage or scrapped, most can be repaired to look and drive like new. Automotive body repairers straighten bent bodies, remove dents, and replace crumpled parts that are beyond repair. They repair all types of vehicles but mostly work on cars and small trucks, although some work on large trucks, buses, or tractor-trailers.

When a damaged vehicle is brought into the shop, body repairers generally receive instructions from a supervisor who determines which parts to restore or replace and how much time the job should take.

Automotive body repairers use special equipment to restore damaged metal frames and body sections. Repairers chain or clamp frames and sections to alignment machines that use hydraulic pressure to align damaged components. "Unibody" vehicles, designs built without frames, must be restored to precise factory specifications for the vehicle to operate correctly. To do so, repairers use bench systems to make accurate measurements of how much each section is out of alignment and hydraulic machinery to return the vehicle back to its original shape.

Body repairers remove badly damaged sections of body panels with a pneumatic metal-cutting gun or by other means and weld in replacement sections. Repairers pull out less serious dents with a hydraulic jack or hand prying bar or knock them out with handtools or pneumatic hammers. They smooth out small dents and creases in the metal, by holding a small anvil against one side of the damaged area, while hammering the opposite side. They also remove very small pits and dimples with pick hammers and punches in a process called metal finishing.

Body repairers also repair or replace the plastic body parts used increasingly on new model vehicles. They remove damaged panels and identify the family and properties of the plastic used on the vehicle. With most types of plastic, repairers can apply heat from a hot-air welding gun or by immersion in hot water and press by hand the softened panel back into its original shape. They replace plastic parts that are badly damaged or very difficult to repair.

Body repairers use plastic or solder to fill small dents that cannot be worked out of the plastic or metal panel. On metal panels, they file or grind the hardened filler to the original shape and clean the surface with a media blaster before painting. In many shops, automotive painters do the painting. (These workers are discussed in the *Handbook* statement on painting and coating machine operators.) In small shops, workers often do both body repairing and painting. A few body repairers specialize in repairing fiberglass car bodies.

In large shops, body repairers may specialize in one type of repair, such as frame straightening or door and fender repair. Some body repairers specialize in installing glass in automobiles and other vehicles. Glass installers remove broken, cracked, or pitted windshields and window glass. Glass installers apply a moisture-proofing compound along the edges of the glass, place it in the vehicle, and install rubber strips around the sides of the windshield or window to make it secure and weatherproof.

Body repair work has variety and challenges—each damaged vehicle presents a different problem. Using their broad knowledge of automotive construction and repair techniques, repairers must develop appropriate methods for each job.

Automotive body repairers use their broad knowledge of automotive construction and repair techniques.

Body repairers usually work alone with only general directions from supervisors. In some shops, helpers or apprentices assist experienced repairers.

Working Conditions

Most automotive body repairers work a standard 40-hour week, although some, including the self-employed, may work 60 or more hours a week. Repairers work indoors in body shops that are noisy, because of hammering against metal and the use of power tools. Most shops are well ventilated to disperse dust and paint fumes. Body repairers often work in awkward or cramped positions, and much of their work is strenuous and dirty. Hazards include cuts from sharp metal edges, burns from torches and heated metal, injuries from power tools, and fumes from paint. However, serious accidents are usually avoided, when the shop is kept clean and orderly and safety practices are observed.

Employment

Automotive body repairers held about 227,000 jobs in 1998. Most repairers worked for automotive repair shops. The next largest number of repairers worked for automobile and truck dealers specializing in body repairs and painting. Others worked for organizations that maintain their own motor vehicles, such as trucking companies and automobile rental companies. Some worked for motor vehicle manufacturers. About 1 automotive body repairer out of 6 was self-employed.

Training, Other Qualifications, and Advancement

Most employers prefer to hire persons who have completed formal training programs in automotive body repair, but these programs supply only a portion of employers' needs. Formal training is highly desirable, because advances in technology have greatly changed the structure, components, and materials used in automobiles. As a result, these new technologies require proficiency in new repair techniques and skills. For example, bodies of newer automobiles are increasingly made of a combination of materials—traditional steel, aluminum, and a growing variety of metal alloys and plastics—each requiring the use of somewhat different techniques to reshape and smooth out dents and small pits. Many high schools, vocational schools, private trade schools, and community colleges offer automotive body repair training programs. Formal training in automotive body repair can enhance chances for employment and speed promotion.

Employers also hire many persons without formal automotive body repair training. These workers learn the trade as helpers, picking up skills on the job from experienced body repairers. For helper jobs, most employers prefer to hire high school graduates who know how to use handtools. Good reading and basic mathematics and computer skills are essential to becoming a fully skilled automotive body repairer. Restoring unibody automobiles to their original form requires such precision that body repairers must follow instructions and diagrams in technical manuals to make very precise three-dimensional measurements of the position of one body section relative to another.

Helpers begin by assisting body repairers in tasks such as removing damaged parts, sanding body panels, and installing repaired parts. They learn to remove small dents and to make other minor repairs. They then progress to more difficult tasks, such as straightening body parts and returning them to their correct alignment. Generally, to become skilled in all aspects of body repair requires 3 to 4 years of on-the-job training.

Certification by the National Institute for Automotive Service Excellence (ASE), though voluntary, is the recognized standard of achievement for automotive body repairers. ASE offers a series of four exams for collision repair professionals twice a year. Repairers may take from one to four ASE Master Collision Repair & Refinish Exams. Repairers who pass at least one exam and have 2 years of hands-on work experience earn ASE certification. Completion of a post-secondary program in automotive body repair may be substituted for 1 year of work experience. Those who pass all four exams become ASE Master Collision Repair & Refinish Technicians. Automotive body repairers must retake the examination at least every 5 years to retain certification.

Continuing education throughout a career in automotive body repair is required. Automotive parts, body materials, and electronics continue to change and become more complex and technologically advanced. To keep up with these technological advances, repairers must continue to gain new skills, read technical manuals, and attend seminars and classes.

An experienced automotive body repairer with supervisory ability may advance to shop supervisor. Some workers open their own body repair shops. Others become automobile damage appraisers for insurance companies.

Job Outlook

Employment of automotive body repairers is expected to increase about as fast as the average for all occupations through the year 2008. Opportunities should be best for persons with formal training in automotive body repair and mechanics.

Demand for qualified body repairers will increase, as the number of motor vehicles in operation continues to grow in line with the Nation's population. With an increase in the number of motor vehicles in use, the number of vehicles damaged in accidents will also increase. New automobile designs increasingly have body parts made of steel alloys, aluminum, and plastics—materials that are more difficult to work with than traditional steel body parts. Also, new, lighter weight automotive designs are prone to greater collision damage than older, heavier designs and, consequently, more time is consumed in repair. The need to replace experienced repairers who transfer to other occupations, retire, or stop working for other reasons will account for the majority of job openings.

The automotive repair business is not very sensitive to changes in economic conditions, and experienced body repairers are rarely laid off. However, although major body damage must be repaired, if a vehicle is to be restored to safe operating condition, repair of minor dents and crumpled fenders can often be deferred during an economic slowdown. During this time, most employers will hire few new workers. In addition, recent business conditions have forced some small, unprofitable body shops to go out of business and have led some dealerships to consolidate body shops, in order to remain viable.

Earnings

Median hourly earnings of automotive body and related repairers, including incentive pay, were $13.18 in 1998. The middle 50 percent earned between $10.23 and $17.71 an hour. The lowest 10 percent earned less than $7.38, and the highest 10 percent earned more than $22.47 an hour. Median hourly earnings in the industries employing the largest number of automotive body and related repairers in 1997 were as follows:

Industry	Earnings
New and used car dealers	$14.20
Automotive repair shops	12.80
Motor vehicles, parts, and supplies	11.40

The majority of body repairers employed by automotive dealers and repair shops are paid on an incentive basis. Under this method, body repairers are paid a predetermined amount for various tasks, and earnings depend on the amount of work assigned to the repairer and how fast it is completed. Employers frequently guarantee workers a minimum weekly salary. Body repairers who work for trucking companies, bus lines, and other organizations that maintain their own vehicles usually receive an hourly wage.

Helpers and trainees usually earn from 30 to 60 percent of the earnings of skilled workers. Helpers and trainees usually receive an hourly rate, until they are skilled enough to be paid on an incentive basis.

Some automotive body repairers are members of unions, including the International Association of Machinists and Aerospace Workers; the International Union, United Automobile, Aerospace and Agricultural Implement Workers of America; the Sheet Metal Workers' International Association; and the International Brotherhood of Teamsters. Most body repairers who are union members work for large automobile dealers, trucking companies, and bus lines.

Related Occupations

Repairing damaged motor vehicles often involves working on mechanical components, as well as vehicle bodies. Automotive body repairers often work closely with individuals in several related occupations, including automotive and diesel mechanics and service technicians, automotive repair service estimators, painting and coating machine operators, and body customizers.

Sources of Additional Information

Additional details about work opportunities may be obtained from automotive body repair shops and motor vehicle dealers; locals of the unions previously mentioned; or local offices of your State employment service. State employment services also are a source of information about training programs.

For general information about automotive body repairer careers, write to:

☛ Automotive Service Association, Inc., 1901 Airport Freeway, Bedford, TX 76021-5732. Internet: **http://www.asashop.org**

☛ National Automobile Dealers Association, 8400 Westpark Dr., McLean, VA 22102.

☛ Inter-Industry Conference On Auto Collision Repair Education Foundation (I-CAR), 3701 Algonquin Rd., Suite 400, Rolling Meadow, IL 60008. Telephone (toll free): 1-888-722-3787.
Internet: **http://www.i-car.com/foundation.html**

For information on how to become a certified automotive body repairer, write to:

☛ ASE, 13505 Dulles Technology Dr., Herndon, VA 20171-3421. Internet: **http://www.asecert.org**

For a directory of certified automotive body repairer programs, contact:

☛ National Automotive Technician Education Foundation, 13505 Dulles Technology Dr., Herndon, VA 20171-3421.
Internet: **http://www.natef.org**

For a directory of accredited private trade and technical schools that offer training programs in automotive body repair, write to:

☛ Accrediting Commission of Career Schools and Colleges of Technology, 2101 Wilson Blvd., Suite 302, Arlington, VA 22201.

For a list of public automotive body repair training programs, contact:

☛ SkillsUSA-VICA, P. O. Box 3000, 1401 James Monroe Hwy., Leesburg, VA 22075. Telephone (toll free): 1-800-321-VICA.
Internet: **http://www.skillsusa.org**

Automotive Mechanics and Service Technicians

(O*NET 85302A and 85302B)

Significant Points

- Opportunities are expected to be very good for persons who complete formal automotive training programs.
- Automotive mechanics and service technicians must be well versed in electronics and mathematics to work on increasingly sophisticated car components and systems.

Nature of the Work

Automotive mechanics and service technicians inspect, maintain, and repair automobiles and light trucks, such as vans and pickups, with gasoline engines. Traditionally, these workers have been called "mechanics." The increasing sophistication of automotive technology now requires workers who can use computerized shop equipment and work with electronic components, while maintaining their skills with traditional handtools. Workers with these new skills are increasingly called "service technicians." (Mechanics and service technicians who work on diesel-powered trucks, buses, and equipment are discussed in the

Handbook statement on diesel mechanics and service technicians. Motorcycle mechanics—who repair and service motorcycles, motorscooters, mopeds, and occasionally small all-terrain vehicles—are discussed in the *Handbook* statement on motorcycle, boat, and small-engine mechanics.)

Anyone whose car or light truck has broken down knows the importance of the jobs of automotive service technicians. The ability to diagnose the source of the problem quickly and accurately—a most valuable skill—requires good reasoning ability and a thorough knowledge of automobiles. Many technicians consider diagnosing hard-to-find troubles one of their most challenging and satisfying duties.

When mechanical or electrical troubles occur, technicians first get a description of the symptoms from the owner or, if they work in a large shop, the repair service estimator who wrote the repair order. To locate the problem, technicians use a diagnostic approach. First, they test to see if components and systems are proper and secure, then they rule out those components or systems that could not logically be the cause of the problem. For example, if an air conditioner malfunctions, technicians' diagnostic approach can pinpoint a problem as simple as a low coolant level or as complex as a bad drivetrain connection that has shorted out the air conditioner. Technicians may have to test drive the vehicle or use a variety of testing equipment, such as on-board and hand-held diagnostic computers or compression gauges to identify the source of the problem. Once the cause of the problem is found, technicians make adjustments or repairs. If a part is damaged, worn beyond repair, or not repairable at a reasonable cost, it is replaced, usually after consultation with the vehicle's owner.

During routine service, technicians inspect and lubricate engines and other components and repair or replace parts before they cause breakdowns. Technicians usually follow a checklist to ensure they examine all important parts. Belts, hoses, plugs, brake and fuel systems, and other potentially troublesome items are among those closely watched.

Service technicians use a variety of tools in their work. They use power tools, such as pneumatic wrenches to remove bolts quickly, machine tools like lathes and grinding machines to rebuild brakes, welding and flame-cutting equipment to remove and repair exhaust systems, and jacks and hoists to lift cars and engines. They also use common handtools like screwdrivers, pliers, and wrenches to work on small parts and in hard-to-reach places.

In the most modern shops of automobile dealers, service technicians use electronic service equipment, such as infrared engine analyzers and computerized diagnostic devices. These devices diagnose problems and make precision adjustments with precise calculations downloaded from large computerized databases. The computerized systems provide automatic updates to technical manuals and unlimited access to manufacturers' service information, technical service bulletins, and other information databases, which allow technicians to keep current on trouble spots and to learn new procedures.

Automotive mechanics and service technicians use a variety of tools, such as pneumatic wrenches to remove bolts quickly.

Automotive service technicians in large shops have increasingly become specialized. For example, *automatic transmission technicians* work on gear trains, couplings, hydraulic pumps, and other parts of automatic transmissions. Extensive training and experience in electronics is needed for the complex components and technology used in new vehicles. *Tune-up technicians* adjust the ignition timing and valves, and adjust or replace spark plugs and other parts to ensure efficient engine performance. They often use electronic test equipment to locate and adjust malfunctions in fuel, ignition, and emissions control systems.

Automotive air-conditioning repairers install and repair air conditioners and service components, such as compressors, condensers, and controls. These workers require special training in Federal and State regulations, governing the handling and disposal of refrigerants. *Front-end mechanics* align and balance wheels and repair steering mechanisms and suspension systems. They frequently use special alignment equipment and wheel-balancing machines. *Brake repairers* adjust brakes, replace brake linings and pads, and make other repairs on brake systems. Some mechanics and technicians specialize in both brake and front-end work.

Automotive-radiator mechanics clean radiators with caustic solutions, locate and solder leaks, and install new radiator cores or complete replacement radiators. They also repair heaters and air-conditioners, and solder leaks in gasoline tanks.

Working Conditions

Most automotive service technicians work a standard 40-hour week, but many self-employed technicians work longer hours. To satisfy customer service needs, many service shops offer evening and weekend service. Generally, service technicians work indoors in well ventilated and lighted repair shops. However, some shops are drafty and noisy. Although some problems can be fixed with simple computerized adjustments, technicians frequently work with dirty and greasy parts, and in awkward positions. They often lift heavy parts and tools. Minor cuts, burns, and bruises are common, but serious accidents are usually avoided when the shop is kept clean and orderly and safety practices are observed.

Employment

Automotive mechanics and service technicians held about 790,000 jobs in 1998. The majority worked for retail and wholesale automotive dealers, independent automotive repair shops, or gasoline service stations. Others found employment in automotive service facilities at department, automotive, and home supply stores. A small number maintained automobile fleets for taxicab and automobile leasing companies; Federal, State, and local governments; and other organizations. Motor vehicle manufacturers employed some technicians to test, adjust, and repair cars at the end of assembly lines. About 22 percent of automotive mechanics and service technicians were self-employed.

Training, Other Qualifications, and Advancement

Automotive technology is rapidly increasing in sophistication, and most training authorities strongly recommend that persons seeking automotive mechanic and service technician jobs complete a formal training program after graduating from high school. However, some automotive mechanics and service technicians still learn the trade solely by assisting and learning from experienced workers.

Many high schools, community colleges, and public and private vocational and technical schools offer automotive service technician training programs. Postsecondary programs usually provide more thorough career preparation than high school programs. High school programs, while an asset, vary greatly in quality. Some programs offer only an introduction to automotive technology and service for the future consumer or hobbyist, whereas others aim to equip graduates with enough skills to get a job as a mechanic's helper or trainee mechanic.

Postsecondary automotive technician training programs vary greatly in format but normally provide intensive career preparation, through a combination of classroom instruction and hands-on practice. Some trade and technical school programs provide concentrated training for 6 months to a year, depending on how many hours the student attends each week. Community college programs normally spread the training over 2 years; supplement the automotive training with instruction in English, basic mathematics, computers, and other subjects; and award an associate degree or certificate. Some students earn repair certificates and opt to leave the program to begin their career, before graduation.

The various automobile manufacturers and their participating dealers sponsor 2-year associate degree programs at postsecondary schools across the Nation. The Accrediting Commission of Career Schools and Colleges of Technology (ACCSCT) currently certifies 48 automotive technology schools and 23 diesel technology schools. Automotive manufacturers provide ASE certified instruction, service equipment, and current model cars on which students practice new skills and learn the latest automotive technology. Curriculums are updated frequently, to reflect changing technology and equipment. Students in these programs typically spend alternate 6- to 12-week periods attending classes full time and working full time in the service departments of sponsoring dealers. At these dealerships, students get practical experience, while assigned to an experienced worker who provides hands-on instruction and time saving tips. Also, some sponsoring dealers provide students with financial assistance for tuition or the purchase of tools.

The National Automotive Technicians Education Foundation (NATEF), an affiliate of the National Institute for Automotive Service Excellence (ASE), certifies automobile service technician, collision repair and refinish technician, engine machinist and medium/heavy truck technician training programs offered by high schools, postsecondary trade schools, technical institutes, and community colleges. While NATEF certification is voluntary, certification does signify that the program meets uniform standards for instructional facilities, equipment, staff credentials, and curriculum. In mid-1998, 1,208 high school and postsecondary automotive service technician training programs had been certified by NATEF, of which 965 trained automobile service technicians, 200 collision specialists, and 43 diesel and medium/heavy truck specialists.

There are more computers aboard a car today than aboard the first spaceship. A new car has from 10 to 15 on-board computers, operating everything from the engine to the radio. As a result, knowledge of electronics has grown increasingly important for automotive mechanics and service technicians. Engine controls and dashboard instruments were among the first components to use electronics; but now electronics are used in brakes, transmissions, steering systems, and a variety of other components. In the past, a specialist usually handled any problems involving electrical systems or electronics. Because electronics are now commonplace, automotive service technicians must be familiar with at least the basic principles of electronics, to recognize when an electronic malfunction may be responsible for a problem. In addition, technicians must be able to test and replace electronic components.

For trainee automotive service technician jobs, employers look for people with strong communication and analytical skills. Good reading, mathematics, and computer skills are needed to study technical manuals, to keep abreast of new technology. People who have a desire to learn new service and repair procedures and specifications are excellent candidates for trainee mechanic jobs. Trainees also must possess mechanical aptitude and knowledge of how automobiles work. Most employers regard the successful completion of a vocational training program in automotive mechanics at a postsecondary institution as the best preparation for trainee positions. Experience working on motor vehicles in the Armed Forces or as a hobby is also valuable. Because of the complexity of new vehicles, a growing number of employers require both completion of high school and additional postsecondary training. Courses in automotive repair, electronics, physics, chemistry, English, computers, and mathematics provide a good educational background for a career as an automotive service technician.

Beginners usually start as trainee technicians, mechanics' helpers, lubrication workers, or gasoline service station attendants and gradually acquire and practice their skills, by working with experienced mechanics and technicians. With a few months' experience, beginners perform many routine service tasks and make simple repairs. It usually takes 2 to 5 years of experience to acquire adequate proficiency to become a journey-level service technician to quickly perform the more difficult types of routine service and repairs. However, graduates of the best postsecondary automotive training programs are often able to earn promotion to the journey level after only a few months on the job. An additional 1 to 2 years' experience familiarizes mechanics and technicians with all types of repairs. Difficult specialties, such as transmission repair, require another year or two of training and experience. In contrast, automotive radiator mechanics and brake specialists, who do not need an all-round knowledge of automotive repair, may learn their jobs in considerably less time.

In the past, many persons have become automotive mechanics through 3- or 4-year formal apprenticeship programs. However, apprenticeships have become rare, as vocational training programs in automotive mechanics have become more common at postsecondary institutions.

At work, the most important possessions of mechanics and technicians are their handtools. Mechanics and technicians usually provide their own tools, and many experienced workers have thousands of dollars invested in them. Employers typically furnish expensive power tools, engine analyzers, and other diagnostic equipment; but hand tools are accumulated with experience.

Employers increasingly send experienced automotive service technicians to manufacturer training centers to learn to repair new models or to receive special training in the repair of components, such as electronic fuel injection or air-conditioners. Motor vehicle dealers may also send promising beginners to manufacturer-sponsored mechanic training programs. Factory representatives visit many shops to conduct short training sessions. Employers, to maintain or upgrade employee skills and increase their value to the dealership, typically furnish this additional training.

The standard credential for automotive mechanics and service technicians is voluntary certification by Automotive Service Excellence (ASE). Certification is available in one or more of eight different service areas, such as electrical systems, engine repair, brake systems, suspension and steering, and heating and air conditioning. For certification in each area, mechanics and technicians must have at least 2 years of experience and pass a written examination. Completion of an automotive mechanic program in high school, vocational or trade school, or community or junior college may be substituted for 1 year of experience. In some cases, graduates of ASE certified programs are certified in up to three specialties. To be certified as a master automotive mechanic, mechanics must be certified in all eight areas. Many dealers must have a required number of mechanics or technicians trained in each specialty. Mechanics and technicians must retake the examination at least every 5 years to maintain their certification.

Experienced technicians who have leadership ability sometimes advance to shop supervisor or service manager. Those who work well with customers may become automotive repair service estimators. Some with sufficient funds open independent repair shops.

Job Outlook

Job opportunities in this occupation are expected to be good for persons who complete automotive training programs in high school, vocational and technical schools, or community colleges. Persons whose training includes basic electronics skills should have the best opportunities. Automotive service technician careers offer an excellent opportunity for well-prepared people with a technical background, because these careers afford the opportunity for good pay and the satisfaction of highly skilled work with vehicles incorporating the latest in high technology. However, persons without formal automotive training are likely to face competition for entry-level jobs.

Employment opportunities for automotive mechanics and service technicians are expected to increase about as fast as the average for all occupations through the year 2008. Employment growth will continue to be concentrated in automobile dealerships, independent automotive repair shops, and specialty car care chains. More national department store chains will provide auto repair services in large shops that employ many technicians to do after-warranty repairs, such as oil changes, brake repair, air conditioner service, and other minor repairs, taking less than 4 hours to complete. Employment of automotive mechanics and service technicians in gasoline service stations will continue to decline, as few stations offer repair services.

The number of automotive mechanics and service technicians will increase, due to the expansion of the driving age population and the number of households with multiple motor vehicles. The growing complexity of automotive technology necessitates that cars be serviced by skilled workers, contributing to the growth in demand for highly trained mechanics and technicians.

More job openings for automotive mechanics and service technicians are expected than for most other occupations, as experienced workers transfer to related occupations, retire, or stop working for other reasons. This large occupation needs a substantial number of entrants each year, to replace the workers who leave the occupation.

Most persons who enter the occupation can expect steady work, because changes in economic conditions have little effect on the automotive repair business. During a downturn, however, some employers may be more reluctant to hire inexperienced workers.

Earnings

Median hourly earnings of automotive mechanics and service technicians, including commission, were $13.16 in 1998. The middle 50 percent earned between $10.02 and $17.14 an hour. The lowest 10 percent earned less than $7.44 and the highest 10 percent earned more than $21.25 an hour. Median annual earnings in the industries employing the largest number of automotive mechanics and service technicians in 1997 were as follows:

Local government, except education and hospitals	$15.19
New and used car dealers	15.03
Automotive repair shops	11.86
Auto and home supply stores	11.31
Gasoline service stations	11.18

Many experienced technicians employed by automotive dealers and independent repair shops receive a commission related to the labor cost charged to the customer. Under this method, weekly earnings depend on the amount of work completed. Employers frequently guarantee commissioned mechanics and technicians a minimum weekly salary. Many master technicians earn from $70,000 to $100,000 annually.

Some automotive service technicians are members of labor unions such as the International Association of Machinists and Aerospace Workers; the International Union, United Automobile, Aerospace and Agricultural Implement Workers of America; the Sheet Metal Workers' International Association; and the International Brotherhood of Teamsters.

Related Occupations

Other workers who repair and service motor vehicles include diesel mechanics and service technicians, automotive body repairers, customizers, repair service estimators, and motorcycle, boat, and small-engine mechanics.

Sources of Additional Information

For more details about work opportunities, contact local automotive dealers and repair shops or the local office of the State employment service. The State employment service also may have information about training programs.

A list of certified automotive technician training programs can be obtained from:

☛ National Automotive Technicians Education Foundation, 13505 Dulles Technology Dr., Herndon, VA 20171-3421.
Internet: **http://www.natef.org**

For a directory of accredited private trade and technical schools that offer programs in automotive technician training, write:

☛ Accrediting Commission of Career Schools and Colleges of Technology, 2101 Wilson Blvd., Suite 302, Arlington, VA 22201.

For a list of public automotive technician training programs, contact:

☛ SkillsUSA-VICA, P.O. Box 3000, 1401 James Monroe Hwy., Leesburg, VA 22075. Telephone (toll free): 1-800-321-VICA.
Internet: **http://www.skillsusa.org**

Information on automobile manufacturer-sponsored 2-year associate degree programs in automotive service technology can be obtained from:

☛ Ford ASSET Program, Ford Customer Service Division, Fairlane Business Park III, 1555 Fairlane Dr., Allen Park, MI 48101. Telephone (toll free): 1-800-272-7218.

☛ Chrysler Corporation, National C.A.P. Coordinator, National Technical Training Center, 2367 Walton Blvd., Auburn Hills, MI 48326. Telephone (toll free): 1-800-626-1523.
Internet: **http://www.CAP.chryslercorp.com**

☛ General Motors Automotive Service Educational Program, National College Coordinator, General Motors Service Technology Group, MC 480-204-001, 30501 Van Dyke Ave., Warren, MI 48090. Telephone (toll free): 1-800-828-6860.

☛ Toyota-Technical Education Network (T-TEN), P.O. Box 4900, Fenton, MO 63026-9842. Telephone (toll free): 1-800-441-5141.
Internet: **http://www.t-ten.com**

Information on how to become a certified automotive service technician is available from:

☛ ASE, 13505 Dulles Technology Dr., Herndon, VA 20171-3421.
Internet: **http://www.asecert.org**

For general information about the work of automotive mechanics and service technicians, write:

☛ Automotive Service Association, Inc., 1901 Airport Freeway, Bedford, TX 76021-5732. Internet: **http://www.asashop.org**

☛ Automotive Service Industry Association, 25 Northwest Point, Elk Grove Village, IL 60007-1035

☛ National Automobile Dealers Association, 8400 Westpark Dr., McLean, VA 22102

Coin, Vending, and Amusement Machine Servicers and Repairers

(O*NET 85947)

Significant Points

- Most workers learn their skills on the job.
- Opportunities should be good for persons with some knowledge of electronics.

Nature of the Work

Coin, vending, and amusement machines are a familiar sight in offices, convenience stores, arcades, and casinos. These coin-operated machines dispense refreshments, test our senses, and spit out lottery tickets nearly everywhere we turn. Coin, vending, and amusement machine servicers and repairers install, service, and stock these machines and keep them in good working order.

Vending machine servicers, often called route drivers, visit coin-operated machines that dispense soft drinks, candy and snacks, and other items. They collect money from the machines, restock merchandise, and change labels to indicate new selections. They also keep the machines clean and appealing.

Vending machine repairers, often called mechanics or technicians, make sure machines operate correctly. When checking complicated electrical and electronic machines, such as beverage dispensers, they make sure that the machines mix drinks properly and that refrigeration and heating units work correctly. On the relatively simple gravity-operated machines, servicers check handles, springs, plungers, and merchandise chutes. They also test coin and change-making mechanisms.

When installing machines, vending machine repairers make the necessary water and electrical connections and check the machines for proper operation. They also make sure installation complies with local plumbing and electrical codes. Because many vending machines dispense food, these workers must comply with State and local public health and sanitation standards.

Amusement machine servicers and repairers work on juke boxes, video games, pinball machines, and slot machines. They make sure the various levers, joysticks, and mechanisms function properly, so that the games remain fair and the juke box selections are accurate. They update selections, repair or replace malfunctioning parts, and rebuild existing equipment. Those who work in the gaming industry must adhere to strict guidelines, because State and Federal agencies regulate many gaming machines.

Preventive maintenance—avoiding trouble before it starts—is a major job of repairers. For example, they periodically clean refrigeration condensers, lubricate mechanical parts, and adjust machines to perform properly.

If a machine breaks down, vending and amusement machine repairers inspect it for obvious problems, such as loose electrical wires, malfunctions of the coin mechanism, and leaks. When servicing electronic machines, repairers test them with hand held diagnostic computers that determine the extent and location of any problem. Repairers may only have to replace a circuit board or other component to fix the problem. However, if the problem cannot be readily located, these workers refer to technical manuals and wiring diagrams and use testing devices, such as electrical circuit testers to find defective parts. Repairers decide if they must replace a part and whether they can fix the malfunction on-site or if they have to send the machine to the repair shop.

In the repair shop, vending and amusement machine repairers use power tools, such as grinding wheels, saws, and drills, as well as voltmeters, ohmmeters, oscilloscopes, and other testing equipment. They also use ordinary repair tools, such as screwdrivers, pliers, and wrenches.

Vending machine servicers and repairers employed by small companies may both fill and fix machines on a regular basis. These combination servicers-repairers stock machines, collect money, fill coin and currency changers, and repair machines when necessary.

Servicers and repairers also do some paper work, such as filing reports, preparing repair cost estimates, ordering parts, and keeping daily records of merchandise distributed. However, new machines with computerized inventory controls reduce the paperwork a servicer must complete.

Working Conditions

Some vending and amusement machine repairers work primarily in company repair shops, but many spend substantial time on the road visiting machines wherever they have been placed. Vending and amusement machines operate around the clock, so repairers often work at night and on weekends and holidays.

Coin, vending, and amusement machine servicers and repairers check handles, springs, plungers, and merchandise chutes on simple gravity-operated machines.

Vending and amusement machine repair shops generally are quiet, well lighted, and have adequate work space. However, when servicing machines on location, the work may be done where pedestrian traffic is heavy, such as in busy supermarkets, industrial complexes, offices, casinos, or arcades. Repair work is relatively safe, although servicers and repairers must take care to avoid hazards such as electrical shocks and cuts from sharp tools and other metal objects. They also must follow safe work procedures, especially when moving heavy vending and amusement machines.

Employment

Coin, vending, and amusement machine servicers and repairers held about 27,000 jobs in 1998. Most repairers work for vending companies that sell food and other items through machines. Others work for soft drink bottling companies that have their own coin-operated machines. A growing number of servicers and repairers work for amusement establishments that own video games, pin-ball machines, juke boxes, slot machines, and similar types of amusement equipment. Although vending and amusement machine servicers and repairers are employed throughout the country, most are located in areas with large populations and many vending and amusement machines.

Training, Other Qualifications, and Advancement

Employers normally prefer to hire high school graduates. New workers are trained to fill and fix machines informally on the job by observing, working with, and receiving instruction from experienced repairers. High school or vocational school courses in electricity, refrigeration, and machine repair are an advantage in qualifying for entry level jobs. Employers usually require applicants to demonstrate mechanical ability, either through work experience or by scoring well on mechanical aptitude tests.

Because coin, vending, and amusement machine servicers and repairers sometimes handle thousands of dollars in merchandise and cash, employers hire persons who have a record of honesty. The ability to deal tactfully with people also is important. A commercial driver's license and a good driving record are essential for most vending and amusement machine servicer and repairer jobs. Some employers require their servicers to be bonded.

As electronics become more prevalent in vending and amusement machines, employers will increasingly prefer applicants who have some training in electronics. Technologically advanced machines with features such as multilevel pricing, inventory control, and scrolling messages extensively use electronics and microchip computers. Some vocational high schools and junior colleges offer 1- to 2-year training programs in basic electronics.

Beginners start training with simple jobs, such as cleaning or stocking machines. They then learn to rebuild machines, by removing defective parts, repairing, adjusting, and testing the machines. Next, they accompany an experienced repairer on service calls, and finally make visits on their own. This learning process takes from 6 months to 3 years, depending on the individual's abilities, previous education, types of machines serviced, and the quality of instruction.

The National Automatic Merchandising Association has a self-study mechanics training program for vending machine repairers. Repairers use manuals for instruction in subjects such as customer relations, safety, electronics, and schematic reading. Upon completion of the program, repairers must pass a written test, to become certified as a journey or master mechanic.

To learn about new machines, repairers and servicers sometimes attend training sessions sponsored by manufacturers that may last from a few days to several weeks. Both trainees and experienced workers sometimes take evening courses in basic electricity, electronics, microwave ovens, refrigeration, and other related subjects to stay on top of new techniques and equipment. Skilled servicers and repairers may be promoted to supervisory jobs or go into business for themselves.

Job Outlook

Employment of coin, vending, and amusement machine servicers and repairers is expected to grow about as fast as the average for all occupations through the year 2008, because of the increasing number of vending and amusement machines in operation.

Establishments are likely to install additional vending machines in industrial plants, hospitals, stores, and other business establishments, to meet the public demand for inexpensive snacks and other food items. The range of products dispensed by machine is expected to increase, as vending machines continue to become increasingly automated and machines are built that include microwave ovens, mini-refrigerators, and freezers. In addition, casinos, arcades, and other amusement establishments are an increasing source of entertainment for baby boomers and young adults. Also, State and multi-State lotteries are increasingly using coin-operated machines, to sell scratch-off tickets in grocery stores and other public places.

Improved technology in newer machines will moderate employment growth, because these machines require maintenance less frequently than older ones. These new machines will need repairing and restocking less often, and contain computers that record sales and inventory data, reducing the amount of time-consuming paperwork. Additionally, some new machines use wireless data transmitters to signal the vending machine company, when these machines need restocking or repairing. This allows servicers and repairers to be dispatched only when needed, instead of their having to check each machine on a regular schedule.

Experienced workers who transfer to other occupations or leave the labor force will create job openings. Persons with some background in electronics should have good job prospects, because electronic circuitry is an important component of vending and amusement machines. If firms cannot find trained or experienced workers for these jobs, they are likely to train qualified route drivers or hire inexperienced people who have acquired some mechanical, electrical, or electronic training by taking high school or vocational courses.

Earnings

Median hourly earnings of coin, vending, and amusement machine servicers and repairers were $11.18 in 1998. The middle 50 percent earned between $8.73 and $13.83 an hour. The lowest 10 percent earned less than $6.80 and the highest 10 percent earned more than $16.56 an hour. Typically, States with some form of legalized gaming have the highest wages.

Most coin, vending, and amusement machine servicers and repairers work 8 hours a day, 5 days a week and receive premium pay for overtime. Some union contracts stipulate higher pay for night work and for emergency repair jobs on weekends and holidays than for regular hours. Some vending machine repairers and servicers are members of the International Brotherhood of Teamsters.

Related Occupations

Other workers who repair equipment with electrical and electronic components include home appliance and power tool repairers, electronic equipment repairers, and general maintenance mechanics.

Sources of Additional Information

Information on job opportunities in this field can be obtained from local vending machine firms and local offices of your State employment service. For general information on vending machine repair, write to:

☛ National Automatic Merchandising Association, 20 N. Wacker Dr., Suite 3500, Chicago, IL 60606-3102.
Internet: **http://www.vending.org**

☛ American Vending Sales, Inc.,750 Morse Ave., Elk Grove Village, IL 60007.

Diesel Mechanics and Service Technicians

(O*NET 85311A)

Significant Points

- A career as a diesel mechanic or service technician offers relatively high wages and the challenge of skilled repair work.
- Opportunities are expected to be good for persons who complete formal training programs.
- National certification is the recognized standard of achievement for diesel mechanics and service technicians.

Nature of the Work

The diesel engine is the workhorse powering the Nation's heavy vehicles and equipment, because it delivers more power per unit of fuel and is more durable than its gasoline-burning counterpart.

Diesel mechanics and service technicians repair and maintain the diesel engines that power transportation equipment, such as heavy trucks, buses, and locomotives. Some diesel mechanics and technicians also work on bulldozers, cranes, road graders, farm tractors, and combines; and a small number repair automobiles or boats. (For information on mechanics and technicians working primarily on automobiles, heavy equipment, or boats, see the *Handbook* statements on automotive, mobile heavy equipment, or motorcycle, boat, and small-engine mechanics.)

Mechanics and technicians who work for organizations that maintain their own vehicles spend most of their time doing preventive maintenance, to ensure that equipment can be operated safely. These workers also eliminate unnecessary wear and damage to parts that could result in costly breakdowns. During a routine maintenance check on a vehicle, technicians follow a checklist that includes the inspection of brake systems, steering mechanisms, wheel bearings, and other important parts. Following an inspection, technicians usually repair or adjust parts that do not work properly and replace parts that cannot be fixed.

In many shops, it is common for workers to do all kinds of repairs. Jobs can vary from working on a vehicle's electrical system one day, to doing major engine repairs the next. In some large shops, technicians specialize in one or two types of work. For example, a shop may have technicians specializing in major engine repair, transmission work, electrical systems, suspension, or brake systems. Diesel maintenance is becoming increasingly complex, as more electronic components are used to control engine operation. In modern shops, diesel mechanics and service technicians use handheld computers to diagnose problems and to adjust engine functions.

Diesel mechanics and service technicians use a variety of tools in their work, including power tools, such as pneumatic wrenches to remove bolts quickly; machine tools, like lathes and grinding machines to rebuild brakes; welding and flame-cutting equipment to remove and repair exhaust systems; and jacks and hoists to lift and move large parts. Common handtools—screwdrivers, pliers, and wrenches—are used to work on small parts and get at hard-to-reach places. Diesel mechanics and service technicians also use a variety of computerized testing equipment to pinpoint and analyze malfunctions in electrical systems and engines.

In large shops, technicians generally receive their assignments from shop supervisors or service managers. Most supervisors and managers are experienced technicians who also assist in diagnosing problems and maintaining quality standards. Technicians may work as a team or be assisted by an apprentice or helper, when doing heavy work, such as removing engines and transmissions.

Working Conditions

Diesel mechanics and service technicians usually work indoors, although they occasionally make repairs to vehicles on the road. Diesel mechanics and service technicians lift heavy parts and tools, handle greasy and dirty parts, and stand or lie in awkward positions to repair vehicles and equipment. Minor cuts, burns, and bruises are common, although serious accidents can usually be avoided, if the shop is kept clean and orderly and safety procedures are followed. Mechanics and technicians normally work in well-lighted, heated, and ventilated areas, however, some shops are drafty and noisy. Many employers provide lockers and shower facilities.

Employment

Diesel mechanics and service technicians held about 255,000 jobs in 1998. Nearly 25 percent serviced trucks and other diesel-powered equipment for customers of vehicle and equipment dealers, leasing companies, or independent automotive repair shops. About 20 percent worked for local and long-distance trucking companies, and another 20 percent maintained the buses and trucks of buslines, public transit companies, school systems, or Federal, State, and local governments. The remaining mechanics and technicians maintained the fleets of trucks and other equipment for manufacturing, construction, or other companies. A relatively small number were self-employed. Nearly every section of the country employs diesel mechanics and service technicians, although most work in towns and cities where trucking companies, bus lines, and other fleet owners have large operations.

Diesel mechanics and service technicians use a variety of testing equipment to pinpoint and analyze malfunctions in electrical systems and engines.

Training, Other Qualifications, and Advancement

Although many persons qualify for diesel mechanic and service technician jobs through years of on-the-job training, authorities recommend the completion of a formal diesel engine training program after graduating from high school. Employers prefer to hire graduates of formal training programs, because of these workers' head start in training and their ability to quickly advance to the journey mechanic level.

Many community colleges and trade and vocational schools offer programs in diesel repair. These 6-month to 2-year programs lead to a certificate of completion or an associate degree. Programs vary in the degree of hands-on training they provide on equipment. Some offer about 30 hours per week on equipment, whereas others offer more lab or classroom instruction. Training provides a foundation in the latest diesel technology and instruction in the service and repair of the vehicles and equipment mechanics and technicians will encounter on the job. These programs also improve the skills needed to interpret technical manuals and communicate with coworkers and customers. Increasingly, employers are working closely with training programs, providing instructors with the latest equipment, techniques, and tools and offering jobs to graduates.

Whereas most employers prefer to hire persons who have completed formal training programs, some mechanics and technicians continue to learn their skills on the job. Unskilled beginners are usually assigned tasks such as cleaning parts, fueling and lubricating vehicles, and driving vehicles into and out of the shop. Beginners are usually promoted to trainee mechanic positions, as they gain experience and as vacancies become available. In some shops, beginners who have experience in automobile service start as trainee mechanics.

Most trainee mechanics perform routine service tasks and make minor repairs after a few months' experience. These workers advance to increasingly difficult jobs, as they prove their ability and competence. After mechanics and technicians master the repair and service of diesel engines, they learn to work on related components, such as brakes, transmissions, and electrical systems. Generally, a technician with at least 3 to 4 years of on-the-job experience will qualify as a journey-level diesel truck or bus mechanic. Completion of a formal training program speeds advancement to the journey level.

For unskilled entry level jobs, employers usually look for applicants who have mechanical aptitude and strong problem solving skills, and who are at least 18 years of age and in good physical condition. Nearly all employers require completion of high school. Courses in automotive repair, electronics, English, mathematics, and physics provide a strong educational background for a career as a diesel mechanic or service technician. A State commercial driver's license is needed to test drive trucks or buses on public roads. Practical experience in automobile repair in a gasoline service station, in the Armed Forces, or as a hobby is also valuable.

Employers often send experienced mechanics and technicians to special training classes conducted by manufacturers and vendors where workers learn the latest technology and repair techniques. Technicians constantly receive updated technical manuals and service procedures outlining changes in techniques and standards for repair. It is essential for technicians to read, interpret, and comprehend service manuals, in order to keep abreast of engineering changes.

Voluntary certification by the National Institute for Automotive Service Excellence (ASE) is recognized as the standard of achievement for diesel mechanics and service technicians. Technicians may be certified as Master Heavy-Duty Truck technicians or in one or more of six different areas of heavy-duty truck repair: Brakes, gasoline engines, diesel engines, drive trains, electrical systems, and suspension and steering. For certification in each area, a technician must pass one or more of the exams and present proof of 2 years of relevant hands-on work experience. Two years of relevant formal training from a high school, vocational or trade school, or community or junior college program may be substituted for up to 1 year of the work experience requirement. To remain certified, technicians must retest every 5 years. This ensures that mechanics and service technicians keep up with changing technology.

A diesel mechanic and service technician may opt for ASE certification as a school bus technician. The certification identifies and recognizes those technicians who possess the knowledge and skills required to diagnose, service, and repair different subsystems of Type A, B, C, and D school buses. The ASE School Bus Technician Test Series includes seven certification exams: Body Systems and Special Equipment (S1), Diesel Engines (S2), Drive Train (S3), Brakes (S4), Suspension and Steering (S5), Electrical/Electronic Systems (S6), and Air Conditioning Systems and Controls (S7). Whereas several of these tests parallel existing ASE truck tests, each one is designed to test knowledge of systems specific to school buses. In order to become ASE certified in school bus repair, technicians must pass one or more of the exams and present proof of 2 years of relevant hands-on work experience. Technicians who pass tests S1 through S6, become ASE-Certified Master School Bus Technicians.

The most important work possessions of mechanics and technicians are their handtools. Mechanics and technicians usually provide their own tools, and many experienced workers have thousands of dollars invested in them. Employers typically furnish expensive power tools, computerized engine analyzers, and other diagnostic equipment; but hand tools are ordinarily accumulated with experience.

Experienced mechanics and technicians with leadership ability may advance to shop supervisors or service managers. Mechanics and technicians with sales ability sometimes become sales representatives. Some open their own repair shops.

Job Outlook

Employment of diesel mechanics and service technicians is expected to increase about as fast as the average for all occupations through the year 2008. Besides employment growth, opportunities will be created by the need to replace those who retire or transfer to other occupations.

Employment of diesel mechanics and service technicians is expected to grow, as freight transportation by truck increases. Additional trucks will be needed for both local and intercity hauling, due to increased production of goods. Due to the greater durability and economy of the diesel engine relative to the gasoline engine, buses and trucks of all sizes are expected to be increasingly powered by diesels. This will create new jobs for diesel mechanics and service technicians.

Careers as diesel mechanics and service technicians attract many, because of the relatively high wages and the challenge of skilled repair work. Opportunities should be good for persons who complete formal training in diesel mechanics at community and junior colleges and vocational and technical schools, but others without formal training may face competition for entry-level jobs.

Most persons entering this occupation can expect steady work, because changes in economic conditions have little effect on the diesel repair business. During a financial downturn, however, some employers may be reluctant to hire new workers.

Earnings

Median hourly earnings of bus and truck mechanics and diesel engine specialists, including incentive pay, were $14.11 in 1998. The middle 50 percent earned between $11.32 and $17.55 an hour. The lowest 10 percent earned less than $9.36 and the highest 10 percent earned more than $20.78 an hour. Median hourly earnings in the industries employing the largest number of bus and truck mechanics and diesel engine specialists in 1997 were as follows:

Industry	Earnings
Local government, except education and hospitals	$16.90
Motor vehicles, parts, and supplies	14.10
Elementary and secondary schools	13.00
Trucking and courier services, except air	12.40
Automotive repair shops	12.30

Beginners usually earn from 50 to 75 percent of the rate of skilled workers and receive increases as they become more skilled, until they reach the rate of a skilled mechanic or service technician.

The majority of mechanics and service technicians work a standard 40-hour week, although some work as many as 70 hours per week, particularly if they are self-employed. A growing number of shops have expanded their hours to better perform repairs and routine service when needed, or as a convenience to customers. Those employed by truck and bus firms providing service around the clock may work evenings, nights, and weekends. These technicians usually receive a higher rate of pay for working non-traditional hours.

Many diesel mechanics and service technicians are members of labor unions, including the International Association of Machinists and Aerospace Workers; the Amalgamated Transit Union; the International Union, United Automobile, Aerospace and Agricultural Implement Workers of America; the Transport Workers Union of America; the Sheet Metal Workers' International Association; and the International Brotherhood of Teamsters.

Related Occupations

Diesel mechanics and service technicians repair trucks, buses, and other diesel-powered equipment. Related mechanic and technician occupations include aircraft mechanics, automotive mechanics and service technicians, boat engine mechanics, farm equipment mechanics, and mobile heavy equipment mechanics.

Sources of Additional Information

More details about work opportunities for diesel mechanics and service technicians may be obtained from local employers such as trucking companies, truck dealers, or bus lines; locals of the unions previously mentioned; and local offices of your State employment service. Local State employment service offices also may have information about training programs. State boards of postsecondary career schools also have information on licensed schools with training programs for diesel mechanics and service technicians.

For general information about a career as a diesel mechanic or service technician, write:

☛ American Trucking Associations, Inc., Maintenance Council, 2200 Mill Rd., Alexandria, VA 22314-4677.

☛ Kenworth Truck Company, Service Coordinator, 700 East Gate Dr., Suite 325, Mt. Laurel, NJ 08054.

☛ Detroit Diesel, Personnel Director, MS B39, 13400 West Outer Dr., Detroit, MI 48239.

Information on how to become a certified medium/heavy-duty diesel mechanic or bus mechanic is available from:

☛ ASE, 13505 Dulles Technology Dr., Herndon, VA 20171-3421. Internet: **http://www.asecert.org**

For a directory of accredited private trade and technical schools with training programs for diesel mechanics and service technicians, contact:

☛Accrediting Commission of Career Schools and Colleges of Technology, 2101 Wilson Blvd., Suite 302, Arlington, VA 22201.

☛ National Automotive Technicians Education Foundation, 13505 Dulles Technology Dr., Herndon, VA 20171-3421.
Internet: **http://www.natef.org**

For a directory of public training programs for diesel mechanics and service technicians, contact:

☛ SkillsUSA-VICA, P.O. Box 3000, 1401 James Monroe Hwy., Leesburg, VA 22075. Telephone: (toll free): 1-800-321-VICA.
Internet: **http://www.skillsusa.org**

Farm Equipment Mechanics

(O*NET 85321)

Significant Points

- Skill in using computerized diagnostic equipment is becoming more important.
- Opportunities should be best for persons who complete post secondary programs in farm equipment or diesel mechanics.
- Jobs are concentrated in small towns and rural areas.

Nature of the Work

Many of today's farms use more sophisticated equipment and advanced business practices than ever before. On average, farms have become larger—although fewer in number—allowing the economical use of specialized farm equipment to increase crop yields even while employing fewer and fewer workers. Specialized farm machinery has grown in size, complexity, and variety, and does everything from tilling the land to milking the cows. To operate efficiently, many farms have several tractors equipped with 40- to 400-horsepower engines. Planters, tillers, fertilizer spreaders, and spray and irrigation equipment help grow the crops and combines, hay balers, swathers, and crop drying equipment aid in harvesting them.

Farm equipment dealers employ most of the farm equipment mechanics. Often called service technicians, these workers service, maintain, and repair farm equipment as well as smaller lawn and garden tractors sold to suburban homeowners. What was typically a general repairer's job around the farm has evolved into a technical career much in demand. Farmers have increasingly turned to farm equipment dealers to service and repair their equipment because the machinery has grown in complexity. Modern equipment uses more electronics and hydraulics making it difficult to perform repairs without some specialized training.

Mechanics work mostly on equipment brought into the shop for repair and adjustment. During planting and harvesting seasons, they may travel to farms to make emergency repairs to minimize delays in farm operations.

Mechanics also perform preventive maintenance on older equipment. Periodically, they test, adjust, clean, and tune engines to keep them in proper working order. The level of service is determined by the difficulty of the problem. In large shops, mechanics usually specialize in certain types of work, such as diesel engine overhaul, hydraulic maintenance, or clutch and transmission repair. Others specialize in certain repairs, such as air-conditioning units often included to cool the cabs of combines and large tractors, or the repair of specific types of equipment such as hay balers. In addition, some mechanics assemble new machinery, do body work, and repair dented or torn sheet metal on tractors or other machinery.

Mechanics use many basic handtools, including wrenches, pliers, hammers, and screwdrivers. They also use precision equipment, such as micrometers and torque wrenches, in addition to welding equipment and power tools to repair broken parts. Increasingly, computerized engine testing equipment, such as dynamometers, engine analysis units, and compression testers, is used to measure engine performance and to find worn piston rings or leaking cylinder valves. Soon, mechanics will have access to computerized diagnostic equipment to monitor and locate malfunctions without turning a wrench.

New technology allows farmers to achieve record crop yields from small plots of land by more precisely tailoring their tillage to accommodate the soil conditions of each. This growing use of site-specific technology or precision farming, as it is known, makes use of the Global Positioning System (GPS), yield monitors, and variable rate applicators. These computerized systems link farmers to satellites and other advanced devices to better monitor their crops and land use. More often than not, farmers rely on their equipment dealer to be their one stop for all repair needs. To better satisfy customer needs, traditional repair shops have begun to service advanced equipment, requiring the mechanic to acquire new skills.

A farm equipment mechanic works on a combine.

Working Conditions

Commonly, farm equipment mechanics work indoors though some do repairs in the field. Most farm equipment mechanics work in well ventilated, lighted, and heated repair shops, but older shops may not offer these amenities; others may work in the farmer's equipment shed or barn where conditions may not be as ideal as in the mechanic's repair shop. Farm equipment mechanics handle greasy and dirty parts and may stand or lie in awkward positions to repair vehicles and equipment. They often lift heavy parts and tools and handle various agricultural chemicals and solutions. Minor cuts, burns, and bruises are common, but serious accidents can be avoided when the shop is kept clean and orderly and safety practices observed.

As with most agricultural occupations, the hours of work for farm equipment mechanics vary according to the season of the year. During the busy planting and harvesting seasons, mechanics often work 6 or 7 days a week, 10 to 12 hours daily. In slow winter months, however, mechanics may work fewer than 40 hours a week.

Employment

Farm equipment mechanics held about 49,000 jobs in 1998. Most mechanics worked in service departments of farm equipment dealers. Others worked in independent repair shops, and in shops on large farms. More than 1 out of 10 farm equipment mechanics was self-employed.

Because nearly every area of the United States has some form of farming, it is common to find farm equipment mechanics employed throughout the country. Employment is concentrated in small towns and rural areas, making this an attractive career choice for people who wish to live away from the big city. However, many mechanics work in the rural fringes of metropolitan areas, so farm equipment mechanics who prefer the conveniences of city life need not live in rural areas.

Training, Other Qualifications, and Advancement

Technical training is becoming more important because of the development of more complex farm machinery, and because of recent efforts to standardize skills within the occupation. Employers prefer to hire trainee farm equipment mechanics who have completed a 1- or 2-year post-secondary training program in agricultural or farm mechanics at a vocational school or community college. However, if these programs are not offered, study of diesel mechanics offers a strong background. Programs in industrial maintenance, which focus on hydraulics, electronics, engine repair, and welding, are also good preparation. Mechanics need knowledge of computers, and must have the aptitude to read circuit diagrams and blueprints in order to make complex repairs to electrical systems.

Most farm equipment mechanics enter the occupation as trainees and become proficient in their trade by assisting experienced mechanics. The length of training varies with the helper's aptitude and prior experience. Usually, 2 years of on-the-job training are necessary for a mechanic to do routine types of repair work efficiently. Highly specialized repair and overhaul jobs usually require additional training.

Many farm equipment mechanics enter this occupation through careers in related occupations. For example, they may have experience working as a diesel mechanic, mobile heavy equipment mechanic, or automotive mechanic. Prior experience in farm work also provides a foundation for the skills and training necessary to become a farm equipment mechanic as farm workers often make minor equipment repairs to save repair costs. Similarly, people with military backgrounds in mechanics have valuable experience and training. Persons who enter from related occupations may start as trainees or helpers, however, they may require less on-the-job training.

Employers look for skilled individuals with the aptitude needed to handle tools and equipment. Occasionally, strength is required to lift, move, or hold heavy parts in place. Difficult repair jobs require problem-solving skills to diagnose the source of the machine's malfunction and choose the correct course of action to fix the problem. The importance of computer skills will increase as many more dealers gain access to computerized diagnostic equipment on a laptop computer. This technology will allow mechanics to simply plug into the farm equipment and do a complete diagnostic check by pushing a button. Experienced mechanics should be able to work independently with minimal supervision.

Farm equipment mechanics may keep abreast of changes in farm equipment technology by going to trade shows, by reading the latest farm equipment literature, and by carefully studying service manuals and analyzing complex diagrams. Many farm equipment mechanics and trainees receive refresher training in short-term programs conducted by farm equipment manufacturers. This is the dealers' way of keeping their employees trained in the latest technology and standards within the industry. A company service representative explains the design, function, and techniques required to repair and maintain new models of farm equipment. In addition, some dealers may send employees to local vocational schools that hold special week-long classes in subjects such as air-conditioning repair or hydraulics. Training courses delivered via satellite and video tapes have become increasingly popular ways to standardize training techniques and to cut expenses needed to reach individual dealers and repair shops.

Mechanics' personal tools are very important to their livelihood. Farm equipment mechanics usually buy their own handtools, although employers furnish power tools and computerized test equipment. Trainee mechanics are expected to accumulate their own tools as they gain experience. Experienced mechanics have thousands of dollars invested in their tools.

Farm equipment mechanics may advance to shop supervisor, service manager, or manager of a farm equipment dealership. Some mechanics open their own repair shops or invest in franchised dealers. A few farm equipment mechanics with strong customer service backgrounds advance to service representatives for farm equipment manufacturers.

Job Outlook

Employment of farm equipment mechanics is expected to decline through the year 2008. Most job openings will arise from the need to replace experienced mechanics who retire. Nevertheless, job opportunities should be good for persons who have completed formal training in farm equipment repair, diesel mechanics, or a similar program. Employers of farm equipment mechanics report difficulty finding qualified candidates to fill available positions because people trained to repair farm equipment have the fundamental skills and knowledge to work as mechanics in industries outside agriculture. Many young people with mechanic training prefer to take jobs as automotive mechanics, diesel mechanics, heavy equipment mechanics, or industry machine repairers, all occupations that offer relatively higher earnings and a wider variety of locations in which to work.

Some consolidation of farmland into fewer and larger farms is expected to continue through 2008. Although farmers may need a smaller stock of equipment in the years ahead, they will keep investing in newer, more efficient and more specialized equipment to till greater acreage more productively and profitably. For example, new planting equipment uses electronics to spread seeds more uniformly. Many modern tractors have large, electronically controlled engines, and air-conditioned cabs, and feature advanced transmissions with many speeds. The new machinery is expensive, usually being designed and manufactured to withstand many years of rugged use. However, it requires periodic service and repairs. The increased complexity of such equipment means that trained mechanics will make repairs rather than the farmers.

Sales of smaller lawn and garden equipment constitute a growing share of the business of most farm equipment dealers. Most large manufacturers of farm equipment now offer a line of smaller tractors to sell through their established dealerships. This equipment, however, is designed for easy home service and only requires a mechanic when major repairs are needed.

The agricultural equipment industry experiences periodic declines in sales. Layoffs of mechanics, however, are uncommon because farmers often elect to repair old equipment rather than purchase new equipment.

Earnings

Median hourly earnings of farm equipment mechanics in 1998 were $10.94. The middle 50 percent earned between $8.86 and $13.20. The lowest 10 percent earned less than $6.96 and the top 10 percent earned more than $16.01. Most farm equipment mechanics also have the opportunity to work overtime during the planting and harvesting seasons, which generally pays time and one-half.

Very few farm equipment mechanics belong to labor unions, but those who do are members of the International Association of Machinists and Aerospace Workers; the International Union, United Automobile, Aerospace and Agricultural Implement Workers of America; and the International Brotherhood of Teamsters.

Related Occupations

Other workers who repair large mobile machinery include aircraft mechanics, automotive mechanics, diesel engine specialists, and mobile heavy equipment mechanics.

Sources of Additional Information

Details about work opportunities may be obtained from local farm equipment dealers and local offices of the State employment service. For general information about the occupation, write to:

☛ North American Equipment Dealers Association, 10877 Watson Rd., St. Louis, MO 63127.

Heating, Air-Conditioning, and Refrigeration Mechanics and Installers

(O*NET 85902A and 85902B)

Significant Points

- Opportunities should be very good for mechanics and installers with technical school or formal apprenticeship training.
- Mechanics and installers need a basic understanding of microelectronics because they increasingly install and service equipment with electronic controls.

Nature of the Work

What would those living in Chicago do without heating, those in Miami do without air-conditioning, or blood banks in all parts of the country do without refrigeration? Heating and air-conditioning systems control the temperature, humidity, and the total air quality in residential, commercial, industrial, and other buildings. Refrigeration systems make it possible to store and transport food, medicine, and other perishable items. Heating, air-conditioning, and refrigeration mechanics and installers, also called technicians, install, maintain, and repair such systems.

Heating, air-conditioning, and refrigeration systems consist of many mechanical, electrical, and electronic components such as motors, compressors, pumps, fans, ducts, pipes, thermostats, and switches. In central heating systems, for example, a furnace heats air that is distributed throughout the building via a system of metal or fiberglass ducts. Technicians must be able to maintain, diagnose, and correct problems throughout the entire system. To do this, they adjust system controls to recommended settings and test the performance of the entire system using special tools and test equipment.

Although they are trained to do both, technicians often specialize in either installation or maintenance and repair. Some specialize in one type of equipment—for example, oil burners, solar panels, or commercial refrigerators. Technicians may work for large or small contracting companies or directly for a manufacturer or wholesaler. Those working for smaller operations tend to do both installation and servicing, and work with heating, cooling, and refrigeration equipment.

Furnace installers, also called *heating equipment technicians*, follow blueprints or other specifications to install oil, gas, electric, solid-fuel, and multiple-fuel heating systems. After putting the equipment in place, they install fuel and water supply lines, air ducts and vents, pumps, and other components. They may connect electrical wiring and controls and check the unit for proper operation. To ensure the proper functioning of the system, furnace installers often use combustion test equipment such as carbon dioxide and oxygen testers.

After a furnace has been installed, technicians often perform routine maintenance and repair work to keep the system operating efficiently. During the fall and winter, for example, when the system is used most, they service and adjust burners and blowers. If the system is not operating properly, they check the thermostat, burner nozzles, controls, or other parts to diagnose and then correct the problem. During the summer, when the heating system is not being used, technicians do maintenance work, such as replacing filters and vacuum-cleaning vents, ducts, and other parts of the system that may accumulate dust and impurities during the operating season.

Air-conditioning and *refrigeration technicians* install and service central air-conditioning systems and a variety of refrigeration equipment. Technicians follow blueprints, design specifications, and manufacturers' instructions to install motors, compressors, condensing units, evaporators, piping, and other components. They connect this equipment to the duct work, refrigerant lines, and electrical power source. After making the connections, they charge the system with refrigerant, check it for proper operation, and program control systems.

When air-conditioning and refrigeration equipment breaks down, technicians diagnose the problem and make repairs. To do this, they test parts such as compressors, relays, and thermostats. During the winter, air-conditioning technicians inspect the systems and do required maintenance, such as overhauling compressors.

When heating, air-conditioning, and refrigeration technicians service equipment, they must use care to conserve, recover, and recycle chlorofluorocarbon (CFC) and hydrochlorofluorocarbon (HCFC) refrigerants used in air-conditioning and refrigeration systems. The release of CFCs and HCFCs contributes to the depletion of the stratospheric ozone layer, which protects plant and animal life from ultraviolet radiation. Technicians conserve the refrigerant by making sure that there are no leaks in the system; they recover it by venting the refrigerant into proper cylinders; and they recycle it for reuse with special filter-dryers.

Heating, air-conditioning, and refrigeration mechanics rely on schematics to keep the equipment operating.

Heating, air-conditioning, and refrigeration technicians are adept at using a variety of tools, including hammers, wrenches, metal snips, electric drills, pipe cutters and benders, measurement gauges, and acetylene torches, to work with refrigerant lines and air ducts. They use voltmeters, thermometers, pressure gauges, manometers, and other testing devices to check air flow, refrigerant pressure, electrical circuits, burners, and other components.

New technology, in the form of cellular "Web" phones that allow technicians to tap into the Internet, may soon affect the way technicians diagnose problems. Computer hardware and software have been developed that allows heating, venting, and refrigeration units to automatically contact the maintenance establishment when problems arise. The maintenance establishment can then notify the technician in the field via cellular phone. The technician then accesss the Internet to "talk" with the unit needing maintenance. While this technology is cutting-edge and not yet widespread, its potential for cost-savings may spur its acceptance.

Other craft workers sometimes install or repair cooling and heating systems. For example, on a large air-conditioning installation job, especially where workers are covered by union contracts, duct work might be done by sheet-metal workers and duct installers; electrical work by electricians; and installation of piping, condensers, and other components by plumbers, pipefitters, and steamfitters. Home appliance repairers usually service room air-conditioners and household refrigerators. (Additional information about each of these occupations appears elsewhere in the *Handbook*.)

Working Conditions

Heating, air-conditioning, and refrigeration mechanics and installers work in homes, stores of all kinds, hospitals, office buildings, and factories—anywhere there is climate-control equipment. They may be assigned to specific job sites at the beginning of each day, or if they are making service calls, they may be dispatched to jobs by radio, telephone, or pagers. Increasingly, employers are using cell phones to coordinate technicians' schedules.

Technicians may work outside in cold or hot weather or in buildings that are uncomfortable because the air-conditioning or heating equipment is broken. In addition, technicians often work in awkward or cramped positions and sometimes are required to work in high places. Hazards include electrical shock, burns, muscle strains, and other injuries from handling heavy equipment. Appropriate safety equipment is necessary when handling refrigerants because contact can cause skin damage, frostbite, or blindness. Inhalation of refrigerants when working in confined spaces is also a possible hazard, and may cause asphyxiation.

Technicians usually work a 40-hour week, but during peak seasons they often work overtime or irregular hours. Maintenance workers, including those who provide maintenance services under contract, often work evening or weekend shifts, and are on call. Most employers try to provide a full workweek the year round by scheduling both installation and maintenance work, and many manufacturers and contractors now provide or even require service contracts. In most shops that service both heating and air-conditioning equipment, employment is very stable throughout the year.

Employment

Heating, air-conditioning, and refrigeration mechanics and installers held about 286,000 jobs in 1998; more than half of these worked for cooling and heating contractors. The remainder were employed in a variety of industries throughout the country, reflecting a widespread dependence on climate-control systems. Some worked for fuel oil dealers, refrigeration and air-conditioning service and repair shops, schools, and department stores that sell heating and air-conditioning systems. Local governments, the Federal Government, hospitals, office buildings, and other organizations that operate large air-conditioning, refrigeration, or heating systems employed others. Approximately 1 of every 7 technicians was self-employed.

Training, Other Qualifications, and Advancement

Because of the increasing sophistication of heating, air-conditioning, and refrigeration systems, employers prefer to hire those with technical school or apprenticeship training. A sizable number of technicians, however, still learn the trade informally on the job.

Many secondary and postsecondary technical and trade schools, junior and community colleges, and the Armed Forces offer 6-month to 2-year programs in heating, air-conditioning, and refrigeration. Students study theory, design, and equipment construction, as well as electronics. They also learn the basics of installation, maintenance, and repair.

Apprenticeship programs are frequently run by joint committees representing local chapters of the Air-Conditioning Contractors of America, the Mechanical Contractors Association of America, the National Association of Plumbing-Heating-Cooling Contractors, and locals of the Sheet Metal Workers' International Association or the United Association of Journeymen and Apprentices of the Plumbing and Pipefitting Industry of the United States and Canada. Other apprenticeship programs are sponsored by local chapters of the Associated Builders and Contractors and the National Association of Home Builders. Formal apprenticeship programs normally last 3 or 4 years and combine on-the-job training with classroom instruction. Classes include subjects such as the use and care of tools, safety practices, blueprint reading, and air-conditioning theory. Applicants for these programs must have a high school diploma or equivalent.

Those who acquire their skills on the job usually begin by assisting experienced technicians. They may begin performing simple tasks such as carrying materials, insulating refrigerant lines, or cleaning furnaces. In time, they move on to more difficult tasks, such as cutting and soldering pipes and sheet metal and checking electrical and electronic circuits.

Courses in shop math, mechanical drawing, applied physics and chemistry, electronics, blueprint reading, and computer applications provide a good background for those interested in entering this occupation. Some knowledge of plumbing or electrical work is also helpful. A basic understanding of microelectronics is becoming more important because of the increasing use of this technology in solid-state equipment controls. Because technicians frequently deal directly with the public, they should be courteous and tactful, especially when dealing with an aggravated customer. They also should be in good physical condition because they sometimes have to lift and move heavy equipment.

All technicians who purchase or work with refrigerants must be certified in their proper handling. To become certified to purchase and handle refrigerants, technicians must pass a written examination specific to the type of work in which they specialize. The three possible areas of certification are: Type I—servicing small appliances, Type II—high pressure refrigerants, and Type III—low pressure refrigerants. Exams are administered by organizations approved by the Environmental Protection Agency, such as trade schools, unions, contractor associations, or building groups.

The Refrigeration Service Engineers Society offers basic self-study courses for individuals with limited experience. In addition to understanding how systems work, technicians must be knowledgeable about refrigerant products, and legislation and regulation that govern their use. The industry recently announced the adoption of one standard for certification of experienced technicians: the Air Conditioning Excellence program, which is offered through North American Technician Excellence, Inc. (NATE).

Advancement usually takes the form of higher wages. Some technicians, however, may advance to positions as supervisor or service manager. Others may move into areas such as sales and marketing. Those with sufficient money and managerial skill can open their own contracting business.

Job Outlook

Job prospects for highly skilled heating, air-conditioning, and refrigeration mechanics and installers are expected to be very good, particularly for those with technical school or formal apprenticeship training to install, remodel, and service new and existing systems. In addition to job openings created by employment growth, thousands of openings will result from the need to replace workers who transfer to other occupations or leave the labor force.

Employment of heating, air-conditioning, and refrigeration mechanics and installers is expected to increase about as fast as the average for all occupations through the year 2008. As the population and economy grow, so does the demand for new residential, commercial, and industrial climate-control systems. Technicians who specialize in installation work may experience periods of unemployment when the level of new construction activity declines, but maintenance and repair work usually remains relatively stable. People and businesses depend on their climate control systems and must keep them in good working order, regardless of economic conditions.

Concern for the environment and energy conservation should continue to prompt the development of new energy-saving heating and air-conditioning systems. An emphasis on better energy management should lead to the replacement of older systems and the installation of newer, more efficient systems in existing homes and buildings. Also, demand for maintenance and service work should increase as businesses and home owners strive to keep systems operating at peak efficiency. Regulations prohibiting the discharge of CFC and HCFC refrigerants and banning CFC production by the year 2000 also should continue to result in demand for technicians to replace many existing systems, or modify them to use new environmentally safe refrigerants. In addition, the continuing focus on improving indoor air quality should contribute to the growth of jobs for heating, air-conditioning, and refrigeration technicians. Also, certain businesses contribute to a growing need for refrigeration. For example, nearly 50 percent of products sold in convenience stores require some sort of refrigeration. Supermarkets and convenience stores have a very large inventory of refrigerated equipment. This huge inventory will also create increasing demand for service technicians in installation, maintenance, and repair.

Earnings

Median hourly earnings of heating, air-conditioning, and refrigeration mechanics and installers were $14.02 in 1998. The middle 50 percent earned between $11.04 and $17.90 an hour. The lowest 10 percent earned less than $8.78 and the top 10 percent earned more than $22.29. Median hourly earnings in the industries employing the largest numbers of heating, air-conditioning, and refrigeration mechanics and installers in 1997 were as follows:

Department stores	$15.00
Local government, except education and hospitals	14.90
Fuel dealers	14.50
Electrical repair shops	13.40
Plumbing, heating, and air conditioning	12.90

Apprentices usually begin at about 50 percent of the wage rate paid to experienced workers. As they gain experience and improve their skills, they receive periodic increases until they reach the wage rate of experienced workers.

Heating, air-conditioning, and refrigeration mechanics and installers enjoy a variety of employer-sponsored benefits. In addition to typical benefits like health insurance and pension plans, some employers pay for work-related training and provide uniforms, company vans, and tools.

Nearly 1 out of every 5 heating, air-conditioning, and refrigeration mechanics and installers is a member of a union. The unions to which the greatest numbers of mechanics and installers belong are the Sheet Metal Workers' International Association and the United Association of Journeymen and Apprentices of the Plumbing and Pipefitting Industry of the United States and Canada.

Related Occupations

Heating, air-conditioning, and refrigeration mechanics and installers work with sheet metal and piping, and repair machinery, such as electrical motors, compressors, and burners. Other workers who have similar skills are boilermakers, electrical appliance servicers, electricians, sheet-metal workers and duct installers, and plumbers, pipefitters, and steamfitters.

Sources of Additional Information

For more information about employment and training opportunities in this trade, contact local vocational and technical schools; local heating, air-conditioning, and refrigeration contractors; a local of the unions previously mentioned; a local joint union-management apprenticeship committee; a local chapter of the Associated Builders and Contractors; or the nearest office of the State employment service or State apprenticeship agency.

For information on career opportunities, training, and technician certification, contact:

☛ Air Conditioning Contractors of America, 1712 New Hampshire Ave., NW., Washington, DC 20009.

For information on technician certification, contact:

☛ North American Technician Excellence (NATE), Suite 300, 8201 Greensboro Drive, McLean, VA 22102.

☛ Air Conditioning Contractors of America, 1712 New Hampshire Ave., NW., Washington, DC 20009.

For information on career opportunities and training, write to:

☛ Associated Builders and Contractors, 1300 North 17th St., Rosslyn, VA 22209.

☛ Refrigeration Service Engineers Society, 1666 Rand Rd., Des Plaines, IL 60016-3552.

☛ Home Builders Institute, National Association of Home Builders, 1090 Vermont Ave. NW., Suite 600, Washington, DC 20005.

☛ National Association of Plumbing-Heating-Cooling Contractors, 180 S. Washington St., P.O. Box 6808, Falls Church, VA 22046.

☛ Mechanical Contractors Association of America, 1385 Piccard Dr., Rockville, MD 20850-4329.

☛ Air Conditioning and Refrigeration Institute, 4301 North Fairfax Dr., Suite 425, Arlington, VA 22203.

Home Appliance and Power Tool Repairers

(O*NET 85711A, 85711B, 85944, and 85999A)

Significant Points

- Although employment of home appliance and power tool repairers is expected to grow slowly, opportunities should be good for skilled repairers.
- Many repairers are high school graduates who are trained on the job.
- Knowledge of basic electronics is becoming increasingly important.

Nature of the Work

If your washer, dryer, or refrigerator has ever broken, you know the importance of a dependable repair person. Home appliance and power tool repairers, often called service technicians, keep your home appliances working and help prevent unwanted breakdowns. Some repairers work specifically on small appliances such as microwaves and vacuum cleaners; others specialize in major appliances such as refrigerators, dishwashers, washers, and dryers. Still others handle power tools or gas appliances.

Repairers visually inspect appliances or power tools and check for unusual noises, excessive vibration, fluid leaks, or loose parts to determine why they fail to operate properly. They use service manuals, troubleshooting guides, and experience to diagnose particularly difficult problems. They disassemble the appliance or tool to examine its internal parts for signs of wear or corrosion. Repairers follow wiring diagrams and use testing devices, such as ammeters, voltmeters, and wattmeters to check electrical systems for shorts and faulty connections.

After identifying problems, they replace or repair defective belts, motors, heating elements, switches, gears, or other items. They tighten, align, clean, and lubricate parts as necessary. Repairers use common hand tools, including screwdrivers, wrenches, files, and pliers, as well as soldering guns and special tools designed for particular appliances. When repairing appliances with electronic parts, they may replace circuit boards or other electronic components.

Many manufacturers incorporate "fuzzy logic" technology into their newer and more expensive appliances. Fuzzy logic technology involves sensors, or inputs, strategically placed inside an appliance to transmit information to an on-board computer. The computer processes this information and adjusts variables such as water and electricity, to optimize appliance performance and reduce wasted resources. Fuzzy logic uses 1 input; "neurofuzzy logic" uses up to 5 inputs; and "chaos logic" uses up to 10 inputs. Dishwashers, washers, and dryers commonly use neurofuzzy logic in their components.

When repairing refrigerators and window air-conditioners, repairers must use care to conserve, recover, and recycle chlorofluorocarbon (CFC) and hydrochlorofluorocarbon (HCFC) refrigerants used in their cooling systems as required by law. Repairers conserve the refrigerant by making sure there are no leaks in the system; they recover the refrigerant by venting it into proper cylinders; and they recycle the refrigerant for reuse with special filter-dryers.

Repairers who service gas appliances may check the heating unit and replace tubing, thermocouples, thermostats, valves, and indicator spindles. They also answer emergency calls for gas leaks. To install gas appliances, repairers may have to install pipes in a customer's home to connect the appliances to the gas line. They measure, lay out, cut, and thread pipe and connect it to a feeder line and to the appliance. They may have to saw holes in walls or floors and hang steel supports from beams or joists to hold gas pipes in place. Once the gas line is in place, they turn on the gas and check for leaks.

Repairers also answer customers' questions about the care and use of appliances. For example, they demonstrate how to load automatic

Home appliance and power tool repairers use service manuals, troubleshooting guides, and experience to diagnose particularly difficult problems.

washing machines, arrange dishes in dishwashers, or sharpen chain saws to maximize performance.

Repairers write up estimates of the cost of repairs for customers, keep records of parts used and hours worked, prepare bills, and collect payments. They also document the capture and disposal of refrigerants.

Working Conditions

Home appliance and power tool repairers who handle portable appliances usually work in repair shops that are generally quiet, well lighted, and adequately ventilated. Those who repair major appliances usually make service calls to customers' homes. They carry their tools and a number of commonly used parts with them in a truck or van for use on their service calls. A repairer may spend several hours a day driving to and from appointments and emergency calls. They may work in clean comfortable rooms such as kitchens, or in damp, dirty, or dusty areas of a home. Repairers sometimes work in cramped and uncomfortable positions when replacing parts in hard-to-reach areas of appliances.

Repairer jobs generally are not hazardous, but they must exercise care and follow safety precautions to avoid electrical shocks and injuries when lifting and moving large appliances. When repairing gas appliances and microwave ovens, they must be aware of the dangers of gas and radiation leaks.

Many home appliance and power tool repairers work a standard 40-hour week. Some repairers work early morning, evening, and weekend shifts. Many repairers remain on-call in case of emergency. Many repairers work overtime and weekend hours in the summer months, when they are in high demand to fix air-conditioners and refrigerators. Repairers of power tools such as saws and drills may also have to work overtime during spring and summer months when use of such tools increases and breakdowns are more frequent.

Home appliance and power tool repairers usually work with little or no direct supervision, a feature of the job that appeals to many people.

Employment

Home appliance and power tool repairers held nearly 51,000 jobs in 1998. More than 15 percent of repairers are self-employed. About one half of salaried repairers worked in retail establishments such as department stores, household appliance stores, and fuel dealers. Others worked for gas and electric utility companies, electrical repair shops, and wholesalers.

Almost every community in the country employs appliance and power tool repairers; a high concentration of jobs are found in more populated areas.

Training, Other Qualifications, and Advancement

Employers generally require a high school diploma for home appliance and power tool repairer jobs. Repairers of small appliances and tools commonly learn the trade on the job; repairers of large household appliances often receive their training in a formal trade school, community college, or directly from the appliance manufacturer. Mechanical aptitude is desirable, and those who work in customers' homes must be courteous and tactful.

Employers prefer to hire people with formal training in appliance repair and electronics. Many repairers complete 1- or 2-year formal training programs in appliance repair and related subjects in high schools, private vocational schools, and community colleges. Courses in basic electricity and electronics are becoming increasingly necessary as more manufacturers install circuit boards and other electronic control systems in home appliances.

Regardless of whether their basic skills are developed through formal training or on the job, trainees usually receive additional training from their employer and manufacturers. In shops that fix portable appliances, they work on a single type of appliance, such as a vacuum cleaner, until they master its repair. Then they move on to others, until they can repair all those handled by the shop. In companies that repair major appliances, beginners assist experienced repairers on service visits. They may also study on their own. They learn to read schematic drawings, analyze problems, determine whether to repair or replace parts, and follow proper safety procedures. Up to 3 years of on-the-job training may be needed for a technician to become skilled in all aspects of repair.

Some appliance and power tool manufacturers and department store chains have formal training programs that include home study and shop classes, in which trainees work with demonstration appliances and other training equipment. Many repairers receive supplemental instruction through 2- or 3-week seminars conducted by appliance and power tool manufacturers. Experienced repairers also often attend training classes and study service manuals. Repairers authorized for warranty work by manufacturers are required to attend periodic training sessions.

The Environmental Protection Agency (EPA) has mandated that all repairers who buy or work with refrigerants must be certified in its proper handling; a technician must pass a written examination to become certified to buy and handle refrigerants. Exams are administered by organizations approved by the EPA, such as trade schools, unions, and employer associations. There are even EPA-approved take-home certification exams. Though no formal training is required for certification, many of these organizations offer training programs designed to prepare workers for the certification examination.

To protect consumers and recognize highly skilled home appliance and power tool repairers, the Association of Home Appliance Manufacturers has instituted the National Appliance Service Technician Certification Program (NASTeC). Together, manufacturers, schools, and field experts write questions that measure the skills of their trade. To become certified, technicians must pass a comprehensive examination testing their competence in the diagnosis, repair and maintenance of major home appliances. The examination is given on demand at locations throughout the country. While there has not previously been standardized certification, growing numbers of employers now encourage repairers to become certified.

The Professional Service Association (PSA) has a certification program with similar goals to the NASTeC program—to recognize skilled repairers. To become certified, technicians must pass an examination. The PSA certification is valid for 4 years, and for renewal the technician must complete at least 12 credit hours of instruction every year during the 4 years. If the technician fails to accumulate the 48 hours of instruction, they must retake the examination.

Repairers in large shops or service centers may be promoted to supervisor, assistant service manager, or service manager. A few repairers advance to managerial positions such as regional service manager or parts manager for appliance or tool manufacturers. Preference is given to those who demonstrate technical competence and show an ability to get along with coworkers and customers. Experienced repairers who have sufficient funds and knowledge of small business management may open their own repair shop.

Job Outlook

Employment of home appliance and power tool repairers is expected to increase slower than the average for all occupations through the year 2008. Prospects should continue to be good for well-trained repairers, particularly those with a strong background in electronics. The number of home appliances and power tools in use is expected to increase with growth in the number of households and businesses and the introduction of new and improved appliances and tools. However, employment growth will be constrained as the frequency of repairs is reduced by increased use of electronic parts such as solid-state circuitry, microprocessors, and sensing devices in appliances. Nevertheless, as appliance and power tool repairers retire or transfer to other occupations, additional job openings will arise.

The availability of manufacturer sponsored training programs could also limit employment growth. Manufacturers often make these programs available only to large equipment dealers, thereby discouraging repairers from becoming self-employed or working for small shops. Many self-employed repairers are forced to join larger shops so that they can stay abreast of developments in the industry.

Jobs are expected to be increasingly concentrated in larger companies as the number of smaller shops and family owned businesses declines. However, those repairers that maintain strong industry relationships may still go into business for themselves.

Employment is relatively steady because the demand for appliance repair services continues even during economic downturns. However, during economic slowdowns some repair shops may lay off repairers.

Earnings

Median annual earnings, including commission, of home appliance and power tool repairers were $26,010 in 1998. The middle 50 percent earned between $20,380 and $34,790 a year. The lowest 10 percent earned less than $15,730 and the highest 10 percent earned more than $42,090 a year.

Earnings of home appliance and power tool repairers vary according to the skill level required to fix equipment, geographic location, and the type of equipment repaired. Because many repairers receive commission along with their salary, earnings increase along with the number of jobs a repairer can complete in a day.

Many larger dealers, manufacturers and service stores offer benefits such as health insurance coverage, sick leave, and retirement and pension programs. Some home appliance and power tool repairers belong to the International Brotherhood of Electrical Workers.

Related Occupations

Other workers who repair electrical and electronic equipment include heating, air-conditioning, and refrigeration mechanics; locksmiths; motorcycle, boat, and small-engine mechanics; office machine and cash register servicers; electronic home entertainment equipment repairers; and coin, vending, and amusement machine servicers and repairers.

Sources of Additional Information

For information about jobs in the home appliance and power tool repair field, contact local appliance repair shops, manufacturers, vocational trade schools, appliance dealers, and utility companies, or the local office of the State employment service.

For general information about the work of home appliance repairers, contact:

☛ Appliance Service News, P.O. Box 809, St. Charles, IL 60174.

☛ National Association of Service Dealers, 10 E. 22nd St., Suite 310, Lombard, IL 60148.

☛ United Servicers Association, Inc., P.O. Box 59707, Dallas, TX 75229.

☛ National Appliance Service Association, 9247 N. Meridian, Suite 216, Indianapolis, IN 46260.

For information on technician certification, as well as general information about the work of home appliance repairers, contact:

☛ National Appliance Service Technician Certification Program (NASTeC), 10 E. 22nd St., Suite 310, Lombard, IL 60148. Telephone (tollfree): 1-888-NASTEC1 (627-8321).
Internet: **http://www.nastecnet.org**

☛ Professional Service Association, 71 Columbia St., Cohoes, NY 12047.

Industrial Machinery Repairers

(O*NET 85112, 85113, 85116C, 85118, 85119A, 85119B, 85128A, and 85128B)

Significant Points

- Workers learn their trade through a 4-year apprenticeship program or informal on-the-job training supplemented by classroom instruction.
- While employment of industrial machinery repairers is projected to grow more slowly than average, applicants with broad skills in machine repair should have favorable job prospects.

Nature of the Work

When production workers encounter problems with the machines they operate, they call industrial machinery repairers. These workers, also called industrial machinery mechanics or maintenance machinists, maintain and repair machinery in a plant or factory. Their work is important not only because an idle machine will delay production, but also because a machine that is not properly repaired and maintained may damage the final product or injure the operator.

Maintenance mechanics must be able to detect and diagnose minor problems and correct them before they become major ones. For example, after hearing a vibration from a machine, the mechanic must decide whether it is due to worn belts, weak motor bearings, or some other problem. Computerized maintenance, vibration analysis techniques, and self-diagnostic systems are making this task easier. Self-diagnostic features on new industrial machinery can determine the cause of a malfunction and, in some cases, alert the mechanic to potential trouble spots before symptoms develop.

After diagnosing the problem, the mechanic disassembles the equipment and repairs or replaces the necessary parts. Once reassembled, the final step is to test the machine to ensure it is running smoothly. When repairing electronically controlled machinery, maintenance mechanics may work closely with electronic repairers or electricians who maintain the machine's electronic parts. However, industrial machinery repairers increasingly need electronic and computer skills to repair sophisticated equipment on their own. (Statements on electronic repairers, commercial and industrial equipment, as well as electricians, appear elsewhere in the *Handbook.*)

Although repairing machines is the most important job of industrial machinery repairers, they also perform preventive maintenance. This includes keeping machines and their parts well oiled, greased, and cleaned. Repairers regularly inspect machinery and check performance. For example, they adjust and calibrate automated manufacturing equipment such as industrial robots, and rebuild components of other industrial machinery. By keeping complete and up-to-date records, mechanics try to anticipate trouble and service equipment before factory production is interrupted.

A wide range of tools may be used when performing repairs or preventive maintenance. Repairers may use a screwdriver and wrench to adjust a motor, or a hoist to lift a printing press off the ground. When replacements for broken or defective parts are not readily available, or when a machine must be quickly returned to production, repairers may sketch a part that can be fabricated by the plant's machine shop. Repairers use catalogs to order replacement parts and often follow blueprints and engineering specifications to maintain and fix equipment.

Industrial machinery repairers maintain and repair machinery in plants or factories.

Installation of new machinery is another responsibility of industrial machinery repairers. As plants retool and invest in new equipment, they increasingly rely on these workers to properly situate and install the machinery. In many plants, this has traditionally been the job of millwrights. (See the statement on millwrights elsewhere in the *Handbook.*) As employers increasingly seek workers who have a variety of skills, industrial machinery repairers are taking on new responsibilities.

Working Conditions

Working conditions for repairers who work in manufacturing are similar to those of production workers. These workers are subject to common shop injuries such as cuts and bruises, and use protective equipment such as hard hats, protective glasses, and safety belts. Industrial machinery repairers may also face additional hazards because they often work on top of a ladder or underneath or above large machinery in cramped conditions.

Because factories and other facilities cannot afford breakdowns of industrial machinery, repairers may be called to the plant at night or on weekends for emergency repairs. Overtime is common among industrial machinery repairers—more than a third work over 40 hours a week.

Employment

Industrial machinery repairers held about 535,000 jobs in 1998. About 7 of every 10 worked in manufacturing industries, primarily food processing, textile mill products, chemicals, fabricated metal products, and primary metals. Others worked for government agencies, public utilities, mining companies, and other establishments in which industrial machinery is used.

Industrial machinery repairers work in a wide variety of plants and are employed in every part of the country. However, employment is concentrated in heavily industrialized areas.

Training, Other Qualifications, and Advancement

Many industrial machinery repairers learn their trade through a 4-year apprenticeship program combining classroom instruction with on-the-job-training. These programs are usually sponsored by a local trade union. Other workers start as helpers and pick up the skills of the trade informally and by taking courses offered by machinery manufacturers and community colleges.

Repairers learn from experienced repairers how to operate, disassemble, repair, and assemble machinery. Classroom instruction focuses on subjects such as shop mathematics, blueprint reading, welding, electronics, and computer training.

Most employers prefer to hire those who have completed high school. High school courses in mechanical drawing, mathematics, blueprint reading, physics, computers, and electronics are especially useful.

Mechanical aptitude and manual dexterity are important characteristics for workers in this trade. Good physical conditioning and agility are also necessary because repairers sometimes have to lift heavy objects or climb to reach equipment located high above the floor.

Opportunities for advancement are limited. Industrial machinery repairers advance either by working with more complicated equipment or by becoming supervisors. The most highly skilled repairers can be promoted to master mechanic or can become machinists or tool and die makers.

Job Outlook

Employment of industrial machinery repairers is projected to grow more slowly than the average for all occupations through 2008. Nevertheless, applicants with broad skills in machine repair should have favorable job prospects. As more firms introduce automated production equipment, industrial machinery mechanics will be needed to ensure these machines are properly maintained and consistently in operation. However, many new machines are capable of self-diagnosis, increasing their reliability and, thus, reducing the need for repairers. As a result, most job openings will stem from the need to replace repairers who transfer to other occupations or leave the labor force.

Unlike many other manufacturing occupations, industrial machinery repairers are not usually affected by seasonal changes in production. During slack periods, when some plant workers are laid off, repairers often are retained to do major overhaul jobs. Although these workers may face layoff or a reduced workweek when economic conditions are particularly severe, they usually are less affected than other workers because machines have to be maintained regardless of production level.

Earnings

Median hourly earnings of industrial machinery repairers were $15.31 in 1998. The middle 50 percent earned between $12.20 and $19.02. The lowest 10 percent earned less than $10.11 and the highest 10 percent earned more than $22.97.

Earnings vary by industry and geographic region. Median hourly earnings in the industries employing the largest numbers of industrial machinery repairers in 1997 are shown below:

Industry	Earnings
Motor vehicles and equipment	$19.80
Metal forgings and stampings	17.70
Blast furnace and basic steel products	17.20
Electronic components and accessories	15.90
Machinery, equipment, and supplies	14.30
Miscellaneous plastics products, not elsewhere classified	14.10
Preserved fruits and vegetables	14.00
Hospitals	12.90
Meat products	12.00

Over 25 percent of industrial machinery mechanics are union members. Labor unions that represent industrial machinery repairers include the United Steelworkers of America; the United Automobile, Aerospace and Agricultural Implement Workers of America; the International Association of Machinists and Aerospace Workers; and the International Union of Electronic, Electrical, Salaried, Machine, and Furniture Workers.

Related Occupations

Other occupations that involve repairing machinery include aircraft mechanics and service technicians; elevator installers and repairers; machinists; millwrights; and automotive, motorcycle, diesel, farm equipment, general maintenance, mobile heavy equipment, and heating, air-conditioning, and refrigeration mechanics.

Sources of Additional Information

Information about employment and apprenticeship opportunities for industrial machinery repairers may be obtained from local offices of the State employment service or from:

☛ United Brotherhood of Carpenters and Joiners of America, 101 Constitution Ave. NW., Washington, DC 20001.

☛ The National Tooling and Machining Association, 9300 Livingston Rd., Fort Washington, MD 20744. Internet: **http://www.ntma.org**

☛ Precision Machined Products Association, 6700 West Snowville Rd., Brecksville, OH 44141. Internet: **http://www.pmpa.org**

Line Installers and Repairers

(O*NET 85702 and 85723)

Significant Points

- Line installer and repairer jobs require a high school diploma and, with experience, provide relatively high earnings.
- Employment is expected to grow due to the expansion of telecommunications networks.
- Line installers and repairers work outdoors under a variety of weather conditions.

Nature of the Work

Vast networks of wires and cables provide customers with electrical power and communications services. Networks of electrical power lines deliver electricity from generating plants to customers. Communications networks of telephone and cable television lines provide voice, video, and other communications services. These networks are constructed and maintained by line installers and repairers.

Line installers, or line erectors, install new lines by constructing utility poles, towers, and underground trenches to carry the wires and cables. Line erectors use a variety of construction equipment including digger derricks, trenchers, and cable plows. Digger derricks are trucks equipped with augers and cranes; the augers dig holes in the ground, and the cranes set utility poles in place. Trenchers and cable plows cut openings in the earth for laying underground cables.

When construction is complete, line installers string cable along the poles, towers, and trenches. For installations on poles and towers, the installers first climb or use truck-mounted buckets to reach the top of the structure. Next, they pull up cable by hand from large reels mounted on trucks. The line is then set in place and pulled so that it contains the correct amount of tension. Finally, the line installers attach the cable to the structure using handtools. When working with electrical powerlines, installers bolt or clamp insulators onto the poles before attaching the cable. Underground cable is laid directly in the trench, or strung through a conduit running through the trench.

Other installation duties include setting up service for customers and installing network equipment. To set up service, line installers string a piece of cable between the customers' premises and the lines running on poles, towers, or in trenches. They place wiring in houses and check that transmission signals are strong. Line installers may also install a variety of equipment. Workers on telephone and cable television lines install amplifiers and repeaters that maintain the strength of communications transmissions. Workers on electrical powerlines install transformers, circuit breakers, switches, and other equipment to control and direct the electrical current.

Line installers connect service to customers' homes.

In addition to installation, line installers and repairers are also responsible for maintenance of electrical, telephone, and cable television lines. The workers periodically travel in trucks, helicopters, and airplanes to visually inspect the wires and cables. Sensitive monitoring equipment can automatically detect malfunctions on the network, such as loss of current flow. When line repairers identify a problem, they travel to the location of the malfunction and repair or replace defective cables or equipment. Bad weather or natural disasters can cause extensive damage to networks. Line installers and repairers must respond quickly to these emergencies in order to restore critical utility and communications services.

Installation and repair work may require splicing, or joining together, separate pieces of cable. Each cable contains numerous individual wires; splicing the cables together requires that each wire in one piece of cable be joined to another wire in the matching piece. Line installers splice cables using small handtools, epoxy, or mechanical equipment. At each splice, they place insulation over the conductor and seal the splice with moisture proof covering.

Many communications networks now use fiber optic cables instead of conventional wire or metal cables. Fiber optic cables are made of thin strands of glass, which transmit pulses of light. These cables can carry more information at higher speeds than conventional cables. The higher transmission capacity of fiber optic cable has allowed communication networks to offer upgraded services, such as high speed Internet access.

Working Conditions

Line installers and repairers must climb and maintain their balance while working on poles and towers. They lift equipment and work in a variety of positions such as stooping or kneeling. Their work often requires that they drive utility vehicles, travel long distances, and work outdoors under a variety of weather conditions. Many line installers and repairers work a 40-hour week; however, emergencies may require overtime work. For example, when severe weather damages electrical and communications lines, line installers and repairers may work long and irregular hours to restore service.

Line installers and repairers encounter serious hazards on their jobs and must follow safety procedures to minimize the potential danger. They wear safety equipment when entering manholes and test for the presence of gas before going underground. Electric powerline workers have the most hazardous jobs. High voltage powerlines can cause electrocution and line installers and repairers must consequently install protective devices when working with live cables. Powerlines are typically higher than telephone and cable television lines, increasing the risk of severe injury due to falls. To prevent these injuries, line installers and repairers must use personal fall protection equipment when working on poles or towers.

Employment

Line installers and repairers held about 279,000 jobs in 1998. Approximately two-thirds were telephone and cable television line installers and repairers; the remainder were electrical powerline workers. Nearly all line installers and repairers worked for telephone, cable television, electric power, or construction companies.

Training, Other Qualifications, and Advancement

Line installers and repairers are trained on the job and most employers generally require only a high school diploma. However, technical knowledge of electricity and electronics obtained through vocational programs, community colleges, or experience in the Armed Forces is preferred. Prospective employees should possess a basic knowledge of math and mechanical ability. Customer service and interpersonal skills are also important. Because the work entails climbing and other physical activity, applicants should have stamina, coordination, and must be unafraid of heights. The ability to distinguish colors is necessary because wires and cables may be coded by color.

Line installers and repairers working for electric power companies generally complete formal apprenticeship or employer training programs. These are sometimes administered jointly by the employer and the union representing the workers. The unions include the International Brotherhood of Electrical Workers, the Communications Workers of America, and the Utility Workers Union of America. Apprenticeship programs last several years and combine formal instruction with on-the-job training.

Line installers and repairers in telephone and cable television companies receive several years of on-the-job training. They may also attend training provided by equipment manufacturers, schools, or industry training organizations. The Society of Cable Television Engineers (SCTE) provides certification programs for line installers and repairers. Applicants for certification must be employed in the cable television industry, and attend training sessions at local SCTE chapters.

Entry-level line installers may be hired as groundmen, helpers, or tree trimmers, who clear branches from telephone and power lines. These workers may advance to positions stringing cable and performing service installations. With experience, they may advance to more sophisticated maintenance and repair positions responsible for increasingly larger portions of the network. Promotion to supervisory or training positions is also possible.

Job Outlook

Overall employment of line installers and repairers is expected to grow about as fast as the average for all occupations through 2008. Much of this increase will result from growth in the telecommunications industry. The introduction of new technologies, such as fiber optic cable, has increased the transmission capacity of telephone and cable television networks. This higher capacity has allowed the creation of new and extremely popular services, such as high-speed Internet access. At the same time, deregulation of the telecommunications industry has reduced barriers to competition. As a result, companies from a variety of industries are installing high capacity networks in order to compete for the increasing demand for telecommunications services. Mergers among highly competitive communications and electrical power companies may result in layoffs; however, these will be offset by growth due to the expansion of telecommunications networks. Besides employment growth, many job openings will result from the need to replace the large number of older workers reaching retirement age.

Employment of telephone and cable television line installers and repairers is expected to grow faster than average. Telephone and cable television companies will create new networks and expand existing ones to provide customers with high-speed access to data, video, and graphics. Line installers and repairers will be needed not only to construct and install networks, but also to maintain the ever-growing systems of wires and cables. Businesses will install extensive private networks as they increasingly use telecommunications lines for access to suppliers and customers. Residential customers will request additional lines to their houses in order to use telephone and Internet communications simultaneously.

The distribution of electrical power has not undergone the same transformation as has occurred in telecommunications, and the need for network expansion is not as great. As a result, the overall employment of electrical powerline installers and repairers should experience little or no growth. However, job openings will arise from the need to replace workers who retire or leave the occupation. Because electrical power companies have reduced hiring and training in recent years, opportunities should be best for workers who possess experience and training.

Earnings

Median hourly earnings for electrical powerline installers and repairers were $20.48 in 1998. The middle 50 percent earned between $16.30 and $23.90. The lowest 10 percent earned less than $11.54 and the highest 10 percent earned more than $33.32. Median hourly earnings in the industries employing the largest numbers of electrical powerline installers and repairers in 1997 are shown below.

Industry	Earnings
Combination utility services	$23.60
Electrical services	20.00
Telephone communications	19.80
Electrical work	17.00
Heavy construction, except highway and street	14.10

Median hourly earnings for telephone and cable television line installers and repairers were $15.75 in 1998. The middle 50 percent earned between $10.97 and $21.42. The lowest 10 percent earned less than $8.85 and the highest 10 percent earned more than $24.54. Median hourly earnings in the industries employing the largest numbers of telephone and cable television line installers and repairers in 1997 are shown below.

Industry	Earnings
Telephone communications	$19.90
Electrical work	12.30
Cable and other pay television services	11.60
Heavy construction, except highway and street	10.60

Most line installers and repairers belong to unions, principally the Communications Workers of America, the International Brotherhood of Electrical Workers, and the Utility Workers Union of America. For these workers, union contracts set wage rates, wage increases, and the time needed to advance from one step to the next.

Related Occupations

Related skilled craft positions include broadcast and sound technicians; electricians; and telecommunications equipment mechanics, installers, and repairers.

Sources of Additional Information

For more details about employment opportunities, contact the telephone, cable television, or electrical power company in your community. For general information on line installer and repairer jobs, write to:

☛ Communications Workers of America, 501 3rd St. NW., Washington, DC 20001.

☛ International Brotherhood of Electrical Workers, Utility Department, 1125 15th St. NW., Washington, DC 20005.

For general information on line installers and repairers and other power plant occupations, write to:

☛ Utility Workers Union of America, 815 16th St. NW., Washington, DC 20006.

For information on training and certification programs in the cable industry, contact:

☛ Society of Cable Telecommunications Engineers, Certification Department, 140 Philips Road, Exton, PA 19341. Internet: **http://www.scte.org**

Maintenance Mechanics, General Utility

(O*NET 85119C and 85132)

Significant Points

- Most general maintenance mechanics are trained on the job; others learn by working as helpers to other repairers or construction workers such as carpenters, electricians, or machinery repairers.

- Despite slower-than-average employment growth resulting from advancements in machinery, job openings should be plentiful due to significant turnover in this large occupation.

Nature of the Work

Most craft workers specialize in one kind of work such as plumbing or carpentry. General maintenance mechanics, however, have skills in many different crafts. They repair and maintain machines, mechanical equipment, and buildings, and work on plumbing, electrical, and air-conditioning and heating systems. They build partitions, make plaster or drywall repairs, and fix or paint roofs, windows, doors, floors, woodwork, and other parts of building structures. They also maintain and repair specialized equipment and machinery found in cafeterias, laundries, hospitals, stores, offices, and factories. Typical duties include troubleshooting and fixing faulty electrical switches, repairing air-conditioning motors, and unclogging drains. New buildings sometimes have computer-controlled systems, requiring mechanics to acquire basic computer skills. For example, new air conditioning systems often can be controlled from a central computer terminal. Additionally, light sensors can be electronically controlled to automatically turn off lights after a set amount of time.

General maintenance mechanics inspect and diagnose problems and determine the best way to correct them, often checking blueprints, repair manuals, and parts catalogs. They obtain supplies and repair parts from distributors or storerooms. They use common hand and power tools such as screwdrivers, saws, drills, wrenches, and hammers, as well as specialized equipment and electronic testing devices. They replace or fix worn or broken parts, where necessary, or make adjustments.

General maintenance mechanics routinely perform preventive maintenance and ensure that machines continue to run smoothly.

These mechanics also do routine preventive maintenance and ensure that machines continue to run smoothly, building systems operate efficiently, and the physical condition of buildings does not deteriorate. Following a checklist, they may inspect drives, motors, and belts, check fluid levels, replace filters, and perform other maintenance actions. Maintenance mechanics keep records of maintenance and repair work.

Mechanics in small establishments, where they are often the only maintenance worker, do all repairs except for very large or difficult jobs. In larger establishments, their duties may be limited to the general maintenance of everything in a workshop or a particular area.

Working Conditions

General maintenance mechanics often do several different tasks in a single day, at any number of locations. They may work inside of a single building or in several different buildings. They may have to stand for long periods, lift heavy objects, and work in uncomfortably hot or cold environments, in awkward and cramped positions, or on ladders. They are subject to electrical shock, burns, falls, cuts, and bruises. Most general maintenance workers work a 40-hour week. Some work evening, night, or weekend shifts, or are on call for emergency repairs.

Those employed in small establishments, where they may be the only maintenance worker, often operate with only limited supervision. Those working in larger establishments often are under the direct supervision of an experienced worker.

Employment

General maintenance mechanics held over 1.2 million jobs in 1998. They were employed in almost every industry. Around 35 percent worked in service industries, mainly in elementary and secondary schools, colleges and universities, hotels, and hospitals and nursing homes. About 16 percent worked in manufacturing industries. Others worked for wholesale and retail firms, government agencies, and real estate firms that operate office and apartment buildings.

Training, Other Qualifications, and Advancement

Most general maintenance mechanics learn their skills informally on the job. They start as helpers, watching and learning from skilled maintenance workers. Helpers begin by doing simple jobs such as fixing leaky faucets and replacing light bulbs, and progress to more difficult tasks such as overhauling machinery or building walls.

Others learn their skills by working as helpers to other repair or construction workers such as carpenters, electricians, or machinery repairers. Necessary skills can also be learned in high school shop classes and postsecondary trade or vocational schools. It generally takes from 1 to 4 years of on-the-job training or school, or a combination of both, to become fully qualified, depending on the skill level required. Because a growing proportion of new buildings rely on computers to control building systems, general maintenance mechanics may need basic computer skills—how to log on to a central computer system and navigate through a series of menus. Usually companies that install computer-controlled equipment provide on-site training for general maintenance mechanics.

Graduation from high school is preferred for entry into this occupation. High school courses in mechanical drawing, electricity, woodworking, blueprint reading, science, mathematics, and computers are useful. Mechanical aptitude, ability to use shop math, and manual dexterity are important. Good health is necessary because the job involves much walking, standing, reaching, and heavy lifting. Difficult jobs require problem-solving ability, and many positions require the ability to work without direct supervision.

Many general maintenance mechanics in large organizations advance to maintenance supervisor or to one of the crafts such as electrician, heating and air-conditioning mechanic, or plumber. Within small organizations, promotion opportunities are limited.

Job Outlook
Job openings should be plentiful. General maintenance mechanics is a large occupation with significant turnover, and many job openings should result from the need to replace workers who transfer to other occupations or stop working for other reasons.

Employment of general maintenance mechanics is expected to grow more slowly than the average for all occupations through 2008. Employment is related to the number of buildings—for example, office and apartment buildings, stores, schools, hospitals, hotels, and factories—and the amount of equipment needing maintenance and repair. As machinery becomes more advanced, however, the need for general mechanics diminishes.

Earnings
Median hourly earnings of general maintenance mechanics were $11.20 in 1998. The middle 50 percent earned between $8.43 and $14.99. The lowest 10 percent earned less than $6.56 and the highest 10 percent earned more than $18.83. Median hourly earnings in the industries employing the largest numbers of general maintenance mechanics in 1997 are shown below:

Local government, except education and hospitals	$11.90
Hospitals	11.30
Real estate agents and managers	9.80
Real estate operators and lessors	9.40
Hotels and motels	8.20

Some general maintenance mechanics are members of unions, including the American Federation of State, County, and Municipal Employees; and the United Automobile Workers.

Related Occupations
Some duties of general maintenance mechanics are similar to those of carpenters, plumbers, industrial machinery repairers, electricians, and heating, air-conditioning, and refrigeration mechanics.

Sources of Additional Information
Information about job opportunities may be obtained from local employers and local offices of the State Employment Service.

Millwrights

(O*NET 85123A and 85123B)

Significant Points

- Training generally lasts 4 to 5 years—through apprenticeship programs that combine on-the-job training with classroom instruction—or through community college coupled with informal on-the-job training.
- Although employment is projected to decline slightly, skilled applicants should have good job opportunities.
- About 58 percent belong to labor unions, one of the highest rates of membership in the economy.

Nature of the Work
Millwrights install, repair, replace, and dismantle the machinery and heavy equipment used in many industries. Responsibilities require a wide range of skills—from blueprint reading and pouring concrete to diagnosing and solving mechanical problems.

The millwright's responsibilities begin when machinery arrives at the job site. New equipment must be unloaded, inspected, and moved into position. To lift and move light machinery, millwrights use rigging and hoisting devices, such as pulleys and cables. In other cases, they require the assistance of hydraulic lift-truck or crane operators to position the machinery. Because millwrights often decide which device to use for moving machinery, they must know the load-bearing properties of ropes, cables, hoists, and cranes.

Millwrights consult with production managers and others to determine the optimal placement of machines in a plant. In some instances, this placement requires building a new foundation. Millwrights either prepare the foundation themselves or supervise its construction, so they must know how to read blueprints and work with building materials, such as concrete, wood, and steel.

When assembling machinery, millwrights fit bearings, align gears and wheels, attach motors, and connect belts, according to the manufacturer's blueprints and drawings. Precision leveling and alignment are important in the assembly process; millwrights must have good mathematical skills, so they can measure angles, material thickness, and small distances with tools such as squares, calipers, and micrometers. When a high level of precision is required, devices such as lasers and ultrasonic measuring tools may be used. Millwrights also work with hand and power tools, such as cutting torches, welding machines, and soldering guns. Some of these workers use metalworking equipment, such as lathes or grinders to modify parts to specifications.

In addition to installing and dismantling machinery, many millwrights repair and maintain equipment. This includes preventive maintenance, such as lubrication and fixing or replacing worn parts. (For further information on machinery maintenance, see the statement on industrial machinery repairers elsewhere in the *Handbook.*)

Increasingly sophisticated automation means more complicated machines for millwrights to install and maintain. For example, millwrights

When assembling machinery, millwrights fit bearings, align gears and wheels, attach motors, and connect belts according to the manufacturer's specifications.

may install and maintain numerical control equipment—computer controlled machine tools that fabricate manufacturing parts. This machinery requires special care and knowledge, so millwrights often work closely with computer or electronics experts, electricians, engineers, and manufacturer's representatives to install it. (Statements on electronics repairers, commercial and industrial equipment, as well as electricians, appear elsewhere in the *Handbook*.)

Working Conditions

Working conditions vary by industry. Millwrights employed in manufacturing often work in a typical shop setting and use protective equipment to avoid common hazards. For example, protective devices, such as safety belts, protective glasses, and hard hats may prevent injuries from falling objects or machinery. Those in construction may work outdoors in uncomfortable weather conditions.

Millwrights may work independently or as part of a team. They must work quickly and precisely, because disabled machinery costs a company time and money. Many millwrights work overtime; nearly half report working more than 40 hours during a typical week. During power outages, millwrights have been assigned overtime and shift work, because of shift requirements.

Employment

Millwrights held about 82,000 jobs in 1998. Most worked in manufacturing, primarily in durable goods industries, such as motor vehicles and equipment and basic steel products. Other millwrights were employed primarily by construction firms and machining and equipment wholesalers; many of these workers are contractors. Although millwrights work in every State, employment is concentrated in heavily industrialized areas.

Training, Other Qualifications, and Advancement

Millwrights are responsible for the mechanical maintenance, repair, overhaul, and installation of machinery, so training is varied and extensive. Millwrights normally train for 4 years—through apprenticeship programs that combine on-the-job training with classroom instruction—or through community college coupled with informal on-the-job training. These programs include training in dismantling, moving, erecting, and repairing machinery. Trainees may also work with concrete and receive instruction in related skills, such as carpentry, welding, and sheet-metal work. Classroom instruction is provided in mathematics, blueprint reading, hydraulics, electricity, computers, and electronics.

Employers prefer applicants with a high school diploma or equivalency and some vocational training or experience. Courses in science, mathematics, mechanical drawing, computers, and machine shop practice are useful. Millwrights are expected to keep their skills up-to-date and may need additional training on technological advances, such as laser shaft alignment and vibration analysis.

Because millwrights assemble and disassemble complicated machinery, mechanical aptitude is very important. Strength and agility also are necessary, because the work can require a considerable amount of lifting and climbing. Millwrights need good interpersonal and communication abilities to work as part of a team and to be able to give detailed instructions to others.

Advancement for millwrights usually takes the form of higher wages. Some advance to supervisor or superintendent, whereas others may become self-employed contractors.

Job Outlook

Employment of millwrights is projected to decline slightly through the year 2008. Nevertheless, skilled applicants should have good job opportunities, because millwrights will be needed to maintain and repair existing machinery, dismantle old machinery, and install new equipment. Job openings will stem from the need to replace experienced millwrights who transfer to other occupations or leave the labor force.

Automation, technological advances, and the growing utilization of lower-paid workers will contribute to the decline in employment. As automation of machinery becomes more widespread, there is a greater need for repair work than for the installation of new machinery. Millwrights are becoming more productive through the use of technologies like hydraulic torque wrenches, ultrasonic measuring tools, and laser shaft alignment, as these technologies allow fewer workers to perform more work. In addition, the demand for millwrights will be adversely affected, as lower-paid workers, such as electronics technicians and industrial machinery mechanics, increasingly assume some installation and maintenance duties. Nevertheless, historical employment of millwrights has been fairly stable, and the growing use of machinery in the Nation's economy should ensure that the employment decline will be small.

Earnings

Median hourly earnings of millwrights were $17.76 in 1998. The middle 50 percent earned between $14.11 and $21.80. The lowest 10 percent earned less than $11.35 and the highest 10 percent earned more than $24.38. Median hourly earnings in the industries employing the largest numbers of millwrights in 1997 are shown below:

Industry	Earnings
Motor vehicles and equipment	$21.60
Paper mills	18.60
Miscellaneous special trade contractors	17.00

Earnings vary by industry and geographic location. About 58 percent of millwrights belong to labor unions, one of the highest rates of membership in the economy.

Related Occupations

To set up machinery for use in a plant, millwrights must know how to use hoisting devices and how to assemble, disassemble, and sometimes repair machinery. Other workers with similar job duties include industrial machinery repairers; aircraft mechanics and service technicians; ironworkers; machine assemblers; and mobile heavy equipment, diesel, and farm equipment mechanics.

Sources of Additional Information

For further information on apprenticeship programs, write to the Apprenticeship Council of your State's labor department, local offices of your State employment service, or local firms that employ millwrights. In addition, you may contact:

☛ The United Brotherhood of Carpenters and Joiners of America, 101 Constitution Ave. NW., Washington DC 20001.

☛ Associated General Contractors of America, 1957 E St. NW., Washington, DC 20006. Internet: **http://www.agc.org**

☛ The National Tooling and Machining Association, 9300 Livingston Rd., Fort Washington, MD 20744. Internet: **http://www.ntma.org**

☛ The Precision Machined Products Association, 6700 West Snowville Rd., Brecksville, OH 44141. Internet: **http://www.pmpa.org**

Mobile Heavy Equipment Mechanics

(O*NET 85314)

Significant Points

- Opportunities should be good for persons with advanced knowledge of electronics and hydraulics.
- This occupation offers relatively high wages and the challenge of skilled repair work.
- National certification is the recognized standard of achievement for mobile heavy equipment mechanics.

Nature of the Work

Mobile heavy equipment is indispensable to construction, logging, surface mining, and other industrial activities. Various types of equipment grade land, lift beams, and dig earth to pave the way for development.

Mobile heavy equipment mechanics repair and maintain the engines, transmissions, hydraulics, and electrical systems powering graders, backhoes, and stripping and loading shovels. (For information on mechanics specializing in diesel engines, see the statement on diesel mechanics and service technicians elsewhere in the *Handbook*.)

Mobile heavy equipment mechanics typically work for construction equipment distributor firms, large construction companies, local and Federal governments, or other organizations operating and maintaining heavy machinery and equipment fleets. They perform routine maintenance checks on diesel engines, transmission components, and brake systems, to ensure safety and longevity of the equipment. Maintenance checks and feedback from equipment operators usually alert mechanics to problems. With modern heavy equipment, hand-held computers can be plugged into on-board computers to diagnose any component needing adjustment or repair. After locating the problem, these technicians rely on their training and experience to use the best possible technique to solve the problem. If necessary, they may partially dismantle the component to examine parts for damage or excessive wear. Then, using hand-held tools, they repair, replace, clean, and lubricate parts, as necessary. After reassembling the component and testing it for safety, mechanics put it back into the equipment and return the equipment to the field.

Many types of mobile heavy equipment use hydraulics to raise and lower movable parts, such as scoops, shovels, log forks, and scraper blades. Repairing malfunctioning hydraulic components is an important responsibility of mobile heavy equipment mechanics. When components lose power, mechanics examine them for hydraulic fluid leaks, ruptured hoses, or worn gaskets on fluid reservoirs. Occasionally, the equipment requires extensive repairs, such as replacing a defective hydraulic pump.

In addition to routine maintenance checks, mobile heavy equipment mechanics perform a variety of other repairs. They diagnose electrical problems and adjust or replace defective electronic components. They also disassemble and repair undercarriages and track assemblies. Occasionally, mechanics weld broken equipment frames and structural parts, using electric or gas welders.

Many mechanics work in repair shops for construction contractors, local government road maintenance departments, or logging and mining companies. They typically perform the routine maintenance and minor repairs necessary to keep equipment in operation. Mechanics in large repair shops—particularly those of mobile heavy equipment dealers and the Federal Government—perform more difficult repairs. These repairs include rebuilding or replacing engines, repairing hydraulic fluid pumps, and correcting electrical problems.

It is common for mechanics in some large shops to specialize in one or two types of work. For example, a shop may have individual specialists in major engine repair, transmission work, electrical systems, and suspension or brake systems. The technology used in heavy equipment is becoming more sophisticated with the increased use of electronic and computer-controlled components. Training in electronics is essential for these mechanics, to make engine adjustments and to diagnose problems. Training in the use of hand-held computers is also necessary, because computers serve as the link between mechanic and vehicle and help mechanics diagnose problems and adjust engine functions.

Mobile heavy equipment mechanics may partially dismantle a component to examine parts for damage or excessive wear.

Mobile heavy equipment mechanics use a variety of tools in their work. They use power tools, such as pneumatic wrenches to remove bolts quickly, machine tools like lathes and grinding machines to rebuild brakes, welding and flame-cutting equipment to remove and repair exhaust systems, and jacks and hoists to lift and move large parts. Common handtools—screwdrivers, pliers, and wrenches—are used to work on small parts and to get at hard-to-reach places. Heavy equipment mechanics also use a variety of computerized testing equipment to pinpoint and analyze malfunctions in electrical systems and engines. For example, they use tachometers and dynamometers to locate engine malfunctions. When working on electrical systems, heavy equipment mechanics use ohmmeters, ammeters, and voltmeters.

Working Conditions

Mobile heavy equipment mechanics usually work indoors, although many make repairs at the work site. Mechanics often lift heavy parts and tools, handle greasy and dirty parts, and stand or lie in awkward positions, to repair vehicles and equipment. Minor cuts, burns, and bruises are common; but serious accidents are normally avoided, when the shop is kept clean and orderly and safety practices are observed. Mechanics usually work in well-lighted, heated, and ventilated areas. However, some shops are drafty and noisy. Many employers provide uniforms, locker rooms, and shower facilities.

When mobile heavy equipment breaks down at a construction site, it may be too difficult or expensive to bring it into a repair shop, so the shop often sends a field service mechanic to the job site to make repairs. Field service mechanics work outdoors and spend much of their time away from the shop. Generally, more experienced mobile heavy equipment mechanics specialize in field service. They usually drive trucks specially equipped with replacement parts and tools. On occasion, they must travel many miles to reach disabled machinery. Field mechanics normally earn a higher wage than their counterparts, because they are required to make on-the-spot decisions necessary to serve their customers.

Employment

Mobile heavy equipment mechanics held about 106,000 jobs in 1998. More than 30 percent were employed by mobile heavy equipment dealers and distributors. Nearly 20 percent worked for construction contractors; and about 18 percent were employed by Federal, State, and local governments. Other mobile heavy equipment mechanics worked for surface mine operators, public utility companies, or heavy equipment rental and leasing companies. Still others repaired equipment for machinery manufacturers, airlines, railroads, steel mills, or oil and gas field companies. Fewer than 1 out of 20 mobile heavy equipment mechanics was self-employed.

Nearly every section of the country employs mobile heavy equipment mechanics, though most work in towns and cities where equipment dealers, equipment rental and leasing companies, and construction companies have repair facilities.

Training, Other Qualifications, and Advancement

Although many persons qualify for heavy equipment mechanic jobs through years of on-the-job training, most employers prefer that applicants complete a formal diesel or heavy equipment mechanic training program after graduating from high school. They seek persons with mechanical aptitude who are knowledgeable about the fundamentals of diesel engines, transmissions, electrical systems, and hydraulics. Additionally, the constant change in equipment technology makes it necessary for mechanics to be flexible and have the capacity to learn new skills quickly.

Many community colleges and vocational schools offer programs in diesel mechanics or automotive repair. Some tailor programs to heavy equipment mechanics. These programs educate the student in the basics of analysis and diagnostic techniques, electronics, and hydraulics. The increased use of electronics and computers makes training in the fundamentals of electronics an essential tool for new mobile heavy equipment mechanics. Some 1- to 2-year programs lead to a certificate of completion, whereas others lead to an associate degree in diesel or heavy equipment mechanics. These programs provide a basic foundation in the components of diesel and heavy equipment technology. These programs also enable trainee mechanics to advance more rapidly to the journey, or experienced worker, level.

A combination of formal and on-the-job training prepares trainee mechanics with the knowledge to efficiently service and repair equipment handled by a shop. Most beginners perform routine service tasks and make minor repairs, after a few months' experience. They advance to harder jobs, as they prove their ability and competence. After trainees master the repair and service of diesel engines, they learn to work on related components, such as brakes, transmissions, and electrical systems. Generally, a mechanic with at least 3 to 4 years of on-the-job experience is accepted as a fully qualified heavy equipment mechanic.

Many employers send trainee mechanics to training sessions conducted by heavy equipment manufacturers. These sessions, which typically last up to 1 week, provide intensive instruction in the repair of a manufacturer's equipment. Some sessions focus on particular components found in all of the manufacturer's equipment, such as diesel engines, transmissions, axles, and electrical systems. Other sessions focus on particular types of equipment, such as crawler-loaders and crawler-dozers. As they progress, trainees may periodically attend additional training sessions. When appropriate, experienced mechanics attend training sessions, to gain familiarity with new technology or with types of equipment they have never repaired.

High school courses in automobile mechanics, physics, chemistry, and mathematics provide a strong foundation for a career as a mechanic. It is also essential for mechanics to be able to read, interpret, and comprehend service manuals, to keep abreast of engineering changes. Experience working on diesel engines and heavy equipment acquired in the Armed Forces also is valuable.

Voluntary certification by the National Institute for Automotive Service Excellence (ASE) is recognized as the standard of achievement for mobile heavy equipment mechanics. Mechanics may be certified as a Master Heavy-Duty Diesel Technician or in one or more of six different areas of heavy-duty equipment repair: Brakes, gasoline engines, diesel engines, drive trains, electrical systems, and suspension and steering. For certification in each area, mechanics must pass a written examination and have at least 2 years' experience. High school, vocational or trade school, or community or junior college training in gasoline or diesel engine repair may substitute for up to 1 year's experience. To remain certified, technicians must retest every 5 years. This ensures that mechanics and service technicians keep up with changing technology.

The most important work possessions of mechanics are their hand tools. Mobile heavy equipment mechanics typically buy their own hand tools, and many experienced mechanics have thousands of dollars invested in them. Employers typically furnish expensive power tools, computerized engine analyzers, and other diagnostic equipment; but hand tools are normally accumulated with experience.

Experienced mechanics may advance to field service jobs, where they have a greater opportunity to tackle problems independently and earn additional pay. Mechanics with leadership ability may become shop supervisors or service managers. Some mechanics open their own repair shops or invest in a franchise.

Job Outlook

Opportunities for heavy equipment mechanic jobs should be good for persons who have completed formal training programs in diesel or heavy equipment mechanics. This is due more to a lack of qualified entrants into the occupation than growth in available jobs. Persons without formal training are expected to encounter growing difficulty entering this occupation.

Employment of mobile heavy equipment mechanics is expected to grow more slowly than the average for all occupations through the year 2008. Increasing numbers of mechanics will be required to support growth in the construction industry, equipment dealers, and rental and leasing companies. As equipment becomes more complex, repairs increasingly must be made by specially trained mechanics.

Because of the nature of construction activity, demand for mobile heavy equipment mechanics follows the Nation's economic cycle. As the economy expands, construction activity increases, resulting in the use of more mobile heavy equipment. More equipment is needed to grade construction sites, excavate basements, and lay water and sewer lines, increasing the need for periodic service and repair. In addition, the construction and repair of highways and bridges also requires more mechanics to service equipment.

Construction and mining are particularly sensitive to changes in the level of economic activity; therefore, mobile heavy equipment may be idled during downturns. In addition, winter is traditionally the slow season for construction activity, particularly in cold regions. Few mechanics may be needed during periods when equipment is used less; however, employers usually try to retain experienced workers. Employers may be reluctant to hire inexperienced workers during slow periods though.

Earnings

Median annual earnings of mobile heavy equipment mechanics were \$31,520 in 1998. The middle 50 percent earned between \$25,050 and \$38,340 a year. The lowest 10 percent earned less than \$20,950 and the highest 10 percent earned more than \$46,500 a year. Median annual earnings in the industries employing the largest number of mobile heavy equipment mechanics in 1997 were as follows:

Industry	Earnings
Federal government	\$34,800
Machinery, equipment, and supplies	29,100
Miscellaneous equipment rental and leasing	28,800
Heavy construction, except highway	28,300
Miscellaneous repair shops	27,000

About one third of all mobile heavy equipment mechanics are members of unions including the International Association of Machinists and Aerospace Workers, the International Union of Operating Engineers, and the International Brotherhood of Teamsters.

Related Occupations

Workers in other occupations who repair and service diesel-powered vehicles and heavy equipment include rail car repairers, farm equipment mechanics, and diesel mechanics and service technicians. Other related occupations include motorcycle, boat, small engine, and heating, air-conditioning, and refrigeration mechanics.

Sources of Additional Information

More details about work opportunities for mobile heavy equipment mechanics may be obtained from local mobile heavy equipment dealers and distributors, construction contractors, and government agencies. Local offices of the State employment service may also have information on work opportunities and training programs.

For general information about a career as a mobile heavy equipment mechanic, contact:

☛ The Equipment Maintenance Counsel, 2020 Lake Shore Ct., Sanger, TX 76266.

☛ Specialized Carriers and Rigging Association, 2750 Prosperity Ave., Suite 620, Fairfax, VA 22031-4312. Internet: **http://www.scranet.org**

☛ The AED Foundation (Associated Equipment Dealers affiliate), 615 W. 22nd St., Oak Brook, IL 60523.
Internet: **http://www.aednet.org/aedf**

For a directory of public training programs for mobile heavy equipment mechanics, contact:

☛ SkillsUSA-VICA, P.O. Box 3000, 1401 James Monroe Hwy., Leesburg, VA 22075. Telephone (toll free): 1-800-321-VICA.
Internet: **http://www.skillsusa.org**

A list of certified diesel mechanic training programs can be obtained from:

☛ National Automotive Technician Education Foundation (NATEF), 13505 Dulles Technology Dr., Herndon, VA 20171-3421.
Internet: **http://www.natef.org**

Information on certification as a heavy-duty diesel mechanic is available from:

☛ Automotive Service Excellence (ASE), 13505 Dulles Technology Dr., Herndon, VA 20171-3421.
Internet: **http://www.asecert.org**

Motorcycle, Boat, and Small-Engine Mechanics

(O*NET 85116B, 85308, 85328A, and 85328B)

Significant Points

- Employment is expected to grow slowly, but persons with formal mechanic training should enjoy good job prospects.
- Because the use of motorcycles, boats, and outdoor power equipment is seasonal in many areas, mechanics may service other types of equipment or work reduced hours in the winter.

Nature of the Work

Though smaller, engines powering motorcycles, boats, and lawn and garden equipment share many characteristics with their larger counterparts, including breakdowns. Motorcycle, boat, and small-engine mechanics repair and service power equipment ranging from racing motorcycles to chain saws.

Small engines, like large engines, require periodic service to minimize the chance of breakdowns and to keep them operating at peak performance. During routine equipment maintenance, mechanics follow a checklist including the inspection and cleaning of brakes, electrical systems, plugs, carburetors, and other parts. Following inspection, mechanics usually repair or adjust parts that do not work properly, or replace unfixable parts. Routine maintenance is normally a major part of the mechanic's work.

When equipment breakdowns occur, mechanics use various techniques to diagnose the source and extent of the problem. The mark of a skilled mechanic is the ability to diagnose mechanical, fuel, and electrical problems, and to make repairs in a minimal amount of time. Quick and accurate diagnosis requires problem-solving ability and a thorough knowledge of the equipment's operation.

In larger repair shops, mechanics may use special computerized diagnostic testing equipment as a preliminary tool in analyzing equipment. These computers provide a systematic performance report of various components to compare them to normal ratings. After pinpointing the problem, the mechanic makes the needed adjustments, repairs, or replacements. Some jobs require minor adjustments or the replacement of a single item, such as a carburetor or fuel pump. In contrast, a complete engine overhaul requires a number of hours to disassemble the engine and replace worn valves, pistons, bearings, and other internal parts. Some highly skilled mechanics use highly specialized components and the latest computerized equipment to customize and tune motorcycles and boats for racing.

Motorcycle, boat, and small-engine mechanics use common handtools such as wrenches, pliers, and screwdrivers. They also use power tools, such as drills and grinders when customized repairs warrant.

Motorcycle, boat, and small engine mechanics follow a checklist, including the inspection and cleaning of engine parts during routine equipment maintenance.

Computerized engine analyzers, compression gauges, ammeters and voltmeters, and other testing devices help mechanics locate faulty parts and tune engines. Hoists may be used to lift heavy equipment such as motorcycles, snowmobiles, or boats. Mechanics often refer to service manuals for detailed directions and specifications while performing repairs.

Motorcycle mechanics repair and overhaul motorcycles, motor scooters, mopeds, and all-terrain vehicles. Besides engines, they may work on transmissions, brakes, and ignition systems, and make minor body repairs. Mechanics usually specialize in the service and repair of one type of equipment, although they may work on closely related products. Mechanics may only service a few makes and models of motorcycles because usually the dealers only service the products they sell.

Boat mechanics, or *marine equipment mechanics*, repair and adjust the engines and electrical and mechanical equipment of inboard and outboard marine engines. Most small boats have portable outboard engines that are removed and brought into the repair shop. Larger craft, such as cabin cruisers and commercial fishing boats, are powered by diesel or gasoline inboard or inboard-outboard engines, which are only removed for major overhauls. Most of these repairs are performed at the docks or marinas. Boat mechanics may also work on propellers, steering mechanisms, marine plumbing, and other boat equipment.

Small-engine mechanics service and repair outdoor power equipment such as lawnmowers, garden tractors, edge trimmers, and chain saws. They may also occasionally work on portable generators and go-carts. In addition, small-engine mechanics in northern parts of the country may work on snowblowers and snowmobiles, but demand for this type of repair is seasonal.

Working Conditions

Motorcycle, boat, and small-engine mechanics usually work in repair shops that are well lighted and ventilated, but are sometimes noisy when testing engines. However, boat mechanics may work outdoors at docks or marinas, and in all weather conditions, when making repairs aboard boats. They may work in cramped, or awkward positions to reach a boat's engine.

During the winter months in the northern United States, mechanics may work fewer than 40 hours a week because the amount of repair and service work declines when lawnmowers, boats and motorcycles are not in use. Many mechanics only work during the busy spring and summer seasons. However, many mechanics schedule time-consuming engine overhauls and work on snowmobiles and snowblowers during winter downtime. Mechanics may work considerably more than 40 hours a week when demand is strong.

Employment

Motorcycle, boat, and small-engine mechanics held about 52,000 jobs in 1998. About 14,000 were motorcycle mechanics, while the remainder specialized in the repair of boats or outdoor power equipment. Two-thirds of all motorcycle, boat, and small-engine mechanics worked for retail hardware and garden stores, or retail dealers of boats, motorcycles, and miscellaneous vehicles. Most of the remainder were employed by independent repair shops, marinas and boat yards, equipment rental companies, wholesale distributors, and landscaping services. About one-third were self-employed.

Training, Other Qualifications, and Advancement

Due to the increasing complexity of motorcycles and boats, most employers prefer to hire mechanics who graduate from formal training programs for motorcycle, marine, or small-engine mechanics. Because the number of these specialized post-secondary programs is limited, most mechanics learn their skills on the job or while working in related occupations. For trainee jobs, employers hire persons with mechanical aptitude who are knowledgeable about the fundamentals of small 2- and 4-stroke engines. Many trainees develop an interest in mechanics and acquire some basic skills through working on automobiles, motorcycles, boats, or outdoor power equipment as a hobby. Others may be introduced to mechanics through vocational automotive training in high school, or one of many post-secondary institutions.

Trainees learn routine service tasks under the guidance of experienced mechanics by replacing ignition points and spark plugs or by taking apart, assembling, and testing new equipment. As trainees gain experience and proficiency, they progress to more difficult tasks such as advanced computerized diagnosis and engine overhauls. Up to 3 years of on the job training may be necessary before a novice worker becomes competent in all aspects of the repair of motorcycle and boat engines.

Employers often send mechanics and trainees to special training courses conducted by motorcycle, boat, and outdoor power equipment manufacturers or distributors. These courses, which can last as long as 2 weeks, upgrade the worker's skills and provide information on repairing new models. They are usually a prerequisite for any mechanic who performs warranty work for manufacturers or insurance companies.

Most employers prefer to hire high school graduates for trainee mechanic positions, but will accept applicants with less education if they possess adequate reading, writing, and arithmetic skills. Many equipment dealers employ students part-time and during the summer, to help assemble new equipment and perform minor repairs. Helpful high school courses include small-engine repair, automobile mechanics, science, and business arithmetic.

Knowledge of basic electronics is essential for motorcycle, boat, and small-engine mechanics. Electronic components control engine performance, instrument displays, and a variety of other functions of motorcycles, boats, and outdoor power equipment. To recognize and fix potential problems, mechanics should be familiar with the basic principles of electronics.

The most important work possessions of mechanics are their hand tools. Mechanics usually provide their own tools and many experienced mechanics have invested thousands of dollars in them. Employers typically furnish expensive power tools, computerized engine analyzers, and other diagnostic equipment, but mechanics accumulate hand tools with experience.

The skills used as a motorcycle, boat, and small-engine mechanic generally transfer to other occupations such as automobile, truck, or heavy equipment mechanics. Experienced mechanics with leadership ability may advance to shop supervisor service manager jobs. Mechanics with sales ability sometimes become sales representatives or open their own repair shops.

Job Outlook

Employment of motorcycle, boat, and small-engine mechanics is expected to grow slower than the average for all occupations through the year 2008. The majority of job openings are expected to be replacement jobs because many experienced motorcycle, boat, and small-engine mechanics leave each year to transfer to other occupations, retire, or stop working for other reasons. Job prospects should be especially favorable for persons who complete mechanic training programs.

Growth of personal disposable income over the 1998-2008 period should provide consumers with more discretionary dollars to buy boats, lawn and garden power equipment, and motorcycles. This will require more mechanics to keep the growing amount of equipment in operation. In addition, routine service will always be a significant source of work for mechanics. While technology will lengthen the interval between check-ups, the need for qualified mechanics to perform this service will increase.

Employment of motorcycle mechanics should increase slowly as the popularity of motorcycles rebounds. Motorcycle usage should continue to be popular with persons between the ages of 18 and 24, an age group which historically has had the greatest proportion of motorcycle enthusiasts. Motorcycles are also increasingly popular with persons over the age of 40. Traditionally, this group has disposable income to spend on recreational equipment such as motorcycles and boats.

Over the next decade, more people will be entering the age group 40 and over; this group is responsible for the largest segment of marine craft purchases. These potential buyers will help expand the market for boats, while helping to maintain the demand for qualified mechanics. Construction of new single-family houses will result in an increase in the lawn and garden equipment in operation, increasing the need for mechanics. However, equipment growth will be slowed by trends toward smaller lawns and contracting out their maintenance to lawn service firms. Growth will also be tempered by the tendency of many consumers to dispose of and replace relatively inexpensive items rather than have them repaired.

Earnings

Median annual earnings of motorcycle mechanics were $23,440 in 1998. The middle 50 percent earned between $18,960 and $29,550 a year. The lowest 10 percent earned less than $13,990 and the highest 10 percent earned more than $36,760 a year.

Median annual earnings of small-engine mechanics were $21,580 in 1998. The middle 50 percent earned between $16,870 and $26,880 a year. The lowest 10 percent earned less than $13,430 and the highest 10 percent earned more than $32,780 a year.

Motorcycle, boat, and small-engine mechanics tend to receive few benefits in small shops, but those employed in larger shops often receive paid vacations, sick leave, and health insurance. Some employers also pay for work related training and provide uniforms.

Related Occupations

Mechanics and repairers who work on other types of mobile equipment powered by internal combustion engines include automotive mechanics and service technicians, diesel mechanics and service technicians, farm equipment mechanics, and mobile heavy equipment mechanics.

Sources of Additional Information

For more details about work opportunities, contact local motorcycle, boat, and lawn and garden equipment dealers, and boat yards and marinas. Local offices of the State employment service may also have information about employment and training opportunities.

General information about motorcycle mechanic careers may be obtained from:

☛ Motorcycle Mechanics Institute, 2844 West Deer Valley Rd., Phoenix, AZ 85027.

☛ American Motorcycle Institute, 3042 West International Speedway Blvd., Daytona Beach, FL 32124. Telephone (toll free): 1-800-874-0645.

General information about boat mechanic careers is available from:

☛ Marine Mechanics Institute, 2844 West Deer Valley Rd., Phoenix, AZ 85027.

☛ American Marine Institute, 3042 West International Speedway Blvd., Daytona Beach, FL 32124. Telephone (toll free): 1-800-874-0645.

General information about small-engine mechanic careers may be obtained from:

☛ Outdoor Power Equipment Institute, 341 South Patrick St., Alexandria, VA 22314.

For a list of public motorcycle, boat, and small-engine mechanic training programs, contact:

☛ SkillsUSA-VICA (Vocational Industry Clubs of America), P.O. Box 3000, 1401 James Monroe Hwy., Leesburg, VA 22075. Telephone (toll free): 1-800-321-VICA. Internet: **http://www.vica.org**

Musical Instrument Repairers and Tuners

(O*NET 85921A, 85921B, 85921C, and 85921D)

Significant Points

- Almost two-thirds of all musical instrument repairers and tuners are self-employed.
- Opportunities should be excellent for persons with formal training in piano technology or brass, woodwind, string, and electronic musical instrument repair.
- Musical instrument repairers and tuners should be able to play the instruments on which they work.

Nature of the Work

Musical instruments provide entertainment and recreation to millions of people everyday. Those who repair and tune instruments combine their love of music with a highly skilled craft to make sure that the next note played is as true as the last. Musical instrument repairers and tuners, often referred to as technicians, work in four specialties: Band instruments, pianos and organs, violins, and guitars. (Repairers and tuners who work on electronic organs are discussed in the *Handbook* statement on electronic home entertainment equipment repairers.)

Band instrument repairers work on woodwind, brass, reed, and percussion instruments damaged through deterioration or accident. Starting with the customer's description of the problem, they examine instruments and determine what must be done to restore them to proper performance levels and established industry specifications. These technicians also regularly tune and adjust instruments.

Brass and wind instrument repairers clean, adjust, and repair trumpets, cornets, french horns, trombones, tubas, clarinets, flutes, saxophones, oboes, and bassoons. They move mechanical parts or play scales to find defects. They may unscrew and remove rod pins, keys, and pistons and remove soldered parts using gas torches. They repair dents in metal instruments using mallets or burnishing tools. They fill cracks in wood instruments by inserting pinning wire and covering it with filler. Repairers also inspect instrument keys and replace worn pads and corks.

Percussion instrument repairers work on drums, cymbals, and xylophones. To repair a drum, technicians remove tension rods by hand or by using a drum key. They cut new drumheads from animal skin, stretch the skin over the rimhoops, and tuck the skin under the hoop using hand tools. To prevent a crack from advancing in a cymbal, gong, or similar instrument, repairers may drill holes at the inside edge of the crack; another technique involves cutting out sections around the cracks using shears or grinding wheels. Percussion repairers also replace the bars and wheels of xylophones.

Piano and organ repairers and tuners locate and correct an assortment of problems associated with thousands of instrument parts made from wood, steel, iron, brass, ivory, felt, and sometimes Teflon. While the piano and organ are each over 300 years old, the basic engineering of today's piano and organ was done almost 100 years ago and the methodology has changed very little since.

To diagnose problems, *piano repairers* talk with customers and examine the parts of the piano. Depending on the severity of the problem, they may replace worn parts, recondition usable parts, or completely rebuild pianos. In some cases, they may reconfigure or

Musical instrument repairers and tuners combine their love of music with a highly skilled craft to ensure that the next note played is as true as the last.

redesign parts to solve a specific problem. For work such as regulating, repining, and restringing, repairers use common hand tools as well as specialty tools. In addition to repair work, piano repairers may also tune pianos.

Piano tuners increase and decrease the tension of piano strings to tune pianos to the proper pitch. A string's pitch is the frequency at which it vibrates, and produces sound, when it is struck by one of the piano's hammers. Pianos are tuned with the aid of either an electric or an acoustic pitch reference. The tuner strikes a key and compares the reference strings' pitch with that of the pitch reference. A tuning hammer (also called a tuning lever) is used to turn a tuning pin to increase or decrease tension on the reference string until its pitch matches that of the pitch reference. The pitch of each of the other strings is set in relation to the reference string. Modern 88-key pianos have over 200 strings and can be tuned in 1 to 2 hours, depending on the condition of the piano and the skill of the repairer.

Generally, piano technicians tune, repair, and rebuild pianos. Some piano technicians provide additional service for pianos with built-in humidity control devices, recording devices, and automatic player-piano devices. These specialty services and repairs require additional training, yet are still considered part of the technician's duties.

Pipe-organ repairers and tuners tune, repair, and install organs that make music by forcing air through flue pipes or reed pipes. The flue pipe sounds when a current of air strikes a metal lip in the side of the pipe. The reed pipe sounds when a current of air vibrates a brass reed inside the pipe.

Pipe-organ repairers locate problems, repair or replace worn parts, and clean pipes. Repairers also assemble organs on site in churches and auditoriums following manufacturer's blueprints. They use hand and power tools to install and connect the air chest, blowers, air ducts, pipes, and other components. They may work in teams or with the assistance of helpers. Depending on the size of the organ, an installation job may take several weeks or even months.

To tune an organ, repairers first match the pitch of the "A" pipes with that of a tuning fork. The pitch of other pipes is set by comparing it to that of the "A" pipes. To tune a flue pipe, repairers move the metal slide that increases or decreases the pipe's "speaking length." To tune a reed pipe, the tuner alters the length of the brass reed. Most organs have hundreds of pipes, so often a day or more is needed to completely tune an organ.

Violin repairers adjust and repair bowed instruments, such as violins, violas, and cellos, using a variety of hand tools. They find defects by inspecting and playing instruments. They replace or repair cracked or broken sections and damaged parts. They also restring instruments and repair damage to the finish of the instruments.

Guitar repairers inspect and play the instrument to determine defects. They replace levels using hand tools, and replace or repair damaged wood or metal parts. They reassemble and string guitars.

Working Conditions

Although they may suffer small cuts and bruises, the work of musical instrument repairers and tuners is relatively safe. Most brass, woodwind, percussion, and string instrument repairers work in repair shops or music stores. Piano and organ repairers and tuners usually work on instruments in homes, schools, colleges and universities, and churches, and may spend several hours a day driving to appointments. Salaried repairers and tuners work out of a shop or store; the self-employed generally work out of their homes.

Recently, musical instrument repairers have switched to using nontoxic chemicals to clean, fill, and mold instruments, instead of the traditional sodium cyanide and chromate solutions. These changes have made workplaces cleaner and safer.

Employment

Musical instrument repairers and tuners held about 13,000 jobs in 1998. Most technicians worked on pianos. About two-thirds were self-employed. About 8 of 10 wage and salary repairers and tuners worked in music stores, and most of the rest worked in repair shops or for musical instrument manufacturers.

Training, Other Qualifications, and Advancement

For musical instrument repairer and tuner jobs, employers prefer people with post high school training in music repair technology. According to a 1997 Piano Technicians Guild membership survey, more than 85 percent of respondents had completed at least some college work; at least 50 percent had a bachelor's degree or higher.

Some musical instrument repairers and tuners learn their trade on the job as apprentices or assistants, but employers willing to provide on-the-job training are difficult to find. A few music stores, large repair shops, and self-employed repairers and tuners hire inexperienced individuals as trainees to learn how to tune and repair instruments under the supervision of experienced workers. Trainees may sell instruments, clean up, or do other routine work. Usually 2 to 5 years of training and practice are needed to become fully qualified.

A small number of technical schools and colleges offer courses in piano technology or brass, woodwind, string, and electronic musical instrument repair. A few music repair schools offer 1- or 2-year courses. There are also home-study (correspondence school) courses in piano technology. Graduates of these courses generally refine their skills by working with an experienced tuner or technician.

Music courses help develop the student's ear for tonal quality. The ability to play an instrument is helpful. Knowledge of woodworking is useful for repairing instruments made of wood.

Repairers and tuners need good hearing, mechanical aptitude, and manual dexterity. For those dealing directly with customers, a neat appearance and a pleasant, cooperative manner are important.

Musical instrument repairers keep up with developments in their fields by studying trade magazines and manufacturers' service manuals. The Piano Technicians Guild helps its members improve their skills through training conducted at local chapter meetings and at regional, national, and international seminars. Guild members can also take a series of tests, one written and two practical, to earn the title Registered Piano Technician. The National Association of Professional Band Instrument Repair Technicians offers similar programs, scholarships, and a trade publication. Its members specialize in the repair of woodwind, brass, string and percussion instruments. Repairers and technicians who work for large dealers, repair shops, or manufacturers can advance to supervisory positions or go into business for themselves.

Job Outlook

Musical instrument repairer and tuner jobs are expected to increase more slowly than the average for all occupations through the year 2008. Replacement needs will provide the most job opportunities as many repairers and tuners near retirement age. The small number of openings, due to both growth and replacement needs, is very low relative to other occupations. Because training is difficult to receive—there are only a few schools that offer training programs and few experienced workers are willing to take on apprentices—opportunities should be excellent for those who do receive training.

Several factors are expected to influence the demand for musical instrument repairers and tuners. The number of people employed as musicians will increase, mainly due to a slight increase in the number of students of all ages playing musical instruments. Because instruments are quite expensive to purchase, growing numbers of instrument repairers will be needed to work on rental equipment leased to students, schools, and other organizations.

Earnings

Median annual earnings of musical instrument repairers and tuners were $23,010 in 1998. The middle 50 percent earned between $17,780 and $29,500 a year. The lowest 10 percent earned less than $13,230 and the highest 10 percent earned more than $38,680 a year. Earnings were generally higher in urban areas.

Related Occupations

Musical instrument repairers need mechanical aptitude and good manual dexterity. Electronic home entertainment equipment repairers, vending machine servicers and repairers, home appliance and power tool repairers, and computer and office machine repairers all require similar talents.

Sources of Additional Information

Details about job opportunities may be available from local music instrument dealers and repair shops.

For general information about piano technicians and a list of schools offering courses in piano technology, write to:

☛ Piano Technicians Guild, 3930 Washington St., Kansas City, MO 64111-2963. Internet: **http://www.ptg.org**

For general information on musical instrument repair, write to:

☛ National Association of Professional Band Instrument Repair Technicians (NAPBIRT), P.O. Box 51, Normal, IL 61761.

Construction Trades Occupations

Boilermakers

(O*NET 89135)

Significant Points

- A formal apprenticeship is the best way to learn this trade.
- Due to the limited number of apprenticeships available and relatively good wages, prospective boilermakers may face competition.

Nature of the Work

Boilermakers and boilermaker mechanics make, install, and repair boilers, vats, and other large vessels that hold liquids and gases. Boilers supply steam to drive huge turbines in electric power plants and to provide heat and power in buildings, factories, and ships. Tanks and vats are used to process and store chemicals, oil, beer, and hundreds of other products.

Boilers and other high-pressure vessels are usually made in sections, by casting each piece out of molten iron or steel. Manufacturers are increasingly automating this process to increase the quality of these vessels. Boiler sections are then welded together, often using automated orbital welding machines, which make more consistent welds than are possible by hand. Small boilers may be assembled in the manufacturing plant; larger boilers are usually assembled on site.

Following blueprints for installing boilers and other vessels, boilermakers locate and mark reference points on the boiler foundation, using straightedges, squares, transits, and tape measures. Boilermakers attach rigging and signal crane operators to lift heavy frame and plate sections and other parts into place. They align sections, using plumb bobs, levels, wedges, and turnbuckles. Boilermakers use hammers, files, grinders, and cutting torches to remove irregular edges so edges fit properly. Then they bolt or weld edges together. Boilermakers align and attach water tubes, stacks, valves, gauges, and other parts and test complete vessels for leaks or other defects. Usually they assemble large vessels temporarily in a fabrication shop to insure a proper fit before final assembly on the permanent site.

Because boilers last a long time—35 years or more—boilermakers regularly maintain them and update components such as burners and boiler tubes to increase efficiency. Boilermaker mechanics maintain and repair boilers and similar vessels. They inspect tubes, fittings, valves, controls, and auxiliary machinery and clean or supervise the cleaning of boilers. They repair or replace defective parts, using hand and power tools, gas torches, and welding equipment, and may operate metalworking machinery to repair or make parts. They also dismantle leaky boilers, patch weak spots with metal stock, replace defective sections, and strengthen joints.

Boilermakers maintain and repair boilers and similar vessels.

Working Conditions

Boilermakers often use potentially dangerous equipment, such as acetylene torches and power grinders, handle heavy parts, and work on ladders or on top of large vessels. Work may be done in cramped quarters inside boilers, vats, or tanks that are often damp and poorly ventilated. To reduce the chance of injuries, boilermakers may wear hardhats, harnesses, protective clothing, safety glasses and shoes, and respirators. Boilermakers usually work a 40-hour week but may experience extended periods of overtime when equipment is shut down for maintenance. Overtime work may also be necessary to meet construction or production deadlines.

Employment

Boilermakers held about 18,000 jobs in 1998. Well over half worked in the construction industry, assembling and erecting boilers and other vessels. About one-fifth worked in manufacturing, primarily in boiler manufacturing shops, iron and steel plants, petroleum refineries, chemical plants, and shipyards. Some also work for boiler repair firms, railroads, or in Navy shipyards and Federal power facilities.

Training, Other Qualifications, and Advancement

Most training authorities recommend a formal apprenticeship to learn this trade. Some people become boilermakers by working as helpers to experienced boilermakers, but generally lack the wide range of skills acquired through an apprenticeship. Apprenticeship programs usually consist of 4 years of on-the-job training, supplemented by about 144 hours of classroom instruction each year in subjects such as set-up and assembly rigging, welding of all types, blueprint reading, and layout. Experienced boilermakers often attend apprenticeship classes to keep their knowledge current.

When an apprenticeship becomes available, the local union publicizes the opportunity by notifying local vocational schools and high school vocational programs. Qualified applicants take an aptitude test administered by the union, specifically designed for boilermaking. The apprenticeship is awarded to the person scoring highest on this test.

When hiring helpers, employers prefer high school or vocational school graduates. Courses in shop, mathematics, blueprint reading, welding, and machine metalworking are useful. Mechanical aptitude and the manual dexterity needed to handle tools also are important.

Some boilermakers advance to supervisory positions. Because of their broader training, apprentices usually have an advantage in promotion.

Job Outlook

Boilermakers is a very small occupation with limited job prospects. Persons who wish to become boilermakers are likely to face competition, due to the limited number of apprenticeships available and the relatively good wages an experienced boilermaker earns. Employment of boilermakers is expected to show little or no change through the year 2008. Most job openings will result from the need to replace experienced workers who leave the occupation.

Growth should be limited by several factors: The trend toward repairing and retrofitting rather than replacing existing boilers, the use of small boilers, which require less on-site assembly, and automation of production technologies.

Most industries that purchase boilers are sensitive to economic conditions. Therefore, during economic downturns, construction boilermakers may be laid off. However, because maintenance and repairs of boilers must continue even during economic downturns, boilermaker mechanics generally have stable employment.

Earnings

In 1998, the median hourly earnings of boilermakers were about $18.45. The middle 50 percent earned between $15.04 and $22.49. The lowest 10 percent earned less than $11.40 and the highest 10 percent earned more than $25.53.

Apprentices generally start at about 60 percent of journey wages, with wages gradually increasing to the journey wage as progress is made in the apprenticeship. However, wages vary greatly around the country, with higher wages in Northeastern, Great Lakes, and Far Western states than in other areas of the country.

Almost one-half of all boilermakers belong to labor unions. The principal union is the International Brotherhood of Boilermakers. Other boilermakers are members of the International Association of Machinists, the United Automobile Workers, or the United Steelworkers of America.

Related Occupations

Workers in a number of other occupations assemble, install, or repair metal equipment or machines. These occupations include assemblers, blacksmiths, instrument makers, ironworkers, machinists, millwrights, patternmakers, plumbers, sheet-metal workers, tool and die makers, and welders.

Sources of Additional Information

For further information regarding boilermaking apprenticeships or other training opportunities, contact local offices of the unions previously mentioned, local construction companies and boiler manufacturers, or the local office of your State employment service.

For information on apprenticeships and the boilermaking occupation, contact:

☛ American Boiler Manufacturing Association, 950 North Glebe Rd., Suite 160, Arlington, VA 22203-1824.

☛ International Brotherhood of Boilermakers, Iron Ship Builders, Blacksmiths, Forgers and Helpers, 753 State Avenue, Suite 570, Kansas City, KS 66101.

Bricklayers and Stonemasons

(O*NET 87302 and 87305B)

Significant Points

- Opportunities should be excellent because job openings are expected to grow faster than the number of workers being trained.
- Work is usually outdoors, requires lifting heavy bricks and blocks, and sometimes involves working on scaffolds.
- Nearly 3 out of every 10 bricklayers and stonemasons are self-employed.

Nature of the Work

Bricklayers and stonemasons work in closely related trades creating attractive, durable surfaces and structures. The work varies in complexity, from laying a simple masonry walkway to installing an ornate exterior of a high-rise building. *Bricklayers*—also called brickmasons—build walls, floors, partitions, fireplaces, chimneys, and other structures with brick, precast masonry panels, concrete block, and other masonry materials. Additionally, bricklayers specialize in installing firebrick linings in industrial furnaces. *Stonemasons* build stone walls, as well as set stone exteriors and floors. They work with two types of stone—natural cut, such as marble, granite, and limestone, and artificial stone made from concrete, marble chips, or other masonry materials. Stonemasons usually work on nonresidential structures, such as houses of worship, hotels, and office buildings.

When building a structure, bricklayers begin by constructing a pyramid of bricks—called a lead—at each corner of a wall, around which the rest of the bricks are laid. Due to the precision needed, these corner leads are time consuming to erect and require the skills of experienced bricklayers. After the corner leads are complete, less experienced bricklayers fill in the wall between the corners, using a line from corner to corner to guide each *course*, or layer, of brick. Because of the expense associated with building corner leads, an increasing number of bricklayers use corner poles, also called masonry guides, that enable them to build an entire wall at the same time. They fasten the corner poles (posts) in a plumb position to define the wall line and stretch a line between them. This line serves as a guide for each course of brick. Bricklayers then spread a bed of mortar (a cement, sand, and water mixture) with a trowel (a flat, bladed metal tool with a handle), place the brick on the mortar bed, and then press and tap the brick into place. Depending on blueprint specifications, bricklayers either cut bricks with a hammer and chisel or saw them to fit around windows, doors, and other openings. Then, mortar joints are finished with jointing tools for a sealed, neat, uniform appearance. Although bricklayers usually use steel supports, or *lintels*, at window and door openings, they sometimes build brick arches instead , which support and enhance the beauty of the brickwork.

Hod carriers, or *helpers*, are workers who assist bricklayers. These workers mix mortar, set up and move scaffolding, and bring bricks and other materials to the bricklayers.

Stonemasons often work from a set of drawings, in which each stone has been numbered for identification. Helpers may locate and carry these prenumbered stones to the masons. A derrick operator using a hoist may be needed to lift large stone pieces into place.

When building a stone wall, masons set the first course of stones into a shallow bed of mortar. They then align the stones with wedges, plumblines, and levels, and adjust them into position with a hard rubber mallet. Masons continue to build the wall by alternating layers of mortar and courses of stone. As the work progresses, masons remove the wedges, fill the joints between stones, and use a pointed metal tool, called a tuck pointer, to smooth the mortar to an attractive finish. To hold large stones in place, stonemasons attach brackets to the stone and weld or bolt these brackets to anchors in the wall. Finally, masons wash the stone with a cleansing solution to remove stains and dry mortar.

When setting stone floors, which often consist of large and heavy pieces of stone, masons first use a trowel to spread a layer of damp mortar over the surface to be covered. Using crowbars and hard rubber mallets for aligning and leveling, they then set the stone in the mortar bed. To finish, workers fill the joints and wash the stone slabs.

Masons use a special hammer and chisel to cut stone. They cut stone along the grain to make various shapes and sizes, and valuable pieces often are cut with a saw that has a diamond blade. Some masons specialize in setting marble which, in many respects, is similar to setting large pieces of stone. Bricklayers and stonemasons also repair imperfections and cracks, and replace broken or missing masonry units in walls and floors.

Most nonresidential buildings are now built with prefabricated panels made of concrete block, brick veneer, stone, granite, marble, tile, or glass. In the past, bricklayers doing nonresidential interior work mostly built block partition walls and elevator shafts. Now, these workers must be more versatile and work with many materials. For example, bricklayers now install light-weight insulated panels used in new skyscraper construction.

Bricklayers use high-speed saws to cut bricks.

Refractory masons are bricklayers who specialize in installing firebrick and refractory tile in high-temperature boilers, furnaces, cupolas, ladles, and soaking pits in industrial establishments. Most of these bricklayers work in steel mills, where molten materials flow on refractory beds from furnaces to rolling machines.

Working Conditions

Bricklayers and stonemasons usually work outdoors. They stand, kneel, and bend for long periods and often have to lift heavy materials. Common hazards include injuries from tools and falls from scaffolds, but these can often be avoided when proper safety practices are followed.

Employment

Bricklayers and stonemasons held about 157,000 jobs in 1998. The vast majority were bricklayers. Workers in these crafts are employed primarily by building, special trade, or general contractors. Bricklayers and stonemasons work throughout the country but, like the general population, are concentrated in metropolitan areas.

Nearly 3 in 10 of all bricklayers and stonemasons were self-employed. Many of the self-employed specialize in contracting small jobs, such as patios, walkways, and fireplaces.

Training, Other Qualifications, and Advancement

Most bricklayers and stonemasons pick up their skills informally, observing and learning from experienced workers. Many others receive training in vocational education schools. However, the best way to learn these skills is through an apprenticeship program, which generally provides the most thorough training.

Individuals who learn the trade on the job usually start as helpers, laborers, or mason tenders. These workers carry materials, move scaffolds, and mix mortar. When the opportunity arises, they learn from experienced craft workers how to spread mortar, lay brick and block, or set stone. As they gain experience, they make the transition to full-fledged craft workers. The learning period on the job normally lasts longer than an apprenticeship program.

Apprenticeships for bricklayers and stonemasons are usually sponsored by local contractors or by local union-management committees. The apprenticeship program requires 3 years of on-the-job training, in addition to a minimum 144 hours of classroom instruction each year in subjects such as blueprint reading, mathematics, layout work, and sketching.

Apprentices often start by working with laborers, carrying materials, mixing mortar, and building scaffolds. This period generally lasts about a month and familiarizes the apprentice with job routines and materials. Next, they learn to lay, align, and join brick and block. Apprentices also learn to work with stone and concrete, which enables them to be certified to work with more than one masonry material.

Applicants for apprenticeships must be at least 17 years old and in good physical condition. A high school education is preferable; and courses in mathematics, mechanical drawing, and shop are helpful. The International Masonry Institute (IMI), a division of the International Union of Bricklayers and Allied Craftsmen, operates training centers in several large cities that help job seekers develop the skills needed to successfully complete the formal apprenticeship program. In addition, the IMI recently opened a national training and education center at Fort Ritchie, Maryland. The national center's programs teach stone, terrazzo, brick, tile, and refractory materials construction, as well as restoration work. Safety and foreman training also are part of the curriculum.

Bricklayers who work in nonresidential construction usually work for large contractors and receive well-rounded training—normally through apprenticeship in all phases of brick or stone work. Those who work in residential construction usually work primarily for small contractors and specialize in only one or two aspects of the job.

Often, experienced workers can advance to supervisory positions or become estimators. They also can open contracting businesses of their own.

Job Outlook

Job opportunities for skilled bricklayers and stonemasons are expected to be excellent, as the growth in job opportunities outpaces the supply of workers trained in this craft. Employment of bricklayers and stonemasons is expected to grow about as fast as the average for all occupations through the year 2008, and additional openings will result from the need to replace bricklayers and stonemasons who retire, transfer to other occupations, or leave the trades for other reasons. The pool of young workers, particularly those between the ages of 16 and 24, available to enter training programs will be increasing slowly; and many in that group are reluctant to seek training for jobs that may be strenuous and have uncomfortable working conditions.

Population and business growth will create a need for new houses, factories, schools, hospitals, offices, and other structures, increasing the demand for bricklayers and stonemasons. Also stimulating demand, will be the need to restore a growing stock of old masonry buildings, as well as the increasing use of brick for decorative work on building fronts and in lobbies and foyers. Brick exteriors should continue to be very popular, as the trend continues toward durable exterior materials requiring little maintenance. However, employment of bricklayers who specialize in refractory repair will decline, along with employment in other occupations in the primary metal industries.

Employment of bricklayers and stonemasons, like that of many other construction workers, is sensitive to changes in the economy. When the level of construction activity falls, workers in these trades can experience periods of unemployment.

Earnings

Median hourly earnings of bricklayers and stonemasons in 1998 were $16.92. The middle 50 percent earned between $12.85 and $21.52. The lowest 10 percent earned less than $9.77 and the highest 10 percent earned more than $27.63. Median hourly earnings in the industries employing the largest number of brickmasons in 1997 are shown below:

Nonresidential building construction	$18.20
Masonry, stonework, and plastering	16.70
Concrete work	14.20
Residential building construction	14.00

Earnings for workers in these trades can be reduced on occasion because poor weather and downturns in construction activity limit the time they can work.

In both of these trades, apprentices or helpers usually start at about 50 percent of the wage rate paid to experienced workers. Pay increases as apprentices gain experience and learn new skills.

Some bricklayers and stonemasons are members of the International Union of Bricklayers and Allied Craftsmen.

Related Occupations
Bricklayers and stonemasons combine a thorough knowledge of brick, concrete block, stone, and marble with manual skill to erect attractive, yet highly durable, structures. Workers in other occupations with similar skills include cement masons, concrete finishers, plasterers, terrazzo workers, and tilesetters.

Sources of Additional Information
For details about apprenticeships or other work opportunities in these trades, contact local bricklaying, stonemasonry, or marble-setting contractors; a local of the union listed above; a local joint union-management apprenticeship committee; or the nearest office of the State employment service or the State apprenticeship agency.

For general information about the work of either bricklayers or stonemasons, contact:

☛ International Union of Bricklayers and Allied Craftsmen, International Masonry Institute Apprenticeship and Training, 815 15th St. NW., Suite 1001, Washington, DC 20005.

Information about the work of bricklayers also can be obtained from:

☛ Associated General Contractors of America, Inc., 1957 E St. NW., Washington, DC 20006.

☛ Brick Institute of America, 11490 Commerce Park Dr., Reston, VA 22091-1525.

☛ Home Builders Institute, National Association of Home Builders, 1201 15th St. NW., Washington, DC 20005.

☛ National Concrete Masonry Association, 2302 Horse Pen Rd., Herndon, VA 22071.

Carpenters

(O*NET 87102A, 87102B, 87102D, 87102F, 87105, and 87121)

Significant Points

- Nearly one-third of carpenters—the largest construction trade in 1998—were self-employed.
- Although employment is expected to grow slowly, job opportunities should be excellent because many carpenters leave the occupation each year.
- Many builders use specialty carpentry subcontractors who do one or two work activities, so versatile carpenters able to switch specialties should have the best opportunities for steady work.

Nature of the Work
Carpenters are involved in many different kinds of construction activity. They cut, fit, and assemble wood and other materials in the construction of buildings, highways, bridges, docks, industrial plants, boats, and many other structures. Carpenters' duties vary by type of employer. Builders increasingly are using specialty trade contractors who, in turn, hire carpenters who specialize in just one or two activities. Some of these activities are setting forms for concrete construction; erecting scaffolding; or doing finishing work, such as installing interior and exterior trim. However, a carpenter directly employed by a general building contractor often must perform a variety of the tasks associated with new construction, such as framing walls and partitions, putting in doors and windows, building stairs, laying hardwood floors, and hanging kitchen cabinets.

Because local building codes often dictate where certain materials can be used, carpenters must know these requirements. Each carpentry task is somewhat different, but most involve the same basic steps. Working from blueprints or instructions from supervisors, carpenters first do the layout—measuring, marking, and arranging materials. They cut and shape wood, plastic, fiberglass, or drywall, using hand and power tools, such as chisels, planes, saws, drills, and sanders. They then join the materials with nails, screws, staples, or adhesives. In the final step, carpenters check the accuracy of their work with levels, rules, plumb bobs, and framing squares and make any necessary adjustments. When working with prefabricated components, such as stairs or wall panels, the carpenter's task is somewhat simpler than above, because it does not require as much layout work or the cutting and assembly of as many pieces. Prefabricated components are designed for easy and fast installation and generally can be installed in a single operation.

Carpenters who remodel homes and other structures must be able to do all aspects of a job—and not just one task. Thus, individuals with good basic overall training are at a distinct advantage, because they can switch from residential building to commercial construction or remodeling work, depending on which offers the best work opportunities.

Carpenters employed outside the construction industry perform a variety of installation and maintenance work. They may replace panes of glass, ceiling tiles, and doors, as well as repair desks, cabinets, and other furniture. Depending on the employer, carpenters install partitions, doors, and windows; change locks; and repair broken furniture. In manufacturing firms, carpenters may assist in moving or installing machinery. (For more information on workers who install machinery, see the sections on industrial machinery repairers and millwrights elsewhere in the *Handbook.*)

Working Conditions
As in other building trades, carpentry work is sometimes strenuous. Prolonged standing, climbing, bending, and kneeling are often necessary. Carpenters risk injury working with sharp or rough materials, using sharp tools and power equipment, and from slips or falls. Additionally, many carpenters work outdoors, which can be uncomfortable.

Some carpenters specialize in framing walls and partitions.

Some carpenters change employers each time they finish a construction job. Others alternate between working for a contractor and working as contractors themselves on small jobs.

Employment

Carpenters, the largest group of building trades workers, held about 1.1 million jobs in 1998. Nearly 4 of every 5 worked for contractors who build, remodel, or repair buildings and other structures. Most of the remainder worked for manufacturing firms, government agencies, wholesale and retail establishments, or schools. Nearly one-third were self-employed.

Carpenters are employed throughout the country in almost every community.

Training, Other Qualifications, and Advancement

Carpenters learn their trade through on-the-job training, as well as formal training programs. Most pick up skills informally by working under the supervision of experienced workers. Many acquire skills through vocational education. Others participate in employer training programs or apprenticeships.

Most employers recommend an apprenticeship as the best way to learn carpentry. Apprenticeship programs are administered by local joint union-management committees of the United Brotherhood of Carpenters and Joiners of America, the Associated General Contractors, Inc., and the National Association of Home Builders. In addition, training programs are administered by local chapters of the Associated Builders and Contractors and by local chapters of the Associated General Contractors, Inc. These programs combine on-the-job training with related classroom instruction.

On the job, apprentices learn elementary structural design and become familiar with common carpentry jobs, such as layout, form building, rough framing, and outside and inside finishing. They also learn to use the tools, machines, equipment, and materials of the trade. Apprentices receive classroom instruction in safety, first aid, blueprint reading, freehand sketching, basic mathematics, and different carpentry techniques. Both in the classroom and on the job, they learn the relationship between carpentry and the other building trades.

Usually, apprenticeship applicants must be at least 17 years old and meet local requirements. For example, some union locals test an applicant's aptitude for carpentry. The length of the program, usually about 3 to 4 years, varies with the apprentice's skill. Because the number of apprenticeship programs is limited, however, only a small proportion of carpenters learn their trade through these programs.

Informal on-the-job training is normally less thorough than an apprenticeship. The degree of training and supervision often depends on the size of the employing firm. A small contractor specializing in home-building may only provide training in rough framing. In contrast, a large general contractor may provide training in several carpentry skills. Although specialization is becoming increasingly common, it is important to try to acquire skills in all aspects of carpentry and to have the flexibility to perform any kind of work.

A high school education is desirable, including courses in carpentry, shop, mechanical drawing, and general mathematics. Manual dexterity, eye-hand coordination, physical fitness, and a good sense of balance are important. The ability to solve arithmetic problems quickly and accurately is also helpful. Employers and apprenticeship committees generally view favorably any training and work experience obtained in the Armed Services or Job Corps.

Carpenters may advance to carpentry supervisors or general construction supervisors. Carpenters usually have greater opportunities than most other construction workers to become general construction supervisors, because carpenters are exposed to the entire construction process. Some carpenters become independent contractors. To advance, these workers should be able to estimate the nature and quantity of materials needed to properly complete a job. In addition, they must be able to estimate, with accuracy, how long a job should take to complete and its cost.

Job Outlook

Job opportunities for carpenters are expected to be plentiful through the year 2008, due primarily to extensive replacement needs. Thousands of job openings will become available each year as carpenters transfer to other occupations or leave the labor force. The total number of job openings for carpenters is usually greater than for other craft occupations, because the carpentry occupation is large and the turnover rate is high. Because there are no strict training requirements for entry, many people with limited skills take jobs as carpenters but eventually leave the occupation because they dislike the work or cannot find steady employment. However, employment of carpenters is expected to increase more slowly than the average for all occupations through the year 2008.

Increased demand for carpenters will create additional job openings. Construction activity should increase slowly, in response to demand for new housing and commercial and industrial plants and the need to renovate and modernize existing structures. Opportunities for frame carpenters should be particularly good.

However, the demand for carpenters will be offset somewhat by expected productivity gains resulting from the increasing use of prefabricated components, such as prehung doors and windows and prefabricated wall panels and stairs, which can be installed very quickly. Prefabricated walls, partitions, and stairs can be lifted into place in one operation; beams—and in some cases entire roof assemblies—can be lifted into place using a crane. As prefabricated components become more standardized, builders may use them more often. In addition, improved adhesives will reduce the time needed to join materials, and lightweight, cordless pneumatic and combustion tools—such as nailers and drills—and sanders with electronic speed controls will make carpenters more efficient.

Carpenters can experience periods of unemployment because of the short-term nature of many construction projects and the cyclical nature of the construction industry. Building activity depends on many factors—interest rates, availability of mortgage funds, government spending, and business investment—that vary with the state of the economy. During economic downturns, the number of job openings for carpenters declines. New and improved tools, equipment, techniques, and materials have vastly increased carpenter versatility. Therefore, carpenters with all-round skills will have better opportunities than those who can only do a few relatively simple, routine tasks.

Job opportunities for carpenters also vary by geographic area. Construction activity parallels the movement of people and businesses and reflects differences in local economic conditions. Therefore, the number of job opportunities and apprenticeship opportunities in a given year may vary widely from area to area.

Earnings

In 1998, median hourly earnings of carpenters were $13.82. The middle 50 percent earned between $10.84 and $18.57. The lowest 10 percent earned less than $8.74 and the highest 10 percent earned more than $23.57. Median hourly earnings in the industries employing the largest numbers of carpenters in 1997 are shown below:

Industry	Earnings
Masonry, stonework, and plastering	$18.20
Nonresidential building construction	15.10
Carpentry and floor work	13.60
Residential building construction	12.40
Personnel supply services	11.40

Earnings can be reduced on occasion, because carpenters lose work time in bad weather and during recessions when jobs are unavailable.

In 1998, median hourly earnings of ceiling tile installers and acoustical carpenters were $15.27. The middle 50 percent earned between $11.88 and $20.50. The lowest 10 percent earned less than $9.68 and the highest 10 percent earned more than $29.57.

Some carpenters are members of the United Brotherhood of Carpenters and Joiners of America.

Related Occupations
Carpenters are skilled construction workers. Workers in other skilled construction occupations include bricklayers, cement masons, concrete finishers, electricians, pipefitters, plasterers, plumbers, stonemasons, and terrazzo workers.

Sources of Additional Information
For information about carpentry apprenticeships or other work opportunities in this trade, contact local carpentry contractors, locals of the union mentioned above, local joint union-contractor apprenticeship committees, or the nearest office of the State employment service or State apprenticeship agency.

For general information about carpentry, contact:

☛ Associated Builders and Contractors, 1300 North 17th St., Rosslyn, VA 22209.

☛ Associated General Contractors of America, Inc., 1957 E St. NW., Washington, DC 20006.

☛ Home Builders Institute, National Association of Home Builders, 1201 15th St. NW., Washington, DC 20005.

☛ United Brotherhood of Carpenters and Joiners of America, 101 Constitution Ave. NW., Washington, DC 20001.

Carpet, Floor, and Tile Installers and Finishers

(O*NET 87308, 87602, 87605, and 87608)

Significant Points

- Over one-half of carpet, floor, and tile installers and finishers are self-employed.
- Working conditions are generally more pleasant than those of other construction trades, because carpet and tile and other floor coverings are installed in finished, or nearly finished, structures.
- Carpet, floor, and tile installers and finishers are less likely than other construction trades to be idled by slowdowns in construction or inclement weather.

Nature of the Work
Carpet, tile, and other types of floor coverings serve an important function in buildings, but their decorative qualities also contribute to the appeal of the buildings. Carpet, floor, and tile installers lay these floor coverings in homes, offices, hospitals, stores, restaurants, and many other types of buildings.

Before installing carpet, *carpet installers* first inspect the surface to be covered to determine its condition and, if necessary, correct any imperfections that could show through the carpet or cause the carpet to wear unevenly. They must measure the area to be carpeted and plan the layout, keeping in mind expected traffic patterns and placement of seams for best appearance and maximum wear.

When installing wall-to-wall carpet without tacks, installers first fasten a tackless strip to the floor, next to the wall. They then install the padded cushion or underlay. Next, they roll out, measure, mark, and cut the carpet, allowing for 2 to 3 inches of extra carpet for the final fitting. Using a device called a "knee kicker", they position the carpet, stretching it to fit evenly on the floor and snugly against each wall and door threshold. They then rough cut the excess carpet. Finally, using a power stretcher, they stretch the carpet, hooking it to the tackless strip to hold it in place. The installer then finishes the edges using a wall trimmer.

Because most carpet comes in 12-foot widths, wall-to-wall installations require installers to tape or sew sections together for large rooms. They join the seams by sewing them with a large needle and special thread or by using heat-taped seams—a special plastic tape made to join seams when activated with heat.

On special upholstery work, such as stairs, carpet may be held in place with staples. Also, in commercial installations, carpet is often glued directly to the floor or to padding that has been glued to the floor.

Carpet installers use handtools such as hammers, drills, staple guns, carpet knives, and rubber mallets. They also may use carpet-laying tools, such as carpet shears, knee kickers, wall trimmers, loop pile cutters, heat irons, and power stretchers.

Tile installers, or *tilesetters*, apply tile to floors, walls, and ceilings. Tile is durable, impervious to water, and easy to clean, making it a popular building material in hospitals, tunnels, lobbies of buildings, bathrooms, and kitchens. To set tile, which generally ranges in size from 1 inch to 12 inches square, tilesetters use cement or "mastic," a very sticky paste. When using cement, tilesetters nail a support of metal mesh to the wall or ceiling to be tiled. They use a trowel to apply a cement mortar—called a "scratch coat"—onto the metal screen and scratch the surface of the soft mortar with a small tool, similar to a rake. After the scratch coat has dried, tilesetters apply another coat of mortar to level the surface and then apply mortar to the back of the tile and place it onto the surface.

To set tile in mastic or a cement adhesive, called "thin set," tilesetters need a flat, solid surface such as drywall, concrete, plaster, or wood. They use a tooth-edged trowel to spread mastic on the surface or apply cement adhesive to the back of the tile and then properly position it.

Because tile varies in color, shape, and size, workers sometimes prearrange tiles on a dry floor according to a specified design. This allows workers to examine the pattern and make changes. In order to cover all exposed areas, including corners and around pipes, tubs, and wash basins, tilesetters cut tiles to fit with a machine saw or a special cutting tool. Once the tile is placed, they gently tap the surface with their trowel handle or a small block of wood to seat the tiles evenly.

When the cement or mastic has set, tilesetters fill the joints with "grout," very fine cement. They then scrape the surface with a rubber-edged device called a "squeegee" to dress the joints and remove excess grout. Before the grout sets, they finish the joints with a damp sponge for a uniform appearance. *Tile finishers* help some tilesetters by supplying and mixing construction materials and doing other tasks such as applying grout and cleaning installed tile.

Floor installers, or *floor layers*, apply blocks, strips, or sheets of shock-absorbing, sound-deadening, or decorative coverings to floors and cabinets using rollers, knives, trowels, sanding machines and other tools. Before installing the floor, floor layers inspect the surface to be covered and, if necessary, correct any imperfections in order to start with a smooth, clean foundation. They measure and cut floor covering materials, such as rubber, linoleum, or cork, and any foundation material, such as felt, according to designated blueprints. Next, they use an adhesive to cement the foundation material to the floor; the foundation helps to deaden sound and prevents the

Carpet installers tape or sew sections together for large rooms.

top floor covering from wearing at board joints. Finally, floor layers install the top covering. They join sections of sheet covering by overlapping adjoining edges and cutting through both layers with a knife to form a tight joint.

Working Conditions

Carpet, floor, and tile installers and finishers generally work indoors and regular daytime hours. However, when carpet installers recarpet stores or offices, they may work evenings and weekends to avoid disturbing customers or employees. Installers and finishers usually work under better conditions than most other construction workers. By the time workers install carpets, flooring, or tile in a new structure, most construction has been completed and the work area is relatively clean and uncluttered. Installing these materials is labor intensive; workers spend much of their time bending, kneeling, and reaching—activities that require endurance. Carpet installers frequently lift heavy rolls of carpet and may move heavy furniture. Safety regulations may require that they wear kneepads or safety goggles when using certain tools.

Although workers are subject to cuts from tools or materials, falls from ladders, and strained muscles, the occupation is not as hazardous as some other construction occupations.

Employment

Carpet, floor, and tile installers and finishers held about 138,000 jobs in 1998. Over one-half of all carpet, floor, and tile installers and finishers were self-employed compared to 1 of every 5 construction workers.

Many carpet installers worked for flooring contractors or floor covering retailers. Most wage and salary tilesetters were employed by tilesetting contractors who work mainly on nonresidential construction projects, such as schools, hospitals, and office buildings. Most self-employed tilesetters work on residential projects.

Although carpet, floor, and tile installers and finishers are employed throughout the Nation, they tend to be concentrated in populated areas where there are high levels of construction activity.

Training, Other Qualifications, and Advancement

The vast majority of carpet, floor, and tile installers and finishers learn their trade informally, on the job, as helpers to experienced workers. Others learn through formal apprenticeship programs, which include on-the-job training as well as related classroom instruction.

Informal training for carpet installers is often sponsored by individual contractors and generally lasts from about 1 1/2 to 2 years. Workers start as helpers, and begin with simple assignments, such as installing stripping and padding, or helping stretch newly installed carpet. With experience, helpers take on more difficult assignments, such as measuring, cutting, and fitting.

Persons who wish to begin a career in carpet installation as a helper or apprentice should be at least 18 years old and have good manual dexterity. Many employers prefer applicants with a high school diploma; courses in general mathematics and shop are helpful. Some employers may require a driver's license and a criminal background check. Because carpet installers frequently deal directly with customers, they should be courteous and tactful.

Many tile and floor layers learn their job through on-the-job training and begin by learning about the tools of the trade. They next learn to mix and apply cement. As they progress, tilesetters and floor layers learn to cut and install tile and floor coverings. Tile setters also learn to apply grout, and do finishing work.

Apprenticeship programs and some contractor-sponsored programs provide comprehensive training in all phases of the tilesetting and floor layer trade. Most apprenticeship programs are union sponsored and consist of weekly classes and on-the-job training usually lasting 3 to 4 years.

When hiring apprentices or helpers for floor layer and tilesetter jobs, employers usually prefer high school graduates who have had courses in general mathematics, mechanical drawing, and shop. Good physical condition, manual dexterity, and a good sense of color harmony also are important assets.

Carpet, floor, and tile installers and finishers may advance to positions as supervisors or become salespersons or estimators. Some carpet installers may become managers for large installation firms. Many carpet, floor, and tile installers and finishers who begin working for a large contractor eventually go into business for themselves as independent subcontractors.

Job Outlook

Employment of carpet, floor, and tile installers and finishers is expected to grow more slowly than the average for all occupations through the year 2008. Growth of carpet installers and floor layers will be due primarily to the continued need to renovate and refurbish existing structures. Carpet as a floor covering continues to be popular and its usage is expected to grow in structures such as schools, offices, hospitals, and industrial plants.

Demand for carpet will also be stimulated by new, more durable fibers that are stain and crush resistant, and come in a wider variety of colors. More resilient carpet needs to be replaced less often, but these attractive new products may induce more people to replace their old carpeting, contributing further to the demand for carpet installers.

Job opportunities for carpet installers are expected to be excellent as the growth in demand outpaces the supply of workers trained in this craft. This occupation is less sensitive to changes in economic conditions than most other construction occupations, because much of the work involves replacing carpet in existing buildings, and renovation work usually allows employment of carpet installers to remain relatively stable. In the many houses built with plywood rather than hardwood floors, wall-to-wall carpeting is a necessity. Similarly, offices, hotels, and stores often cover concrete floors with wall-to-wall carpet, which must be periodically replaced.

Demand for tilesetters will stem from population and business growth, which should result in more construction of shopping malls, hospitals, schools, restaurants, and other structures where tile is used extensively. Tile is expected to continue to increase in popularity as a building material and be used more extensively, particularly in more expensive homes, whose construction is expected to increase. In more modestly priced homes, however, the use of tile substitutes, such as plastic or fiberglass tub and shower enclosures, is expected to increase, slowing the growth in demand for tilesetters.

Job opportunities for tilesetters will not be as plentiful as in other construction occupations because the occupation is small and turnover is relatively low.

Earnings

In 1998, the median hourly earnings of carpet installers were $12.73. The middle 50 percent earned between $9.91 and $18.77. The lowest 10 percent earned less than $6.94 and the top 10 percent earned more than $24.05. Median hourly earnings in the industries employing the largest numbers of carpet installers in 1997 are shown below:

Industry	Earnings
Carpentry and floor work	$13.90
Furniture and home furnishings stores	10.90

Carpet installers are paid either on an hourly basis, or by the number of yards of carpet installed. The rates vary widely depending on the geographic location and whether the installer is affiliated with a union.

Median hourly earnings of tilesetters were $16.26 in 1998. The middle 50 percent earned between $11.97 and $20.68. The lowest 10 percent earned less than $8.92 and the top 10 percent earned more than $25.52. Earnings of tilesetters also vary greatly by geographic location and by union membership.

In 1998, the median hourly earnings of all other full-time carpet, floor, and tile installers and finishers were $12.42.

Apprentices and other trainees usually start out earning about half of what an experienced worker earns, though their wage rate increases as they advance through the training program.

Some carpet installers, floor layers, and tilesetters belong to the United Brotherhood of Carpenters and Joiners of America. Some tilesetters also belong to the International Union of Bricklayers and Allied Craftsmen, while some carpet installers belong to the International Brotherhood of Painters and Allied Trades.

Related Occupations

Carpet, floor, and tile installers and finishers measure, cut, and fit materials to cover a space. Workers in other occupations involving similar skills but using different materials, include bricklayers, carpenters, cement masons, concrete finishers, drywall installers and finishers, marblesetters, painters and paperhangers, roofers, sheet-metal workers, stonemasons, and terrazzo workers.

Sources of Additional Information

For details about apprenticeships or work opportunities, contact local flooring or tilesetting contractors or retailers; locals of the unions previously mentioned; or the nearest office of the State apprenticeship agency or the State employment service.

For general information about the work of carpet installers and floor layers, contact:

☛ Floor Covering Installation Contractors Association, P.O. Box 948, Dalton, GA 30722-0948.

Additional information on training for carpet installers and floor layers is available from:

☛ International Brotherhood of Painters and Allied Trades, 1750 New York Ave. NW., Washington, DC 20006.

For general information about the work of tilesetters and finishers, contact:

☛ International Union of Bricklayers and Allied Craftsmen, International Masonry Institute, Apprenticeship and Training, 815 15th St. NW., Washington, DC 20005.

For information concerning training of carpet installers, floor and tile setters, and finishers contact:

☛ United Brotherhood of Carpenters and Joiners of America, 101 Constitution Ave. NW., Washington, DC 20001.

Cement Masons, Concrete Finishers, and Terrazzo Workers

(O*NET 87311)

Significant Points

- Employment of cement masons, concrete finishers, and terrazzo workers will increase slowly as new technology makes these workers more productive.
- Most learn their trade on the job, either through formal 3-year apprenticeship programs or by working as helpers.
- Jobs are often outdoors and require a lot of bending and kneeling.

Nature of the Work

Cement masons, concrete finishers, and terrazzo workers all work with concrete, one of the most common and durable materials used in construction jobs. Once set, concrete—a mixture of Portland cement, sand, gravel, and water—becomes the foundation for everything from decorative patios and floors to huge dams or miles of roadways.

Cement masons place and finish the concrete. They may also color concrete surfaces, expose aggregate (small stones) in walls and sidewalks, or fabricate concrete beams, columns, and panels. In preparing a site for placing concrete, cement masons first set the forms for holding the concrete to the desired pitch and depth and properly align them. They then direct the casting of the concrete and supervise laborers who use shovels or special tools to spread it. Masons then guide a straightedge back and forth across the top of the forms to "screed," or level, the freshly placed concrete. Immediately after leveling the concrete, masons carefully smooth the concrete surface with a "bull float," a long-handled tool about 8 by 48 inches that covers the coarser materials in the concrete and brings a rich mixture of fine cement paste to the surface.

After the concrete has been leveled and floated, *concrete finishers* press an edger between the forms and the concrete and guide it along the edge and the surface. This produces slightly rounded edges and helps prevent chipping or cracking. They use a special tool called a "groover" to make joints or grooves at specific intervals that help control cracking. Next, finishers trowel the surface using either a powered or a hand trowel, a small, smooth, rectangular metal tool.

Sometimes, cement masons perform all steps of laying concrete, including the finishing. As the final step, masons retrowel the concrete surface back and forth with powered and hand trowels to create a smooth finish. For a coarse, nonskid finish, masons brush the surface with a broom or stiff-bristled brush. For a pebble finish, they embed small gravel chips into the surface. They then wash any excess cement from the exposed chips with a mild acid solution. For color, they use colored premixed concrete. On concrete surfaces that will remain exposed after forms are stripped, such as columns, ceilings, and wall panels, cement masons cut away high spots and loose concrete with hammer and chisel, fill any large indentations with a Portland cement paste and smooth the surface with a rubbing carborundum stone. Finally, they coat the exposed area with a rich Portland cement mixture using either a special tool or a coarse cloth to rub the concrete to a uniform finish.

Throughout the entire process cement masons must monitor how the wind, heat, or cold effects the curing of the concrete. They must have a thorough knowledge of concrete characteristics so that by using sight and touch they can determine what is happening to the concrete and take measures to prevent defects.

Terrazzo workers create attractive walkways, floors, patios, and panels by exposing marble chips and other fine aggregates on the surface of finished concrete. Much of the preliminary work of terrazzo workers is similar to that of cement masons.

When laying sidewalks, concrete masons carefully smooth the surface.

Attractive, marble-chip terrazzo requires three layers of materials. First, cement masons or terrazzo workers build a solid, level concrete foundation that is 3 to 4 inches deep. After the forms are removed from the foundation, workers add a 1-inch layer of sandy concrete. Before this layer sets, terrazzo workers partially embed metal divider strips into the concrete wherever there is to be a joint or change of color in the terrazzo. These strips separate the different designs and colors of the terrazzo panels and help prevent cracks. For the final layer, terrazzo workers blend and place into each of the panels a fine marble chip mixture that may be color-pigmented. They then hand trowel each panel until it is level with the tops of the ferrule strips. While the mixture is still wet, workers toss additional marble chips of various colors into each panel and roll a lightweight roller over the entire surface.

When the terrazzo is thoroughly dry, helpers grind it with a terrazzo grinder, which is somewhat like a floor polisher, only much heavier. Slight depressions left by the grinding are filled with a matching grout material and hand troweled for a smooth, uniform surface. Terrazzo workers then clean, polish, and seal the dry surface for a lustrous finish.

Working Conditions

Concrete or terrazzo work is fast-paced and strenuous and requires continuous physical effort. Because most finishing is done at floor level, workers must bend and kneel a lot. Many jobs are outdoors and work is generally halted during inclement weather. The work, either indoor or outdoor, may be in areas that are muddy, dusty, and dirty. To avoid chemical burns from uncured concrete and sore knees from frequent kneeling, many workers wear kneepads. Workers usually wear water-repellent boots while working in wet concrete.

Employment

Cement masons, concrete finishers, and terrazzo workers held about 139,000 jobs in 1998; terrazzo workers accounted for a very small proportion of the total. Most cement masons and concrete finishers worked for concrete contractors or for general contractors on projects such as highways, bridges, shopping malls, or large buildings such as factories, schools, and hospitals. A small number were employed by firms that manufacture concrete products. Most terrazzo workers worked for special trade contractors who install decorative floors and wall panels.

Only about 1 out of 20 cement masons, concrete finishers, and terrazzo workers was self-employed, a smaller proportion than in other building trades. Most self-employed masons specialized in small jobs, such as driveways, sidewalks, and patios.

Training, Other Qualifications, and Advancement

Cement masons, concrete finishers, and terrazzo workers learn their trades either through on-the-job training as helpers, by attending trade or vocational/technical schools, or through 3-year apprenticeship programs. Many masons and finishers first gain experience as construction laborers.

When hiring helpers and apprentices, employers prefer high school graduates who are at least 18 years old and in good physical condition and who have a driver's license. The ability to get along with others also is important because cement masons frequently work in teams. High school courses in general science, shop mathematics, blueprint reading, or mechanical drawing provide a helpful background.

On-the-job training programs consist of informal instruction from experienced workers in which helpers learn to use the tools, equipment, machines, and materials of the trade. They begin with tasks such as edging and jointing and using a straightedge on freshly placed concrete. As they progress, assignments become more complex, and trainees can usually do finishing work within a short time.

Three-year apprenticeship programs, usually jointly sponsored by local unions and contractors, provide on-the-job training in addition to a recommended minimum of 144 hours of classroom instruction each year. A written test and a physical exam may be required. In the classroom, apprentices learn applied mathematics, blueprint reading, and safety. Apprentices generally receive special instruction in layout work and cost estimating.

Cement masons, concrete finishers, and terrazzo workers should enjoy doing demanding work. They should have pride of craftsmanship and be able to work without close supervision.

Experienced cement masons, concrete finishers, or terrazzo workers may advance to become supervisors or contract estimators. Some open their own concrete businesses.

Job Outlook

Employment of cement masons, concrete finishers, and terrazzo workers is expected to grow more slowly than the average for all occupations through the year 2008. In addition to job openings that will stem from the rising demand for the services of these workers, other openings will become available as experienced workers transfer to other occupations or leave the labor force.

The demand for cement masons, concrete finishers, and terrazzo workers will rise as the population and the economy grow. They will be needed to build highways, bridges, subways, factories, office buildings, hotels, shopping centers, schools, hospitals, and other structures. In addition, the increasing use of concrete as a building material—particularly in nonresidential construction—will add to the demand. More cement masons also will be needed to repair and renovate existing highways, bridges, and other structures.

Employment growth of cement masons, concrete finishers, and terrazzo workers, however, will not keep pace with the growth of these construction projects. Workers' productivity will increase through use of improved concrete pumping systems, continuous concrete mixers, quicker setting cement, troweling machines, prefabricated masonry systems, and other improved materials, equipment, and tools.

Despite expected slow job growth, opportunities for skilled cement masons, concrete finishers, and terrazzo workers are expected to be excellent as the increase in demand outpaces the supply of workers trained in this craft. The pool of young workers, particularly those between the ages of 16 and 24, available to enter training programs will also increase slowly, and many in that group will be reluctant to seek training for jobs that may be strenuous and have uncomfortable working conditions.

Employment of cement masons, concrete finishers, and terrazzo workers, like that of many other workers, is sensitive to the fluctuations of the economy. Workers in these trades may experience periods of unemployment when the level of nonresidential construction falls. On the other hand, shortages of these workers may occur in some areas during peak periods of building activity.

Earnings

In 1998, the median hourly earnings of cement masons, concrete finishers, and terrazzo workers were $12.39. The middle 50 percent earned between $9.99 and $16.65. The top 10 percent earned over $22.04 and the bottom 10 percent earned less that $7.92. Median hourly earnings in the industries employing the largest numbers of cement masons, concrete finishers, and terrazzo workers in 1997 are shown below:

Industry	Earnings
Highway and street construction	$12.80
Concrete work	12.40
Heavy construction, except highway	12.30
Nonresidential building construction	11.40
Miscellaneous special trade contractors	11.20

Earnings for workers in these trades may be reduced on occasion, because poor weather and downturns in construction activity limit the time they can work. Cement masons often work overtime, with premium pay, because once concrete has been placed, the job must be completed.

Many cement masons, concrete finishers, and terrazzo workers belong to the Operative Plasterers' and Cement Masons' International Association of the United States and Canada, or to the International

Union of Bricklayers and Allied Craftsmen. Some terrazzo workers belong to the United Brotherhood of Carpenters and Joiners of the United States. According to the limited information available, average hourly earnings—including benefits—for cement masons who belonged to a union and worked full time, ranged between $15.40 and $46.80 in 1998. Cement masons in New York, Boston, San Francisco, Chicago, Los Angeles, Philadelphia, and other large cities received the highest wages. Nonunion workers generally have lower wage rates than union workers. Apprentices usually start at 50 to 60 percent of the rate paid to experienced workers.

Related Occupations
Cement masons, concrete finishers, and terrazzo workers combine skill with knowledge of building materials to construct buildings, highways, and other structures. Other occupations involving similar skills and knowledge include bricklayers, form builders, marble setters, plasterers, stonemasons, and tilesetters.

Sources of Additional Information
For information about apprenticeships and work opportunities, contact local concrete or terrazzo contractors; locals of unions previously mentioned; a local joint union-management apprenticeship committee; or the nearest office of the State employment service or State apprenticeship agency.

For general information about cement masons, concrete finishers, and terrazzo workers, contact:

☛ Associated General Contractors of America, Inc., 1957 E St. NW., Washington, DC 20006.

☛ International Union of Bricklayers and Allied Craftsmen, International Masonry Institute Apprenticeship and Training, 815 15th St. NW., Suite 1001, Washington, DC 20005.

☛ Operative Plasterers' and Cement Masons' International Association of the United States and Canada, 14405 Laurel Place, Suite 300, Laurel, MD 20707.

☛ National Terrazzo and Mosaic Association, 101 E. Market St., Suite 2004, Leesburg, VA 20176-3122.

☛ Portland Cement Association, 5420 Old Orchard Rd., Skokie, IL 60077.

☛ United Brotherhood of Carpenters and Joiners of America, 101 Constitution Ave. NW., Washington, DC 20001.

Construction Equipment Operators

(O*NET 87708, 97938, and 97956)

Significant Points

- Most acquire their skills on the job, but some construction equipment operators complete formal apprenticeship programs.
- Employment is expected to grow slowly due to slow overall growth in the construction industries.
- Workers in these occupations often have high pay rates, but many cannot work in inclement weather, thus reducing earnings.

Nature of the Work
Construction equipment operators use machinery to move construction materials, earth, and other heavy materials and to apply asphalt and concrete to roads and other substructures. Operators control equipment by moving levers or foot pedals, operating switches, or turning dials. The operation of much of this equipment is becoming more complex as a result of computerized controls. Construction equipment operators may also set up and inspect equipment, make adjustments, and perform minor repairs.

Construction equipment operators include grader, bulldozer, and scraper operators, operating engineers, and paving, surfacing, and tamping equipment operators. *Grader, bulldozer, and scraper operators* gouge out, distribute, level, and grade earth with vehicles equipped with a concave blade attached across the front. In addition to the familiar bulldozers, they operate trench excavators, road graders, and similar equipment. Operators maneuver the equipment in successive passes to raise or lower terrain to a specific grade. They may uproot trees and move large rocks while preparing the surface.

Operating engineers are unique in that they operate several different types of power construction equipment such as cranes, derricks, shovels, tractors, scrapers, pumps and hoists. They may operate cranes and derricks that lift materials, machinery, or other heavy objects from the ground. They extend or retract a horizontally mounted boom to lower, or raise a hook attached to the loadline, often in response to hand signals and radioed instructions from other workers. They also may operate excavation and loading machines equipped with scoops, shovels, or buckets that dig sand, gravel, earth, or similar materials and load it into trucks or onto conveyors. Sometimes they may drive and control industrial trucks or tractors equipped with a forklift or boom for lifting materials or hitches for pulling trailers. They also may operate and maintain air compressors, pumps, and other power equipment at construction work sites.

Paving and surfacing equipment operators use levers and other controls to operate machines that spread and level asphalt or spread and smooth concrete for roadways or other substructures. *Asphalt paving machine operators* turn valves to regulate the temperature and flow of asphalt onto the roadbed. They must watch that the machine distributes the paving material evenly and without voids and make sure there is a constant flow of asphalt going into the hopper. *Concrete paving machine operators* move levers and turn handwheels to lower an attachment that spreads, vibrates, and levels wet concrete within forms. They must observe the surface of concrete to point out low spots for workers to add concrete. They use other attachments to the machine to float the surface of the concrete, spray on a curing compound, and cut expansion joints. *Tamping equipment operators* operate tamping machines that compact earth and other fill materials for roadbeds. They also may operate machines with interchangeable hammers to cut or break up old pavement and drive guardrail posts into earth.

Working Conditions
Many construction equipment operators work outdoors, in nearly every type of climate and weather condition. Some machines, including bulldozers, scrapers, and particularly tampers, are noisy and shake or jolt the operator. As with most machinery, accidents generally can be avoided by observing proper operating procedures and safety practices.

Many construction equipment operators work outdoors in hot and cold weather and sometimes in rain or snow.

Some operators work in remote locations on large construction projects, such as highways and dams, or in factory or mining operations.

Employment

Construction equipment operators held about 321,000 jobs in 1998. Jobs were distributed as follows:

Operating engineers	126,000
Grader, bulldozer, and scraper operators	122,000
Paving, surfacing, and tamping equipment operators	74,000

About 3 out of every 5 construction equipment operators worked in the construction industry. Many equipment operators worked in heavy construction building structures such as bridges or railroads, and substructures such as highways and streets. About one-fourth of all construction equipment operators worked in State and local government. Others, mostly grader, bulldozer, and scraper operators, worked in mining. Some also worked in manufacturing and for utility companies. A few construction equipment operators were self-employed.

Construction equipment operators work in every section of the country.

Training, other qualifications and advancement

Construction equipment operators usually learn their skills on the job. Operators need a good sense of balance, the ability to judge distance, and good eye-hand-foot coordination. Employers of construction equipment operators generally prefer to hire high school graduates, although some employers may train persons having less education to operate some types of equipment.

The more technologically advanced construction equipment has computerized controls, which require different operating skills than in the past. Operators of such equipment may need more training and some understanding of electronics. Mechanical aptitude and high school training in automobile mechanics are helpful because workers may perform some maintenance on their machines. Experience operating related mobile equipment, such as farm tractors or heavy equipment in the Armed Forces, is an asset.

Beginning construction equipment operators handle light equipment under the guidance of an experienced operator. Later, they may operate heavier equipment such as bulldozers and cranes. Some construction equipment operators, however, train in formal 3-year operating engineer apprenticeship programs administered by union-management committees of the International Union of Operating Engineers and the Associated General Contractors of America. Because apprentices learn to operate a wider variety of machines than other beginners, they usually have better job opportunities. Apprenticeship programs consist of at least 3 years, or 6,000 hours, of on-the-job training and 144 hours a year of related classroom instruction.

Private vocational schools offer instruction in the operation of certain types of construction equipment. Completion of such a program may help a person get a job as a trainee or apprentice. However, persons considering such training should check the reputation of the school among employers in the area.

Job Outlook

Overall employment of construction equipment operators is expected to increase more slowly than the average for all occupations through the year 2008. About 60 percent of these workers are concentrated in the construction industry, which is projected to grow slowly over the next ten years. Although demand for most construction equipment operators should keep pace with growth of the construction industry, increased spending on improving the Nation's infrastructure of highways, bridges, and dams should result in slightly stronger demand for paving, surfacing, and tamping equipment operators. In addition to employment growth in this occupation, many jobs openings will arise because of the need to replace experienced workers who transfer to other occupations or leave the labor force.

Equipment improvements are also expected to continue to raise workers' productivity and moderate demand for skilled operators. Technological advances in hydraulics and electronics have led to better equipment that requires more skill to operate than was previously necessary. Precision computerized controls and robotics are automating many crane and tower operator and hoist and winch operator positions, slowing employment growth for operating engineers.

Employment of construction equipment operators is sensitive to fluctuations in the economy. Workers in these trades may experience periods of unemployment when the level of nonresidential construction activity falls.

Earnings

Earnings for construction equipment operators vary. In 1998, median hourly earnings of operating engineers were $16.95. The middle 50 percent earned between $12.72 and $22.34. The lowest 10 percent earned less than $10.32 and the highest 10 percent earned more than $31.09. Median hourly earnings in the industries employing the largest number of operating engineers in 1997 were:

Highway and street construction	$20.60
Heavy construction, except highway	19.90
Miscellaneous special trade contractors	19.20
Local government, except education and hospitals	13.50
State government, except education and hospitals	11.70

Median hourly earnings of grader, bulldozer, and scraper operators in 1998 were $12.94. The middle 50 percent earned between $10.64 and $17.07. The lowest 10 percent earned less than $8.94 and the highest 10 percent earned more than $21.83. Median hourly earnings in the industries employing the largest number of grader, bulldozer, and scraper operators in 1997 were:

Bituminous coal and lignite mining	$17.00
Highway and street construction	12.70
Miscellaneous special trade contractors	12.50
Heavy construction, except highway	12.00

Median hourly earnings of paving, surfacing, and tamping equipment operators in 1998 were $11.78. The middle 50 percent earned between $9.55 and $15.81. The lowest 10 percent earned less than $7.59 and the highest 10 percent earned more than $19.91. Median hourly earnings in the industries employing the largest number of paving, surfacing, and tamping equipment operators in 1997 were:

Highway and street construction	$12.00
Local government, except education and hospitals	11.30
Concrete work	11.10

Pay scales generally are higher in metropolitan areas. Annual earnings of some workers may be lower than hourly rates would indicate, because the amount of time they work may be limited by bad weather.

Related Occupations

Other workers who operate heavy mechanical equipment include truck and bus drivers, manufacturing equipment operators, logging equipment operators, and farmers and farm workers.

Sources of Additional Information

For further information about apprenticeships or work opportunities for construction equipment operators, contact a local of the International Union of Operating Engineers; a local apprenticeship committee; or the nearest office of the State apprenticeship agency. In addition, the local office of the State employment service may provide information about apprenticeship and other training programs.

For general information about the work of construction equipment operators, contact:

☛ National Center for Construction Education and Research, University of Florida, P.O. Box 141104, Gainesville, FL 32614-1104.

☛ Associated General Contractors of America, Inc., 1957 E St. NW., Washington, DC 20006.
☛ International Union of Operating Engineers, 1125 17th St. NW., Washington, DC 20036.

Drywall Installers and Finishers

(O*NET 87108, 87111, and 87114)

Significant Points

- Employment is projected to grow slowly, but thousands of job openings will arise annually because turnover is high.
- Inclement weather seldom interrupts work, but workers may be idled when downturns in the economy slow new construction activity.
- Most drywall installers and finishers learn the trade on the job, either by working as helpers or through a formal apprenticeship.

Nature of the Work

Drywall consists of a thin layer of gypsum between two layers of heavy paper. It is used today for walls and ceilings in most buildings because it is both faster and cheaper to install than plaster.

There are two kinds of drywall workers: installers and finishers. *Installers*, also called *applicators*, fasten drywall panels to the inside framework of residential houses and other buildings. *Finishers*, or *tapers*, prepare these panels for painting by taping and finishing joints and imperfections.

Because drywall panels are manufactured in standard sizes—usually 4 feet by 8 or 12 feet—installers must measure, cut, and fit some pieces around doors and windows. They also saw or cut holes in panels for electrical outlets, air-conditioning units, and plumbing. After making these alterations, installers may glue, nail, or screw the wallboard panels to the wood or metal framework. Because drywall is heavy and cumbersome, a helper generally assists the installer in positioning and securing the panel. A lift is often used when placing ceiling panels.

After the drywall is installed, finishers fill joints between panels with a joint compound. Using the wide, flat tip of a special trowel, they spread the joint compound into and along each side of the joint with brushlike strokes. They immediately use the trowel to press a paper tape—used to reinforce the drywall and to hide imperfections—into the wet compound and to smooth away excess material. Nail and screw depressions also are covered with this compound, as are imperfections caused by the installation of air-conditioning vents and other fixtures. On large commercial projects, finishers may use automatic taping tools that apply the joint compound and tape in one step. Finishers apply second and third coats, sanding the treated areas after each coat to make them as smooth as the rest of the wall surface. This results in a very smooth and almost perfect surface. Some finishers apply textured surfaces to walls and ceilings with trowels, brushes, or spray guns.

Drywall installers must measure, cut, and fit some drywall pieces around doors and windows.

Working Conditions

As in many other construction trades, drywall work sometimes is strenuous. Installers and finishers spend most of the day on their feet, either standing, bending, or kneeling. Some finishers use stilts to tape and finish ceiling and angle joints. Installers have to lift and maneuver heavy panels. Hazards include falls from ladders and scaffolds, and injuries from power tools. Because sanding joint compound to a smooth finish creates a great deal of dust, some finishers wear masks for protection.

Employment

Drywall installers and finishers held about 163,000 jobs in 1998. Most worked for contractors specializing in drywall installation; others worked for contractors doing many kinds of construction. Nearly 42,000 were self-employed independent contractors.

Most installers and finishers are employed in populated areas. In other areas, where there may not be enough work to keep a drywall installer employed full time, carpenters and painters usually do the drywall work.

Training, Other Qualifications, and Advancement

Most drywall workers start as helpers and learn their skills on the job. Installer helpers start by carrying materials, lifting and holding panels, and cleaning up debris. Within a few weeks, they learn to measure, cut, and install materials. Eventually, they become fully experienced workers. Finisher apprentices begin by taping joints and touching up nail holes, scrapes, and other imperfections. They soon learn to install corner guards and to conceal openings around pipes. At the end of their training, drywall installers and finishers learn to estimate the cost of installing and finishing drywall.

Some drywall installers and finishers learn their trade in an apprenticeship program. The United Brotherhood of Carpenters and Joiners of America, in cooperation with local contractors, administers an apprenticeship program in carpentry that includes instruction in drywall installation. In addition, local affiliates of the Associated Builders and Contractors and the National Association of Home Builders conduct training programs for nonunion workers. The International Brotherhood of Painters and Allied Trades conducts a 2-year apprenticeship program for drywall finishers.

Employers prefer high school graduates who are in good physical condition, but they frequently hire applicants with less education. High school or vocational school courses in carpentry provide a helpful background for drywall work. Regardless of educational background, installers must be good at simple arithmetic.

Drywall workers with a few years' experience and leadership ability may become supervisors. Some workers start their own contracting businesses.

Job Outlook

Replacement needs will account for almost all job openings for drywall installers and finishers through the year 2008. Thousands of jobs will open up each year because of the need to replace workers who transfer to jobs in other occupations or leave the labor force. Turnover in this occupation is very high, reflecting the lack of formal training requirements and the fluctuations of the business cycle, to which the construction industry is very sensitive. Because of their relatively weak attachment to the occupation, many workers with limited skills leave the occupation when they find they dislike the work or because they can't find steady employment.

Additional job openings will be created by the rising demand for drywall work. Employment is expected to grow more slowly than the average for all occupations, reflecting the slow growth of new construction and renovation. In addition to traditional interior work, the growing acceptance of insulated exterior wall systems will provide additional jobs for drywall workers.

Despite the growing use of exterior panels, most drywall installation and finishing is done indoors. Therefore, these workers lose less work time because of inclement weather than some other construction workers. Nevertheless, they may be unemployed between construction projects and during downturns in construction activity.

Earnings

In 1998, the median hourly earnings of drywall installers and finishers were $14.38. The middle 50 percent earned between $11.34 and $19.22. The lowest 10 percent earned less that $9.04 and the highest 10 percent earned more than $24.47.

Trainees usually started at about half the rate paid to experienced workers and received wage increases as they became more highly skilled.

Some contractors pay these workers according to the number of panels they install or finish per day; others pay an hourly rate. A 40-hour week is standard, but sometimes the workweek may be longer. Those who are paid hourly rates receive premium pay for overtime.

Related Occupations

Drywall installers and finishers combine strength and dexterity with precision and accuracy to make materials fit according to a plan. Other occupations that require similar abilities include carpenters, floor covering installers, form builders, insulation workers, and plasterers and stucco masons.

Sources of Additional Information

For information about work opportunities in drywall application and finishing, contact local drywall installation contractors; a local of the unions previously mentioned; a local joint union-management apprenticeship committee; a State or local chapter of the Associated Builders and Contractors; or the nearest office of the State employment service or State apprenticeship agency.

For details about job qualifications and training programs in drywall application and finishing, write to:

☛ Associated Builders and Contractors, Inc., 1300 North 17th St., Rosslyn, VA 22209.

☛ Home Builders Institute, National Association of Home Builders, 1201 15th St. NW., Washington, DC 20005.

☛ International Brotherhood of Painters and Allied Trades, 1750 New York Ave. NW., Washington, DC 20006.

☛ United Brotherhood of Carpenters and Joiners of America, 101 Constitution Ave. NW., Washington, DC 20001.

Electricians

(O*NET 87202A and 87202C)

Significant Points

- Job opportunities are expected to be very good for qualified electricians.
- Most electricians acquire their skills by completing a formal 4-or 5-year apprenticeship program.
- In contrast to other construction trades, about one-third of all electricians work in industries other than construction.

Nature of the Work

Electricity is essential for light, power, air-conditioning, and refrigeration. Electricians install, connect, test, and maintain electrical systems for a variety of purposes, including climate control, security, and communications. They also may install and maintain the electronic controls for machines in business and industry. Although most electricians specialize in either construction or maintenance, a growing number do both.

Electricians work with blueprints when they install electrical systems in factories, office buildings, homes, and other structures. Blueprints indicate the location of circuits, outlets, load centers, panel boards, and other equipment. Electricians must follow the National Electric Code and comply with State and local building codes when they install these systems. In factories and offices, they first place conduit (pipe or tubing) inside designated partitions, walls, or other concealed areas. They also fasten to the wall small metal or plastic boxes that will house electrical switches and outlets. They then pull insulated wires or cables through the conduit to complete circuits between these boxes. In lighter construction, such as residential, plastic-covered wire usually is used rather than conduit.

Regardless of the type of wire used, electricians connect it to circuit breakers, transformers, or other components. They join the wires by twisting ends together with pliers, and covering the ends with special plastic connectors. When stronger connections are required, electricians may use an electric "soldering gun" to melt metal onto the twisted wires, which they then cover with durable electrical tape. After they finish the wiring, they use testing equipment, such as ohmmeters, voltmeters, and oscilloscopes, to check the circuits

Electricians need color vision because wires are usually identified by color.

for proper connections, ensuring electrical compatibility and safety of components.

In addition to wiring a building's electrical system, electricians may install coaxial or fiber optic cable for computers and other telecommunications equipment. A growing number of electricians installs telephone, computer wiring and equipment, and fire alarm and security systems. They also may connect motors to electrical power and install electronic controls for industrial equipment.

Maintenance work varies greatly, depending on where the electrician is employed. Electricians who specialize in residential work may rewire a home and replace an old fuse box with a new circuit breaker to accommodate additional appliances. Those who work in large factories may repair motors, transformers, generators, and electronic controllers on machine tools and industrial robots. Those in office buildings and small plants may repair all types of electrical equipment.

Maintenance electricians spend much of their time in preventive maintenance. They periodically inspect equipment, and locate and correct problems before breakdowns occur. Electricians may also advise management on whether continued operation of equipment could be hazardous or not. When needed, they install new electrical equipment. When breakdowns occur, they must make the necessary repairs as quickly as possible in order to minimize inconvenience. Electricians may replace items such as circuit breakers, fuses, switches, electrical and electronic components, or wire. When working with complex electronic devices, they may work with engineers, engineering technicians, or industrial machinery repairers. (For information about each of these occupations, see the statements located elsewhere in the *Handbook*.)

Electricians use handtools such as screwdrivers, pliers, knives, and hacksaws. They also use power tools and testing equipment such as oscilloscopes, ammeters, and test lamps.

Working Conditions

Electricians' work is sometimes strenuous. They may stand for long periods of time and frequently work on ladders and scaffolds. Their working environment varies, depending on the type of job. Some may work in dusty, dirty, hot, or wet conditions, or in confined areas, ditches or other uncomfortable places. Electricians risk injury from electrical shock, falls, and cuts; to avoid injuries, they must follow strict safety procedures. Some electricians may have to travel to job sites, which may be up to 100 miles away.

Most electricians work a standard 40-hour week, although overtime may be required. Those in maintenance work may have to work nights, on weekends, and be on call. Companies that operate 24 hours a day may employ three shifts of electricians. Generally, the first shift is primarily responsible for routine maintenance, while the other shifts perform preventive maintenance.

Employment

Electricians held about 656,000 jobs in 1998. About two-thirds were employed in the construction industry. Others worked as maintenance electricians and were employed in virtually every industry. In addition, about 1 out of 10 electricians was self-employed.

Because of the widespread need for electrical services, jobs for electricians are found in all parts of the country.

Training, Other Qualifications, and Advancement

Most people learn the electrical trade by completing a 4- or 5-year apprenticeship program. Apprenticeship gives trainees a thorough knowledge of all aspects of the trade and generally improves their ability to find a job. Although more electricians are trained through apprenticeship than workers in other construction trades, some still learn their skills informally, on the job.

Large apprenticeship programs are usually sponsored by joint training committees made up of local unions of the International Brotherhood of Electrical Workers, and local chapters of the National Electrical Contractors Association. Training may also be provided by company management committees of individual electrical contracting companies and by local chapters of the Associated Builders and Contractors and the Independent Electrical Contractors. Because of the comprehensive training received, those who complete apprenticeship programs qualify to do both maintenance and construction work.

The typical large apprenticeship program provides at least 144 hours of classroom instruction each year, and 8,000 hours of on-the-job training over the course of the apprenticeship. In the classroom, apprentices learn blueprint reading, electrical theory, electronics, mathematics, electrical code requirements, and safety and first aid practices. They also receive specialized training in welding, communications, fire alarm systems, and cranes and elevators. On the job, under the supervision of experienced electricians, apprentices must demonstrate mastery of the electrician's work. At first, they drill holes, set anchors, and set up conduit. Later, they measure, fabricate, and install conduit, as well as install, connect, and test wiring, outlets, and switches. They also learn to set up and draw diagrams for entire electrical systems.

Those who do not enter a formal apprenticeship program can begin to learn the trade informally by working as helpers for experienced electricians. While learning to install conduit, connect wires, and test circuits, helpers also learn safety practices. Many helpers supplement this training with trade school or correspondence courses.

Regardless of how one learns the trade, previous training is very helpful. High school courses in mathematics, electricity, electronics, mechanical drawing, science, and shop provide a good background. Special training offered in the Armed Forces and by postsecondary technical schools also is beneficial. All applicants should be in good health and have at least average physical strength. Agility and dexterity also are important. Good color vision is needed because workers must frequently identify electrical wires by color.

Most apprenticeship sponsors require applicants for apprentice positions to be at least 18 years old and have a high school diploma or its equivalent. For those interested in becoming maintenance electricians, a background in electronics is increasingly important because of the growing use of complex electronic controls on manufacturing equipment.

Most localities require electricians to be licensed. Although licensing requirements vary from area to area, electricians usually must pass an examination that tests their knowledge of electrical theory, the National Electrical Code, and local electric and building codes.

Electricians periodically take courses offered by their employer or union to keep abreast of changes in the National Electrical Code, materials, or methods of installation.

Experienced electricians can become supervisors and then superintendents. Those with sufficient capital and management skills may start their own contracting business, although this may require an electrical contractor's license.

Job Outlook

Job opportunities for skilled electricians are expected to be very good as the growth in demand outpaces the supply of workers trained in this craft. There is expected to be a shortage of skilled workers during the next decade because of the anticipated smaller pool of young workers entering training programs.

Employment of electricians is expected to increase about as fast as the average for all occupations through the year 2008. Nearly two-thirds of wage and salaried electricians are concentrated in the construction industry, which is expected to grow more slowly than the average for all industries. Nevertheless, as the population and economy grow, more electricians will be needed to install and maintain electrical devices and wiring in homes, factories, offices, and other structures. New technologies also are expected to continue to stimulate the demand for these workers. Increasingly, buildings will be prewired during construction to accommodate use of computers and telecommunications equipment. More and more factories will be using robots and automated manufacturing systems. Installation of this equipment, which is expected to increase, should also stimulate demand for electricians. Additional jobs will be created by rehabilitation and retrofitting of existing structures.

In addition to jobs created by increased demand for electrical work, many openings will occur each year as electricians transfer to other occupations, retire, or leave the labor force for other reasons. Because of their lengthy training and relatively high earnings, a smaller proportion of electricians than other craft workers leave their occupation each year. The number of retirements is expected to rise, however, as more electricians reach retirement age.

Employment of construction electricians, like that of many other construction workers, is sensitive to changes in the economy. This results from the limited duration of construction projects and the cyclical nature of the construction industry. During economic downturns, job openings for electricians are reduced as the level of construction declines. Apprenticeship opportunities also are less plentiful during these periods.

Although employment of maintenance electricians is steadier than that of construction electricians, those working in the automotive and other manufacturing industries that are sensitive to cyclical swings in the economy may be laid off during recessions. Also, efforts to reduce operating costs and increase productivity through the increased use of contracting out for electrical services may limit opportunities for maintenance electricians in many industries. However, this should be partially offset by increased demand by electrical contracting firms.

Job opportunities for electricians also vary by area. Employment opportunities follow the movement of people and businesses among States and local areas, and reflect differences in local economic conditions. The number of job opportunities in a given year may fluctuate widely from area to area. Some parts of the country may experience an oversupply of electricians, for example, while others may have a shortage.

Earnings

In 1998, median hourly earnings of electricians were $16.98. The middle 50 percent earned between $12.69 and $22.34. The lowest 10 percent earned less than $10.07 and the highest 10 percent earned more than $30.99. Median hourly earnings in the industries employing the largest number of electricians in 1997 are shown below:

Industry	Earnings
Motor vehicles and equipment	$21.50
Local government, except education and hospitals	18.30
Electrical work	16.20
Personnel supply services	12.60

Depending on experience, apprentices usually start at between 30 and 50 percent of the rate paid to experienced electricians. As they become more skilled, they receive periodic increases throughout the course of the apprenticeship program. Many employers also provide training opportunities for experienced electricians to improve their skills.

Many construction electricians are members of the International Brotherhood of Electrical Workers. Among unions organizing maintenance electricians are the International Brotherhood of Electrical Workers; the International Union of Electronic, Electrical, Salaried, Machine, and Furniture Workers; the International Association of Machinists and Aerospace Workers; the International Union, United Automobile, Aerospace and Agricultural Implement Workers of America; and the United Steelworkers of America.

Related Occupations

To install and maintain electrical systems, electricians combine manual skill and knowledge of electrical materials and concepts. Workers in other occupations involving similar skills include air-conditioning mechanics, cable installers and repairers, electronics mechanics, and elevator installers and repairers.

Sources of Additional Information

For details about apprenticeships or other work opportunities in this trade, contact the offices of the State employment service, the State apprenticeship agency, local electrical contractors or firms that employ maintenance electricians, or local union-management electrician apprenticeship committees. This information may also be available from local chapters of the Independent Electrical Contractors, Inc.; the National Electrical Contractors Association; the Home Builders Institute; the Associated Builders and Contractors; and the International Brotherhood of Electrical Workers.

Additional information on apprenticeships is available from:

- The National Joint Apprenticeship and Training Committee for the Electric Industry, 301 Prince Georges Blvd., Suite D, Upper Marlboro, MD 20744.

For general information about the work of electricians, contact:

- Independent Electrical Contractors, Inc., 2010-A Eisenhower Avenue Alexandria, VA 22314.
- National Electrical Contractors Association (NECA), 3 Metro Center, Suite 1100, Bethesda, MD 20814. Internet: **http://www.recant.org**
- International Brotherhood of Electrical Workers (IBEW), 1125 15th St. NW., Washington, DC 20005. Internet: **http://www.IBEW.org**
- Associated Builders and Contractors, 1300 North 17th St., Rosslyn, VA 22209.
- Homebuilders Institute, National Association of Home Builders, 1201 15th St. NW., Washington, DC 20005.

Elevator Installers and Repairers

(O*NET 85932)

Significant Points

- Elevator installers and repairers learn the trade through years of on-the-job training, usually through a program run by their union.
- Almost 75 percent of elevator installers and repairers are union members—a greater proportion than nearly any other occupation.
- The combination of slow employment growth and the high pay these workers earn should continue to result in low job turnover and relatively few job openings.

Nature of the Work

Elevator installers and repairers—also called *elevator constructors* or *elevator mechanics*—assemble, install, and replace elevators, escalators, dumbwaiters, moving walkways, and similar equipment in new and old buildings. Once the equipment is in service, they maintain and repair it, as well. They are also responsible for modernizing older equipment.

To install, repair, and maintain modern elevators, which are almost all electronically controlled, elevator installers and repairers must have a thorough knowledge of electronics, electricity, and hydraulics. Many elevators today are installed with microprocessors, which are programmed to constantly analyze traffic conditions to dispatch elevators in the most efficient manner. With these computer controls, it is now possible to get the greatest amount of service with the least number of cars.

When installing a new elevator, installers and repairers begin by studying blueprints to determine the equipment needed to install rails, machines, car enclosures, motors, pumps, cylinders, and plunger foundations. Once this has been determined, they begin equipment installation. Working on scaffolding or platforms, installers bolt or weld steel rails to the walls of the shaft to guide the elevator.

Elevator installers put in electrical wires and controls by running tubing, called conduit, along a shaft's walls from floor to floor. Once in place, mechanics pull plastic-covered electrical wires through the conduit. They then install electrical components and related devices required at each floor and at the main control panel in the machine room.

Installers bolt or weld together the steel frame of an elevator car at the bottom of the shaft, install the car's platform, walls, and doors, and attach guide shoes and rollers to minimize the lateral motion of the car, as it travels through the shaft. They also install the outer doors and door frames at the elevator entrances on each floor.

For cabled elevators, these workers install geared or gearless machines with a traction drive wheel that guides and moves heavy steel cables connected to the elevator car and counterweight. (The counterweight moves in the opposite direction from the car and aids in its swift and smooth movement.) Elevator installers also install elevators in which a car sits on a hydraulic plunger that is driven by a pump. The plunger pushes the elevator car up from underneath, similar to a lift in an auto service station.

Installers and repairers also install escalators. They put in place the steel framework, the electrically powered stairs, and the tracks and install associated motors and electrical wiring. In addition to elevators and escalators, they also may install devices such as dumbwaiters and material lifts—which are similar to elevators in design—moving walkways, stair lifts, and wheelchair lifts.

The most highly skilled elevator installers and repairers, called "adjusters," specialize in fine-tuning all the equipment after installation. Adjusters make sure that an elevator is working according to specifications, such as stopping correctly at each floor within a specified time. Once an elevator is operating properly, it must be maintained and serviced regularly to keep it in safe working condition. Elevator maintenance mechanics generally do preventive maintenance—such as oiling and greasing moving parts, replacing worn parts, testing equipment with meters and gauges, and adjusting equipment for optimal performance. They also troubleshoot and may be called in to do emergency repairs.

Elevator installers need a working knowledge of electronics, electricity, and hydraulics.

A service crew usually handles major repairs—for example, replacing cables, elevator doors, or machine bearings. This may require cutting torches or rigging equipment—tools a maintenance mechanic would not normally carry. Service crews also do major modernization and alteration work, such as moving and replacing electrical motors, hydraulic pumps, and control panels.

Elevator installers and repairers usually specialize in installation, maintenance, or repair work. Maintenance and repair workers generally need more knowledge of electricity and electronics than installers do, because a large part of maintenance and repair work is troubleshooting. Similarly, construction adjusters need a thorough knowledge of electricity, electronics, and computers, to ensure that newly installed elevators operate properly.

Working Conditions

Most elevator installers and repairers work a 40-hour week. However, maintenance and service mechanics often work overtime when repairing essential elevator equipment and are sometimes on 24-hour call. Maintenance mechanics, unlike most elevator installers, are on their own most of the day and typically service the same elevators periodically.

Elevator installers lift and carry heavy equipment and parts and may work in cramped spaces or awkward positions. Hazards include falls, electrical shock, muscle strains, and other injuries related to handling heavy equipment. Because most of their work is performed indoors in buildings under construction or in existing buildings, elevator installers and repairers lose less work time due to inclement weather than other building trades workers.

Employment

Elevator installers and repairers held about 30,000 jobs in 1998. Most were employed by special trade contractors. Others were employed by field offices of elevator manufacturers, wholesale distributors, small, local elevator maintenance and repair contractors, or by government agencies or businesses that do their own elevator maintenance and repair.

Training, Other Qualifications, and Advancement

Most elevator installers and repairers apply for their jobs through a local of the International Union of Elevator Constructors. Applicants for trainee positions must be at least 18 years old, have a high school diploma or equivalent, and pass an aptitude test. Good physical condition and mechanical aptitude also are important.

Elevator installers and repairers learn their trade in a program administered by local joint educational committees representing the employers and the union. These programs, through which the trainee learns everything from installation to repair, combine on-the-job training with classroom instruction in electrical and electronic theory, mathematics, applications of physics, and safety. In nonunion shops they may complete training programs sponsored by independent contractors.

Generally, trainees or helpers must complete a 6-month probationary period. After successful completion, they work toward becoming fully qualified mechanics within 4 to 5 years. To be classified as a fully qualified mechanic, union trainees must pass a standard mechanics examination administered by the National Elevator Industry Educational Program. Most States and cities also require elevator constructors to pass a licensing examination.

Most trainees or helpers assist experienced elevator installers and repairers. Beginners carry materials and tools, bolt rails to walls, and assemble elevator cars. Eventually, trainees learn more difficult tasks, such as wiring, which requires knowledge of local and national electrical codes.

High school courses in electricity, mathematics, and physics provide a useful background. As elevators become increasingly sophisticated, workers may find it necessary to acquire more advanced formal education—for example, in postsecondary technical school or junior college—with an emphasis on electronics. Workers with more formal education usually advance more quickly than their counterparts.

Many elevator installers and repairers also receive training to become familiar with a company's particular equipment from their employers or through manufacturers. Retraining is very important to keep abreast of technological developments in elevator repair. In fact, union elevator constructors typically receive continual training throughout their careers, either through correspondence courses, seminars, or formal classes. Although voluntary, this training greatly improves one's chances for promotion.

Some installers may receive further training in specialized areas and advance to mechanic-in-charge, adjuster, supervisor, or elevator inspector. Adjusters, for example, may be picked for the position because they possess particular skills or are seen to be electronically inclined. Other workers may move into management, sales, or product design jobs.

Job Outlook

Employment of elevator installers and repairers is expected to increase as fast as the average for all occupations through the year 2008, but relatively few new job opportunities will be generated because the occupation is small. Replacement needs, another source of jobs, also will be relatively low. This is, in part, because a substantial amount of time is invested in specialized training that yields high earnings, so workers tend to remain in these jobs. The job outlook for new workers is largely dependent on activity in the construction industry, and opportunities may vary from year to year as conditions within the industry change. Job prospects should be best for those with postsecondary training in electronics or more advanced formal education.

Demand for elevator installers and repairers will increase as equipment ages and needs repairs and as the construction of new buildings with elevators and escalators increases. Growth also should be driven by the need to continually update and modernize old equipment, including improvements in appearance and the installation of increasingly sophisticated equipment and computerized controls. Because it's desirable that equipment be always kept in good working condition, economic downturns will have less of an effect on employment of elevator maintenance and repair mechanics than on other occupations. The need for people to service elevators and escalators should increase, as equipment becomes more intricate and complex.

Earnings

Median hourly earnings of elevator installers and repairers in 1998 were $23.01. The middle 50 percent earned between $18.41 and $32.20. The lowest 10 percent earned less than $14.22 and the top 10 percent earned more than $40.70.

In addition to free continuing education, elevator installers and repairers receive basic benefits enjoyed by most other workers.

The proportion of elevator installers and repairers who are union members is higher than nearly any other occupation. Almost 75 percent of elevator installers and repairers are members of a union, compared to 14 percent in all occupations, and 22 percent for other craft and repair occupations. Most elevator installers and repairers belong to the International Union of Elevator Constructors.

Related Occupations

Elevator installers and repairers combine electrical and mechanical skills with construction skills, such as welding, rigging, measuring, and blueprint reading. Other occupations that require many of these skills are boilermaker, electrician, industrial machinery repairer, millwright, sheet metal worker, and structural and reinforcing metal workers.

Sources of Additional Information

For further details about opportunities as an elevator installer and repairer, contact elevator manufacturers, elevator repair and maintenance contractors, a local of the International Union of Elevator Constructors, or the nearest local public employment service office.

Glaziers

(O*NET 87811)

Significant Points

- Glaziers learn the trade on the job, either through a formal apprenticeship or by working as helpers to experienced glaziers.
- Glazier employment is expected to increase slowly due to the slow growth anticipated in construction.

Nature of the Work

Glass serves many uses in modern buildings. Insulated and specially treated glass keeps in warmed or cooled air, and provides good condensation and sound control qualities; tempered and laminated glass makes doors and windows more secure. In large commercial buildings, glass panels give skyscrapers a distinctive look while reducing the need for artificial lighting. The creative use of large windows, glass doors, skylights, and sun room additions make homes bright, airy, and inviting.

Glaziers are the workers responsible for selecting, cutting, installing, replacing, and removing all types of glass. They generally work on one of several types of projects. Residential glazing involves work such as replacing glass in home windows, installing glass mirrors, shower doors and bathtub enclosures, and glass for table tops and display cases. On commercial interior projects, glaziers install items such as heavy, often etched, decorative room dividers and windows with speak holes and security glazing. Glazing projects may also involve replacement of storefront windows for establishments such as, supermarkets, auto dealerships, and banks. In the construction of large commercial buildings, glaziers build metal framework extrusions and install glass panels or curtainwalls.

Besides working with glass, glaziers may also work with plastics, granite, marble, and similar materials used as glass substitutes. They may mount steel and aluminum sashes or frames and attach locks and hinges to glass doors. For most jobs, the glass is precut and mounted in frames at a factory or a contractor's shop. It arrives at the job site ready for glaziers to position and secure it in place. They may use a crane or hoist with suction cups to lift large, heavy pieces of glass. They then gently guide the glass into position by hand.

Once glaziers have the glass in place, they secure it with mastic, putty, or other pastelike cement, or with bolts, rubber gaskets, glazing compound, metal clips, or metal or wood molding. When they secure glass using a rubber gasket—a thick, molded rubber half-tube with a split running its length—they first secure the gasket around the perimeter within the opening, then set the glass into the split side of the gasket, causing it to clamp to the edges and hold the glass firmly in place.

When they use metal clips and wood molding, glaziers first secure the molding to the opening, place the glass in the molding, and then force spring-like metal clips between the glass and the molding. The clips exert pressure and keep the glass firmly in place.

When a glazing compound is used, glaziers first spread it neatly against and around the edges of the molding on the inside of the opening. Next, they install the glass. Pressing it against the compound on the inside molding, workers screw or nail outside molding that loosely holds the glass in place. To hold it firmly, they pack the space between the molding and the glass with glazing compound and then trim any excess material with a glazing knife.

For some jobs, the glazier must cut the glass manually at the job site. To prepare the glass for cutting, glaziers rest it either on edge on a rack or "A-frame," or flat against a cutting table. They then measure and mark the glass for the cut.

Glaziers cut glass with a special tool that has a very hard metal wheel about 1/6 inch in diameter. Using a straightedge as a guide, the glazier presses the cutter's wheel firmly on the glass, guiding and rolling it carefully to make a score just below the surface. To help the cutting tool move smoothly across the glass, workers brush a thin layer of oil

Glaziers constantly lift, bend, and kneel.

along the line of the intended cut or dip the cutting tool in oil. Immediately after cutting, the glazier presses on the shorter end of the glass to break it cleanly along the cut.

In addition to handtools such as glass cutters, suction cups, and glazing knives, glaziers use power tools such as saws, drills, cutters, and grinders. An increasing number of glaziers use computers in the shop or at the job site to improve their layout work and reduce the amount of glass that is wasted.

Working Conditions

Glaziers often work outdoors, sometimes in inclement weather. At times, they work on scaffolds at great heights. They do a considerable amount of bending, kneeling, lifting, and standing. Glaziers may be injured by broken glass or cutting tools, falls from scaffolds, or from improperly lifting heavy glass panels.

Employment

Glaziers held about 44,000 jobs in 1998. About 3 out of every 5 glaziers worked for glazing contractors engaged in new construction, alteration, and repair. About 1 out of 5 worked in retail glass shops that install or replace glass and for wholesale distributors of products containing glass. Others worked in automotive repair stores.

Training, Other Qualifications, and Advancement

Many glaziers learn the trade informally on the job. They usually start as helpers, carrying glass and cleaning up debris in glass shops. They often practice cutting on discarded glass. After a while, they are given an opportunity to cut glass for a job. Eventually, helpers assist experienced workers on simple installation jobs. By working with experienced glaziers, they eventually acquire the skills of a fully qualified glazier.

Employers recommend glaziers learn the trade through a formal apprenticeship program that lasts 3 to 4 years. Apprenticeship programs, which are administered by the National Glass Association and local union-management committees or local contractors' associations, consist of on-the-job training, as well as 144 hours of classroom instruction or home study each year. On the job, apprentices learn to use the tools and equipment of the trade; handle, measure, cut, and install glass and metal framing; cut and fit moldings; and install and balance glass doors. In the classroom, they are taught basic mathematics, blueprint reading and sketching, general construction techniques, safety practices, and first aid. Learning the trade through an apprenticeship program usually takes less time and provides more complete training than acquiring skills informally on the job, but opportunities for apprenticeships are declining.

Local apprenticeship administrators determine the physical, age, and educational requirements needed by applicants for apprenticeships and for helper positions. In general, applicants must be in good physical condition and at least 17 years old. High school or vocational school graduates are preferred. In some areas, applicants must take mechanical aptitude tests. Courses in general mathematics, blueprint reading or mechanical drawing, general construction, and shop provide a good background.

Standards for acceptance into apprenticeship programs are rising to reflect changing requirements associated with new products and equipment. Glaziers need a basic understanding of electricity and electronics in order to be able to install electrochromatic glass and electronically controlled glass doors. In addition, the growing use of computers in glass layout requires more and more that glaziers be familiar with personal computers.

Because many glaziers do not learn the trade through a formal apprenticeship program, the National Glass Association (NGA) offers a series of written examinations which certify an individual's competency to perform glazier work at three progressively more difficult levels of proficiency. These levels include Level I, Glazier; Level II, Commercial Interior/Residential Glazier or Storefront/Curtainwall Glazier; and Level III, Master Glazier.

Advancement generally consists of increases in pay for most glaziers; some advance to supervisory jobs or become contractors or estimators.

Job Outlook

Employment of glaziers is expected to increase more slowly than the average for all occupations through the year 2008, as a result of anticipated slow growth in residential and non-residential construction.

Demand for glaziers will be spurred by the continuing need to modernize and repair existing structures and the popularity of glass in bathroom and kitchen design. Improved glass performance in insulation, privacy, safety, condensation control, and noise reduction are also expected to contribute to the demand for glaziers in both residential and nonresidential remodeling. Recent innovations include electrochromatic glass, water-shedding glass, distortion-free and high visibility glass, and self-tinting glass. A continuing emphasis on energy management, which encourages people to replace their old windows and doors with high efficiency products, will also spur the demand for glaziers. In addition to jobs due to employment growth, the need to replace experienced glaziers who retire or leave the occupation for other reasons is expected to create numerous openings.

People wishing to become construction glaziers should expect to experience periods of unemployment resulting from the limited duration of construction projects and the cyclical nature of the construction industry. During bad economic times, job openings for glaziers are reduced as the level of construction declines. Because construction activity varies from area to area, job openings, as well as apprenticeship opportunities, fluctuate with local economic conditions. Consequently, some parts of the country may experience an oversupply of these workers while others may have a shortage. Employment and apprenticeship opportunities should be greatest in metropolitan areas, where most glazing contractors and glass shops are located.

Earnings

In 1998, median hourly earnings of glaziers were $12.70. The middle 50 percent earned between $10.26 and $16.45. The lowest 10 percent earned less than $7.91 and the highest 10 percent earned more than $21.91. Median hourly earnings in the industries employing the largest number of glaziers in 1997 are shown below:

Miscellaneous special trade contractors	$12.50
Paint, glass, and wallpaper stores	11.20

Glaziers covered by union contracts generally earn more than their non-union counterparts. According to the limited information available, average hourly earnings—including benefits—for glaziers who belonged to a union and worked full time, ranged between $15.70 and $43.00 in 1998. Glaziers in New York, Boston, San Francisco, Chicago, Los Angeles, Philadelphia, and other large cities received the highest wages. Apprentice wage rates usually start at 50 to 60 percent of the rate paid to experienced glaziers and increase every 6 months. Because glaziers can lose time due to weather conditions and fluctuations in construction activity, their overall earnings may be lower than their hourly wages suggest.

Many glaziers employed in construction are members of the International Brotherhood of Painters and Allied Trades.

Related Occupations

Glaziers use their knowledge of construction materials and techniques to install glass. Other construction workers whose jobs also involve skilled, custom work are bricklayers, carpenters, floor layers, paperhangers, terrazzo workers, and tile setters.

Sources of Additional Information

For more information about glazier apprenticeships or work opportunities, contact local glazing or general contractors; a local of the International Brotherhood of Painters and Allied Trades; a local joint union-management apprenticeship agency; or the nearest office of the State employment service or State apprenticeship agency.

For general information about the work of glaziers, contact:

☛ International Brotherhood of Painters and Allied Trades, 1750 New York Ave. NW., Washington, DC 20006.

For information concerning training for glaziers contact:

☛ National Glass Association, Education and Training Department, 8200 Greensboro Dr., 3rd floor, McLean, VA 22102.

☛ Glass Association of North America, White Lakes Professional Building, 3310 Southwest Harrison St., Topeka, KS 66611-2279.

Hazardous Materials Removal Workers

(O*NET 87999 and 97989B)

Significant Points

- Formal education beyond high school is not required, but good mathematics skills are important to job performance.
- Employment is expected to grow about as fast as average; job openings will be available in all disciplines, especially lead abatement and decontamination jobs.

Nature of the Work

Increased public awareness and Federal and State regulations require the removal of hazardous materials from buildings, facilities and the environment to avoid further contamination of natural resources and to promote public health and safety. Hazardous materials removal workers identify, remove, package, transport and dispose of various hazardous materials, including asbestos, lead, and radioactive and nuclear materials. The removal of hazardous materials, or "hazmats," from public places and the environment is also called abatement, remediation and decontamination.

Hazardous materials removal workers use a variety of tools and equipment, depending on the work at hand. Equipment ranges from brooms to personal protective suits that are totally contained to avoid exposure. Depending on the threat of contamination, equipment required can include disposable or reusable coveralls, gloves, hard hats, shoe covers, safety glasses or goggles, chemical resistant clothing, face shields and hearing protection. Most workers are also required to wear respirators while working to protect them from airborne particles. These respirators range from simple versions that cover only the mouth and nose to self-contained suits with their own oxygen supply.

Asbestos is a material used in the past for fireproofing roofing, flooring and heat insulation and a variety of other uses. While materials containing asbestos are rarely used in buildings anymore, there are still structures containing the material. Fairly harmless when imbedded in materials, asbestos, when airborne, can cause several lung diseases, including lung cancer and asbestiosis.

Lead was a common building component found in paint and plumbing fixtures and pipes until the late 1970's. Because lead is easily absorbed into the bloodstream, it can travel to vital organs and build up there. The health risks associated with lead poisoning include fatigue, loss of appetite, miscarriage, and learning disabilities and decreased IQ in children. Due to these risks, it has become necessary to remove lead-based products and asbestos from buildings and structures.

Asbestos abatement and *lead abatement workers* remove these and other materials from buildings scheduled to be renovated or demolished. They use a variety of hand and power tools, such as vacuums and scrapers, to remove asbestos and lead from surfaces. The vacuums used by asbestos abatement workers have special, highly efficient filters designed to trap the asbestos, which is later disposed of or stored. During the abatement, special monitors for asbestos and lead content sample the air to protect the workers; lead abatement workers also wear a personal air monitor that indicates how much lead the worker has been exposed to. Workers also use monitoring devices to identify the asbestos, lead and other materials that need to be removed from the surfaces of walls and structures.

A typical residential lead abatement project involves using a chemical to strip the lead-based paint from the walls of the home. Lead abatement workers apply the compound with a putty knife and allow it to dry. Then they scrape the hazardous material into an impregnable container for transport and storage. They also use sandblasters and high-pressure water sprayers to remove lead from large structures.

Radioactive materials are classified as either high- or low-level wastes. High-level wastes primarily are nuclear reactor fuels used to produce electricity. Low-level wastes include any radioactively contaminated protective clothing, tools, filters, medical equipment, and other items. *Decontamination technicians* perform duties similar to janitors and cleaners. They use brooms, mops and other tools to clean exposed areas and remove exposed items for decontamination or disposal. With experience these workers can advance to *radiation protection technician* jobs and use radiation survey meters to locate and evaluate materials, operate high pressure cleaning equipment for decontamination, and package radioactive materials for transportation or disposal.

Decommissioning and decontamination (D&D) workers remove and treat radioactive materials generated by nuclear facilities and power plants. They use a variety of hand-tools to break down contaminated items such as "gloveboxes," which are used to process radioactive materials. At decommissioning sites the workers clean and decontaminate the facility, as well as remove any radioactive or contaminated materials.

Treatment, storage and disposal (TSD) workers transport and prepare materials for treatment or disposal. To insure proper treatment of materials, laws require workers in this field be able to verify shipping manifests. At incinerator facilities, these workers transport materials from the customer or service center to the incinerator. At landfills, they follow a strict procedure for the processing and storage of hazardous materials. They organize and track the location of items in the fill and may help change the state of a material from liquid to solid in preparation for its storage. These workers typically operate heavy machinery such as forklifts, earth moving machinery and large trucks and rigs.

Hazardous materials removal workers, whether working in asbestos and lead abatement or in radioactive decontamination, must stand, stoop and kneel for long periods of time. Workers may also be required to construct scaffolding or erect containment areas prior to the abatement or decontamination. Government regulation, in most cases, dictates that hazardous materials removal workers are closely supervised on the work site. The standard is usually one supervisor to every 10 workers. The work is very structured, planned out sometimes years in advance and team oriented. There is a great deal of cooperation among supervisors and coworkers. Due to the nature of the materials being removed, work areas are restricted to licensed hazardous materials removal workers, minimizing exposure to the public.

Working Conditions

Hazardous materials removal workers face different working conditions depending on their area of expertise. Although many work a standard 40-hour week, overtime and shift work is not uncommon, especially in asbestos and lead abatement. Asbestos and lead abatement workers tend to work primarily in buildings and other structures, such as office buildings and schools. Because they are under pressure to complete their work and must work around the schedules of others, completing projects often requires night and weekend work.

Treatment, storage and disposal workers are employed primarily at facilities such as landfills, incinerators, boilers and industrial furnaces. These facilities are often located in remote areas due to the kinds of work being done. As a result, workers employed by treatment, storage or disposal facilities may commute long distances to work.

Decommissioning and decontamination workers, decontamination technicians and radiation protection technicians work at nuclear facilities and electrical power plants. These sites, like treatment, storage and disposal facilities, also are often far from urban areas. They may need to use sharp tools to dismantle contaminated objects, often in cramped conditions. A hazardous materials removal worker must have great self-control and a level head to cope with the daily stress associated with working with hazardous materials.

A hazardous materials removal worker sprays to minimize dust during an asbestos abatement.

Hazardous materials removal employees work in a highly structured environment to minimize danger. Each phase of an operation is planned out in advance and workers are trained to deal with safety breaches and hazardous situations. Crew and supervisors take every precaution to insure the work site is safe. Some hazardous materials removal workers must wear fully enclosed personal protective suits for several hours at a time, which may be hot and uncomfortable and cause some individuals to experience claustrophobia.

Hazardous materials removal workers may be required to travel outside their normal working area in order to respond to emergency situations. These emergency cleanups sometimes take several days or weeks to complete and workers usually are away from home for the duration of the project.

Employment

Hazardous materials removal workers held about 38,000 jobs in 1998. About two-thirds were employed by special trade contractors, primarily in asbestos and lead abatement. The next largest industry of employment was sanitary services, including treatment, storage and disposal facilities. A small number worked in electric services at nuclear and electric plants as decommissioning and decontamination workers and radiation safety and decontamination technicians.

Training, Other Qualifications, and Advancement

Formal education beyond a high school diploma is not required to become a hazardous materials removal worker. However, workers must be able to perform basic mathematical conversions and calculations, manipulating readings for consideration during the abatement. To perform the job duties, workers should also have good physical strength and manual dexterity.

Federal regulations require a license to work as a hazardous materials removal worker. Most employers provide technical training on the job, but a formal 32- to 40-hour training program must be completed to be licensed to work as an asbestos and lead abatement worker or a treatment, storage, and disposal worker. The program covers health hazards, personal protective equipment and clothing, site safety, hazard recognition and identification, and decontamination. In some cases, workers will discover one hazardous material while abating another. If the workers are not licensed to work with the newly discovered material they cannot continue to work. Many experienced workers opt to take courses in additional disciplines to counteract this problem. Some employers prefer to hire workers licensed in multiple disciplines.

For decommissioning and decontamination workers employed at nuclear facilities, training is more extensive. In addition to the standard 40-hour training course in asbestos, lead, and hazardous waste, workers must take courses on regulations governing nuclear materials and radiation safety. These courses add up to approximately three months of training, though most are not taken consecutively. Many agencies, organizations and companies throughout the country provide training programs that are approved by the Environmental Protection Agency, the Department of Energy, and other regulatory bodies. Workers in all fields are required to take refresher courses every year to maintain their license.

Job Outlook

Overall employment in this occupation is expected to grow about as fast as the average for all occupations through the year 2008. Employment of the largest group of workers, asbestos and lead abatement workers, is expected to grow as fast as other occupations in special trade contractors, but opportunities will be best in lead abatement. Unlike other occupations in construction trades, employment for these workers is little affected by slowdowns in the economy.

Employment of decontamination technicians, radiation safety technicians, and decommissioning and decontamination workers is expected to grow due to increased pressure for safer and cleaner nuclear and electric generator facilities. In addition, the number of closed facilities that need decommissioning may continue to grow due to federal legislation. These workers are less affected by fluctuations in the economy because the facilities they work in must operate regardless of the state of the economy.

Earnings

Median hourly earnings of hazardous materials removal workers were $13.28 in 1998. The middle 50 percent earned between $10.76 and $17.85 per hour. The lowest 10 percent earned less than $9.26 per hour and the highest 10 percent earned more than $22.14 per hour.

According to the limited data available, treatment, storage and disposal workers usually earn slightly more than asbestos and lead abatement workers or decontamination technicians. Decontamination and decommissioning workers and radiation protection technicians, though comprising the smallest group, tend to earn the highest wages.

Related Occupations

Asbestos and lead abatement workers share similar skills with other construction trades workers, including bricklayers and stonemasons, concrete masons and terrazzo workers, insulation workers, and sheetmetal workers. Treatment, storage and disposal workers, decommissioning and decontamination workers, and decontamination and radiation safety technicians work closely with plant and system operators such as electric power generating plant operators and water and wastewater treatment plant operators.

Sources of Additional Information

For more information on hazardous materials removal workers, including training information, contact:

☛ Laborers-AGC Education and Training Fund, 37 Deerfield Rd., P.O. Box 37, Promfret, CT 06259.

Insulation Workers

(O*NET 87802)

Significant Points

- Opportunities for insulation workers are expected to be favorable because of high turnover.
- Most insulation workers learn informally on the job; others complete formal apprenticeship programs.

Nature of the Work

Properly insulated buildings reduce energy consumption by keeping heat in during the winter and out in the summer. Refrigerated storage rooms, vats, tanks, vessels, boilers, and steam and hot water pipes also are insulated to prevent the wasteful transfer of heat. Insulation workers install the materials used to insulate buildings and equipment.

Insulation workers cement, staple, wire, tape, or spray insulation. When covering a steam pipe, for example, insulation workers measure and cut sections of insulation to the proper length, stretch it open along a cut that runs the length of the material, and slip it over the pipe. They fasten the insulation with adhesive, staples, tape, or wire bands. Sometimes they wrap a cover of aluminum, plastic, or canvas over it and cement or band the cover in place. Insulation workers may screw on sheet metal around insulated pipes to protect the insulation from weather conditions or physical abuse.

When covering a wall or other flat surface, workers may use a hose to spray foam insulation onto a wire mesh. The wire mesh provides a rough surface to which the foam can cling, and adds strength to the finished surface. Workers may then install drywall or apply a final coat of plaster for a finished appearance.

In attics or exterior walls of uninsulated buildings, workers blow in loose-fill insulation. A helper feeds a machine with fiberglass, cellulose, or rock wool insulation while another worker blows the insulation with a compressor hose into the space being filled.

Insulation workers remove asbestos from buildings.

In new construction or major renovations, insulation workers staple fiberglass or rockwool batts to exterior walls and ceilings before drywall, paneling, or plaster walls are put in place. In major renovations of old buildings or when putting new insulation around pipes and industrial machinery, insulation workers often must first remove the old insulation. In the past, asbestos—now known to cause cancer in humans—was used extensively in walls and ceilings and for covering pipes, boilers, and various industrial equipment. Because of this danger, U.S. Environmental Protection Agency regulations require that asbestos be removed before a building undergoes major renovations or is demolished. When asbestos is present, specially trained workers must remove the asbestos before insulation workers can install the new insulating materials. (See the statement on hazardous materials removal workers elsewhere in the *Handbook*.)

Insulation workers use common handtools—trowels, brushes, knives, scissors, saws, pliers, and stapling guns. They use power saws to cut insulating materials, welding machines to join sheet metal or secure clamps, and compressors for blowing or spraying insulation.

Working Conditions

Insulation workers generally work indoors. They spend most of the workday on their feet, either standing, bending, or kneeling. Sometimes, they work from ladders or in tight spaces. The work requires more coordination than strength. Insulation work is often dusty and dirty, and the summer heat can make the insulation worker very uncomfortable. The minute particles from insulation materials, especially when blown, can irritate the eyes, skin, and respiratory system. Workers follow strict safety guidelines to protect themselves from the dangers of insulating irritants, keeping work areas well ventilated, wearing protective suits, masks, and respirators, and taking decontamination showers when necessary.

Employment
Insulation workers held about 67,000 jobs in 1998. The construction industry employed 9 out of 10; most worked for insulation or other construction trades contractors. Small numbers of insulation workers held jobs in the Federal Government, in wholesale trade, and in shipbuilding and other manufacturing industries that have extensive installations for power, heating, and cooling. Most worked in urban areas. In less populated areas, carpenters, heating and air-conditioning installers, or drywall installers may do insulation work.

Training, Other Qualifications, and Advancement
Most insulation workers learn their trade informally on the job, although some workers complete formal apprenticeship programs. For entry jobs, insulation contractors prefer high school graduates who are in good physical condition and licensed to drive. High school courses in blueprint reading, shop math, sheet-metal layout, and general construction provide a helpful background. Applicants seeking apprenticeship positions must have a high school diploma or its equivalent, and be at least 18 years old.

Trainees who learn on the job receive instruction and supervision from experienced insulation workers. Trainees begin with simple tasks, such as carrying insulation or holding material while it is fastened in place. On-the-job training can take up to 2 years, depending on the work. Learning to install insulation in homes generally requires less training than insulation application in commercial and industrial settings. As they gain experience, trainees receive less supervision, more responsibility, and higher pay.

In contrast, trainees in formal apprenticeship programs receive in-depth instruction in all phases of insulation. Apprenticeship programs may be provided by a joint committee of local insulation contractors and the local union of the International Association of Heat and Frost Insulators and Asbestos Workers, to which many insulation workers belong. Programs normally consist of 4 years of on-the-job training coupled with classroom instruction, and trainees must pass practical and written tests to demonstrate knowledge of the trade.

Skilled insulation workers may advance to supervisor, shop superintendent, insulation contract estimator, or set up their own insulation business.

Job Outlook
Opportunities for insulation workers are expected to be favorable. Employment of insulation workers is expected to increase more slowly than the average for all occupations through the year 2008, but replacement needs are usually high due to the many workers who transfer to other occupations. Concerns about the efficient use of energy to heat and cool buildings will result in growth in demand for insulation workers in the construction of new residential, industrial, and commercial buildings. In addition, renovation and efforts to improve insulation in existing structures also will increase demand.

Despite growth in demand, replacement needs will account for most job openings. Each year thousands of jobs will become available as insulation workers transfer to other occupations or leave the labor force. There are no strict training requirements for entry, and many people with limited skills work as insulation workers for a short time and then move on to other types of work, creating many job openings.

Insulation workers in the construction industry may experience periods of unemployment because of the short duration of many construction projects and the cyclical nature of construction activity. Workers employed in industrial plants generally have more stable employment because maintenance and repair must be done on a continuing basis. Most insulation is applied after buildings are enclosed.

Earnings
In 1998, median hourly earnings of insulation workers were $12.25. The middle 50 percent earned between $9.71 and $15.94. The lowest 10 percent earned less than $7.52 and the highest 10 percent earned more than $22.62. Median hourly earnings in the industries employing the largest number of insulation workers in 1997 are shown below:

Miscellaneous special trade contractors	$12.90
Masonry, stonework, and plastering	10.80

According to the limited information available, average hourly earnings—including benefits—for insulation workers who belonged to a union and worked full time, ranged between $22.10 and $48.70 in 1998. Insulation workers in New York, Boston, San Francisco, Chicago, Los Angeles, Philadelphia, and other large cities received the highest wages. Insulation workers doing commercial and industrial work earn substantially more than those working in residential construction, which does not require as much skill.

Related Occupations
Insulation workers combine their knowledge of insulation materials with the skills of cutting, fitting, and installing materials. Workers in occupations involving similar skills include carpenters, carpet installers, drywall installers and finishers, floor layers, roofers, and sheet-metal workers and duct installers.

Sources of Additional Information
For information about training programs or other work opportunities in this trade, contact a local insulation contractor; a local chapter of the International Association of Heat and Frost Insulators and Asbestos Workers; the nearest office of the State employment service or State apprenticeship agency, or:

☛ International Association of Heat and Frost Insulators and Asbestos Workers, 1776 Massachusetts Ave. NW., Suite 301, Washington, DC 20036

☛ National Insulation Contractors Association, 99 Canal Center Plaza, Suite 222, Alexandria, VA 22314.

☛ Insulation Contractors Association of America, 1321 Duke St., Suite 303, Alexandria, VA 22314.

Painters and Paperhangers

(O*NET 87402A and 87402B)

Significant Points

- Painters and paperhangers are one of the larger construction occupations.
- Most painters and paperhangers learn their craft informally on the job as helpers to experienced painters.
- Opportunities for jobs should be good due to high job turnover in the occupation.

Nature of the Work
Paint and wall coverings make surfaces clean, attractive and bright. In addition, paints and other sealers protect outside walls from wear caused by exposure to the weather. Although some people do both painting and paperhanging, each requires different skills.

Painters apply paint, stain, varnish, and other finishes to buildings and other structures. They choose the right paint or finish for the surface to be covered, taking into account durability, ease of handling, method of application, and customers' wishes. Painters first prepare the surfaces to be covered so the paint will adhere properly. This may require removing the old coat by stripping, sanding, wire brushing, burning, or water and abrasive blasting. Painters also wash walls and trim to remove dirt and grease, fill nail holes and cracks, sandpaper rough spots,

Painters prepare the surfaces to be covered so the paint will adhere properly.

and brush off dust. On new surfaces, they apply a primer or sealer to prepare the surface for the finish coat. Painters also mix paints and match colors, relying on knowledge of paint composition and color harmony. In large paint shops or hardware stores, this function is automated.

There are several ways to apply paint and similar coverings. Painters must be able to choose the right paint applicator for each job, depending on the surface to be covered, the characteristics of the finish, and other factors. Some jobs only need a good bristle brush with a soft, tapered edge; others require a dip or fountain pressure roller; still others can best be done using a paint sprayer. Many jobs need several types of applicators. The right tools for each job not only expedite the painter's work but also produce the most attractive surface.

When working on tall buildings, painters erect scaffolding, including "swing stages," scaffolds suspended by ropes, or cables attached to roof hooks. When painting steeples and other conical structures, they use a "bosun chair," a swinglike device.

Paperhangers cover walls and ceilings with decorative wall coverings made of paper, vinyl, or fabric. They first prepare the surface to be covered by applying "sizing," which seals the surface and makes the covering stick better. When redecorating, they may first remove the old covering by soaking, steaming, or applying solvents. When necessary, they patch holes and take care of other imperfections before hanging the new wall covering.

After the surface has been prepared, paperhangers must prepare the paste or other adhesive. Then they measure the area to be covered, check the covering for flaws, cut the covering into strips of the proper size, and closely examine the pattern to match it when the strips are hung.

The next step is to brush or roll the adhesive onto the back of the covering, then to place the strips on the wall or ceiling, making sure the pattern is matched, the strips are hung straight, and the edges butted together to make tight, closed seams. Finally, paperhangers smooth the strips to remove bubbles and wrinkles, trim the top and bottom with a razor knife, and wipe off any excess adhesive.

Working Conditions

Most painters and paperhangers work 40 hours a week or less; about 1 out of 10 works part time. Painters and paperhangers must stand for long periods. Their jobs also require a considerable amount of climbing and bending. These workers must have stamina because much of the work is done with their arms raised overhead. Painters often work outdoors, but seldom in wet, cold, or inclement weather.

Painters and paperhangers risk injury from slips or falls off ladders and scaffolds. They may sometimes work with materials that can be hazardous if masks are not worn or if ventilation is poor. Some painting iobs can leave a worker covered with paint.

Employment

Painters and paperhangers held about 476,000 jobs in 1998; most were painters. Almost 2 out of every 3 painters and paperhangers work for contractors engaged in new construction, repair, restoration, or remodeling work. In addition, organizations that own or manage large buildings, such as apartment complexes, employ maintenance painters, as do some schools, hospitals, factories, and government agencies.

Self-employed independent painting contractors accounted for over 40 percent of all painters and paperhangers, significantly greater than the proportion of building trades workers in general.

Training, Other Qualifications, and Advancement

Painting and paperhanging are learned through apprenticeship or informal, on-the-job instruction. Although training authorities recommend completion of an apprenticeship program as the best way to become a painter or paperhanger, most painters learn the trade informally on the job as a helper to an experienced painter. Few opportunities for informal training exist for paperhangers because few paperhangers have a need for helpers.

The apprenticeship for painters and paperhangers consists of 3 to 4 years of on-the-job training, in addition to 144 hours of related classroom instruction each year. Apprentices receive instruction in color harmony, use and care of tools and equipment, surface preparation, application techniques, paint mixing and matching, characteristics of different finishes, blueprint reading, wood finishing, and safety.

Whether a painter learns the trade through a formal apprenticeship or informally as a helper, on-the-job instruction covers similar skill areas. Under the direction of experienced workers, trainees carry supplies, erect scaffolds, and do simple painting and surface preparation tasks while they learn about paint and painting equipment. Within 2 or 3 years, trainees learn to prepare surfaces for painting and paperhanging, to mix paints, and to apply paint and wall coverings efficiently and neatly. Near the end of their training, they may learn decorating concepts, color coordination, and cost-estimating techniques. In addition to learning craft skills, painters must become familiar with safety and health regulations so their work is in compliance with the law.

Apprentices or helpers generally must be at least 16 years old and in good physical condition. A high school education or its equivalent, with courses in mathematics, is usually required to enter an apprenticeship program. Applicants should have good manual dexterity and good color sense.

Painters and paperhangers may advance to supervisory or estimating jobs with painting and decorating contractors. Many establish their own painting and decorating businesses.

Job Outlook

Employment of painters and paperhangers is expected to grow more slowly than the average for all occupations through the year 2008, as the level of new construction increases slowly and the stock of buildings and other structures that require maintenance and renovation grows. Painting is very labor intensive and not suitable to the kinds of technological changes that might make workers more productive and restrict employment growth.

In addition to job openings created by rising demand for the services of these workers, thousands of jobs will become available each year as painters and paperhangers transfer to other occupations or leave the labor force. There are no strict training requirements for entry, so many people with limited skills work as painters or paperhangers for a short time and then move on to other types of work, creating many job openings. Many fewer openings will occur for paperhangers because the number of these jobs is comparatively small.

Because there are no strict training requirements, prospects for jobs as painters or paperhangers should be favorable. However, job seekers considering these occupations should expect some periods of unemployment, especially until they become fully skilled. Many construction projects are of short duration, and construction activity is cyclical and seasonal in nature. Remodeling, restoration, and maintenance projects, however, often provide many jobs for painters and paperhangers even when new construction activity declines. The most versatile painters and skilled paperhangers generally are most able to keep working steadily during downturns in the economy.

Earnings

In 1998, median hourly earnings of painters and paperhangers were $12.07. The middle 50 percent earned between $9.81 and $16.16. The lowest 10 percent earned less than $7.50 and the highest 10 percent earned more than $21.40. Median hourly earnings in the industries employing the largest numbers of painters and paperhangers in 1997 are shown below:

Industry	Earnings
Local government, except education and hospitals	$16.90
Painting and paper hanging	11.60
Miscellaneous special trade contractors	11.40
Residential building construction	10.70
Real estate operators and lessors	9.20

In general, paperhangers earn more than painters. Earnings for painters may be reduced on occasion because of bad weather and the short-term nature of many construction jobs.

Hourly wage rates for apprentices usually start at 40 to 50 percent of the rate for experienced workers and increase periodically.

Some painters and paperhangers are members of the International Brotherhood of Painters and Allied Trades. Some maintenance painters are members of other unions.

Related Occupations

Painters and paperhangers apply various coverings to decorate and protect wood, drywall, metal, and other surfaces. Other occupations in which workers apply paints and similar finishes include billboard posterers, metal sprayers, undercoaters, and transportation equipment painters.

Sources of Additional Information

For details about painting and paperhanging apprenticeships or work opportunities, contact local painting and decorating contractors; a local of the International Brotherhood of Painters and Allied Trades; a local joint union-management apprenticeship committee; or an office of the State apprenticeship agency or State employment service.

For general information about the work of painters and paperhangers, contact:

☛ Associated Builders and Contractors, 1300 North 17th St., Rosslyn, VA 22209.

☛ International Brotherhood of Painters and Allied Trades, 1750 New York Ave. NW., Washington, DC 20006.

☛ Home Builders Institute, National Association of Home Builders, 1201 15th St. NW., Washington, DC 20005.

Plasterers and Stucco Masons

(O*NET 87317)

Significant Points

- Plasterers and stucco masons are projected to be one of the fastest growing occupations in construction trades, increasing about as fast as the average for all occupations.
- The use of plaster in new building construction is regaining popularity because of its durability, finish, and fire-retardant qualities.
- Plastering usually is learned on the job, either through a formal apprenticeship program or by working as a helper.

Nature of the Work

Plastering—one of the oldest crafts in the building trades—is enjoying resurgence in popularity because of the introduction of newer, less costly materials and techniques. Plasterers apply plaster to interior walls and ceilings to form fire-resistant and relatively soundproof surfaces. They also apply plaster veneer over drywall to create smooth or textured abrasion-resistant finishes. In addition, plasterers install prefabricated exterior insulation systems over existing walls—for good insulation and interesting architectural effects—and cast ornamental designs in plaster. Stucco masons apply durable plasters, such as polymer-based acrylic finishes and stucco to exterior surfaces. Drywall workers and lathers, a related occupation, use drywall instead of plaster, when erecting interior walls and ceilings. (See the section on drywall workers and lathers elsewhere in the *Handbook*.)

When plasterers work with interior surfaces such as cinder block and concrete, they first apply a brown coat of gypsum plaster that provides a base, followed by a second or finish coat—also called "white coat"—which is a lime-based plaster. When plastering metal lath (supportive wire mesh) foundations, they apply a preparatory, or "scratch coat," with a trowel. They spread this rich plaster mixture into and over the metal lath. Before the plaster sets, plasterers scratch its surface with a rake-like tool to produce ridges, so the subsequent brown coat will bond tightly.

Laborers prepare a thick, smooth plaster for the brown coat. Plasterers spray or trowel this mixture onto the surface, then finish by smoothing it to an even, level surface.

Plasterers apply durable plasters such as polymer-based acrylic finishes and stucco to exterior surfaces.

For the finish coat, plasterers prepare a mixture of lime, plaster of Paris, and water. They quickly apply this onto the brown coat using a "hawk"—a light, metal plate with a handle—trowel, brush, and water. This mixture, which sets very quickly, produces a very smooth, durable finish.

Plasterers also work with a plaster material that can be finished in a single coat. This "thin-coat" or gypsum veneer plaster is made of lime and plaster of Paris and is mixed with water at the job site. This plaster provides a smooth, durable, abrasion resistant finish on interior masonry surfaces, special gypsum baseboard, or drywall prepared with a bonding agent.

Plasterers create decorative interior surfaces as well. They do this by pressing a brush or trowel firmly against a wet plaster surface and using a circular hand motion to create decorative swirls.

For exterior work, stucco masons usually apply stucco—a mixture of Portland cement, lime, and sand—over cement, concrete, masonry, or lath. Stucco may also be applied directly to a wire lath with a scratch coat followed by a brown coat and then a finish coat. Stucco masons may also embed marble or gravel chips into the finish coat to achieve a pebblelike, decorative finish.

Increasingly, plasterers apply insulation to the exteriors of new and old buildings. They cover the outer wall with rigid foam insulation board and reinforcing mesh and then trowel on a polymer-based or polymer-modified base coat. They may apply an additional coat of this material with a decorative finish.

Plasterers sometimes do complex decorative and ornamental work that requires special skill and creativity. For example, they may mold intricate wall and ceiling designs. Following an architect's blueprint, plasterers pour or spray a special plaster into a mold and allow it to set. Workers then remove the molded plaster and put it in place, according to the plan.

Working Conditions

Most plastering jobs are indoors; however, plasterers and stucco masons work outside when applying stucco or exterior wall insulation and decorative finish systems. Sometimes plasterers work on scaffolds high above the ground.

Plastering is physically demanding, requiring considerable standing, bending, lifting, and reaching overhead. The work can be dusty and dirty, soiling shoes and clothing, and can irritate the skin and eyes.

Employment

Plasterers and stucco masons held about 40,000 jobs in 1998. Most plasterers and stucco masons work on new construction sites, particularly where special architectural and lighting effects are part of the work. Some repair and renovate older buildings. Many plasterers and stucco masons are employed in Florida, California, and the Southwest, where exterior plasters with decorative finishes are very popular.

Most plasterers and stucco masons work for independent contractors. About 1 out of every 6 plasterers and stucco masons is self-employed.

Training, Other Qualifications, and Advancement

Although most employers recommend apprenticeship as the best way to learn plastering, many people learn the trade by working as helpers to experienced plasterers and stucco masons. Those who learn the trade informally as helpers usually start by carrying materials, setting up scaffolds, and mixing plaster. Later they learn to apply the scratch, brown, and finish coats.

Apprenticeship programs, sponsored by local joint committees of contractors and unions, generally consist of 2 or 3 years of on-the-job training, in addition to at least 144 hours annually of classroom instruction in drafting, blueprint reading, and mathematics for layout work.

In the classroom, apprentices start with a history of the trade and the industry. They also learn about the uses of plaster, estimating materials and costs, and casting ornamental plaster designs. On the job, they learn about lath bases, plaster mixes, methods of plastering, blueprint reading, and safety. They also learn how to use various tools, such as hand and powered trowels, floats, brushes, straightedges, power tools, plaster-mixing machines, and piston-type pumps. Some apprenticeship programs allow individuals to obtain training in related occupations, such as cement masonry and bricklaying.

Applicants for apprentice or helper jobs normally must be at least 17 years old, in good physical condition, and have good manual dexterity. Applicants who have a high school education are preferred. Courses in general mathematics, mechanical drawing, and shop provide a useful background.

Plasterers and stucco masons may advance to supervisors, superintendents, or estimators for plastering contractors or may become self-employed contractors.

Job Outlook

Employment of plasterers and stucco masons is expected to increase about as fast as the average for all occupations through the year 2008. In addition to job openings due to rising demand for plastering and stuccowork, jobs will open as plasterers and stucco masons transfer to other occupations or leave the labor force.

In past years, employment of plasterers declined as more builders switched to drywall construction. This decline has halted, however, and employment of plasterers is expected to continue growing as a result of the appreciation for the durability and attractiveness troweled finishes provide. Thin-coat plastering—or veneering—in particular, is gaining wide acceptance as more and more builders recognize its ease of application, durability, quality of finish, and fire-retarding qualities. An increasing use of prefabricated wall systems as well as new polymer-based or polymer-modified acrylic exterior insulating finishes is also gaining popularity. This is not only because of their durability, attractiveness, and insulating properties but also because of their relatively low cost. These wall systems and finishes are growing in popularity particularly in the South and Southwest regions of the country. In addition, plasterers will be needed to renovate plasterwork in old structures and to create special architectural effects, such as curved surfaces, which are not practical with drywall materials.

Most plasterers and stucco masons work in construction, where prospects fluctuate from year to year due to changing economic conditions. Bad weather affects plastering less than other construction trades because most work is indoors. On exterior surfacing jobs, however, plasterers and stucco masons may lose time because materials cannot be applied under wet or freezing conditions. Best employment opportunities should continue to be in Florida, California, and the Southwest, where exterior plaster and decorative finishes are expected to remain popular.

Earnings

In 1998, median hourly earnings of plasterers and stucco masons were $14.13. The middle 50 percent earned between $11.20 and $18.22. The lowest 10 percent earned less than $9.05 and the top 10 percent earned more than $23.69.

According to the limited information available, average hourly earnings—including benefits—for plasterers and stucco masons who belonged to a union and worked full time ranged between $14.70 and $39.90 in 1998. Plasterers in New York, Boston, Chicago, San Francisco, Los Angeles, and other large cities received the highest hourly earnings. Apprentice wage rates start at about half the rate paid to experienced plasterers and stucco masons. Annual earnings for plasterers and stucco masons and apprentices can be less than the hourly rate would indicate, because poor weather and periodic declines in construction activity can limit work time.

Many plasterers and stucco masons are members of unions. They are represented by the Operative Plasterers' and Cement Masons' International Association of the United States and Canada, or the International Union of Bricklayers and Allied Craftsmen.

Related Occupations

Other construction workers who use a trowel as their primary tool include drywall installers and finishers, bricklayers, cement masons, concrete finishers, marble setters, stonemasons, terrazzo workers, and tilesetters.

Sources of Additional Information

For information about apprenticeships or other work opportunities, contact local plastering contractors, locals of the unions previously mentioned, a local joint union-management apprenticeship committee, or the nearest office of your State apprenticeship agency or your State employment service.

For general information about the work of plasterers and stucco masons, contact:

☛ International Union of Bricklayers and Allied Craftsmen, 815 15th Street, NW., Washington, DC 20005.

☛ Operative Plasterers' and Cement Masons' International Association of the United States and Canada, 14405 Laurel Place, Suite 300, Laurel, MD 20707.

Plumbers, Pipefitters, and Steamfitters

(O*NET 87502A and 87502B)

Significant Points

- Although employment is projected to increase slowly, job opportunities should be excellent because not enough people are seeking training as plumbers, pipefitters, and steamfitters.
- Most workers learn the trade through a formal 4 to 5-year apprenticeship program.
- Plumbers, pipefitters, and steamfitters are one of the largest and highest paid construction occupations.

Nature of the Work

Most people are familiar with plumbers who come to their home to unclog a drain or install an appliance. In addition to these activities, however, plumbers, pipefitters, and steamfitters install, maintain, and repair many different types of pipe systems. For example, some systems move water to a municipal water treatment plant and then to residential, commercial, and public buildings. Other systems dispose of waste, provide gas to stoves and furnaces, or supply air-conditioning. Pipe systems in power plants carry the steam that powers huge turbines. Pipes also are used in manufacturing plants to move material through the production process.

Although plumbing, pipefitting, and steamfitting sometimes are considered a single trade, workers generally specialize in one of these three areas. *Plumbers* install and repair the water, waste disposal, drainage, and gas systems in homes and commercial and industrial buildings. Plumbers also install plumbing fixtures—bathtubs, showers, sinks, and toilets—and appliances such as dishwashers and water heaters. *Pipefitters* install and repair both high and low-pressure pipe systems used in manufacturing, in the generation of electricity, and in heating and cooling buildings. They also install automatic controls that are increasingly being used to regulate these systems. Some pipefitters specialize in only one type of system. *Steamfitters*, for example, install pipe systems that move liquids or gases under high pressure. *Sprinklerfitters* install automatic fire sprinkler systems in buildings.

Plumbers, pipefitters, and steamfitters use many different materials and construction techniques, depending on the type of project. Residential water systems, for example, use copper, steel, and plastic pipe that can be handled and installed by one or two workers. Municipal sewerage systems, on the other hand, are made of large cast iron pipes; installation normally requires crews of pipefitters. Despite these differences, all plumbers, pipefitters, and steamfitters must be able to follow building plans or blueprints and instructions from supervisors, lay out the job, and work efficiently with the materials and tools of the trade. Increasingly, computers are used to create blueprints and plan layouts.

When construction plumbers install piping in a house, for example, they work from blueprints or drawings that show the planned location of pipes, plumbing fixtures, and appliances. They first lay out the job to fit the piping into the structure of the house with the least waste of material and within the confines of the structure. They then measure and mark areas where pipes will be installed and connected. Construction plumbers also check for obstructions such as electrical wiring and, if necessary, plan the pipe installation around the problem.

Sometimes plumbers have to cut holes in walls, ceilings, and floors of a house. For some systems, they may have to hang steel supports from ceiling joists to hold the pipe in place. To assemble a system, plumbers—using saws, pipe cutters, and pipe-bending machines—cut and bend lengths of pipe. They connect lengths of pipe with fittings with the method depending on the type of pipe used. For plastic pipe, plumbers connect the sections and fittings with adhesives. For copper pipe, they slide fittings over the end of the pipe and solder the fitting in place with a torch.

After the piping is in place in the house, plumbers install the fixtures and appliances and connect the system to the outside water or sewer lines. Finally, using pressure gauges, they check the system, to insure the plumbing works properly.

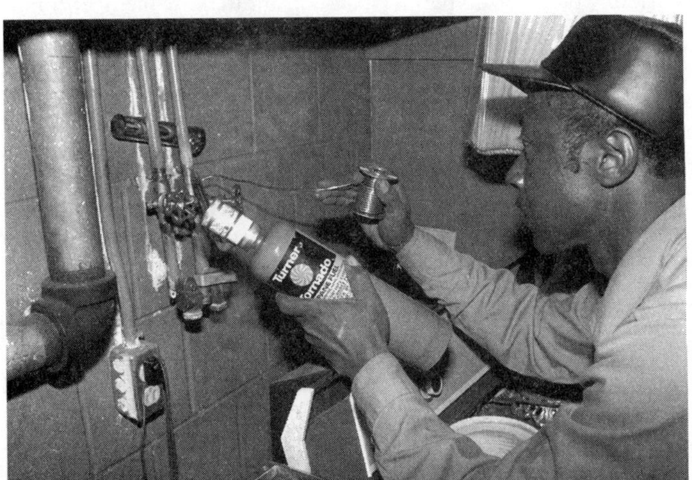

Plumbers install and repair waste disposal systems in homes.

Working Conditions

Because plumbers, pipefitters, and steamfitters frequently must lift heavy pipes, stand for long periods, and sometimes work in uncomfortable or cramped positions, they need physical strength as well as stamina. They also may have to work outdoors in inclement weather. In addition, they are subject to possible falls from ladders, cuts from sharp tools, and burns from hot pipes or soldering equipment.

Plumbers, pipefitters, and steamfitters engaged in construction generally work a standard 40-hour week; those involved in maintaining pipe systems, including those who provide maintenance services under contract, may have to work evening or weekend shifts, as well as be on call. These maintenance workers may spend quite a bit of time traveling to and from work sites.

Employment

Plumbers and pipefitters held about 426,000 jobs in 1998. About two-thirds worked for mechanical and plumbing contractors engaged in new construction, repair, modernization, or maintenance work. Others did maintenance work for a variety of industrial, commercial, and government employers. For example, pipefitters were employed as maintenance personnel in the petroleum and chemical industries, where manufacturing operations require the moving of liquids and gases through pipes. Almost 1 of every 5 plumbers, pipefitters, and steamfitters was self-employed.

Jobs for plumbers, pipefitters, and steamfitters are distributed across the country in about the same proportion as the general population.

Training, Other Qualifications, and Advancement

Virtually all plumbers, pipefitters, and steamfitters undergo some type of apprenticeship training. Many programs are administered by local union-management committees made up of members of the United Association of Journeymen and Apprentices of the Plumbing and Pipefitting Industry of the United States and Canada, and local employers who are members of either the Mechanical Contractors Association of America, Inc., the National Association of Plumbing-Heating-Cooling Contractors, or the National Fire Sprinkler Association, Inc.

Nonunion training and apprenticeship programs are administered by local chapters of the Associated Builders and Contractors, the National Association of Plumbing-Heating-Cooling Contractors, the American Fire Sprinkler Association, or the Home Builders Institute of the National Association of Home Builders.

Apprenticeships—both union and nonunion—consist of 4 to 5 years of on-the-job training, in addition to at least 144 hours annually of related classroom instruction. Classroom subjects include drafting and blueprint reading, mathematics, applied physics and chemistry, safety, and local plumbing codes and regulations. On the job, apprentices first learn basic skills such as identifying grades and types of pipe, using the tools of the trade, and safely unloading materials. As apprentices gain experience, they learn how to work with various types of pipe and how to install different piping systems and plumbing fixtures. Apprenticeship gives trainees a thorough knowledge of all aspects of the trade. Although most plumbers, pipefitters, and steamfitters are trained through apprenticeship, some still learn their skills informally on the job.

Applicants for union or nonunion apprentice jobs must be at least 18 years old and in good physical condition. Apprenticeship committees may require applicants to have a high school diploma or its equivalent. Armed Forces training in plumbing and pipefitting is considered very good preparation. In fact, persons with this background may be given credit for previous experience when entering a civilian apprenticeship program. Secondary or post secondary courses in shop, plumbing, general mathematics, drafting, blueprint reading, computers, and physics also are good preparation.

Although there are no uniform national licensing requirements, most communities require plumbers to be licensed. Licensing requirements vary from area to area, but most localities require workers to pass an examination that tests their knowledge of the trade and of local plumbing codes.

Some plumbers, pipefitters, and steamfitters may become supervivors for mechanical and plumbing contractors. Others go into business for themselves.

Job Outlook

Job opportunities for skilled plumbers, pipefitters, and steamfitters are expected to be excellent, as growth in demand outpaces the supply of workers trained in this craft. Employment of plumbers, pipefitters, and steamfitters is expected to grow more slowly than the average for all occupations through the year 2008. However, the pool of young workers available to enter training programs will also be increasing slowly, and many in that group are reluctant to seek training for jobs that may be strenuous and have uncomfortable working conditions.

Construction activity—residential, industrial, and commercial—is expected to grow slowly over the next decade. Demand for plumbers will stem from building renovation, including the increasing installation of sprinkler systems; repair and maintenance of existing residential systems; and maintenance activities for places having extensive systems of pipes, such as power plants, water and wastewater treatment plants, pipelines, office buildings, and factories. However, the growing use of plastic pipe and fittings, which are much easier to install and repair than other types; increasingly efficient sprinkler systems; and other new technologies will mean employment will not grow as fast as it has in past years. However, several thousand positions will become available each year from the need to replace experienced workers who retire or leave the occupation for other reasons.

Traditionally, many organizations with extensive pipe systems have employed their own plumbers, pipefitters, or steamfitters to maintain the equipment and keep everything running smoothly. But, to reduce labor costs, many of these firms no longer employ a full-time in-house plumber or pipefitter. Instead, when they need a plumber, they rely on workers provided under service contracts by plumbing and pipefitting contractors.

Construction projects provide only temporary employment so when a project ends, plumbers, pipefitters, and steamfitters working on the project may experience bouts of unemployment. Because construction activity varies from area to area, job openings, as well as apprenticeship opportunities, fluctuate with local economic conditions. However, employment of plumbers, pipefitters, and steamfitters is generally less sensitive to changes in economic conditions than some of the other construction trades. Even when construction activity declines, maintenance, rehabilitation, and replacement of existing piping systems, as well as the growing installation of fire sprinkler systems, provide many jobs for plumbers, pipefitters, and steamfitters.

Earnings

In 1998, median hourly earnings of plumbers, pipefitters, and steamfitters were $16.67. The middle 50 percent earned between $12.81 and $22.18. The lowest 10 percent earned less than $10.16 and the highest 10 percent earned more than $30.99. Median hourly earnings in the industries employing the largest numbers of plumbers, pipefitters, and steamfitters in 1997 are shown below:

Motor vehicles and equipment	$21.70
Plumbing, heating, and air conditioning	16.10
Heavy construction, except highway	15.60
Nonresidential building construction	15.20
Local government, except education and hospitals	14.00

Apprentices usually begin at about 50 percent of the wage rate paid to experienced plumbers, pipefitters, and steamfitters. Wages increase periodically as skills improve. After an initial waiting period, apprentices receive the same benefits as experienced plumbers, pipefitters, and steamfitters.

Many plumbers, pipefitters, and steamfitters are members of the United Association of Journeymen and Apprentices of the Plumbing and Pipefitting Industry of the United States and Canada.

Related Occupations

Other occupations in which workers install and repair mechanical systems in buildings are boilermakers; stationary engineers; electricians; elevator installers and repairers; industrial machinery repairers; millwrights; sheet-metal workers and duct installers; and heating, air-conditioning, and refrigeration mechanics and installers.

Sources of Additional Information

For information about apprenticeships or work opportunities in plumbing, pipefitting, and steamfitting, contact local plumbing, heating, and air-conditioning contractors; a local or State chapter of the National Association of Plumbing, Heating, and Cooling Contractors; a local chapter of the Mechanical Contractors Association; a local chapter of the United Association of Journeymen and Apprentices of the Plumbing and Pipefitting Industry of the United States and Canada; or the nearest office of your State employment service or State apprenticeship agency. This information is also available from:

☛ The Home Builders Institute, National Association of Home Builders, 1201 15th St. NW., Washington, DC 20005.

For general information about the work of plumbers, pipefitters, and sprinklerfitters, contact:

☛ National Association of Plumbing-Heating-Cooling Contractors, 180 S. Washington St., P.O. Box 6808, Falls Church, VA 22040.

☛ Associated Builders and Contractors, 1300 North 17th St., Rosslyn, VA 22209.

☛ National Fire Sprinkler Association, Robin Hill Corporate Park, Rt. 22, Box 1000, Patterson, NY 12563.

☛ American Fire Sprinkler Association, Inc., 12959 Jupiter Rd., Suite 142, Dallas, TX 75238-3200.

☛ Mechanical Contractors Association of America, 1385 Piccard Dr., Rockville, MD 20850.

Roofers

(O*NET 87808)

Significant Points

- Jobs for roofers should be plentiful through the year 2008, because roofing work is hot, strenuous, and dirty, making job turnover high.
- Demand for roofers is less susceptible to downturns in the economy than some of the other construction trades because the majority of roofing work is repair and reroofing.
- Roofing has the highest accident rate of all construction occupations.

Nature of the Work

A leaky roof can damage ceilings, walls, and furnishings. To protect buildings and their contents from water damage, roofers repair and install roofs made of tar or asphalt and gravel; rubber or thermoplastic; metal; or shingles made of asphalt, slate, fiberglass, wood, tile, or other material. Repair and reroofing—replacing old roofs on existing buildings—provide many job opportunities for these workers. Roofers also may waterproof foundation walls and floors.

There are two types of roofs, flat and pitched (sloped). Most commercial, industrial, and apartment buildings have flat or slightly sloping roofs. Most houses have pitched roofs. Some roofers work on both types; others specialize.

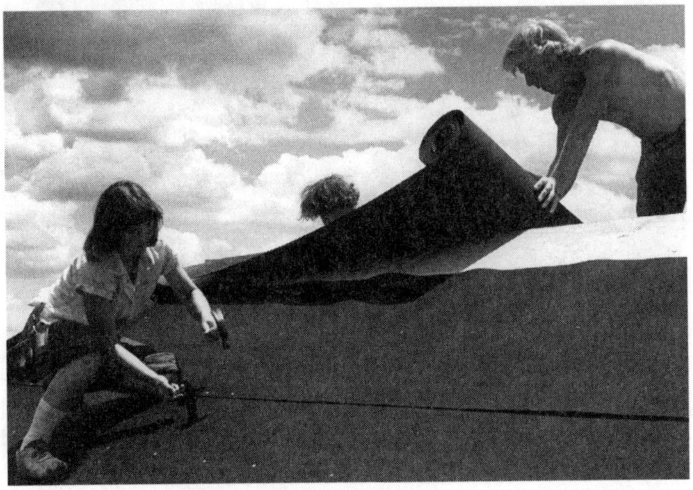

Roofers work outdoors in all types of weather.

Most flat roofs are covered with several layers of materials. Roofers first put a layer of insulation on the roof deck. Over the insulation, they then spread a coat of molten bitumen, a tar-like substance. Next, they install partially overlapping layers of roofing felt—a fabric saturated in bitumen—over the insulation surface. Roofers use a mop to spread hot bitumen over the surface and under the next layer. This seals the seams and makes the surface watertight. Roofers repeat these steps to build up the desired number of layers, called "plies." The top layer is either glazed to make a smooth finish or has gravel embedded in the hot bitumen for a rough surface.

An increasing number of flat roofs are covered with a single-ply membrane of waterproof rubber or thermoplastic compounds. Roofers roll these sheets over the roof's insulation and seal the seams. Adhesive, mechanical fasteners, or stone ballasts hold the sheets in place. The building must be of sufficient strength to hold the ballast.

Most residential roofs are covered with shingles. To apply shingles, roofers first lay, cut, and tack 3-foot strips of roofing felt lengthwise over the entire roof. Then, starting from the bottom edge, they nail overlapping rows of shingles to the roof. Workers measure and cut the felt and shingles to fit intersecting roofs and to fit around vent pipes and chimneys. Wherever two roof surfaces intersect or shingles reach a vent pipe or chimney, roofers cement or nail flashing-strips of metal or shingle over the joints to make them watertight. Finally, roofers cover exposed nailheads with roofing cement or caulking to prevent water leakage.

Some roofers also waterproof and dampproof masonry and concrete walls and floors. To prepare surfaces for waterproofing, they hammer and chisel away rough spots or remove them with a rubbing brick before applying a coat of liquid waterproofing compound. They may also paint or spray surfaces with a waterproofing material or attach waterproofing membrane to surfaces. When dampproofing, they usually spray a bitumen-based coating on interior or exterior surfaces.

Working Conditions

Roofing work is strenuous. It involves heavy lifting, as well as climbing, bending, and kneeling. Roofers work outdoors in all types of weather, particularly when making repairs. These workers risk injuries from slips or falls from scaffolds, ladders, or roofs or from burns from hot bitumen. In addition, roofs become extremely hot during the summer. In fact, of all construction industries, the roofing industry has the highest accident rate.

Employment

Roofers held about 158,000 jobs in 1998. Almost all wage and salary roofers worked for roofing contractors. About 1 out of every 3 roofers was self-employed. Many self-employed roofers specialize in residential work.

Training, Other Qualifications, and Advancement

Most roofers acquire their skills informally by working as helpers for experienced roofers. They start by carrying equipment and material and erecting scaffolds and hoists. Within 2 or 3 months, trainees are taught to measure, cut, and fit roofing materials, and later, to lay asphalt or fiberglass shingles. Because some roofing materials are used infrequently, it can take several years to get experience working on all the various types of roofing applications.

Some roofers train through 3-year apprenticeship programs administered by local union-management committees representing roofing contractors and locals of the United Union of Roofers, Waterproofers, and Allied Workers. The apprenticeship program generally consists of a minimum of 2,000 hours of on-the-job training annually, plus 144 hours of classroom instruction a year in subjects such as tools and their use, arithmetic, and safety. On-the-job training for apprentices is similar to that for helpers, except the apprenticeship program is more structured. Apprentices also learn to dampproof and waterproof walls.

Good physical condition and good balance are essential for roofers. A high school education or its equivalent is helpful, as are courses in mechanical drawing and basic mathematics. Most apprentices are at least 18 years old.

Roofers may advance to supervisor or estimator for a roofing contractor, or become contractors themselves.

Job Outlook

Jobs for roofers should be plentiful through the year 2008, primarily because of the need to replace workers who transfer to other occupations or leave the labor force. Turnover is high—roofing work is hot, strenuous, and dirty, and a significant number of workers treat roofing as a temporary job until something better comes along. Some roofers leave the occupation to go into other construction trades.

Employment of roofers is expected to grow about as fast as the average for all occupations through the year 2008. Roofs deteriorate faster than most other parts of buildings and periodically need to be repaired or replaced. About 75 percent of roofing work is repair and reroofing, a higher proportion than in most other construction work. As a result, demand for roofers is less susceptible to downturns in the economy than some of the other construction trades. In addition to repair and reroofing work on the growing stock of buildings, new construction of industrial, commercial, and residential buildings will add to the demand for roofers. However, many innovations and advances in materials, techniques, and tools have made roofers more productive than before and will restrict the growth of employment—at least to some extent. Jobs should be easiest to find during spring and summer, when most roofing is done.

Earnings

In 1998, median hourly earnings of roofers were $12.18. The middle 50 percent earned between $9.72 and $16.47. The lowest 10 percent earned less than $7.56 and the highest 10 percent earned more than $21.77.

Some roofers are members of the United Union of Roofers, Waterproofers & Allied Workers. According to the limited information available, average hourly earnings—including benefits—for roofers who belonged to a union and worked full time, ranged between $15.30 and $41.20 in 1998. Roofers in New York, Boston, San Francisco, Chicago, Los Angeles, Philadelphia, and other large cities received the highest wages.

Apprentices usually start at about 40 percent of the rate paid to experienced roofers and receive periodic raises as they acquire the skills of the trade. Earnings for roofers are reduced on occasion because poor weather often limits the time they can work.

Related Occupations

Roofers use shingles, bitumen and gravel, single-ply plastic or rubber sheets, or other materials to waterproof building surfaces. Workers in other occupations who cover surfaces with special materials for protection and decoration include carpenters, cement masons, concrete finishers, drywall installers and finishers, floor covering installers, plasterers and stucco masons, terrazzo workers, and tilesetters.

Sources of Additional Information

For information about roofing apprenticeships or job opportunities in this trade, contact local roofing contractors; a local chapter of the roofers union; a local joint union-management apprenticeship committee; or the nearest office of your State employment service or State apprenticeship agency.

For information about the work of roofers, contact:

☛ National Roofing Contractors Association, 10255 W. Higgins Rd., Rosemont, IL 60018-5607

☛ United Union of Roofers, Waterproofers and Allied Workers, 1660 L St. NW., Suite 800, Washington, DC 20036.

Sheet Metal Workers and Duct Installers

(O*NET 89132)

Significant Points

- Job prospects should be good for persons who complete apprenticeship programs.
- Sheet metal work tends to be steadier than some other construction crafts, because maintenance and replacement work in existing buildings can compensate for slack in new construction.
- Unlike most construction craft occupations, few sheet metal workers and duct installers are self-employed.

Nature of the Work

Sheet metal workers and duct installers make, install, and maintain air-conditioning, heating, ventilation, and pollution control duct systems; roofs; siding; rain gutters; downspouts; skylights; restaurant equipment; outdoor signs; and many other building parts and products made from metal sheets. They may also work with fiberglass and plastic materials. Although some workers specialize in fabrication, installation, or maintenance, most do all three jobs. (Workers employed in the mass production of sheet metal products in manufacturing are not included in this statement.)

Sheet metal workers usually fabricate their products at a shop away from the construction site. They first study plans and specifications to determine the kind and quantity of materials they will need. They then measure, cut, bend, shape, and fasten pieces of sheet metal to make duct work, counter tops, and other custom products. In an increasing number of shops, sheet metal workers use computerized metalworking equipment. This enables them to experiment with different layouts and to select the one that results in the least waste of material. They cut or form parts with computer-controlled saws, lasers, shears, and presses.

In shops without computerized equipment, and for products that cannot be made on such equipment, sheet metal workers use hand calculators to make the required calculations and use tapes, rulers, and other measuring devices for layout work. They then cut or stamp the parts on machine tools.

Before assembling pieces, sheet metal workers check each part for accuracy and, if necessary, finish it by using hand, rotary, or squaring

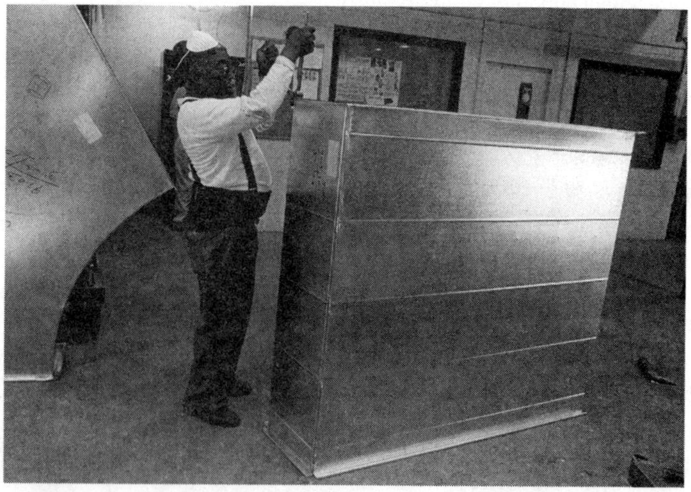

Sheet-metal workers usually fabricate their products at a shop away from the construction site.

shears and hacksaws. After the parts have been inspected, workers fasten seams and joints together with welds, bolts, cement, rivets, solder, specially formed sheet metal drive clips, or other connecting devices. They then take the parts to the construction site where they further assemble the pieces as they install them. These workers install ducts, pipes, and tubes by joining them end to end and hanging them with metal hangers secured to a ceiling or a wall. They also use shears, hammers, punches, and drills to make parts at the work site or to alter parts made in the shop.

Some jobs are done completely at the job site. When installing a metal roof, for example, sheet metal workers measure and cut the roofing panels that are needed to complete the job. They secure the first panel in place and interlock and fasten the grooved edge of the next panel into the grooved edge of the first. Then they nail or weld the free edge of the panel to the structure. This two-step process is repeated for each additional panel. Finally, they fasten machine-made molding at joints, along corners, and around windows and doors for a neat, finished effect.

In addition to installation, some sheet metal workers specialize in testing, balancing, adjusting, and servicing existing air-conditioning and ventilation systems to make sure they are functioning properly and to improve their energy efficiency.

Working Conditions

Sheet metal workers and duct installers usually work a 40-hour week. Those who fabricate sheet metal products work in shops that are well-lighted and well-ventilated. However, they stand for long periods and lift heavy materials and finished pieces. Sheet metal workers must follow safety practices because working around high-speed machines can be dangerous. They are also subject to cuts from sharp metal, burns from soldering and welding, and falls from ladders and scaffolds. They usually wear safety glasses but must not wear jewelry or loose-fitting clothing that could easily be caught in a machine.

Those doing installation work do considerable bending, lifting, standing, climbing, and squatting, sometimes in close quarters or in awkward positions. Although installing duct systems and kitchen equipment is done indoors, the installation of siding, roofs, and gutters involves much outdoor work, requiring sheet metal workers to work in various kinds of weather.

Employment

Sheet metal workers and duct installers held about 122,000 jobs in the construction industry in 1998. Nearly three-fourths worked for plumbing, heating, and air-conditioning contractors; most of the rest worked for roofing and sheet metal contractors. Some worked for other special trade contractors and for general contractors engaged in residential and commercial building. Unlike many other construction trades, few sheet metal workers are self-employed.

Jobs for sheet metal workers are distributed throughout the country in about the same proportion as the total population.

Training, Other Qualifications, and Advancement

Sheet metal contractors consider apprenticeship the best way to learn this trade. The apprenticeship program consists of 4 or 5 years of on-the-job training and a minimum of 144 hours per year of classroom instruction. Apprenticeship programs provide comprehensive instruction in both sheet metal fabrication and installation. They are administered by local joint committees composed of the Sheet Metal Workers' International Association, local chapters of the Sheet Metal and Air-Conditioning Contractors National Association.

On the job, apprentices learn the basics of pattern layout and how to cut, bend, fabricate, and install sheet metal. They begin with basic ductwork and gradually advance to more difficult jobs, such as making more complex ducts, fittings, and decorative pieces. They also use materials such as fiberglass, plastics, and other non-metallic materials.

In the classroom, apprentices learn drafting, plan and specification reading, trigonometry and geometry applicable to layout work, the use of computerized equipment, welding, and the principles of heating, air-conditioning, and ventilating systems. Safety is stressed throughout the program. In addition, apprentices learn the relationship between sheet metal work and other construction work.

A relatively small number of persons pick up the trade informally, usually by working as helpers to experienced sheet metal workers. Most begin by carrying metal and cleaning up debris in a metal shop while they learn about materials and tools and their uses. Later, they learn to operate machines that bend or cut metal. In time, helpers go out on the job site to learn installation. Those who acquire their skills this way often take vocational school courses in mathematics or sheet metal fabrication to supplement their work experience. To be promoted to the journey level, helpers usually must pass the same written examination as apprentices.

Applicants for jobs as apprentices or helpers should be in good physical condition and have mechanical and mathematical aptitude. Good eye-hand coordination, spatial and form perception, and manual dexterity are also important. Local apprenticeship committees require a high school education or its equivalent. Courses in algebra, trigonometry, geometry, mechanical drawing, and shop provide a helpful background for learning the trade, as does related work experience obtained in the Armed Services.

It is important for experienced sheet metal workers to keep abreast of new technological developments, such as the growing use of computerized layout and laser cutting machines. Workers often take additional training provided by the union or by their employer, to improve existing skills or to acquire new ones.

Sheet metal workers and duct installers may advance to supervisory jobs. Some of these workers take additional training in welding and do work that is more specialized. Others go into the contracting business for themselves. Because a sheet metal contractor must have a shop with equipment to fabricate products, this type of contracting business is more expensive to start than other types of construction contracting.

Job Outlook

Job prospects are expected to be favorable for sheet metal workers and duct installers over the long run, because the number of skilled workers is likely to be insufficient to meet demand, due to job growth and the need to replace workers who leave the occupation. Opportunities should be particularly good for individuals who acquire apprenticeship training. Employment of sheet metal workers and duct installers in construction is expected to increase faster than the average for all occupations, reflecting growth in the demand for sheet metal installations as more industrial, commercial, and residential structures are built. Growing demand for additional energy-efficient air-conditioning, heating, and ventilation systems in the growing stock of old buildings, as well as other types of renovation and maintenance work, also should boost employment. In addition, the popularity of decorative sheet metal products and increased architectural restoration are expected to add to the demand for sheet metal workers and duct installers. Despite this growth in demand, most job openings will result from the need to replace workers who retire or leave the occupation for other reasons.

Workers may experience periods of unemployment, when construction projects end and economic conditions reduce the amount of construction activity. Because local economic conditions can vary widely, there can be shortages of experienced workers in some areas and an oversupply in other parts of the country. The availability of training slots also fluctuates with economic conditions, so the number of openings may vary from year to year and by geographic area. Nevertheless, employment of sheet metal workers and duct installers is less sensitive to declines in new construction than employment of some other construction workers, such as carpenters. Maintenance of existing equipment—which is less affected by economic fluctuations than new construction—makes up a large part of the work done by sheet metal workers. Installation of new air-conditioning and heating systems in existing buildings continues during construction slumps, as individuals and businesses seek more energy-efficient equipment to cut utility bills. In addition, a large proportion of sheet metal installation and maintenance is done indoors, so these workers usually lose less work time due to bad weather than other construction workers do.

Earnings

In 1998, median hourly earnings of sheet metal workers and duct installers employed in all industries were $13.48. The lowest 10 percent of all sheet metal workers and duct installers earned less than $7.96 and the highest 10 percent earned more than $24.97. Sheet metal workers who work in the construction industry generally have the highest earnings.

According to the limited information available, average hourly earnings—including benefits—for sheet metal workers who belonged to a union and worked full time ranged between $19.20 and $49.40 in 1998.

Apprentices normally start at about 40 percent of the rate paid to experienced workers. As apprentices acquire more skills of the trade throughout the course of the apprenticeship program, they receive periodic increases until their pay approaches that of experienced workers. In addition, union workers in some areas receive supplemental wages from the union when they are on layoff or shortened workweeks. Almost 40 percent of all sheet metal workers and duct installers are members of the Sheet Metal Workers' International Association.

Related Occupations

To fabricate and install sheet metal products, sheet metal workers and duct installers combine metalworking skills and knowledge of construction materials and techniques. Other occupations in which workers lay out and fabricate metal products include layout workers, machinists, metal fabricators, metal patternmakers, shipfitters, and tool and die makers. Construction occupations requiring similar skills and knowledge include heating, air-conditioning, and refrigeration technicians, and glaziers.

Sources of Additional Information

For more information about apprenticeships or other work opportunities, contact local sheet metal contractors or heating, refrigeration, and air-conditioning contractors; a local of the Sheet Metal Workers; a local of the Sheet Metal and Air Conditioning Contractors National Association; a local joint union-management apprenticeship committee; or the nearest office of your State employment service or apprenticeship agency.

For general information about sheet metal workers and duct installers, contact:

☛ The International Training Institute , 601 N. Fairfax St., Suite 240, Alexandria, VA 22314.

☛ The Sheet Metal and Air Conditioning Contractors National Association, 4201 Lafayette Center Dr., Chantilly, VA 20151-1209.

☛ The Sheet Metal Workers International Association, 1750 New York Ave. NW., Washington, DC 20006.

Structural and Reinforcing Metal Workers

(O*NET 87314, 87814, and 91714)

Significant Points

- Structural and reinforcing metal workers earn high pay but often can't work during inclement weather.
- These workers are among the most likely to be put out of work when downturns in the economy slow new construction.
- Most people enter this occupation through a formal 3-year apprenticeship.

Nature of the Work

Builders use materials made from iron, steel, aluminum, fiberglass, precast concrete, brass, and bronze to construct highways, bridges, office and other large buildings, and power transmission towers. These structures have frames made of steel columns, beams, and girders. In addition, reinforced concrete—concrete containing steel bars or wire fabric—is an important material in buildings, bridges, and other structures, as the steel gives the concrete additional strength. Moreover, metal stairways, catwalks, floor gratings, ladders, and window frames—as well as lampposts, railings, fences, and decorative ironwork—increase these structures functionality and attractiveness. Structural and reinforcing metal workers fabricate, assemble, and install these metal products. They also repair, renovate, and maintain older buildings and structures, such as steel mills, utility plants, automobile factories, highways, and bridges.

Before construction can begin, metal workers must erect steel frames and assemble the cranes and derricks that move structural steel, reinforcing bars, buckets of concrete, lumber, and other materials and equipment around the construction site. The structural metal arrives at the construction site in sections. There, it is lifted into position by a mobile crane. Metal workers then connect the sections and set the cables to do the hoisting.

Once this job has been completed, *structural metal workers* begin to connect steel columns, beams, and girders according to blueprints and instructions from supervisors and superintendents. Structural steel, reinforcing rods, and ornamental iron generally come to the construction site ready for erection—cut to the proper size, with holes drilled for bolts and numbered for assembly. Metal workers do this pre-construction site work in fabricating shops usually located away from the construction site. In these fabrication shops, metal workers lay out the raw steel received from a steel mill and cut, bend, drill, bolt, and weld each piece according to the specifications for that particular job. Metal workers at the construction site unload and stack the fabricated steel so it can be hoisted easily when needed.

To hoist the steel, metal workers attach cables from a crane or derrick. One worker directs the hoist operator with hand signals. Another worker holds a rope (tag line) attached to the steel to prevent it from swinging. The crane or derrick hoists steel into place in the framework where several workers, using spud wrenches, position the steel with connecting bars and jacks. Workers using drift pins or the handle of a spud wrench—a long wrench with a pointed handle—align the holes in the steel with the holes in the framework. Then they temporarily bolt the piece in place; check vertical and

Reinforcing workers wire reinforcing bars.

horizontal alignment with plumb bobs, laser equipment, transits, or levels; and then bolt or weld the piece permanently in place.

Reinforcing metal workers set the bars in the forms that hold concrete, following blueprints showing the location, size, and number of reinforcing bars. They then fasten the bars together by tying wire around them with pliers. When reinforcing floors, workers place blocks under the reinforcing bars to hold the bars off the deck. Although these materials usually arrive ready to use, metal workers occasionally must cut bars with metal shears or acetylene torches, bend them by hand or machine, or weld them with arc-welding equipment. Some concrete is reinforced with welded wire fabric. Using hooked rods, workers cut and fit the fabric and, while a concrete crew places the concrete, metal workers properly position the fabric in the concrete.

Workers install ornamental ironwork and related pieces after the exterior of the building has been completed. As they hoist pieces into position, metal workers bring them into position, make sure they fit correctly and bolt, braze, or weld them for a secure fit.

Metal fabricators fabricate and assemble structural metal products, such as metal tanks used to store petroleum, water, or other fluids and assemble metal parts for bridges and prefabricated metal buildings, according to plans or specifications.

Working Conditions

Structural and reinforcing metal workers usually work outside in all kinds of weather. However, those who work at great heights do not work when it is wet, icy, or extremely windy. Because the danger of injuries due to falls is great, ironworkers use safety devices, such as safety belts, scaffolding, and nets to reduce risk.

Employment

Structural and reinforcing metal workers held about 87,000 jobs in the construction industry in 1998. About 1 out of every 2 worked for structural steel erection contractors. Most of the remainder worked for contractors specializing in the construction of homes; factories; commercial buildings; churches; schools; bridges and tunnels; and water, sewer, communications, and power lines.

Structural and reinforcing metal workers are employed in all parts of the country, but most work in metropolitan areas, where most commercial and industrial construction takes place.

Training, Other Qualifications, and Advancement

Most employers recommend apprenticeship as the best way to learn this trade. The apprenticeship consists of 3 or 4 years of on-the-job training and a minimum of 144 hours a year of classroom instruction. Apprenticeship programs are usually administered by joint union-management committees made up of representatives of local unions of the International Association of Bridge, Structural, Ornamental and Reinforcing Iron Workers and local chapters of contractors' associations.

Metal workers must be at least 18 years old. A high school diploma may be preferred by employers and may be required by some local apprenticeship committees. High school courses in general mathematics, mechanical drawing, and shop are helpful. Because materials used in metal working are heavy and bulky, metal workers must be in good physical condition. They also need good agility, balance, eyesight, and depth perception to safely work at great heights on narrow beams and girders. Metal workers should not be afraid of heights or suffer from dizziness.

In the classroom, apprentices study blueprint reading; mathematics for layout work; the basics of structural erecting, rigging, reinforcing, welding and burning; ornamental erection; and assembling. Apprentices also study the care and safe use of tools and materials. On the job, apprentices work in all aspects of the trade, such as unloading and storing materials at the job site, rigging materials for movement by crane or derrick, connecting structural steel, and welding.

Some metal workers learn the trade informally on the job without completing an apprenticeship. These workers generally do not receive classroom training, although some large contractors have extensive training programs. On-the-job trainees usually begin by assisting experienced ironworkers by doing simple jobs, like carrying various materials. With experience, trainees perform more difficult tasks like cutting and fitting different parts. Learning through work experience alone may not provide training as complete as an apprenticeship program, however, and usually takes longer.

Some experienced workers become supervisors. Others may go into the contracting business for themselves.

Job Outlook

Employment of structural and reinforcing metal workers is expected to increase more slowly than the average for all occupations through the year 2008, largely because of the continued slow growth in industrial and commercial construction. The rehabilitation and maintenance of an increasing number of older buildings, factories, power plants, and highways and bridges is expected to increase, mitigating somewhat slower employment growth. In addition, more metal workers will be needed to build incinerators and other structures to contain hazardous materials as part of ongoing toxic waste cleanup. Although employment growth will create many new jobs for structural and reinforcing metal workers, most openings will result from the need to replace experienced metal workers who transfer to other occupations or leave the labor force.

The number of job openings fluctuates from year to year as economic conditions and the level of construction activity change. During economic downturns, metal workers can experience high rates of unemployment. Similarly, job opportunities for metal workers may vary widely by geographic area. Job openings for metal workers usually are more abundant during the spring and summer months, when the level of construction activity increases.

Earnings

In 1998, median hourly earnings of structural and reinforcing metal workers in all industries were $15.81. The middle 50 percent earned between $11.66 and $21.94. The lowest 10 percent earned less than $9.17 and the highest 10 percent earned more than $26.64. Median hourly earnings in the industries employing the largest number of structural and reinforcing metal workers in 1997 were:

Miscellaneous special trade contractors	$16.50
Nonresidential building construction	12.40

In 1997, median hourly earnings of metal fabricators of structural metal products working for miscellaneous special trade contractors were about $13.00.

Many workers in this trade are members of the International Association of Bridge, Structural, Ornamental, and Reinforcing Iron Workers. According to the limited information available, average hourly earnings—including benefits—for structural and reinforcing metal workers who belonged to a union and worked full time, ranged between $14.90 and $48.30 in 1998. Structural and reinforcing metal workers in New York, Boston, San Francisco, Chicago, Los Angeles, Philadelphia, and other large cities received the highest wages.

Apprentices generally start at about 50 to 60 percent of the rate paid to experienced journey workers. They receive periodic increases throughout the course of the apprenticeship program, as they acquire the skills of the trade, until their pay approaches that of experienced workers.

Earnings for metal workers may be reduced on occasion because work can be limited by bad weather, the short-term nature of construction jobs, and economic downturns.

Related Occupations

Structural and reinforcing metal workers play an essential role in erecting buildings, bridges, highways, powerlines, and other structures. Others who also work on these construction jobs are operating engineers, cement masons and concrete finishers, and welders.

Sources of Additional Information

For more information on apprenticeships or other work opportunities, contact local general contractors; a local of the International Association of Bridge, Structural, Ornamental, and Reinforcing Iron Workers Union; a local joint ironworkers' union-management apprenticeship committee; a local or State chapter of the Associated Builders and Contractors, or the nearest office of your State employment service or apprenticeship agency.

For general information about metalworkers, contact:

☛ Associated General Contractors of America, Inc., 1957 E St. NW., Washington, DC 20006.

☛ International Association of Bridge, Structural, Ornamental, and Reinforcing Iron Workers, 1750 New York Ave. NW., Suite 400, Washington, DC 20006.

☛ National Erectors Association, 1501 Lee Hwy., Suite 202, Arlington, VA 22209.

☛ National Association of Reinforcing Steel Contractors, 10382 Main St., Suite 300, P.O. Box 280, Fairfax, VA 22030.

Production Occupations

Assemblers

Precision Assemblers

(O*NET 87102C, 93102B, 93102C, 93102D, 93105, 93108, 93111A, 93111B, 93114, 93117, 93197A, and 93197C)

Significant Points

- Virtually all precision assemblers work in plants that manufacture durable goods.
- Most precision assemblers are promoted from the ranks of workers in lesser skilled jobs.
- Projected slower-than-average employment growth reflects increasing automation and the internationalization of production.

Nature of the Work

Precision assemblers are highly skilled workers who assemble a wide range of finished products from manufactured parts or subassemblies. They produce intricate manufactured products, such as aircraft, automobiles, computers, and small electrical and electronic components. Unlike some assemblers who perform simple, repetitive tasks, precision assemblers generally perform a series of more complex tasks.

Precision assemblers may work on subassemblies or the final assembly of finished products or components of an array of products. For example, precision electrical and electronic equipment assemblers put together or modify missile control systems, radio or test equipment, computers, machine-tool numerical controls, radar, sonar, and appliances, and prototypes of these and other products. Precision electromechanical equipment assemblers prepare and test equipment or devices such as dynamometers, ejection-seat mechanisms, and tape drives. Precision machine builders construct, assemble, or rebuild engines and turbines, and office, agricultural, construction, oil field, rolling mill, textile, woodworking, paper, printing, and food wrapping machinery. Precision aircraft assemblers put together and install parts of airplanes, space vehicles, or missiles, such as wings or landing gear. Precision structural metal fitters align and fit structural metal parts according to detailed specifications prior to welding or riveting.

Precision assemblers involved in product development read and interpret engineering specifications from text, drawings, and computer-aided drafting systems. They may also use a variety of tools and precision measuring instruments. Some experienced assemblers work with engineers and technicians, assembling prototypes or test products.

As technology changes, so too does the manufacturing process. For example, flexible manufacturing systems include the manufacturing applications of robotics, computers, programmable motion control, and various sensing technologies. These systems change the way goods are made, and affect the jobs of those who make them. The concept of cellular manufacturing, for example, places a greater premium on the communication and teamwork of "cells" than it does on the old assembly line process. As the U.S. manufacturing sector continues to evolve in the face of growing international competition and changing technology, the nature of precision assembly will change along with it.

Working Conditions

The working conditions for precision assemblers vary, from plant to plant and from industry to industry. Conditions may be noisy and many assemblers may have to sit or stand for long periods of time. Electronics assemblers, for example, sit at tables in rooms that are clean, well lit, and free from dust. Assemblers of aircraft and industrial machinery, however, usually come in contact with oil and grease, and their working areas may be quite noisy. They may also have to lift and fit heavy objects. In many cases, the increased use of robots or other pneumatically powered machinery has improved working conditions by lowering the overall noise level of the facility.

Most full-time assemblers work a 40-hour week, although overtime and shift work is fairly common in some industries. Work schedules of assemblers may vary at plants with more than one shift.

Employment

Virtually all of the 422,000 precision assembler jobs in 1998 were in plants that manufacture durable goods; 48 percent were electrical and electronic equipment assemblers. The distribution of employment among the various types of precision assemblers was as follows.

Precision assemblers produce intricate manufactured products such as small electrical and electronic components.

Electrical and electronic equipment assemblers	201,000
Machine builders and other precision machine assemblers	74,000
Electromechanical equipment assemblers	50,000
Fitters, structural metal	17,000
Aircraft assemblers	17,000
All other precision assemblers	64,000

Assembly of electronic and electrical machinery, equipment, and supplies, including electrical switches, welding equipment, electric motors, lighting equipment, household appliances, and radios and television sets accounted for 33 percent of all jobs. Industrial machinery assembly of diesel engines, steam turbine generators, farm tractors, mining and construction machinery, office machines, and the like accounted for 29 percent of all jobs. Other industries that employ many precision assemblers were transportation equipment (aircraft, autos, trucks, and buses) and instruments manufacturing.

The following list shows the wage and salary employment of precision assemblers in durable goods manufacturing in 1998 by industry.

Electronic and other electrical equipment manufacturing	137,000
Industrial machinery and equipment manufacturing	122,000
Transportation equipment manufacturing	63,000
Instruments and related products manufacturing	61,000
Fabricated metal products manufacturing	22,000
All other industries	2,200

Training, Other Qualifications, and Advancement

Most precision assemblers are promoted from the ranks of workers in lesser skilled jobs in the same establishment. The ability to do accurate work at a rapid pace is a key job requirement. A high school diploma is preferred.

Applicants need specialized training for some precision assembly jobs. For example, employers may require that applicants for electrical or electronic assembler jobs be technical school graduates or have equivalent military training. Some companies may also provide extensive on-the-job training or classroom instruction on the broad range of assembly duties that employees may be required to perform.

Good eyesight, with or without glasses, is required for assemblers who work with small parts. Plants that make electrical and electronic products may test applicants for color vision, because many of their products contain many differently colored wires. Manual dexterity and the ability to carry out complex, repetitive tasks quickly and methodically are also important.

As precision assemblers become more experienced, they may progress to jobs that require more skill and be given more responsibility. Experienced assemblers may become product repairers if they have learned the many assembly operations and understand the construction of a product. These workers fix assembled articles that operators or inspectors have identified as defective. Assemblers also can advance to quality control jobs or be promoted to supervisor. Experienced precision assemblers also may become members of research and development teams, working with engineers and other project designers to design, develop, and test new product models. In some companies, assemblers can become trainees for one of the skilled trades. Those with a background in math, science, and computers may advance to programmers or operators of more highly automated production equipment.

Job Outlook

Job growth among precision assemblers is expected to be slower than the average for all occupations through the year 2008, reflecting increasing automation and the internationalization of production. As manufacturers strive for greater precision and productivity, work that can be performed more economically or more efficiently by automated equipment will be transferred to these machines. In addition to jobs stemming from growth, many job openings will result from the need to replace workers transferring to other occupations or leaving the labor force.

Recent advancements have made robotics more applicable and more affordable in manufacturing. The introduction of robots should continue raising the productivity of assembly workers and adversely affecting their employment.

The effects of automation will be felt more acutely in some industries than in others. Flexible manufacturing systems are expensive, and a large volume of repetitive work is required to justify their purchase. Also, where the assembly parts involved are irregular in size or location, new technology is only now beginning to make inroads. For example, much precision assembly in the aerospace industry is done in hard-to-reach locations unsuited for robots—inside airplane fuselages or gear boxes, for example—and replacement of these workers by automated processes will be slower and less comprehensive than replacement of other workers such as welders and painters. On the other hand, automation will continue to make more inroads in the precision assembly of electronic goods, where a significant number of these workers are employed.

Many producers send their subassembly or component production functions to countries where labor costs are lower. This growing internationalization of production, promoted by more liberal trade and investment policies, results in shifts in the composition of this country's manufacturing workforce. For example, decisions by American corporations to relocate assembly in other nations may lead to employment reductions for precision assemblers in some industries. A freer trade environment will lead to growth in the export of goods assembled in the United States and will result in the creation of additional jobs in other industries.

Earnings

Earnings vary by industry, geographic region, skill, educational level, and complexity of the machinery operated. In 1998, median hourly earnings were $18.46 for aircraft assemblers, $12.59 for fitters, and $11.18 for electromechanical equipment assemblers.

Median hourly earnings of machine builders were $14.06 in 1998. The middle 50 percent earned between $11.11 and $17.24. The lowest 10 percent earned less than $9.02 and the highest 10 percent earned $21.29. Median hourly earnings in the manufacturing industries employing the largest numbers of machine builders in 1997 are shown below:

Motor vehicles	$16.60
Engines and turbines	14.80
Metalworking machinery	14.30
Construction and related machinery	13.50
Special industrial machinery	13.40
General industrial machinery	12.90

Median hourly earnings of electrical and electronic equipment assemblers were $10.45 in 1998. The middle 50 percent earned between $8.35 and $13.41. The lowest 10 percent earned less than $6.80 and the highest 10 percent earned more than $16.55. Median hourly earnings in the manufacturing industries employing the largest number of electrical and electronic equipment assemblers in 1997 are shown below:

Aircraft and parts	$13.40
Computer and office equipment	11.20
Search and navigation equipment	10.90
Communications equipment	9.90
Electronic components and accessories	8.70

Many precision assemblers are members of labor unions. These unions include the International Association of Machinists and Aerospace Workers; the United Electrical, Radio and Machine Workers of America; the United Automobile, Aerospace and Agricultural Implement Workers of America; the International Brotherhood of Electrical Workers; and the United Steelworkers of America.

Related Occupations

Other occupations that involve operating machines and tools and assembling products include welders, ophthalmic laboratory technicians, and machine operators.

Sources of Additional Information

Information about employment opportunities for assemblers is available from local offices of the State employment service and from locals of the unions mentioned earlier.

Blue-Collar Worker Supervisors

(O*NET 81002, 81005A, 81005B, 81008, 81011, and 81017)

Significant Points

- Although many workers with high school diplomas still rise through the ranks, employers increasingly seek applicants with postsecondary training.
- Employment in manufacturing is expected to decline, reflecting the increasing use of computers, the implementation of self-directed work teams, and leaner management structures.
- In construction and most other nonmanufacturing industries, employment of managers and the workers they supervise is expected to increase.
- Supervisors in the highly cyclical construction industry may be laid off when construction activity declines.

Nature of the Work

For the millions of workers who assemble manufactured goods, service electronics equipment, work in construction, load trucks, or perform thousands of other activities, a blue-collar worker supervisor is the boss. In addition to "the boss," blue-collar worker supervisors go by many other titles. The most common are first-line supervisor or foreman and forewoman, but titles vary according to the industry in which these workers are employed. In the textile industry, for example, these supervisors may be referred to as second hands; on ships, they may be called boatswains. In the construction industry, supervisors can be referred to as superintendents, crew chiefs, or foremen and forewomen, depending upon the type and size of their employer. Toolpushers or gang pushers are common terms used to describe blue-collar supervisors in the oil drilling business.

Although the responsibilities of blue-collar worker supervisors are as varied as the titles they hold, their primary task is to ensure that workers, equipment, and materials are used properly to maximize productivity. To accomplish this, they perform many duties. Supervisors make sure machinery is set up correctly, schedule or perform repairs and maintenance work, create work schedules, keep production and employee records, monitor employees, and ensure that work is done correctly and on time. In addition, they organize workers' activities, make necessary adjustments to ensure that work continues uninterrupted, train new workers, and ensure the existence of a safe working environment.

The means by which supervisors perform these duties have changed dramatically in recent years as companies have restructured their operations for maximum efficiency. Supervisors now use computers to schedule work flow, monitor the quality of workers' output, keep track of materials, update the inventory control system, and perform other supervisory tasks. In addition, new management philosophies that emphasize fewer levels of management and greater employee power in decisionmaking have altered the role of these supervisors. In the past, supervisors exercised their authority to direct the efforts of blue-collar workers; increasingly, supervisors are assuming the role of a facilitator for groups of workers, aiding in group decisionmaking and conflict resolution.

Because they serve as the main conduit of information between management and blue-collar workers, supervisors have many interpersonal tasks related to their job. They inform workers about company plans and policies; recommend good performers for wage increases, awards, or promotions; and deal with poor performers by outlining expectations, counseling workers in proper methods, issuing warnings, or recommending disciplinary action. They also meet on a regular basis with their managers, reporting any problems and discussing possible solutions. Supervisors may often meet among themselves to discuss goals, company operations, and performance. In companies with labor unions, supervisors must follow all provisions of labor-management contracts.

Working Conditions

Blue-collar worker supervisors work in a range of settings based on the industry in which they are employed. Many supervisors work on the shop floor. This can be tiring if they are on their feet most of their shift or working near loud and dangerous machinery. Other supervisors, such as those in construction and oil exploration and production, sometimes work outdoors in severe weather conditions.

Supervisors may be on the job before other workers arrive and often stay after others leave. Some supervisors work in plants that operate around the clock, so they may work any one of three shifts, as well as weekends and holidays. In some cases, supervisors work all three shifts on a rotating basis; in others, shift assignments are made on the basis of seniority.

Because organizational restructuring and downsizing have required many blue-collar worker supervisors to oversee more workers and departments in recent years, longer hours and added responsibilities have increased on-the-job stress for many supervisors.

Employment

Blue-collar worker supervisors held about 2.3 million jobs in 1998. Although salaried supervisors are found in almost all industries, 2 of every 5 work in manufacturing. Other industries employing blue-collar worker supervisors include wholesale and retail trade, public utilities, repair shops, transportation, and government. The vast majority of the 230,000 self-employed workers in this occupation are employed in construction.

Training, Other Qualifications, and Advancement

When choosing supervisors, employers generally look for experience, job knowledge, organizational skills, and leadership qualities. Employers also emphasize the ability to motivate employees, maintain high morale, and command respect. In addition, well-rounded applicants who are able to deal with different situations and a diverse work force are desired. Communication and interpersonal skills are also extremely important attributes in this occupation.

Motivating employees is an important function of blue-collar worker supervisors.

Completion of high school is often the minimum educational requirement to become a blue-collar worker supervisor, but workers generally receive training in human resources, computer software, and management before they advance to these positions. Although many workers with high school diplomas still rise through the ranks, employers increasingly seek applicants with postsecondary technical degrees. In high-technology industries, such as aerospace and electronics, employers may require a bachelor's degree or technical school training. Large companies usually offer better opportunities for promotion to blue-collar worker supervisor positions than do smaller companies.

In most manufacturing companies, a degree in business or engineering, combined with in-house training, is needed to advance from supervisor to department head or production manager. In the construction industry, supervisors increasingly need a degree in construction management or engineering if they expect to advance to project manager, operations manager, or general superintendent. Some use their skills and experience to start their own construction contracting firms. Supervisors in repair shops may open their own businesses.

Job Outlook

Employment of blue-collar worker supervisors is expected to grow more slowly than the average for all occupations through 2008. As the number of workers in the economy increases, so will the need to supervise these workers. Organizational restructuring and new developments in technology, however, will moderate employment growth. In addition to growth, many openings will arise from the need to replace workers who transfer to other occupations or leave the labor force.

Projected job growth varies by industry. In manufacturing, employment of supervisors is expected to show little to no change despite an increase in manufacturing jobs as each supervisor is expected to oversee more workers. This trend reflects the increasing use of computers to meet supervisory responsibilities, such as production analysis and scheduling, greater involvement of production workers in decisionmaking, and the formation of self-directed work teams. These developments are not as prevalent in construction and most other nonmanufacturing industries, where the employment of blue-collar worker supervisors is expected to rise along with employment of the workers they supervise.

Because of their skill and seniority, blue-collar worker supervisors often are protected from layoffs during a recession. However, some supervisors in the highly cyclical construction industry may be laid off when construction activity declines.

Earnings

Median annual earnings for blue-collar worker supervisors were $37,180 in 1998. The middle 50 percent earned between $28,210 and $48,290. The lowest 10 percent earned less than $21,910, and the highest 10 percent earned over $71,320. Most supervisors earn significantly more than the workers they supervise. Although most blue-collar workers are paid by the hour, the majority of supervisors receive an annual salary. Some supervisors receive extra pay when they work overtime. Median annual earnings in the industries employing the largest number of blue-collar worker supervisors in 1997 were:

Industry	Earnings
Nonresidential building construction	$39,700
Motor vehicle dealers	37,500
Local government, except education and hospitals	36,500
Residential building construction	35,800
Miscellaneous plastics products (manufacturing)	31,500

Related Occupations

Other workers with supervisory duties include those who supervise professional, technical, sales, clerical, and service workers. Some of these are retail store or department managers, sales managers, clerical supervisors, bank officers, head tellers, hotel managers, postmasters, head cooks, head nurses, and surveyors.

Sources of Additional Information

For information on management development programs for blue-collar worker supervisors, contact:

☛ American Management Association, 1601 Broadway, New York, NY 10019. Internet: **http://www.amanet.org**

☛ National Management Association, 2210 Arbor Blvd., Dayton, OH 45439. Internet: **http://www.nma1.org**

☛ American Institute of Constructors, 1300 N. 17th St., Suite 830, Rosslyn, VA 22209.

☛ AIC Constructor Certification Commission, 466 94th Ave. North, St. Petersburg, FL 33702. Internet: **http://www.aicnet.org**

Fishers and Fishing Vessel Operators

(O*NET 79999E)

Significant Points

- The proportion of self-employed workers is among the highest in the workforce.
- Many jobs require strenuous work, long hours, and provide only seasonal employment.
- Employment is projected to decline, due to depletion of fish stocks and new Federal and State laws restricting fishing.

Nature of the Work

Fishers and fishing vessel operators catch and trap various types of marine life for human consumption, animal feed, bait, and other uses. (Aquaculture—the raising and harvesting for commercial purposes of fish and other aquatic life in ponds or confined bodies of water—is covered in the *Handbook* statement on farmers and farm managers.)

Fishing hundreds of miles from shore with commercial fishing vessels—large boats capable of hauling a catch of tens of thousands of pounds of fish—requires a crew including a captain, or skipper, a first mate and sometimes a second mate, boatswain, and deckhands with specialized skills.

The *captain* plans and oversees the fishing operation—the fish to be sought, the location of the best fishing grounds, the method of capture, the duration of the trip, and the sale of the catch.

The captain ensures the fishing vessel is seaworthy; oversees the purchase of supplies, gear, and equipment such as fuel, netting, and cables and hires qualified crew members and assigns their duties. The captain plots the vessel's course, using navigation instruments such as compasses, sextants, and charts. Additionally, vessels are equipped with electronic navigational equipment such as autopilots, loran systems, and satellite navigation systems. Ships also use radar to avoid obstacles and depth sounders to indicate the water depth and the existence of marine life between the vessel and sea bottom. The captain directs the fishing operation through the officers, and records daily activities in the ship's log. Upon returning to port, the captain arranges for the sale of the catch—directly to buyers or through a fish auction—and ensures each crew member receives the prearranged portion of adjusted net proceeds from the sale of the catch. Some captains have begun buying and selling fish via the Internet; and as electronic commerce grows as a method to find buyers for fresh catch, more captains may use computers.

The *first mate*—the captain's assistant, who must be familiar with navigation requirements and the operation of all electronic equipment—assumes control of the vessel when the captain is off duty. Duty shifts, called watches, usually last 6 hours. The mate's regular duty, with the help of the boatswain and under the captain's oversight, is to direct the fishing operations and sailing responsibilities of the deckhands. These include the operation, maintenance, and repair of the vessel and the gathering, preservation, stowing, and unloading of the catch.

The *boatswain*, a highly experienced deckhand with supervisory responsibilities, directs the *deckhands* as they carry out the sailing and fishing operations. Before departure, the boatswain directs the deckhands to load equipment and supplies, either by hand or with hoisting equipment, and to untie lines from other boats and the dock. When necessary, boatswains repair fishing gear, equipment, nets, and accessories. They operate the fishing gear, letting out and pulling in nets and lines. They extract the catch such as pollock, flounder, menhaden, and tuna, from the nets or lines' hooks. Deckhands use dip nets to prevent the escape of small fish and gaffs to facilitate the landing of large fish. They then wash, salt, ice, and stow away the catch. Deckhands must also ensure that decks are clear and clean at all times and the vessel's engines and equipment are kept in good working order. Upon return to port, they secure the vessel's lines to and from the docks and other vessels. Unless *lumpers*, or laborers, are hired, the deckhands unload the catch.

Large fishing vessels that operate in deep water generally have technologically advanced equipment, and some may have facilities on board where the fish are processed and prepared for sale. Such vessels are equipped for long stays at sea and can perform the work of several smaller boats.

Some full-time and many part-time fishers work on small boats in relatively shallow waters, often in sight of land. Navigation and communication needs are modest, and there is little need for much electronic equipment or provisions for long stays at sea. Crews are small—usually only one or two people collaborate on all aspects of the fishing operation. This may include placing gill nets across the mouths of rivers or inlets, entrapment nets in bays and lakes, or pots and traps for shellfish such as lobsters and crabs. Dredges and scrapes are sometimes used to gather shellfish such as oysters and scallops. A very small proportion of commercial fishing is conducted as diving operations. Depending upon the water's depth, divers—wearing regulation diving suits with an umbilical (air line) or a scuba outfit and equipment—use spears to catch fish and use nets and other equipment to gather shellfish, coral, sea urchins, abalone, and sponges. In very shallow waters, fish are caught from small boats having an outboard motor, from rowboats, or by wading. Fishers use a wide variety of hand-operated equipment—for example, nets, tongs, rakes, hoes, hooks, and shovels—to gather fish and shellfish; catch amphibians and reptiles such as frogs and turtles; and harvest marine vegetation, such as Irish moss and kelp.

Fishers may spend long shifts at sea.

Although most fishers are involved with commercial fishing, some captains and deckhands are primarily employed in sport or recreational fishing. Typically, a group of people charter a fishing vessel—for periods ranging from several hours to a number of days—for sport fishing, socializing, and relaxation and employ a captain and possibly several deckhands.

Working Conditions

Fishing operations are conducted under various environmental conditions, depending on the region of the country and the kind of species sought. Storms, fog, and wind may hamper fishing vessels. Divers are affected by murky water and unexpected shifts in underwater currents.

Fishers and fishing vessel operators work under hazardous conditions, and often help is not readily available. Malfunctioning navigation or communication equipment may lead to collisions or shipwrecks. Malfunctioning fishing gear poses the danger of injury to the crew, who also must guard against entanglement in fishing nets and gear, slippery decks resulting from fish processing operations, ice formation in the winter, or being swept overboard—a fearsome situation. Also, treatment for any serious injuries may have to await transfer to a hospital. Divers must guard against entanglement of air lines, malfunction of scuba equipment, decompression problems, and attacks by predatory fish.

Fishers and fishing vessel operators face strenuous outdoor work and long hours. Commercial fishing trips may require a stay of several weeks, or even months—hundreds of miles away from home port. The pace of work varies, from intense, while netting and hauling the catch aboard, to relatively relaxed, while traveling between home port and the fishing grounds. However, lookout watches are a regular responsibility, and crew members must be prepared to stand watch at prearranged times of the day or night. Although fishing gear has improved, and operations have become more mechanized, netting and processing fish are strenuous activities. Whereas newer vessels have improved living quarters and amenities, such as television and shower stalls, crews still experience the aggravations of confined conditions, continuous close personal contact, and the absence of family.

Employment

Fishers and fishing vessel operators held an estimated 51,000 jobs in 1998. About 6 out of 10 were self-employed. Nearly half worked variable schedules, to accommodate sudden changes in weather or fish migration patterns. Besides fishing conducted primarily to harvest food, some jobs involved sport fishing activities.

Training, Other Qualifications, and Advancement

Fishers usually acquire occupational skills on the job, many as members of families involved in fishing activities. No formal academic requirements exist. Operators of large commercial fishing vessels are required to complete a Coast Guard-approved training course. Students can expedite their entrance into these occupations by enrolling in 2-year vocational-technical programs offered by secondary schools. In addition, some community colleges and universities offer fishery technology and related programs that include courses in seamanship, vessel operations, marine safety, navigation, vessel repair and maintenance, health emergencies, and fishing gear technology. Courses include hands-on experience. Secondary and postsecondary programs are normally offered in or near coastal areas.

Experienced fishers may find short-term workshops offered through various postsecondary institutions especially useful. These programs provide a good working knowledge of electronic equipment used in navigation and communication and the latest improvements in fishing gear.

Captains and mates on large fishing vessels of at least 200 gross tons must be licensed. Captains of sport fishing boats used for charter, regardless of size, must also be licensed. Crew members on certain fish processing vessels may need a merchant mariner's document. The U.S. Coast Guard issues these documents and licenses to individuals who meet the stipulated health, physical, and academic requirements. (For information about merchant marine occupations, see the statement on water transportation occupations elsewhere in the *Handbook*.)

Fishers must be in good health and possess physical strength. Good coordination and mechanical aptitude are necessary to operate, maintain, and repair equipment and fishing gear. Fishers need perseverance to work long hours at sea, often under difficult conditions. On large vessels, they must be able to work as members of a team. Fishers must be patient, yet always alert, to overcome the boredom of long watches, when not engaged in fishing operations. The ability to assume any deckhand's functions, on short notice, is important. As supervisors, mates must be able to assume all duties, including the captain's, when necessary. The captain must be highly experienced, mature, decisive, and possess the business skills needed to run business operations.

On fishing vessels, most fishers begin as deckhands. Deckhands whose experience and interests are in ship engineering—maintenance and repair of ship engines and equipment—can eventually become licensed chief engineers on large commercial vessels, after meeting the Coast Guard's experience, physical, and academic requirements. Divers in fishing operations can enter commercial diving activity—for example, repairing ships or maintaining piers and marinas—usually after completion of a certified training program sponsored by an educational institution or industry association. Experienced, reliable deckhands who display supervisory qualities may become boatswains. Boatswains may, in turn, become second mates, first mates, and finally captains. Almost all captains become self-employed, and the overwhelming majority eventually own, or have an interest in, one or more fishing ships. Some may choose to run a sport or recreational fishing operation. When their seagoing days are over, experienced individuals may work in or, with the necessary capital, own stores selling fishing and marine equipment and supplies. Some captains may assume advisory or administrative positions in industry trade associations or government offices, such as harbor development commissions or in teaching positions in industry-sponsored workshops or educational institutions.

Job Outlook

Employment of fishers and fishing vessel operators is expected to decline through the year 2008. These occupations depend on the natural ability of fish stock to replenish itself through growth and reproduction, as well as on governmental estimates of the health of fisheries. Many operations are currently at or beyond maximum sustainable yield, and the number of workers who can earn an adequate income from fishing is expected to decline. Job openings will arise from the need to replace workers who retire or leave the occupation. Some fishers and fishing vessel operators leave the occupation, because of the strenuous and hazardous nature of the job and the lack of steady, year-round income.

In many areas, particularly the North Atlantic, pollution and excessive fishing have adversely affected the stock of fish and, consequently, the employment opportunities for fishers. In some areas, States have greatly reduced permits to fishers, to allow stocks of fish and shellfish to replenish themselves, idling many fishers. Other factors contributing to the projected decline in employment of fishers include the use of sophisticated electronic equipment for navigation, communication, and fish location; improvements in fishing gear, which have greatly increased the efficiency of fishing operations; and the use of highly automated *floating processors*, where the catch is processed aboard the vessel. Sport fishing boats will continue to provide some job opportunities.

Earnings

Median weekly earnings of full-time fishers and fishing vessel operators were about $386 in 1998. The middle 50 percent earned between $292 and $641. The highest paid 10 percent earned over $785, whereas the lowest paid 10 percent earned less than $194.

Earnings of fishers and fishing vessel operators normally are highest in the summer and fall—when demand for services peaks and environmental conditions are favorable—and lowest during the winter. Many full-time and most part-time workers supplement their income by working in other activities during the off-season. For example, fishers may work in seafood processing plants, establishments selling fishing and marine equipment, or in construction.

Earnings of fishers vary widely, depending upon the specific occupational function, size of the ship, and the amount and value of the catch. The costs of the fishing operation—operating the ship, repair and maintenance of gear and equipment, and the crew's supplies—are deducted from the sale of the catch. Net proceeds are distributed among the crew members in accordance with a prearranged percentage. Generally, the ship's owner—usually its captain—receives half of the net proceeds, which covers any profit as well as the depreciation, maintenance, and replacement costs of the ship.

Related Occupations

Numerous occupations involve outdoor activities similar to those of fishers and fishing vessel operators. Among these are fishing and hunting guides, fish hatchery and aquaculture workers, game wardens, harbor pilots, merchant marine officers and seamen, and wildlife management specialists.

Sources of Additional Information

For information on licensing requirements to fish in a particular area, contact:

☛ National Marine Fisheries Service, NMFS Scientific Publications Office, 7600 Sand Point Way NE., Seattle, WA 98115.

Names of postsecondary schools offering fishing and related marine educational programs are available from:

☛ Marine Technology Society, 1828 L St. NW., Suite 906, Washington, DC 20036-5104.

Information on licensing of fishing vessel captains and mates, and requirements for merchant mariner documentation, is available from the U.S. Coast Guard Marine Inspection Office or Marine Safety Office in your State, or:

☛ Office of Compliance, Commandant (G-MOC-3) 2100 Second St. SW., Washington, DC 20593.

☛ Licensing and Pilotage Branch, National Maritime Center, 4200 Wilson Blvd., Suite 510, Arlington, VA 22203-1804.

Food Processing Occupations

Butchers and Meat, Poultry, and Fish Cutters

(O*NET 65023, 89802, and 93938)

Significant Points

- Workers in meatpacking plants have among the highest incidences of injury and illness of all workers.
- Length of training ranges from a few days for some cutters to 1 or 2 years for highly skilled butchers.
- Job growth will be concentrated among lower skilled meat, poultry, and fish cutters, as more meat cutting and processing shifts from retail stores to food processing plants.

Nature of the Work

Butchers and meat, poultry, and fish cutters are employed at different stages in the process that converts animal carcasses into manageable pieces of meat suitable for sale to wholesales or consumers. Meat, poultry, and fish cutters commonly work in meatpacking or fish and poultry processing plants, while butchers are usually employed at the retail level. As a result of this distinction, the nature of these jobs varies significantly.

In meatpacking plants, *meatcutters* slaughter cattle, hogs, goats, and sheep and cut the carcasses into large wholesale cuts, such as rounds, loins, ribs, and chucks to facilitate the handling, distribution, and marketing of meat. In some of these plants, meatcutters also further process these primal parts into cuts that are ready for retail use. These workers also produce hamburger meat and meat trimmings, which are used to prepare sausages, luncheon meats, and other fabricated meat products. Meatcutters usually work on assembly lines, with each individual responsible for only a few of the many cuts needed to process a carcass. Depending on the type of cut, they use knives, cleavers, meat saws, bandsaws, or other, often dangerous, equipment.

In grocery stores, wholesale establishments that supply meat to restaurants, and institutional food service facilities, *butchers* separate wholesale cuts of meat into retail cuts or individual size servings. They cut meat into steaks and chops, shape and tie roasts, and grind beef for sale as chopped meat. Boneless cuts are prepared using knives, slicers, or power cutters, while bandsaws are required to carve bone-in pieces. Butchers in retail food stores may also weigh, wrap, and label the cuts of meat, arrange them in refrigerated cases for display, and prepare special cuts of meat to fill unique orders.

Poultry cutters slaughter and cut up chickens, turkeys, and other types of poultry. Although the poultry processing industry is becoming increasingly automated, many jobs such as trimming, packing, and deboning are still done manually. As in the meatpacking industry, most poultry cutters perform routine cuts on poultry as it moves along production lines.

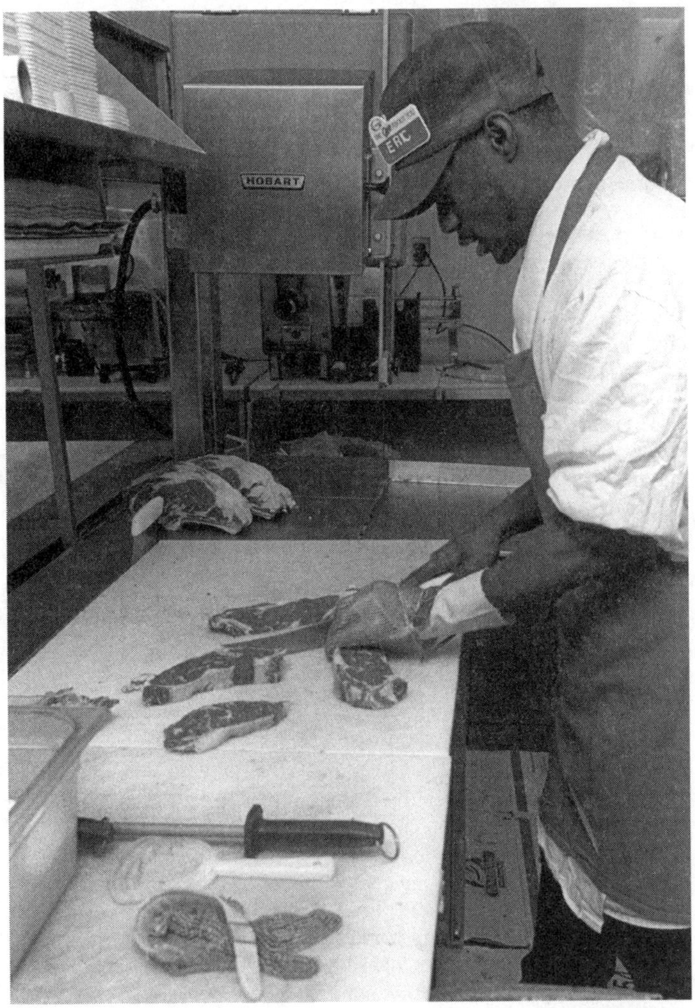

Butchers separate wholesale cuts of meat into retail cuts or individual-size servings.

Unlike the occupations listed above, *fish cutters,* also called *fish cleaners*, are likely to be employed in both manufacturing and retail establishments. These workers primarily cut, scale, and dress fish by removing the head, scales, and other inedible portions and cutting the fish into steaks or boneless fillets. In retail markets, they may also wait on customers and clean fish to order.

Meat, poultry, and fish cutters also prepare ready-to-heat foods. This often entails filleting meat or fish or cutting it into bite-sized pieces, preparing and adding vegetables, or applying sauces or breading.

Working Conditions

Working conditions vary by type and size of establishment. In meatpacking plants and large retail food establishments, butchers and meatcutters work in large meatcutting rooms equipped with power machines and conveyors. In small retail markets, the butcher or fish cleaner may work in a space behind the meat counter. To avoid viral and bacterial infections, work areas must be clean and sanitary.

Butchers and meat, poultry, and fish cutters often work in cold, damp rooms, which are refrigerated to prevent meat from spoiling and are damp because meat cutting generates large amounts of blood, condensation, and fat. Cool damp floors increase the likelihood of slips and falls. In addition, the low temperature, combined with the need to stand for long periods of time and perform physical tasks, makes the work tiring. As a result, butchers and meat, poultry, and fish cutters are more susceptible to injury than most other workers. In fact, meatpacking plants had the highest incidence of work-related injury and illness of any industry in 1997. Nearly 1 in 3 employees experienced a work-related injury or illness during that year.

Injuries include cuts, and even amputations, that occur when knives, cleavers, and power tools are used improperly. Also, repetitive slicing and lifting often lead to cumulative trauma injuries, such as carpal tunnel syndrome. To reduce the incidence of cumulative trauma disorders, some employers have reduced workloads, redesigned jobs and tools, and increased awareness of early warning signs. Nevertheless, workers in this occupation still face the serious threat of disabling injuries.

Employment

Butchers and meat, poultry, and fish cutters held about 359,000 jobs in 1998. Nearly 60 percent worked in meatpacking or poultry and fish processing plants, while most others in this occupation were employed at the retail level in grocery stores, meat and fish markets, restaurants, or hotels. The majority of the 216,000 skilled butchers and meatcutters worked in retail grocery stores, while nearly all meat, poultry, and fish cutters worked in meatpacking or poultry and fish processing plants.

Highly skilled butchers and meatcutters are employed in almost every city and town in the Nation, while lower skilled meat, poultry, and fish cutter jobs are concentrated in communities with food processing plants.

Training, Other Qualifications, and Advancement

Most butchers and meat, poultry, and fish cutters acquire their skills on the job through formal and informal training programs. The length of training varies significantly in this occupation, with simple cutting operations requiring a few days to learn, while more complex tasks, like eviscerating, generally require about a month to learn. The training period for a highly skilled butcher at the retail level may be a 1 or 2 years.

Generally, on-the-job trainees begin by doing less difficult jobs, such as simple cuts or removing bones. Under the guidance of experienced workers, trainees learn the proper use of tools and equipment and how to prepare various cuts of meat. After demonstrating skill with various meatcutting tools, they learn to divide carcasses into wholesale cuts and wholesale cuts into retail and individual portions. Trainees may also learn to roll and tie roasts, prepare sausage, and cure meat.

Those employed in retail food establishments often are taught operations such as inventory control, meat buying, and record keeping. In addition, growing concern about the safety of meats has led employers to offer extensive training in food safety to employees.

Skills important in meat, poultry, and fish cutting are manual dexterity, good depth perception, color discrimination, and good hand-eye coordination. Physical strength is often needed to lift and move heavy pieces of meat. Butchers and fish cleaners who wait on customers should have a pleasant personality, a neat appearance, and the ability to communicate clearly. In some States, a health certificate is required for employment.

Butchers and meat, poultry, and fish cutters in retail or wholesale establishments may progress to supervisory jobs, such as meat or seafood department managers in supermarkets. A few of these workers become meat or seafood buyers for wholesalers or supermarket chains. Some open their own meat or fish markets. In processing plants, meat, poultry, and fish cutters may advance to supervisory positions or become team leaders.

Job Outlook

Overall employment of butchers and meat, poultry, and fish cutters is expected to grow more slowly than the average for all occupations through 2008. Job growth will be concentrated among lower skilled meat, poultry, and fish cutters, as more meat cutting and processing shifts from retail stores to food processing plants. Nevertheless, job opportunities should be available at all levels of the occupation due to the need to replace experienced workers who transfer to other occupations or leave the labor force.

As the Nation's population grows, the demand for meat, poultry, and seafood should continue to increase. Successful marketing by the poultry industry is likely to increase demand for rotisserie chicken and ready-to-heat products. Similarly, the development of lower-fat and ready-to-heat products promises to stimulate the consumption of red meat. Although per capita consumption of fish and other seafood has been constant over the previous decade, population growth is expected to push consumption to record levels in coming years.

Employment growth of lower skilled meat, poultry, and fish cutters—who work primarily in meatpacking, poultry, and fish processing plants—is expected to increase faster than the average for all occupations in coming years. Although much of the production of poultry and fabricated poultry products is performed by machines, the growing popularity of labor-intensive, ready-to-heat goods promises to spur demand for poultry workers. Meat and fish cutters also will be in demand, as the task of preparing ready-to-heat meat and fish goods slowly shifts from retail stores to processing plants. Although the supply of edible ocean fish is limited, advances in fish farming, or "aquaculture," should help meet the growing demand for fish and produce ample opportunities for fish cutters.

Employment of more highly skilled butchers and meatcutters, who work primarily in retail stores, is expected to gradually decline. New automation and the consolidation of the meatpacking and poultry processing industries are enabling employers to transfer employment from higher-paid butchers to lower-wage meatcutters in meatpacking plants. At present, most red meat arrives at grocery stores partially cut up, but a growing share of meat is being delivered pre-packaged, with additional fat removed, to wholesalers and retailers. This trend is resulting in less work for retail butchers and a declining demand for their employment.

Earnings

Butchers and meatcutters had median annual earnings $20,420 in 1998. The middle 50 percent earned between $16,380 and $26,400. The highest paid 10 percent earned more than $34,460 annually, while the lowest 10 percent earned less than $13,140. Butchers and slaughterers who worked at the manufacturing level in the meat products industry earned $18,100 in 1997. Butchers and meatcutters employed at the retail level typically earn more than those in manufacturing. Median hourly earnings in the retail industries employing the largest number of butchers and meatcutters in 1997 were:

Industry	Earnings
Grocery stores	$22,700
Meat and fish markets	19,300
Groceries and related products (wholesale trade)	19,200
Eating and drinking places	15,000

Meat, poultry, and fish cutters typically earn less than butchers and meatcutters. In 1998, average annual earnings for these lower-skilled workers were $16,270, with the middle 50 percent earning between $14,280 and $18,390, the top 10 percent earning over $20,760, and the lowest decile less than $12,780. Meat, poultry, and fish cutters in the meat products industry earned $15,600 in 1997, while those working in miscellaneous food and kindred products earned $12,200.

Butchers and meat and fish cutters generally received typical benefits, including pension plans for those who were union members or employed by grocery stores. However, poultry workers rarely earned substantial benefits. Many butchers and meat, poultry, and fish cutters are members of the United Food and Commercial Workers International Union. In 1998, nearly a third of all butchers and meatcutters were union members or covered by a union contract.

Related Occupations

Butchers and meat, poultry, and fish cutters must be skilled at both hand and machine work and must have some knowledge of processes and techniques involved in handling and preparing food. Other occupations in food preparation that require similar skills and knowledge include bakers, chefs and cooks, and food preparation workers.

Sources of Additional Information

Information about work opportunities can be obtained from local employers or local offices of the State employment service. For information on training and other aspects of this trade, contact:

☛ United Food and Commercial Workers International Union, 1775 K St. NW., Washington, DC 20006.

Forestry, Conservation, and Logging Occupations

(O*NET 73002, 73005, 73011, 73099A, 73099B, 73099C, 73099D, 73099E, 79002A, 79002B, and 79008)

Significant Points

- Workers spend all their time outdoors, sometimes in poor weather and often in isolated areas.
- These jobs are physically demanding and hazardous.
- A small decline is expected in overall employment of forestry and logging occupations.

Nature of the Work

The Nation's forests are a rich natural resource, providing beauty and tranquillity, varied recreational areas, and wood for commercial use. Managing forests and woodlands requires many different kinds of workers. Forest and conservation workers help develop, maintain, and protect these forests by growing and planting new tree seedlings, fighting insects and diseases that attack trees, and helping to control soil erosion. Timber cutting and logging workers harvest thousands of acres of forests each year for the timber that provides the raw material for countless consumer and industrial products.

Generally working under the direction of a professional forester, *forestry technicians* compile data on the size, content, and condition of forest land tracts. These workers travel through sections of forest to gather basic information, such as species and population of trees, disease and insect damage, tree seedling mortality, and conditions that may cause fire danger. Forestry technicians also train and lead forest and conservation workers in seasonal activities, such as planting tree seedlings, putting out forest fires, and maintaining recreational facilities.

Forest workers are less skilled workers who perform a variety of tasks to reforest and conserve timberlands and maintain forest facilities, such as roads and campsites. Some forest workers, called tree planters, use digging and planting tools called "dibble bars" and "hoedads" to plant tree seedlings to reforest timberland areas. Forest workers also remove diseased or undesirable trees with a powersaw or handsaw and spray trees with insecticides or herbicides to kill insects and to protect against disease. Forest workers in private industry usually work for professional foresters and paint boundary lines, assist with prescribed burning, and aid in tree marking and measuring by keeping a tally of the trees examined and counted. Those who work for Federal and State governments also clear away brush and debris from jurisdictional camp trails, roadsides, and camping areas. Some clean kitchens and rest rooms at recreational facilities and campgrounds.

Other forest and conservation workers work in forest nurseries, sorting out tree seedlings and discarding those that do not meet prescribed standards of root formation, stem development, and foliage condition.

Some forest workers are employed on tree farms, where they plant, cultivate, and harvest many different kinds of trees. Duties vary depending on the type of tree farm. Those who work on specialty farms, such as those growing Christmas or ornamental trees for nurseries, are responsible for shearing tree tops and limbs to control growth, increase limb density, and improve tree shape. In addition, duties include planting, spraying to control surrounding weed growth and insects, and harvesting.

Other forest workers gather, by hand or using hand tools, products from the woodlands such as decorative greens, tree cones and barks, moss, and other wild plant life. Still others tap trees for sap to make syrup or to produce chemicals.

The timber cutting and logging process is carried out by a variety of workers who make up a logging crew. *Fallers* cut down trees with axes or hand-held power chain saws. Usually using gas-powered chain saws, *buckers* trim off the tops and branches and buck (cut) the resulting logs into specified lengths.

Choke setters fasten chokers (steel cables or chains) around logs to be skidded (dragged) by tractors or forwarded by the cable yarding system to the landing or deck area where logs are separated by species and loaded onto trucks. *Rigging slingers* and *chasers* set up and dismantle the cables and guy wires of the cable yarding system. *Log sorters*, *markers*, *movers*, and *debarkers* sort, mark, and move logs, based on species, size, and ownership, and tend machines that debarks logs.

Logging equipment operators on a logging crew perform a number of duties. They drive crawler or wheeled tractors called skidders, or forwarders, which drag or transport logs from the felling site in the woods to the log landing area for loading. They operate grapple loaders, which lift and load logs into trucks, and tree fellers or shears, which cut the trees. They use tree harvesters to shear the tops off of trees, cut and limb the trees, and then cut the logs into desired lengths. Some logging equipment operators use tracked or wheeled equipment similar to a fork lift to load logs and pulpwood off trucks or gondola railroad cars, usually in a sawmill or pulpmill woodyard.

Log graders and *scalers* inspect logs for defects, measure logs to determine their volume, and estimate the marketable content or value of logs or pulpwood. These workers often use hand-held data collection terminals to enter data about individual trees, which can later be downloaded or sent, via modem, from the scaling area to a central computer.

Other timber cutting and logging workers have a variety of responsibilities. Some workers hike through forests to assess logging conditions. Laborers clear areas of brush and other growth to prepare for logging activities or to promote growth of desirable species of trees.

The timber cutting and logging industry is characterized by a large number of small crews of 4 to 8 workers. A typical crew might consist of one or two fallers or one feller machine operator, one bucker, two logging tractor operators to drag cut trees to the loading deck, and one equipment operator to load the logs onto trucks. Most crews work for self-employed logging contractors who possess substantial logging experience, the capital to purchase equipment, and skills needed to run a small business successfully. Most contractors work alongside their crews as working supervisors and often operate one of the logging machines, such as the grapple loader or the tree harvester. Many manage more than one crew and function as owner-supervisors.

Although timber cutting and logging equipment has greatly improved and operations are becoming increasingly mechanized, many logging jobs are still labor intensive. These jobs require various levels of skill, ranging from the unskilled task of manually moving logs, branches, and equipment to skillfully using chain saws, peavies (hooked poles), and log jacks to cut and position logs for further processing or loading. To keep costs down, some timber cutting and logging workers maintain and repair the equipment they use. A skillful, experienced logger is expected to handle a variety of logging operations.

Working Conditions

Forestry and logging jobs are physically demanding. These workers spend all their time outdoors, sometimes in poor weather and often in isolated areas. A few lumber camps in Alaska house workers in bunkhouses or company towns. Workers in sparsely populated western

Forest workers perform a variety of tasks to reforest timberlands and maintain forest facilities such as roads and campsites.

States commute long distances between their homes and logging sites. In the more densely populated eastern and southern States, commuting distances are much shorter.

Most logging occupations involve lifting, climbing, and other strenuous activities. Loggers work under unusually hazardous conditions. Falling trees and branches are a constant menace, as are the dangers associated with log handling operations and use of sawing equipment, especially delimbing devices. Special care must be taken during strong winds, which can even halt operations. Slippery or muddy ground and hidden roots or vines not only reduce efficiency but also present a constant danger, especially in the presence of moving vehicles and machinery. Poisonous plants, brambles, insects, snakes, and heat and humidity are minor annoyances. If safety precautions are not taken, the high noise level of sawing and skidding operations over long periods of time may impair hearing. Experience, exercise of caution, and use of proper safety measures and equipment—such as hardhats, eye and ear protection, and safety clothing and boots—are extremely important to avoid injury.

The jobs of forest and conservation workers are generally much less hazardous. It may be necessary for some forestry aides or forest workers to walk long distances through densely wooded areas to do their work.

Employment

Forestry conservation and logging workers held about 120,000 jobs in 1998, distributed among the following occupations:

Occupation	Jobs
Forest and conservation workers	33,000
Logging equipment operators	56,000
Fallers and buckers	18,000
All other timber cutting and related logging occupations	13,000

Most wage and salary logging workers are employed in the logging camps and logging contractors industry. Others work in sawmills and planing mills or for services specializing in the care and maintenance of ornamental trees. Although logging operations are found in most States, the Southeast employs the most, about 40 percent of all logging workers, followed by the Northwest, which employs 25 percent.

Self-employed logging workers account for 1 of every 4 logging workers—a much higher proportion of self-employment than for most occupations.

Most forest and conservation workers are employed by government at some level. Of these workers, about 14,000 are employed by the Federal Government, mostly in the U.S. Department of Agriculture's Forest Service; about 9,000 work for State governments, and 6,000 work for local governments. Most of the remainder work for companies that operate timber tracts, tree farms, or forest nurseries, or for establishments that supply forestry services. Although forest and conservation workers are located in every State, employment is concentrated in the West and Southeast where many national and private forests and parks are located.

Seasonal demand for forestry and logging workers varies by region. For example, in the northern States, winter work is common because the frozen ground facilitates logging. In the Southeast, logging and related activities occur year round.

Training, Other Qualifications, and Advancement

Most forestry and logging workers develop skills through on-the-job training with instruction coming primarily from experienced workers. Logging workers must familiarize themselves with the character and potential dangers of the forest environment and the operation of logging machinery and equipment. However, large logging companies and trade associations, such as the Northeastern Loggers Association and the American Pulpwood Association, offer special programs, particularly for workers training to operate large, expensive machinery and equipment. Often, a representative of the manufacturer or company spends several days in the field explaining and overseeing the operation of newly purchased machinery. Safety training is a vital part of instruction for all logging workers.

Many State forestry or logging associations provide training sessions for fallers, whose job duties require more skill and experience than other positions on the logging team. Sessions may take place in the field, where trainees, under the supervision of an experienced logger, have the opportunity to practice various felling techniques. Fallers learn how to manually cut down extremely large or expensive trees safely and with minimal damage to the felled or surrounding trees.

Training programs for loggers are becoming common in many States, in response to a collaborative effort by the American Forest and Paper Association and others in the forestry industry, to encourage the health and productivity of the Nation's forests. Logger training programs vary by State, but generally include some type of classroom or field training in a number of areas—best management practices, safety, endangered species, reforestation, and business management. Some programs lead to logger certification.

Experience in other occupations can expedite entry into some logging occupations. For example, equipment operators, such as truckdrivers and bulldozer and crane operators, can assume skidding and yarding functions. Some loggers have worked in sawmills or on family farms with extensive wooded areas. Some logging contractors were formerly crew members of family-owned businesses operated over several generations.

Generally, little formal education is required for most forestry and logging occupations. The minimum requirement for a forestry technician or aide is a high school education. Many secondary schools, including vocational and technical schools, and some community colleges offer courses or a 2-year degree in general forestry, wildlife, conservation, and forest harvesting, which could be helpful in obtaining a job. A curriculum that includes field trips to observe or participate in forestry or logging activities provides a particularly good background. There are no educational requirements for forest worker jobs. Many of these workers are high school or college students who are hired on a part-time or seasonal basis to perform short-term, labor-intensive tasks, such as planting tree seedlings.

Forestry and logging workers must be in good health and able to work outdoors every day. They must also be able to work as part of a team. Many logging occupations require physical strength and stamina. Maturity and good judgment are important in making quick, intelligent decisions in dealing with hazards as they arise. Mechanical aptitude and coordination are necessary qualities for operators of machinery and equipment, who often are responsible for repair and maintenance as well. Initiative and managerial and business skills are necessary for success as a self-employed logging contractor.

Experience working at a nursery or as a laborer can be useful in obtaining a job as a forest worker. Logging workers generally advance from occupations involving primarily manual labor to those involving the operation of expensive, sometimes complicated, machinery and other equipment. Inexperienced entrants usually begin as laborers, who carry tools and equipment, clear brush, and load and unload logs and brush. For some, familiarization with logging operations may lead to jobs such as log handling equipment operator. Further experience may lead to jobs involving the operation of more complicated machinery and yarding towers to transport, load, and unload logs. Those who have the motor skills required for the efficient use of power saws and other equipment may become fallers and buckers.

Job Outlook

Employment of forestry, conservation, and logging workers is expected to decline slightly through the year 2008. Any job openings will result from replacement needs. Many logging workers transfer to other jobs that are less physically demanding and dangerous. In addition, many forestry workers are young workers who are not committed to the occupation on a long-term basis. Some take jobs to earn money for school; others only work in this occupation until they find a better-paying job.

Employment of timber cutting and logging occupations is expected to decline slightly. Despite steady demand for lumber and other wood products, increased mechanization of logging operations and improvements in logging equipment will continue to depress demand for workers. In addition, forest conservation efforts may restrict the volume of public timber available for harvesting, particularly in Federal forests in the West and Northwest, further dampening demand for timber cutting and logging workers.

Little or no change is expected in the employment of forest and conservation workers. Environmental concerns may spur the demand for workers who maintain and conserve our woodlands, especially at the State and local government levels; however, budgetary constraints within the Federal Government and in many State governments are expected to suppress job growth.

Increasing mechanization will have different effects on timber cutting and logging workers. Employment of fallers, buckers, choke setters, and other workers whose jobs are labor intensive should decline, as safer, labor-saving machinery and other equipment are increasingly used. Employment of machinery and equipment operators, such as logging tractor and log handling equipment operators, should be less adversely affected.

Weather can force curtailment of logging operations during the muddy spring season and cold winter months, depending on the geographic region. Changes in the level of construction, particularly residential construction, also affect logging activities in the short term. In addition, logging operations must be relocated when timber harvesting in a particular area has been completed. During prolonged periods of inactivity, some workers may stay on the job to maintain or repair logging machinery and equipment; others are forced to find jobs in other occupations or be without work.

Earnings

Earnings vary depending on the particular forestry or logging occupation and experience, ranging from the minimum wage in some beginning laborer positions to about $25.00 an hour for some experienced fallers. Median hourly earnings in 1998 for forestry, conservation, and logging occupations were as follows:

All other timber cutting and related logging workers	$11.65
Fallers and buckers	11.30
Forest and conservation workers	11.13
Logging equipment operators	11.13

Generally, earnings of more skilled workers, such as yarder operators, are higher than those of less skilled workers, such as laborers and choke setters.

Earnings of logging workers vary by size of establishment and by geographic area. Workers in the largest establishments earn more than those in the smallest establishments. Workers in Alaska and the Northwest earn more than those in the South, where the cost of living is generally lower.

In 1999, forestry technicians and aides who worked for the Federal Government averaged about $31,300 a year.

Forest and conservation workers who work for Federal, State, and local governments and large private firms generally enjoy more generous benefits than workers in smaller firms. Small logging contractors generally offer timber cutting and logging workers few benefits. However, some employers offer full-time workers basic benefits, such as medical coverage, and provide safety apparel and equipment.

Related Occupations

Other occupations concerned with the care of trees and their environment include arborist, groundskeeper, landscaper, nursery worker, and soil conservation technician. Logging equipment operators have skills similar to material moving equipment operators, such as industrial truck and tractor operators and crane and tower operators.

Sources of Additional Information

For information about forestry jobs with the Federal Government, contact:

☛ Chief, U.S. Forest Service, U.S. Department of Agriculture, 14th St. and Independence Ave., SW., Washington, DC 20013.

For information about timber cutting and logging careers and secondary and postsecondary programs offering training for logging occupations, contact:

☛ Northeastern Loggers Association, P.O. Box 69, Old Forge, NY 13420.

☛ Timber Producers Association of Michigan and Wisconsin, P.O. Box 39, Tomahawk, WI 54487.

☛ American Pulpwood Association, Inc., 600 Jefferson Plaza, Suite 350, Rockville, MD 20852.

The school of forestry at your State land-grant college or university should also be able to provide useful information.

A list of State forestry associations and other forestry-related State associations is available at most public libraries.

Inspectors, Testers, and Graders

(O*NET 21911K, 21911M, 21911N, 83002A, 83002B, 83002C, 83002D, 83005A, 83008A, 83008C, 83008D, and 83099)

Significant Points

- For workers who perform relatively simple tests of products, a high school diploma is sufficient; experienced production workers fill more complex precision inspecting positions.
- Like many other occupations concentrated in manufacturing, employment is expected to decline, reflecting the growth of automated inspection and the redistribution of quality control responsibilities from inspectors to other production workers.

Nature of the Work

Inspectors, testers, and graders ensure that your food will not make you sick, your car will run properly, and your pants will not split the first time you wear them. These workers monitor quality standards for virtually all manufactured products, including foods, textiles, clothing, glassware, motor vehicles, electronic components, computers, and structural steel. As quality has become a more central focus in many production firms, daily duties of inspectors have changed. In some cases, their titles also have changed to "quality control inspector" or a similar name, reflecting the growing importance of quality. (A separate statement on construction and building inspectors appears elsewhere in the *Handbook.*)

Regardless of title, all inspectors, testers, and graders work to guarantee the quality of the goods their firms produce. Specific job duties vary across the wide range of industries in which these workers are found. For example, they may check products by sight, sound, feel, smell, or even taste to locate imperfections, such as cuts, scratches, bubbles, missing pieces, misweaves, or crooked seams. These workers also may verify dimensions, color, weight, texture, strength, or other physical characteristics of objects. Machinery testers generally verify that parts fit, move correctly, and are properly lubricated; check the pressure of gases and the level of liquids; test the flow of electricity; and do a test run to check for proper operation. Some jobs involve only a quick visual inspection; others require a longer, detailed one.

Inspectors, testers, and graders are involved at every stage of the production process. Some inspectors examine materials received from a supplier before sending them to the production line. Others inspect components, subassemblies, and assemblies or perform a final check on the finished product. Depending on the skill level of the inspectors, they may also set up and test equipment, calibrate precision instruments, or repair defective products.

Inspectors, testers, and graders rely on a number of tools to perform their jobs. Many use micrometers, calipers, alignment gauges, and other instruments to check and compare the dimensions of parts against the parts' specifications. They may also operate electronic equipment, such as measuring machines, which use sensitive probes to measure a part's dimensional accuracy. Inspectors testing electrical devices may use voltmeters, ammeters, and oscilloscopes to test insulation, current flow, and resistance.

Inspectors mark, tag, or note problems. They may reject defective items outright, send them for repair or correction, or fix minor problems themselves. If the product checks out, they may screw on a nameplate, tag it, stamp a serial number, or certify it in some other way. Inspectors, testers, and graders record the results of their inspections, compute the percentage of defects and other statistical parameters, and prepare inspection and test reports. Some electronic inspection equipment automatically provides test reports containing these inspection results. When defects are found, inspectors notify supervisors, and help analyze and correct the production problems.

Recent emphasis on quality control in manufacturing has meant that inspection is becoming more fully integrated into the production process. For example, some companies have set up teams of inspection and production workers to jointly review and improve product quality. In addition, many companies now use self-monitoring production machines to ensure that the output is produced within quality standards. Self-monitoring machines can alert inspectors to production problems, and automatically repair defects in some cases. Many firms have completely automated inspection with the help of advanced vision systems, using machinery installed at one or several points in the production process. Inspectors in these firms calibrate and monitor the equipment, review output, and perform random product checks.

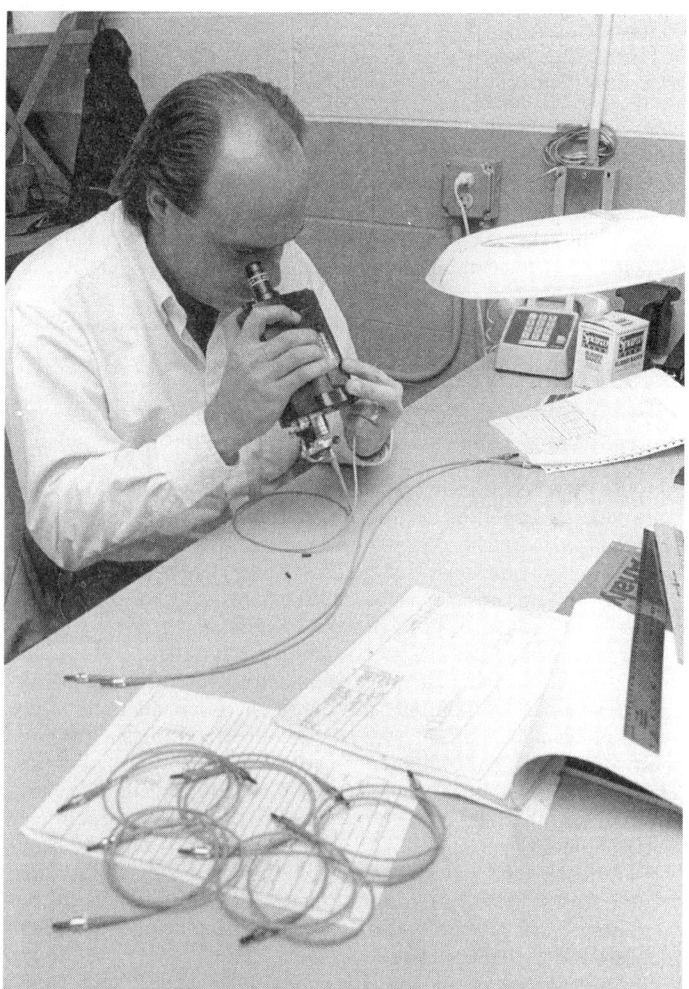

Inspectors, testers, and graders check products for imperfections.

Working Conditions

Working conditions vary by industry and establishment size. As a result, some inspectors examine similar products for an entire shift, whereas others examine a variety of items. In manufacturing, most inspectors remain at one work station; in transportation, some travel from place to place to do inspections. Inspectors in some industries may be on their feet all day and may have to lift heavy objects, whereas in other industries they sit during most of their shift and do little strenuous work. Workers in heavy manufacturing plants may be exposed to the noise and grime of machinery; in other plants, inspectors work in clean, air-conditioned environments, suitable for carrying out controlled tests.

Some inspectors work evenings, nights, or weekends. In these cases, shift assignments generally are made on the basis of seniority. Overtime may be required to meet production goals.

Employment

Inspectors, testers, and graders held about 689,000 jobs in 1998. About 2 out of 3 worked in manufacturing establishments that produced such products as industrial machinery and equipment, motor vehicles and equipment, aircraft and parts, primary and fabricated metals, electronic components and accessories, food, textiles, and apparel. Inspectors, testers, and graders also were found in temporary help services, transportation, wholesale trade, engineering and management services, and government agencies.

Training, Other Qualifications, and Advancement

Training requirements vary, based on the responsibilities of the inspector, tester, or grader. For workers who perform simple "pass/fail" tests of products, a high school diploma is preferred and may be required for some jobs. Simple jobs may be filled by beginners provided with inhouse training. Training for new inspectors may cover the use of special meters, gauges, computers, or other instruments; quality control techniques; blueprint reading; safety; and reporting requirements. There are some postsecondary training programs in testing, but many employers prefer to train inspectors on the job.

Complex precision inspecting positions are filled by experienced assemblers, machine operators, or mechanics who already have a thorough knowledge of the products and production processes. To advance to these positions, experienced workers may need training in statistical process control, new automation, or the company's quality assurance policies. As automated inspection equipment becomes more common, computer skills are increasingly important.

In general, inspectors, testers, and graders need mechanical aptitude, math skills, and good hand-eye coordination and vision. Advancement for these workers frequently takes the form of higher pay. They also may advance to inspector of more complex products, supervisor, or to related positions, such as purchaser of materials and equipment.

Job Outlook

Like many other occupations concentrated in the manufacturing sector, employment of inspectors, testers, and graders is expected to decline through the year 2008. The projected decline stems primarily from the growth of automated inspection and the redistribution of quality control responsibilities from inspectors to production workers. In spite of declining employment, a large number of job openings will arise due to turnover in this large occupation. Many of these jobs, however, will be available only to experienced production workers with advanced skills.

Employment of inspectors, testers, and graders will be significantly affected by the increasing focus on quality in American industry. The emphasis on quality is leading manufacturers to invest in automated inspection equipment and to take a more systematic approach to quality inspection. Continued improvements in technologies, such as spectrophotometers and computer-assisted visual inspection systems, allow firms to effectively automate simple inspection tasks, increasing worker productivity and reducing the demand for inspectors. As the price of these technologies continues to decrease, they will become more cost-effective for firms and will be more widely implemented in a broad range of industries.

Apart from automation, firms are improving quality by building it into the production process. This has led firms to redistribute many inspection duties from inspectors, testers, and graders to other production workers who monitor quality at every stage of the process. In addition, the growing implementation of statistical process control is resulting in "smarter" inspection. Using this system, firms survey the sources and incidence of defects so these firms can better focus their efforts and reduce production of defective products.

In many industries, however, automation is not being aggressively pursued as an alternative to manual inspection. When key inspection elements are oriented to size, such as length, width, or thickness, automation may play some role in the future. But when taste, smell, texture, appearance, or product performance are important, inspection will probably continue to be done by humans. Employment of inspectors, testers, and graders is expected to increase in fast-growing industries, such as wholesale trade, and in business services as more manufacturers and industrial firms hire temporary inspectors to increase the flexibility of their staffing strategies.

Earnings

Median hourly earnings of inspectors, testers, and graders were $11.28 in 1998. The middle 50 percent earned between $8.63 and $15.53 an hour. The lowest 10 percent earned less than $6.78 an hour; the highest 10 percent earned more than $20.40 an hour. Median hourly earnings of transportation inspectors in the railroad industry were $18.10 in 1997.

Related Occupations

Workers who inspect products or services include construction and building inspectors, who examine a variety of structures, and inspectors and compliance officers, who inspect and enforce rules on matters such as health, safety, food, licensing, or finance.

Sources of Additional Information

For general information about inspectors, testers, and graders, contact:

☛ The National Tooling and Machining Association, 9300 Livingston Rd., Fort Washington, MD 20744. Internet: **http://www.ntma.org**

☛ The American Society for Quality, 611 East Wisconsin Ave., P.O. Box 3005, Milwaukee, WI 53201-3005. Internet: **http://www.asq.org**

Metalworking and Plastics-Working Occupations

Jewelers and Precious Stone and Metal Workers

(O*NET 89123A, 89123B, 89126C, 89126E, 89126K, and 89926A)

Significant Points

- About one-third of all jewelers were self-employed; many operated their own store or repair shop, and some specialized in designing and creating custom jewelry.
- Slightly over half of all salaried jewelers worked in retail establishments, while one-third were employed in manufacturing plants.
- Although employment is expected to decline slightly, prospects should be excellent as more people retire or leave the occupation.

Nature of the Work

Jewelers design, manufacture, repair, and adjust rings, necklaces, bracelets, earrings, and other jewelry. They use a variety of common and specialized handtools to mold and shape metal and set gemstones. Increasingly, jewelers use computers to design jewelry and lasers to perform very delicate and intricate work.

Jewelers usually specialize in one or more areas: Designing and manufacturing new pieces of jewelry, gem cutting, setting and polishing stones, or repairing broken items. Jewelers who are knowledgeable about the quality, characteristics, and value of gemstones also sell jewelry and provide appraisal services. In small retail or repair shops, jewelers may be involved in all aspects of the work. Jewelers who own or manage stores or shops also hire and train employees; order, market, and sell merchandise; and perform other managerial duties.

The work of jewelers requires a high degree of skill, precision, and attention to detail regardless of the type of establishment or work setting. Typical repair work includes enlarging or reducing ring sizes, resetting stones, and replacing broken clasps and mountings. Some jewelers also design or make their own jewelry. Following their own designs, or those created by designers or customers, they begin by shaping the metal or carving wax to make a model for casting the metal. The individual parts are then soldered together, and the jeweler may mount a diamond or other gem, or engrave a design into the metal. Although jewelers mainly use computers for inventory control, some jewelry designers also use them to design and create customized pieces according to their customers' wishes. With the aid of computers, customers visualize different combinations of styles, cuts, shanks, sizes, and stones to create their own pieces.

In manufacturing, jewelers usually specialize in a single operation. Some may make models or tools for the jewelry that is to be produced. Others do finishing work, such as setting stones, polishing, or engraving. A growing number of jewelers use lasers for cutting and improving the quality of stones, intricate engraving or design work, and ID inscription. Some manufacturing firms use CAD/CAM (computer-aided design and manufacturing) to facilitate product design and automate some steps in the mold and model-making process. As such systems become more affordable, their use should increase. In larger manufacturing establishments, jewelers may be required to perform several tasks as new manufacturing processes make their way through the industry.

Working Conditions

A jeweler's work involves a great deal of concentration and attention to detail. Working on precious stones and metals, while trying to satisfy customers' and employers' demands for speed and quality, can cause fatigue or stress. However, the use of more ergonomically correct jewelers' benches has eliminated the strain and discomfort formerly caused by spending long periods bending over a workbench in one position. In larger manufacturing plants and some smaller repair shops, chemicals, sharp or pointed tools, and jewelers' torches pose potential safety threats and may cause injury if proper care is not taken.

In repair shops, jewelers usually work alone with little supervision. In retail stores, on the other hand, they may talk with customers about repairs, perform custom design work, and even do some sales work.

Jewelers and precious stone and metal workers use a variety of handtools to mold metal and set gemstones.

Because many of their materials are very valuable, jewelers must observe strict security procedures. These include locked doors that are only opened by a buzzer, barred windows, burglar alarms, and, for large jewelry establishments, the presence of armed guards.

Employment

Jewelers and precious stone and metal workers held about 30,000 jobs in 1998. About one-third of all these workers were self-employed; many operated their own store or repair shop, and some specialized in designing and creating custom jewelry.

One-half of all salaried jewelers worked in retail establishments, while one-third were employed in manufacturing plants. Although jewelry stores and repair shops can be found in every city and many small towns, most job opportunities are in larger metropolitan areas. Many jewelers employed in manufacturing work in Rhode Island, New York, and Los Angeles.

Training, Other Qualifications, and Advancement

Jewelers' skills usually are learned in vocational or technical schools, through correspondence courses, or informally on the job. Colleges and art and design schools also offer programs that can lead to a bachelor's or master's degree of fine arts in jewelry design. Formal training in the basic skills of the trade enhances one's employment and advancement opportunities. Many employers prefer jewelers with design, repair, and sales skills. Some aspiring jewelers begin working as clerks in department stores, and transfer to jobs in jewelry shops or manufacturing firms after gaining experience.

For those interested in working in a jewelry store or repair shop, vocational and technical schools or courses offered by local colleges are the best sources of training. In these programs, which vary in length from 6 months to 1 year, students learn the use and care of jewelers' tools and machines and basic jewelry making and repairing skills, such as design, casting, stone setting, and polishing. Technical school courses also cover topics including blueprint reading, math, and shop theory. To enter most technical school or college programs, a high school diploma or its equivalent is required. Because computer-aided design is used increasingly in the jewelry field, it is recommended that students—especially those interested in design and manufacturing—obtain training in CAD.

The Gemological Institute of America (GIA) offers programs lasting about 6 months and self-paced correspondence courses that may last longer. The GIA offers the graduate gemologist (G.G.) and graduate jeweler (G.J.) diplomas, along with a variety of courses in gemology and jewelry manufacturing and design. Advanced programs cover a wide range of topics, including the identification and grading of diamonds and gemstones.

Most employers feel that vocational and technical school graduates need several more years of supervised, on-the-job training to refine their repair skills and learn more about the operation of the store or shop. In addition, some employers encourage workers to improve their skills by enrolling in short-term technical school courses such as sample making, wax carving, or gemology. Many employers pay all or part of the cost of this additional training.

In jewelry manufacturing plants, workers traditionally develop their skills through informal apprenticeships and on-the-job training. This training lasts 3 to 4 years, depending on the difficulty of the specialty. Training usually focuses on casting, stonesetting, modelmaking, or engraving. In recent years, a growing number of technical schools and colleges have begun to offer training designed for jewelers working in manufacturing. Like employers in retail trade, though, those in manufacturing now prefer graduates of these programs because they are familiar with the production process, requiring less on-the-job training.

The precise and delicate nature of jewelry work requires finger and hand dexterity, good hand-eye coordination, patience, and concentration. Artistic ability and fashion consciousness are major assets because jewelry must be stylish and attractive. Those who work in jewelry stores have frequent contact with customers and should be neat, personable, and knowledgeable about the merchandise. In addition, employers require someone of good character because jewelers work with very valuable materials.

Advancement opportunities are limited and greatly dependent on an individual's skill and initiative. In manufacturing, some jewelers advance to supervisory jobs, such as master jeweler or head jeweler, but for most, advancement takes the form of higher pay doing the same job. Jewelers who work in jewelry stores or repair shops may become managers; some open their own businesses.

For those interested in starting their own business, they first should establish themselves and build a reputation for their work within the jewelry trade. Then, they can obtain sufficient credit from jewelry suppliers and wholesalers to acquire the necessary inventory. Also, because the jewelry business is highly competitive, jewelers who plan to open their own store should have experience in selling, as well as knowledge of marketing and business management. Courses in these areas often are available from technical schools and community colleges.

Job Outlook

Employment of jewelers and precious stone and metal workers is expected to decline through 2008. Employment opportunities, however, should be excellent, reflecting current shortages in the occupation and the need to replace jewelers who retire or leave the labor force for other reasons.

The demand for jewelry largely depends on the amount of disposable income people have. Therefore, the increasing number of affluent individuals, working women, double-income households, and fashion conscious men are expected to keep jewelry sales strong. Traditionally, job opportunities for jewelers depended largely on jewelry sales and demand for jewelry repair services, which makes up approximately half of a retail jewelry store's revenues. Now, however, non-traditional jewelry marketers, such as discount stores, mail-order catalogue companies, and television shopping networks have limited the growth of sales from traditional jewelers. These types of establishments require fewer jewelers, thus limiting job opportunities. Demand for jewelers who specialize in repair work, however, should remain steady or even increase as jewelry sales increase because non-traditional vendors typically do not offer repair services.

Opportunities in jewelry stores and repair shops will be best for graduates from a jeweler or gemologist training program. Demand for repair workers will be strong because maintaining and repairing jewelry is an ongoing process, even during economic slowdowns. In fact, demand for jewelry repair may increase during recessions as people repair or restore existing pieces rather than purchase new ones.

Within manufacturing, increasing automation will adversely affect employment of low-skilled occupations, such as assembler and polisher. Automation will have a lesser impact on more creative, highly skilled positions, such as mold and model maker. Furthermore, small manufacturers, which typify the industry, will have an increasingly difficult time competing with the larger manufacturers when it comes to supplying large retailers. Because of recent international trade agreements, exports are increasing modestly as manufacturers become more competitive in foreign markets. However, imports from foreign manufacturers are increasing more rapidly than exports due to these same agreements.

Earnings

Median annual earnings for jewelers and precious stone and metal workers were $23,820 in 1998. The middle 50 percent earned between $17,110 and $32,540. The lowest 10 percent earned less than $12,670 and the highest 10 percent earned over $41,160.

According to the Manufacturing Jewelers and Suppliers of America, the median average hourly wage of jewelers in companies with more than 10 employees was $13.62 in 1998. Beginners in jewelry factories usually start at considerably less pay than experienced workers do. As they become more proficient, they receive raises.

Most jewelers enjoy a variety of benefits including reimbursement from their employers for work-related courses and discounts on jewelry purchases.

Related Occupations

Jewelers and precious stone and metal workers do precision handwork. Other skilled workers who do similar jobs include polishers, dental laboratory technicians, hand engravers, and watch makers and repairers.

Sources of Additional Information

Information on job opportunities and training programs for jewelers is available from:

☛ Gemological Institute of America, 5345 Armada Dr., Carlsbad, CA 92008.

☛ California Institute of Jewelry Training, 5800 Winding Way, Carmichael, CA 95608.

General career information is available from:

☛ Jewelers of America, 1185 Avenue of the Americas, 30th Floor, New York, NY 10036.

☛ Manufacturing Jewelers and Suppliers of America, 1 State St., 6th Floor, Providence, RI 02908-5035.

To receive a list of technical schools accredited by the Accrediting Commission of Career Schools and Colleges of Technology which have programs in jewelry design, contact:

☛ Accrediting Commission of Career Schools and Colleges of Technology, 2101 Wilson Blvd., Suite 302, Arlington, VA 22201.

Machinists and Numerical Control Machine Tool Programmers

(O*NET 25111 and 89108)

Significant Points

- Formal training in high schools, vocational schools, or community colleges is typical; many entrants have previously worked as machine tool operators or setters.
- Job opportunities will be excellent, as employers continue to report difficulties in finding workers with the necessary skills and knowledge.

Nature of the Work

Machinists use machine tools, such as lathes, drill presses, and milling machines to produce precision metal parts. Although they may produce large quantities of one part, precision machinists often produce small batches or one-of-a-kind items. They use their knowledge of the working properties of metals and their skill with machine tools to plan and carry out the operations needed to make machined products that meet precise specifications.

Before they machine a part, machinists must carefully plan and prepare the operation. These workers first review blueprints or written specifications for a job. Next, they calculate where to cut or bore into the workpiece, how fast to feed the metal into the machine, and how much metal to remove. They then select tools and materials for the job, plan the sequence of cutting and finishing operations, and mark the metal stock to show where cuts should be made.

After this layout work is completed, machinists perform the necessary machining operations. They position the metal stock on the machine tool—drill presses, lathes, milling machines, or others—set the controls, and make the cuts. During the machining process, they must constantly monitor the feed and speed of the machine. Machinists also ensure that the workpiece is being properly lubricated and cooled, because the machining of metal products generates a significant amount of heat.

Some machinists, often called production machinists, may produce large quantities of one part, especially parts requiring complex operations and great precision. For unusually sophisticated procedures, expensive machinery is used. Usually, however, large numbers of parts requiring more routine operations are produced by metalworking and plastics-working machine operators. (See the statement on metalworking and plastics-working machine operators elsewhere in the *Handbook.*) Other machinists do maintenance work—repairing or making new parts for existing machinery. To

It takes several years to become a highly skilled machinist.

repair a broken part, maintenance machinists may refer to blueprints and perform the same machining operations that were needed to create the original part.

Increasingly, the machine tools used to produce metal parts are computer numerically controlled (CNC)—that is, they contain computer controllers that direct the machine's operations. The controller reads a program—a coded list of the steps necessary to perform a specific machining job—and runs the machine tool's mechanisms through the steps. The introduction of CNC machine tools has changed the nature of the work of machinists. These machines enable machinists to be more productive and to produce parts with a level of precision that is not possible with traditional machining techniques. Furthermore, because precise movements are recorded in a program that can be saved and used again in the future, they allow this high level of precision to be consistently repeated. CNC machine tools also allow various functions to be performed with one setup, thereby reducing the need for additional, labor-intensive setups.

The quality of the products these machines produce depends largely on the programs, which may be produced by machinists or by CNC machine tool programmers (CNC programmers). CNC programmers begin as machinists do—by analyzing blueprints, computing the size and position of the cuts, determining the sequence of machine operations, selecting tools, and calculating the machine speed and feed rates. They then write the program in the language of the machine's controller and store it. Skilled machinists may also do programming. In fact, as computer-aided manufacturing (CAM) software becomes more user-friendly and CNC machines are more widely used, machinists are increasingly expected to perform this function.

Machinists work alone or with CNC programmers to check new programs and ensure that machinery will function properly and the output will meet specifications. Because a problem with the program could damage costly machinery and cutting tools, computer simulations may be used instead of a trial run to check the program. If errors are found, the program must be changed and re-tested until the problem is resolved. In addition, growing connectivity between computer-aided design software and CNC machine tools is raising productivity by automatically translating designs into instructions, which are understood by the computer controller on the machine tool. These new CAM technologies enable programs to be easily modified for use on other jobs with similar specifications, thereby reducing time and effort.

Working Conditions

Most machine shops are well lit and ventilated. Nevertheless, working around high-speed machine tools presents certain dangers, and workers must follow safety precautions. Machinists wear protective equipment such as safety glasses to shield against bits of flying metal and earplugs to dampen machinery noise. They must also exercise caution when handling hazardous coolants and lubricants. The job requires stamina, because machinists stand most of the day and at times may need to lift moderately heavy workpieces.

CNC programmers work in offices that typically are near, but separate from, the shop floor. These work areas are usually clean, well lit, and free of machine noise.

Most machinists and CNC programmers work a 40-hour week. Evening and weekend shifts are becoming more common as companies justify investments in more expensive machinery by extending hours of operation. Overtime is common during peak production periods.

Employment

Machinists and CNC programmers held about 434,000 jobs in 1998, with the vast majority being machinists. Most machinists work in small machining shops or in manufacturing firms that produce durable goods, such as metalworking and industrial machinery, aircraft, or motor vehicles. Maintenance machinists work in most industries that use production machinery. Although machinists and CNC programmers work in all parts of the country, jobs are most plentiful in the Northeast, Midwest, and West Coast where manufacturing is concentrated.

Training, Other Qualifications, and Advancement

A high school or vocational school education, including courses in mathematics, blueprint reading, metalworking, and drafting, is generally a prerequisite for becoming a machinist or CNC programmer. Basic knowledge of computers and electronics is also helpful because of the increased use of computer-controlled machine tools. Experience with machine tools is extremely important. In fact, many entrants to these occupations have previously worked as machine tool operators or setters. Persons interested in becoming machinists or CNC programmers should be mechanically inclined, able to work independently, and able to do highly accurate work that requires concentration and physical effort.

Machinist training varies from formal apprenticeship and postsecondary programs to informal on-the-job training. Apprentice programs consist of shop training and related classroom instruction. In shop training, apprentices learn filing, handtapping, and dowel fitting, as well as the operation of various machine tools. Classroom instruction includes math, physics, blueprint reading, mechanical drawing, and shop practices. In addition, as machine shops have increased their use of computer-controlled equipment, training in the operation and programming of CNC machine tools has become essential. Such formal apprenticeships are relatively rare, however, as a growing number of machinists and CNC programmers receive most of their formal training from community or technical colleges.

To boost the skill level of machinists and to create a more uniform standard of competency, a number of training facilities and colleges have recently begun implementing curriculums incorporating national skills standards developed by the National Institute of Metalworking Skills (NIMS). After completing such a curriculum and passing a performance requirement and written exam, a NIMS credential is granted to trainees, providing formal recognition of competency in a metalworking field. This designation can lead to advancement or confirmation of skills during a job search.

Qualifications for CNC programmers vary widely depending upon the complexity of the job. Basic requirements parallel those of machinists. Employers often prefer skilled machinists or those with technical school training. For some specialized types of programming, such as with complex parts for the aerospace or shipbuilding industries, employers may prefer individuals with a degree in engineering.

For those entering CNC programming directly, a basic knowledge of computers and electronics is necessary, and experience with machine tools is extremely helpful. Classroom training includes an introduction to numerical control, the basics of programming, and more complex topics, such as computer-aided manufacturing. Trainees start writing simple programs under the direction of an experienced programmer. Although machinery manufacturers are trying to standardize programming languages, there are numerous languages in use. Because of this, CNC programmers should be able to learn new programming languages.

As new automation is introduced, machinists and CNC programmers normally receive additional training to update their skills. This training is usually provided by a representative of the equipment manufacturer or a local technical school. Some employers offer tuition reimbursement for job-related courses.

Machinists and CNC programmers can advance in several ways. Experienced machinists may become CNC programmers, and some are promoted to supervisory or administrative positions in their firms. A few open their own shops.

Job Outlook

Despite slower than average employment growth, job opportunities will be excellent for machinists, as employers continue to report difficulties in finding workers with the necessary skills and knowledge to fill machining and CNC programming openings. Many job openings will arise each year from the need to replace experienced machinists and programmers who transfer to other occupations or retire. The number of openings for machinists is expected to be greater than the number of openings for CNC programmers, primarily because the machinist occupation is larger.

Employment of machinists and CNC programmers is expected to grow more slowly than the average for all occupations through 2008. In spite of a robust economy, rising productivity among machinists and CNC programmers will limit their employment growth. Productivity gains are resulting from the expanded use of computer-controlled machine tools and new technologies, such as high-speed machining, which reduce the time required for machining operations. This allows fewer machinists to accomplish the same amount of work previously performed by more workers. Technology is not expected to affect the employment of machinists as significantly as most other production occupations, however, because many of the unique operations performed by machinists cannot be efficiently automated. In addition, firms are likely to retain their most skilled workers to operate expensive new machinery.

Despite increased use of CNC machine tools on shop floors, CNC programmers are also projected to grow more slowly than the average for all occupations through 2008. As advanced machine tool technology allows some programming and minor adjustments to be performed on the shop floor by machinists, tool and die makers, and machine operators, fewer CNC programmers will be needed. In addition, the demand for CNC programmers will be negatively affected by the increasing use of software that automatically translates part and product designs into CNC machine tool instructions.

Employment levels in these occupations are influenced by economic cycles—as the demand for machined goods falls, machinists and CNC programmers involved in production may be laid off or forced to work fewer hours. Employment of machinists involved in plant maintenance, however, is often more stable, because proper maintenance and repair of costly equipment remain vital concerns, even when production levels fall.

Earnings

Median annual earnings of machinists were $28,860 in 1998. The middle 50 percent earned between $22,670 and $36,100. The lowest 10 percent had earnings of less than $17,800, while the top 10 percent earned over $42,480. Median annual earnings in the manufacturing industries employing the largest number of machinists in 1997 were:

Aircraft and parts	$32,200
Metalworking machinery	28,300
Industrial machinery, not elsewhere classified	26,500

Median annual earnings of CNC programmers were about $40,490 in 1998. The middle 50 percent earned between $33,230 and $49,620. The lowest 10 percent had earnings of less than $27,170, whereas the top 10 percent earned over $72,290.

Related Occupations

Occupations most closely related to that of machinist and CNC programmer are other machining occupations. These include tool and die maker, metalworking and plastics-working machine operator, tool planner, and instrument maker. Workers in other occupations that require precision and skill in working with metal include blacksmiths, gunsmiths, locksmiths, metal patternmakers, and welders.

CNC programmers apply their knowledge of machining operations, metals, blueprints, and machine programming to write programs that run machine tools. Computer programmers also write detailed programs to meet precise specifications.

Sources of Additional Information

For general information about this occupation, contact:

☛ The Precision Machined Products Association, 6700 West Snowville Rd., Brecksville, OH 44141. Internet: **http://www.pmpa.org**

☛ The National Tooling and Machining Association, 9300 Livingston Rd., Fort Washington, MD 20744. Internet: **http://www.ntma.org**

Metalworking and Plastics-Working Machine Operators

(O*NET 89132, 91102, 91105, 91108, 91111, 91114A, 91114B, 91117, 91302, 91305, 91308, 91311, 91314, 91317, 91321, 91502, 91505, 91508, 91714, 91902, 91905, 91908, 91911, 91917, 91921, 91923, 91926, 91928, 91932, and 91938)

Significant Points

- A few weeks of on-the-job training is sufficient for most workers to learn basic machine operations, but several years are required to become a skilled operator.
- Projected employment change varies by type of job. Employment of most manual machine tool operators is expected to decline, while that of multiple and computer-controlled machine tool operators will grow.

Nature of the Work

Consider the parts of a toaster, such as the metal or plastic housing or the lever that lowers the toast. These parts, and many other metal and plastic products, are produced by metalworking and plastics-working machine operators. In fact, machine tool operators in the metalworking and plastics industries play a major part in producing most of the consumer products on which we rely daily.

In general, these workers can be separated into two groups—those who set up machines for operation and those who tend the machines during production. Set-up workers prepare the machines prior to production and may adjust the machinery during operation. Operators and tenders, on the other hand, primarily monitor the machinery during operation, sometimes loading or unloading the machine or making minor adjustments to the controls. Many workers set up and operate equipment. Because the set-up process requires an understanding of the entire production process, setters usually have more training and are more highly skilled than those who simply operate or tend machinery. As new automation simplifies the setup process, however, less skilled workers are also increasingly able to set up machines for operation.

Setters, operators, tenders, and set-up operators are usually identified by the type of machine with which they work. Some examples of specific titles are screw machine operator, plastics-molding machine set-up operator, punch press operator, and lathe tender. Job duties usually vary based on the size of the firm and on the type of machine being operated. Although some workers specialize in one or two types of machinery, many are trained to set up or operate a variety of machines.

Metalworking machine setters and operators set up and tend machines that cut and form all types of metal parts. Traditionally, set-up workers plan and set up the sequence of operations according to blueprints, layouts, or other instructions. They adjust speed, feed, and other controls, choose the proper coolants and lubricants, and select the instruments or tools for each operation. Using micrometers, gauges, and other precision measuring instruments, they may also compare the completed work with the tolerance limits stated in the specifications.

Although there are many different types of metalworking machine tools that require specific knowledge and skills, most operators perform similar tasks. Whether tending grinding machines that remove excess material from the surface of machined products or presses that extrude metal through a die to form wire, operators usually perform simple, repetitive operations that can be learned quickly. Typically, these workers place metal stock in a machine on which the operating specifications have already been set. They may watch one or more machines and make minor adjustments according to their instructions. Regardless of the type of machine they operate, machine tenders usually depend on skilled set-up workers for major adjustments when the machines are not functioning properly.

Plastics-working machine operators set up and tend machines that transform plastic compounds—chemical-based products that can be produced in powder, pellet, or syrup form—into a wide variety of consumer goods such as toys, tubing, and auto parts. These products are manufactured using various methods, of which injection molding is the most common. The injection molding machine heats a plastic compound and forces it into a mold. After the part has cooled and hardened, the mold opens and the part is released. Many common kitchen products are produced using this method.

To produce long parts such as pipes or window frames, an extruding machine is usually employed. These machines force a plastic compound through a die that contains an opening of the desired shape of the final product. Yet another type of plastics working technique is blow molding. Blow-molding machines force hot air into a mold which contains a plastic tube. As the air moves into the mold, the plastic tube is inflated to the shape of the mold and a plastic container is formed. The familiar 2-liter soft drink bottles are produced using this method.

Regardless of the process used, plastics-working machine operators check the materials feed, the temperature and pressure of the machine, and the rate at which the product hardens. Depending on the type of equipment in use, they may also load material into the machine, make minor adjustments, or unload and inspect the finished products. Plastics-working machine operators also remove clogged material from molds or dies. Because molds and dies are quite costly, operators must exercise care to avoid damaging them.

Metalworking machine operators increasingly use numerically controlled (NC) equipment. These machine tools have two major components—an electronic controller and a machine tool. Today, most NC machines are computer numerically controlled (CNC), which means that the controllers are computers. The controller directs the mechanisms of the machine tool through the positioning and machining described in the program or instructions for the job. A program could contain, for example, commands that cause the controller to move a drill bit to certain spots on a workpiece and drill a hole at each spot.

CNC machine tools are often used in computer-integrated manufacturing systems. In these systems, automated material handling equipment moves workpieces through a series of stations where machining processes are computer numerically controlled. In some cases, the workpiece is stationary and the tools change automatically. Although the machining is done automatically, CNC machine tools must be set up and used properly in order to obtain the maximum benefit from their use. These tasks are the responsibility of CNC machine-tool operators or, in some instances, machinists. (See the statement on machinists and numerical control machine tool programmers elsewhere in the *Handbook*.)

Like the duties of manual metal and plastics machine operators, the duties of numerical-control machine-tool operators vary. Working from given instructions, CNC operators load programs that are usually stored on disks into the controller. They also securely position the workpiece, attach the necessary tools, and check the coolants and lubricants. Many CNC machines are equipped with automatic tool changers, so operators may also load several tools in the proper sequence. This entire process may require a few minutes or several hours, depending on the size of the workpiece and the complexity of the job.

A new program often must be adjusted to obtain the desired results. If the tool moves to the wrong position or makes a cut that is too deep, the program must be changed so the job is done properly. A machinist or machine tool programmer usually performs this function, occasionally with the assistance of a computer automated design program that simulates the operation of machine tools. However, a new generation of machine tool technology, known as direct numerical control, allows operators to make changes to the program and enter new specifications using minicomputers on the shop floor.

Because CNC machine tools are very expensive, operators monitor machinery to prevent situations that could result in costly damage to the cutting tools or other parts. The extent to which the operator performs this function depends on the type of job as well as the type of equipment being used. Some CNC machine tools automatically monitor and adjust machining operations. When the job has been properly set up and the program has been checked, the operator may only need to monitor the machine as it operates. These operators often set up and monitor more than one machine. Other jobs require frequent loading and unloading, tool changing, or programming. Operators may check the finished part using micrometers, gauges, or other precision inspection equipment to ensure that it meets specifications. Increasingly, however, this function is being performed by NC machine tools that are able to inspect products as they are produced.

Operating computerized machine tools is increasingly common.

CNC machines are changing the nature of the work that machine setters and operators perform. Computer-controlled machines simplify setups by using formerly tested computer programs for new workpieces. If a workpiece is similar to one previously produced, small adjustments can be made to the old program instead of developing a new program from scratch. Also, a growing number of CNC machine tools are able to inspect products as they are manufactured. As a result of these developments, CNC machine tool operators tend to have less physical interaction with the machinery or materials than manual machine tool operators. They primarily act as "troubleshooters," monitoring machines on which the loading, forming, and unloading processes are often controlled by computers.

Working Conditions

Most metalworking and plastics-working machine operators work in areas that are clean, well lit, and well ventilated. Nevertheless, many operators require stamina because they are on their feet much of the day and may do moderately heavy lifting. Also, these workers operate powerful, high-speed machines that can be dangerous if strict safety rules are not observed. Most operators wear protective equipment, such as safety glasses and earplugs to protect against flying particles of metal or plastic and noise from the machines. Other required equipment varies by work setting and machine. For example, workers in the plastics industry who work near materials that emit dangerous fumes or dust must wear face masks or self-contained breathing apparatuses.

Most metal and plastics-working machine operators work a 40-hour week, but overtime is common during periods of increased production. Because many metalworking and plastics-working shops operate more than one shift daily, some operators work nights and weekends

Employment

Metalworking and plastics-working machine operators held about 1,509,000 jobs in 1998. Of these, 1,421,000 were manual machine operators, and 88,000 were NC machine operators. About 8 out of every 10 metalworking and plastics-working machine operators are found in five manufacturing industries—fabricated metal products, industrial machinery and equipment, miscellaneous plastic products, transportation equipment, and primary metals. The following tabulation shows the distribution of employment of metalworking and plastics-working machine operators by detailed occupation.

Cutting and forming machine tool setters and operators	726,000
Molding machine setters and operators	229,000
Sheet metal workers and duct installers, non-construction	102,000
Combination machine tool setters and operators	107,000
Numerical control machine operators	88,000
Plating machine setters and operators	45,000
Metal fabricators, structural metal products, non-construction	36,000
Heat treating machine setters and operators	23,000
All other metal and plastics-working machine operators	148,000

Training, Other Qualifications, and Advancement

Metalworking and plastics-working machine operators learn their skills on the job. Trainees begin by observing and assisting experienced workers, sometimes in formal training programs. Under supervision they may supply material, start and stop the machine, or remove finished products from the machine. They then advance to more difficult tasks such as adjusting feed speeds, changing cutting tools, or inspecting a finished product for defects. Eventually they become responsible for their own machines.

The complexity of equipment largely determines the time required to become an operator. Most operators learn the basic machine operations and functions in a few weeks, but they may need several years to become skilled operators or to advance to the more highly skilled job of set-up operator.

Set-up operators normally need a thorough knowledge of the machinery and of the products being manufactured because they often plan the sequence of work, make the first production run, and determine which adjustments need to be made. Strong analytical abilities are particularly important to perform this job. Some companies have formal training programs for set-up operators that combine classroom instruction with on-the-job training.

CNC machine tool operators undergo similar training. Working under a supervisor or an experienced operator, trainees learn to set up and run one or more types of numerically controlled machine tools. They usually learn the basics of their jobs within a few months. However, the length of the training period varies with the number and complexity of the machine tools the operator will run and with the individual's ability. If the employer expects operators to write programs, trainees may attend programming courses offered by machine tool manufacturers or technical schools.

Although no special education is required for most operating jobs, employers prefer to hire applicants with good basic skills. Many require employees to have a high school education and to read, write, and speak English. This is especially true for NC machine operators, who may need constant retraining as the company introduces new equipment. Because machinery is becoming more complex and shop floor organization is changing, employers increasingly look for persons with good communication and interpersonal skills. Mechanical aptitude, manual dexterity, and experience working with machinery are also helpful. Those interested in becoming metalworking or plastics-working machine operators can improve their employment opportunities by completing high school courses in shop and blueprint reading and by gaining a working knowledge of the properties of metals and plastics. A solid math background including courses in algebra, geometry, trigonometry, and basic statistics is also useful.

Job opportunities and advancement can also be enhanced by becoming certified in a particular machining skill. The National Institute for Metalworking Skills has developed standards for metalworking machine operators. After taking a course approved by the organization and passing a written exam and performance requirement, a credential is issued that formally recognizes the person as competent in a specific machining operation. The Society of Plastics Industry, Inc., the national trade association representing plastics manufacturers, also certifies workers in the plastics industry. To achieve machine operator certification, two year's experience operating a plastics processing machine is recommended, and one must pass a computer-based exam.

Advancement for operators usually takes the form of higher pay, although there are some limited opportunities for operators to advance to new positions as well. For example, they can become multiple machine operators, set-up operators, or trainees for the more highly skilled positions of machinist or tool and die maker. Manual machine operators can move on to CNC equipment when it is introduced in their establishments. Some set-up workers and CNC operators may advance to supervisory positions. CNC operators who have substantial training in CNC programming may advance to the higher-paying job of numerical control machine tool programmer. (See the statements on machinists and numerical control machine tool programmers, and tool and die makers elsewhere in the *Handbook*.)

Job Outlook

Divergent employment trends are expected over the 1998-2008 period among the various metalworking and plastics-working machine operators. In general, employment of these workers will be affected by the rate of technological implementation, the demand for the goods they produce, the effects of trade, and the reorganization of production processes. These trends are expected to spur employment growth among NC machine operators, combination machine tool operators, plastics molding machine operators, and a number of miscellaneous operating positions. On the other hand, employment is projected to decline in some of the more traditional operator occupations, such as manual cutting and forming machine tool operators, and sheet metal workers. Despite differing rates of employment change, a large number of metalworking and plastics-working machine operator jobs will become available due to an expected surge in retirements as the first of the baby boomers become eligible for retirement in the next decade.

One of the most important factors influencing employment change in this occupation is the implementation of labor-saving machinery. In order to remain competitive by improving quality and lowering production costs, many firms are adopting new technologies, such as computer-controlled machine tools and robots. Computer-controlled equipment allows operators to simultaneously tend a greater number of machines and often makes setup easier, thereby reducing the amount of time set-up workers spend on each machine. Robots are being used to load and unload parts from machines. For these reasons, the lower-skilled positions of manual machine tool operators and tenders are more likely to be eliminated by these new technologies because the functions they perform are more easily automated. The spread of new automation will lead to rising employment, however, for NC machine tool operators.

The demand for metalworking and plastics-working machine operators largely mirrors the demand for the parts they produce. Recent growth in the domestic economy, for example, has led to rebounding employment in a number of machine tool operating occupations. In addition, the consumption of plastic products has grown as they have been substituted for metal goods in many consumer and manufacturing products in recent years. Although the rate of substitution may slow in the future, this process is likely to continue and should result in stronger demand for machine operators in plastics than in metalworking.

Both industries, however, face stiff foreign competition that is limiting the demand for domestically-produced parts. One way that larger U.S. producers have responded to this competition is by moving production operations to other countries where labor costs are lower. These moves are likely to continue and will further reduce employment opportunities for many metalworking and plastics-working machine tool operators in the United States.

Workers with a thorough background in machine operations, exposure to a variety of machines, and a good working knowledge of the properties of metals and plastics will be best able to adjust to this changing environment. In addition, new shop floor arrangements will reward workers with good basic mathematics and reading skills, good communication skills, and the ability and willingness to learn new tasks. As workers are called upon to adapt to new production methods and to operate more machines, the number of combination machine tool operators will continue to rise.

Earnings

Earnings for machine operators can vary based on a number of different factors. The most important are the size of the company, whether the shop is union or nonunion, the industry, and skill level and experience of the operator. Also, temporary employees, who are being hired in greater numbers, usually get paid less than company-employed workers. The median annual earnings in 1998 for a variety of metalworking and plastics-working operators were:

Lathe and turning machine setters and set-up operators	$28,250
Sheet metal workers and duct installers	28,030
Numerical control machine operators	27,110
Heat treating machine setters and operators	25,160
Metal molding machine setters and operators	24,870
Grinding machine operators	24,740
Machine tool cutting operators	24,510
Metal fabricators, structural metal products	24,070
Combination machine tool setters and operators	23,860
Punching machine setters and operators	23,270
Electrolytic plating machine setters and operators	21,210
Machine forming operators	20,170
Plastic molding machine setters and operators	18,580

Approximately one-third of these workers are union members, about double the rate for other workers in the economy. Metalworking industries have a higher rate of unionization than the plastics industry.

Related Occupations

Workers in occupations closely related to metalworking and plastics-working machine operators include machinists, tool and die makers, extruding and forming machine operators producing synthetic fibers, woodworking machine operators, and metal patternmakers. Numerical-control machine-tool operators may program CNC machines or alter existing programs, which are functions closely related to those performed by NC machine tool programmers.

Sources of Additional Information

For general information about the metalworking trades, contact:

☛ The National Tooling and Machining Association, 9300 Livingston Rd., Fort Washington, MD 20744. Internet: **http://www.ntma.org**

☛ The Precision Machined Products Association, 6700 West Snowville Rd., Brecksville, OH 44141. Internet: **http://www.pmpa.org**

☛ The Society of Plastics Industry, 1801 K St. NW, Suite 600K, Washington, DC 20006.
Internet: **http://www.socplas.org** and **http://www.certifyme.org**

Tool and Die Makers

(O*NET 89102)

Significant Points

- Tool and die makers learn their trade through 4 or 5 years of education and training in formal apprenticeships, postsecondary programs, or informal on-the-job training.
- Advancements in automation and increased imports of precision metal products will contribute to the projected decline in employment; nevertheless, jobseekers with the appropriate skills and background should enjoy excellent opportunities.

Nature of the Work

Tool and die makers are among the most highly skilled production workers in the economy. These workers produce tools, dies, and special guiding and holding devices that enable machines to manufacture a variety of products we use daily—from clothing and furniture to heavy equipment and parts for aircraft.

Toolmakers craft precision tools which are used to cut, shape, and form metal and other materials. They also produce jigs and fixtures (devices that hold metal while it is bored, stamped, or drilled) and gauges and other measuring devices. Diemakers construct metal forms (dies) that are used to shape metal in stamping and forging operations. They also make metal molds for diecasting and for molding plastics, ceramics, and composite materials. In addition to developing, designing and producing new tools and dies, these workers may also repair worn or damaged tools, dies, gauges, jigs, and fixtures.

To perform these functions, tool and die makers employ many types of machine tools and precision measuring instruments. They must also be familiar with the machining properties, such as hardness and heat tolerance, of a wide variety of common metals and alloys. As a result, tool and die makers usually must have a much broader knowledge of machining operations, mathematics, and blueprint reading than most other machining workers.

Working from blueprints or instructions, tool and die makers first must plan the sequence of operations necessary to manufacture the tool or die. Next, they measure and mark the pieces of metal that will be cut to form parts of the final product. At this point, tool and die makers cut, drill, or bore the part as required, checking to ensure that the final product meets specifications. Finally, these workers assemble the parts and perform finishing jobs such as filing, grinding, and polishing surfaces.

Modern technology is helping to change the ways that tool and die makers perform their jobs. For example, these workers increasingly use computer-aided design (CAD) to develop products and parts. Specifications entered into computer programs can be used to electronically develop drawings for the required tools and dies. The electronic drawings are then processed by a computer-aided manufacturing (CAM) program to calculate cutting tool paths and the sequence of operations. Once these instructions are developed, computer numerically controlled (CNC) machines usually are used to produce the die. Programs can also be electronically stored and adapted for future use, saving time and increasing worker productivity.

Working Conditions

Tool and die makers usually work in toolrooms. These areas are quieter than the production floor because there are fewer machines in use at one time. They are also generally clean and cool to accommodate the growing number of computer-operated machines. To minimize the exposure of workers to moving parts, machines have guards and shields. Tool and die makers must also follow safety rules and wear protective equipment, such as safety glasses to shield against bits of flying metal, earplugs to protect against noise, and gloves and masks to reduce exposure to hazardous lubricants and cleaners. These workers also

Tool and die makers must be mechanically inclined and able to solve problems independently.

need stamina because they often spend much of the day on their feet and may do moderately heavy lifting.

Companies employing tool and die makers have traditionally operated only one shift per day. However, as the cost of new machinery and technology has increased, many employers now have more than one shift. Overtime and weekend work are common, especially during peak production periods.

Employment

Tool and die makers held about 138,000 jobs in 1998. Most worked in industries that manufacture metalworking machinery and equipment, motor vehicles, aircraft, plastics products, telecommunications equipment, and medical instruments. Although they are found throughout the country, jobs are most plentiful in the Midwest, Northeast, and West Coast, where many of the metalworking industries are located.

Training, Other Qualifications, and Advancement

Tool and die makers learn their trade through 4 or 5 years of education and training in formal apprenticeships, postsecondary programs, or informal on-the-job training. The best way to learn all aspects of tool and die making, according to most employers, is a formal apprenticeship program that combines classroom instruction and job experience. These programs are rare, however. A growing number of tool and die makers receive most of their formal classroom training from community and technical colleges.

Tool and die maker trainees learn to operate milling machines, lathes, grinders, and other machine tools. They also learn to use handtools for fitting and assembling gauges, and other mechanical and metal-forming equipment. In addition, they study metalworking processes such as heat treating and plating. Classroom training usually consists of mechanical drawing, tool designing, tool programming, blueprint reading, and mathematics courses, including algebra, geometry, trigonometry, and basic statistics. Tool and die makers increasingly must have good computer skills to work with CAD technology and CNC machine tools.

Workers who become tool and die makers without completing formal apprenticeships generally acquire their skills through a combination of informal on-the-job training and classroom instruction at a vocational school or community college. They often begin as machine operators and gradually take on more difficult assignments. Many machinists become tool and die makers. In fact, tool and die makers are often considered highly specialized machinists. (See the statement on machinists and machine tool programmers elsewhere in the *Handbook*.)

Because tools and dies must meet strict specifications—precision to one ten-thousandth of an inch is common—the work of tool and die makers requires a high degree of patience and attention to detail. Good eyesight is essential. Persons entering this occupation should also be mechanically inclined, able to work and solve problems independently, and capable of doing work that requires concentration and physical effort.

There are several ways for skilled workers to advance. Some move into supervisory and administrative positions in their firms; some obtain their college degree and go into engineering; others become tool designers or machine tool programmers; and many start their own shops.

Job Outlook

Employment of tool and die makers is expected to decline through 2008. Nevertheless, jobseekers with the appropriate skills and background should enjoy excellent opportunities as employers across the Nation report difficulties in finding qualified workers to fill these positions. Moreover, many openings will be created each year by tool and die makers who retire. As more of these highly skilled workers retire, employers in certain parts of the country, who are already facing a shortage of workers, may face even more pronounced shortages, which will contribute to declining employment in the occupation.

Apart from a shortage of new entrants, the projected decline in employment reflects advancements in automation, including CNC machine tools and computer-aided design. CNC machine tools have made tool and die makers more productive, while CAD and CAM have allowed some functions previously performed by these workers to be carried out by a computer and CNC programmer. Because precision metal products are a primary component of manufacturing machinery, increased imports of finished goods and precision metal products, including tools and dies, may lessen the demand for tool and die makers. However, these workers are highly skilled and play a key role in the operation of many firms. As firms invest in new equipment, modify production techniques, and implement product design changes more rapidly, they will continue to rely heavily on skilled tool and die makers for retooling. This fact, coupled with a growing demand for motor vehicles, aircraft, machinery, and other products that use machined metal parts, should help to moderate the decline in employment.

Earnings

Median annual earnings of tool and die makers were $37,250 in 1998. The middle 50 percent earned between $29,910 and $45,240. The lowest 10 percent had earnings of less than $23,960, while the top 10 percent earned over $51,160. Median annual earnings in the manufacturing industries employing the largest number of tool and die makers in 1997 are shown below.

Industry	Earnings
Motor vehicles and equipment	$43,400
Aircraft and parts	39,800
Metal forgings and stampings	39,600
Miscellaneous plastics products	35,700
Metalworking machinery	34,600

Related Occupations

The occupations most closely related to the work of tool and die makers are other machining occupations. These include machinist, mold maker, instrument maker, metalworking and plastics-working machine operator, and machine tool programmer.

Other occupations that require precision and skill in working with metal include blacksmith, gunsmith, locksmith, metal patternmaker, and welder.

Sources of Additional Information

For information about careers in tool and die making, contact:

- The National Tooling and Machining Association, 9300 Livingston Rd., Ft. Washington, MD 20744. Internet: **http://www.ntma.org**
- Precision Metalforming Association, Tool & Die Division, 6363 Oak Tree Blvd., Independence, OH 44131-2500. Internet: **http://www.metalforming.com**
- Tooling and Manufacturing Association, 1177 South Dee Rd., Park Ridge, IL 60068. Internet: **http://www.tmanet.com**

Welders, Cutters, and Welding Machine Operators

(O*NET 91702, 91705, 93914A, 93914B, and 93914C)

Significant Points

- Training for welders can range from a few weeks of school or on-the-job training for low skilled positions to several years of combined school and on-the-job training for high skilled jobs.
- Job prospects should be excellent, as employers report a shortage of qualified applicants.

Nature of the Work

Welding is the most common way of permanently joining metal parts. In this process, heat is applied to metal pieces, melting and fusing them to form a permanent bond. Because of its strength, welding is used in shipbuilding, automobile manufacturing and repair, aerospace applications, and thousands of other manufactured products. Welding is also used to join beams when constructing buildings, bridges, and other structures, and to join pipes in pipelines, power plants, and refineries.

Welders and welding machine operators use many types of welding equipment in a variety of positions, such as flat, vertical, horizontal, and overhead. They may perform manual welding, in which the work is entirely controlled by the welder, or semi-automatic welding, in which the welder uses machinery, such as a wire feeder, to help perform welding tasks. Skilled welders generally plan work from drawings or specifications or by using their knowledge of welding and metals to analyze damaged metal parts. These workers then select and set up welding equipment and examine welds, to insure they meet standards or specifications. Some welders have more limited duties, however. They perform routine jobs that have already been planned and laid out and do not require extensive knowledge of welding techniques.

Automated welding is used in an increasing number of production processes. In these instances, a machine or robot performs the welding tasks, while monitored by a welding machine operator. Welding machine operators set up and operate welding machines, as specified by layouts, work orders, or blueprints. Operators must load parts correctly and constantly monitor the machine to ensure that it produces the desired weld.

The work of arc, plasma, and flame cutters is closely related to that of welders. However, instead of joining metals, cutters use the heat from burning gases or an electric arc to cut and trim metal objects to specific dimensions. Cutters also dismantle large objects, such as ships, railroad cars, automobiles, or aircraft. Some operate and monitor cutting machines similar to those used by welding machine operators.

Working Conditions

Welders and cutters are often exposed to a number of potential hazards, including the intense light created by the arc, hazardous fumes, and burns. To protect themselves, they wear safety shoes, goggles, hoods with protective lenses, and other devices designed to prevent burns and eye injuries and for protection from falling objects. Automated welding machine operators are not exposed to as many dangers, however, and a face shield or goggles usually provides adequate protection for these workers.

Welders and cutters may work outdoors in inclement weather or indoors, sometimes in a confining area designed to contain sparks and glare. When outdoors, they may work on a scaffold or platform high off the ground. In addition, they may be required to lift heavy objects and work in a variety of awkward positions, having to make welds while bending, stooping, or working overhead.

Although the majority of welders work a 40-hour week, overtime is common, and some welders work up to 70 hours per week. Welders may also work in shifts as long as 12 hours.

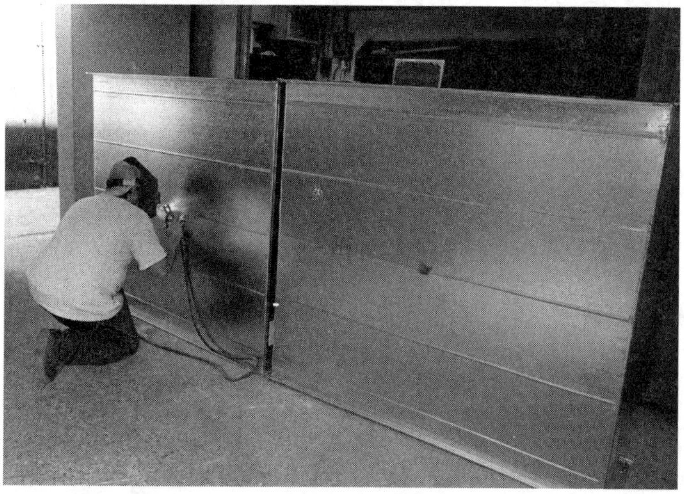

Welders must be able to concentrate for long periods and have good hand-eye coordination.

Employment

Welders, cutters, and welding machine operators held about 477,000 jobs in 1998. Of these jobs, 3 of every 4 were held by welders and cutters, who worked mostly in manufacturing and services. The majority of those in manufacturing were employed in the transportation equipment, industrial machinery and equipment, or fabricated metal products industries. Those employed in the service sector worked mainly in repair shops and for personnel supply agencies. All welding machine operators were employed in manufacturing industries, primarily fabricated metal products, machinery, and motor vehicles.

Training, Other Qualifications, and Advancement

Training for welders can range from a few weeks of school or on-the-job training for low skilled positions to several years of combined school and on-the-job training for highly skilled jobs. Formal training is available in high schools, vocational schools, and post secondary institutions, such as vocational-technical institutes, community colleges, and private welding schools. The Armed Forces operate welding schools as well. Some employers provide training to help welders improve their skills. Courses in blueprint reading, shop mathematics, mechanical drawing, physics, chemistry, and metallurgy are helpful. Knowledge of computers is gaining importance, especially for welding machine operators, as some welders are becoming responsible for the programming of computer-controlled welding machines, including robots.

Some welders become certified, a process whereby the employer sends a worker to an institution, such as an independent testing lab or technical school, to weld a test specimen to specific codes and standards required by the employer. Testing procedures are based on the standards and codes set by one of several industry associations with which the employer may be affiliated. If the welding inspector at the examining institution determines that the worker has performed according to the employer's guidelines, the inspector will then certify the welder being tested as able to work with a particular welding procedure.

Welders and cutters need good eyesight, hand-eye coordination, and manual dexterity. They should be able to concentrate on detailed work for long periods and be able to bend, stoop, and work in awkward positions. In addition, welders increasingly need to be willing to receive training and perform tasks in other production jobs.

Welders can advance to more skilled welding jobs with additional training and experience. For example, they may become welding technicians, supervisors, inspectors, or instructors. Some experienced welders open their own repair shops.

Job Outlook

Despite projected slower-than-average employment growth, job prospects should be excellent for welders with the right skills, as many employers report difficulties in finding qualified applicants. In addition, openings will arise as workers retire or leave the occupation for other reasons.

Employment of welders, cutters, and welding machine operators is expected to grow more slowly than the average for all occupations through 2008, reflecting rising automation and productivity in many of the industries that employ these workers. The major factor affecting employment of welders is the health of the industries in which they work. Because almost every manufacturing industry uses welding at some stage of manufacturing or in the repair and maintenance of equipment, a strong economy will keep demand for welders high. A downturn affecting such industries as auto manufacturing, construction, or petroleum, however, would have a negative impact on the employment of welders in those areas and could cause some layoffs. Government funding levels for infrastructure repairs and improvements is also expected to be an important determinant of future welding jobs.

Regardless of the state of the economy, the shortage of welders and drive to increase productivity and cut costs is leading many companies to invest more in automation, especially computer-controlled and robotically-controlled welding machinery. This may affect the demand for low-skilled manual welders, as the jobs that are currently being automated are the simple, repetitive ones. The growing use of automation, however, should increase demand for welding machine operators. Welders working on construction projects or in equipment repair will not be as affected, because their jobs are not as easily automated.

Technology is helping to improve welding and create more uses for welding in the workplace. For example, new ways are being developed to weld dissimilar materials and nonmetallic materials, such as plastics, composites, and new alloys. Also, laser beam welding and other techniques are improving the results of welding and making it applicable to a wider assortment of jobs. The effect of technological innovation on the overall use of welding is unclear, however, because other processes designed to replace welding and make welders more productive, such as new adhesive technologies and high-speed machining, will contribute to decreasing demand for these workers.

Earnings

Median annual earnings of welders and cutters were $25,810 in 1998. The middle 50 percent earned between $21,440 and $32,020. The lowest 10 percent had earnings of less than $17,550, while the top 10 percent earned over $39,650. Median annual earnings in the industries employing the largest number of welders and cutters in 1997 were:

Ship and boat building and repairing	$27,200
Construction and related machinery	25,300
Motor vehicles and equipment	24,700
Fabricated structural metal products	23,800
Miscellaneous repair shops	22,600

Median annual earnings of welding machine operators were $25,010 in 1998. The middle 50 percent earned between $20,820 and $31,270. The lowest 10 percent had earnings of less than $16,870, while the top 10 percent earned over $39,710. Median annual earnings in the industries employing the largest number of welding machine operators in 1997 were:

Construction and related machinery	$26,100
Metal forgings and stampings	24,100
Motor vehicles and equipment	23,700
Fabricated structural metal products	22,400
Miscellaneous fabricated metal products	20,500

More than one-fourth of welders belong to unions. Among these are the International Association of Machinists and Aerospace Workers; the International Brotherhood of Boilermakers, Iron Ship Builders, Blacksmiths, Forgers and Helpers; the International Union, United Automobile, Aerospace and Agricultural Implement Workers of America; the United Association of Journeymen and Apprentices of the Plumbing and Pipe Fitting Industry of the United States and Canada; and the United Electrical, Radio, and Machine Workers of America.

Related Occupations

Welders and cutters are skilled metal workers. Other metal workers include blacksmiths, forge shop workers, machinists, machine-tool operators, tool and die makers, millwrights, sheet-metal workers, boilermakers, and metal sculptors.

Welding machine operators run machines that weld metal parts. Others who run metalworking machines include lathe and turning, milling and planing, punching and stamping press, and rolling machine operators.

Sources of Additional Information

For information on training opportunities and jobs for welders, cutters, and welding machine operators, contact local employers, the local office of the State employment service, or schools providing welding training.

Information on careers in welding is available from:

☛ American Welding Society, 550 N.W. Lejeune Rd., Miami, FL 33126-5699. Internet: **http://www.aws.org**

Plant and Systems Operators

Electric Power Generating Plant Operators and Power Distributors and Dispatchers

(O*NET 95021, 95023, 95026, and 95028)

Significant Points

- Overall employment of operators, distributors, and dispatchers is expected to decline, as deregulation and increasing competition cause the electric utility industry to restructure and cut jobs.
- Job losses will not be offset by new power plants because their greater automation requires fewer operators, and plant construction is expected to slow due to concerns about electric power generating overcapacity.
- Shrinking employment and low turnover of operator positions will decrease advancement opportunities for helpers and laborers.

Nature of the Work

Electricity is vital for most of our everyday activities. From the moment you flip the first switch each morning, you are connecting to a huge network of people, electric lines, and generating equipment. Electric power generating plant operators control the machinery that generates electricity. Power distributors and dispatchers control the flow of electricity, from the power plant over a network of transmission lines to industrial plants and substations, and finally over distribution lines to residential users.

Electric power generating plant operators control and monitor boilers, turbines, generators, and auxiliary equipment in power generating plants. Operators distribute power demands among generators, combine the current from several generators, and monitor instruments to maintain voltage and regulate electricity flows from the plant. When power requirements change, these workers start or stop generators and connect or disconnect them from circuits. They may use computers to keep records of switching operations and loads on generators, lines, and transformers. Operators may also use computers to prepare reports of unusual incidents, malfunctioning equipment, or maintenance performed during their shift.

Operators in plants with automated control systems work mainly in a central control room and usually are called *control room operators* and *control room operator trainees* or *assistants*. In older plants, the controls for the equipment are not centralized, and *switchboard operators* control the flow of electricity from a central point, whereas *auxiliary equipment operators* work throughout the plant, operating and monitoring valves, switches, and gauges.

The Nuclear Regulatory Commission (NRC) licenses operators of nuclear power plants. *Reactor operators* are authorized to control equipment that affects the power of the reactor in a nuclear power plant. In addition, an NRC-licensed *senior reactor operator* acts as the supervisor of the plant for each shift and supervises operation of all controls in the control room.

Power distributors and dispatchers, also called *load dispatchers* or *systems operators*, control the flow of electricity through transmission lines to industrial plants and substations that supply residential electric needs. They operate current converters, voltage transformers, and circuit breakers. Dispatchers monitor equipment and record readings at a pilot board, which is a map of the transmission grid system showing the status of transmission circuits and connections with substations and industrial plants.

Dispatchers also anticipate power needs, such as those caused by changes in the weather. They call control room operators to start or stop boilers and generators, to bring production into balance with needs. They handle emergencies such as transformer or transmission line failures and route current around affected areas. They also operate and monitor equipment in substations, which step up or step down voltage, and operate switchboard levers to control the flow of electricity in and out of substations.

Working Conditions

Because electricity is provided around the clock, operators, distributors, and dispatchers usually work one of three daily 8-hour shifts or one of two 12-hour shifts on a rotating basis. Shift assignments may change periodically, so all operators can share duty on less desirable shifts. Work on rotating shifts can be stressful and fatiguing, because of the constant change in living and sleeping patterns. Operators, distributors, and dispatchers who work in control rooms generally sit or stand at a control station. This work is not physically strenuous but requires constant attention. Operators who work outside the control room may be exposed to danger from electric shock, falls, and burns.

Plant operators often use computers to keep records of switching operations and loads on generators, lines, and transformers.

Nuclear power plant operators are subject to random drug and alcohol tests, as are most workers at nuclear power plants.

Employment

Electric power generating plant operators and power distributors and dispatchers held about 45,000 jobs in 1998. Jobs are located throughout the country. About 92 percent worked for utility companies and government agencies that produced electricity. Others worked for manufacturing establishments that produce electricity for their own use.

Training, Other Qualifications, and Advancement

Employers seek high school graduates for entry level operator, distributor, and dispatcher positions. They prefer candidates with strong math and science skills. College level courses or prior experience in a mechanical or technical job may be helpful. Employers increasingly require computer proficiency, as computers are used to keep records, generate reports, and track maintenance. Most entry-level positions are helper or laborer jobs, such as powerline construction. Depending on the results of aptitude tests, worker preferences, and availability of openings, workers may be assigned to train for one of many utility positions.

Workers selected for training as a power distributor or power plant operator at a fossil-fueled power plant undergo extensive on-the-job and classroom training. Several years of training and experience are required to become a fully qualified control room operator or power distributor. With further training and experience, workers may advance to shift supervisor. Utilities generally promote from within; therefore, opportunities to advance by moving to another employer are limited.

Extensive training and experience are necessary to pass the Nuclear Regulatory Commission (NRC) examinations for licensed reactor operators and senior reactor operators. To maintain their license, licensed reactor operators must pass an annual practical plant operation exam and a biennial written exam administered by their employer. Training may include simulator and on-the-job training, classroom instruction, and individual study. Entrants to nuclear power plant operator trainee jobs must have strong math and science skills. Experience in other power plants or with Navy nuclear propulsion plants also is helpful. With further training and experience, reactor operators may advance to senior reactor operators.

In addition to preliminary training as a power plant operator or power distributor or dispatcher, most workers are given periodic refresher training. Nuclear power plant operators are given frequent refresher training. This training is usually taken on plant simulators designed specifically to replicate procedures and situations that might be encountered working at the trainee's plant.

Job Outlook

People who want to become electric power generating plant operators and power distributors and dispatchers are expected to encounter keen competition for these high-paying jobs. Declining employment and low turnover in this occupation will result in few job opportunities for the large number of eligible candidates.

Employment of electric power generating plant operators and power distributors and dispatchers is expected to decline slightly through the year 2008, as the industry restructures in response to deregulation and increasing competition. The Energy Policy Act of 1992 has had a tremendous impact on the organization of the utilities industry. This legislation enabled increased competition in power generating utilities, by allowing independent power producers to sell power directly to industrial and other wholesale customers. Utilities, historically operated as regulated local monopolies, are restructuring operations to reduce costs and compete effectively, resulting in fewer jobs at all levels and reduced job security.

The pace of new plant construction and equipment upgrading will also limit opportunities for electric power generating plant operators, distributors, and dispatchers. Expansion of power-generating capacity is expected to gradually slow through the year 2008, as utilities strive to avoid overcapacity. In addition, the increasing use of automatic controls and more efficient equipment in new plants should require fewer operators.

Earnings

Median annual earnings of power generating and reactor plant operators were $44,840 in 1998. The middle 50 percent earned between $37,190 and $50,940 a year. The lowest 10 percent earned less than $29,000 and the highest 10 percent earned more than $73,090 a year. Median annual earnings of power generating plant operators in 1997 were $43,800 in electric services.

Median annual earnings of power distributors and dispatchers were $45,690 in 1998. The middle 50 percent earned between $37,350 and $56,810 a year. The lowest 10 percent earned less than $29,620 and the highest 10 percent earned more than $78,060 a year.

According to information from union surveys, average annual earnings for fossil fuel power plant operators were about $46,500 in 1999. Nuclear power plant operators earned an average of about $56,200 annually in 1998. Senior or chief operators earned 10 to 15 percent more than operators did. Over half of all electric power generating plant operators and power distributors and dispatchers were union members.

Related Occupations

Other workers who monitor and operate plant and systems equipment include stationary engineers, water and wastewater treatment plant operators, waterworks pumpstation operators, chemical plant and system operators, and refinery operators.

Sources of Additional Information

For information about employment opportunities, contact local electric utility companies, locals of unions mentioned below, and an office of the State employment service.

For general information about power plant and nuclear reactor operators and power distributors and dispatchers, contact:

☛ International Brotherhood of Electrical Workers, 1125 15th St. NW., Washington, DC 20005.

☛ Utility Workers Union of America, 815 16th St. NW., Washington, DC 20006.

Stationary Engineers

(O*NET 95032)

Significant Points

- Job opportunities will be best for workers with computer training.
- Stationary engineers usually acquire their skills through a formal apprenticeship program or informal on-the-job training supplemented by courses at a trade or technical school.
- A license to operate boilers, ventilation, air conditioning, and other equipment is required in most States and cities.

Nature of the Work

Heating, air-conditioning, and ventilation systems keep large buildings comfortable all year long. Industrial plants often have facilities to provide electrical power, steam, or other services. Stationary engineers operate and maintain these systems, which can include boilers, air-conditioning and refrigeration equipment, diesel engines, turbines, generators, pumps, condensers, and compressors. The equipment stationary engineers operate is similar to equipment operated by locomotive or marine engineers, except it is not on a moving vehicle.

Stationary engineers start up, regulate, and shut down equipment. They ensure that it operates safely, economically, and within established limits by monitoring meters, gauges, and computerized controls. They manually control equipment and, if necessary, make adjustments. They use hand and power tools to perform repairs and maintenance ranging from a complete overhaul to replacing defective valves, gaskets, or bearings. They also record relevant events and facts concerning operation and maintenance in an equipment log. On steam boilers, for example, they observe, control, and record steam pressure, temperature, water level and chemistry, power output, fuel consumption, and emissions. They watch and listen to machinery and routinely check safety devices, identifying and correcting any trouble that develops.

Increasingly, stationary engineers use computers to operate the mechanical systems of new buildings and plants. Engineers monitor, adjust, and diagnose these systems from a central location or from a laptop computer linked into the buildings' communications network.

Routine maintenance, such as lubricating moving parts, replacing filters, and removing soot and corrosion that can reduce operating efficiency, is a regular part of the work of stationary engineers. They test boiler water and add chemicals to prevent corrosion and harmful deposits. They also may check the air quality of the ventilation system and make adjustments to keep within mandated guidelines.

In a large building or industrial plant, a stationary engineer may be in charge of all mechanical systems in the building. Engineers may supervise the work of assistant stationary engineers, turbine operators, boiler tenders, and air-conditioning and refrigeration operators and mechanics. Some perform other maintenance duties, such as carpentry, plumbing, and electrical repairs. In a small building or industrial plant, there may be only one stationary engineer.

Stationary engineers increasingly use computers to operate the mechanical systems of new buildings and plants.

Working Conditions

Stationary engineers generally have steady, year-round employment. The average workweek is 40 hours. In facilities that operate around the clock, an engineer usually works one of three daily 8-hour shifts on a rotating basis. Weekend and holiday work often is required.

Engine rooms, power plants, and boiler rooms usually are clean and well lighted. Even under the most favorable conditions, however, some stationary engineers are exposed to high temperatures, dust, dirt, and high noise levels from the equipment. General maintenance duties may also require contact with oil, grease, or smoke. Workers spend much of their time on their feet. They may also have to crawl inside boilers and work in crouching or kneeling positions to inspect, clean, or repair equipment.

Stationary engineers work around potentially hazardous machinery such as boilers and electrical equipment. They must follow procedures to guard against burns, electric shock, and exposure to hazardous materials such as asbestos or certain chemicals.

Employment

Stationary engineers held about 31,000 jobs in 1998. They worked in a variety of places, including factories, hospitals, hotels, office and apartment buildings, schools, and shopping malls. Some are employed as contractors to a building or plant.

Stationary engineers work throughout the country, generally in the more heavily populated areas where large industrial and commercial establishments are located.

Training, Other Qualifications, and Advancement

Stationary engineers usually acquire their skills through a formal apprenticeship program or informal on-the-job training supplemented by courses at a trade or technical school. In addition, valuable experience can be obtained in the Navy or the Merchant Marine because marine-engineering plants are similar to many stationary power and heating plants. Most employers prefer to hire persons with at least a high school diploma or its equivalent due to the increasing complexity of the equipment engineers work with. Many stationary engineers have some college education. Mechanical aptitude, manual dexterity, and good physical condition also are important.

The International Union of Operating Engineers sponsors apprenticeship programs and is the principal union for stationary engineers. In selecting apprentices, most local labor-management apprenticeship committees prefer applicants with education or training in mathematics, computers, mechanical drawing, machine-shop practice, physics, and chemistry.

An apprenticeship usually lasts 4 years and includes 8,000 hours of on-the-job training. In addition, apprentices receive 600 hours of classroom instruction in subjects such as boiler design and operation, elementary physics, pneumatics, refrigeration, air conditioning, electricity, and electronics.

Those who acquire their skills on the job usually start as boiler tenders or helpers to experienced stationary engineers. This practical experience may be supplemented by postsecondary vocational training in computerized controls and instrumentation. However, becoming a stationary engineer without completing a formal apprenticeship program usually requires many years of work experience.

Most large and some small employers encourage and pay for skill-improvement training for their employees. Training is almost always provided when new equipment is introduced or when regulations concerning some aspect of their duties change.

Most States and cities have licensing requirements for stationary engineers. Applicants usually must be at least 18 years of age, reside for a specified period in the State or locality, meet experience requirements, and pass a written examination. A stationary engineer who moves from one State or city to another may have to pass an examination for a new license due to regional differences in licensing requirements.

There are several classes of stationary engineer licenses. Each class specifies the type and size of equipment the engineer can operate without supervision. A licensed first-class stationary engineer is qualified to run a large facility, supervise others, and operate equipment of all types and capacities. An applicant for this license may be required to have a high school education, apprenticeship or on-the-job training, and several years of experience. Licenses below first class limit the types or capacities of equipment the engineer may operate without supervision.

Stationary engineers advance by being placed in charge of larger, more powerful, or more varied equipment. Generally, engineers advance to these jobs as they obtain higher class licenses. Some stationary engineers advance to boiler inspectors, chief plant engineers, building and plant superintendents, or building managers. A few obtain jobs as examining engineers or technical instructors.

Job Outlook

Persons wishing to become stationary engineers may face competition for job openings. Employment opportunities will be best for those with apprenticeship training or vocational school courses covering systems operation using computerized controls and instrumentation.

Employment of stationary engineers is expected to decline through the year 2008. Continuing commercial and industrial development will increase the amount of equipment to be operated and maintained. However, automated systems and computerized controls are making newly-installed equipment more efficient, thus reducing the number of jobs needed for their operation. Some job openings will arise from the need to replace experienced workers who transfer to other occupations or leave the labor force. However, turnover in this occupation is low, partly due to its high wages. Consequently, relatively few replacement openings are expected.

Earnings

Median annual earnings of stationary engineers were $38,270 in 1998. The middle 50 percent earned between $31,560 and $46,390 a year. The lowest 10 percent earned less than $24,910 and the highest 10 percent earned more than $55,730 a year.

Related Occupations

Other workers who monitor and operate stationary machinery include nuclear reactor operators, power station operators, water and wastewater treatment plant operators, waterworks pump-station operators, chemical plant and system operators, and refinery operators. Often, workers who operate and maintain all of the equipment in a building or plant are called general maintenance mechanics.

Sources of Additional Information

Information about apprenticeships and vocational training or work opportunities is available from local offices of State employment services, locals of the International Union of Operating Engineers, vocational schools, and from State and local licensing agencies.

Specific questions about this occupation should be addressed to:

☛ International Union of Operating Engineers, 1125 17th St. NW., Washington, DC 20036. Internet: **http://www.iuoe.org**

☛ National Association of Power Engineers, Inc., 1 Springfield St., Chicopee, MA 01013. Internet: **http://www.powerengineers.com**

☛ Building Owners and Managers Institute International, 1521 Ritchie Hwy., Arnold, MD 21012. Internet: **http://www.bomi-edu.org**

Water and Wastewater Treatment Plant Operators

(O*NET 95002A)

Significant Points

- Employment is concentrated in local government and private water supply and sanitary services companies.
- Although completion of high school continues to be sufficient for most jobs, postsecondary training is increasingly an asset as new water pollution control standards make treatment plants more complex.

- In 49 States, operators must pass exams certifying that they are capable of overseeing various treatment processes.

Nature of the Work

Clean water is essential for good health, recreation, fish and wildlife, and industry. *Water treatment plant operators* treat water so that it is safe to drink. *Wastewater treatment plant operators* remove harmful pollutants from domestic and industrial wastewater so that it is safe to return to the environment.

Water is pumped from wells, rivers, and streams to water treatment plants where it is treated and distributed to customers. Wastewater travels through customers' sewer pipes to wastewater treatment plants where it is treated and returned to streams, rivers, and oceans, or reused for irrigation and landscaping. Operators in both types of plants control processes and equipment to remove or destroy harmful materials, chemical compounds, and microorganisms from the water. They also control pumps, valves, and other processing equipment to move the water or wastewater through the various treatment processes, and dispose of the removed waste materials.

Operators read, interpret, and adjust meters and gauges to make sure plant equipment and processes are working properly. They operate chemical-feeding devices, take samples of the water or wastewater, perform chemical and biological laboratory analyses, and adjust the amount of chemicals, such as chlorine, in the water. They use a variety of instruments to sample and measure water quality, and common hand and power tools to make repairs. Operators also make minor repairs to valves, pumps, and other equipment.

Water and wastewater treatment plant operators increasingly rely on computers to help monitor equipment, store sampling results, make process control decisions, schedule and record maintenance activities, and produce reports. When problems occur, operators may use their computers to determine the cause of the malfunction and its solution.

Occasionally operators must work under emergency conditions. A heavy rainstorm, for example, may cause large amounts of wastewater to flow into sewers, exceeding a plant's treatment capacity. Emergencies also can be caused by conditions inside a plant, such as chlorine gas leaks or oxygen deficiencies. To handle these conditions, operators are trained in emergency management response using special safety equipment and procedures to protect public health and the facility. During these periods, operators may work under extreme pressure to correct problems as quickly as possible. These periods may create dangerous working conditions and operators must be extremely cautious.

The specific duties of plant operators depend on the type and size of plant. In smaller plants, one operator may control all machinery, perform tests, keep records, handle complaints, and do repairs and maintenance. A few operators may handle both a water treatment and a wastewater treatment plant. In larger plants with many employees, operators may be more specialized and only monitor one process. The staff may also include chemists, engineers, laboratory technicians, mechanics, helpers, supervisors, and a superintendent.

Water pollution standards have become increasingly stringent since adoption of two major Federal environmental statutes: the Clean Water Act of 1972, which implemented a national system of regulation on the discharge of pollutants; and the Safe Drinking Water Act of 1974, which established standards for drinking water. Industrial facilities sending their wastes to municipal treatment plants must meet certain minimum standards to ensure the wastes have been adequately pretreated and will not damage municipal treatment facilities. Municipal water treatment plants also must meet stringent drinking water standards. The list of contaminants regulated by these statutes has grown over time. For example, the 1996 Safe Drinking Water Act Amendments include standards for the monitoring of cryptosporidium and giardia, two biological organisms that cause health problems. Operators must be familiar with the guidelines established by Federal regulations and how they affect their plant. In addition to Federal regulations, operators also must be aware of any guidelines imposed by the State or locality in which the plant operates.

Water and wastewater treatment plant operators increasingly rely on computers.

Working Conditions

Water and wastewater treatment plant operators work both indoors and outdoors and may be exposed to noise from machinery and unpleasant odors. Operators have to stoop, reach, and climb and sometimes get their clothes dirty. They must pay close attention to safety procedures for they may be confronted with hazardous conditions, such as slippery walkways, dangerous gases, and malfunctioning equipment. Plants operate 24 hours a day, 7 days a week; therefore, operators work one of three 8-hour shifts and weekends and holidays on a rotational basis. Whenever emergencies arise, operators may be required to work overtime.

Employment

Water and wastewater treatment plant operators held about 98,000 jobs in 1998. Most worked for local governments. Some worked for private water supply and sanitary services companies, which increasingly provide operation and management services to local governments on a contract basis. About half worked as water treatment plant operators and half worked as wastewater treatment plant operators.

Water and wastewater treatment plant operators are employed throughout the country, but most jobs are in larger towns and cities. Although nearly all work full time, those who work in small towns may only work part time at the treatment plant—the remainder of their time may be spent handling other municipal duties.

Training, Other Qualifications, and Advancement

A high school diploma commonly is required for water and wastewater treatment plant operator jobs. Operators need mechanical aptitude and should be competent in basic mathematics, chemistry, and biology. They must have the ability to apply data to formulas of treatment requirements, flow levels, and concentration levels. Some basic familiarity with computers also is necessary because of the trend toward computer-controlled equipment and more sophisticated instrumentation. Certain positions—particularly in larger cities and towns—are covered by civil service regulations. Applicants for these positions may be required to pass a written examination testing elementary mathematics skills, mechanical aptitude, and general intelligence.

Completion of an associate degree or 1-year certificate program in water quality and wastewater treatment technology increases an applicant's chances for employment and promotion because plants are becoming more complex. Offered throughout the country, these programs provide a good general knowledge of water and wastewater treatment processes as well as basic preparation for becoming an operator.

Trainees usually start as attendants or operators-in-training and learn their skills on the job under the direction of an experienced operator. They learn by observing and doing routine tasks such as recording meter readings; taking samples of wastewater and sludge; and performing simple maintenance and repair work on pumps, electric motors, valves, and other plant equipment. Larger treatment plants generally combine this on-the-job training with formal classroom or self-paced study programs.

In 49 States, operators must pass an examination to certify that they are capable of overseeing wastewater treatment plant operations. A voluntary certification program is in effect in the remaining State. There are different levels of certification depending on the operator's experience and training. Higher certification levels qualify the operator for a wider variety of treatment processes. Certification requirements vary by State and by size of treatment plants. Although relocation may mean having to become certified in a new location, many States accept other States' certifications.

Presently a nationally mandated certification program for operators does not exist. However, the Safe Drinking Water Act Amendments of 1996 require that within 2 years the Environmental Protection Agency specify minimum standards for drinking water operator certification, and that States implement those standards within another 2 years.

Most State drinking water and water pollution control agencies offer training courses to improve operators' skills and knowledge. These courses cover principles of treatment processes and process control, laboratory procedures, maintenance, management skills, collection systems, safety, chlorination, sedimentation, biological treatment, sludge treatment and disposal, and flow measurements. Some operators take correspondence courses on subjects related to water and wastewater treatment, and some employers pay part of the tuition for related college courses in science or engineering.

As operators are promoted, they become responsible for more complex treatment processes. Some operators are promoted to plant supervisor or superintendent; others advance by transferring to a larger facility. Postsecondary training in water and wastewater treatment coupled with increasingly responsible experience as an operator may be sufficient to qualify for superintendent of a small plant, where a superintendent also serves as an operator. However, educational requirements are rising as larger, more complex treatment plants are built to meet new drinking water and water pollution control standards. With each promotion, the operator must have greater knowledge of Federal, State, and local regulations. Superintendents of large plants generally need an engineering or science degree.

A few operators get jobs with State drinking water or water pollution control agencies as technicians, who monitor and provide technical assistance to plants throughout the State. Vocational-technical school or community college training generally is preferred for technician jobs. Experienced operators may transfer to related jobs with industrial wastewater treatment plants, water or wastewater treatment equipment and chemical companies, engineering consulting firms, or vocational-technical schools.

Job Outlook

Employment of water and wastewater treatment plant operators is expected to grow as fast as the average for all occupations through the year 2008. Because the number of applicants in this field is normally low, job prospects will be good for qualified applicants.

The increasing population and growth of the economy are expected to increase demand for essential water and wastewater treatment services. As new plants are constructed to meet this demand, employment of water and wastewater treatment plant operators will increase. In addition, some job openings will occur as experienced operators transfer to other occupations or leave the labor force.

Local governments are the largest employers of water and wastewater treatment plant operators. However, industry deregulation has increased reliance on private firms specializing in the operation and management of water and wastewater treatment facilities. As a result, employment in privately owned facilities will grow much faster than the average. Increased pre-treatment activity by manufacturing firms will also create new job opportunities.

Earnings

Median annual earnings of water and liquid waste treatment plant and system operators were $29,660 in 1998. The middle 50 percent earned between $23,210 and $36,680. The lowest 10 percent earned less than $18,500 and the highest 10 percent earned more than $44,710. Median annual earnings of water and liquid waste treatment plant and systems operators in 1997 were $28,700 in local government, except education and hospitals.

In addition to their annual salaries, water and wastewater treatment plant operators usually receive benefits that include health and life insurance, a retirement plan, and educational reimbursement for job-related courses.

Related Occupations

Other workers whose main activity consists of operating a system of machinery to process or produce materials include boiler operators, gas-compressor operators, power plant operators, power reactor operators, stationary engineers, turbine operators, chemical plant and system operators, and petroleum refinery operators.

Sources of Additional Information

For information on employment opportunities, contact State or local water pollution control agencies, State water and wastewater operator associations, State environmental training centers, or local offices of the State employment service.

For information on certification, contact:

☛ Association of Boards of Certification, 208 Fifth St., Ames, IA 50010-6259. Internet: **http://www.abccert.org**

For educational information related to a career as a water treatment plant operator, contact:

☛ American Water Works Association, 6666 West Quincy Ave., Denver, CO 80235.

☛ Water Environment Federation, 601 Wythe St., Alexandria, VA 22314.

Printing Occupations

Bindery Workers

(O*NET 89721, 92525, and 92546)

Significant Points

- Most bindery workers train on the job.
- Opportunities for hand bookbinders are limited because of the small number of establishments that do this highly specialized work.
- Employment of bindery workers is expected to grow more slowly than average, reflecting increasingly productive bindery operations.

Nature of the Work

The process of combining printed sheets into finished products such as books, magazines, catalogs, folders, directories, or product packaging is known as "binding." Binding involves cutting, folding, gathering, gluing, stapling, stitching, trimming, sewing, wrapping, and other finishing operations. Bindery workers operate and maintain the machines that perform these various tasks.

Job duties depend on the kind of material being bound. In firms that do *edition binding*, for example, workers bind books produced in large numbers, or "runs." *Job binding* workers bind books produced in smaller quantities. In firms specializing in *library binding*, workers repair books and provide other specialized binding services to libraries. *Pamphlet binding* workers produce leaflets and folders, and *manifold binding* workers bind business forms such as ledgers and books of sales receipts. *Blankbook binding* workers bind blank pages to produce notebooks, checkbooks, address books, diaries, calendars, and note pads.

Some types of binding and finishing consist of only one step. Preparing leaflets or newspaper inserts, for example, require only folding. Binding of books and magazines, on the other hand, requires a number of steps.

Bookbinders assemble books and magazines from large, flat, printed sheets of paper. Skilled bookbinders operate machines that first fold printed sheets into "signatures," which are groups of pages arranged sequentially. Bookbinders then sew, stitch, or glue the assembled signatures together, shape the book bodies with presses and trimming machines, and reinforce them with glued fabric strips. Covers are created separately, and glued, pasted, or stitched onto the book bodies. The books then undergo a variety of finishing operations, often including wrapping in paper jackets.

A small number of bookbinders work in hand binderies. These highly skilled workers design original or special bindings for limited editions, or restore and rebind rare books. The work requires creativity, knowledge of binding materials, and a thorough background in the history of binding. Hand bookbinding gives individuals the opportunity to work in the greatest variety of jobs.

Bindery workers in small shops may perform many binding tasks, while those in large shops are usually assigned only one or a few operations, such as operating complicated manual or electronic guillotine paper cutters or folding machines. Others specialize in adjusting and preparing equipment, and may perform minor repairs as needed.

Working Conditions

Binderies are often noisy and jobs can be fairly strenuous, requiring considerable lifting, standing, and carrying. They may also require stooping, kneeling, and crouching. Binding often resembles an assembly line where workers perform repetitive tasks.

Employment

In 1998, bindery workers held about 96,000 jobs, including about 6,600 working as skilled bookbinders and approximately 90,000 working as lesser skilled bindery machine operators.

Although large libraries and book publishers employ some bindery workers, the majority of jobs are in commercial printing plants. Another large employer of bindery workers are bindery trade shops, which specialize in providing binding services for printers without binderies or whose printing production exceeds their binding capabilities. Few publishers maintain their own manufacturing facilities, so most contract out the printing and assembly of books to commercial printing plants or bindery trade shops.

Most bindery workers train on the job.

Bindery jobs are concentrated near large metropolitan areas such as New York, Chicago, Washington, DC, Los Angeles, Philadelphia, and Dallas.

Training, Other Qualifications, and Advancement

Most bindery workers learn the craft through on-the-job training. Inexperienced workers are usually assigned simple tasks such as moving paper from cutting machines to folding machines. They learn basic binding skills, including the characteristics of paper and how to cut large sheets of paper into different sizes with the least amount of waste. As workers gain experience, they advance to more difficult tasks and learn to operate one or more pieces of equipment. Usually, it takes one to three months to learn to operate the simpler machines but it can take up to one year to become completely familiar with more complex equipment, such as computerized binding machines.

Formal apprenticeships are not as common as they used to be, but are still offered by some employers. Apprenticeships provide a more structured program that enables workers to acquire the high levels of specialization and skill needed for some bindery jobs. For example, a 4-year apprenticeship is usually necessary to teach workers how to restore rare books and to produce valuable collectors' items.

Employers prefer to hire experienced individuals, but will train workers with some basic knowledge of binding operations. High school students interested in bindery careers should take shop courses or attend a vocational-technical high school. Occupational skill centers, usually operated by labor unions, also provide an introduction to the bindery career. To keep pace with ever-changing technology, retraining will become increasingly important for bindery workers.

Bindery workers need basic mathematics and language skills. Bindery work requires careful attention to detail so accuracy, patience, neatness, and good eyesight are also important. Manual dexterity is essential in order to count, insert, paste, and fold. Mechanical aptitude is needed to operate the newer, more automated equipment. Artistic ability and imagination are necessary for hand bookbinding.

Training in graphic arts can also be an asset. Vocational-technical institutes offer postsecondary programs in the graphic arts, as do some skill updating or retraining programs, and community colleges. Some updating and retraining programs require students to have bindery experience; other programs are available through unions for members. Four-year colleges also offer programs, but their emphasis is on preparing people for careers as graphic artists, educators, or managers in the graphic arts field.

Without additional training, advancement opportunities outside of bindery work are limited. In large binderies, experienced bookbinders may advance to supervisory positions.

Job Outlook

Employment of bindery workers is expected to grow about as fast as the average for all occupations through 2008 as demand for printed material grows, but productivity in bindery operations increases. Most job openings for bindery workers will result from the need to replace experienced workers who change jobs or leave the labor force.

Growth of the printing industry will continue to spur demand for bindery workers by commercial printers. The volume of printed material should grow due to increased marketing of products through catalogs, newspaper inserts, and direct mail advertising. Book publishing is expected to grow slowly. Rising school enrollments and the expanding middle-aged and older population—age groups that do the most leisure reading—will account for most of this growth. At the same time, the growth of product packaging, such as that required for

CD-ROM, videos, and other business and educational products, will contribute to the relative stability of binding services. The packaging of these items typically involves folding, gluing, finishing, and shrink-wrapping.

Binding is becoming increasingly mechanized as computers are attached to or associated with binding equipment. New "in-line" equipment performs a number of operations in sequence, beginning with raw stock and ending with a complete finished product. Technological advances such as automatic tabbers, counters, palletizers, and joggers reduce labor and improve the appearance of the finished product. These improvements are increasingly inducing printing companies to invest in in-house binding and finishing equipment. However, growth in demand for specialized bindery workers who assist skilled bookbinders will be slowed as binding machinery continues to become more efficient.

The small number of establishments that do this highly specialized work limits opportunities for hand bookbinders. Experienced bindery workers will have the best opportunities.

Earnings

Median hourly earnings of bookbinders were $9.95 in 1998. The middle 50 percent earned between $7.65 and $13.94 an hour. The lowest 10 percent earned less than $6.35, and the highest 10 percent earned more than $17.56.

Median hourly earnings of bindery machine and set-up operators were $9.91 in 1998. The middle 50 percent earned between $7.55 and $13.39 an hour. The lowest 10 percent earned less than $6.26, and the highest 10 percent earned more than $17.25. Workers covered by union contracts usually had higher earnings.

Related Occupations

Other workers who set up and operate production machinery include papermaking machine operators, printing press operators, and various precision machine operators.

Sources of Additional Information

Information about apprenticeships and other training opportunities may be obtained from local printing industry associations, local bookbinding shops, local offices of the Graphic Communications International Union, or local offices of the State employment service.

For general information on bindery occupations, write to:

☛ Graphic Communications International Union, 1900 L St. NW., Washington, DC 20036. Internet: **http://www.gciu.org**

For information on careers and training programs in printing and the graphic arts, contact:

☛ Education Council of the Graphic Arts Industry, 1899 Preston White Dr., Reston, VA 20191. Internet: **http://www.npes.org**

☛ PIA—Printing Industries of America, Inc., 100 Daingerfield Rd., Alexandria, VA 22314. Internet: **http://www.printing.org**

☛ The Graphic Arts Technical Foundation, 200 Deer Run Road, Sewickley, PA 15143. Internet: **http://www.gatf.org**

Prepress Workers

(O*NET 89702, 89705, 89706, 89707, 89712, 89713, 89715, 89717, 89718, 89719A, 89719B, 89799B, 92541, and 92545)

Significant Points

- Most workers train on-the-job; some complete formal graphics arts programs or other postsecondary programs in printing technology.
- Increased use of computers in typesetting and page layout has greatly changed the nature of work and may eliminate many prepress jobs.

Nature of the Work

The printing process has three stages—prepress, press, and binding or postpress. Prepress workers prepare material for printing presses. They perform a variety of tasks involved with transforming text and pictures into finished pages and making printing plates of the pages.

Advances in computer software and printing technology continue to change prepress work. Customers, as well as prepress workers, use their computers to produce material that looks like the desired finished product. Customers, using their own computers, increasingly do much of the typesetting and page layout work formerly done by prepress workers. This process, called "desktop publishing," poses new challenges for the printing industry. Instead of receiving simple typed text from customers, prepress workers get the material on a computer disk. Because of this, customers are increasingly likely to have already settled on a format on their own, rather than relying on suggestions from prepress workers. Furthermore, the printing industry is rapidly moving toward complete "digital imaging," by which customers' material received on computer disks is converted directly into printing plates. Other innovations in prepress work are digital color page makeup systems, electronic page layout systems, and off-press color proofing systems.

Typesetting and page layouts have also been affected by technological changes. The old "hot type" method of text composition—which used molten lead to create individual letters, paragraphs, and full pages of text—is nearly extinct. Today, composition work is done with computers and "cold type" technology. Cold type, which is any of a variety of methods creating type without molten lead, has traditionally used "phototypesetting" to ready text and pictures for printing. Although this method has many variations, all use photography to create images on paper. The images are assembled into page format and rephotographed to create film negatives from which the actual printing plates are made. However, newer cold type methods are becoming more common. These automate the photography or make printing plates directly from electronic files.

In one common form of phototypesetting, text is entered into a computer programmed to hyphenate, space, and create columns of text. Typesetters or data entry clerks may do keyboarding of text at the printing establishment or, increasingly, authors do this work before the job is sent out for composition. The coded text is then transferred to a typesetting machine, which uses photography, a cathode-ray tube, or a laser to create an image on typesetting paper or film. Once it has been developed the paper or film is sent to a lithographer who makes the actual printing plate.

Desktop publishing specialists use a keyboard to enter and select the size and style of type, the column width, and appropriate spacing, and to store it in the computer. The computer then displays and arranges columns of type on a screen resembling a television screen. An entire newspaper, catalog, or book page, complete with artwork and graphics, can be made up on the screen exactly as it will appear in print. Operators transmit the pages for production into film and then into plates or directly into plates. *Preflight technicians* edit the work of the desktop publishing specialists and ensure the overall quality of the finished product before it is delivered to the customer. In small shops, *job printers* may be responsible for composition and page layout, reading proofs for errors and clarity, correcting mistakes, and printing.

New technologies also affect the roles of other composition workers. Improvements in desktop publishing software allow customers to do more of their own typesetting. "Imagesetters" read text from computer memory and then "beam" it directly onto film, paper, or plates, bypassing the slower photographic process traditionally used.

With traditional photographic processes, the material is arranged and typeset, and then passed on to workers who further prepare it for the presses. *Camera operators* are usually classified as line camera operators, halftone operators, or color separation photographers. Line camera operators start the process of making a lithographic plate by photographing and developing film negatives or positives of the material to be printed. They adjust light and expose film for a specified length of time, and then develop film in a series of chemical baths. They may load exposed film in machines that automatically develop and fix the image.

The use of film in printing will decline, as electronic imaging becomes more prevalent. With decreased costs and improved quality, electronic imaging has become the method of choice in the industry.

The litographic printing process requires that images be made up of tiny dots coming together to form a picture. Photographs cannot be printed without them. When normal "continuous-tone" photographs need to be reproduced, halftone camera operators separate the photograph into pictures containing the dots. Color separation photography is more complex. In this process, camera operators produce four-color separation negatives from a continuous-tone color print or transparency.

Most of this separation work is done electronically on scanners. *Scanner operators* use computerized equipment to create film negatives or positives of photographs or art. The computer controls the color separation of the scanning process, and with the help of the operator, corrects for mistakes, or compensates for deficiencies in the original color print or transparency. Each scan produces a dotted image, or halftone, of the original in one of four primary printing colors—yellow, magenta, cyan, and black. The images are used to produce printing plates that print each of these colors, with transparent colored inks, one at a time. These produce "secondary" color combinations of red, green, blue, and black which can be combined to produce the colors and hues of the original photograph.

Scanners that can perform color correction during the color separation procedure are rapidly replacing *lithographic dot etchers,* who retouch film negatives or positives by sharpening or reshaping images. They work by hand, using chemicals, dyes, and special tools. Dot etchers must know the characteristics of all types of paper and must produce fine shades of color. Like camera operators, they are usually assigned to only one phase of the work, and may have job titles such as dot etcher, retoucher, or letterer.

Prepress work continues to change due to advances in computer software and printing technology.

New technology is also lessening the need for *film strippers,* who cut the film to the required size and arrange and tape the negatives onto "flats"—or layout sheets used by platemakers to make press plates. When completed, flats resemble large film negatives of the text in its final form. In large printing establishments such as newspapers, arrangement is done automatically.

Platemakers use a photographic process to make printing plates. The film assembly or flat is placed on top of a thin metal plate coated with a light-sensitive resin. Exposure to ultraviolet light activates the chemical in parts not protected by the film's dark areas. The plate is then developed in a solution that removes the unexposed non-image area, exposing bare metal. The chemical on areas of the plate exposed to the light hardens and becomes water repellent. The hardened parts of the plate form the text.

A growing number of printing plants use lasers to directly convert electronic data to plates without any use of film. Entering, storing, and retrieving information from computer-aided equipment require technical skills. In addition to operating and maintaining the equipment, lithographic platemakers must make sure that plates meet quality standards.

During the printing process, the plate is first covered with a thin coat of water. The water adheres only to the bare metal non-image areas, and is repelled by the hardened areas that were exposed to light. Next, the plate comes in contact with a rubber roller covered with oil-based ink. Because oil and water do not mix, the ink is repelled by the water-coated area and sticks to the hardened areas. The ink covering the hardened text is transferred to paper.

Although computers perform a wider variety of tasks, printing still involves text composition, page layout, and plate making, so printing will still require prepress workers. As computer skills become increasingly important, these workers will need to demonstrate a desire and an ability to benefit from the frequent retraining required by rapidly changing technology.

Working Conditions

Prepress workers usually work in clean, air-conditioned areas with little noise. Some workers, such as typesetters and compositors, may develop eyestrain from working in front of a video display terminal, or musculoskeletal problems such as backaches. Lithographic artists and film strippers may find working with fine detail tiring to the eyes. Platemakers, who work with toxic chemicals, face the hazard of skin irritations. Workers are often subject to stress and the pressures of short deadlines and tight work schedules.

Prepress employees usually work an 8-hour day. Some workers—particularly those employed by newspapers—work night shifts, weekends, and holidays.

Employment

Prepress workers held about 135,000 jobs in 1998. Employment was distributed as follows:

Prepress precision workers	
Desktop publishing specialists	26,000
Film strippers, printing	23,000
Job printers	17,000
Platemakers	15,000
Compositors and typesetters	14,000
Camera operators	9,200
Paste-up workers	9,000
Photoengravers	2,700
All other precision printing workers	17,000
Prepress machine operators	
Typesetting and composing machine operators	13,000
Photoengraving and lithographic machine operators	6,800

Most prepress jobs were found in firms that handle commercial or business printing, and in newspaper plants. Commercial printing firms print newspaper inserts, catalogs, pamphlets, and advertisements, while business form establishments print material such as sales receipts. A large number of jobs are also found in printing trade service firms and "in-plant" operations. Establishments in printing trade services typically perform custom compositing, platemaking, and related prepress services.

The printing and publishing industry is one of the most geographically dispersed in the United States, and prepress jobs are found throughout the country. However, job prospects may be best in large metropolitan cities such as New York, Chicago, Los Angeles, Philadelphia, Washington DC, and Dallas.

Training, Other Qualifications, and Advancement

Most prepress workers train on the job; the length of training varies by occupation. Some skills, such as typesetting, can be learned in a few months, but they are the most likely to be automated in the future. Other skills, such as stripping (image assembly), require years of experience to master. However, these workers should also expect to receive intensive retraining.

Workers often start as helpers who are selected for on-the-job training programs after demonstrating their reliability and interest in the occupation. They begin with instruction from an experienced craft worker and advance based on their demonstrated mastery of skills at each level. All workers should expect to be retrained from time to time to handle new, improved equipment. As workers gain experience, they advance to positions with greater responsibility. Some move into supervisory positions.

Apprenticeship is another way to become a skilled prepress worker, although few apprenticeships have been offered in recent years. Apprenticeship programs emphasize a specific craft—such as camera operator, film stripper, lithographic etcher, scanner operator, or platemaker—but apprentices are introduced to all phases of printing.

Usually, most employers prefer to hire high school graduates who possess good communication skills, both oral and written. Prepress workers should be able to deal courteously with people, because in small shops they may take customer orders. They may also add, subtract, multiply, divide, and compute ratios to estimate job costs. Persons interested in working for firms using advanced printing technology need to know the basics of electronics and computers. Mathematical skills are also essential for operating many of the software packages used to run modern, computerized prepress equipment.

Prepress workers need good manual dexterity, and they must be able to pay attention to detail and work independently. Good eyesight, including visual acuity, depth perception, field of view, color vision, and the ability to focus quickly, are also assets. Artistic ability is often a plus. Employers also seek persons who are even-tempered and adaptable, important qualities for workers who often must meet deadlines and learn how to operate new equipment.

Formal graphic arts programs, offered by community and junior colleges and some 4-year colleges, are a good way to learn about the industry. These programs provide job-related training, which will help when seeking full-time employment. Bachelor's degree programs in graphic arts are usually intended for students who may eventually move into management positions, and 2-year associate degree programs are designed to train skilled workers.

Courses in various aspects of printing are also available at vocational-technical institutes, industry-sponsored update and retraining programs, and private trade and technical schools.

As workers gain experience, they may advance to positions with greater responsibility. Some move into supervisory positions.

Job Outlook

Overall employment of prepress workers is expected to decline through 2008. Demand for printed material should continue to grow, spurred by rising levels of personal income, increasing school enrollments, higher levels of educational attainment, and expanding markets. However, increased use of computers in desktop publishing should eliminate many prepress jobs.

Technological advances will have a varying effect on employment among the prepress occupations. Employment of desktop publishing specialists is expected to grow much faster than average. This reflects the increasing proportion of page layout and design that will be performed using computers. In contrast, a decline in prepress machine operators is expected as the duties these workers perform manually become increasingly automated. Paste-up, composition and typesetting, photoengraving, platemaking, film stripping, and camera operator occupations are expected to experience declines as handwork becomes automated.

Job prospects also will vary by industry. Changes in technology have shifted many employment opportunities away from the traditional printing plants into advertising agencies, public relations firms, and large corporations. Many companies are turning to in-house typesetting or desktop publishing, as personal computers with elaborate graphic capabilities have become common. Corporations are finding it more profitable to print their own newsletters and other reports than to send them out to trade shops. In addition, press shops themselves have responded to desktop publishers' needs by sending their own staff into the field to help customers prepare an electronic product that will live up to the customer's expectations once it has been printed.

Compositors and typesetters should find competition extremely keen in the newspaper industry. Computerized equipment allowing reporters and editors to specify type and style, and to format pages at a desktop computer terminal, has already eliminated many typesetting and composition jobs; more may disappear in the years ahead.

Many new jobs for prepress workers are expected to emerge in commercial printing establishments. New equipment should reduce the time needed to complete a printing job, and allow commercial printers to make inroads into new markets that require fast turnaround. Because small establishments predominate, commercial printing should provide the best opportunities for inexperienced workers who want to gain a good background in all facets of printing.

Most employers prefer to hire experienced prepress workers. Among persons without experience, however, opportunities should be best for those with computer backgrounds who have completed postsecondary programs in printing technology. Many employers prefer graduates of these programs because the comprehensive training they receive helps them learn the printing process and adapt more rapidly to new processes and techniques.

Earnings

Wage rates for prepress workers vary according to occupation, level of experience, training, location, and size of the firm, and whether they are union members. The following tabulation shows the range of median hourly earnings of workers in various prepress occupations for 1998.

Occupation	Earnings
Film strippers, printing	$15.53
All other printing workers, precision	14.63
Desktop publishing specialists	14.00
Platemakers	13.75
Photoengravers	13.67
Camera operators	11.72
Job printers	11.58
Photoengraving and lithographic machine operators and tendors	11.52
Typesetting and composing machine operators and tendors	11.08
Compositors and typesetters, precision	10.85
Paste-up workers	9.53

Of the unionized prepress workers, scanner operators earned an hourly wage of $23.20 in 1998, and film strippers earned $19.45 per hour, according to the Graphic Communications International Union, the principal union for prepress workers.

Related Occupations

Prepress workers use artistic skills in their work. These skills are also essential for sign painters, jewelers, decorators, engravers, and graphic artists. In addition to typesetters, other workers who operate machines equipped with keyboards include typists and data entry keyers.

Sources of Additional Information

Details about apprenticeship and other training programs may be obtained from local employers such as newspapers and printing shops, or from local offices of the State employment service.

For information on careers and training in printing and the graphic arts, write to:

☛ PIA—Printing Industries of America, Inc., 100 Daingerfield Rd., Alexandria, VA 22314. Internet: **http://www.printing.org**

☛ Education Council of the Graphic Arts Industry, 1899 Preston White Dr., Reston, VA 20191. Internet: **http://www.npes.org**

☛ Graphic Communications International Union, 1900 L St. NW., Washington, DC 20036. Internet: **http://www.gciu.org**

☛ The Graphic Arts Technical Foundation, 200 Deer Run Rd., Sewickley, PA 15143. Internet: **http://www.gatf.org**

Printing Press Operators

(O*NET 89799A, 92512, 92515, 92519, 92524, 92529D, 92529E, 92543, and 92549)

Significant Points

- Most are trained informally on the job while working as assistants or helpers; basic computer skills are necessary for operators of newer presses.
- Employment growth will be slowed by the increasing use of new, more efficient computerized printing presses.
- Jobseekers are likely to face keen competition.

Nature of the Work

Printing press operators prepare, operate, and maintain the printing presses in a pressroom. Duties of press operators vary according to the type of press they operate—offset lithography, gravure, flexography, screen printing, or letterpress. Offset lithography, which transfers an inked impression from a rubber-covered cylinder to paper or other material, is the dominant printing process. With gravure, the recesses on an etched plate or cylinder are inked and pressed to paper. Flexography is a form of rotary printing in which ink is applied to the surface by a flexible rubber printing plate with a raised image area. Gravure and flexography should increase in use, but letterpress, in which an inked, raised surface is pressed against paper, will be phased out. In addition to the major printing processes, plateless or nonimpact processes are coming into general use. Plateless processes—including electronic, electrostatic, and ink-jet printing—are used for copying, duplicating, and document and specialty printing, usually by quick and in-house printing shops.

To prepare presses for printing, press operators install and adjust the printing plate, adjust pressure, ink the presses, load paper, and adjust the press to the paper size. Press operators ensure that paper and ink meet specifications, and adjust margins and the flow of ink to the inking rollers accordingly. They then feed paper through the press cylinders and adjust feed and tension controls.

While printing presses are running, press operators monitor their operation and keep the paper feeders well stocked. They make adjustments to correct uneven ink distribution, speed, and temperatures in the drying chamber, if the press has one. If paper jams or tears and the press stops, which can happen with some offset presses, operators quickly correct the problem to minimize downtime. Similarly, operators working with other high-speed presses constantly look for problems, making quick corrections to avoid expensive losses of paper and ink. Throughout the run, operators occasionally pull sheets to check for any printing imperfections.

In most shops, press operators also perform preventive maintenance. They oil and clean the presses and make minor repairs.

Press operators' jobs differ from one shop to another because of differences in the kinds and sizes of presses. Small commercial shops are operated by one person and tend to have relatively small presses, which print only one or two colors at a time. Operators who work with large presses have assistants and helpers. Large newspaper, magazine, and book printers use giant "in-line web" presses that require a crew of several press operators and press assistants. These presses are fed paper in big rolls, called "webs," up to 50 inches or more in width. Presses print the paper on both sides; trim, assemble, score, and fold the pages; and count the finished sections as they come off the press.

Most plants have or will soon have installed printing presses with computers and sophisticated instruments to control press operations, making it possible to set up for jobs in less time. Computers allow press operators to perform many of their tasks electronically. With this equipment, press operators monitor the printing process on a control panel or computer monitor, which allows them to adjust the press electronically.

Working Conditions

Operating a press can be physically and mentally demanding, and sometimes tedious. Press operators are on their feet most of the time. Often, operators work under pressure to meet deadlines. Most printing presses are capable of high printing speeds, and adjustments must be made quickly to avoid waste. Pressrooms are noisy, and workers in certain areas wear ear protectors. Working with press machinery can be hazardous, but accidents can be avoided when safe work practices are observed. The threat of accidents is less with newer computerized presses because operators make most adjustments from a control panel. Many press operators work evening, night, and overtime shifts.

Employment

Press operators held about 253,000 jobs in 1998. Employment was distributed as follows:

Occupation	Jobs
Printing press machine setters and operators	142,000
Offset lithographic press operators	63,000
Screen printing machine setters and setup operators	28,000
Letterpress operators	10,000
All other printing press setters and set-up operators	9,500

Most press operator jobs were in newspaper plants or in firms handling commercial or business printing. Commercial printing firms print newspaper inserts, catalogs, pamphlets, and the advertisements found in mailboxes, and business form establishments print items such as business cards, sales receipts, and paper used in computers. Additional jobs were in the "in-plant" section of organizations and businesses that do their own printing—such as banks, insurance companies, and government agencies.

The printing and publishing industry is one of the most geographically dispersed in the United States, and press operators can find jobs throughout the country. However, jobs are concentrated in large printing centers such as New York, Los Angeles, Chicago, Philadelphia, Washington, DC, and Dallas.

Training, Other Qualifications, and Advancement

Although completion of a formal apprenticeship or a postsecondary program in printing equipment operation continue to be the best ways to learn the trade, most printing press operators are trained informally on the job while working as assistants or helpers to experienced operators. Beginning press operators load, unload, and clean presses. With time, they move up to operating one-color sheet-fed presses and eventually advance to multicolor presses. Operators are likely to gain experience on many kinds of printing presses during the course of their career.

Printing press operators prepare, operate, and maintain the printing presses in a pressroom.

Apprenticeships for press operators in commercial shops take 4 years. In addition to on-the-job instruction, apprenticeships include related classroom or correspondence school courses. Once the dominant method for preparing for this occupation, apprenticeships are becoming less prevalent.

In contrast, formal postsecondary programs in printing equipment operation offered by technical and trade schools and community colleges are growing in importance. Some postsecondary school programs require 2 years of study and award an associate degree, but most programs can be completed in 1 year or less. Postsecondary courses in printing are increasingly important because they provide the theoretical knowledge needed to operate advanced equipment.

Persons who wish to become printing press operators need mechanical aptitude to make press adjustments and repairs. Oral and writing skills are also required. Operators should possess the mathematical skills necessary to compute percentages, weights, and measures, and to calculate the amount of ink and paper needed to do a job. Because of technical developments in the printing industry, courses in chemistry, electronics, color theory, and physics are helpful.

Technological changes have had a tremendous effect on the skills needed by press operators. New presses now require operators to possess basic computer skills. Even experienced operators periodically receive retraining and skill updating. For example, printing plants that change from sheetfed offset presses to weboffset presses have to retrain the entire press crew because skill requirements for the two types of presses are different. Weboffset presses, with their faster operating speeds, require faster decisions, monitoring of more variables, and greater physical effort. In the future, workers are expected to need to retrain several times during their career.

Press operators may advance in pay and responsibility by working on a more complex printing press. Through experience and demonstrated ability, for example, a one-color sheetfed press operator may become a four-color sheetfed press operator. Others may advance to pressroom supervisor and become responsible for the an entire press crew.

Job Outlook

Persons seeking jobs as printing press operators are likely to face keen competition from experienced operators and prepress workers who have been displaced by new technology, particularly those who have completed retraining programs. Opportunities to become printing press operators are likely to be best for persons who qualify for formal apprenticeship training or who complete postsecondary training programs.

Employment of press operators is expected to grow little through 2008. Although demand for printed materials will grow, employment growth will be slowed by the increased use of new, more efficient computerized printing presses. However, employment growth will vary among press operator jobs. Employment of screen printing machine setters and set-up operators and printing press machine setters, operators, and tenders will increase, while employment of offset lithograhic and letterpress operators will decline sharply. Most job openings will result from the need to replace operators who retire or leave the occupation.

Most new jobs will result from expansion of the printing industry as demand for printed material increases in response to demographic trends, U.S. expansion into foreign markets, and growing use of direct mail by advertisers. Demand for books and magazines will increase as school enrollments rise, and as substantial growth in the middle-aged and older population spurs adult education and leisure reading. Additional growth should stem from increased foreign demand for domestic trade publications, professional and scientific works, and mass-market books such as paperbacks.

Continued employment in commercial printing will be spurred by increased expenditures for print advertising materials to be mailed directly to prospective customers. New market research techniques are leading advertisers to increase spending on messages targeted to specific audiences, and should continue to require the printing of a wide variety of newspaper inserts, catalogs, direct mail enclosures, and other kinds of print advertising.

Other printing, such as newspapers, books, and greeting cards, will also provide jobs. Experienced press operators will fill most of these jobs because many employers are under severe pressure to meet deadlines and have limited time to train new employees.

Earnings

The basic wage rate for a press operator depends on the type of press being run and the geographic area in which the work is located. Workers covered by union contracts usually had higher earnings. The following tabulation shows the range of median hourly earnings of various press operators for 1998.

Occupation	Earnings
Offset lithographic press operators	$14.91
Letterpress operators	13.76
All other printing press setters and set-up operators	13.33
Printing press machine setters, operators and tenders	12.51
Screen printing machine setters and set-up operators	9.08

Related Occupations

Other workers who set up and operate production machinery include papermaking, shoemaking, bindery, and various precision machine operators.

Sources of Additional Information

Details about apprenticeships and other training opportunities may be obtained from local employers such as newspapers and printing shops, local offices of the Graphic Communications International Union, local affiliates of Printing Industries of America, or local offices of the State employment service.

For general information about press operators, write to:

☛ Graphic Communications International Union, 1900 L St. NW., Washington, DC 20036. Internet: **http://www.gciu.org**

For information on careers and training in printing and the graphic arts, write to:

☛ PIA—Printing Industries of America, Inc., 100 Daingerfield Rd., Alexandria, VA 22314. Internet: **http://www.printing.org**

☛ Education Council of the Graphic Arts Industry, 1899 Preston White Dr., Reston, VA 20191. Internet: **http://www.npes.org**

☛ The Graphic Arts Technical Foundation, 200 Deer Run Rd., Sewickley, PA 15143. Internet: **http://www.gatf.org**

Textile, Apparel, and Furnishings Occupations

Apparel Workers

(O*Net 89502A, 89502D, 89505A, 89505B, 92717, 92721, 92728, 93921, 93923B, and 93926E)

Significant Points

- Most workers are trained on the job; those in firms that emphasize teamwork are trained in all operations performed by their team.
- Employment of apparel workers is expected to decline due to increased imports, offshore assembly, and laborsaving machinery.
- Earnings of most apparel workers are low.

Nature of the Work

Apparel workers help keep us warm, comfortable, and in style. They play this important role in our lives by transforming cloth, leather, and fur into clothing and other consumer products. Many apparel workers also repair and alter these products. (Some items that we think of as apparel, such as socks or pantyhose, are produced in knitting mills. Workers who are employed in these factories are classified as textile rather than as apparel workers. A separate statement on textile machinery operators is presented in this section of the *Handbook*.)

Apparel production begins with a designer's creation that has been made into a sample product. Because many apparel items are mass-produced, the sample must be converted into a pattern, a step which is usually done with the aid of a computer. After a design is made, sample makers produce the sample garment for the designer. (A separate statement on designers is presented elsewhere in the *Handbook*.)

Once the pattern has been created, the fabric must be spread and cut. Many layers of material may be spread on the cutting table, depending on the quantity being produced and the type of material. Workers known as markers must determine the best arrangement or layout of the pattern pieces to minimize waste. In many plants, this step depends on the judgment of the worker, but computers increasingly determine the optimum arrangement of the pattern pieces.

Using an electric knife or other cutting tool, other workers cut out the various pieces of material following the outline of the pattern. On especially delicate or valuable items, this may be done by hand. Workers must pay close attention to detail because a mistake in the cutting process can ruin many yards of material. In more automated firms, electronic copies of layouts are sent to computer-controlled cutting machines that are monitored by cutting machine operators.

Once the material has been cut, it is ready to be sewn together into a shirt, knapsack, dress, or other product. Most sewing is done by sewing machine operators, who are classified by the type of machine and product on which they work. The most basic division is between sewing machine operators who produce clothing and those who produce nongarment items such as towels, sheets, and curtains. Both garment and nongarment machine operators usually specialize in a single operation, such as bindings, collars, or hems. Because each product requires a variety of sewing operations that cannot be done on the same machine, companies producing apparel have many types of specialized sewing machines.

Some materials may be sewn by hand rather than by machine due to their value and delicacy. Hand sewers may specialize in a particular operation, such as sewing buttonholes or adding lace or other trimming. They also work with the designer to make a sample of a new product. When sewing operations have been completed, workers remove loose threads, basting stitching, and lint from the finished product.

Although final inspection of the product is usually done at this time, inspectors are found in all stages of the production process. They mark defects in uncut fabric so that layout workers can position the pattern to avoid them. When they find defects in semi-finished garments, they may repair the garments themselves or send them back to be mended. (For a more detailed discussion, see the statement on inspectors, testers, and graders elsewhere in the *Handbook*.)

Pressers ensure that finished products are free of wrinkles. Some pressers specialize in a particular garment part; others do the final pressing before the product is shipped to the store. Specially designed steam-pressing machines, which are much more productive than hand pressing, usually do the final pressing.

A large number of apparel workers are employed by small firms that lack the resources to invest in new, more efficient equipment. Because of this and the difficulty of automating the assembly process, the nature of the work for many apparel workers has remained relatively unchanged. Nevertheless, in larger firms with modern facilities, some operations are computerized, and many product-moving operations are performed by automated material handling systems.

In addition, many firms now use another workplace innovation—the modular manufacturing system—to increase product quality while reducing production time. In this system, operators work together in a module or team. Although each worker in the modular system usually

Apparel workers must pay close attention to details.

specializes in one operation, most are trained to perform all of the operations performed by their team so that they can substitute for other workers. Not only do operators communicate more with other workers in the new system, they are given added responsibilities, such as correcting problems, scheduling, and monitoring standards.

Because some people require or prefer clothing made especially for them, not all apparel goods are mass-produced. For these people, custom tailors make garments from start to finish by taking measurements and helping the customer select the right fabric and design. These workers are highly skilled and must be capable in all phases of clothing production.

Many other custom tailors and sewers work in retail outlets, including laundries and dry-cleaning establishments, where they make alterations and adjustments to ready-to-wear clothing. In some establishments, these workers specialize in one function, such as altering jackets or shortening pants. They may also perform other duties, such as taking measurements or pressing garments.

Working Conditions

Working conditions in apparel production vary by establishment and by occupation. Older factories tend to be congested and poorly lit and ventilated, but more modern facilities are usually better planned, have more work space, and are well-lit and ventilated. Due to the nature of the work and the machinery being used, sewing and pressing are usually noisy and occasionally hot, whereas patternmaking and spreading areas are quieter. Laundries and dry-cleaning establishments are often hot and noisy; retail stores, on the other hand, tend to be relatively quiet and comfortable.

Most persons in apparel occupations work a standard 5-day, 35- to 40-hour week. Some apparel manufacturers add second shifts to justify the expense of new machinery. Those employed in retail stores and in laundry and dry-cleaning establishments may work evenings and weekends.

Work in apparel production can be physically demanding. Some workers sit for long periods, and others spend many hours on their feet, leaning over tables and operating machinery. In some instances, new machinery and production techniques have decreased the physical demands upon workers. For example, newer pressing machines are now operated by foot pedals or computer controls and do not require much strength to operate. Although there are no life-threatening dangers or health hazards associated with work in apparel, operators must be attentive while running equipment such as sewing machines, pressers, and automated cutters. A few workers wear protective devices such as gloves.

While much of the work in apparel is still based on a piecework system that allows for little interpersonal contact, some apparel firms are placing more emphasis on teamwork and cooperation. In this new system, individuals work closely with one another and each team or module often has managerial authority over itself, increasing the overall responsibility of each operator.

Employment

Apparel workers held 730,000 jobs in 1998. The following tabulation shows that about 7 out of 10 were sewing machine operators:

Occupation	Jobs
Garment sewing machine operators	369,000
Nongarment sewing machine operators	137,000
Custom tailors	74,000
Pressing machine operators	69,000
Hand cutters and trimmers	42,000
Patternmakers and layout workers	16,000
Hand pressers	13,000
Hand sewers	10,000

Production jobs are concentrated in California, New York, North Carolina, Pennsylvania, Tennessee, and Georgia. Most of these jobs are in the apparel and textile industries, except for pressers and custom tailors. Although pressing operations are an integral part of the apparel production process, more than one-half of all pressers are employed in the laundry and dry-cleaning industry. More than one-half of all custom tailors work in retail clothing establishments, and many others are self-employed. For both of these occupations, jobs are found in every part of the country.

Training, Other Qualifications, and Advancement

Training requirements vary by industry. Few employers in the apparel industry require production workers to have a high school diploma or previous work experience. Nevertheless, entrants with secondary or postsecondary vocational training or previous work experience in apparel production usually have a better chance of getting a job and advancing to a supervisory position.

Retailers prefer to hire custom tailors and sewers with previous experience in apparel manufacture, design, or alterations. Knowledge of fabrics, design, and construction is very important. Although laundries and dry cleaners prefer entrants with previous work experience, they routinely hire inexperienced workers.

In general, apparel workers need good hand-eye coordination and the ability to perform repetitive tasks for long periods. Knowledge of fabrics and their characteristics is sometimes required.

Regardless of setting, workers usually begin by performing simple tasks. As they gain experience, they are assigned more difficult operations. Further advancement is limited, however. Some production workers may become first-line supervisors, but the majority remains on the production line. Occasionally, a patternmaker may advance to designer, but usually only after additional training at a design school. Some experienced custom tailors open their own tailoring shop. Custom tailoring is a very competitive field, however, and training in small business operations can mean the difference between success and failure.

Machine operators are usually trained on the job by more experienced employees or by machinery manufacturers' representatives. As machinery in the industry continues to become more complex, some apparel workers will need training in the basics of computers and electronics. In addition, the trend toward cross-training of operators will increase the time needed to learn different machines, and the rise of modular manufacturing will require workers to acquire the interpersonal skills necessary to work effectively as part of a team.

Job Outlook

Employment of apparel workers is expected to decline through 2008. Apparel workers have been among the most rapidly declining occupational groups in the economy, and increasing imports, the use of offshore assembly, and greater productivity through new automation will contribute to additional job losses. Because of the large size of this occupation, however, many thousands of job openings will arise each year from the need to replace persons who transfer to other occupations, retire, or leave the occupation for other reasons.

Employment in the domestic apparel industry has declined in recent years as foreign producers have gained a greater share of the U.S. market. Imports now account for roughly half of domestic apparel consumption, and this share is expected to increase as the U.S. market is opened further by the North American Free Trade Agreement (NAFTA) and the Agreement on Textiles and Clothing (ATC) of the World Trade Organization. NAFTA allows apparel produced in Mexico and Canada to be imported, duty-free, to the United States. A number of apparel companies have already moved their production facilities to Mexico to reduce costs, and this trend is expected to continue. The ATC will result in the elimination of quotas and a reduction in tariffs for many apparel products. As this agreement is phased in through 2005, domestic production will continue to move abroad and imports into the U.S. market will increase, causing further decline in employment of apparel workers in the United States.

To avoid losing more of the market, domestic manufacturers are developing the ability to take advantage of their proximity to the U.S. market by responding more quickly to changes in market demand. This is especially important in high-fashion items with rapidly changing demand. U.S. producers are able to use computers and electronic data interchange to closely monitor the sales of the items that they produce and to respond quickly to diminishing inventories. They are, therefore, able to keep retailers stocked with the most popular items and to reduce production of apparel that is not selling well. Because of fierce competition in the market for apparel and the growing demands of large retailers, however, apparel firms will continue to be under intense pressure to cut costs and produce more with fewer workers.

Despite advances in technology, it has been difficult to use automated equipment extensively in the apparel industry due to the soft properties of textile products. In addition, it is time consuming and expensive to adapt existing technology to the wide variety of items produced and the frequent style and seasonal changes. However, some larger firms and those that produce standardized items have automated pre-sewing functions, material handling, and some simple sewing procedures. Technological developments, such as computer-aided marking and grading, computer-controlled cutters, semiautomatic sewing and pressing machines, and automated material handling systems have increased output while reducing the need for some workers in larger firms. As the apparel industry continues to restructure and consolidate, more of the smaller, less efficient producers will lose market share to larger firms and foreign producers.

Another practice that will influence employment levels is the use of offshore assembly. A provision in U.S. tariff regulations reduces tariffs on apparel imports from Caribbean nations that are assembled from pieces of fabric which were cut in the United States. This enables the most labor-intensive step in the production process—assembly—to be performed at much lower wage rates. This trend is expected to continue and will curtail job opportunities for sewing machine operators in the United States. Because many pre-sewing functions such as design will continue to be done domestically, however, workers who perform these functions will not be as adversely affected.

Custom tailors and sewers, the most skilled apparel workers, are also expected to experience declining employment. Demand for their services will continue to lessen as consumers are increasingly likely to buy new, mass-produced apparel instead of purchasing custom-made apparel or having clothes altered or repaired.

Earnings

Earnings of apparel workers vary by industry and occupation. Median hourly earnings of the largest group of apparel workers—garment sewing machine operators—were $7.09 in 1998. Most of these workers earned between $5.99 and $8.43. Median hourly earnings in the industries that employed the most garment sewing machine operators in 1997 were:

Knitting mills	$7.32
Miscellaneous fabricated textile products	7.22
Men's and boys' furnishings	6.99
Women's and children's undergarments	6.34
Women's and misses' outerwear	6.07

Sewing machine operators who assembled nongarment items had slightly higher earnings in 1998. Median hourly earnings were $8.17, with most of these workers earning between $6.67 and $9.84. Earnings in the industries that employed the largest number of nongarment sewing machine operators in 1997 were:

Household furniture	$8.99
Miscellaneous fabricated textile products	7.86

Earnings also varied among other apparel workers. Pressing machine operators had median hourly earnings of $7.28 in 1998, while patternmakers and layout workers earned about $10.38. Among hand workers, cutters and trimmers earned $8.23, pressers earned $7.09, and sewers earned $7.46 an hour. Finally, custom tailors earned a median annual income of $18,630 in 1998. Because many production workers in apparel manufacturing are paid according to the number of acceptable pieces they or their group produce, their total earnings depend on skill, speed, and accuracy.

Benefits also vary. A few large employers, for example, include child care in their benefits package. Apparel workers in retail trade also may receive a discount on their purchases. In addition, some of the larger manufacturers operate company stores, where employees can purchase apparel products at significant discounts. Some small firms, however, offer only limited benefits. In addition to employer-sponsored benefits, the principal union—the Union of Needletrades, Industrial, and Textile Employees (UNITE)—provides benefits to its members.

Related Occupations

The duties of apparel workers vary from those requiring very little skill and training to those that are highly complex, requiring several years of training. Workers operating machinery and equipment, such as pressing or sewing machine operators, perform duties similar to metalworking and plastics-working, textile, and shoe sewing machine operators. Other workers who perform handwork are precision woodworkers, precision assemblers, upholsterers, and shoe and leather workers.

Sources of Additional Information

Information regarding careers in apparel is available from numerous technical institutes that offer specialized textile and apparel programs. A list of these can be found in college guides. In addition, the local office of the State employment service or an apparel manufacturer can provide information on job opportunities in a specific area.

For general information on the apparel industry, contact:

- American Apparel Manufacturers Association, 2500 Wilson Blvd., Suite 301, Arlington, VA 22201. Internet: **http://www.americanapparel.com**

Shoe and Leather Workers and Repairers

(O*Net 89511)

Significant Points

- Workers generally learn their craft on the job; trainees become fully skilled in 6 months to 2 years.
- Employment is expected to decline, reflecting increases in imports, laborsaving machinery, and business costs.

Nature of the Work

Shoe and leather workers create stylish and durable leather products, such as boots, saddles, and luggage. Although they produce different goods, shoe and leather workers share many tasks. For example, they first check the texture, color, and strength of the leather. They then place a pattern of the item being produced on the leather, trace the pattern onto the leather, cut along the outline, and sew the pieces together. Other steps may vary according to the type of good being produced.

Orthopedic and therapeutic shoemakers, for instance, make or modify footwear according to a doctor's prescription. These workers attach the insoles to shoe lasts (a wooden form shaped like a foot), affix the shoe uppers, and apply heels and outsoles. These shoemakers then shape the heels with a knife and sand them on a buffing wheel for smoothness. Finally, they dye and polish the shoes. Custom shoe workers also may modify existing footwear for people with foot problems and special needs. This can involve preparing inserts, heel pads, and lifts from casts of customers' feet.

In addition to the common steps listed above, *saddlemakers* often apply leather dyes and liquid top coats to produce a gloss finish on a saddle. They may also decorate the saddle surface by hand stitching or by stamping the leather with decorative patterns and designs. *Luggage makers* fasten leather to a frame and attach handles and other hardware. They also cut and secure linings inside the frames and sew or stamp designs onto the luggage exterior.

Shoe and leather repairers use their knowledge of leatherworking to extend the lives of worn leather goods. The most common type of shoe repair is replacing soles and heels. Repairers place the shoe on a last and remove the old sole and heel with a knife or pliers or both. They then attach new soles and heels to shoes either by stitching them in place or by using cement or nails. Leather repairers also work with other leather goods, such as suitcases or handbags, that may need seams to be re-sewn or handles and linings replaced.

All leather workers and repairers use handtools and machines. The most commonly used handtools are knives, hammers, awls (used to poke holes in leather to make sewing possible), and skivers (for splitting leather). Power-operated equipment includes sewing machines, heel nailing machines, sanding machines, hole punching machines, sole stitchers, and computerized machinery to analyze foot needs and conditions.

Depending on the size of the factory or shop, a leather worker may perform one or more of the steps required to complete or repair a product. In smaller factories or shops, workers generally perform several tasks, while those in larger facilities tend to specialize. Most leather workers, however, eventually learn the different skills involved in producing leather goods as they move from one task to another.

Self-employed shoe repairers and owners of custom-made shoe and leather shops have managerial responsibilities in addition to their regular duties. They must maintain good relations with their customers, make business decisions, and keep accurate records.

Working Conditions

Working conditions of leather workers vary according to the type of work performed, the size of the factory or business, and the practices of each shop. Workers employed in custom leather goods manufacturing establishments generally work a regular 40-hour week. Those in repair shops work nights and weekends and often work irregular hours. For those who own repair shops, long hours are common.

Shoe and leather workers and repairers need to pay close attention when working with machines to avoid punctures, lacerations, and abrasions. Although there are few health hazards if precautions are followed, work areas can be noisy and odors from leather dyes and stains are often present.

Employment

Shoe and leather workers and repairers held about 23,000 jobs in 1998. Wage and salary workers held about 17,000 jobs. About half of these wage and salary workers were employed in the manufacture of footwear products; one-fifth were employed in the production of leather goods such as luggage, handbags, and apparel; and another fifth worked in shoe repair and shoeshine shops. Self-employed individuals, who typically own and operate small shoe repair shops or specialty leather manufacturing firms, held about 6,000 jobs.

Shoe and leather workers typically learn their skills on the job.

Training, Other Qualifications, and Advancement

Precision shoe and leather workers and repairers generally learn their craft on the job, either through in-house training programs or working as helpers to experienced workers. Helpers usually begin by performing simple tasks and progressing to more difficult jobs like cutting or stitching leather. Trainees typically become fully skilled in 6 months to 2 years; the length of training varies according to the nature of the work and the aptitude and dedication of the individual.

A limited number of schools and national shoe repair chains offer training in shoe repair and leather work. These programs may last from a few weeks to 1 year and impart basic skills including leather cutting, stitching, and dyeing. Students learn shoe construction, practice shoe repair, and study the fundamentals of running a small business. Graduates are encouraged to gain additional training by working with an experienced leather worker or repairer.

Shoe repairers need to keep their skills up-to-date to work with rapidly changing footwear styles. Some repairers do this by attending trade shows and receiving training from product manufacturers. Others attend specialized training seminars and workshops in custom shoe making, shoe repair, and other leather work sponsored by national and regional associations.

Pedorthists—who produce or modify prescription footwear—may receive certification from the Pedorthic Footwear Association. These workers become certified after completing 120 hours of training and passing an exam.

Manual dexterity and the mechanical aptitude to work with handtools and machines are important in the shoe repair and leatherworking occupations. Shoe and leather workers who produce custom goods should have artistic ability as well. These workers should have self-discipline to work alone under little supervision. In addition, leather workers and repairers who own shops must have knowledge of business practices and management, as well as a pleasant manner when dealing with customers.

Many individuals begin as workers or repairers and advance to salaried supervisory and managerial positions. Some may open their own shop or business.

Job Outlook

Employment of shoe and leather workers is expected to decline through 2008, primarily because of the growing number of imported shoes and other leather goods which have displaced domestic production. In addition, inexpensive imports have made the cost of replacing shoes and leather goods cheaper or more convenient than repairing them, thereby reducing the demand for shoe and leather repairers.

These workers are also adversely affected by other factors, such as the rising cost of leather and higher rents in the high-traffic areas in which more shoe repairers are relocating. Moreover, shoe repair shops that offer "while-you-wait" service are investing in new machinery which is making repairers more productive and helping to reduce the demand for these workers. Some of the more expensive, fine leather products will continue to be repaired, however, and this demand will moderate the employment decline of shoe and leather repairers. In the future, though, most job openings in this occupation will arise from the need to replace experienced workers who transfer to other occupations or leave the work force.

Prospects for workers employed in the manufacture and modification of custom-made molded or orthopedic shoes are better than those for most other leather workers. This reflects rapid growth in the elderly population and an increasing emphasis on preventive foot care. The employment effects of these trends may be limited, however, because the demand for orthopedic footwear is increasingly filled by manufactured shoes that are modified to specification instead of completely custom made.

Earnings

Median hourly earnings of shoe and leather workers and repairers were \$7.99 in 1998. Half earned between \$6.50 and \$9.84. The bottom 10 percent earned less than \$5.79, while the top 10 percent earned over \$11.47. Those employed in the non-rubber footwear industry earned an average of $7.73 an hour in 1997. Owners of shoe repair and custom shoe manufacturing shops typically earn substantially more than beginning salaried workers.

Related Occupations

Other workers who make or repair items using handtools and machinery include dressmakers, custom tailors and sewers, designers and patternmakers, and furriers.

Sources of Additional Information

For information about the custom-made prescription shoe business and training opportunities in this field, contact:

☛ Pedorthic Footwear Association, 7150 Columbia Gateway Dr., Suite G, Columbia, MD 21046. Internet: **www.pedorthics.org**

Textile Machinery Operators

(O*Net 92702, 92705, 92708, 92711, and 92714)

Significant Points

- Employment is expected to decline, primarily due to more productive machinery and open international trade.
- Because the textile industry is highly automated, persons with technical skills and some computer training will have the best opportunities.
- Night and weekend shifts are common, because many textile and fiber mills operate 24 hours a day.
- Earnings are low.

Nature of the Work

Textile machinery operators tend machines that manufacture a wide range of textile products. Most people know that textiles are used to make hosiery, towels, and socks; but many are surprised to learn that textile products are used in such things as roofs, tires, and roads. Textile machinery operators play an important part in producing all these goods, by controlling equipment that cleans, cards, combs, and draws fiber; spins fiber into yarn; and weaves, knits, or tufts yarn into textile products. These workers are responsible for numerous machines that they start, stop, clean, and monitor for proper functioning.

There are many phases in the textile production process, and operators' duties depend on the product and type of machinery used. The process begins with the preparation of synthetic or natural fibers for spinning. Fibers are cleaned and aligned through processes called carding and combing. To prepare the fiber for spinning, very short fibers and foreign matter are removed, and the fibers are drawn into a substance called sliver. During this process, different types of fibers may be combined, to give products a desired texture, durability, or other characteristics. Operators constantly monitor their machines during this stage, checking the movement of the fiber, removing and replacing cans of sliver, repairing breaks in the sliver, and making minor repairs to the machinery. The full cans of sliver are then taken to the spinning area, where they are drawn and twisted onto bobbins to produce yarn. (This is an automated version of the old fashion spinning wheel.)

In contrast to the process described above, some workers oversee machinery that makes fibers from wood pulp or chemicals. To produce this fiber, wood pulp or chemical compounds are melted or dissolved in a liquid, which is then extruded, or forced, through holes in a metal plate, called a spinneret. The sizes and shapes of the holes in the spinneret determine the shape and uses of the fiber. Workers adjust the flow of fiber base through the spinneret, repair breaks in the fiber, and make minor adjustments to the machinery. Because this fiber is created through a chemical process, chemical companies, not textile mills, employ the majority of these workers.

Whether natural or manufactured, finished yarn is then taken to be woven, knitted, tufted, or bonded with heat or chemicals. Each of these processes creates a different type of textile product and requires a different type of machine. Woven fabrics are made on looms that interlace the yarn. Knit products, such as socks or women's hosiery, are produced by intermeshing loops of yarn. Carpeting is made through the tufting process, in which the loops of yarn are pushed through a backing material. Although the processes are now highly automated, these concepts have been used for many centuries to produce textile products.

Once the yarn has been woven, knitted, or tufted, the resulting fabric is ready to be dyed and finished—either at the textile mill or at a plant specializing in textile finishing. Depending on the end use of the yarn, it may be dyed before or after it is woven, knitted, or tufted. Some fabric is treated before it is dyed, to remove other chemical additives that could affect the quality of the finished product. Products are often finished by treating them to prevent excessive shrinkage, provide strength, make them stain-resistant, or give them a silky luster. In the production of hosiery and socks, for example, the stocking or sock is placed on a form and then exposed to steam and heat to give it shape.

Textile machinery operators play a vital role in all of the various processes described above. In spite of this wide range of processes, operators share many responsibilities. Most prepare their machinery prior to a production run and help maintain the equipment, by adjusting the timing on a machine, threading the harnesses that create patterns in textile goods, and repairing machinery. Each operator oversees numerous machines, performing such duties as repairing breaks in the yarn and monitoring its supply. Because highly automated machinery is used in textile mills, computers control many of the processes, making it possible for each operator to monitor a large area or number of machines. The complexity of many machines often requires operators to specialize in a particular type of machine.

Working Conditions

Most textile machine operators work in textile mills or chemical plants. Working conditions in these facilities depend on the age and degree of modernization of the factory. New facilities usually offer ventilation and climate control that reduce potential problems caused by airborne fibers and fumes. In a few old facilities, workers in areas with high levels of airborne materials often use protective glasses and masks that cover their noses and mouths.

Although some new machinery is relatively quiet, a number of workers still wear ear protection. Many machines operate at high speeds, and workers must be careful not to wear clothing or jewelry that could get caught in moving parts. In addition, many extruding and

Textile production is highly automated.

forming machine operators wear protective shoes and clothing, when working with certain chemical compounds.

Most textile machinery operators work a standard 40-hour week. Night and weekend shifts are common, because many textile and fiber mills operate 24 hours a day. Employers often use a rotating schedule of shifts, however, so operators do not consistently work nights or weekends.

Employment

Textile machinery operators held about 277,000 jobs in 1998. Most of these workers were employed in weaving, finishing, yarn, and thread mills; but knitting mills and manufactured fiber producers also employed a significant share. Most extruding and forming machine operators were employed in chemical plants.

North Carolina, Georgia, and South Carolina were the leading States in the employment of textile workers. Most of the remaining workers were employed in other southern States, California, and the Northeast.

Training, Other Qualifications, and Advancement

Although not required for all machine-operating positions, a high school diploma or its equivalent is becoming common for entry-level positions in many mills. Some mills prefer applicants to possess a high school diploma and additional technical training. This training may be obtained, in part, at a formal training institution, such as a technical school. Experienced workers or representatives of machinery manufacturers may offer extensive on-the-job training.

As the textile industry becomes more highly automated, some operators will need to understand complex machinery and be able to diagnose problems. Because textile machinery is increasingly controlled electronically, jobseekers will benefit from a basic knowledge of computers and electronics.

Physical stamina and manual dexterity are important attributes for these jobs. In addition, self-direction and interpersonal skills are becoming important for textile machinery operators, as organizational changes that promote teamwork and encourage few levels of management are leading operators to assume increasing responsibility and to take initiative.

Textile machinery operators can advance in several ways. Some workers become instructors and train new employees. Others advance by taking positions requiring additional skills and increased responsibility. A number of experienced operators are promoted to first-line supervisory positions.

Job Outlook

Employment of textile machinery operators is expected to decline over the 1998-2008 period. The most important factors influencing the employment outlook will be increased worker productivity through the introduction of laborsaving machinery and an open trading environment. In spite of the projected decline, many openings will be created annually, as workers change occupations or leave the labor force. Because the textile industry is highly automated, persons with technical skills and some computer training will have the best opportunities.

Employment is expected to decline, as textile firms respond to growing competition in coming years by investing in new equipment, reorganizing work practices, and consolidating. New machinery, such as faster air jet looms and computer-integrated manufacturing technology, will increase productivity and allow each operator to monitor a large number of machines. Many factories are also reorganizing production floors to further increase productivity and to give workers additional responsibility. Also, textile firms are merging to benefit from economies of scale and to pool resources to invest in new equipment. Although each of the above practices should make the textile industry increasingly competitive, these practices will adversely affect the employment outlook for many machine operators.

Another major uncertainty for textile workers is the future of trade. Recent trade initiatives, like the North American Free Trade Agreement and the Agreement on Textiles and Clothing of the World Trade Organization, will help to open export markets for textiles produced in the United States. At the same time, they will dismantle much of the protection that has been provided to the industry for decades, leading to more textile imports and relocation of textile mills to other countries. While the textile industry will be able to compete in many product lines, the labor-intensive U.S. apparel industry will be more adversely affected by these trade initiatives. This, in turn, will negatively affect the demand for textile machinery operators, because the apparel industry is the largest consumer of American-made textiles.

In contrast to other textile machine operating occupations, extruding machine operators, who produce synthetic fibers are expected to experience growing employment in coming years. Because this occupation is small, however, growth is projected to create only a small number of new openings.

Earnings

Median hourly earnings of textile draw-out and winding machine operators, who account for about two-thirds of textile machinery operators, were $9.37 in 1998. The middle 50 percent earned between $7.84 and $10.62. The lowest 10 percent had earnings of less than $6.61, whereas the top 10 percent earned over $12.20.

Median hourly earnings for other textile machinery operators in 1998 were $13.43 for extruding and forming machine operators, $10.40 for textile machine setters and set-up operators, and $9.31 for textile bleaching and dyeing machine operators. In general, earnings vary significantly, depending on the type of mill, job specialty, shift, and seniority. In addition to typical benefits, some firms provide on-site daycare facilities, educational benefits, and employee discounts in company-owned outlet stores.

Related Occupations

Metalworking and plastics-working machine operators perform similar duties and have many of the same entry and training requirements as extruding and forming machine operators and tenders, textile machine operators and tenders, and textile bleaching and dyeing machine operators. Setters and setup operators in other industries—metal fabrication and plastics manufacturing, for example—perform duties comparable to those of textile machine setters and setup operators.

Sources of Additional Information

Information about job opportunities in textile and synthetic fiber production is available from local employers and local offices of the State employment service.

For general information on careers, technology, and trade regulations in the textile industry, contact:

☛ American Textile Manufacturers Institute, Inc., 1130 Connecticut Ave. NW., Suite 1200, Washington, DC 20036-3954. Internet: **http://www.atmi.org**

☛ Institute of Textile Technology, 2551 Ivy Rd., Charlottesville, NC 22903-4614. Internet: **http://www.itt.edu**

Upholsterers

(O*NET 89508)

Significant Points

- About 1 out of 3 is self-employed—triple the average for all craft workers.
- Most upholsterers gain experience through on-the-job training.
- Opportunities for experienced upholsterers should be good, because few people enter the occupation and few shops offer training.

Nature of the Work

Upholsterers make our lives more comfortable and aesthetically pleasing by adding upholstery to new furniture and renewing existing upholstered furniture. In addition, some upholsterers repair or replace automobile upholstery and convertible and vinyl tops. In either case, these workers need an extensive knowledge of fabrics, materials, and upholstery techniques.

Although the many fabrics and other materials used in an upholstered product have changed considerably over time, the basic process of constructing and assembling a piece of furniture has remained much the same. This process always starts with the frame. For both new and reconditioned pieces of upholstered furniture, the upholsterer examines the frame for wood defects, loose sections, and finish. Upholsterers may make minor repairs, such as regluing or refinishing, but major repairs, such as modifications to etched or intricate items, are typically referred to a general furniture repairer or a highly skilled craftsperson.

When restoring a piece, upholsterers first discard the old, worn coverings by using a hammer or tack puller to remove staples, tacks, or other fasteners. Worn sections of padding are then removed, but upholsterers try to reuse as much of the padding as possible, to preserve the shape of the item. After removing all materials and exposing the bare frame, the upholsterer examines the frame for bent and broken springs, repairing or replacing old ones, as necessary. The webbing, which is a strong cloth mat that holds the springs, is also checked for wear. If it is too weak to hold the springs properly and support the upholstered sections, new webbing is installed. Upholsterers do this by tightly stretching the webbing (typically made of nylon, jute, or cotton) from one side of the frame to the other, securely tacking it on both ends. Additional webbing is layered onto the first and attached to the frame forming a new mat.

The upholsterer then positions the springs, either sinuous-wire or hand-tied coils, on the mat, so they conform to it and compress evenly. The coils are then sewn or stapled to the mat or frame and tied to each other. Burlap or a pad of compressed fiber is stretched over the springs to hold their shape, then cut, smoothed, and tacked to the frame. The next step is preparing the frame with cardboard to fill in open areas or give curve to the frame. Upholsterers then cover the springs with filler, such as foam or a polyester batt or similar fibrous batting material, to form a smooth, rounded surface.

Upholsterers also measure and cut fabric for arms, backs, and other furniture sections, leaving as little waste as possible. Using a basting stitch, fabric pieces are sewn together, to ensure a tight, smooth fit. The cover is removed, and any necessary adjustments are made. The final upholstered item is sewn together and tacked, stapled, or glued to the frame. Finally, upholsterers attach any ornaments, such as fringes, buttons, or rivets.

When performing these tasks, upholsterers use common hand tools, such as tack hammers, staple guns, tack and staple removers, pliers, and shears. They also employ specialized equipment like webbing stretchers and upholstery needles. In addition, most upholsterers use sewing machines.

Upholsterers involved in custom work must be highly skilled.

The nature of an upholsterer's work often varies with work setting. Those who produce new furniture in factories typically perform a limited range of skilled, often repetitive, tasks. Upholsterers doing reupholstery or custom work, however, perform a broader range of highly skilled upholstery tasks. In addition to other tasks, upholsterers who work in upholstery shops may pick up and deliver furniture or help customers select new coverings. Those who manage shops also order supplies and equipment and keep business records.

Working Conditions

Most upholsterers work in a shop or factory. Working conditions in these facilities typically vary according to size. Although many shops and factories are spacious, have adequate lighting, and are well ventilated and heated, some may be cramped and dusty.

Upholstery work is not dangerous, but upholsterers usually wear protective gloves and clothing when using sharp tools and lifting and handling furniture or springs. Upholsterers stand most of the workday and may do a lot of bending and heavy lifting. They also may work in awkward positions for short periods of time.

Employment

Furniture upholsterers held about 66,000 jobs in 1998. About 1 out of 3 was self-employed—triple the average for all craft workers. Companies that manufacture furniture and shops that reupholster and repair furniture employed most upholsters. Others worked in shops specializing in reupholstering the seats of automobiles and other vehicles.

Training, Other Qualifications, and Advancement

Most upholsterers gain the skills necessary to become an experienced worker through on-the-job training. In a furniture factory, this training usually lasts about 6 weeks, but it may be supplemented by an additional 3 years of training, to become fully qualified in skilled production work. It may take as many as 8 to 10 years of experience and progressively more difficult work, however, for an upholsterer to reach the top of the trade. Generally, these highly skilled upholsterers work on custom-made and re-upholstered pieces at the high end of the market.

When hiring helpers, employers generally prefer people with some knowledge of the trade. Inexperienced persons may receive basic training in upholstery in high school, vocational and technical schools, and some community colleges. These programs include sewing machine operation, measuring, cutting, springing, frame repair, tufting, and channeling, as well as business and interior design courses. Additional training and experience are usually required, before graduates become fully proficient in their trade.

Upholsterers should have manual dexterity, good coordination, and, in some cases, the strength needed to lift heavy furniture. An eye for detail, a flair for color, and a creative use of fabrics also are helpful.

The primary forms of advancement for upholsterers are opening their own shop or moving into management. It is relatively easy to open a shop, because a small investment in hand tools and a sewing machine are all that is needed. The upholstery business is extremely competitive, however, so operating a shop successfully is difficult. In large shops and factories, experienced or highly skilled upholsterers may become supervisors or sample makers.

Job Outlook

Job opportunities for experienced upholsterers should be good. The number of upholsterers with experience is limited, because few young people enter the occupation and few shops offer training.

Little or no change in the employment of upholsterers is expected through 2008. The increasing manufacture of new, relatively inexpensive upholstered furniture is expected to reduce the demand for reupholstery, solidifying employment at the current level. Nevertheless, a steady demand will continue to exist for upholsterers to restore very valuable furniture. Unlike many other production occupations, automation is not expected to reduce employment opportunities substantially in this occupation, because most upholstery work is labor-intensive and is not easily automated.

Employment of upholsterers in automobile repair has been declining for some time, although the rate of decline should slow. The widespread use of more durable fabrics for automobile seat covers, soft-tops, and convertibles is responsible, in part, for the loss of workers in this industry. This decline may be partially offset in coming years by the reemergence of the luxury automobile, especially those with leather upholstery and convertible tops. Despite little or no change in overall employment of upholsterers, job openings should arise from the need to replace experienced workers who transfer to other occupations or leave the labor force.

Earnings

Median annual earnings of upholsterers were $22,050 in 1998; the middle 50 percent earned between $17,800 and $26,920. The lowest 10 percent earned less than $14,160, while the top 10 percent earned over $33,150. Median annual earnings in the household furniture industry were $21,300, and workers performing reupholstery and furniture repair received a median annual salary of $22,500 in 1997. Earnings of self-employed upholsterers depend on the size and location of the shop and on the number of hours worked.

Related Occupations

Other workers who combine manual skills and knowledge of materials such as fabrics and wood are fur cutters, furniture finishers, pattern and model makers, and casket coverers.

Sources of Additional Information

For details about work opportunities for upholsterers in your area, contact local upholstery shops or the local office of the State employment service.

To receive a list of technical schools with accredited programs in upholstery, contact:

☛ Accrediting Commission of Career Schools and Colleges of Technology, 2101 Wilson Blvd., Suite 302, Arlington, VA 22201. Internet: **http://www.accsct.org**

Woodworking Occupations

(O*NET 89302A, 89302C, 89305, 89308, 89311, 89314, 89397A, 89397B, 89398, 92302, 92305, 92308, 92311, and 92314)

Significant Points

- Overall employment is projected to decline; increasing automation and imports will result in a decrease among woodworking machine operators, while demand for customized wood products will spur minimal growth among precision woodworkers.
- Job prospects will be best for highly skilled workers and those with knowledge of computer-controlled machine tool operation.
- Most woodworkers are trained on the job; basic machine operations may be learned in a few months, but becoming a skilled woodworker often requires 2 or more years.

Nature of the Work

In spite of the development of sophisticated composites and alloys, the demand for wood products continues unabated. Helping to meet this demand are production and precision woodworkers. Production woodworkers can be found in primary industries, such as sawmills and plywood mills, as well as in secondary industries that manufacture furniture, kitchen cabinets, musical instruments, and other fabricated wood products. Precision woodworkers, on the other hand, usually work in small shops that make architectural woodwork, furniture, and many other specialty items.

Production workers usually set up, operate, and tend woodworking machines—such as power saws, planers, sanders, lathes, jointers, and routers—to cut and shape components from lumber, plywood, and other wood panel products. Working from blueprints, supervisors' instructions, or shop drawings that woodworkers themselves produce, woodworkers first determine the best method of shaping and assembling parts. Before cutting, they must often measure and mark the materials. They also verify dimensions to adhere to specifications and may trim parts using handtools such as planes, chisels, wood files, or sanders to insure a tight fit. Most production woodworkers operate a specific woodworking machine, but some are responsible for a variety of machines. Lower skilled operators may merely press a switch on a woodworking machine and monitor the automatic operation, whereas more highly skilled operators set up equipment, cut and shape wooden parts, and verify dimensions using a template, caliper, or rule. In sawmills, machine operators cut logs into planks, timbers, or boards. In veneer mills, they cut veneer sheets for making plywood from logs. And in furniture plants, woodworkers make furniture components, such as table legs, drawers, rails, and spindles.

The next step in the manufacturing process is the production of subassemblies using fasteners and adhesives. The pieces are then brought together to form a complete unit. The product is then finish sanded, stained, and if necessary, coated with a sealer, such as lacquer or varnish. Woodworkers may perform this work in teams or be assisted by a helper.

All woodworkers are employed at some stage of the process through which logs of wood are transformed into finished products. Some of these workers produce the structural elements of buildings; others mill hardwood and softwood lumber; still others assemble finished wood products. They operate machines that cut, shape, assemble, and finish raw wood to make the doors, windows, cabinets, trusses, plywood, flooring, paneling, molding, and trim that are components of most homes. Others may fashion home accessories, such as beds, sofas, tables, dressers, and chairs. In addition to these household goods, woodworkers also make sporting goods, including baseball bats, racquets, and oars, as well as musical instruments, toys, caskets, tool handles, and thousands of other wooden items.

Woodworkers have been greatly affected by the introduction of computer-controlled machinery. This technology has raised worker productivity, by allowing one operator to simultaneously tend a greater number of machines. With computerized numerical controls, an operator can program a machine to perform a sequence of operations automatically, resulting in greater precision and reliability. The integration of computers with equipment has improved production speeds and capabilities, simplified setup and maintenance requirements, and increased the demand for workers with computer skills.

While this costly equipment has had a great impact on workers in the largest, most efficient firms, precision or custom woodworkers—who generally work in smaller firms—have continued to employ the same production techniques they have used for many years. These workers—

such as cabinetmakers, model makers, wood machinists, and furniture and wood finishers—work on a customized basis, often building one-of-a-kind items. Precision woodworkers usually perform a complete cycle of tasks, cutting, shaping, surface preparation, and assembling prepared parts of complex wood components into a finished wood product. For this reason, these workers normally need substantial training and an ability to work from detailed instructions and specifications. In addition, they often are required to exercise independent judgment when undertaking an assignment.

Precision woodworkers produce many varieties of woods from basic household furniture to custom office furniture. Making furniture by hand is a demanding and time-consuming endeavor, but one that can award great gratification. Wood is a vastly rich material and comes in many different colors, patterns, and textures, requiring different methods of working. Whether creating simple, classic pieces or sculptured furnishings, precision woodworkers discover the many facets of wood.

Working Conditions

Working conditions vary by industry and specific job duties. In primary industries, such as logging and sawmilling, working conditions are physically demanding, due to the handling of heavy, bulky material. Workers in these industries may also encounter excessive noise and dust and other air pollutants. However, using earplugs and respirators may somewhat control these factors. Also, rigid adherence to safety precautions minimizes risk of injury from contact with rough woodstock, sharp tools, and power equipment. The risk of injury is also lowered by the installation of computer-controlled equipment, which reduces the physical labor and hands-on contact with the machine.

In secondary industries, such as furniture and kitchen cabinet manufacturing, working conditions also depend on the industry and the particular job. Employees who operate machinery must often wear ear and eye protection, follow operating safety instructions, and use safety shields or guards to prevent accidents. Those who work in the finishing area must either be provided with an appropriate dust or vapor mask, a complete protective safety suit, or work in a finishing environment that removes all vapors and particle matter from the atmosphere. Prolonged standing, lifting, and fitting heavy objects are common characteristics of the job.

Employment

Woodworkers held about 372,000 jobs in 1998. Self-employed woodworkers, mostly cabinetmakers and furniture finishers, accounted for 43,000 of these jobs. Employment was distributed as follows:

Woodworkers, precision	229,000
Woodworking machine setters and operators	143,000
Head sawyers	64,000
Woodworking machine operators	79,000

Woodworkers may use sanders to cut and shape components from lumber, plywood, and other wood panel products.

Nearly 82 percent of salaried woodworkers were employed in manufacturing industries. Among these woodworkers, 29 percent were found in establishments fabricating household and office furniture and fixtures and almost 50 percent worked in lumber and wood products, manufacturing a variety of raw, intermediate, and finished woodstock. Wholesale and retail lumber dealers, furniture stores, reupholstery and furniture repair shops, and construction firms also employ woodworkers.

Woodworking jobs are found throughout the country. However, production jobs are concentrated in the South and Northwest, close to the supply of wood, whereas furniture makers are more prevalent in the East. Custom shops can be found everywhere, but are generally concentrated in or near highly populated areas.

Training, Other Qualifications, and Advancement

Most woodworkers are trained on the job, picking up skills informally from experienced workers. Some acquire skills through vocational education or by working as carpenters on construction jobs. Others may attend colleges or universities that offer training in areas including wood technology, furniture manufacturing, wood engineering, and production management. These programs prepare students for positions in production, supervision, engineering, and management.

Beginners usually observe and help experienced machine operators. They may supply material to or remove fabricated products from machines. Trainees also do simple machine operating jobs, while at first closely supervised by experienced workers. As beginners gain experience, they perform more complex jobs with less supervision. Some may learn to read blueprints, set up machines, and plan the sequence of the work. Most woodworkers learn basic machine operations and job tasks in a few months, but becoming a skilled woodworker often requires 2 or more years.

Employers increasingly seek applicants with a high school diploma or the equivalent, because of the growing sophistication of machinery and the constant need for retraining. Persons seeking woodworking jobs can enhance their employment and advancement prospects by completing high school and receiving training in mathematics, science, and computer applications. Other important qualities for entrants in this occupation include mechanical ability, manual dexterity, and the ability to pay attention to detail.

Advancement opportunities are often limited and depend upon availability, seniority, and a worker's skills and initiative. Sometimes experienced woodworkers become inspectors or supervisors responsible for the work of a group of woodworkers. Production workers can often advance into these positions by assuming additional responsibilities and by attending workshops, seminars, or college programs. Those who are highly skilled may set up their own woodworking shops.

Job Outlook

Employment of woodworkers is expected to decline through the year 2008. Whereas employment of lesser-skilled woodworking machine operators is expected to decline, limited growth is expected among higher-skilled precision woodworkers. However, thousands of openings will arise each year because of the need to replace experienced woodworkers who transfer to other occupations or leave the labor force.

Demand for woodworkers will stem from increases in population, personal income, and business expenditures, in addition to the continuing need for repair and renovation of residential and commercial properties. Therefore, opportunities should be particularly good for woodworkers who specialize in such items as moldings, cabinets, stairs, and windows. Prospects will be best for highly skilled woodworkers with knowledge of computer-controlled machine tool operation.

Several factors may limit the growth of woodworking occupations. Technological advances, like robots and computerized numerical control machinery, will prevent employment from rising as fast as the demand for wood products, particularly in the mills and manufacturing plants where many processes can be automated. In addition, some jobs in the United States will be lost, as imports continue to grow and as U.S. firms move some production to other countries. Also, the demand for wood may be reduced somewhat, as materials such as metal, plastic, and fiberglass continue to be used in many products as alternatives to wood. Environmental measures designed to control various pollutants used in, or generated by, woodworking processes may also impact employment, especially in secondary industries, such as household furniture. Because of these trends, employment opportunities in primary wood industries could be more limited than those in secondary industries.

Employment in all woodworking occupations is highly sensitive to economic cycles; and during economic downturns, workers are subject to layoffs or a reduction in hours.

Earnings

Median annual earnings of wood machinists were $19,980 in 1998. The middle 50 percent earned between $16,170 and $23,920. The lowest 10 percent earned less than $13,380 and the highest 10 percent earned more than $28,590. Median annual earnings in the industries employing the largest numbers of wood machinists in 1997 are shown below:

Millwork, plywood, and structural members	$19,500
Household furniture	19,000

Median annual earnings of cabinetmakers and bench carpenters were $22,390 in 1998. The middle 50 percent earned between $17,870 and $28,250. The lowest 10 percent earned less than $14,260 and the highest 10 percent earned more than $35,880. Median earnings in the industries employing the largest numbers of cabinetmakers and bench carpenters in 1997 are shown below:

Residential building construction	$26,400
Partitions and fixtures	23,700
Carpentry and floor work	22,600
Millwork, plywood, and structural members	21,300
Furniture and homefurnishings stores	21,200
Household furniture	18,500

Median annual earnings of woodworking machine operators and tenders, setters and set-up operators were $19,260 in 1998. The middle 50 percent earned between $15,600 and $22,910. The lowest 10 percent earned less than $13,260 and the highest 10 percent earned more than $27,060. Median annual earnings in the industries employing the largest numbers of woodworking machine operators and tenders, setters and set-up operators in 1997 are shown below:

Millwork, plywood, and structural members	$19,500
Sawmills and planing mills	18,500
Household furniture	18,300
Miscellaneous wood products	17,000

Earnings vary by industry, geographic region, skill, educational level, and complexity of machinery operated. In 1998, median annual earnings were $19,490 for head sawyers and sawing machine operators and tenders; $19,880 for furniture finishers; and $22,430 for all other precision woodworkers.

Some woodworkers, such as those in logging or sawmills, who are engaged in processing primary wood and building materials, are members of the International Association of Machinists. Others belong to the United Furniture Workers of America or the United Brotherhood of Carpenters and Joiners of America.

Related Occupations

Many woodworkers follow blueprints and drawings and use machines to shape and form raw wood into a final product. Workers who perform similar functions working with other materials include precision metalworkers, metalworking and plastics-working machine operators, metal fabricators, molders and shapers, and leather workers.

Sources of Additional Information

For information about woodworking occupations, contact local furniture manufacturers, sawmills and planing mills, cabinetmaking or millwork firms, lumber dealers, a local of one of the unions mentioned above, or the nearest office of the State employment service.

For general information about furniture woodworking occupations, contact:

☛ American Furniture Manufacturers Association, Manufacturing Services Division, P.O. Box HP-7, High Point, NC 27261. Internet: **http://www.afmahp.org**

Miscellaneous Production Occupations

Dental Laboratory Technicians

(O*NET 89921)

Significant Points

- Employment should increase slowly, as the public's improving dental health requires fewer dentures but more bridges and crowns.
- Dental laboratory technicians need artistic aptitude for detailed and precise work, a high degree of manual dexterity, and good vision.

Nature of the Work

Dental laboratory technicians fill prescriptions from dentists for crowns, bridges, dentures, and other dental prosthetics. First, dentists send a specification of the item to be fabricated, along with an impression (mold) of the patient's mouth or teeth. Then dental laboratory technicians, also called dental technicians, create a model of the patient's mouth, by pouring plaster into the impression and allowing it to set. Next, they place the model on an apparatus that mimics the bite and movement of the patient's jaw. The model serves as the basis of the prosthetic device. Technicians examine the model, noting the size and shape of the adjacent teeth, as well as gaps within the gumline. Based upon these observations and the dentist's specifications, technicians build and shape a wax tooth or teeth model, using small hand instruments called wax spatulas and wax carvers. They use this wax model to cast the metal framework for the prosthetic device.

Once the wax tooth has been formed, dental technicians pour the cast and form the metal, and using small hand-held tools, prepare the surface to allow the metal and porcelain to bond. They then apply porcelain in layers, to arrive at the precise shape and color of a tooth. Technicians place the tooth in a porcelain furnace to bake the porcelain onto the metal framework, then adjust the shape and color, with subsequent grinding and addition of porcelain to achieve a sealed finish. The final product is a near exact replica of the lost tooth or teeth.

In some laboratories, technicians perform all stages of the work, whereas in other labs, each technician does only a few. Dental laboratory technicians can specialize in one of five areas: Orthodontic appliances, crowns and bridges, complete dentures, partial dentures, or ceramics. Job titles can reflect specialization in these areas. For example, technicians who make porcelain and acrylic restorations are called *dental ceramists*.

Working Conditions

Dental laboratory technicians generally work in clean, well lighted, and well-ventilated areas. Technicians usually have their own workbenches, which can be equipped with Bunsen burners, grinding and

A dental laboratory technician examines a patient's model, noting the size and shape of the adjacent teeth as well as gaps within the gumline.

polishing equipment, and hand instruments, such as wax spatulas and wax carvers.

The work is extremely delicate and time consuming. Salaried technicians usually work 40 hours a week, but self-employed technicians frequently work longer hours.

Employment

Dental laboratory technicians held about 44,000 jobs in 1998. Most jobs were in commercial dental laboratories, which usually are small, privately owned businesses with fewer than five employees. However, some laboratories are large; a few employ over 50 technicians.

Some dental laboratory technicians worked in dentists' offices. Others worked for hospitals providing dental services, including Department of Veterans Affairs' hospitals. Some technicians work in dental laboratories in their homes, in addition to their regular job. Approximately 1 technician in 5 is self-employed, a higher proportion than in most other occupations.

Training, Other Qualifications, and Advancement

Most dental laboratory technicians learn their craft on the job. They begin with simple tasks, such as pouring plaster into an impression, and progress to more complex procedures, such as making porcelain crowns and bridges. Becoming a fully trained technician requires an average of 3 to 4 years, depending upon the individual's aptitude and ambition; but it may take a few years more to become an accomplished technician.

Training in dental laboratory technology is also available through community and junior colleges, vocational-technical institutes, and the Armed Forces. Formal training programs vary greatly both in length and the level of skill they impart.

In 1998, 34 programs in dental laboratory technology were approved (accredited) by the Commission on Dental Accreditation in conjunction with the American Dental Association (ADA). These programs provide classroom instruction in dental materials science, oral anatomy, fabrication procedures, ethics, and related subjects. In addition, each student is given supervised practical experience in a school or an associated dental laboratory. Accredited programs normally take 2 years to complete and lead to an associate degree.

Graduates of 2-year training programs need additional hands-on experience to become fully qualified. Each dental laboratory owner operates in a different way, and classroom instruction does not necessarily expose students to techniques and procedures favored by individual laboratory owners. Students who have taken enough courses to learn the basics of the craft are usually considered good candidates for training, regardless of whether they have completed a formal program. Many employers will train someone without any classroom experience.

The National Board offers certification, which is voluntary, in five specialty areas: crowns and bridges, ceramics, partial dentures, complete dentures, and orthodontic appliances.

In large dental laboratories, technicians may become supervisors or managers. Experienced technicians may teach or take jobs with dental suppliers in such areas as product development, marketing, and sales. Still, for most technicians, opening one's own laboratory is the way toward advancement and higher earnings.

A high degree of manual dexterity, good vision, and the ability to recognize very fine color shadings and variations in shape are necessary. An artistic aptitude for detailed and precise work is also important. High school students interested in becoming dental laboratory technicians should take courses in art, metal and wood shop, drafting, and sciences. Courses in management and business may help those wishing to operate their own laboratories.

Job Outlook

Job opportunities for dental laboratory technicians should be favorable, despite very slow growth in the occupation. Employers have difficulty filling trainee positions, probably because of relatively low entry-level salaries and lack of familiarity with the occupation.

Although job opportunities are favorable, little or no change in the employment of dental laboratory technicians is expected through the year 2008, due to changes in dental care. The overall dental health of the population has improved because of fluoridation of drinking water, which has reduced the incidence of dental cavities, and greater emphasis on preventive dental care since the early-1960s. As a result, full dentures will be less common, as most people will need only a bridge or crown. However, during the last few years, demand has arisen from an aging public that is growing increasingly interested in cosmetic prosthesis. For example, many dental laboratories are filling orders for composite fillings that are white and look like a natural tooth to replace older, less attractive fillings.

Earnings

Median annual earnings of salaried precision dental laboratory technicians were $25,660 in 1998. The middle 50 percent earned between $19,410 and $34,600 a year. The lowest 10 percent earned less than $14,720 and the highest 10 percent earned more than $45,980 a year. Median annual earnings of dental laboratory technicians in 1997 were $24,100 in medical and dental laboratories and $25,500 in offices and clinics of dentists.

In general, earnings of self-employed technicians exceed those of salaried workers. Technicians in large laboratories tend to specialize in a few procedures, and, therefore, tend to be paid a lower wage than those employed in small laboratories that perform a variety of tasks.

Related Occupations

Dental laboratory technicians fabricate artificial teeth, crowns and bridges, and orthodontic appliances, following specifications and instructions provided by dentists. Other workers who make medical devices include arch-support technicians, orthotics technicians (braces and surgical supports), prosthetics technicians (artificial limbs and appliances), opticians, and ophthalmic laboratory technicians.

Sources of Additional Information

For a list of accredited programs in dental laboratory technology, contact:

☛ Commission on Dental Accreditation, American Dental Association, 211 E. Chicago Ave., Chicago, IL 60611. Internet: **http://www.ada.org**

General information on grants and scholarships is available from dental technology schools.

For information on requirements for certification, contact:

☛ National Board for Certification in Dental Technology, 8201 Greensboro Dr., Suite 300, McLean VA 22101.

For information on career opportunities in commercial laboratories, contact:

☛ National Association of Dental Laboratories, 8201 Greensboro Dr., Suite 300, McLean VA 22101. Internet: **http://www.nadl.org**

Electronic Semiconductor Processors

(O*NET 92902A, 92902B, 92902C, 92902D, 92902E, and 92902G)

Significant Points

- Electronic semiconductor processors is the only manufacturing occupation expected to grow much faster than the average for all occupations.
- A 1-year certificate in semiconductor technology is good preparation for semiconductor processor operator positions; for more highly skilled technician positions, an associate degree in electronics technology or a related field is necessary.

Nature of the Work

Semiconductors—also known as computer chips, microchips, or integrated chips—are the miniature but powerful brains of high technology equipment. They are comprised of a myriad of tiny aluminum wires and electric switches, which manipulate the flow of electrical current. Electronic semiconductor processors are responsible for many of the steps necessary to manufacture each semiconductor that goes into a personal computer, missile guidance system, and a host of other electronic equipment.

Semiconductor processors manufacture semiconductors in disks about the size of dinner plates. These disks, called wafers, are thin slices of silicon on which the circuitry of the microchips is layered. Each wafer is eventually cut into dozens of individual chips.

Semiconductor processors make wafers using photolithography, a printing process for creating plates from photographic images. Operating automated equipment, workers imprint precise microscopic patterns of the circuitry on the wafers, etch out the patterns with acids, and replace the patterns with silicon and other materials. Then the wafers receive a chemical bath to make them smooth, and the imprint process begins again on a new layer with the next pattern. Wafers usually have from 8 to 20 such layers of microscopic, three-dimensional circuitry.

Semiconductors are produced in semiconductor fabricating plants, or "fabs". Within fabs, the manufacture and cutting of wafers to create semiconductors takes place in "clean rooms." Clean rooms are production areas that must be kept free of any airborne matter, because the least bit of dust can damage a semiconductor. All semiconductor processors working in clean rooms—both operators and technicians—must wear special lightweight outer garments known as "bunny suits." Bunny suits fit over clothing to prevent lint and other particles from contaminating semiconductor processing worksites.

Operators, who make up the majority of the workers in clean rooms, start and monitor the sophisticated equipment that performs the various tasks during the many steps of the semiconductor production sequence. They spend a great deal of time at computer terminals, monitoring the equipment. They transfer wafer carriers from one development station to the next. Once begun, production of semiconductor wafers is continuous: Operators work to the pace of the machinery that has largely automated the production process. Operators are responsible for keeping the automated machinery at proper operating parameters.

Technicians account for a smaller percentage of the workers in clean rooms, but they trouble-shoot production problems and make equipment adjustments and repairs. They also take the lead in assuring quality control and in maintaining equipment. In order to prevent the need for repairs, technicians perform diagnostic analyses and run computations. For example, technicians may determine if a flaw in a chip is due to contamination and peculiar to that wafer, or if the flaw is inherent in the manufacturing process.

Working Conditions

The work pace in clean rooms is deliberately slow. Limited movement keeps the air in clean rooms as free as possible of dust and other particles, which can destroy semiconductors during production. Because the machinery sets operators' rate of work in the largely automated production process, workers keep an easy-going pace. Although workers spend some time alone monitoring equipment, operators and technicians spend much of their time working in teams.

Technicians are on their feet most of the day, walking through the clean room to oversee production activities. Operators spend a great deal of time sitting or standing at work stations, monitoring computer readouts and gauges. Sometimes, they must retrieve wafers from one station and take them to another. To minimize the risk of dropping expensive wafers and semiconductors, transportation of wafer carriers between work stations is usually automated.

The temperature in the clean rooms must be kept within narrow ranges, usually a comfortable 72 degrees Fahrenheit. The temperature inside bunny suits stays fairly constant as well. However, workers in bunny suits face some restrictions because entry and exit from each clean room are controlled to minimize contamination.

An electronic semiconductor processor inspects the quality of the wafers containing microchips.

The work environment of semiconductor fabricating plants is one of the safest in any industry. Measures taken to avoid contamination of the wafers lead to more than just antiseptically clean rooms: they result in a work environment nearly free of conditions that cause occupational illnesses and accidents.

Semiconductor fabricating plants operate around the clock. For this reason, night and weekend work is common. In some plants, workers maintain standard 8-hour shifts, 5 days a week. In other plants, employees work 12-hour shifts to minimize the disruption of clean room operations brought about by shift changes. Managers in some plants allow workers to alternate schedules for equitable distribution of the "graveyard" shift.

Employment

Electronic semiconductor processors held 63,000 jobs in 1998. Nearly all of them were employed in facilities that manufacture electronic components and accessories, though a small percentage worked in plants that primarily manufacture computers and office equipment.

Training, Other Qualifications, and Advancement

People interested in becoming semiconductor processors, either operators or technicians, need a solid background in mathematics and physical sciences. In addition to their application to the field, math and science knowledge are essentials for pursuing higher education in semiconductor technology—and knowledge of both subjects is one of the best ways to advance in the semiconductor fabricating field.

Semiconductor processor workers must also be able to think analytically and critically to anticipate problems and avoid costly mistakes. Communication skills are also vital, as workers must be able to convey their thoughts and ideas both orally and in writing.

A high school diploma or equivalent is the minimum requirement for entry-level operator jobs in semiconductor fabrication plants. Technicians must have at least an associate degree in electronics technology or a related field. Although completion of a 1-year certificate program in semiconductor technology offered by some community colleges is an asset, employers prefer to hire persons who have completed associate degree programs.

Degree or certificate candidates who get hands-on training while attending school look even more attractive to prospective employers. Semiconductor technology programs in a growing number of community colleges include an internship at a semiconductor fabricating plant; many students in these programs already hold full- or part-time jobs in the industry and work toward semiconductor technology in their spare time to upgrade or update their skills. In addition, to ensure that operators and technicians keep their skills current, most employers provide 40 hours of formal training annually. Some employers also provide financial assistance to employees who want to earn associate and bachelor's degrees.

Those who live near a semiconductor processing plant may have another option for getting started in the field: summer and part-time employment. Students often are hired to work during the summer, and some students are allowed to continue working part time during the school year. Students in summer and part-time semiconductor processor jobs learn what education they need to prosper in the field. They also gain valuable experience that may lead to full-time employment after graduation.

Some semiconductor processing technicians transfer to sales engineer jobs with suppliers of the machines that manufacture the semiconductors or become field support personnel.

Job Outlook

Between 1998 and 2008, employment of electronic semiconductor processors is projected to increase much faster than the average for all occupations. Besides the creation of new jobs, additional openings will result from the need to replace workers who leave the occupation. Growing demand for semiconductors and semiconductor processors will stem from the many existing and future applications for semiconductors in computers, vehicles, telecommunications, appliances, and other equipment.

The electronic components and accessories industry is projected to be one of the most rapidly growing manufacturing industries. Moreover, industry development of semiconductors made from better materials means that semiconductors will become even smaller, more powerful, and more durable. For example, the industry is researching a new generation of microchips, made with copper rather than aluminum wires, which will better conduct electricity. Also, technology to develop chips based on plastic, rather than on silicon, will make laptop computers durable enough to take to worksites where these computers could not easily have been used previously, such as construction sites. These technological developments will lead to new applications in commercial markets, resulting in employment growth in the industry.

Job prospects should be best for people with postsecondary education in electronics or semiconductor technology. Prospects should also be favorable for high school graduates with a strong science background, particularly for those who are willing to work toward a postsecondary degree while employed.

Earnings

Median hourly earnings of electronic semiconductor processors were \$11.93 in 1998. The middle 50 percent earned between \$9.76 and \$14.25 an hour. The lowest 10 percent earned less than \$8.43 and the top 10 percent earned more than \$17.70 an hour.

Technicians with an associate degree in electronics or semiconductor technology generally started at higher salaries than those with less education.

Related Occupations

Electronic semiconductor processors do production work that resembles the work of precision assemblers of electrical and electronic equipment. Also, many electronic semiconductor processors have academic training in semiconductor technology, which emphasizes scientific and engineering principles. Other occupations that require some college or postsecondary vocational training emphasizing such principles are electrical and electronic technicians and science technicians.

Sources of Additional Information

For more information on semiconductor processor careers, contact:

☛ Semiconductor Industry Association, 4300 Stevens Creek Blvd., No. 271, San Jose, CA 95129.

☛ SEMATECH, 2706 Montopolis Dr., Austin, TX 78741. Internet: **http://www.4chipjobs.com**

☛ Maricopa Advanced Technology Education Center (MATEC), 2323 West 14th St., Suite 402, Tempe, AZ 85281. Internet: **http://matec.org**

Ophthalmic Laboratory Technicians

(O*NET 89917A and 89917D)

Significant Points

- Although some lenses are still produced by hand, technicians increasingly use automated equipment to make lenses.
- Nearly all ophthalmic laboratory technicians learn their skills on the job.
- The number of job openings will be low because the occupation is small and slow growth in employment is expected.

Nature of the Work

Ophthalmic laboratory technicians—also known as manufacturing opticians, optical mechanics, or optical goods workers—make prescription eyeglass lenses. Prescription lenses are curved in such a way that light is correctly focused onto the retina of the patient's eye, improving vision. Some ophthalmic laboratory technicians manufacture lenses for other optical instruments, such as telescopes and binoculars. Ophthalmic laboratory technicians cut, grind, edge, and finish lenses according to specifications provided by dispensing opticians, optometrists, or ophthalmologists, and may insert lenses into frames to produce finished glasses. Although some lenses are still produced by hand, technicians increasingly use automated equipment to make lenses.

Ophthalmic laboratory technicians should not be confused with workers in other vision care occupations. Ophthalmologists and optometrists are "eye doctors" who examine eyes, diagnose and treat vision problems, and prescribe corrective lenses. Ophthalmologists are physicians who perform eye surgery. Dispensing opticians, who may also do work described here, help patients select frames and lenses, and adjust finished eyeglasses. (See the statement on physicians, which includes ophthalmologists, and the statements on optometrists and dispensing opticians elsewhere in the *Handbook.*)

Ophthalmic laboratory technicians read prescription specifications, then select standard glass or plastic lens blanks and mark them to indicate where the curves specified on the prescription should be ground. They place the lens into the lens grinder, set the dials for the prescribed curvature, and start the machine. After a minute or so, the lens is ready to be "finished" by a machine that rotates it against a fine abrasive to grind it and smooth out rough edges. The lens is then placed in a polishing machine with an even finer abrasive, to polish it to a smooth, bright finish.

Next, the technician examines the lens through a lensometer, an instrument similar in shape to a microscope, to make sure the degree and placement of the curve is correct. The technician then cuts the lenses and bevels the edges to fit the frame, dips each lens into dye if the prescription calls for tinted or coated lenses, polishes the edges, and assembles the lenses and frame parts into a finished pair of glasses.

Ophthalmic laboratory technicians make prescription eyeglass lenses.

In small laboratories, technicians usually handle every phase of the operation. In large ones, technicians may be responsible for operating computerized equipment where virtually every phase of operation is automated. Technicians also inspect the final product for quality and accuracy.

Working Conditions

Ophthalmic laboratory technicians work in relatively clean and well-lighted laboratories and have limited contact with the public. Surroundings are relatively quiet despite the humming of machines. At times, technicians wear goggles to protect their eyes, and may spend a great deal of time standing.

Most ophthalmic laboratory technicians work a 5-day, 40-hour week, which may include weekends, evenings, or occasionally, some overtime. Some work part time.

Ophthalmic laboratory technicians need to take precautions against the hazards associated with cutting glass, handling chemicals, and working near machinery.

Employment

Ophthalmic laboratory technicians held about 23,000 jobs in 1998. Thirty-three percent were in retail optical stores that manufacture and sell prescription glasses. A little over 31 percent were in optical laboratories. These laboratories manufacture eyewear for sale by retail stores that fabricate prescription glasses, and by ophthalmologists and optometrists. Most of the rest were in wholesalers or in optical laboratories that manufacture lenses for other optical instruments, such as telescopes and binoculars.

Training, Other Qualifications, and Advancement

Nearly all ophthalmic laboratory technicians learn their skills on the job. Employers filling trainee jobs prefer applicants who are high school graduates. Courses in science, mathematics, and computers are valuable; manual dexterity and the ability to do precision work are essential.

Technician trainees producing lenses by hand start on simple tasks such as marking or blocking lenses for grinding, then progress to lens grinding, lens cutting, edging, beveling, and eyeglass assembly. Depending on individual aptitude, it may take up to 6 months to become proficient in all phases of the work.

Technicians using automated systems will find computer skills valuable. Training is completed on the job and varies in duration depending on the type of machinery and individual aptitude.

Some ophthalmic laboratory technicians learn their trade in the Armed Forces. Others attend the few programs in optical technology offered by vocational-technical institutes or trade schools. These programs have classes in optical theory, surfacing and lens finishing, and the reading and applying of prescriptions. Programs vary in length from 6 months to 1 year, and award certificates or diplomas.

Ophthalmic laboratory technicians can become supervisors and managers. Some technicians become dispensing opticians, although further education or training is generally required.

Job Outlook

Overall employment of ophthalmic laboratory technicians is expected to grow more slowly than average through the year 2008. Employment is expected to increase slowly in manufacturing as firms invest in automated machinery. In retail trade, employment is expected to decline.

Demographic trends make it likely that many more Americans will need vision care in the years ahead. Not only will the population grow, but also the proportion of middle-aged and older adults is projected to increase rapidly. Middle age is a time when many people use corrective lenses for the first time, and elderly persons require more vision care, on the whole, than others.

Fashion, too, influences demand. Frames come in a variety of styles and colors—encouraging people to buy more than one pair. Demand is also expected to grow in response to the availability of new technologies that improve the quality and look of corrective lenses, such as anti-reflective coatings and bifocal lenses without the line visible in traditional bifocals.

Most job openings will arise from the need to replace technicians who transfer to other occupations or leave the labor force. Only a small number of total job openings will occur each year because the occupation is small.

Earnings

Median hourly earnings of ophthalmic laboratory technicians were $9.39 in 1998. The middle 50 percent earned between $7.56 and $11.58 an hour. The lowest 10 percent earned less than $6.48 and the highest 10 percent earned more than $15.74 an hour. Median hourly earnings of ophthalmic laboratory technicians in 1997 were $8.60 in ophthalmic goods and $8.30 in retail stores, not elsewhere classified.

Related Occupations

Workers in other precision production occupations include biomedical equipment technicians, dental laboratory technicians, orthodontic technicians, orthotics technicians, prosthetics technicians, and instrument repairers.

Sources of Additional Information

For general information about a career as an ophthalmic laboratory technician and a list of accredited programs in ophthalmic laboratory technology, contact:

☛ Commission on Opticianry Accreditation, 10111 Martin Luther King, Jr. Hwy., Suite 100, Bowie, MD 20720-4299.
Internet: **http://www.coaccreditation.com**

Painting and Coating Machine Operators

(O*NET 92947, 92951, and 92953)

Significant Points

- Most workers acquire their skills on the job; for most operators, training lasts from a few days to several months, but becoming skilled in all aspects of automotive painting usually requires 1 to 2 years.
- Slower-than-average growth is projected through 2008, but job prospects should be favorable.

Nature of the Work

Millions of items ranging from cars to candy are covered by paint, plastic, varnish, chocolate, or some other type of coating solution. Often the protection provided by the paint or coating is essential to the product, as with the coating of insulating material covering wires and other electrical and electronic components. Many paints and coatings have dual purposes, such as the paint finish on an automobile, which heightens the visual appearance of the vehicle while providing protection from corrosion.

Painting and coating machine operators control the machinery that applies these paints and coatings to a wide range of manufactured products. Perhaps the most straightforward technique is simply dipping an item in a large vat of paint or other coating. This is the technique used by *dippers*, who immerse racks or baskets of articles in vats of paint, liquid plastic, or other solutions using a power hoist. Similarly, *tumbling barrel painters* deposit articles made of porous materials in a barrel of paint, varnish, or other coating, which is then rotated to insure thorough coverage.

Another familiar technique is spraying products with a solution of paint or other coating. *Spray-machine operators* use spray guns to coat metal, wood, ceramic, fabric, paper, and food products with paint and other coating solutions. Following a formula, operators fill the equipment's tanks with a mixture of paints or chemicals, adding prescribed amounts of solution. They adjust nozzles on the spray guns to obtain the proper dispersion of the spray and hold or position the guns to direct the spray onto the article. Operators also check the flow and viscosity of the paint or solution and visually inspect the quality of the coating. When products are drying, these workers must often regulate the temperature and air circulation in drying ovens.

Painting and coating machine operators use various types of spray machines to coat a range of products. Often, their job title reflects the specialized nature of the machine or the coating being applied. For example, *enrobing machine operators* coat, or "enrobe," confectionery, bakery, and other food products with melted chocolate, cheese, oils, sugar, or other substances. *Paper coating machine operators* spray "size" on rolls of paper to give it its gloss or finish. And *silvering applicators* spray silver, tin, and copper solutions on glass in the manufacture of mirrors.

In response to concerns about air pollution and worker safety, manufacturers increasingly use new types of paints and coatings on their products instead of high-solvent paints. Water-based paints and powder coatings are two of the most common. These compounds do not emit as many volatile organic compounds into the air and can be applied to a variety of products. Powder coatings are sprayed much like liquid paints and then heated to melt and cure the coating.

The adoption of new types of paints is often accompanied by a conversion to more automated painting equipment that the operator sets and monitors. When using these machines, operators position the automatic spray guns, set the nozzles, and synchronize the action of the guns with the speed of the conveyor carrying articles through the machine and drying ovens. The operator may also add solvents or water to the paint vessel that prepares the paint for application. During operation, these workers tend painting machines, observe gauges on the control panel, and randomly check articles for evidence of any variation from specifications. The operator then uses a spray gun to "touch up" spots where necessary.

Although the majority of painting and coating machine operators are employed in manufacturing, the best known group of these workers refinish old and damaged cars, trucks, and buses in automotive body repair and paint shops. *Automotive painters* are among the most highly skilled manual spray operators because they perform intricate, detailed work and mix paints to match the original color, a task that is especially difficult if the color has faded.

To prepare a vehicle for painting, automotive painters or their helpers use power sanders and sandpaper to remove the original paint or

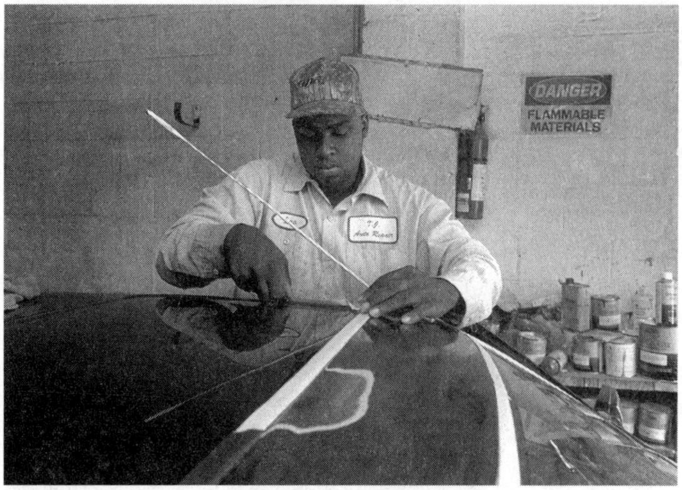

A painting and coating machine operator carefully prepares a car before painting.

rust, and then fill small dents and scratches with body filler. They also remove or mask parts they do not want to paint, such as chrome trim, headlights, windows, and mirrors. Automotive painters use a spray gun to apply several coats of paint. They apply lacquer, enamel, or water-based primers to vehicles with metal bodies, and flexible primers to newer vehicles with plastic body parts. Controlling the spray gun by hand, they apply successive coats until the finish of the repaired sections of the vehicle matches that of the original undamaged portions. To speed drying between coats, they may place the freshly painted vehicle under heat lamps or in a special infrared oven. After each coat of primer dries, they sand the surface to remove any irregularities and to improve the adhesion of the next coat. Final sanding of the primers may be done by hand with a fine grade of sandpaper. A sealer is then applied and allowed to dry, followed by the final topcoat. When lacquer is used, painters or their helpers usually polish the finished surface after the final coat has dried.

Working Conditions

Painting and coating machine operators work indoors and may be exposed to dangerous fumes from paint and coating solutions. Although painting is usually done in special ventilated booths, many operators wear masks or respirators that cover their noses and mouths. In addition, the Clean Air Act of 1990 has led to a decrease in workers' exposure to hazardous chemicals by regulating emissions of volatile organic compounds from paints and other chemicals. This legislation has also led to increasing use of more sophisticated paint booths and fresh air systems which provide a safer work environment.

Operators have to stand for long periods of time and, when using a spray gun, they may have to bend, stoop, or crouch in uncomfortable positions to reach different parts of the article. Most operators work a normal 40-hour week, but self-employed automotive painters sometimes work more than 50 hours a week, depending on the number of vehicles customers want repainted.

Employment

Painting and coating machine operators held about 171,000 jobs in 1998. Lesser skilled operators accounted for about 3 out of 4 jobs, while more skilled transportation equipment painters accounted for about 1 out of 4. More than 85 percent of jobs for salaried workers were found in manufacturing establishments, where they applied coatings to items such as fabricated metal products, motor vehicles and related equipment, industrial machines, household and office furniture, and plastics, wood, and paper products. Other workers included automotive painters employed by independent automotive repair shops and body repair and paint shops operated by retail motor vehicle dealers. About 6 percent of painting and coating machine operators were self-employed; most of these were automotive painters.

Training, Other Qualifications, and Advancement

Most painting and coating machine operators acquire their skills on the job, usually by watching and helping experienced operators. For most operators, training lasts from a few days to several months. Coating and painting machine operators who modify the operation of computer-controlled equipment during operation may require additional training in computer operations and minor programming.

Similar to painting and coating machine operators, most automotive painters start as helpers and gain their skills informally on the job. Becoming skilled in all aspects of automotive painting usually requires 1 to 2 years of on-the-job training. Beginning helpers usually remove trim, clean and sand surfaces to be painted, mask surfaces that they do not want painted, and polish finished work. As helpers gain experience, they progress to more complicated tasks, such as mixing paint to achieve a good match and using spray guns to apply primer coats or final coats to small areas.

Painters should have keen eyesight and a good sense of color. Completion of high school is generally not required but is advantageous. Additional instruction is offered at many community colleges and vocational or technical schools. Such programs enhance one's employment prospects and can speed promotion to the next level.

Some employers sponsor training programs to help their workers become more productive. This training is available from manufacturers of chemicals, paints, or equipment or from other private sources. It may include safety and quality tips and knowledge of products, equipment, and general business practices. Some automotive painters are sent to technical schools to learn the intricacies of mixing and applying different types of paint.

Voluntary certification by the National Institute for Automotive Service Excellence (ASE) is recognized as the standard of achievement for automotive painters. For certification, painters must pass a written examination and have at least 2 years of experience in the field. High school, trade or vocational school, or community or junior college training in automotive painting and refinishing may substitute for up to 1 year of experience. To retain certification, painters must retake the examination at least every 5 years.

Experienced painting and coating machine operators with leadership ability may become team leaders or supervisors. Those who acquire practical experience or college or other formal training may become sales or technical representatives for chemical or paint companies. Eventually, some automotive painters open their own shops.

Job Outlook

Job prospects should be favorable for skilled automotive painters and new entrants with vocational school training in this specialty, as numerous employers have reported difficulties in locating qualified applicants. Overall employment of painting and coating machine operators is expected to grow more slowly than the average for all occupations through the year 2008. Employment growth for highly skilled transportation painters and automotive refinishers is projected to be slightly faster than for lesser skilled painting and coating machine operators. In addition to job growth, several thousand jobs will become available each year as employers replace experienced operators who transfer to other occupations or leave the labor force.

An increasing population demanding more manufactured goods will spur employment growth among painting and coating machine operators. Employment growth will be limited, however, by improvements in the automation of paint and coating applications that will raise worker productivity. For example, operators will be able to coat goods more rapidly as they use increasingly sophisticated industrial robots that move and aim spray guns more like humans; as the cost of robots continues to fall, they will be more widely used. The Clean Air Act of 1990, which sets limits on the emissions of ozone-forming volatile organic compounds, also is expected to impede the employment growth of operators in manufacturing because firms tend to introduce more efficient automation as they switch to water-based and powder coatings to comply with the law.

Because the detailed work of refinishing automobiles in collision repair shops and motor vehicle dealerships does not lend itself to automation, painters employed in these establishments are projected to experience more rapid growth. As the demand for refinishing continues to grow, slower productivity growth among these workers will lead to employment increases more in line with the growing demand for their services.

The number of job openings for painting and coating machine operators may fluctuate from year to year due to cyclical changes in economic conditions. When demand for manufactured goods lessens, production may be suspended or reduced, and workers may be laid off or face a shortened workweek. Automotive painters, on the other hand, can expect relatively steady work because automobiles damaged in accidents require repair and refinishing regardless of the state of the economy.

Earnings

Median hourly earnings of coating, painting, and spraying machine operators, tenders, setters, and set-up operators were $10.49 in 1998. The middle 50 percent earned between $8.49 and $12.90 an hour. The lowest 10 percent earned less than $6.93 and the highest 10 percent earned more than $15.62 an hour.

Median hourly earnings of transportation equipment painters were $14.00 in 1998. The middle 50 percent earned between $10.86 and $18.95 an hour. The lowest 10 percent earned less than $8.50 and the highest 10 percent earned more than $23.37 an hour. Median hourly earnings of transportation equipment painters in 1997 were $13.30 in automotive repair shops and $15.50 in motor vehicle and equipment manufacturing.

Many automotive painters employed by motor vehicle dealers and independent automotive repair shops receive a commission based on the labor cost charged to the customer. Under this method, earnings depend largely on the amount of work a painter does and how fast it is completed. Employers frequently guarantee commissioned painters a minimum weekly salary. Helpers and trainees usually receive an hourly rate until they become sufficiently skilled to work on commission. Trucking companies, bus lines, and other organizations that repair and refinish their own vehicles usually pay by the hour.

Many painting and coating machine operators belong to unions. Most union operators work for manufacturers and the larger motor vehicle dealers.

Related Occupations

Other occupations in which workers apply paints and coatings include construction and maintenance painters, electrolytic metal platers, and hand painting, coating, and decorating occupations.

Sources of Additional Information

For more details about work opportunities, contact local manufacturers, automotive-body repair shops, motor vehicle dealers, and vocational schools; locals of unions representing these workers; or the local office of the State employment service. The State employment service also may be a source of information about training programs.

Information on how to become a certified automotive painter is available from:

☛ National Institute for Automotive Service Excellence (ASE), 13505 Dulles Technology Dr., Suite 2, Herndon, VA 20171-3421. Internet: **http://www.asecert.org**

Photographic Process Workers

(O*NET 89914A, 89914B, 89914C, 89914D, and 92908)

Significant Points

- Employment opportunities for photographic process workers are expected to decline as digital photography becomes commonplace.
- Most photographic process workers receive on-the-job training from their companies, manufacturers' representatives, and experienced workers.

Nature of the Work

Both amateur and professional photographers rely heavily on photographic process workers to develop film, make prints or slides, and do related tasks, such as enlarging or retouching photographs. *Photographic processing machine operators and tenders* operate various machines, such as mounting presses and motion picture film printing, photographic printing, and film developing machines. *Precision photographic process workers* perform more delicate tasks, such as retouching photographic negatives and prints to emphasize or correct specific features.

Photographic processing machine operators and tenders often have specialized jobs. *Film process technicians* operate machines that develop exposed photographic film or sensitized paper in a series of chemical and water baths to produce negative or positive images. First, technicians mix developing and fixing solutions, following a formula. They then load the film in the machine, which immerses the exposed film in a developer solution. This brings out the latent image. The next steps include immersing the negative in a stop-bath to halt the developer action, transferring it to a hyposolution to fix the image, and then immersing it in water to remove the chemicals. The photographic process worker then dries the film. In some cases, these steps are performed by hand.

Color printer operators control equipment that produces color prints from negatives. These workers read customer instructions to determine processing requirements. They load film into color printing equipment, examine negatives to determine equipment control settings, set controls, and produce a specified number of prints. Finally, they inspect the finished prints for defects, remove any that are found, and insert the processed negatives and prints into an envelope for return to the customer.

Paper process technicians develop strips of exposed photographic paper; *takedown sorters* sort processed film; and *automatic mounters* operate equipment that cuts and mounts slide film into individual transparencies.

Precision photographic process workers, sometimes known as *digital imaging technicians*, use computer images of conventional negatives and specialized computer software to vary the contrast of images, remove unwanted background, or combine features from different photographs. The use of computers and digital technology is replacing much manual work, but some precision photographic process

Photographic process workers develop film, make prints or slides, and enlarge or retouch photographs.

workers who work in portrait studios still perform many specialized tasks by hand directly on the photo or negative: *airbrush artists* restore damaged and faded photographs, and may color or shade drawings to create photographic likenesses using an airbrush; *photographic retouchers* alter photographic negatives, prints, or images to accentuate the subject; *colorists* apply oil colors to portrait photographs to create natural, lifelike appearances; and *photographic spotters* remove imperfections on photographic prints and images.

Working Conditions

Photographic process workers generally spend their work hours in clean, appropriately lighted, well-ventilated, and air-conditioned offices, photofinishing laboratories, or 1-hour minilabs. In recent years, more commercial photographic processing has been done on computers than in darkrooms; and this trend is expected to continue. At peak times, portrait studios may hire individuals who work outside the studio to retouch negatives.

Photographic process machine operators must do repetitive work at a rapid pace without any loss of accuracy. Precision process workers do detailed tasks, such as airbrushing and spotting, which can contribute to eye fatigue.

Some photographic process workers are exposed continuously to the chemicals and fumes associated with developing and printing. These workers must wear rubber gloves and aprons and take precautions against these hazards.

Many photo laboratory employees work a 40-hour week, including weekends, and may work overtime during peak seasons.

Employment

Photographic process workers held about 63,000 jobs in 1998; almost three quarters of the jobs were for machine operators and tenders. Photofinishing laboratories and 1-hour minilabs employed about two-thirds. About 1 out of 7 worked for portrait studios and commercial laboratories that specialize in processing the work of professional photographers for advertising and other industries.

Employment fluctuates somewhat over the course of the year. Typically, employment peaks during school graduation and summer vacation periods, and again during the winter holiday season.

Training, Other Qualifications, and Advancement

Most photographic process workers receive on-the-job training from their companies, manufacturers' representatives, and experienced workers. New employees gradually learn to use the machines and chemicals that develop and print film.

Employers prefer applicants who are high school graduates or those who have some experience in the field. Computer skills; proficiency in mathematics, art, and chemistry; and photography courses that include instruction in film processing are all valuable preparation for precision work. Such courses are available through high schools, vocational-technical institutes, private trade schools, and colleges and universities.

On-the-job training in photographic processing occupations can range from just a few hours for print machine operators to several months for precision workers like airbrush artists and colorists. Some workers attend periodic training seminars to maintain a high level of skill. Manual dexterity, good hand-eye coordination, and good vision, including normal color perception, are important qualifications for precision photographic process workers. They must also be comfortable with computers and able to adapt to technological advances.

Photographic process machine workers can sometimes advance from jobs as machine operators to supervisory positions in laboratories or to management positions within retail stores.

Job Outlook

Overall employment of photographic process workers is expected to decline through the year 2008. Most openings will result from replacement needs, which tend to be higher for machine operators than for precision process workers.

In recent years, the use of digital cameras, which use electronic memory rather than film to record images, has grown rapidly among professional photographers and advanced amateurs. As the cost of digital photography drops, the use of such cameras will become more widespread among amateur photographers, reducing the demand for traditional photographic processing machine operators and tenders. However, conventional cameras, which use film to record images, are expected to continue to be the camera of choice among most casual photographers. Population growth and the popularity of amateur and family photography will contribute to an ongoing need for photographic process workers to process the film used in conventional cameras. This need will prevent what otherwise would be an even larger decline in the numbers of these workers.

Digital cameras and imaging are also expected to reduce the need for precision photographic process workers. Using digital technology, consumers who have a personal computer and the proper software will be able to download and view pictures on their computer, as well as manipulate, correct, and retouch their own photographs. No matter what improvements occur in camera technology though, there will be some precision processing tasks that require skillful manual treatment. Portrait studios, in particular, will continue to use colorists and airbrush artists, who work directly on actual photographs or negatives.

Earnings

Earnings of photographic process workers vary greatly depending on skill level, experience, and geographic location. Median hourly earnings for precision photographic process workers in 1998 were $10.39. The middle 50 percent earned between $7.69 and $13.20. The lowest 10 percent earned less than $6.15 and the highest 10 percent earned more than $18.49.

Median hourly earning for photographic processing machine operators and tenders in 1998 were $8.56. The middle 50 percent earned between $7.08 and $10.96. The lowest 10 percent earned less than $6.05 and the highest 10 percent earned more than $14.84. Median hourly earning in the industries employing the largest number of photographic processing machine operators and tenders in 1997 are shown below:

Miscellaneous business services	$8.30
Photographic studios, portrait	8.00

Precision photographic process workers generally earn more as their skill level and the complexity of the tasks they perform increase.

Related Occupations

Precision photographic process workers need a specialized knowledge of the photodeveloping process. Other workers who apply specialized technical knowledge include chemical laboratory technicians, crime laboratory analysts, food testers, medical laboratory assistants, metallurgical technicians, quality control technicians, engravers, and some of the printing occupations, such as photolithographer.

Photographic process machine operators perform work similar to that of other machine operators, such as computer, peripheral equipment, and printing press operators.

Sources of Additional Information

For information about employment opportunities in photographic laboratories and schools that offer degrees in photographic technology, contact:

☛ Photo Marketing Association International, 3000 Picture Place, Jackson, MI 49201.

Transportation and Material Moving Occupations

Busdrivers

(O*NET 97108 and 97111)

Significant Points

- Opportunities should be good, particularly for school busdriver jobs.
- A commercial driver's license is required to operate on interstate bus routes.
- Busdrivers must posses strong customer service skills, including communication skills and the ability to manage large groups of people.

Nature of the Work

Millions of Americans every day leave the driving to busdrivers. Busdrivers are essential in providing passengers with an alternative to their automobiles or other forms of transportation. Intercity busdrivers transport people between regions of a State or of the country; local transit busdrivers, within a metropolitan area or county; motorcoach drivers, on charter excursions and tours; and school busdrivers, to and from schools and related events.

Drivers pick up and drop off passengers at bus stops, stations, or, in the case of students, at regularly scheduled neighborhood locations based on strict time schedules. Drivers must operate vehicles safely, especially when traffic is heavier than normal. However, they cannot let light traffic put them ahead of schedule so that they miss passengers.

Intercity and *local transit busdrivers* report to their assigned terminal or garage, where they stock up on tickets or transfers and prepare trip report forms. In some firms, maintenance departments are responsible for keeping vehicles in good condition. In others, drivers may check their vehicle's tires, brakes, windshield wipers, lights, oil, fuel, and water supply, before beginning their routes. Drivers usually verify that the bus has safety equipment, such as fire extinguishers, first aid kits, and emergency reflectors in case of an emergency.

During the course of their shift, intercity and local transit busdrivers collect fares; answer questions about schedules, routes, and transfer points; and sometimes announce stops. Intercity busdrivers may make only a single one-way trip to a distant city or a round trip each day. They may stop at towns just a few miles apart or only at large cities hundreds of miles apart. Local transit busdrivers may make several trips each day over the same city and suburban streets, stopping as frequently as every few blocks.

Local transit busdrivers submit daily trip reports with a record of trips made, significant schedule delays, and mechanical problems. Intercity drivers who drive across State or national boundaries must comply with U.S. Department of Transportation regulations. These include completing vehicle inspection reports and recording distances traveled and the periods of time they spend driving, performing other duties, and off duty.

Motorcoach drivers transport passengers on charter trips and sightseeing tours. Drivers routinely interact with customers and tour guides to make the trip as comfortable and informative as possible. They are directly responsible for keeping to strict schedules, adhering to the guidelines of the tours' itinerary, and the overall success of the trip. Trips frequently last more than 1 day, and if they are assigned to an extended tour, they may be away for a week or more. As with all drivers who drive across State or national boundaries, motorcoach drivers must comply with U.S. Department of Transportation regulations.

School busdrivers usually drive the same routes each day, stopping to pick up pupils in the morning and return them to their homes in the afternoon. Some school busdrivers also transport students and teachers on field trips or to sporting events.

Busdrivers must be alert to prevent accidents, especially in heavy traffic or in bad weather, and to avoid sudden stops or swerves that jar passengers. School busdrivers must exercise particular caution when children are getting on or off the bus. They must maintain order on their bus and enforce school safety standards by allowing only students to board. In addition, they must know and enforce rules regarding student conduct used throughout the school system.

School busdrivers do not always have to report to an assigned terminal or garage. In some cases, school busdrivers often have the choice of taking their bus home, or parking it in a more convenient area. School busdrivers do not collect fares. Instead, they prepare weekly reports on the number of students, trips or runs, work hours, miles, and the amount of fuel consumption. Their supervisors set time schedules and routes for the day or week.

Working Conditions

Driving a bus through heavy traffic while dealing with passengers is not physically strenuous, but can be stressful and fatiguing. On the other hand, many drivers enjoy the opportunity to work without direct supervision, with full responsibility for their bus and passengers.

Many busdrivers enjoy the opportunity to work without direct supervision, with full responsibility for their bus and passengers.

Intercity busdrivers may work nights, weekends, and holidays and often spend nights away from home, where they stay in hotels at company expense. Senior drivers with regular routes have regular weekly work schedules, but others do not have regular schedules and must be prepared to report for work on short notice. They report for work only when called for a charter assignment or to drive extra buses on a regular route. Intercity bus travel and charter work tends to be seasonal. From May through August, drivers may work the maximum number of hours per week that regulations allow. During winter, junior drivers may work infrequently, except for busy holiday travel periods, and may be furloughed for periods of time.

School busdrivers work only when school is in session. Many work 20 hours a week or less, driving one or two routes in the morning and afternoon. Drivers taking field or athletic trips or who also have midday kindergarten routes may work more hours a week.

Regular local transit busdrivers usually have a 5-day workweek; Saturdays and Sundays are considered regular workdays. Some drivers work evenings and after midnight. To accommodate commuters, many work "split shifts," for example, 6 a.m. to 10 a.m. and 3 p.m. to 7 p.m., with time off in between.

Tour and charter bus drivers may work any day and all hours of the day, including weekends and holidays. Their hours are dictated by the charter trips booked and the schedule and prearranged itinerary of tours. However, like all busdrivers, their weekly hours must be consistent with the Department of Transportation's rules and regulations concerning hours of service. For example, a long-distance driver may not work more than 60 hours in any 7-day period and drivers must rest 8 hours for every 10 hours of driving.

Employment

Busdrivers held about 638,000 jobs in 1998. More than a third worked part time. About two-thirds of all drivers worked for school systems or companies providing school bus services under contract, as shown in the accompanying chart. Most of the remainder worked for private and local government transit systems; some also worked for intercity and charter buslines.

Training, Other Qualifications, and Advancement

Busdriver qualifications and standards are established by State and Federal regulations. All drivers must comply with Federal regulations and any State regulations that exceed Federal requirements.

Most busdrivers operate school buses.

Distribution of wage and salary employment, 1998

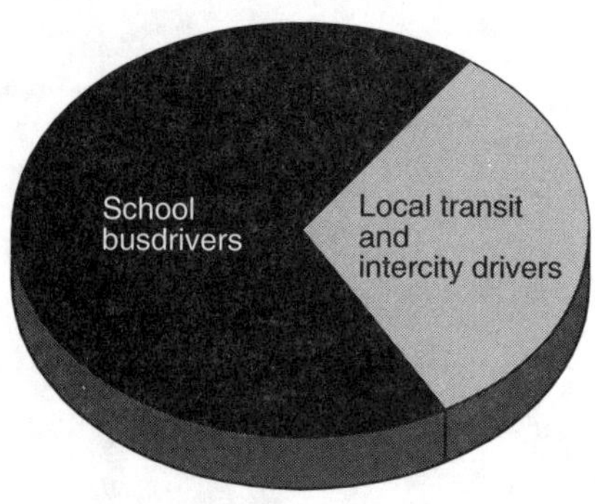

Federal regulations require drivers who operate vehicles designed to transport 16 or more passengers to hold a commercial driver's license (CDL) from the State in which they live.

To qualify for a commercial driver's license, applicants must pass a written test on rules and regulations and then demonstrate they can operate a bus safely. A national data bank permanently records all driving violations incurred by persons who hold commercial licenses. A State may not issue a commercial driver's license to a driver who already has a license suspended or revoked in another State. A driver with a CDL must accompany trainees until they get their own CDL. Information on how to apply for a commercial driver's license may be obtained from State motor vehicle administrations.

While many States allow those who are 18 years and older to drive buses within State borders, the U.S. Department of Transportation establishes minimum qualifications for busdrivers engaged in interstate commerce. Federal Motor Carrier Safety Regulations require drivers to be at least 21 years old and pass a physical examination once every 2 years. The main physical requirements include good hearing, 20/40 vision with or without glasses or corrective lenses, and a 70 degree field of vision in each eye. Drivers must not be color blind. Drivers must be able to hear a forced whisper in one ear at not less than 5 feet, with or without a hearing aide. Drivers must have normal use of arms and legs and normal blood pressure. Drivers may not use any controlled substances, unless prescribed by a licensed physician. Persons with epilepsy or diabetes controlled by insulin are not permitted to be interstate busdrivers. Federal regulations also require employers to test their drivers for alcohol and drug use as a condition of employment, and require periodic random tests while on duty. In addition, a driver must not have been convicted of a felony involving the use of a motor vehicle; a crime involving drugs; driving under the influence of drugs or alcohol; or hit-and-run driving which resulted in injury or death. All drivers must be able to read and speak English well enough to read road signs, prepare reports, and communicate with law enforcement officers and the public. In addition, drivers must take a written examination on the Motor Carrier Safety Regulations of the U.S. Department of Transportation.

Many employers prefer high school graduates and require a written test of ability to follow complex bus schedules. Many intercity and public transit bus companies prefer applicants who are at least 24 years of age; some require several years of bus or truck driving experience. In some States, school busdrivers must pass a background investigation to uncover any criminal record or history of mental problems.

Because busdrivers deal with passengers, they must be courteous. They need an even temperament and emotional stability because driving in heavy, fast-moving, or stop-and-go traffic and dealing with passengers can be stressful. Drivers must have strong customer service skills, including communication skills and the ability to coordinate and manage large groups of people.

Most intercity bus companies and local transit systems give driver trainees 2 to 8 weeks of classroom and "behind-the-wheel" instruction. In the classroom, trainees learn U.S. Department of Transportation and company work rules, safety regulations, State and municipal driving regulations, and safe driving practices. They also learn to read schedules, determine fares, keep records, and deal courteously with passengers.

School busdrivers are also required to obtain a commercial driver's license from the State in which they live. Many persons who enter school busdriving have never driven any vehicle larger than an automobile. They receive between 1 and 4 weeks of driving instruction plus classroom training on State and local laws, regulations, and policies of operating school buses; safe driving practices; driver-pupil relations; first aid; disabled student special needs; and emergency evacuation procedures. School busdrivers must also be aware of school systems rules for discipline and conduct for busdrivers and the students they transport.

During training, busdrivers practice driving on set courses. They practice turns and zigzag maneuvers, backing up, and driving in narrow lanes. Then they drive in light traffic and, eventually, on congested highways and city streets. They also make trial runs, without passengers, to improve their driving skills and learn the routes. Local transit trainees memorize and drive each of the runs operating out of their assigned garage. New drivers begin with a "break-in" period. They make regularly scheduled trips with passengers, accompanied by an experienced driver who gives helpful tips, answers questions, and evaluates the new driver's performance.

New intercity and local transit drivers are usually placed on an "extra" list to drive charter runs, extra buses on regular runs, and special runs (for example, during morning and evening rush hours and to sports events). They also substitute for regular drivers who are ill or on vacation. New drivers remain on the extra list, and may work only part time, perhaps for several years, until they have enough seniority to receive a regular run.

Senior drivers may bid for runs they prefer, such as those with more work hours, lighter traffic, weekends off, or, in the case of intercity busdrivers, higher earnings or fewer workdays per week.

Opportunities for promotion are generally limited. However, experienced drivers may become supervisors or dispatchers, assigning buses to drivers, checking whether drivers are on schedule, rerouting buses to avoid blocked streets or other problems, and dispatching extra vehicles and service crews to scenes of accidents and breakdowns. In transit agencies with rail systems, drivers may become train operators or station attendants. A few drivers become managers. Promotion in publicly owned bus systems is often by competitive civil service examination. Some motorcoach drivers purchase their own equipment and go in to business for themselves.

Job Outlook

Persons seeking jobs as busdrivers over the 1998-2008 period should encounter good opportunities. Many employers have recently had difficulty finding qualified candidates to fill vacancies left by departing employees. Opportunities should be best for individuals with good driving records who are willing to start on a part-time or irregular schedule, as well as for those seeking jobs as school busdrivers in rapidly growing metropolitan areas. Those seeking higher paying intercity and public transit busdriver positions may encounter competition.

Employment of busdrivers is expected to increase about as fast as average for all occupations through the year 2008, primarily to meet the transportation needs of a growing school-age population and local environmental concerns. Thousands of additional job openings are expected to occur each year because of the need to replace workers who take jobs in other occupations, retire, or leave the occupation for other reasons.

School busdriving jobs should be easiest to acquire because most are part time positions with high turnover and minimal training requirements. The number of school busdrivers is expected to increase as a result of growth in elementary and secondary school enrollments. In addition, as more of the Nation's population is concentrated in suburban areas—where students generally ride school buses—and less in the central cities—where transportation is not provided for most pupils—more school busdrivers will be needed.

Employment of local transit and intercity drivers will grow as bus ridership increases. Local and intercity bus travel is expected to increase as the population and labor force grows. However, more individual travelers will opt to travel by airplane or automobile rather than by bus. Most growth in intercity drivers will probably be in group charter travel, rather than scheduled intercity bus services. There may continue to be competition for local transit and intercity busdriver jobs in some areas because many of these positions offer relatively high wages and attractive benefits. The most competitive positions will be those offering regular hours and steady driving routes.

Full-time busdrivers are rarely laid off during recessions. However, hours of part-time local transit and intercity busdrivers may be reduced if bus ridership decreases because fewer extra buses would be needed. Seasonal layoffs are common. Many intercity busdrivers with little seniority, for example, are furloughed during the winter when regular schedule and charter business falls off; school busdrivers seldom work during the summer or school holidays.

Earnings

Median hourly earnings of transit and intercity busdrivers were $11.72 in 1998. The middle 50 percent earned between $8.58 and $16.04 an hour. The lowest 10 percent earned less than $6.66 and the highest 10 percent earned more than $19.18 an hour. Median hourly earnings in the industries employing the largest numbers of transit and intercity busdrivers in 1997 were as follows:

Industry	Earnings
Local government, except education and hospitals	$14.20
Intercity and rural bus transportation	10.50
Local and suburban transportation	10.20
School buses, contract	10.20
Bus charter service	8.80

Median hourly earnings of school busdrivers were $9.05 in 1998. The middle 50 percent earned between $6.33 and $11.44 an hour. The lowest 10 percent earned less than $5.59 and the highest 10 percent earned more than $14.00 an hour. Median hourly earnings of school busdrivers in 1997 were $9.20 in contract school buses and $8.60 in elementary and secondary schools.

According to the American Public Transit Association, in early 1999 local transit busdrivers in metropolitan areas with more than 2 million inhabitants were paid an average top hourly wage rate of about $17.90 by companies with over 1,000 employees, and about $16.00 by those with fewer than 1,000 employees. In smaller metropolitan areas, they had an average top hourly wage rate of about $14.70 in areas with between 250,000 and 500,000 residents, and about $12.60 in areas with resident populations below 50,000. Generally, drivers can reach the top rate in 3 or 4 years.

The benefits busdrivers receive from their employers vary greatly. Most intercity and local transit busdrivers receive paid health and life insurance, sick leave, and free bus rides on any of the regular routes of their line or system. Drivers who work full time also get as much as 4 weeks of vacation annually. Most local transit busdrivers are also covered by dental insurance and pension plans. School busdrivers receive sick leave, and many are covered by health and life insurance and pension plans. Because they generally do not work when school is not in session, they do not get vacation leave. In a number of States, local transit and school busdrivers employed by local governments are covered by a State-wide public employee pension system.

Most intercity and many local transit busdrivers are members of the Amalgamated Transit Union. Local transit busdrivers in New York and several other large cities belong to the Transport Workers Union of America. Some drivers belong to the United Transportation Union and the International Brotherhood of Teamsters.

Related Occupations

Other workers who drive vehicles on highways and city streets are taxi drivers, truckdrivers, and chauffeurs.

Sources of Additional Information

For further information on employment opportunities, contact local transit systems, intercity buslines, school systems, or the local offices of the State employment service.

General information on busdriving is available from:

☛ American Bus Association, 1100 New York Avenue NW., Suite 1050, Washington, DC 20005. Internet: **http://www.buses.org**

General information on school busdriving is available from:

☛ National School Transportation Association, P.O. Box 2639, Springfield, VA 22152. Internet: **http://www.schooltrans.com**

General information on local transit busdriving is available from:

☛ American Public Transit Association, 1201 New York Ave. NW., Suite 400, Washington, DC 20005. Internet: **http://www.apta.com**

General information on motorcoach driving is available from:

☛ United Motorcoach Association, 113 S. West St., 4th Floor, Alexandria, VA 22314. Telephone (toll free): 1-800-424-8262. Internet: **http://www.uma.org**

Material Moving Equipment Operators

(O*NET 97902, 97905, 97908, 97911, 97914, 97917, 97921, 97923A, 97923B, 97926, 97928, 97932, 97935, 97941, 97944, 97947, 97951, 97953, and 97989A)

Significant Points

- Most workers acquire their skills on the job.
- Workers in these occupations often have high pay rates, but seasonal work may reduce earnings.

Nature of the Work

Material moving equipment operators use machinery to move construction materials, earth, petroleum products, and other heavy materials. Generally, they move materials over short distances—around a construction site, factory, or warehouse. Some move materials on or off trucks and ships. Operators control equipment by moving levers or foot pedals, operating switches, or turning dials. They may also set up and inspect equipment, make adjustments, and perform minor repairs when needed.

Material moving equipment operators are classified by the type of equipment they operate. Each piece of equipment requires different skills to move different types of loads. (For information on *operating engineers, paving and surfacing equipment operators, and grader, bulldozer, and scraper operators* see the statement on construction equipment operators, elsewhere in the *Handbook.*)

Industrial truck and tractor operators drive and control industrial trucks or tractors equipped with lifting devices, such as a forklift or boom, and trailer hitches. A typical industrial truck, often called a forklift or lift truck, has a hydraulic lifting mechanism and forks. Industrial truck operators use these forks to carry loads on a skid, or pallet, around a factory or warehouse. They also pull trailers loaded with materials, goods, or equipment within factories and warehouses, or around outdoor storage areas.

Excavation and loading machine operators dig and load sand, gravel, earth, or similar materials into trucks or onto conveyors using machinery equipped with scoops, shovels, or buckets. Construction and mining industries employ virtually all *excavation and loading machine operators.*

Crane and tower operators lift materials, machinery, or other heavy objects. They extend or retract a horizontally mounted boom to lower or raise a hook attached to the loadline. Most operators coordinate their maneuvers in response to hand signals and radioed instructions. Operators position the loads from the on-board console or from a remote console at the site. While crane and tower operators are noticeable at office building and other construction sites, the biggest group works in primary metal, metal fabrication, and transportation equipment manufacturing industries that use heavy, bulky materials.

Hoist and winch operators control movement of cables, cages and platforms to move workers and materials for construction, manufacturing, logging and other industrial operations. They also lube and maintain the drum and cables and make other minor repairs. One half of all jobs for hoist and winch operators were found in manufacturing or mining industries.

Other material moving equipment operators tend air compressors or pumps at construction sites, or operate oil or natural gas pumps and compressors at wells and on pipelines. Some operate ship loading and unloading equipment, conveyors, hoists, and other specialized material handling equipment such as mine or railroad tank car unloading equipment.

Material moving equipment operators may keep records of materials moved, and do some manual loading and unloading. They also may clean, fuel, and service their equipment.

Working Conditions

Many material moving equipment operators work outdoors in every type of climate and weather condition. Industrial truck and tractor operators work mainly in warehouses or manufacturing plants. Some machines are noisy and shake or jolt the operator. These jobs have become much safer with overhead guards on forklift trucks and other safety equipment. As with most machinery, most accidents can be avoided by observing proper operating procedures and safety practices.

Employment

Material moving equipment operators held about 808,000 jobs in 1998. They were distributed among the detailed occupation groups as follows:

Occupation	Jobs
Industrial truck and tractor operators	415,000
Excavation and loading machine operators	106,000
Crane and tower operators	49,000
Hoist and winch operators	11,000
All other material moving equipment operators	228,000

Material moving equipment operators move materials around a construction site, factory, or warehouse.

The largest proportion—36 percent—of material moving equipment operators worked in manufacturing. Most of these were industrial truck and tractor operators. Over 33 percent of all material moving equipment operators worked in transportation, public utilities, wholesale trade or retail trade industries. Significant numbers of material moving equipment operators also worked in construction, mining, and service industries. A few material moving equipment operators were self-employed.

Material moving equipment operators work in every part of the country. Some work in remote locations on large construction projects, such as highways and dams, or in factory or mining operations.

Training, Other Qualifications, and Advancement
Material moving equipment operators usually learn their skills on the job. Operators need a good sense of balance, distance judgment, and eye-hand-foot coordination. Employers of material moving equipment operators prefer high school graduates, although some equipment may require less education to operate. Mechanical aptitude and high school training in automobile or diesel mechanics are helpful because workers may perform some maintenance on their machines. Experience operating mobile equipment, such as farm tractors or heavy equipment in the Armed Forces, is an asset.

As part of an on-the-job apprenticeship, beginning material moving equipment operators handle light equipment under the guidance of an experienced operator. Later, they may operate heavier equipment such as cranes.

Private vocational schools offer instruction in the operation of certain types of material moving equipment. Completion of such a program may help a person get a job as a trainee or apprentice. However, persons considering such training should check the reputation of the school among employers in the area.

Job Outlook
Employment of material moving equipment operators will increase slower than the average for all occupations through 2008. The expected growth stems from an expanding economy and increased spending on the Nation's infrastructure of highways, bridges, and dams. However, equipment improvements, including the growing automation of material handling in factories and warehouses, continue to raise productivity and moderate the demand for skilled operators. In addition to employment growth in this large occupation, many jobs will open up because of the need to replace experienced workers who transfer to other occupations or leave the labor force.

Job growth for material moving equipment operators largely depends on growth in the industries employing them. Employment of operators in manufacturing will decline in tandem with overall industry employment. Employment in construction will grow faster than the average for all occupations, due to the demand for construction related excavation and loading machine operators who prepare new sites for construction. Employment will also grow rapidly in temporary help organizations and companies that lease equipment.

Growth of industrial truck and tractor operators, the largest occupation in this group, will be slower than the average for all occupations. Growth of industrial truck and tractor operators will be constrained by technological improvements. Some firms use computerized dispatching or onboard data communication devices to enable industrial truck and tractor operators to move and track goods more efficiently. In other firms, industrial trucks and tractors may be replaced by computer-controlled conveyor systems, overhead handling systems, or automated vehicles that do not require operators. Employment of hoist and winch operators will grow slowly and crane and tower operators will have little or no growth as precision computerized controls and robotics automate their work in manufacturing and some other industries.

Both construction and manufacturing are very sensitive to changes in economic conditions, so the number of job openings for operators in these industries may fluctuate from year to year.

Earnings
Median annual earnings of industrial truck and tractor operators were $23,360 in 1998. The middle 50 percent earned between $19,170 and $29,760 a year. The lowest 10 percent earned less than $15,410 and the highest 10 percent earned more than $37,670 a year. Median annual earnings in the industries employing the largest number of industrial truck and tractor operators in 1997 were as follows:

Motor vehicles and equipment	$35,300
Trucking and courier services, except air	26,600
Groceries and related products	22,800
Public warehousing and storage	21,300
Personnel supply services	20,700

Median annual earnings of excavation and loading machine operators were $27,090 in 1998. The middle 50 percent earned between $22,240 and $35,580 a year. The lowest 10 percent earned less than $18,620 and the highest 10 percent earned more than $46,140 a year.

Median annual earnings of crane and tower operators were $30,510 in 1998. The middle 50 percent earned between $24,340 and $38,270 a year. The lowest 10 percent earned less than $20,560 and the highest 10 percent earned more than $46,680 a year.

Median annual earnings of hoist and winch operators were $28,030 in 1998. The middle 50 percent earned between $21,120 and $36,400 a year. The lowest 10 percent earned less than $17,370 and the highest 10 percent earned more than $45,260 a year.

Pay usually is higher in metropolitan areas. Seasonal work may reduce earnings.

Related Occupations
Other workers who operate mechanical equipment include railroad yard workers, truck and bus drivers, construction equipment operators, and farm equipment operators.

Sources of Additional Information
Local State employment service offices may provide information about job opportunities and training programs.

Information on industrial truck and tractor operators is available from:

☛ Industrial Truck Association, 1750 K St. NW., Suite 460, Washington, DC 20006.

☛ Specialized Carriers and Rigging Association, 2750 Prosperity Ave., Suite 620, Fairfax, VA 22301.

Rail Transportation Occupations

(O*NET 97302, 97305, 97308, 97311, 97314, 97317A, 97317B, 97399A, and 97399B)

Significant Points

- Overall employment in the railroad transportation industry is expected to decline due to productivity gains.
- Employment of locomotive engineers and subway and streetcar operators is projected to grow slowly, and in all other rail transportation occupations it is projected to decline.
- Over 8 out of 10 rail transportation workers are members of unions and many have relatively high earnings.

Nature of the Work

More than a century ago, freight and passenger railroads were the ties binding the Nation together and the engine driving the economy. Today, rail transportation remains a vital link in our Nation's transportation network and economy. Railroads deliver thousands of travelers and over 1.8 billion tons of freight to destinations throughout the Nation, while subways and streetcars transport millions of passengers within metropolitan areas.

Locomotive engineers are among the most experienced and skilled workers on the railroad. Locomotive engineers operate large trains carrying cargo and passengers between stations. Most engineers run diesel locomotives, while a few operate electrically powered locomotives.

Before and after each run, engineers check their locomotives for mechanical problems. Minor adjustments are made on the spot, while the engine shop supervisor handles any major problems. Engineers receive starting instructions from conductors and move controls such as throttles and air brakes to drive the locomotive. They monitor gauges and meters that measure speed, amperage, battery charge, and air pressure both in the brake lines and in the main reservoir.

Both on the open road and in the yard, engineers confer with conductors and traffic control center personnel via radiophone to issue or receive information concerning stops, delays, or oncoming trains. They interpret train orders, railroad rules and regulations, and train signals indicating track obstructions, other train movements, and speed limits. They must have a thorough knowledge of the signaling systems, yards, and terminals in addition to their routes. Engineers must be constantly aware of the condition and makeup of their train. This is extremely important because trains react differently to acceleration, braking, and curves, depending on the number of cars, the ratio of empty to loaded cars, and the amount of slack in the train.

Traditionally, freight train crews included either one or two brake operators—one in the locomotive with the engineer and another who rode with the conductor in the rear car. In an effort to reduce costs and take advantage of new technology, most railroads are phasing out *assistant engineers* and *brake operators*. Assistant engineers help monitor locomotive instruments and signals and observe the track for obstructions. Brake operators work under the direction of conductors and do the physical work involved in adding and removing cars at railroad stations and assembling and disassembling trains in railroad yards. Now, most freight trains only use an engineer and a conductor, stationed with the engineer, because new visual instrumentation and monitoring devices have eliminated the need for crewmembers located on the rear of the train.

Railroad conductors coordinate the activities of freight and passenger train crews. Railroad conductors assigned to freight trains review schedules, switching orders, way bills, and shipping records to obtain cargo loading and unloading information. Conductors assigned to passenger trains ensure passenger safety and comfort. They collect tickets and fares, and coordinate crew activities to provide boarding, porter, maid, and meal services. Most passenger trains also employ *assistant conductors* to help collect tickets and assist passengers.

Before a train leaves the terminal, the conductor and engineer discuss instructions received from the dispatcher concerning the train's route, timetable, and cargo. While underway, conductors receive additional information by radio. This may include information about track conditions or instructions to pull off at the next available stop and let another train pass. During the run, conductors use two-way radios and cellular phones to communicate with dispatchers, engineers and conductors of other trains.

Conductors receive information from dispatch or electronic monitoring devices that relay any equipment problems on the train or the rail. They may arrange for defective cars to be removed from the train for repairs at the nearest station or stop. Additionally, alternative routes may be discussed if there is a defect or obstruction on the rail. They inform dispatchers of any problems using a radio or wayside telephone.

Yardmasters coordinate activities of workers engaged in railroad traffic operations. These activities include the makeup or breakup of trains and switching inbound or outbound traffic to a specific section of the line. Some cars are sent to unload their cargo on special tracks, while other cars are moved to other tracks to await assemblage into new trains destined for different cities. Yardmasters tell engineers the make-up of trains and where to move the cars. Computerized switches divert the locomotive or cars to the proper track for coupling and uncoupling.

Other *railroad yard workers* perform a variety of activities such as inspecting couplings and air-hoses. They may operate track switches to route cars to different sections of the yard, signal engineers and set warning signals, or help couple and uncouple rolling stock to make up or break up trains. *Rail yard engineers, dinkey operators, and hostlers* drive switching or other locomotive or small "dinkey" engines within railroad yards, industrial plants, mines and quarries, or construction projects.

In contrast to other rail transportation workers, subway and streetcar operators generally work for public transit authorities instead of railroads. *Subway operators* control trains that transport passengers throughout a city and its suburbs. The trains run on rail-guided tracks in underground tunnels, on the surface or elevated above streets. Operators start, slow, or stop the train and must stay alert to observe signals along the track that indicate when they must slow or stop their train to avoid obstructions or other trains ahead. They also make announcements to riders, may open and close the doors, and ensure that passengers get on and off the subway safely.

To meet predetermined schedules, operators must control the train's speed and the amount of time spent at each station. Increasingly, however, these functions are controlled by computers and not by the operator. When breakdowns or emergencies occur, operators contact their dispatcher or supervisor and may have to evacuate cars.

Streetcar operators drive electric-powered streetcars or trolleys that transport passengers in metropolitan areas. Some tracks may be recessed in city streets or have grade crossings, so operators must observe traffic signals and cope with car and truck traffic. Operators start, slow, and stop their cars so passengers may get on or off with ease. They may collect fares, and issue change and transfers. They also answer questions from passengers concerning fares, schedules, and routes.

Working Conditions

Because trains operate 24 hours a day, 7 days a week, many rail transportation employees often work nights, weekends, and holidays. On

Conductors collect tickets and fares and coordinate boarding, porter, maid, and meal services.

some days, operators work multiple shifts. Seniority usually dictates who receives the more desirable shifts.

Most freight trains are unscheduled, and few workers on these trains have scheduled assignments. Instead, their names are placed on a list and they must await their turn to work. Jobs are usually handed out on short notice and often at odd hours. Because road service personnel often work on trains operating between stations that are hundreds of miles apart, they may spend several nights at a time away from home.

Workers on passenger trains ordinarily have more regular and reliable shifts. The appearance, temperature, and accommodations of the passenger trains are also more comfortable than freight trains.

Freight and yard conductors spend most of their time outdoors in varying weather. The work of operators on local runs, where trains frequently stop at stations to pick up and deliver cars, is physically demanding. Climbing up and down and getting off moving cars is strenuous and can be dangerous.

Employment

Rail transportation workers held 85,000 jobs in 1998—including 33,000 locomotive engineers; 25,000 conductors and yardmasters; and 14,000 brake, signal, and switch operators. Subway and streetcar operators accounted for 3,300 jobs. Railroads employ more than 90 percent of all rail transportation workers. The rest work for State and local governments as subway and streetcar operators, and for mining and manufacturing establishments operating their own locomotives and dinkey engines that move rail cars containing ore, coal, and other bulk materials.

Training, Other Qualifications, and Advancement

Most railroad transportation workers begin as yard laborers, and later may have the opportunity to train for engineer or conductor jobs. Railroads require that applicants have a minimum of a high school diploma or equivalent. Applicants must have good hearing, eyesight, and color vision, as well as good hand-eye coordination, manual dexterity, and mechanical aptitude. Physical stamina is required for brake operator jobs. Employers require railroad transportation job applicants to pass a physical examination and drug and alcohol screening. In addition, under Federal law all members of train crews are subject to random drug and alcohol testing while on duty.

On most railroads, entry-level employees help assemble and disassemble trains in the yard. After these operators gain experience, they may have the opportunity for road assignments, although trains now carry brake operators only when they pick up and drop off a lot of cars en route. On most railroads, new brake operators undergo extensive on-the-job training and classroom instruction, including instruction in signaling, coupling and uncoupling cars, throwing switches, and boarding moving trains.

Applicants for locomotive engineer jobs must be at least 21 years old. Frequently, employers fill engineer positions with workers who have experience in other railroad operating occupations. Federal regulations require beginning engineers to complete a formal engineer training program, including classroom, simulator, and hands-on instruction in locomotive operation. The instruction is usually administered by the rail company. At the end of the training period, they must pass qualifying tests covering locomotive equipment, air brake systems, fuel economy, train handling techniques, and operating rules and regulations. The company issues the engineer a license after the applicant successfully passes the examinations. Other conditions and rules may apply to entry-level engineers, and these rules usually vary between railroads.

Engineers undergo periodic physical examinations and drug and alcohol testing to determine their fitness to operate locomotives. Unannounced safety and efficiency tests are also given to judge their overall conduct of operations. In some cases, engineers who fail to meet these physical and conduct standards are restricted to yard service; in other instances, they may be disciplined, trained to perform other work, or discharged.

Conductor jobs are generally filled from the ranks of experienced brake operators who have passed tests covering signals, timetables, operating rules, and related subjects. Some companies require these tests to be passed within the first 2 years of employment. Seniority usually is the main factor in determining promotion from brake operator to conductor. There is a great deal of competition for conductor positions because their earnings are substantially higher than entry-level occupations. Most railroads maintain separate seniority lists for road service and yard service conductors. On some railroads, conductors start in the yards, then move to freight or passenger service. Some conductors advance to managerial or administrative positions.

Newly trained brake operators, engineers, and conductors, are placed on the "extra board" until permanent positions become available. Extra board workers only receive assignments when the railroad needs substitutes for regular workers who are absent because of vacation, illness, or other personal reasons. On most railroads, conductors on the extra board, for example, may work as brake operators if there are not enough conductor-runs available that month. Extra board workers frequently must wait years until they accumulate enough seniority to get a regular assignment. Seniority rules may also allow workers with greater seniority to select their type of assignment. For example, an engineer may move from an initial regular assignment in yard service to road service.

For subway and streetcar operator jobs, subway transit systems prefer applicants with a high school education. Applicants must also be in good health, have good communication skills, and be able to make quick, responsible judgments.

New operators are generally placed in training programs that last from a few weeks to 6 months. At the end of the period of classroom and on-the-job training, operators usually must pass qualifying examinations covering the operating system, troubleshooting, and evacuation and emergency procedures. Some operators with sufficient seniority can advance to station managers or other supervisory positions.

Job Outlook

Competition for available opportunities is expected to be keen. Many persons qualify for rail transportation occupations because education beyond high school is generally not required. Many more desire employment than can be hired because the pay is good and the work steady.

Employment for a majority of railroad transportation occupations is expected to decline through the year 2008, with only locomotive engineers and subway and streetcar operators expected to grow. The need to replace workers who transfer to other occupations or retire will be the only source of job openings. A limited number of total job openings is expected, because the attractive pay, tenure, and job security results in relatively few rail transportation workers leaving their jobs. In addition, not all the workers who leave the occupations will be replaced, further reducing job openings. The industry continues to reduce its workforce because of productivity gains, mergers, and divestiture-related cutbacks.

Demand for railroad freight service will grow as the economy and the intermodal transportation of goods expand and railroads become more efficient. Intermodal systems use trucks to pick-up and deliver the shippers' sealed trailers or containers, and trains to transport them long distance. This saves customers time and money by efficiently carrying goods across country. Intermodalism is the fastest growing type of railroad transportation. For railroads, the benefit has been the increased efficiency of equipment use, allowing increases in the number of runs each train makes in a year. In order to compete with other modes of transportation such as trucks, ships and barges, and aircraft, railroads are improving delivery times and on-time service while reducing shipping rates.

As a result, businesses are expected to increasingly use railroads to carry their goods.

However, growth in the number of railroad transportation workers will generally be adversely affected by innovations such as larger, faster, more fuel-efficient trains and computerized classification yards that make it possible to move freight more economically. Computers are used to keep track of freight cars, match empty cars with the closest loads, and dispatch trains. Computer-assisted devices alert engineers to train malfunctions and new work rules have become widespread allowing trains to operate with two- or three-person crews instead of the traditional five-person crews. Employment of locomotive and yard engineers should grow as the industry expands to high-speed service in various corridors in the country.

Subway and streetcar operator employment is expected to grow as metropolitan areas build new rail systems and add new lines to existing systems. State and local governments support new construction because population growth in metropolitan areas has increased automobile traffic, making streets and highways more congested. Improved rail systems offer an alternative to automobile transportation that can reduce road congestion and, by reducing automobile use, contribute to government mandated improvements in air quality.

Earnings

Median hourly earnings of locomotive engineers were $19.14 in 1998. The middle 50 percent earned between $15.07 and $23.81 an hour. The lowest 10 percent earned less than $12.22 and the highest 10 percent earned more than $35.65 an hour.

Median hourly earnings of railroad conductors and yardmasters were $18.51 in 1998. The middle 50 percent earned between $16.24 and $23.47 an hour. The lowest 10 percent earned less than $13.60 and the highest 10 percent earned more than $35.27 an hour.

Median hourly earnings of railroad brake, signal, and switch operators were $17.57 in 1998. The middle 50 percent earned between $15.50 and $19.44 an hour. The lowest 10 percent earned less than $12.86 and the highest 10 percent earned more than $24.16 an hour.

Median hourly earnings of subway and streetcar operators were $20.83 in 1998. The middle 50 percent earned between $19.04 and $22.60 an hour. The lowest 10 percent earned less than $16.23 and the highest 10 percent earned more than $23.66 an hour.

Most railroad workers in road service are paid according to miles traveled or hours worked; whichever leads to higher earnings. Full-time employees have steadier work, more regular hours, increased opportunities for overtime work, and higher earnings than do those assigned to the extra board. In 1998, a third of all rail transportation employees worked 40 hours a week. About another third worked in excess of 40-hours and received extra pay for overtime.

According to the National Railroad Labor Conference in 1997, the average annual earnings for engineers ranged from $55,100 for yard-freight engineers, to $69,000 for local-freight engineers. For conductors, earnings ranged from $51,700 for yard-freight conductors, up to $65,200 for passenger conductors. The NRLC reported that brake operators averaged from $42,400 for yard-freight operators, up to $57,700 for local-freight operators.

According to data from the American Public Transit Association, in early 1999 the top-rate full-time hourly earnings of operators for commuter rail ranged from $17.50 to $28.70; operators for heavy rail from $17.50 to $26.00; and operators for light rail from $13.60 to $21.90. Transit workers in the northeastern United States typically had the highest wages.

More than 80 percent of railroad transportation workers are members of unions. Many different railroad unions represent various crafts on the railroads. Most railroad engineers are members of the Brotherhood of Locomotive Engineers, while most other railroad transportation workers are members of the United Transportation Union. Many subway operators are members of the Amalgamated Transit Union, while others belong to the Transport Workers Union of North America.

Sources of Additional Information

To obtain information on employment opportunities for railroad transportation workers, contact the employment offices of the various railroads and rail transit systems, or State employment service offices.

For general information about the rail transportation industry, contact:

☛ Association of American Railroads, 50 F St. NW., Washington, DC 20001. Internet: **http://www.aar.org.**

☛ Federal Railroad Administration, 400 7th St. SW., Washington, DC 20590. Internet: **http://www.fra.dot.gov**

For general information about career opportunities in passenger transportation, contact:

☛ American Public Transit Association, 1201 New York Ave. NW., Suite 400, Washington, DC 20005. Internet: **http://www.apta.com**

General information on rail transportation occupations and career opportunities as a locomotive engineer is available from:

☛ Brotherhood of Locomotive Engineers, 1370 Ontario Ave., Cleveland, OH 44113-1702. Internet: **http://www.ble.org**

For information on certification and training programs, contact:

☛ National Association of Railroad Sciences, Johnson County Community College, 12345 College Blvd., Overland Park, KS 66210. Internet: **http://www.jccc.net/orgs/nars**

Taxi Drivers and Chauffeurs

(O*NET 97114)

Significant Points

- Taxi drivers and chauffeurs can work all schedules, including full-time, part-time, night, evening, and weekend work.
- Many people work in these jobs for short periods, so job opportunities will be good because replacement needs are high.
- Many taxi drivers and chauffeurs like the independent, unsupervised work of driving their automobile.

Nature of the Work

Anyone who has been in a large city knows the importance of taxi and limousine drivers. These drivers help passengers get to and from their homes, workplaces, and recreational pursuits such as dining, entertainment, and shopping. They also help out-of-town business people and tourists get around in new surroundings.

Taxi drivers, also known as cab drivers, usually spend most of their time cruising the streets to pick up fares. They drive taxicabs, which are most frequently large, conventional automobiles modified for commercial passenger transport.

At the start of their driving shift, taxi drivers usually report to a taxicab service or garage where they are assigned a vehicle. They record their name, work date, and cab identification number on a trip sheet. Drivers check the cab's fuel and oil levels, and make sure the lights, brakes, and windshield wipers are in good working order. Drivers adjust rear and side mirrors and their seat for comfort. Any equipment or part not in good working order is reported to the dispatcher or company mechanic.

Taxi drivers pick up passengers in one of three ways: cruising the streets to pick up random passengers; prearranged pickups; and pickups from taxi stands established in highly trafficked areas. The majority of passengers hail or "wave down" drivers cruising the streets, especially in urban areas. Customers may also prearrange a pickup by calling a cab company and giving a location, approximate pick up time, and destination. The cab company dispatcher then relays the information to a driver by two-way radio, cellular telephone, or on-board computer. Drivers also pick up passengers waiting at cabstands or in taxi lines at airports, train stations, hotels, and other places where people frequently seek taxis.

Some drivers transport individuals with special needs, such as those with disabilities and the elderly. They operate specially equipped vehicles designed to accommodate a variety of needs in non-emergency situations. Although special certification is not necessary, some additional training on the equipment and passenger needs may be required.

Drivers should be familiar with streets in the areas they serve so they can use the most efficient route to destinations. They should know the locations of frequently requested destinations, such as airports, bus and railroad terminals, convention centers, hotels, and other points of interest. In case of emergency, the driver should also know the location of fire and police stations and hospitals.

Upon reaching the destination, drivers determine the fare and announce it to the rider. Fares often consist of many parts. In many taxicabs, a taximeter measures the fare based on the length of the trip and the amount of time the trip took. Drivers turn the taximeter on when passengers enter the cab and turn it off when they reach the final destination. The fare may also include a surcharge for additional passengers, a fee for handling luggage, or a drop charge—an additional flat fee added for the use the cab. Passengers generally add a tip or gratuity to the fare. The amount of the gratuity depends on the passengers' satisfaction with the quality and efficiency of the ride and courtesy of the driver. Drivers issue receipts upon request from the passenger. They enter onto the trip sheet all information regarding the trip, including the place and time of pick-up and drop-off and the total fee. These logs help check the driver's activity and efficiency. Drivers also must fill out accident reports when necessary.

Chauffeurs operate limousines, vans, and private cars for limousine companies, private businesses, government agencies, and wealthy individuals. Many chauffeurs transport customers in large vans between hotels and airports, bus, or train terminals. Others drive luxury automobiles, such as limousines, to business events, entertainment venues, and social events. Still others provide full time personal transportation for wealthy families and private companies.

At the start of the workday, chauffeurs ready their automobiles or vans for use. They inspect the vehicle for cleanliness and, when needed, vacuum the interior and wash the exterior body, windows, and mirrors. They check fuel and oil levels and make sure the lights, tires, brakes, and windshield wipers work. Chauffeurs may

Taxi drivers should be familiar with frequently requested destinations in the areas they serve.

perform routine maintenance and make minor repairs, such as changing tires or adding oil and other fluids when needed. If a vehicle requires more complicated repair, they take it to a professional mechanic.

Chauffeurs cater to passengers with attentive customer service and a special regard for detail. They help riders into the car by holding open doors, holding umbrellas when raining, and loading packages and luggage into the trunk of the car. They may perform errands for their employers such as delivering packages or picking up clients arriving at airports. Many chauffeurs offer conveniences and luxuries in their limousines to insure a pleasurable ride, such as newspapers, magazines, music, drinks, televisions, and telephones. A growing number of chauffeurs work as full-service executive assistants, simultaneously acting as driver, secretary, and itinerary-planner.

Working Conditions

Taxi drivers and chauffeurs occasionally have to load and unload heavy luggage and packages. Driving for long periods can be tiring and uncomfortable, especially in densely populated urban areas. Drivers must be alert to conditions on the road, especially in heavy and congested traffic or in bad weather. They must take precautions to prevent accidents and avoid sudden stops, turns, and other driving maneuvers that would jar passengers. Taxi drivers also risk robbery because they work alone and often carry large amounts of cash.

Work hours of taxi drivers and chauffeurs vary greatly. Some jobs offer full-time or part-time employment with work hours that can change from day to day or remain the same every day. It is often necessary for drivers to report to work on short notice. Chauffeurs who work for a single employer may be on call much of the time. Evening and weekend work are common for limousine and taxicab services.

The needs of the client or employer dictate the work schedule for chauffeurs. The work of taxi drivers is much less structured. Working free from supervision, they may break for a meal or a rest whenever their vehicle is unoccupied. This occupation is attractive to individuals seeking flexible work schedules, such as college and post-graduate students. Similarly, other service workers such as ambulance drivers and police officers often consider moonlighting as taxi drivers and chauffeurs.

Full-time taxi drivers usually work one shift a day, which may last from 8 to 12 hours. Part-time drivers may work half a shift each day, or work a full shift once or twice a week. Drivers must be on duty at all times of the day and night, because most taxi companies offer services 24 hours a day. Early morning and late night shifts are common. Drivers work long hours during holidays, weekends, and other special events to support heavier demand for their services. Independent drivers, however, often set their own hours and schedules.

Design improvements in newer cabs have reduced stress and increased the comfort and efficiency of drivers. Many regulators require standard amenities such as air conditioning. Modern taxicabs are also sometimes equipped with sophisticated tracking devices, fare meters, and dispatching equipment. Satellites and tracking systems link many of these state-of-the-art vehicles with company headquarters. In a matter of seconds, dispatchers can deliver directions, traffic advisories, weather reports, and other important communications to drivers anywhere in the transporting area. The satellite link-up also allows dispatchers to track vehicle location, fuel consumption, and engine performance. Drivers can easily communicate with dispatchers to discuss delivery schedules and courses of action should there be mechanical problems. When threatened with crime or violence, drivers may have special "trouble lights" to alert authorities of emergencies and guarantee that help arrives quickly.

Taxi drivers and chauffeurs meet many different types of people. Dealing with rude customers and waiting for passengers requires patience. Many municipalities and taxicab and chauffeur companies require taxi drivers to wear clean and neat clothes. Many chauffeurs wear more formal attire; such as a tuxedo, a coat and tie, a dress, or a uniform and cap.

Employment

Taxi drivers and chauffeurs held about 132,000 jobs in 1998. About two-thirds were wage and salary workers employed by a company or business. Of these, over one half worked for local and suburban passenger transportation and taxicab companies. Others worked for service oriented companies such as automotive rental dealerships, hotels, health care facilities, and funeral homes. About a third were self-employed.

Training, Other Qualifications, and Advancement

Local governments set license standards and requirements for taxi drivers and chauffeurs. Although requirements vary, most municipalities have minimum qualifications for driving experience and training. Many taxi and limousine companies set higher standards than required by law. It is common for companies to review applicants' medical, credit, criminal, and driving records. In addition, many companies require a higher minimum age and prefer that drivers be high school graduates.

Persons interested in driving a limousine or taxicab must first have a regular automobile driver's license. They also must acquire a chauffeur or taxi driver's license, commonly called a "hack" license. Local authorities generally require applicants for a hack license to pass a written exam or complete a training program. To qualify through either an exam or a training program, applicants must know local geography, motor vehicle laws, safe driving practices, regulations governing taxicabs, and display some aptitude for customer service. Many training programs include a test on English proficiency, usually in the form of listening comprehension; applicants who do not pass the English exam must take an English course along with the formal driving program. Many taxicab or limousine companies sponsor applicants and give them a temporary permit that allows them to drive, although they may not yet have finished the training program or passed the test. However, some jurisdictions, such as New York City, have discontinued this practice and now require driver applicants to complete the licensing process before operating a taxi or limousine.

Some taxi and limousine companies give new drivers on-the-job training. They show drivers how to operate the taximeter and communications equipment, and how to complete paperwork. Other topics covered may include driver safety and popular sightseeing and entertainment destinations. Many companies have contracts with social service agencies and transportation services to transport elderly and disabled citizens in non-emergency situations. To support these services, new drivers may get special training on how to handle wheelchair lifts and other mechanical devices.

Taxi drivers and chauffeurs should be able to get along with many different types of people. They must be patient when waiting for passengers or when dealing with rude customers. It is also helpful for drivers to be tolerant and have even tempers when driving in heavy and congested traffic. Drivers should be dependable because passengers rely on them to be picked up at a prearranged time and taken to the correct destination. To be successful, drivers must be responsible and self-motivated because they work with little supervision. Increasingly, companies encourage drivers to develop their own loyal customer base to improve their businesses.

The majority of taxi drivers and chauffeurs are called "lease drivers." Lease drivers pay a daily, weekly, or monthly fee to the company allowing them to lease their vehicle. In the case of limousines, leasing also allows the driver access to the company's dispatch system. The fee may also include a charge for vehicle maintenance, insurance, and a deposit on the vehicle. Lease drivers may take their cars home with them when they are not on duty.

Opportunities for advancement are limited for taxi drivers and chauffeurs. Experienced drivers may obtain preferred routes or shifts. Some advance to dispatcher or manager jobs; others may start their own limousine company. On the other hand, many drivers like the independent, unsupervised work of driving their automobile.

In small and medium size communities, drivers are sometimes able to buy their taxi, limousine, or other type of automobile and go into business for themselves. These independent owner-drivers require an additional permit allowing them to operate their vehicle as a company. Some big cities limit the number of operating permits. In these cities, drivers become owner-drivers by buying permits from owner-drivers who leave the business. Although many owner-drivers are successful, some fail to cover expenses and eventually lose their permit and automobile. Good business sense and courses in accounting, business, and business arithmetic can help an owner-driver become successful. Knowledge of mechanics enables owner-drivers to perform routine maintenance and minor repairs to cut expenses.

Job Outlook

Persons seeking jobs as taxi drivers and chauffeurs should encounter good opportunities. Thousands of job openings will occur each year as drivers transfer to other occupations or leave the labor force. However, driving jobs vary greatly in terms of earnings, work hours, and working conditions. Opportunities should be best for persons with good driving records and the ability to work flexible schedules.

Employment of taxi drivers and chauffeurs is expected to grow as fast as the average for all occupations through the year 2008 as local and suburban travel increases with population growth. Opportunities should be best in rapidly growing metropolitan areas.

Job opportunities can fluctuate from season to season and from month to month. Extra drivers may be hired during holiday seasons and peak travel and tourist times. During economic slowdowns, drivers are seldom laid off but they may have to increase their working hours, and earnings may decline somewhat.

Earnings

Earnings of taxi drivers and chauffeurs vary greatly, depending on the number of hours worked, customers' tips, and other factors. Median hourly earnings of taxi drivers and chauffeurs, excluding tips, were $7.48 in 1998. The middle 50 percent earned between $6.02 and $9.79 an hour. The lowest 10 percent earned less than $5.55 and the highest 10 percent earned more than $12.44 an hour. Median hourly earnings in the industries employing the largest number of taxi drivers and chauffeurs in 1997 were as follows:

Local and suburban transportation	$8.30
Taxicabs	7.10
Automotive rentals, no drivers	6.40

According to limited information available, the majority of self-employed taxi owner-drivers earned from about $20,000 to $30,000 annually, including tips. However, professional drivers with a regular clientele often earn more. Many chauffeurs who worked full time earned from about $25,000 to $50,000, including tips. Earnings were generally higher in urban areas.

Related Occupations

Other workers who have similar jobs include personal attendants, tour and travel guides, busdrivers, truckdrivers, and subway and streetcar operators.

Sources of Additional Information

Information on licensing and registration of taxi drivers and chauffeurs is available from offices of local governments regulating taxicabs. For information about work opportunities as a taxi driver or chauffeur, contact local taxi or limousine companies or State employment service offices.

For general information about the work of taxi drivers and the taxi industry, contact:

☛ International Taxicab and Livery Association, 3849 Farragut Ave., Kensington, MD 20895. Internet: **http://www.taxinetwork.com**

For general information about the work of limousine drivers, contact:

☛ National Limousine Association, 900 North Pitt St., Suite 220, Alexandria, VA 22314. Telephone (toll free): 1-800-652-7007.

Truckdrivers

(O*NET 97102A, 97102B, 97105, and 97117)

Significant Points

- Opportunities in truckdriving should be good because this occupation has among the greatest number of job openings each year.
- Competition is expected for jobs offering the highest earnings or most favorable work schedules.
- A commercial drivers' license is required to operate most larger trucks.

Nature of the Work

Truckdrivers are a constant presence on the Nation's highways and interstates, delivering everything from automobiles to canned foods. Due to their ability to link up with ships, trains, and airplanes, trucks usually make the initial pickup and final delivery of goods. Trucks carry nearly all goods at some point in their journey from producer to consumer.

Before leaving the terminal or warehouse, truckdrivers check their trucks for fuel and oil. They also inspect the trucks to make sure the brakes, windshield wipers, and lights are working and that a fire extinguisher, flares, and other safety equipment are aboard and in working order. Drivers make sure their cargo is secure and adjust their mirrors so that both sides of the truck are visible from the driver's seat. Equipment that does not work, is missing, or not loaded properly is reported to the dispatcher.

Once underway, drivers must be alert to prevent accidents. Because drivers of large tractor-trailers sit higher than cars, pickups, and vans, they can see farther down the road. They seek traffic lanes that allow them to move at a steady speed, while keeping sight of varying road conditions.

The length of deliveries varies according to the merchandise being transported and the final destination of the goods. Local drivers may provide daily service for a specific route, while other drivers make inter-city and interstate deliveries that take longer and may vary from job to job. The driver's responsibilities and assignments change according to the time spent on the road and the type of payloads transported.

Short haul or *local truckdrivers* may be assigned short "turnarounds" to deliver a shipment to a nearby city, pick up another loaded trailer, and drive it back to their home base the same day. They usually load or unload the merchandise at the customer's place of business. Drivers may have helpers if there are many deliveries to make during the day or if the load requires heavy moving. Typically, before the driver arrives for work, material handlers load the trucks and arrange items in order of delivery to minimize handling of the merchandise. Customers must sign receipts for goods and pay drivers the balance due on the merchandise if there is a cash-on-delivery arrangement. At the end of the day, drivers turn in receipts, money, records of deliveries made, and any reports on mechanical problems with their trucks.

The work of local truckdrivers varies depending on the product they transport. Produce truckers usually pick up a loaded truck early in the morning and spend the rest of the day delivering produce to many different grocery stores. Lumber truckdrivers, on the other hand, make several trips from the lumber yard to one or more construction sites. Gasoline tank truckdrivers attach the hoses and operate the pumps on their trucks to transfer the gasoline to gas stations' storage tanks.

Some local truckdrivers have sales and customer relations responsibilities. The primary responsibility of *driver-sales workers*, or *route drivers*, is to deliver their firm's products and represent the company in a positive manner. Their response to customer complaints and requests for special services can make the difference between a large order and a lost customer. Route drivers also use their selling ability to increase sales and gain additional customers.

The duties of driver-sales workers vary according to their industry, the policies of their particular company, and the emphasis placed on their sales responsibility. Most have wholesale routes that deliver to businesses and stores rather than homes. For example, wholesale bakery driver-sales workers deliver and arrange bread, cakes, rolls, and other baked goods on display racks in grocery stores. They estimate the amount and variety of baked goods to stock by paying close attention to the items that sell well, and those sitting on the shelves. They may recommend changes in a store's order or may encourage the manager to stock new bakery products. Driver-sales workers employed by laundries that rent linens, towels, work clothes, and other items visit businesses regularly to replace soiled laundry. From time to time, they solicit new orders from businesses along their route.

Vending machine driver-sales workers service machines in factories, schools, and other buildings. They check items remaining in the machines, replace stock, and remove money deposited in the cash boxes. They also examine each vending machine to make minor repairs, clean machines, and to see merchandise and change are dispensed properly.

After completing their route, driver-sales workers order items for the next delivery based on what products have been selling well, the weather, time of year, and any customer feedback.

Long haul truckdrivers may haul loads from city to city for a week or more before returning home. Some companies use two drivers on very long runs—one drives while the other sleeps in a berth behind the cab. "Sleeper" runs may last for days, or even weeks, usually with the truck stopping only for fuel, food, loading, and unloading.

Some long-distance drivers who have regular runs transport freight to the same city on a regular basis. Other drivers perform unscheduled runs because shippers request varying service to different cities every day. Dispatchers tell these drivers when to report for work and where to haul the freight.

Truckdrivers make sure cargo is secure before departing for their destination.

After long-distance truckdrivers reach their destination or complete their operating shift, the U.S. Department of Transportation requires they complete reports detailing the trip, the condition of the truck, and the circumstances of any accidents. In addition, Federal regulations require employers to subject drivers to random alcohol and drug tests while on duty.

Long-distance truckdrivers spend most of their working time behind the wheel but may load or unload their cargo after arriving at the final destination. This is especially common when drivers haul specialty cargo, because they may be the only one at the destination familiar with this procedure or certified to handle the materials. Auto-transport drivers, for example, drive and position cars on the trailers and head ramps and remove them at the dealerships. When picking up or delivering furniture, drivers of long-distance moving vans hire local workers to help them load or unload.

Working Conditions

Truckdriving has become less physically demanding because most trucks now have more comfortable seats, better ventilation, and improved ergonomically designed cabs. Although these changes make the work environment more attractive, driving for many hours at a stretch, unloading cargo, and making many deliveries can be tiring. Local truckdrivers, unlike long-distance drivers, usually return home in the evening. Some self-employed long distance truckdrivers who own and operate their trucks spend most of the year away from home.

Design improvements in newer trucks reduce stress and increase the efficiency of long-distance drivers. Many of the newer trucks are virtual mini-apartments on wheels, equipped with refrigerators, televisions, and bunks. Satellites and Global Positioning Systems (GPS) link many of these state-of-the-art vehicles with company headquarters. Troubleshooting, directions, weather reports, and other important communications can be delivered to the truck anywhere in the country within seconds. Drivers can easily communicate with the dispatcher to discuss delivery schedules and courses of action in the event of mechanical problems. The satellite link-up also allows the dispatcher to track the truck's location, fuel consumption, and engine performance.

The U.S. Department of Transportation governs work hours and other working conditions of truckdrivers engaged in interstate commerce. For example, a long-distance driver cannot work more than 60 hours in any 7-day period. Federal regulations also require that truckers rest 8 hours for every 10 hours of driving. Many drivers, particularly on long runs, work close to the maximum time permitted because they are typically compensated by the number of miles or hours they drive. Drivers on long runs may face boredom, loneliness, and fatigue. Drivers frequently travel at night, on holidays, and weekends to avoid traffic delays and deliver cargo on time.

Local truckdrivers frequently work 50 or more hours a week. Many who handle food for chain grocery stores, produce markets, or bakeries work long hours starting late at night or early in the morning. Although most drivers have a regular route, some have different routes each day. Many local truckdrivers, particularly driver-sales workers, load and unload their own trucks. This requires considerable lifting, carrying, and walking each day.

Employment

Truckdrivers held about 3.3 million jobs in 1998. Most truckdrivers find employment in large metropolitan areas where major trucking, retail, and wholesale companies have distribution outlets. Some drivers work in rural areas providing specialized services, such as delivering milk to dairies or coal to a railroad.

Trucking companies employed about 30 percent of all truckdrivers in the United States. Thirty-five percent worked for companies engaged in wholesale or retail trade, such as auto parts stores, oil companies, lumber yards, or distributors of food and grocery products. The remaining truckdrivers were distributed across many industries, including construction, manufacturing, and services.

Fewer than 1 out of 10 truckdrivers were self-employed. Of these, a significant number were owner-operators who either serve a variety of businesses independently or lease their services and trucks to a trucking company.

Training, Other Qualifications, and Advancement

State and Federal regulations govern the qualifications and standards for truckdrivers. All drivers must comply with Federal regulations and any State regulations exceeding Federal requirements. Truckdrivers must have a driver's license issued by the State in which they live, and most employers require a clean driving record. Drivers of trucks designed to carry at least 26,000 pounds—including most tractor-trailers as well as bigger straight trucks—must obtain a commercial driver's license (CDL) from the State in which they live. All truckdrivers who operate trucks transporting hazardous materials must obtain a CDL regardless of truck size. Federal regulations governing the CDL exempt certain groups including farmers, emergency medical technicians, firefighters, some military drivers, and snow and ice removers. In many States, a regular driver's license is sufficient for driving light trucks and vans.

To qualify for a commercial driver's license, applicants must pass a written test on rules and regulations, and then demonstrate they can operate a commercial truck safely. A national data bank permanently records all driving violations incurred by persons who hold commercial licenses. A State will check these records and not issue a commercial driver's license to a driver who already has a license suspended or revoked in another State. Licensed drivers must accompany trainees until they get their own CDL. Information on how to apply for a commercial driver's license may be obtained from State motor vehicle administrations.

While many States allow those who are 18 years and older to drive trucks within State borders, the U.S. Department of Transportation establishes minimum qualifications for truckdrivers engaged in interstate commerce. Federal Motor Carrier Safety Regulations require drivers to be at least 21 years old and pass a physical examination once every 2 years. The main physical requirements include good hearing, 20/40 vision with or without glasses or corrective lenses, and a 70 degree field of vision in each eye. Drivers can not be color blind. Drivers must be able to hear a forced whisper in one ear at not less than 5 feet, with or without a hearing aide. Drivers must have normal use of arms and legs and normal blood pressure. Drivers can not use any controlled substances, unless prescribed by a licensed physician. Persons with epilepsy or diabetes controlled by insulin are not permitted to be interstate truckdrivers. Federal regulations also require employers to test their drivers for alcohol and drug use as a condition of employment, and require periodic random tests while on duty. In addition, a driver must not have been convicted of a felony involving the use of a motor vehicle; a crime using drugs; driving under the influence of drugs or alcohol; or hit-and-run driving which resulted in injury or death. All drivers must be able to read and speak English well enough to read road signs, prepare reports, and communicate with law enforcement officers and the public. Also, drivers must take a written examination on the Motor Carrier Safety Regulations of the U.S. Department of Transportation.

Many trucking operations have higher standards than those described. Many firms require that drivers be at least 25 years old, be able to lift heavy objects, and have driven trucks for 3 to 5 years. Many prefer to hire high school graduates and require annual physical examinations.

Driver-training courses are a desirable method of preparing for truckdriving jobs and for obtaining a commercial driver's license. High school courses in driver-training and automotive mechanics may also be helpful. Many private and public technical-vocational schools offer tractor-trailer driver training programs. Students learn to maneuver large vehicles on crowded streets and in highway traffic. They also learn to inspect the trucks and freight for compliance with Federal, State, and local regulations. Some programs provide only a limited amount of actual driving experience, and completion of a program does not assure a job. Persons interested in attending one of these schools should check with local trucking companies to make sure the school's training is acceptable.

Some States require prospective drivers to complete a training course in basic truckdriving before being issued their CDL. In Maine, for instance, prospective applicants must complete an 8-week course from a school certified by the Professional Truck Drivers Institute (PTDI). PTDI-certified schools provide training that meets Federal Highway Administration guidelines for training tractor-trailer drivers. Illinois requires the skills standards but drivers do not have to attend a certified school.

Drivers must get along well with people because they often deal directly with customers. Employers seek driver-sales workers who speak well and have self-confidence, initiative, tact, and a neat appearance. Employers also look for responsible, self-motivated individuals able to work with little supervision.

Training given to new drivers by employers is usually informal, and may consist of only a few hours of instruction from an experienced driver, sometimes on the new employee's own time. New drivers may also ride with and observe experienced drivers before assignment of their own runs. Drivers receive additional training to drive special types of trucks or handle hazardous materials. Some companies give 1 to 2 days of classroom instruction covering general duties, the operation and loading of a truck, company policies, and the preparation of delivery forms and company records. Driver-sales workers also receive training on the various types of products they carry so they will be more effective sales workers and better able to handle customer requests.

Very few people enter truckdriving professions directly out of school; most truckdrivers previously held jobs in other occupations. Driving experience in the Armed Forces can be an asset. In some instances, a person may also start as a truckdriver's helper, driving part of the day and helping to load and unload freight. Senior helpers receive promotion when driving vacancies occur.

Although most new truckdrivers are assigned immediately to regular driving jobs, some start as extra drivers, substituting for regular drivers who are ill or on vacation. They receive a regular assignment when an opening occurs.

New drivers sometimes start on panel, or other small "straight" trucks. As they gain experience and show competent driving skills, they may advance to larger and heavier trucks, and finally to tractor-trailers.

Advancement of truckdrivers is generally limited to driving runs that provide increased earnings or preferred schedules and working conditions. For the most part, a local truckdriver may advance to driving heavy or special types of trucks, or transfer to long-distance truckdriving. Working for companies that also employ long-distance drivers is the best way to advance to these positions. A few truckdrivers may advance to dispatcher, manager, or traffic work—for example, planning delivery schedules.

Some long-distance truckdrivers purchase a truck and go into business for themselves. Although many of these owner-operators are successful, some fail to cover expenses and eventually go out of business. Owner-operators should have good business sense as well as truckdriving experience. Courses in accounting, business, and business mathematics are helpful, and knowledge of truck mechanics can enable owner-operators to perform their own routine maintenance and minor repairs.

Job Outlook

Opportunities should be favorable for persons interested in truckdriving. This occupation has among the largest number of job openings each year. Although growth in demand for truckdrivers will create thousands of openings, the majority will occur as experienced drivers transfer to other fields of work, retire, or leave the labor force for other reasons. Jobs vary greatly in terms of earnings, weekly work hours, number of nights spent on the road, and in the quality of equipment operated. Because truckdriving does not require education beyond high school, competition is expected for jobs with the most attractive earnings and working conditions.

Employment of truckdrivers is expected to increase about as fast as the average for all occupations through the year 2008 as the economy grows and the amount of freight carried by trucks increases. The increased use of rail, air, and ship transportation requires truckdrivers to pick up and deliver shipments. Growth of long-distance drivers may slow as rail cars increasingly ship loaded trailers across country, but long-distance truckdrivers will continue to haul perishable and other time-sensitive goods.

Average growth of local and long-distance truckdriver employment will outweigh the slow growth in driver-sales worker jobs. The number of truckdrivers with sales responsibilities is expected to increase slower than the average for all other occupations because companies are increasingly splitting their responsibilities among other workers. They will shift sales, ordering, and customer service tasks to sales and office staffs, and use regular truckdrivers to make deliveries to customers.

Job opportunities may vary from year to year, because the strength of the economy dictates the amount of freight moved by trucks. Companies tend to hire more drivers when the economy is strong and deliveries are in high demand. Consequently, when the economy slows, employers hire fewer drivers or even lay off drivers. Independent owner-operators are particularly vulnerable to slowdowns. Industries least likely to be affected by economic fluctuation tend to be the most stable places for employment.

Earnings

Median hourly earnings of drivers of light and heavy trucks were $11.67 in 1998. The middle 50 percent earned between $8.80 and $15.57 an hour. The lowest 10 percent earned less than $6.51 and the highest 10 percent earned more than $19.14 an hour. Median annual earnings in the industries employing the largest numbers of heavy or tractor-trailer truckdrivers in 1997 were as follows:

Industry	Earnings
Trucking and courier services, except air	$14.10
Groceries and related products	13.30
Local government, except education and hospitals	11.60
Highway and street construction	11.40
Concrete, gypsum, and plaster products	11.20

Median annual earnings in the industries employing the largest number of light truckdrivers, including delivery and route workers, in 1997 were as follows:

Industry	Earnings
Air transportation, scheduled	$14.10
Trucking and courier services, except air	10.90
Groceries and related products	10.60
Motor vehicles, parts, and supplies	7.30
Eating and drinking places	5.70

Median hourly earnings of driver-sales workers, including commission, were $9.29 in 1998. The middle 50 percent earned between $6.13 and $13.06 an hour. The lowest 10 percent earned less than $5.58 and the highest 10 percent earned more than $17.41 an hour. Median annual earnings in the industries employing the largest number of driver-sales workers in 1997 were as follows:

Industry	Earnings
Laundry, cleaning, and garment services	$12.20
Groceries and related products	11.20
Nonstore retailers	9.30
Motor vehicles, parts, and supplies	7.00
Eating and drinking places	5.60

As a general rule, local truckdrivers receive an hourly wage and extra pay for working overtime, usually after 40 hours. Employers pay long-distance drivers primarily by the mile. Their rate per mile can vary greatly from employer to employer and may even depend on the type of cargo. Typically, earnings increase with mileage driven, seniority, and the size and type of truck driven. Most driver-sales workers receive a commission based on their sales in addition to an hourly wage.

Most self-employed truckdrivers are primarily engaged in long-distance hauling. After deducting their living expenses and the costs associated with operating their trucks, earnings of $20,000 to $25,000 a year are common.

Many truckdrivers are members of the International Brotherhood of Teamsters. Some truckdrivers employed by companies outside the trucking industry are members of unions representing the plant workers of the companies for which they work.

Related Occupations

Other driving occupations include ambulance driver, busdriver, chauffeur, and taxi driver.

Sources of Additional Information

Information on truckdriver employment opportunities is available from local trucking companies and local offices of the State employment service.

Information on career opportunities in truckdriving may be obtained from:

☛ American Trucking Associations, Inc., 2200 Mill Rd., Alexandria, VA 22314. Internet: **http://www.truckline.com**

☛ American Trucking Association Foundation, 660 Roosevelt Ave., Pawtucket, RI 02860

The Professional Truck Driver Institute of America, a nonprofit organization established by the trucking industry, manufacturers, and others, certifies truckdriver training programs meeting industry standards. A free list of certified tractor-trailer driver training programs may be obtained from:

☛ Professional Truck Driver Institute, 2200 Mill Rd., Alexandria, VA 22314, or by calling (703) 838-8842. Internet: **http://www.ptdia.org**

Water Transportation Occupations

(O*NET 97502A, 97505, 97508, 97514, 97517, and 97521)

Significant Points

- Many jobs in water transportation occupations require a merchant mariner's document or a license from the U.S. Coast Guard.
- Merchant mariners on ocean going ships are hired for periods ranging from a single voyage to several continuous voyages and may be away from home continuously for months.
- Jobs aboard ocean going vessels have high pay but competition for them remains keen and merchant mariners might have to wait months between work opportunities.

Nature of the Work

Movement of huge amounts of cargo, as well as passengers, between nations and within our nation depends on workers in water transportation occupations. They operate and maintain deep sea merchant ships, tugboats, towboats, ferries, dredges, excursion vessels, and other waterborne craft on the oceans, the Great Lakes, in harbors, on rivers and canals, and on other waterways. (Workers who operate water craft used in commercial fishing are described in the section on fishers and fishing vessel operators elsewhere in the *Handbook.*)

Captains or *masters* are in overall command of the operation of a vessel and they supervise the work of any other officers and crew. They determine the course and speed, maneuver to avoid hazards, and continuously monitor the vessel's position using charts and navigational aides. They either direct or oversee crew members who steer the vessel, determine its location, operate engines, communicate to other vessels, perform maintenance, handle lines, or operate vessel equipment. Captains and their department heads insure that proper procedures and safety practices are followed; check that machinery and equipment are in good working order; and oversee the loading and discharging of cargo or passengers. They also maintain logs and other records tracking the ships' movements, efforts at controlling pollution, and cargo/passenger carrying history.

Deck officers or *mates* perform the work for captains on vessels when they are on duty. Mates also supervise and coordinate activities for the crew aboard the ship. They inspect the cargo holds during loading to ensure the load is stowed according to specifications. Mates supervise crew members engaged in maintenance and the primary up-keep of the vessel. All mates stand watch for specified periods, usually 4 hours on and 8 hours off. However, on smaller vessels, there may be only one mate (called a pilot on some inland vessels) who alternates watches with the captain. The mate would assume command of the ship if the captain became incapacitated. When more than one mate is necessary aboard a ship, they are typically designated Chief Mate or First Mate, Second Mate, and Third Mate.

Marine or *ship engineers* operate, maintain, and repair propulsion engines, boilers, generators, pumps, and other machinery. Merchant marine vessels usually have four engineering officers: A chief engineer, and a first, second, and third assistant engineer. Assistant engineers stand periodic watches, overseeing the safe operation of engines and machinery.

Seamen, also called *deckhands* (particularly on inland waters), operate the vessel and its deck equipment under the direction of the ship's officers, and keep the non-engineering areas in good condition. They stand watch, looking out for other vessels and obstructions in the ship's path and navigational aids such as buoys and lighthouses. They also steer the ship, measure water depth in shallow water, and maintain and operate deck equipment such as lifeboats, anchors, and cargo-handling gear. When docking or departing, they handle lines. They also perform routine maintenance chores such as repairing lines, chipping rust, and painting and cleaning decks or other areas. Seamen may also load and unload cargo, if necessary. On vessels handling liquid cargo, they hook up hoses, operate pumps, and clean tanks. Deckhands on tugboats or tow vessels tie barges together into tow units, inspect them periodically, and disconnect them when the destination is reached. Larger vessels usually have a *boatswain* or head seaman.

Qualified members of the engine department, or QMED's, work in the engine spaces below decks under the direction of the ship's engineering officers. They lubricate gears, shafts, bearings, and other moving parts of engines and motors, read pressure and temperature gauges and record data, and may assist with repairs and adjust machinery.

A typical deep sea merchant ship has a captain, three deck officers or mates, a chief engineer and three assistant engineers, plus six or more non-officers, such as deck seamen, QMED's, and cooks or foodhandlers. The size and service of the ship determine the number of crew for a particular voyage. Small vessels operating in harbors, rivers, or along the coast may have a crew comprised only of a captain and one deckhand. The cooking responsibilities usually fall under the deckhands' duties. On larger coastal ships, the crew may include a captain, a mate or pilot, an engineer, and seven or eight seamen. Non-licensed positions on a large ship may include a full-time cook, an electrician, machinery mechanics, and a radio officer.

Water transportation workers move barges though locks on the Mississippi River.

Pilots guide ships in and out of harbors, through straits, and on rivers and other confined waterways where a familiarity with local water depths, winds, tides, currents, and hazards such as reefs and shoals are of prime importance. Pilots on river and canal vessels are usually regular crew members, like mates. Harbor pilots are generally independent contractors, who accompany vessels while they enter or leave port. They may pilot many ships in a single day.

Working Conditions

Merchant mariners spend extended periods at sea, and earn leave. Most are hired for one or more voyages that last for several months, although there is no job security after that voyage. Merchant marine officers and seamen, both veterans and beginners, are hired for voyages through union hiring halls or directly by shipping companies. Hiring halls prioritize the candidates by the length of time the person has been out of work, and fill open slots accordingly. Hiring halls are typically found in major seaports.

At sea, these workers usually stand watch for 4 hours and are off for 8 hours, 7 days a week. Those employed on Great Lakes ships work 60 days and have 30 days off, but do not work in the winter when the lakes are frozen. Workers on rivers, canals, and in harbors are more likely to have year-round work. Some work 8- or 12-hour shifts and go home every day. Others work steadily for a week or month and then have an extended period off. When working, they are usually on duty for 6 or 12 hours and are off for 6 or 12 hours.

People in water transportation occupations work in all weather conditions. Although merchant mariners try to avoid severe storms while at sea, working in damp and cold conditions is often inevitable. While it is uncommon nowadays for vessels to suffer sea disasters such as fire, explosion, or a sinking, workers face the possibility that they may have to abandon their craft on short notice if it collides with other vessels or runs aground. They also risk injury or death from falling overboard, and hazards associated with working with machinery, heavy loads, and dangerous cargo.

Most newer vessels are air-conditioned, soundproofed from noisy machinery, and equipped with comfortable living quarters. Nevertheless, some mariners dislike the long periods away from home and the confinement aboard ship, and consequently leave the industry.

Employment

Water transportation workers held about 56,000 jobs in 1998. The total number who worked at some point in the year was somewhat higher because many merchant marine officers and seamen worked only part of the year. The following tabulation shows employment in the occupations that make up this group:

Able seamen, ordinary seamen, and deckhands	23,000
Ship captains and pilots	19,000
Ship, boat, and barge mates	8,000
Ship engineers	6,000

Over 2,900 of the captains and pilots were self-employed, operating their own vessel, or were pilots who were independent contractors.

About 30 percent of all water transportation workers were employed on board merchant marine ships or U.S. Navy Military Sealift ships operating on the oceans or Great Lakes. Another 47 percent were employed in water transportation services, working on tugs, towboats, ferries, dredges, and other watercraft in harbors, on rivers and canals, and other waterways. Others worked in water transportation services such as piloting vessels in and out of harbors, operating lighters and chartered boats, and in marine construction, salvaging, and surveying. The remaining water transportation workers were employed on vessels that carry passengers, such as cruise ships, casino boats, sightseeing and excursion boats, and ferries.

Training and Other Qualifications

Entry, training, and educational requirements for most water transportation occupations are established and regulated by the U.S. Coast Guard, an agency of the U.S. Department of Transportation. All officers and operators of watercraft must be licensed by the U.S. Coast Guard, which offers various kinds of licenses, depending on the position and type of craft.

To qualify for a deck or engineering officer's license, applicants usually must have graduated from the U.S. Merchant Marine Academy, or one of the six State academies, and pass a written examination. Federal regulations also require that an applicant pass a physical examination and a drug screening before being considered. Persons without formal training can be licensed if they pass the written exam and possess at least 3 years of appropriate sea experience. However, it is difficult to pass the examination without substantial formal schooling or independent study. Also, because seamen may work 6 months a year or less, it can take 5 to 8 years to accumulate the necessary experience. The academies offer a 4-year academic program leading to a bachelor of science degree, a license as a third mate (deck officer) or third assistant engineer (engineering officer) issued by the U.S. Coast Guard, and a commission as ensign in the U.S. Naval Reserve, Merchant Marine Reserve, or the Coast Guard Reserve. With experience and additional training, third officers may qualify for higher rank. Because of keen competition, however, officers may have to take jobs below the grade for which they are licensed.

For employment in the merchant marine as an unlicensed seaman, a merchant mariner's document issued by the U.S. Coast Guard is needed. Most of the jobs must be filled by U.S. citizens. However, a small percentage of applicants for merchant mariner documents do not need to be U.S. citizens, but must at least be aliens legally admitted into the U.S. and holding a green card. A medical certificate of excellent health and a certificate attesting to vision, color perception, and general physical condition may be required for higher-level deckhands. While no experience or formal schooling is required, training at a union-operated school is the best source. Beginners are classified as ordinary seamen and may be assigned to any of the three unlicensed departments: deck, engine, or steward. With experience at sea, and perhaps union-sponsored training, an ordinary seaman can pass the able seaman exam and move up with 3 years of service.

No special training or experience is needed to become a seaman or deckhand on vessels operating in harbors or on rivers or other waterways. Newly hired workers are generally given a short introductory course and then learn skills on the job. After sufficient experience, they are eligible to take a Coast Guard exam to qualify as a mate, pilot, or captain. Substantial knowledge gained through experience, courses taught at approved schools, and independent study are needed to pass the exam.

Harbor pilot training is usually an extended apprenticeship with a towing company or a pilot association. Entrants may be able seamen or licensed officers.

Job Outlook

Keen competition is expected to continue for jobs in water transportation occupations. Overall, employment in water transportation occupations is projected to grow more slowly than the average for all occupations through the year 2008. Opportunities will vary by sector.

Employment in deep sea shipping for American mariners is expected to stabilize after several years of decline. New international regulations have raised shipping standards with respect to safety, training, and working conditions. Consequently, competition from ships that sail under foreign flags of convenience (FOCs) should lessen as insurance rates rise for ships that don't meet the new standards. Insuring ships under industrialized countries' flags, including that of the United States, should become less expensive, increasing the amount of international cargo carried by U.S. ships. A fleet of deep sea U.S. flagged ships is considered to be vital to the Nation's defense, so some receive Federal support through a maritime security subsidy and other provisions in laws limit certain Federal cargoes to ships that fly the U.S. flag.

Newer ships are designed to be operated safely by much smaller crews. Innovations include automated controls and computerized monitoring systems in navigation, engine control, watchkeeping, ship management, and cargo handling. Possible future developments include "fast ships," ocean-going cargo vessels that use jet propulsion, which would decrease ocean-crossing times significantly. If such plans are successful, the industry will benefit in terms of increased business and employment. As older vessels are replaced, crew responsibilities will change. Seamen will need to learn new skills to be able to handle these varied duties.

Vessels on rivers and canals and on the Great Lakes carry mostly bulk products such as coal, iron ore, petroleum, sand and gravel, grain, and chemicals. Though shipments of these products are expected to grow through the year 2008, current imports of steel are dampening employment on the Lakes. Employment in water transportation services is likely to rise, however.

Growth is also expected in the cruise line industry within U.S. waters. Vessels that operate between U.S. ports are required by law to be U.S. flagged vessels. The building and staffing of several new cruise ships over the next 3 to 4 years will create new opportunities for employment at sea in the cruise line industry, which is composed mostly of foreign flagged ships.

Nevertheless, openings within the traditional industrial sectors for mariners, though expanding slightly, will remain tight. Many experienced merchant mariners may continue to go for periods of time without work. As a result, unions have been traditionally slow to accept new members. However, this situation appears to be changing, as the demand for non-licensed personnel has been on the rise. Also, many maritime academy graduates have not found licensed shipboard jobs in the U.S. merchant marine, although most do find jobs in related industries. Because they are commissioned as ensigns in the U.S. Naval or Coast Guard Reserve, some are selected for active duty in the Navy or Coast Guard. Some find jobs as seamen on U.S. flagged or foreign flagged vessels, tugboats, other watercraft, or enter civilian jobs with the U.S. Navy. Some take land-based jobs with shipping companies, marine insurance companies, manufacturers of boilers or related machinery, or other related jobs.

Earnings

Earnings vary widely depending on the particular water transportation position and experience, ranging from the minimum wage in some beginning seamen or mate positions to more than $35.00 an hour for some experienced captains and ship engineers. The following tabulation presents 1998 median hourly earnings for water transportation occupations:

Occupation	Earnings
Captains and pilots	$19.81
Ship engineers	19.31
Ship, boat, and barge mates	14.09
Able seamen, ordinary seamen, and deckhands	11.40

Related Occupations

Workers in occupations having duties and responsibilities similar to these occupations include fishing vessel captains, ferryboat operators, and longshoremen.

Sources of Additional Information

Information on merchant marine careers, training, and licensing requirements is available from:

☛ Maritime Administration, U.S. Department of Transportation, 400 7th St. SW., Room 7302, Washington, DC 20590.

☛ Seafarers' International Union, 5201 Auth Way, Camp Springs, MD 20746.

☛ Paul Hall Center for Maritime Training and Education, P.O. Box 75, Piney Point, MD 20674-0075.

☛ U.S. Coast Guard National Maritime Center, Licensing and Evaluation Branch, 4200 Wilson Boulevard, Suite 510, Arlington, VA 22203.

Individuals interested in attending a merchant marine academy should contact:

☛ Admissions Office, U.S. Merchant Marine Academy, Steamboat Rd., Kings Point, NY 11024.

Handlers, Equipment Cleaners, Helpers, and Laborers

(O*NET 93956, 93997, 93998, 93999, 97805, 97808, 98102, 98311, 98312, 98313, 98314, 98315, 98319, 98323, 98502, 98702, 98705, 98799A, 98799B, 98902A, 98905, 98999A, and 98999B)

Significant Points

- Job openings should be numerous because the occupation is very large and turnover is relatively high.
- Most jobs require no work experience or specific training, but earnings are low.

Nature of the Work

Employers in almost all industries hire entry level workers to do tasks requiring little training, or to assist more skilled production, construction, operating, and maintenance workers. These entry level workers perform a broad array of material mover, helper, or laborer jobs, ranging from moving boxes and feeding machines, to cleaning equipment and work areas. Many do tasks that are needed to make the work of more skilled employees flow smoothly. Handlers, equipment cleaners, helpers, and laborers often do routine physical work under close supervision. They generally follow oral or written instructions from supervisors or more experienced workers, and have little opportunity to make decisions. To perform their jobs effectively, helpers and laborers must be familiar with the duties of the workers they help, as well as with the materials, tools, and machinery they use.

Freight, stock, and material hand movers move materials to and from storage and production areas, loading docks, delivery vehicles, ships, and containers. They move materials either manually, or with forklifts, dollies, handtrucks, or carts. Their specific duties vary by industry and work setting. Specialized workers within this group include stevedores, who load and unload ships; baggage and cargo handlers, who work in transportation industries; and furniture movers. In factories, they may move raw materials, components, and finished goods between loading docks, storage areas, and work areas. They receive and sort materials and supplies and prepare them according to work orders for delivery to work or storage areas.

Hand packers and *packagers* manually pack, package or wrap a variety of materials. They may inspect items for defects, label cartons, stamp information on products, keep records of items packed, and stack packages on loading docks. This group also includes order fillers, who pack materials for shipment, as well as grocery store courtesy clerks. In grocery stores, they may bag groceries, carry packages to customers' cars, and return shopping carts to designated areas.

Machine feeders and *offbearers* feed materials into or remove materials from automatic equipment or machines tended by other workers.

Service station attendants fill fuel tanks and wash windshields on automobiles, buses, trucks, and other vehicles. They may perform simple service and repair tasks under the direction of a mechanic, such as change oil, repair tires, and replace belts, lights, windshield wipers, and other accessories. They may also collect payment for services and supplies.

Refuse and *recyclable material collectors* gather trash, garbage, and recyclables from homes and businesses along a regularly scheduled route, and deposit the refuse in their truck for transport to a dump, landfill, or recycling center. They lift and empty garbage cans or recycling bins by hand, or operate a hydraulic lift truck that picks up and empties dumpsters.

Vehicle washers and *equipment cleaners* clean machinery, vehicles, storage tanks, pipelines, and similar equipment using water and other cleaning agents, vacuums, hoses, brushes, cloths, and other cleaning equipment.

Parking lot attendants assist customers in parking their cars in lots or storage areas and collect fees from customers.

Helpers assist skilled construction trades workers, mechanics and repairers, and workers in production and extractive occupations. (Statements on these occupations appear elsewhere in the *Handbook*.) They aid machine operators and tenders by moving materials, supplies, and tools to and from work areas. Some may tend machines if an operator is not available. Helpers may sort finished products, keep records of machine processes, report malfunctions to operators, and clean machinery after use. Mechanics' helpers assist mechanics and service technicians who repair motor vehicles, industrial machinery, and electrical, electronic, and other equipment. They may fetch tools, materials, and supplies; hold materials or tools; take apart defective equipment; remove rivets; prepare replacement parts; or clean work areas. Construction trades' helpers carry tools, materials, and equipment to carpenters, electricians, plasterers, masons, painters, plumbers, roofers, and other construction trades workers.

Freight, stock, and material movers handle a variety of materials, including furniture.

Construction craft laborers are skilled workers who provide much of the physically demanding labor at construction projects, tunnel and shaft excavations, hazardous waste removal projects, and demolition sites. They clean and prepare sites, dig trenches, mix and place concrete, and set braces to support the sides of excavations. At hazardous waste removal projects, they perform material and atmospheric sampling; build, clean, and decontaminate enclosure structures; and package and transport hazardous materials. Other highly specialized tasks include operating laser guidance equipment to place pipes, and setting explosives for tunnel, shaft, and road construction. In addition to these duties, construction craft laborers may assist other craft workers.

Construction craft laborers operate a variety of equipment including pavement breakers; jackhammers; earth tampers; concrete, mortar, and plaster mixers; guided boring machines; small mechanical hoists; laser beam equipment; and surveying and measuring equipment.

Working Conditions

Most handlers, equipment cleaners, helpers, and laborers do repetitive, physically demanding work. They may lift and carry heavy objects, and stoop, kneel, crouch, or crawl in awkward positions. Some work at great heights, or outdoors in all weather conditions. Some jobs expose workers to harmful materials or chemicals, fumes, odors, loud noise, or dangerous machinery. To avoid injury, these employees wear safety clothing, such as gloves and hard hats, and devices to protect their eyes, mouth, or hearing.

Handlers, equipment cleaners, helpers, and laborers generally work 8-hour shifts, though longer shifts are also common. In many industries, handlers, equipment cleaners, helpers, and laborers work evening or "graveyard" shifts. Service station and parking lot attendants may work at night because these establishments may be open at all hours; handlers in grocery stores may stock shelves at night when stores are closed. Refuse and recyclable material collectors often work early morning shifts, starting at 5:00 or 6:00. Construction helpers and construction craft laborers may only work during certain seasons, when the weather permits construction activity.

Employment

Handlers, equipment cleaners, helpers, and laborers held about 5.1 million jobs in 1998. Their employment was distributed among the following detailed occupations:

Occupation	Jobs
Hand packers and packagers	984,000
Freight, stock, and material movers, hand	822,000
Helpers, construction trades	576,000
Cleaners of vehicles and equipment	288,000
Machine feeders and offbearers	213,000
Service station attendants	141,000
Refuse and recyclable materials collectors	99,000
Parking lot attendants	86,000
All other helpers, laborers, and material movers, hand	1,934,000

Handlers, equipment cleaners, helpers, and laborers are employed throughout the country in virtually all industries, with the greatest numbers concentrated in manufacturing, construction, wholesale and retail trade, and personnel supply services. Nearly 1 out of 4 works part time. A growing number are employed on a temporary or contract basis, many through firms providing personnel supply services. For example, companies that only need a laborer for a few days to move materials or clean up a site may contract with temporary help agencies specializing in providing this type of worker on a short-term basis.

Training, Other Qualifications, and Advancement

For most handler, equipment cleaner, helper, and laborer jobs, employers hire people without work experience or specific training. Some require a high school diploma, while others do not. Most employers, however, require workers to be at least 18 years old and physically able to perform the work. For those jobs requiring physical exertion, employers may require that applicants pass a physical exam. Some employers also require drug testing or background checks prior to employment. These workers are often younger than workers in other occupations—reflecting the limited training but significant physical requirements of many of these jobs.

For all of these jobs, employers look for people who are reliable and hard working. For those jobs that involve dealing with the public, such as grocery store helpers and service station or parking lot attendants, workers should be pleasant and courteous. Most jobs require reading and basic mathematics skills to read procedures manuals, billing, and other documents, and to collect payment for services from customers.

Handlers, equipment cleaners, helpers, and laborers generally learn skills informally, on the job from more experienced workers or supervisors. However, workers who use dangerous equipment or handle toxic chemicals usually receive specialized training in safety awareness and procedures.

Formal apprenticeship programs provide more thorough preparation for jobs as construction craft laborers. Local apprenticeship programs are operated under guidelines established by the Laborers-Associated General Contractors of America (AGC) Education and Training Fund. Programs include at least 4,000 hours of on-the job training, with 144 hours of classroom training. Most union contractors and laborer unions require some training before an apprentice is placed on the job. Apprentices are instructed in the correct use of numerous tools and equipment that must be mastered before they complete the program.

Experience in many of these jobs may allow workers to qualify or become trainees for other skilled positions as construction trades workers, machine operators, assemblers, or other production workers; transportation, material moving equipment, or vehicle operators; or mechanics or repairers. In fact, many employers prefer to promote qualified handlers, equipment cleaners, helpers, and laborers as openings arise. Some may eventually advance to become supervisors.

Job Outlook

Employment of handlers, equipment cleaners, helpers, and laborers is expected to grow about as fast as the average for all occupations through the year 2008. Job openings should be numerous because the occupation is very large and turnover is relatively high—characteristic of occupations requiring little formal training. Many openings will arise from the need to replace workers who retire, transfer to other occupations, or who leave the labor force for other reasons.

Projected employment growth varies by detailed occupation. Among service station attendants and machine feeders and offbearers, employment is expected to decline slightly. Employment of freight, stock, and other material hand movers is expected to experience little change. Slower-than-average growth is expected for refuse and recyclable materials collectors and construction trades helpers. Finally, driven largely by rapid growth in the industries in which they are most concentrated, faster-than-average growth is expected for vehicle washers and equipment cleaners, hand packers and packagers, and parking lot attendants.

Overall, demand for handlers, equipment cleaners, helpers, and laborers depends not only on growth in the industries employing these workers, but also on growth among the skilled workers whom they assist. Slower-than-average growth among construction trades helpers, for example, is directly related to expectations of employment growth among construction trades workers. However, growth of helper and construction craft laborer employment will be spurred by continuing emphasis on hazardous waste cleanup and other environmental projects, and on rebuilding infrastructure—roads, bridges, tunnels, and communications facilities, for example.

Employment growth will also be affected by automation. Some of these jobs are repetitive and, therefore, easily replaced by new machines and equipment that improve productivity and quality control. Automated ticketing equipment, for example, reduces the need for parking lot attendants to issue tickets by hand. Some helper, handler, and hand packer and packaging jobs will be eliminated by automated material handling equipment, such as conveyor belts and computer-controlled lift mechanisms, and machines that automatically load, unload, and package materials. As more skilled jobs, such as those of assemblers, become automated, demand for these types of employees who assist them will decline.

Many employers have also begun combining job responsibilities or contracting out labor. Job combinations may lead to displacement of handlers, equipment cleaners, helpers, and laborers because their tasks may be assumed by more highly skilled workers. In other cases, a helper may assist more than one type of worker, reducing the number of helpers needed. In addition, these occupations may increasingly be staffed by contingent workers as more employers turn to hiring temporary handlers, equipment cleaners, helpers, and laborers.

Earnings

Median hourly earnings of hand packers and packagers in 1998 were $6.99. The middle 50 percent earned between $5.90 and $8.65 an hour. The lowest 10 percent earned less than $5.54 an hour; the highest 10 percent earned more than $10.74. Median hourly earnings in 1997 in the industries employing the largest numbers of hand packers and packagers are shown below:

Meat products	$8.20
Miscellaneous plastics products, not elsewhere classified	8.00
Miscellaneous business services	6.80
Personnel supply services	6.40
Grocery stores	5.70

In 1998, median hourly earnings were $8.88 for freight, stock, and material movers, hand. The middle 50 percent earned between $7.09 and $11.23 an hour. The lowest 10 percent earned less than $5.99 an hour; the highest 10 percent earned more than $14.79.

Median hourly earnings of construction trades helpers were $9.38 in 1998. The middle 50 percent earned between $7.50 and $11.49 an hour. The lowest 10 percent earned less than $6.34 an hour; the highest 10 percent earned more than $15.68.

Median hourly earnings for other handlers, equipment cleaners, helpers, and laborers in 1998 are shown below:

Refuse and recyclable material collectors	$10.51
Machine feeders and offbearers	9.04
Cleaners of vehicles and equipment	6.99
Service station attendants	6.90
Parking lot attendants	6.69

Construction craft laborers generally have higher weekly earnings than other workers in this group. However, they may be more likely to lose work time because of bad weather and the cyclical nature of construction work.

About 1 in 5 handlers, equipment cleaners, helpers, and laborers are members of a union. Many belong to the Laborers' International Union of North America.

Related Occupations

Other entry level workers who perform mostly physical work include roustabouts in the oil industry, certain timber cutting and logging occupations, and groundskeepers. The jobs of handlers, equipment cleaners, helpers, and laborers are often similar to those of the more experienced workers they assist, including machine operators, construction craft workers, assemblers, mechanics, and repairers.

Sources of Additional Information

For information about jobs as handlers, equipment cleaners, helpers, and laborers, contact local building or construction contractors, manufacturers, and wholesale and retail establishments, or the local office of the State employment service.

For general information about the work of construction craft laborers, contact:

☛ Laborers' International Union of North America, 905 16th St. NW., Washington, DC 20006. Internet: **http://www.liuna.org**

For general information about the work of vehicle cleaners, contact:

☛ International Carwash Association, 401 N. Michigan Ave., Chicago, IL 60611. Internet: **http://www.carwashes.com**

Job Opportunities in the Armed Forces

(O*NET 99003)

Significant Points

- Opportunities should be good in all branches of the Armed Forces for applicants who meet designated standards.
- Enlisted personnel need at least a high school diploma, while officers need a bachelor's or advanced degree.
- Hours and working conditions can be arduous and vary substantially.
- Some training and duty assignments are hazardous, even in peacetime.

Nature of the Work

Maintaining a strong national defense encompasses such diverse activities as running a hospital, commanding a tank, programming computers, operating a nuclear reactor, or repairing and maintaining a helicopter. The military provides training and work experience in these fields and many others for over 1.2 million people who serve in the active Army, Navy, Marine Corps, Air Force, and Coast Guard, their Reserve components, and the Air and Army National Guard.

The military distinguishes between enlisted and officer careers. Enlisted personnel comprise about 85 percent of the Armed Forces and carry out the fundamental operations of the military in areas such as combat, administration, construction, engineering, health care, and human resources. Officers, who make up the remaining 15 percent of the Armed Forces, are the leaders of the military. They supervise and manage activities in every occupational specialty in the military.

The following sections discuss the major occupational groups for enlisted personnel and officers.

Enlisted occupational groups:

Administrative careers include a wide variety of positions. The military must keep accurate information for planning and managing its operations. Paper and electronic records are kept on equipment, funds, personnel, supplies, and other property of the military. Enlisted administrative personnel record information, type reports, and maintain files to assist military offices. Personnel may work in a specialized area such as finance, accounting, legal, maintenance, or supply.

Combat specialty occupations refer to those enlisted specialties, such as infantry, artillery, and special forces, that operate weapons or execute special missions during combat situations. They normally specialize by the type of weapon system or combat operation. These personnel maneuver against enemy forces, and position and fire artillery, guns, and missiles to destroy enemy positions. They may also operate tanks and amphibious assault vehicles in combat or scouting missions. When the military has difficult and dangerous missions to perform, they call upon special operations teams. These elite combat forces stay in a constant state of readiness to strike anywhere in the world on a moment's notice. Special operations forces team members conduct offensive raids, demolitions, intelligence, search and rescue, and other missions from aboard aircraft, helicopters, ships, or submarines.

Construction occupations in the military include personnel who build or repair buildings, airfields, bridges, foundations, dams, bunkers, and the electrical and plumbing components of these structures. Enlisted personnel in construction occupations operate bulldozers, cranes, graders, and other heavy equipment. Construction specialists may also work with engineers and other building specialists as part of military construction teams. Some personnel specialize in areas such as plumbing or electrical wiring. Plumbers and pipe fitters install and repair the plumbing and pipe systems needed in buildings, on aircraft, and ships. Building electricians install and repair electrical wiring systems in offices, airplane hangars, and other buildings on military bases.

Electronic and electrical equipment repair personnel repair and maintain electronic and electrical equipment used in the military today. Repairers normally specialize by type of equipment being repaired, such as avionics, computer, communications, or weapons systems. For example, avionics technicians install, test, maintain, and repair a wide variety of electronic systems including navigational and communications equipment on aircraft. Weapons maintenance technicians maintain and repair weapons used by combat forces, most of which have electronic components and systems that assist in locating targets, aiming weapons, and firing them.

The military has many *engineering, science, and technical* occupations that require specific knowledge to operate technical equipment, solve complex problems or to provide and interpret information. Enlisted personnel normally specialize in an area such as information technology, space operations, environmental health and safety, or intelligence. Information technology specialists, for example, develop software programs and operate computer systems. Space operations specialists use and repair spacecraft ground control command equipment, including electronic systems that track spacecraft location and operation. Environmental health and safety specialists inspect military facilities and food supplies for the presence of disease, germs, or other conditions hazardous to health and the environment. Intelligence specialists gather and study information using aerial photographs and various types of radar and surveillance systems.

Health care personnel assist medical professionals in treating and providing services for patients. They may work as part of a patient service team in close contact with doctors, dentists, nurses, and physical therapists to provide the necessary support functions within a hospital or clinic. Health care specialists normally specialize in a particular area. They may provide emergency medical treatment, operate diagnostic equipment such as X-ray and ultrasound equipment, conduct laboratory tests on tissue and blood samples, maintain pharmacy supplies, or maintain patient records.

Human resource development specialists recruit and place qualified personnel, and provide the training programs necessary to help people perform their jobs effectively. Personnel in this career area normally specialize by activity. Recruiting specialists, for example, provide information about military careers to young people, parents, schools, and local communities. They explain service employment and training opportunities, pay and benefits, and the nature of service life. Personnel specialists collect and store information about people's careers in the military, including training, job assignment, promotion, and health information. Training specialists and instructors provide military personnel with the knowledge needed to perform their jobs.

Machine operator and production careers include occupations that require the operation of industrial equipment, machinery, and tools to fabricate and repair parts for a variety of items and structures. They may operate boilers, turbines, nuclear reactors, and portable generators aboard ships and submarines. Personnel often specialize by type of work performed. Welders, for instance, work with various types of metals to repair or form the structural parts of ships, submarines, buildings, or other equipment. Other specialists inspect, maintain, and repair survival equipment such as parachutes and aircraft life support equipment.

Media and public affairs careers include those occupations that are involved in the public presentation and interpretation of military information and events. Enlisted media and public affairs personnel take and develop photographs; film, record, and edit audio and video programs; present news and music programs; and produce graphic artwork, drawings, and other visual displays. Other public affairs specialists act as interpreters and translators to convert written or spoken foreign languages into English or other languages.

Protective service personnel enforce military laws and regulations and provide emergency response to natural and man made disasters. Personnel normally specialize by function. Specialists in emergency management implement response procedures for all types of disasters, such as floods, earthquakes, hurricanes, or enemy attack. Military police control traffic, prevent crime, and respond to emergencies. Other law enforcement and security specialists investigate crimes committed on military property and guard inmates in military correctional facilities. Firefighters put out, control, and help prevent fires in buildings, aircraft, and aboard ships.

Support services occupations include subsistence services and occupations that support the morale and well-being of military personnel and their families. Food service specialists prepare all types of food in dining halls, hospitals, and ships. Counselors help military personnel and their families to overcome social problems. They work as part of a team that may include social workers, psychologists, medical officers, chaplains, personnel specialists, and commanders. The military also provides chaplains and religious program specialists to help meet the spiritual needs of its personnel. Religious program specialists assist chaplains with religious services, religious education programs, and administrative duties.

Transportation and material handling specialists ensure the safe transport of people and cargo. Most personnel within this occupational group are classified according to mode of transportation (i.e. aircraft, automotive vehicle, or ship). Air crew members operate equipment on board aircraft during operations. Vehicle drivers operate all types of heavy military vehicles including fuel or water tank trucks, semi-tractor trailers, heavy troop transports, and passenger buses. Boat operators navigate and pilot many types of small water craft, including tugboats, gunboats, and barges. Cargo specialists load and unload military supplies and material using equipment such as forklifts and cranes.

Vehicle and machinery mechanics conduct preventive and corrective maintenance on aircraft, automotive and heavy equipment, heating and cooling systems, marine engines, and powerhouse station equipment. They typically specialize by the type of equipment that they maintain. Aircraft mechanics inspect, service, and repair helicopters and airplanes. Automotive and heavy equipment mechanics maintain and repair vehicles such as jeeps, cars, trucks, tanks, self-propelled missile launchers, and other combat vehicles. They also repair bulldozers, power shovels, and other construction equipment. Heating and cooling mechanics install and repair air conditioning, refrigeration, and heating equipment. Marine engine mechanics repair and maintain gasoline and diesel engines on ships, boats, and other water craft. They also repair shipboard mechanical and electrical equipment. Powerhouse mechanics install, maintain, and repair electrical and mechanical equipment in power-generating stations.

Many occupations in the Armed Forces are becoming increasingly technical.

Officer occupational groups:

Combat specialty officers plan and direct military operations, oversee combat activities, and serve as combat leaders. This category includes officers in charge of tanks and other armored assault vehicles, artillery systems, special forces, and infantry. They normally specialize by type of unit that they lead. Within the unit, they may specialize by the type of weapon system. Artillery and missile system officers, for example, direct personnel as they target, launch, test, and maintain various types of missiles and artillery. Special forces officers lead their units in offensive raids, demolitions, intelligence gathering, and search and rescue missions.

Engineering, science, and technical officers have a wide range of responsibilities based on their area of expertise. They lead or perform activities in areas such as information technology, environmental health and safety, and engineering. These officers may direct the operations of communications centers or the development of complex computer systems. Environmental health and safety officers study the air, ground, and water to identify and analyze sources of pollution and its effects. They also direct programs to control safety and health hazards in the work place. Other personnel work as aerospace engineers to design and direct the development of military aircraft, missiles, and spacecraft.

Executive, administrative, and managerial officers oversee and direct military activities in key functional areas such as finance, accounting, health administration, logistics, and supply. Health services administrators, for instance, are responsible for the overall quality of care provided at the hospitals and clinics they operate. They must ensure that each department works together to provide the highest quality of care. As another example, the military buys billions of dollars worth of equipment, supplies, and services from private industry each year. Purchasing and contracting managers negotiate and monitor contracts for purchasing equipment, materials, and services.

Health care officers provide health services at military facilities based on their area of specialization. Officers who examine, diagnose, and treat patients with illness, injury, or disease include physicians, registered nurses, and dentists. Other health care officers provide therapy, rehabilitative treatment, and other services for patients. Physical and occupational therapists plan and administer therapy to help patients adjust to disabilities, regain independence, and return to work. Speech therapists evaluate and treat patients with hearing and speech problems. Dietitians manage food service facilities and plan meals for hospital patients and outpatients who need special diets. Pharmacists manage the purchasing, storing, and dispensing of drugs and medicines.

Human resource development officers manage recruitment, placement, and training strategies and programs in the military. Personnel in this area normally specialize by activity. Recruiting managers direct recruiting efforts and provide information about military careers to young people, parents, schools, and local communities. Personnel managers direct military personnel functions such as job assignment, staff promotion, and career counseling. Training and education directors identify training needs and develop and manage educational programs designed to keep military personnel current in the skills they need to perform their jobs.

Support services officers include personnel who manage food service activities and perform services in support of the morale and well being of military personnel and their families. Food service managers oversee the preparation and delivery of food services within dining facilities located on military installations and vessels. Social workers focus on improving conditions that cause social problems, such as drug and alcohol abuse, racism, and sexism. Chaplains conduct worship services for military personnel and perform other spiritual duties covering beliefs and practices of all religious faiths.

Media and public affairs officers oversee the development, production, and presentation of information or events for the public. These officers may produce and direct motion pictures, videotapes, and TV and radio broadcasts that are used for training, news, and entertainment. Some plan, develop, and direct the activities of military bands. Public affairs officers respond to inquiries about military activities and prepare news releases and reports to keep the public informed.

Protective service officers are responsible for the safety and protection of individuals and property on military bases and vessels. Emergency management officers plan and prepare for all types of natural and man made disasters. They develop warning, control, and evacuation plans to be used in the event of a disaster. Law enforcement and security officers enforce applicable laws on military bases and investigate crimes when the law has been transgressed.

Officers in *transportation* occupations manage and perform activities related to the safe transport of military personnel and material by air, road, rail, and water. Officers normally specialize by mode of transportation or area of expertise since, in many cases, there are licensing and certification requirements. Pilots in the military fly various types of specialized airplanes and helicopters to carry troops and equipment and execute combat missions. Navigators use radar, radio and other navigation equipment to determine their position and plan their route of travel. Officers on ships and submarines work as a team to manage the various departments aboard their vessels. Transportation officers must also direct the maintenance of transportation equipment.

Many professionals are needed to serve the medical needs of the Armed Forces.

Employment

In 1999, over 1.2 million individuals were on active duty in the Armed Forces—about 445,000 in the Army, 272,000 in the Navy, 343,000 in the Air Force, 143,000 in the Marine Corps, and 26,000 in the Coast Guard. Table 1 shows the occupational composition of enlisted personnel in 1999, while table 2 presents similar information for officer personnel.

Table 1. Military enlisted personnel by broad occupational category and branch of military service, 1999

Occupational Group—Enlisted	*Army*	*Air Force*	*Coast Guard*	*Marine Corps*	*Navy*	*Total, all services*
Administrative occupations	17,124	16,599	1,834	11,078	13,569	60,204
Combat specialty occupations	105,811	214	—	30,009	1,926	137,960
Construction occupations	4,214	5,732	2,181	3,972	2,775	18,874
Electronic and electrical repair occupations	25,431	51,900	3,075	12,876	43,879	137,161
Engineering, science, and technical occupations	39,362	47,091	2,193	15,705	34,726	139,077
Health care occupations	28,933	21,770	688	0[1]	23,090	74,481
Support services occupations	12,994	7,210	1158	3,109	8,654	33,125
Machine operator and precision work occupations	2,295	7,066	1,501	1,940	18,807	31,609
Media and public affairs occupations	8,001	6,393	125	1,831	2,985	19,335
Protective service occupations	24,562	18,602	180	6,315	7,038	56,697
Transportation and material handling occupations	53,556	31,582	4,244	27,876	28,524	145,782
Vehicle machinery mechanic occupations	46,783	47,807	2,392	15,796	39,541	152,319
Human resource development occupations	14,504	10,376	348	1,672	12,459	39,359
Total, by service[2]	383,570	272,342	19,919	132,179	237,973	1,045,983

[1]The Marine Corps employs no medical personnel. Their medical services are provided by the Navy.
[2]Sum of individual items may not equal totals because personnel on temporary assignment are not included in these occupational classifications.

SOURCE: U.S. Department of Defense, Defense Manpower Data Center East

Table 2. Military officer personnel by broad occupational category and branch of service, 1999

Occupational Group—Officer	*Army*	*Air Force*	*Coast Guard*	*Marine Corps*	*Navy*	*Total, all services*
Combat specialty occupations	19,470	5,951	42	1,102	2,232	28,797
Engineering, science, and technical occupations	16,106	15,840	1,392	1,706	7,924	42,968
Executive, administrative, and managerial occupations	8,259	8,905	349	1,290	6,321	25,124
Health care occupations	11,055	11,073	8	0[1]	7,332	29,468
Support services occupations	1,211	1,636	—	45	1155	4,047
Media and public affairs occupations	50	1,570	18	142	335	2,115
Protective service occupations	1671	1,446	374	330	786	4,607
Transportation occupations	1,851	19,890	3341	5,017	13,140	43,239
Human resource development occupations	1,256	4,093	265	1,673	4,136	11,423
Total, by service[2]	60,929	70,404	5,789	11,305	43,361	191,788
Total (Enlisted and Officer)[2]	444,499	342,746	25,708	143,484	281,334	1,237,771

[1]The Marine Corps employs no medical personnel. Their medical services are provided by the Navy.
[2]Sum of individual items may not equal totals because personnel on temporary assignment are not included in these occupational classifications.

SOURCE: U.S. Department of Defense, Defense Manpower Data Center East

Military personnel are stationed throughout the United States and in many countries around the world. More than a third of military jobs are located in California, Texas, North Carolina, or Virginia. About 258,000 individuals were stationed outside the United States in 1998, including those assigned to ships at sea. Over 116,000 of these were stationed in Europe, mainly in Germany, and another 96,000 assigned to East Asia and the Pacific area, mostly in Japan and the Republic of Korea.

Qualifications, Training, and Advancement

Enlisted personnel. In order to join the services, enlisted personnel must sign a legal agreement called an enlistment contract, which usually involves a commitment to 8 years of service. Depending on the terms of the contract, 2 to 6 years are spent on active duty and the balance are spent in the reserves. The enlistment contract obligates the service to provide the agreed-upon job, rating, pay, cash bonuses for enlistment in certain occupations, medical and other benefits, occupational training, and continuing education. In return, enlisted personnel must serve satisfactorily for the specified period of time.

Requirements for each service vary, but certain qualifications for enlistment are common to all branches. In order to enlist, one must be between the ages of 17 and 35, be a U.S. citizen or immigrant alien holding permanent resident status, not have a felony record, and possess a birth certificate. Applicants who are 17 must have the consent of a parent or legal guardian before entering the service. Air Force enlisted personnel must enter active duty before their 28th birthday. Applicants must pass both a written examination—the Armed Services Vocational Aptitude Battery—and meet certain minimum physical standards such as height, weight, vision, and overall health. All branches require high school graduation or its equivalent for certain enlistment options. In 1999, over 9 out of 10 volunteers were high school graduates. Single parents are generally not eligible to enlist.

People thinking about enlisting in the military should learn as much as they can about military life before making a decision. This is especially important if you are thinking about making the military a career. Speaking to friends and relatives with military experience is a good idea. Determine what the military can offer you and what it will expect in return. Then talk to a recruiter, who can determine if you qualify for enlistment, explain the various enlistment options, and tell you which military occupational specialties currently have openings. Bear in mind that the recruiter's job is to recruit promising applicants into their branch of military service, so the information he or she gives you is likely to stress the positive aspects of military life in the branch in which the recruiter serves.

Ask the recruiter for the branch you have chosen to assess your chances of being accepted for training in the occupation or occupations of your choice, or, better still, take the aptitude exam to see how well you score. The military uses the aptitude exam as a placement exam, and test scores largely determine an individual's chances of being accepted into a particular training program. Selection for a particular type of training depends on the needs of the service, your general and technical aptitudes, and your personal preference. Because all prospective recruits are required to take the exam, those who do so before committing themselves to enlist have the advantage of knowing in advance whether they stand a good chance of being accepted for training in a particular specialty. The recruiter can schedule you for the Armed Services Vocational Aptitude Battery without any obligation. Many high schools offer the exam as an easy way for students to explore the possibility of a military career, and the test also provides insight into career areas where the student has demonstrated aptitudes and interests.

If you decide to join the military, the next step is to pass the physical examination and sign an enlistment contract. This involves choosing, qualifying, and agreeing on a number of enlistment options such as length of active duty time, which may vary according to the enlistment option. Most active duty programs have enlistment options ranging from 3 to 6 years, although there are some 2-year programs. The contract will also state the date of enlistment and other options such as

Pay and benefits in all branches of the Armed Forces are determined by grade and years of service.

bonuses and types of training to be received. If the service is unable to fulfill its part of the contract, such as providing a certain kind of training, the contract may become null and void.

All services offer a "delayed entry program" by which an individual can delay entry into active duty for up to 1 year after enlisting. High school students can enlist during their senior year and enter a service after graduation. Others choose this program because the job training they desire is not currently available but will be within the coming year or because they need time to arrange personal affairs.

Women are eligible to enter most military specialties. Although many women serve in medical and administrative support positions, women also work as mechanics, missile maintenance technicians, heavy equipment operators, fighter pilots, and intelligence officers. Only occupations involving direct exposure to combat are excluded.

People planning to apply the skills gained through military training to a civilian career should first determine how good the prospects are for civilian employment in jobs related to the military specialty which interests them. Second, they should know the prerequisites for the related civilian job. Many occupations require a license, certification, or a minimum level of education. In such cases, it is important to determine whether military training is sufficient to enter the civilian equivalent or, if not, what additional training will be required. Other *Handbook* statements discuss the job outlook for civilian occupations for which military training is helpful. Additional information often can be obtained from school counselors.

Following enlistment, new members of the Armed Forces undergo recruit training, which is better known as "basic" training. Recruit training provides a 6 to 11-week introduction to military life with courses in military skills and protocol. Days and nights are carefully structured and include rigorous physical exercises designed to improve strength and endurance and build unit cohesion.

Following basic training, most recruits take additional training at technical schools that prepare them for a particular military occupational specialty. The formal training period generally lasts from 10 to 20 weeks, although training for certain occupations—nuclear power plant operator, for example—may take as long as a year. Recruits not assigned to classroom instruction receive on-the-job training at their first duty assignment.

Many service people get college credit for the technical training they receive on duty, which, combined with off-duty courses, can lead to an associate degree through community college programs such as the Community College of the Air Force. In addition to on-duty training, military personnel may choose from a variety of educational programs. Most military installations have tuition assistance programs for people wishing to take courses during off-duty hours. These may be correspondence courses or degree programs offered by local colleges or universities. Tuition assistance pays up to 75 percent of college costs. Also available are courses designed to help service personnel earn high school equivalency diplomas. Each service branch provides opportunities for full-time study to a limited number of exceptional applicants. Military personnel accepted into these highly competitive programs receive full pay, allowances, tuition, and related fees. In return, they must agree to serve an additional amount of time in the service. Other very selective programs enable enlisted personnel to qualify as commissioned officers through additional military training.

Warrant officers. Warrant officers are technical and tactical leaders who specialize in a specific technical area; for example, one group of warrant officers is Army aviators. The Army Warrant Officer Corps comprises less than 3 percent of the total Army. Although small in size, their level of responsibility is high. They receive extended career opportunities, worldwide leadership assignments, and increased pay and retirement benefits. Selection to attend the Warrant Officer Candidate School is highly competitive and restricted to those with the rank of E5 or higher (see table 3).

Officers. Officer training in the Armed Forces is provided through the Federal service academies (Military, Naval, Air Force, and Coast Guard); the Reserve Officers Training Corps (ROTC) offered at many colleges and universities; Officer Candidate School (OCS) or Officer Training School (OTS); the National Guard (State Officer Candidate School programs); the Uniformed Services University of Health Sciences; and other programs. All are very selective and are good options for those wishing to make the military a career.

Federal service academies provide a 4-year college program leading to a Bachelor of Science degree. Midshipmen or cadets are provided free room and board, tuition, medical care, and a monthly allowance. Graduates receive regular or reserve commissions and have a 5-year active duty obligation, or longer if entering flight training.

To become a candidate for appointment as a cadet or midshipman in one of the service academies, most applicants obtain a nomination from an authorized source (usually a member of Congress). Candidates do not need to know a member of Congress personally to request a nomination. Nominees must have an academic record of the requisite quality, college aptitude test scores above an established minimum, and recommendations from teachers or school officials; they must also pass a medical examination. Appointments are made from the list of eligible nominees. Appointments to the Coast Guard Academy, however, are made strictly on a competitive basis. A nomination is not required.

ROTC programs train students in about 950 Army, 60 Navy and Marine Corps, and 550 Air Force units at participating colleges and universities. Trainees take 2 to 5 hours of military instruction a week in addition to regular college courses. After graduation, they may serve as officers on active duty for a stipulated period of time. Some may serve their obligation in the Reserves or Guard. In the last 2 years of a ROTC program, students receive a monthly allowance while attending school and additional pay for summer training. ROTC scholarships for 2, 3, and 4 years are available on a competitive basis. All scholarships pay for tuition and have allowances for subsistence, textbooks, supplies, and other fees.

College graduates can earn a commission in the Armed Forces through OCS or OTS programs in the Army, Navy, Air Force, Marine Corps, Coast Guard, and National Guard. These officers generally must serve their obligation on active duty. Those with training in certain health professions may qualify for direct appointment as officers. In the case of health professions students, financial assistance and internship opportunities are available from the military in return for specified periods of military service. Prospective medical students can apply to the Uniformed Services University of Health Sciences, which offers free tuition in a program leading to a Doctor of Medicine (M.D.) degree. In return, graduates must serve for 7 years in either the military or the Public Health Service. Direct appointments also are available for those qualified to serve in other special duties, such as the judge advocate general (legal) or chaplain corps. Flight training is available to commissioned officers in each branch of the Armed Forces. In addition, the Army has a direct enlistment option to become a warrant officer aviator.

Tradition and ceremony are important in the Armed Forces.

Each service has different criteria for promoting personnel. Generally, the first few promotions for both enlisted and officer personnel come easily; subsequent promotions are much more competitive. Criteria for promotion may include time in service and grade, job performance, a fitness report (supervisor's recommendation), and written examinations. People who are passed over for promotion several times generally must leave the military. The following table shows the officer, warrant officer, and enlisted ranks by service.

Job Outlook

Opportunities should be good for qualified individuals in all branches of the Armed Forces through 2008. Many military personnel retire after 20 years of service with a pension while still young enough to start a new career. About 365,000 enlisted personnel and officers must be recruited each year to replace those who complete their commitment or retire. Since the end of the draft in 1973, the military has met its personnel requirements through volunteers. When the economy is good, it is more difficult for all the services to meet their quotas, while it is much easier to do so in times of recession.

America's strategic position is stronger than it has been in decades. Although there were reductions in personnel due to the reduction in the threat from Eastern Europe and Russia, the number of active duty personnel is now expected to remain about constant through 2008. The Armed Forces' goal is to maintain a sufficient force to fight and win two major regional conflicts occurring at the same time. Political events, however, could cause these plans to change.

Educational requirements will continue to rise as military jobs become more technical and complex. High school graduates and applicants with a college background will be sought to fill the ranks of enlisted personnel, while virtually all officers will need at least a bachelor's degree and, in some cases, an advanced degree as well.

Earnings, Allowances, and Benefits

The earnings structure for military personnel are shown in table 4. Most enlisted personnel started as recruits at Grade E-1 in 1999; however, those with special skills or above-average education started as high as Grade E-4. Most warrant officers started at Grade W-1 or W-2, depending upon their occupational and academic qualifications and the branch of service, but these individuals all had previous military service and this is not an entry-level occupation. Most commissioned officers started at Grade O-1; while some highly trained officers—for example, physicians, engineers, and scientists—started as high as Grade O-3 or O-4.

Table 3. Military rank and employment for active duty personnel, March 1999

Grade	*Rank and title* Army	Navy and Coast Guard	Air Force	Marine Corps	Total DOD Employment
Commissioned officers:					
O-10	General	Admiral	General	General	38
O-9	Lieutenant General	Vice Admiral	Lieutenant General	Lieutenant General	114
O-8	Major General	Rear Admiral Upper	Major General	Major General	287
O-7	Brigadier General	Rear Admiral Lower	Brigadier General	Brigadier General	446
O-6	Colonel	Captain	Colonel	Colonel	11,423
O-5	Lieutenant Colonel	Commander	Lieutenant Colonel	Lieutenant Colonel	28,428
O-4	Major	Lieutenant Commander	Major	Major	43,027
O-3	Captain	Lieutenant	Captain	Captain	69,358
O-2	1st Lieutenant	Lieutenant (JG)	1st Lieutenant	1st Lieutenant	28,096
O-1	2nd Lieutenant	Ensign	2nd Lieutenant	2nd Lieutenant	22,038
Warrant officers:					
W-5	Chief Warrant Officer	Chief Warrant Officer	—	Chief Warrant Officer	459
W-4	Chief Warrant Officer	Chief Warrant Officer	—	Chief Warrant Officer	2,123
W-3	Chief Warrant Officer	Chief Warrant Officer	—	Chief Warrant Officer	4,019
W-2	Chief Warrant Officer	Chief Warrant Officer	—	Chief Warrant Officer	6,455
W-1	Warrant Officer	Warrant Officer	—	Warrant Officer	2,402
Enlisted personnel:					
E-9	Sergeant Major	Master Chief Petty Officer	Chief Master Sergeant	Sergeant Major	10,241
E-8	1st Sergeant/Master Sergeant	Sr. Chief Petty Officer	Senior Master Sergeant	Master Sergeant/1st Sergeant	26,014
E-7	Sergeant First Class	Chief Petty Officer	Master Sergeant	Gunnery Sergeant	99,201
E-6	Staff Sergeant	Petty Officer 1st Class	Technical Sergeant	Staff Sergeant	163,075
E-5	Sergeant	Petty Officer 2nd Class	Staff Sergeant	Sergeant	232,854
E-4	Corporal/Specialist	Petty Officer 3rd Class	Senior Airman	Corporal	264,757
E-3	Private First Class	Seaman	Airman 1st Class	Lance Corporal	186,647
E-2	Private	Seaman Apprentice	Airman	Private 1st Class	98,115
E-1	Private	Seaman Recruit	Airman Basic	Private	57,961

SOURCE: U.S. Department of Defense

In addition to basic pay, military personnel receive free room and board (or a tax-free housing and subsistence allowance), medical and dental care, a military clothing allowance, military supermarket and department store shopping privileges, 30 days of paid vacation a year (referred to as leave), and travel opportunities. Other allowances are paid for foreign duty, hazardous duty, submarine and flight duty, and employment as a medical officer. Athletic and other recreational facilities such as libraries, gymnasiums, tennis courts, golf courses, bowling centers, and movies are available on many military installations. Military personnel are eligible for retirement benefits after 20 years of service.

The Veterans Administration (VA) provides numerous benefits to those who have served at least 2 years in the Armed Forces. Veterans are eligible for free care in VA hospitals for all service-related disabilities regardless of time served; those with other medical problems are eligible for free VA care if they are unable to pay the cost of hospitalization elsewhere. Admission to a VA medical center depends on the availability of beds, however. Veterans are also eligible for certain loans, including home loans. Veterans, regardless of health, can convert a military life insurance policy to an individual policy with any participating company in the veteran's State of residence. In addition, job counseling, testing, and placement services are available.

Veterans who participate in the New Montgomery GI Bill Program receive educational benefits. Under this program, Armed Forces personnel may elect to deduct from their pay up to $100 a month to put toward their future education for the first 12 months of active duty. Veterans who serve on active duty for three years or more, or two years active duty plus four years in the Selected Reserve or National Guard, will receive $427.87 a month in basic benefits for 36 months. Those who enlist and serve for less than 3 years will receive $347.65 a month. In addition, each service provides its own additional contributions for future education. This sum becomes the service member's educational fund. Upon separation from active duty, the fund can be used to finance educational costs at any VA-approved institution. VA-approved schools include many vocational, correspondence, business, technical, and flight training schools; community and junior colleges; and colleges and universities.

Job opportunities in the Armed Forces should be good for qualified people.

Table 4. Military basic monthly pay by grade for active duty personnel, January 1, 1999

Years of service						
Grade	**Less than 2**	**Over 4**	**Over 8**	**Over 12**	**Over 16**	**Over 20**
O-9	6,947.10	7,281.00	7,466.10	7,776.90	8,425.80	8,892.60
O-8	6,292.20	6,634.50	7,129.20	7,466.10	7,776.90	8,425.80
O-7	5,228.40	5,583.90	5,834.40	6,172.50	7,129.20	7,619.70
O-6	3,875.10	4,536.60	4,536.60	4,536.60	5,432.40	5,834.40
O-5	3,099.60	3,891.00	3,891.00	4,224.30	4,845.00	5,277.90
O-4	2,612.40	3,393.30	3,608.70	4,071.90	4,444.80	4,566.60
O-3	2,427.60	3,210.60	3,484.80	3,855.30	3,949.50	3,949.50
O-2	2,117.10	2,871.30	2,930.40	2,930.40	2,930.40	2,930.40
O-1	1,838.10	2,312.10	2,312.10	2,312.10	2,312.10	2,312.10
W-5	—	—	—	—	—	4,221.30
W-4	2,473.20	2,714.10	2,962.80	3,303.00	3,577.80	3,792.00
W-3	2,247.90	2,469.90	2,681.70	2,930.40	3,114.00	3,335.70
W-2	1,968.90	2,192.10	2,438.40	2,623.80	2,809.50	2,993.10
W-1	1,640.40	2,037.90	2,221.50	2,407.20	2,591.70	2,777.70
E-8	—	—	2,412.60	2,547.30	2,682.90	2,811.30
E-7	1,684.80	1,952.10	2,082.90	2,216.70	2,382.60	2,480.40
E-6	1,449.30	1,715.40	1,844.10	2,010.00	2,140.20	2,172.60
E-5	1,271.70	1,514.70	1,680.30	1,811.10	1,844.10	1,844.10
E-4	1,185.90	1,428.60	1,485.30	1,485.30	1,485.30	1,485.30
E-3	1,179.80	1,274.70	1,274.70	1,274.70	1,274.70	1,274.70
E-2	1,075.80	1,075.80	1,075.80	1,075.80	1,075.80	1,075.80
E-1 >4mos	959.40	959.40	959.40	959.40	959.40	959.40

SOURCE: U.S. Department of Defense—Defense Finance and Accounting Service

Sources of Additional Information

Each of the military services publishes handbooks, fact sheets, and pamphlets describing entrance requirements, training and advancement opportunities, and other aspects of military careers. These publications are widely available at all recruiting stations, most State employment service offices, and in high schools, colleges, and public libraries. Information on educational and other veterans' benefits is available from VA offices located throughout the country.

In addition, the *Military Career Guide Online* is a compendium of military occupational, training, and career information presented by the Defense Manpower Data Center, a Department of Defense agency which is designed for use by students and jobseekers. This information is available on the Internet:

http://www.militarycareers.com

Data for Occupations Not Studied in Detail

Employment in the 253 occupations covered in detail in the main body of the *Handbook* accounts for about 122 million or 87 percent of all jobs in the economy. Although occupations covering the full spectrum of work are included, those requiring lengthy education or training are generally given the most attention.

This chapter presents summary data on 72 additional occupations, for which employment projections are prepared, but for which detailed occupational information is not developed. These occupations account for about 4 percent of all jobs. For each occupation, a brief description of the nature of work, the number of jobs in 1998, a phrase describing the projected employment change from 1998 to 2008, and the most significant source of training are presented. For guidelines on interpreting the description of projected employment change, refer to a chapter in the front of the *Handbook*, Occupational Information Included in the *Handbook*.

The approximately 9 percent of all jobs not covered either in the detailed occupational descriptions in the main body of the *Handbook* or in the summary data presented in this chapter are mainly residual categories, such as "all other management support workers," for which little meaningful information could be developed.

Executive, Administrative, and Managerial Occupations

Communications, transportation, and utilities operations managers

Plan, organize, direct, control, or coordinate activities related to: Communications by telephone, telegraph, radio, or television; transporting people or goods by air, highway, railway, water, or pipeline; managing transportation facilities, such as airports, harbors, or terminals; managing warehousing and storage facilities; or supplying electricity, gas, water, steam, or sanitation services. General managers of large establishments or operations should be reported as general managers and top executives.

1998 employment: 196,000
Projected 1998-2008 employment change: About as fast as average
Most significant source of training: Work experience plus bachelor's or higher degree

Credit analysts

Analyze current credit data and financial statements of individuals or firms to determine the degree of risk involved in extending credit or lending money. Prepare reports with this credit information for use in decision-making.

1998 employment: 42,000
Projected 1998-2008 employment change: About as fast as average
Most significant source of training: Bachelor's degree

Postmasters and mail superintendents

Direct and coordinate operational, administrative, management, and supportive services of a U.S. post office; or coordinate activities of workers engaged in postal and related work in assigned post office.

1998 employment: 26,000
Projected 1998-2008 employment change: Slower than average
Most significant source of training: Work experience in a related occupation

Tax examiners, collectors, and revenue agents

Determine tax liability or collect taxes from individuals or business firms according to prescribed laws and regulations.

1998 employment: 62,000
Projected 1998-2008 employment change: Slower than average
Most significant source of training: Bachelor's degree

Professional and Technical Occupations

Athletes, coaches, umpires, and related workers

Participate in competitive professional athletic events as a player, coach, manager, umpire, or judge. Include athletic trainers, scouts, official scorers, and timekeepers.

1998 employment: 52,000
Projected 1998-2008 employment change: Faster than average
Most significant source of training: Long-term on-the-job training

Assessors

Appraise real and personal property to determine its fair value. May assess taxes in accordance with prescribed schedules.

1998 employment: 22,000
Projected 1998-2008 employment change: About as fast as average
Most significant source of training: Bachelor's degree

Directors, religious activities and education

Direct and coordinate activities of a denominational group to meet religious needs of students. Plan, organize, and direct religious school programs designed to promote religious education among members of religious institution. Provide counseling and guidance relative to marital, health, financial, and religious problems.

1998 employment: 112,000
Projected 1998-2008 employment change: Faster than average
Most significant source of training: Bachelor's degree

Farm and home management advisors

Advise, instruct, and assist individuals and families engaged in agriculture, agricultural related processes, or home economics activities. Demonstrate procedures and apply research findings to solve problems; instruct and train in product development, sales, and the utilization of machinery and equipment to promote general welfare. Include county agricultural agents, feed and farm management advisers, home economists, and extension service advisers.

1998 employment: 10,000
Projected 1998-2008 employment change: A decline
Most significant source of training: Bachelor's degree

Psychiatric technicians

Provide nursing care to mentally ill, emotionally disturbed, or mentally retarded patients. Participate in rehabilitation and treatment programs. Help with personal hygiene. Administer oral medications and hypodermic injections, following physician's prescriptions and hospital procedures. Monitor patient's physical and emotional well-being and report to medical staff.

1998 employment: 66,000
Projected 1998-2008 employment change: About as fast as average
Most significant source of training: Postsecondary vocational training

Radiation therapists

Provide radiation therapy to patients as prescribed by a radiologist according to established practices and standards. Duties may include reviewing prescription and diagnosis; acting as liaison with physician and supportive care personnel; preparing equipment, such as immobilization, treatment, and protection devices; and maintaining records, reports, and files. May assist in dosimetry procedures and tumor localization.

1998 employment: 12,000
Projected 1998-2008 employment change: About as fast as average
Most significant source of training: Associate degree

Residential counselors

Coordinate activities for residents of care and treatment institutions, boarding schools, college fraternities or sororities, children homes, or similar establishments. Work includes developing or assisting in the development of program plans for individuals, maintaining household records, and assigning rooms. Counsel residents in identifying and resolving social or other problems. Order supplies and determine need for maintenance, repairs, and furnishings.

1998 employment: 190,000
Projected 1998-2008 employment change: Much faster than average
Most significant source of training: Bachelor's degree

Tax preparers

Prepare tax returns for individuals or small businesses but do not have the background or responsibilities of an accredited accountant or certified public accountant. May work for established tax return firm.

1998 employment: 79,000
Projected 1998-2008 employment change: About as fast as average
Most significant source of training: Moderate-term on-the-job training

Title examiners, abstractors, and searchers

Title examiners: Search public records and examine titles to determine legal condition of property title. Copy or summarize (abstracts) recorded documents which affect condition of title to property (e.g., mortgages, trust deeds, and contracts). May prepare and issue policy that guarantees legality of title. *Abstractors*: Summarize pertinent legal or insurance details or sections of statutes or case law from reference books for purpose of examination, proof, or ready reference. Search out titles to determine if title deed is correct. *Searchers*: Compile list of mortgages, deeds, contracts, judgments, and other instruments pertaining to title by searching public and private records of real estate or title insurance company.

1998 employment: 30,000
Projected 1998-2008 employment change: A decline
Most significant source of training: Moderate-term on-the-job training

Veterinary technologists and technicians

Perform medical tests in a laboratory environment for use in the treatment and diagnosis of diseases in animals. Prepare vaccines and serums for prevention of diseases. Prepare tissue samples, take blood samples, and execute laboratory tests such as urinalysis and blood counts. Clean and sterilize instruments and materials and maintain equipment and machines.

1998 employment: 32,000
Projected 1998-2008 employment change: About as fast as average
Most significant source of training: Associates degree

Marketing and Sales Occupations

Parts salespersons

Sell spare and replaceable parts and equipment from behind counter in agency, repair shop, or parts store. Determine make, year, and type of part needed by observing damaged part or listening to a description of malfunction. Read catalogue to find stock number, price, etc., and fill customer's order from stock. Exclude workers whose primary responsibilities are to receive, store, and issue materials, equipment, and other items from stockroom.

1998 employment: 300,000
Projected 1998-2008 employment change: Little or no change
Most significant source of training: Moderate-term on-the-job training

Real estate appraisers

Appraise real property to determine its value for purchase, sales, investment, mortgage, or loan purposes.

1998 employment: 48,000
Projected 1998-2008 employment change: About as fast as average
Most significant source of training: Bachelor's degree

Administrative Support Occupations, Including Clerical

Court clerks

Perform clerical duties in courts of law; prepare docket of cases to be called; secure information for judges; and contact witnesses, attorneys, and litigants to obtain information for court.

1998 employment: 51,000
Projected 1998-2008 employment change: About as fast as average
Most significant source of training: Short-term on-the-job training

Duplicating, mail, and other office machine operators

Duplicating machine operators: Operate one of a variety of office machines such as photocopying, photographic, mimeograph, and duplicating machines to make copies. Exclude blueprinting machine operators and operators of offset printing machines and presses. *Mail machine operators*: Operate machines that emboss names, addresses, and other matter onto metal plates for use in addressing machines; print names, addresses, and similar information onto items such as envelopes, accounting forms, and advertising literature; address, fold, stuff, seal, and stamp mail; and open envelopes. Exclude workers who prepare incoming and outgoing mail for distribution by hand.

1998 employment: 197,000
Projected 1998-2008 employment change: Little or no change
Most significant source of training: Short-term on-the-job training

Insurance appraisers, auto damage

Appraise automobile or other vehicle damage to determine cost of repair for insurance claim settlement and seek agreement with automotive repair shop on cost of repair. Prepare insurance forms to indicate repair cost or cost estimates and recommendations.

1998 employment: 10,000
Projected 1998-2008 employment change: About as fast as average
Most significant source of training: Long-term on-the-job training

License clerks

Issue licenses or permits to qualified applicants. Obtain necessary information; record data; advise applicants on requirements; collect fees; and issue licenses. May conduct oral, written, visual, or performance testing.

1998 employment: 24,000
Projected 1998-2008 employment change: About as fast as average
Most significant source of training: Short-term on-the-job training

Municipal clerks

Draft agendas and bylaws for town or city council; record minutes of council meetings; answer official correspondence; keep fiscal records and accounts; and prepare reports on civic needs.

1998 employment: 25,000
Projected 1998-2008 employment change: About as fast as average
Most significant source of training: Short-term on-the-job training

Proofreaders and copy markers

Read transcript or proof type setup to detect and mark for correction any grammatical, typographical, or compositional errors. Exclude workers whose primary duty is editing copy. Include proofreaders of Braille.

1998 employment: 41,000
Projected 1998-2008 employment change: A decline
Most significant source of training: Short-term on-the-job training

Statistical clerks

Compile and compute data according to statistical formulas for use in statistical studies. May perform actuarial computations using algebra and trigonometry and compile charts and graphs for use by actuaries. Include actuarial clerks.

1998 employment: 72,000
Projected 1998-2008 employment change: A decline
Most significant source of training: Moderate-term on-the-job training

Service Occupations

Ambulance drivers and attendants, except emergency medical technicians

Drive ambulance or assist ambulance driver in transporting sick, injured, or convalescent persons. Assist in lifting patients and rendering first aid. May be required to have Red Cross first-aid training certificate.

1998 employment: 19,000
Projected 1998-2008 employment change: Faster than average
Most significant source of training: Short-term on-the-job training

Amusement and recreation attendants

Perform any of a variety of attending duties at amusement or recreation facility. Schedule use of recreation facilities, allocate equipment to participants of sporting events or recreational pursuits, collect fees for games played, or operate carnival rides and amusement concessions.

1998 employment: 337,000
Projected 1998-2008 employment change: Faster than average
Most significant source of training: Short-term on-the-job training

Baggage porters and bellhops

Carry baggage for travelers at transportation terminals or for guests at hotels or similar establishments. Additional duties include assisting handicapped persons, running errands, delivering ice, and directing people to their desired destinations.

1998 employment: 40,000
Projected 1998-2008 employment change: About as fast as average
Most significant source of training: Short-term on-the-job training

Crossing guards

Guide or control vehicular or pedestrian traffic at such places as street and railroad crossings and construction sites.

1998 employment: 54,000
Projected 1998-2008 employment change: Slower than average
Most significant source of training: Short-term on-the-job training

Ushers, lobby attendants, and ticket takers

Assist patrons at entertainment events, such as sporting events, motion pictures, or theater performances. Collect admission tickets and passes from patrons. May assist in finding seats, searching for lost articles, and locating such facilities as rest rooms and telephones.

1998 employment: 84,000
Projected 1998-2008 employment change: About as fast as average
Most significant source of training: Short-term on-the-job training

Mechanics, Installers, and Repairers

Bicycle repairers

Repair and service bicycles using hand tools.

1998 employment: 11,000
Projected 1998-2008 employment change: Faster than average
Most significant source of training: Moderate-term on-the-job training

Camera and photographic equipment repairers

Repair and adjust cameras and photographic equipment, including motion picture cameras and equipment, using specialized tools and testing devices.

1998 employment: 9,000
Projected 1998-2008 employment change: Slower than average
Most significant source of training: Moderate-term on-the-job training

Locksmiths and safe repairers

Repair and open locks; make keys; change locks and safe combinations; and install and repair safes.

1998 employment: 27,000
Projected 1998-2008 employment change: About as fast as average
Most significant source of training: Moderate-term on-the-job training

Medical equipment repairers
Test, adjust, and repair electromedical equipment using hand tools and meters.

1998 employment: 11,000
Projected 1998-2008 employment change: About as fast as average
Most significant source of training: Long-term on-the-job training

Precision instrument repairers
Install, test, repair, maintain, and adjust indicating, recording, telemetering, and controlling instruments used to measure and control variables such as pressure, flow, temperature, motion, force, and chemical composition. Include instrument repairers who repair, calibrate, and test instruments such as voltmeters, ammeters, and galvanometers.

1998 employment: 33,000
Projected 1998-2008 employment change: A decline
Most significant source of training: Long-term on-the-job training

Riggers
Set up or repair rigging for ships and shipyards, manufacturing plants, logging yards, construction projects, and for the entertainment industry. Select cables, ropes, pulleys, winches, blocks, and sheaves according to weight and size of load to be moved. Coordinate and direct other workers and the movement of equipment to accomplish the task.

1998 employment: 11,000
Projected 1998-2008 employment change: Little or no change
Most significant source of training: Long-term on-the-job training

Tire repairers and changers
Repair and replace tires, tubes, treads, and related products on automobiles, buses, trucks, and other vehicles. Duties include mounting tires on wheels, balancing tires and wheels, and testing and repairing damaged tires and inner tubes.

1998 employment: 83,000
Projected 1998-2008 employment change: About as fast as average
Most significant source of training: Short-term on-the-job training

Watch repairers
Repair, clean, and adjust mechanisms of instruments such as watches, time clocks, and timing switches using hand tools and measuring instruments.

1998 employment: 8,400
Projected 1998-2008 employment change: A decline
Most significant source of training: Long-term on-the-job training

Construction Trades Occupations

Highway maintenance workers
Maintain highways, municipal and rural roads, airport runways, and rights-of-way in safe condition. Duties include patching broken or eroded pavement, and erecting and repairing guard rails, highway markers, and snow fences using a posthole digger, shovel, axe, saw, hammer and nails, or power tools. May also clear brush or plant trees along rights-of-way.

1998 employment: 155,000
Projected 1998-2008 employment change: About as fast as average
Most significant source of training: Short-term on-the-job training

Mining, quarrying, and tunneling occupations
Rock splitters, quarry: Separate blocks of rough dimension stone from quarry mass using jackhammer, wedges, and feathers. *Roof bolters*: Operate self-propelled machine to install roof support bolts in underground mine. *Mining machine operators*: Operate mining machines, such as self-propelled or truck-mounted drilling machines, continuous mining machines, channeling machines, and cutting machines to extract coal, metal and nonmetal ores, rock, stone, or sand from underground or surface excavation. Exclude truck, shovel, and conveyor operators. *Continuous mining machine operators*: Operate self-propelled mining machines that rip coal, metal and nonmetal ores, rock, stone, or sand from the face and load it onto conveyors or into shuttle cars in a continuous operation. *Mine cutting and channeling machine operators*: Operate machines that cut or channel along the face or seams of coal mines, stone quarries, or other mining surfaces to facilitate blasting, separating, or removing minerals or materials from mines or from the earth's surface. Include shale planers.

1998 employment: 23,000
Projected 1998-2008 employment change: A decline
Most significant source of training: Long-term on-the-job training

Pipelayers and pipelaying fitters
Pipelayers: Lay glazed or unglazed clay, concrete, plastic, or cast-iron pipe for storm or sanitation sewers, drains, water mains, and oil or gas lines. Perform any combination of the following tasks: Grade trenches or culverts, position pipe, or seal joints. *Pipelaying fitters*: Align pipeline section in preparation of welding. Signal tractor driver for placement of pipeline sections in proper alignment. Insert steel spacer.

1998 employment: 57,000
Projected 1998-2008 employment change: Slower than average
Most significant source of training: Moderate-term on-the-job training

Roustabouts, oil and gas
Perform a variety of assigned tasks in or around an oil field such as assembling or repairing equipment, digging drainage trenches, and loading or unloading trucks.

1998 employment: 30,000
Projected 1998-2008 employment change: A decline
Most significant source of training: Short-term on-the-job training

Production Occupations

Bakers, manufacturing
Mix and bake ingredients according to recipes to produce breads, pastries, and other baked goods. Goods are produced in large quantities for sale through establishments such as grocery stores. Generally, high-volume production equipment is used.

1998 employment: 55,000
Projected 1998-2008 employment change: Slower than average
Most significant source of training: Moderate-term on-the-job training

Boiler operators and tenders, low pressure

Operate or tend low-pressure stationary steam boilers and auxiliary steam equipment, such as pumps, compressors and air-conditioning equipment, to supply steam heat for office buildings, apartment houses, or industrial establishments; to maintain steam at specified pressure aboard marine vessels; or to generate and supply compressed air for operation of pneumatic tools, hoists, and air lances.

1998 employment: 16,000
Projected 1998-2008 employment change: A decline
Most significant source of training: Moderate-term on-the-job training

Cannery workers

Perform a variety of routine tasks in canning, freezing, preserving, or packing food products. Duties may include sorting, grading, washing, peeling, trimming, or slicing agricultural produce.

1998 employment: 50,000
Projected 1998-2008 employment change: A decline
Most significant source of training: Short-term on-the-job training

Cement and gluing machine operators and tenders

Operate or tend cementing and gluing machines to join together items to form a completed product or to form an article for further processing. Processes include: Joining veneer sheets into plywood; gluing paper to glass wool, cardboard or paper; joining rubber and rubberized fabric parts, plastic, simulated leather, and other materials.

1998 employment: 35,000
Projected 1998-2008 employment change: A decline
Most significant source of training: Moderate-term on-the-job training

Chemical equipment controllers, operators, and tenders

Controllers and operators: Control or operate equipment to control chemical changes or reactions in the processing of industrial or consumer products. Exclude operators who control equipment centrally controlled through panel boards. *Tenders*: Tend equipment in which a chemical change or reaction takes place in the processing of industrial or consumer products. Typical equipment used are: Devulcanizers, batch stills, fermenting tanks, steam-jacketed kettles, and reactor vessels.

1998 employment: 100,000
Projected 1998-2008 employment change: About as fast as average
Most significant source of training: Moderate-term on-the-job training

Chemical plant and system operators

Control and operate an entire chemical process or system of machines, such as reduction pots and heated air towers, through the use of panelboards, control boards, or semiautomatic equipment.

1998 employment: 43,000
Projected 1998-2008 employment change: About as fast as average
Most significant source of training: Long-term on-the-job training

Coil winders, tapers, and finishers

Wind wire coils used in electrical components, such as resistors and transformers, and in electrical equipment and instruments, such as field cores, bobbins, armature cores, electrical motors, generators, and control equipment. May involve the use of coil-winding and coil-making machines.

1998 employment: 22,000
Projected 1998-2008 employment change: Slower than average
Most significant source of training: Short-term on-the-job training

Cooking and roasting machine operators and tenders, food and tobacco

Cooking machine operators and tenders: Operate or tend cooking equipment, such as steam cooking vats, deep fry cookers, pressure cookers, kettles, and boilers, to prepare food products, such as meats, sugar, cheese, and grain. Exclude food roasting, baking, and drying machine operators and tenders. *Roasting, baking, and drying machine operators and tenders*: Operate or tend roasting, baking, or drying equipment to: Reduce moisture content of food or tobacco products, such as tobacco, cocoa and coffee beans, macaroni, and grain; roast grain, nuts, or coffee beans; bake bread or other bakery products; or process food preparatory to canning. These machines include hearth ovens, kiln driers, roasters, char kilns, steam ovens, and vacuum drying equipment.

1998 employment: 31,000
Projected 1998-2008 employment change: A decline
Most significant source of training: Moderate-term on-the-job training

Crushing, grinding, mixing, and blending machine operators and tenders

Crushing, grinding, and polishing machine operators and tenders: Operate or tend machines to crush or grind any of a wide variety of materials, such as coal, glass, plastic, dried fruit, grain, stone, chemicals, food, or rubber; or operate or tend machines that buff and polish materials or products, such as stone, glass, slate, plastic or metal trim, bowling balls, or eyeglasses. *Mixing and blending machine operators and tenders*: Operate or tend machines to mix or blend any of a wide variety of materials, such as spices, dough batter, tobacco, fruit juices, chemicals, livestock feed, food products, color pigments, or explosive ingredients.

1998 employment: 150,000
Projected 1998-2008 employment change: Slower than average
Most significant source of training: Moderate-term on-the-job training

Cutting and slicing machine setters, operators, and tenders

Operators and tenders: Operate or tend machines to cut or slice any of a wide variety of products or materials, such as tobacco, food, paper, roofing slate, glass, stone, rubber, cork, and insulating material. Exclude metal, wood, and plastic sawing machine operators and tenders, and textile cutting machine operators and tenders. *Setters and setup operators*: Set up or set up and operate machines that cut or slice materials, such as glass, stone, cork, rubber, crepe, wallboard, and fibrous insulating board, to specified dimensions for further processing. Exclude wood sawyers, metal or plastic sawyers, shear or slitter operators, and textile setters and set-up operators.

1998 employment: 96,000
Projected 1998-2008 employment change: Slower than average
Most significant source of training: Moderate-term on-the-job training

Dairy processing equipment operators, including setters

Set up, operate, or tend continuous flow or vat-type equipment to process milk, cream, or other dairy products, following specified methods and formulas.

1998 employment: 15,000

Projected 1998-2008 employment change: A decline
Most significant source of training: Moderate-term on-the-job training

Electrical and electronic assemblers

Perform electrical and electronic assembly work at a level less than that required of precision assemblers. Include electronic wirers, armature connectors, electric motor winders, skein winders, carbon brush assemblers, battery and battery parts assemblers, electric sign assemblers, and electrical and electronic subassemblers.

1998 employment: 246,000
Projected 1998-2008 employment change: Slower than average
Most significant source of training: Short-term on-the-job training

Extruding and forming machine setters, operators, and tenders

Operators and tenders: Operate or tend machines to shape and form any of a wide variety of manufactured products, such as glass bulbs, molded food and candy, rubber goods, clay products, wax products, tobacco plugs, cosmetics, or paper products, by means of extruding, compressing or compacting. *Setters and setup operators*: Set up or set up and operate machines, such as glass forming machines, plodder machines, and tuber machines, to manufacture any of a wide variety of products, such as soap bars, formed rubber, glassware, food, brick, and tile, by means of extruding, compressing, or compacting.

1998 employment: 126,000
Projected 1998-2008 employment change: Slower than average
Most significant source of training: Moderate-term on-the-job training

Farm workers

Food and fiber crops: Manually plant, cultivate, and harvest food and fiber products such as grains, vegetables, fruits, nuts, and field crops (e.g., cotton, mint, hops, and tobacco). Use hand tools such as shovels, trowels, hoes, tampers, pruning hooks, shears, and knives. Duties may include tilling soil and applying fertilizers; transplanting, weeding, thinning, or pruning crops; applying fungicides, herbicides, or pesticides; and packing and loading harvested products. May construct trellises, repair fences and farm buildings, or participate in irrigation activities. Include workers involved in expediting pollination and those who cut seed tuber crops into sections for planting. *Farm and ranch animals*: Attend to live farm or ranch animals that may include cattle, sheep, swine, goats, and poultry produced for animal products such as meat, fur, skins, feathers, milk, and eggs. Duties may include feeding, watering, herding, grazing, castrating, branding, debeaking, weighing, catching, and loading animals. May maintain records on animals; examine animals to detect diseases and injuries; assist in birth deliveries; and administer medications, vaccinations, or insecticides as appropriate. May clean and maintain animal housing areas. Include workers who tend dairy milking machines, shear wool from sheep, collect eggs in hatcheries, place shoes on animals' hooves, and tend bee colonies.

1998 employment: 851,000
Projected 1998-2008 employment change: A decline
Most significant source of training: Short-term on-the-job training

Foundry mold assembly and shakeout workers

Prepare molds for pouring. Duties include: Cleaning and assembling foundry molds, and tending machine that bonds cope and drag together to form completed shell mold.

1998 employment: 9,300
Projected 1998-2008 employment change: Little or no change
Most significant source of training: Moderate-term on-the-job training

Furnace, kiln, oven, drier, or kettle operators and tenders

Operate or tend heating equipment other than basic metal or plastic processing equipment. *Oven operators or tenders*: Bake fiberglass or painted products, fuse glass or enamel to metal products, carbonize coal, or cure rubber or other products. *Furnace operators or tenders*: Anneal glass, roast sulfur, convert chemicals, or process petroleum. *Kettle operators and tenders*: Boil soap, or melt antimony or asphalt materials. *Drier operators and tenders*: Remove moisture from paper, chemicals, ore, clay products, or slurry. *Kiln operators and tenders*: Heat minerals, dry lumber, fire greenware, anneal glassware, or bake clay products.

1998 employment: 25,000
Projected 1998-2008 employment change: A decline
Most significant source of training: Moderate-term on-the-job training

Furnace operators and tenders

Operate or tend furnaces, such as gas, oil, coal, electric-arc or electric induction, open-hearth, or oxygen furnaces, to melt and refine metal before casting or to produce specified types of steel. Exclude heat-treating and related furnace operators.

1998 employment: 23,000
Projected 1998-2008 employment change: A decline
Most significant source of training: Moderate-term on-the-job training

Gas and petroleum plant and systems occupations

Gaugers: Gauge and test oil in storage tanks. Regulate flow of oil into pipelines at wells, tank farms, refineries, and marine and rail terminals, following prescribed standards and regulations. *Petroleum refinery and control panel operators*: Analyze specifications and control continuous operation of petroleum refining and processing units. Operate control panel to regulate temperature, pressure, rate of flow, and tank level in petroleum refining unit, according to process schedules. *Gas plant operators*: Distribute or process gas for utility companies and others. Distribute gas for an entire plant or process, often using panelboards, control boards, or semi-automatic equipment. *Petroleum pump systems operators*: Control or operate manifold and pumping systems to circulate liquids through a petroleum refinery. Exclude workers who do not operate entire manifold or pumping systems. Exclude oil pumpers who operate pipelines running outside of the refinery.

1998 employment: 38,000
Projected 1998-2008 employment change: A decline
Most significant source of training: Long-term on-the-job training

Grinders and polishers, hand

Grind and polish, using hand tools or hand-held power tools, a wide variety of metal, stone, clay, plastic, and glass objects or parts. Include grinders and chippers, polishers and buffers, metal sanders and finishers, glass grinders and polishers, and plastic buffers and finishers. Exclude precision-level workers.

1998 employment: 81,000
Projected 1998-2008 employment change: Slower than average
Most significant source of training: Short-term on-the-job training

Laundry and drycleaning machine operators and tenders, except pressing

Operate or tend washing or dry-cleaning machines to wash or dry-clean commercial, industrial, or household articles, such as cloth garments, suede, leather, furs, blankets, draperies, fine linens, rugs, and carpets.

1998 employment: 167,000
Projected 1998-2008 employment change: About as fast as average
Most significant source of training: Moderate-term on-the-job training

Machine assemblers
Perform assembly work at a level less than that required of precision assemblers. Include air-conditioning coil assemblers, ball bearing ring assemblers, fuel injection assemblers, and subassemblers.

1998 employment: 67,000
Projected 1998-2008 employment change: Slower than average
Most significant source of training: Short-term on-the-job training

Motion picture projectionists
Set up and operate motion picture projection and sound reproduction equipment.

1998 employment: 9,300
Projected 1998-2008 employment change: A decline
Most significant source of training: Short-term on-the-job training

Packaging and filling machine operators and tenders
Operate or tend machines, such as filling machines, casing-running machines, ham rolling machines, preservative filling machines, baling machines, wrapping machines, and stuffing machines, to prepare industrial or consumer products, such as gas cylinders, meat and other food products, tobacco, insulation, ammunition, stuffed toys, and athletic equipment for storage or shipment.

1998 employment: 377,000
Projected 1998-2008 employment change: About as fast as average
Most significant source of training: Moderate-term on-the-job training

Painting, coating, and decorating workers, hand
Paint, coat, and decorate, using handtools or hand-held power tools, a wide variety of manufactured items, such as furniture, glass and plateware, lamps, jewelry, books, or leather products. Include inlayers, stainers, enamelers, and decal appliers.

1998 employment: 39,000
Projected 1998-2008 employment change: About as fast as average
Most significant source of training: Short-term on-the-job training

Paper goods machine setters and setup operators
Set up or set up and operate paper goods machines that perform a variety of functions, such as converting, sawing, corrugating, banding, wrapping, boxing, stitching, forming, or sealing paper or paperboard sheets into products, such as toilet tissue, towels, napkins, bags, envelopes, tubing, cartons, wax rolls, and containers.

1998 employment: 62,000
Projected 1998-2008 employment change: A decline
Most significant source of training: Moderate-term on-the-job training

Separating, filtering, clarifying, precipitating, and still machine operators and tenders
Operate or tend machines such as filter presses, shaker screens, centrifuges, condenser tubes, precipitator tanks, fermenting tanks, evaporating tanks, scrubbing towers, and batch stills. These machines extract, sort, or separate liquids, gases, or solid materials from other materials in order to recover a refined product or material. Exclude workers who operate equipment to control chemical changes or reactions.

1998 employment: 28,000
Projected 1998-2008 employment change: A decline
Most significant source of training: Moderate-term on-the-job training

Shipfitters
Lay out and fabricate metal structural parts, such as plates, bulkheads, and frames. Brace them in position within hull of ship for riveting or welding. May prepare molds and templates for fabrication of nonstandard parts.

1998 employment: 8,700
Projected 1998-2008 employment change: A decline
Most significant source of training: Long-term on-the-job training

Shoe sewing machine operators and tenders
Operate or tend single, double, or multiple-needle stitching machines to join or decorate shoe parts, to reinforce shoe parts, or to attach buckles.

1998 employment: 6,500
Projected 1998-2008 employment change: A decline
Most significant source of training: Moderate-term on-the-job training

Solderers and brazers
Use hand soldering and brazing equipment to join together metal parts or components of metal products, or to fill holes, indentations, and seams of fabricated metal products.

1998 employment: 35,000
Projected 1998-2008 employment change: About as fast as average
Most significant source of training: Short-term on-the-job training

Soldering and brazing machine operators and setters
Operators and tenders: Operate or tend soldering and brazing machines that braze, solder, or spot weld fabricated metal products or components as specified by work orders, blueprints, and layout specifications. *Setters and setup operators*: Set up or set up and operate soldering or brazing machines to bronze, solder, heat treat, or spot weld fabricated metal products or components as specified by work orders, blueprints, and layout specifications.

1998 employment: 12,000
Projected 1998-2008 employment change: Slower than average
Most significant source of training: Moderate-term on-the-job training

Supervisors, farming, forestry, and agricultural-related occupations
Directly supervise and coordinate the activities of agricultural, forestry, fishing, and related workers. May supervise helpers assigned to these workers.

1998 employment: 92,000
Projected 1998-2008 employment change: Slower than average
Most significant source of training: Work experience in a related occupation

Tire building machine operators
Operate machines such as collapsible drum devices to build pneumatic tires from rubber components, such as beads, ply stock, tread, and sidewalls.

1998 employment: 18,000
Projected 1998-2008 employment change: A decline
Most significant source of training: Moderate-term on-the-job training

Assumptions and Methods Used in Preparing Employment Projections

Occupational statements in the *Handbook* use one of six adjectives to describe projected change in employment (see page 19) The adjectives are based on numerical projections developed using the Bureau's employment projections model system. Projections of occupational employment comprise the sixth and final step in the system; the six steps are listed in the discussion of methods below. A full description, including numerical projections of employment, appears in the November 1999 *Monthly Labor Review*, BLS *Handbook of Methods*, and in *Employment Outlook: 1998-2008,* BLS Bulletin 2522. The Winter 1999-2000 *Occupational Outlook Quarterly* presents the projections in a series of charts.

The projections reflect the knowledge and judgment of staff in the Bureau's Office of Employment Projections and of knowledgeable people from other offices in the Bureau, other government agencies, colleges and universities, industries, unions, professional societies, and trade associations, who furnished data and information, prepared reports, or reviewed the projections. The Bureau takes full responsibility, however, for the projections.

Assumptions. The information in the *Handbook* is based on an economic projection, which is characterized by a labor force growing at the same rate as during the past 10-year period (1988-98), faster productivity growth, a constant unemployment rate, increasing trade deficits, and a Federal budget surplus. Other assumptions include moderate growth in Federal spending programs and above average growth in consumer spending on durable goods. Spending on food and beverages will grow more slowly than the average for all consumer expenditures, while spending on health care and other services, such as entertainment, recreation, and financial services, will grow faster. Investment in production equipment—including factory automation, communication, and computer items—will grow rapidly. Residential construction will grow with the population while nonresidential construction will make a comeback from depressed levels over the previous 10-year period.

Although the Bureau considers these assumptions reasonable, the economy may follow a different course, resulting in a different pattern of occupational growth. Real growth could also be different because most occupations are sensitive to a much wider variety of factors than those considered in the various models. Unforeseen changes in consumer, business, or government spending patterns and in the way goods and services are produced could greatly alter the growth of individual occupations.

Methods. This section summarizes the steps by which the Bureau arrives at projections of employment by occupation. BLS uses Bureau of the Census projections of the population by age, gender, and race, combined with projections of labor force participation rates—the percent of the specified group of the population working or seeking work—to arrive at estimates of the civilian labor force for the projected year.

BLS projections are developed in a series of six steps, each of which is based on separate projection procedures and models and various related assumptions. These six steps, or system components, deal with:

- The size and demographic composition of the labor force
- The growth of the aggregate economy
- Final demand or gross domestic product (GDP)
- Interindustry relationships (input—output)
- Industry output and employment
- Occupational employment

These components provide the overall analytical framework needed to develop detailed employment projections. Each component is developed in order, with the results of each used as input for successive components and with some results feeding back to earlier steps. Each step is repeated a number of times to ensure internal consistency as assumptions and results are reviewed and revised.

The projections of the labor force and assumptions about other demographic variables, fiscal policy, foreign economic activity, and energy prices and availability form the input to the macroeconomic model. This model projects GDP (sales to all final consuming sectors in the economy) and the distribution of GDP by its major demand components (consumer expenditures, investment, government purchases, and net exports). Estimating the intermediate flows of goods and services—for example, the steel incorporated into automobiles—is the next step in the projections process. The resulting estimates of demand for goods and services are used to project industry output of final products as well as total output by industry.

Industry output of goods and services is then converted to industry employment. Studies of trends in productivity and technology are used to estimate future output per worker hour, and regression analysis is used to estimate worker hours. These estimates, along with output projections, are used to develop the final industry employment projections.

An industry-occupation matrix is used to project employment for wage and salary workers. The matrix shows occupational staffing patterns—each occupation as a percent of the work force in every industry. The matrix covering the 1998-2008 period includes 262 detailed industries and 521 detailed occupations. Data for current staffing patterns in the matrix come from the Bureau's Occupational Employment Statistics surveys, which collect data from employers on a 3-year cycle.

The occupational staffing patterns for each industry were projected based on anticipated changes in the way goods and services are produced, then applied to projected industry employment, and the resulting employment was summed across industries to get total wage and salary employment by occupation. Using this method, rapid employment growth is projected for health care workers while employment of railroad transportation workers is expected to decline, reflecting the projected change in the health care and railroad transportation industries, respectively.

Employment in an occupation also may grow or decline as a result of many other factors. For example, rapid growth is expected among teacher aides and educational assistants as increasing attention to the quality of education leads schools to hire more support staff. Rapid growth is also expected among computer systems analysts as technology advances and organizations place more emphasis on network applications and maximizing the efficiency of their computer systems. On the other hand, automation, the expanding use of computers, and developments in computer software will result in limited growth or declining employment among many clerical workers, machine operators, and assemblers. The projected-year matrix incorporates these expected changes.

Data on self-employed workers in each occupation come from the Current Population Survey. Self-employed workers were projected separately.

Replacement needs. In most occupations, replacement needs provide more job openings than growth. Replacement openings occur as people leave occupations. Some individuals transfer to other occupations as a step up the career ladder or to change careers; some stop working temporarily, perhaps to return to school or care for a family; other workers—retirees for example—leave the labor force permanently. A discussion of replacements and the methodology used to prepare estimates is presented in *Occupational Projections and Training Data, 2000-01 Edition,* BLS Bulletin 2521.

Standard Occupational Classification and Occupational Information Network Coverage

The 1998 *Standard Occupational Classification* (SOC), with 822 detailed occupations, reflects the current occupational structure in the United States and was designed to provide a universal occupational classification system. All Federal agencies that collect occupational data will adhere to the new SOC. Information on the 1998 SOC, including its occupational structure, is available online. Internet: **http://stats.bls.gov/soc/soc_home.htm**

The 1998 *Occupational Information Network* (O*NET), with over 1,100 occupations, replaces the *Dictionary of Occupational Titles* and will be used by public employment service offices to classify and place jobseekers. For most occupations where the SOC and O*NET do not match, the O*NET provides more detail; in some cases, the SOC provides more detail. The 1998 O*NET was developed by job analysts. Future information on job duties, knowledge and skills, education and training, and other occupational characteristics will come directly from workers and employers. Information on O*NET is available from O*NET Project, DOL Office of Policy Research/ETA/O*NET, 200 Constitution Ave. NW, MS N5637, Washington, DC 20210. Telephone (202) 219-7161. Fax (202) 219-9186. Internet: **http://www.doleta.gov/programs/onet.**

Nearly all occupational statements in this 2000-01 edition of the *Handbook* list the *O*NET* codes that relate to or match the definitions used in the Bureau's 1998 Occupational Employment Statistics (OES) survey—the principal source of occupational employment data in the *Handbook.* All numbers listed also appear in the table below. The table is arranged by 1998 SOC code, followed by the associated 1998 O*NET code—also known as the occupational unit (OU) code—and title, and the page on which the corresponding *Handbook* statement begins.

Notes

In 1999, the occupational classification in the Bureau's OES survey began to reflect the 1998 SOC. As a result, occupational statements in the 2002-03 edition of the *Handbook*, which is expected to be published in early 2002, will list the O*NET codes that relate to or match the SOC-based definitions used in the 1999 OES survey.

Comparability with older classification systems is important for analyzing long-term trends in employment and other worker characteristics. To simplify historical comparisons, BLS economists have developed a crosswalk showing the relationship between occupations in the 1998 OES survey and the 1999 SOC-based OES survey. The crosswalk is available from the Bureau of Labor Statistics, Office of Employment and Unemployment Statistics, Division of Occupational and Administrative Statistics, Room 4840, 2 Massachusetts Ave. NE, Washington, DC 20212.

SOC Code	*O*NET Code*	*O*NET Title*	*Page*
11-1011	19005A	Government service executives	51
11-1011	19005B	Private sector executives	50
11-1021	19005A	Government service executives	51
11-1021	19005B	Private sector executives	50
11-1031	19005A	Government service executives	51
11-2011	13011A	Advertising and promotions managers	25
11-2021	13011C	Marketing managers	25
11-2022	13011B	Sales managers	25
11-2031	13011D	Fundraising directors	25
11-3011	13014B	Administrative services managers	23
11-3021	13017C	Computer and information systems managers	41
11-3031	13002A	Treasurers, controllers, and chief financial officers	45
11-3031	13002B	Financial managers, branch or department	45
11-3041	13005A	Human resources managers	57
11-3042	13005B	Training and development managers	57
11-3049	13005A	Human resources managers	57
11-3049	13005C	Labor relations managers	57
11-3051	15014	Industrial production managers	61
11-3061	13008	Purchasing managers	73
11-3071	15023A	Transportation managers	521
11-3071	15023D	Storage and distribution managers	521
11-9011	15017A	Landscaping managers	331
11-9011	15031	Nursery and greenhouse managers	331
11-9011	79999K	Agricultural crop farm managers	43
11-9011	79999L	Livestock production managers	43
11-9011	79999M	Fish hatchery managers	43
11-9012	79999C	Horticultural specialty growers	43
11-9012	79999D	Farmers	43
11-9012	79999G	Aqua-culturists	43
11-9012	79999J	Gamekeepers	43
11-9021	15017B	Construction managers	31
11-9031	15005B	Educational program directors	36
11-9032	15005B	Educational program directors	36
11-9033	15005A	College and university administrators	36
11-9039	15005B	Educational program directors	36
11-9041	13017A	Engineering managers	41
11-9051	15026B	Food-service managers	76
11-9061	39011	Funeral directors and morticians	48
11-9081	15026A	Lodging managers	55
11-9111	15008A	Nursing directors	53
11-9111	15008B	Medical and health services managers	53
11-9121	13017B	Natural sciences managers	41
11-9131	15002	Postmasters and mail superintendents	521
11-9141	15011B	Property, real estate, and community association managers	71
11-9199	15023B	Communications managers	521
11-9199	15023C	Utilities managers	521
13-1021	21305A	Purchasing agents and buyers, farm products	73
13-1022	21302	Wholesale and retail buyers, except farm products	73
13-1023	21308A	Purchasing agents and contract specialists	73
13-1031	21921	Claims examiners, property and casualty insurance	285
13-1031	53302	Insurance adjusters, examiners, and investigators	285
13-1032	53305	Insurance appraisers, auto damage	523
13-1041	21911B	Environmental compliance inspectors	63
13-1041	21911C	Immigration and customs inspectors	366
13-1041	21911D	Licensing examiners and inspectors	63
13-1041	21911F	Equal opportunity representatives and officers	63
13-1041	21911H	Government property inspectors and investigators	63
13-1041	21911L	Pressure vessel inspectors	63
13-1041	21911P	Coroners	63
13-1051	21902	Cost estimators	34
13-1051	85305D	Automotive body repair estimators	34
13-1071	21508	Employment interviewers, private or public employment service	39
13-1071	21511B	Employer relations and job development specialists	57
13-1071	21511E	Personnel recruiters	57
13-1072	21511A	Job and occupational analysts	57

SOC Code	O*NET Code	O*NET Title	Page
13-1073	21511D	Employee training specialists	57
13-1079	13005E	Employee assistance specialists	57
13-1079	21511C	Employee relations specialists	57
13-1079	21511F	Labor relations specialists	57
13-1111	21905	Management analysts	69
13-2011	21114A	Accountants	20
13-2011	21114B	Auditors	20
13-2021	21917	Assessors	521
13-2021	43011	Appraisers, real estate	522
13-2031	21117	Budget analysts	27
13-2041	21105	Credit analysts	521
13-2053	21102	Underwriters	65
13-2061	21911J	Financial examiners	63
13-2071	21108	Loan officers and counselors	67
13-2072	21108	Loan officers and counselors	67
13-2081	21914	Tax examiners, collectors, and revenue agents	521
13-2082	21111	Tax preparers	522
15-1021	25105	Computer programmers	113
15-1031	22127	Computer engineers	109
15-1032	22127	Computer engineers	109
15-1041	25104	Computer support specialists	109
15-1051	25102	Systems analysts, electronic data processing	109
15-1061	25103A	Database administrators	109
15-1081	25199A	Data communications analysts	109
15-1099	21114C	Data processing auditors	109
15-2011	25313	Actuaries	107
15-2021	25319A	Mathematicians	116
15-2031	25302	Operations and systems researchers and analysts, except computer	118
15-2041	25312	Statisticians	120
15-2099	25319B	Weight analysts	116
15-2099	25319C	All other mathematical scientists	116
15-3011	25323	Mathematical technicians	139
17-1011	22302	Architects, except landscape and marine	98
17-1012	22308	Landscape architects	102
17-1021	22311A	Cartographers and photogrammetrists	105
17-1021	25103B	Geographic information system specialists	105
17-1022	22311B	Surveyors	105
17-2011	22102	Aerospace engineers	85
17-2011	22102	Aerospace engineers	88
17-2021	22123	Agricultural engineers	85
17-2041	22114	Chemical engineers	85
17-2041	22114	Chemical engineers	89
17-2051	22121	Civil engineers, including traffic	90
17-2051	22121	Civil engineers, including traffic	85
17-2061	22127	Computer engineers	109
17-2071	22126A	Electrical engineers	85
17-2071	22126A	Electrical engineers	90
17-2072	22126B	Electronics engineers, except computer	90
17-2072	22126B	Electronics engineers, except computer	85
17-2111	22132A	Industrial safety and health engineers	85
17-2111	22132B	Fire-prevention and protection engineers	85
17-2111	22132C	Product safety engineers	85
17-2112	22128	Industrial engineers, except safety	91
17-2112	22128	Industrial engineers, except safety	85
17-2121	22138	Marine engineers	85
17-2121	22305	Marine architects	85
17-2131	22105A	Ceramic engineers	92
17-2131	22105A	Ceramic engineers	85
17-2131	22105B	Metallurgists	85
17-2131	22105B	Metallurgists	92
17-2131	22105C	Welding engineers	85
17-2131	22105C	Welding engineers	92
17-2131	22105D	Materials engineers	92
17-2131	22105D	Materials engineers	85
17-2141	22135	Mechanical engineers	85
17-2141	22135	Mechanical engineers	93
17-2151	22108	Mining engineers, including mine safety	93
17-2151	22108	Mining engineers, including mine safety	85
17-2161	22117	Nuclear engineers	85
17-2161	22117	Nuclear engineers	94
17-2171	22111	Petroleum engineers	85
17-2171	22111	Petroleum engineers	95
17-2199	21308B	Procurement engineers	85
17-2199	22197	Production engineers	85
17-3011	22514A	Architectural drafters	100
17-3011	22514C	Civil drafters	100
17-3012	22514B	Electronic drafters	100
17-3012	22517	Estimators and drafters, utilities	100
17-3013	22514D	Mechanical drafters	100
17-3021	22599C	Aerospace engineering technicians	96
17-3022	22502	Civil engineering technicians	96
17-3023	22505A	Electronics engineering technicians	96
17-3023	22505B	Calibration and instrumentation technicians	96
17-3023	22505C	Electrical engineering technicians	96
17-3023	22599G	All other engineering and related technicians	96
17-3024	93111B	Electromechanical technicians	443
17-3024	93111B	Electromechanical technicians	96
17-3026	22508	Industrial engineering technicians and technologists	96
17-3027	22511	Mechanical engineering technicians and technologists	96
17-3029	22599B	Metallurgical technicians	96
17-3029	22599D	Agricultural engineering technicians	96
17-3029	22599E	Chemical engineering technicians	96
17-3031	22521A	Surveying technicians	105
17-3031	22521B	Mapping technicians	105
19-1011	24305A	Animal scientists	122
19-1012	24305C	Food scientists	122
19-1013	24305B	Plant scientists	122
19-1013	24305D	Soil scientists	122
19-1021	24308A	Biochemists	124
19-1021	24308C	Biophysicists	124
19-1022	24308E	Microbiologists	124
19-1023	24308H	Zoologists	124
19-1029	24308B	Biologists	124
19-1029	24308D	Botanists	124
19-1029	24308F	Geneticists	124
19-1029	24308G	Physiologists and cytologists	124
19-1029	24308J	Toxicologists	124
19-1031	24302B	Soil conservationists	127
19-1031	24302D	Range managers	127
19-1031	24302E	Park naturalists	127
19-1032	24302A	Foresters	127
19-1032	24302C	Wood technologists	127
19-1041	24311	Medical scientists	124
19-1042	24311	Medical scientists	124
19-2011	24102B	Astronomers	136
19-2012	24102A	Physicists	136
19-2021	24108	Atmospheric and space scientists	129
19-2031	24105	Chemists, except biochemists	131
19-2042	24111A	Geologists	133
19-2042	24111B	Geophysicists	133
19-2043	24111B	Geophysicists	133
19-3011	27102A	Economists	148
19-3021	27102B	Market research analysts	148
19-3031	27108D	Educational psychologists	150
19-3031	27108G	Clinical psychologists	150
19-3031	27108H	Counseling psychologists	150
19-3032	27108J	Industrial-organizational psychologists	150
19-3039	27108A	Developmental psychologists	150
19-3039	27108C	Experimental psychologists	150
19-3039	27108E	Social psychologists	150
19-3041	27199B	Sociologists	154
19-3051	27105	Urban and regional planners	153
19-3091	27199C	Anthropologists	154
19-3091	27199H	Archeologists	154
19-3092	24199A	Geographers	154
19-3093	27199E	Historians	154
19-3093	27199G	Genealogists	154
19-3094	27199A	Political scientists	154
19-3099	27199D	Linguistic scientists	154
19-3099	27199F	Intelligence specialists	154
19-4011	24502A	Biological and agricultural technologists	139
19-4011	24502B	Artificial breeding technicians	139
19-4011	24505B	Food science technicians	139
19-4021	24502C	Biological and agricultural technicians	139
19-4021	24502D	Biology specimen technicians	139
19-4031	24505A	Chemical technicians	139
19-4041	24505C	Assayers	139
19-4041	24511B	Geological data technicians	139
19-4041	24511E	Geological sample test technicians	139
19-4051	24508A	Nuclear equipment operation technicians	139
19-4051	24508B	Nuclear monitoring technicians	139
19-4091	24505E	Environmental science technicians	139

SOC Code	O*NET Code	O*NET Title	Page
19-4092	24599B	Criminalists and ballistics experts	139
19-4093	79002B	Forester aides	450
19-4099	22599F	Laser technicians	139
19-4099	24505D	Textile science technicians	139
19-4099	24599A	Meteorological technicians	139
19-4099	24599C	Scientific helpers	139
21-1011	27302	Social workers, medical and psychiatric	161
21-1012	31514	Vocational and educational counselors	175
21-1014	27302	Social workers, medical and psychiatric	161
21-1015	31514	Vocational and educational counselors	175
21-1019	31514	Vocational and educational counselors	175
21-1021	27305A	Community organization social workers	161
21-1021	27305B	Social workers	161
21-1022	27302	Social workers, medical and psychiatric	161
21-1023	27302	Social workers, medical and psychiatric	161
21-1029	27305B	Social workers	161
21-1092	27305C	Probation and correctional treatment specialists	161
21-1093	27308	Human services workers	157
21-2011	27502	Clergy	167
21-2011	27502	Clergy	164
21-2011	27502	Clergy	164
21-2011	27502	Clergy	166
21-2021	27505	Directors, religious activities and education	521
23-1011	28108	Lawyers	141
23-1021	28105	Adjudicators, hearings officers, and judicial reviewers	141
23-1022	28105	Adjudicators, hearings officers, and judicial reviewers	141
23-1023	28102	Judges and magistrates	141
23-2011	28305	Paralegals and legal assistants	145
23-2091	55302A	Stenotype operators	295
23-2093	28308	Title searchers	522
23-2093	28311	Title examiners and abstractors	522
25-1011	31202	Life sciences teachers-postsecondary	173
25-1021	31226	Computer science teachers-postsecondary	173
25-1022	31224	Mathematical sciences teachers-postsecondary	173
25-1031	31299	All other postsecondary teachers	173
25-1032	31222	Engineering teachers-postsecondary	173
25-1041	31202	Life sciences teachers-postsecondary	173
25-1042	31202	Life sciences teachers-postsecondary	173
25-1043	31202	Life sciences teachers-postsecondary	173
25-1051	31209	All other physical science teachers-postsecondary	173
25-1052	31204	Chemistry teachers-postsecondary	173
25-1053	31202	Life sciences teachers-postsecondary	173
25-1054	31206	Physics teachers-postsecondary	173
25-1061	31210	Social science teachers-postsecondary	173
25-1062	31210	Social science teachers-postsecondary	173
25-1063	31210	Social science teachers-postsecondary	173
25-1064	31299	All other postsecondary teachers	173
25-1065	31210	Social science teachers-postsecondary	173
25-1066	31210	Social science teachers-postsecondary	173
25-1067	31210	Social science teachers-postsecondary	173
25-1069	31210	Social science teachers-postsecondary	173
25-1071	31212	Health specialties teachers-postsecondary	173
25-1072	31114	Nursing instructors-postsecondary	173
25-1081	31299	All other postsecondary teachers	173
25-1082	31299	All other postsecondary teachers	173
25-1111	31299	All other postsecondary teachers	173
25-1112	31299	All other postsecondary teachers	173
25-1113	31299	All other postsecondary teachers	173
25-1121	31218	Art, drama, and music teachers-postsecondary	173
25-1122	31299	All other postsecondary teachers	173
25-1123	31216	English and foreign language teachers-postsecondary	173
25-1124	31216	English and foreign language teachers-postsecondary	173
25-1125	31210	Social science teachers-postsecondary	173
25-1126	31299	All other postsecondary teachers	173
25-1192	31299	All other postsecondary teachers	173
25-1193	31299	All other postsecondary teachers	173
25-1194	31314	Teachers and instructors, vocational education and training	168
25-1199	31299	All other postsecondary teachers	173
25-2011	31303	Teachers, preschool	353
25-2012	31304	Teachers, kindergarten	183
25-2021	31305	Teachers, elementary school	183
25-2022	31308	Teachers, secondary school	183
25-2023	31308	Teachers, secondary school	183
25-2031	31308	Teachers, secondary school	183
25-2032	31308	Teachers, secondary school	183
25-2041	31311A	Special education vocational training teachers	187
25-2041	31311B	Teachers-emotionally impaired, mentally impaired, and learning disabled	187
25-2041	31311C	Teachers-physically, visually, and hearing impaired	187
25-2042	31311A	Special education vocational training teachers	187
25-2042	31311B	Teachers-emotionally impaired, mentally impaired, and learning disabled	187
25-2042	31311C	Teachers-physically, visually, and hearing impaired	187
25-2043	31311A	Special education vocational training teachers	187
25-2043	31311B	Teachers-emotionally impaired, mentally impaired, and learning disabled	187
25-2043	31311C	Teachers-physically, visually, and hearing impaired	187
25-3011	31317	Instructors, nonvocational education	168
25-3021	31317	Instructors, nonvocational education	168
25-4011	31511B	Archivists	170
25-4012	31511A	Curators	170
25-4013	31511C	Museum research workers	170
25-4013	31511D	Museum technicians and conservators	170
25-4021	31502A	Librarians	179
25-4021	31502B	Library research workers	179
25-4031	31505	Technical assistants, library	182
25-9021	31323	Farm and home management advisors	521
25-9041	31521	Teacher aides, paraprofessional	326
25-9041	53905	Teacher aides and educational assistants, clerical	326
27-1011	34038E	Art directors	251
27-1012	39999H	All other professional, paraprofessional, and technical workers	251
27-1013	34035A	Painters and illustrators	251
27-1013	34035B	Sketch artists	251
27-1013	34035E	Sculptors	251
27-1014	34035D	Cartoonists and animators	251
27-1014	39999H	All other professional, paraprofessional, and technical workers	251
27-1019	39999E	Taxidermists	251
27-1021	34038B	Commercial and industrial designers	246
27-1022	34038A	Fashion designers	246
27-1023	34038F	Floral designers	246
27-1024	34035C	Graphic designers	251
27-1025	34041	Interior designers	246
27-1026	34044	Merchandise displayers and window trimmers	246
27-1027	34038C	Set designers	246
27-1027	34038D	Exhibit designers	246
27-1029	39999H	All other professional, paraprofessional, and technical workers	246
27-2011	34056A	Actors and performers	254
27-2012	34056F	Producers	254
27-2012	34056G	Directors-stage, motion pictures, television, and radio	254
27-2012	34056H	Program directors	254
27-2012	34056J	Talent directors	254
27-2012	34056K	Technical directors/managers	254
27-2021	34058C	Professional athletes	521
27-2021	34058E	Motor racers	521
27-2021	34058F	Jockeys and sulky drivers	521
27-2022	31321	Instructors and coaches, sports and physical training	178
27-2022	34058A	Coaches and scouts	521
27-2023	34058L	Umpires, referees, and other sports officials	521
27-2031	34053A	Dancers	256
27-2032	34053B	Choreographers	256
27-2041	34047A	Music directors	258
27-2041	34047B	Music arrangers and orchestrators	258
27-2041	34047E	Composers	258
27-2042	34047C	Singers	258
27-2042	34051	Musicians, instrumental	258
27-2099	34047F	Prompters	254
27-2099	34056B	Extras/stand-ins	254
27-2099	34056D	Amusement entertainers	254
27-2099	34056E	Equestrian performers	254
27-3011	34017	Announcers, radio and television	236

SOC Code	*O*NET Code*	*O*NET Title*	*Page*
27-3012	34021	Announcers, except radio and television	236
27-3021	34014	Broadcast news analysts	239
27-3022	34002A	Columnists, critics, and commentators	239
27-3022	34011	Reporters and correspondents	239
27-3031	34008	Public relations specialists and publicity writers	241
27-3041	34002D	Editors	243
27-3041	34002E	Managing editors	243
27-3041	34002F	Programming and script editors and coordinators	243
27-3041	34002G	Book editors	243
27-3041	34002M	Dictionary editors	243
27-3042	34005	Technical writers	243
27-3043	34002B	Poets and lyricists	243
27-3043	34002C	Creative writers	243
27-3043	34002J	Caption writers	243
27-3043	34002L	Copy writers	243
27-4012	34028B	Broadcast technicians	237
27-4012	34028C	Transmitter engineers	237
27-4014	22599A	Sound engineering technicians	237
27-4021	34023A	Professional photographers	249
27-4021	34023B	Photographers, scientific	249
27-4031	34026	Camera operators, television and motion picture	249
29-1011	32113	Chiropractors	189
29-1021	32105B	Dentists	191
29-1022	32105G	Oral and maxillofacial surgeons	191
29-1023	32105D	Orthodontists	191
29-1024	32105F	Prosthodontists	191
29-1029	32105A	Oral pathologists	191
29-1031	32521	Dietitians and nutritionists	200
29-1041	32108	Optometrists	192
29-1051	32517	Pharmacists	203
29-1061	32102F	Anesthesiologists	193
29-1062	32102A	Doctors of medicine (MD)	193
29-1063	32102A	Doctors of medicine (MD)	193
29-1064	32102A	Doctors of medicine (MD)	193
29-1065	32102A	Doctors of medicine (MD)	193
29-1066	32102E	Psychiatrists	193
29-1067	32102J	Surgeons	193
29-1069	32102B	Doctors of osteopathy (DO)	193
29-1069	32102U	Pathologists	193
29-1071	32511	Physician's assistants	207
29-1081	32111	Podiatrists	196
29-1111	32502	Registered nurses	210
29-1121	32314	Speech-language pathologists and audiologists	214
29-1122	32305	Occupational therapists	202
29-1123	32308	Physical therapists	205
29-1124	32913	Radiation therapists	522
29-1125	32317	Recreational therapists	209
29-1126	32302	Respiratory therapists	213
29-1127	32314	Speech-language pathologists and audiologists	214
29-1131	32114A	Veterinary scientists	197
29-1131	32114B	Veterinarians	197
29-1131	32114C	Veterinary inspectors	197
29-2011	32902	Medical and clinical laboratory technologists	218
29-2012	32905	Medical and clinical laboratory technicians	218
29-2021	32908	Dental hygienists	220
29-2031	32925	Cardiology technologists	217
29-2032	32919	Radiologic technologists	233
29-2033	32914	Nuclear medicine technologists	228
29-2034	32919	Radiologic technologists	233
29-2034	32921	Radiologic technicians	233
29-2041	32508	Emergency medical technicians	223
29-2052	32518	Pharmacy technicians	231
29-2053	32931	Psychiatric technicians	521
29-2055	32928	Surgical technologists and technicians	234
29-2056	39999H	All other professional, paraprofessional, and technical workers	522
29-2061	32505	Licensed practical nurses	227
29-2071	32911	Medical records technicians	225
29-2081	32514	Opticians, dispensing and measuring	229
29-2099	32923	Electroneurodiagnostic technologists	222
29-2099	32926	Electrocardiograph technicians	217
29-9011	21911A	Public health officers and inspectors	63
29-9011	21911E	Industrial and occupational safety and health inspectors	63
29-9011	21911T	Radiation-protection specialists	63
29-9091	34058B	Athletic trainers	521
31-1011	66011	Home health aides	351
31-1012	66008	Nursing aides, orderlies, and attendants	343
31-1013	66014	Psychiatric aides	343
31-2011	66021	Occupational therapy assistants and aides	345
31-2012	66021	Occupational therapy assistants and aides	345
31-2021	66017	Physical and corrective therapy assistants and aides	346
31-2022	66017	Physical and corrective therapy assistants and aides	346
31-9091	66002	Dental assistants	341
31-9092	66005	Medical assistants	342
31-9094	55302A	Stenotype operators	295
31-9095	32518	Pharmacy technicians	231
31-9096	79806	Veterinary assistants	357
31-9099	66099A	Morgue attendants	342
31-9099	66099D	Phlebotomists	218
33-1011	61009E	All other service supervisors and manager/supervisors	359
33-1012	61005	Police and detective supervisors	366
33-1021	61002A	Municipal fire fighting and prevention supervisors	361
33-1021	61002B	Forest fire fighting and prevention supervisors	361
33-1099	63026	United states marshals	366
33-2011	63008A	Municipal fire fighters	361
33-2011	63008B	Forest fire fighters	361
33-2021	63002A	Fire inspectors	361
33-2021	63002B	Fire investigators	361
33-2022	63005	Forest fire inspectors and prevention specialists	361
33-3011	63023	Bailiffs	366
33-3012	63017	Correction officers and jailers	359
33-3021	63011A	Police detectives	366
33-3021	63011B	Police identification and records officers	366
33-3021	63028A	Criminal investigators and special agents	366
33-3021	63028B	Child support, missing persons, and unemployment insurance fraud investigators	366
33-3031	63041	Fish and game wardens	366
33-3041	63021	Parking enforcement officers	366
33-3051	63014A	Police patrol officers	366
33-3051	63014B	Highway patrol pilots	366
33-3051	63032	Sheriffs and deputy sheriffs	366
33-3052	63038	Railroad and transit police and special agents	366
33-9021	63035	Detectives and investigators, except public	369
33-9032	63047	Guards and watch guards	364
33-9091	63044	Crossing guards	523
35-2011	65032	Cooks, specialty fast food	336
35-2012	65028	Cooks, institution or cafeteria	336
35-2013	69999E	All other service workers	355
35-2014	65026	Cooks, restaurant	336
35-2015	65035	Cooks, short order	336
35-2021	65038A	Food preparation workers	336
35-3011	65005	Bartenders	338
35-3021	65041	Combined food preparation and service workers	338
35-3022	65017	Counter attendants-lunchroom, coffee shop, or cafeteria	338
35-3031	65008A	Waiters/waitresses	338
35-3041	65011	Food servers, outside	338
35-9011	65014	Dining room and cafeteria attendants, and bartender helpers	338
35-9021	65038B	Kitchen helpers	336
35-9021	69999E	All other service workers	336
35-9031	65002	Hosts and hostesses-restaurant, lounge or coffee shop	338
35-9099	65008B	Wine stewards/stewardesses	338
35-9099	65099A	Vending machine attendants	338
35-9099	65099B	Food order expediters	338
37-1011	61008	Housekeeping supervisors	330
37-1012	15032	Lawn service managers	331
37-1012	72002A	First-line supervisors and manager/supervisors-agricultural crop workers	527
37-1012	72002B	First-line supervisors and manager/supervisors-animal husbandry workers	527
37-1012	72002C	First-line supervisors and manager/supervisors-animal care workers, except livestock	527
37-1012	72002D	First-line supervisors and manager/supervisors-landscaping workers	527

SOC Code	O*NET Code	O*NET Title	Page
47-4041	87999	All other construction and extractive workers, except helpers	428
47-4051	87711	Highway maintenance workers	524
47-5041	87941	Continuous mining machine operators	524
47-5042	87943	Mine cutting and channeling machine operators	524
47-5049	87949A	Mining machine operators and tenders	524
47-5049	87949B	Oil and gas well-pumping and blending-equipment operators	524
47-5051	87908	Rock splitters, quarry	524
47-5061	87923	Roof bolters	524
47-5071	87921	Roustabouts	524
47-5081	98323	Helpers-extractive workers	511
49-1011	81002	First-line supervisors and manager/ supervisors-mechanics, installers, and repairers	445
49-1011	81005A	First-line supervisors and manager/ supervisors-construction trades workers	445
49-1011	81005B	First-line supervisors and manager/ supervisors-extractive workers	445
49-1011	81008	First-line supervisors and manager/ supervisors-production and operating workers	445
49-1011	81011	First-line supervisors and manager/ supervisors-transportation and material moving machine and vehicle operators	445
49-1011	81017	First-line supervisors and manager/ supervisors-helpers, laborers, and material movers, hand	445
49-2011	85705	Data processing equipment repairers	372
49-2011	85926	Office machine and cash register servicers	372
49-2021	85514	Radio mechanics	376
49-2022	85502	Central office and pbx installers and repairers	376
49-2022	85505	Frame wirers, central office	376
49-2022	85508	Telegraph and teletype installers and maintainers	376
49-2022	85599A	Communication equipment mechanics, installers, and repairers	376
49-2022	85599B	Telecommunications facility examiners	376
49-2022	85599C	Sound technicians	376
49-2022	85726	Station installers and repairers, telephone	376
49-2091	85728A	Aircraft electricians	378
49-2092	85711A	Electric home appliance and power tool repairers	394
49-2094	85717A	Electronics mechanics and technicians	375
49-2097	85708	Electronic home entertainment equipment repairers	374
49-3011	85323A	Airframe-and-power-plant mechanics	378
49-3011	85326	Aircraft engine specialists	378
49-3021	85305B	Automotive body repairers	380
49-3021	85305C	Truck and trailer body repairers	380
49-3022	85305A	Automotive glass installers and repairers	380
49-3023	85302A	Automotive master mechanics	382
49-3023	85302B	Automotive specialty technicians	382
49-3031	85311A	Diesel engine mechanics	387
49-3041	85321	Farm equipment mechanics	389
49-3042	85314	Mobile heavy equipment mechanics, except engines	402
49-3051	85328A	Motorboat mechanics	405
49-3052	85308	Motorcycle mechanics and repairers	405
49-3053	85328B	Small engine mechanics	405
49-3091	85951	Bicycle repairers	523
49-3093	85953	Tire repairers and changers	524
49-9021	85902A	Heating and air conditioning mechanics	391
49-9021	85902B	Refrigeration mechanics	391
49-9031	85711B	Home appliance installers	394
49-9031	85944	Gas appliance repairers	394
49-9041	85112	Machinery maintenance mechanics, textile machines	396
49-9041	85113	Machinery maintenance mechanics, sewing machines	396
49-9041	85118	Machinery maintenance mechanics, water or power generation plant	396
49-9041	85119A	Machinery maintenance mechanics	396
49-9041	85119B	Machinery maintenance repairers	396
49-9041	85119C	All other machinery maintenance mechanics	396
49-9042	85132	Maintenance repairers, general utility	399
49-9043	85128A	Machinery maintenance servicers	396
49-9043	85128B	Oilers	396
49-9044	85123A	Manufacturer's service representatives and technicians	401
49-9044	85123B	Millwrights	401
49-9051	85723	Electrical powerline installers and repairers	397
49-9052	85702	Telephone and cable television line installers and repairers	397
49-9061	85914	Camera and photographic equipment repairers	523
49-9062	85908	Electromedical and biomedical equipment repairers	524
49-9063	85921A	Keyboard instrument repairers and tuners	407
49-9063	85921B	Stringed instrument repairers and tuners	407
49-9063	85921C	Reed or wind instrument repairers and tuners	407
49-9063	85921D	Percussion instrument repairers and tuners	407
49-9064	85917	Watchmakers	524
49-9069	85905	Precision instrument repairers	524
49-9091	85947	Coin and vending machine servicers and repairers	385
49-9094	85923	Locksmiths and safe repairers	523
49-9096	85935	Riggers	524
49-9098	98102	Helpers-mechanics and repairers	511
49-9099	85116B	Marine engine mechanics	405
49-9099	85116C	Marine services technicians	396
49-9099	85323B	Aircraft body and bonded structure repairers	378
49-9099	85717B	Test card and circuit board repairers	375
49-9099	85999A	Hand and portable power tool repairers	394
49-9099	87202C	Electrical utility trouble shooters	422
51-1011	81002	First-line supervisors and manager/ supervisors-mechanics, installers, and repairers	445
51-1011	81005A	First-line supervisors and manager/ supervisors-construction trades workers	445
51-1011	81005B	First-line supervisors and manager/ supervisors-extractive workers	445
51-1011	81008	First-line supervisors and manager/ supervisors-production and operating workers	445
51-1011	81011	First-line supervisors and manager/ supervisors-transportation and material moving machineand vehicle operators	445
51-1011	81017	First-line supervisors and manager/ supervisors-helpers, laborers, and material movers, hand	445
51-2011	93102B	Aircraft structure assemblers, precision	443
51-2011	93102C	Aircraft systems assemblers, precision	443
51-2011	93102D	Aircraft rigging assemblers	443
51-2021	93908	Coil winders, tapers, and finishers	525
51-2022	93114	Electrical and electronic equipment assemblers-precision	443
51-2022	93905A	Battery assemblers	526
51-2022	93905B	Electronic components assemblers	526
51-2022	93905C	Electric motor assemblers	526
51-2022	93905D	Electrical components assemblers	526
51-2023	93111A	Electromechanical equipment assemblers-precision	443
51-2023	93111B	Electromechanical technicians	443
51-2023	93111B	Electromechanical technicians	96
51-2031	85311B	Diesel engine erectors and fitters	527
51-2031	93105	Machine builders and other precision machine assemblers	443
51-2031	93902	Machine assemblers	527
51-2041	91714	Metal fabricators, structural metal products	459
51-2041	91714	Metal fabricators, structural metal products	527
51-2041	91714	Metal fabricators, structural metal products	440
51-2041	93108	Fitters, structural metal-precision	443
51-2093	93117	Watch, clock, and chronometer assemblers, adjusters, and calibrators-precision	443
51-2099	87102C	Tank builders and coopers	443
51-2099	89302C	Jig builders	484
51-2099	89502D	Hat patternmakers	477
51-2099	93197A	Musical instrument makers, metalworking	443
51-2099	93197C	All other precision assemblers	443
51-3011	65021	Bakers, bread and pastry	336
51-3011	89805	Bakers, manufacturing	524
51-3021	65023	Butchers and meat cutters	448

SOC Code	*O*NET Code*	*O*NET Title*	*Page*
51-6064	92711	Textile draw-out machine operators and tenders	481
51-6091	92708	Extruding and forming machine operators and tenders, synthetic or glass fibers	481
51-6092	89502A	Fabric and apparel patternmakers	477
51-6092	89502B	Embroidery patternmakers and designers	477
51-6093	89508	Upholsterers	482
51-7011	89308	Wood machinists	484
51-7011	89311	Cabinetmakers and bench carpenters	484
51-7021	89314	Furniture finishers	484
51-7031	89302A	Patternmakers and model makers, wood	484
51-7032	89302A	Patternmakers and model makers, wood	484
51-7041	92302	Sawing machine setters and set-up operators	484
51-7041	92305	Head sawyers	484
51-7041	92308	Sawing machine operators and tenders	484
51-7042	92311	Woodworking machine setters and set-up operators, except sawing	484
51-7042	92314	Woodworking machine operators and tenders, except sawing	484
51-7099	89305	Woodworking layout workers	484
51-7099	89397A	Custom precision woodworkers, musical instruments	484
51-7099	89397B	Custom precision woodworkers	484
51-7099	89398	Standard precision woodworkers	484
51-8011	95026	Power reactor operators	465
51-8012	95028	Power distributors and dispatchers	465
51-8013	95021	Power generating plant operators, except auxiliary equipment operators	465
51-8013	95023	Auxiliary equipment operators, power	465
51-8021	92926	Boiler operators and tenders, low pressure	525
51-8021	95032	Stationary engineers	467
51-8031	95002A	Water treatment plant and system operators	468
51-8091	95008	Chemical plant and system operators	525
51-8092	95005A	Gas processing plant operators	526
51-8092	95005B	Gas distribution plant operators	526
51-8093	95011	Petroleum pump system operators	526
51-8093	95014	Petroleum refinery and control panel operators	526
51-8093	95017	Gaugers	526
51-9011	92935	Chemical equipment controllers and operators	525
51-9011	92938	Chemical equipment tenders	525
51-9012	92932	Dairy processing equipment operators, including setters	525
51-9012	92962	Separating, filtering, clarifying, precipitating, and still machine operators and tenders	527
51-9012	92965	Crushing, grinding, mixing, and blending machine operators and tenders	525
51-9021	92965	Crushing, grinding, mixing, and blending machine operators and tenders	525
51-9022	93953	Grinding and polishing workers, hand	526
51-9023	92965	Crushing, grinding, mixing, and blending machine operators and tenders	525
51-9031	93926B	Rock splitters	477
51-9031	93926D	Glass cutters and finishers	477
51-9031	93926E	Cutters and trimmers, hand	477
51-9032	92941A	Fiber product cutting machine setters and set-up operators	525
51-9032	92941B	Stone sawyers	525
51-9032	92941D	Glass cutting machine setters and set-up operators	525
51-9032	92944	Cutting and slicing machine operators and tenders	525
51-9041	92968	Extruding, forming, pressing, and compacting machine setters and set-up operators	526
51-9041	92971	Extruding, forming, pressing, and compacting machine operators and tenders	526
51-9051	92923	Furnace, kiln, oven, drier, or kettle operators and tenders	526
51-9061	83002A	Materials inspectors	453
51-9061	83002B	Mechanical inspectors	453
51-9061	83002C	Precision devices inspectors and testers	453
51-9061	83002D	Electrical and electronic inspectors and testers	453
51-9061	83005A	Production inspectors, testers, graders, sorters, samplers, weighers	453
51-9061	83099	All other inspectors, testers and related workers	453
51-9071	89123A	Jewelers	455
51-9071	89123B	Silversmiths	455
51-9071	89126C	Model and mold makers, jewelry	455
51-9071	89126E	Bench workers, jewelry	455
51-9071	89126K	Pewter casters and finishers	455
51-9071	89926A	Gem and diamond workers	455
51-9081	89921	Precision dental laboratory technicians	486
51-9083	89917A	Precision lens grinders and polishers	489
51-9083	89917D	Optical instrument assemblers	489
51-9111	92974	Packaging and filling machine operators and tenders	527
51-9111	93935	Cannery workers	525
51-9121	92951	Coating, painting, and spraying machine setters and set-up operators	491
51-9121	92953	Coating, painting, and spraying machine operators and tenders	491
51-9122	92947	Painters, transportation equipment	491
51-9123	93947B	Bakery and confectionery decorating workers	527
51-9131	89914A	Photographic retouchers and restorers	493
51-9131	89914B	Photographic reproduction technicians	493
51-9131	89914C	Photographic hand developers	493
51-9131	89914D	Film laboratory technicians	493
51-9132	92908	Photographic processing machine operators and tenders	493
51-9141	92902A	Electronic semiconductor processors	488
51-9141	92902B	Electronic semiconductor wafer etchers and engravers	488
51-9141	92902C	Electronic semiconductor test and development technicians	488
51-9141	92902D	Electronic semiconductor crystal-growing technicians and equipment operators	488
51-9141	92902E	Electronic semiconductor sawyers, abraders, and polishers	488
51-9141	92902G	Electronic semiconductor wafer breakers, mounters, and packagers	488
51-9191	92956	Cementing and gluing machine operators and tenders	525
51-9192	93935	Cannery workers	525
51-9196	92914	Paper goods machine setters and set-up operators	527
51-9197	92911	Tire building machine operators	527
51-9198	98999A	Production laborers	511
51-9198	98999B	Production helpers	511
51-9199	93956	Assemblers and fabricators-except machine, electrical, electronic, and precision	511
51-9199	93997	Intermediate hand workers	511
51-9199	93998	Elemental hand workers	511
51-9199	93999	All other hand workers	511
53-1021	81002	First-line supervisors and manager/supervisors-mechanics, installers, and repairers	445
53-1021	81005A	First-line supervisors and manager/supervisors-construction trades workers	445
53-1021	81005B	First-line supervisors and manager/supervisors-extractive workers	445
53-1021	81008	First-line supervisors and manager/supervisors-production and operating workers	445
53-1021	81011	First-line supervisors and manager/supervisors-transportation and material moving machine and vehicle operators	445
53-1021	81017	First-line supervisors and manager/supervisors-helpers, laborers, and material movers, hand	445
53-1031	81002	First-line supervisors and manager/supervisors-mechanics, installers, and repairers	445
53-1031	81005A	First-line supervisors and manager/supervisors-construction trades workers	445

SOC Code	O*NET Code	O*NET Title	Page
53-1031	81005B	First-line supervisors and manager/supervisors-extractive workers	445
53-1031	81008	First-line supervisors and manager/supervisors-production and operating workers	445
53-1031	81011	First-line supervisors and manager/supervisors-transportation and material moving machine and vehicle operators	445
53-1031	81017	First-line supervisors and manager/supervisors-helpers, laborers, and material movers, hand	445
53-2011	97702B	Commercial airplane pilots	80
53-2011	97702D	Flight instructors	80
53-2011	97702E	Flight navigators	80
53-2011	97702H	Flight engineers	80
53-2012	97702B	Commercial airplane pilots	80
53-2012	97702C	Small aircraft pilots	80
53-2012	97702D	Flight instructors	80
53-2012	97702E	Flight navigators	80
53-2012	97702H	Flight engineers	80
53-2012	97702J	Commercial helicopter pilots	80
53-2021	39002	Airplane dispatchers and air traffic controllers	83
53-3011	66023	Ambulance drivers and attendants, except emergency medical technicians	523
53-3021	97108	Bus drivers	495
53-3022	97111	Bus drivers, school	495
53-3031	97117	Driver/sales workers	505
53-3032	97102A	Truck drivers, heavy	505
53-3032	97102B	Tractor-trailer truck drivers	505
53-3033	97105	Truck drivers, light-including delivery and route workers	505
53-3041	97114	Taxi drivers and chauffeurs	502
53-4011	97305	Locomotive engineers	499
53-4012	97311	Locomotive firers	499
53-4013	97308	Rail yard engineers, dinkey operators, and hostlers	499
53-4021	97317A	Train crew members	499
53-4021	97317B	Railroad yard workers	499
53-4031	97302	Railroad conductors and yardmasters	499
53-4041	97314	Subway and streetcar operators	499
53-4099	97399A	On-track mobile equipment operators	499
53-4099	97399B	Railroad control tower switching and car retarding operators	499
53-5011	97514	Able seamen	508
53-5011	97517	Ordinary seamen and marine oilers	508
53-5021	97502A	Ship and boat captains	508
53-5021	97505	Mates-ship, boat, and barge	508
53-5021	97508	Pilots, ship	508
53-5031	97521	Ship engineers	508
53-6021	97808	Parking lot attendants	511
53-6031	97805	Service station attendants	511
53-6051	21911K	Aviation inspectors	453
53-6051	21911M	Public transportation inspectors	453
53-6051	21911N	Marine cargo inspectors	453
53-6051	83008A	Railroad inspectors	453
53-6051	83008C	Motor vehicle inspectors	453
53-6051	83008D	Freight inspectors	453
53-7011	97923B	Aerial tram tenders	498
53-7011	97951	Conveyor operators and tenders	498
53-7021	97944	Crane and tower operators	498
53-7031	97928	Dredge operators	498
53-7032	97923A	Excavating and loading machine operators	498
53-7032	97926	Dragline operators	498
53-7033	97932	Loading machine operators, underground mining	498
53-7041	97941	Hoist and winch operators	498
53-7051	97947	Industrial truck and tractor operators	498
53-7061	98905	Vehicle washers and equipment cleaners	511
53-7062	98702	Stevedores, except equipment operators	511
53-7062	98799A	Grips and set-up workers, motion picture sets, studios, and stages	511
53-7062	98799B	Freight, stock, and material movers, hand	511
53-7063	98502	Machine feeders and offbearers	511
53-7064	98902A	Packers and packagers, hand	511
53-7071	97917	Gas pumping station operators	498
53-7071	97921	Gas compressor operators	498
53-7072	97908	Oil pumpers, except well head	498
53-7072	97914	Main line station engineers	498
53-7072	97953	Pump operators	498
53-7073	97911	Well head pumpers	498
53-7081	98705	Refuse and recyclable material collectors	511
53-7111	97935	Shuttle car operators	498
53-7121	97905	Tank car and truck loaders	498
53-7199	97902	Longshore equipment operators	498
53-7199	97989A	All other material moving equipment operators	498
53-7199	97989B	Irradiated-fuel handlers	428
55-0000	99003	Military	514

Reprints

All the occupational statements in the 2000-01 *Occupational Outlook Handbook* are available in reprint form. Reprints are especially useful for jobseekers who want to know about a single field and for counselors who need to stretch the contents of a single *Handbook* among many students.

The bulletin numbers and titles of all 20 reprints along with an index to the reprints are listed below. Prices for individual reprints or for a complete set of reprints as well as an order form are accessible on the Internet: **http://stats.bls.gov/emphome.htm**

Bulletin No.	*Title*
2520-1	Tomorrow's Jobs
2520-2	Business and Managerial Occupations
2520-3	Engineering, Scientific, and Related Occupations
2520-4	Computer and Mathematics-Related Occupations
2520-5	Social Scientists and Legal Occupations
2520-6	Education and Social Service Occupations and Clergy
2520-7	Health Diagnosing Occupations and Assistants
2520-8	Dietetics, Nursing, Pharmacy, and Therapy Occupations
2520-9	Health Technologists and Technicians
2520-10	Communications, Design, Performing Arts, and Related Occupations
2520-11	Technologists and Technicians, Except Health
2520-12	Sales Occupations
2520-13	Clerical and Other Administrative Support Occupations
2520-14	Protective Service Occupations and Compliance Inspectors
2520-15	Service Occupations: Cleaning, Food, Health, and Personal
2520-16	Mechanics, Equipment Installers, and Repairers
2520-17	Construction Trades and Extractive Occupations
2520-18	Metalworking, Plastics-Working, and Woodworking Occupations
2520-19	Production Occupations
2520-20	Transportation and Forestry, Fishing, and Related Occupations

If you want information about: — *order Bulletin No. 2520-*

E

F

G

H

I

J

L

M

N

O

P

R

S

T

U

V

W

Index

C

D

E

I

J

K

L

N

O

P

Q

R

S

T

U

V

W

X

Z